Lecture Notes in Computer Science 2519

Edited by G. Goos, J. Hartmanis, and J. van Leeuwen

W0106145

Springer-Verlag Berlin Heidelberg GmbH

Robert Meersman
Zahir Tari et al. (Eds.)

On the Move to Meaningful Internet Systems 2002: CoopIS, DOA, and ODBASE

Confederated International Conferences
CoopIS, DOA, and ODBASE 2002
Proceedings

 Springer

Series Editors

Gerhard Goos, Karlsruhe University, Germany
Juris Hartmanis, Cornell University, NY, USA
Jan van Leeuwen, Utrecht University, The Netherlands

Volume Editors

Robert Meersman
DOA Institute
p/a Leeuwlantstraat 83, 2100 Antwerp, Belgium
E-mail: Robert.Meersman@vub.ac.be

Zahir Tari
RMIT University
School of Computer Science and IT
GPO Box 2476V, VIC 3001, Melbourne, Australia
E-mail: zahirt@cs.rmit.edu.au

Cataloging-in-Publication Data applied for

Bibliographic information published by Die Deutsche Bibliothek
Die Deutsche Bibliothek lists this publication in the Deutsche Nationalbibliografie;
detailed bibliographic data is available in the Internet at http://dnb.ddb.de

CR Subject Classification (1998): H.2, C.2, H.3, H.4, H.5, I.2, D.2.12, K.4

ISBN 978-3-540-00106-5   ISBN 978-3-540-36124-4 (eBook)
DOI 10.1007/978-3-540-36124-4

http://www.springer.de

© Springer-Verlag Berlin Heidelberg 2002
Originally published by Springer-Verlag Berlin Heidelberg New York in 2002.

Typesetting: Camera-ready by author, data conversion by PTP Berlin, Stefan Sossna
Printed on acid-free paper   SPIN 10871047   06/3142   5 4 3 2 1 0

Volume Editors

Robert Meersman
Zahir Tari

CoopIS 2002

Stefano Spaccapietra
Calton Pu

DOA 2002

Rachid Guerraoui
Joe Loyall
Douglas C. Schmidt

ODBASE 2002

Karl Aberer
Ling Liu

Message from General Co-chairs

As large, complex and networked yet intelligent information systems become the focus and norm for computing, software issues covering a wide range of issues such as data and web semantics, distributed objects, web services, databases, workflow, cooperation, ubiquity, interoperability, and mobility for the development of internet- and intranet-based systems in organizations and for e-business need to be addressed in a fundamental way. This federated conference event is unique in that it provides an opportunity for researchers and practitioners to understand these recent developments within their respective as well as broader contexts. It colocated for the first time three related, complementary and successful conferences: DOA, covering infrastructure-enabling technologies, distributed objects, Internet computing, protocols, etc.; ODBASE, covering web semantics, XML databases, ontologies etc.; and, finally, CoopIS, covering interoperation, workflow systems, knowledge management, etc. Each of these conferences treats its topics along multiple axes of theory (i.e., underlying theoretical solutions), design and development (e.g., technical and conceptual solutions), and applications (e.g., case studies and industrial solutions).

The three conferences share the distributed and ubiquity aspects of modern computing systems, and the resulting application/pull created by the Internet and the so-called "Semantic Web". For DOA 02 the primary emphasis is on the distributed object infrastructure; for ODBASE 02 it is on the knowledge bases and methods required for enabling semantical use; and for CoopIS 02 it is on the interaction of such technologies and methods within an organization or network of organizations. As they must, these subject areas overlap and, in fact, the organizers specifically looked for submissions in any of the areas that also emphasized the envisaged mutual impact among relevant issues. To stimulate this "cross-pollination," a common program of representative keynote speakers, a joint tutorial program, and a common Industry Track that ran parallel to the entire event were assembled.

We received many submissions for the three conferences (293 in total: 111 for CoopIS 02, 106 for DOA 02, and 76 for ODBASE 02). Not only can we claim much success in attracting so many scientific papers, but from this harvest it was possible to compose a high-quality and representative cross-section of research worldwide in the different areas covered by the federated event. Among these submitted papers, indeed only a small number could be selected (i.e., around a 25% acceptance rate). The reviewing process was excellent and each paper was reviewed by at least three experts.

On behalf of the organization committee, we really would like to thank all the people who were directly or indirectly involved in the setup of these federated conferences and therefore made it a success. We must in particular be grateful to our seven PC co-chairs who, together with their many PC members, did an excellent job in selecting the best papers. Of course handling the submission, reviewing, and notification of such a large number of papers today is not possible without suitable software and we need to thank our CyberChair expert, Kwong Lai. We would like to thank especially Ugur Cetintemel, the Publicity Chair, who made this federated event known to a very large public. Finally, our particular thanks go to Jan Demey (who built the registration system) and Daniel Meersman (who is running the conference secretariat).

We do hope that you enjoyed this federated event and that we may see you all again next year in Europe.

August 2002   Robert Meersman
                                                             Zahir Tari
                                                       Michael Papazoglou

CoopIS 02 PC Co-chairs' Message

Welcome to the Proceedings of the Tenth International Conference on Cooperative Information Systems (CoopIS 02). This year, CoopIS was part of a federated conference in Irvine, California, jointly with the International Symposium on Distributed Objects and Applications (DOA) and the International Conference on Ontologies, Databases, and Applications of Semantics for large-scale Information Systems (ODBASE). The theme of the 2002 Federated Conference was "On the Move to Meaningful Internet Systems and Ubiquitous Computing."

We received a large number of submissions this year and we had to reject many good ones. Of the 111 papers reviewed by the program committee, 30 papers were accepted for presentation and publication. In addition, 12 submissions were accepted as poster papers in the proceedings, with a short presentation at the conference.

We are happy to report that cooperative information systems continues to be a vigorous area of research for our "core" community in databases and related areas. In addition, several "new" areas of interest (new to CoopIS) are emerging. Examples of traditional CoopIS areas of interest include query processing, interoperability, workflow, work process, and business/transactions. There are examples of increasing overlap between cooperative information systems and other areas of research in mobility, agents, data and system quality issues, peer-to-peer, and ubiquitous environments. We believe this successful "broadening" of CoopIS points to the increasing relevance of the research area as well as the corresponding growth of the community.

We would like to acknowledge a number of people who made CoopIS such a growing success. First, we want to thank the authors of all the submitted papers and conference attendees, since they are the representatives of the CoopIS community. Without a vigorous community there cannot be a successful conference. Second, we thank the PC members who reviewed the papers and provided valuable feedback to the authors. Third, we would like to thank the federated conference organizers for the professional management of the electronic paper submission and review process. In particular, we recognize the efforts of Prof. Zahir Tari and Kwong Yuen Lai of RMIT University, Australia.

Thank you and we hope you enjoyed the conference and the papers.

August 2002

Stefano Spaccapietra
Calton Pu

DOA 02 PC Co-chairs' Message

Welcome to the Proceedings of the Fourth International Symposium on Distributed Objects and Applications (DOA). There is increasing consensus among IT researchers and practitioners about the importance and potential of distributed object computing (DOC) technologies. It's also clear that there have been significant intellectual and commercial advances in this area in recent years. DOC technologies provide capabilities for use in various application domains, including aerospace, banking, process control, telecommunications, medical systems, and many other domains. They are also now offering practical, real-life production solutions to a host of technical problems, including quality-of-service enforcement and interoperability across different software, hardware, and network platforms. DOC systems are being built according to different paradigms and architectures, such as OMG's CORBA, Sun's J2EE, Microsoft's .Net, and other request broker principles and implementations, and contingent technologies such as Sun's Java-based active objects and messaging services, to provide a basis for building complex distributed applications.

Among the 106 submissions to DOA 2002, 28 papers were selected for inclusion in the technical program of the conference and 24 papers were selected for presentation in an interactive poster session at the conference. Every paper was reviewed by at least three members of the program committee. Each paper was judged according to its technical merit, originality, presentation quality, and relevance to the conference topics. The final program spans the following topics related to DOC technologies:

- Object request broker enhancements
- Web services
- Distributed object scalability and heterogeneity
- Dependability, security, and assurance
- Reflection and reconfiguration
- Mobility
- Real-time scheduling and performance
- Component-based applications

We would like to express our deepest appreciation to the authors of the submitted papers, the program committee members for their diligence in reviewing the submissions, the attendees for their participation, and finally to the members of the organizing committee for their efforts towards making DOA 2002 a successful conference.

August 2002

Rachid Guerraoui
Joe Loyall
Douglas Schmidt

ODBASE 02 PC Co-chairs' Message

Welcome to the First International Conference on Ontologies, Databases, and Applications of Semantics for Large-Scale Information Systems (ODBASE 02). ODBASE conferences present a new forum for addressing semantic issues in large-scale networked information systems, such as internet and intranet systems. ODBASE 02 has a special interest in gathering researchers and practitioners from multiple disciplines (such as web semantics, databases, knowledge management, and ontologies) and exchanging ideas and research results on semantic issues and their roles in ubiquitous computing. As the world heads towards larger-scale repositories of structured, semistructured, and unstructured information, the need to understand, capture, and utilize the semantics of these data is of growing interest. The first ODBASE conference was dedicated towards building more meaningful internet systems.

We were pleased to present a high-quality technical program. Seventy-six papers were submitted to ODBASE this year. The submissions were from more than 10 countries. Of these, only 21 full papers were accepted as the regular research papers. We were fortunate to have 40 program committee members who assisted us by giving very detailed reviews. A key aspect of ODBASE 02 was that we brought the worlds of semantic webs, ontologies, and databases together in a single high-quality forum. In addition to the regular papers, we accepted 4 poster papers where authors were able to give brief descriptions of their research. Finally, we would like to thank Kwong Yuen Lai who did an amazing amount of work in facilitating the online PC meeting, reviews, and technical program development.

August 2002   Karl Aberer
                                                                          Ling Liu

Organization Committee

CoopIS 02, DOA 02 and ODBASE 02 were organized by RMIT University (School of Computer Science and Information Technology), UCI, Vrije University of Brussels (Department of Computer Science) and the University of California at Irvine (Department of Computer and Electrical Engineering).

Executive Committee

Conference Co-chairs:	Robert Meersman (Vrije University of Brussels, Belgium), Michael Papazoglou (Tilburg University, The Netherlands), and Zahir Tari (RMIT University, Australia)
CoopIS 02 PC Co-chairs:	Calton Pu (Georgia Tech., USA) and Stefano Spaccapietra (EPFL, Switzerland)
DOA 02 PC Co-chairs:	Rachid Guerraoui (EPFL, Switzerland), Joe Loyall (BBN Technologies, USA), and Douglas Schmidt (UCI, USA)
ODBASE 02 PC Co-chairs:	Karl Aberer (EPFL, Switzerland) and Ling Liu (Georgia Tech., USA)
Organizing Chair:	Angelo Corsaro (UCI, USA)
Tutorials:	Vipul Kashyap (NIH, USA)
Publicity Chair:	Ugur Cetintemel (Brown University, USA)

CoopIS 02 Program Committee

D. Abel
C. Batini
K. Becker
M. Bowman
A. Buchmann
O. Bukhres
M.S. Chen
P. Cohen
P. Constantopoulos
U. Dayal
A. Di Leva
A. Doucet
M.C. Fauvet
T. Finin
A. Gal
L. Gong

J.L. Hainaut
A. Hofstede
M. Huhns
R. Hull
Y. Kambayashi
L. Kerschberg
M. Kitsuregawa
D. Kotz
S. Laufmann
D.L. Lee
M. Luck
S. Madnick
T. Masui
D. McLeod
C. Medeiros
J. Mylopolos

C. Neuman
S. Nishio
M. Norrie
M.E. Orlowska
M. Panti
C. Parent
B. Pernici
L. Raschid
T. Risch
M. Rusinkiewicz
F. Saltor
J. Scholtz
T. Starner
W.M.P. van der Aalst
K.Y. Wang
M. Wooldridge

J. Yang
M. Yoshikawa

DOA 02 Program Committee

S. Baker
D.E. Bakken
R. Baldoni
Z. Bellahsene
G. Blair
A. Bloesch
J. Cross
P. Eugster
C. Gokey
A. Gokhale
D. Hagimont
A. Jacobsen
R. Klefstad
J. Kienzle
R. King
B. Krämer
D. Lea
F. Manola
K. Mazouni

T.Y. Meng
P. Narasimhan
F. Pacull
D. Sharp
R. Soley
R. Schantz
E. Shokri
M. van Steen
J.-B. Stefani
G. Thaker
N. Venkatasubramanian
S. Yajnik
S. Vinoski
A. Watson
D. Wells
A. Zomaya
A. Zaslavsky
G. Zhijing

ODBASE 02 Program Committee

C. Bussler
T. Catarci
A. Chen
V. Christophides
T. Critchlow
S. Decker
T. Dillon
J. Euzenat
D. Fensel
A. Gal
J. Geller
D. Georgakopoulos
N. Guarino
K. Karlapalem
V. Kashyap
M. Koubarakis

M. Lenzerini
T.W. Ling
A. Maedche
L. Mark
L. Mazzucchelli
A. Mendelzon
M. Missikoff
J. Mylopoulos
S. Navathe
E. Neuhold
M.E. Orlowska
A. Ouksel
M. Papazoglou
Q. Li
M. Scholl
A. Sheth

K. Siau   T.C. Tang
J. Sowa   H. Weigand
K. Sycara   J. Zeleznikow

Sponsors

Boeing, USA
OntoWeb, The Netherlands
Telecordia Technologies, USA

Table of Contents

COOPIS 2002 FULL PAPERS

Interoperability

Workflow

Mobility

Agents

P2P & Ubiquitous

Work Process

Business & Transactions

Infrastructure

Query Processing

Quality Issues

COOPIS 2002 POSTERS

Agents & Middlewares

Cooperative Systems

DOA 2002 FULL PAPERS

ORB Enhancements

Web Services

Distributed Object Scalability and Heterogeneity

Dependability, Security, Assurance

Reflection and Reconfiguration

Mobility

Real-Time Scheduling and Performance

Component Based Applications

ODBASE 2002 FULL PAPERS

Ontology Languages

Conceptual Modelling and Ontologies

Ontology Management

Ontology Development and Engineering

XML and Data Integration

Tools for Intelligent Web

ODBASE 2002 Posters

Object Security Attributes: Enabling Application-Specific Access Control in Middleware

Konstantin Beznosov

Quadrasis, Hitachi Computer Products (America), Inc., Waltham, MA
konstantin.beznosov@quadrasis.com

Abstract. This paper makes two primary contributions toward establishing support for application-specific factors in middleware security mechanisms. First, it develops a simple classification framework for reasoning about the architecture of the security mechanisms in distributed applications that follow the decision-enforcement paradigm of the reference monitor. It uses the framework to demonstrate that the existing solutions lack satisfying tradeoffs for a wide range of those applications that require application-specific factors to be used in security decisions while mediating access requests.
Second, by introducing attribute function in addition to decision and enforcement functions, it proposes a novel scheme for clean separation among suppliers of middleware security, security decision logic, and application-logic, while supporting application-specific protection policies. To illustrate the scheme on a concrete example, we describe its mapping into CORBA Security.

1 Introduction

The employment of application-specific factors in security decisions is not new, one example being target ADI in OSI access control framework [1]. Most current commercial distributed application security systems [2-5] provide various levels of support for application-specific information in policy decisions. What is missing, though, is a systematic inclusion of the support for these factors in the architecture of access control and other security mechanisms of middleware systems.

This void results in a lack of adequate architectural provisions in middleware security, leading to ad-hoc solutions. Although some efforts are under way to develop support for object security metadata in authorization policies [6], the present analysis did not reveal any notable in support of application-specific factors in the security mechanisms of distributed applications. Systematic support for application-specific factors is necessary, but it is missing in the architecture of distributed applications.

In this paper, we propose a schema for systematic support of application-specific factors in security mechanisms for distributed applications. To facilitate analysis of the existing solutions for supporting such factors, as well as to describe the proposed solution, we develop a framework for reasoning about those security mechanisms in distributed

R. Meersman, Z. Tari (Eds.): CoopIS/DOA/ODBASE 2002, LNCS 2519, pp. 693–710, 2002.

applications that follow decision-enforcement paradigm, e.g. access control, audit, and quality of message protection. The framework allows for classifying all solutions into four major schemes.

We use the framework to introduce our solution, which has two primary components: 1) generic representation of application-specific security-related factors in the form of object security attributes and 2) additional function for retrieving them at the time of access request mediation by the security sub-system. Being conceptually simple, the approach enables the use of application-specific factors in security policy decisions without coupling evaluation engines and target objects, while maintaining underlying middleware security application-neutral. Therefore, the security decision function can be provided by a third-party, while the enforcement function stays in the middleware, thus freeing the application owner from implementing either. To substantiate a relatively abstract explanation of the proposed solution, we show its translation into a concrete architecture of CORBA Security.

The reminder of the paper is organized as follows. The problem to be addressed is stated in Section 2. The framework is introduced and the available solutions are discussed in section 3. section 4 presents our solution in generic form. Its concrete application to CORBA Security is discussed in section 5. Discussion is provided in section 6 and conclusions are drawn in section 7.

2 Problem Motivation

The problem raises because of the conflict of the following forces. On the one hand, a capable implementation of middleware security typically involves a complex and expensive piece of machinery, and is somewhat similar in its generality to operating system security. As a consequence of its critical nature, middleware security needs to be carefully designed, implemented, tested, assured, and tuned for performance and scalability. It is thus essential for the producers of middleware security to avoid alterations to their products and yet apply them to diverse application domains.

On the other hand, there is strong and natural interest among owners of distributed applications in making security decisions, mainly authorization ones, based on factors specific to the applications and organizational workflow, which is sometimes referred as object security metadata, as in Bonatti et al. [6].

2.1 What Are Application-Specific Factors

Unlike a resource security attribute, an application-specific factor is a certain characteristic or property of an application's resource, produced, modified and processed in the course of normal application execution and not for the sole purpose of a security policy decision. In OO middleware and other distributed systems, application objects are such resources. A remote analogy is resource access control decision information (ADI), defined as a description of the resource's security-relevant properties, in an ISO access control framework [1]. The difference between ADI and application-specific factors is that the former could be administered and utilized for the sole purpose of making access control decisions.

2.2   Examples

To illustrate the needs of user organizations, consider the following real-life examples from the banking and telecommunication domains. Several people could be associated with each bank account, each having different rights. For example, the primary holder can do everything, including deleting the account, whereas the secondary holders, depending on the loyalty of the primary holder, could have different levels of limited access, such as withdrawing limited amounts and reviewing activities. All others can only deposit to the account. Implementation of such policies requires dynamic evaluation of the relationship between the accessing subject and an account. A list of account holders and their "rank" (e.g. primary and secondary) are such application-specific factors.

Security policies that U.S. long distance telephone carriers need to enforce depend on the state (e.g. Florida, Pennsylvania) in which a particular account is located. At the same time, accounts change phone numbers (and therefore possibly state) due to the relocations of their owners. Appearing to be a small and relatively infrequently occurring task, manually re-associating an account object with the corresponding state's policy becomes a resource-consuming operation for carriers with millions of subscribers (relocating, on average, every 5 years over 5,000 per day for 10^6 subscribers). Instead, the policy could be determined using the first 6 digits of the phone number, which becomes one of the application-specific factors to be used in security policy decisions.

2.3   Objective

Also advocated by others [6] and identified as one of the input types for access decision function in [1], this demand for the use of application-specific information in authorization and other security decisions has a clear rationale. The more application or workflow information is used in security decisions, the better is the integration between security and application administration, which leads to low administration costs and fewer errors of application and security administrators. More importantly, enforcement of application-specific policies in the middleware frees developers from coding such policies in their applications, thus making systems less complex, quicker to build, and easier to evolve. These two factors result in significant long-term savings for application developers and owners.

At the same time, a number of enterprise-scale authorization products first appeared on the market of web servers security, and then expanded into application servers. These systems are good candidates for providing authorization services to distributed applications and the underlying middleware security. However, as we will show in the next section, there are technical obstacles in integrating them with both the former and the latter.

A question arises as to whether there a way to keep middleware security services generic and yet allow for enforcement of security policies specific to different application domains, possibly with the use of enterprise authorization systems.

3   Available Solutions

For the purpose of analyzing solutions to the problem, we differentiate all approaches to security policy decisions and enforcement in distributed systems based on two factors: the nature of policy decision and enforcement functions. Roughly, each of these functions can be provided by the distributed application itself or by the security subsystem of the underlying distribution infrastructure, i.e. middleware security. Using acro-

Table 1: Acronyms for different locations of security policy decisions and enforcement

	Decision Function	Enforcement Function
Middleware	MD	ME
Application	AD	AE

nyms defined in Table 1, we have four possible combinations of decision and enforcement: MDME, ADME, ADAE and MDAE. In the following subsections, we explain each scheme and use this classification to assert that the available solutions do not provide desirable trade-offs.

3.1   MDME – Everything Is Done by Middleware

The first case, the most obvious, occurs when both functions of security decision and its enforcement are provided by the middleware security, as shown in Figure 1. This is

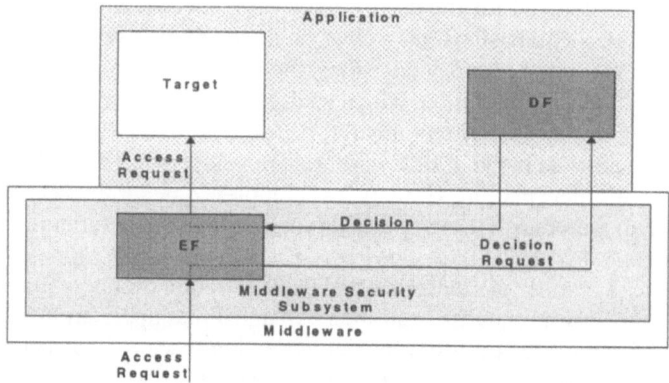

Fig. 1. MDME schema

what practical middleware security systems implement. Being generic, both decision and enforcement functions come with the security subsystem. Applications are security-unaware, and therefore, are easier to design, develop, test, deploy and support. In addition, since the reference monitor is not "spilled" over into the application layer, assurance efforts are limited to the middleware layer and those below. This is why the MDME schema is considered to be the best for the purpose of enterprise security integration. However, with this approach no application-specific factors can be used for security policy decisions. Consequently, the MDME schema is of no use for addressing the stated problem.

3.2   ADME – Application Decisions Are Enforced in Middleware

A better way is to externalize application-specific security logic into a separate service or module and make the middleware security subsystem to obtain policy decisions from it. This ADME schema is illustrated in Figure 2.

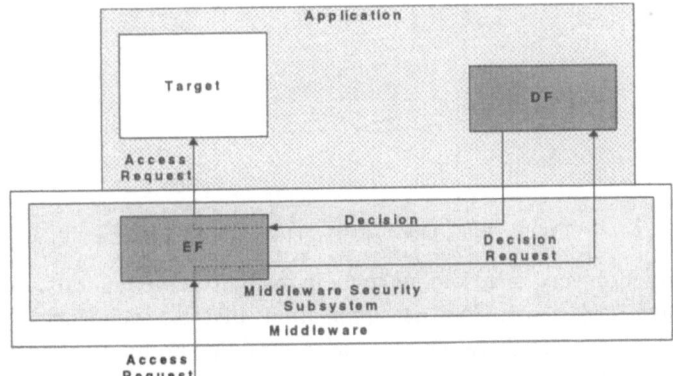

Fig. 2. ADME schema

The schema has been realized in a number of middleware architectures. For example, CORBA Security [7] has replaceable AccessDecision and other interfaces. Java authentication and authorization service (JAAS) [8, 9], which recently became a part of J2SE v1.4, has replaceable interface *Policy* that serves authorization decisions. Although appearing to be versatile, the ADME schema comes with two major drawbacks.

Firstly, even being application-specific, the decision function (DF) still has the same generic interface for the enforcement function (EF) to query it because the latter remains generic. The interface protocols are not capable of communicating application-specific information between EF and DF. For instance, operation *access_allowed()* in COR-BA's replaceable *AccessDecision* interface takes subject's credentials, reference to the target object (just "target" for short), target type, and operation on it. Java's *Policy::get-Permissions()* accepts, as input parameters, information representing the original location of the code and the public keys of its signer. Microsoft's .NET security model, although not currently well documented, appears to have a security architecture similar to Java in this regard. Clearly, neither of them provide for application-specific factors to be communicated from enforcement to decision point.

And, even if the DF interface supported communication of application-specific factors, the means of retrieving such factors in the EF are not defined. Thus, a custom implementation of DF would have to employ a back door to go back to the target object (or a data repository) and retrieve application-specific factors from there, as shown in Figure 3.

When a back door is provided by a target object, the main drawback of the technique is due to the performance hit. Specifically, in some applications, it could be expensive to

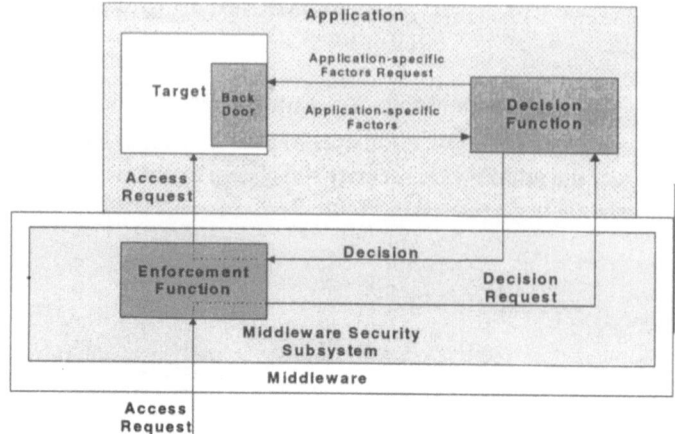

Fig. 3. Back Doors to Target in ADME Schema

restore the target objects' state and make them ready to serve requests, including those coming through back doors. Consider applications that use secondary or even tertiary storage for the object state between sessions. It could be prohibitively expensive to restore an object, obtain some data through its back door, and make an authorization decision just to find that access has been denied. Performing expensive re-incarnation of target objects for making security decisions also creates a vulnerability for denial of service attacks.

Despite DF having a potential to be specific to the application domain, ADME schema allows enforcement of only those run-time pre-requisites, such as (dynamic) conditions in [10, 11] and [6], obligations in XACML [12] and provisions in [13], that are non-specific to application domains (such as CPU load). This limitation is due to EF being part of the generic middleware layer.

Secondly, being an all-or-nothing solution, the use of the application-specific decision function forces the new logic to re-implement authorization decisions completely, which is prohibitively complex and difficult to do correctly for distributed large scale systems, thus rendering this approach unrealistic for most user organizations with the needs in application-specific authorization and other security logic. End-user organizations do not want to be in the business of implementing authorization and other security policy evaluation engines, which is required if application-specific factors were to be used in security policy evaluation.

3.3   ADAE – Security-Aware Applications

ADAE schema is more flexible for making security decisions based on application-specific factors then the previous two. The intent is to let an application-provided EF to call the DF (also provided by the application), thus obviating the problem of obtaining application-specific factors by a generic EF. The schema is illustrated in Figure 4. Although generic, the protocol of supplying necessary information to a DF and retrieving decisions from it can be used for communicating application-specific factors.

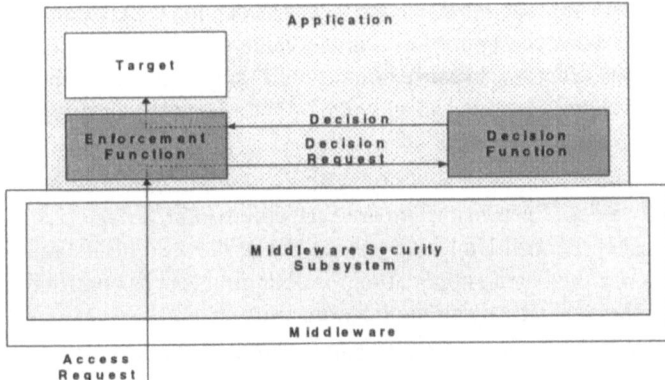

Fig. 4. ADAE schema: general case

The general case (Figure 4) of this schema, when EF is external to targets, although being employed in some research systems [14-17], is not known to be popular in real-life solutions. We believe this is because it requires a proxy object implementing EF to "wrap" each target, and it does not allow enforcement of fine-grain policies because EF is outside of the target.

3.3.1   ADAE with Target Implementing EF

However, a particular case of ADAE – when EF is implemented in the target – as shown in Figure 5, is widely used. It is popular in distributed application systems con-

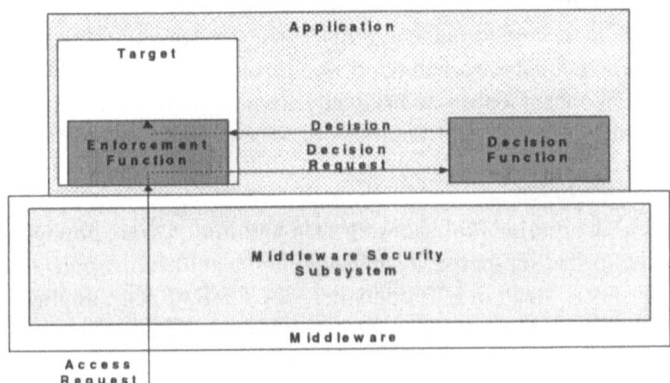

Fig. 5. ADAE schema: target implements EF

structed on top of limited middleware security technologies, e.g., those lacking access control enforcement, such as Kerberos [18] and SESAME [19]) or implementations. Other reasons for employing ADAE schema with EF implemented in targets are the capability to enforce fine-grain security policies and the ease of obtaining application-specific factors because of the collocation of the business and enforcement functions.

One example of the approach is Resource Access Decision (RAD) architecture [20, 21], where a resource name, composed of a name-value pair list, can be used for encoding application-specific factors. In our example with long distance telephone carriers, account's phone number, encoded in the name of the resource in question, can be now used during policy evaluation.[1]

Other examples of middleware security systems in which the enforcement function is implemented by an application system are Praesidium [22], Adage [23], GAA API [10, 11, 24] and Access Control Unit in [6]. As in RAD, these solutions feature an authorization function invoked by an application for obtaining access control decisions, which are expected to be enforced by an application.

Unfortunately, this active role of the target in composing queries to DF and enforcing decisions results in a number of disadvantages, the most salient one being the necessity for security-related code to be mixed with business logic, thus making targets security-aware. As we argue in [25], this security awareness by target objects makes them more complex and prone to security vulnerabilities. It also makes it more difficult to perform security assurance, and forces application developers to be experts in security programming, despite externalizing security decision logic.

Being the best and sometimes the only viable solution for particular cases with complex, application-specific, or fine-grain security policies, programming EF inside of target objects is still a sub-optimal approach for those application domains where a combination of a general purpose security decision function with application-specific attributes could suffice.

3.4   MDAE Schema

We are not aware of any solutions that employ MDAE schema. This is not surprising, since application-executed enforcement of security decisions made by the middleware security subsystem does not seem to bring any advantage over any other scheme, while having all the disadvantages and limitations of MDME schema and some of ADAE.

3.5   Real-Life Hybrids

Several commercial solutions for securing web and middleware applications [2-5, 26] implement an authorization server. It can be queried by either an application itself (ASP or JSP in a web server, bean in EJB container, or CORBA/COM application object) or a middleware-specific enforcement function (web server filter, EJB container, or CORBA security interceptor). Although widely employed in large organizations, neither of these usages introduces any novel solution to the stated problem. The former is an instance of ADAE and the latter, ADME schemas.

4   Generic Solution – ADME/AF Schema

We introduce a new approach, here, that enjoys the advantages of ADME schema and yet enables the use of application-specific factors in security policy decisions without coupling evaluation engines and target objects. Therefore, DF can be provided by a

---

[1] Clearly, this requires appropriate programming of the decision function.

third-party company, including an authorization product vendor, while EF stays in the middleware, thus freeing the application owner from implementing either.

As we discussed in section 3.2, though allowing security decision logic to be application-specific, the original ADME schema suffers from a lack of the means: a) to communicate application-specific factors to DF and, most importantly b) to obtain them, given the target object in question.

We address the first, simpler, problem by introducing generic representation for application-specific factors. These, object security attributes (OSA), as we refer to them, can be expressed in a number of formats, varying in complexity from name-value pairs to arbitrary XML-based structures. The semantic interpretation of an OSA is completely up to the processing entity -- DF. In our example with a telecommunication carrier, for each account object there could be an OSA "holding" the current phone number of the account. More than one OSA can be associated with a target object, comprising a collection of OSAs.

We resolve the second issue, obtaining OSAs for the corresponding target object, by introducing additional function in the ADME schema -- the attribute retrieving function, or attribute function (AF), as shown in Figure 6. This function has simple syntax: it ac-

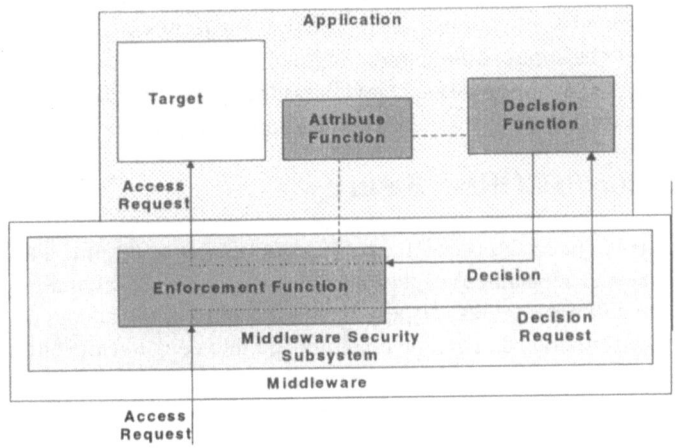

Fig. 6. Attribute function in ADME schema

cepts (middleware-specific) data that are necessary for identifying the state of the target object and returns a set of OSAs for that object. The target object state is necessary for retrieving such object metadata as its OSAs. Since OSA semantics are very specific to the application being protected, AF is provided by the application and not by the middleware or security layers.

The function that obtains OSAs via AF is very dependent on the particular implementation of the approach. In some circumstances, EF could be in better position to make an invocation to AF; in others, DF could be in a better position to do so. Moreover, some implementations could make EF and DF to perform this step together. For example, in section 5, we show how CORBA-specific realization of ADME/AF schema splits AF into two objects, one of which is invoked by EF and the other by DF.

There are a number of advantages if AF is invoked by EF. First, data, necessary for identifying the target state that EF has at its disposal at the invocation point, are very specific to the middleware technology and the type of the particular object adapter that hosts the target. Therefore, for a DF to obtain OSAs from AF, EF would have to pass such data to DF. Second, since DF is usually a COTS, which serves authorization decisions in other schemas, such as ADAE, and for different middleware systems, decision interface to it is too generic to support target state data. Third, there could be more than one DF -- one for each type of security policy, e.g., authorization, audit, quality of protection, and non-repudiation -- invoked at every access to a target. It seems beneficial to minimize the number of potentially expensive invocations on AF by obtaining OSAs once per access request.

On the other hand, postponing invocation of AF allows for lazy strategy, i.e., OSAs are retrieved only if some DF is going to use them. Moreover, a DF could require only particular OSA(s). Retrieving only needed OSA(s) is simple to implement when invocation to AF is done by DF.

This introduction of OSAs as a way to represent target metadata related to security decisions in distributed applications, and a function for retrieving them, AF, enables security decisions to be application-specific, while keeping EF in the middleware security layer and using COTS authorization, as well as other security policy decision functions, systems without modifications. We refer to this approach as ADME/AF schema.

5   Application to CORBA Security

Thus far, we have stated the problem, analysed available solutions, and presented our approach in a form independent of any particular middleware technology. Further, we generalized the solution so that it is applicable not only to the access control, but also to other security functions that can be decomposed into decision and enforcement phases on each access request. Now, we move on to consider a particular middleware security technology -- CORBA security -- and demonstrate how the general solution applies to it.

5.1   CORBA Architecture

This section provides a description, adopted from [27, 28], of CORBA ORB architecture. The architecture consists of several primary components, as illustrated in Figure 7 and described below.

Target object or object -- a CORBA programming entity that consists of an adapter-specific identity, an interface, and an implementation, which is known as a Servant. Servant is an implementation programming language entity that defines the operations that support a CORBA IDL interface. Servants can be written in a variety of languages, including C, C++, Java, Smalltalk, and Ada.

Client -- the program entity that invokes an operation on an object implementation using **object reference** (OR). Accessing the services of a remote object should be transparent to the caller. Ideally, it should be as simple as calling a method on an object, i.e.,

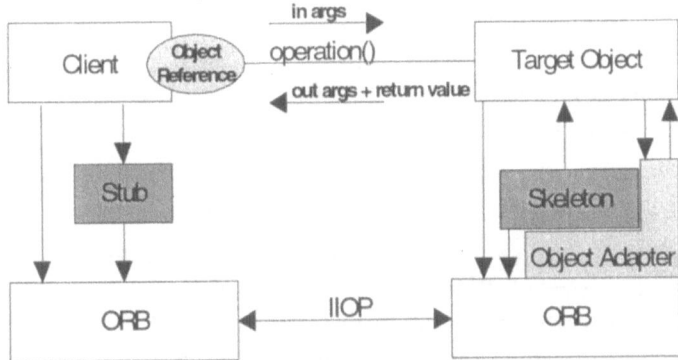

Fig. 7. CORBA ORB architecture

obj->op(args). The remaining components in Figure 7 help to support this level of transparency.

Object Request Broker (ORB) provides a mechanism for transparently communicating client requests to target object implementations. It simplifies distributed programming by decoupling the client from the details of the method invocations, thus making client requests appear to be local procedure calls. When a client invokes an operation, the client and target ORBs are responsible for finding the object implementation, transparently activating it if necessary, delivering the request to the object, and returning any response to the caller. An ORB is a logical entity that may be implemented in various ways, such as through one or more processes or a set of libraries. To decouple applications from implementation details, the CORBA specification defines an abstract interface for an ORB, which provides various helper functions.

CORBA IDL **stubs** and **skeletons** serve as the "glue" between the client and server applications, respectively, and the ORB. The transformation between CORBA IDL definitions and the target programming language is automated by a CORBA IDL compiler. The use of a compiler reduces the potential for inconsistencies between client stubs and server skeletons and increases opportunities for automated compiler optimizations.

Object Adapter (OA) assists the ORB in delivering requests to the object and with activating the object. More importantly, an object adapter associates object implementations with the ORB. Object adapters can be specialized to provide support for certain object implementation styles, e.g., OODB object adapters for persistence and library object adapters for non-remote objects. The ORB and the OA cooperate to allow client applications to invoke requests on CORBA objects and to ensure that each valid CORBA object is mapped to a servant. In addition, the ORB and the OA cooperate to transparently locate and invoke the proper servants given the addressing information stored in CORBA object references.

The primary type of OA used in current CORBA applications is portable object adapter (POA) [29]. A server application can have multiple POAs nested within it. An application might want to create multiple POAs to support various types of CORBA objects and/or different kinds of servant styles. For example, the application might have two POAs, one that supports transient objects and one that supports persistent objects.

A nested POA can be created by invoking a factory operation on another POA. All servers have at least one POA, the Root POA. To create a POA nested under the Root POA, the application invokes the *create* POA operation on the Root POA. The object reference for the Root POA is available from the ORB. The characteristics of each POA, other than the Root POA, are controlled at POA-creation time using different POA policies.

5.2   Run-Time CORBA Security

CORBA Security service (CS) [7] defines interfaces to a collection of objects for enforcing a range of security policies using diverse security mechanisms. It provides abstraction from an underlying security technology so that CORBA-based applications can be independent from the particular security infrastructure provided by the user enterprise computing environment. Due to its general nature, CS is not tailored to any particular access control model. Instead, it defines a general mechanism that is supposed to be adequate for the majority of cases and could be configured to support various access control models. The CS model comprises the following functionalities, among others, visible to application developers and security administrators: identification and authentication, authorization and access control, auditing, integrity and confidentiality protection, authentication of clients and target objects, optional non-repudiation, and administration of security policies.

One of the objectives of CS is to be totally unobtrusive to application developers. Security-unaware target objects should be able to run securely on a secure ORB without any active involvement on their site. Meanwhile, it must be possible for security-aware objects to exercise stricter security policies than those enforced by CS. In the CS model, all object invocations are mediated by the appropriate security functions in order to enforce various security policies such as access control. Those functions are part of CS and are tightly integrated with the ORB and the corresponding OAs.

Security policies are enforced completely outside of an application system at the ORB level. Everything, including obtaining information necessary for making policy decisions, such as access control, is accomplished before the method invocation is dispatched to the target object. As Figure 8 shows, policy enforcement code is executed inside the CORBA Security enforcement sub-system, when a message from client application to a target object is passed through the ORB. Executed at the client ORB as well as at the target ORB, the enforcement code uses the following three sources of information for making policy decisions to enforce:

- The policy of the domain(s) to which the target belongs.
- The information from credentials of the client. In case of access control policy enforcement, these are client privilege attributes, such as access identity, group membership, roles and clearance. Whereas for audit policy enforcement, security attribute of type *AuditId* is used.
- The access request itself.

Although a CORBA security sub-systems can be, and usually is, integrated with the ORB and OAs using proprietary means, for the sake of simplicity, we conceptualize its enforcement function as a security interceptor.

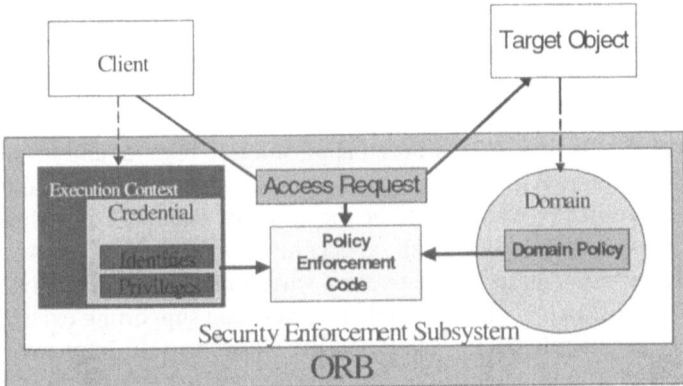

Fig. 8. Enforcement of policies in CORBA Security subsystem

5.3   Attribute Retrieval Function

In our solution to the domain of CORBA Security, the closest analogy to AF is interface *AttributeRetriever*. This interface provides the following operations for retrieving OSAs:

- get_attributes_by_type(type: AttributeType) : AttributeValueList
- get_all_attributes() : ObjectAttributeList

Having its operations implicitly tied into particular target object, the interface constitutes only part of AF, which is invoked by DF. However, there is another part of AF invoked by EF. This is due to the problem of invoking adapter-specific AF by adapter-neutral DF. AF has to be specific to the type of object adapter because, as in most middleware technologies, the notion of object universal identity is not well developed in CORBA architecture.[2] But object-specific identity is sufficiently strong in the context of a particular object adapter, i.e., the adapter has a sufficient amount of information to dispatch an access request to the right object servant, which is responsible for processing application requests for the object in question. On the other hand, it is highly undesirable to have decision functions specific to the adapter type.

This is why an additional level of indirection via interface *Manager*, the other part of AF, has been introduced. Adapter-specific derivatives of Manager locate *AttributeRetriever* objects and return them to the EF, which is implemented in the form of a security interceptor. Being adapter-specific, such an interceptor takes control over the access requests, as well as obtains and enforces policy decisions. Before a security interceptor invokes DFs, it obtains a local reference to the correct *AttributeRetriever* object from the corresponding *Manager*, and places it on *Current* object that serves as a thread-specific placeholder for OSA-related information. Later, when the interceptor calls *Access-Decision* and other objects, their implementations can obtain OSAs from *AttributeRetriever* via its OR available off *Current* object. This lazy strategy of making *AttributeR-*

---

[2] See [30] for detailed discussion on the shortcomings of object identity in middleware security.

etriever available for subsequent queries by DFs allows for retrieval of OSAs only if necessary. If OSAs are required more than once per access request, an *AttributeRetriever* could cache results of time expensive retrieval operation.

5.4   Registering and Discovering Managers

Another issue involves the means for an application to register and for the interceptor to obtain a local reference to a *Manager*. Along with this, an additional issue required a resolution, specifically what should be the scope of *Manager*, i.e., should one *Manager* serve *AttributeRetrievers* for all objects in a given application. And, if not, then how should a security interceptor determine what *Manager* serves a given object? We saw certain benefits in making the solution flexible and supporting existence of several *Managers* for each application. This flexibility allows various implementations of *AttributeRetrievers* in one application. Moreover, since adapter-specific derivatives of *Manager* must be used, the limitation to only one *Manager* instance would prevent different object adapters from co-existing in the same application.

However, it turned out to be difficult to find a way to share multiple *Managers* among process collocated objects. The essence of the problem is the lack of a placement for the information associating an object with a *Manager*. An object adapter appeared to be the only appropriate place to store such information with good chances to retrieve it efficiently at the time of mediating an access request. The associating information is stored in the form of *ManagerPolicy*. This lightweight object holds a reference to the *Manager* instance. The use of *ManagerPolicy* follows the design philosophy exercised in the design of POA, where configuration of a particular POA instance is encoded in the form of POA policies "attached" to the adapter at the time of its creation.

The relationships between target objects, *Managers*, *ManagerPolicies* and object adapters is illustrated in Figure 9. Access requests for any given object are originally

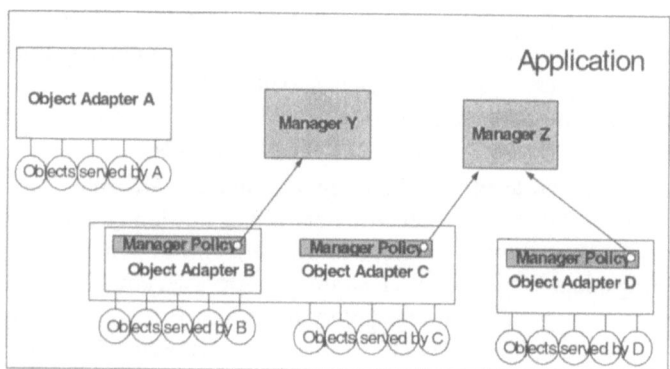

Fig. 9. Relationships among objects, object adapters, OSA Managers, and *ManagerPolicies*

pre-processed and then dispatched by the corresponding object adapter (OA) to the object's servant. OAs can constitute hierarchies with one root, unlimited child and corresponding parent adapters. For each OA, there could be no more than one *Manager* that serves OSAs for all objects under the adapter. That *Manager* is said to serve the OA. The same *Manager* can serve more that one OA, as in the case of object adapters C and D and *Manager* Z, as seen in Figure 9.

Each OA could contain an instance of *ManagerPolicy*, which holds an object reference to the *Manager* serving the adapter. If an application provides a *Manager* for the given OA, it sets ManagerPolicy (containing a reference to the *Manager*) on the adapter using mechanisms specific to the adapter type. For example, such a policy, among others, is passed to the adapter's parent at the child's creation time in the case of POA. If no *ManagerPolicy* is set on an OA, as for adapter A (Figure 9), then no *Manager* serves this adapter, which is equivalent to the lack of OSAs associated with the adapter's objects.

The diagram in Figure 10 depicts a sequence of invocations that an application performs

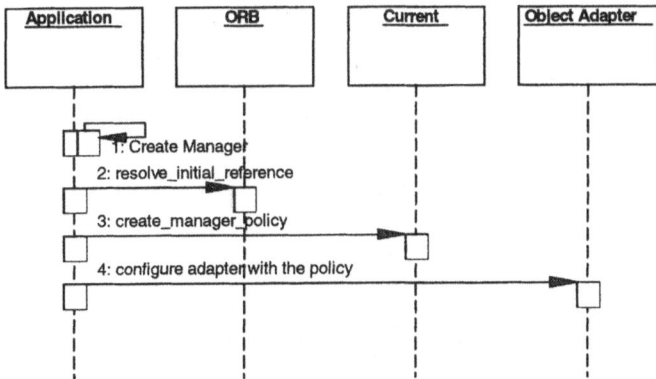

Fig. 10. Sequence of Steps Done by an Application for Registering a Manager

for registering its *Manager* implementation with an OA. After creating an implementation of adapter-specific *Manager* sub-interface (invocation 1 in the sequence diagram), the application obtains a reference to the Current from the ORB by invoking *ORB::resolve_initial_references()* with argument "ObjectSecurityAttributeCurrent" (invocation 2). Then, the application uses a factory operation on the *Current* interface, to which it supplies a valid OR for the *Manager*, for creating an instance of a *ManagerPolicy* (invocation 3). While processing the invocation, *Current* creates an instance of *ManagerPolicy* and returns it to the caller.

The final step (invocation 4) is to "hand" the *ManagerPolicy* to the OA using the OA-specific mechanisms. In the case of POA, for example, an instance of *ManagerPolicy* is inserted, with other *CORBA::Policy* objects, in the list of policies provided to the parent POA as an argument of factory operation *PortableServer::POA::create_POA()* for creating the POA that will serve the same objects as the *Manager* referred in the *ManagerPolicy* will.

Detailed architecture of the solution in the realm of CORBA Security is provided in [31]. The work presented in this section became a CORBA standard adopted by the Object Management Group, and it is currently on finalization track.

6   Discussion

ADME/AF schema is not the ideal and does not work for all cases. Fore examples, being derived from ADME, it would not work for applications that require fine grain protection, because its granularity is not finer than methods exposed by a target object. It also does not support application-specific pre-requisites.

Further, if a DF has to call an AF, then its implementation becomes specific to AF interface; yet additional DF wrapping could help. Some middleware technologies, such as COM+ [32], do not provide mechanisms for implementing ADME schemas, which limits the applicability of this approach. Those rare applications in which security policies are difficult to express using application-specific factors, fall out of the applicability scope as well.

While having these limitations and disadvantages, the ADME/AF schema offers all the flexibility of embedding decision functions in the target without requiring the target to be security aware, for those applications whose security policies have moderate granularity requirements, can be expressed using OSAs, and need only decisions enforceable by generic EF.

Our solution enables the process of implementing secure distributed applications to be cleanly separated among:

- middleware security suppliers, who implement EF,
- security logic suppliers, who implement DF,
- application suppliers, who implement target objects, and possibly AF, and
- application owners who, having possibly AF implemented, configure EF, AF and DF to work together and enforce application-specific protection.

While we deliberately limited the proposed approach to the domain of distributed applications, it may be useful to investigate its applicability and utility for operating systems, as an example.

7   Conclusions

In this paper, we described the problem of supporting application-specific factors in security mechanisms in the field of distributed application systems. In order to address the problem, we first created a framework for reasoning about those security mechanisms in distributed applications that follow decision-enforcement paradigm. Employing the framework, we showed that all cases can be partitioned into one of four schemas, depending on whether middleware security or application provides decision and/or enforcement functions. Although offering the most promising solution for the stated problem, ADME schema nonetheless lacks the means of obtaining and communicating application-specific factors to DF. In the described solution, we introduced the notion of an object security attribute (OSA) as a generic way to represent security-related information about the application object being accessed. More importantly, we proposed attribute retrieval function (AF) that serves attributes to DFs, as a new element to the updated schema. By introducing ADME/AF schema, we made the initial step toward systematic support for application-specific factors in middleware access control mechanisms.

To illustrate the concepts of OSAs and AF on a concrete technology, we described their realization for CORBA Security. The described application of ADME/AF schema to CORBA domain has been adopted by the Object Management Group as part of SDMM specification [31] in November 2001, and it is currently on finalization track.

Acknowledgements

The concept of object security attributes was prompted by a conversation with Ron Monzillo at an OMG TC meeting in 2000. Their specific architecture and realization for CORBA Security have their origins from the work on SDMM specification that has undergone numerous discussions. Some individuals who contributed most to these discussions and helped with their critiques of OSA architecture are Ted Burghart, Fred Dushin, Don Flinn, Bret Hartman, Polar Humenn, Tadashi Kaji, Jishnu Mukerji, Mindy Rudell and Kent Salmond.

Thanks to Bret Hartman for reviewing the paper in its early stage and for providing helpful comments.

References

[1]   OSI, "Information Technology -- Open Systems Interconnection -- Security frameworks in open systems -- Part 3: Access control," ISO/IEC JTC1 10181-3, 1994.

[2]   G. Karjoth, "The Authorization Service of Tivoli Policy Director," presented at Annual Computer Security Applications Conference (ACSAC), New Orleans, Louisiana, 2001.

[3]   Netegrity, "SiteMinder Concepts Guide," Netegrity, Waltham, MA 2000.

[4]   Entegrity, "Entegrity AssureAccess™ - Technical Overview," Entegrity Solutions, September 2000.

[5]   Securant, "Unified Access Management: A Model For Integrated Web Security," Securant Technologies, June 25 1999, http://www.cleartrust.com.

[6]   P. A. Bonatti, E. Damiani, S. D. C. d. Vimercati, and P. Samarati, "A Component-based Architecture for Secure Data Publication," presented at ACSAC, New Orleans, Louisiana, 2001.

[7]   OMG, "CORBAservices: Common Object Services Specification, Security Service Specification v1.7," document formal/01-03-08 2001, http://www.omg.org/cgi-bin/doc?formal/01-03-08.

[8]   C. Lai, L. Gong, L. Koved, A. Nadalin, and R. Schemers, "User Authentication And Authorization In The Java Platform," presented at ACSAC, Phoenix, Arizona, USA, 1999, http://java.sun.com/security/jaas/doc/acsac.html.

[9]   Sun, "Java Authentication and Authorization Service (JAAS)," Sun Microsystems, 2001.

[10] T. Ryutov and C. Neuman, "Access Control Framework for Distributed Applications (Work in Progress)," IETF, Internet Draft draft-ietf-cat-acc-cntrl-frmw-03, March 9 2000.

[11] T. Ryutov and C. Neuman, "Representation and Evaluation of Security Policies for Distributed System Services," presented at DARPA Information Servability Conference Exposition, Healton Head, South Carolina, 2000.

[12]   XACML-TC, "OASIS eXtensible Access Control Markup Language (XACML), Committee Draft," OASIS May 9 2002, http://www.oasis-open.org/committees/xacml/docs/.

[13]   M. Kudo and S. Hada, "XML Document Security Based on Provisional Authorization," presented at ACM Conference on Computer and Communications Security, Athenes, Greece, 2000.

[14]   B. Hailpern and H. Ossher, "Extending Objects to Support Multiple Interfaces and Access Control," *IEEE Transactions on Software Engineering*, vol. 16, pp. 1247-1257, 1990.

[15]   J. Barkley, "Implementing Role-based Access Control Using Object Technology," presented at The First ACM Workshop on Role-Based Access Control (RBAC), Fairfax, Virginia, USA, 1995.

[16]   R. Filman and T. Linden, "SafeBots: a Paradigm for Software Security Controls," presented at New Security Paradigms Workshop, Lake Arrowhead, CA USA, 1996.

[17]   T. Riechmann and F. J. Hauck, "Meta Objects for Access Control: A Formal Model for Role-based Principals," presented at New Security Paradigms Workshop, Charlottesville, VA USA, 1998.

[18]   IETF, "RFC 1510, The Kerberos Network Authentication Service, V5," Internet Engineering Task Force, 1993.

[19]   T. Parker and D. Pinkas, "SESAME V4 - Overview," SESAME, December 1995.

[20]   OMG, "Resource Access Decision Facility," OMG, document number: formal/2001-04-01, August 2001, http://www.omg.org/cgi-bin/doc?formal/2001-04-01.

[21]   K. Beznosov, Y. Deng, B. Blakley, C. Burt, and J. Barkley, "A Resource Access Decision Service for CORBA-based Distributed Systems," presented at ACSAC, Phoenix, Arizona, USA, 1999.

[22]   HP, "HP Adds Value to DCE Security Framework with Praesidium Authorization Server," in *DCE Application Development Trends Magazine*, 1996.

[23]   R. Simon and M. E. Zurko, "Adage: An Architecture for Distributed Authorization," OSF Research Institute, Cambridge 1997, http://www.osf.org/www/adage/adage-arch-draft/adage-arch-draft.ps.

[24]   T. Ryutov and C. Neuman, "Generic Authorization and Access control Application Program Interface: C-bindings," IETF, draft-ietf-cat-gaa-bind-03, March 9 2000.

[25]   B. Hartman, D. J. Flinn, and K. Beznosov, *Enterprise Security With EJB and CORBA*. New York: John Wiley & Sons, Inc., 2001.

[26]   Encommerce, "getAccess Design and Administration Guide," Encommerce, September 20 1999, http://www.encommerce.com.

[27]   D. C. Schmidt, "Overview of CORBA," 2001, http://www.cs.wustl.edu/~schmidt/corba-overview.html.

[28]   D. C. Schmidt and S. Vinoski, "Object Adapters: Concepts and Terminology," in *SIGS C++ Report*, vol. 9, 1997.

[29]   OMG, "Specification of the Portable Object Adapter (POA)," OMG document # formal/01-09-48, 2001.

[30]   U. Lang, D. Gollmann, and R. Schreiner, "Verifiable Identifiers in Middleware Security," presented at ACSAC, New Orleans, Louisiana, 2001.

[31]   OMG, "Security Domain Membership Management Service, Final Submission," document # orbos/2001-07-20, July 11 2001.

[32]   K. Brown, *Programming Windows Security*, First ed. Upper Saddle River, NJ: Addison-Wesley, 2000.

Integrating Optimistic Virtual Synchrony to a CORBA Object Group Service

Gláucia de Oliveira Dias and Alba Cristina Magalhaes Alves de Melo

Department of Computer Science, Campus Universitario - Asa Norte, Caixa Postal 4466,
University of Brasilia, Brasilia – DF, CEP 70910-900, Brazil
{glaucia,albamm}@cic.unb.br

Abstract. In dynamic object groups, objects are allowed to join or leave the group at any time during the group lifetime. Each time the number of members in a group changes, a new view is created. Virtual synchrony is an useful property in dynamic groups which guarantees that if two processes stay in the same view after a view change, the same set of messages will be delivered to them. Most of the protocols that implement virtual synchrony stop regular message activity while a view change is under way. Optimistic virtual synchrony (OVS) allows messages to be sent and received while a view is changing by estimating which members would be present in the next view. If the estimation is wrong, messages are „rolled back". In this paper, we propose and evaluate an approach to integrate OVS to a CORBA group service called OGS. Our results show that OVS provides very good performance improvements during view changes when compared with other protocols that guarantee virtual synchrony.

1   Introduction

Object Groups are a powerful abstraction that allows a collection of objects to be invoked as a single unit. Rather than sending messages to invoke specific objects, the application sends messages to the group and the group service is responsible to multicast them to all members in a consistent way. Thus, groups provide a powerful and easy to use programming interface and, more important than that, they are particularly useful to build fault-tolerant distributed applications.

Object Groups are usually dynamic, i.e., objects can join or leave the group at any moment during the group lifetime. In this scenario, a group membership service is needed to keep track of the current active members of the group. Each time the set of currently active members change, by joining or leaving the group, a new view is created.

Usually, group communication services provide some variation of virtual synchrony semantics, by interleaving membership notifications with regular messages. In virtual synchrony, an event is always associated with the view in which it occurs [8]. Thus, in traditional implementations, regular message activity stops whenever a view change is under way.

Most of the existing membership services decide about a new view by running a consensus protocol [1,7]. Since the time overhead associated with consensus is non-negligible, as in the general case decision is made in at least two rounds [2], the time

R. Meersman, Z. Tari (Eds.): CoopIS/DOA/ODBASE 2002, LNCS 2519, pp. 711–722, 2002.

in which message activity is suspended in group servers that provide virtual synchrony can be considered high.

Optimistic Virtual Synchrony (OVS) was proposed by [12] and aims to reduce message delivery latency by allowing a new kind of messages, called optimistic messages, to be sent and received while a view is changing. Optimistic messages are sent or received by a set of members which the group server estimates will be present in the next view. Once the next view is established, the system decides if optimistic messages must be delivered by evaluating an application-defined predicate. If this predicate is evaluated to false, messages are discarded and the application that sent the message is notified. Otherwise, messages are promptly delivered to the application.

OVS was already integrated by [12] to a group communication service named Transis [6]. The results presented in this work are very similar to our results. Nonetheless, Transis originally ran only on Sun machines and it is not built upon CORBA. This poses many problems concerning portability and execution across multiple platforms.

In this paper, we propose the integration between OVS and an existing CORBA group service to evaluate the benefits of providing optimistic virtual synchrony. OVS was integrated to Object Group Service for CORBA (OGS) [7]. OGS provides three multicast ordering semantics: unordered, FIFO and total order. Among these semantics, only the last one assures that a message is delivered in the same view it is sent. OVS was implemented in OGS as an additional execution mode whose goal is to reduce message delivery latency while a view is changing. As far as we know, this is the first attempt to integrate OVS in an object group server based on CORBA.

Our results show that, for a group with initially three members and some view changes while one of the members constantly sends messages, a reduction of 42% on the total execution time, for 4KB messages, were obtained when compared with some OGS original protocols. In addition, we observed that the execution time of applications using OVS was not so susceptible to the frequency of view changes as do the applications using the native protocols.

The remainder of this paper is organized as follows. In Section 2, object groups are briefly described. Section 3 presents Optimistic Virtual Synchrony. The Object Group Service is presented in section 4 and section 5 describes how OVS was integrated to OGS. Some experimental results are discussed in section 6. Finally, section 7 concludes the paper and presents some future work.

2   Distributed Object Groups

A group is a collection of processes (or objects) that act together in some system or user-specified way [13]. Group communication services manage groups of objects and provide primitives for sending messages to all members of a group [14]. Messages can be sent to a group without having to know the number, identity, or location of individual members.

Groups can be classified according to various characteristics:

1. Static or dynamic groups: static groups are created with a fixed number of members that doesn't change during the group's lifetime. Dynamic groups are groups whose members change over time; members can join and leave the group anytime.
2. Closed or open groups: in closed groups only members can send a message to their group. In open groups, any process or object in the system can send to the group.
3. Peer or hierarchical groups: in peer groups, all processes are equal and all decisions are made collectively. In hierarchical groups, decisions are made by one process that is called the coordinator.

Group communication systems typically integrate two types of services: *group membership* and *group multicast* [12].

The aim of *group multicast* is to permit each object to receive copies of the messages sent to the group with delivery guarantees. These guarantees include agreement on the set of messages that every process in the group should receive and on the delivery ordering across the group members [5].

Group multicast must provide well-defined semantics concerning the ordering in which messages are delivered. The common ordering semantics are total ordering, causal ordering and FIFO ordering [5]. In a generic way, *multicast(g,m)* is the operation which sends the message *m* to all process of the group *g*.

1. *FIFO ordering*: If a correct process issues *multicast(g,m)* and then *multicast(g,m')*, then every correct process that delivers *m'* will deliver *m* before *m'*.
2. *Causal ordering*: If *multicast(g,m)* → *multicast(g,m')*, where → is the happened-before relation [9] induced only by messages sent between the members of *g*, then any correct process that delivers *m'* will deliver *m* before *m'*.
3. *Total ordering*: If a correct process delivers message *m* before it delivers *m'*, then any other correct process that delivers *m'* will deliver *m* before *m'*.

Figure 1 illustrates these orderings for the case of three processes (P, Q and R).

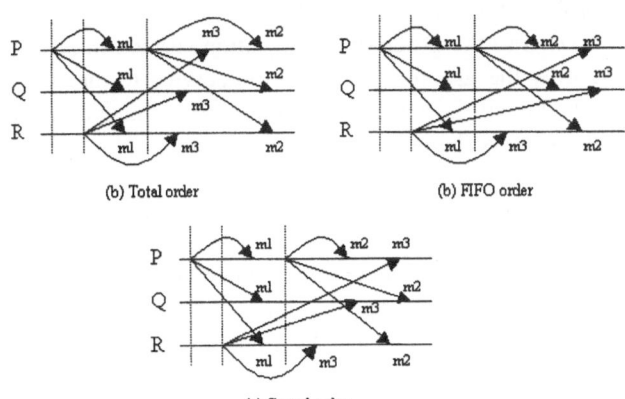

(b) Total order   (b) FIFO order

(c) Causal order

Fig. 1. Some usual orderings of multicast messages: total order, FIFO and causal order

A *group membership service* maintains a listing of the currently active and connected group members. Each time a member joins or is removed from the group, a *view* is created. A new view contains the active group members in a specific moment.

In a group communication service, send and receive events occur within the context of views. Several group communication systems generally provide virtual synchrony semantics. Virtual synchrony requires two processes that participate in the same two consecutive views to deliver the same set of messages in previous view [12,14].

Nearly all variants of virtual synchrony specify that a message must be delivered in the same view that it was sent. This property has been called *group awareness* [12] and *Sending View Delivery* [14]. Group awareness is important to applications that desire to reduce the amount of context information sent with each message and the amount of computation time needed to process a message.

3   Optimistic Virtual Synchrony

In order to provide group awareness, most group communication systems block processes from sending messages during a view change until the new view is delivered to the application [12]. Such blocking can cause an expensive waste of valuable computation and network resources.

Optimistic Virtual Synchrony (OVS) is a form of group communication that provides group awareness decreasing this waste of resource using an optimistic approach [12]. OVS allows applications to send messages during periods in which existing group communication services usually block. Each view event is preceded by an optimistic view event, which provides the application with an estimate of the next view. After this event, applications may send optimistic messages that would be delivered in the next view. If the optimistic messages cannot be delivered, they are discarded and the sending application is informed.

Usually, group communication services interact with their applications via an interface consisting of three types of events [12]: *send, receive,* and *view.* A send event is sent by the application to the group communication service to send a message. A receive event is sent by the group communication service to the application to deliver the message. A view event is sent by the group communication service to notify the application that the view is changing.

There is an event that occurs after the application receives a message. It is called *deliver event* and it is executed by the application to process the message.

To block sending messages while view changes occur, *block* and *flush* events are added to this interface. A *block event* is sent by the service to the application to inform it that a view change is under way. The application answers with a *flush event* [14].

With OVS, the block event is replaced by an optimistic view event, *optView,* which contains an estimate of the set of members that would be present in the next view [12]. When the application receives the *optView event,* it sends a *flush event* and enters into *optimistic mode.* In this mode, applications still receive messages that were sent in the view that they are leaving and may send optimistic messages to be delivered in the next view. When the group communication service delivers a new view to the application, the application returns to *normal mode* and sends a *viewAck event* to the group communication service to denote the end of the optimistic mode. In the normal mode, the application sends regular messages to be delivered in the same view.

When the new view is delivered, the group communication service checks whether the optimistic messages should be delivered in the new view or not. This is checked by applying a predicate, *MessageCondition*, to each optimistic message. If the predicate is evaluated to true, the message is delivered. Otherwise, the message is discarded and a *discardedMessage event* is sent to the application.

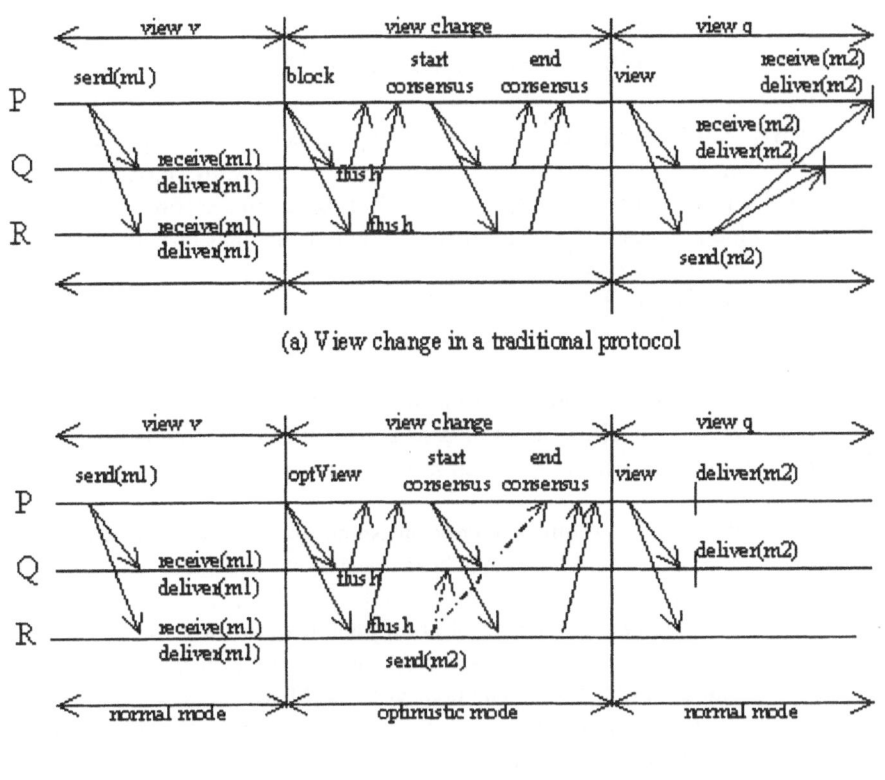

(a) View change in a traditional protocol

(b) View change in OVS

Fig. 2. Behavior of view change in two protocols that provide group awareness

Figure 2 illustrates the difference between a system that provides group awareness in a traditional way (2.a) and a system that uses optimistic virtual synchrony. Initially, the active view is view v. Once a view is established, processes can send and receive messages that are immediately delivered to the application.

When process P notifies a view change (figure 2.a) it sends a *block event* for each member. Then, the members answer with *flush event*. After this moment, no process can send messages and the consensus is initialized by process P to decide the new view. Usually, the consensus is executed in the group communication systems to decide a new view. After the ending of the consensus, the processes receive the new view and processes can send messages between themselves.

In figure 2.b, process P notifies a view change by sending an *optview event* to the members. The group communication members enter in the optimistic mode. In this mode, the members can send messages which are marked as optimistic. This means that the messages will be received by the processes, however will not be delivered [12]. After the ending of the consensus, the processes receive the new view and return to normal mode. At this instant, the received messages, for which message condition is true, are delivered for the application.

4   The CORBA Object Group Service (OGS)

The CORBA Object Group Service (OGS) was proposed by [7]. It provides solutions to the problem of object group in object-based middleware environments using CORBA [11]. The architecture proposed in OGS is based in the concept of component integration, which consists of several distinct components that provide various facilities for reliable distributed computing.

The OGS components include [7]:

1. *Messaging Service*: implements non-blocking reliable point-to-point and multi-cast communication.
2. *Monitoring Service*: monitors objects and detects failures.
3. *Consensus Service*: allows a set of objects to reach a common decision.
4. *Group Service*: provides the group multicast abstraction and membership management.

In the rest of this section, only the consensus and group services will be presented in detail, since the optimistic virtual synchrony design in OGS involved these services. Further information about the other services can be found in [7].

· The *Consensus Service* allows a set of group members to solve the distributed consensus problem [3]. The consensus permits that various objects reach agreement in a decision related to an initial value. The consensus problem can be defined in terms of two primitives: *propose*(v) and *decide*(v), where v is a value. All correct participants can propose an initial value, and must agree on some final value related to the proposed values.

The implementation of the OGS consensus service is based on the algorithm of Chandra and Toueg [4]. The algorithm is based on the rotating coordinator paradigm [2] and proceeds in asynchronous rounds. In every round, a different process plays the role of the coordinator.

The figure 3 shows a running of the consensus algorithm with three participating processes. The members (Q, R) send an estimate to the coordinator member (P). The member (P) proposes a value and send to the other members. These members, after agreeing on the proposal, send an ack to P and, finally, P sends the final decision to Q and R.

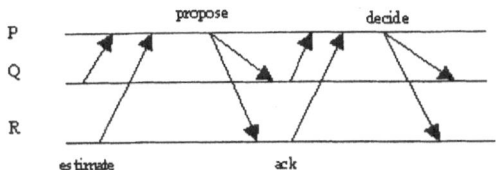

Fig. 3. Running of the consensus algorithm in OGS

OGS provides also an optimized version of the original consensus. In the *optimized consensus*, the coordinator doesn't wait for a majority of propositions, but simply takes his own estimate and proposes it [7]. If the coordinator's estimate is wrong, the traditional consensus protocol is executed.

OGS uses the consensus service to implement totally ordered group multicast and group membership management. Each consensus instance decides on a totally ordered set of messages to deliver and a set of suspect members to remove from current view.

The *Group Service* is the core of the OGS. It implements two functionalities: *group multicast* and *group membership* [7].

Group multicast provides support for sending multicast messages to all the members of the group. It has primitives for sending invocations to a group instead of singleton objects. OGS implements open and closed groups. Multicast primitives in OGS can be classified according to their degree of *reliability* and their *ordering guarantees*.

Reliable multicast means that all correct group members deliver the same set of messages [2]. OGS provides unreliable and reliable multicast primitives. Reliable multicast, in itself, does not ensure that group consistency is preserved; it is generally combined with an ordering guarantee.

Concerning the ordering guarantees, the current version of OGS provides the following multicast primitives:

1. *Unordered*: does not provide an ordering of messages neither group awareness.
2. *FIFO*: provides an ordering of messages sent by the same object, but does not provide group awareness.
3. *Total Order*: provides an ordering of messages and ensures group awareness.

Thus, among these primitives, only the total order implements a form of virtual synchrony.

The *Group membership* service manages objects of the group. OGS supports dynamic groups, so new members can join or leave an existing group, or may be implicitly removed from the group because of a failure. Objects that want to join a group do so by contacting the membership service, which updates the list of group members. Dynamic group membership involves two kinds of protocols: *view change* and *state transfer*.

A *view change protocol* is run each time the composition of a group changes. It ensures that every correct member of the group receives a new list indicating the current members of the group. View changes are totally ordered with each other.

A *state transfer protocol* is an atomic operation that happens during view change, when a new member joins an existing group. It consists in obtaining the state from a current group member, and giving it to the new member. This protocol ensures that the state of all group members is kept consistent upon membership changes. The view change protocol can terminate only after a state transfer is completed [7].

5   Integrating Optimistic Virtual Synchrony to OGS

In order to integrate Optimistic Virtual Synchrony to the CORBA Object Group Service (OGS) [7], the following modifications were made to OGS:

1. Modification of the message's structure to include the identification of optimistic messages.
2. Addition of code to identify normal and optimistic modes.
3. Addition of treatment for optimistic messages.

1. *Modification of the message's structure*: In OGS, internally, messages are sent in a structure, which is composed by the message identification, sender identification, reply's number, ordering semantics, version and data. A new field was included, message type, which allows the system to distinguish an optimistic message from a normal message. This field is also used when the membership service tells the members to change from normal mode to optimistic mode or vice-versa. The new type of the message structure is shown below.

```
/* Definition of Message Type. Included for optimistic  messages */
    enum MessageType{
        NORMAL,
        OPTIMISTIC,
        CHANGE_OPTIMISTIC,
        CHANGE_NORMAL
    };

/* Internal message. */
    struct Message {
        MessageId id_;
        GroupAccessManager sender_;
        NumReplies nb_replies_;
        Ordering ordering_;
        MessageType type_;
        unsigned long view_version_;
        any data_;
    };
```

2. *Identification of normal and optimistic modes*: in the original OGS, when a view change is recognized, a totally ordered message is sent to the members of the group. At this moment, consensus is initiated to decide upon new view. In our proposal, members start in a normal mode. Once the members receive the view change message, they enter in optimistic mode. After consensus finishes, members change to normal mode again (figure 4).

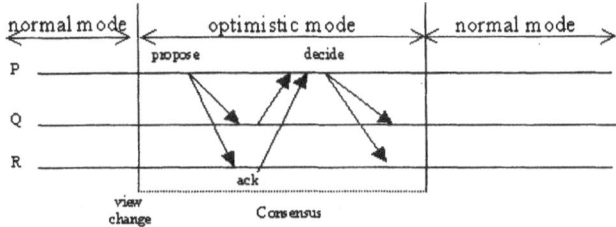

Fig. 4. Inclusion of the optimistic mode in OGS

3. *Treatment of optimistic messages*:

    3.1 To send a message, a process verifies if it is in optimistic mode and, if so, the message type is set to optimistic.

    3.2 When a message is received by a process, three situations can arise: (a) if the message type is normal, it is treated normally; (b) if the member is in the optimistic mode, the optimistic message is enqueued in a buffer for optimistic messages; (c) if the member is in the normal mode and an optimistic message is received, the method *boolean message_condition (newView, optView, msg)* is executed. With this method, the application defines if the message can be delivered or not.

    3.3 When a new view is delivered, each message in the optimistic message buffer is checked to see if the sender is a member of the new view. If so, the method *boolean message_condition (newView, optView, msg)* is applied. Otherwise, the message is discarded and the sender application is notified.

6   Experimental Results

OVS was implemented using JDK 1.1.8 and Visibroker for Java 3.2 and integrated to OGS. OGS runs on top of Microsoft Windows NT 4.0.

To evaluate our proposal, we ran our experiments on 4 machines: 3 Athlon 900MHz, with 128MB RAM and a Pentium II 550 MHz that worked exclusively as a name server. All machines were connected by a 10Mb/sec Ethernet hub and ran our tests in dedicated mode.

Our test was made to evaluate two characteristics: the overhead introduced by OVS when no view changes occur and its performance gains as long as the frequency of view changes become higher. To do so, we measured the total execution time for a client to send 50 messages to a group composed by 3 members without view changes occurring simultaneously and we also measured the cases for two and three interleaved view changes. The protocols considered in our tests were OGS total order (TO), OGS total order with optimized consensus (OTO) and optimistic virtual synchrony (OVS). The results obtained for message sizes of 4KB and 8KB are shown in tables 1 and 2, respectively. Figures 5 and 6 show these results in a graphic.

Table 1. Execution time (ms) for sending 50 messages to 3 members with 2 interleaved view changes (message size = 4KB).

Message Ordering Semantics	Number of view changes		
	Zero	2	3
Total Order (TO)	13229	22072	26398
Optimized Total Order (OTO)	7581	19107	25947
Optimistic Virtual Synchrony (OVS)	13250	14872	15071

Table 2. Execution time (ms) for sending 50 messages to 3 members with 2 interleaved view changes (message size = 8KB).

Message Ordering Semantics	Number of view changes		
	Zero	2	3
Total Order (TO)	19157	27049	29232
Optimized Total Order (OTO)	14410	24996	27029
Optimistic Virtual Synchrony (OVS)	19257	22503	26508

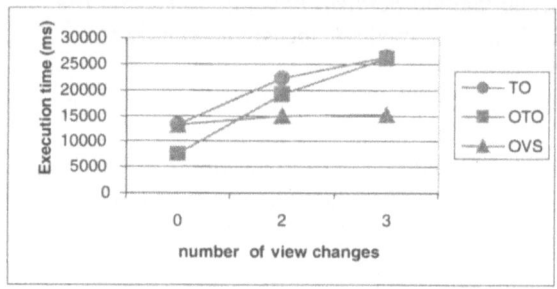

Fig. 5. Execution time x number of view changes for 4KB messages

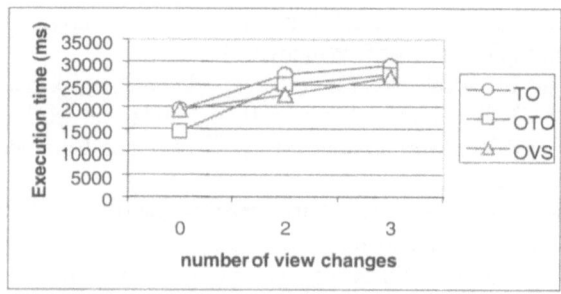

Fig. 6. Execution time x number of view changes for 8KB messages

The results presented in figures 5 and 6 show that OVS has a better performance than the other two protocols when view changes are considered. This behavior can be easily explained since, in total order and extended total order, message activity is suspended while a view change is being decided. On the other hand, with OVS, messages can be sent and received while a view is changing; only message delivery is postponed.

It can also be seen in figure 6 that OVS presents a lower increase in the execution time as long as the frequency of view changes becomes higher. The other two protocols are more sensitive to the number of view changes and, for that reason, less appropriate when scalability is considered.

The performance improvement achieved by OVS for 8KB messages (figure 6) was lower than in the precedent case (figure 5). Analyzing this scenario, it can be observed that the message size is the double of the precedent case and the time needed to reach a consensus on a new view remains the same. Therefore, less optimistic messages are sent while a view is changing and, consequently, the performance improvement of OVS decreases, but still exists.

7   Conclusions and Future Work

In this paper, we discussed and evaluated one approach to integrate optimistic virtual synchrony to a CORBA object group server (OGS). We claim that, by allowing messages to proceed while a view is changing, optimistic virtual synchrony provides a good compromise between performance and the guarantees offered to the application.

Optimistic virtual synchrony was defined as a new execution mode in OGS. Modifications were made in a modular way, making only minor modifications to the original structure of OGS. Our results show very good performance improvements when our approach is compared with the original OGS message ordering semantics that provide group awareness: total order and extended total order.

As future work, we intend to implement a distributed near-video-on-demand service on top of our approach since we think it can take a great advantage of optimistic virtual synchrony. Also, we intend to investigate what modifications must be done in our approach in order to make it possible for OGS+OVS to run in a wireless environment. Particularly we must study how OVS can be used consistently in a partitioned network, by incorporating the concept of extended virtual synchrony [10].

Acknowledgements. This work is partially supported by FINATEC and Capes/PAEP.

References

1.   Agarwal, D. A., Chevassut, O., Thompson, M. R., Tsudik, G.: An Integrated Solution for Secure Group Communication in Wide-Area Networks. In Proceedings of the 6th IEEE Symposium on Computers and Communications, Hammamet, Tunisia (July 2001)
2.   Attiya, H., Welch, J.: Distributed Computing: Fundamentals, Simulations and Advanced Topics. McGraw Hill Pub Co., England (1998) 451
3.   Barborak, M., Malek, M., Dahbura, A.: The consensus problem in distributed computing. ACM Computing Surveys, Vol.25(2). (June 1993) 171-220

4. Chandra, T. D., Toueg, S.: Unreliable failure detectors for reliable distributed systems. Journal of the ACM, Vol.43(2). (1996) 225-267
5. Coulouris, G., Dollimore,J., Kindberg, T.: Distributed Systems Concepts and Design. (2000) 153-158, 436-451, 556-565
6. Dolev, D., Malki, D.: The Transis Approach to High Availability Cluster Communication. Communications of the ACM (April 1996)
7. Felber, P.: The CORBA Object Group Service. Lausanne, EPFL (1998)
8. Keidar, I., Khazan,R.: A Client-Server Approach to Virtually Synchronous Group Multicast: Specifications and Algorithms. Proc. of the Int. Conf. on Distributed Computing Systems (2000)
9. Lamport, L.: Time, Clocks and the Ordering of Events in a Distributed System. Comunications of the ACM, Vol.21. (July 1978) 558-564.
10. Moser, L.E., Amir, Y., Melliar-Smith, P.M., Agarwal, D.A.: Extended Virtual Synchrony. The 14th IEEE International Conference on Distributed Computing Systems (ICDCS) (June 1994) 56-65.
11. OMG: The Common Object Request Broker: Architecture and Specification. OMG (February 1998)
12. Sussman, J., Keidar, I., Marzullo, K.: Optimistic Virtual Synchrony. MIT Technical Report MIT-LCS-TR –792 (November 1999)
13. Tanenbaum, A. S.: Distributed Operating Systems (1995) 99-115
14. Vitenberg, R., Keidar, I., Chockler, G. V., Dolev, D.: Group Communication Specifications: A Comprehensive Study. MIT Technical Report MIT-LCS-TR-790 (September 1999)

Implementing a CORBA-Based Architecture for Leveraging the Security Level of Existing Applications

D. Cotroneo, A. Mazzeo, L. Romano, and S. Russo

University of Naples Federico II
Dipartimento di Informatica e Sistemistica
Via Claudio 21
80125 Napoli, Italy
{cotroneo, mazzeo, lrom, sterusso}@unina.it

Abstract. This work presents an implementation technique which exploits separation of concerns and reuse in a CORBA-based, multi-tier architecture to improve the security (availability, integrity, and confidentiality) level of an existing application. Functional properties are guaranteed via wrapping of the existing software modules. All security mechanisms are handled by the business logic of the middle-tier. Availability and integrity are achieved via replication of the functional modules. Confidentiality is obtained via cryptography. The technique is presented with regard to a case study application. We describe the conceptual model behind the architecture, discuss implementation issues, and present technical solutions.

1 Introduction

Security has become a key requirement for the vast majority of current applications. Ideally, a secure system is one which always enables authorized users to access system services, and never allows unauthorized users to do so. Security is thus a composite attribute, which takes into account the following features [1]:

- Availability - A system is available if it is providing the expected service;
- Integrity - Avoids that messages and stored data be tampered with by someone braking into the system;
- Confidentiality - Provides privacy for messages, services, and stored data by hiding information.

As systems are being opened to the Internet, commercial traders, financial institutions, service providers, and consumers are exposed to a variety of potential damages, which are often referred to as electronic risks [2]. These may include direct financial loss resulting from fraud, theft of valuable confidential information, loss of business opportunity through disruption of service, unauthorized use of resources, loss of customer confidence or respect, and costs resulting from

R. Meersman, Z. Tari (Eds.): CoopIS/DOA/ODBASE 2002, LNCS 2519, pp. 723–736, 2002.
© Springer-Verlag Berlin Heidelberg 2002

uncertainty. In order to mitigate risks and promulgate the deployment of information systems in open networked environments, applications must guarantee high security levels.

However, there is a great deal of existing applications around, which were not designed with the objective of providing high security, since they were supposed to operate in protected environments, which were immune from the threats of most open networked environments. These applications are thus inadequate to operate in modern Internet and intranet scenarios. Nevertheless, they are often a valuable heritage, since they i) fully satisfy system functional requirements, ii) have been thoroughly tested during years long operation, and iii) are strongly coupled with the rest of the enterprise information and production infrastructure. It is foreseeable that in the next years there will be an increasing need for security oriented application-integration actions aiming at improving the security level of many existing applications.

In this work, we present a CORBA-based, multi-tier architecture which leverages the security level of an existing software application[1]. This provides the opportunity to value the investment in legacy applications, while reducing the risk of security breaches.

In this context, by legacy application we mean a software program for which maintenance actions - other than wrapping - are either impossible or prohibitively costly.

The proposed architecture has been developed by exploiting separation of concerns and reuse, and it is based on a multi-tier architecture. Functional properties are guaranteed by incorporating the existing software modules. Availability and integrity are achieved via replication of the functional modules. By using replication, we are able to deliver system services to (authorized) users, also in the presence of failures and/or intrusions affecting the legacy modules. Confidentiality is obtained via cryptography. All security mechanisms are handled by the business logic of the middle-tier.

This approach can be extremely effective in minimizing the development cost of a secure system, for two fundamental reasons:

1. Code writing activity is minimized, since system functions are implemented via reuse of existing software;
2. System testing activity is reduced, since only security-related functions and interactions between individual components need to be tested.

The rest of the paper is organized as follows. Section 2 illustrates the objectives of our research. Section 3 illustrates the assumptions we make. Section 4 describes the architecture of the overall system, and the interactions between individual system components. Section 5 deals with the implementation of the middle-tier server, which represents the core of the system and gives some preliminary experimental results about the performance of the system. Section 6 concludes the paper with some final remarks about results achieved and lessons learned.

---

[1] Since we focus on a specific class of existing applications, namely legacy applications, we will use the terms existing application and legacy application interchangeably throughout the paper.

2   Objectives

Before we present the objectives of our work, we need to define some terms we use in the rest of the paper. Definitions are taken from [3] and [1]. A **fault** is the adjudged cause of an **error**, which in turn may lead to a **failure**, i.e. to a deviation from the specified service, where the service specification is an agreed upon description of the expected service. We focus on two specific categories of faults:

- Faults, whose nature is accidental, and which are originated by physical phenomena. We will call these faults **Accidental Faults**, or simply **Faults**;
- Faults, whose nature is deliberate and malicious, and and which are human made. We will call these faults **Deliberate Faults**, or **Intrusions**.

The proposed CORBA-based architecture acts as new system, which - in addition to providing the same functions as the legacy applications - satisfies the following security requirements:

1. Availability - The service must be **available** to authorized users and **not available** to unauthorized users;
2. Integrity - Messages delivered to authorized users must not be tampered with, i.e. their contents must not be modified;
3. Confidentiality - Messages delivered to authorized users must not be disclosed, i.e. their contents must not be revealed to others.

In order to do so, the new system must be able to avoid/tolerate Faults and Intrusions. More precisely, our objective is to avoid that a fault or an intrusion affecting a module running in the back-end propagates through the tiers, and eventually leads to a failure of the overall system, as illustrated in figure 1.

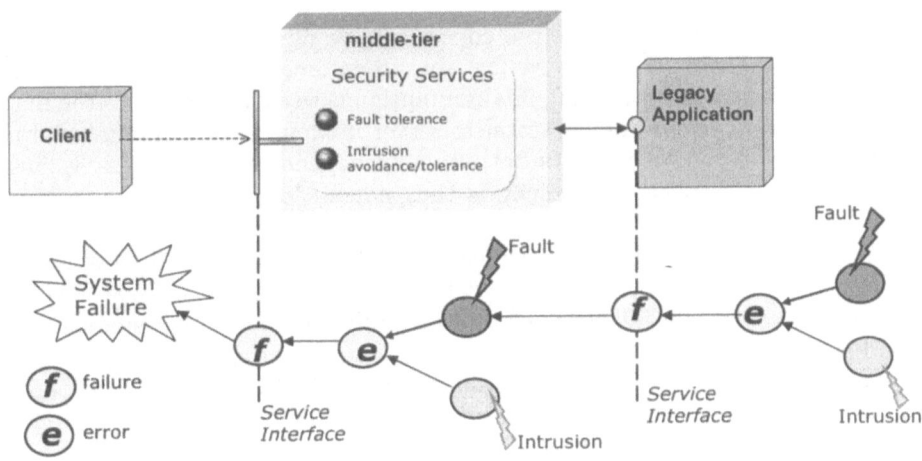

Fig. 1. Propagation of faults and intrusions.

Legacy server failures (middle-tier server Faults) can be of two different types:

1. **Timing Failure (Timeout Fault)** – That means the legacy code fails to produce any output within a predefined amount of time. This may be originated by a variety of causes, including:
   - Process/Host Performance fault - The legacy application process or host is too busy for delivering the requested service within the predefined timeout;
   - Process/Host crash/hung - The legacy application process/host is down or hung, i.e. it does not reply to external stimuli;
   - Network failure - The quality of the connection to the machine hosting the legacy application is too poor, or the machine can not be reached at all;
   - Unavailability of crucial system resources - This typically occurs when the system is under a Denial Of Service (DOS) attack [7].
2. **Value Failure (Value Fault)** – That means the legacy application does provide a reply, but this is incorrect, i.e. it contains errors. This may be originated by a variety of causes, including:
   - Hardware-induced software errors – These are errors in the application due to faults affecting the underlying hardware [6];
   - Communication errors - Such errors occur when data gets corrupted while traversing the network infrastructure. Unless "leaky" communication protocols [8]² are adopted, this kind of errors are fairly unlikely to happen;
   - Erroneous system state/configuration - This may be the consequence of naturally occurring phenomena (such as process aging) or of intentional attacks.

3   Assumptions

As far as the legacy application is concerned, we assume that its state be deterministic. If this is the case, we are able to enforce consistency of individual replicas. It should be noted that this assumption is weaker than the (often made) stateless server assumption. A stateless server implements a combinatorial machine, i.e. at any given time its outputs only depend on the current values of the inputs, and replica consistency is thus not an issue at all. The technique we present can be extended to legacy applications which do not satisfy the deterministic state assumption, provided that all sources of non-determinism be dealt with. Common sources of non-determinism are multi-threaded execution in the replicas, system calls (especially when different operating systems host individual replicas), and more. How to deal with non determinism when managing replica consistency is a widely investigated research topic, but it is beyond the scope of this work. The interested reader can refer to [10].

---

² Most network protocols, also the so called unreliable ones, protect data with Cyclic Redundancy Codes (CRC) information. Corrupted data is most likely detected (and dropped) than delivered. A leaky protocol is instead a protocol that allows corrupted information to be delivered to the destination.

As far as the middle-tier server and the underlying infrastructure are concerned, we do not address issues related to faults and intrusions affecting them, since we concentrate on faults and intrusions in the back-end application. We thus assume that the middle-tier server and the infrastructure supporting it are immune from faults and intrusions. We want to explicitly note that most research projects in the field of middleware infrastructures and frameworks also make this assumption. To the best of our knowledge, no research project in the field of dependable distributed environments currently takes explicitly into consideration the problem of the dependability of the supporting infrastructure. This also applies to major research projects, such as AQuA [9], Eternal [5], and OGS [12]. We are only aware of a fault injection study conducted on the Chameleon system [4], where injections are performed both to the protected applications and to the supporting infrastructure.

As far as the local network infrastructure is concerned, we assume a Local Area Network (LAN) connects the distributed objects which implement the middle-tier server between them, and to the replicas running in the back-end. Such a connection will be considered reliable, i.e. messages are always delivered without errors, and with a limited delay. This is not a very strong assumption for currently available LAN technologies.

4   Overall System Architecture

The solution we propose relies on a three-tier architecture which replicates and secures the legacy application, and on Commercial-Off-The-Shelf (COTS) technologies. The overall system architecture is depicted in figure 2.

The figure shows the clients, the middle-tier server, and the group of replicated legacy application instances. Replicas are added/removed as they become available/unavailable. Clients access the services via the Service Proxy. Communication between Clients and the Proxy is over a protected channel. The administrator can set system parameter according to security and performance requirements.

The middle-tier server is a CORBA distributed application, consisting of several interacting components, which communicate over a secure CORBA platform. The middle-tier adds security to the legacy application which runs in the back-end. In the following, the roles of individual components of the middle-tier are described.

4.1   Service Proxy

The Proxy scheme is quite a flexible mechanism, when third party services must be encapsulated - possibly enhanced - and exported. The Service Proxy provides different behaviors, depending on configuration settings of the system, such as the replication level currently available, and the specific adjudication strategy chosen. Clients are unaware of which specific objects are actually providing the service, and of what their internal mechanisms are.

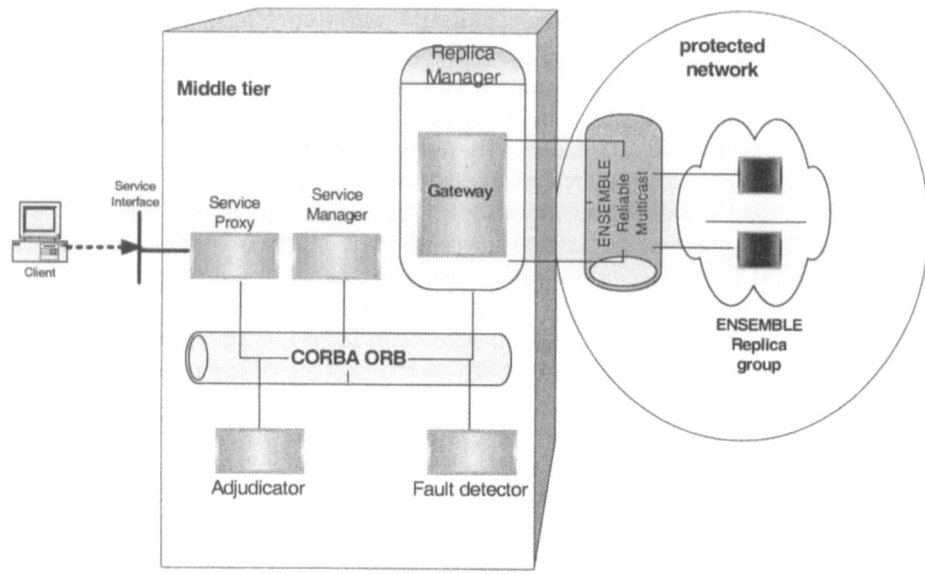

Fig. 2. Conceptual system architecture

4.2   Service Manager

The **Service Manager** component is in charge of configuring all the others. It must provide functions to customize the behavior of individual objects (such as the the specific strategy which must be used to build the reply to be sent to the client, and the transports which are to be used for data transmission and for signaling), and to set system configuration parameters (such as the key length and value, the number of replicas to be launched, the number of threads in the thread pools, and so on).

4.3   Fault Detector

As illustrated in figure 1, in a three tier structure, failures of the back end components represent faults of the middle-tier. We will thus use the terms failure and fault to describe the same phenomenon, depending on the specific observation point used, i.e., the legacy system or the middle-tier server, respectively. The **Fault Detector** is in charge of detecting both Value Faults and Timeout Faults. The concepts of Value Faults and Timeout Faults were defined in section 2.

4.4   Replica Manager

The **Replica Manager** is in charge of enforcing replica consistency, i.e. of ensuring that all replica be in the same state at any time. To this end, it handles the following events:

- *Group view changes* - One or more replicas have failed/have recovered from a failure, and are to be removed from/added to the group of active replicas;
- *Recoveries* - Due to a failure, the state of a replica must be restored, in order to be allow it to be re-integrated in the system at a later time; recovered from a failure, and are to be removed from/added to the group of active replicas;
- *Reconfigurations* - Due to a group view change, the system must modify its operation mode.

The `Gateway` is a key sub-component of the `Replica Manager`, since it wraps the server module of the legacy application, in order to allow the middle-tier to use its functions. Multicast connectivity was achieved by means of Ensemble, an application-level multicast package developed at Cornell University [13]. To this end, the `Gateway` must perform the following tasks:

- It must handle Ensemble multicast communication needed to ensure that all replicas are kept in a consistent state;
- It must handle all synchronization-related issues;
- It must handle all format-related issues. In fact, research has demonstrated that, in order for data comparison procedures to work properly, "smart" data interpretation capabilities are needed [14]. The `Gateway` is thus in charge of purifying the data from application-specific and platform-related dependencies, before data is handed over to the `Adjudicator`.

4.5 Adjudicator

The `Adjudicator` builds a single reply to be sent to the client from the multiple replies of currently available replicas. In order to do so, it interacts with the `Gateway` and with the `Fault Detector`. It determines the reply based on the specific choices made by the administrator via the `Service Manager` interface. Alternative strategies are implemented, which are described in detail in section 5. All strategies are based on threshold mechanisms, but with different values of the threshold.

5   Implementation Details

In this section, we provide technical details about the implementation of the system.

As far as specific technologies are concerned, the middle-tier Server and the client have been developed using Java. Java libraries are also used for SSL communication [16]. We used IAIK [15] Java libraries to handle X509 certificates [17]. The objects communicate over a secure CORBA infrastructure, namely Orbix 2000 with SSL/TLS [18]. The Service Proxy communicates with the client over a protected connection.

5.1 Case Study Application

The case study application is a software module for the execution of crypto-graphic procedures. It is written in C and runs on a Sun Workstation, equipped with Solaris 2.6 OS. The application consists of a client and a server module, which communicate over a TCP socket channel. The client sends the file to be signed to the server. The server computes a digest of the file and signs it with its private key. The algorithm used to compute the message digest is SHA1 [19], and the algorithm used for the digital signature is RSA [20]. For performance reasons, the private key used for signing is kept in RAM. Only the signature is returned to the client.

5.2 Gateway

As already mentioned, the Gateway object is a key sub-component of the Replica Manager. It wraps the server module of the case study application, in order to allow the middle-tier to use its functions. Multicast connectivity was achieved by means of Ensemble [13]. Sub-roles were identified and mapped to two sub-components. These are:

- *Request* - This object encapsulates the request to be sent to the legacy system and provides a post interface which multicasts the request to all replicas, which are currently in the group;
- *Reply* - This object is a list, which contains all replies from individual server replicas;
- *View_state* - This object encapsulates information from Ensemble View.state and View.local records. This information describes the current configuration of the replica group, and it is used by the Adjudicator to decide which actions should be taken.

Since we decided to use Ensemble for multicast communication. We thus had to attach Ensemble to the Gateway object (at one end) and to the server replicas (at the other end). The former task was straightforward: we just had to link the Ensemble library to the Gateway code. The latter task was quite more complex. In fact, the legacy application came with a TCP/IP socket based interface. We had to intercept TCP calls, and redirect them to Ensemble. In order to do so, we developed a virtual device driver within the Solaris Kernel of the node which hosted the legacy server. The overall communication schema is depicted in figure 3.

Solaris 2.6, which derives from Unix System V family, provides a power-ful I/O mechanism, the STREAMS framework [21]. This mechanism consists of a set of system calls, kernel resources, and kernel routines. STREAMS pro-vides an effective environment for kernel services and drivers requiring mod-ularity. The fundamental STREAMS unit is the Stream. A Stream is a full-duplex bi-directional data-transfer path between a process in the user space and a STREAMS driver in the kernel space. It is composed of a Stream head, zero or more modules, and a driver. Data on a Stream are passed in the form of messages. Each Stream's module has its own pair of queues, one for read-ing and one for writing. Queues are the basic elements by which the Stream

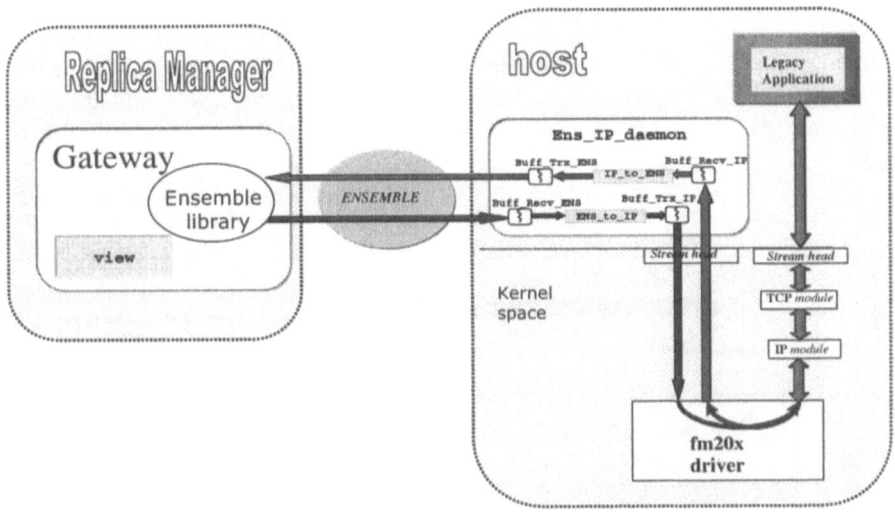

Fig. 3. Communication between the gateway and the group of legacy applications

head, modules, and drivers are connected. We implemented a loop-back pseudo-device driver [22]. Such a driver is able to route messages between two different Streams. More precisely, the driver implements a sort of full-duplex pipe between two Streams: one is attached to an Ensemble-enabled daemon process (namely, Ens_IP_daemon), the other is attached to the legacy application. The Ens_IP_daemon receives and transmits messages using the Ensemble communication library. The legacy application is connected to a virtual IP address which is mapped to the implemented device-driver. In other words, the driver acts as a virtual network interface card for the legacy application.The daemon process, namely Ens_IP_daemon, is structured as a multithreaded process. Two threads, namely Buff_Tx_ENS and Buff_Rx_ENS, are in charge of handling Ensemble communication with the Gateway component and other two threads, namely Buff_Tx_IP and Buff_Rx_IP, are in charge of handling the communication with the pseudo device-driver. The Buff_Rx_ENS thread is responsible of receiving multicast messages sent by the Gateway and the Buff_Tx_ENS is in charge of transmitting packets to the driver. They interact by means of a circular queue, namely ENS_to_IP, according to the producer-consumer paradigm. The Buff_Tx_ENS thread is in charge of transmitting packets to the Gateway by using a UDP unicast communication and the Buff_Rx_ENS thread is in charge of receiving packets from the driver. They interact by means of a circular queue, namely IP_to_ENS, according to the producer-consumer paradigm.

Preliminary experimental results are about the performance of our driver. Tests were executed over a 100 Mbit/s fast-ethernet switched LAN. The Gateway sub-component was on a commodity PC (PIII 800Mhz with 256 Mbyte of RAM) running Linux. The legacy application was on a Sun workstation (Ultra 1 with 128 Mbyte of RAM) running Solaris 2.6. Figure 4 shows the throughput, as a

732 D. Cotroneo et al.

function of the packet size, between the Gateway and the legacy application in the following contexts: i) the Gateway was connected to a single instance of the legacy application replica by means of the standard socket library (plain IP); ii) the Gateway was connected to a single instance of the legacy application replica by means of the Ensemble communication library, and the pseudo-device driver fm20x.

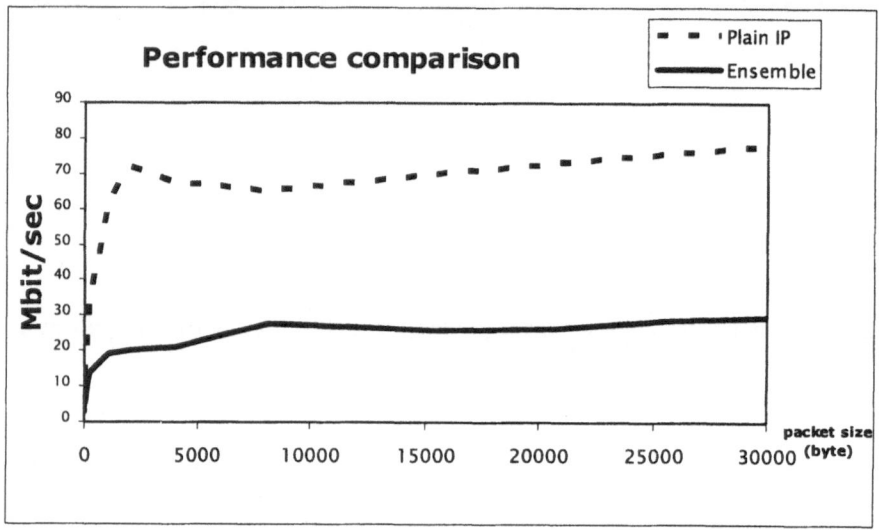

Fig. 4. Performance Comparison

As the figure shows, using the proposed communication scheme has an average throughput of 25 Mbit/sec. against 80 Mbit/sec. for the socket-based communication. It is evident from the results that replicating legacy application is fairly costly. This is not surprising, since we introduced an additional tier in the communication chain and an additional protocol stack (the Stream connected to the driver).

5.3 Replica Manager

The overall architecture of the Replica Manager component is depicted in figure 5.

Server responses are encapsulated in the Reply Object, and sent to the Adjudicator component via the ORB. In order to decouple the communication between the Gateway and the Adjudicator component the CORBA Event service is exploited. The Gateway acts as an event supplier and it adopts a push paradigm, i.e. as soon as it has the Reply it creates an event and sends it to the CORBA Event channel. The Adjudicator acts as an event consumer and it adopts a pull model, i.e. as soon as it has finished to process the previous

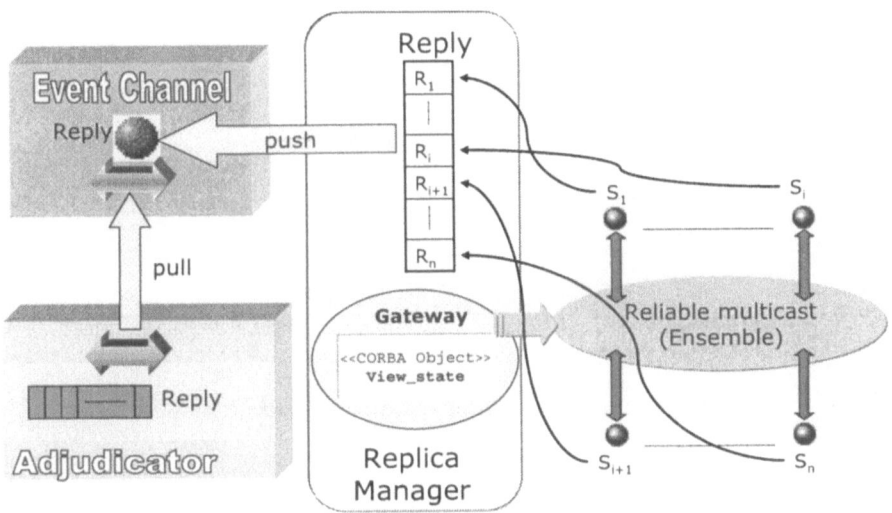

Fig. 5. The Replica Manager component and its interface with the Adjudicator

reply it can retrieve the next one form the CORBA Event channel. Information about the current state of the system is made available to the `Adjudicator` via a CORBA stub of the `View_state` object.

5.4 Adjudicator

The `Adjudicator` component implements two of the functions described in the conceptual system architecture, namely the `Adjudicator` itself and the `Fault Detector`. These functions were implemented in the same component, because they are tightly coupled to each other. The `Adjudicator` has the capability of detecting Value Faults and of building a (hopefully) correct reply to be sent to the client. Figure 6 depicts the implementation the `Adjudicator` component.

It implements two alternative voting strategies: *most dependable* and *fail silent*. The former implements a majority voting scheme. For instance, if the system manages three replicas, it exhibits a 2 out of 3 behavior, i.e. if at least two replicas agree on a value, that value becomes the output of the overall system. By using the latter scheme, the system delivers an output if all units agree on the results, otherwise the system do not exhibit any response at all. In our context, we decided to privilege fail silent behavior, i.e. in the case of a tie, no reply is produced. Fail silent is a preferred failure mode in all applications for which no reply is a better option, as compared to an incorrect reply. We believe security critical applications belong to such a class of applications.

The `Adjudicator` obtains from the CORBA Event Channel the Reply Event Object. Such an object is composed of n responses, $R_1..R_n$. The state of the system is known from the `View_state` Object, held by the `Gateway`. Such an

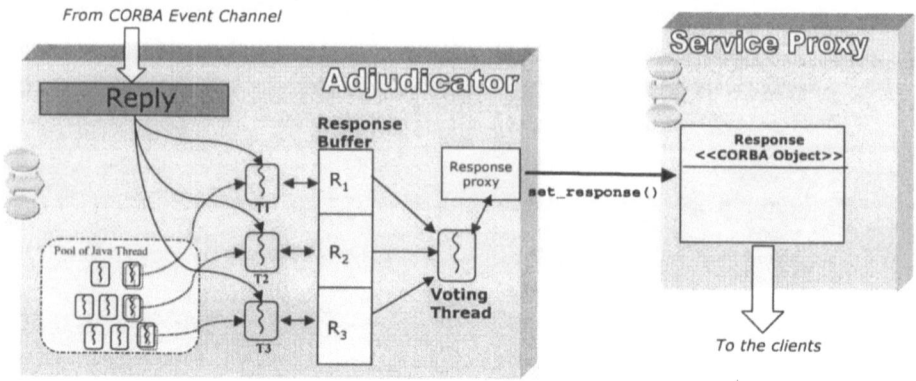

Fig. 6. The Adjudicator component

object can be accessed via the CORBA ORB. The voting process is applied to the n responses which compose the Reply Object.

Since it is expensive to create a new thread for each incoming response, a pool of Java Threads is created at initialization time. A Java Thread is then assigned on the fly to each response. The administrator can set the number of threads which make up the pool. This should be done in accordance with the characteristics of the hardware platform. As an example, on systems where memory is scarce, it is better to limit the number of threads in the pool. Figure 6 describes the voting process of the Adjudicator Component in the case of the Reply Event Object is composed of three responses, and three is also the number of replicas currently in the system. Three threads are allocated from the pool and they are in charge of getting responses from the Reply object and copying them in the Response Buffer. As soon as they are done, the component is ready to pull another Reply object. The Voting Thread is in charge of implementing the adjudication strategy, according to the settings performed by the administrator via the Service Manager interface . As soon as the voting has been done, the voting thread sets the Response via the ORB, calling setresponse() method on the Reponse CORBA stub, which acts as a stub for the Response CORBA Object. A sort of pipeline is so set-up between the Gateway, which push Reply Objects, and the Service Proxy, which delivers the Response to the client.

6   Conclusions and Future Work

This work presented an implementation technique, which relies on a CORBA-based Multi-Tier architecture, capable of adding security to an existing legacy application. The proposed technique is ideally suited for cost-effective development of secure/high-available applications where backward compatibility is an issue.

A system prototype has been developed and tested on a distributed heterogeneous platform. The prototype incorporates a legacy cryptographic application module and replicates it. Security is achieved by means of the business logic of the Middle Tier component. The legacy software is integrated in the new system without changing it at all. By doing so, legacy services are delivered at a higher security level - as compared to one of the original application- in a transparent way.

As far as development costs are concerned, our experience suggests that this approach makes it possible to: i) improve the security of the delivered service in a transparent way, since the service has a polymorph implementation of a unified interface , and ii) minimize the development effort, since full reuse of existing software is achieved. The objective of future activity will be thorough evaluation of the effectiveness of the approach, both in terms of fault resilience and performance. To this aim, we plan to conduct massive fault injection experiments.

Acknowledgements. This work has been partially carried out under the financial support of Italian Ministry for University and Science and Technology Research (MURST)within the project "MUSIQUE: Infrastructure for QoS in Web Multimedia Services with Heterogeneous Access" and "LABNET 2". Authors want to acknowledge the contribution of Andrea Bondavalli for his suggestions and comments.

References

1. Y. Deswarte, K. Kanoun, and J. C. Laprie, "Diversity against Accidental and Deliberate faults", in Computer Security, Dependability, and Assurance, P. Amman, B.H. Barnes, S. Jajodia, E.H. Sibley, eds, IEEE Computer Society Press, 1999
2. D. Atkins, et al., "Internet Security Professional Reference". 2nd edn. New Riders Publishing, Indianapolis, 1997
3. J. C. Laprie, "Dependable Computing and Fault Tolerance: Concepts and Terminology", in *Proc. of 15th International Symposium on Fault Tolerant Computing*,IEEE Computer Society,, pp. 2-11, Ann Arbor, MI, 1985.
4. Z.T. Kalbarczyk, S. Bagchi, K. Whisnant, and R.K. Iyer, "Chameleon: A software Infrastructure for Adaptive Fault Tolerance", in *IEEE Transactions on Parallel and Distributed Systems*, vol.10, no.6, June 1999.
5. L.E. Moser, P.M. Melliar-Smith, P. Narasimhan, L. Tewksbury and V. Kalogeraki, "The Eternal System: An Architecture for Enterprise Applications", in *Proc. of International Enterprise Distributed Object Computing Conference* ,University of Mannheim, Germany (September 1999), pp. 214-222
6. K.K. Goswami, R.K. Iyer, "Simulation of Software Behavior Under Hardware Faults", in *Proc. of the 23rd Annual International Symposium on Fault-Tolerant Computing*, Toulouse, France, June 1993.
7. John D. Howard, An Analysis of Security Incidents on the Internet 1989-1995, Apr. 1997, Pittsburgh, Pennsylvania, USA.
   http://www.cert.org/research/JHThesis/Start.html
8. R. Han, D. Messerschmitt, A progressively reliable transport protocol for interactive wireless multimedia, in Multimedia Systems 7: pp. 141–156, 1999
9. M. Cukier et al., "AQuA: An Adaptive Architecture that Provides Dependable Distributed Objects", in *Proc. of the 17th IEEE Symposium on Reliable Distributed Systems (SRDS'98)*, West Lafayette, Indiana, USA, October 23, 1998, pp. 245–253.

10. P. Narasimhan, L. E. Moser, P.M. Melliar-Smith, "Replica Consistency of Objects in Partitionable Distributed Systems", in *Distributed Systems Engineering*, vol.4, no.3, September 1997, pp. 139–150.

11. J.C. Fabre and T. Pèrennou, "A Metaobject Architecture for Fault-Tolerant Distributed Systems: The FRIENDS Approach",in *IEEE Transactions on Computers*, vol. 47, no. 1, January 1998.

12. P. Felber, R. Guerraoui, A. Schiper, "The Implementation of a Object Group Service", in *Theory and Practice of Object Systems (TAPOS)*,Wiley&Sons, Vol. 4, No. 2, 1998.

13. Ken Birman, Robert Constable, Mark Hayden, Christopher Kreitz, Ohad Rodeh, Robbert van Renesse, Werner Vogels,The Horus and Ensemble Projects: Accomplishments and Limitations, in Proceedings of the DARPA Information Survivability Conference & Exposition (DISCEX '00), January 25-27 2000 in Hilton Head, South Carolina

14. D.E. Bakken, Z. Zhan, C.C. Jones, D.A. Karr, Middleware Support for Voting and Data Fusion, in: The 2001 International Conference on Dependable Systems and Networks, IEEE-CS, 2001, pp. 453–462.

15. Institute for Applied Information Processing and Communications, March 2001 http://jcewww.iaik.tu-graz.ac.at/jce/jce.htm.

16. IONA Technologies PLC, "Orbix 2000 SSL/TLS Programmer's Guide". December 2000 available on http://www.iona.com.

17. R. Housley, W. Ford, W. Polk, D. Solo, Internet X.509 Public Key Infrastructure Certificate and CRL Profile, RFC 2459, January 1999.

18. IONA Technologies PLC, "Orbix 2000 Programmer's Guide Java Edition". December 2000 available on http://www.iona.com.

19. National Institute of Standards and Technology: Secure Hash Standard, FIPS PUB 180-1, Federal Information Processing Standards Pubblication, 1995 (available online at http://www.itl.nist.gov/fipspubs/fips180-1.htm)

20. R. Rivest, The MD5 Message-Digest Algorithm, RFC 1321, MIT LCS & RSA Data Security Inc., April 1992.

21. Uresh Vahalia, UNIX Internals, The new frontiers, Prentice Hall International, 1996.

22. Driver Developer Site AnswerBook, Solaris 2.6 Writing Device Driver, SunSoft Inc, Mountain View CA., 1997 (http://docs.sun.com).

Reconciling Replication and Transactions for the End-to-End Reliability of CORBA Applications

Pascal Felber[1] and Priya Narasimhan[2]

[1] Institut EURECOM, 2229 route des Crêtes, BP 193
06904 Sophia Antipolis, France
`pascal.felber@eurecom.fr`
[2] ISRI, School of Computer Science, Carnegie Mellon University
Pittsburgh, PA 15213-3890
`priya@cs.cmu.edu`

Abstract. The CORBA standard now incorporates support for reliability through two distinct mechanisms — replication (using the Fault Tolerant CORBA standard) and transactions (using the CORBA Object Transaction Service). Transactions represent a roll-back reliability mechanism, and handle a fault by reverting to the last committed state, and by discarding operations that were in progress at the time of the fault. Replication represents a roll-forward reliability mechanism, and handles a fault by re-playing any operations that were in progress at another operational replica of the crashed server. Most of today's enterprise applications have a three-tier structure, with simple clients in the first tier, servers in the middle-tier to perform the processing, and databases in the third tier to store information. For such applications, replication is required to protect the middle-tier processing, while transactions are required to protect the third-tier data. This requires the reconciliation of roll-forward and roll-back reliability mechanisms in order to protect both data and processing, and to provide consistent end-to-end reliable operation. This paper looks at the issues of integrating replication with transactions for three-tier enterprise CORBA applications, with particular emphasis on reconciling the Fault Tolerant CORBA standard and the CORBA Object Transaction Service.

1 Introduction

The emergence of Internet-based enterprise computing and Web-based electronic commerce has led to the development of system architectures with advanced features to address technical and quality-of-service (QoS) issues such as security, data integrity, high-availability, reliability, scalability, atomicity, and session management. Reliability, in particular, forms the cornerstone of every enterprise, with the market becoming increasingly intolerant of downtime, and with enterprise server crashes leading to bad publicity, prohibitive financial losses, reduction in stock prices, and loss of customers. With its adverse impact on the economy [4] and on our quality of life, the lack of fault tolerance is increasingly

R. Meersman, Z. Tari (Eds.): CoopIS/DOA/ODBASE 2002, LNCS 2519, pp. 737–754, 2002.

more unacceptable, particularly for enterprise applications. Therefore, continuous perceived uptime and reliability are key requirements of electronic commerce servers.

There are several approaches to providing fault tolerance. Hardware redundancy solutions are insufficient because they focus primarily on detecting, and tolerating, hardware defects. Enterprise systems contain a lot of software, for the most part, and use both hardware and software components that can fail, thereby disrupting service. To provide the necessary degree of availability, these systems must use hot swappable components (to replace a failed component on-the-fly with a working component) and failover (to switch all clients to working with the replaced component, instead of the old failed one). There are two distinct aspects of fault tolerance for enterprise systems — protection of the data and protection of the processing (operations that are in progress) when a fault occurs. To protect against the loss or the corruption of data, databases and transaction processing systems are often employed. To protect against the loss of operations or processing, the servers that perform the processing are often replicated, so that there exist redundant servers to perform the computing and redundant network resources for running the distributed application.

Most of today's enterprise applications have a three-tier structure, with simple front-end clients (usually browsers) in the first tier, servers (business logic) in the middle-tier to perform the processing, and databases and legacy applications in the third tier to store information. Different technologies form the basis for each of the three tiers — for instance, application servers are usually the environment of choice for the middle-tier business logic components. The architecture of most enterprise applications is based on client-server middleware, where a client requests services across the network, and a server performs the services and returns results to the client.

Middleware platforms such as the Common Object Request Broker Architecture (CORBA) [8] are increasingly being adopted because they simplify client-server application programming by rendering transparent the low-level details of networking, distribution, physical location, hardware, operating systems, and byte order. However, despite their many attractive features, middleware platforms have still not found favor for deployment in applications that have high reliability requirements. Recognizing this deficiency, the Object Management Group (OMG), the CORBA standards body, has attempted to incorporate specifications for reliability into the CORBA middleware standard. The reliability support within CORBA takes two different forms: (i) the CORBA Object Transaction Service (OTS) [10], and (ii) the recently adopted Fault Tolerant CORBA (FT-CORBA) standard [9].

Unfortunately, both of these specifications were developed independently, and it is, in fact, difficult to reconcile replications and transactions in general. The reason for this is that replication represents a *roll-forward* mechanism, where a fault (crash of a server) is tolerated by switching over to a backup replica of the server, and re-doing, or moving forward with, the operations in progress at the failed server. On the other hand, transactions represent a *roll-back* mechanism, where the crash of a server is tolerated by discarding all of the operations in progress at the failed server, and by reverting to the last well-known, or committed, state persisted in a database. Clearly, the focus of each reliability mechanism differs — transactions focus on protecting data, while replication focuses on protecting processing. Stated another way, a roll-forward mechanism promotes *liveness*, while a roll-back mechanism promotes *safety*.

For true reliability, enterprise applications clearly require elements of both roll-forward and roll-back reliability strategies, in order to protect *both* data and processing. In fact, each of the two complementary strategies stands to benefit greatly from the other. However, in today's state-of-the-art and state-of-the-practice, this is challenging to achieve.

There exist two orthogonal, but equally essential, properties in building mission-critical distributed systems: *availability* and *consistency*. Availability provides clients with the abstraction of a continuous service, despite the failure of some server components, and is generally achieved using the replication of critical resources, so that the failure of the copy of a critical component can be masked by another copy. Consistency guarantees informally that the system will always remain in a coherent state, despite the occurrence of faults. The partial execution of an operation might lead to the violation of the consistency property. For instance, when money is transferred from one bank account to another, the system is in an incoherent state if the money is withdrawn from the source account, but not deposited in the destination account. Consistency is generally maintained through the use of transactional facilities. By integrating replication and transactions, we can achieve two additional objectives: we provide stronger consistency to replicated systems by supporting non-deterministic operation, and we provide higher availability and failure transparency to transactional systems.

In this paper, we explore the underlying problems in composing the roll-forward capability provided by replication with the roll-back capability provided by transactional systems, in order to achieve end-to-end reliability for distributed enterprise CORBA systems. We have chosen CORBA as our vehicle for exploring the research problems of integrating replication and transactions because of our prior experience[1] with building replication-based CORBA systems, and also because CORBA is unique in being the only middleware that currently incorporates specifications for both replication (FT-CORBA) and transactions (OTS). It is our hope that the ideas in this paper will lay the foundations for reconciling these two separate specifications and, thereby, for deriving more powerful capability by combining FT-CORBA with OTS. It is not our intention, in this paper, to invent novel protocols, but rather to present a pragmatic approach for leveraging the best of the transactional and replication worlds, and for combining their power to achieve both reliability and availability for critical CORBA applications.

---

[1] The co-authors of this paper have independently developed fault-tolerant CORBA systems [2,7], well before the FT-CORBA standard was approved. In addition, both co-authors have contributed to, and participated in, the FT-CORBA standardization process.

The rest of this paper is organized as follows: Section 2 introduces the necessary background concepts, and presents the fundamental system models that
we consider in the rest of this paper. Section 3 describes and compares roll-back
and roll-forward reliability in greater detail. Section 4 outlines our novel scheme
for integrating the best of the FT-CORBA and the OTS mechanisms to achieve
end-to-end availability and consistency. Section 5 discusses other research efforts that are relevant to our work in this area. Finally, Section 6 presents some
concluding remarks.

2   Background

The architectures that form the focus of this paper are three-tier distributed
enterprise middleware applications. Thin first-tier clients communicate with application servers that implement the application's logic, typically using a middleware component model such as Enterprise JavaBeans (EJB) [14] or the CORBA
Component Model (CCM) [11]. These middle-tier servers are transactional and
have access to back-end systems, which are typically highly available parallel
database servers. Figure 1 illustrates such a three-tier configuration in which
multiple application servers are used to process requests from possibly thousands of thin clients.

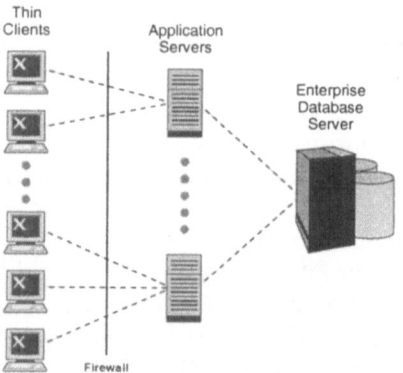

Fig. 1. A Typical Three-tier Architecture

Although communication between clients and servers can happen over various
protocols, such as HTTP, HTTP/S, RMI-IIOP or SSL, in this paper, the focus
is on the use of CORBA for distributed first-to-second tier client-server interactions. Similarly, we assume that communication between the middle-tier application servers and the third-tier database system are performed using CORBA.
Thus, for the rest of this text, we assume that the communication between the
various tiers of this distributed client-server architecture occurs over CORBA's

Internet Inter-ORB Protocol (IIOP). However, the mechanisms discussed in this paper are generic, and can be readily extended to other middleware and protocols, as well as to additional levels of nesting (n-tier architectures).

In the rest of this section, we describe the current support for transactions and fault tolerance within the CORBA standard.

2.1 The CORBA Object Transaction Service

CORBA incorporates support for roll-back reliability through the Object Transaction Service (OTS) [10]. OTS forms a part of the rich suite of services (such as Naming, Events, Notification, etc.) that CORBA incorporates, and that vendors provide, in order to free CORBA programmers from having to write such commonly-used functionality themselves.

OTS essentially specifies interfaces for synchronizing a transaction across the elements of a distributed client-server application, as shown in Figure 2. A transaction satisfies the four so-called ACID properties: Atomicity, i.e., transactions executes completely or not at all; Consistency, i.e., transactions are a correct transformation of state; Isolation, i.e., even though transactions execute concurrently, it appears for each transaction, T, that other transactions execute either before T, or after T, but not both; and Durability, i.e., modifications performed by completed transactions survive failures.

In OTS, a transaction is typically initiated by a client, and can involve multiple objects performing multiple requests. The scope of the transaction is defined by a transaction context, which is shared by the participating objects. The transaction context is logically bound to the thread of the client that initiated the transaction, and is implicitly associated with subsequent requests that the client issues, until the client decides to terminate the transaction. If no fault occurs for the duration of the transaction, the changes produced as a consequence of the client's requests are committed, or preserved, in accordance with the durability property above. In case a fault occurs during the transaction, any changes to data that have occurred within the duration and scope of the current transaction are rolled back and discarded.

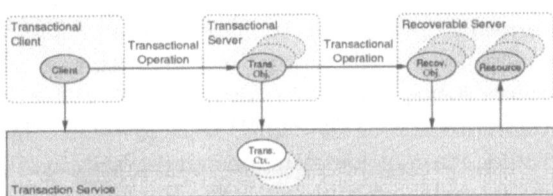

Fig. 2. Architectural Overview of OTS

Apart from the transactional client and the transaction context, a distributed transaction typically involves three other kinds of objects — transactional, recoverable and resource objects. *Transactional objects* are CORBA objects whose behavior and/or state is affected by being invoked within the scope of a transaction (e.g., objects that refer to persistent data that can be modified by transactional requests). *Recoverable objects* are transactional objects that explicitly participate in the transaction service protocols. They do so by registering *resource objects* with the OTS which, in turn, drives the commit protocol by issuing requests to the resources registered for the transaction. Transactional (recoverable) objects are hosted in transactional (recoverable) servers, which participate to the two-phase commit protocol executed upon completion of a distributed transaction.

OTS implements roll-back reliability in the sense that the effect of the requests issued in the context of a failed transaction are undone on all recoverable servers. Roll-back might be implicitly triggered on the occurrence of a fault, or explicitly requested by a transactional object. Upon roll-back, the client might re-try the transaction or take some other appropriate action.

2.2   The Fault-Tolerant CORBA Standard

Support for roll-forward reliability in CORBA is provided by the recently adopted fault-tolerant CORBA (FT-CORBA) [9] specification. FT-CORBA implements reliability by replicating critical objects: if a server replica fails while processing a client's request, then another replica can take over the processing of the request, generally without the client noticing the failure.

The FT-CORBA specification includes minimal fault-tolerant mechanisms to be included in any CORBA implementation, as well as interfaces for more advanced management facilities intended to be provided by a fault-tolerant CORBA implementation. FT-CORBA implementors are free to use proprietary mechanisms (such as reliable multicast protocols) for their actual implementation, as long as the resulting system complies with the interfaces defined in the specification, and the behavior expected from those interfaces.

The client-side mechanisms to be included in all CORBA implementations — regardless of whether they implement FT-CORBA or not — have been intentionally kept minimal. They essentially specify object references that can contain multiple profiles, each of which designates a replica (multi-profile IORs[2]), and simple rules for iterating through the profiles in case of failure. These mechanisms ensure that unreplicated clients can interact with replicated FT-CORBA servers in a fault-tolerant manner.

The server-side components of FT-CORBA are shown in Figure 3. The Replication Manager handles the creation, deletion and replication of both the application objects and the infrastructure objects. The Replication Manager replicates objects and distributes the replicas across the system. Although each replica of

---

[2] An Interoperable Object Reference (IOR) is a standardized form of a reference to a CORBA object, and can contains one or more profiles. Each profile contains sufficient information to contact the object using some protocol, usually TCP/IP; this information often includes the host name, port number, and object key associated with the CORBA object.

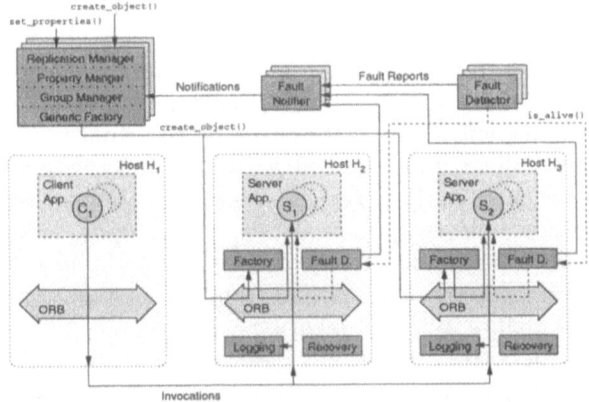

Fig. 3. Architectural Overview of FT-CORBA

an object has an individual object reference, the Replication Manager fabricates an object group reference that clients use to contact the replicated object. The Replication Manager's functionality is achieved through the Property Manager, the Generic Factory, and the Object Group Manager.

Host, process, and object faults are detected by the Fault Detector. The occurrence of faults are reported to the Fault Notifier, which filters them and distributes fault event notifications to the Replication Manager. Based on these notifications, the Replication Manager initiates appropriate actions to enable the system to recover from faults.

3   Reliability Strategies

In this section, we compare the replication-based and transaction-based reliability strategies introduced in the previous section, with particular focus on their respective benefits and drawbacks.

3.1   Replication-Based Reliability

Replication is intended at protecting computational resources through the use of redundancy: if a processor fails, then another processor can take over the processing of the failed processor.

In distributed systems, the two best-known replication styles are *active* [13] and *primary-backup* [1] (or *passive*) replication. A replicated object is often represented by an object group, with the replicas of the object forming the members of the group. The object group membership may be static or dynamic. Static membership implies that the number, and the identity, of the replicas do not change over the lifetime of the replicated object; on the other hand, dynamic replication allows replicas to be added or removed at run-time.

With active replication, all of the replicas of the object play the same role: every active replica receives each request, processes it, updates its state, and sends a response back to the client. Because the client's invocations are always sent to, and processed by, every server replica, the failure of any of the server replicas can be made transparent to the client. With primary-backup replication, one of the server replicas is designated as the primary, while all of the other replicas serve as backups. A client typically sends its request only to the primary, which executes the request, updates it own state, updates the states of the backups, and sends the response to the client. The periodic state updates from the primary to the backups serve to synchronize the states of all of the server replicas at specific points in their execution.

Replication implements *roll-forward* recovery mechanisms that promote liveness by continuing processing where it had been left at the time of the failure. In active replication, in the event of a fault (one of the active replicas crashes), the other replicas continue processing the current request, regardless, thereby implicitly implementing a roll-forward mechanism. In primary-backup replication, in the event of a fault (the primary replica crashes), one of the backup replicas takes over as the new primary and re-processes any requests that the previous primary was performing before it failed. If a backup replica crashes, then, there is no loss in processing. Thus, the roll-forward mechanism is explicitly implemented in the re-election of a new primary replica, and the re-processing of requests by the new primary. Consistency is maintained for both active and primary-backup replication by guaranteeing that partial request execution will not harm since the request will be eventually completed (by "rolling forward").

A major limitation of replication-based system is that consistency may not be preserved in the presence of non-determinism. Indeed, a frequent assumption in building replicated CORBA systems is that each CORBA object is deterministic in behavior. Determinism implies that if distinct distributed replicas of the object, starting from the same initial state, receive and process the same set of operations in the same order, they will all reach the same final state. It is this reproducible behavior of the application that lends itself so well to reliability. Unfortunately, pure deterministic behavior is rather difficult to achieve, except for very simple applications. Common sources of non-determinism include the use of local timers, multi-threading, operating system-specific calls, processor-specific functions, shared memory primitives, etc.

Non-deterministic behavior is an inevitable and challenging problem in the development of fault-tolerant systems. For active replication, determinism is crucial to maintaining the consistency of the states of the replicas of the object. Passive replication is often perceived to be the solution for non-deterministic applications. There is some truth in this perception because, with passive replication, invocations are processed only by the primary, and the primary's state is captured and then used to update the states of the backup replicas. If the primary fails while processing an invocation, any partial execution is discarded, and the invocation is processed afresh by the new primary. Because the state updates happen only at one of the replicas, namely, at the primary replica, the results of any non-deterministic behavior of the replicated object are completely contained, and do not wreak havoc with the consistency of the object.

There exist situations, however, where passive replication is not sufficient to deal with non-determinism. This is particularly true of scenarios where the non-deterministic behavior of a passively replicated object is not contained because the behavior has "leaked" to other replicated objects in the system. Consider the case where the primary replica invokes another server object based on some non-deterministic decision (e.g., for load balancing, the primary replica randomly chooses one of n servers to process a credit-card transaction). If the primary replica fails after issuing the invocation, there is no guarantee that the new primary will select the same server as the old primary; thus, the system will now be in an inconsistent state because the old and the new primary replicas have communicated with different servers, both of whose states might be updated.

For passive replication to resolve non-deterministic behavior, there should be no persistent effect (i.e., no lingering "leakage" of non-determinism) resulting from the partial execution of an invocation by a failed replica. This is possible if the passively replicated object does not access external components based on non-deterministic inputs, or if all accesses are performed in the context of a transaction aborted upon failure. Sources of non-determinism (such as thread scheduling) can also be controlled by careful programming. In general, however, passive replication is no cure for non-determinism.

3.2 Transaction-Based Reliability

Unlike replication, transaction processing systems essentially aim at protecting data. When a failure occurs in the context of a transaction, the objects involved in the transaction are reverted to their state just prior to the beginning of the transaction. All of the state updates and all of the processing that occurred during the transaction are discarded, often with no trace left in the system. Some systems support nested transactions, where a new (child) transaction can be initiated within the scope of an existing (parent) transaction. If the nested (child) transaction fails, the enclosing (parent) transaction needs not automatically roll back; the application can attempt to correct the problem, and subsequently retry the nested transaction. However, if the enclosing transaction encounters a fault, then all the nested transactions roll back, along with the enclosing transaction.

Transactions use roll-back recovery mechanisms that guarantee consistency by undoing partial request processing. Data is protected from the undesirable side-effects of failures, but computational resources may become unavailable for arbitrary durations. Transactions are thus an effective mechanism for preserving consistency, but not for achieving high availability, as they sometimes trade liveness for safety.

3.3 Roll-Back vs. Roll-Forward

Consider a simple three-tier bank application. A client C issues a transfer request to a passively replicated bank object B, which in turn withdraw money from a bank account X and deposit it on another account Y (see Figure 4). The bank is essentially a stateless object that coordinates the money transfer between stateful bank account objects, typically hosted in a database server. As the data

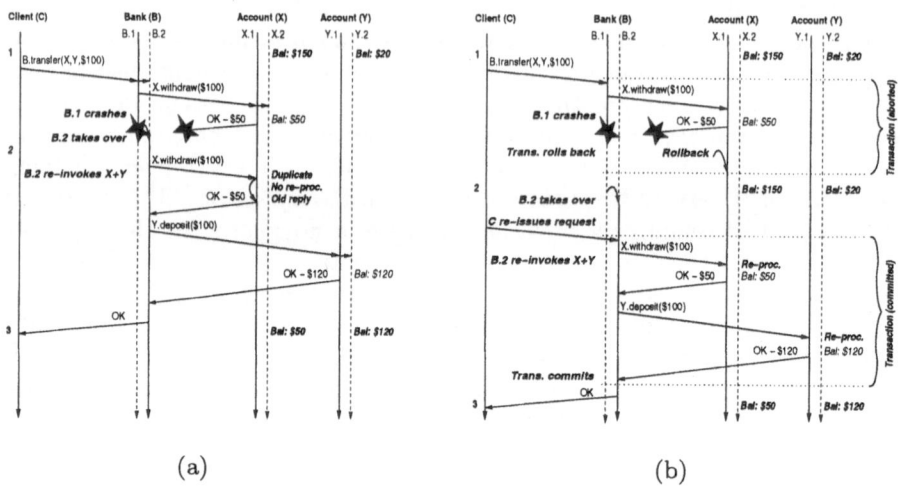

Fig. 4. Reliability in Multi-tier Applications. (a) Roll-forward. (b) Roll-back.

pertaining to the bank accounts is possibly managed by distinct entities, e.g., different branches, the account objects execute on different servers and are not co-located with the bank object. Any of the bank or account objects can therefore fail independently.

If the primary bank object B_1 fails while performing a transfer, neither the invoker C, nor the backup B_2 generally know at what point B_1 failed — whether it was before/while invoking X, between invocations to X and Y, or after/while invoking Y. Roll-forward and roll-back reliability strategies adopt two approaches to address this problem, as illustrated in Figure 4, where the flow of requests/replies is represented by arrows, and the flow of time occurs downward, toward the bottom of the figure.

With roll-forward reliability strategies, invocations are traditionally sent using reliable multicast (also known as reliable group communication), so that all of the replicas of an object receive every request. This is evident in an active replication configuration, where a client does not need to re-issue the request if one of the active server replicas fails (in fact, the client is typically not even aware of this failure). In a primary-backup setting, when the primary has finished processing a request, it multicasts both the response and a state update to the backups before returning the response to the client. The state update allows the backups to synchronize their state with that of the primary. The response is also cached by the backups for retrieval, should the primary fail. If the primary fails, then a backup assumes the role of the new primary transparently. If the primary fails before returning a response to the client, the client will re-issue the request to one of the backups (now the new primary); if the new primary has a cached response and the last state update of the old primary, it can readily return a response; if it doesn't have the cached response, it will re-process the request.

In Figure 4 (a), B_1 fails after having successfully invoked X, but before invoking Y and replying to C. When taking over as the new primary, B_2 does not know when B_1 failed, and it re-processes the request. If we assume that objects have a deterministic behavior, B_2 will re-invoke X and Y. Unless these invocations are idempotent (i.e., repeated executions of the invocation leave the state of the invoked object unaltered), re-processing these requests will corrupt the state of X. Thus, such duplicate processing of requests should not be allowed to occur. To guarantee this behavior, using FT-CORBA, the invoker embeds a request identifier within each request. This identifier is used at the invoked server X to detect a duplicate invocation, and to return previously cached replies instead of re-processing the entire request. The invocation to Y is normally processed and, finally, B_2 sends a reply to C. Note that, for C, the server moves from one consistent state (1) to another consistent state (3); the intermediary inconsistent state (2) is note exposed to C.

With roll-back reliability strategies, an invocation is typically sent using point-to-point communication and, upon failure of the invoked server, all effects of the invocation are first wiped out from the system, and the invoker then re-issues the request to a backup server. This retransmission is generally performed transparently by the middleware infrastructure, without the knowledge of the client application. However, the roll-back phase of the recovery requires mechanisms to enable a component to undo some changes to its state, and any effects of processing an invocation, in order to avoid inconsistencies. This can be achieved using transactional facilities to reset the component to a previous well-known committed state if the transaction aborts.

Roll-back becomes more interesting when the participants in the transaction are distributed entities. In such distributed transactions, it is possible to roll back the actions even on remote components that have been invoked in the context of the transaction. In Figure 4 (b), B_1 starts a new transaction before processing the request from C, and fails just after having successfully invoked X. Since B_1 did not commit the transaction, the actions performed on X as part of this transaction are undone, and the state of the system (i.e., the balance of the accounts) is reset to what it was prior to the the invocation of B_1. With this roll-back strategy, the entire invocation sub-chain whose root is the crashed object is reverted to its previous consistent state. Since C does not receive a reply, it eventually re-issues the request to B_2. If no fault occurs, invocations to X and Y are then processed normally, and a reply is returned to C. Note that, if C does not re-issue its request, the server will be left in a consistent state (2), identical to the initial state (1); after re-invocation, the server reaches a consistent final state (3).

Because of their potential for faster recovery (there is no roll-back phase prior to the retry-recovery phase), roll-forward approaches are well suited to systems that have real-time requirements or that need predictable response times, such as embedded systems or supervision and control applications. In particular, when roll-forward recovery is used with active replication, recovery time can be significantly faster than with roll-back recovery. On the other hand, roll-back approaches are well adapted to transactional systems where the integrity of data far outranks the recovery time, such as electronic commerce and banking applications.

Because each reliability strategies have distinct properties, critical distributed application can significantly benefit from combining their particular strengths (strong consistency with transactions and high availability with replication) while simultaneously alleviating their respective limitations (deterministic behavior with replications and unpredictable response time with transactions).

4   Combining Replication and Transactions

In this section, we outline a protocol to provide end-to-end reliability between clients and replicated servers. It supports non-deterministic servers and nested invocations, and can be used in transactional environments, such as enterprise application servers. Although we illustrate this protocol in the context of a three-tier architecture, it extends naturally to n-tier systems.

With this protocol, the client can issue a request (remote invocation) to a "highly available" server. The outcome of the request is preserved, despite the failure of the client, network, or server. In the event of a failure, the client can re-issue the same request to obtain a reply, without worrying about duplicate processing and its potential for the corruption of the server state.

The protocol makes use of FT-CORBA and OTS to replicate computational resources and to maintain consistency. It also assumes that servers have access to a logging infrastructure — similar to the logging mechanisms specified by FT-CORBA — for storing, and retrieving, information. The log must be accessible by all the replicas of an object and support transactional operation. It can be implemented by various mechanisms, such as a database, or communication primitives that guarantee atomic exchange of data among replicas at commit time.

The important feature of this architecture is the fact that the middle-tier servers perform the core processing, and initiate transactions on the third-tier database servers, which store and persist the data. We exploit the FT-CORBA infrastructure to handle the server replication and client-side failover. We then exploit the OTS mechanisms to enable the servers to perform their processing (to handle a client request) in the scope of nested transactions that they initiate. Thus, as emphasized in the following sections, we "marry" the best of the OTS and FT-CORBA mechanisms to achieve end-to-end reliability and availability all the way from the first-tier client to the third-tier database.

4.1   Client-Side Mechanisms

Server objects are passively replicated and hosted by an FT-CORBA infrastructure. A replicated server is represented by a multi-profile CORBA Interoperable Object Reference (IOR), with each profile enumerating the address (host name, port number, object key) of a server replica. A non-replicated first-tier client addresses the middle-tier primary server replica using this fault-tolerant object reference.

On its part, the client does not need to perform any additional processing, apart from conforming to the client-side FT-CORBA specification. According to the FT-CORBA standard, the client-side ORB runtime first invokes the primary server replica. If the primary is suspected to have failed, then, the client-side ORB runtime transparently iterates through the addresses contained in the multi-profile IOR, invoking each address in search of an operational server replica.

A `ServiceContext` field,[3] embedded within the request by the client-side ORB runtime, contains a unique request identifier that permits the middle-tier servers to detect if the request is a duplicate, i.e., it has been seen before. This allows the server-side ORB runtimes to detect, and discard, duplicate requests and, therefore, to prevent the server state from being corrupted. Note that the client's invocation does *not* need to execute in the context of a transaction, or use OTS at all (thereby eliminating the need for embedding transactional service context within the client's request). Thus, the only service context information carried in the request from the first-tier to the middle-tier is that for FT-CORBA duplicate-request detection.

4.2   Server-Side Mechanisms

On the server side, the protocol relies on OTS and FT-CORBA to achieve both consistency and availability. Consistency is implemented not only through the OTS' mechanisms, but also through the server-side fault-tolerant ORB runtime. If a client mistakenly invokes a backup replica (rather than the primary replica), the server-side FT-CORBA runtime intercepts the request (before it reaches the server replica), and transparently notifies the client of the primary's identity using a LOCATION_FORWARD reply message. The client-side ORB runtime can use the address embedded within that message to contact the real primary replica. The client request is never executed on a non-primary replica, thereby ensuring that the states of the server replicas are not rendered inconsistent by accidental diversion of requests to the wrong server replica.

On receiving a request from a first-tier client, the primary first checks in the log to see if the request has already been processed (the unique duplicate-detection context embedded in the client's request is used precisely for this purpose). If the current client request is a duplicate, the primary returns the previously generated (and cached) reply. If this is a fresh non-duplicate request, the primary server replica initiates an OTS transaction. Note that, in a multi-tier architecture, this might be a nested transaction, if the incoming request was already part of another transaction. The scope of the transaction encloses all the operations performed by the replica, including any interactions with other components.

The client's request is then processed within the scope of this server-initiated transaction. By hosting the middle-tier servers over an FT-CORBA infrastruc-

---

[3] CORBA allows a client to propagate additional information to the server, in order to influence the processing of a specific invocation. This additional information is embedded into the `ServiceContext` field of an IIOP invocation message, and is interpreted by the server-side ORB runtime.

ture that is OTS-enabled, the servers can initiate transactions, while benefiting from the FT-CORBA mechanisms. This allows us to handle both stateless and stateful servers in the middle-tier, as opposed to most three-tier enterprise architectures, which typically handle only stateless servers. If the server object is stateful, then, the state (or state update) is retrieved from the primary replica through the `Checkpointable` (or `Updateable`) interface that every object must support, according to the FT-CORBA standard. This state is written to the log, together with the response for the client. The replica then commits the transaction and returns the response to the client.

If the primary fails before committing, the transaction rolls back and undoes all of the operations performed by the failed replica (the complete invocation chain whose root is the failed primary is "rolled back", including data written to the log). If the primary fails after committing, the reply is available at the backup replicas, one of which is elected as the new primary and will return this reply if the invocation is encountered again.

This protocol applies recursively to further tiers. Thanks to the use of nested transactions, a failure can be contained into just one branch of the invocation tree and a roll-forward strategy can be used within the scope of that branch.

This scheme is best illustrated by an example. Consider the bank application introduced in Section 3.3. Figure 5 shows a run of the protocol with two failures. The client C first sends a transfer request to the replicated bank object B. The primary replica, B_1, starts an transaction TX_1 and sends a request for withdrawal to account X. In turn, the primary replica of the account, X_1, starts a transactions $TX_{1.1}$ nested within TX_1, performs the withdrawal, logs the state update and the response, commits the transaction, and returns the response to B_1, which fails before receiving the response. As B_1 fails before committing TX_1, the transaction rolls back. As a consequence, nested transaction $TX_{1.1}$ also rolls back and the state of the account is reverted to its previous value. At the time B_2 takes over, the global state of the system is consistent thanks to the roll-back recovery mechanism of OTS.

The client runtime of the FT ORB at C detects the failure of B_1 and transparently re-issue the transfer request to the second profile in the IOR, B_2. This roll-forward mechanism effectively shields the client from the failure of the server. B_2 notices that the transfer request has not yet been processed — there is no associated entry in the log. Therefore, B_2 initiates a new top-level transaction TX_2 and invokes the primary replica X_1. X_1 performs a withdrawal in the context of a new nested transaction $TX_{2.1}$, returns a reply, and fails (after committing the transaction). Note that, in this scenario, the failure occurs at a 3rd tier server and transaction $TX_{2.1}$ does not roll-back. The FT ORB runtime at B detects the failure and re-issues the request to the backup server X_2, again using a roll-forward mechanism. Since transaction $TX_{2.1}$ completed successfully, X_2 detects that the request has already been processed, fetches the state update and the reply from the log, updates its state, and returns the previous reply to B_2. Finally, B_2 performs the deposit on account Y, logs the response, commits transaction TX_2, and returns the response to the client.

The key idea here is the combination of the replication and transaction models. The beauty of the server-initiated OTS transaction scope is that any fault

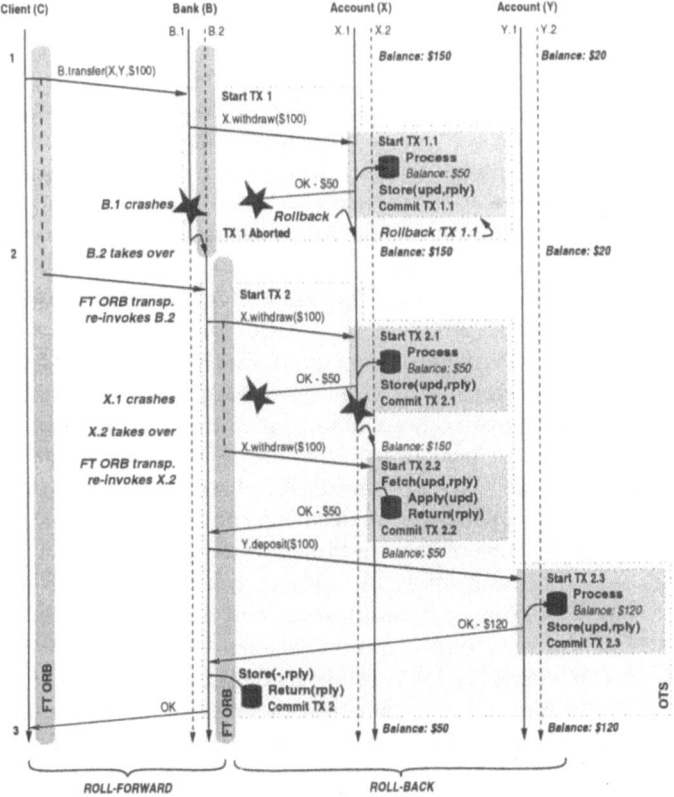

Fig. 5. Protocol Run with Failures in the 2nd and 3rd Tiers.

that occurs during the server's processing of the client's request will not violate data consistency (because it merely triggers a roll-back of the processing and state changes). At the same time, because the server is replicated, and the client-side ORB runtime is equipped with the FT-CORBA failover infrastructure, the crash of a server replica does not lead to loss of availability, either. Thus, the best of both worlds — replication for availability (liveness) and transactions for consistency (safety) — is achieved.

5   Related Work

There exist several commercial implementations and research prototypes of the FT-CORBA specification, as well as of the OTS specification. These implementations employ either the roll-back or the roll-forward reliability strategies, but do not attempt to reconcile the two different approaches. Because our focus in this paper is on the *integration* of the two approaches, and not on systems that satisfy only one of the two approaches, we will not discuss the merits and drawbacks of the various FT-CORBA and OTS implementations.

Instead, we will highlight other research efforts that have attempted to solve specific aspects of this integration problem, albeit from a different viewpoint. Related efforts include research on integrating transactional protocols with group communication protocols, where group communication forms the foundation for maintaining consistency in most replication-based systems.

GroupTransactions [12] aim to take advantage of both group communication and transactions through a new transactional model, where transactional servers can, in fact, be groups of processes. This allows for transactional applications to be built on top of computer clusters.

An e-Transaction [3] is one that executes exactly once despite failures, and is targeted at three-tier enterprise architectures with stateless middle-tier servers that are replicated. This overcomes the limitations of current transactional technologies that, for the most part, ensure at-most-once request processing, which is not sufficiently reliable. The e-Transaction abstraction builds upon an asynchronous replication scheme that provides both the liveness feature of replication, as well as the safety feature of transactions.

Another CORBA-related effort [6] aims to compare the two different kinds of systems — one with group communication and no transactions, and the other with transactions and no group communication — from the viewpoint of replicating objects for availability. Their study leads them to conclude that although transactions are effective in their own right, using group communication infrastructures to support transactional applications can lead to benefits, such as faster failover in the event of a fault.

While all of the above replication schemes refer to objects or servers, the notion of integrating group communication into a transactional model has been extended to the replication of the entire database itself [5]. This work attempts to eliminate the centralized and, therefore, unreliable approach that databases adopt today. The proposed family of replication protocols exploit group communication semantics to eliminate deadlocks, improve performance, and enhance reliability.

IBM Research's Dependency-Spheres [15] aims to integrate (asynchronous) messaging and (synchronous) transactions for distributed objects, with the intention of increasing the level of reliability provided for enterprise Web Services. Dependency-Spheres provide a new kind of global transaction context that allows both synchronous and asynchronous distributed messaging style exchanges to occur within a single transaction-like operation.

To the best of our knowledge, our research represents the first use of transactional mechanisms to implement replication, and to address the determinism problem of nested interactions between replicated objects.

6   Conclusion

Today's enterprise applications have a three-tier structure, with simple clients in the first tier, servers in the middle-tier to perform the processing, and databases in the third tier to store information. For such enterprise applications, replication is required to protect the middle-tier processing, while transactions are required to protect the third-tier data. The CORBA middleware standard now incorporates support for reliability through these two distinct mechanisms — roll-forward replication (using the new Fault Tolerant CORBA standard) and roll-forward transactions (using the CORBA Object Transaction Service). In the current state-of-the-art and state-of-the-practice, it is difficult to reconcile these two techniques.

For true reliability, however, enterprise applications clearly require elements of both roll-forward reliability (to protect processing, and for liveness) and roll-back reliability (to protect data, and for safety). In this paper, we presented a novel combination of replication and transactions to achieve the best of both worlds, and to obtain end-to-end consistency and availability all the way from the first-tier client to the third-tier database.

We exploit the FT-CORBA infrastructure to handle the server replication and client-side failover. We then exploit the OTS mechanisms to enable the servers to perform their processing in the scope of nested transactions that they initiate. To our knowledge, this is the first use of transactional mechanisms to implement replication and to address the determinism problem of nested interactions between replicated objects. Although our solution has been presented in the context of CORBA, it is equally applicable to other transactional environments.

Early results from experimental evaluation with off-the-shelf ORBs demonstrate that little effort is required to combine replication and transaction in a real-world application, and the overhead remains small under normal operation. In the presence of failures, the performance of the replication and recovery mechanisms strongly depends on where and when the failures occur — a failure occurring in the context of a top-level transaction will force a roll-back, which might be costly when many resources are involved in the transaction. In addition, the overhead of recovery is highly dependent of the quality of the FT-CORBA and OTS implementations, and in particular the performance and accuracy of their monitoring mechanisms.

References

1. N. Budhiraja, K. Marzullo, F. Schneider, and S. Toueg. *Distributed Systems*, chapter 8: The Primary-Backup Approach, pages 199–216. 2nd edition, 1993.
2. P. Felber. *The CORBA Object Group Service: A Service Approach to Object Groups in CORBA*. PhD thesis, Swiss Federal Institute of Technology, Lausanne, Switzerland, 1998.
3. S. Frølund and R. Guerraoui, "Implementing e-Transactions with Asynchronous Replication," *IEEE Transactions on Parallel and Distributed Systems*, vol. 12, no. 2, pp. 133-146 (2001).
4. IBM Global Services. *Improving Systems Availability*, 1998.
5. B. Kemme and G. Alonso, "A Suite of Database Replication Protocols Based on Group Communication Primitives," *Proceedings of the IEEE International Conference on Distributed Computing Systems*, Amsterdam, pp. 156-163 (May 1998).

6. M. C. Little and S. K. Shrivastava, "Integrating Group Communication with Transactions for Implementing Persistent Replicated Objects," *Lecture Notes in Computer Science*, vol 1752, Springer-Verlag, 2000.

7. P. Narasimhan. *Transparent Fault Tolerance for CORBA*. PhD thesis, Department of Electrical and Computer Engineering, University of California, Santa Barbara, December 1999.

8. Object Management Group. *The Common Object Request Broker: Architecture and Specification*, 2.6 edition, OMG Technical Committee Document formal/02-01-02, January 2002.

9. Object Management Group. *Fault Tolerant CORBA*, OMG Technical Committee Document formal/01-12-29, December 2001.

10. Object Management Group. *Object Transaction Service Specification*, OMG Technical Committee Document formal/01-11-03, May 2001.

11. Object Management Group. *The CORBA Component Model*, OMG Technical Committee Document ptc/01-11-02, January 2002.

12. M. Patino-Martinez, R. Jimenez-Peris and S. Arevalo, "Group Transactions: An Integrated Approach to Transactions and Group Communication," *Concurrency in Dependable Computing*, Kluwer Academic Publishers, 2002.

13. F. Schneider. *Distributed Systems*, chapter 7: Replication Management using the State-Machine Approach, pages 169–197. 2nd edition, 1993.

14. Sun Microsystems. *Enterprise Java Beans*, version 2.0.

15. S. Tai, T. A. Mikalsen, I. Rouvellou and S. M. Sutton, Jr., "Dependency-Spheres: A Global Transaction Context for Distributed Objects and Messages", *Proceedings of the 5th IEEE International Enterprise Distributed Object Computing Conference*, Seattle, WA (September 2001).

Runtime Performance Modeling and Measurement of Adaptive Distributed Object Applications

John Zinky, Joseph Loyall, and Richard Shapiro

BBN Technologies, 10 Moulton Street, Cambridge, MA USA
{jzinky, jloyall, rshapiro}@bbn.com

Abstract. Distributed applications that can adapt at runtime to changing quality of service (QoS) require a *model* of the expected QoS and of the possible application adaptations. QoS models in turn require runtime measurements, both in-band and out-of-band, from across the application's components. As the comprehensiveness of the model increases, so does the quality of adaptation. But eventually the increasing comprehensiveness becomes too complex for the QoS Designer to deal with effectively. In addition, performance models of any complexity are expensive to create and maintain at runtime. The QoS Designer therefore needs a set of distributed-QoS tools to assist in the construction of models, the handling of quality vs. complexity tradeoffs, and the efficient maintenance of models at runtime. This paper describes the Quality Objects (QuO) middleware support that provides for developing a performance model; collecting and organizing run-time measurements of a system, both in-band and out-of-band; and maintaining the model at runtime in an efficient way.

1   Introduction

Many distributed object application domains, such as military, financial, and health care, have stringent quality of service (QoS) requirements. Hosting these applications on wide-area networks, with their unpredictable and changing resource availability, and in embedded environments, with their constrained resources, requires applications to be aware of the resources in their environment and able to adapt in multiple ways to changes in resource availability. Based on these two requirements, an *adaptation strategy* must be developed that chooses an application behavior for any given environmental situation. The design of this strategy is the job of the *QoS Designer*, a role which is distinct from, and complementary to, that of the Application Designer who develops the functional algorithmic code of the application.

A *performance model* predicts how the application will behave given the usage patterns, underlying resources, QoS requirements, and adaptation strategy. The appropriate level of detail in the model depends on the available adaptations and resource parameters, and on the price the application is willing to pay for adaptivity. A more detailed model provides finer-grained control over the application's QoS behavior, but also requires more effort to construct at design time and to keep current at runtime. The examples will illustrate the tradeoffs between complex fine-grained modeling and simpler but coarser models.

R. Meersman, Z. Tari (Eds.): CoopIS/DOA/ODBASE 2002, LNCS 2519, pp. 755–772, 2002.

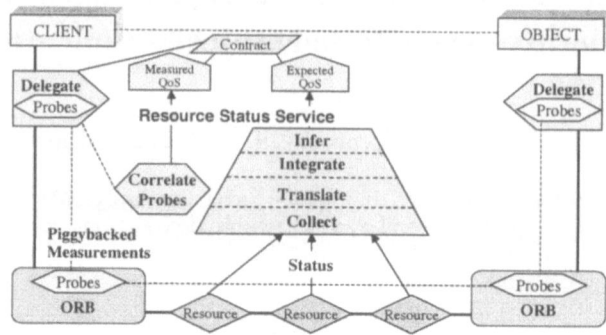

Fig. 1. In-band and out-of-band measures

This paper describes the support that QuO middleware provides for collecting runtime measurements of the system, for developing a performance model of the application and its environment, and for maintaining the performance model at runtime. Maintaining this model and its data is an important part of the QoS Designer's work in creating an adaptive strategy. One of the major recent advances in the QuO middleware is the development of the *Resource Status Service (RSS)*, a distributed service for measuring, aggregating, and disseminating resource information in a distributed system. In this paper, we describe the RSS and its use in creating and maintaining performance models of runtime systems.

Figure 1 shows how QuO runtime supports both in-band measurements and out-of-band expectations of QoS parameters. *In-band* measurements are inserted directly into the function call tree. This provides actual end-to-end QoS measurements of remote function calls using specific resources. *Out-of-band* measurements monitor the system resources and try to infer expected QoS. Integrating these two kinds of measurements is at the heart of any adaptation strategy.

The paper is organized as follows. Section 2 provides a brief overview of the QuO middleware. This section may be skipped if you're already familiar with QuO. Section 3 introduces an example distributed object application, an image server system developed using QuO, which is part of our open-source software toolkit and will serve as a running example throughout the rest of the paper. Section 4 describes QuO's support for gathering in-band measurements. Section 5 describes QuO's support for out-of-band measurements, including the RSS. Section 6 describes QuO support for creating efficient runtime models. Finally, Section 7 describes how to calibrate the performance models, by combining in-band performance measurements and resource capacity measurements. Each section includes examples based on the image server application.

2   The QuO Framework for Adaptive Applications

The Quality Objects (QuO) framework is an extension to traditional distributed object middleware, such as CORBA and RMI, which manage the functional interactions between objects. In ideal circumstances, CORBA and RMI can give the illusion that remote objects are local. Where resources are limited and QoS requirements are stringent, this illusion is impossible to maintain. In the traditional approach, the algorithms for managing adaptation to constrained resources are entangled with the application's functional algorithms. This results in overly complicated code that's very difficult to maintain and extend. QuO provides support for programming QoS measurement, control, and adaptation in the middleware layer, separating the system specific and adaptive code from the functional code of the client and object implementations. In this way, QuO supports reuse of adaptive code and eases the application programmer's burden of programming system issues.

As illustrated in Figure 2, a QuO application extends the traditional distributed object computing (DOC) model with the following components:

QuO contracts summarize an application's current operating mode, expected resource utilization, rules for transition among operating states, and means for notifying applications of changes in QoS or in system status. Contract specifications are written in a high-level specification language called CDL and preprocessed into Java or C++ by the QuO code generator.

System condition objects (Sysconds) provide interfaces to system resources, mechanisms, and managers. They provide high-level reusable interfaces to measure, manipulate, and control lower-level real-time control and measurement capabilities. They export values that describe facets of system status, such as the current memory utilization or priority of a running thread, and provide interfaces to control system characteristics, such as modifying the processor clock rate or scheduling priorities.

QoS-aware Delegates are adaptive components that modify the system's runtime behavior along the paths of method calls and returns. QuO delegates are implemented as wrappers on method stubs or skeletons, thereby inserting behavior between the client and server. Delegates are written in a high-level aspect language called ASL and converted into Java or C++ by the QuO code generator.

Qoskets pull together contracts, delegates, and system conditions into reusable components that are independent of any specific functional interfaces. Combining a functional interface with a Qosket makes a new object that implements the functional interface and manages some QoS aspect.

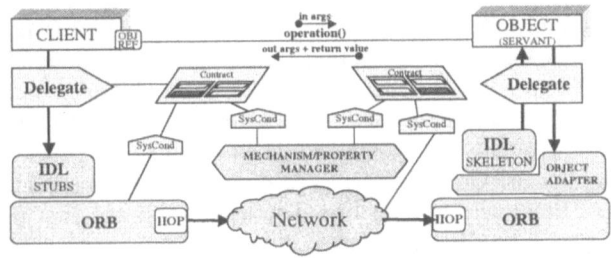

Fig. 2. The execution model of an adaptive application using QuO

Fig. 3. The image server can produce images that are big or small, processed or unprocessed with different resource usage characteristics

In summary, QuO includes high-level specification languages, a code generator, a runtime kernel, libraries of reusable qoskets and system condition objects, QoS property managers. These components are described in detail in other papers [8, 14, 15, 17], as is the application of QuO to properties such as security [18] and dependability [1]. In this paper we concentrate on QuO's support for developing a performance model of an application and its environment, and for maintaining the performance model at runtime.

3   An Example: Data Dissemination in a Wide-Area Network

As a running example in this paper, we will use an image server application that we have developed using the QuO adaptive middleware and which serves as the basis for many of our example and experimental applications. It consists of a remote data server maintaining a database of images and a client requesting images from the remote server. The data server has the capability of producing versions of the images of different sizes and of different quality as illustrated in Figure 3. The image server exposes interfaces enabling the client to request pictures that are "big" or "small", "processed" or "unprocessed." Big pictures use more CPU resources to display and more bandwidth to transmit than small pictures do. Processed pictures use more CPU resources on the server side to improve the image quality.

The challenge for the QoS designer is to program into the application an adaptive tradeoff between timeliness and quality. The user wants the best picture, but is not willing to wait very long. Better pictures (bigger and processed) take longer to transmit because they take more resources. The application needs to measure the timeliness of image delivery, and when round-trip image delivery and processing slows, the application needs to gather enough information to determine whether the source of the slowdown is network or CPU degradation and adapt accordingly.

As a basic example of adaptation, we use a qosket, called Bottleneck, which partitions the operating environment along the dimensions of bandwidth and CPU resources. Bottleneck's contract has four regions with high and low server CPU along one dimension and high and low network bandwidth along the other. The Bottleneck qosket also includes system condition objects for determining the status of the runtime environment, used by the contract to determine the high and low regions. The qosket encapsulates all the behavior needed to measure the relevant system resources and to determine whether the constrained resource is the network, the CPU, or both. Note that the qosket is completely independent of the application and is therefore reusable.

When the QoS designer combines the Bottleneck qosket with the image server application, he specifies a binding of the contract regions to method calls on the remote object using QuO's *Adaptation Specification Language, ASL* [12]. The QuO code generator creates a delegate that calls the appropriate server methods based on the Bottleneck contract region. While the functional application continues to call the original remote `read` method, the delegate will transparently substitute calls to other methods, depending on the state of the resources. When there are no resource bottlenecks, `readBigProcessed` is used because it gives the best picture. When both CPU and bandwidth resources are scarce, `readSmallUnprocessed` is used because it reduces the time to process and transmit the picture. Likewise, `readSmall-Processed` is used when the Network is the only bottleneck and `readBigUnprocessed` is used when the CPU is the only bottleneck. This is a simple strategy for trading off timeliness and quality with respect to the system constraints.

The image server application is typical of several of our experimental and transitioned applications, differing in the images they provide, the system in which they are hosted, and the adaptation choices they offer to maintain QoS. For example, in the avionics example described in [9], the image server delivers *virtual target folders*, which contain map images with notations and other information. The client and server are embedded in separate aircraft and communicate through a wireless link. Because of the extremely constrained bandwidth of the wireless link and the large size of the data images, the server offers the choice to break each image into smaller tiles, which are delivered separately and reassembled by the client, and to choose the quality of each tile. Higher quality tiles use more bandwidth and CPU.

In the dependable server application described in [10], the image server provides two interfaces, one that authenticates requests and services them with a secure server and another that does not authenticate requests. In this application, the client has the option to tradeoff security for speed, since the authenticating server requires extra data (and thus uses more bandwidth) for the authentication and more time and CPU to validate the identity of the requester.

The QoS designer can design many schemes to resolve the tradeoff between picture quality and call latency. The cleverness and appropriateness of the specific adaptation scheme developed is irrelevant to this discussion. What is important is the kind of adaptation schemes that are possible and how well QuO mechanisms support them. In the following sections, we will show how additional system information made available by measurement and modeling can be used to help refine the adaptation.

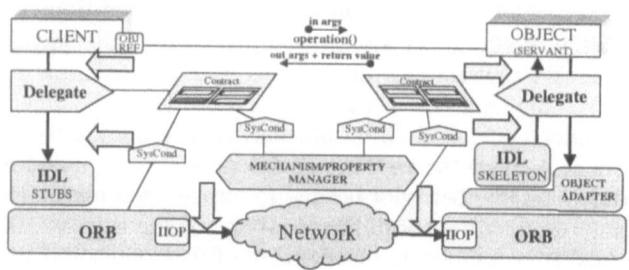

Fig. 4. QuO's in-band instrumentation gathers information along the remote method call and return

4   In-Band Instrumentation

The basic idea of in-band instrumentation is to insert measurement points along the call path from the client to the server and back. This instrumentation gathers measurements along the method call and return as illustrated in Figure 4, measuring things such as the number of calls; round trip latency; the time spent in the network; or the effective capacity of some underlying resource. The problem with adding instrumentation in traditional applications is that the code has to be placed at many places along the path and the results gathered together for processing and dissemination. Adding instrumentation code breaks the normal boundaries/interfaces as defined by the functional decomposition of the distributed system. Special support is needed to add this code and use its results without creating a tangled mess.

CORBA provides some support for inserting instrumentation into the data path between the client and server. CORBA interceptors [11] allow requests and replies to be intercepted at several points during the transmission of a remote call. CORBA Pluggable Protocols [7] allow new transport protocols to be used instead of the default IIOP protocol over TCP. The new transport protocols can add instrumentation to the messages to measure QoS properties and can provide control over network resources using RSVP [19] or Diffserv [5].

Other distributed object middleware, such as Java RMI, do not have CORBA's open implementation, so instrumentation must be added above or below the equivalent of the ORB. For instrumentation below the ORB, QuO uses a Gateway Shell [14], which can intercept method calls and manage their QoS as request and reply messages are transmitted over the network resources.

QuO supports above the ORB instrumentation for both CORBA and RMI. QuO's ASL language and code generator uses aspect-oriented programming (AOP) techniques to weave code inside methods for both the client-side and server-side delegates. Instrumentation code often needs to be added to all methods in an interface, e.g., adding a timer call before and after each remote method call. Features of native languages, such as Java and C++, do not readily support code that cross-cuts many methods, although Java's class reflection [16] could be used to query an object for a list of all its methods and construct an instrumentation delegate at runtime. QuO uses an approach to support instrumentation in many methods similar to those in other aspect-oriented languages, such as AspectJ. However, unlike AspectJ, QuO supports both Java and C++, and supports weaving code across distributed systems.

4.1   Example: Client-Side Latency Measurement

Suppose that the QoS designer needs to keep the latency of a call in the image server application below a threshold, so that delivery of images is smooth. If the latency is too high, the `read` method could downshift to a remote method that uses fewer resources, such as from `readBigProcessed` to `readBigUnprocessed`, to `readSmallUnprocessed`. The QoS designer can create a contract that implements the downshift as a state machine, but needs access to a measure of the latency to trigger the downshift.

QuO's contract evaluation mechanism includes support for measuring method latency. Usually, a QuO contract is evaluated before and after a remote method is called. QuO provides a Probe Syscond class, illustrated in Figure 2, which catches the contract evaluation signal and measures the method latency. Different types of Probe Syscond can process the raw latency into statistical metrics, such as the average latency over the last ten calls.

When the contract downshifts to a new region, the latency is expected to go down, but the averaging mechanism still remembers old values. To avoid controlling based on old values, the new behavior must be locked in until the statistics converge to a meaningful value. QuO contracts support locking the contract into the current region until the statistics have stabilized.

4.2   Example: Correlated Server and Client Latency

Suppose the QoS designer needs to determine which resource is the bottleneck. In the last example, the downshift behavior arbitrarily chose to reduce the server load (adapting to `readBigUnprocessed`). But the cause of the latency problem could just as well have been the network. The client side can measure end-to-end QoS characteristics, such as the overall latency or the sizes of requests and replies, but cannot determine which sub-components are contributing to the latency. To determine the relative contribution of sub-components, timers must be set and read as the call enters and leaves each component (identified by the yellow arrows in Figure 4). The measurements can be compared to differentiate between components. The approach is to pass a trace record from the client to the server and back, so that the client can determine the amount of time spent using different resources, such as network bandwidth and server-side CPU.

The ASL for adding a trace record is more complicated than adding simple behavior calls, because it needs to add an additional parameter to the interface to carry the trace record between the client and server. But if the interface is being changed at the client, the server must also change its interface to support the new trace record parameter. The consequence is that the remote object now has two interfaces, the normal interface and one with the instrumentation parameter. QuO includes a reusable qosket that manages adding a trace record and processing the results to get the relative network and server latency.

4.3   Example: Regression for Resource Capacity

Suppose the QoS designer needs to know the capacity of a resource such as the network bandwidth. The measured bandwidth could be used as a threshold to determine if the network capacity is high or low. The QoS designer can use ASL to invoke statistical processing of the trace record when it's returned to the client. QuO has a default linear regression library that can be used to fit a curve for resource capacity, based on the measured latency and load. Note that the ASL and regression library are not application specific. This set of tools can therefore be configured as a reusable qosket.

4.4   Example: Detecting a Drop in Effective Bandwidth

Suppose the QoS designer needs to detect a drop in the effective capacity of a resource, for example due to a sudden increase in cross traffic on the network link between the client and server. The contract could select small or big pictures based on a threshold for a resource's capacity. But the QoS designer does not want the selection to thrash when the effective capacity is close to the threshold. One solution is to use hysteresis, where the threshold value going down is lower than the threshold value going up. QuO contracts support hysteresis by locking the contract in a region until some condition is true. The QoS designer can use the statistical properties of the fitted capacity to make the threshold even more robust. The upper error bound can be used for going down and the lower error bound can be used for going up. When the fit is poor the error bounds spread out making the system harder to transition between regions.

When the underlying system changes abruptly, detecting the absolute magnitude of the change is difficult. Since the fit for effective capacity is based on past measurements, during a transition there are samples from both the old capacity and the new capacity. Figure 5 shows a capacity prediction using a box car filter of the last 10 image transfers. The small graphs show the fit for the effective capacity before, during, and after the onset of the traffic spike. Notice the left and right scatter plots: the slopes of the points accurately estimate the effective capacity and there are no outliers. The center scatter plot shows measurements during a transition between regions. It has measurements from both regions and therefore a less clear slope. The fit can have any value, based on the usage pattern during the transition; in this case, the fit underestimates the effective capacity. During a transition it is best to ignore the fit and lock down the contract region until the fit consists only of measurements of the new capacity.

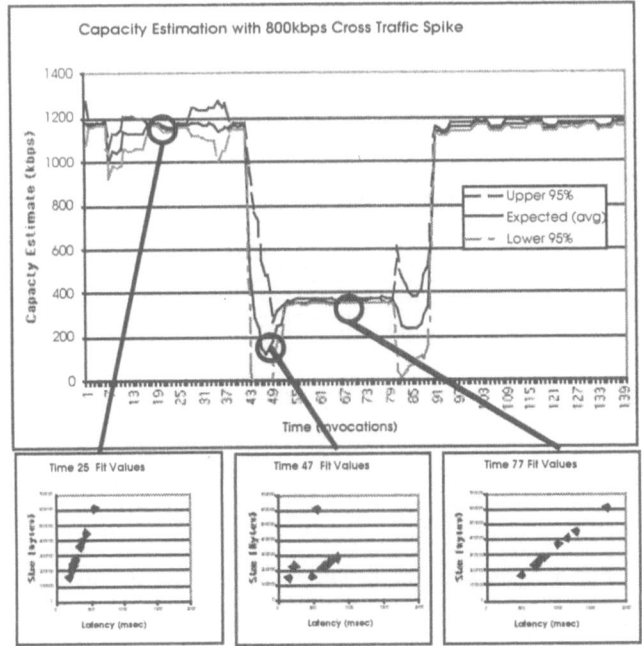

Fig. 5. Estimating bandwidth during a quick change

5   Out-of-Band Instrumentation

Out-of-band instrumentation gathers performance information about the underlying system outside the context of remote method calls. Information is collected from the resources along the path between the client and the remote object. The information from different resources is integrated and translated into a consistent representation. Given a model of how the application uses the resources, the expected QoS can then be inferred (Figure 1).

Out-of-band information is traditionally used by centralized network and system management applications. But here, we want this information disseminated to the applications themselves. The applications become aware of the underlying resources and can use this information to adapt, i.e., they become network-aware applications. CMU's Remos [3] is an example of a collection system specifically designed to collect and integrate data from networks and hosts and disseminate them to applications. The Remos modeler is capable of representing individual resources or aggregate capacity, such as the bandwidth along a path in the network. Other resource managers also fill this role, such as the Globus Resource Monitor [6] and Desiderata Resource Manager [13].

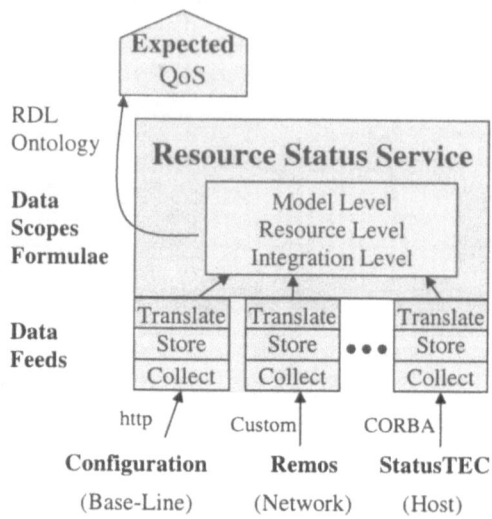

Fig. 6. Architecture of the Resource Status Service Architecture

5.1   QuO Resource Status Service

QuO's Resource Status Service (RSS) extends the idea of network-aware application by supporting both a resource model and a high-level application model. QuO's RSS has an open implementation, with several well-defined integration points at which different types of out-of-band collectors can be added. Remos is an example of such collector. Figure 6 shows the QuO RSS architecture and its integration points.

RSS is a completely distributed service; each application process effectively gets its own RSS server, which gathers information needed by the process. The RSS can be integrated into the application process (currently Java only) or can be located nearby as an independent CORBA server (currently necessary for C++).

The local RSS server maintains a representation of the status of each resource used by the application process. The status is updated independently of the application even when the resource is remote. These status values are used to make adaptive decisions in critical data paths, which can't afford to query for remote status on demand. The local status representation is the *current best guess* for the remote status.

Any given RSS value can subscribe to other RSS values, in which case it will be updated whenever any of its dependant values changes. QuO system condition objects can also subscribe to RSS values. This data-driven forward chaining follows all the data dependencies and can ultimately trigger adaptation by means of the system condition objects. For example, a remote poller can detect a change in the status of a resource and disseminate the status change to all interested RSS servers. Inside an RSS server the status value can propagate through internal formulas resulting in a change to the value of system condition objects. QuO contracts are evaluated when their observed system condition objects change value, which might result in a transition between contract regions. The transition code can trigger an application adaptation. Note that the forward chaining is asynchronous and independent of the operation of the application, which may or may not be using the resource at the time.

The asynchronous forward chaining in RSS also improves cache consistency for ordinary system conditions. For example, a QuO delegate requests a contract evaluation in order to dispatch the appropriate adaptive behavior. Contract evaluations use the value of system condition objects, which by design are always available. So the evaluation returns quickly, because the system condition objects were being updated in anticipation of their being used.

The RSS implementation has other mechanisms for ensuring that the status representation is updated, including support for backward chaining, in which data queries can trigger further queries for supporting data.

5.2   Data Values

Data in the RSS is represented as a multi-field record. As the value is processed, meta-data is added to help with integrating data from several sources. In the current implementation that meta-data fields consist of a timestamp, a source stamp, a credibility rating and a units tag.

One of the key features of the RSS is the integration of several raw data values into a single integrated value or best guess. When new raw data arrives, the RSS must decide if the new raw value changes the current integrated value (since changes to integrated values trigger forward chaining). This decision is derived from the following considerations. The results are summarized in the integrated data's credibility-rating.

- **Aggregation**: the time period over which the observations were made.
- **Staleness**: how old the data is;
- **Source type**: the method used to collection the data
- **Trust or Collector Authority**: whether the collector of the information is trusted or the information is just hearsay.
- **Sensitivity**: Whether a key component of the data has low credibility.

5.3   Data Feeds

No universally accepted standard exists for data collection, so the RSS takes the pragmatic approach of adding an integration point, called a Data Feed, for interfacing with different collection systems.

A Data Feed is responsible for moving the data from a collection system into the RSS. Besides having to implement the collector's data transfer protocol, the Data Feed must also manage which status values to collect and how often. Some collectors push data to the client, which matches well with the RSS's internal publish and subscribe mechanisms. Other collectors must be polled. Also, the collector's data format needs to be translated into the internal RSS format, which may include semantic as well as syntactic translation, such as adding credibility meta-data.

QuO 3.0 comes with three flavors of Data Feeds: static data via http (e.g. resource configurations); ad hoc dynamic data using special-purpose protocols (e.g. bandwidth information from Remos); and mixed static and dynamic data using a CORBA

TypedEventChannel (e.g. host probes). QuO 3.0 comes with a CORBA TypedEventChannel (TEC) to disseminate status information from remote collectors [21].

5.4   Example: Dynamic Calculation of Expected Resource Capacity

Suppose the QoS Designer wants to detect denial of service attacks. Since these kinds of attacks consume excessive resources, one indication would be a mismatch between measured and expected resource capacity. In-band measurement with regression (described in Section 4) can determine the current effective resource capacity but cannot offer any notion of what the capacity of the resource *should be*. One technique for computing expectation is to use historic in-band measurements, i.e. take "baseline" measurements over past runs of the application. But for highly dynamic environments, such as mobile networks, history is a bad predictor of the present. Other techniques are needed to calculate the expected resource capacity.

The RSS manages the gathering of out-of-band measurements from which the expected capacity for resources can be calculated. It integrates the data from all the Data Feeds that are available. Some of these feeds are static (e.g. configuration data on a web page), some are dynamic (bandwidth capacity calculations from Remos), and the integration formulas must accommodate both. For example, if only the static web data is available, the RSS will use those values, but assign them a low credibility. If a Remos collector becomes available, the RSS will use those dynamic values instead of the static data and will increase the credibility correspondingly. The integration formulas can also calculate specific values from more general ones, for example by narrowing configuration information about bandwidth between subnets into an expected bandwidth between hosts on those subnets.

6   Runtime Performance Models

For the purposes of this paper, a runtime performance model is a shadow-representation of the running application, including representations of the underlying resources, the static structure of the application, and a specific application' instance. QuO RSS allows the explicit creation of such models.

The model of underlying resources represents both the resources and their interconnections (topology). The resource model is analogous to a network management system with an internal model-object for each host and network connection. Network and System management modeling is a fairly mature technology and has extensive ontologies for classifying resources and their relationships [2]. The current RSS modeling of resources is a medium-grain implementation based on these ontologies.

The representation of the application's structure is also an explicit part of the model. In this case the model-objects represent "interesting" classes from the application's class hierarchy. Currently, the application models are hand coded. We plan to automate this process using the QuO code generators or existing representations of application models such as UML.

A model of an application instance combines both the resource representation and application structure representation. The application's dynamic call tree is represented and has *HasA* links to the resources and *IsA* links to the application structure. The resulting model is a skeleton on which specific QoS predictors can be attached. Figure 7 shows how a predictor for method latency was added to the skeleton representing the application structure (Class), resources (Host) and call tree (Method).

To support efficient runtime construction of model-objects, QuO RSS has two kinds of modeling components with rich meta-data (reflectivity). Data Scopes represent model-objects and their relationships. Data Formulas represent dynamic attributes of the model-objects.

Model construction happens in two phases. The first step is creation of the model-objects (Data Scopes), their attributes (Data-Formulas) and their relationships. Setting up the Data Scopes is a fairly expensive operation because resolving relationships involves walking many data structures. Setting up the Data Scopes is analogous to the application binding a client to a remote object. This operation usually happens only once and changes infrequently during the application's life cycle. Likewise Data Scopes are rarely created, but frequently evaluated.

The second step is evaluating the Data Formulas. This operation is very efficient because dependencies and caches are established when Data Scopes are created.

6.1 Data Scopes

Data Scopes are a class of objects which have additional meta-data to allow reflectivity at runtime. The main feature of a Data Scope is that existence of its attributes is resolved at runtime and depends on the inter-relationships among Data Scopes. When a Data Scope is given an attribute name to resolve, it searches its local attributes and the attributes of other Data Scopes for which it has relationships. The search scheme is completely programmable by the QoS Designer, but some basic relationships are supported. The containment relationship (HasA) allows parents to share their attributes with their children. For example, if an object is contained in a host, the object has all the attributes of the host. Another relationship is *proto-type*, which can set the default values for types of objects. Also, the relationship *reference* describes how remote objects are hooked together. Figure 7 illustrates a graphical representation of an object served by a specific host.

6.2 Data Formulas

Data Formulas are a class of objects allowing for forward and backward chaining of calculations. Data Formulas manage a mathematical formula and keep track of the formula's dependencies. Data Formulas are part of a publish and subscribe mesh. When a formula value changes all the formulas that depend on the changed formula are reevaluated. Data Formulas can also handle other issues, such as data credibility, unit conversion, caching, and snapshotting. For example, Data Formulas allow for automatically handling missing or low credibility data.

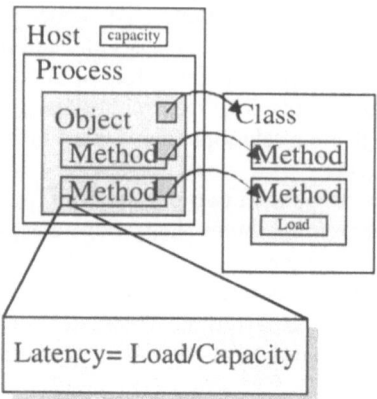

Fig. 7. A model of method latency using Data Scopes and Data Formulas

Figure 7 shows a Data Formula for latency being attached as an attribute for a Method Data Scope. The Latency Formula depends on other formulas that can be resolved in the context of the Method Scope. The resolution is done when the Latency Formula is created. The publish and subscribe mesh updates the Latency Formula when its dependent formulas change value.

6.3   Example: Predicting Object Latency

Suppose the QoS Designer wants to choose the fastest server to request a picture. The contract could pick the server based on a prediction of end-to-end latency, which includes object latency and network latency. The server-side method latency is the amount of time taken above the orb to process the picture. Network latency is the time to transmit the request and reply messages from the client to the server, including marshaling and transmission time. For this example we will predict just the server-side method latency.

Server-side method latency depends solely on the server CPU resources. Method latency is longer if the picture is larger or if the CPU resources decrease. A model for the processing time of a picture is: *latency is the number of instructions needed to process a picture divided by the effective capacity of the server CPU*. The number of instructions is the size of the picture times the number of instructions it takes to process a byte.

The effective capacity of a server depends on its raw CPU capacity and the competition from other processes. Linux exports an estimate of CPU capacity called *BogoMips* and an estimate of competing load called *LoadAverage*. The effect of CPU LoadAverage for Linux is a hard metric to model [4]. A simple model would be that when the server process is not greedy and the read processing is small, the read request sneaks in and gets the whole CPU regardless of the LoadAverage. If the object is greedy, the CPU scheduler will multiplex the CPU between the waiting processes including the server. So the Load Average reduces the capacity. Also, the number of CPUs on the server reduces the effect of load average.

```
MethodLatency =
((   ReplySize * ReplyInstructionsPerByte
   + RequestSize*RequestInstructionsPerByte)
 /(CPUMips/Max(1,(LoadAverage/NumberCPUs)))
```

Note this formula assumes that there are no queuing effects due to other method calls waiting to use the object. Also the formula assumes that the per-invocation load is negligible, i.e., the load is independent of picture size. The QoS designer can add more comprehensive formulas.

Note that this formula is reuseable, i.e. this formula could be used to model the latency of any method call on any object instance. But the parameters of the formula are relative to the object's context. For example, each object instance is hosted on a different server, and each method on the object has a different ReplyInstPerByte. When the MethodLatency's Formula is bound to a method's Scope, the relative references are resolved by the Scope. For example, to find the BogoMips the method's Scope would follow its containment relationships until it found a BogoMips formula on its host scope. To find ReplyInstPerByte, the Scope would follow the proto-type relationships, because this is a characteristic of this type of method. Allowing Scopes to dynamically resolve the parameter bindings is a powerful tool for reusing formulas. Also, because the RSS integrates data from many sources and picks the most credible, the formula is robust even if some of the data sources are missing.

7   Calibration of Models

In the Method Latency Formula of the last example, an application specific parameter appeared called ReplyInstructionsPerByte. This parameter is different for each method called on the server object. Separating out this parameter allows the Latency Formula to be decoupled from a specific type of hardware. But how does the QoS Designer determine this characteristic of a specific object implementation?

One way to calibrate models is to run off-line performance experiments over a wide variety of hardware and software configurations. The results of these experiments can be used to fit parameters of the model. The QoS designer can use QuO instrumentation (described in Sections 4 and 5) to collect latency and load (picture size) measurements. QuO instrumentation can log this information to a file. After several runs of the application using different resources and load mixes the raw data can be fed to a regression program. The QoS designer must use knowledge of how the application is structured to determine the right kind of model to fit and the parameters needed. In the above example, a linear model based on picture size was used and gave adequate results. Higher order models or non-linear models can also be used as dictated by application implementation.

Once the calibration parameters are determined, they need to be loaded into the performance model at runtime. The QuO RSS Data Feed service allows the parameters to be published. Because the calibration is specific to an application implementa-

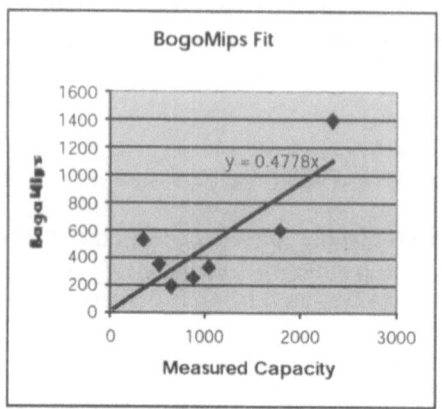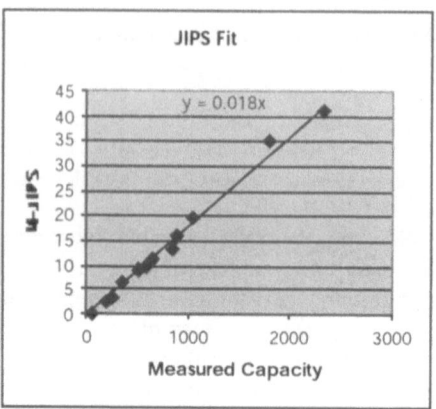

Fig. 8. JIPS micro benchmark predicts CPU capacity over a wide range of processor types

tion it should be stored with the application's static structure which is published as part of the configuration database on a central web page.

Besides the calibration results being published using the RSS, the raw calibration data could also be published by the applications. We plan to investigate automatic calibration where different instances of the application publish the raw data and a central calibration service can process this data. One run of the application usually does not cover enough of the range of resources and usage patterns to get a good fit. So using data from multiple runs at different times and users may cover more than enough range. Also, having the applications publish raw measurements allows a summary of expected usage patterns which can be correlated by user and group.

7.1   Example: Comparing Benchmarks BogoMips vs JIPS

One of the problems in calibrating applications is determining the capacity of the host resources. Linux publishes an estimate of host capacity called BogoMips, which is based on the processor clock frequency and a fudge factor of the architecture type. But using just BogoMips is not good enough to predict application performance. When running Java on our test bed machines we have observed a factor of 100 difference between hosts, from old Sparc IPCs running JDK 1.1.7 to Xeon PCs running Java 1.3 with JIT. Besides the version of Java, the machine architecture and OS also changes the host's capacity to run Java applications. So we developed a simple Java benchmark that estimates the Java Instructions per Second (JIPS), which includes the effects of the Java VM, OS and host architecture.

Figure 8 shows the results of calibrating the image server application against BogoMips and JIPS. All measurements used the same version of Java, but different processor types. The JIPS benchmark had a good fit with the image server application, whereas the BogoMips had outliers for non-Pentium II/III processors.

The JIPS benchmark measures the processing time in a tight loop doing integer arithmetic, which matches well to image processing. This type of loop does not take advantage of the large cache of the Xeon processor or the fast bus speed of the Sun server. These machines perform well at other tasks such as compiling, but showed disappointing performance for the JIPS benchmarks. We plan to investigate using several types of JIPS benchmarks that can be compared to the application. When the application is calibrated, it can specify which benchmark best predicts the perform-ance of the applications.

8   Conclusions

The QoS designer needs help. Adding adaptive behavior to existing systems is diffi-cult. While QuO middleware supports developing reusable adaptive behaviors and adding them to existing applications, useful adaptation requires awareness and meas-urement of the dynamic conditions of the system. In this paper, we described several ways to gather runtime measurements useful in triggering adaptive behavior. These included both in-band measurements gathered in the path of object interactions and out-of-band measurements gathered by direct observations of the system independent of application operation. We described the support that QuO provides for in-band and out-of-band measurements and for creating runtime performance models of the sys-tem, which help organize the awareness of resources. QuO's RSS is a powerful reus-able service that can be used to integrate available information into a coherent view of the underlying resources in a system. Accurate runtime performance models and dy-namic system measurement are important to creating efficient adaptive behavior for a performance critical application. We illustrated our results in the context of a distrib-uted image server application. The QuO software and the applications described in this paper are available open-source at http://quo.bbn.com.

References

1. Cukier M, Ren J, Sabnis C, Henke D, Pistole J, Sanders W, Bakken D, Berman M, Karr D, Schantz R. "AQuA: An Adaptive Architecture that Provides Dependable Distributed Ob-jects," *Proceedings of the 17th IEEE Symposium on Reliable Distributed Systems*, October 1998.
2. DMTF, "Common Information Model (CIM) Standard. http://www.dmtf.org/standards/standard_cim.php
3. Dinda P, Gross T, Karrer, R Lowekamp B, Miller N, Steenkiste P, and Sutherland S, *The Architecture of the Remos System*, 10th IEEE Symposium on High-Performance Distrib-uted Computing (HPDC'01), IEEE, August 2001, San Francisco.
4. Dinda P, Lowekamp B, Kallivokas L, O'Hallaron D, *The Case For Prediction-based Best-effort Real-time Systems*, 7th International Workshop on Parallel and Distributed Real-time Systems (WPDRTS 1999),
5. IETF RFC 2475 "An Architecture for Differentiated Services"
6. Czajkowski, Foster, Karonis, Kesselman, Martin, Smith, Tuecke. "A Resource Manage-ment Architecture for Metacomputing Systems" *Proc. IPPS/SPDP '98 Workshop on Job Scheduling Strategies for Parallel Processing*, pp. 62-82, 1998.

7. Kuhns F, O'Ryan, Schmidt D, Othman 0, Parsons J, "The Design and Performance of a Pluggable Protocols Framework for Object Request Broker Middleware", IFIP workshop on Protocols for High-speed Networks, Aug 1999.
8. Loyall J, Bakken D, Schantz R, Zinky J, Karr D, Vanegas R, Anderson K. "QoS Aspect Languages and Their Runtime Integration," *Lecture Notes in Computer Science*, 1511, Springer-Verlag. *Proceedings of the Fourth Workshop on Languages, Compilers, and Run-time Systems for Scalable Computers (LCR98)*, Pittsburgh, Pennsylvania, 28-30 May 1998.
9. Loyall JL, Gossett JM, Gill CD, Schantz RE, Zinky JA, Pal P, Shapiro R, Rodrigues C, Atighetchi M, Karr D. "Comparing and Contrasting Adaptive Middleware Support in Wide-Area and Embedded Distributed Object Applications," *Proceedings of the 21st IEEE International Conference on Distributed Computing Systems (ICDCS-21)*, April 16-19, 2001, Phoenix, Arizona.
10. Loyall JP, Pal PP, Schantz RE, Webber F. "Building Adaptive and Agile Applications Using Intrusion Detection and Response," *Proceedings of NDSS 2000, the Network and Distributed System Security Symposium*, February 2-4 2000, San Diego, CA.
11. Object Management Group, "Portable Interceptors Specification" (orbos/99-12-01), http://www.omg.org
12. QuO Toolkit Users' and Reference Guides. http://www.dist-systems.bbn.com/tech/QuO/release/
13. Ravindan B, Welsh L, Brugggerman C, Shirazi B, Cavanaugh C, "A Resource Management Model for Dynamic, Scalable, Dependble, Real-time Systems, IEEE Real-time Technology and Applications Symposium.
14. Schantz R, Zinky J, Karr D, Bakken D, Megquier J, Loyall J. "An Object-level Gateway Supporting Integrated-Property Quality of Service," *Proceedings of The 2nd IEEE International Symposium on Object-oriented Real-time distributed Computing (ISORC 99)*, May 1999.
15. Schantz RE, Loyall JP, Atighetchi M, Pal PP. "Packaging Quality of Service Control Behaviors for Reuse," *Proceedings of the 5th IEEE International Symposium on Object-oriented Real-time distributed Computing (ISORC 2002)*, April 29 - May 1, 2002, Washington, DC.
16. Sun Microsystems. Java Language Specification. "Dynamic Proxies" jdk 1.3.
17. Vanegas R, Zinky J, Loyall J, Karr D, Schantz R, Bakken D. "QuO's Runtime Support for Quality of Service in Distributed Objects," *Proceedings of Middleware 98, the IFIP International Conference on Distributed Systems Platform and Open Distributed Processing*, September 1998.
18. Webber F, Pal P, Schantz R, and Loyall J. "Defense-Enabled Applications," *Proceedings of the Second DARPA Information Survivability Conference and Exposition (DISCEX II)*, Anaheim, CA, 12-14 June 2001.
19. Zhang L, et al. "RSVP: a New Resource Protocol," *IEEE Network*, 7(6), September 1993.
20. Zinky J, Bakken D, Schantz R. "Architectural Support for Quality of Service for CORBA Objects," *Theory and Practice of Object Systems* 3(1), 1997.
21. Zinky J, Bakken D, Krishnaswamy V, Ahamad M. "PASS - A Service for Efficient Large Scale Dissemination of Time Varying Data Using CORBA," IEEE ICDCS 1999.

An Infrastructure for Adaptable Middleware*

Pierre-Charles David and Thomas Ledoux

École des Mines de Nantes
Département Informatique
4, rue Alfred Kastler – BP 20722
F-44307 Nantes Cedex 3, France
{pcdavid,ledoux}@emn.fr

Abstract. Today's software systems have to deal with an increasing diversity and complexity of execution environments. Next generation applications will have to deal with the unknown, with execution conditions which can not be predicted at the time they are written: they must be *adaptable*. In this paper, we present our current answer to this problem, in the form of an infrastructure for adaptable middleware. This infrastructure distinguishes functional components from non-functional services and enables dynamic reconfiguration of the associations between them. These associations are controlled by an *adaptation engine* which monitors both the execution environment and the application, and adapts the associations according to *adaptation policies*.

1 Introduction

Today's software systems have to deal with an increasing diversity and complexity of execution environments. New types of computing platforms appear regularly like Personal Digital Assistants and mobile phones, each with different processors, operating systems, hardware devices, etc. This context makes applications development more and more difficult: programmers need to deal with a wide spectrum of hardware platforms, each with dynamically varying – and generally unpredictable and uncontrollable – resources, and which all have to work together. Next generation applications will have to deal with the unknown, with execution conditions which can not be predicted at the time they are written: they must be able to adapt their behavior to fit the dynamically evolving environment.

Adding ad-hoc support for dynamic reconfiguration and adaptation in an application is not a trivial task. It can result in very complex systems where the real business features are hidden by all the mechanisms introduced to allow appropriate dynamic reconfigurations. In our opinion, the most promising approach to solve this problem is to build an insulation layer, the *middleware*, between the applications and their environment. This layer provides common abstractions and services for applications developers to write their programs, and, most importantly for our problem, factors all the environment-specific code

---

* This research is supported by the RNTL project ARCAD (http://arcad.essi.fr)

R. Meersman, Z. Tari (Eds.): CoopIS/DOA/ODBASE 2002, LNCS 2519, pp. 773–790, 2002.
© Springer-Verlag Berlin Heidelberg 2002

outside from the main – functional – code. This is a first step towards a solution for dynamic adaptation, because changes in the execution environment now mostly impact the middleware layer instead of the whole application. The next step is to make this middleware more flexible, and able to be adapted – or even better to adapt itself – to environmental changes. Although current industrial middleware implementations ([1,2,3]) do not take into account the dynamic execution conditions, previous works on *adaptable middleware* [4,5] have shown the viability of this approach.

In this context, the goal of our work is to make it easy for the application developers to build adaptable applications, and to provide the required infrastructure and tools to actually adapt them. The solution we propose in this paper is to make explicit the separation between what depends on the changing environment (non-functional, middleware services) and what does not (functional, business components). Then, the associations between these two kinds of code can be modified at run-time in a way that depends on dynamic execution conditions, to adapt the application to this environment.

This paper is organized as follows: first we present a simple, concrete example of an application that will be used as an illustration throughout the paper (Sect. 2). Then, we describe the general architecture of our infrastructure (Sect. 3) before detailing each of its subsystems (Sections 4 to 6) and showing how the current prototype is used in practice (Sect. 7). Finally, we compare our approach to other related works (Sect. 8), before concluding (Sect. 9).

2   Running Example

This section describes an example application which will be used throughout the paper to illustrate our proposition.

The application is a client/server based bookstore system. A bookstore company provides its customers a Java-based graphical client to allow them to browse and search the catalog, to order books and to manage their accounts. The company expects its customers to use the clients in all kinds of situations and on different platforms (desktop computers, laptops, even PDAs), and wants their experience to be as smooth as possible. To enable this, both the server and the client must be able to adapt to the evolutions of the execution environment. For example, the bandwidth of a wireless connection on a typical PDA can undergo variations which must be taken into account by the distribution mechanisms to provide a correct Quality of Service.

The business model developed for the application contains classes such as `Catalog`, `Book`, `Order` and `Customer`. Using these core classes, the company programmers create two applications. The first one is a server designed to be used internally to manage the catalog and follow customers' orders. The second one is the graphical client that is shipped to customers. None of these two programs contain any reference to middleware-type services like server-side persistence or distribution mechanisms; these will be added separately to enable their dynamic adaptation, as will be shown in the rest of the paper.

3   Proposed Architecture

In this section, we give a brief overview of the architecture we propose to enable application adaptation using a middleware-level infrastructure. More details on each of the subsystems introduced here can be found in the next sections (Sect. 4, Sect. 5 and Sect. 6).

From a very abstract perspective, we can consider any software system as being the implementation of a *solution* to a given *problem* (specification documents and functional requirements) in a particular *context* (available resources, non-functional requirements). This means that our system depends both on the problem specification and on the execution context. The problem definition tends to stabilize over the time, even though it is never completely frozen. On the other hand, the execution context is constantly changing, and at different rates: from macroscopic evolutions (new hardware platforms with specific characteristics appearing every few months), to microscopic changes (resources availability with evolutions in the order of a second or less).

The biggest challenge is thus to design and build software systems so that they can be adapted to dynamically varying resources, and this is why we have chosen to concentrate our work on this kind of adaptations. As we said in the introduction, we think that middleware approaches, with the explicit separation of *functional code* (resulting from the problem specification) and *non-functional code* (low level services dealing with the execution context) are a natural target for adaptations to the execution conditions.

The architecture we propose (see Fig. 1) roughly consists of three parts, corresponding to its three main functions: observation (of the environment and of the application), decision taking, and action (on the running system). A simple *monitoring framework* (Sect. 5) is used to detect changes in the execution environment, and introspection is used to observe the application. When a significant change is detected, an *adaptation engine* is notified. This component is in charge of deciding what modification is necessary to adapt the system, based on *adaptation policies* written in a custom language (Sect. 6). Finally, the decision taken by the adaptation engine is implemented on the running system by modifications of the associations between functional, business-level components and non-functional components implementing middleware-type services (Sect. 4).

The following sections present theses three subsystems in more details.

4   Application Model and Available Actions

This section describes the application model from the user's point of view, and the possible reconfigurations enabled by this model.

We consider that the application is composed of two kinds of components: functional ones (derived directly from the problem specification, in our example Customers and Books for instance), and non-functional ones (providing execution mechanisms and services adapted to a particular environment, for example distribution using RMI or SOAP). The modifications our system can perform

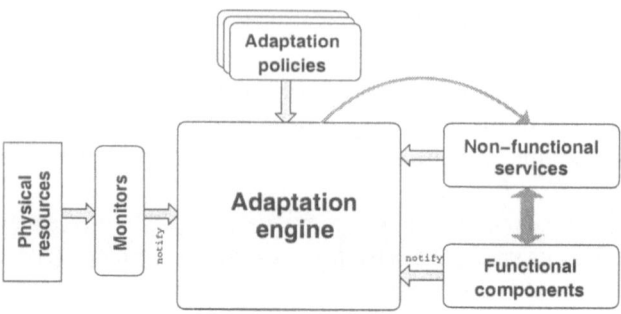

Fig. 1. Global architecture

concern the run-time associations between functional and non-functional components.

4.1 Functional Components

Because we didn't want to impose any unnecessary constraints to the application programmer, what we call functional components here are actually simple, completely standard Java objects. At least, from the user's point of view. When he develops his business code, the application programmer does not need to do anything special like implementing required interfaces, or conforming to any standard or conventions (like EJB's requirements for explicit interfaces specification). If we take the example presented in Section 2, the Catalog, Book, Customer and Order classes would be completely standard Java, without any reference to external libraries.

However, in order to be able to adapt the behavior of these objects, our infrastructure needs to get some control over their execution. Reflection and metaprogramming techniques [6,7] provide us exactly the kind of control we need. Every functional component thus gets associated with a metalevel controller which intercepts and interprets all objects creation, method receptions and fields accesses. The metalevel infrastructure uses the RAM Metaobject Protocol [8]. The metalevel controller associated to each functional component is an instance of Container, a subclass of RAM's default MetaObject class (see Figure 2 to get an idea of MetaObject's interface). The Container class, named so because of its similarities in role with Enterprise Java Beans containers [1], adds to this default metaobject class the support required for dynamic composition of services and is described in section 4.2.

In order to introduce the indirection to the metalevel into the standard Java code written by application programmers, we provide a special compiler described in [9] (actually a source preprocessor using AspectJ [10]) which transforms classes written by the user into RAM ReflectiveObjects. The transformation consists in the addition of a new field (the link to the metalevel Container), and the redirection of every method call, object creation and field

```
public class MetaObject implements Serializable {
    public Object create(ReflectiveObject creationRequestor,
                         Constructor constructor, Object[] initArgs);
    public void initialize(ReflectiveObject base, Object[] parameters);
    public Object invokeMethod(ReflectiveObject receiver, Method method, Object[] args);
    public Object getField(ReflectiveObject target, String fieldName);
    public Object setField(ReflectiveObject target, String fieldName,
                           Object oldValue, Object newValue);
    public void deserialize(ReflectiveObject obj, ObjectInputStream in);
    public void serialize(ReflectiveObject obj, ObjectOutputStream out);
}
```

Fig. 2. Outline of the RAM MetaObject protocol

access to this metaobject (the original methods are renamed and made transparently accessible from the metalevel).

To summarize, from the point of view of the application programmer functional components are standard Java objects, except that they must be compiled
using a special compiler. Behind the scene, this compilation adds reflective features to these objects using the RAM Metaobject Protocol, so that their behavior
can be observed and controlled at run-time.

4.2   Non-functional Components: Services & Roles

The second part of our application model deals with non-functional components.
These are meant to implement middleware-type services, like distribution and
persistence, and to be applied to functional components.

Figure 3 shows the classes used to model non-functional components in our
system.

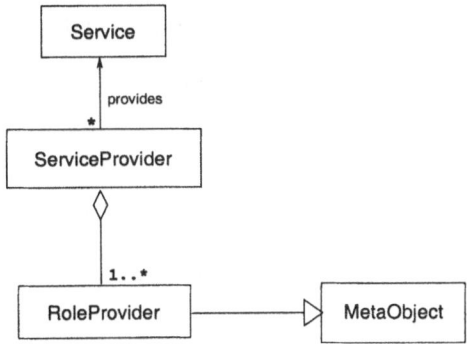

Fig. 3. Services and roles

Service Represents an abstract non-functional service, identified by a name.
Objects of this class currently serve only as identifiers and do not contain

any implementation. This allows for multiple implementations of the same service, each of which can have different properties. *Examples*: `replication`, `distribution`, `persistence`.

`ServiceProvider` Represents a specific implementation of a service. For example, a distribution service for our bookstore example application, implemented using RMI, would include an `RMIProvider` class specializing `ServiceProvider` which would declare implementing the `distribution` service.

`RoleProvider` Metaobjects providing the actual service implementation.

Although for very simple services like tracing only one component is concerned, for most services a cooperation between multiple components is necessary. For example, in a remote message sending service, at least two components must cooperate: a server and a proxy. Our system sees a service as a set of cooperating roles. Each of these roles is implemented by a specific `RoleProvider` metaobject, and these are coordinated by the corresponding `ServiceProvider`. In the previous example, the `RMIProvider` service defines two roles, named `server` and `proxy`. The usage of this service implies the use of both roles.

The `Container` attached to every functional component is a "generic" metaobject in the sense that it does not in itself modify the default interpretation of the messages it intercepts. However, it provides the ability to compose multiple `RoleProviders` (which are metaobjects) and to modify this composition dynamically[1]. To do this, `Containers` manage a dynamic list of `RoleProviders` attached to them, and provide a simple protocol to allow the dynamic manipulation of this list (see Fig. 4). This allows a fine-grained adaptation, because every single functional component can be adapted independently, as opposed to system-wide adaptations found in [5] for example, or even class-wide adaptations. When a `Container` intercepts a message sent to its underlying component, it reroutes the message to all the roles currently attached. Each non-functional component can then process the message in order to implement the non-functional service it corresponds to.

```
public interface Container {
  ...
  RoleProvider getRoleProvider(Service service, String role);
  void attach(RoleProvider rp);
  RoleProvider detach(Service service, String role);
  ...
}
```

Fig. 4. Roles manipulation protocol of the `Container` interface

---

[1] Currently, we do not handle the problem of the roles composition; they are simply chained and each one is called in turn. We plan to investigate existing works on this subject, like [11], to provide a more sophisticated solution in the future.

The result of this system is that the behavior of each functional component can be modified at runtime by attaching or detaching the appropriate
RoleProvider to its Container.

5 Observation

Adaptation must be guided by a good knowledge both of the execution environment and of the system itself. The observation framework described in this
section has two roles: to expose enough information to the adaptation engine to
allow it to take educated decisions, and to detect meaningful changes in these
informations. Of course, which changes are meaningful depends heavily on the
semantics of each application, so the framework itself is generic and is configured
for each application using information given in adaptation policies.

Concerning the environment, the system manages a hierarchy of objects of
class MonitoredResource accessible from a unique ResourcesManager. The top-
level node, named 'host', represents the local machine. Intermediary nodes
represent categories ('storage' for example), and leafs represent individual resources (for example, 'hda' representing the first hard drive). Each of these
nodes is described through *attributes* attached to them, which are simple *name*
/ *value* pairs. The values of these attributes can change dynamically and hence
represent the current state of the resource they are attached to. Figure 5 summarizes this organization.

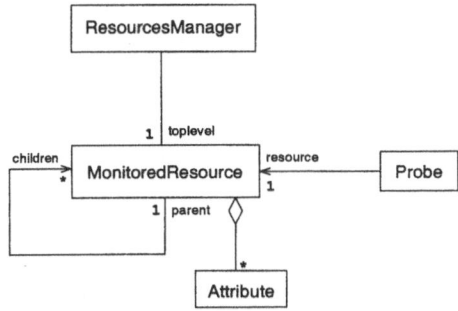

Fig. 5. MonitoredResources and Attributes

A particular resource can be designated using a syntax similar to Unix paths:
'/host/storage/permanent/hda' designates the node representing the first
hard drive. Accessing the value of an attribute is as simple: '/host/storage-
/permanent/hda.total_capacity_kb' represents the capacity of the hard drive.
The attributes attached to individual resources are called *primitive attributes*.
Another kind of attributes, called *synthesized attributes* can be attached to intermediary nodes. Their values are the result of arbitrary computations over the

attributes attached to sub-nodes. This allows for example to summarize information in order to get a higher-level view of the system. Currently, this requires the creation of a subclass of `MonitoredResource` in order to implement the necessary processing in Java.

The exact structure of the tree and the values of the node attributes are managed by instances of class `Probe`. Probes are active objects responsible for gathering information about the execution condition (for example the current load, battery status...). The information reflected by the `MonitoredResource` hierarchy is updated asynchronously by the different probes, and is always available to the adaptation engine through a query interface. Furthermore, `MonitoredRe-sources` implement a notification protocol, so that the adaptation engine can ask to be notified when a given attribute value changes or when a resource appears or disappears (which would happen for example if a new USB device is hot-plugged or unplugged in a computer).

This system gives the adaptation engine a dynamic view of the current execution context, but this is not enough to allow adaptation; the engine also needs a good knowledge of the program to be adapted itself. As we said earlier in section 4, the components constituting the application are represented indirectly in our system by generic `Containers`. To allow different components to be distinguished by the adaptation engine, we use the same technique as for resources: arbitrary attributes can be attached to containers to describe their underlying component. The system defines a small set of generic attributes which are added automatically to every container, like the `className` attribute, whose value is the name of the class of the underlying component. It is also possible to tell the system to automatically "export" as attributes the fields of the underlying component. For example, instances of class `Order` from our bookstore application example could export the value of their `totalAmount` field as an attribute to enable adaptations according to this information (cf 6.2). Container attributes support the same access protocols as resources attributes (explicit query and change notification).

6   Decision

This section describes how the adaptation engine works, and how it is configured.

The adaptation engine is the heart of our system. It is the link between the two other functionalities: observation and action. When the observation framework detects a meaningful change either in the execution environment or in the application itself, it notifies the engine, whose role is to decide what action is necessary to adapt the application, and then to implement this action using the operations made available by containers (attachment or detachment of roles).

The adaptation engine is designed to be completely independent of an application domain. However, adaptation decisions are highly dependent on the nature and semantics of the applications: a banking application does not have the same constraints as a multimedia one for example. Thus, the engine must be "specialized" for each application; this is done by configuring the engine using *adaptation policies.* Actually, adaptation policies can be thought of as adaptation programs written in a specific language. The adaptation engine is then an interpreter for these programs. Our long-term goal is for the language(s) used to write adaptation policies to be as high-level and declarative as possible, in order to ease the work of application programmers and administrators.

We decided to split adaptation policies in two parts: one designed to be written by application programmers and free from low-level considerations, and the other more oriented towards system administrators. The goal is to simplify the work of application programmers, and to allow them to ignore as much as possible platform-specific issues. These issues can be dealt separately by specialists. This split results in two kinds of adaptation policies, expressed at different levels of abstraction: low-level *system policies* and higher-level *application policies*, both of which are complementary and necessary to configure the adaptation engine.

6.1   System Policies

System policies are low-level policies, whose role is to define adaptation rules independently of application semantic. They are normally written by system specialists and they can be reused in different applications. Concretely, a system policy is a named set of rules of the form *condition ⇒ actions*, where the *condition* is a boolean expression concerning the execution environment (as reflected by the resources hierarchy described in Sect. 5), and *actions* is a list of actions, each describing the attachment or detachment of a particular role of a service (as described in Sect. 4). The adaptation engine uses the notification interface of the resources hierarchy to listen to the appropriate conditions. When such a condition occurs, it evaluates the set of corresponding actions.

In the current prototype, the policies are written using a Scheme-like syntax (easy to parse and flexible). The language is not a complete Scheme however, and the primitives available to define the condition part of a rule include only basic numerical operations and comparisons, string comparison and logical operators. As for the second part of the rule, it is not directly interpreted as an action *per se*. It actually tells the adaptation engine that a particular role must be attached (with appropriate parameters) or detached. When the rule is activated, the engine will determine if this implies an attachment, a reconfiguration or a removal of the mentioned role. For example, if the rule says that role `some.role` must be attached and that it already is, the engine does not need to do anything (except perhaps a reconfiguration if attachment parameters differ).

Application to the Example. Figure 6 shows four different (but related) system policies, which could be used in our bookstore example application to manage server-side and client-side distribution. The first two are generic server-side and client-side policies, comprised of only one rule. They are always active. Their corresponding action is to attach a `distribution.rpc.server` (resp. `distribution.rpc.client`) to functional objects, enabling simple remote message calls. The third policy is designed to be used by clients with a wireless network connection. Because this kind of connection tends to provide highly variable bandwidth, the policy adds a role implementing asynchronous method calls with transparent futures; this way the client is never blocked by a sudden drop in bandwidth, enhancing the user experience. The second rule adds a proxy.caching role (local caching of remote objects fields) to save bandwidth when it becomes too low[2]. Finally the last policy is to be used by mobile hosts relying on a battery: when the autonomy drops below 5 minutes, we add a persistence role to make sure we will not loose data in case of power failure.

```
(def-policy "distribution.server"
  (when #t (ensure-attached "distribution.rpc.server")))

(def-policy "distribution.default-client"
  (when #t (ensure-attached "distribution.rpc.client"
                            ((server . "pollux.info.emn.fr")))))

(def-policy "distribution.wireless-client"
  (when (= (attr "/host/network.connection-type") "wireless")
    (ensure-attached "invocation.asynchronous.future"))
  (when (and (= (attr "/host/network.connection-type") "wireless")
             (< (attr "/host/network.available-bandwidth_kbs") 5)
    (ensure-attached "proxy.caching"))))

(def-policy "distribution.mobile-client"
  (when (and (not (attr "/host/battery.charging"))
             (< (attr "/host/battery.autonomy_s") 300))
      (ensure-attached "persistence")))
```

Fig. 6. Examples of a system policies

In our example application, the first policy could be installed on the enterprise server to enable remote access to the catalog. The second one would be installed on a customer's desktop computer, while the second, third and fourth would all be deployed on his laptop. When the laptop is used as a desktop, using AC power and connected on the LAN, the rules defined in the distribution.wireless-client and distribution.mobile-client are inactive, and both client hosts behave in the same way.

---

[2] If the bandwidth varies a lot around 5 kb/s, this can lead to unstable states where the service is constantly attached and detached. This can be solved using less naive conditions, for example relative to synthesized attributes implementing a hysteresis mechanism.

6.2   Application Policies

Application policies are higher-level than system ones and, as their name implies, are designed to be written by programmers specifically for an application (*i.e.* they are not reusable). System policies answer two questions: *When?* (the condition part of the rules) and *What?* (the action part). However, they do not say *to whom* to apply these actions. This is the role of application policies: they tell the adaptation engine which of the functional components present in the system must be affected by which system policy.

To fulfill this goal, application policies define two things:

1. *components groups*, designating "similar" functional components, that must be adapted the same way;
2. and *bindings* between these groups and previously defined system policies (or specific services).

As we said earlier when describing components and containers (see Sect. 4), the only things that can be used to distinguish functional components are the attributes attached to their containers. Groups are hence defined according to the values of these attributes. More specifically, a component group is defined by three things: a name, a *super-group* and a filtering predicate expressed over components attributes. The members of the group are then all the members of the super-group for which the predicate evaluates to true. A special group, named **all** and containing every functional component in the system is used to "bootstrap" this definition mechanism. Of course, the attributes of components are dynamic, and can appear, disappear or change during the program execution. The system uses the notification interface of component attributes, combined with incremental evaluation of the predicates in order to track the dynamic composition of all the groups.

For each of these dynamic groups, the application policy then defines bindings to system policies. These provide the missing link between system policies and application policies. The semantic is simple: when a system policy is bound to a group, every adaptation rule in this policy applies to the members of this group. Instead of binding a whole system policy, it is also possible to bind a specific role, including configuration parameters for the role.

Application to the Example. Figure 7 shows examples of application policies which could be used with our bookstore example application. The first two policies are intended to be deployed on the server to supplement the system policies already presented. The first one simply identifies the functional components which will be affected by the **distribution.server** system policies (and hence be accessible remotely). The second policy defines a dynamic group of functional components, consisting of all the **Orders** of more than $ 500. These components are bound to a **logging** policy, not presented here but which logs all the activities on these components. The group it defines, **logged-components**, is dynamic in the sense that its filtering predicate depends on the **totalAmount** attribute, which reflects a field in the underlying Order Java object, and hence can change dynamically.

The third policy, remote-components.desktop, binds the default distri-bution.default-client to the functional components, making them simple proxies for the components living on the server. The last policy is almost the same, but is intended for laptops, and adds the corresponding system policies we described earlier.

```
;; Enterprise Server
(def-group "distributed-components" :parent "all"
   (select (or (= (attr "className") "com.mycompany.Catalog")
               (= (attr "className") "com.mycompany.Customer")
               (= (attr "className") "com.mycompany.Book")
               (= (attr "className") "com.mycompany.Order")))
   (bind "distribution.server"))

(def-group "logged-components" :parent "all"
   (select (and (= (attr "className") "com.mycompany.Order")
                (> (attr "totalAmount") 500)))
   (bind "logging"))

;; Desktop Client
(def-group "remote-components.desktop" :parent "all"
   (select (or (= (attr "className") "com.mycompany.Catalog")
               (= (attr "className") "com.mycompany.Customer")
               (= (attr "className") "com.mycompany.Book")
               (= (attr "className") "com.mycompany.Order")))
   (bind "distribution.default-client"))

;; Laptop Client
(def-group "remote-components.laptop" :parent "all"
   (select (or (= (attr "className") "com.mycompany.Catalog")
               (= (attr "className") "com.mycompany.Customer")
               (= (attr "className") "com.mycompany.Book")
               (= (attr "className") "com.mycompany.Order")))
   (bind "distribution.default-client" "distribution.wireless-client"
         "distribution.mobile-client"))
```

Fig. 7. Example of an application policy.

Now that both the system policies and the corresponding application poli-cies have been presented, we can have a closer look at how the system would react in a concrete situation. Consider a typical user working on his desktop computer. During a break, he launches the bookstore client application, starts to browse the catalog and selects some interesting titles. The application policy installed on his desktop machine is remote-components.desktop, which uses a very simple distribution mechanism (plain RMI); this is appropriate because the corporate network provides a high and stable bandwidth. After a while, the user realizes that an important meeting is scheduled in a few minutes, so he closes the client (without loosing any information, as it contained only proxy objects), takes his laptop with him and goes to the meeting room (which is equiped with a wireless network access point). The meeting taking more time than expected, our user decides to launch the bookstore client on his laptop to finish his order. The version installed on the laptop contains *exactly* the same Java code (`.class` files), the only difference being in the adaptation policies deployed (the laptop has the `remote-components.laptop` application policy and the system policies it requires). Because the state of his order has always stayed on the server, the user can restart his shopping at the point he stopped it on his desktop. At the beginning, because the conditions are close enough to the ones on the desktop, the additional policies have only one effect: the addition of an asynchronous messaging service (with transparent futures). However, as time goes by, the available bandwidth starts to drop (maybe his colleagues got bored also and started to browse the web). The monitoring system detects it and triggers the corresponding rule in the `distribution.wireless-client` policy, resulting in the addition of a service implementing local caching of object values in smart proxies. If the user's shopping basket contains more than $ 500 of books, the `logged-components` policy deployed on the server will make sure all the operations on the server-side `Order` object will get logged (for future analysis by marketing for example).

As this scenario shows, our system allows the exact same (binary) code to be adapted to different execution environments (server, various clients), and more importantly to *dynamically adapt* the behavior of this code to fit the evolution of these environments, or of the application itself.

6.3   Interpreting Adaptation Policies

Once both kinds of adaptation policies are loaded into the adaptation engine, they are merged together in a common internal model easier to interpret (see figure 8).

For each group, a `GroupBindings` object is created. Then, for each system policy bound to this group (in the application policy), each rule it defines is translated into a `Condition` and a `ServiceBinding` (including optional parameters). The resulting *conditional binding* is managed by the `GroupBindings` object.

The `Group` itself is only responsible to track its content (which functional components enter and leave it). The `GroupBindings` is the heart of the adaptation engine: it is responsible to implement the conditional binding for all the elements in the group, and only them. Concretely this means that at every instant, all the components currently in the group must have attached to them all the roles defined by the active bindings (the ones whose `Condition` is currently `true`).

To do this, the `GroupBindings` registers as a listener both from the group itself and from the condition. When it detects that a condition's value changes, it

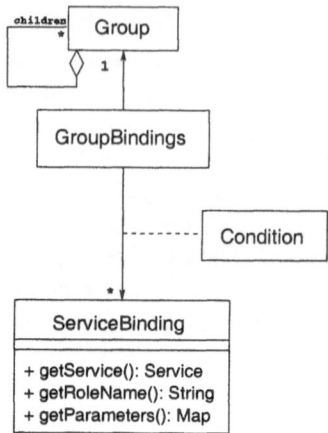

Fig. 8. Internal model used by the adaptation engine

attaches (if it became **true**) or detaches (if it became **false**) the corresponding role to/from every component currently in the group. Symmetrically, when the Group's content changes, all the currently active bindings are attached to the new components and detached from the ones who leave the group.

The performance and threading issues are not handled in the current model and prototype: detection of changes and modification of the system happen asynchronously and the platform offers no guarantee on the order of the operations. Lots of other issues remain unhandled currently, like detection and correction of conflicts between policies, and consistency guarantees that components reconfigurations do not interfere with their normal execution. All these issues are part of our planned future work; the current implementation focused on providing a simple proof of concept.

7   Prototype Usage

Concretely, our current prototype of this architecture consists of two elements: a special compiler used to make the application classes reflective [9] and an application launcher.

During the development phase, the application programmer only has to develop the business objects required for his application, and to compile them with the provided tool which builds reflective classes. Then, he must determine which non-functional services he wants for his components and encode this decision in an application policy. The rest of the development can be handled by someone else at deployment time.

The job of the deployer is to install the application on a specific host. To do this, he needs to write or reuse system policies required by the application policies, and adapted to the host. He also needs the actual probes and services implementations, but it should be possible to develop these completely independently of a specific application, and hence to get a high degree of reuse. From a more concrete point of view, the files needing to be installed include: the application code,the adaptation engine itself (currently about 300k of Java bytecode), the library of probes (specific to the deployment host), the adaptation policies (Scheme-like files), and the implementations of the services required by these policies. The difference between a client and a server will only come from the policies used to configure them and from the actual services used (in our bookstore example, `distribution.server` and `distribution.default-client`).

To actually run the application on a specific host, we provide an application launcher (included in the engine code). This launcher is given as parameter a set of configuration files (system and application policies), and the name of the main program to run. Its task is to setup the probes (part of the monitoring framework, Sect. 5), to discover the available services, and to configure the adaptation engine with the supplied policies. When this is done, it simply starts the application program. From then on, the engine becomes passive, and only reacts to notifications. These notifications can come either from the monitoring framework or from the application itself. When it receives such a notification, the engine interprets the appropriate policies and applies the required modification, before going passive again.

Using loose coupling between all the elements of our system (functional and non-functional components, system and application policies), our architecture allows a strong separation of the different roles: each of these tasks can be handled separately by specialists.

8   Related Work

This section discusses some of the other research projects in the field of adaptable middleware, and their relations to our work.

Open-ORB [12,4] is a project whose goal is to define an architecture for adaptable middleware, particularly in the domain of multimedia applications. It is based on a component model which includes explicit dependencies and interaction between components, support for continuous media (streaming), and an event notification model. This model is used both for base-level components and for a structured metalevel of components (called *metaspace models*). Adaptation is done through specialization of components at the metalevel, affecting the behavior of base-level components. Open-ORB has a lot of similarities with our model, but it does not put the same emphasis on how the adaptation decisions are taken (they must basically be programmed "by hand").

DART [13] is a platform allowing the development of distributed applications. It uses reflection techniques to enable dynamic adaptation, both at the base level and at the meta level, using mechanisms similar to a *Strategy* pattern [14] where the method lookup mechanism is extended to take into account the external execution conditions. The mechanisms it provides are very sophisticated and powerful, but actually using these mechanisms requires explicit programming of the adaptation policies.

The dynamicTAO ORB [5] is an extension of the CORBA compliant TAO ORB. TAO is a free ORB designed in a very modular way, so that it is possible to build (statically) custom versions of the ORB by choosing among different implementations for each part of the ORB engine. dynamicTAO makes it possible to use these reconfiguration capabilities at runtime. It uses a *Strategy* pattern [14] to organize the available implementations of ORB elements, and a monitoring service can be used to switch at runtime between these implementations, based on the changing execution conditions. The main problem with this approach is that the changes are system-wide; it is not possible to adapt independently different parts of the system.

MolèNE [15] is a framework designed to ease the development of adaptable applications in the domain of large scale mobile systems. It uses a reflective architecture where the adaptation code is written at the metalevel. When MolèNE's *Detection and Notification Framework* (similar to ours but more sophisticated) detects a change in this environment, it notifies the *adaptive components* constituting the application. These components are able to switch at runtime between different implementations (suited to different execution conditions). The adaptation strategies are encoded in an automata associated to adaptive components. The MolèNE framework is quite complete and sophisticated, but it handles only functional adaptation, and it requires multiple implementations of every functional components.

[16] describes an architecture designed to ease the adaptation of applications to changing execution conditions. The model considers different layers (operating system, middleware, application, and user), each of which is described using metadata in order to ease their collaborations. When the application invokes a service, the middleware uses both the application metadata and the metadata reflecting the execution conditions to decide how to implement this service. Applications can also ask the middleware to be notified when specific execution conditions occurs. This system allows fine adaptation of applications, but it requires that service calls are coded explicitly in the applications. Although we agree with the authors that complete transparency is not possible if we want adaptation (which requires awareness), we tried with our approach to untangle the core application code (not adapted directly in our system) from non-functional services (our main subject of adaptation).

9   Conclusion

In this paper, we presented an infrastructure which can be used to make middleware platforms dynamically adaptable to changing execution environment (Sect. 3). It uses a simple observation framework to reify the state of the execution environment and of the program itself, and metaprogramming techniques to modify the application programs by dynamically attaching or detaching non-functional services to functional components. Its main advantage over existing solutions is that all the adaptation code is expressed in *adaptation policies* using two special-purpose languages which are interpreted at run-time by an *adapta-*

tion engine. One of these languages is low-level and designed to be written by system administrators and deployers. The other is higher-level and designed for application programmers. Loose coupling between the elements of our system enables a strong separation of the different roles in application development, and the potential for reuse of code like probes and services.

9.1   Future Work

Future works are planned to improve the individual parts of our system, but without modifying the general architecture. The adaptation policies and the adaptation engine executing them will evolve toward a higher level of abstraction, with more declarative languages. We also want to study the relationships between our approach and Aspect-Oriented Programming and aspect languages [17].

A global formalization of the model and of its execution semantics – including concurrency – will also need to be developed. Concerning performance, we will investigate the use of partial evaluation techniques at different stages in the development process; for example, it should be possible using tools like AspectJ to statically weave non-functional aspects with functional components at deployment-time if we can detect (analyzing adaptation policies) that some bindings will never be changed. Finally, an important research direction will concern how multiple instances of our system can collaborate in a large-scale distributed application, where no one has a complete control or knowledge over the services and policies used by other parties.

References

[1] DeMichiel, L., mit Yal inalp, L., Krishnan, S.: Enterprise JavaBeans^{TM} Specification. SUN Microsystems. (2001) Version 2.0, Final Release.

[2] Object Management Group: Common object request broker architecture (CORBA/IIOP), version 2.5. OMG Document formal/2001-09-01 (2001)

[3] Sessions, R.: COM+ and the battle for the Middle Tier. Wiley (2000)

[4] Blair, G.S., Coulson, G., Andersen, A., Blair, L., Clarke, M., Costa, F., Duran, H., Parlavantzas, N., Saikoski, K.B.: A principled approach to supporting adaptation in distributed mobile environments. In: 5th International Symposium on Software Engineering for Parallel and Distributed Systems (PDSE-2000), Limerick, Ireland (2000)

[5] Kon, F., Rom n, M., Liu, P., Mao, J., Yamane, T., Magalh es, L.C., Campbell, R.H.: Monitoring, security, and dynamic configuration with the dynamicTAO reflective ORB. In: Proceedings of Middleware 2000, International Conference on Distributed Systems Platforms, New York, USA. Volume 1795 of LNCS., Springer-Verlag (2000) 121–143

[6] Maes, P.: Concepts and experiments in computational reflection. In: Proceedings of OOPSLA'87, New York, USA, ACM SIGPLAN, ACM Press (1987) 147–155

[7] Kiczales, G., des Rivi res, J., Bobrow, D.G.: The art of the Meta-Object Protocol. MIT Press (1991)

[8] Bouraqadi-Sa dani, N.M.N., Ledoux, T., S dholt, M.: A reflective infrastructure for coarse-grained strong mobility and its tool-based implementation. In: Invited presentation at the *International Workshop on "Experiences with reflective systems"* (held in conjunction with Reflection 2001). (2001)

[9] David, P.C., Ledoux, T., Bouraqadi-Sa dani, M.N.: Two-step weaving with reflection using AspectJ. In: OOPSLA 2001 Workshop on Advanced Separation of Concerns in Object-Oriented Systems, Tampa, USA (2001)

[10] Kiczales, G., Hilsdale, E., Hugunin, J., Kersten, M., Palm, J., Griswold, W.G.: An overview of AspectJ. In Knudsen, J.L., ed.: ECOOP 2001. Volume 2072 of LNCS., Springer-Verlag (2001) 327–353

[11] Pawlak, R., Seinturier, L., Duchien, L., Florin, G.: JAC: A flexible and efficient solution for aspect-oriented programming in Java. In: Reflection 2001. Volume 2192 of LNCS., Springer-Verlag (2001) 1–24

[12] Andersen, A., Blair, G.S., Eliassen, F.: OOPP: A reflective component-based middleware. In: NIK 2000, Bodø, Norway (2000)

[13] Raverdy, P.G., Lea, R.: Reflection support for adaptive distributed applications. In: Proceedings of the 3rd International Enterprise Distributed Object Computing Conference (EDOC '99). (1999)

[14] Gamma, E., Helm, R., Johnson, R., Vlissides, J.: Design Patterns. Professional Computing Series. Addison-Wesley (1994)

[15] Malenfant, J., Segarra, M.T., Andr , F.: Dynamic adaptability: the Mol NE experiment. In Yonezawa, A., Matsuoka, S., eds.: Proceedings of Reflection 2001, The Third International Conference on Metalevel Architectures and Separation of Crosscutting Concerns, Kyoto, Japan. LNCS 2192, AITO, Springer-Verlag (2001) 110–117

[16] Capra, L., Emmerich, W., Mascolo, C.: Reflective middleware solutions for context-aware applications. In Yonezawa, A., Matsuoka, S., eds.: Proceedings of Reflection 2001, The Third International Conference on Metalevel Architectures and Separation of Crosscutting Concerns, Kyoto, Japan. LNCS 2192, AITO, Springer-Verlag (2001) 126–133

[17] Kiczales, G., Lamping, J., Mendhekar, A., Maeda, C., Lopes, C.V., Loingtier, J.M., Irwin, J.: Aspect-oriented programming. In: Proceedings of the European Conference on Object-Oriented Programming (ECOOP). Volume 1241 of LNCS, Springer-Verlag (1997)

A Reflective Middleware Framework for Communication in Dynamic Environments

Sebastian Gutierrez-Nolasco[1] and Nalini Venkatasubramanian[1]

University of California, Irvine, Irvine, CA 92697-3430 USA
{seguti,nalini}@ics.uci.edu

Abstract. The goal of a flexible communication framework is to allow dynamic customization of complex communication protocols without compromising the overall system performance. However, the communication protocols provided in successful middleware frameworks are usually tailored to specific and/or static requirements are not suitable for dynamic environments. In dynamic environments, applications must be able to customize communication protocols on-the-fly in order to respond to change requirements while protecting the system from reaching inconsistent states that can lead to deadlocks, livelocks and incorrect execution semantics. Hence, there is a need to identify interprotocol and protocol-(middleware) service interactions in order to ensure safe flexibility of the system. The work described here proposes a reflective communication framework (RCF) capable of expressing different levels of dynamic customization of communication protocols while ensuring safe customization of communication protocols.

1 Introduction

Current advances in storage and networking technologies such as wireless communication, mobile computing and real-time system support have enabled a new class of applications that require ubiquitous access to information, anywhere, anyplace and anytime. Such applications demand a high degree of flexibility and adaptability in order to deal with (a)changes in application requirements and (b)changes in the computational and communication environment. In order to ensure cost-effective system performance and provide a high degree of flexibility and adaptability in such environments, dynamic communication customization is required. In this paper, we develop a customizable communication framework where interactions between application components can be dynamically reconfigured to adapt to changing application, network and system conditions.

Middleware abstracts communication services, allowing the development of network transparent distributed applications. Although current middleware platforms provide mechanisms to enhance application behavior transparently at runtime [30], communication services provided are tailored to specific and usually static requirements. Such static communication frameworks are not well suited in dynamic asynchronous environments, where the communication framework must be able to automatically reconfigure itself in order to respond to changes

R. Meersman, Z. Tari (Eds.): CoopIS/DOA/ODBASE 2002, LNCS 2519, pp. 791–808, 2002.

in the computational and communication environments, such as resource and service restrictions, or changing network conditions and/or network availability.

For example, financial applications use time sensitive information to forecast and represent the stock market accurately. These applications usually run in private networks, which guarantee certain degree of reliability and security. In order to be able to access this information in a ubiquitous fashion (i.e. anywhere, anytime) via a handheld device, we require a communication environment that provides support for continuous flow of time sensitive information in the presence of varying network and system conditions. In order to achieve this, we assume that every message has a predefined valid time span, which defines the message lifetime. This time span is defined by the application and may vary over time. Thus, the communication framework will try to deliver the message before reaching the end of the time period by using a timed delivery protocol with priorities timeouts and selected retransmission based on the application time span. If the environment becomes also insecure, a secure communication protocol is required to guarantee message integrity, secrecy and possibly authenticity. Intuitively, layering the timed delivery protocol on top of the security protocol will not work, because the protocol was not designed to deal with an insecure medium, which may corrupt or fake messages. For instance, the header of the protocol will remain unprotected and may be modified. However, layering the security protocol on top of the timed delivery protocol may not work either since encryption is an intensive computational task that may significantly alter the message time span.

When two or more communication protocols are composed in order to obtain their combined benefits, their guarantees (desirable properties, e.g. security and timed delivery) are not always preserved. Preservation of protocol guarantees may crucially depend on the composition order and their interaction parameters.

Furthermore, the presence of middleware services may further complicate the communication between them. e.g. object mobility is used to exploit locallity and provide a certain degree of fault tolerance, but it also adds location uncertainity, which may impact the performance and correctness of the communication framework.

In this paper, we propose a reflective communication framework (RCF) using a meta-architectural approach to allow for dynamic customization and reconfiguration of communication protocols. The RCF is based on a formal model that allows for us to reason about the correctness of customizability. Specifically, we analyze issues with inter-protocol interactions, protocol-service interactions and show how multiple communication protocols and middleware services can be safely and dynamically reconfigured using the proposed architecture.

Our objective is to build an efficient framework that realizes the formal model and preserves the correctness properties. Furthermore, the basic RCF architecture can be integrated into generic distributed computing environment or middleware framework. To illustrate the feasibility of this approach, we have integrated the RCF model into a reflective middleware architecture, CompOSE|Q [24], currently being developed at the University of California, Irvine.

The remainder of this paper is organized as follows. In Section 2, we discuss the basic theoretical model of a flexible distributed environment. In Section 3, we describe the basic RCF framework. Composability and interaction issues are discussed in Section 4. We describe implementation issues encountered while developing an RCF and discuss initial performance results in Section 5. We describe related work and conclude in Section 6 with future research directions.

2   The Two Level Meta Architectural Model

Since the actor model of computation [11] incorporates the notion of encapsulation and interaction only via message passing, it offers a clear, flexible and simple semantic approach to describe distributed systems based on incoming communications [12]. The system is modeled as a group of self contained and independent autonomous objects, called actors, which communicate via asynchronous (buffered) message passing. On receiving a communication, an actor processes the message in a manner determined by its current behavior. As a result, the actor may: (1) Create new actors, (2) Change its behavior and (3) Send messages to itself or to other (existing) actors. Since mail addresses may be communicated in messages the configuration of the communication is dynamic and the activation order (one message activates another if the latter is sent during the processing of the former) determines communication patterns.

The two level actor machine (TLAM) model refines the actor model to specify, compose and reason about resource management services in open distributed systems[28]. In the TLAM model, a system is composed of two kinds of actors, base actors and meta actors, distributed over a network of processing nodes. Base actors carry out application level computation, while meta actors are part of the run-time system, which manages system resources and controls the run-time behavior of the base level. Meta actors communicate with each other via message passing as do base actors, and they may also examine and modify the state of the base actors located on the same node. Base level actors and messages have associated run-time annotations that can be set and read by meta actors. The annotations are invisible to base level computation. Actions which result in a change of base level state, are called events and meta actors may react to them if they occur on their node.

A TLAM configuration has a set of base and meta level actors and a set of undelivered messages. The actors are distributed over the TLAM nodes. Each actor has a unique name (actor identifier) and the configuration associates a current state to each actor name. The undelivered messages are distributed over the network (some are traveling along communication links and others are held in node buffers).

CompOSE|Q [24] is a a reflective middleware framework based on the TLAM model that facilitates the specification and reasoning about the dynamic composition and concurrent execution of resource management policies in open distributed systems. To ensure non-interference and manage the complexity of reasoning about components of open distributed environments in general, the

TLAM strategy is to identify key system services where non-trivial interactions between the application and system occur, i.e. base-meta interactions. We refer to these key services as *core services* (see Figure 1). Core services are then used in specifying and implementing more complex activities within the framework as purely meta-level interactions. e.g. a QoS Brokerage service in [27], a logger service in [25] and a distributed garbage collector service in [26].The development of suitable non-interference requirements allows us to reason about composition of multiple system services; these services have constraints that must be obeyed to maintain composability. We have identified three core activities:

- **Remote Creation:** - Recreation of services/data at a remote site. Remote creation can be used as the basis for designing algorithms for activities such as migration, replication and load balancing.
- **Distributed Snapshot:** Capturing information at multiple nodes/sites used as a basis for distributed garbage collection
- **Directory Services:** Interactions with a global repository. Directory services can be used to provide access control and implement group communication protocols.

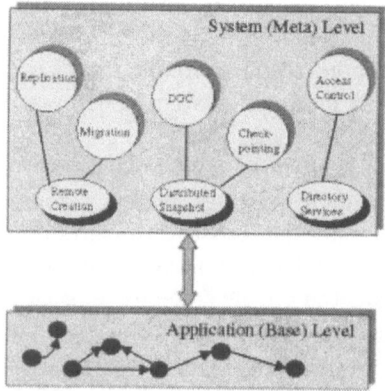

Fig. 1. Classification of core services

3   A Reflective Communication Framework

In this section, we describe a meta level communication framework that (a)provides run-time flexibility in the composition of communication protocols while ensuring their correctness and (b)ensures correctness of the resource management services (e.g. garbage collection, migration, etc.) in the presence of the flexible communication layer. To achieve this, the communication framework must distinguish and handle different types of messages and communication protocols among objects (actors) in the system.

In order to provide correct composition of communication protocols in a transparent and scalable fashion, the TLAM model is extended with a reflective communication framework (RCF), which customizes the base level communication as follows (see Figure 2). Each base level actor has a meta level actor, called *messenger*, which serves as the customized and transparent mail queue for that base level actor. There is one *communication manager* in every node of the distributed system, which implements and controls the correct composition of communication protocols specified by messengers on that node. A messenger has four message queues:

- The *up* queue is used as the (base level) actor's send buffer.
- The *down* queue is used to deliver messages to the (base level) actor, serving as its customized mail queue.
- The *in* queue is used for interaction with the communication manager, requesting communication services of the incoming messages (to the base level actor).
- The *out* queue is used for interaction with the communication manager, requesting communication services for the outgoing messages (from the base level actor).

Hence, the *up* and *down* queues hold messages with no communication protocols attached to them (i.e. raw messages), while the *in* and *out* queues hold messages with communication protocols attached to them (i.e. processed messages). The *in* and *out* queues allow us to support timing QoS constraints through message priority, since messages may be reordered and served according to their priority.

The communication manager has a set of communication protocol actors, each of them implementing a particular communication protocol provided by the framework (e.g. reliable, in-order or security). This scheme allows us to abstract a core set of communication protocols and share it between the different messengers on a node, simplifying the synchronization and composition process. Furthermore, it encourages separation of concerns in the process of message transmission and reception. However, in purely reflective architectures, reasoning about the semantics of correct communication composition may be complicated; moreover, its implementation may be inefficient.

In order to maintain accurate semantics and provide an efficient implementation of the architecture, the communication manager implements a set of meta level entities, called communication message coordinators (or simply *message coordinators*).Every message requiring a communication protocol is assigned a message coordinator and at any instance, a message coordinator handles the composition of the communication protocols requested by a messenger for an individual message. The message coordinator assures the correct order of composition of required protocols and provides a coordination mechanism between the messenger and the protocols that provide it. This concept of reusable message coordinators is an efficient way to handle the service request of each messenger without having to pay the bottleneck associated with the centralization of the services in the node communication manager and allows us to process concurrently multiple messages.

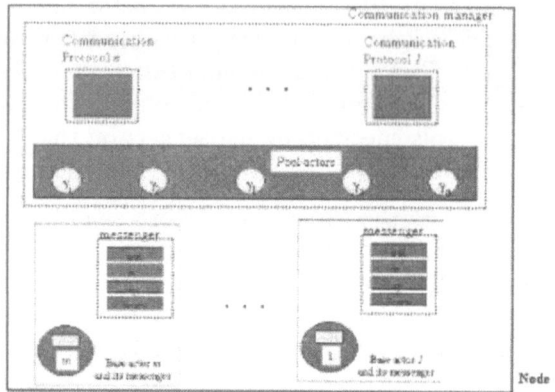

Fig. 2. The reflective communication framework model

In the RCF model, a communication protocol may be explicitly requested (at any instance) by the sender or implicitly specified by its messenger, in case the sender and the receiver previously agreed to use a particular communication protocol. In order to provide dynamic customization of communication protocols (potentially on a per message basis), the RCF model separates specification, composition and implementation of communication protocols.

The specification is handled by the messenger through a message service list (*msl*), which determines the set of communication protocols to be used in the communication of a specific message to its target. The communication protocols required by a communication may be explicitly specified or constructed by the messenger using target-actor information within the message. The messenger also assigns every outgoing message a unique message identifier (*msgid*), which is a unique sequence of values assigned to every message to be sent. The *msgid* is composed by concatenating the communication manager identifier (*cmid*), an application identifier (*appid*), a communication manager sequence number (*cms*) and a local time stamp (*ts*) defined by Lamport's happened-before relation [17]. The protocols themselves are implemented by independent communication protocol actors. This scheme allows us to add (*plug in*) or remove (*plug out*) communication protocols dynamically.

4   Protocol Interactions and Interference

Issues of correctness can be quite subtle and complex in dynamic asynchronous environments, where fluctuations in the communication environment may interfere with the execution of communication protocols and middleware services. For a long time, customization of communication protocols has been seen as an isolated communication protocol composition problem and its interactions with other resource management (middleware) services underestimated. We have identified two common aspects that must be constrained in order to achieve safe flexibility while providing customization of communication services: Protocol interference and Protocol-Service interactions.

4.1 Protocol Interference

In order to support customization, the communication framework may need to alter the set of currently executing protocols. A newly chosen protocol set must be composed. This in turn implies that the composition order of the combined protocols be constrained in order to preserve their communication guarantees and obtain their combined benefits. Although the problem of determining the correct composition order of communication protocols has not been completely solved, several useful techniques have been developed. In particular, Horus [32] and Ensemble [22] provide a finite set of ready-to-use protocol stacks for group communication, each one of them implementing a specific set of properties. BAST [3] is more flexible and presents an extensible set of communication protocols to provide fault tolerance that can be combined at run-time. Unfortunately, protocol composition goes far beyond the mere layering order of the protocols due to subtle interaction properties that must be clearly spelled out.

Let us assume that we have an application server *svr* running in a private network and three mobile objects *a,b* and *c* that want to access time sensitive information from *svr* and communicate with each other in an ubiquitous reliable fashion. Since the communication environment may lack support for continuous flow of information, due to unpredictable network conditions, a timed delivery protocol *TD1* may be selected (transparent to the end user) to provide timed reliable delivery of messages within a certain period of time, using message counters and selected retransmission.

Assuming that *a,b* and *c* are moving towards an insecure environment, they may decide to add a secure communication protocol *S1* (in addition to the *TD1* protocol already provided), in order to ensure message integrity,secrecy and possibly authenticity.

As we previously described, mere layering *TD1* after *S1* or *S1* after *TD1* will not work, because *TD1* was not designed to deal with an insecure medium, which may corrupt or fake messages and the algorithm used in *S1* may increase the processing time required to encrypt/decrypt a message far beyond the message time span. Furthermore, most security protocols work under the assumption of a session based communication that may not hold in dynamic environments, where a frequent re-keying operation may need to be executed. Thus, messages may face temporary delays due to re-keying, contributing to further communication overhead. Under these circumstances, the framework should be able to select a more suitable security protocol *S2* (based on message digests, for instance) in order to reduce the overhead and comply with the application timing requirement.

As can be observed, the time span (or deadline) is an interaction parameter that constrains communication protocol behaviors in order to achieve an application requirement (i.e. timed delivery). Usually, interaction parameters are entwined in the protocol functionality, for example, the message time-out values in a reliable delivery protocol.

We believe that for communication to be truly customizable, protocols must be encoded to separately specify (a) protocol functionality and (b) interaction properties and parameters. This will provide us the ability to determine what interaction parameters are affected when protocols are composed and allow us to modify these parameters independently if necessary. Furthermore, the chosen protocols may exhibit dependencies on other protocols or micro-protocols. Protocol dependency schemes have been researched and we have been able to integrate and leverage dependence relationships between protocols studied in other projects [4] [22].

This provides us with an initial sample set of communication protocols to uncover interaction properties that we are use in the development of a generic rule base. The rule base is used as an oracle using which the RCF determines which protocol implementation is more suitable to use for a particular application in terms of actual requirement coverage and efficiency.

Within the RCF, each protocol specification is enhanced with (i)a list of prerequisites (dependencies) *prlst*, (ii)a list of restrictions *rstlst* and (iii)a list of interaction parameters *iplst*. The *prlst* specifies requirements of the protocol in terms of other protocols; while the *rstlst* specifies restrictions on protocol composability (e.g. protocol *cp1* can not be executed with protocol *cp4*)[1]. The *iplst* specifies the parameters that might be adjusted in order to ensure safe composition of protocols.

Using the modular specifications described above, the message coordinator ensures safe protocol composition by coordinating and possibly constraining protocol execution order at the sender side as follows:

1. Extracts the *prlst* and *rstlst* of each protocol listed in the message service list (*msl*).
2. Creates a master list of *prlst* and *rstlst* by eliminating protocol redundancies in the individual *prlst* and *rstlst* lists.
3. Extracts from the message payload the application requirements.
4. Determines the required interaction parameters by using the information encoded in the *iplst* lists, the application requirements and the predefined rule base strategy.
5. Generates a composition order list *ordl* by cross referencing and using the information encoded in the *prlst* and *rstlst* master lists.
6. Verifies that the composition order obeys the interaction constraints and adjusts the required interaction parameters.

---

[1] The mechanisms for creation and formal verification of prerequisites and restrictions are beyond the scope of this paper

7. Serializes execution order if it is required to assure safe composition.
8. Coordinates communication protocol execution by enforcing execution constraints.

The above steps are mainly required at the sender side where a message is composed. Handling messages delivered at the receiver end is simple since the specific communication protocol set applied to the message payload must only be unwrapped.

4.2   Protocol-Service Interactions

In this section, we briefly illustrate protocol-service interaction issues that can arise when communication protocols (e.g. a reliable delivery protocol) and a middleware service (e.g. a migration service) interact. Here, we use the term *protocol* as an implementation of a particular semantic property (or property variant) in the communication environment, and *middleware service* as an activity on the end-point nodes to implement specific application requirements or tasks. Usually, middleware (resource management) services make assumptions about the underlying communication environment. If these assumptions are not satisfied by the communication subsystem, correctness violations, such as inconsistent states and incorrect execution semantics may occur. Let us consider the interaction between the migration service and the communication subsystem in dynamic environments. The migration service allows actor relocation for easier access, availability and load balancing. Let us further consider a specific implementation of the actor migration service that uses a 3 phase approach: (1)Phase C_0 determines the computation to be migrated by suspending the actor computation and noting its current description, (2)Phase C_1 creates a new remote actor with the current actor description in the desired node and (3)Phase C_3 establishes transparent access to the migrated actor by changing the original actor's behavior to a *forwarder* that redirects all the incoming messages to the new actor location. When an actor migrates every so often, a forwarder actor chain is built to redirect incoming messages The forwarder chain may contain cycles and does not provide information about the current actor location. The migration process can be enhanced to detect when an actor returns to a previously visited location and reconciliate the cycle to avoid unnecessary loops. This implies that the local migration manager on a node (which executes the cycle detection and reconciliation algorithm) has access to the entire history, i.e. forwarder chain of objects, of the migrating object.

Traversing this forwarder chain may take an unpredictable amount of time, especially if the actor is migrating during the traversal process.

Let us now assume that a reliable message delivery protocol is integrated into this framework. Since determining where the target actor of a message currently resides can possibly take an unpredictable amount of time, the timeout values encoded into the reliable delivery protocol may be meaningless. This can destroy message delivery guarantees even when the underlying transport layer is reliable. i.e. In the extreme case, if an actor is continuously migrated from one location to another, a message sent to it may be continuously forwarded to the previous actor location, but never reaches the actor due to the frequent actor migration. In fact the problem is worse. It is complex for a sender to distinguish between a message that is in transit chasing its migrating destination and a message that is lost due to unreliable delivery.

Figure 3 illustrates this problem. Actors A and B on nodes N1 and N2 respectively exchange messages (m_1,m_2), then A decides to migrate to node N3(becoming actorA') and a forwarder chain (dashed line) is established between the actor's previous location (depicted as A) and its current location (depicted as A'). If B sent a message m_3 to A (at any point in time during or after the migration), m_3 will be forwarded to the new actor location (A') as soon as the migration has completed; meanwhile A' may decide to migrate again to node N4, now becoming A'' and the forwarder chain is updated. Since m_3 must now traverse the forwarder chain, it is possible that the original timeout value may expire. B now sends another message m_4 (which could possibly be a retransmission of m3). Meanwhile, the actor continues to migrate asynchronously to node N5 (object A''') and then to node N6 (object A'''') without any knowledge that messages m_3 and m_4 are chasing it. In fact, the problem get more complicated if B starts to migrate (which may be the case in actual applications). In this case we have acknowledgements chasing a migrating sender.

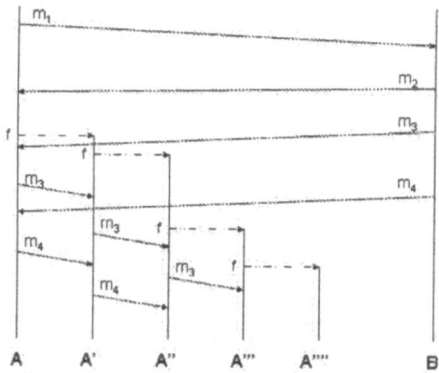

Fig. 3. Interaction diagram of the composition problem between a reliable delivery protocol and a migration service

A naive solution is the use of a flooding mechanism such as broadcast or multicast whereby every reliable message is broadcast to every node; the messaging layer can then determine if a current incarnation of the object resides on its node. Apart from being excessive in terms of messaging overhead, this solution requires that each object maintain the entire history of all possible previous names; it also requires that the messaging layer traverse the history chain of potentially every object on its node. We dismiss this solution due to the excessive overhead that will result in highly dynamic message-based environments with frequent object migrations.

A conservative solution is to constrain actor mobility in order to guarantee message delivery. A pessimistic approach may serialize the migration and reliable messaging sending processes (e.g by publishing well known intervals when objects may migrate) [2].

We propose a conservative (yet not fully pessimistic) solution where we constrain actor migration only during the time required to ensure message delivery to that specific object. This solution requires that some node in the forwarder chain realizes when a reliable message must be delivered to a local object and restrains the migration process until the desired messages are delivered. Assuming that we are able to reconcile forwarder chains, the overhead of successful message delivery is upper bounded by $O(NP)$ where N is the total number of nodes in the system and P is maximum number of protocols that need to be applied to the message. That is, in the worst case, the actor may visit every node in the system before being notified that it cannot migrate until the chasing messages are delivered to it.

We now add a timed delivery requirement to this process. The above solution proposed can only ensure the worst case timing guarantees due to the fact that traversing a forwarder chain may take a significant amount of time, especially if the actor migrates frequently during the traversal process, the number of nodes in the network is huge and/or the protocol processing overheads are high.

We propose a more reasonable approach to enforcing timing constraints where we can upper bound message delivery overhead to be $OC + P$ where C is a constant representing the DS overhead. In this solution, a directory service always maintains the current location of the object (this is a feature already implemented in CompOSE|Q to ensure composability of middleware services). A timed (reliable) messaging protocol will now consult the DS to determine the current actor location. As a side effect, the DS entry is annotated with a *disable-migration* action. If a migration has already been initiated (but not completed) before the message from timed-delivery protocol reaches the DS, the existing (to become stale) location is returned to the timed-delivery protocol. The current migration is allowed to proceed asynchronously and succeed, a forwarder is established and a subsequent migration from the new location is stalled until the desired message has been acknowledged to be delivered. The timed reliable message will now need to traverse at most one forwarder link. The worst case time taken for reliable delivery is now the sum of a DS access time (constant) and the overhead of traversing one forwarder link. Note, however that this solution requires suitable enhancements to the reliable delivery protocol, the directory management modules and the migration service. The RCF modules can adaptively choose to traverse the forwarder chains or consult the DS based on the

---

[2] Note that placing strong constraints on actor behavior (ability to migrate in this case) can be overly restrictive and prevent adaptation to system and application criteria. In fact, they may be used by an arbitrary (malicious) actor to produce byzantine failures.

timeliness requirements of the reliable message and some information on the frequency of migration of the object under consideration. For further details on the correctness reasoning of the above protocol-service composition, refer to[34].

5   Implementation and Performance

In order to provide an implementation environment of the RCF, we constrain the *Java* programming language to achieve actor semantics [28][33][6]. Since a messenger may have multiple communication request in its queues at any point in the execution, our objective is to exploit maximal concurrency in the processing of messages without violating actor semantics. This in term requires that access to the multiple messenger queues be appropriately synchronized.

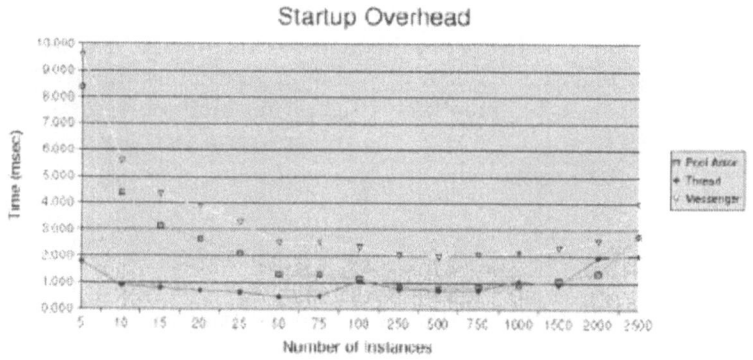

Fig. 4. Thread, Pool Actor and Messenger creation overhead

We adopt a *pipelined* approach to execute multiple communication operations within a messenger. we also provide for the activation of external (new or pre-existing) actors within messages, thereby supporting a continuation pattern style (CPS) implementation [5]. To achieve this, we extend the *Active Object pattern* appropriately [31] and instantiate CPS execution via the *command pattern* [8]. The main advantage of this approach is that the individual operations on a messenger need not be strictly sequential. In fact, the only synchronization necessary is in the messenger's queues, since more than one message coordinator, the runtime transport layer and the messenger itself might try to dequeue a message from the same queue or from an empty queue or enqueue a message into the same queue. To facilitate this, we developed a blocking queue mechanism based on a linked list implementation (see Table 2), in order to ensure correct execution. Although the overhead in Java for synchronized access to the messenger queues is quite expensive; we have observed that it is a fixed cost that can be amortized by pipelining as the number of messages in the system increases. This amortization is bounded by the available heap space allocated to the runtime environment.

Table 1. Creation overhead of the RCF: The Communication manager has three communication protocols and a pool size of ten message coordinators. The Messenger creation is slightly more expensive because it has 4 queues that must be initialized

Creation Overhead	μsec
Communication Manager Pool (10) (9960) Protocols(3) (2990)	12950
Message Coordinator	996
Messenger	1203

The platform used to measure the performance of the RCF model are Sun Ultra5 workstations (333Mhz UltraSPARC IIi with 256KB external cache and 128 MB RAM) running Solaris 2.7 connected via a 100Mb/s Ethernet link. The performance metric results presented below were obtained without timing *inlined JVM* internal calls using JDK-1.2.2 with green threads:

1. **RCF Startup Overhead:** The amount of time required for the communication manager startup is dependent of the number of protocols initially implemented and the size of the (message coordinator) pool specified. Initially, we decided to model 3 protocols and a pool size of 10 message coordinators (Table 1). Although expensive at startup in terms of system resources, the pool really improves the performance at run-time because message coordinators are awakened when needed instead of being created at run-time, which can be quite expensive as Figure 4 shows. Note that the high cost paid by the messenger and message coordinators at the beginning is due to the initialization of the blocking queues, four for every messenger and one for each message coordinator. Unfortunately, messenger creation happens at run-time, which may decrease system performance. An alternative solution would be to create a pool of messengers at startup and link them at run-time.

2. **Messenger Management Overhead:** During messenger creation, 4 blocking queues are created and initialized. Queue initialization is expensive due to the linked list implementation and the spin lock required to avoid race conditions in message dequeue operations. Table 2 shows the blocking queue overhead in terms of its common operations.

Table 2. Blocking Queue Operations:

Blocking Queue Operations	μsec
Initialization	1136
Enqueue	308
Dequeue	325
Flush	160

Since every messenger has 4 blocking queues that can hold either raw messages (*i.e.*, messages without protocol services attached to it) or processed messages, and it must be able to inspect the contents of enqueued messages without dequeueing them, messenger management overhead becomes critical (Table 3).

Table 3. Message Operations:

Message Operations	μsec
Message Inspection	223
Raw Message Enqueue	489
Raw Message Dequeue	466
Processed Message Enqueue	1710
Processed Message Dequeue	1801

3. **Total Message Overhead:** In order to measure the end-to-end message overhead, we use $CompOSE|Q$ as our underlying run-time environment, which consists of a set of runtime kernels that run on individual nodes of the distributed system and middleware components that provide the required distributed services (*i.e.* object migration, directory services or distributed garbage collection). The node runtime kernel is a substrate on which actors execute. The principal components of a node runtime kernel are:

   a) A *node manager* actor, which manages and coordinates various components in a node.
   b) A *node info manager* actors, which manages information needed by local actors and interfaces with a global (logically centralized) directory service.
   c) A transport subsystem that handles messages between actors. It provides a framework for sending the the outgoing messages to the appropriate node (routing) and resolving incoming messages to their appropriate actor queues (message resolution).

As we can see in Table 4, the end-to-end message overhead is measured by categorizing the different overheads involved in the process. First we measured the message transmission and reception overheads of the underlying transport layer. Then, we integrated our model into the framework and measured the time needed to send a raw message and a message tunneled through the RCF. Finally, we send processed messages using a reliable secure customization.

   a) **Raw Message Overhead:** During system startup a *communication manager* is instantiated in each node of the system. When an actor is created and protocol composition services are not desired or required, a corresponding *messenger* is not created; the actor sends and receives raw messages using the underlying message transport layer.
   b) **RCF Tunneling Overhead:** When flexible communication is required or desired, an independent *messenger* is created for every base level actor

and the entire RCF functionality is invoked. Since an actor can potentially communicate differently (using different protocols or not using any protocol) with each of its acquaintances at any time, the overhead of the RCF model must be minimized in the case of communications with no protocols attached. In this scenario, we tunnel raw messages through the actor's *messenger* directly to the underlying message transport layer.

c) **Processed Message Overhead:**Because most of the protocols need to add some information to the message (in the form of headers), its execution contributes to some processing overhead, which increases the total time by one order of magnitude. Reducing the overhead of protocol layering is a difficult task; fortunately, this cost is almost neglected in terms of remote communication due to the roundtrip delay, which is estimated to be between 20-41 milliseconds. Our actual implementation is suboptimal since a naive implementation of the protocol results in the protocol overhead being around 0.622 milliseconds. Possible optimizations may be obtained if we replicate stateless protocols[3], and improve current protocol implementations.

Table 4. Message Transmission (Tx) and Reception (Rx) Overhead:

Message Overhead	Tx (μsec)	Rx (μsec)
Raw Message	181	141
RCF Tunneling	670	607
Processed Message	1891	1942

6   Related Work and Concluding Remarks

Traditional reflective languages aim at providing a customizable execution of concurrent systems. Former approaches to composition of communication services [13] [20][7][21] assume point-to-point communication and do not impose formal restrictions on the structure and semantics of basic communication primitives. Basically, they use the onion skin model as a conceptual foundation for separation of concerns. [15] presents a formal specification of communication services in rewriting theory. However, they do not deal with dynamic installation of communication services and they synchronize each object with its meta object. A Similar approach is taken in [18], where they use the concept of *weaving* to deal with the problems posed by composition of distributed (point-to-point) communication services. Similarly, [14] provides a meta level architecture at the language level to support a limited fault tolerant system mechanisms, in particular replication.

---

[3] Stateless protocols do not need to keep softstate information about every message sent or received

Commercially available distributed middleware infrastructures have incorporated the notion of reflection in order to provide the desired level of configurability and openness in a controlled manner [9][2]. However, they do not provide semantics that accurately describe the composition of communication services and they do not deal with the implication of composing services and communication protocols. *e.g.* The pluggable protocol framework [1] addresses the lack of support for multiple inter-ORB protocols and deals with integration and use of multiple ORB messaging and transport protocols, not with the composition of the protocols itself. DynamicTAO [10] explore ways to make the various components of an ORB dynamically configurable as well as componentizing them to achieve minimal footprint for small applications [19].

In recent years, several group communication systems (GCS) have been developed to provide additional flexibility of communication services by allowing for dynamic composition of communication protocols [16] [32] [22] [23]. Specification and formal characterization of group communication services has been developed in the context of *I/O Automata* [29]. Often, the communication mechanisms are built into the architecture; dynamic installation and revocation of communication protocols on-the-fly to deal with such changes are cumbersome and error-prone.

The designed communication framework provides flexibility in composition and dynamic installation of communication protocols, and provides the first step in an effort to provide a cost-effective communication framework capable of addressing adaptive environments with evolving policies. However, the integration of the RCF with reflective middleware services requires further investigation; the overall middleware environment must allow the service and protocol implementations to adapt themselves based on existing system conditions and application requirements.

Future work includes the development of an extensive suite of interaction properties for various communication protocols that implement application requirements and the creation of a generic rule base strategy to manage interprotocol interactions.

References

[1] Alexander Arulanthu, Carlos O'Ryan, Douglas C Schmidt, Michael Kircher and Jeff Parsons. The Design and Performance of a Scalable ORB Architecture for CORBA Asynchronous Messaging. In *Proceedings of the IFIP/ACM Middleware 2000*, 2000.

[2] Ashish Singhai, Aamod Sane and Roy Campbel. Reflective ORBs: supporting robust, time-critical distribution. In *Proceedings of the European Conference on Object-Oriented Programing*, 1997.

[3] Benoit Garbinato and Rachid Guerraoui. Using the Strategy Design Pattern to Compose Reliable Distributed Protocols. In *Usenix Conference on Object-Oriented Technologies and Systems*, 1997.

[4] Benoit Garbinato and Rachid Guerraoui. Flexible Protocol Composition in BAST. In *IEEE International Conference on Distributed Computing Systems*, 1998.

[5] Carlos Varela and Gul Agha. Linguistic Support for Actors, First-Class Token-Passing Continuations and Join Continuations. In *Midwest Society for Programming Languages and Systems Workshop*, 1999.

[6] Carlos Varela and Gul Agha. Programming Dynamically Reconfigurable Open Systems with SALSA. In *Object-Oriented Programming, Systems, Languages and Applications (OOPSLA), Intriguing Technology Track*, 2001.

[7] Daniel Sturman. *Modular Specification of Interaction of Interaction Policies in Distributed Computing*. PhD thesis, University of Illinois at Urbana-Champaing, 1996.

[8] Erich Gamma, Richard Helm, Ralp Johnson and John Vlissides. *Design Patterns: Elements of Reusable Object-Oriented Software*. Addison-Wesley, 1994.

[9] Fabio Costa, Gordon Blairand Geoff Coulson. Experiments with Reflective Middleware. Technical Report MPG-98-11, Lancaster University, 1998.

[10] Fabio Kon, Manuel Román, Ping Liu, Jina Mao, Tomonori Yamane, Luiz C Magalhães and Roy Campbell. Monitoring and Security and Dynamic Configuration with the dynamicTAO Reflective ORB. In *Proceedings of the IFIP/ACM Middleware 2000*, 2000.

[11] Gul Agha. *Actors: A model of Concurrent Computation in Distributed Systems*. MIT Press, 1986.

[12] Gul Agha and Ian A Mason and Scott F Smith and Carolyn Talcott. A Foundation for Actor Computation. *Functional Programming*, 1993.

[13] Gul Agha, Svend Frolund, Rajendra Panwar and Daniel Sturman. A Linguistic Framework for Dynamic Composition of Dependability Protocols. In *Dependable Computing and Fault Tolerant Systems*, 1993.

[14] Jean-Charles Fabre and Tanguy Perennou. A Metaobject Architecture for Fault-tolerant Distributed Systems: The FRIENDS Approach. In *IEEE Transactions on Computers, (47):78-95*, 1998.

[15] Jose Meseguer, Carolyn Talcott and Denker G. Rewriting Semantics of Meta-Objects and Composable Distributed Services. SRI International, 1999.

[16] Larry Peterson, Norm Hutchinson, Sean O'Malley and Mark Abbot. RPC in the x-Kernel: Evaluating New Design Techniques. In *Proceedings of the 14th ACM Symposium on Operating System Principles*, 1993.

[17] Leslie Lamport. Time and clocks and the ordering of events in a distributed system. *Communications of the ACM*, 21(7):558-565, 1978.

[18] Lynne Blair and Gordon Blair. The Impact of Aspect-Oriented Programming on Formal Methods. In *Proceedings of the European Conference on Object-Oriented Programing*, 1998.

[19] Manuel Roman, Dennis Mickunas, Fabio Kon and Roy Campbell. LegORB and Ubiquitous CORBA. In *Proceedings of the IFIP/ACM Workshop on Reflective Middleware 2000*, 2000.

[20] Mark Astley and Gul Agha. Customization and Composition of Distributed Objects: Middleware Abstractions for Policy Management. In *6th International Symposium on the foundation of Software Engineering*, 1998.

[21] Mark Astley, Daniel Sturman and Gul Agha. Customizable Middleware for Distributed Software. Communication of the ACM, 2000.

[22] Mark Garland Hayden. *The Ensemble System*. PhD thesis, Cornell University, 1998. Department of Computer Science.

[23] Matti A. Hiltunen, Vijaykumar Immanuel and Richard D. Schlichting. Supporting Customized Failure Models for Distributed Software. In *Distributed System Engineering, (6):103-111*, 1999.

[24] Nalini Venkatasubramanian. ComPOSE—Q - A QoS-enabled Customizable Middleware Framework for Distributed Computing. In *Proceedings of the IEEE International Conference on Distributed Computing Systems*, 1999.

[25] Nalini Venkatasubramanian and Carolyn Talcott. A Semantic Framework for Modeling and Reasoning about Reflective Middleware. In *IEEE Distributed Systems Online, 2(6)*, 2001.

[26] Nalini Venkatasubramanian and Carolyn Talcott. A Formal Correctness Proof for the Hierarchical Distributed Garbage Collection Algorithm. Technical Report TR-Stanford, Stanford University, 2002.

[27] Nalini Venkatasubramanian, Carolyn Talcott and Gul Agha. A Formal Model for Reasoning about Adaptive QoS-Enabled Middleware. In *Formal Methods Europe (FME 2001)*, 2001.

[28] Nalini Venkatasubramanian, Mayur Deshpande, Shivjit Mohapatra, Sebastian Gutierrez-Nolasco and Jehan Wickramasuriya. Design and Implementation of a Composable Reflective Middleware Framework. In *International Conference on Distributed Computer Systems*, 2001.

[29] Nancy Lynch and M R Tuttle. An Introduction to Input/Output Automata. *CWI Quarterly*, 2(3):219-246, 1989.

[30] Priya Narasimhan, Luise E Moser and P M Melliar-Smith. Using Interceptors to Enhance CORBA. *IEEE Computer Magazine*, 1999.

[31] R.G. Lavender and Douglas C. Schmidt. Active Object: an Object Behavioral Pattern for Concurrent Programming. In *Pattern Languages of Program Design*, 1996.

[32] Robbert van Renesse, Kenneth Birman and Silvano Maffeis. Horus: A Flexible Group Communication System. *Communication of the ACM*, 39(4):76-83, 1996.

[33] Sebastian Gutierrez-Nolasco and Nalini Venkatasubramanian. Design Patterns for Safe Reflective Middleware. In *OOPSLA, Workshop Towards Patterns and Pattern Languages for Object-Oriented Distributed Real-Time and Embedded Systems*, 2001.

[34] Sebastian Gutierrez-Nolasco and Nalini Venkatasubramanian. Reliable Communication with Mobile Objects in Faulty Environments. Technical Report TR-DSM-01-04, University of California, Irvine, 2001.

A Dynamic Proxy Based Architecture to Support Distributed Java Objects in a Mobile Environment

G. Biegel, V. Cahill, and M. Haahr

Distributed Systems Group
Department of Computer Science
University of Dublin, Trinity College
Dublin 2, Ireland
{Greg.Biegel, Vinny.Cahill, Mads.Haahr}@cs.tcd.ie

Abstract. Java Remote Method Invocation (RMI), as a distributed object technology, has poor existing support for operation in wireless mobile computing environments. The use of RMI in a mobile environment poses a number of problems related to hardware mobility and the characteristics of wireless networks. This paper describes an implementation of an architecture supporting RMI client and server applications in a wireless mobile environment. Mobility support is provided for in two major components. Connectivity management manages wireless connections and hides the inherent unreliability of wireless media from higher layers. Location management addresses the difficulty of correctly locating and invoking RMI server objects hosted by mobile devices. The implementation is evaluated in terms of transparency and the associated cost of introducing mobility support for RMI applications.

1 Introduction

Java Remote Method Invocation (RMI) [1] permits the invocation of methods on Java objects residing in remote address spaces. As well as being an important distributed object technology in its own right, other platforms such as Enterprise Java Beans (EJB) [2] and JINI [3] use RMI for communication. The widespread adoption of Java technology has led to an increasing number of small mobile computing devices with built in Java capability. RMI was designed primarily for use in static wired networks and in its present form, RMI does not support operation in mobile computing environments well.

Mobile computing environments [4] have a number of constraints not present in wired networks which need to be accounted for when providing support for applications in such environments -

Device Constraints: Mobile devices, by definition, are smaller and lighter than their static counterparts and have more limited display, processing, and power capabilities.

R. Meersman, Z. Tari (Eds.): CoopIS/DOA/ODBASE 2002, LNCS 2519, pp. 809–826, 2002.
© Springer-Verlag Berlin Heidelberg 2002

Network Constraints: Mobile devices rely on wireless communications which are presently characterised by low bandwidths, high latencies, and intermittent connectivity. The Architecture for Location-Independent Computing Environments (ALICE) [5] was designed to provide mobility support for a range of client/server application protocols through the introduction of connectivity management addressing the characteristics of wireless networks such as high latency and low bandwidth. ALICE is independent of application protocols and hence may be maintained across different distributed object technologies.

Location Management: Mobile devices change their point of connection to the network frequently, and this may invalidate references held to objects resident on these devices. This invalidation of references poses a problem to clients attempting to contact objects on such devices. In this paper, we present a solution to the problem of location management of RMI servers in mobile environments based on dynamic proxies. We demonstrate how dynamic proxies may be used to redirect method invocations between fixed and mobile devices in a manner that is largely transparent to the client, and does not dramatically impact on the time taken per method invocation.

The resulting implementation permits the transparent operation of both RMI clients and servers within a mobile environment.

2   Roadmap

The remainder of this paper describes our solution for supporting RMI applications in mobile environments. Section 3 provides some background. Section 4 examines the integration of the application protocol independent module of ALICE into the RMI runtime in order to support mobile RMI clients. Section 5 presents our solution, based on dynamic proxies, to the problem of location management for the operation of mobile RMI servers. Section 6 describes our implementation, whilst Sect. 7 presents a performance evaluation. Section 8 introduces related work and finally Sect. 9 presents our conclusions.

3   Background

This section provides some background on the the mobile environment and the ALICE architecture, Java RMI, and dynamic proxies.

3.1   The ALICE Architecture

ALICE is an architectural framework that provides mobility support for a range of application-level client/server protocols [5]. The ALICE architecture allows such application-level protocols to provide their own mobility support through location management, disconnected operation support, and connectivity management. ALICE permits the operation of mobile servers with no centralised location register to keep track of the whereabouts of the servers. The physical

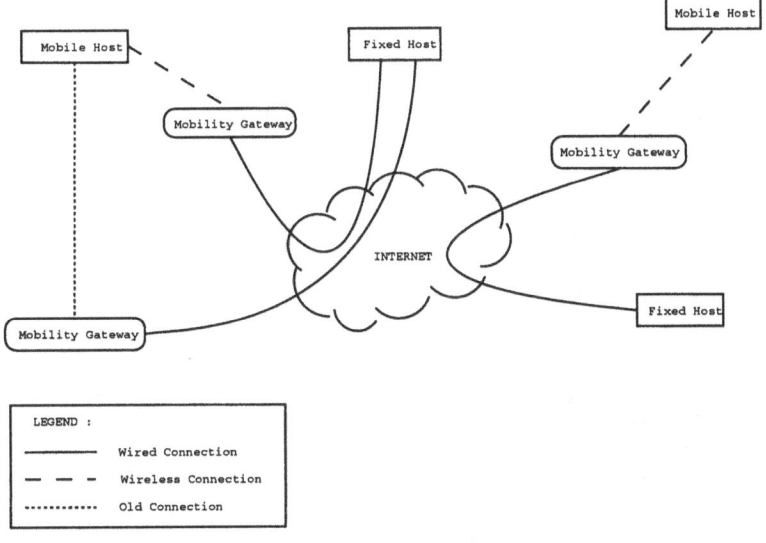

Fig. 1. The mobile environment

environment for which the ALICE framework was developed is illustrated in Fig.
1. Mobile Hosts (MH) are mobile computing devices with wireless network interfaces. These MHs are connected to stationary Mobility Gateways (MG) that
maintain both wireless and wired network interfaces and act as the entry point
from the wireless network into the wired network. Fixed Hosts (FH) are stationary computing devices that communicate with the MHs via the MGs. The
MHs are physically mobile and may change their point of connection from one
MG to another during a procedure known as handoff. ALICE provides mobility
support in the form of a layered architecture, with each ALICE layer solving
specific problems introduced by the mobile environment.

- The *Mobility Layer* manages connections between the MH and the MG,
  hiding the complexity of the wireless network characteristics from higher
  layers
- The *Swizzling Layer* supports server mobility by translating server references
  to refer to a MG rather than directly to an MH
- The *Disconnected Operation Layer* allows clients to cache server functionality
  during periods when an MH becomes disconnected

3.2 Java RMI

RMI is part of the Java Distributed Object Model [6] and provides the illusion
of invoking a method on a local object, whilst in fact the method may be invoked on an object in a different address space. RMI was designed specifically
to be language dependent and hence able to take advantage of the existing Java

Object Model. Java's Garbage Collection mechanism has also been extended to encompass remote objects.

RMI makes use of a proprietary protocol on the wire known as the Java Remote Method Protocol (JRMP), which in turn operates on top of TCP/IP. An important feature of RMI is the ability to replace standard TCP sockets with programmer-defined socket types through the specification of custom socket factories.

3.3 Dynamic Proxies

Dynamic proxies are a feature of the Java 2 Platform since version 1.3. A dynamic proxy class is a class that implements a set of interfaces specified at runtime in order to provide a type-safe proxy through which an invocation of an interface method, on the proxy, is dispatched to another object. Invocations on the proxy are dispatched to a single `invoke()` method in the proxy class. This method is then free to do anything with the invocation, including dispatch it to another object, before returning the result of the invocation to the client.

The fact that the proxy class is developed against an interface ensures the proxy is totally transparent to the client and lends the dynamic proxy class towards use within an RMI application since remote objects in RMI applications are required to be coded against an interface. Consequently, a dynamic proxy representation may be created for any remote object without requiring any additional representation of the remote object. Importantly, no pre-generation of the proxy class is required, further aiding the transparency of the process.

4   Mobile Host as Client

When the MH is acting as a client, connectivity management between the MH and the MG is provided for in ALICE by the Mobility Layer (ML) which manages the wireless connection and hides the inherent unreliability of the medium from higher layers. Connectivity management takes the form of transparent reconnection of broken transport layer connections, as well as tunneling of existing connections after a MH has moved from one MG to another. The ML was designed to operate independently of any application-level protocol issues, and thus may be used across a range of distributed object technologies [5].

4.1 Mobility Layer

The ML, which is implemented in C, consists of a superset of standard BSD sockets, known as *sockets+* [5]. Replacements of the standard socket functions are provided, as well as functions to manage callbacks from the ML to the application. Such callbacks may be used to notify the application of changes in state of connectivity. Their use requires that the application be aware of its mobility, but application use of callbacks is optional.

4.2 Replacing the Java Socket Implementation

The Java Native Interface (JNI) is the native programming interface for Java, allowing access to native code from Java code. There are two ways in which the ML could be integrated into RMI using JNI in combination with custom socket implementations, and although both ways alter the underlying socket implementation used by RMI, there are differences in how the socket replacement classes are integrated into RMI.

The Java networking package provides the `java.net.Socket` and `java.net.-ServerSocket` classes which provide client and server communication endpoint functionality respectively. By default JRMP uses instances of these socket classes to provide communication between remote objects, although it is possible to specify extensions of these classes to be used by RMI.

Both the `java.net.Socket` and `java.net.ServerSocket` classes contain a reference to a `java.net.SocketImpl`, which is an abstract class representing the socket implementation. The socket implementation defaults to the `java.net.Plain-SocketImpl` class. This socket implementation class handles the dispatch of calls to the socket functions implemented in native code. This is done through JNI calls made by the `java.net.PlainSocketImpl` class and dispatched to a shared library, (e.g., `libnet.so` on Linux, `net.dll` on Windows).

Given the way in which sockets are implemented in Java, the two ways in which the ML socket functions may be integrated into RMI at the native library level are as follows.

Creating a Custom Socket Implementation. Firstly, it is possible to write a custom socket implementation class other than the default `java.net.PlainSocket-Impl`, say `alice.rmi.ALICESocketImpl`, which accesses a custom shared library, say `libALICEnet.so`. The shared library would be constructed from the ML socket functions with appropriate JNI method signatures, to present a similar interface to the standard Java `libnet.so` library.

The major difference between the `java.net.PlainSocketImpl` class and the `alice.rmi.ALICESocketImpl` class is the additional functions for the management of callbacks to the application layer that are part of the `alice.rmi.ALICESocket-Impl` class. Another difference between the implementations occurs in the loading of the shared library. The call to load the native shared library containing the platform-specific socket functions is altered to rather load the ML socket functions, thus providing these to the RMI runtime in place of standard system sockets.

Replacing the Shared Library at Runtime. Another approach to replacing the standard native socket calls is to create a shared library with the same exposed external interface as the default `libnet.so` library, but which delegates calls to the ML socket functions rather than the standard native socket functions. It is possible to specify, to the Java runtime library loader, the path from which to load libraries. By altering this path to load the altered `libnet.so` library at runtime, the standard socket functions may effectively be replaced by the ALICE socket replacement functions.

The advantage of this approach is that the standard socket functions could be replaced with the ALICE ML socket functions transparently to the application, without the need to alter legacy code. This approach does however have significant disadvantages in that the ALICE ML does permit for mobile aware operation and provides an extended API (sockets+) for mobile-aware operation. The sockets+ API would not be exposed by simply replacing the `libnet.so` library.

4.3   Chosen Approach

The method used to integrate the ALICE ML into the RMI runtime system is the creation of a custom socket implementation. This approach is considered the most closely aligned with the goals of the Java language, where new socket implementations are expected to be developed to fulfill certain requirements. Following this approach, the custom `Socket` and `ServerSocket` classes will maintain a socket implementation attribute of the type `alice.rmi.ALICESocketImpl`.

The connectivity management support offered to the RMI runtime system by the ML is sufficient when the MH is acting as a client of a remote server object.

5   Mobile Host as Server

Addressing problems arise when an RMI object resident on a MH acts as a server. Servers traditionally export references to themselves so that clients know where they may be contacted. RMI servers export references of type `java.rmi.server.-RemoteRef`. These references contain an IP address and port number combination referring to the machine on which the server object is hosted. In the mobile environment assumed by ALICE, a MH is not directly contactable and all communication to and from it must pass through a MG. Thus, if a server is hosted on a MH and exports a reference based on the MH's address, the reference is invalid (since the host is not directly contactable at this address) and any attempts to invoke the server using this reference will fail. ALICE introduced the Swizzling Layer to overcome the problem of location management for CORBA, through the changing of the endpoint of a server reference to point to the MG rather than the MH. Swizzling object references was not considered appropriate for RMI due to differences in the way RMI implements remote object referencing, and we rather adopt an invocation redirection mechanism for location management which relays invocations between the MG and MH.

5.1   Remote Object Referencing in Java

The way in which an RMI server object (`ServerImpl`) is related to the address space in which it is resident is illustrated in Fig. 2. The `rmiregistry` is a simple, non-persistent, bootstrap name server from which a reference to a remote object on a given host may be obtained by a client.

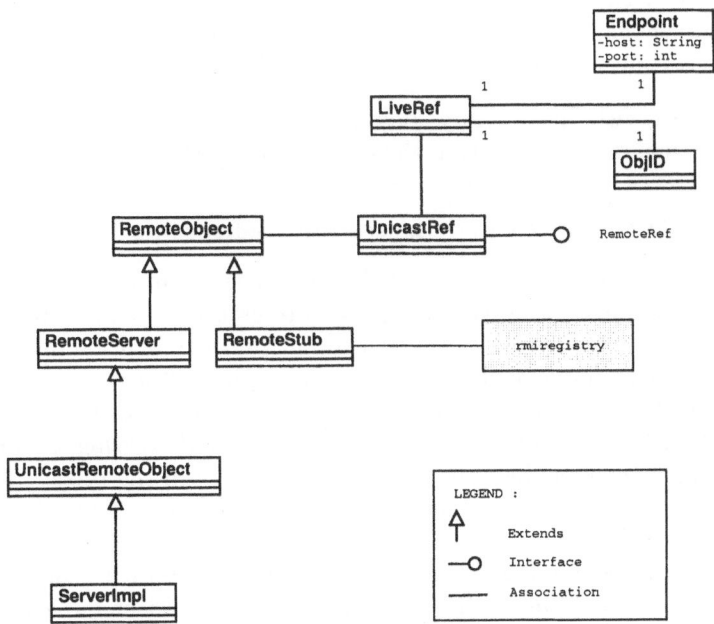

Fig. 2. Class hierarchy for remote objects in RMI

The reference that a client receives from the registry is in most cases actually to a stub and not the object itself [1]. As illustrated in Fig. 2, the stub contains a `sun.rmi.server.UnicastRef` attribute, which in turn contains a `sun.rmi.-transport.LiveRef` attribute, that contains a `sun.rmi.transport.Endpoint`, giving the hostname and port number at which the object resides, and a unique identifier in the form of an object ID.

In addition to the retrieval of a remote object reference by way of lookup on an `rmiregistry`, there are two further ways by which an RMI client may obtain a reference to a remote object:

– **As the return value from a method invocation**
A method invoked by a client on a remote object may return, as a result of the method invocation, a reference to a remote object. The client may then invoke methods on this object as if it resided locally. The registry lookup essentially obtains a reference as a result of the invocation of the `lookup()` method.

---

[1] If the server resides in the same virtual machine as the client, a reference to the actual object will be returned rather than a stub

– **As an argument to a method called on the client**
The third way in which a client may obtain a reference to a remote object, is as an argument to a method invoked on the client, by the server. This case arises when the client is also an RMI server object. In such a scenario, an RMI server may make a callback to the client and may potentially pass it a reference to a further remote object.

As is the case with the registry lookup, what is in most cases returned is a reference to the stub representing the object, rather than the object itself.

5.2   Using Dynamic Proxy Classes for Redirection

Dynamic proxies provide the basis of the invocation redirection mechanism developed. It is possible using dynamic proxies to create a proxy representation of a class, which implements a set of interfaces, at runtime. Method invocations are then handled by an implementation of the `java.lang.reflect.InvocationHandler` interface, which if present on the MG, could forward the invocation onto the MH attached to it. It is possible to remove all knowledge of creating the proxy from the client code which enables client-side transparency in the process.

Following the dynamic proxy approach, a proxy class, say a `ServerProxy`, is developed which implements the `java.lang.reflect.InvocationHandler` interface. This class takes a generic `Object` as an argument to its constructor and then uses reflection to determine what interfaces the object implements. Each object hosted on a MH needs to bind to the registry running on the MG that it is currently connected to. What is actually bound to the registry, however, is a dynamic proxy object transparently implementing the same remote interface as the remote object. This `ServerProxy` object is bound to the registry on the MG and is what is actually returned to clients performing a lookup against the remote object name. The `ServerProxy` also maintains a reference to the MG from which it originated and any invocations made on the proxy are propagated firstly to the MG and then on to the actual remote object, the location of which is known to the MG. Invocation responses are likewise propagated back through the MG. Figure 3 presents the operation of the scheme in more detail. In the scenario shown, a client obtains a reference to a remote object by way of a registry lookup.

The dynamic proxy based scheme operates as follows :

1. The MG process binds to the Mobility Registry daemon on the MG, using a well-known name.
2. A remote object resident on a MH performs a lookup, against the well-known name, on the MG to which it is attached.
3. A reference to the MG process is returned to the remote object.
4. The remote object invokes the `register()` method on the Mobility Gateway process, passing itself as a parameter.
5. The registration process creates a `ServerProxy` object on the MG which implements the same set of interfaces as the remote object. This completes the set up process.

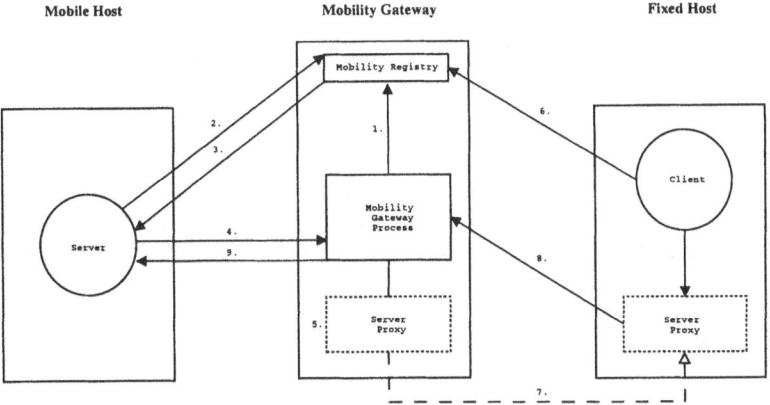

Fig. 3. Dynamic proxy architecture

6. A client performs a lookup against the server name, on the MG.
7. A reference to the `ServerProxy` object, rather than to the actual remote object is returned to the client.
8. Any invocations made against this reference are forwarded to a single method within the `ServerProxy` object and then onto the MG process.
9. The MG process then forwards the invocation onto the actual remote object resident on the MH, and returns the result along the same path back to the client.

This approach is achievable with no changes to the existing RMI architecture and therefore is one of the most attractive solutions to the location management problem.

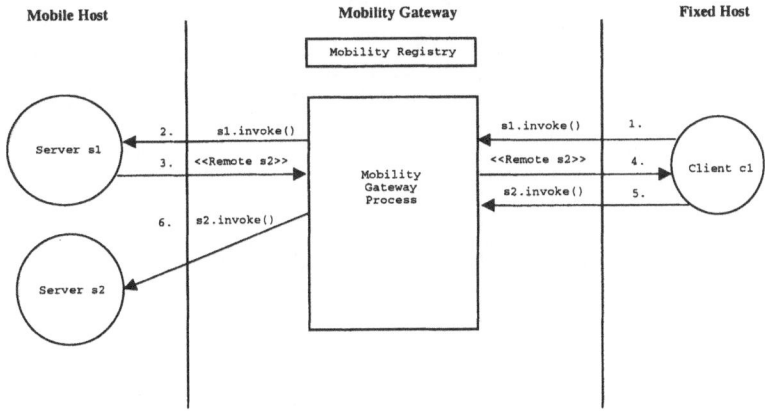

Fig. 4. Reference obtained from invocation

Reference obtained as return value of invocation. The case where a FH receives a reference to a remote object by way of the return value of a method invocation, is illustrated in Fig. 4 and operates in a similar manner except that the value returned by the invocation in step 3 of Fig. 4 is inspected at the MG. If it is a reference to a remote object, a dynamic proxy representing the object is created and registered with the MG and a reference to the proxy object is returned to the client in step 4. The rmiregistry is not necessarily involved in the process, although it may have been involved in obtaining the reference to s1.

Reference obtained by argument. A similar scheme is employed to detect whether a reference to a remote object is passed as an argument in a callback from a MH to a FH. Each argument is inspected at the MG and if a remote reference is being passed, a proxy representation is created at the MG, and a reference to this proxy replaces the original argument.

6   Implementation

This section describes the implementation of our solution to connectivity management and location management for mobile RMI. We use the same layer notation and terminology as in [5]. When referring to an entire layer, either the full name (the *Mobility Layer*) or its abbreviated form (the *ML*) will be used. When referring to a single component of a layer, the location of the component will be subscripted. For instance, the component of the ML residing on the MG will be referred to as ML_{MG}. The position of each of the components implemented is illustrated in Fig. 5.

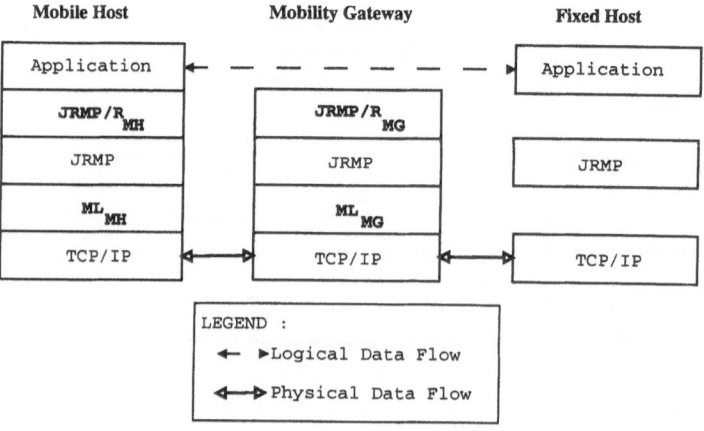

Fig. 5. Software architecture

6.1   Connectivity Management

Connectivity management is achieved through integration of the ML into RMI by the specification of alternative socket factories to RMI as discussed in Sect. 4.2.

ML$_{MH}$ Component. The ML$_{MH}$ component is the component of the ML present on the MH. It is this component that provides the ALICE socket replacement functions and the sockets+ API (for mobile-aware applications) to layers above it, and which replaces the TCP transport layer in mobile-enabled applications. The ML$_{MH}$ component also contains a daemon, the mlmhd, which multiplexes applications' connections onto a single transport connection to the MG.

In terms of RMI, socket functions are not accessed explicitly by the application programmer, but rather by the RMI runtime system which creates sockets through the standard API as they are needed for communication. Consequently, it is for this API that an interface to Java needs to be constructed.

ML$_{MG}$ Component. The ALICE ML$_{MG}$ component consists of a daemon, the mlmgd, which executes on the MG. The mlmgd daemon is connected to the mlmhd daemon running on a MH and is responsible for relaying connections between the MG and the MHs. Since this part of the ML is a daemon process and does not require any interaction with the application programmer, there is no need to provide an interface to it from Java.

Integration into RMI. The integration of the ML into the RMI runtime entails a number of steps, discussed below.

- **The creation of a custom Shared Object Library**
  We created a file named ALICESocketImpl.c, which was functionally equivalent to the PlainSocketImpl.c file, but contained additional methods for the sockets+ API, and linked this file against the ALICE Mobility Layer socket replacement functions, to produce a shared object file called libALICEnet.so.

- **The creation of a custom Socket Implementation**
  The next step was to create a custom Java socket implementation class, extending from the java.net.SocketImpl class and making calls to libALICEnet.

- **The creation of custom Socket classes**
  Up until this point, there has been no distinction between Socket and ServerSocket types, as both use the same implementation class. The creation of custom socket classes realises this distinction and two separate socket classes are created, alice.rmi.ALICESocket and alice.rmi.ALICEServerSocket.

- **The creation of a custom Socket Factory**
  The final step is the creation of client socket factory and server socket factory objects which RMI uses to supply instances of `alice.rmi.ALICESocket` and `alice.rmi.ALICEServerSocket` respectively for communication.

6.2   Location Management

A new layer, named the Java Remote Method Protocol Redirect (JRMP/R) Layer, was developed using dynamic proxy objects to provide location management for mobile RMI servers.

The JRMP/R layer consists of two components, that component resident on the MH, JRMP/R$_{MH}$, and that resident on the MG, JRMP/R$_{MG}$.

JRMP/R$_{MH}$ Component. The JRMP/R$_{MH}$ component consists of a modified version of the `java.rmi.Naming` class. The `alice.rmi.Naming` class maintains a reference to the current MG to which the MH is connected. When mobility support is required, RMI server objects use the `alice.rmi.Naming` class to register themselves with the RMI runtime. This class presents the same API to the application programmer as the `java.rmi.Naming` class.

The `alice.rmi.Naming` class overrides a subset of the methods in the `java.-rmi.Naming` class and introduces some additional methods. The most important change introduced by the `alice.rmi.Naming` class is the overriding of the `bind()` and `rebind()` methods. The overridden methods still take the same arguments as the methods in `java.rmi.Naming`, that is a `String` name for the object, and the remote reference to the object. The `java.rmi.Naming` class causes the binding of the remote reference and the name of the object in a table within the rmiregistry subject to the condition that a remote object may only register with an rmiregistry running in the same address space as itself.

The overridden `bind()` method, rather than causing the binding of the name and remote reference to a registry in the same address space, causes the registration of the reference with the JRMP/R$_{MG}$ component on the MG. Registration with this component effectively causes the instantiation of a proxy representation of the server and its binding to an rmiregistry running on the MG (in a separate address space). In this way, the semantics of RMI are changed slightly in that calling the `bind()` method in one address space causes the binding of the object (at least a proxy representing the object) in a different address space.

JRMP/R$_{MG}$ Component. The JRMP/R$_{MG}$ component of the JRMP/R layer consists of the following objects that collectively work together to transparently intercept invocations on server objects as described in Sect. 5.2.

- **Mobility Gateway Process**
  The MG process executes on the MG itself and provides a set of methods to the JRMP/R$_{MH}$ component to allow the registration and deregistration

of remote objects resident on a MH that is connected to the gateway. The MG process is involved with server handoff.

– **Mobility Registry**
  The Mobility Registry is an rmiregistry running on the MG and providing a lookup service for clients wishing to obtain a reference to a server hosted by a MH. The Mobility Registry contains the name of the server object bound to a proxy representation of the object created upon registration.

– **Proxy objects**
  Each remote object that registers with the MG has a dynamic proxy object, implementing the same remote interface, created on the gateway. This proxy object is an instantiation of the `alice.rmi.ServerProxy` class, which is part of the JRMP/R_{MG} component.

7 Evaluation

This section evaluates our dynamic proxy based location management scheme for mobile RMI applications in terms of performance and transparency of the solution.

7.1 Performance

The performance evaluation first compared the cost of standard one-hop RMI with that of standard one-hop RMI with the introduction of a dynamic proxy at the server. This indicated the overhead introduced by dynamic proxies for standard one-hop RMI. Since mobile RMI introduces an extra hop per invocation, we then compared the cost of standard two-hop RMI via an MG, with that of standard two-hop RMI via an MG using dynamic proxies to determine the cost of introducing dynamic proxies in this scenario. Finally, this was compared with the cost of introducing full JRMP/R support for mobile RMI to determine the cost of introducing full JRMP/R functionality.

Parameterless Invocation (Type 1). For one-hop RMI between a client and a server, the introduction of a dynamic proxy that simply forwarded the invocation to the real remote object, resulted in a marginal increase of 3.6% in the time taken to perform a remote invocation as illustrated in Fig. 6. This increase is due to the use of reflection by the dynamic proxy.

For mobile RMI, the use of dynamic proxies introduced additional overhead into this type of invocation, leading to an increase of 14.6% in the time taken, over that of standard two-hop RMI. The extra time is due to the high costs of reflection which is used by dynamic proxies in Java to determine which method has been invoked on the proxy.

The operation of full JRMP/R support for this type of invocation led to an increase of 5.1% in the time taken over that of using dynamic proxies, and

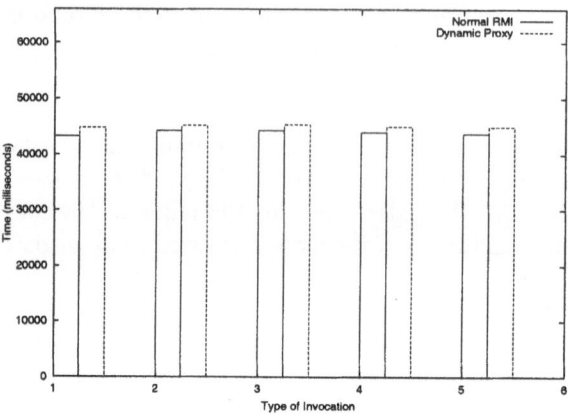

Fig. 6. Invocation times for 10 000 remote method invocations in one-hop RMI for 5 types of invocation

an increase of 20.5% in the time taken over standard two-hop RMI. This is illustrated in Fig. 7. The additional time taken to perform an invocation using full JRMP/R support is introduced by the need to use additional reflection at the MG in order to determine the method to be invoked at the server due to the non-serialisability of the Method type. Since the method being invoked is both void and parameterless, there is no need for the replacement of parameters or return types with proxy representations at the gateway.

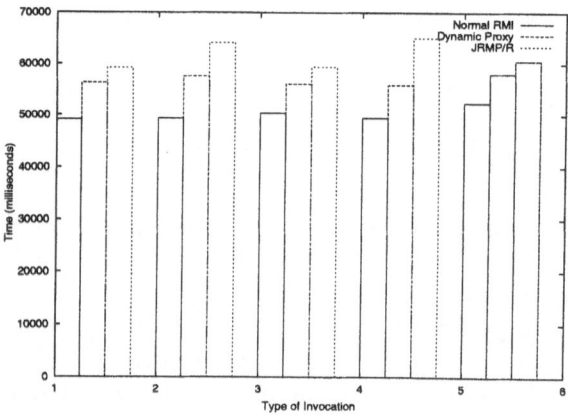

Fig. 7. Invocation times for 10 000 remote method invocations in two-hop RMI for 5 types of invocation

Primitive Parameter (Type 2). Once again, the introduction of dynamic proxies between client and server in standard, one-hop RMI led to a slight increase of 2% in the time taken to perform an invocation, as illustrated in Fig. 6.

For RMI in a mobile environment, the invocation of a void method with a primitive parameter (an integer in this case) was once again least expensive at the level of standard RMI. The introduction of dynamic proxies led to an increase in the time taken to perform an invocation of 16.6% which is comparable to the increase observed in the void parameterless invocation and has the same explanation.

Full JRMP/R operation in this type of invocation led to an increase of 11.4% in the time taken over that using only dynamic proxies, and an increase of 30% over that using standard RMI. The increase is illustrated in Fig. 7.

The significant increase in the time taken over that using standard RMI is due in part to the need to perform reflection at the MG in order to determine the method type, and due in part to the need to inspect the method parameter at the MG. The inspection of the parameter is needed in order to determine whether a reference to a remote object is being passed as a parameter, in which case a proxy representation is required (see Sect. 5.2). The process of inspection utilises reflection which accounts for the additional time introduced into the invocation.

Object Parameter (Type 3). A marginal increase of 2.3% in the time taken to perform a remote method invocation is observed with the introduction of a dynamic proxy in one-hop RMI as illustrated in Fig. 6.

Similarly, for mobile RMI, the passing of a Java object as a parameter to a method is least expensive when using standard RMI. The use of dynamic proxies in the architecture led to an increase of 11.3% in the time taken to perform an invocation, which is similar to the previous two scenarios.

Additional overhead is introduced by reflection at the MG in order to determine both the method type and in order to inspect the parameter type to see whether a reference to a remote object is being passed. In this case, the method type determination and parameter inspection together resulted in an increase of 5.9% in the time taken to perform an invocation, over that of just using dynamic proxies, and an increase of 17.8% over standard RMI (see Fig. 7). This is significantly less than the overhead introduced by the inspection of primitive parameters at the MG. This may be explained by the fact that object creation is an expensive operation in Java. For the primitive parameter scenario (Type 2), an object representation of the primitive data type needs to be constructed so that it may be serialised for the RMI call. For example, if the parameter is an int, then an object of type Integer must be created to represent this integer.

Primitive Return (Type 4). For one-hop RMI an increase of 2.3% in the time taken to invoke a remote method is observed with the introduction of dynamic proxies (Fig. 6), due to the reflection performed by the dynamic proxy.

For mobile RMI, the invocation of a method with no parameters, but a primitive return type (an integer in this case) was least expensive under standard RMI, with an additional 13.1% being introduced into the time taken to perform an invocation with the introduction of dynamic proxies.

The operation of the full JRMP/R Layer led to an increase of 16.4% in the time taken over that of RMI using dynamic proxies, and an increase of 31.6% over standard RMI. This is illustrated in Fig. 7.

Once again,the additional cost of making an RMI call may be accounted for by the need to determine the method type and inspect the return value of the invocation.

Object Return (Type 5). The introduction of a dynamic proxy to one-hop RMI for this type of invocation increased the time taken to invoke a remote method by 2.7% as shown in Fig. 7.

For mobile RMI, the invocation of a method with no parameters, but which returns a Java object is the most costly type of invocation in terms of standard RMI. This is due to the need to serialise the return value of the method.

The use of dynamic proxies for this type of invocation increases the time taken to invoke such a method by 10.8% due to the cost of reflection. Full JRMP/R Layer support increases the time taken to invoke a method of this type by 4.3% over the use of dynamic proxies and an overall increase of 15.6% over standard RMI (see Fig. 7).

Client Side Transparency. The incorporation of the location management support offered to mobile RMI servers by the JRMP/R Layer is almost completely transparent to the client of a mobile RMI server, barring the need to perform certain bootstrap remote reference lookups on a different host (the MG, rather than the MH itself). Whilst this may require the alteration of hard-coded host addresses in certain legacy applications, in most cases it should simply require the change of the host parameter provided at runtime to the client.

Server Side Transparency. The introduction of the JRMP/R layer at the server side is not (and should not be) completely transparent to the application programmer. The use of an alternative to the `java.rmi.Naming` class is required for mobile servers, but the alternative `Naming` class does present the same API and use of it is syntactically identical to the standard RMI Naming class.

8   Related Work

The problems of host mobility addressed by our architecture are also addressed by Mobile IP [7] at the network layer. However, the Mobile IP solution to host mobility requires all hosts to use a modified network protocol and requires the maintenance of a centralised location register. An element of routing indirection is also introduced in Mobile IP. Our architecture does not require the replacement of the existing IP protocol, nor the maintenance of a centralised location register. Previous work has been carried out on the extension of the ALICE architecture to RMI [8], resulting in a Java version of the ML. Our architecture improves upon this approach through re-use of the existing ML component, dealing with all possible ways that a client may obtain a remote reference and by making mobility support transparent to the client by removing the need to hand code proxy classes.

Software mobility of RMI remote objects in a network has been addressed by [9] resulting in enhanced remote objects which are able to migrate between different address spaces.

A number of projects have examined the operation of RMI over a wireless link from the perspective of the efficiency of the communication mechanisms employed by RMI [10,11]. These projects deal with aspects of connectivity management of a wireless connection with specific reference to the operation of RMI over such a connection. Location management of mobile clients and servers is not dealt with in these projects. [12] addresses the operation of Remote Procedure Call in a mobile environment.

Work has been carried out on interceptors for RMI utilising dynamic proxies, custom socket implementations and replacement of shared libraries [13] to intercept RMI method invocations. The RMI Proxy [14] is a commercial application protocol which makes use of dynamic proxies to provide an approach to allow controlled penetration of firewalls by RMI clients and servers.

9   Conclusion

This paper discussed the provision of support to RMI applications in a mobile environment including connectivity management, in the form of management of the wireless connection and insulation of RMI applications from the inherent unreliability of the medium, and location management using dynamic proxies to support RMI servers on mobile hosts.

Connectivity management was provided for RMI applications through the re-use of the application protocol independent Mobility Layer module of ALICE and provided for the full operation of mobile RMI clients.

A location management scheme for RMI based on dynamic proxies was developed to provide invocation redirection via a gateway between the wireless and wired networks, and permitted the operation of mobile RMI servers.

The mobility support provided by our architecture enabled the full operation of both RMI clients and server objects within a mobile environment. Mobility support was provided on top of the existing network (IP) protocols, with a high degree of transparency and a low degree of overhead and without the need for a centralised location register.

Acknowledgements. Gregory Biegel was in receipt of a Beit Fellowship at the time of this research and is very grateful to the Beit Trust for their generous support.

References

1. Sun Microsystems, Java Remote Method Invocation Specification Revision 1.7, http://java.sun.com/products/jdk/rmi, December 1999.
2. Sun Microsystems, Enterprise JavaBeans 2.0 Specification, http://java.sun.com/products/ejb, August 2001.
3. Sun Microsystems, JINI v1.1 Specification, http://java.sun.com/jini, October 2000.
4. George H. Forman and John Zahorjan The Challenges of Mobile Computing IEEE Computer Journal, April 1994
5. Mads Haahr, Raymond Cunningham and Vinny Cahill, Towards a Generic Architecture for Mobile Object-Oriented Applications, In *SerP 2000: Workshop on Service Portability*, December 2000.
6. Roger Biggs, Ann Wollrath and Jim Waldo, A Distributed Object Model for the Java System, In *USENIX 1996 Conference on Object Oriented Technologies (COOTS)*, pp. 219–231.
7. Charles E. Perkins, Mobile IP IEEE Communications Magazine, Vol. 35, No. 5, pp. 84-99, May 1997
8. Tom Wall, Mobile RMI : Supporting Remote Access to Java Server Objects on Mobile Hosts, In *Proceedings, International Symposium on Distributed Objects and Applications*, pp. 41–51, September 2001
9. Avvenuti et al., MobileRMI: a ToolKit to Enhance Java RMI with Mobility, In *6th ECOOP Workshop On Mobile Object Systems: Operating System Support, Security and Programming Languages*, June 2000.
10. Stefano Campadello, Oskari Koskimies and Kimmo Raatikainen, Wireless Java RMI, In *4th International Enterprise Distributed Object Computing Conference*, pp. 114–123, September 2000.
11. Vijaykumar Krishnaswamy and Dan Walther and Sumeer Bhola and Ethendranath Bommaiah and George Riley and Brad Topol and Mustaque Ahamad, Efficient Implementations of Java Remote Method Invocation (RMI), In *Proceedings of the 4th USENIX Conference on Object-Oriented Technologies and Systems (COOTS '98)* pp. 19–35 April 1998.
12. Ajay Bakre and B.R. Badrinath, M-RPC: A Remote Procedure Call Service for Mobile Clients, In *Proceedings of the 1st ACM Mobicom Conference* pp. 2–11, 1995.
13. N. Narasimhan, L.E Moser and P.M Melliar-Smith, Interceptors for Java Remote Method Invocation, *Java Grande - Concurrency : Practice and Experience* 2000.
14. Esmond Pitt and Neil Belford, The RMI Proxy White Paper, http://www.rmiproxy.com March 2001.

A CORBA-Based Workflow Management System for Wireless Communication Environments

Leonardo Hartleben Reinehr and Maria Beatriz Felgar de Toledo

Computing Institute, State University of Campinas,
PO Box 6176, 13083-970, Campinas, Brazil
{reinehr, beatriz}@ic.unicamp.br
http://www.ic.unicamp.br

Abstract. This paper addresses the problem of developing Workflow Management Systems in wireless communication environments, where connections are unstable and non-permanent. In such an environment, users should be able to perform tasks independently from location and type of connection. The proposed model aims at meeting these requirements through task reservation and anticipated transfer of data and applications to the mobile computer, increasing its autonomy. Moreover, the paper describes the prototype implementation based on CORBA.

Keywords: Workflow Management System, Mobile Computing, Wireless Communication, CORBA.

1 Introduction

Workflow Management Systems (WFMS) have attracted much interest as they increase the efficiency of an organization by automating organizational processes. Many WFMS have been developed and successfully used. However, these systems still have some limitations, such as low interoperability among different WFMS, insufficient support for failure recovery and low flexibility [1] [5] [6] [8] [9] [10].

WMFS's usually require that the users are connected to wired networks, restricting user's mobility. With the appearance of wireless networks and portable devices, it has become important to allow flexible use of WFMS's. Thus a user, from his laptop or other portable device, will be able to execute tasks independent from location and connection type.

Consider the following example. A maintenance firm defines a process, managed by a WFMS, consisting of various tasks, one of them is VisitCustomer. This task is executed by a maintenance technician, who gets a service order and visits the respective customer. In a traditional WFMS, in the beginning of the day the technician gets the service orders assigned to him and visits each customer. When visiting a client, after figuring out what is the problem (e.g., some part p of an equipment is broken), the technician calls the firm and asks

R. Meersman, Z. Tari (Eds.): CoopIS/DOA/ODBASE 2002, LNCS 2519, pp. 827–844, 2002.
© Springer-Verlag Berlin Heidelberg 2002

about the availability of p. The inventory is then checked; if the part is not available, the technician requests its purchase. Then, when the part has arrived, the technician returns at the customer and finishes the service.

On the other hand, if the WFMS provides mobility support, when the technician detects that the part p is broken, instead of calling the firm he connects to the WFMS (using a laptop and a cell phone) and queries the system about the availability of p. If the part is not found, the technician starts a workflow to purchase p. From this point, the technician can, at any time and location (even when he is on the road), connect to the WFMS and check the status of this workflow (if the purchasing order was already dispatched, if the part is on its way, and so on). When the workflow is completed, the technician can take the part on the firm and return to the customer, finishing the service.

This example shows how operation through wireless networks expands a WFMS flexibility, besides increasing its efficiency and increasing system automation. However, supporting this kind of operation requires some changes in the workflow system. When the user is always connected to the WFMS, he can be constantly monitored and can get new task assignments at any time. In a wireless environment this is not possible anymore, because the user may stay long periods disconnected. Moreover, communication failures may occur more frequently. Thus, new control mechanisms are necessary, in order to preserve the mobile machine autonomy but, at the same time, guarantee that the processes are executed according to their specifications.

In this paper, we present the WorkToDo, a WFMS for wireless communication environments. The WorkToDo allows users to execute tasks while disconnected or when communication failures, typical of wireless environments, occur.

The paper is organized as follows. Section 2 compares our work to other research projects. Section 3 describes the workflow model used in WorkToDo and Section 4 describes the system architecture. Section 5 contains aspects related to the system operation. Section 6 describes the developed prototype, followed by an example and some results. Finally, Section 7 presents the conclusions of the paper.

2   Related Work

The Exotica Project [1] allows planned disconnection. The user can select a group of tasks to be executed (through the *lock* operation, which removes the tasks from other users' worklists), causing the related data to be copied to the user's machine. During disconnected operation the user can execute the selected tasks. Upon reconnection the data is copied back to the WFMS.

In the INCAS model [2], the entities that execute tasks can communicate through wireless links. The INCAS only requires that entities are capable of receiving an INCA, executing the requested operations and redirect the INCA to the next entity. However, there are some implementation issues related to the last requirement for which no solutions have been proposed yet (e.g., if an entity

X must redirect an INCA to another entity Y, what X should do if Y can not be contacted for a long time?).

Bussler [3] presents a list of requirements to incorporate disconnected operation into conventional WFMS and proposes the *mobile worklists* concept to meet these requirements. There is not, however, any reference to some implementation. Finally, Jing *et al.* [8] discuss the prefetching technique for mobile environments.

The integration between CORBA and WFMS's is also explored by some projects, such as METEOR [4]. There is an implementation of the METEOR model using CORBA, called ORBWork, in which each component of the model is mapped to a CORBA server. However, METEOR does not explore the system usage in wireless environments.

Our approach aims not only to propose a model and architecture considering wireless communication environments, but also to validate the model presenting a CORBA-based prototype. The developed WFMS focus on the aspects related to wireless environments, supporting semi-connected and disconnected operation. As Exotica, we have used the locking approach for the selection of tasks to be executed in disconnected mode. Moreover, we have incorporated some of the requirements pointed out by Bussler, such as local management of task deadlines. But unlike previous works, which are focused only on disconnected operation, our system also focuses on the issues of wireless environments, such as partition failures and low network bandwidth. Communication failures are masked by asynchronous operations such as prefetching and postponed propagation of results.

3   Process Model

When modeling a process we define the following aspects: which tasks should be executed, in which sequence, by whom and with what data. These are known as functional, behavioral, organizational and informational aspects of a process, respectively [5] [7].

Figure 1 shows a representation of the model used in WorkToDo. A process is a set of activities and dependences among them; each activity has a set of input and output data and a processing entity responsible for its execution.

The WorkToDo uses the concept of *Process Types*. When modeling a process, one actually defines a process type, which can be instantiated several times, creating particular executions (instances) of that type.

3.1   Activities

A process consists of a set of activities which defines the process functional aspect. After their execution, the process is considered complete. Activities can be tasks or sub-processes. Tasks are elementary actions, while sub-processes are other processes.

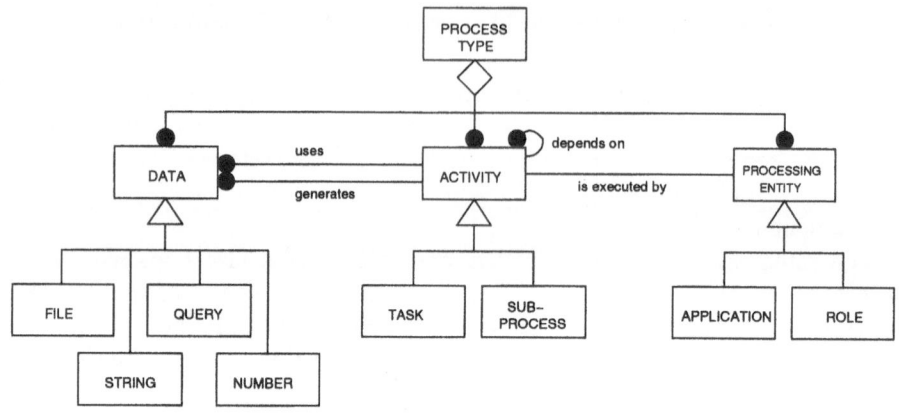

Fig. 1. The WorkToDo process model.

WorkToDo defines five possible states for a given activity: NOT_READY – the activity cannot be executed because one or more conditions for its execution have not been reached yet; READY – all the conditions required for the activity execution have been reached; RUNNING – the activity is being executed; SUCCEEDED – the activity has been executed with success; FAILED – an error occurred during activity execution.

Transitions between states are shown in Figure 2. NOT_READY is the initial state, SUCCEEDED and FAILED are the final states. In a given moment, an activity has one and only one state.

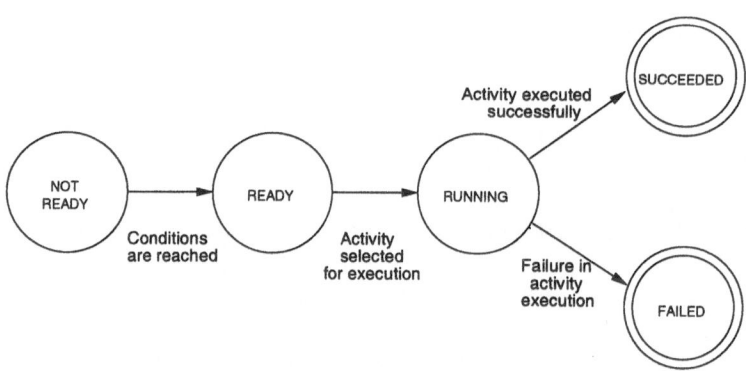

Fig. 2. State transition diagram for an activity.

3.2   Tasks

Tasks are those activities that cannot be decomposed (e.g., copying a file, executing a transaction on a database). They are defined by *Task Models*, which are used to create tasks during a process execution. The task data are specified in the process definition, in such a way that each task instance uses its own data. Tasks are classified in three types:

Automatic. Tasks which are executed by a software invoked automatically by the WFMS (e.g., accessing a database, copying a file).

Semi-automatic. Tasks which are executed by a human assisted by a software (e.g., writing a document using a text editor, scanning a photograph).

Manual. Tasks which are executed exclusively by a human (e.g., filling in a form, sending a letter).

Moreover, among other characteristics (e.g., priority and description), a task can be defined as allowable to be executed disconnected or not.

3.3   Dependence Rules

WorkToDo uses dependence rules to model the behavioral aspect of a process. A dependence rule contains the conditions that must be reached to allow the execution of an activity. These conditions are described in terms of activity state transitions. A rule is composed by zero or more terms containing an activity name and a state. These terms may be operands of boolean operators (**and, or**). An example of dependence rule is shown below:

$$\text{and } (A_1 \rightarrow \text{SUCCEEDED}, \ A_2 \rightarrow \text{SUCCEEDED})$$

In this example, the activity associated with the rule will be executed only when activities A_1 and A_2 reach the SUCCEEDED state. The dependence rule has two terms: $A_1 \rightarrow$ SUCCEEDED and $A_2 \rightarrow$ SUCCEEDED, which are operands of an **and** operation. Valid states for terms are those valid for activities, as seen in Section 3.1. Activities with empty dependence rules can be executed immediately.

3.4   Processing Entities

Every task has a processing entity responsible for its execution. Processing entities model the organizational aspect of a process and are specified in the task models. The WorkToDo defines two types of processing entities:

Applications. These are the processing entities of automatic tasks. When the task is initiated, the correspondent application must be invoked (possibly with parameters and/or input/output data). Each automatic task has an associated application.

Users. Users are the processing entities of semi-automatic and manual tasks. Tasks are assigned to users through a role mechanism. A *Role* is a group of users with some set of characteristics. The task definition specifies a role R, allowing any user belonging to R to execute the task.

3.5   Data

Tasks can use input data and generate output data; data specification corresponds to the informational aspect of a process. In WorkToDo, data may be:
Files – files stored on disk; Queries – SQL (Simple Query Language) expressions
which are queries on databases that return a set of tuples; Strings – alphanu-
merical values; and Numbers – integer or real values.

Each process in execution has a private area, called *Process Context*, to store
its data. When a task needs to read or write data, it accesses this area. The
context of a process instance P can be accessed only by the tasks that belong to
P, isolating each instance data and avoiding interferences among the executions
of different processes.

3.6   Definition Language

WorkToDo provides a *Workflow Definition Language* (WDL) to allow the definition of process types, task models and applications. A process type definition
contains a list of activities and, for each activity, its input and output data, its
dependences and its processing entity. A task model specifies the task characteristics, such as type and priority. An application definition contains the application characteristics, such as size and operating system on which it can be
executed.

4   Architecture

WorkToDo has a distributed architecture, shown in Figure 3. As each component
can be executed on a different host, the communication can be achieved by a
distributed platform, such as RPC (Remote Procedure Call), Sockets, CORBA
(Common Object Request Broker Architecture) or RMI (Remote Method Invocation). In the prototype implemented we used CORBA, as will be shown in
Section 6.

4.1   User and Role Manager

The User and Role Manager (URM) is responsible for managing users and roles.
It provides the following operations: insertion/removal of users to/from roles,
retrieval of a user's roles, retrieval of users in a role, among others. The URM
controls two repositories:

Users. This repository contains information about system users, such as name,
password, status (connected or not to the WFMS), and time of the last
connection.

Roles. This repository stores existing roles, together with a list of users belonging to each role. A user may assume zero or more roles.

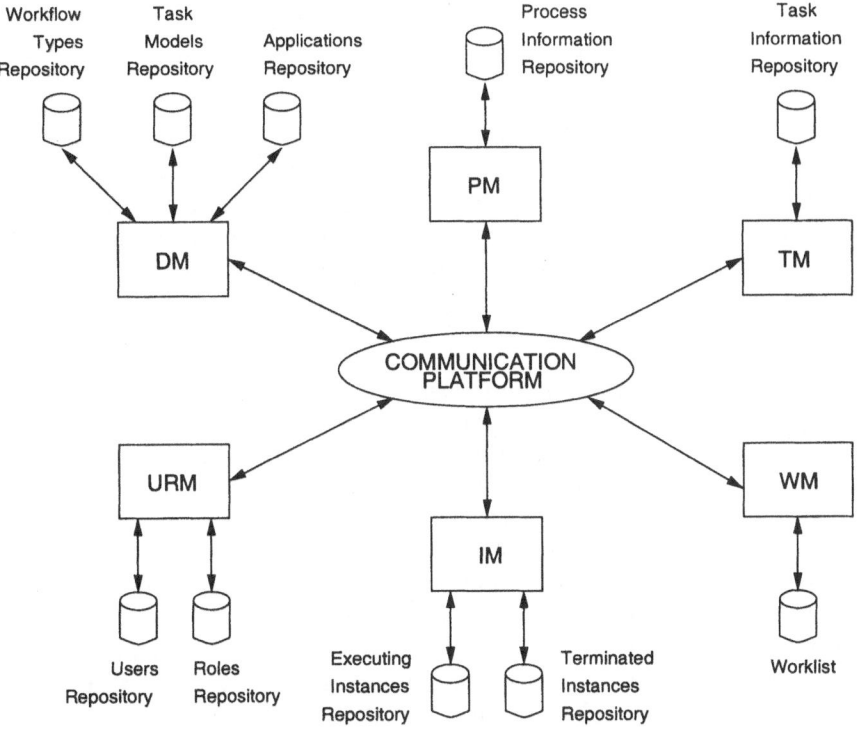

Fig. 3. WorkToDo distributed architecture.

4.2 Definition Manager

The Definition Manager (DM) manages process types, task models and applications definitions. The DM provides operations for retrieval of existing definitions and insertion/removal of definitions. The DM manages three repositories which stores process types, task models and applications definitions.

When a process type is inserted into the type repository, the DM asks for a role name. This role is called the type *Creator Role*. Instances of this type can be created only by users belonging to the type creator role.

4.3 Instance Manager

The Instance Manager (IM) maintains information about the process instances in execution, as well as those already executed. The IM is also responsible for creating a Process Manager for each new instance; at creation time, the IM transfers a copy of the process type definition to the Process Manager. The IM maintains two repositories:

Processes. This repository stores information about executing instances, such as name, type and host from where it is being managed.

Completed Processes. This repository stores information about terminated instances, such as instance name, final state, start and end time, and the final state of each one of its tasks.

The IM is also responsible for managing eventual failures of the Process Managers. In such cases, the IM can create a new Process Manager in another host, initializing it with the last consistent state of the failed Process Manager. The Process Manager state is recovered from the process repository, which is updated periodically with the new states of Process Managers.

4.4   Process Manager

The Process Manager (PM) is responsible for coordinating a process execution. The PM verifies which tasks are ready to execute, initiates their execution and collects their results, verifying if these results allow the execution of other tasks. There is one PM for each executing process instance.

The PM maintains a list with the tasks that compose the process, called *Tasklist*. The tasklist stores all the information needed for the execution of the tasks, such as name, type, input and output data, processing entity and current state. This information is called *Task Definition*. The tasklist consists, therefore, of a list of task definitions. The PM also maintains a repository which stores the current state of the instance, containing information such as the instance name, its start and end time and its tasklist.

The PM contains two sub-components:

Scheduler. This component evaluates the conditions for the execution of the tasks. Every time a state transition of a task T occurs, the Scheduler reevaluates the dependence rules of the tasks related to T. When the conditions of a dependence rule are all satisfied, the task state is modified to READY.

Dispatcher. This component prepares the tasks for execution. The Dispatcher periodically checks the tasklist for ready tasks. When a ready task is found, the Dispatcher executes one of the following actions: if the task is automatic, it creates a Task Manager to manage the task execution; if the task is semi-automatic or manual, it notifies the users belonging to the task role about its availability.

In the case of semi-automatic and manual tasks, the users to be notified are chosen according to a *Notification Policy* (which is defined at instance creation time and may be modified during its execution):

1. All users belonging to the role;
2. The first n users who belong to the role and have less assigned tasks;
3. The first n users who belong to the role and have less selected tasks;
4. The first n users who belong to the role and have connected to the WFMS more recently.

It is also responsibility of the PM to manage possible failures of the Task Managers. In these cases, the PM can create a new Task Manager, on the same host or another, initializing it with the last known consistent state of the failed Task Manager.

4.5 Task Manager

The function of the Task Manager (TM) is to control the execution of an automatic task. The TM is created by a PM and initialized according to the respective task definition. The TM then invokes the application responsible for the execution of the task (with the necessary data) and monitors its execution. When it is finished, the TM notifies the correspondent PM, returning the task termination type (with success or with failure). If a task execution fails, the TM can execute the task again until it succeeds or it reaches a maximum number of retries (specified in the task model).

4.6 Worklist Manager

The Worklist Manager (WM) controls and maintains a list with all the tasks that can be executed by a given user. This list is called *worklist* and the tasks are called *workitems*.

Each workitem corresponds to some process task. Thus, every time a workitem state changes, the state of the corresponding task is also changed. This guarantees that the changes made by users on the workitems are reflected on tasks (and consequently on processes). The workitems always correspond to semi-automatic or manual tasks, since automatic tasks are managed in a different way (through TMs) and are not added to worklists.

There is one and only one WM for each user, that is executed on the user's machine.

5 System Operation

This section describes the functional aspects of WorkToDo, emphasizing the operation in wireless communication environments.

5.1 User-System Interaction

Users interact with the WFMS through the worklist, invoking the following actions:

Visualize workitems. The worklist shows the user's workitems, listed according to one of four ordering types: by arrival time, by priority, by deadline and by size of related data. A user can also move workitems to any position in the worklist.

Select workitems. When the user wants to execute a workitem, he must select it. The correspondent PM receives a notification, passing it to the other WMs that also received this workitem; the WMs remove the workitem from their users' worklists. The user who selected the workitem is then authorized to execute the workitem. This selection mechanism prevents a workitem to be executed by more than one user.

Lock workitems. When the user wants to execute a workitem in disconnected mode, he must lock it (as will be seen in Section 5.4). Thus, the workitem is removed from the worklists of the other users of that role, in a similar way as if the workitem had been selected. A workitem can only be locked if its correspondent task was defined as allowed to be executed disconnected.

Moreover, a user can check which processes are executing and query the state of the processes he participates. The user is also allowed to create instances of a process when he belongs to the creator role of this process type.

To the WFMS, users can be *active* or *inactive*. An active user is connected to the WFMS, being able to receive new ready tasks, to select tasks for execution, to create process instances and query instance states, among other operations. An inactive user is not connected to the WFMS, being restricted to interactions with the Worklist Manager, as will be seen in Section 5.4.

WorkToDo defines two kinds of special users:

Administrator. An administrator has some privileges of administrative and management nature, being able to query and modify information about users, roles, process types, task models and applications. The administrator is actually a role which can be assumed by many users.

User-in-charge. Every process instance has a user-in-charge, who must take certain decisions when necessary. The WFMS notifies this user about task deadlines, task execution failures, and start and end time of instances execution; the user in charge decides what to do in such situations (e.g., re-execute a failed task).

5.2   Task Deadlines

Tasks may have deadlines, which represent the time limit to their execution. The deadline of a task is specified in the task model definition. If a task deadline is reached, the user-in-charge of the process instance decides if the instance execution should be interrupted or not.

The WFMS notifies users periodically when the deadline is approaching. Moreover, when the deadline reaches 24 hours, the task is assigned to the user-in-charge, even if the task has been selected by some other user (in this case the workitem related to the task is removed from the user's worklist). This mechanism guarantees task execution within the deadline even if the original user is unable to finish it.

The deadline of a task is controlled by the PM to which the task belong. However, if a user locks a task and becomes disconnected, his WM will control the deadline instead of the PM. The task assignment to the user-in-charge is still carried out by the PM.

5.3   Prefetching

The prefetching technique consists of copying to the user's machine a workitem that later may be executed in disconnected mode (Section 5.4). Thus, when this workitem is locked, all information required for its execution will be already available, minimizing the delay from the user's point of view. The prefetching is always made in background, transparently to the user, using available bandwidth.

The prefetching occurs as follows: while the user is connected to the WFMS, the WM periodically checks if the worklist contains some workitem which can be executed in disconnected mode. If it does, the WM copies the workitem to the user's machine. By copying a workitem we mean copying both data and application related to the workitem (if they exist). When the copying is completed, the workitem is said to be *transferred*.

All workitems that can be executed in disconnected mode are included in the prefetching, and the order in which they are prefetched is given by its ordering in the worklist. However, a locked workitem gains priority over non-locked ones.

5.4   Disconnected Operation

In WorkToDo, a user participating in a process can execute tasks without being connected to the WFMS. The user chooses one or more workitems, disconnects from the system and, after executing the workitems (minutes, hours or days later), connects again to the WFMS to notify the execution results.

The WorkToDo supports planned disconnected operations, requiring the user to notify the system prior to disconnection. Users reserve workitems to execute in disconnected mode through a *locking* mechanism.

During disconnected operation a user can visualize and modify his worklist normally, besides executing workitems in the same way that when connected. The only difference is that, in disconnected mode, the worklist shows only those workitems locked before disconnection; the remaining workitems get disabled.

In order to execute a workitem in disconnected mode all data related to the workitem must be available locally. Therefore, these data are copied to the user's machine at disconnection time (or before, if we consider prefetching). Moreover, when the user reconnects, the WFMS must be notified about the results of workitem executions. The protocols for user's disconnection and reconnection are described below.

Disconnection Protocol

1. The user notifies his WM that he wants to disconnect from the WFMS, specifying the maximum time he can wait until disconnection;
2. The WM checks if the user has some selected workitem. In this case the WM asks the user if disconnection should proceed;
3. The WM notifies the URM about the user's disconnection;
4. The URM sets the user's status to inactive;
5. The WM calculates the size of each locked and non-transferred workitem, defined as the sum of the size of the application and the data related to the workitem (if they exist). The application is only considered if it is not installed on the user's machine;

6. The WM calculates the amount of data to transfer, defined as the sum of the sizes of all locked and non-transferred workitems;

7. The WM verifies if the network bandwidth supports the transfer of the required data within the time specified by the user. In negative case, the system indicates the required time and allows the user to unlock some workitem(s), returning to step 5;

8. The WM verifies if there is enough free disk space on the user's machine to store the required data. In negative case, the system asks the user to correct the problem (e.g., freeing disk space) or to unlock some workitem(s), returning to step 5;

9. The WM copies each locked and non-transferred workitem;

10. The WM disables all non-locked workitems;

11. The WFMS notifies the user when the machine is finally disconnected.

At any time during the protocol execution disconnections may occur (both by the user's decision or by failures). After reconnection the data transfer is continued from where it has stopped. Moreover, a transferred workitem can be executed in disconnected mode even if the disconnection protocol has not been executed entirely, as long as the workitem has already been locked (avoiding other users to execute it) and its data is locally available.

Reconnection Protocol

1. The user notifies his WM that he wants to connect to the WFMS;

2. The WM notifies the URM about the user's connection;

3. The URM sets the user's status to active;

4. The WFMS notifies the user that he is connected and that the results of the workitem executions will be transferred to the WFMS;

5. The WM enables all workitems;

6. For each workitem executed in disconnected mode, the WM:

   a) In background, transfers to the correspondent PM the data generated by the workitem execution;

   b) Removes the workitem from the worklist.

In the moment of disconnection, all non-locked workitems are disabled; step 5 enables them again. Some of these workitems may have already been selected, locked or even executed by other users. Therefore, the worklist is updated in the next interaction between WM and PM or when the user attempts to select a workitem. As with the previous protocol, this protocol execution may be interrupted by failures and resumed upon reconnection.

It is important to say that, even if disconnected operation is supported, not all tasks should be executed in disconnected mode [3]. Some aspects must be considered, such as the size of data and applications and the delay in tasks and processes execution (because of the inherent delay of disconnected operation). Thus, it is necessary a trade-off analysis before defining a task as allowable to be executed disconnected.

5.5   Semi-connected Operation

Semi-connected (or weakly-connected) operation occurs when a user interacts with the system through a wireless link. Users see no difference from operation through a conventional connection, except for system response that is slower.

During semi-connected operation there may exist periods when there is little or even no communication between the user's machine and the WFMS. These periods are used for prefetching, taking as much advantage as possible of the network bandwidth. Thus, when the user selects a workitem, its data may be already available locally. In this case, it may be less expensive to execute the workitem locally instead of remotely, avoiding communication with another machine and thus masking possible failures.

When the user selects a workitem in semi-connected mode, the WM verifies if the workitem has already been transferred. In positive case, the user may choose between using local or remote data in the workitem execution. Local execution avoids remote communication, but after execution the data must be copied back to the WFMS. If the workitem execution has a high number of data accesses, the local execution will probably be better; on the other hand, if the execution generates a large amount of data, the time to transfer the results to the WFMS will be too high. This tradeoff must be considered by the user to maximize efficiency.

If a connection breaks, the WM disables all non-locked workitems as well as the locked but non-transferred, keeping enabled only those workitems that are locked and transferred. Thus, the user may keep working on these workitems exactly as in planned disconnection. If the user has some workitem being executed when the failure occurs, there are three cases to be considered:

1. If the workitem was being executed over local data, its execution may proceed normally, as if the workitem were being executed in disconnected mode. The execution results will be transferred to the WFMS upon user's reconnection;
2. If the workitem uses remote data, its execution is temporarily stopped. When the user reconnects and the data is available again, the execution is resumed;
3. If the workitem uses a remote application, after reconnection the user may restart the application and resume the task execution.

6   Prototype

This Section describes some characteristics of the WorkToDo prototype built to test the system. Furthermore, the Section contains an example of a process and the results obtained from the tests.

6.1   CORBA & Java

The WorkToDo can be implemented using any programming language and any distributed platform that supports remote communication. In this prototype, we used CORBA (IONA's CORBA implementation OrbixWeb 3.1) and Java (JDK 1.2).

The choice for Java was motivated by its property to be multiplatform, allowing the system execution on different hardware and operating systems. This is an important aspect in a workflow system, where many users access the system from various machines.

CORBA was chosen because it provides transparent remote object access, making the development of distributed applications easier. Furthermore, it is a relatively stable technology and has been used successfully in many contexts.

The components of the architecture were all implemented as CORBA servers, communicating through a Local Area Network (LAN). The only exception is the Worklist Manager, which may use a wireless link.

The OrbixWeb extends the basic ORB functionalities, providing a set of additional services. Some of them were used in the prototype to improve efficiency and are described below:

Persistent objects. This service allows the state of an object to be recovered and saved automatically when the object is activated and deactivated, respectively.

Multithreaded servers. This service allows a server to process many requests simultaneously. Each time the server receives a request, a separate thread is created to process the request, freeing the server to receive other requests.

Timeout for servers. Through this service, it is possible to establish for how long a server will stay active after processing a request. After a certain amount of time without receiving any requests, the server is automatically deactivated. This amount of time may be specified when the server is created.

Multithreaded servers were used to minimize the response time for clients, since a multithreaded server is much faster in processing simultaneous requests than a single-threaded one. The timeout for servers provides memory savings: if a server do not get any requests during a certain period of time, it is deactivated, freeing memory (although there will be an extra overhead when the server receives a request, since it will have to be reactivated). The timeout for servers in the tests was 10 minutes. Persistent objects were used together with timeouts to automatically save servers state periodically.

6.2   Example of Use

To illustrate the use of WorkToDo, we will considerate the example described previously, in which a maintenance firm attending a set of customers creates a process to manage its services. The specification of such process in the WorkToDo Workflow Definition Language is the following (other tasks are omitted due to space limitations):

```
WORKFLOW Maintenance {
    FILE ServiceOrder {
```

```
          NAME "/processes/files/ServiceOrder.doc";
      }
      ⋮

      TASK VisitCustomer:FillForm {
          ROLE Technician;
          IN_CONTEXT ServiceOrder;
          OUT_CONTEXT ServiceOrder;
          DEPENDS CreateServiceOrder -> SUCCEEDED;
          DESCRIPTION "Fill in fields 'Services' and
                          'Materials' from Service Order";
      }
      ⋮

  }
```

The process, named **Maintenance**, contains the task **VisitCustomer**, which is an instance of the task model **FillForm**. The role **Technician** is responsible for this task execution and the task will only be executed if the task **CreateServiceOrder** is executed successfully. The only input and output data for **VisitCustomer** is the file **ServiceOrder.doc**, identified by **ServiceOrder** and found at the path **/processes/files/**. The specification also contains a description of what must be done to execute the task.

The task model **FillForm** is defined as follows:

```
  TASK FillForm {
      TYPE Semi-automatic;
      APPLICATION TextEditor;
      PRIORITY 10;
      DEADLINE 48 HOURS;
      DISCONNECTED_OPERATION true;
  }
```

The task is semi-automatic and its related application is **TextEditor** (whose characteristics are defined separately). The definition also includes the task priority and deadline. The clause **DISCONNECTED_OPERATION** indicates if the task may be executed in disconnected mode (**true**) or not (**false**).

Let us suppose that there is an instance of the process **Maintenance** in execution and that the task **CreateServiceOrder** has been executed successfully. In this case, the task **VisitCustomer** may be executed, because its dependences are satisfied. As it is a semi-automatic task, the Dispatcher inserts a workitem corresponding to the task in the worklist of all users belonging to the role **Technician** (or some of these users, according to the chosen notification policy).

Figure 4 shows the worklist of a user who belongs to the role **Technician**. In this worklist there are tasks of several instances of process **Maintenance**, as well as of process **wf2**. The worklist belongs to the user **Paulo** (which is connected to the WFMS) and contains five workitems: three of them corresponding to **VisitCustomer** tasks from different instances of process **Maintenance**; and the other two corresponding to **task_1** tasks from instances of **wf2**. The first workitem is ready to be executed, the second and third are selected and the fourth is locked. Workitems that have the same task name are uniquely identified in the worklist by the name of the instance to which their respective tasks belong.

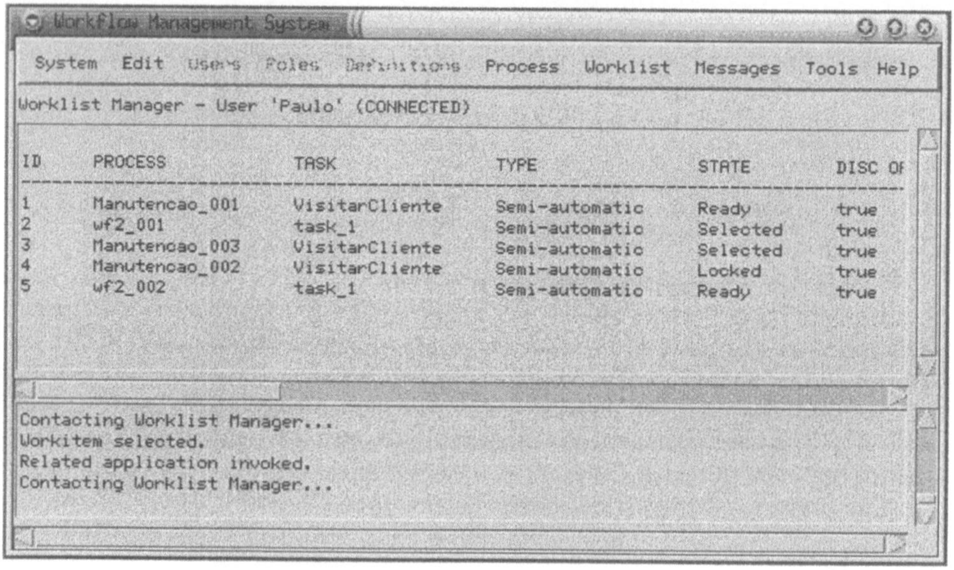

Fig. 4. Example of a Worklist.

As shown, the worklist contains other information about the workitems, such as the respective task and process instance name, the workitem type, current state and disconnected execution availability. Through the menu the user can interact with the worklist, the workitems and the WFMS.

6.3   Results

During the tests execution, the URM, DM and IM were executed at distinct hosts. The host of each PM was chosen at instance creation time, the TMs were created in the hosts indicated by the application correspondent to the automatic task and the hosts of the WMs were their user's hosts.

Disconnected and semi-connected operation have proved to be feasible and the system to be stable in the face of communication failures, without generating inconsistencies. When a communication failure occurs, if some PM can not contact a user's WM after a certain number of tries (5 in the tests), that user is considered inactive. When this WM interacts with some other component, the user is considered active again.

Using the prefetching technique, the execution time of the disconnection protocol has become very small, consisting mainly of the remote call to the

URM. This happens because the transfer of the locked workitems, the protocol step which consumes more time, has already been executed.

We plan to execute performance tests for the prototype, such as memory and processor usage (especially by the WM, on the mobile computer), and minimum bandwidth required to achieve a satisfactory performance in semi-connected operation, among others.

CORBA Evaluation. CORBA has fit well into the workflow system. The provided transparency is clearly a great benefit, separating the application functional aspects from the distribution aspect.

However, the required memory to run a server object is relatively high, limiting the use of CORBA in mobile devices with little memory, such as PDAs. Moreover, the processing complexity and storage capacity needed to support CORBA does not seem suitable for these kind of devices. These problems could be avoided, maybe, using *minimumCORBA*[1].

CORBA IORs. There is a problem with respect to the CORBA IORs of some objects (the WMs, which are executed on mobile hosts). When a mobile host moves to another cell, it receives a new IP address, invalidating all IORs. One way to solve this problem is to store the WM state into the URM before moving, to instantiate a new WM recovering this state and to inform the new address to the URM. In order to achieve this, the WM must know when the mobile host moves to a new cell.

7   Conclusions

In this paper we presented the WorkToDo, a WFMS for wireless communication environments. With this system, the users can execute tasks from their laptop or other portable device without any mobility restriction. Moreover, the users can execute tasks even disconnected from the system, using a locking mechanism to reserve the tasks to be executed in disconnected mode. Prior to disconnection the WorkToDo executes a protocol which copies all task data to the user's machine. The tasks are then executed using local data. Upon reconnection another protocol is executed, which transfers back to the WorkToDo the execution results.

We have considered aspects such as local task deadline management (controlled by the WM) and the copy of data and results (made by the WM in the disconnection and reconnection protocols). The WorkToDo also implements the prefetching technique to optimize the copy of workitems. While the user is connected to the WFMS, the WM copies (in background) the workitems that can

---

[1] minimumCORBA is a subset of CORBA, targeted to the development of applications on devices with limited computing resources. It does not include aspects such as dynamic facilities for creating and activating objects and for serving requests.

be executed in disconnected mode. If the user locks these workitems, their data will already be available locally.

Asynchronous techniques such as prefetching and postponed propagation of results can also optimize the use of available bandwidth and mask eventual communication failures.

Finally, the model was validated by a prototype implementation written in Java and using OrbixWeb-ORB as the communication platform.

Acknowledgments. We would like to thank the CNPq (National Council for Scientific and Technological Development) and the SAI (Advanced Information Systems) project of PRONEX-MCT for the financial support of our research.

References

1. Alonso, G., Agrawal, D., El Abbadi, A., Gunthor, R., Kamath, M., Mohan, C.: Exotica/FMDC: Handling Disconnected Clients in a Workflow Management System. In: Proceedings of the 3rd International Conference on Cooperative Information Systems. Vienna, Austria (1995) 99–110
2. Barbara, D., Mehrotra, S., Rusinkiewicz, M.: INCAS: A Computation Model for Dynamic Workflows in Autonomous Distributed Environments. Technical Report, Department of Computer Science, University of Houston, USA (1994)
3. Bussler, C.: User Mobility in Workflow Management Systems. In: Proceedings of the Telecommunication Information Networking Architecture Conference (TINA). Melbourne, Australia (1995)
4. Das, S., Kochut, K., Miller, J., Sheth, A., Worah, D.: ORBWork: A Reliable Distributed CORBA-based Workflow Enactment System for METEOR. Technical Report, Department of Computer Science, University of Georgia, USA (1997)
5. Eder, J., Groiss, H., Liebhart, W.: Workflow Management and Databases. In: Proceedings of the 2nd Forum International d'Informatique Appliquee. Tunis, Tunisia (1996)
6. Georgakopoulos, D., Hornick, M., Sheth, A.: An Overview of Workflow Management: From Process Modeling to Workflow Automation Infrastructure. In: Distributed and Parallel Databases, Vol. 3 (1995) 119–153
7. Jablonski, S.: Functional and Behavioral Aspects of Process Modelling in Workflow Systems. In: Chroust, G., Benczur, A. (eds.): CON 94 Workflow Management: Challenges, Paradigms and Products. R. Oldenburg (1994) 113–133
8. Jing, J., Huff, K., Sinha, H., Hurtwitz, B., Robinson, B.: Workflow and Application Adaptations in Mobile Environments. In: Proceedings of the 2nd IEEE Workshop on Mobile Computing Systems and Applications. New Orleans, Louisiana, USA (1999)
9. Kamath, M., Ramamritham, K.: Bridging the Gap Between Transaction Management and Workflow Management. In: Proceedings of NSF Workshop on Workflow and Process Automation in Information Systems. Athens, Georgia (1996)
10. Veijalainen, J., Lehtola, A., Pihlajamaa, O.: Research Issues in Workflow Systems. Technical Report, VTT Information Technology, Finland (1995)

Customizable Deployment, Composition, and Hosting of Distributed Java Applications

Stefan Paal [1], Reiner Kammüller [2], and Bernd Freisleben [3]

[1] Fraunhofer Institute for Media Communication
Schloss Birlinghoven, D-53754 St. Augustin, Germany
stefan.paal@imk.fraunhofer.de
[2] Department of Electrical Engineering and Computer Science, University of Siegen
Hölderlinstr. 3, D-57068 Siegen, Germany
kammueller@pd.et-inf.uni-siegen.de
[3] Department of Mathematics and Computer Science, University of Marburg
Hans-Meerwein-Strasse, D-35032 Marburg, Germany
freisleb@informatik.uni-marburg.de

Abstract. Deploying and running Java applications on a single host is covered by standard approaches. However, when applications are dynamically deployed on distributed hosts, the situation is quite different. In this context, applications are likely to be composed of classes, located in remote repositories and possibly related to identical class names. Hence, the typical class loader approach is no longer feasible to resolve the right byte code. Moreover, the native *Java Runtime Environment (JRE)* has originally not been designed to host more than one application concurrently within a single *Java Virtual Machine (JVM)*. Thus, there are also unresolved issues concerning hosting distributed applications. In this paper, we present a new approach for a customizable Java application middleware with respect to the topics of *application deployment, composition and hosting*. Finally, the application of the approach within a distributed middleware platform is presented, wherein applications are *customizably* deployed, *dynamically* composed and *concurrently* hosted.

1 Introduction

In contrast to other, native programming languages like C++, Java does not only come with a programming environment but also with a runtime environment, the so called *Java Runtime Environment (JRE)*. It shields the application from the underlying system environment and provides access to its resources, independently of the current operating system or hardware. One part of the JRE is the *Java Virtual Machine (JVM)* which hosts the Java application and is responsible for locating and loading the related byte code and finally starting the execution of the application. In this sense, the JRE can be regarded as a quite simple application framework which is able to host a single application.

Before a Java application can be started by the JVM, the related byte code of the application classes must be located, loaded and resolved. The latter means that loaded classes may refer to other classes which must also be loaded before the referring class can be used [1]. For this purpose, the native JVM delegates usually the class loading request to the so called *system class loader* that locates the byte code using an environment variable CLASSPATH and the *fully-qualified class name (FQCN)* of the required classes, which is composed of the package name and the class name itself [2,3]. In addition, there may be other class loaders which are *user-defined* and are free in the way the byte code is located and loaded [4,5].

However, common to all class loaders is that each can load the same class only once during its lifetime, whereby two classes are assumed to be the same class when their FQCNs are equal. Due to this fact and the fact that Java applications are usually composed of many classes, the deployed classes are organized in tree-like organized packages, whose names are prepended to the class name, forming the FQCN.

Obviously, this kind of application deployment eases class localization and loading, but on the other hand, this feature makes it nearly impossible to select byte code depending on other properties than the class name, such as implementation version or debug variant of the class. Of course, many application frameworks instantiate a user-defined class loader and introduce a new loading mechanism, but they usually change the way classes are *loaded* and sometimes also how they are *located*, but not how they are *selected*. As a consequence, it is not possible to instruct existing application frameworks which classes should actually be used when composing a certain application. Instead, the application framework loads needed classes as they are requested, while it is assumed that these classes are found somehow during runtime [3].

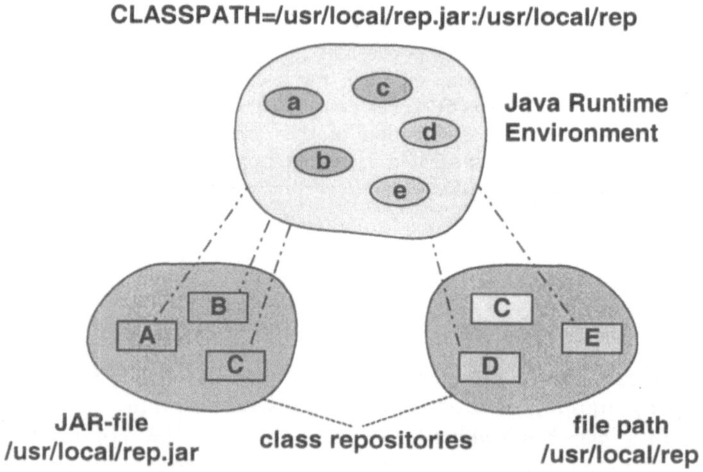

CLASSPATH=/usr/local/rep.jar:/usr/local/rep

Fig. 1. Class loading with two conflicting class repositories

As shown in fig. 1, assuming the CLASSPATH contains two locations from where requested classes should be loaded. Beside of class C, only one byte code for each class can be found. But class C is available in two different variants. Thus, when the class loader is requested to load a class, it can only determine by its name where to find the related byte code. Hence, it will load the byte code for C always from the JAR-file, since it is specified in CLASSPATH before the file path. As a result, the major problem in application composition and deployment still remains, namely how to build an application framework that can be customized, not only statically but even dynamically during runtime, which classes of the deployed ones are needed, should be selected and used to compose the application?

Apart from the class *selection* problem, there is another related problem concerning class *hosting*. The native JVM and its system class loader have been designed to host only a single application and are run by the underlying operating system within a single process. Therefore, further Java applications have to be started in additional JVMs. Although this is well-suited for stand-alone applications running on a single machine, it causes problems when a multi-application environment like a server platform should be configured to run more than one application, requiring the same classes in different variants concurrently and wanting to share data within the border of a JVM. As mentioned above, the problems are caused by the fact that class loaders can load a certain class only once during their lifetime. In detail, all loaded classes are put within so called *namespaces*, each associated with one class loader, wherein no two classes with the same FQCN can co-exist.

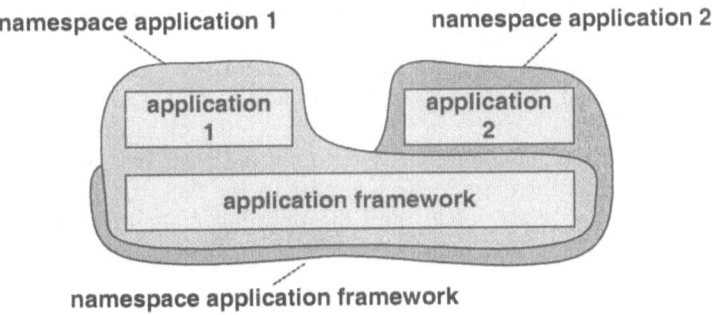

Fig. 2. Application hosting with separated application namespaces

There are implementations using more than one classloader, each managing its own namespace. That way, they can host the same application in different variants and are even able to reload dynamically the application code when it has been changed in the byte code repository. Although this resolves the multi-application problem, it raises another problem, since it separates all application code completely and makes it difficult to share data directly among each other, as illustrated in fig. 2.

There are three class loaders and their associated namespaces, each for the applications and the framework itself. After starting the application framework, applications 1 and 2 are dynamically loaded and placed in two different namespaces, so that their classes are shielded against each other. Though this is necessary for concurrent application hosting when using classes with the same FQCN, the applications can only interact by using classes located in the framework namespace.

To understand the problem in more detail, it is useful to regard some class loading details, extracted from [2,3]. Beside of the provided class loaders like the *bootstrap class loader* and *system class loader*, application developers are able to define further so called *user-defined* class loaders. Like any other class loader, they are ordinary Java objects, instantiated from a class that is inherited from *java.lang.ClassLoader*. In order to customize the class loading process, the user-defined class loader has to override the appropriate methods of *java.lang.ClassLoader*, typically *findClass* respectively *loadClass*. Then, after a related class loader object has been instantiated with *new*, it can be used to load a class by calling the method *loadClass* with the appropriate class name. Moreover, each loaded class is assigned to the namespace of the used class loader and subsequent class loading requests issued by its objects will be automatically passed to that class loader. Thus, a user-defined class loader is hooked into the system simply by using it to load an initial class with *loadClass*.

Furthermore, each class loader has exactly one parent class loader which is assigned upon its creation and that can not be changed afterwards. If no parent class loader is given, then the *system class loader* is automatically assigned as parent. This leads to a *parent-delegation model* and forms a class loader tree with the system class loader at the root. With that, the class loaders are usually implemented in such a manner that they delegate class loading requests at first to their parent and will not try to load the class, if the parent returns the requested class. But in the case the parent class loader is not able to load the requested class, for example it is not accordingly configured or an error occurs, the parent raises an exception and the request is returned to its child. Finally, if even the firstly called class loader at the end of the chain is also not able to load the class, a *ClassNotFoundException* is raised and it is up to the application to handle the exception.

Within this context, there are two kinds of class loader associated with a loaded class instance, so called *initiating class loaders* and so called *defining class loaders*. While each loaded class instance has only one defining class loader that is actually loading the related byte code and finally defining the class instance, there might be several associated initiating class loaders, simply by the fact that they are in the chain between the requesting class loader and the defining class loader. An illustrating example is shown in fig. 3, where three class loaders CL1, CL2 and CL3 are shown.

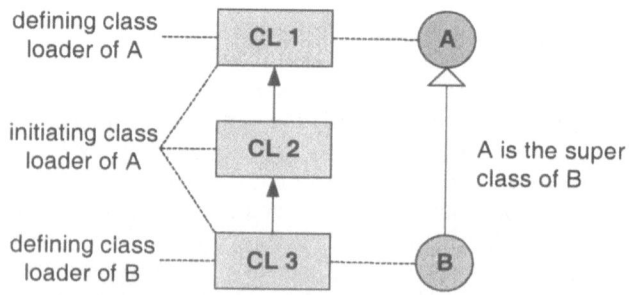

Fig. 3. Initiating and defining class loaders

Assuming the class loader CL1 is able to load class A and CL3 can load class B, which is inherited from A. When CL3 is requested to load B, it must first load its super class A. Since it is not able to load A, it delegates the request up to its parent CL2, which in turn delegates the request to CL1. Finally, CL1 loads A and becomes the defining class loader of A. The other participating class loaders become initiating class loaders of A.

The namespace of a class loader can now be defined more precisely: it is simply a list of classes, for which the class loader has served as an initiating class loader. All classes within this list can *see* and use only the other classes in that list or loaded classes from their parent class loader, but not from any other class loader, located elsewhere.

Due to this fact, objects in two namespaces can only share data and collaborate, if they *see* the associated classes, or in other words, if the methods of the object stem from classes or interfaces, which are loaded from the same parent class loader. In fig. 4, B and C have been put in different, separated namespaces, since they are loaded and defined by CL2 and CL3, which are not chained. In turn, class A, the super class of B, is loaded and defined by CL1, which is the parent class loader of CL2 and CL3. Assuming that object o1 and o2 have been created and object o2 gets the reference of o1. Then, object o2 is able to downcast the reference of o1 to A, but not to B, since B is in another namespace and not visible to o2. Therefore, it can only call methods of o1, defined in A.

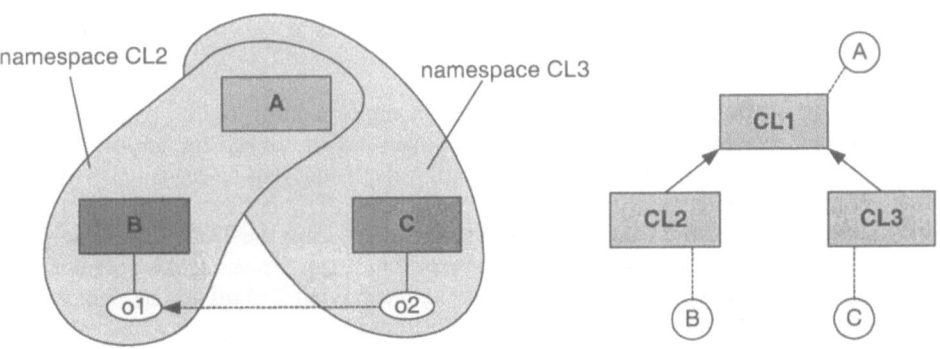

Fig. 4. Calling methods from objects in another namespace

Similar to the class loading problem mentioned above, the existing approaches do not offer the ability to *select* which classes should be put in separated namespaces and which can be kept in common namespaces nor how this task can be customized dynamically and individually for each application. This is especially important for a multi-application environment, when two unknown, dynamically loaded applications want to share common data with each other or with the application framework itself.

In this paper, we present a customizable Java application middleware to solve the illustrated problems. For this purpose, we introduce so called *Java Class Spaces*, which manage namespaces and the loaded classes in a customizable manner, enabling the application middleware to host different applications concurrently. Second, we propose so called *Java Class Collections*, which group classes individually and decorate them with additional properties. In contrast to the ordinary Java class loading approach, where classes are selected, located and organized within the JVM just by using their class names, we introduce a customizable way of how classes are selected and organized dynamically, namely also with respect to certain properties like version information or application demands. This decouples the mechanism of *application-based class selection* and *deployment-dependent class location*, supporting the development as well as the customizable deployment, composition and hosting of distributed applications.

The paper is organized as follows. Section 2 discusses features of Java application frameworks with respect to *application development, composition, deployment and hosting*. In section 3, our approach to develop a customizable Java application middleware is presented. In section 4, the application of our approach is illustrated, and section 5 concludes the paper with an outline of future work.

2 Java Application Framework

There are various approaches to application frameworks running on top of a native JRE, which claim to ease the development and which support more or less *deployment, composition* and *hosting* of applications. In the following, we outline these tasks and how they are accomplished by existing approaches.

2.1 Application Development

The major task of an application developer is implementing the so called *business logic* of the application. But since a Java application can not run on its own, it has to follow the guidelines for writing an application itself that can be executed within the used runtime environment. Considering the native JRE, it has to provide a static method *main*, where the execution is started after creating the JVM. Conversely, the application can direct the JRE to load application classes by using the operator *new*. In addition, the application wants to access the underlying system and its resources as well as utilizing existing application code. For these purposes, the *Java Development Kit (JDK)* comes with a lot of classes that can be used to access the system resources and ease application development by providing ready-to-use classes for many purposes. In particular, the JDK offers methods how an application can be extended during runtime, requesting additional classes dynamically for example with the static method *forClass* or using the *reflection* API.

There are several specialized application frameworks that provide certain development support [6]. A widely used implementation for Internet applications is *Jakarta Tomcat*, which is used to host so called *Java servlets*, a specialized kind of application, and expects as the execution start point the method *init* within the servlet class [7]. It also comes with many classes, which assist the developer in implementing HTTP request handling and serving HTML pages.

2.2 Application Deployment

Besides application development as supported by the *programming environment*, the application must also be deployed in the actual *runtime environment* before it can be executed. At first, the application framework should support the concurrent deployment of the same class in different implementation variants like debug or multi-threading releases. Though this is quite simple for stand-alone applications, it is getting rather complex when running a multi-application environment like *Jakarta Tomcat*, dealing with various installed class files.

Second, the original class loading approach of Java has a quite limited way to locate and load classes dynamically from sources other than the file system. The obvious way to extend this capability is the provision of user-defined class loaders which can access class files individually, e.g. over the network [8]. In this scenario, the user-defined class loader focuses usually on the task how the requested classes can be loaded. But some of them also deal with the question how to locate the requested class and use their own mechanism to resolve the location of the class. This allows to place the classes elsewhere, assuming there is a class loader to handle the related location and loading issues. An example of an Internet-based deployment approach is described in [9], where application code is spread over the Internet and dynamically loaded using particular class loaders.

2.3   Application Composition

A further important feature of Java application frameworks is the composition of applications from deployed classes, even dynamically configured during runtime. While the *application developer* defines within the application code *which* classes should be loaded, the *application composer* configures from *where* to load the requested classes. Within a native JRE the latter task is originally fulfilled by defining the environment setting CLASSPATH, specifying file paths or so called JAR files containing the needed classes. The *system class loader* provided by the JRE evaluates that setting to load classes, but it is only capable to access local file systems.

While this scenario is quite widely used, it inherits some essential weak points with respect to the origin idea of application composition. First, it is not possible to exclude single classes from a given path or JAR file, therefore classes with the same name located within two specified file paths are selected by the order in the CLASSPATH setting, leading to strange behaviors when not properly handled. An example are the Java classes of *Apache Xerces* [10], which accompany the latest SUN JDK 1.4.0 [11], but are also part of existing program installations like *Apache Cocoon* [12]. Due to evolving releases, there are conflicts which can not be always handled by appropriate orderings in CLASSPATH. This has even forced some installations to modify delivered JAR files for proper execution!

Second, in our opinion applications are not just composed by specifying the location of single classes or JAR files. Moreover, the latter are often packaged rather simply by the application deployer, which has grouped related and non-related classes within a single file for easy delivery. In contrast to that, applications are rather composed by the fact that groups of certain classes represent a particular needed functionality. These groups can span different JAR files or just be parts of them. As a result, application composition has to be separated from application deployment. Or in other words, *functionality driven class composition* should be independent of *installation based class deployment*. But this can not be achieved just by evaluating the environment setting CLASSPATH, since it is used to define concurrently which concrete classes can be loaded and from where they are retrieved.

There are several application frameworks which extend the ordinary class loading approach and overcome some of the depicted limitations. They often use additional configuration files, enabling the specification of certain dynamically loaded classes independently of their location. Examples are plugins or handlers which provide certain exchangeable functionality like in *Java Database Connectivity (JDBC)*, whose database connectors can by selected transparently to the application, depending on the actually used database. Another example is *Jakarta Tomcat* that allows to define dynamically loaded protocol interceptors.

2.4   Application Hosting

As described above, the native JRE is not capable to host more than one application. However, there are approaches for multi-application environments which overcome this limitation and are able to host different applications concurrently within a single JVM. They share commonly used resources like code libraries, memory space, network or database connections, thus improving greatly the utilization of these resources in contrast to the usage of a single JVM per application [13,14]. This is facilitated in a particular manner, since the applications do not need to cross the borders of their JVM for that purpose and can collaborate directly without using RMI [15], CORBA [16] or similar solutions [17]. Particularly in multi-user environments like Internet-enabled application servers, when many applications share the same resources, these features may be quite important [18,19].

Another objective in this context is the dynamic loading and unloading of applications. For example, it is usually not allowed to shutdown a JVM which hosts several web services due to the reload of one single service. For this purpose and to ensure the proper execution of applications in the presence of other hosted applications, each application is placed in a new namespace in which an application can load its own classes separately from classes loaded by other applications, except for the classes loaded by the framework. This is ensured by the fact that each class loader delegates class loading requests at first to their parents. That way, parent class loaders get always the first chance to load the class before their childs, and all applications can share data using classes from the framework.

To summarize, there are various tasks and requirements an application framework has to deal with, namely it has to support the development of applications as well as their deployment, composition and hosting. Although there are many approaches which handle these tasks, they are mostly not customizable in the way they do that. They often introduce new features which are used to overcome existing limitations, but at the same time introduce other constraints, for example, to the structure of the Java application to be hosted, such as *Enterprise Java Beans (EJB)* [20], *Apache Avalon* [21], or *SUN ONE* [22]. Thus, they are not generally suitable for legacy Java applications. Moreover, most of them are not available stand-alone, but part of another framework like *Jakarta Tomcat* [7]. What is still missing is the seamless support of legacy applications, which benefit transparently from introduced features regarded above, not only in a predefined way, but in a customizable manner.

3   Customizable Java Application Middleware

In the following, we present a customizable *Java Application Middleware* which accomplishes the depicted tasks, not only by adding new features, but by customizing existing features concerning *deployment*, *composition* and *hosting* of Java applications. In contrast to conventional frameworks, our approach does neither force developers nor end-users to deal with a new development or runtime environment. In fact, the middleware mediates transparently between the underlying runtime environment and the application on top. Thus, it is also able to run on legacy Java runtime environments, originally delivered by SUN, and to host legacy applications, which transparently benefit from the customizable features.

3.1   Objectives

The objectives of a customizable Java application middleware are presented in the following:

Transparent Handling of Legacy Application Code and Class Repositories
An application framework which forces the developer or deployer to change existing and moreover running application code to be executable within the framework will of course not be accepted widely. Therefore, a keystone of a customizable application framework is the transparent handling of new features, allowing the developer to focus on actual tasks and enabling the integration of legacy application code.

Customizable Resource Registration during Runtime
The native class loader concept of Java expects the specification of class repositories like JAR-files and file path in the environment variable CLASSPATH. Though this is fairly well-suited for standalone applications which are managed by a single developer and deployer, it limits the way how applications can be composed when new resources like classes or resource bundles are added dynamically. Thus, a customizable application framework should not only support the registration of classes by the deployer before starting the framework but also by the application during runtime.

Definition of Class Dependencies on the Composition and Deployment Level
Usually, applications are composed of dozens of classes, each having certain dependencies on other classes. They are resolved by loading the required classes in the case they are not already in memory. Though one could try to manage each class separately, this is not convenient. It would be better to group classes together with respect to their functionality and define dependencies between these groups, thus reducing the complexity of the configuration. The declaration of the groups can be used to specify how and from where to load the associated classes. As a result, the application developer and composer could specify *which* classes are needed, and the application deployer could configure *where* to find the appropriate classes and how to resolve their dependencies.

Dynamic Configuration of Shared and Separated Classes
Certain application developers want their applications to use special features of the framework. Particularly with regard to loading concurrent classes, the configuration of shared and separated classes should be customizable by the application. This enables the dynamic extension with additional functionalities and plugins during runtime and eases the resolution of occurring conflicts.

Decoration of Classes with Custom Properties for Conditional Class Selection
Ordinary class loaders *locate* and *load* the requested classes by using the given class name. This is sufficient as long as there is no need to *select* the correct class out of a bunch of classes with the same name, e.g. representing different implementation variants of the same class. For this purpose, additional properties of the requested class should be used to determine which class variant actually to load. However, existing application frameworks and their class loader do not support the specification of further parameters other than the class name.

Determining the Required Classes before an Application Starts
After a Java application has been started, the JRE loads missing classes into memory step by step as they are requested. In case a class can not be found, the JRE throws a *ClassNotFoundException* and the program is usually aborted. Due to this sequence, an application deployer is not able to track down a missing class before the exception occurs or even to configure the environment appropriately to avoid the exception at all. This is even getting worse when the deployer has to configure an application framework, wherein many applications should be hosted, increasing the complexity of class dependencies. Therefore, a framework should indicate missing classes before the application is started.

No Modification of Legacy Applications and Class Repositories
A further important issue is the compatibility with existing legacy applications. This should not only be valid for applications where the source code is available, but also for legacy applications that can not be re-compiled or even modified. Furthermore, deployed class repositories like Java Archives should be usable without adaptation or repackaging.

3.2 Architectural Approaches

Regarding the defined features of a customizable Java application framework, the first task is to introduce a new *composition paradigm*. Although a Java application developer uses classes to implement an application and packages in which all classes are placed *logically*, they do not contain any *composition information*, neither which classes belong together nor which classes are required by the application during runtime. Therefore, our first architectural approach is the introduction of so called *class collections*, which are used to compose applications in a new way as follows.

In contrast to ordinary application frameworks, where application composition is quite weakly defined by naming required classes and packages and providing locations where to find *potentially* needed classes, class collections refine this by defining explicitly which classes can be loaded by the application and which can not be loaded; even more, the application framework can determine *before* an application is started whether all classes are available. This is especially important in dynamically changing deployment scenarios like Internet environments or peer-to-peer architectures. Furthermore, they offer the decoration of certain classes with additional properties. Thus, an application framework can be customized dynamically not to load the debug variant of the class, but the release variant. This can be done without changing the deployment settings, just by defining the composition of the application while it is started.

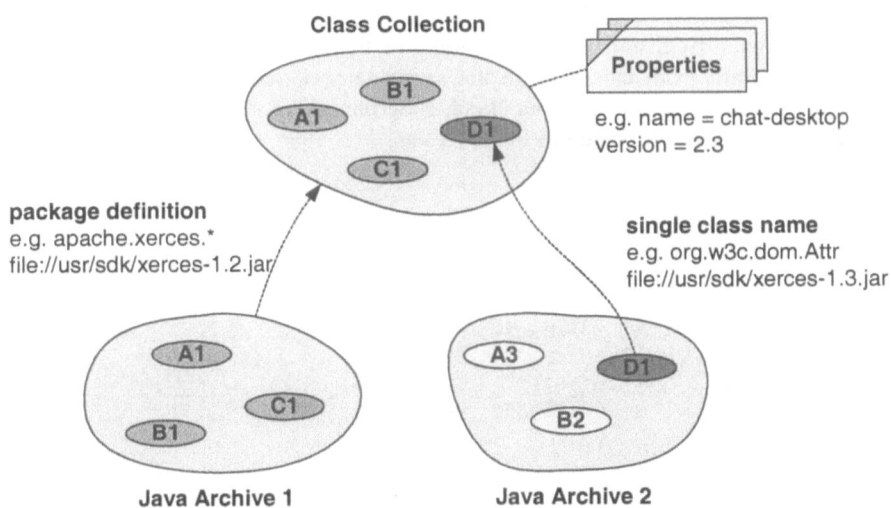

Fig. 5. Definition of a Class Collection, its properties and location of the related classes

Fig. 5 illustrates an example of a class collection. It contains properties, package and class names as well as the locations where the classes can be found, but not the byte code itself. All information is encapsulated within a configuration file, which can be browsed and searched by specifying the name and properties the searched collection should meet. This way, one could create a registry of class collection definitions, each associating classes and properties. An application framework can use this registry to request information where to find the appropriate classes and to compose applications with different class variants as it is needed by the application.

Even though class collections itself represent an essential improvement of how applications can be composed and deployed, there are still other features which are needed by a customizable application middleware. Based on class collections, we introduce another architectural approach, so called *class spaces*, which define the *layout of application code* within the application framework. Usually, all classes of an application are placed within a single namespace. But even if there is no conflict with classes using the same class name, some applications ask the framework to reload or exchange some portion of the application code like plugins. For this purpose, new namespaces are created in which the new classes can be placed. The old namespaces exist further, but are no longer used. This is done in a rather proprietary manner, and there is no way to define where the loaded classes have to be put, e.g. in the parent namespace or in the current namespace. However, this feature is required when two applications want to share data as illustrated above. Thus, we wrap *class spaces* around namespaces. They are able to monitor, which class should be loaded and can delegate customizably class loading requests to other class spaces.

In fig. 6, there is a class space SCS and two further class spaces UCS1 and UCS2 as children of the first. All objects, created by classes in UCS1 will have the class loader of UCS1 associated. In the case, one of these objects wants to create an object from a new class, the class loader is asked to load the byte code of the newly requested class. For this purpose, it determines wether the related class space, in this case UCS1, is configured to load the class. If not, it delegates the request up to its parent class space SCS and its class loader. In this example, objects in UCS1 and UCS2 can be built from classes with the same name C, but could rely on different class implementations. On the other hand, they can share data and collaborate with each other, using classes located in SCS.

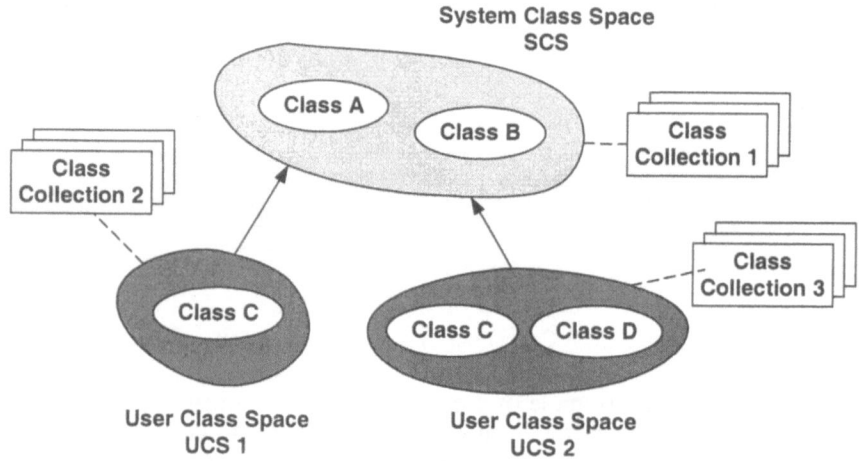

Fig. 6. Class Spaces

Another view on a more virtual level arises from the separation of objects due to the discrete, exclusive class layout. Chained class spaces, starting from a leaf class space following up the path to the system class space, load exclusively configured classes. In other words, there are no two class spaces in the chain, configured to load the same class. This is particularly important for casting objects, since an object can only be casted to a class or an interface which is loaded by a class loader on the path from its class loader up to the system class loader. As a result, though there are different class loaders loading classes from which objects are created, the objects can interact as if their classes are loaded by a single class loader. Thus, the usage of different class loaders is virtually hidden and the collectivity of these objects is enclosed within a so called *object space*. Within this context, the smallest object space is rather trivial and is only associated with one class loader. In comparison to *namespaces*, which are associated with an *initiating class loader* and represents a lists of classes passed through the loader, *object spaces* are orthogonal to that. They do not represent a list of classes, but rather a list of objects which can interact.

In fig. 7, there are four class spaces, which are chained as illustrated. Furthermore, there are three non-trivial object spaces, containing several class spaces. The object space *A* contains class spaces *application1*, *root* and *system*, whereby object space *B* contains class spaces *application2*, *root* and *system*. The third object space *C* contains just *root* and *system*. Consequently, *application1* and *application2* can only interact using objects with related classes located in *root* and *system*.

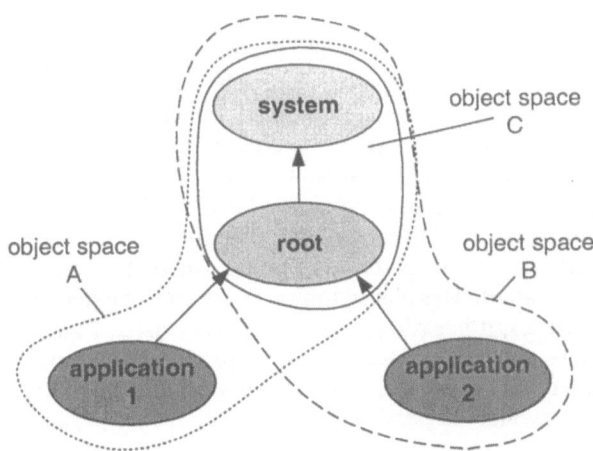

Fig. 7. Object Spaces

In addition, the configuration of a class space and its classes that can be loaded is combined with information where to find the related byte code. Although one is able to register separately each loadable class in a class space, it is much more convenient to use the introduced *class collections* for registration. With that, a class space can be configured to hold a whole bunch of classes in a particular variant at once.

A further special issue at this point is the question how the system should resolve registration conflicts between parent and child class space, if both want to register the same class. The answer is quite simple: all registrations must be checked against the registration in the chained class spaces, and if there is already a chained class space which handles the class, the registration is denied. Thus, concurrent classes could be managed up to a certain degree if the class spaces are configured properly by the application middleware.

Finally, the layout of application code, shared and separated classes is defined *without* modifying existing application code. The configuration process of class spaces and the arrangment of newly loaded classes are completely transparent to the application.

3.3   Realization

After presenting the basic ideas of our approach, its realization and its characteristics are illustrated in detail.

Class Collections. A class collection represents a virtual group of classes, which should be linked and associated with certain properties like version or debug information. The term *virtual* means, those classes are not really re-packaged and placed in a new JAR-file, but rather they remain completely in existing JAR-files or directory structures. The definition of class collections is done with an XML configuration file. An example of it can be seen in fig. 8, which shows a sample configuration for the *Apache-Xalan* classes. The first part groups classes of the release 1.2.2 together by specifying a property *version* beside the collection name *apache-xalan*. In the second part, the same is defined for classes of the release 2.2. For flexibility and efficiency, the declaration is done with regular expressions, thus it is easy to address various classes with few statements.

Though the example is quite short, it shows how simple ordinary class repositories can be disposed in class collections without changing any existing file. With it, an application framework can easily be configured where to find classes and which classes can be loaded at all. The configuration is arbitrarily extensible with additional properties and JAR-files; it is even possible to group classes from different JAR-files within a single class collection. That way, we are able to define *composition-based grouping* independently of *deployment-dependant packaging* of JAR-files.

```
<collection name="apache-xalan">
   <variant>
      <property name="version" value="1.2.2" />
      <file location="/sdk/apache-xalan-1.2.2/xalan.jar">
         <resource name="org/apache/xalan/.*" />
      </file>
   </variant>
   <variant>
      <property name="version" value="2.2" />
      <compatible name="apache-xalan">
         <property name="version" value="1.2.2" />
      </compatible>
      <file location="/sdk/apache-xalan-2.2/xalan.jar">
         <resource name="javax/xml/transform/.*" />
         <resource name="org/apache/xalan/.*" />
         <resource name="org/apache/xpath/.*" />
      </file>
   </variant>
</collection>
```

Fig. 8. Definition of class collections

Class Spaces. As introduced above, each class space encapsulates a class loader and its related namespace, whereby class spaces can be configured which classes they can load and which requests should be delegated to the parent class space. The configuration of class spaces can be done dynamically by the application itself as shown in fig. 9. At first, a new class space *app* is created with the class space *system* as parent. Then, a new resource is registered in the class space, specifying that all classes, whose names start with *javax.xml.parsers* will be found in the given JAR-file and the class space should be able to load them. Another dynamic variant is shown after that using class collections with given properties. The class space is hereby configured to host classes defined in the collection *sun-javamail* with the version *1.2*. In contrast to the first variant, the usage of class collections defers the concrete configuration which classes can be loaded and where to find the byte code. The deployer is able to redefine that by modifying the configuration of the collections.

```
IClassSpace app = null;
app = getClassMgr().createClassSpace("app", "system");
app.registerResource("javax/xml/parsers/.*",
                        "/xerces-1.4.4/xerces.jar");
HashSet props = new HashSet();
props.add("version", "1.2");
app.registerCollection("sun-javamail", props);
Class parser = app.getClassLoader().loadClass
("org.apache.xerces.parsers.DOMParser ");
Class mail = app.getClassLoader().loadClass
                        ("javax.mail.Message");
```

Fig. 9. Dynamic Class Space Configuration

Finally, at the end of the example, the class space is requested to load two classes; hence, the classes are injected into the class space. All subsequent class loading requests initiated by them will now be handled by the class space *app*. At this point, it should be stressed, that the class space does not load any class without a request.

An example for a static class space configuration is shown in fig. 10. A class space called *application* is defined with the class space *system* as parent. It is also configured to host classes from the collections *jakarta-tomcat* and *sun-javamail* with the given version numbers. The class space *application* is not automatically created, but whenever the application opens a class space with that name, the configuration files is read and the class space is configured respectively. In this context, the usage of class collections eases and enables the concrete composition by the deployer, who is able to redefine this by modifying the related configuration files.

```
<space name="application" parent="system">
  <collection id="jakarta-tomcat">
    <property name="version" value="3.2.3" />
  </collection>
  <collection id="sun-javamail">
    <property name="version" value="1.2" />
  </collection>
</space>
```

Fig. 10. Static Class Space Configuration

Object Spaces. As described above, *object spaces* are virtual entities, grouping objects together, which can interact as if they are loaded by one single class loader. This is quite important, in the case of casting or comparing objects, which might have been instantiated by two classes, having the same FQCN, but are loaded within two class spaces. Therefore, the application framework offers methods to determine, whether two objects belong to one object space. Moreover, an object can belong to several object spaces, which can be also retrieved as shown in fig. 11.

```
Class c1 = system.getClassLoader().loadClass
                              ("java.util.HashMap");
Class c2 = app.getClassLoader().loadClass
                ("org.apache.xerces.parsers.DOMParser");
Object o1 = c1.newInstance();
Object o2 = c2.newInstance();
boolean fSame = getClassMgr().sameObjectSpace(o1,o2);
HashSet objSpaces = getClassMgr().getObjectSpaces(o1);
```

Fig. 11. Using Object Spaces

3.4   Discussion

The presented approach is completely transparent to legacy application code and existing class repositories, no recompilation, rewriting or repackaging are needed. Instead, the concerns of *application composition, hosting* and *deployment* are separated using additional configuration files for *class spaces* and *class collections* as described. Certainly, they have to be set up appropriately according to the *composition* and *hosting* requirements of the applications and the class *deployment* on the platform. But with that, legacy applications are completely unaware to reside within *class spaces* or to be composed using *class collections*. The related application class spaces are created before the applications are started and the first class of the application is loaded into the related class space by the framework. In this context, the approach benefits from the automatic connection of loaded classes and the used class loader to hook itself transparently into the system for all subsequent class loading requests of the application. Indeed, this can only be guaranteed as long as the application does not create a user-defined class loader itself, which may break the configured class separation. Another topic is the overhead by using our approach in contrast to a legacy runtime environment. At this point, it should be stressed, that there is no overhead once the requested classes are loaded, since the classes are cached and no particular lookup into the introduced configuration files is needed. On the other hand, the first loading request of a class imposes some overhead regarding the lookup which class space may handle the class and which class collection contains the requested class. But this can be minimized using regular expressions to keep the configuration of class collections small. Furthermore, the hierarchy of class spaces will usually be rather tiny, typically less than five levels. Thus, only few delegations between childs and their parents occur. And in the case a parent can not load a class, it returns control to its childs using boolean return values instead of exceptions; hence speeding up the delegation. Compared to other middleware solutions, our approach does not force developers to use a new programming model or technique. It does not propose how to add new functionality or aspects to a Java program like *Aspect-*

Oriented Programming (AOP) [23], but rather it presents a new way to *deploy*, *compose* and *host* Java applications transparently with regard to their implementation.

4 Application of the Approach

The presented approach has been developed as part of the *middleware platform ODIN* [24], which is currently being used in several ongoing research projects like *netzspannung.org* [25,26] and *Awake* [27]. Its major goal is the provision of an open, multi-platform programming and runtime environment for distributed applications. It supports multi-application hosting within a single JVM, which improves the utilization of resources and eases the inter-application communication. For that purpose, it has to shield each hosted application against each other, but also to enable collaboration between them. The Java implementation of ODIN uses the presented approach to achieve these goals and its application is now presented in the following.

4.1 Java Application Middleware

The JRE contains a JVM, which enables users to run Java Applications on each supported platform, independent of the operating system. In this context, the native JVM is usually only able to host one application at the same time. But in contrast to that, the presented approach is used by ODIN to form a *Java Application Middleware (JAM)* that enables multi-application hosting within a single JVM.

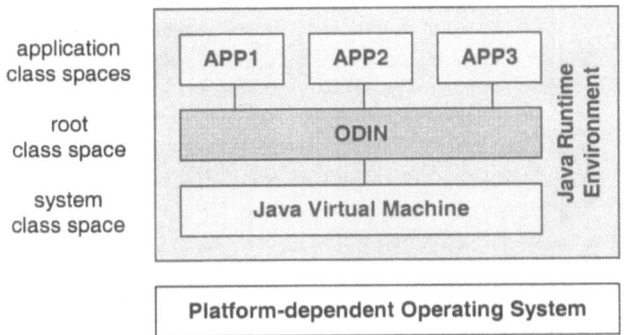

Fig. 12. Application Middleware

This is achieved by placing ODIN between the hosted applications and the JVM, as shown in fig. 12, and is also feasible for legacy applications without any modification of the related byte code. For this purpose, ODIN manages loaded classes using *Java Class Spaces (JCS)* as described in the presented approach above and intercepts class loading requests as follows. For running an application, the JAM has to be started first. It establishes a *system layer*, wherein all basic classes like *java.lang.** will be loaded into the related *system class space*. On top of this layer, the *ODIN framework layer* resides with its *root class space* that is created as a child class space of the *system class space*. It handles all framework related classes of ODIN. Afterwards, an *application class space* is created for each hosted application, in the example for *app1*, *app2*, and *app3* with the *root class space* as parent. Finally, the classes containing the method *main* of the applications are loaded using the user-defined class loader associated with the corresponding application class space. Thus, the application class space represents the *initiating class loader* of the application classes; hence all subsequent class loading requests of the application are transparently handled by the class space as described in the presented approach. This can be done dynamically by requesting applications on the fly or statically as depicted in fig. 13 for *app1*, *app2* and *app3*. The parameters *classReg* and *classSpaceReg* define where to find the configurations files for *class collections* and *class spaces*.

```
java MainStarter -classReg=file:///etc/collections.xml\
-classSpaceReg=file:///etc/spaces.xml app1 app2 app3
```

Fig. 13. Starting the Application Middleware ODIN and the hosted applications

4.2   Distributed Application Systems

Generally, the origin JRE has not been designed for distributed scenarios, where applications are dynamically composed of classes, retrieved from remote repositories.

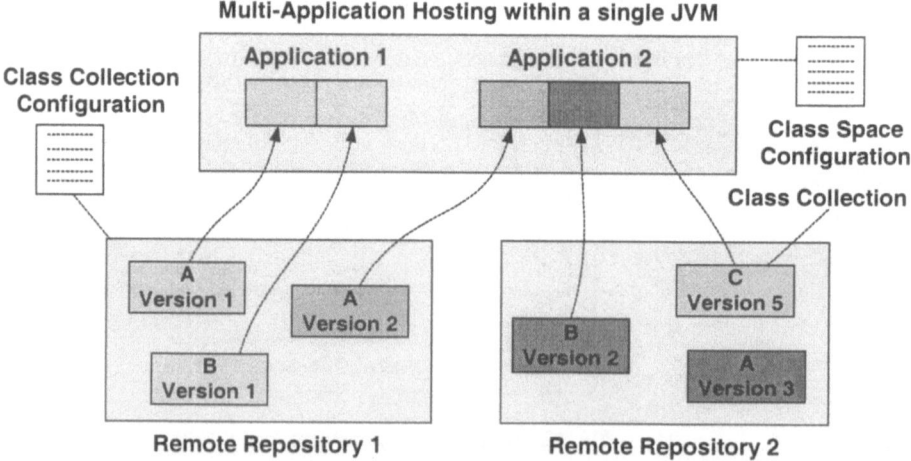

Fig. 14. Remote Repositories and Application Hosting

But this is quite important when distributed applications like *agents* are dynamically deployed on several computers, which are neither previously configured to host the application nor contain the appropriate classes to run the application. But since different applications request possibly different variants of the same class, each variant has to be installed and selectable by each application individually. Therefore, we use the presented approach of *Java Class Collections (JCC)* in ODIN to define the *logical* grouping of Java classes required by each application, independently of the *physical* location of Java classes as shown in fig. 14. The *Java Class Spaces (JCS)*, wherein the applications should be hosted, are configured with the appropriate JCC, containing the correct variants of the required classes. With that, applications could request classes without any knowledge from which remote repository the classes are actually retrieved. Thus, the *application configuration* is completely decoupled from the *platform configuration*. This is especially useful for deploying distributed applications, since one can specify the required classes of the application independent of the deployment scenario of the host, where it should run.

5 Conclusions

In this paper, we have presented a customizable application middleware, which enables the separate configuration of *application composition* and *application deployment*. Along with that, we have showed the customization of *application hosting*, managing different implementations of the same class concurrently and how to shield and share these classes for hosting multi-applications within a single JVM. In this context, we have introduced so called *class collections*, *class spaces* and *object spaces* which are heavily based on the decoration of Java classes with additional properties, but also on the managed separation of loaded classes and objects within the JVM. Finally, after the illustration of the implementation issues, we depicted the application of the approach in the middleware platform ODIN.

Based upon the presented approach, there are various issues for future work. Actually, we use static configuration files to configure the class spaces and the required class collections of an application. But this could be done dynamically, evaluating the related class files and considering the current configuration of the framework. Though, it is not difficult to handle that manually, it would help to integrate dynamically legacy applications coming from elsewhere, e.g. dynamically loaded from the Internet. Even more complex is the dynamic reconfiguration of the application environment, if new classes have to be loaded. As long as there are only few class spaces, one could easily track down the relationship between them and provide an appropriate configuration. However, an Internet platform hosting many dynamic services reaches very fast dozens of class spaces. This complicates their proper arrangement, which is important for shielding and sharing loaded classes and applications.

Another interesting issue is the *dynamic resolving* of missing classes. Beside of the *static prevention* used in an ordinary JVM, the class space could catch the *ClassNotFoundException* and try to locate the requested class *on the fly*, pretending the class has been found. This would open a new way how classes are resolved and loaded, e.g. one could interpose a *class loading interceptor* and defer the decision *which* implementation of the class is used until running the application.

Acknowledgements. The presented approach has been evaluated and used in the implementation of the Internet platform *netzspannung.org* [25]. The related project CAT [28] is funded by the German Federal Ministry for Education and Research and is conducted by the research group MARS from the Fraunhofer Institute for Media Communication, St. Augustin in cooperation with the University of Siegen, Germany.

References

1. Lindholm, T., Yellin, F. The Java Virtual Machine Specification. Addison-Wesley. 1999.
2. Venners, B. Inside The Java 2 Virtual Machine. McGraw-Hill. 1999.
3. Eckel, B. Thinking in Java. Prentice Hall. 2000.
4. Liang, S., Bracha, G. Dynamic Class Loading In The Java Virtual Machine. Proc. of the Conference on Object-Oriented Programming, Systems, Languages, and Applications (OOPSLA). Canada 1998. pp. 36-44.
5. Gong, L. Secure Java Class Loading. IEEE Internet Computing, Vol. 2, Nr. 6, pp. 56-61. 1998.
6. Expresso – Application Development Framework. http://www.jcorporate.com/html/products/expresso.html. 2002.
7. Jakarta Tomcat - Servlet Engine. http://jakarta.apache.org/tomcat/index.html
8. Java Web Start. http://java.sun.com/products/javawebstart. 2002.
9. Paal, S., Kammüller, R., Freisleben, B. Distributed Extension of Internet Information Systems. In Proc. of the 13th International Conference on Parallel and Distributed Computing and Systems (PDCS 2001). Anaheim, USA. IASTED 2001. pp. 38-43.
10. Apache Xerces – Java XML Parser. http://xml.apache.org/xerces2-j. 2002
11. SUN Java Development Kit. http://java.sun.com/products/j2se/1.4/index.html. 2002.
12. The Apache Software Foundation. Apache XML Cocoon. 2001. http://xml.apache.org/cocoon/xsp.html
13. Fayad, M. E., Schmidt, D. C., Johnson, R. E. Implementing Application Frameworks: Object-Oriented Frameworks at Work. John Wiley & Sons. 1999.
14. Lewis, T. Object Oriented Application Frameworks. Manning Publications Co. 1995.
15. Grosso, W. Java RMI. O'Reilly & Associates. 2001.
16. Orfali, R., Harkey, D. Client/Server Programming with Java and Corba. John Wiley & Sons, Inc. 1998.
17. Marvic, R., Merle, P., Geib, J.-M. Towards a Dynamic CORBA Component Platform. Proc. of 2nd International Symposium on Distributed Objects and Applications (DOA). Antwerpen, Belgium. IEEE 2000. pp. 305-314.
18. Latteier, A. Bobo and Principia: An Object-Based Web Application Platform. WebTechniques, February 1999.
19. Little, M. C., Wheater, S. M. Building Configurable Applications in Java. Proc. of the 4th International Conference on Configurable Distributed Systems. Annapolis, Maryland. 1998. pp. 172-179.
20. Monson-Haefel, R. Enterprise Java Beans. O'Reilly & Associates. 2000.
21. Apache Server Framework Avalon. http://jakarta.apache.org/avalon/framework/index.html
22. Sun Open Network Environment (ONE). http://www.sun.com/sunone. 2002
23. Kiczales, G., Lamping, J., Mendhekar, A., Maeda, C., Videira Lopes C., Loingtier, J.-M., and Irwin, J. Aspect-Oriented Programming. Proc. of the European Conference on Object-Oriented Programming (ECOOP), Finland. Springer-Verlag LNCS 1241. June 1997.
24. Open Distributed Network Environment. http://odin.informatik.uni-siegen.de
25. netzspannung.org, Communication Platform for Digital Art and Media Culture. http://netzspannung.org

26. Fleischmann, M., Strauss, W., Novak, J., Paal, S., Müller, B., Blome, G., Peranovic, P., Seibert, C. netzspannung.org – An Internet Media Lab for Knowledge Discovery in Mixed Realities. In Proc. of 1st Conference on Artistic, Cultural and Scientific Aspects of Experimental Media Spaces (CAST01). St. Augustin, Germany. 2001. pp. 121-129.
27. AWAKE - Networked Awareness for Knowledge Discovery. 2002. http://awake.imk.fraunhofer.de
28. Fleischmann, M., Strauss, W. Communication of Art and Technology (CAT). IMK/ MARS, GMD St. Augustin. http://imk.gmd.de/images/mars/files/Band_1_download.pdf

Resource Discovery for Pervasive Environments

Andry Rakotonirainy and Greg Groves

School of Information Technology and Electrical Engineering
University of Queensland - Australia
andry@itee.uq.edu.au, ggroves@dstc.edu.au

Abstract. Pervasive computing will mean a marked change in the way people use and interact with computers. Access to information and services will no longer be restricted to desktop or laptop computers. Mobile services will co-operate seamlessly and in a transparent way to provide the required information without any user intervention. Resource discovery will play an integral role in the future of pervasive systems but there are many significant problems yet to be overcome. This paper investigates and analyses the deficiencies of the current resource discovery protocols; identifies the key problems and presents a solution. We present a distributed and adaptable architecture that addresses the identified deficiencies. It uses technologies such as XML and J2ME CLDC. A significantly different approach to that of previous attempts has been taken in order to present a flexible and adaptable resource discovery system, which will be required to underpin the future pervasive computing environment. A prototype, using a Palm Pilot Vx on which the system operates, has been implemented and tested.[1]

1 Introduction

Pervasive computing aims at pushing computational services from conventional desktop interfaces to the surrounding environment in a form that is transparent to the user [9,27]. A user will no longer access information and services via a stationary desktop interface; the interface will surround the user and be accessible via small informational devices co-operating with one another as well as all available devices and systems to provide information and services to the user.

Small informational mobile devices will be of vital importance to the realization of this vision. Mobile devices are very resource limited. In order to reduce the significance of these limitations they should be able to discover and use the resources of surrounding devices.

Resource Discovery (RD) in the mobile environment has many challenges. RD must take place over the whole range of available devices. This spans an enormous number of devices and is constantly growing. Devices of all different types,

---

[1] The work reported in this paper has been funded in part by the Co-operative Research Centre Program through the Department of Industry, Science and Tourism of the Commonwealth Government of Australia

R. Meersman, Z. Tari (Eds.): CoopIS/DOA/ODBASE 2002, LNCS 2519, pp. 866–883, 2002.

manufacturers, operating systems and capabilities must be covered. Examples include mobile phones, pagers, personal data assistants (PDAs) and embedded devices. This means that all these devices with all their different capabilities must support a RD system.

Most current RD systems have been designed with desktop and server systems in mind. These often require complex protocols that are not supported by mobile devices. Consequently they are not suitable for use by mobile devices in realistic scenarios and do not support ad hoc or peer to peer networking, which is prevalent in pervasive environments. Pervasive computing requires that devices work seamlessly with whatever other resources are available, including RD systems. This means that mobile devices should be able to take advantage of RD systems available on desktop and server systems as well as among other mobile devices.

This paper focuses on the issues relating to RD protocols the ad hoc networks in which pervasive devices operate. It investigates and determines the key issues that need to be resolved in order to have an adaptable and flexible RD protocol suitable for use in a pervasive computing environment.

Section 2 presents a survey and evaluation of discovery protocols. Section 3, evaluates existing RD protocols and defines important requirements. Section 4 details the architecture of a RD protocol. An implementation of the proposed protocol and efficiency tests are described in Section 5. A summary of contributions and outlines is described in conclusion.

2   Survey of Discovery Protocols

A mobile computing device can simply be defined as a computing device that has limited processor, memory and battery life, different input/output methods (multimodal) when compared with desktops and built-in networking capability to create ad hoc networks. An ad hoc network is one that is established dynamically among devices and is maintained by them for their communication needs. The devices themselves act as network nodes routing the traffic. Our survey covers protocols at the middleware layer (e.g. Jini, UDDI) as well as services at transport layer (e.g. Bluetooth, HAVi ...)[3].

2.1   Survey

Service Location Protocol (SLP) from Sun Microsystems is an IETF standard for the spontaneous discovery of services [12]. The SLP architecture utilises three types of agents. It consists of User Agents, Service Agents and Directory Agents. These refer to clients, services and directories respectively. User Agents acquire service handles for user applications; Service Agents advertise service handles and Directory Agents collect service information. Multiple Directory Agents can be used to provide redundancy or a hierarchy or graph of domains. SLP can be decomposed into two main components and three subsidiary functions. The two main functions are obtaining service handles for User Agents and maintaining the directory of advertised services. The subsidiary functions are discovering available service attributes, Directory Agents and types of Service Agents

Jini, from Sun Microsystems, is designed to federate groups of devices and software components into a single dynamic distributed system [8]. The Jini protocol is based on leases with expiry. Consequently, entities that crash are automatically removed from all Lookup Services when the lease expires. Leases ensure that Jini recovers from crashed entities, and that the global state is rebuilt in case of a Lookup Service failure. The Jini Lookup Service also provides notification of the arrival and departure of entities, as well as notification to the entity itself when it is discovered. This enables the runtime composition of services and allows the construction of sophisticated services to manage a dynamic environment. The Jini protocol enables Lookup Services to be federated in arbitrary topologies, theoretically enabling the protocol to scale to large systems. More recently, Sun Microsystems released JXTA technology [25]. It is a set of open protocols that allow any connected device on the network ranging from cell phones and wireless PDAs to PCs and servers to communicate and collaborate in a P2P manner. It enables discovery of peers and resources on the network even across firewalls.

The Jini Mobile Edition (JiniME) [16] research proposal aims to develop a version of Jini designed to run on wireless mobile computing devices, specifically those using the Java 2 Micro Edition (J2ME) Connected, Limited Device Configuration (CLDC) and PDA profile [24]. The technical underpinnings of Jini aim to be provided by JiniME, namely: serialized objects, downloaded codebases, dynamically loaded classes, remote invocation of services, lookup services and bootstrapping discovery protocols.

JiniME aims to adhere to the same principles as standard Jini. However JiniME has a different design center from that of standard Jini. It is based on limited capabilities, the devices are battery powered and have limited amounts of memory available. The devices have wireless network connectivity, less bandwidth, and may not support full TCP/IP. The architecture of a JiniME federation includes JiniME capable mobile devices, each having its own classfile server and lookup service advertising the services offered by the device. It also specifies a Jini Bridge that joins a JiniME federation to a standard Jini federation.

Universal Plug and Play (UPnP) is a standard for spontaneous discovery from Microsoft Corporation [6]. UPnP handles network address resolution, and with the IETF proposal Simple Service Discovery Protocol (SSDP), it provides service discovery [11]. The UPnP architecture is similar to that of SLP and Salutation.

SSDP enables devices and services to announce their presence to the network as well as discover available devices and services. SSDP can operate with or without a directory service. If a directory service or proxy is available then the devices will use it, otherwise they will use a proxy-less operation. Advertisement is done by a local broadcast announcement. Services are described by extended URLs similar, but not compatible with SLP. The URL is for an XML file with a description of the device. Using this URL, SSDP defines a web-based discovery protocol-using HTTP over both unicast and multicast UDP. The registration and query process sends and receives data in HTTP format. Services are described in XML. The XML can be a complete abstract description of the type of service, and interface to a specific instance of the service or the state of a service.

Universal Description, Discovery and Integration (UDDI) is a specification for distributed web-based services from IBM and Microsoft Corporation [15]. It is a set of publicly accessible specifications that allows businesses to register information about the web services that they offer so other businesses can find them. A web service is defined as specific business functionality exposed by a company for the purpose of providing a way for another company or software program to use the service. The UDDI approach relies upon a distributed registry of businesses and service descriptions implemented in a common XML format. UDDI business registration is used to describe a business entity and its web services. The registration consists of three components; "white pages", "yellow pages" and "green pages". The UDDI specification describes a conceptual cloud of web services and an interface that defines a simple framework for describing any kind of web service. It is an upper layer in a stack of web services. UDDI uses standards based technologies. In descending order, these are Simple Object Access Protocol (SOAP)[5] XML, HTTP and TCP/IP.

The Salutation protocol is an open specification for the spontaneous config- uration of network devices and services [20]. The architecture uses an abstract model with three components; client, server and Salutation Manager (SLM). SLMs co-ordinate with one another, acting like agents on behalf of their clients. Data transfer between devices is mediated through SLMs. The architecture pro- vides call-backs into the devices to notify of events. An event may be data arriving or a device becoming unavailable. Registration is done with the local or closest available SLM. SLMs discover other SLMs and exchange registra- tion information. Data exchange is provided using transport-dependent modules called Transport Managers. Transport Managers may communicate with those on different transport media. Transport Managers may use broadcast RPC to broadcast internally. Data descriptions follow the Abstract Syntax Notation One (ASN.1) encoding standard from OSI. A service description is a collection of functional unit descriptions containing a collection of attributes records. These records are queried during the discovery process with an API. The discovery request is sent to the local SLM, which it redirects to other SLMs. The SLMs communicate using Remote Procedure Calls (RPCs) developed by Sun.

The Secure Service Discovery Service (SSDS) is part of the University of Cali- fornia, Berkeley Ninja research project [7]. SSDS is implemented in Java and uses XML for service description and location, rather than Java objects. The SSDS architectural model is made up of clients, services and Secure Discovery Service (SDS) servers. Service availability is announced by periodic authenticated multi- casts from the SDS server. This announcement contains URLs for available SDS servers. The SDS servers and clients may cache information for efficiency, but the state of the system can be reconstructed from the multicasts. SSDS uses Java Re- mote Method Invocation (RMI). The protocol exchanges XML documents and service location is achieved by matching XML tags. The Ninja project is exploring the inter-operability of spontaneous networking and heterogeneous devices. Theoretically, automatic mapping of interfaces between protocols using XML descriptions is possible. SSDS provides strong mandatory security, as all parties are authenticated and message traffic is encrypted. Authentication and encrypted communication is provided by a custom re-implementation of the Java RMI protocol. SDS servers are hierarchically organised allowing additional servers to be added dynamically and enables the detection and restarting of a failed server. The IBM Universal Information Appliance (UIA) has been strongly influenced by the Ninja project and SSDS [10].

Bluetooth is short range wireless transmission technology [4]. The Bluetooth protocol stack contains a Service Discovery Protocol (SDP) which is used to locate services provided by or available to a Bluetooth device. Bluetooth SDP has been designed to suit the dynamic nature of ad hoc networks. It addresses service discovery for this environment, supporting searching by service type, attributes and browsing, without a prior knowledge of the service characteristics. Commands and responses are sent to and received from lower layers of the protocol stack. SDP communication is between an SDP server located on the remote device and an SDP client on the local device. The server maintains a list of records describing the characteristics of all the services associated with the server. A client retrieves a record by issuing an SDP request. All the information about a service is maintained in a single service record by an SDP service. SDP uses a request/response model with each transaction consisting of a Protocol Data Unit (PDU), either a request or response. Bluetooth SDP does not provide functionality for accessing services. Once services are discovered they may be used by other protocols. Bluetooth SDP may co-exist with other discovery protocols but does not require them.

The Home Audio/Video Inter-operability (HAVi) Device Discovery uses the Self Describing Device (SDD) data to discover a device in the network [13]. SDD data contains information to provide an embedded software entity called Device Control Module (DCM). This enables the registration of device capabilities with the HAVi registry allowing applications to infer the basic set of command messages that can be sent to the device. To access device capabilities, HAVi provides a Messaging System along with DCMs. This allows applications to issue requests to and receive replies from devices. The application sends messages to DCMs and the DCMs exchange information in proprietary communication between devices in a well defined set of messages that must be supported by all devices of a particular class. Since any device can query the registry, an application can determine the message set supported by the DCM. Similarly, since any application has access to the Messaging System, any application can interact with the DCM of any device.

MOCA is an adaptable service framework targeting mobile computing devices from IBM [2]. MOCA is based on the notion of services and the assumption that applications are composed of sets of co-operating services. A service is a software component, encapsulating or exposing a function. The MOCA architecture consists of a registry and a set of essential services. A service may be active or passive. The essential services are: local file cache, file loader, application manager. Access to services may be restricted by a user-specified security policy. Services and applications may reside locally on the device or be dynamically downloaded. The service registry performs two roles; a central service repository and life-cycle management. Services are dynamically registered using a service descriptor containing an interface name, an implementation name and a URL. To bind to a service an object asks the registry to perform a lookup, returning a reference to an object implementing the required interface. The requester may use the service by the exposed interface methods. A lazy loading approach enables a service to be registered without a service being installed or downloading on the device. The communication may be implemented by a custom or standard protocol. Registered services have an associated period of validity (lease). When the validity expires the service is removed.

Table 1. Summary of protocols

Protocol	Centralised and Distributed	Complexity Code size suit Mobility	Network Transport independence	Language independence	OS and platform independence	Code Mobility	Service attributes searchable Protocol	Inter connectivity
SLP	Partial	v.1	TCP/IP	Yes	No	No	Yes	No
Jini	Partial	No	Yes	Java	Yes	Yes	Yes	No
UPnP (SSDP)	Partial	No	No	Yes	No	No	XML	XML
UDDI	Centralised only	No	TCP/IP	Yes	Yes	No	XML	XML
Salutation	Both	Suitable	Yes	Yes	No	No	ASN.1	ASN.1
SSDS	Partial	No	Yes	Java	Yes	No	XML	XML
Bluetooth SDP	Yes	Suitable	Yes	Yes	No	No	No	No
MOCA	Distributed	Suitable	Yes	Java	Yes	Yes	No	No
HAVi	Partial	Suitable	Yes	Yes	No	No	No	No
JiniME	Partial	Suitable J2ME (CLDC)	Yes	Java (J2ME CLDC)	Yes	Yes	Yes	No
JXTA	Distributed	Suitable	Yes	Yes	Yes	Yes	Yes	No

3 Evaluation

This section uses five criterion to evaluate the cited architectures. The criterion are (i) support for distributed/centralised discovery, (ii) network transport support, (iii) functionality, (iv) service description/filtering, and (v) support for interoperability. A summary of the evaluation is shown in Table 1.

3.1 Support for Distributed/Centralized Discovery

The architectures under consideration vary in support of both centralised and distributed or peer-to-peer environments. The support can be classified into three areas; architecture that requires or only supports a centralised or directory centric approach, architecture that only supports a distributed discovery mechanism also called peer-to-peer and architecture that supports both.

Jini, UDDI and SSDS belong to the first category. They only support a centralised approach. MOCA and Bluetooth SDP are the only protocols reviewed that uses a purely distributed registry approach. Maintained separately on each device, SLP, UPnP (SSDP), Salutation, and HAVi provide differing notions of support for both centralised and distributed approaches. We call it "partial" support for centralized and distributed as some "light" version of these protocols could provide centralized and distributed directory.

The common approach used by protocols supporting both centralised and peer-to-peer architectures is to operate with a full feature set when a centralised directory service is available. When this service is no longer available a directory-less configuration allows the protocol to function with a reduction in features and efficiency. This is usually achieved by local broadcast where clients can locate services directly. This configuration is used in SLP, Salutation and UPnP (SSDP), while both Bluetooth SDP and HAVi use a similar implementation with minor changes that are dictated by their close reliance on other protocols, namely the Bluetooth protocol stack and SDD data definition.

A discovery protocol for use in the mobile environment needs to be able to move between different configurations without significant degradation of services or functionality. Therefore protocols that support both centralised and distributed (peer-to-peer) approaches are more suitable than those that are limited by one approach.

3.2   Network Transport Support

SLP and Jini are constructed to work over TCP/IP. They need the basic IP protocols, TCP and/or UDP, and preferably DHCP (Dynamic Host Configuration Protocol) to be available on the network. In addition Jini requires Java RMI, object serialisation and a service browser if a client wishes to use a service. Both the client and server must run Java with the Jini extension installed. SLP is operating system independent.

UPnP SSDP uses UDP and TCP based HTTP to discover services in IP-based networks. UPnP does not define a specific programming model making it device, operating system and program language independent. Devices interact with one another using specific APIs. The use of APIs mean that devices running different operating systems can interact and it also allows the use of different transport mediums. This means that the discovery protocol does not have to use IP-based transport mediums. Alternatives such as IEEE 1394 Firewire, USB and several more [6] are available, although IP-based networks are the most common. Since devices use HTTP servers to send information about the device in the form of an XML document with XSL, HTTP and XML must be supported.

UDDI is a specification for distributed Web-based information registries of Web services" [15]. The UDDI specification requires existing common internet protocols HTTP, TCP/IP, XML and SOAP.

One of the key features of Salutation is transport protocol independence. It does, however, use Sun's RPC to communicate between SLMs. It defines

APIs for clients to invoke these operations. Salutation also uses ASN.1 for data descriptions.

SSDS uses Java RMI and XML for descriptions. SSDS provides mandatory strong security. It uses a custom re-implementation of the RMI protocol [7]. Bluetooth SDP is specifically designed for the Bluetooth environment. It requires lower layers of the Bluetooth protocol stack.

HAVi uses command sets to define devices of a particular class. The requirements of different classes vary greatly and the method of communication is proprietary, and may vary from class to class. This means that the requirements can vary dramatically between devices of different classes. However a basic level of functionality is consistent across all classes, providing a description mechanism with very limited prerequisites.

MOCA is implemented as a framework on top of a JVM. The global architecture is defined as a set of applications that use services, both optional and essential, which use a registry which is constructed using e-Java libraries on top of a JVM.

Jini, SSDS, MOCA and JiniME, to some extent, depend on the Java programming language. The remaining protocols reviewed, SLP, UPnP, UDDI, Salutation, Bluetooth SDP and HAVi, are not dependent on a particular programming language. They are however dependent on the particular operating system and platform for which the protocol is developed. The Java based protocols are platform and operating system independent in the respect they will operate anywhere a JVM or in the case of JiniME a J2ME CLDC JVM is available.

Protocols such as SLP, UDDI and Bluetooth SDP require specific network transport protocols. Protocols may have prerequisites other than transport protocol, programming language, operating system and platform. SSDS, UDDI and UPnP have an additional prerequisite due to their use of XML.

3.3   Functionality Provided

Functionality is evaluated in the following areas: support for the usage of services, code mobility, leasing concept and security.

The majority of reviewed protocols support the usage of services. The exceptions being SLP and Bluetooth SDP which both may be used to discover services but rely on another mechanism to make use of the discovered services. The remaining protocols reviewed, Jini, UPnP, UDDI, Salutation, SSDS, HAVi, MOCA and JiniME, support both the discovery and use of services. Code mobility is often supported by the use of Java, therefore only those protocols implemented in Java have the option of supporting mobile code (as opposed to a proper use of standard agent technology). Those protocols that support mobile code are Jini, JiniME and MOCA. Code mobility transfers services between devices for later use. However the original device relies on the underlying correctness of the JVM in which security problems have been highlighted.

Code mobility could be a disadvantage. Firstly, the advantages offered by transferring a service is offset by the disadvantages imposed on the device. A device would require the space to download each service. What would happen if there was not adequate space? Would another service be sacrificed? This creates many problems on top of the security concerns previously mentioned. Another disadvantage arises from the usage pattern of users of mobile devices. When using a mobile device users want to access a service immediately. This service may be within local context, for example, using a local printer. Downloading this service for later use would not be very beneficial to a mobile user. The leasing concept is advantageous in mobile environments, especially in ad hoc networks. It provides a "self-healing" approach that can make a system very robust without manual intervention. Protocols supporting this approach are SLP, Jini, JiniME, UPnP.

Security issues such as authentication and encryption are often overlooked in mobile environments. However, they must be considered. The desire for a protocol to be automatic, lightweight and minimise network usage has seen the focus on very simple schemes. The user should have permission before they can use a service and the transmission should not be able to be intercepted by unauthorised parties. A prime focus of SSDS is security. It provides strong mandatory security. All parties are authenticated and all message traffic is encrypted. In SLP, UPnP and UDDI security is optional and IP-based. Jini, JiniME and MOCA provide security via the underlying JVM. Bluetooth SDP and HAVi do not cover any security issues, security must be provided by some external architecture. Salutation provides a basic authentication mechanism, but the security is weak due to the weaknesses of the underlying SunRPC.

3.4   Service Description and Filtering

A discovery service should be able to locate instances of specifically desired services. This means that a protocol should support filtering of service requests. As the number and variety of available services increases the more important filtering will become. Another closely related problem is the bootstrap problem for spontaneous configuration. Client and server must share enough common semantics to establish communication and negotiate. Designing and implementing the meta-protocol is difficult for open, dynamic networks in which the parties may have never encountered one another before, and cannot assume shared code or architectures.

XML is the technology of choice for this task. It is general enough to express the required concepts, rigorously specified and widely accepted and deployed. XML is specifically designed to support automatic translation and transformation between XML languages. This provides the capability for interoperation between multiple services and devices. XML is supported by UPnP, UDDI and SSDS. It should be noted that while XML may solve the problem of delivering service descriptions, it cannot address the fundamental conceptual issues that must be shared between different designs and models.

3.5   Support for Protocol Inter-operability

Many of the protocols reviewed are logically compatible, and could be mapped and bridged. Protocols supporting XML, UPnP, UDDI and SSDS, provide an underlying architecture that may support inter-operability, which may be seen in future development iterations [17]. Salutation has made an effort to support protocol bridging in wireless environments with bindings for IrDA [19] and Bluetooth. Unfortunately this approach is inadequate, as discovery should be universal. It should not be necessary to implement equivalent protocols or have multi-protocol proxies. This is especially evident in mobile devices, which do not have the resources to support the kind of complex code that would be needed. The remaining protocols (SLP, Jini, Bluetooth SDP, HAVi, MOCA, Jxta and JiniME) have no explicit mechanism supporting protocol inter-operability.

4   Architecture

To address the above key problems, a protocol is required that is able to work with many other types of RD protocols. Not only must a device be able to advertise any service that it may be offering it must be able to offload RD and management to other systems that are not constrained by the same limitations or even limited to the same extent. This problem is two fold.

First, the device must be able to use a discovery server when available and return to its own RD and management when it is no longer available. A device must also be able to find out the capabilities of other devices. This stops a device from offloading RD and management to another device that is less able to do the job than it is.

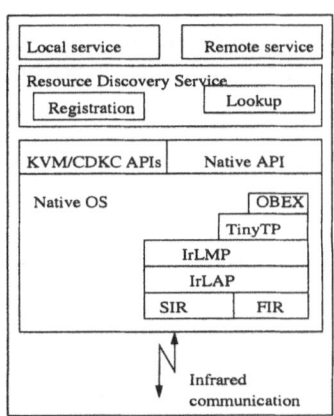

Fig. 1. Architecture

This section presents the design of our service discovery protocol. The design was driven by eight requirements: (i) the ability of a device to announce its presence to the network (ii) Spontaneous discovery of devices and services available (iii) The ability of discovery protocols to enable self-configuration (iv) The ability of a device to describe its capabilities and query and understand the capabilities of other devices. (v) Self-configuration without human administrative intervention (vi) Inter-operability across manufacturers and platforms (vii) Provide inter-operability solutions that overcome challenges presented by the growing number of service discovery protocols. (viii) Automatic adaptation to mobility and sporadic availability. Our architecture, for small devices, consists of three layers as shown in Figure1. The Native Operating System provides the communication mechanisms. A Java virtual machine (KVM), CDLC API and Native API allow us to access the OS calls. The KVM provides remote invocation mechanisms. The RD protocol is the middle layer. It consists of a registration and lookup service. These services are offered to local and remote services.

The Object Exchange protocol OBEX layer provides object exchange facilities for beaming data between devices. It is installed by default in any Palm Vx. OBEX is similar to the HyperText Transport Protocol (HTTP) although scaled down to provide a bridge between HTTP servers and small devices using IrDA OBEX. The OBEX layer is built on top of other layers in the IrDA protocol stacks as shown in Figure 1. The Serial Infrared (SIR) layer and the Fast Infrared (FIR) layer are the hardware portions of the IrDA protocol stack. SIR supports speeds up to 115,200 kbps and the FIR up to 4Mbps. The Infrared Link Access Protocol (IrLAP) layer provides a data pipe between IrDA devices. The Infrared Link Management Protocol (IrLMP) layer manages multiple IrLAP sessions and the Tiny Transport Protcol (TinyTP) layer provides a lightweight transfer protocol for higher-level IrDA layers such as the OBEX layer.

4.1   Resource Discovery Protocol

The RD protocol has two distinct modes of operation: centralised and distributed. When in contact with a server, or a system that identifies itself as a server, the protocol will enter centralised mode and attempt to maximise the use of this server system. When a server entity is unavailable or is no longer reachable the protocol enters distributed mode.

In distributed mode the protocol continues to actively and efficiently advertise, use, register and de-register services amongst peer devices. Figure 2 presents an overview of the design. Centralised and distributed modes of operation are shown. Also shown is a device using an application that acts as a router, communicating with a discovery server while also exporting services. In this configuration all exported services are available by all the communicating devices. Each device is uniquely identified by an IP address (note that we do not necessarily use the IP protocol). Our protocol assumes

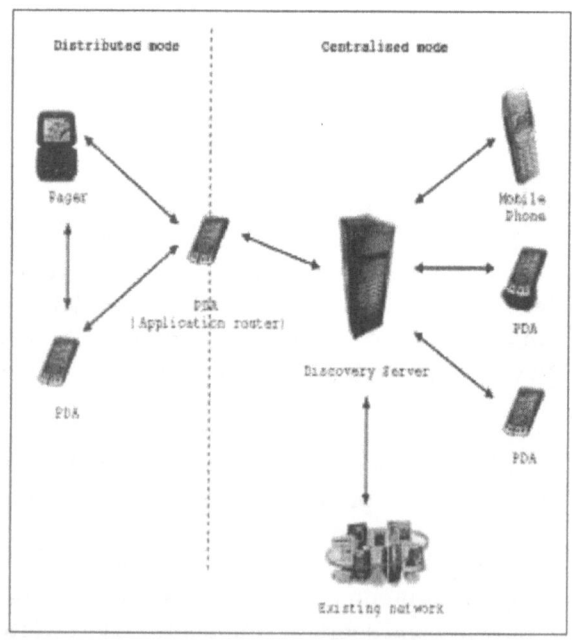

Fig. 2. Architecture overview

that these have been previously assigned and are unique. A device description is stored in each device. By using a device identification number (device ID) a device type can be referred to and identified without requiring a full description at each interaction. XML is used to define messages and device definitions as XML tools are widely available. XML is used to describe message type and structure.

Despite the fact that we are testing our discovery protocol on top of OBEX, the discovery protocol is not designed with a dependence on any particular network transport protocol. However, it is oriented towards use in a broadcast transmission system. Leases are used to determine when devices are no longer reachable and the availability of services offered by a device. When a device starts offering a service or changes a service it calculates a timestamp that is used in a service advertisement. A remote device uses this to check whether it has up to date service information from that device.

4.2   Service Description and Messages Types

Services are described by their signature. Our service signature is very similar CORBA IDL description. We use XML to have a more complete description. The description includes information such as type of the operation, textual description, timestamp and expiry date. We plan to use WSDL (Web Service Definition Language) in the future [28]. Annexe 1 shows an example description of an "add" service that we used as basis for our tests.

The protocol makes use of typed messages. Each message contains a header that corresponds to common control information described in XML. The header contains: local IP address, message sequence number, optional message acknowledgement number, destination IP address or addresses and message type identification, indicating which of the previously defined types the message is. Example:

```
<control>
      <ip>172.16.0.1</ip>
      <seq>8</seq>
      <ack>10</ack>
      <destIp>172.16.0.10</destIp>
      <destIp>172.16.0.15</destIp>
      <type>Message_type</type>
</control>
```

The protocol exchanges the following type of messages.

1. Advertisement message is used to notify all devices within range that it has a service to offer. Only those devices that offer services send a message of this type.
2. Acknowledgement message type is used to inform a device that it has received a message.
3. Registration request is a request for details. A request may be made for a device description or a service description, or both.
4. Registration reply is a response to a registration request. It may contain a device description, service description or both.
5. Service request is a request by an application to use a remote service. It contains input information and identifies the service requested.

6. Service reply is a response to a service request. It contains the output of the requested service.
7. Update message provides a mechanism for updating device descriptions, particularly in relation to device status, and services and service description.
8. Renew request is made when a service's leases expires. It is a request for a new lease, which, if possible, will be extended by an update message.

The following sections illustrate the interaction between entities involved in discovery mechanism. Diagrams are used to describe the interactions between devices. Messages are typed. E.g. $ack(32, 5)$ is an acknowledgement message, the first parameter is the sequence number, the second is acknowledgment number.

4.3   Selecting Mode of Operation

Centralised mode depends on the availability of a system willing to provide the functionality of a discovery server. It also depends on whether the local device wishes to use this remote system. The centralised mode of operation is a service, and is used and managed in a manner similar to other services. The service has a lease mechanism and therefore an expiry time. On its expiry the local device will return to the distributed mode of operation. Likewise, if the system or remote device that provides the service is no longer reachable the service is no longer available and the local device returns to the distributed mode of operation.

4.4   Centralised and Distributed Mode Behaviour

Distributed mode represents the behaviour of the protocol when it can communicate with one or many devices using this protocol to share services. The protocol may export services, when available, or just make use of the services of surrounding devices. Figure 3-b describes the interaction between two devices. Device A is exporting a service and device B chooses to use the service provided by device A when it is made available. When examining this interaction it is important to note that the ordering of messages is not strict. For example the advertisements, registration request and registration replies could occur in a different or even interleaved ordering. As long as the sequence and acknowledgement numbers are correct and the messages arrive before the timeout for their arrival is reached the ordering in not important.

The protocol changes to centralised mode in the presence of a discovery server. Devices can offer additional services to a discovery server. Figure 3-a describes centralised interaction between a device A, exporting services and a discovery server. Device A provides the discovery server with a new service, which then updates the current list of services available. It also shows what happens when device A is no longer available and the discovery server removes the service.

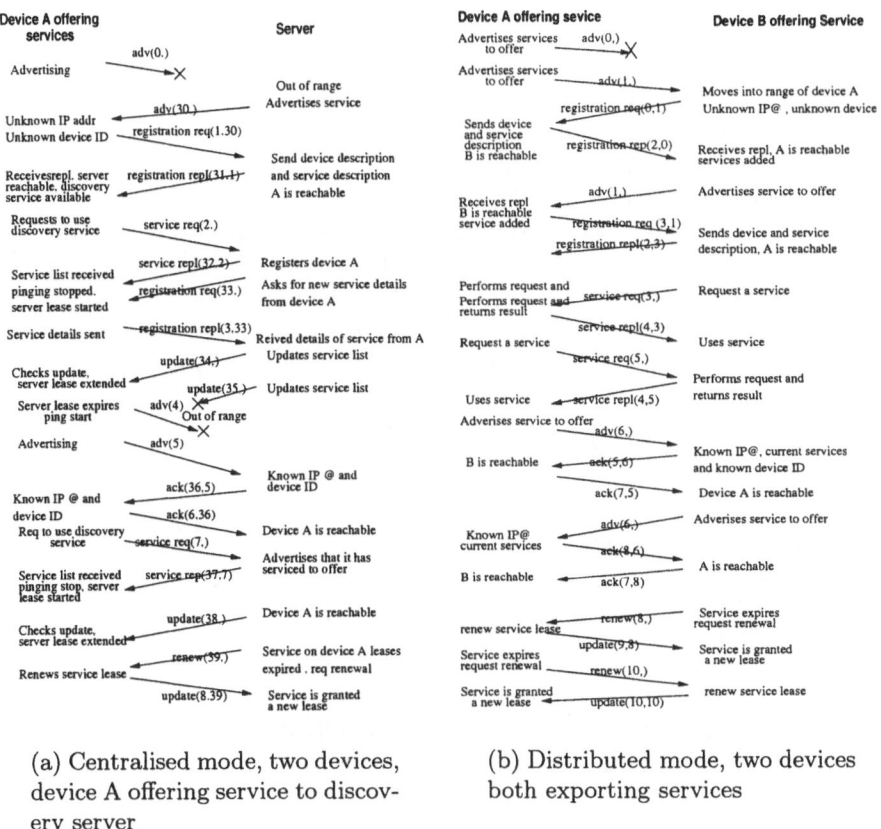

(a) Centralised mode, two devices, device A offering service to discovery server

(b) Distributed mode, two devices both exporting services

Fig. 3. Centralised and Distributed protocol

5 Performance Testing

5.1 Environment and Application Testing

This project makes use of Java 2 Platform Micro Edition (J2ME) Connected Limited Device Configuration (CLDC) under development by Sun Microsystems. This environment aims to integrate development of applications on informational appliances with existing Java technology. kXML was chosen as the most suitable XML parser for use in the prototype. The footprint of kXML is 52K. The performance testing consists of testing the responsiveness of a simple application communicating with IrDA (115.2 Kbps).

We implemented four test applications: add, subtract, multiply and divide. The applications use the described discovery protocol to offer servers and use the services of others in various combinations. Four modules contain the functionality of the four test applications: Add.java, Subtract.java, Multiply.java and Divide.java. The XML parsing application is contained in ParseXML.java.

PalmDB.java contains methods that use the persistent memory of the devices used and DeviceType.java provides a XML definition of the devices used (The DeviceType module provides a mapping between a deviceID and the device definition as described in an XML document). DemoApp.java contains the GUI implementation, RD and management threads, initialisation, shutdown and controlling methods. We wrote less than 800 lines of Java code (including GUI,service parser) to perform the test.

The testing of application responsiveness involved measuring the time taken for the application to load (not including Palm startup time). From Table 2, Test A indicates a significant delay from when the application is selected and it is ready for use. Test C shows that this time increases when there are services stored in the Palm database that have to be retrieved and parsed.

Table 2. Application responsiveness results

	Test	Palm Vx
A	Pre-verification and initialisation	11.24 s
B	Shutdown	2.20 s
C	Pre-verification, initialisation and DB parse of one service	13.82 s
D	Shutdown including writing one service to DB	1.98 s

The main cause of the delay is the J2ME CLDC KVM. Although it does significantly less pre-verification than J2SE does, it still must do some and this is very noticeable when the clock speed is around 16Mhz. The initialisation of the GUI part of the application is also a contributing factor to the observed delay. During development of the prototype, kAWT, an abstract windowing toolkit for the KVM, was initially tried. While the implementation of the GUI was significantly easier, the start-up time was more than doubled which made the application responsiveness unacceptable.

The current application responsiveness is considered satisfactory, considering the use of the J2ME CLDC KVM and the significant size of the prototype application.

5.2 Comparative Analysis Remote/Central

Table 3 shows the time taken to use both local and remote services when available. It shows a significant delay when using a remote service due to the message transfer incurred and the time taken to parse the messages, construct a reply and use the results.

5.3 XML Parsing Times

The time taken to parse an XML document is of importance to the scalability of the protocol. Each message must be parsed. The following tests use XML

Table 3. Service request times

Test	Palm Vx
Using a local service	0.32 s
Using a remote service	11.91 s
Two devices exchange and use services	15.33 s

documents (less than 10 lines) to time the speed of the XML parser parsing each message on Palm Vx, a desktop system (CPU clock speed of 800Mhz). The results of the parsing tests of the reference XML documents are shown in Table 4. These results show that the XML parsing is not a significant delay when compared with the total time taken to perform requests. The combination of factors such as the time taken to write to and read from the infrared port and for the user to accept the input of data as currently required by the KVM are much more significant factors. Once these issues are addressed the time taken for requests to be processed will drop and the usability will increase.

Table 4. XML parsing times in milliseconds

XML Document	Desktop	Palm Vx
Advertisement	50	1460
Acknowledgement	40	1090
Registration request	50	1000
Registration reply	60	5030
Service request	50	1640
Service reply	50	1380
Update	50	3920
Renew	40	1320

6 Conclusions

Complexity and code size are very important when considering suitability of a protocol for use in mobile environments. Currently protocols such as Jini, UPnP, UDDI and SSDS require resources greater than are currently available in mobile devices to function effectively. We have reviewed existing RD systems, defined the key problems and have addressed the means by which these problems may be overcome. We designed a RD protocol specifically targeted for use by mobile devices in ad hoc networks. Applications and a prototype have been implemented and tested to validate the proposed solution. We have demonstrated that an XML based RD protocol can be implemented using mobile computing devices in ad hoc networks. The discovery protocol features (i) centralised and distributed modes of operation (ii) integral device descriptions (iii) use of leases and timestamping of services and (iv) support for protocol inter-operability. The prototype was written in Java using J2ME CLDC platform. We did some performance measurements and showed the most process consuming function in the protocol. We plan to compare and contrast our protocol against various surveyed protocols.

References

1. Abowd, G., Software Engineering Issues for Ubiquitous Computing. Proc. of ICSE'99, 1999.
2. Beck, J., Geffaut, A., Islam, N., MOCA: A Service Framework for Mobile Computing Devices. 1999 http://acm.org/pub/citations/proceedings/com/313300/p62-beck.
3. Bettstetter, C., Renner, C., A comparison of service discovery protocols and implentation of the service location protocol. 2000, Institute of Commerical Networks: Munich, Germany. p. 4.
4. Bluetooth Consortium, Bluetooth Protocol Architecture. Bluetooth White Paper, 2001. 2001(31 August). http://www.bluetooth.com.
5. Box, D., Ehnebuske, D., Kakivaya, G., Layman, A., Mendelsohn, N., Frystyk, H., Thatte, S., Winer, D, Simple bject Access Protocol (SOAP) 1.1. 2000. http://www.w3.org/TR/SOAP.
6. Christensson, B. and O. Larsson, Universal Plug and Play Connects Smart Devices. WinHEC 99, 1999.
7. Czerwinski, S., Zhao, B., Hodes, T., Todd, D., Joseph, A., Katz, R., An Architecture for a Secure Service Discovery Service. Mobicom'99, 1999.
8. Edwards, W.K., Core JINI. 1999, Sun Microsystems press JAVA series. NJ: Prentice Hall.
9. Esler, M., Hightower, J., Anderson, T., Borriello, G., Next century Challenges: Data-centric Networking for Invisible Computing. The Portolano Project at the University of Washingtion. Proc. of the fifth ACM/IEEE Intl. Conf. on Mobile Networking and Computing, 1999.
10. Eustice, K., Lehman, T., Morales, A., Munson, M., Edlund, S., Guillen, M., A universal information appliance. IBM Systems Journal, 1999. 38(4).
11. Goland, Y., Cai, T., Leach, P., Gu, Y., Albright, S., Simple Service Discovery Protocol. IETF Draft, 1999. Draft-cai-ssdp-v1-03.
12. Guttman, E., Service Location Protocol: Automatic Discovery of IP Network Services. IEEE Internet Computing, 1999. 4(4): p. 71-80.
13. HAVi Consortium, HAVi V1.0 Specification. 2000. http://www.havi.org/home.html.
14. Hodes, T., Katz, R., A Document-based Framework for Internet Application Control. Second USENIX Symposium on Internet Technologies and Systems, 1999.
15. IBM and Microsoft, UDDI Technical White Paper. 2000. http://www.uddi.org/.
16. Kaminsky, A., JiniME: Jini Connection Technology for Mobile Devices. 2000. http://www.cs.rit.edu/~anhinga/whitepapers/JiniMEWhitePaper.
17. Miller, B., Mapping Salutation Architecture APIs to Bluetooth Service Discovery Layer. Bluetooth Consortium 1.C.118/1.0, 1999.
18. Miller, B., Pascoe, R., Salutation Service Discovery in Pervasive Computing Environments. 2000, IBM Pervasive Computing White Papers.
19. Pascoe, R., Salutation-Lite. 1999, The Salutation Consortium. http://www.salutation.org/whitepaper.Sal-Lite.PDF.
20. Salutation Consortium, Salutation Architecture Specification Version 2.1. 1999. http://www.salutation.org.

21. Shoemaker, P., et al., JSR75 PDA Profile for the J2ME Platform. 2001. `http://jcp.org/jsr/detail/75.jsp`.
22. Sun Microsystems, Java 2 Platform, Micro Edition (J2ME Platform). 2001. `http://java.sun.com/j2me`
23. Sun Microsystems, Java 2 Platform, Micro Edition (J2ME Platform). 2001. p. 10. `http://java.sun.com/j2me`.
24. Sun Microsystems, J2ME CLDC Kjava/Palm "Add-On" Package, K Virtual Machine (KVM) . 2001. `http://java.sun.com/people/shommel/KVM/index.html`.
25. Sun Microsystems JXTA `http://www.jxta.org` 2002.
26. Wahl, M., Howes, T., Kille, S., Lightweight Directory Access Protocol (v3). IETF RFC 2251, 1997.
27. Weiser, M., Some computer science issues in ubiquitous computing. Communications of the ACM, 1993. 36(7): p. 75-84.
28. WSDL Web Service Definition Language - W3C Note 15 March 2001. `http://www.w3.org/TR/wsdl`.

APPENDIX A

Registration reply message structure: A registration reply message contains an XML optional description of:

1. a service description, which contains a count of the number of services that are described by this service description (one if ommited). Each service described contains: A name, the IP address of the device offering the service, a description, an execution identifier, which is invoked by the offering application when it receives a service request, number of input arguments, argument descriptions for each of the input arguments required, a description of the output type, a timestamp in milliseconds which indicates when the service was registered and a lease in milliseconds.

```
<serviceDefn>
  <name>add</name>
  <description> adds two integers </description>
  <execution>add</execution>
          <args>2</args>
              <arg1>int</arg1>
              <arg2>int</arg2>
          <out>int</out>
  <timestamp> 9998532157  </timestamp>
  <expiry> 5000 </expiry>
</serviceDefn>
```

2. a device description that contains: device ID, device name, display information (number of pixels, colour depth), optional CPU processor speed in MHz, memory size in bytes, secondary storage size in bytes and status information, battery status as a percentage.

An Adaptive Scheduling Service for Real-Time CORBA

Alexandre Cervieri[1], Rômulo Silva de Oliveira[2], and Cláudio F. Resin Geyer[1]

[1]Universidade Federal do Rio Grande do Sul - UFRGS
Instituto de Informática - Av. Bento Gonçalves, 9500 – Bloco IV
Porto Alegre, RS – Brasil
{cervieri, geyer}@inf.ufrgs.br
[2]Departamento de Automação e Sistemas - DAS-CTC-UFSC
Caixa Postal 476 - CEP 88040-900
Florianópolis, SC – Brasil
romulo@das.ufsc.br

Abstract. CORBA is an important standard middleware used in the development of distributed applications. It has also been used with distributed real-time applications, through its extension for real-time systems, RT-CORBA. RT-CORBA includes many mechanisms to reduce the non-determinism associated with ordinary CORBA. These mechanisms can be used to provide guarantees for hard real-time systems if the right support from the operating system and network protocols is available. RT-CORBA mechanisms can also be used to improve the timing behavior of soft real-time applications, when the lower layers are not able to provide guarantees. This paper proposes an adaptive scheduling service in the context of RT-CORBA to support the implementation of distributed soft real-time applications. The proposal is based on the adaptation of task periods, so as to reduce system load while still trying to meet the original deadline of all tasks. This is a best-effort approach that dynamically provides graceful degradation in case of overload. The adaptive service proposed in this paper is validated by a set of experiences based on mechanisms of RT-CORBA and TAO, the ORB implementation used.

1 Introduction

The large-scale availability of computer networks has motivated the search for ways to facilitate and to accelerate the development of applications in distributed systems. CORBA (Common Object Request Broker Architecture), created as an initiative of OMG (Object Management Group), is a middleware that provides a high degree of language and platform independence for the application [1] [2].

However, CORBA at first had no mechanisms to define and guarantee temporal behavior, as well as QoS requirements. These initial limitations made CORBA not appropriate for real-time applications. In order to overcome these deficiencies, OMG started an effort to define a real-time extension to CORBA denominated RT-CORBA [3] [4].

RT-CORBA is still a standard under development. It includes interfaces and mechanisms to allow the definition and the execution of a great variety of real-time applications. Even so, many of the mechanisms that try to maintain the predictability

R. Meersman, Z. Tari (Eds.): CoopIS/DOA/ODBASE 2002, LNCS 2519, pp. 884–899, 2002.

of the applications depend on another aspects such as support from the operating system to guarantee time requirements, a more predictable communication system, scheduling policies and mechanisms that guarantee the execution of tasks at the correct moment [5].

RT-CORBA still has many opened questions on this latter aspect. One of the essential points for the development of a real-time system is the choice of the correct scheduling policy for a given class of applications. Hard real-time applications do not allow deadline misses. Consequently, they demand a scheduling policy capable of providing off-line guarantees. Soft real-time applications allow a run-time scheduling approach, by the use of best-effort policies. In this case some quality degradation is accepted in order to satisfy deadlines, and even delays are allowed to same degree.

The aim of this work is to present an adaptive scheduling service in the context of RT-CORBA to support the implementation of distributed real-time applications. The proposal is based on the adaptation of task periods, with the objective of minimizing system load while still trying to satisfy the deadlines of all tasks. The adaptive service proposed in this paper is validated by a set of experiences based on mechanisms of the RT-CORBA standard and of TAO, the specific ORB implementation used.

This paper is organized so that in section 2 we make a brief revision of standard CORBA and RT-CORBA besides presenting some characteristics of TAO, the implementation used. Section 3 is a small revision of the literature on adaptive mechanisms in real-time systems. Finally, section 4 describes the adaptive scheduling service proposed. Its implementation is presented in section 5 and section 6 shows the results of the experiences. Final remarks appear in section 7.

2   RT – CORBA

Defined by OMG, CORBA is nowadays one of the most complete architectures for the development of distributed systems applications. Many of the benefits associated with CORBA stand in the use of an independent language (IDL – Interface Definition Language) to define object interfaces. It is possible to integrate applications not written for distributed systems and event legacy software in these systems because of the existence of IDL mappings for several languages used in the market.

The OMA (Object Management Architecture) is defined as a reference model for the technology of objects. The development of that architecture followed certain technical objectives so that it brought benefits to the management of objects, such as: conformity, distribution transparency, good performance in remote and local operations, expandable and dynamic behavior, architecture based on name service, access control, concurrency control, among others. OMG (Object Management Group) used the OMA to describe a generalization, a more abstract model, that is to say, a model of higher level, which is implemented by CORBA. It can be said that OMA serves as a "type" and CORBA as an "instance" of that type [6].

The ORB (Object Request Broker) is the communication middleware that allows client objects to send request and receive replies from server objects, which can execute locally or remotely in relation to the client. They have defined mappings of IDL to several languages to allow the access to the ORB, while not defining details about its implementation. That guarantees some freedom for the developers and assures that a program specified for an ORB will be partially portable to any other

ORB that is compliant with CORBA definitions. The Object Adapter, for its time, has the function of controlling the life cycle of the servers. It is responsible for server creation, activation and destruction [7].

Clients and servers can also access ORB services and the CORBA standard services defined by OMG. We can highlight, for its importance in this work: (i) the name service, whose function is to identify an object based on its name, returning its reference, and vice-versa; (ii) the event service, which defines a generic interface for sending messages between multiple sources and multiple destinations. The event service includes an event channel that allows the generation of events without consumers and suppliers having to communicate directly. Two forms of interaction are offered: (i) push, the supplier is active and sends events to the channel; (ii) pull, the consumer is active and tries to receive an event from the channel (this operation may be blocking or not) [1].

In spite of the advantages that it brings to the development of distributed applications, CORBA 2.x does not satisfy all the demands of high performance and real-time applications, mainly because of the following reasons [8] [9]: lack of interfaces to define QoS (Quality of Service), lack of guarantees of QoS, lack of programming characteristics suitable for real-time and lack of optimizations for high performance.

Due to the CORBA drawbacks in supporting real-time applications, OMG have created in 1995 a work group with the objective of extending CORBA specifications. In October 1998, the five proposals presented were united in a single document [8], RT-CORBA (included in the specification of CORBA 2.4). It is nowadays in a process of developing version 2, which will integrate CORBA 3.

RT-CORBA identifies capacities that can be vertically (from the network layer to the application layer and vice-versa) and horizontally (end to end) integrated and managed by an ORB to guarantee the predictability about activities between CORBA clients and servers. Some of those capacities are:

- **Management of the communication infrastructure**: RT-CORBA should provide polices and mechanisms for the management of the communication infrastructure, from the choice of a connection to the exploration of advanced QoS characteristics, including threads interface, thread pools, explicit binding and others;
- **Operating system scheduling mechanisms**: ORBs explore the mechanisms of the operating system to schedule activities at the application level. RT-CORBA considers mainly real-time systems based on fixed priorities. In that way, these mechanisms correspond to the management of priorities of the threads scheduled by the operating system;
- **Real-time ORB**: a real-time ORB should provide standardized interfaces to allow applications to specify their demands of resources to the ORB, besides supporting communication between clients and servers in a transparent way;
- **Real-time services and applications**: a real-time ORB should also create an efficient environment, with end-to-end predictability, for high-level services and applications.

Since OMG does not supply an implementation of CORBA and RT-CORBA, there are alternatives to be analyzed. Among CORBA implementations and, more specifically, RT-CORBA implementations, TAO (The ACE ORB) is an important one. TAO can be considered more than just an ORB to support real-time communication, it is a complete architecture for execution of real-time applications, with as much hard as soft deadlines. The architecture of TAO contains the following characteristics and elements [10]: a real-time I/O sub-system, RT-ORB, protocol GIOP for real-time, RT-POA, optimized IDL compiler and presentation layer, optimizations of the memory management by minimizing the copy of data and means for QoS specification.

TAO is one of the ORBs that presents the most complete implementation of RT-CORBA. However, its implementation of some services differs from the standard definitions. One of those services is scheduling. The TAO scheduling service is responsible for allocating system resources in order to guarantee the needs of the applications. It was designed for hard real-time applications and its main objective is to guarantee that the demands for resources will be satisfied. It is divided in an off-line component and a run-time component. First, the possibility of a correct scheduling of all the operations is analyzed and their priorities are assigned. Run-time components offer fast access to priorities values and coordinate mode change operations.

Another TAO service that was improved for the use in real-time applications was the event service. Basically the method of interaction push was affected [11]: (i) consumers and suppliers of events can specify their demand and execution characteristics using QoS parameters; (ii) correlation and filtering mechanisms are centralized in the event channel; (iii) consumers can specify time-out dependent events.

3 Adaptation Mechanisms for Real-Time Applications

Even in computer systems specifically built for the execution of real-time applications there are many opportunities for adaptation. This can happen because of the load generated by the application not having a well-known limit that can be analyzed off-line. Even if the load has a well characterized demand for resources, it may not be economically feasible to guarantee its behavior in a worst-case scenario.

Although most of the real-time literature is about adaptation through quality of service negotiation, adaptation can also be a unilateral action. In the case of a unilateral adaptation the following scenarios are possible:

- A variation in the application behavior triggers an adaptation of the support.
- A variation in the support behavior triggers an adaptation of the support itself.
- A variation in the application triggers an adaptation of the application itself. In systems where the application can reserve resources, the application itself must manage reserved resources.
- A variation in the support behavior triggers an adaptation of the application. This situation is very common in distributed systems, where variations of the response time can be associated with sending messages on the network.

Real-time applications in a distributed environment are subject to variations in the response time of its tasks. Those variations can be caused by delays in message transmissions on the network or changes in some processing node used by the application. There is the need for a continuous adaptation during the application lifetime. Adaptation mechanisms described in the literature that can be used in this context will be examined in this section:

- **Delaying a task.** The simplest and more frequent form of adaptation is simply to relax the deadline concept. One of the first papers proposing this approach appears in Jensen et. al. [12]. They propose that the conclusion of each task contributes to the system with a benefit and the value of this benefit can be expressed as a function of the instant of task conclusion (time-value function).
- **Changes in the task period.** In a real-time application a lot of tasks are executed periodically. In general, these tasks have their period defined off-line. A way to provide adaptability in the application is to allow this period to vary dynamically during its execution. This way, the quality of the application, represented here by the period of its tasks, would be adapted to the performance of the platform where it executes.
- **Canceling a task execution.** A more radical form of flexibilization is simply not to execute some tasks when the performance is below the desired level. In the case of applications with repetitive tasks, it is possible to cancel a specific task activation or to cancel the task completely.
- **Changes in the task execution time.** In this adaptation mechanism, tasks are scheduled so they respect their respective deadlines. In case of overload, the task execution time is reduced. In order to implement that, it is necessary for each task to have options of the type quality versus execution time. This approach is usually known as Imprecise Computation [13].

There are several proposals in the literature about how to measure system quality and how to act on the system to maximize its quality. For example, in Lu et. al. [14] the quality of a system is measured by the deadline miss rate and by the rate of system utilization in a given measuring window. Control is implemented by changing the operation mode of tasks and by deciding to accept or reject tasks for execution. Beccari et. al. [15] also identifies overloads in the system through the processor utilization and the control is implemented through graceful degradation of task periods. Other works found in the literature that follow the same direction can be found in Welch et. al. [16], Shin & Meissner [17] and Abdelzaher et. al. [18] [19].

Table 1 presents a qualitative analysis of some adaptive approaches in the literature.

4   Adaptive Scheduling Service

In the previous section many adaptation mechanisms were introduced. Considering that a lot of real-time applications have its structure based on periodic activities, we opted for an approach directed to this type of activity. The proposal of this work was inspired by Lu et. al. [14] and other works that use a feedback loop to control the system during overloads.

In the same way of Lu et. al. [14], our control of the system is based on information collected from all activities that compose the system. This information is analyzed by a periodic process, which will be called as AdaptiveService in this work. Lu et. al. [14] includes adaptation in the system by considering the utilization rate of the system ($U(t)$) and the deadline miss rate ($MR(t)$, miss ratio function) of the tasks inside a measuring window (MW miss-ratio window). The measure of deadline miss-

Table 1. Some adaptive techniques in the literature

Proposal	Measuring	Acting	Experiences	Platform
Lu et. al. [14]	Deadline miss rate and system usage within a measuring window.	Changes in the task operation mode and take the decision when accept or reject new tasks.	Simulation	Single processor.
Brandt et. al. [15]	System usage.	CPU usage determines the system operation mode (requirements and relative benefit).	Linux/UNIX systems.	Single processor.
Beccari et. al. [20]	System usage.	Changes in the period of soft real time tasks (hard real time tasks are not affected), graceful degradation.	Simulation and prototype still under development for a VME-based system.	Single processor.
Shin & Meissner [17]	System quality (each task has a benefit value depending on the period).	Changes in the period of tasks and/or tasks relocation.	Simulation (random tasks and sample application)	Multi processor.
Abdelzaher et. al. [19]	Throughput in packets per second.	Changes in the QoS level (communication) required by the tasks.	The Open Group (TOG) 7.2 kernel	Client/Server (comm. system)
Abdelzager et. al. [18]	The system benefit is calculated when every new task arrives.	Accept or reject the execution of tasks modules or the whole task, following the QoS level negotiated.	RTPOOL implemented over OSF Mach RT-mk7.2	Multi processor.

ratio is quite adapted for systems with firm deadlines, where there is no benefit in concluding a task after its deadline.

Unlike the approach used by [14], which was created for a monoprocessor, we deal with the execution of soft real-time tasks on a distributed system. We decided to quantify the system quality by comparing the deadlines and the response times of the real-time tasks. This quality measure will be denominated delay profile (DY(t)), which is observed within a measuring window called delay window (DW). In this work it is assumed that the deadline of each task is equal to the nominal period of the same task (D=P). Therefore, DY(t) can be expressed as:

$$DY(t) = \sum_{t-DW}^{t} \frac{(R_i - D_i)}{N}$$

(1)

t: current instant of time

DW: delay window, the time window used for calculation of DY(t)

R_i: response time of task i for a certain activation

D_i: task deadline

N: number of conclusions (of all tasks) within window DW

Actuation is done on the task periods. This actuation could be made for each task in a specific way. For example, there could be an adaptation factor especially calculated for each task by considering each task importance. In this work it is assumed that all tasks have the same importance. DY(t) is used for the calculus of an actuation factor on the period of each task in the following way:

$$factor = K_P * E(t) \Rightarrow$$
$$factor = K_P * (DY(t) - SDY) \Rightarrow$$
$$factor = K_P DY(t) - K_P SDY$$

(2)

where E(t) denotes the value of the error in a certain instant and it can be expressed by DY(t)-SDY, where SDY is the desirable average delay for the system. K_p (proportional constant) and SDY are values defined by the designer and/or programmer of the system according to mathematical calculations or previous experimentation. A small value for K_p will define a smooth actuation on the system.

The factor is used by the AdaptiveService for the calculus of the effective period of each task by:

$$P_{effective} = P_{min} + factor(P_{max} - P_{min})$$

(3)

Besides the values of K_p, SDY and DW, the mechanism for the designer/programmer to specify the actuation also includes the values of P_{min} (minimum period) and P_{max} (maximum period) of each task. According to the equation above, the AdaptiveService is capable of varying the period of each task (the effective period) according to the factor calculated previously, but always within the limits established by the minimum and maximum period of each task.

The computation of DY(t) along the time considers that the deadline is always equal to the nominal period of each task. Along the execution, the effective period can be altered according to the adaptation factor calculated by the adaptive service. Even so, it is always used the same deadline for each task, which is equal to the respective nominal period. The adaptation is achieved by varying the task period and not the task deadline.

5 Adaptive Scheduling Service Implementation on TAO

The proposed adaptation mechanism is designed for applications composed by periodic tasks. Applications can also contain aperiodic tasks and passive objects. The class diagram of one possible implementation of the mechanism can be seen in figure 1. The main elements of figure 1 are detailed in the next paragraphs.

Task

It represents aperiodic tasks and passive objects. It is implemented as a servant that will incarnate a CORBA object. At the moment of its creation it registers a name with the name server (NamingService) so that the active objects can find them and make method invocations.

Each task is a CORBA object and it is activated in its own POA, configured with the PriorityModelPolicy as ClientPropagated, in order to respect the priority of the objects that make the invocation.

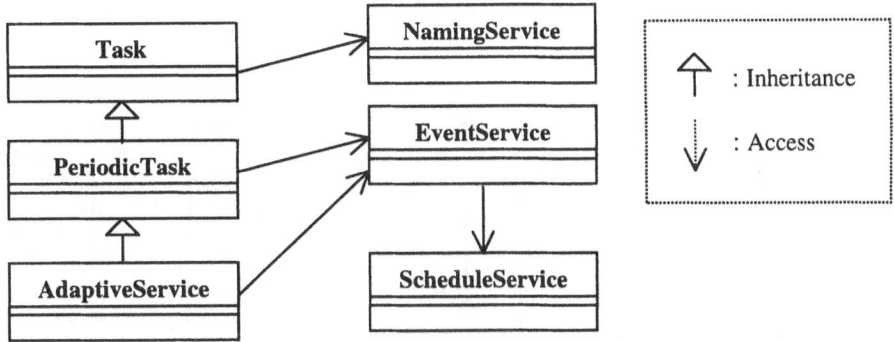

Fig. 1. Class diagram of the adaptive model implementation

PeriodicTask
It represents the periodic tasks. This class is abstract and cannot be directly instantiated. It requires the definition of a derived class. A periodic task (PeriodicTask) is, ultimately, a consumer that enrolls in the event service (EventService) of TAO to receive time-out events in specific time intervals. This time interval is the period defined in the RT_Info of the task during the off-line phase of the scheduling.

Each PeriodicTask also have an own POA and it is configured with PriorityModelPolicy as ServerDeclared (to use the priority defined in its RT_Info) and a ThreadPool with the number of static and dynamic threads defined by the programmer at the moment instances are created.

AdaptiveService
The adaptive service (AdaptiveService) is implemented as a periodic task that needs to be described as an RT_Info in the off-line phase of scheduling. Its period must be equal to DW and can be configured in the RT_Info.

The adaptive service is responsible for collecting data from the periodic tasks (the aperiodic tasks will not be considered by the service) and for posterior actuation on the system. This process can be seen in figure 2.

In order to use the scheduling service of TAO it is necessary to divide the work in two phases: off-line and run-time. At the off-line phase the timing properties of each task (including the adaptation service itself) are registered by using data structures called RT_Infos.

At the beginning of the run-time phase each periodic task should obtain a reference for the adaptation service. It then should invoke an adaptation service method to enroll itself, also informing the values of minimum and maximum period. Each periodic task must be implemented as an instance of a subclass of PeriodicTask. That class provides mechanisms to obtain the task response time by using timers and then to invoke automatically the method mark of the adaptation service in order to inform the value measured.

The adaptation service has, therefore, the function of calculating the value of $DY(t)$ at each activation (time interval DW) and of calculating the value of the adaptation factor to be applied to the periods of all periodic tasks. The effective period calculated for each task is then used to request to the event service a new connection to each task

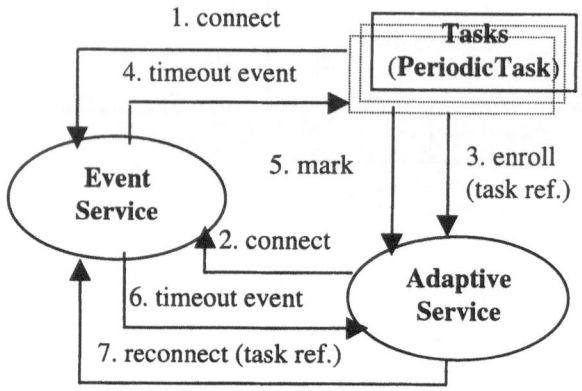

1. Each task connects to the event service to receive timeout events in intervals defined by the period configured in the RT_Info in the off-line stage of the application.
2. The adaptive service also connects to the event service to receive timeout events in accordance to the required period.
3. Each task enrolls itself in the adaptive service informing Pmax, Pmin and also its reference.
4. After all tasks being connected, the event service starts generating timeout events in intervals defined by the tasks periods (which are present in the RT_Info).

5. After each task execution, the response time is measured and sent to the adaptive service.
6. In each activation, the adaptive service calculates the value of DY(t) within the DW window and the new factor.
7. In case of the actual factor is different of the last one, the Adaptive Service requires the the event service reconnect all the tasks sending the new effective period.

Fig. 2. Operation of the adaptive scheduling service

for time-out events, but with this new value as time interval between successive activations. The response time of the adaptation service to load increases is, therefore, dependent of the response time of the event service to re-connecting the consumers for new intervals of time-out events. Situations that demand immediate response to sudden increases of load would need a fast event service when dealing with the reconnections of consumers.

6   Experiences

6.1   Application Structure

There are many classes of distributed real-time applications that could be used to test the adaptation mechanism proposed in this work.

A class of real-time applications that presents many possibilities for studying is the class of industrial automation systems. This kind of system has many different types of tasks, aperiodic, sporadic, periodic, with different levels of importance.

This work sought to identify and to represent some of the types of tasks found in this type of system.

- **Sensor** and **Actuator** were the elements of automation applications chosen to represent passive objects. They are derived from class Task and they have methods defined in IDL that can be invoked by active elements of the system.
- We identified three possible types of periodic tasks in automation systems. They will be defined as subclasses of PeriodicTask: (i) **Logger** represents the tasks that are responsible for the collection of data in order to log the system status along the time, it has a period reasonably high (one second); (ii) **Operator** represents monitoring processes (collection and presentation of the information) that interact with a human operator; (iii) class **Alarm** represents monitoring processes that can identify problems in the system and they are supposed to have a period smaller than that of other tasks in order to be always updated with the last data collected in the system.

The application created simulates the behavior of each class defined above and reproduces the oneway or twoway dependencies. The next section presents details on the registering of these tasks, their temporal restrictions and dependencies.

6.2 Conditions of the Experiences

In order to validate the proposed adaptation mechanism, we made several experiments considering the same test scenario. After considering the application class used as test base (industrial automation), where in most cases the initial configuration is seldom altered, we assumed the same number of tasks and the same number of hardware equipments (computers, sensors, actuators, etc.) for all experiments. Experiments differ only about the details of the proposed adaptation mechanism.

For all the experiments described in this section, a network formed by two machines was assumed, with the hardware and software configuration presented in table 2.

Table 2. Hardware and software configuration for the experiments

Machine	Hardware	Software
Node 1	Pentium III 650MHz 128MB RAM	Windows 2000 Advanced Server operating system Visual C++ 6.0 compiler ACE version 5.2 TAO version 1.2
Node 2	AMD K7 Duron 750MHz 128MB RAM	Windows 2000 Advanced Server operating system Visual C++ 6.0 compiler ACE version 5.2 TAO version 1.2

Tasks were distributed among the computers in a static and arbitrary way. Table 3 shows the task allocation used in all experiments, as well as their execution times, period, dependencies registered with the TAO scheduling service and the respective priority calculated by that TAO service.

Table 3. Task allocation to nodes

| Machine | Tasks | | | | | | |
| | Time | Worst Exec. Time (ms) | Period (ms) | Dependencies | | Priority | |
				oneway	twoway	CORBA[1]	Win 2k
Node 1	sensorA	10	-	-	-	2	1
	actuatorA	20	-	-	-	0	15
	actuatorB	20	-	-	-	0	15
	alarm1	20	100	actuatorA actuatorB	sensorA sensorB	0	15
	operator1	300	500	-	sensorA sensorB	1	2
Node 2	sensorB	10	-	-	-	2	1
	alarm2	20	100	actuatorA actuatorB	sensorA sensorB	0	15
	operator2	300	500	-	sensorA sensorB	1	2
	logger1	500	1000	-	sensorA sensorB	2	1
	logger2	500	1000	-	sensorA sensorB	2	1
	Adaptive Service	40	1000	-	-	2	1
	Naming Service	-	-	-	-	-	-
	Event Service	-	-	-	-	-	-
	Schedule Service	-	-	-	-	-	-

6.3 Measured Results

Initially we executed the application without the adaptive scheduling service (AdaptiveService), but we had calculated DY(t) for each period during its execution. Table 4 shows the averages of period and delay for each periodic task and figure 3 shows the evolution of DY(t) along the time for executions of two minutes.

By analyzing table 4 and figure 3 one observes that there are significant delays affecting specially the two tasks with larger priority (alarm1 and alarm2). In spite of possessing the largest priority, those tasks are also the most demanding in terms of processor time. They end up suffering delays for this reason, for the blocking caused by Windows and also for the characteristics of the TCP/IP protocol that maintains sending queues based on the FIFO police.

---

[1] The value zero represents the higher priority and the higher value the lower priority.

Table 4. Average values for period and delay without adaptation

Task	Period Mean (P)	Delay Mean (R-D)^2
alarm1	104,58 ms	1248,34 ms
alarm2	103,14 ms	226,56 ms
operator1	500,07 ms	-230,78 ms
operator2	500,08 ms	-348,12 ms
logger1	1000,3 ms	-780,59 ms
logger2	1000,71 ms	-732,34 ms

The negative values for the delay in table 4 indicate that the task finished before its deadline.

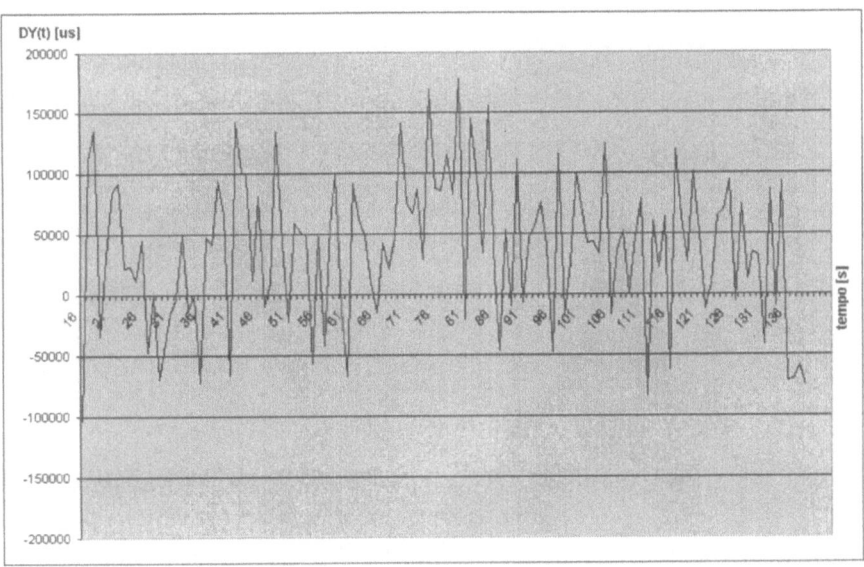

Fig. 3. DY(t) for a system without adaptation

Table 5. Average values with adaptation, initial parameters

Task	Period Mean (P)	Delay Mean (R-D)
alarm1	115,82 ms	34,50 ms
alarm2	115,47 ms	24,78 ms
operator1	687,87 ms	-348,11 ms
operator2	687,16 ms	-321,7 ms
logger1	1668,80 ms	-713,25 ms
logger2	1659,74 ms	-640,37 ms

---

^{2} R is the response time of a task in a specific activation and D is the task deadline. We consider the deadline equal to the nominal period of a task (D=P).

One of the first tests with the adaptive service used K_p=1/250000 and SDY=-50000 us. The results can be seen in table 5 and figure 4. The delays are a little smaller (but still existent) than those found before, but the adaptation is still unstable. It has oscillations around the value determined for SDY. Besides, it is noticed that the delay decreased even with the tasks (alarm1 and alarm2) executing with smaller average periods.

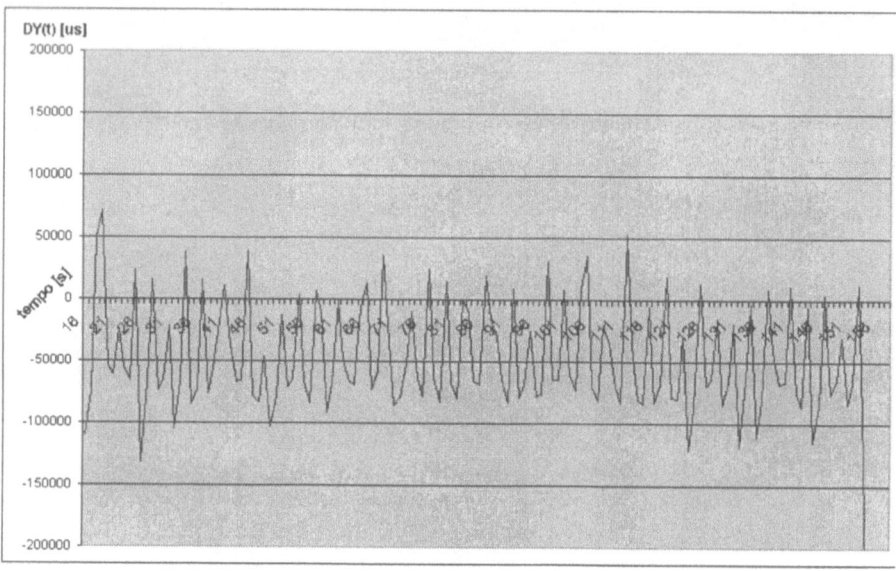

Fig. 4. DY(t) for a system with adaptation, initial parameters

The stability of the control implemented by the adaptation mechanism depends on the values of K_p and SDY. The adjustment of these constants could be made through mathematical calculus from control engineering, since we use a simple proportional control. Even so, it was not an objective of this work to deepen the study in this area. It was sought, through experimentation, to alter the values of constant K_p and SDY so that the actuation on the system becomes smooth. In the case of small oscillations, we would like to maintain the values of DY(t) negative.

After some tests we arrived at the values of K_p=1/420000 and SDY=-60000 us, whose results can be seen in table 6 and figure 5.

Table 6. Average values for a system with adaptation, final parameters

Task	Period Mean (P)	Delay Mean (R-D)
alarm1	113,84 ms	9,81 ms
alarm2	112,44 ms	7,98 ms
operator1	709,66 ms	-339,85 ms
operator2	705,81 ms	-339,99 ms
logger1	1733,3 ms	-734,04 ms
logger2	1720,36 ms	-649,03 ms

It can be observed in figure 5 an increased stability of the system. After the initial peak of load the system acts in a way to improve DY(t). The consequence of making SDY more negative (in the case, -60000 us) is the maintenance of value DY(t) close to value SDY due to the works of the adaptation service. Then, the average delay (showed in table 6) were smaller than what was observed in the system without adaptation. In short, every task was able to have a response time close to their respective deadlines, with only a small change in its period.

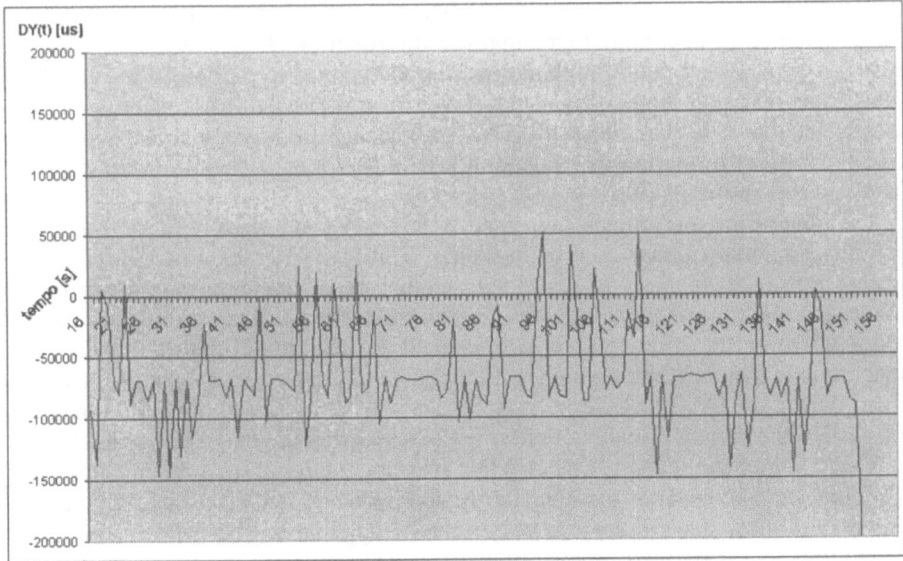

Fig. 5. DY(t) for a system with adaptation, final parameters

The values of the constants K_p and SDY depend on the conditions of each application. As said previously, the control engineer or the system designer must define the appropriate values for those parameters according to mathematical models or experimental measurement done specifically about the application considered.

The results presented in this section show that the proposed adaptation mechanism could be used with real applications as long as the necessary configurations for each application are resolved.

7   Conclusions

CORBA brought advantages for the development of distributed applications. Even so, it presents some drawbacks for real-time applications that impelled the definition of a specific extension, RT-CORBA, which is still under development. Existing implementations try to follow its recommendations, but many times they create their own solutions to make its ORB more predictable and with some extra facilities to create real-time applications.

The most important aspect to be taken into consideration is that CORBA and its extension RT-CORBA are a middleware. They depend much on the operating system and on the hardware used. Because of that, no matter how much RT-CORBA (or, more specifically, an implementation of it, like TAO) tries to solve its definition deficiencies to provide deadline and QoS guarantees, it is dependent of the operating system and network.

This paper presented an adaptive scheduling service for RT-CORBA to be used with real-time applications that tolerate a best-effort approach.

The main focus of concern was periodic tasks with timing requirements. Although the approach presented here will not be feasible for absolutely all applications, it can be used whenever there is some flexibility about the period of tasks. Actuation is based on a feedback loop that supplies information about response times to an adaptive service. We have implemented the adaptation by varying the period of the tasks. The variation of the period is derived from the calculus of what was denoted $DY(t)$, delay profile. The delay profile is the measure of how much early or late each task finished with relation to its deadline (period) within a specific measure window (DW, delay window).

The idea of the mechanism presented in this paper is basically to sacrifice the task period to maintain under control its delay. This way it is exercised a control over system behavior in case of overload. Unlike most systems, where an overload generates random degradation, the approach proposed here allows a controlled degradation in the moments of overload. It is also important to notice that the adaptation is dynamic, which means it is capable of answering to load oscillations that occur during the execution of the system. The mechanism automatically obtains from the system the largest possible quality, while respecting the deadlines of the tasks.

Validation of the proposed mechanism was made through its implementation using RT-CORBA mechanisms and scheduling and event services available in ORB TAO. The results show that for a given experimental application the mechanism improved system quality, as defined by the comparison between response time and deadline of each task.

The adaptation mechanism used acts in a homogeneous way on the tasks, so the same adaptation factor is used with the period of all tasks. Improvements may be obtained by the calculation of a specific adaptation factor for each task, also considering each task importance. The choice of the common minimum multiple of the task periods as the period of the adaptation service was ad-hoc, although many works in the literature do the same. It is an open question if this choice is the best for any application. Possible work in the future include experiences to verify those aspects and also to analyze the scalability of the solution, since the tests described in this paper used only two computers. The replacement of TAO event service for another specifically designed to generate periodic events and to make fast changes in established connections may improve the response time of the adaptive service as a whole.

References

1. Mowbray, Thomas J.; Ruh, William A.; Inside CORBA: Distributed Object Standards and Applications. USA: Addison-Wesley, 1998.
2. Orfali, Robert; Harkey, Dan; Client/Server Programming with JAVA and CORBA, 2. ed. USA: Wiley Computer Publishing, 1998.

3. Feng, W.; Syyid, U.; Liu, J. W.-S. Providing for an Open, Real-Time CORBA. Disponível por WWW em http://www.researchindex.com (Dez. 2000).

4. O'Ryan, Carlos; Schmidt, Douglas C.; Kuhns, Fred; Spivak, Marina; Parsons, Jeff; Pyarali, Irfan; Levine, David L. Evaluating Policies and Mechanisms to Support Distributed Real-Time Applications with CORBA. Disponível por WWW em http://www.cs.wustl.edu/~schmidt/corba-research-realtime.html (Nov. 2000).

5. Gill, Christopher D.; Levine, David L.; Schmidt, Douglas C. The Design and Performance of a Real-Time CORBA Scheduling Service. Disponível por WWW em http://www.researchindex.com (Dez. 2000).

6. Pope, Alan; The CORBA Reference Guide: Understanding the Common Object Request Broker Architecture. USA: Addison-Wesley, 1998.

7. Henning, Michi; Vinoski, Steve; Advanced CORBA Programming with C++. USA: Addison-Wesley, 1999.

8. OMG; Realtime CORBA. Alcatel; Hewlett-Packard Company; Lucent Technologies, Inc.; Object-Oriented Concepts, Inc.; Sun Microsystems, Inc.; Tri-Pacif. OMG Document orbos/98-01-08. Disponível por WWW em http://www.cs.wustl.edu/~schmidt/PDF (Oct. 2000)

9. Schmidt, Douglas C.; Levine, David L.; Cleeland, Chris. Architectures and Patterns for Developing High-performance, Real-time ORB Endsystems. Setembro, 1998. Disponível por WWW em http://www.cs.wustl.edu/~schmidt/corba-research-realtime.html (Oct. 2000)

10. Schmidt, Douglas C.; Levine, David L.; Mungee, Sumedh. The Design of the TAO Real-Time Object Request Broker. Computer Communications Journal, 1997. Disponível por WWW em http://www.researchindex.com (Dez. 2000).

11. Harrison, Timothy H.; Levine, David L.; Schmidt, Douglas C.; The Design and Performance of a Real-Time CORBA Event Service. Object-Oriented Programming Systems, Languages and Applications (OOPSLA), Outubro 1997. Disponível por WWW em http://www.researchindex.com (Aug. 2001).

12. Jensen, E. D.; Locke, C. D.; Tokuda, H.; A Time-Driven Scheduling Model for Real-Time Operating Systems. Proceedings of the IEEE Real-Time Systems Symposium, pp. 112-122, Dez. 1985.

13. Liu, J. W. S. et. al., Algorithms for Scheduling Imprecise Computations. IEEE Computer, pp.58-68, May 1991.

14. Lu, Chenyang; Stankovic, John A.; Abdelzaher, Tarek F.; Tao, Gang; Son, Sang H.; Marley, Michael; Performance Specifications and Metrics for Adaptive Real-Time Systems. 21st IEEE Real-Time Systems Symposium, Nov. 2000.

15. Beccari, G.; Caselli, S.; Reggiani, M.; Zanichelli, F.; Rate Modulation of Soft Real-Time Tasks in Autonomous Robot Control Systems. 11th Euromicro Conference on Real-Time Systems, England, June 1999.

16. Welch, L. R.; Shirazi, B. A.; Ravindran, B.; Adaptive Resource Management for Scalable, Dependable Real-Time Systems: Middleware Services and Applications to Shipboard Computing Systems. IEEE Real-time Technology and Applications Symposium, June 1998.

17. Shin, K.G.; Meissner, C. L.; Adaptation and Graceful Degradation of Control System Performance by Task Reallocation and Period Adjustment. 11th EuroMicro Conference on Real-Time Systems, June 1999.

18. Abdelzaher, T. F.; Atkins, E. M.; Shin, K. G.; QoS negotiation in real-time systems and its application to automatic flight control. IEEE Real-Time Technology and Applications Symposium, June 1997.

19. Abdelzaher, E. M.; Shin, K. G.; End-host Architecture for QoS-Adaptive Communication. IEEE Real-Time Technology and Applications Symposium, June 1998.

20. Beccari, G.; Caselli, S.; Reggiani, M.; Zanichelli, F.; Rate Modulation of Soft Real-Time Tasks in Autonomous Robot Control Systems. 11th Euromicro Conference on Real-Time Systems, England, June 1999.

The Design and Performance of the jRate Real-Time Java Implementation

Angelo Corsaro and Douglas C. Schmidt

Electrical and Computer Engineering Department,
University of California, Irvine, CA 92697
{corsaro, schmidt}@ece.uci.edu

Abstract. Over 90 percent of all microprocessors are now used for real-time and embedded applications. Since the behavior of these applications is often constrained by the physical world, it is important to devise higher-level programming languages and middleware that robustly and productively enforce real-time constraints, as well as meeting conventional functional requirements. This paper provides two contributions to the study of programming languages and middleware for real-time and embedded applications. We first present how we are applying generative programming techniques to develop jRate, which is an open-source ahead-of-time-compiled implementation of the Real-time Specification for Java (RTSJ). The goal of jRate is to provide developers the ability to generate RTSJ implementations that are customized for their needs. We then show performance results of jRate that illustrate how well it performs compared to the TimeSys RTSJ Reference Implementation (RI).

1 Introduction

1.1 Current Challenges

The vast majority of all microprocessors are now used for embedded systems, in which computer processors control physical, chemical, or biological processes or devices in real-time. Examples of such systems include telecommunication networks (*e.g.*, wireless phone services), tele-medicine (*e.g.*, remote surgery), manufacturing process automation (*e.g.*, hot rolling mills), and defense applications (*e.g.*, avionics mission computing systems). These real-time embedded systems are increasingly being connected via wireless and wireline networks. Designing real-time embedded systems that implement their required capabilities, are dependable and predictable, and are parsimonious in their use of limited computing resources is hard; building them on time and within budget is even harder. Moreover, due to global competition for marketshare and engineering talent, companies are now also faced with the problem of developing and delivering new products in short time frames. It is therefore essential that the production of real-time embedded systems can take advantage of languages, tools, and methods that enable higher software productivity.

R. Meersman, Z. Tari (Eds.): CoopIS/DOA/ODBASE 2002, LNCS 2519, pp. 900–921, 2002.

1.2 The State of the Art

Many real-time embedded systems are still developed in C, and increasingly also in C++. While writing in C/C++ is more productive than assembly code, they are not the most productive or error-free programming languages. A key source of errors in C/C++ stems from their *memory management* mechanisms, which require programmers to allocate and deallocate memory manually. Moreover, C++ is a feature rich, complex language with a steep learning curve, which makes it hard to find and retain experienced real-time embedded developers who are trained to use it well.

Real-time embedded software should ultimately be synthesized from high-level specifications expressed with domain-specific modeling tools [1]. Until those tools mature, however, a considerable amount of real-time embedded software still needs to be programmed by software developers. Ideally, these developers should use a programming language that shields them from many accidental complexities, such as type errors, memory management, and steep learning curves. The Java [2] programming language has become an attractive choice for the following reasons:

- It has a large and rapidly growing programmer base and is taught in many universities.
- It is simpler than C++, yet programmers experienced in C++ can learn it easily.
- It has a virtual machine architecture—the Java Virtual Machine (JVM)—that allows Java applications to run on any platform that supports a JVM.
- It has a powerful, portable standard library that can reduce programming time and costs.
- It offloads many tedious and error-prone programming details, particularly memory management, from developers into the language runtime system.
- It has desirable language features, such as strong typing, dynamic class loading, and reflection/introspection.
- It defines portable support for concurrency and synchronization.
- Its bytecode representation is more compact than native code, which can reduce memory usage for embedded systems.

Conventional Java implementations are unsuitable for developing real-time embedded systems, however, due to the following problems:

- The scheduling of Java threads is purposely underspecified to make it easy to develop JVMs for new platforms.
- The Java Garbage Collector (GC) has higher execution eligibility that any other Java thread, which means that a thread could experience unbounded preemption latency while waiting for the GC to run.
- Java provides coarse-grained control over memory allocation and access, *i.e.*, it allows applications to allocate objects on the heap, but provides no control over the type of memory in which objects are allocated.
- Due to its interpreted origins, the performance of JVMs has historically lagged that of equivalent C/C++ programs by an order of magnitude or more.

To address these problems, the Real-time Java Experts Group has defined the Real-Time Specification for Java (RTSJ) [3], which provides the following capabilities:

- New memory management models that can be used in lieu of garbage collection.
- Access to raw physical memory.
- A higher resolution time granularity suitable for real-time systems.
- Stronger guarantees on thread semantics when compared to regular Java, *i.e.*, the most eligible runnable thread is always run.

Until recently, there was no implementation of the RTSJ, which hampered the adoption of Java in real-time embedded systems. It also hampered systematic empirical analysis of the pros and cons of the RTSJ programming model. Several implementations of RTSJ are now available, however, including the RTSJ Reference Implementation (RI) from TimeSys [4].

1.3 The Road Ahead

While the RTSJ represents an ambitious step toward improving the state of the art in embedded and real-time system development, there are a number of open issues. In particular, the RTSJ was designed with generality in mind. While this is a laudable goal, generality is often at odds with the resource constraints of embedded systems. Moreover, providing developers with an overly general API can actually increase the learning curve and introduce accidental complexity in the API itself.

For example, the scheduling API in RTSJ was designed to match any scheduling algorithm, including RMS, EDF, LLF, RED, MUF, etc. While this generality covers a broad range of alternatives, it may be overly complicated for an application that simply needs a priority preemptive scheduler. But can we do any better then this? Can we provide the needed flexibility and extensibility, without putting undue burden on developers?

We believe that the answer is affirmative, based on our experience to date using Generative Programming (GP) [5] techniques, such as Aspect-Oriented Programming (AOP) [6], Meta-Programming (MP) [7], Component-Oriented Programming (COP) [8], and Model-Integrated Computing (MIC) [1]. Generative programming makes it possible to develop middleware systems that are amenable to customization of behavior and protocols (*e.g.*, APIs), via automatic code generation and composition.

Using a GP approach, the development of middleware, such as RTSJ or Real-time CORBA [9], need not lead to a single implementation. Instead, it can provide a set of components and configuration knowledge that can be used to generated a specific implementation based on user-defined specifications. If we consider the RTSJ scheduling API example, for instance, application developers that need a simple priority preemptive scheduler could use generative programming to specify this as a requirement. The outcome of the generation process would then be a Real-time Java platform that exposed only the API needed for a priority-based scheduler and whose implementation was also optimized for priority-based schedulers.

1.4 Paper Organization

The remainder of the paper is organized as follows: Section 2 provides a brief overview of the RTSJ; Section 3 describes the architecture and design rationale of jRate; Section 4 presents empirical results obtained by benchmarking jRate and the TimeSys RTSJ

Reference Implementation (RI) using our RTJPerf [10] benchmarking suite; Section 5 compares our work on jRate with related research; and Section 6 summarizes the results we obtained and outlines how they can be used to improve the support of next-generation implementations of RTSJ for real-time embedded software.

2 Overview of the Real-Time Specification for Java

The RTSJ extends the Java API and refines the semantics of certain constructs to support the development of real-time systems. The guiding principles followed by the expert group who created the RTSJ specification included [3]:

- Backward compatibility with the Java 2 platform
- No syntactic extension to the Java language, *i.e.* no new keywords
- Write once carefully, run anywhere conditionally
- Enable predictable execution and
- Balance between current practice and advanced features.

Below, we present an overview of the extensions provided by the RTSJ.

2.1 Memory

The RTSJ extends the Java memory model by providing memory areas other than the heap. These memory areas are characterized by the lifetime the objects created in the given memory area and/or by their allocation time. *Scoped memory areas* provide guarantees on allocation time. Each real-time thread is associated with a *scope stack* that defines its allocation context and the *history* of the memory areas it has entered. Figure 1 shows how the scope stack for threads T_1 and T_2 evolve while moving from one memory area to another.

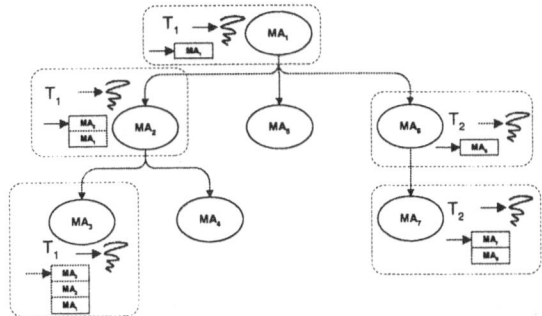

Fig. 1. Thread Scope Stack in the RTSJ Memory Model

As shown in Figure 2, the RTSJ specification provides scoped memories with linear and variable allocation times (LTMemory, LTPhysicalMemory and VTMemory, VTPhysicalMemory, respectively).

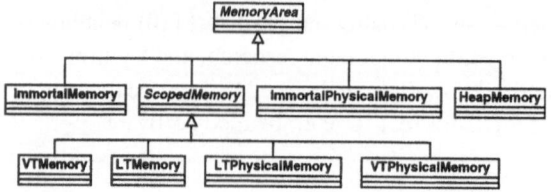

Fig. 2. Hierarchy of Classes in the RTSJ Memory Model

For linear allocation time scoped memory, the RTSJ requires that the time needed to allocate the $n > 0$ bytes to hold the class instance must be bounded by a polynomial function $f(n) \leq Cn$ for some constant $C > 0$.[1] The RTSJ also introduces the concept of *Immortal Memory*. Objects allocated within this memory area have the same lifetime of the JVM, *i.e* are never collected. Another addition to the Java memory model provided by the RTSJ allows direct access to raw memory, as well as to allocate Java objects at specific memory locations.

2.2   Threads

The RTSJ extends the existing Java threading model with two new types of real-time threads: RealtimeThread and NoHeapRealtimeThread. The relation of these new classes with respect to the regular Java thread class is depicted in Figure 3.

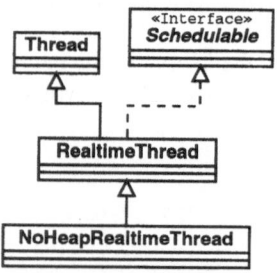

Fig. 3. RTSJ Real-time Thread class Hierarchy

The NoHeapRealtimeThread can have execution eligibility higher than the garbage collector.[2] Therefore, a NoHeapRealtimeThread can neither allocate nor reference any heap objects. The scheduler controls the *execution eligibility*[3] of the instances of this class by using the SchedulingParameters associated with it.

---

[1] This bound does not include the time taken by an object's constructor or a class's static initializers.

[2] The RTSJ v1.0 specification states that the NoHeapRealtimeThread always has execution eligibility higher than the GC, but this has been changed in the v1.01.

[3] Execution eligibility is defined as the position of a schedulable entity in a total ordering established by a scheduler over the available entities [11]. The total order depends on the scheduling policy. The only scheduler required by the RTSJ is a priority scheduler, which uses the

2.3 Scheduling

The RTSJ introduces the concept of a Schedulable object. The execution of Schedulable entities is managed by the scheduler that holds a reference to them. The RTSJ provide a scheduling API that is sufficiently general to implement commonly used scheduling algorithms, such as RMS, EDF, LLF, RED, MUF, etc. However, the only required scheduler for a RTSJ-compliant implementation is a priority preemptive scheduler that can distinguish 28 different priorities.

2.4 Asynchrony

The RTSJ defines mechanisms to bind the execution of program logic to the occurrence of internal and/or external events. In particular, the RTSJ provides a way to associate an asynchronous event handler to some application-specific or external events.

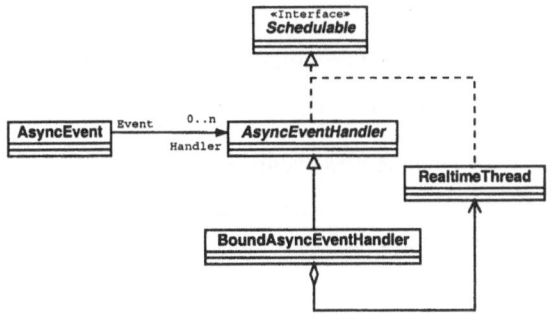

Fig. 4. RTSJ Asynchronous Event Class Hierarchy

As shown in Figure 4, there are two types of asynchronous event handlers defined in RTSJ:

- The AsyncEventHandler class, which does not have a thread permanently bound to it—nor is it guaranteed that there will be a separate thread for each AsyncEventHandler. The RTSJ simply requires that after an event is fired the execution of all its associated AsyncEventHandlers will be dispatched.
- The BoundAsyncEventHandler class, which has a real-time thread associated with it permanently. The associated real-time thread is used throughout its lifetime to handle event firings.

Event handlers can also be specified a *no-heap*, which means that the thread used to handle the event must be a NoHeapRealtimeThread.

The RTSJ also introduces the concept of *Asynchronous Transfer of Control* (ATC), which allows a thread to asynchronously transfer the control from a locus of execution to another.

PriorityParameters to determine the execution eligibility of a Schedulable entity, such as threads or event handlers.

2.5   Time and Timers

Real-time embedded systems often use timers to perform certain actions at a given time in the future, as well as at periodic future intervals. For example, timers can be used to sample data, play music, transmit video frames, etc.

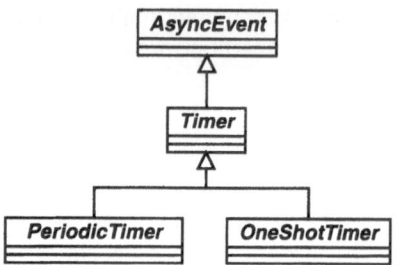

Fig. 5. RTSJ Timer Class Hierarchy

As shown in Figure 5, the RTSJ provides two types of timers:

- OneShotTimer, which generates an event at the expiration of its associated time interval and
- PeriodicTimer, which generates events periodically.

OneShotTimers and PeriodicTimers events are handled by AsyncEventHandlers. The RTSJ also supports high resolution timers and high resolution clocks.

3   jRate Overview

jRate is an open-source RTSJ-based real-time Java implementation that we are developing at the University of California, Irvine (UCI). jRate extends the open-source the GNU Compiler for Java (GCJ) runtime system [12] to provide an ahead-of-time compiled platform for the development of RTSJ-compliant applications.

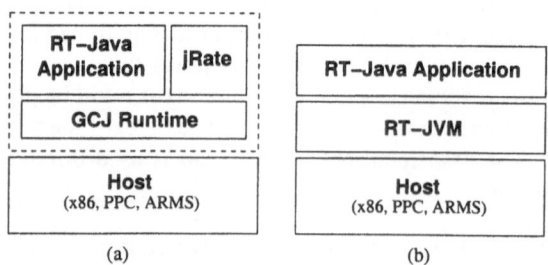

Fig. 6. The jRate Architecture

The jRate architecture shown in Figure 6(a) differs from the JVM model shown in Figure 6(b) since there is no JVM interpreting the Java bytecode. Instead, jRate ahead-of-time compiles RTSJ applications into native code. The Java and RTSJ services, such as garbage collection, real-time threads, and scheduling, are accessible via the GCJ and jRate runtime systems, respectively.

One downside of ahead-of-time compiled RTSJ implementations like jRate is that they can hinder portability since applications must be recompiled each time they are ported to a new architecture. In practice, however, embedded and real-time software developers should find this a small price to pay for the substantial performance benefits, compared to Java implementations based on interpreters or just-in-time (JIT) compilers.

3.1   Current jRate Capabilities

The RTSJ features currently supported by jRate are described next.

Memory Areas. jRate supports scoped memory and immortal memory. It provides a strategy to decide which type of memory, such as linear time memory or variable time memory, should be used as immortal memory. The RTSJ does not specify the immortal memory implementation, but since we believe it is important to specify the type of memory used, jRate can configure it at application launch time. The scoped memory implementation exposes an additional non-standard extension that allows the use of non-thread safe allocators. This extension allows threads to avoid unnecessary locks if a memory area will always be accessed by one thread.

jRate also provides a new type of scoped memory called CTMemory, which trades off allocation time for the memory area creation time. This memory area is zeroed at initialization time and the amount used is also zeroed each time the memory reference count[4] drops to zero. This feature provides constant time allocation for objects created within the CTMemory.

The internal organization of the CTMemory is depicted in Figure 7.

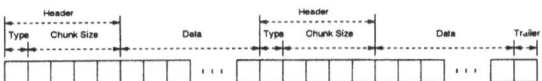

Fig. 7. The jRate CTMemory Structure

The *type* field distinguishes different types of objects. In fact, there are different types of objects that must be treated slightly differently, *e.g.*, some must be finalized, whereas others need not be finalized.

Real-Time Threads and Scheduling. jRate currently supports real-time threads of the type RealtimeThread (*i.e.* it does not yet support NoHeapRealtimeThread), using a basic priority preemptive scheduler. This implementation simply relies upon the underlying real-time operating system priority preemptive scheduler.

---

[4] The reference count associated with a scoped memory is represented by the number of real-time thread that are currently active in it, *i.e.* have entered the scoped memory, but have not exited yet.

Asynchrony. jRate provides a robust and efficient asynchronous event handling implementation, as shown by the empirical results in Section 4.2. This implementation avoids any source of priority inversion and provides lock free dispatch on most platforms.[5] jRate uses the priority queues ordered by the execution eligibility of the handlers for the event dispatching. Execution eligibility is the ordering mechanism used throughout jRate, *e.g.*, it is used to achieve total ordering of schedulable entities whose QoS are expressed in various ways. This approach is an application of the formalisms presented in [11].

High Resolution Time and Clock. jRate implements the RTSJ high resolution time API. Different implementations of real-time clocks are provided. Depending on the underlying hardware and OS platform, resolution from nanoseconds up to microseconds can be obtained.

3.2   Next Steps: A Chameleonic Real-Time Java Implementation

jRate is intended to be a "chameleonic" Real-time Java implementation. We use the analogy since jRate is designed to its target environment, just as a chameleon adapts to its surrounding environment. In jRate, the adaptation process is obtained via generative programming techniques. Our ultimate goal is to provide a set of core reusable components, along with the appropriate configuration tools, so application developers can automatically generate a customized Real-time Java implementation that precisely meets their needs. Our work to date has focused on manually generating high performance and small footprint implementations of the RTSJ specification.

Figure 8 shows a typical generative programming approach.

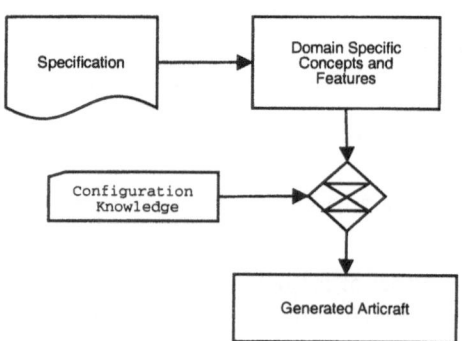

Fig. 8. Generative Programming Approach

In this approach, the *feature profile* provided by application developers is used to select the set of features that must be present in the generated Real-time Java implementation. Generative tools are used to compose the different parts, check dependencies, and optimize the generated system.

---

[5] On certain platforms, such as Compaq Alpha, the assumptions that we rely upon to avoid locking do not hold, so for those platforms jRate must use locks.

For instance, in the context of jRate, a given *feature profile* might designate the following:

- A priority-based scheduler with no support for feasibility analysis
- Raw memory access is not needed, and
- A particular style of scoped memory must be used.

This information is then used by generators to provide an instance of jRate that is optimized for this particular use case. The generated API could be simplified since the user only wants to use priority-based scheduler and does not need any feasibility analysis support.

The tools we are applying to make jRate a *generative* real-time Java implementations include AspectJ [13] and AspectC++ [14], along with other techniques that are commonly used in generative programming, such as:

- **Static crosscutting** to compose APIs. Static crosscutting is an AOP technique that allows "meta-programmers" to modify the static structure of a class, *e.g.*, by adding methods or changing an inheritance hierarchy.
- **Dynamic crosscutting** is used to customize and compose run-time behaviors. Dynamic crosscutting is another AOP technique that allows the execution of aspect code at specific points in the application, known as *join-points*, such as method invocations, data member assignments, etc.

4   jRate Performance

This section presents jRate's performance results for the primary RTSJ features. All experiments were conducted using RTJPerf, which is an open-source benchmarking suite for RTSJ available at http://tao.doc.wustl.edu/~corsaro/periscope.html, see [10,15] for in-depth coverage of the RTJPerf benchmark suite and a comparison of jRate's performance with a range of Java implementations, including CVM, the TimeSys RTSJ Reference Implementation (RI), and Sun's JDK 1.4.

The test results reported in this section were obtained on an Intel Pentium III 733 MHz with 256 MB RAM, running Linux RedHat 7.2 with the TimeSys Linux/RT 3.0 GPL[6] kernel [16]. jRate was compared against the TimeSys RTSJ RI [4], to provide a baseline to compare jRate against. The RI is based on a Java 2 Micro Edition (J2ME) JVM and supports only an interpreted execution mode *i.e.*, there is no just-in-time (JIT) compilation. The *efficiency* of the RI was intentionally not optimized since its main goal was *predictable* real-time behavior and RTSJ-compliance. The RI runs on all Linux platforms, but the priority inversion control mechanisms are available to the RI only when running under TimeSys Linux/RT [16], *i.e.*, the commercial version.

4.1   jRate Memory Subsystem Performance

Scoped Memory Allocation Time Test. RTJPerf provides a test that measures the allocation time for different types of scoped memory. The results obtained for the jRate's and RI implementation of scoped memory are presented and analyzed below.

---

[6] This OS is the freely available version of TimeSys Linux/RT and is available under the GNU Public License (GPL).

Test Settings. To measure the average allocation time incurred by the RI implementation of LTMemory and VTMemory, we ran the RTJPerf allocation time test for allocation sizes ranging from 32 to 16,384 bytes. Each test samples 1,000 values of the allocation time for the given allocation size. This test also measured the average allocation time of jRate's CTMemory implementation. Figure 9 shows how jRate's CTMemory implementation relates to the memory areas defined by the RTSJ, which are depicted in Figure 2.

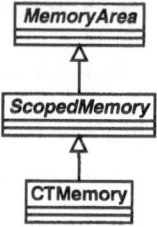

Fig. 9. CTMemory Class Hierarchy

Test Results. The data obtained by running the allocation time tests were processed to obtain an average, dispersion, and worst-case measure of the allocation time. We compute both the average and dispersion indexes since they indicate the following information:

- How predictable is the implementation
- How much variation in allocation time can occur and
- How the worst-case behavior compares to the average-case and to the case that provides a 99% upper bound.[7]

Figure 10 shows the resulting average allocation time for the different test runs and Figure 11 shows the standard deviation of the allocation time measured in the various test settings.

Figure 12 shows the performance ratio between jRate's CTMemory and the RI LTMemory. This ratio indicates how many times smaller the CTMemory average allocation time is compared to the average allocation time for the RI LTMemory.

Results Analysis. We now analyze the results of the tests that measured the average and worst-case allocation times, along with the dispersion for the different test settings:

- **Average Measures.** As shown in Figure 10, both LTMemory and VTMemory provide linear time allocation with respect to the allocated memory size. Matching results were found for the other measured statistical parameter, based on this, we infer that the RI implementation of LTMemory and VTMemory are similar, so we mostly focus on the LTMemory since our results also apply to VTMemory. jRate has an average allocation time that is independent of the allocated chunk, which helps analyze the timing of real-time Java code, even without knowing the amount of memory that will be needed. Figure 12 shows that for small memory chunks the jRate memory

---

[7] By "99% upper bound" we mean that value that represents an upper bound for the measured values in the 99th percentile of the cases.

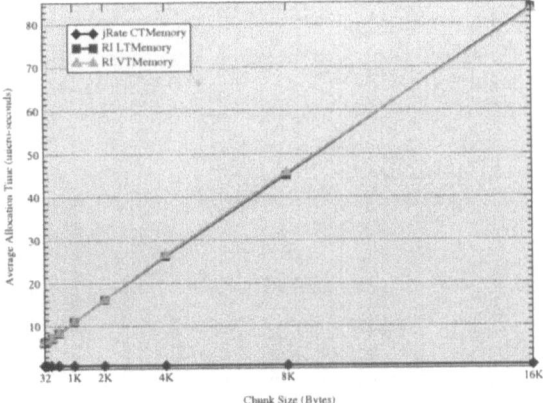

Fig. 10. Average Allocation Time.

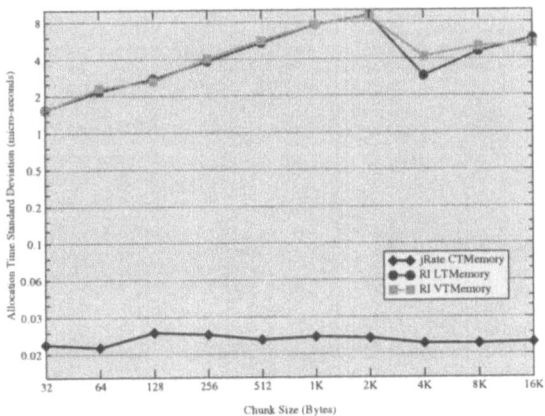

Fig. 11. Allocation Time Standard Deviation.

allocator is nearly ten times faster than RI's LTMemory. For the biggest chunk we tested, jRate's CTMemory is ~95 times faster RI's LTMemory.

– **Dispersion Measures.** The standard deviation of the different allocation time cases is shown in Figure 11. This deviation increases with the chunk size allocated for both LTMemory and VTMemory until it reaches 4 Kbytes, where it suddenly drops and then it starts growing again. On Linux, a virtual memory page is exactly 4 Kbytes, but when an array of 4 Kbytes is allocated the actual memory is slightly larger to store freelist management information. In contrast, the CTMemory implementation has the smallest variance and the flattest trend.

The plots in Figure 13 show the cumulative relative frequency distribution of the allocation time for some of the different cases discussed above. These graphs illustrate how the allocation time is distributed for different types of memory and different allocation sizes. For any given point t on the x axis, the value on the y axis indicates the relative frequency of allocation time for which $AllocationTime \leq t$.

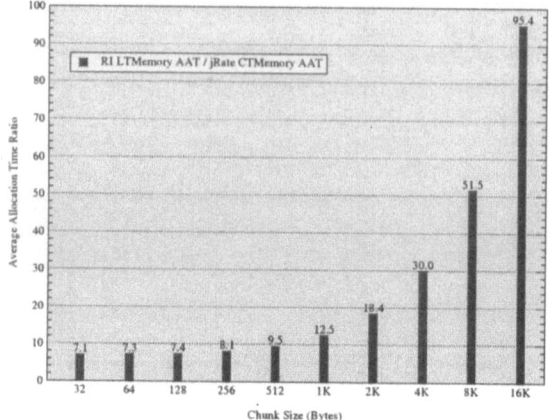

Fig. 12. Speedup of the CTMemory Average Allocation Time Over the LTMemory Average Allocation Time.

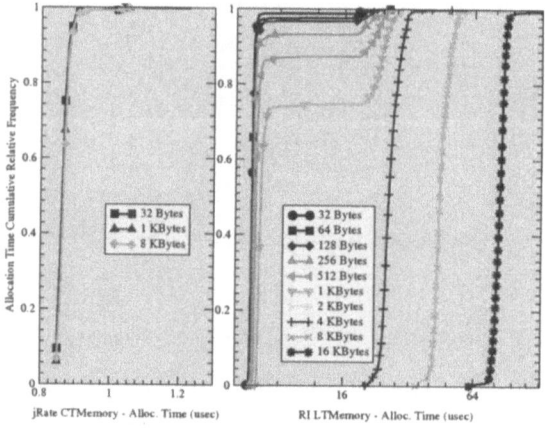

Fig. 13. Allocation Time Cumulative Relative Frequency Distribution.

This graph, along with Figure 11 that shows the standard deviation, provides insights on how the measured allocation time is dispersed and distributed.

- **Worst-case Measures.** Figure 14 and Figure 15 show the bounds on the allocation time for jRate's CTMemory and the RI LTMemory. Each of these graphs depicts the worst, best, and average allocation times, along with the 99% upper bound of the allocation time. Figure 14 illustrates how the worst-case execution time for jRate's CTMemory is at most ~1.4 times larger than its average execution time.

  Figure 15 shows how the maximum, average, and the 99% case, for the RI LTMemory, converge as the size of the allocated chunk increases. The minimum ratio between the worst-case allocation time and the average-case is ~1.6 for a chunk size of 16K. Figure 14, Figure 15 and Figure 13 also characterize the distribution of the allocation time. Figure 13 shows how for some allocation sizes, the allocation time for the RI LTMemory is centered around two points.

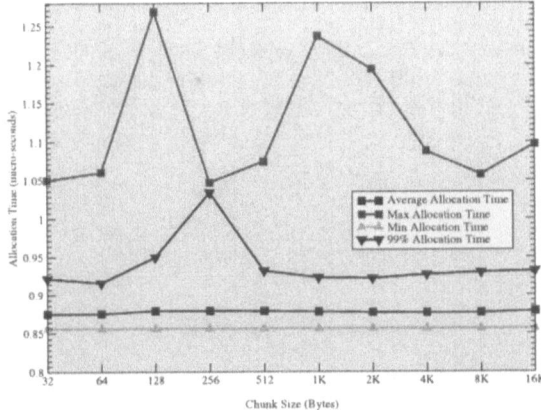

Fig. 14. CTMemory Worst, Best, Average and 99% Allocation Time.

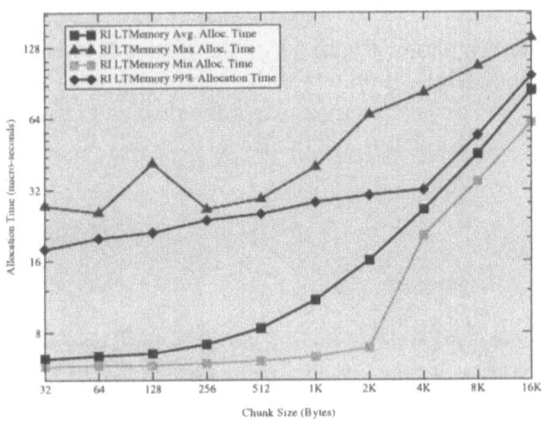

Fig. 15. LTMemory Worst, Best, Average and 99% Allocation Time.

4.2   jRate's Asynchronous Event Handler Performances

Asynchronous Event Handler Dispatch Delay Test. RTJPerf provides a test that measures the dispatch latency of the two types of RTSJ asynchronous event handlers, which are the BoundAsyncEventHandler and the AsyncEventHandler. The results we obtained are presented and analyzed below.

Test Settings. To measure the dispatch latency provided by different types of asynchronous event handlers defined by the RTSJ, we ran the asynchrony tests provided by RTJPerf, and described in [10,15], with a fire count of 2,000 for both RI and jRate. To ensure that each event firing causes a complete execution cycle, we ran the test in "lockstep mode," where one thread fires an event and only after the thread that handles the event is done is the event fired again. To avoid the interference of the GC while performing the test, the real-time thread that fires and handles the event uses scoped memory as its current memory area.

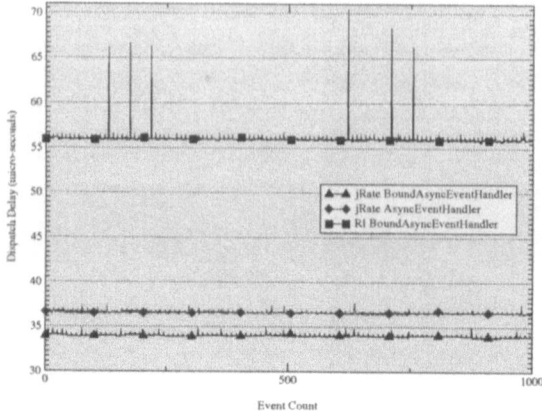

Fig. 16. Dispatch Latency Trend for Successive Event Firing.

Test Results. Figure 16 shows the trend of the dispatch latency for successive event firings.[8] The data obtained by running the dispatch delay tests were processed to obtain average worst-case and dispersion measure of the dispatch latency. Table 1 and Table 2 shows the results found for jRate and the RI respectively.

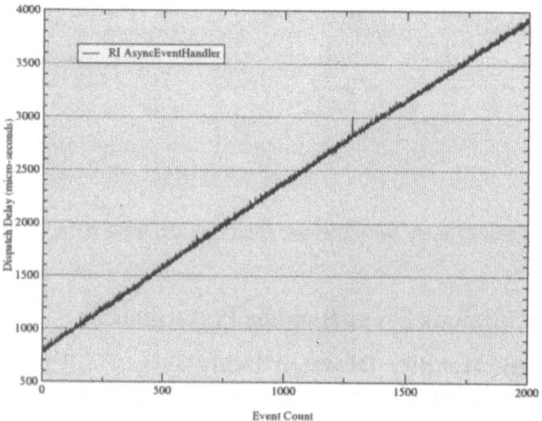

Fig. 17. AsyncEventHandler Dispatch Latency Trend.

Results Analysis. Below we analyze the results of the tests that measure the average-case and worst-case dispatch latency, as well as its dispersion, for the different test settings:

---

[8] Since The RI's AsyncEventHandler trend is completely off the scale, it is omitted in this figure and depicted separately in Figure 17.

Table 1. jRate Event Handler's Dispatch Latency statistics for the Different Settings

	AsycnEventHandler	BoundAsycnEventHandler
Avg.	36.574 μs	34.004 μs
Std. Dev.	0.113 μs	0.148 μs
Max	39.400 μs	35.555 μs
99%	36.945 μs	34.472 μs

Table 2. RI Event Handler's Dispatch Latency Statistics for the Different Settings

	AsycnEventHandler	BoundAsycnEventHandler
Avg.	2373.0 μs	56.100 μs
Std. Dev.	909.92 μs	0.848 μs
Max	3950.8 μs	70.462 μs
99%	3892.5 μs	56.692 μs

- **Average Measures.** Table 2 illustrates the large average dispatch latency incurred by the RTSJ RI AsyncEventHandler. The results in Figure 17 show how the actual dispatch latency increases as the event count increases. By tracing the memory used when running the test using heap memory, we found that not only did memory usage increased steadily, but even invoking the GC explicitly did not free any memory. These results reveal a problem with how the RI manages the resources associated to threads. The RI's AsyncEventHandler creates a new thread to handle a new event, and the problem appears to be a memory leak in the underlying RI memory manager associated with threads, rather than a limitation with the model used to handle the events. In contrast, the RI's BoundAsyncEventHandler performs quite well, *i.e.*, its average dispatch latency is slightly less than twice as large as the average dispatch latency for jRate.
  Figure 16 and Table 1 show that the average dispatch latency of jRate's AsyncEventHandler is the same order of magnitude as its BoundAsyncEventHandler. The difference between the two average dispatch latency stems from jRate's AsyncEventHandler implementation, which uses an *executor* [17] thread from a pool of threads to perform the event firing, rather than having a thread permanently bound to the handler.
- **Dispersion Measures.** The results in Table 2, Table 1, Figure 16, and Figure 18 illustrate how jRate's BoundAsyncEventHandler dispatch latency incurs the least jitter. The dispatch latency value dispersion for the RTSJ RI BoundAsyncEventHandler is also quite good, though its jitter is higher than jRate's AsyncEventHandler and BoundAsyncEventHandler. The higher jitter in RI may stem from the fact that the RI stores the event handlers in a java.util.Vector. This data structure achieves thread-safety by synchronizing all method that get(), add(), or remove() elements from it, which acquires and releases a lock associated with the vector for each method.
  To avoid this locking overhead, jRate uses a data structure that associates the event handler list with a given event and allows the contents of the data structure to be read without acquiring/releasing a lock. Only modifications to the data structure must be serialized. As a result, jRate's AsyncEventHandler dispatch latency is relatively predictable, even though the handler has no thread bound to it permanently. The

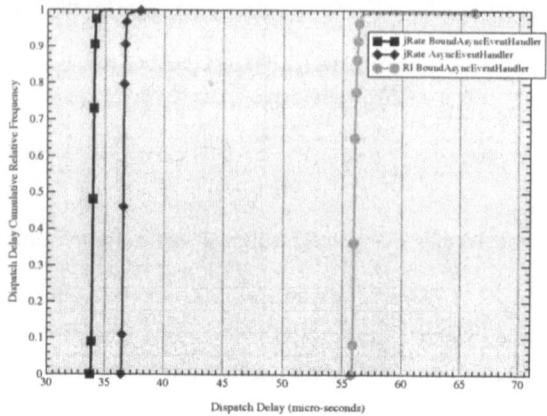

Fig. 18. Cumulative Dispatch Latency Distribution.

jRate thread pool implementation uses LIFO queues for its executor, *i.e.*, the last executor that has completed executing is the first one reused. This technique is often applied in thread pool implementations to leverage cache affinity benefits [18].
– **Worst-case Measures.** Table 1 illustrates how the jRate's BoundAsyncEventHandler and AsyncEventHandler have worst-case execution time that is close to its average-case. The worst-case dispatch delay provided by the RI's BoundAsyncEventHandler is not as good as the one provided by jRate, due to differences in how their event dispatching mechanisms are implemented. The 99% bound differs only on the first decimal digit for both jRate and the RI (clearly we do not consider the RI's AsyncEventHandler since no bound can be put on its behavior).

Asynchronous Event Handler Priority Inversion Test. This test measures how the dispatch latency of an asynchronous event handler H is influenced by the presence of N others event handlers, characterized by a lower execution eligibility than H. In the ideal case, H's dispatch latency should be independent of N, and any delay introduced by the presence of other handlers represents some degree of priority inversion. The results we obtained are presented and analyzed below.

Test Settings. This test uses the same settings as the asynchronous event handler dispatch delay test. Only the BoundAsyncEventHandler performance is measured, however, because the RI's AsyncEventHandlers are essentially unusable since their dispatch latency grows linearly with the number of event handled (see Figure 17), which masks any priority inversions. Moreover, jRate's AsyncEventHandler performance is similar to its BoundAsyncEventHandler performance, so the results obtained from testing one applies to the other. The current test uses the following two types of asynchronous event handlers:

– The first is identical to the one used in the previous test, *i.e.*, it gets a time stamp after the handler is called and measures the dispatch latency. This logic is associated with H.

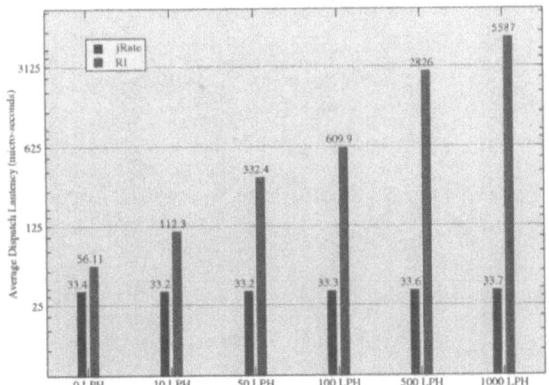

Fig. 19. *H*'s Average Dispatch Latency.

– The second does nothing and is used for the lower priority handlers.

Test Results. Table 3 and Table 4 report how the average, standard deviation, maximum and 99% bound of the dispatch delay changes for *H* as the number of low-priority handlers increase. Figure 19 and Figure 20 provide a graphical representation for the average and dispersion measures.

Table 3. jRate's Dispatch Delay Statistics.

	Avg.	Std. Dev.	Max	99%
0 LP	33.375 μs	0.124 μs	34.877 μs	34.116 μs
10 LP	33.154 μs	0.134 μs	34.903 μs	33.797 μs
50 LP	33.205 μs	0.161 μs	36.063 μs	33.825 μs
100 LP	33.264 μs	0.147 μs	35.959 μs	33.851 μs
500 LP	33.632 μs	0.180 μs	37.149 μs	34.283 μs
1000 LP	33.739 μs	0.199 μs	37.565 μs	34.458 μs

Table 4. RI's Dispatch Delay Statistics.

	Avg.	Std. Dev.	Max	99%
0 LP	56.106 μs	0.887 μs	70.462 μs	56.706 μs
10 LP	112.33 μs	1.346 μs	133.90 μs	122.18 μs
50 LP	332.41 μs	2.396 μs	353.17 μs	344.86 μs
100 LP	609.92 μs	3.410 μs	631.51 μs	624.96 μs
500 LP	2826.4 μs	12.005 μs	2884.0 μs	2862.1 μs
1000 LP	5587.0 μs	23.768 μs	5672.7 μs	5650.3 μs

Results Analysis. Below, we analyze the results of the tests that measure average-case and worst-case dispatch latency, as well as its dispersion, for jRate and the RI.

– **Average Measures.** Figure 19 and Tables 3 and 4 illustrate that the average dispatch latency experienced by *H* is essentially constant for jRate, regardless of the number

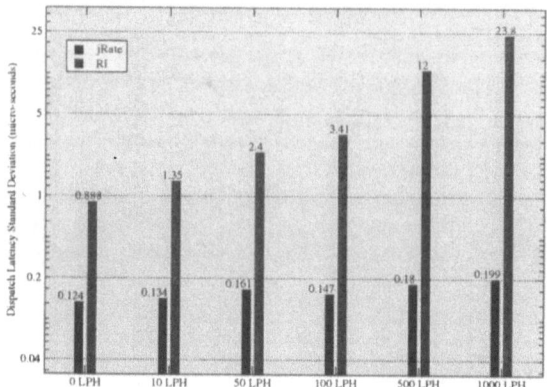

Fig. 20. *H* Dispatch Latency's Standard Deviation.

of low-priority handlers. It grows rapidly, however, as the number of low-priority handlers increase for the RI. The RI's event dispatching priority inversion is problematic for real-time systems and stems from the fact that its queue of handlers is implemented with a `java.util.Vector`, which is not ordered by the *execution eligibility*. In contrast, the priority queues in jRate's event dispatching are ordered by the execution eligibility of the handlers.

Execution eligibility is the ordering mechanism used throughout jRate. For example, it is used to achieve total ordering of schedulable entities whose QoS are expressed in different ways. This approach is an application of the formalisms presented in [11].

- **Dispersion Measures.** Figure 20 and Tables 3 and 4 illustrate how *H*'s dispatch latency dispersion grows as the number of low-priority handlers increases in the RI. The dispatch latency incurred by *H* in the RI therefore not only grows with the number of low-priority handlers, but its variability increases *i.e.*, its predictability decreases. In contrast, jRate's standard deviation increases very little as the low-priority handlers increase. As mentioned in the discussion of the average measurements above, the difference in performance stems from the proper choice of priority queue.

- **Worst-Case Measures.** Tables 3 and 4 illustrate how the worst-case dispatch delay is largely independent of the number of low-priority handlers for jRate. In contrast, worst-case dispatch delay for the RI increases as the number of low-priority handlers grows. The 99% bound is close to the average for jRate and relatively close for the RI.

5   Related Work

Although the RTSJ was adopted fairly recently [3], there are already a number of research projects related to our work on jRate and RTJPerf. The following projects are particularly interesting:

- The **FLEX** [19] provides a Java compiler written in Java, along with an advanced code analysis framework. FLEX generates native code for StrongARM or MIPS processors, and can also generate C code. It uses advanced analysis techniques to automatically detect the portions of a Java application that can take advantage of certain real-time Java features, such as memory areas or real-time threads.

- The OVM [20] project is developing an open-source JVM framework for research on the RTSJ and programming languages. The OVM virtual machine is written entirely in Java and its architecture emphasizes customizability and pluggable components. Its implementation strives to maintain a balance between performance and flexibility, allowing users to customize the implementation of operations such as message dispatch, synchronization, field access, and speed. OVM allows dynamic updates of the implementation of instructions on a running VM.
- Work on real-time storage allocation and collection [21] is being conducted at Washington University, St. Louis. The main goal of this effort is to develop new algorithms and architectures for memory allocation and garbage collection that provide worst-case execution bounds suitable for real-time embedded systems.

There are several ways in which we plan to leverage our work on jRate and the work being done in the FLEX, OVM, and real-time allocator projects outlined above. For instance, the jRate RTSJ library implementation could become the library used by the OVM. This is possible because jRate has been designed to port easily from one Java platform to another. jRate could be used as the RTSJ library on which FLEX relies. Likewise, the work on real-time allocators and garbage collectors could be to implement jRate's scoped memory with different characteristics than its current CTMemory design.

6   Concluding Remarks and Future Directions

This paper presented an overview of jRate, which is an ahead-of-time compiled implementation of RTSJ. We analyzed the results of systematic benchmarks of jRate and the TimeSys RTSJ RI based on the RTJPerf benchmarking suite [10]. RTJPerf is one of the first open-source benchmarking suites designed to evaluate RTSJ-compliant Java implementations empirically. The RTJPerf results shown in Section 4 underscore that jRate is both efficient and predictable since its use of ahead-of-time compilation (1) improves its performance and (2) limits the sources of overhead and jitter introduced by interpreted or just-in-time (JIT) compiled execution.

Although jRate implements many core RTSJ features, the following omissions will be addressed in our future work:

- Add support for the remaining RTSJ features, such as timers, POSIX signal handling, periodic and no-heap real-time threads, and physical memory access. Some feature that we don't plan to implement in the first release of jRate is the memory reference checking, and the Asynchronous transfer control. Since jRate will be the primary Real-Time Java platform used by ZEN [22], jRate's implementation is being driven by the features that are most important for real-time ORBs.
- Provide a user-level scheduling framework that leverages the simple priority-based scheduling provided by the underlying real-time operating systems to provide advanced scheduling services.
- Focus on applying generative programming techniques to jRate. This will involve completely partitioning the Java and C++ parts of jRate into sets of aspects that can

be woven together at compile-time to configure custom real-time Java implementations that are tailored for specific application needs.

– Provide a meta-object protocol as one of the aspects to support both computational and structural reflection. Reflection is useful for real-time applications that must manage resources dynamically. Moreover, it enables developers to customize the behavior of jRate's implementation at run-time.

Our long-term goal is to create not just a single RTSJ implementation, but a set of components that allow users to generate custom Real-time Java implementation tailored for particular requirements and environments. Developer therefore will not have to pay the cost and accidental complexity for features that they do not use.

The first alpha version of jRate was released to the public in mid July 2002. Information on its current status and availability can be found at http://tao.doc.wustl.edu/~corsaro/jRate. Since jRate is an open-source project, we encourage researchers and developers to provide us feedback and help improve its quality and capabilities. jRate will use the same open-source model we use for ACE [23] and TAO [24], which has proved to be successful to produce high-quality open-source middleware.

References

1. Sztipanovits, J., Karsai, G.: Model-Integrated Computing. IEEE Computer **30** (1997) 110–112
2. Arnold, K., Gosling, J., Holmes, D.: The Java Programming Language. Addison-Wesley, Boston (2000)
3. Bollella, Gosling, Brosgol, Dibble, Furr, Hardin, Turnbull: The Real-Time Specification for Java. Addison-Wesley (2000)
4. TimeSys: Real-Time Specification for Java Reference Implementation. www.timesys.com/rtj (2001)
5. Czaenwcki, K., Eisenecker, U.W.: Generative Programming: Methods, Tools, and Applications. Addison-Wesley, Reading, Massachusetts (2000)
6. Kiczales, G., Lamping, J., Mendhekar, A., Maeda, C., Lopes, C.V., Loingtier, J.M., Irwin, J.: Aspect-Oriented Programming. In: Proceedings of the 11th European Conference on Object-Oriented Programming. (1997)
7. Kiczales, G., des Rivieres, J., Bobrow, D.G.: The Art of The Metaobject Protocol. The MIT Press, Cambridge, Massachusetts (1991)
8. Heineman, G.T., Councill, B.T.: Component-Based Software Engineering: Putting the Pieces Together. Addison-Wesley, Reading, Massachusetts (2001)
9. Schmidt, D.C., Kuhns, F.: An Overview of the Real-time CORBA Specification. IEEE Computer Magazine, Special Issue on Object-oriented Real-time Computing **33** (2000)
10. Corsaro, A., Schmidt, D.C.: Evaluating Real-Time Java Features and Performance for Real-time Embedded Systems. In: Proceedings of the 8th IEEE Real-Time Technology and Applications Symposium, San Jose, IEEE (2002)
11. Corsaro, A., Schmidt, D.C., Cytron, R.K., Gill, C.: Formalizing Meta-Programming Techniques to Reconcile Heterogeneous Scheduling Disciplines in Open Distributed Real-Time Systems. In: Proceedings of the 3rd International Symposium on Distributed Objects and Applications., Rome, Italy, OMG (2001) 289–299
12. GNU is Not Unix: GCJ: The GNU Complier for Java. http://gcc.gnu.org/java (2002)

13. The AspectJ Organization: Aspect-Oriented Programming for Java. `www.aspectj.org` (2001)
14. The AspectC++ Organization: Aspect-Oriented Programming for C++. `www.aspectc.org` (2001)
15. Corsaro, A., Schmidt, D.C.: Evaluating Real-Time Java Features and Performance for Real-time Embedded Systems. Technical Report 2002-001, University of Califoria, Irvine (2002)
16. TimeSys: TimeSys Linux/RT 3.0. `www.timesys.com` (2001)
17. Lea, D.: Concurrent Programming in Java: Design Principles and Patterns, Second Edition. Addison-Wesley, Boston (2000)
18. Salehi, J.D., Kurose, J.F., Towsley, D.: The Effectiveness of Affinity-Based Scheduling in Multiprocessor Networking. In: IEEE INFOCOM, San Francisco, USA, IEEE Computer Society Press (1996)
19. M. Rinard et al.: FLEX Compiler Infrastructure.
    `http://www.flex-compiler.lcs.mit.edu/Harpoon/` (2002)
20. OVM/Consortium: OVM An Open RTSJ Compliant JVM. `http://www.ovmj.org/` (2002)
21. Donahue, S.M., Hampton, M.P., Deters, M., Nye, J.M., Cytron, R.K., Kavi, K.M.: Storage allocation for real-time, embedded systems. In Henzinger, T.A., Kirsch, C.M., eds.: Embedded Software: Proceedings of the First International Workshop, Springer Verlag (2001) 131–147
22. Klefstad, R., Schmidt, D.C., O'Ryan, C.: The Design of a Real-time CORBA ORB using Real-time Java. In: Proceedings of the International Symposium on Object-Oriented Real-time Distributed Computing, IEEE (2002)
23. Schmidt, D.C.: The ADAPTIVE Communication Environment (ACE).
    www.cs.wustl.edu/~schmidt/ACE.html (1997)
24. Center for Distributed Object Computing: The ACE ORB (TAO).
    www.cs.wustl.edu/~schmidt/TAO.html (Washington University)

Empirical Differences between COTS Middleware Scheduling Strategies*

Christopher D. Gill[1], Fred Kuhns[1], Douglas C. Schmidt[2], and Ron K. Cytron[1]

[1] Department of Computer Science, Washington University, St. Louis
{cdgill, fredk, cytron}@cs.wustl.edu
[2] Department of Electrical and Computer Engineering, University of California, Irvine
schmidt@uci.edu

Abstract. The proportion of complex distributed real-time embedded (DRE) systems made up of commercial-off-the-shelf (COTS) hardware and software is increasing significantly in response to the difficulty and expense of building DRE systems entirely from scratch. In previous work, we showed how applying different scheduling strategies in middleware can allow COTS-based solutions to provide both assurance and optimization of real-time constraints for important classes of mission-critical DRE systems. There are few empirical studies, however, that help developers of COTS-based DRE systems to make crucial distinctions between strategies that appear similar in policy, but whose run-time effects may differ in practice.

This paper provides two contributions to the study of real-time quality of service (QoS) assurance and performance in COTS-based DRE systems. First, we examine in detail two hybrid static/dynamic scheduling strategies that should behave similarly according to policy alone, but that in fact produce different results under the same conditions, both in utilization and in meeting real-time assurances. Second, we offer recommendations based on these results for developers of mission-critical DRE systems, such as the Boeing Bold Stroke platform used in the Adaptive Software Flight Demonstration (ASFD) program under which our experiments were conducted. These contributions address and highlight the importance of the following issues to real-time scheduling in COTS environments: (1) careful mapping of scheduling policies into implementation mechanisms and (2) benchmarking and analysis of actual systems in representative operational environments.

Keywords: Dynamic Scheduling Algorithms and Analysis, Real-Time Assurance and Optimization, Distributed Real-time and Embedded Systems, Mission Critical Systems, Quality of Service Issues, Middleware and APIs.

* This work was supported in part by Boeing, DARPA ITO, DARPA contract F33615-00-C-1697 (PCES) and AFRL contracts F3615-97-D-1155/DO (WSOA) and F33645-97-D-1155 (ASTD/ASFD).

R. Meersman, Z. Tari (Eds.): CoopIS/DOA/ODBASE 2002, LNCS 2519, pp. 922–947, 2002.

1   Introduction

1.1   Motivation: Distributed Real-Time and Embedded Systems

Distributed, real-time, and embedded (DRE) systems are becoming increasingly widespread and important. Examples of DRE systems include *autonomous agent teams*, *e.g.*, multi-robot environment mapping, *manufacturing process automation, e.g.*, high-performance assembly lines, and *defense systems, e.g.*, avionics mission computing systems. Although there are many types of DRE systems, they must all achieve the following capabilities:

- Managing connections and data transfer between distinct endsystems
- Offering predictable and efficient control over end-to-end system resources and
- Operating within resource limitations imposed by weight, cost, and power constraints.

Designing DRE systems that can offer strong assurances of real-time predictability, and yet are parsimonious in their use of limited computing resources is hard; building them on time and within budget is even harder. Therefore, studying real-time policies and mechanisms within commercial-off-the-shelf (COTS) systems empirically is essential to ensure mission-critical DRE systems can be built and maintained in a cost-effective manner.

Our previous work [1,2] has quantified the benefits of applying multiple scheduling paradigms in COTS middleware to support the quality of service (QoS) demands of mission-critical DRE systems that possess a mix of hard and soft real-time requirements, such as avionics mission computing systems [3], mission-critical distributed audio/video processing [4,5], and real-time robotic systems [6]. However, our previous work also showed that when more than one strategy is plausible for a given system based on policy alone, the best choice of which strategy to apply may not be obvious.[1] This paper therefore presents additional empirical results and analysis of multi-paradigm COTS middleware to offer insights into a canonical choice between two hybrid static/dynamic scheduling strategies. We suggest guidelines for choosing between the strategies examined in this research, and posit a model and hypotheses to test that model for further investigation of these issues as future work.

The research presented in this paper was conducted in the context of a real-world mission-critical DRE application: a research operational flight program (OFP) designed for technology transfer to production avionics mission computing systems. This paper can therefore be viewed as a case study of the application of scheduling strategies in middleware for next-generation DRE systems. The results it presents apply to a class of DRE systems that cross-cuts application domains that manage both critical and non-critical real-time requirements.

---

[1] We distinguish the *policy* of a scheduling strategy, *i.e.*, the *algorithm* for ordering operations it schedules, from the *mechanisms* used to implement that policy, *e.g.*, prioritized threads, queues, and timers.

1.2   Context: Real-Time CORBA Middleware

DRE systems have historically been custom developed in an *ad hoc* and inflexible manner. While many operational systems have been built this way, this development process failed to address the following challenges adequately: (1) reducing total ownership costs, (2) providing portable QoS management, and (3) tailoring resource provisioning to assure *critical* system requirements are met in the worst case, while recovering resources appropriately to improve *non-critical* performance in the average case. In recent years, the following technologies have converged to address these challenges:

Distributed Object Computing (DOC) Middleware. DOC middleware is systems software that resides between the applications and the underlying operating systems, network protocol stacks, and hardware [7]. It offers clients portable language-independent and location-transparent invocation of methods on target object implementations [8]. DOC middleware simplifies application development by off-loading the tedious and error-prone aspects of distributed computing from application developers to middleware developers.

Real-Time CORBA. Real-time CORBA [9] is a DOC middleware standard that adds capabilities that support end-to-end predictability for remote operations to the original CORBA specification. It improves system predictability and bounds or avoids priority inversions, by supporting end-to-end management of system resources. To implement Real-time CORBA effectively, an Object Request Broker (ORB) must provide run-time support for many DRE features, such as connection management, marshaling/demarshaling, demultiplexing, language and OS independence, resource scheduling and load balancing. However, first-generation ORBs did not provide features or optimizations to support DRE systems with stringent QoS requirements.

The ACE ORB (TAO). To meet the stringent QoS requirements of DRE systems, researchers at Washington University in St. Louis and the University of California, Irvine have developed a second-generation ORB called TAO [10], which is an open-source implementation of Real-time CORBA that supports efficient, predictable, and flexible DRE computing. Prior work on TAO has explored many dimensions of high-performance and real-time ORB design and performance, including scalable event processing [11], request demultiplexing [12], I/O subsystem [13] and protocol [14] integration, connection architectures [15], asynchronous [16] and synchronous [17] concurrent request processing, adaptive load balancing [18], meta-programming mechanisms [19], and IDL stub/skeleton optimizations [20].

Kokyu Multi-paradigm Scheduling Framework. To increase responsiveness to varying operational environments, we have recently [2] extended our prior research on static [10] and dynamic [3] scheduling for Real-time CORBA by incorporating a *strategized scheduling framework* called *Kokyu*[2] within the TAO Real-Time Event Service. Kokyu addresses the challenge that no *single* scheduling paradigm performs best in

---

[2] Kokyu is a Japanese word meaning literally "breath", but also implying timing and coordination.

all environments, by enabling the configuration and empirical evaluation of multiple scheduling paradigms, including:

- **Static** scheduling strategies, *e.g.*, rate monotonic scheduling (RMS) [21],
- **Dynamic** scheduling strategies, *e.g.*, earliest deadline first (EDF) [21] and minimum laxity first (MLF) [6], and
- **Hybrid static/dynamic** scheduling strategies, *e.g.*, maximum urgency first (MUF) [6] and RMS+MLF [22].

This paper focuses on the hybrid static/dynamic MUF [6] and RMS+MLF [22] strategies, which were demonstrated in our recent work [2] to be preferable in COTS-based middleware when the total system load is infeasible but the critical subset of that load is still feasible. Specifically, both MUF and RMS+MLF were able to (1) *partition* critical and non-critical resource utilization using static mechanisms (such as thread priorities in COTS-based systems), and then (2) dynamically schedule single *operations*[3] within one [22] or more [6] of the partitions. The results in this paper illustrate how the Kokyu framework can provide adaptability across product families, operating systems, and most importantly environmental conditions, while preserving the rigorous scheduling guarantees and testability offered by prior work on statically scheduled CORBA operations [10, 23,24] and multi-paradigm scheduling [2].

1.3 Performance Differences between Similar Strategies

A crucial question for developers of mission-critical DRE systems is whether the differences *in policy alone* between alternative scheduling strategies are sufficient to distinguish which strategy (or sequence of alternative strategies) should be used *in practice* under a given set of system and environmental conditions. This paper presents empirical evidence that policy alone is *not* sufficient. Careful prototyping, modeling, analysis, and optimization of the actual behavior of the enforcement mechanisms themselves is therefore necessary to ensure good choices.

The work described in this paper is motivated by empirical results from our work on multi-paradigm scheduling [2]. Our results revealed differences in the performance of two scheduling strategies, RMS+MLF and MUF, that might have been expected to perform more similarly under the conditions of the experiment. Specifically, in terms of policy alone, the RMS+MLF and MUF strategies might not be expected to show meaningful differences in actual real-time performance. Our reasoning is presented below:

1. Under the experimental conditions described in Section 3, the sequence of resource requests for both critical and non-critical operations was identical in our experiments under the RMS+MLF and MUF scheduling strategies.
2. The pseudo-random sequence of jitter added to critical and non-critical operations was identical for RMS+MLF and MUF.

---

[3] We term the short-lived computation performed each time an event is pushed to a component an *operation*.

3. Since both RMS+MLF and MUF monotonically prioritize critical requests ahead of non-critical ones, the availability of the CPU to non-critical processing, as a function of time, should have been identical.
4. Since the RMS+MLF and MUF strategies both use laxity to order non-critical requests in a lowest-priority queue, the order in which non-critical requests were serviced should have been identical for the two strategies as well.

Clearly, policy alone is insufficient to explain the results we saw in our recent work with Kokyu. These results indicate the need to consider how that policy model might be extended to account for variations in the performance due to properties of the mechanisms used to implement the policies. This paper therefore presents new analysis of data obtained from our earlier experiments, and identifies newly discovered correlations within those data. For future work we offer a plausible model for the observed behavior of the RMS+MLF and MUF scheduling strategies and suggest additional hypotheses and experiments as to verify that model.

1.4 Paper Organization

The remainder of this paper is organized as follows: Section 2 describes the application, middleware, OS, and hardware configurations that comprise the open experimentation platform used for our empirical studies; Section 3 summarizes the experimental design factors relevant to the performance differences between scheduling strategies in our previous work; Section 4 presents new findings based on further analysis of the data; Section 5 summarizes our observations and makes recommendations based on our results, identifies a plausible model for variability in the scheduling strategies, and suggests hypotheses and experiments for future work; Section 6 compares our research on Kokyu with related work; Finally, Section 7 offers concluding remarks.

2 Open Experimentation Platform

This paper focuses on experiments conducted under the Adaptive Software Flight Demonstration (ASFD) program [25] on a mission-critical system that is representative of an important class of DRE systems: *the operational flight program (OFP) in an avionics mission computing system*. An operational flight program (OFP) manages sensors and operator displays, navigates the aircraft's course, and controls on-board equipment. The avionics system used for those experiments consisted of operational flight program (OFP) components hosted on the *Bold Stroke* domain-specific middleware infrastructure, which in turn is built using the distribution middleware capabilities and common middleware services provided by the TAO Real-time CORBA Object Request Broker (ORB).

Figure 1 [2] illustrates the following OS/hardware, middleware, and application layers of the open experimentation platform:[4]

---

[4] This platform, and the studies conducted on it, were supported under the Adaptive Software Flight Demonstration (ASFD) program hosted by the Boeing Phantom Works Open Systems Architecture organization. This work was administered by the Embedded Systems Branch of the

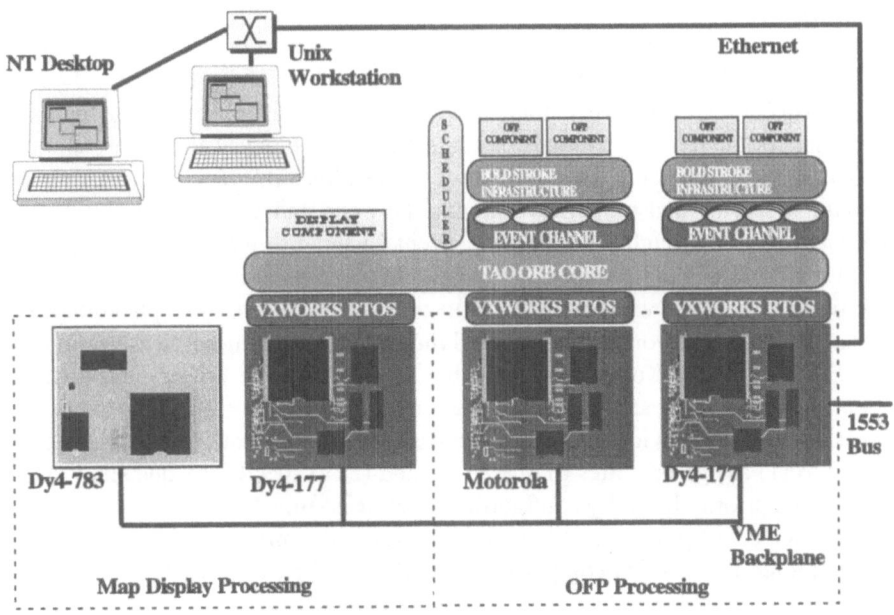

Fig. 1. Open Experimentation Platform Hardware and Software

COTS OS/Hardware. The COTS hardware and operating system used in the experiments described in Section 3 consisted of a commercial VME-64 chassis with four commercial processor cards, a desktop computer running Windows NT 4.0 used for data gathering and visualization, and a portable UNIX workstation used to load executable programs onto the boards in the VME chassis and as a file server for a digital map display.

Two COTS processor cards, a Dy4-783 and a Dy4-177, performed the map display function. The Dy4-783 card had a memory-mapped display processor and the Dy4-177 card hosted an application component that ran the map display algorithms. The operational flight program (OFP) system was distributed across the remaining two processor cards. The first system card was a 200 MHz, PowerPC 604, Motorola card, which ran the experimental system on the VxWorks [26] 5.3.1 real-time operating system. The second system card was a 100 MHz, PowerPC 603, Dy4-177 card. This card contained a MIL-STD-1553 MUX bus interface card and the Ethernet interface for the VME chassis. All external communication, *e.g.*, over the 1553 bus to connected sensors and actuators (called *remote terminals*) in the aircraft, or over the VME backplane to diagnostic and debug systems, went through this card. This card also controlled timing for frame sequencing and display updates, upon which operation rates on the Motorola card depended.

Information Directorate, Air Force Research Labs (AFRL), Wright-Patterson Air Force Base, Dayton, Ohio. Portions of the TAO ORB and the Bold Stroke open experimentation platform were developed under support from DARPA ITO.

DOC Middleware. The COTS distributed object computing middleware used for the Adaptive Software Flight Demonstration (ASFD) demonstration was based on the TAO 1.2 implementation of Real-time CORBA [10,9]. The TAO Real-time Event Channel [11] is a publish/subscribe service that mediates communication between components acting as proxies for (1) remote terminals that interact with the physical environment and (2) the operations that process the data. Sensor proxies flush relevant data to a Bold Stroke *replication service* that propagates the data between endsystems. The sensor proxies then *push* events through the Real-time Event Channel to the processing operations[5]. Operation deadlines in the experimental system correspond to the points in time when their respective output values must be delivered and flushed to the replication service.

The Kokyu framework provides scheduling and dispatching services to TAO's Real-time Event Channel. Kokyu is responsible for (1) isolating critical processing from non-critical processing and (2) making the remaining CPU time available to non-critical processing. Kokyu provides these services via a scheduling strategy with which it is configured to (1) assign priorities to operations and (2) to specify the queueing discipline used at each priority level. By configuring TAO's Real-time Event Channel according to the specified set of priorities and queue disciplines, the middleware services described above enforce the mission computing system's real-time QoS assurances and performance.

Bold Stroke Domain-Specific Middleware. The open experimentation platform for our work is based on the Bold Stroke domain-specific middleware [23,24]. Bold Stroke uses COTS hardware and middleware to produce a standards-based component architecture for military avionics mission computing capabilities, such as navigation, data link management, and weapons control. A driving objective of Bold Stroke is to support reusable product-line applications, leading to a highly configurable application component model and supporting reusable middleware services, such replication and persistence services.

Bold Stroke has been developed and deployed using DOC middleware components and services based on the TAO Real-time ORB, the TAO Real-time Event Channel, and the Kokyu framework. Bold Stroke uses TAO's Real-time Event Channel atop the TAO Object Request Broker (ORB) to communicate between components (1) on the same endsystem and (2) distributed across different endsystems. The Kokyu scheduler maintains information required for priority-preserving dispatching, which in the experimental framework described in Section 3 was performed in dispatching queues within the TAO Real-time Event Channel.

OFP Application. The operational flight program (OFP) application used as the basis of our multi-paradigm scheduling experiments provides avionics mission computing capabilities for an AV-8B (Harrier) aircraft. It is a distributed operational flight program (OFP) implemented in C++ using the Boeing AV-8 Open Systems Core Avionics Requirements airframe [27] and the Boeing Bold Stroke domain-specific middleware. All major operational flight program (OFP) components were implemented as periodically invoked operations, executed by event consumers. Each operation belongs to one of two equivalence classes:

---

[5] Event channels are used in Bold Stroke to minimize coupling between application components.

- **Hard real-time (HRT) for critical operations**—Critical operations in the HRT class are those whose failure to meet any given deadline has potentially significant consequences for the correctness of the application.
- **Soft real-time (SRT) for non-critical operations**—Deadline success for the non-critical SRT operations is desirable but not strictly mandatory.

There were five pre-defined rates of execution in the system: 40 Hz, 20 Hz, 10 Hz, 5 Hz, and 1 Hz. Each operation ran at one of these rates. For the Adaptive Software Flight Demonstration (ASFD) open experimentation platform, new 20 Hz SRT functions were added to the operational flight program (OFP), including routes and steering components, as well as a digital map display.

3 Relevant Experimental Characteristics

This section outlines experimental factors relevant to analysis and modeling of the observed performance differences between Maximum Urgency First (MUF) [6], and Rate Monotonic Scheduling (RMS)+Minimum Laxity First (MLF) [22] under representative environmental conditions with varying *load* and *load jitter* on the open experimentation platform described in Section 2. The remainder of this section describes the new hypotheses we investigated for this paper, the variables that were controlled, and the variables that were measured in our studies.

3.1 Hypotheses

The hypotheses explored in these studies are shown in Table 1. This table also notes how we conducted our analysis to evaluate each hypothesis. To test these hypotheses

Table 1. Hypotheses Studied and Analysis Approaches

Hypothesis	Analysis
The efficiency and effectiveness of each scheduling strategy are sensitive to *environmental* factors, *i.e.*, load and load jitter.	We examine both efficiency and effectiveness across widely varying load and load jitter conditions.
Performance differences between similar scheduling strategies may correlate more strongly with mechanism-level factors than policy-level factors.	We examine performance of similar strategies in conditions under which behavior is expected to be similar by policy alone.
Performance differences show meaningful correlation to a plausible model for mechanism-level behavior.	We compare fine-grain differences in performance data to differences in mechanisms and their plausible responses to variations in environmental conditions, *i.e.*, load and load jitter.

through study of the empirical differences between the similar RMS+MLF and MUF hybrid static/dynamic scheduling strategies, we examined detailed operation dispatching success and failure data collected on the experimentation platform described in Section 2.

The data came from identical trials using each of the following canonical scheduling strategies:

– **Rate Monotonic Scheduling (RMS)** [21], which is a purely static strategy that assigns priorities in rate order and manages requests at each priority level in first-in-first-out (FIFO) order. We examined RMS performance for comparison as it gives insight into the bounds of sensitivity to increasing load and load jitter.
– **Maximum Urgency First (MUF)** [6], which is a hybrid static/dynamic strategy that assigns static priorities by operation criticality, and schedules within each static priority by minimum laxity.
– **Rate Monotonic Scheduling (RMS)+Minimum Laxity First (MLF)** [22], is also a hybrid static/dynamic strategy, which first schedules critical operations according to rate and then non-critical operations at lower priority according to laxity.

We selected these strategies for further analysis since our earlier work [2] showed them to be the most applicable to operational flight program (OFP) application requirements to support both hard real-time (HRT) and soft real-time (SRT) operations under a range of load and load jitter conditions.

3.2   Controlled Variables

To manage the effects of varying load and load jitter in the more diverse operating environments in which they are being asked to run, many next-generation DRE systems must satisfy resource demands that

1. vary overall at longer time-scales across a series of stable epochs of operation and
2. produce different degrees of execution time jitter in invocation-to-invocation demands across shorter time-scales within each epoch.

To model variations in both overall processing load and the degree of execution time jitter imposed by these types of demands, the experiments on which the analysis presented here is based added operations to a sequence of twelve epochs of operation, each representing a distinct *operating region* [4] numbered 0–11, as shown in Figure 2 [2]. In this section, we

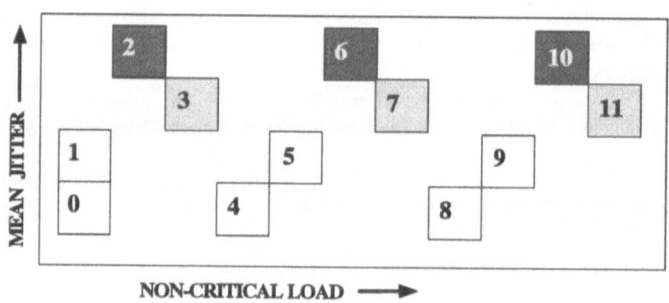

Fig. 2. Operating Regions

summarize the experimental characteristics of these operating regions[6] to characterize the observed differences between the RMS+MLF and MUF scheduling strategies.

As we discussed in Section 1.3, the following experimental characteristics are relevant to examine the differences in performance between the RMS+MLF and MUF scheduling strategies:

– The sequence of resource requests for both critical and non-critical operations
– The pseudo-random sequence of jitter added to critical and non-critical operations
– The relative ordering of critical and non-critical request partitions and
– The ordering of non-critical operations.

We now consider each of these characteristics in turn:

Sequence of Resource Requests. Resource requests were made at each of the following rates: 20 Hz, 10 Hz, 5 Hz, and 1 Hz. The phasing of application operations was organized to reduce contention for the CPU overall, and to provide regular windows of low contention for the CPU, in which to extract collected data without interfering with the experiment itself. Figure 3 [2] shows the resulting framing of operations in the executing operational flight program (OFP).

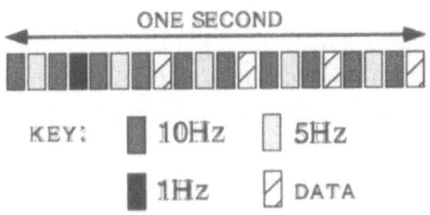

Fig. 3. Framing of Operation Requests and Metrics Data Extraction Points

In addition to the fixed operational flight program (OFP) operations, which were present and active in each operating region, we introduced chains of additional 20 Hz soft real-time (SRT) navigation route leg[7] updates to each operating region. Computing route legs was implemented with each route segment successfully completed requesting the next segment, up to the length of the chain. We varied the length of the request chain to move from lowest to highest *fundamental* non-critical load. We did this incrementally from region 1 to region 11, while keeping the fundamental critical load constant across operating regions. We kept the non-critical load the same in region 0 and region 1 to ensure that we compared the effects of two different levels of jitter with no change in fundamental load in at least one case.

---

[6] The operating regions selected for these experiments are designed to provide a representative but manageable set of distinct combinations of load and execution jitter, across a range of load and jitter of interest to the avionics mission computing application.

[7] A route leg is a segment of a navigation route computed in one operation invocation.

The key observation regarding the analysis presented in this paper is that both the RMS+MLF and MUF scheduling strategies used the same framing sequence (shown in Figure 3) and the same sequence of load. The same load in both critical and non-critical operations was therefore offered for each strategy, so we can meaningfully compare the performance differences between the strategies.

Pseudo-Random Jitter Sequence. To examine the effects of (1) varying levels of load jitter across similar fundamental loads and (2) similar levels of jitter across varying non-critical loads, we added an additional hard real-time (HRT) event consumer to the second Dy4-177 card at each of the following rates: 10 Hz, 5 Hz, and 1 Hz hard real-time (HRT). In these experiments, the additional operations acted as surrogates for the workload variation that would normally be associated with a distributed production operational flight program (OFP) in a variable environment. The CPU utilization by these additional hard real-time (HRT) event consumers was randomized across a given range in each operating region, with the range of variation cycling every four regions through the following:

1. 0 msec (lowest mean and lowest variance)
2. 0–5 msec (medium-low mean, medium variance)
3. 5–10 msec (highest mean, medium variance)
4. 0–10 msec (medium-high mean, highest variance)

Table 2 summarizes the hard real-time (HRT) execution jitter added to each operating region. *Average* jitter was thus lowest in regions 0, 4, and 8, higher in regions 1, 5, and 9, higher still in regions 3, 7, and 11, and highest in regions 2, 6, and 10. The *range* of jitter variability was lowest in regions 0, 4, and 8, was comparable in odd-numbered regions, and was highest in regions 2, 6, and 10.

Table 2. Load Jitter For Each Operating Region

Regions	Variable HRT Execution
0,4,8	0 msec
1,5,9	0 to 5 msec
2,6,10	5 to 10 msec
3,7,11	0 to 10 msec

The key observation for the analysis presented in this paper is that the execution time variability within each range was implemented as a pseudo-random sequence initialized with the same seed for each strategy. The load and load jitter were therefore identical for the RMS+MLF and MUF strategies.

Relative Ordering of Request Partitions. By policy, both the RMS+MLF and MUF scheduling strategies (1) partition critical operations from non-critical operations, and (2) schedule operations in the critical partition in preference to operations in the non-critical partition. Moreover, these policies were implemented using thread priorities from a preemptive multi-tasking real-time OS (VxWorks) as described in Section 2. The relative ordering of request partitions was therefore also the same for RMS+MLF and MUF.

Ordering of Non-Critical Operations. By policy, both RMS+MLF and MUF place all non-critical operations in a lowest-priority queue managed by operation laxity. The same values for relevant operation characteristics (*i.e.*, period and execution time) were used for each operation under each strategy. The non-critical operations were therefore handled the same way under the RMS+MLF and MUF strategies.

3.3   Measured Variables

Section 3.2 showed that at a policy level the RMS+MLF and MUF strategies were indistinguishable under the *controlled* variables of the experiment. Below, we examine the *measured* variables of the experiment, which distinguish the behavior of the RMS+MLF and MUF strategies. We also offer insights into the possible reasons for those differences in Section 5.

To measure the response of each strategy to the varying load and load jitter described in Section 3.2, we instrumented the application and middleware using lightweight, high-resolution time stamps to characterize system behavior. We focus here on the missed and made operation deadlines.

The missed and made operation deadlines offer two kinds of information. First, we can assess the real-time *effectiveness*[8] of a scheduling strategy by measuring the number (and category) of deadlines made. Our definition of real-time effectiveness differs from conventional notions of throughput: within a sample, each SRT operations is counted only if it made its deadline, and no HRT operation deadlines were missed in the entire sample. The higher the total number of soft real-time (SRT) deadlines that were made without missing any hard real-time (HRT) deadlines, the higher the level of performance of the strategy. Second, we can assess the real-time *efficiency* of the scheduling strategies by also examining the *fraction* of SRT operation deadlines that were made. Efficiency as we define it is simply the SRT effectiveness divided by the total number of SRT operations, *i.e.*, the *offered load*. The higher the fraction of soft real-time (SRT) operation deadlines that were made, again without missing any hard real-time (HRT) deadlines, the higher the efficiency of a strategy.

In general, the measured efficiency is most divergent when the offered load has significance, *i.e.*, when the SRT and HRT operations together exceed the feasible utilization bound for the CPU, as in operating regions 7 through 11. Otherwise, the effectiveness measure is sufficient to distinguish the behaviors of the scheduling strategies. The distribution of efficiency values, as shown in Section 4.2, provides insight into the finer-grained behavior of each strategy. In aggregate, this information can be used to profile the response of a strategy to the offered load and load jitter in each operating region.

---

[8] The definition of effectiveness used here is that of the avionics mission computing application studied: although other definitions are possible, we do not consider them in this paper.

4   Empirical Results

We now present results from new analysis of the trials described in Section 3, using the open experimental platform described in Section 2. Specifically, we systematically examine the hypotheses described in Table 1 and note how our observations do or do not support the hypothesis in each case. We thus empirically evaluate the differences between the RMS+MLF and MUF strategies in practice. In the process, we also uncover insights relevant to developers of mission-critical DRE systems.

4.1   Efficiency and Effectiveness of SRT Operation Dispatching

Hypothesis. The efficiency and effectiveness of each scheduling strategy are sensitive to *environmental* factors, *i.e.*, load and load jitter.

Overview of the Analysis. To evaluate this hypothesis, we examine how the efficiency and effectiveness of each strategy varied with changing load and load jitter. In addition to RMS+MLF and MUF (which are similar hybrid static/dynamic strategies), we also examine the behavior of the canonical RMS static strategy for purposes of comparison.

Synopsis of Results. Figure 4 shows the relative sensitivity of RMS, RMS+MLF, and MUF to variations in load and load jitter, such as might be expected to occur from variations in a next-generation DRE system's environment. The vertical axis in Figure 4 shows an average weighted soft real-time (SRT) performance function, over the different operating regions described in Section 3.2, which are shown on the horizontal axis. For each sample, a value of zero was assigned if any hard real-time (HRT) deadlines were missed in that sample, or otherwise the value was the number of soft real-time (SRT) deadlines made. An average was then taken over those values in each operating region, for each strategy.

The RMS strategy showed increasing performance across operating regions 0 through 6. It then rapidly decreased through operating region 7 to minimal performance in operating regions 8 through 11. The RMS+MLF and MUF strategies both showed cyclic patterns of performance across operating regions 0 through 11, with the cycle spanning four operating regions.

In addition to the SRT performance differences indicated in Figure 4, we note that while RMS offered the best SRT performance in operating regions 0 through 7, in operating region 7 RMS showed 5 samples with missed HRT deadlines (in operating regions 8 through 11 RMS showed missed HRT deadlines in each sample). We also note that while MUF performed slightly better than RMS+MLF in operating region 9, MUF had a single sample with a single missed HRT deadline late in the operating region.

Analysis of Results. Figure 4 shows strong correlation between the performance of scheduling strategies and environmental factors. More interestingly, the results discussed above correlate with different factors for RMS than the RMS+MLF or MUF, and correlate with the same factor for RMS+MLF and MUF. In particular, the RMS performance correlated strongly with varying total load, but had no observable correlation with the variations in load jitter. RMS+MLF and MUF performance showed strong correlation

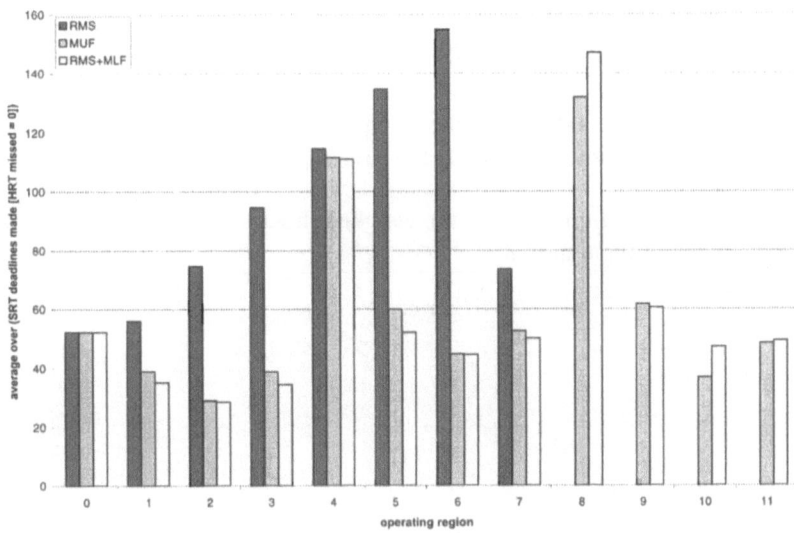

Fig. 4. Relative Performance of RMS, RMS+MLF, and MUF

with load jitter, but only weak correlation (*i.e.*, amplitude of the performance cycle) with variations in system load. Moreover, the *difference* in performance between RMS+MLF and MUF varied meaningfully as a function of the additional jitter in resource request execution times, although the offered load and load jitter of resource requests were kept the same for the two strategies in each operating region of our experiments.

Summary. The results above support the hypothesis that the efficiency and effectiveness of each scheduling strategy are sensitive to *environmental* factors, and refine the hypothesis with respect to which factors are the most relevant to each of the strategies studied. In the ASFD program, we collaborated with DRE system developers to identify canonical scheduling strategies and important environmental factors and to examine the sensitivities of those in realistic operating environments. Furthermore the results presented above identify which strategies performed best under different environmental conditions. In Section 5 we extend these observations and make observations for mission-critical COTS-based DRE systems in general, to ensure environmental factors are adequately addressed in selecting middleware scheduling strategies.

4.2   Mechanism-Level Correlation

Hypothesis. Performance differences between similar scheduling strategies may correlate more strongly with mechanism-level factors than policy-level factors.

Overview of the Analysis. To evaluate this hypothesis, we examine how differences in mechanism-level factors correlated with differences in the performance of each strategy. We focus on the extent to which each strategy meets non-critical deadlines under different conditions of load and load jitter where policy differences do not distinguish the strategies. As we argued in Section 1.3, there is no meaningful correlation between policy in RMS+MLF and MUF and the observed performance differences, under the experimental conditions described in Section 3.2. We therefore focus on whether meaningful correlation can be established between differences in the mechanisms used to implement RMS+MLF and MUF and the observed performance.

Synopsis of Results. Figure 5 shows the weighted fraction of SRT deadlines made for each sample in operating region 8.

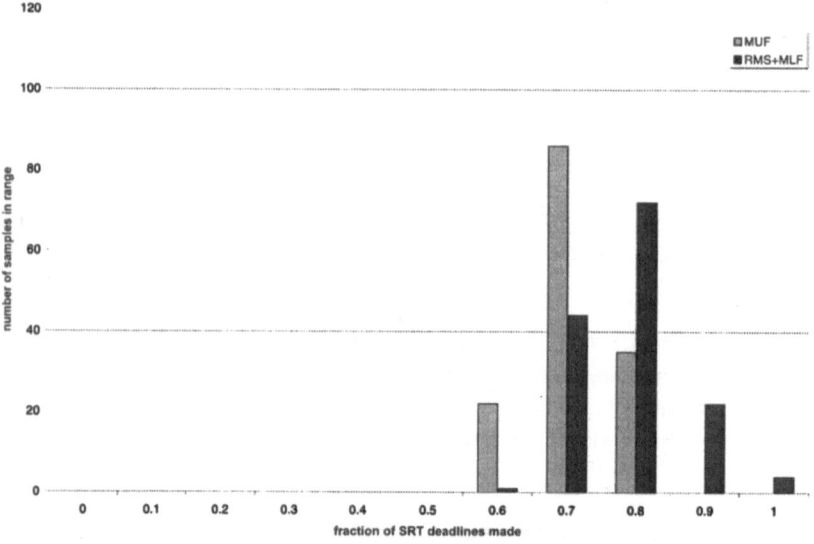

Fig. 5. Weighted SRT Fraction in Operating Region 8

We note two main characteristics of operating region 8:

1. As with each of the operating regions 7 through 11, the total load is above the feasible threshold, while the critical load remains feasible. Figure 5 illustrates two important similarities between performance of the RMS+MLF and MUF strategies under these conditions. First, both strategies achieved high *levels* of SRT deadline success, with no missed HRT deadlines.
2. The *distribution* of values is similar and is reasonably well bounded in each case. MUF showed slightly more variation in its SRT performance values, and consistently exhibited slightly lower levels of success than RMS+MLF.

Figure 6 shows the weighted fraction of SRT deadlines made for each sample in operating region 9. Operating region 9 had slightly higher total load than region 8, but more importantly had an additional medium-low (0-5 msec) level of load jitter.

Under these conditions, both strategies showed lower average levels of SRT deadline success, and a wider range of values overall. Interestingly, while the overall ranges of values were similar, MUF showed a much more continuous distribution of values than RMS+MLF. Interestingly, while MUF had slightly lower minimum and maximum values, its performance on average was better than that of RMS+MLF. We also note a single sample in which MUF missed one HRT deadline, toward the end of the time spent in operating region 9.

Analysis of Results. In each of the graphs in this section, the level and distribution of SRT performance values distinguish the strategies in ways that map well to mechanism-level differences. For MUF, the ordering of HRT operations in a dynamic queue necessarily adds overhead compared to the best-case performance of multiple FIFO queues at different thread priorities, which is how RMS+MLF manages its HRT operations. As discussed previously, the policy differences in the absence of other factors indicate the type of similar performance seen in Figure 5, albeit with a downward shift in the MUF values due to mechanism-level dynamic scheduling overhead.

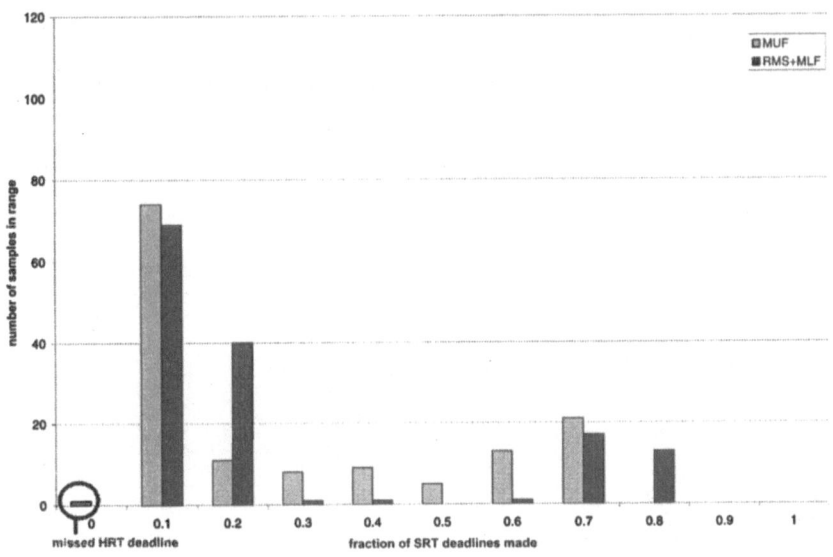

Fig. 6. Weighted SRT Fraction in Operating Region 9

Consider the pacing of operation dispatch requests under conditions of little or no load jitter, and the handling of requests in priority order. These factors offer evidence that in Figure 5 we do in fact see the best-case mechanism-level performance of the RMS+MLF strategy, where in each 20Hz frame the highest priority operations all run to completion, then the next highest priority, and so forth. In figure 6, we see evidence that the performance differences indicates pulses of preemption overhead, contributing to higher overhead on average in RMS+MLF. We note especially the reasonably periodic and bi-modal distribution of the RMS+MLF performance values. This suggests that the medium-low level of load jitter in operating region 9 resulted in non-optimal arrival patterns with lower priority requests arriving immediately before a higher priority request. In practice systems are architected to avoid realizing the worst case request arrival patterns which result in a critical instant [21]. The degree to which one succeeds is affected by variations in job arrival and processing times.

Summary. The results above support the hypothesis that performance differences between similar scheduling strategies may correlate more strongly with mechanism-level factors than policy-level factors. We focused our attention on implementation mechanisms of scheduling strategies in the ASFD operating environment. In doing so, we correlated different mechanism-level responses to environmental factors with real-time behvaior. We found that benchmarking canonical scheduling strategies in the ASFD operating environment was essential to evaluate our middleware scheduling implementation. Section 5 describes recommendations to developers of next-generation DRE systems based on these observations.

4.3   Correlation with a Plausible Model

Hypothesis. Performance differences show meaningful correlation to a plausible model for mechanism-level behavior.

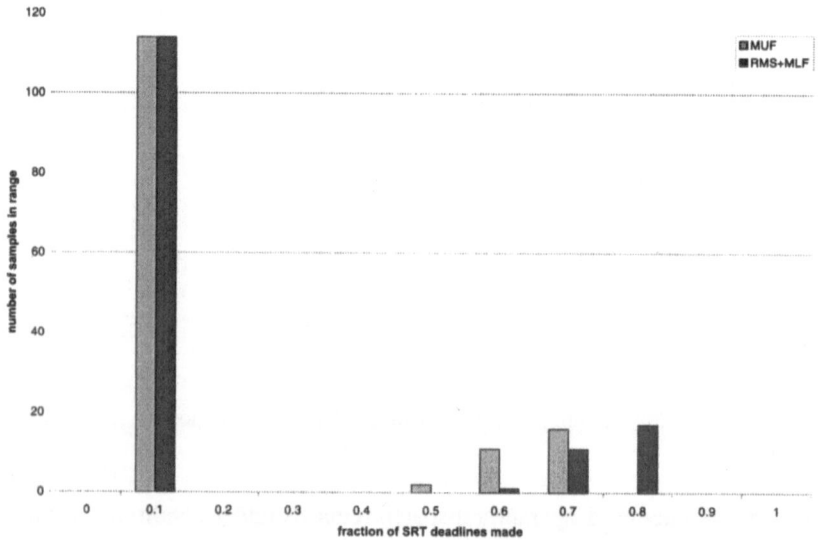

Fig. 7. Weighted SRT Fraction in Operating Region 10

Overview of the Analysis. To evaluate this hypothesis, we compare fine-grain differences in performance data to differences in mechanisms and their plausible responses to variations in environmental conditions, *i.e.*, load and load jitter. In particular, we examine weighted SRT performance in operating regions 8 through 11, each of which represents a canonical case of load and load jitter conditions.

Synopsis of Results. Figure 7 shows the weighted fraction of SRT deadlines made for each sample in operating region 10. A similar relationship between high jitter and low jitter to performance of the strategies is shown in operating regions 8 and 10. MUF values are offset slightly downward in region 10, and the overall distributions of values are narrow, albeit at lower levels than in region 8.

Figure 8 shows the weighted fraction of SRT deadlines made for each sample in operating region 11. A similar relationship between medium-low and medium-high jitter to performance of the strategies is shown in operating region 11. MUF values are distributed more continuously than those of RMS+MLF.

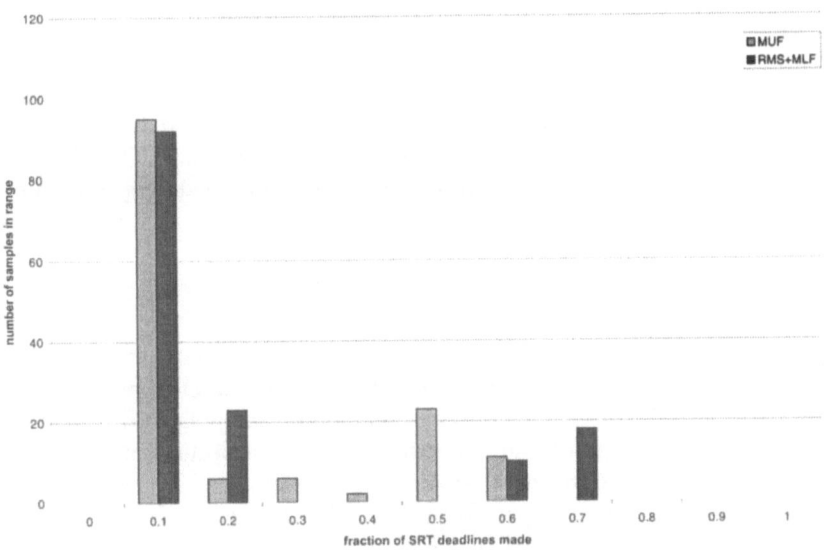

Fig. 8. Weighted SRT Fraction in Operating Region 11

Analysis of Results. In each of the graphs in this section, and those shown in Section 4.2, the performance differences between the strategies correlate strongly with the expected response of mechanism-level factors to the load and load jitter conditions in each operating region. Specifically, it appears that a phasing effect in the pacing of HRT operations due to jitter is responsible for these results, with RMS+MLF suffering little preemption overhead in the zero-jitter regions (0,4,8), higher preemption overhead in the regions with medium-low or medium-high jitter (1,3,5,7,9,11), and then low preemption overhead again in the high-jitter regions (2,6,10).

Summary. The results above support the hypothesis that performance differences show meaningful correlation to a plausible model for mechanism-level behavior. Our observations suggest that intermediate levels of jitter introduced experiments described in Section 3 led to greater overhead of the RMS+MLF mechanisms. We attribute this effect to greater preemption and context switching overhead as a result of a form of phasing in the arrival of HRT dispatch requests–as the jitter was increased or decreased away from medium levels, RMS+MLF showed less distribution in its SRT deadline success values overall. In Section 5, we offer recommendations based on our experiences establishing the empirical basis for (and constructing) this model, identify key elements of the model, and suggest further hypotheses and experiments to validate the model as future work.

5   Lessons Learned and Future Research

Below, we present key observations and recommendations based on our empirical results from Section 4. These observations and recommendations apply both to the particular avionics mission computing application we have studied and to a larger family of mission-critical DRE systems. While our work focused on event channel mediated interactions between distributed objects, we expect our results to be reasonably applicable to a broader class of interactions based on periodic priority-based CORBA scheduling models. We also describe future work to validate a model for scheduling variability based on our observations.

5.1   Summary of Lessons Learned

As we noted in Section 1.1, the use of COTS operating systems and middleware is highly desirable for building and maintaining mission-critical DRE systems in a cost-effective manner. However, COTS software cannot simply be applied to applications with specialized processing requirements, without careful empirical study of the implications of the specific policies and mechanisms employed within those systems. In particular, real-time applications have stringent requirements that may vary with environmental stimuli, system load or operator intervention.

Fundamental difficulties in providing predictable behavior of complex systems when they are under moderate to heavy loads can compound this problem. Individual policies and mechanisms, such as those for the scheduling strategies we have studied, may exhibit differing overheads and sensitivities to environmental conditions. However, with judicious use of COTS building blocks and armed with a core understanding of the underlying mechanisms it is possible to build high-performance, real-time applications. Our research has identified several key areas where developers can improve system behavior and predictability:

• **Observation.** The efficiency and effectiveness of each scheduling strategy are sensitive to *environmental* factors.

- **Recommendation.** Middleware researchers and DRE system developers should collaborate to ensure that (1) the environmental sensitivities of particular scheduling strategies are well characterized in realistic operating environments, and (2) the factors present in a particular DRE system's particular operating environment are used to choose between scheduling strategies for that system.

- **Observation.** Performance differences between similar scheduling strategies may correlate more strongly with mechanism-level factors than policy-level factors. In particular, it is not valid to base selection of a scheduling policy on a model of scheduling behavior unless the model, the application requirements, and the actual behavior of mechanisms used to implement the model are sufficiently coherent.

- **Recommendation.** *Middleware researchers* should focus attention on mechanism-level implementation details of scheduling strategies in COTS-based environments, to offer (1) robust real-time assurances and (2) control over trade-offs for optimization. Moreover, *developers* of COTS-based DRE systems should benchmark their scheduling strategies in operationally meaningful environments, to evaluate the extent to which a particular middleware implementation has addressed these issues.

- **Observation.** Performance differences between the RMS+MLF and MUF strategies show meaningful correlation to a plausible model for mechanism-level behavior. Specifically, our results suggest that preemption and queue overhead effects are crucial factors for modeling the performance differences between these strategies.

- **Recommendation.** Middleware researchers and developers of COTS-based mission-critical DRE systems should collaborate to construct, extend, and empirically evaluate detailed models for *mechanism-level* scheduling and dispatching behavior in COTS hardware and software environments. Moreover, these models should be evaluated rigorously in terms of critical assurances and non-critical performance. In particular, as preferred models emerge from this effort, additional attention should be paid to refining, cross-validating models across applications and domains, and unifying models where possible to attain a more coherent picture of COTS-based real-time QoS management. This larger-scale effort will in turn lead to higher-quality models and techniques for managing real-time QoS in mission-critical COTS-based DRE systems.

5.2   Future Work

Our experimental results in Section 4 validated the ability of scheduling frameworks to adapt strategies to changing load and operation mode. However, they also raised issues related to the sensitivity of the mechanisms used in the operational environment. It is common practice when designing real-time systems to select a strategy based on worst-case analysis. However, our results show that this is not necessarily optimal nor desirable. In practice, different policies and their implementation exhibit varying overheads and sensitivities to environmental conditions.

For example, in theory, we would expect that partitioning the HRT and SRT operations by scheduling priority would protect the critical operations, thus ensuring they always meet their deadlines. This is not the case, however, as shown by the missed critical deadline in operating region 9 for MUF (see Section 4.2). We would also suspect that given a feasible schedule for the critical tasks the use of a non-preemptive dispatching strategy for the critical operations as provided by the MUF implementation would result in overall lower overhead as the overhead of preemption is not necessary nor will queue depths be large for our structured environment. While this appears to be true for operating regions 0 through 7, under heavy loads it breaks down.

These observations lead to the identification of several key aspects of the system that contribute to variability of the results:

- Operation scheduling parameters
- Preemption model based on thread priorities and request arrival
- Queueing discipline for ordering within each thread priority level and
- Mechanism overhead in response to the above factors.

We propose these factors as the basis for a mechanism-level model for variability of different scheduling strategies, which we will evaluate as future work. Specifically, we will examine the following hypotheses regarding the MUF and RMS+MLF strategies–and the experiment following each hypothesis–to validate this middleware scheduling model:

• **Hypothesis 1.** *Overhead differences in the middleware and OS can be shown to account for the observed latency differences between the strategies.* To validate this hypothesis, we are devising experiments to measure and compare key sources of overhead, such as queue depths, queue ordering cost, thread context switch cost, degree of preemption, in the middleware and OS under experimental conditions comparable to those described in Section 3.

• **Hypothesis 2.** *The question of whether (a) thread preemption and context switching overhead or (b) overhead from ordering operations in a dynamic queue is greater under each distinct set of load and load jitter conditions, can be shown to account for the performance differences between the RMS+MLF and MUF strategies under those conditions.* To validate this hypothesis, we are devising experiments to measure and compare the complete preemption timeline for all operations to the measured middleware and OS overhead factors under comparable experimental conditions to those described in Section 3.

6   Related Work

Distributed real-time and embedded (DRE) computing is an emerging field of study. An increasing number of research efforts are focusing on end-to-end quality of service (QoS) properties, such as timeliness, by integrating quality of service (QoS) management policies and mechanisms, *e.g.*, real-time scheduling into standards-based middleware, such as Real-time CORBA. Pioneering efforts are beginning to extend this field by providing meta-capabilities, such as configuration flexibility, reflection, and ultimately adaptation, while still meeting strict quality of service (QoS) assurances. This section describes representative work that is related to our Kokyu framework.

Avionics Platform Research. The following two branches of research are endeavoring to make quality of service (QoS)-managed system infrastructure a prevalent feature of avionics computing systems:

• **Avionics Domain Platform Research.** Standardized avionics platforms, such as the ARINC Avionics Application Software Standard Interface (APEX) for Integrated Modular Avionics (IMA) [28], provide quality of service (QoS) assurances for systems in the avionics domain. McElhone [29] examines the question of how to support operations with soft real-time constraints and possibly long running or variable length computations, in canonical avionics-specific platforms, such as IMA.

• **Open Systems Avionics Research.** Sharp, Doerr, *et al.* [23,24] address the challenge of retaining key quality of service (QoS) assurances in avionics systems, while improving modularity, reuse, cycle times, and cost across families of flight software applications. The Bold Stroke avionics domain-specific middleware described in Section 2 has emerged and evolved through that work. Our research on flexible and adaptive real-time scheduling and dispatching was conducted within the context of the Bold Stroke infrastructure, and has contributed to its evolution.

CORBA-Related QoS Middleware Research. There is a growing body of work related to CORBA-based quality of service (QoS) middleware. We focus below on related CORBA middleware research efforts that address scheduling or other forms of adaptive quality of service (QoS) management.

• **Standard Specifications.** The OMG Real-Time CORBA 1.0 [30] specification includes interfaces for an optional scheduling service that can be implemented readily using Kokyu's flexible scheduling and dispatching capabilities. We plan to release an implementation of this service built using the Kokyu framework. Emerging COTS middleware standards, such as Dynamic Scheduling Real-Time the Common Object Request Broker Architecture (CORBA) 2.0 (DSRTCORBA) [31], as well as the non-CORBA Real-Time Specification for Java^{TM} (RTSJ) [32], generalize the possible range of scheduler implementations, rather than specifying a particular scheduling approach.

• **BBN QuO.** The *Quality Objects* (QuO) distributed object middleware is developed at BBN Technologies [33]. QuO is based on CORBA and provides the following support for agile applications running in wide-area networks: (1) *run-time performance tuning and configuration* through the specification of *quality of service (QoS) regions*, behavior alternatives, and reconfiguration strategies that allows the QuO run-time to adaptively trigger reconfiguration as system conditions change (represented by transitions between operating regions) and (2) *feedback* across software and distribution boundaries based on a control loop in which client applications and server objects request levels of service and are notified of changes in service. We have integrated Kokyu with the QuO framework, as described in [4].

- **UCSB Realize.** The Realize project at UCSB has developed an approach based on object migration and replication, to improve performance of soft real-time distributed systems [34,35]. This approach constitutes a higher level of adaptive control for soft real-time quality of service (QoS) management, and is complementary to Kokyu.

- **UCI TMO.** The Time-triggered Message-triggered Objects (TMO) project [36] at the University of California, Irvine, supports the integrated design of distributed OO systems and real-time simulators of their operating environments. The TMO model provides structured timing semantics for distributed real-time object-oriented applications by extending conventional invocation semantics for object methods, *i.e.*, CORBA operations, to include (1) invocation of time-triggered operations based on system times and (2) invocation and time bounded execution of conventional message-triggered operations. TMO, Kokyu, and TAO are complementary technologies because (1) TMO and Kokyu extend and generalize TAO's existing time-based invocation capabilities and (2) TAO provides a configurable and dependable connection infrastructure needed by the TMO CNCM service.

Non-CORBA QoS Research. In addition to CORBA-related quality of service (QoS) middleware research, our work on Kokyu is also related to the following quality of service (QoS) research conducted outside CORBA:

- **Utah CRM.** Regehr and Lepreau [37] propose the CPU Resource Manager (CRM), a middleware service for managing processor allocation using scheduling abstractions provided by Commercial off-the-shelf (COTS) operating systems. They examine different kinds of quality of service (QoS) reservations and propose a unifying low-level middleware abstraction layer to shield developers from accidental complexities produced by variations in scheduling abstractions at the operating system level. Our approach focuses on *encapsulation* of scheduling and dispatching policies, and providing flexible infrastructure to allow arbitrary composition of heuristics. Rather than enclosing a known set of common abstractions, our aim is to provide flexible support for diverse and possibly unanticipated combinations of scheduling requirements, mechanisms, and policies in middleware.

- **UCI RED-Linux Scheduling Framework.** Wang, *et al.* [38], at the University of California, Irvine, have proposed a general scheduling framework to unify three distinct kinds of scheduling approaches: *priority-based*, *time-based*, and *share-based*. They decompose scheduling behavior into policy (*allocator*) and mechanism (*dispatching*) components, which are similar to the Kokyu scheduling service framework. They have implemented the dispatching portion of this framework in their real-time extensions to the Linux kernel, called RED-Linux.

- **Feedback Control Scheduling.** One of the most important areas of related work is the pioneering research on feedback control real-time scheduling (FCS), conducted by Stankovic, Lu, *et al.*, at the University of Virginia. FCS applies control theory to real-time scheduling [39,40,41,42,43,44] for soft real-time systems, to reduce the number of missed deadlines at run-time. We consider the FCS work highly complementary to our efforts to model, and distinguish through empirical study, strategies for real-time assurance and performance optimization.

7   Concluding Remarks

New increasingly non-deterministic types of processing, such as video and imaging [4], are being targeted for transition to existing mission-critical distributed real-time and embedded (DRE) systems. In recent work [2], we showed how Kokyu's ability to manage variations in execution load and load jitter through alternative scheduling strategies increases the applicability of these techniques to DRE systems built using COTS software architectures. This paper extended those results by further analysis that offers more exact guidance on choice of scheduling strategies to developers of mission-critical DRE systems. In particular, this paper presented new empirical evidence that the observed performance differences between the RMS+MLF and MUF strategies are due to mechanism-level effects in the face of load jitter, rather than policy-level differences in the capabilities of the scheduling strategies.

Acknowledgments. We gratefully acknowledge the support and direction of the AFRL program manager for ASFD, Kenneth Littlejohn, and of Boeing Bold Stroke Principal Investigators Bryan Doerr and David Sharp. In addition, we would like to thank Greg Holtmeyer for his contributions to this research.

References

1. C. D. Gill, R. Cytron, and D. C. Schmidt, "Middleware Scheduling Optimization Techniques for Distributed Real-Time and Embedded Systems," in *Proceedings of the 7th Workshop on Object-oriented Real-time Dependable Systems*, (San Diego, CA), IEEE, Jan. 2002.
2. C. Gill, D. C. Schmidt, and R. Cytron, "Multi-Paradigm Scheduling for Distributed Real-Time Embedded Computing," *IEEE Proceedings Special Issue on Modeling and Design of Embedded Software*, Oct. 2002.
3. C. D. Gill, D. L. Levine, and D. C. Schmidt, "The Design and Performance of a Real-Time CORBA Scheduling Service," *Real-Time Systems, The International Journal of Time-Critical Computing Systems, special issue on Real-Time Middleware*, vol. 20, Mar. 2001.
4. J. Loyall, J. Gossett, C. Gill, R. Schantz, J. Zinky, P. Pal, R. Shapiro, C. Rodrigues, M. Atighetchi, and D. Karr, "Comparing and Contrasting Adaptive Middleware Support in Wide-Area and Embedded Distributed Object Applications," in *Proceedings of the 21st International Conference on Distributed Computing Systems (ICDCS-21)*, pp. 625–634, IEEE, Apr. 2001.
5. D. A. Karr, C. Rodrigues, Y. Krishnamurthy, I. Pyarali, and D. C. Schmidt, "Application of the QuO Quality-of-Service Framework to a Distributed Video Application," in *Proceedings of the 3rd International Symposium on Distributed Objects and Applications*, (Rome, Italy), OMG, Sept. 2001.
6. D. B. Stewart and P. K. Khosla, "Real-Time Scheduling of Sensor-Based Control Systems," in *Real-Time Programming* (W. Halang and K. Ramamritham, eds.), Tarrytown, NY: Pergamon Press, 1992.

7. R. E. Schantz and D. C. Schmidt, "Middleware for Distributed Systems: Evolving the Common Structure for Network-centric Applications," in *Encyclopedia of Software Engineering* (J. Marciniak and G. Telecki, eds.), New York: Wiley & Sons, 2002.
8. M. Henning and S. Vinoski, *Advanced CORBA Programming with C++*. Reading, MA: Addison-Wesley, 1999.
9. Object Management Group, *The Common Object Request Broker: Architecture and Specification, Revision 2.6*, Dec. 2001.
10. D. C. Schmidt, D. L. Levine, and S. Mungee, "The Design and Performance of Real-Time Object Request Brokers," *Computer Communications*, vol. 21, pp. 294–324, Apr. 1998.
11. T. H. Harrison, D. L. Levine, and D. C. Schmidt, "The Design and Performance of a Real-time CORBA Event Service," in *Proceedings of OOPSLA '97*, (Atlanta, GA), pp. 184–199, ACM, Oct. 1997.
12. A. Gokhale and D. C. Schmidt, "Measuring and Optimizing CORBA Latency and Scalability Over High-speed Networks," *Transactions on Computing*, vol. 47, no. 4, 1998.
13. F. Kuhns, D. C. Schmidt, C. O'Ryan, and D. Levine, "Supporting High-performance I/O in QoS-enabled ORB Middleware," *Cluster Computing: the Journal on Networks, Software, and Applications*, vol. 3, no. 3, 2000.
14. C. O'Ryan, F. Kuhns, D. C. Schmidt, O. Othman, and J. Parsons, "The Design and Performance of a Pluggable Protocols Framework for Real-time Distributed Object Computing Middleware," in *Proceedings of the Middleware 2000 Conference*, ACM/IFIP, Apr. 2000.
15. D. C. Schmidt, S. Mungee, S. Flores-Gaitan, and A. Gokhale, "Software Architectures for Reducing Priority Inversion and Non-determinism in Real-time Object Request Brokers," *Journal of Real-time Systems, special issue on Real-time Computing in the Age of the Web and the Internet*, vol. 21, no. 2, 2001.
16. A. B. Arulanthu, C. O'Ryan, D. C. Schmidt, M. Kircher, and J. Parsons, "The Design and Performance of a Scalable ORB Architecture for CORBA Asynchronous Messaging," in *Proceedings of the Middleware 2000 Conference*, ACM/IFIP, Apr. 2000.
17. C. O'Ryan, D. C. Schmidt, F. Kuhns, M. Spivak, J. Parsons, I. Pyarali, and D. L. Levine, "Evaluating Policies and Mechanisms to Support Distributed Real-Time Applications with CORBA," *Concurrency and Computing: Practice and Experience*, vol. 13, no. 2, pp. 507–541, 2001.
18. O. Othman, C. O'Ryan, and D. C. Schmidt, "An Efficient Adaptive Load Balancing Service for CORBA," *IEEE Distributed Systems Online*, vol. 2, Mar. 2001.
19. N. Wang, D. C. Schmidt, O. Othman, and K. Parameswaran, "Evaluating Meta-Programming Mechanisms for ORB Middleware," *IEEE Communication Magazine, special issue on Evolving Communications Software: Techniques and Technologies*, vol. 39, Oct. 2001.
20. A. Gokhale and D. C. Schmidt, "Optimizing a CORBA IIOP Protocol Engine for Minimal Footprint Multimedia Systems," *Journal on Selected Areas in Communications special issue on Service Enabling Platforms for Networked Multimedia Systems*, vol. 17, Sept. 1999.
21. C. Liu and J. Layland, "Scheduling Algorithms for Multiprogramming in a Hard-Real-Time Environment," *JACM*, vol. 20, pp. 46–61, Jan. 1973.
22. J.-Y. Chung, J. W.-S. Liu, and K.-J. Lin, "Scheduling Periodic Jobs that Allow Imprecise Results," *IEEE Transactions on Computers*, vol. 39, pp. 1156–1174, Sept. 1990.
23. D. C. Sharp, "Reducing Avionics Software Cost Through Component Based Product Line Development," in *Proceedings of the 10th Annual Software Technology Conference*, Apr. 1998.
24. B. S. Doerr and D. C. Sharp, "Freeing Product Line Architectures from Execution Dependencies," in *Proceedings of the 11th Annual Software Technology Conference*, Apr. 1999.
25. W.-P. A. F. B. Air Force Research Labs, "Adaptive Software Flight Demonstration (ASFD)." Delivery Order 003 of the WSSTS contract to The Boeing Company, number F33615-97-D-1155, 1999.

26. Wind River Systems, "VxWorks 5.3." www.wrs.com/products/html/vxworks.html.
27. T. B. Company, "Open Systems Core Avionics Requirement (OSCAR)."
    http://www.acq.osd.mil/osjtf/pdf/oscar.pdf.
28. ARINC Incorporated, Annapolis, Maryland, USA, *Document No. 653: Avionics Application
    Software Standard Inteface (Draft 15)*, Jan. 1997.
29. C. McElhone, "Soft Computations within Integrated Avionics Systems," in *Proceedings of
    the IEEE National Aerospace and Electronics Conference (NAECON 2000)*, Oct. 2000.
30. Object Management Group, *Real-time CORBA Joint Revised Submission*, OMG Document
    orbos/99-02-12 ed., Mar. 1999.
31. Object Management Group, *Dynamic Scheduling Real-Time CORBA 2.0 Joint Final Submis-
    sion*, OMG Document orbos/2001-06-09 ed., Apr. 2001.
32. Bollella, Gosling, Brosgol, Dibble, Furr, Hardin, and Turnbull, *The Real-Time Specification
    for Java*. Addison-Wesley, 2000.
33. J. A. Zinky, D. E. Bakken, and R. Schantz, "Architectural Support for Quality of Service for
    CORBA Objects," *Theory and Practice of Object Systems*, vol. 3, no. 1, pp. 1–20, 1997.
34. V. Kalogeraki, P. M. Melliar-Smith, and L. E. Moser, "Dynamic Migration Algorithms for Dis-
    tributed Object Systems," in *21st IEEE International Conference on Distributed Computing
    Systems (ICDCS)*, (Phoenix AZ), IEEE, Apr. 2001.
35. V. Kalogeraki, P. M. Melliar-Smith, and L. E. Moser, "Dynamic Scheduling of Distributed
    Method Invocations," in *21st IEEE Real-Time Systems Symposium*, (Orlando, FL), IEEE,
    Nov. 2000.
36. K. H. K. Kim, "Object Structures for Real-Time Systems and Simulators," *IEEE Computer*,
    pp. 62–70, Aug. 1997.
37. J. Regehr and J. Lepreau, "The Case for Using Middleware to Manage Diverse Soft Real-Time
    Schedulers," in *Proceedings of the International Workshop on Multimedia Middleware (M3W
    '01)*, (Ottawa, Canada), Oct. 2001.
38. Y.-C. Wang and K.-J. Lin, "Implementing A General Real-Time Scheduling Framework in
    the RED-Linux Real-Time Kernel," in *IEEE Real-Time Systems Symposium*, pp. 246–255,
    IEEE, Dec. 1999.
39. C. Lu, J. A. Stankovic, G. Tao, and S. H. Son, "Feedback Control Real-Time Scheduling:
    Framework, Modeling, and Algorithms," *Journal of Real-Time Systems, Special Issue on
    Control-Theoretical Approaches to Real-Time Computing*, 2002, to appear.
40. C. Lu, *Feedback Control Real-Time Scheduling*. PhD thesis, University of Virginia, Char-
    lottesville, VA, May 2001.
41. J. A. Stankovic, T. He, T. F. Abdelzaher, M. Marley, G. Tao, S. H. Son, and C. Lu, "Feedback
    Control Scheduling in Distributed Systems," in *The 22nd IEEE Real-Time Systems Symposium
    (RTSS '01)*, (London UK), Dec. 2001.
42. C. Lu, J. A. Stankovic, T. F. Abdelzaher, G. Tao, S. H. Son, and M. Marley, "Performance
    Specifications and Metrics for Adaptive Real-Time Systems," in *The 21st IEEE Real-Time
    Systems Symposium (RTSS '00)*, (Orlando FL), Dec. 2000.
43. C. Lu, J. A. Stankovic, G. Tao, and S. H. Son, "Design and Evaluation of a Feedback Control
    EDF Scheduling Algorithm," in *The 20th IEEE Real-Time Systems Symposium (RTSS '99)*,
    (Phoenix AZ), Dec. 1999.
44. J. A. Stankovic, C. Lu, S. H. Son, and G. Tao, "The Case for Feedback Control Real-Time
    Scheduling," in *11th EuroMicro Conference on Real-Time Systems*, (York UK), June 1999.

Adding Business Rules and Constraints in Component Based Applications[1]

Antonio Coronato[1], Marco Cinquegrani[1], and Giuseppe De Pietro[2]

Progetto Mezzogiorno, Consiglio Nazionale delle Ricerche, Via Castellino 111, 80131
Napoli, Italy
{coronato.a, cinquegrani.m@irsip.na.cnr.it}
[2]Centro di Ricerca sui Calcolatori Paralleli e i Supercalcolatori, Consiglio Nazionale delle
Ricerche, Via Castellino 111, 80131 Napoli, Italy
{depietro.g@cps.na.cnr.it}

Abstract. Models have demonstrated to be the most efficient tool to formalize
system properties that have to be developed. Currently, designers are able to
accurately specify high-level as well as low-level system details by means of
visual UML models. In the case of component based applications, after having
produced UML visual models, designers have to describe component interfaces.
This task is accomplished by means of the standard Interface Definition
Language (IDL). Unfortunately, IDL does not allow designers to take into
account system properties like object constraints, relations, and business rules,
as reported by UML models. Therefore, no trace of such properties is kept into
skeletons of source code automatically generated by idl compilers so that their
implementation is completely in charge of software programmers. In this paper
a process for adding object constraints and business rules in component based
applications is presented. In particular, we provide: i) a constraint language to
produce models, in addition to idl interfaces, for specifying object constrains
and business rules; ii) some implementation patterns for turning constraints and
rules in source code; and iii) a preliminary tool able to interpret the constraint
language and then to add rules and constraints in the skeletons of software
components generated by a commercial idl compiler.

1   Introduction

From some years now, modeling activities have been assuming ever more relevance
in software production processes. As matter of fact, models have resulted in the best
way to handle the growing complexity of software systems. This has made the
Unified Modeling Language (UML) [5] an essential tool for developing high quality,
possibly error-free, complex systems or, from another point of view, the potentialities
of the UML to produce highly accurate models have let modeling activities assume a
crucial role in any software production processes. In addition, the OMG is defining a

---

[1] This research has been partly supported by the "Nuove tecnologie per la conoscenza, lo
studio e la gestione dei beni artistici e culturali: il patrimonio museale della Provincia di
Catania" project.

R. Meersman, Z. Tari (Eds.): CoopIS/DOA/ODBASE 2002, LNCS 2519, pp. 948–964, 2002.

new way to conceive complex systems, namely the Model Driven Architecture [1], which relies on two levels of models (Platform Independent Models and Platform Dependent Models) defined by means of particular UML dialects also called profiles [6].

Definitely, designers take great care in modeling activities. As a result, these activities produce several accurate visual UML models that efficiently specify high-level as well as low-level system details.

Nevertheless, the implementation of several system properties is completely in charge of software developers. Indeed, in the case of component based applications, once system properties have been formalized by UML diagrams, designers have to produce component interfaces using the IDL language [4][10]. Afterwards, such interfaces are processed by IDL compilers in order to generate skeletons of software components. Unfortunately, the IDL language does not allow to formalize features like constraints, relations, and business rules; thus no trace of such properties is kept in the skeletons of software components generated by IDL compilers, and their implementation is completely in charge of programmers who have to refer to visual UML models as documentation. On the contrary, the possibility of having tools and processes for mapping all modeled system properties in source code would remarkably ease the development phase and shrink the software error probability.

This paper presents a development process and a preliminary tool which allow to automatically produce enhanced skeletons of software components. In particular, we focused on the implementation of object constraints and some kinds of business rules in CORBA based applications.

The process consists of the following steps: 1) Formalizing component interfaces by means of the IDL language; 2) Expressing rules and constraints using a constrain language; 3) Compiling idl interfaces to produce skeletons of software components; 4) Compiling rules and constraints to improve the components produced at the previous step; 5) Filling the components with their own business logic.

It is worth to note that steps 1 and 3 are those fulfilled in ordinary development processes; steps 2 and 4 are completely new; step 5 gets easier in the proposed approach.

Step 2 is accomplished by formalizing rules and constraints in textual models that are produced using a constraint language. The constraint language that we adopted is an extended version of the Object Constraint Language (OCL) [2][3], which is an emerging formal language proposed by the OMG to complete UML class diagrams with invariant constraints, pre-conditions, and post-conditions. Moreover, this language has been extended to model further system properties not specifiable neither by means of the standard IDL language nor by means of the basis OCL language.

Step 4 is automatically fulfilled by a tool that we developed to transform rules and constraints in source code. Transformations rely on some implementation patterns also presented in the paper.

Step 5 is the one accomplished by software developers. The proposed approach relieves developers of implementing the system features already automatically developed in the previous steps.

The rest of the paper is organized as follow. Section 2 describes the constraint language. Section 3 deals with the implementation patterns. Section 4 describes the tool architecture. Section 5 presents a case study. Section 6 discusses some related works. Section 7 concludes the paper with some remarks and directions for future research.

2   The Constraint Language

The main objective of our work was to provide designers and developers with tools for automatically and efficiently implementing business rules in component based applications. Since most business rules, in each application field, can be formalized by specifying constraints that must hold on system's entities, we concentrated on implementing invariant conditions, pre-conditions, post-conditions, and guards.

In order to rich our target, a modeling language – by means of which to specify constraints – must be provided. In particular, such a modeling language should allow to model those structural system properties, already formalized in UML diagrams, which can not be expressed in IDL interfaces. Moreover, it should produce textual models that could be processed either by a specific tool or by an enhanced idl compiler.

Currently, the OMG is proposing the OCL as an emerging standard language to formally model object constraints, which are not clearly specifiable in a UML class diagram. The OCL has interesting properties. Indeed, it is formal, but it is also quite friendly because it does not rely on particularly complex mathematical constructs. Moreover, it allows to produce textual models.

However, it is important to note that OCL was devised to enhance the understanding of UML class diagrams, but IDL models are semantically poorer than UML ones. As a consequence, coupling the OCL and the IDL as they are would not work because of the existing semantic gap between IDL models and UML class diagram models; thus, to reduce such a gap, the OCL has been properly extended. By this way, the resulting semantic gap between the couple <UML class diagram, standard OCL> and the couple <IDL, extended OCL> is almost null.

Table 1 shows the major language keywords, brief descriptions, and the indication whether they are part of the standard OCL language or not.

Table 1. Language keywords

Keyword	Description	OCL extension
Context	This keyword indicates the class or the operation to which the rule is referred to	
INV	This keyword indicates an invariant condition	
PRE	This keyword indicates a pre condition	
POST	This keyword indicates a post condition	
GUARD	This keyword indicates a guard waiting for a condition	✓
ASSOCIATION	This keyword indicates an association between two classes	✓
Toward	This keyword indicates the end point of an association	✓
AGGREGATION	This keyword indicates an aggregation between two classes	✓
Aggregate	This keyword indicates what are the aggregated object in an aggregation	✓
Aggregatedto	This keyword indicates what is the aggregated object in an aggregation	✓
COMPOSITION	This keyword indicates a composition between two classes	✓
Compose	This keyword indicates what is the composed object in a composition	✓
Composed	This keyword indicates what are the composing objects in a composition	✓
Multiplicity	This keyword indicates the multiplicity of a relation	✓

Self	This keyword indicates the current instance of a class	
Execute	This keyword indicates an operation to execute	✓
@PRE	This keyword indicates the previous value of a variable	

Figure 1 depicts an example of UML class diagram with several constraints expressed in natural language. Figure 2 reports the model produced using the constraint language so far described. It is important to note that such a model is not exhaustive, but it must be coupled to IDL models that describe interfaces for components *A, A1, A2, B*, and *B1*.

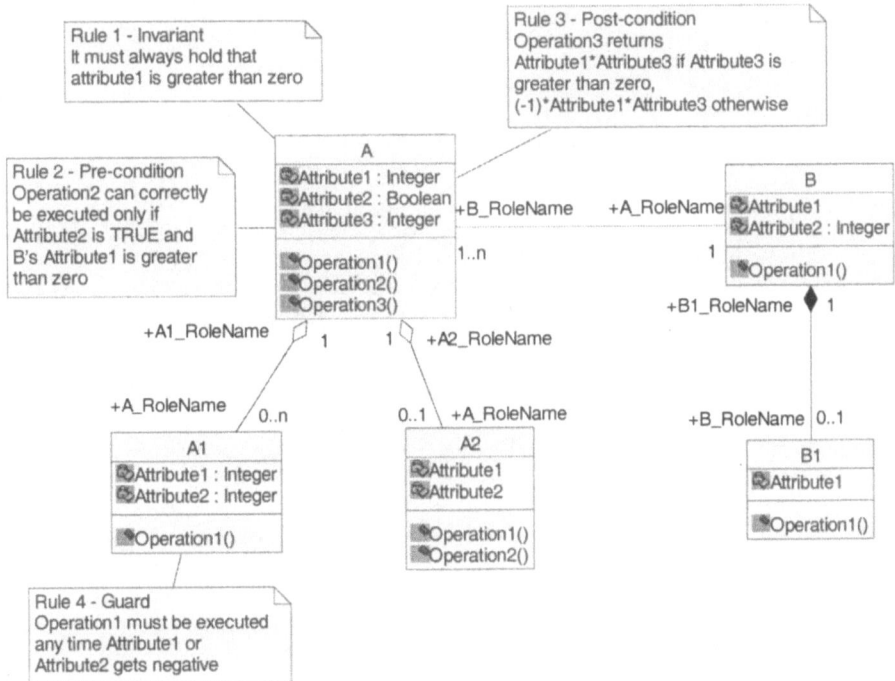

Fig. 1. UML class diagram

3   Patterns for Implementing Business Rules

This section presents patterns to translate some kinds of object constraints in source code. In particular, we focus on invariant conditions, pre-conditions, post-conditions, and guards that are applied to inner component attributes. No object navigation has been taken into account yet.

Implementation has been referred to C++ components. It has also been supposed that each component attribute is always updated by means of the *set* operation.

```
-- Constraints model
Context A                                    -- Class A
INV:    self.Attribute1 > 0                  -- Rule 1: Invariant constraint over Attribute1

ASSOCIATION: A_RoleName multiplicity 1 toward B
                                             -- Association between class A and class B from
                                             -- the A side
AGGREGATION: A_RoleName multiplicity 0 to many aggregate A -- Aggregation between class A
                                             -- and class A1 from the A side
AGGREGATION: A_RoleName multiplicity 0 to 1 aggregate A2    -- Aggregation between class A
                                             -- and class A2 from the A side
Context A::operation2()                       -- Class A, operation: operation2
PRE:    ((self.Attribute2 == TRUE) and (self.B.Attribute1 > 0))  -- Pre-condition over operation2

Context A::operation3()                       -- Class A, operation: operation3
POST:  if (self.attribute3 > 0)               -- Post-condition over operation3
              return  self.Attribute1* self.Attribute3
       else
              return  (-1)* self.Attribute1* self.Attribute3

Context A1                                    -- Class A1
GUARD: if (self.Attribute1 < 0) or (self.Attribute2 < 0) execute self.operation1() -- Rule 4: Guard
                                             -- to execute operation1

AGGREGATION: A1_RoleName multiplicity 1 aggregatedto A    -- Aggregation between class A1
                                             -- and class A from the A1 side

Context A2                                    -- Class A2
AGGREGATION: A2_RoleName multiplicity 1 aggregatedto A    -- Aggregation between class A2
                                             -- and class A from the A2 side

Context B                                     -- Class B
ASSOCIATION: B_RoleName multiplicity 1 to many toward A   -- Association between class A and
       -- class B from the B side
COMPOSITION: B_RoleName multiplicity 0 to 1 composedby B1  -- Composition between class
                                             -- B and class B1 from the B side

Context B1                                    -- Class B1
COMPOSITION: B1_RoleName multiplicity 1 compose B    -- Composition between class B1 and
                                             -- class B from the B1 side
```

Fig. 2. Constraint model

3.1 Invariant Constraints

An invariant constraint is a condition that must always hold as long as the system operates. It typically constraints the value of an attribute, thus it can conveniently be implemented by modifying the attribute *set* operation, which should evaluate the condition before changing the attribute value. Figure 3 shows the modifications suggested for implementing the constraint formalized in the following model:

```
-- Constraint model

Context A                                     -- Class A
INV:    self.Attribute1 > 0                   -- Invariant constraint over Attribute1
```

Implementation consists of:

1. Defining a new operation, namely *inv_attribute1,* to check the invariant condition
2. Modifying the set operation in order either to change the attribute value if the invariant condition is valid or to throw an exception otherwise

```
class A
{
private:
    int Attribute1;



public:
    void set_Attribute1(int value)
    {
        Attribute1 = value;
    }



}
```

```
class A
{
private:
    int Attribute1;



public:
    void set_Attribute1(int value)
    {
        if(inv_Attribute1(value))
            Attribute1 = value;
        else
            throw Exception("INV NOT HOLD);
    }

    bool inv_Attribute1(int value)
    {
        if(value > 0)
            return true;
        else
            return false;
    }



}
```

Fig. 3. Invariant constraint implementation

3.2 Pre-conditions

A pre condition is a condition that must hold before executing an operation. It typically evaluates one or more attributes. Figure 4 shows the modifications suggested for implementing the following constraint:

```
-- Constraint model

Context A::operation2()                                    -- Class A, operation: operation2
PRE:    ((self.Attribute2 == TRUE) and (self.Attribute1 > 0)) -- Pre-condition over operation2
```

In this case, a new operation (namely pre_operation2) is defined to verify whether the pre-condition is hold or not. In addition, the *operation2* is modified to execute the *pre_operation2* before any other statement.

```
void A::operation2()
{
    // Business logic
}
```

```
void A::operation2()
{
    if ( pre_operation2() )
    {
        // Business logic
    }
    else
        throw Exception("PRE NOT HOLD!")
}

bool A::pre_operation2()
{
    if ( (Attribute2 == true) && (Attribute1 > 0) )
        return true;
    else
        return false;
}
```

Fig. 4. Pre-condition implementatio

3.3 Post-conditions

A post condition defines either the return value of a method or modifications on the value of component attributes that must be performed. Figure 5 shows a post condition and its implementation.

```
-- Constraint model

Context A::operation3()                        -- Class A, operation: operation3
POST:  if (self.attribute3 > 0)                -- Post-condition over operation3
            return self.Attribute1* self.Attribute3
       else
            return (-1)* self.Attribute1* self.Attribute3
```

```
int A::operation3()
{
    // Business logic
}
```

```
int A::operation3()
{
    if ( Attribute3 > 0 )
        return Attribute1*Attribute3;
    else
        return (-1)*Attribute1*Attribute3;
}
```

Fig. 5. Post-condition implementation

It is important to note that in the case of pre and post conditions, the operation business logic section is partly (sometimes completely) filled. However, the real objective is not to specify the method behavior, but it is to provide tools for automatically implementing business rules. This involves the specification of constraints, which, as a consequence, affect the behavior of components' operations. In any case, designers continue to focus on components' interfaces and implementation details are kept hidden as long as development is performed by automatic tools. In addition, they have tools for specifying and developing further system's properties.

3.4 Guards

Guards force the execution of operations any time triggers get a specific state. Triggers are all attributes involved in the guard condition. Thus, referring to the guard reported in the following, triggers are *Attribute1* and *Attribute2*. This means that any time one of those attribute is updated, the guard condition must be evaluated.

```
-- Constraint model

Context A1
Class A1
GUARD: if (self.Attribute1 < 0) or (self.Attribute2 < 0) execute self.operation1()   -- Rule 4: Guard
condition

to execute operation1
```

As depicted in figure 6, implementation consists of:
1. Defining a new operation, namely *guard_ name,* to check the guard condition;
2. Modifying the *set* operation for each trigger in order to check the guard condition whenever the trigger is updated.

4   Tool Architecture

The proposed approach relies on the use of either an enhanced idl compiler, which should be able to process constraints models as well, or a specific tool which should process constraints models and then act over skeletons of components generated by regular idl compilers.

This section briefly describes a preliminary tool that can enhance C++ components generated by the IONA Orbix2000™ idlgen compiler [11]. The development process is shown in figure 7. IDL interfaces are compiled by the Orbix2000™ compiler. Afterwards, the previously generated C++ components and the constraints files are processed by the tool to obtain enhanced C++ components.

At the moment, the tool processes constraints that must hold on attributes and operations belonging of singular components, i.e. constraints must not involve external object navigation because the tool is an early release, which is not able to handle component relations yet.

The tool operates in three phases:
1. Constraint file analysis;
2. Data structures construction ;
3. Source code modification.

```
void A::set_Attribute1(int value)              void A::set_Attribute1(int value)
{                                              {
    Attribute1 = value;                            Attribute1 = value;

}                                                  guard1();

void A::set_Attribute2(int value)              }
{
    Attribute2 = value;                        void A::set_Attribute2(int value)
                                               {
}                                                  Attribute2 = value;

void A::operation1()                               guard1();
{
    // Business logic                          }
}
                                               void A::guard1()
                                               {
                                                   if( (Attribute1 < 0) || (Attribute2 < 0))
                                                       operation2();
                                               }

                                               void A::operation1()
                                               {
                                                   // Business logic
                                               }
```

Fig. 6. Guard implementation

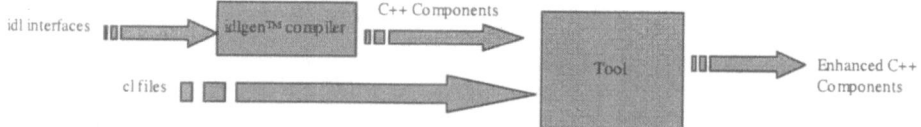

Fig. 7. Development process

During the constraint file analysis, a very simple syntax check is performed. In the data structures construction phase, a few data structures are build. Finally, during the third phase, source code is modified. Modifications are performed using the data structures so far constructed and the patterns described in the previous section. Moreover, such modifications must be properly nested into the source code. In particular, the tool implements invariant conditions as first. Next, pre and post conditions are coded. Finally, guard conditions are inserted.

5   Case Study

This section presents a simple case study in order to show an application of the proposed approach. In particular, we considered a system that must offer cataloguing and exposing functions for relics owned by an archeological museum.

Relics are classified by age, epoch, style, and type. A cataloguing card that includes technical descriptions and pictures is associated to each relic. Relics are also periodically verified in order to establish whether to restore them or not. Verifications as well as restorations are performed in specialized laboratories. Any time a relic is restored or verified, a verification timeout is set to establish how long to wait before having the next verification operation. Such a verification timeout must always range between maximum and minimum values (suppose 6 months and 24 months respectively) established for relic classes by means of generic criteria.

Museums can lend/borrow relics to/from other museums to organize special events. Relics can be lent only if they are available (not on verification/restoration). Likewise, relics can be verified/restored only if the verification timeout is expired and they have not been lent (they are currently available).

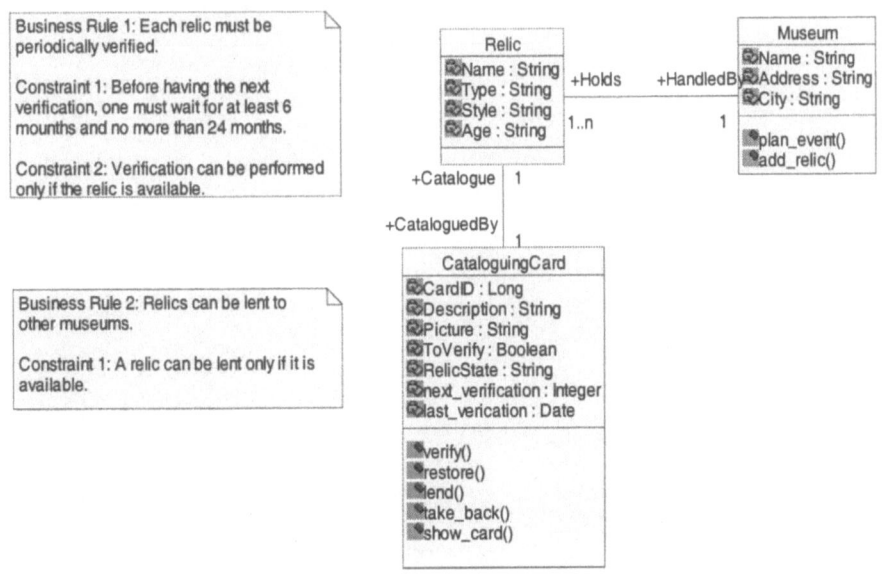

Fig. 8. UML class diagram

Figure 8 depicts a UML model describing the system being constructed. In such a model, we have designed three components (namely *Relic*, *Museum*, *CataloguingCard*). *Relic* is the component containing relic objects, which are owned by a museum (in turn described by the *Museum* component). *CataloguingCard* stores information about the associated relic. In addition, operations like verification, restoration, and so on, are registered in the *CataloguingCard*. It has also been supposed to have a background procedure that periodically checks the verification timeouts and sets the *ToVerify* attribute when the timeout has expired. The verification timeout is implemented by the *next_verification* attribute, which memorizes the number of months to wait for the next verification. The model also reports the two main business rules and some related constraints.

After having produced a UML visual model, we accomplished the five steps described previously.

Step 1

This step consists of developing IDL interfaces. IDL interfaces for the case study are reported in figure 9.

```
module CaseStudy {
    struct Date {
            short Day;
            short Month;
            long Year;
    };

    interface Relic
    {
            attribute string Name;
            attribute string Type;
            attribute string Style;
            attribute long Age;
    };

    interface CataloguingCard
    {
            attribute long CardID;
            attribute string Description;
            attribute string PictureURL;
            attribute boolean ToVerify;
            attribute string RelicState;
            attribute long next_verification;
            attribute Date last_verification;

            void verify( );
            void restore( );
            void lend( );
            void take_back( );
            void show_card( );
    };

    interface Museum
    {
            attribute string Name;
            attribute string Address;
            attribute string City;

            void plan_event( );
            void add_relic( );
    };
};
```

Fig. 9. IDL interfaces for system's components

Step 2

After having specified components' interface, designers can formalize business rules and components' constraints. In the case study, new object constraints have been derived to formalize business rules in addition to the ones already specified in the UML class diagram.

In particular, rule 1 is implemented by a guard that executes the *verify* operation any time the executing condition gets true. Rule 2 is implemented by the *lend* operation, which can be executed only if the relic is available. Moreover, the *lend* operation must set the relic state to LENT. Similar constraints must hold for *restore* and *take_back* operations. Finally, an invariant constraint has been set over the *next_verification* attribute in order to assure correct updates.

```
-- Constraints model

Context CataloguingCard                          -- Class CataloguingCard,
INV: (self.next_verification => 6) and (self.next_verification <= 24) -- next_verification invariant
condition

GUARD: if (self.ToVerify == TRUE) and (self.State == AVAILABLE)    -- Guard condition
```

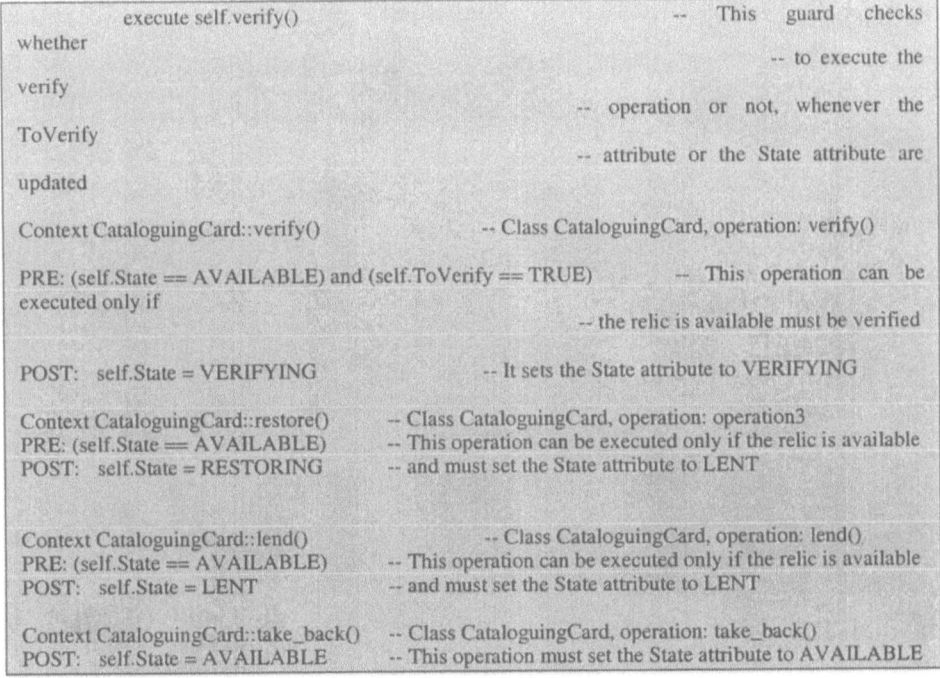

Fig. 10. Constraint model

It is worth to note that the constraints model does not include any relation between components because the tool is not able to process them yet, thus we conceived a case study with rules and constraints concentrated on a specific component. For this reason, we will focus only on the *CataloguingCard* component, which is the one affected by constraints.

Step 3
Step 3 is the first one of the development phase, i.e. the design phase can be considered finished at the end of step 2.

During this step, component skeletons are generated by the IDL compiler. Figure 11 shows the *CataloguingCard* component skeleton generated by the ORBIX2000™ idlgen compiler. In the figure, some comment lines have been eliminated to reduce the dimension of the figure itself.

```
virtual ~CaseStudy_CataloguingCardImpl();

// _create() -- create a new servant.
// Hides the difference between direct inheritance and tie servants.
static POA_CaseStudy::CataloguingCard*
_create(PortableServer::POA_ptr);

// IDL operations
          virtual void        verify();
          virtual void        restore();
          virtual void        lend();
          virtual void        take_back();
          virtual void        show_card();

// IDL attributes
          virtual CORBA::Long CardID() IT_THROW_DECL((CORBA::SystemException));
          virtual      void        CardID(CORBA::Long              _new_value)
IT_THROW_DECL((CORBA::SystemException));
          virtual char* Description() IT_THROW_DECL((CORBA::SystemException));
          virtual      void        Description(const      char*      _new_value)
IT_THROW_DECL((CORBA::SystemException));
          virtual char* PictureURL() IT_THROW_DECL((CORBA::SystemException));
          virtual      void        PictureURL(const      char*      _new_value)
IT_THROW_DECL((CORBA::SystemException));
          virtual CORBA::Boolean ToVerify() IT_THROW_DECL((CORBA::SystemException));
          virtual      void        ToVerify(CORBA::Boolean           _new_value)
IT_THROW_DECL((CORBA::SystemException));
          virtual char* RelicState() IT_THROW_DECL((CORBA::SystemException));
          virtual      void        RelicState(const      char*      _new_value)
IT_THROW_DECL((CORBA::SystemException));
          virtual              CORBA::Long              next_verification()
IT_THROW_DECL((CORBA::SystemException));
          virtual      void     next_verification(CORBA::Long        _new_value)
IT_THROW_DECL((CORBA::SystemException));
          virtual              CaseStudy::Date           last_verification()
IT_THROW_DECL((CORBA::SystemException));
          virtual      void     last_verification(const CaseStudy::Date&  _new_value)
IT_THROW_DECL((CORBA::SystemException));

private:
// Instance variables for attributes.
          CORBA::Long          m_CardID;
          CORBA::String_var    m_Description;
          CORBA::String_var    m_PictureURL;
          CORBA::Boolean       m_ToVerify;
          CORBA::String_var    m_RelicState;
          CORBA::Long          m_next_verification;
          CaseStudy::Date      m_last_verification;
// The following are not implemented
CaseStudy_CataloguingCardImpl(const CaseStudy_CataloguingCardImpl &);
CaseStudy_CataloguingCardImpl& operator=(const CaseStudy_CataloguingCardImpl &);
};
#endif
```

Fig. 11. Class CataloguingCard as generated by the ORBIX2000 idlgen compiler.

Step 4

In this phase, the generated component skeletons are modified by the tool. Figure 12 shows the new methods (bold lines) added to the *CataloguingCard* component.

```
class CaseStudy_CataloguingCardImpl :

{
private:

        bool inv_m_next_verification(CORBA::Long value);
        bool pre_verify();
        bool pre_restore();
        bool pre_lend();
        bool pre_take_back();
        void guard1();
```

Fig. 12. Added operation

Figure 13 depicts the implementation of the added methods and the changes done on the other methods in accordance to the developing patterns described previously.

```
// verify() -- Implements IDL operation "CaseStudy::CataloguingCard::verify".
void CaseStudy_CataloguingCardImpl::verify()
{
        if(pre_verify())
                m_RelicState = "AVAILABLE";
        else
                throw Exception("PRE NOT HOLD");
}

bool CaseStudy_CataloguingCardImpl::pre_verify()
{
        if(m_RelicState == "AVAILABLE" && m_ToVerify == true)
                return true;
        else
                return false;
}

// restore() -- Implements IDL operation "CaseStudy::CataloguingCard::restore".
void CaseStudy_CataloguingCardImpl::restore()
{
        if(pre_restore())
                m_RelicState = "RESTORING";
        else
                throw Exception("PRE NOT HOLD");
}

bool CaseStudy_CataloguingCardImpl::pre_restore()
{
        if(m_RelicState == "AVAILABLE")
                return true;
        else
                return false;
}

// lend() -- Implements IDL operation "CaseStudy::CataloguingCard::lend".
```

```
void CaseStudy_CataloguingCardImpl::lend()
{
        if(pre_lend())
                m_RelicState = "LENT";
        else
                throw Exception("PRE NOT HOLD");
}

bool CaseStudy_CataloguingCardImpl::pre_lend()
{
        if(m_RelicState == "AVAILABLE")
                return true;
        else
                return false;
}

// take_back() -- Implements IDL operation "CaseStudy::CataloguingCard::take_back".
void CaseStudy_CataloguingCardImpl::take_back()
{
        m_RelicState = "AVAILABLE";
}

void CaseStudy_CataloguingCardImpl::guard1()
{
        if ((RelicState == "AVAILABLE") && (ToVerify == true))
                        verify();
}

// ToVerify() -- Modifier for IDL attribute "CaseStudy::CataloguingCard::ToVerify".
void CaseStudy_CataloguingCardImpl::ToVerify(CORBA::Boolean _new_value)
IT_THROW_DECL((CORBA::SystemException))
{
    // Copy the new value into the attribute's instance variable.
    m_ToVerify = _new_value;

    guard1();
}

// RelicState() -- Modifier for IDL attribute "CaseStudy::CataloguingCard::RelicState".
void CaseStudy_CataloguingCardImpl::RelicState(const char* _new_value)
IT_THROW_DECL((CORBA::SystemException))
{
    // Copy the new value into the attribute's instance variable.
    m_RelicState = CORBA::string_dup(_new_value);

    guard1();
}
```

Fig. 13. Method implementations.

Step 5

During this phase, developers adds business logic to the component skeletons. This phase is not of interest for the present paper, thus we will not describe it. However, it must be noted that developers have not only to fill operations (like *show_card*, *plan_event*, and *add_relic*) that have not been affected by constraints, but also they generally have to complete the behavior of those operations for which pre-conditions and/or post-conditions have been specified. This is due to the fact that post-conditions and even more pre-conditions do not specify the entire operation behavior, but only constraints that must hold to assure a correct execution.

6   Related Works

A similar approach has been proposed in [8]. The author suggest to formalize invariant conditions, pre-conditions, and post-conditions as comment lines in Java source code. Then, such comment lines are processed by a pre-compiler (pre-processor) that implements the specified constraints. In this case, a non standard constraint language is adopted. Moreover, guards conditions are not taken into account. Finally, constraints are specified directly into the source code; thus, designers have no tool for the design phase.

The Larch/C++ [7] is a Larch-style behavioral interface specification language by means of which one specifies both the interface of a procedure or abstract data type and its behavior. However, the specification of the behavior of a procedure that can include the definition of pre and post conditions is accomplished by providing logical assertions using a mathematical vocabulary, which has a formal meaning specified, in part by the user of Larch/C++, in the Larch Shared Language (LSL). Again, a formal non standard constraint language is adopted, guard conditions are not taken into account, and specifications can not be issued until the development phase.

The Eiffel language [9] provides the support for designing by contract but, it seems to have the same weaknesses of the previous approaches.

Finally, all presented solutions are not component oriented.

7   Conclusions

Major contributions provided by the present paper are: i) An extended version of the OCL language that can be used in the modeling activity to formalize business rules and to complete the idl interfaces models; ii) Some patterns for implementing business rules in C++ programs, but different implementations would not significantly change; iii) a preliminary tool able to modify the source code generated by a commercial IDL compiler to automatically implement the formalized rules and constraints.

Future work will aim to verify a larger set of business rules. The tool will also be improved: it has to handle object relations as well as rules that require inter-object navigation. Finally, it should be better understood how rules may interfere each other while generating code in a more complex scenario.

References

1   R. Soley, *"Model Driven Architecture"*, available at www.omg.org
2   J. Warmer and A. Kleppe, *"The Object Constraint Language: Precise Modeling with UML"*, Addison-Wesley publishing, 1999

3   OMG, *"Object Constrait Specifications"*, available at www.omg.org

4   ISO/IEC 14750 standard.

5   Hans-Erik Eriksson and Magnus Penker, *"UML toolkit"*, Wiley publishing.

6   OMG, *"Unified Modeling Language Specifications"*, v1.4, chapter 4, available at www.omg.org

7   G. T. Leavens, "Larch/C++" reference manual, available at http://www.cs.iastate.edu/~leavens/larchc++.html

8   R. Kramer, "iContract – the Java Design by Contract tool", in proc. of International Conference of Object Oriented Language and Systems (TOOLS 26, USA'98), IEEE Computer Society Press.

9   M. Bertrand, "Eiffel: The Language", Object Oriented Series, Prentice Hall publishing, 2nd edition 1992.

10 Jon Siegel, *"CORBA - Fundamentals and Programming"* John Wiley & Sons Publishing.

11 *"ORBIX 2000 Tutorial"*, available at http://www.iona.com/docs.

Configuring the Communication Middleware to Support Multi-user Object-Oriented Environments*

Sandra Teixeira, Pedro Vicente, Alexandre Pinto, Hugo Miranda, Luis Rodrigues[1], Jorge Martins, and António Rito-Silva[2]

[1] Universidade de Lisboa
{steixeira,pedrofrv,apinto,hmiranda,ler}@di.fc.ul.pt
[2] INESC-ID
{Jorge.B.Martins,Rito.Silva}@inesc-id.pt

Abstract. Distributed multi-user interactive systems have a rich and complex set of requirements. A promising approach to tackle the complexity of these systems is to rely on configurable architectures that are able to support component re-utilization and composition.
The MOOSCo project, Multi-user Object-Oriented environments with Separation of Concerns, addresses the difficulties in applying a component-based approach in a vertical and integrated manner, from analysis to implementation, to the design of this class of systems. To support communication among distributed components, the project uses a configurable group communication system called *Appia*. The paper discusses the role of *Appia* in the MOOSCo architecture and shows how it makes possible to derive, in a simple and elegant way, the most appropriate protocol composition depending on the objects shared by the multi-user object-oriented environment.

1 Introduction

Distributed multi-user interactive systems represent an extremely relevant research area. Applications such as virtual environments, distributed simulation, computer supported collaborative work (CSCW), multi-user games or dungeons (MUDs), and multi-user object-oriented environments (MOOs) [5] are becoming increasingly pervasive. From the analysis, software engineering and system support point-of-view, these applications are extremely challenging due to its unique requirements for dependability, scalability, adaptability, usability, non-functional domains to be considered, and efficiency.

The MOOSCo project [1] [12], Multi-user Object-Oriented environments with Separation of Concerns, addresses the difficulties in applying a component-based approach in a vertical and integrated manner, from analysis to implementation,

---

* This work was partially supported by Fundação para a Ciência e Tecnologia, POCTI/ C/ EEI/1 33127/ 1999 MOOSCo.

R. Meersman, Z. Tari (Eds.): CoopIS/DOA/ODBASE 2002, LNCS 2519, pp. 965–980, 2002.

to the design of this class of systems. The MOOSCo project addresses the several concerns involved in the development of MOOs, such as object interaction, awareness management, distributed communication, information sharing and so forth. A promising approach to tackle the complexity of these systems is to rely on configurable architectures that are able to support component re-utilization and composition. The MOOSCo architecture is based on component composition and addresses three abstraction layers: user models, middleware abstractions, and communication protocols. Due to the compositional characteristics of the architecture, it is possible to use middleware abstractions and communication protocols tailored to the specific user models needed in each case. To support this fine-grain level of composition, including at the level of the communication protocols, the project is relying on a framework for protocol composition and execution called *Appia* [11].

In this paper we show the advantages of using *Appia* as a composition framework for MOOs with particular emphasis on distributed communication and information sharing concerns. Using a concrete example of a virtual space with different shared objects, we show how the application designer may select a different composition of communication protocols for each attribute of a shared object and how it can enforce inter-channel constraints. Moreover, this configuration can be performed using a configuration file. This allows the application to be configured during its deployment, not only as a function of the objects being shared but also of the properties of the network infrastructure.

The paper is structured as follows. The different configuration requirements of the MOOSCo system are introduced in Section 2. Section 3 makes a brief introduction to the *Appia* system and shows how it is used in MOOSCo. The comparative performance of the resulting system is presented in 4. Section 5 presents related work. The advantages and difficulties of the approach are discussed in Section 6. Section 7 concludes the paper.

2 Configurable Multi-user Environments

2.1 Multi-user Environments

Multi-user virtual environments, such as MOOs, support real-time interaction between several geographically distributed users. To achieve this, MOOs offer linked virtual shared spaces, usually following a *virtual room* metaphor. It is within these virtual rooms that users may share data and multimedia information (such as graphics, images and sounds).

MOOs offer the mechanisms for a user to enter or leave a virtual room, watch other users activities while they happen and interact with other users in the environment. These systems allow the creation and modification of the virtual environment by change, addition and removal of objects.

Naturally, information sharing is a central aspect in the environment implementation. There are several types of information shared by the MOO users. First of all, the users have to be aware of other users in the same virtual room and of the operations performed by these. This implies that whenever a user enters or leaves the room, all other users are informed. Secondly, users must perceive and be able to interact with the objects in the room. This implies that the adding or removing of any object must be indicated to all users in the room. Furthermore the users must be aware of objects' changes: Each object is characterized by one or more attributes (for example, position, speed, sound, etc) that can be changed independently and one or more actions (for example rotate, play, etc) that can be performed at will. Finally, the communication requirements to propagate the changes of these attributes or actions may be completely different (for example, the data propagation protocols are different from the audio propagation protocols).

Although each object attribute places different demands on the communication protocols, the dissemination of attribute information must respect a global coherence so that every user has the same perception of the environment. This means that the MOOs communication support must allow the configuration of the quality of service required for a specific attribute, but also allow the configuration of the coherence relations between different attributes.

2.2   Monolithic Solutions *versus* Configurable Solutions

As just described, there is not a unique and best solution in the context of MOOs. Solutions should be contextual. On the other hand, the overall satisfaction of MOO requirements for consistency, adaptability, scalability, and efficiency, is not easy and may result in conflicting and inconsistent solutions. For instance, due to latency, messages might arrive in different orders at different machines. This results in a consistency problem: different users get different views of the environment.

To solve this sort of problems most MOOs resort to a given, pre-defined, non-configurable strategy. For instance, some approaches rely on a centralized server to serialize messages. Such solution does not scale to a large number of users. Other approaches use a decentralized approach, that rely on communication protocols that provide total ordering and causal ordering for messages in the system. Such approaches may perform well in local-area networks but also exhibit scalability limitations in large-scale networks due to the number of messages that may need to be exchanged. In addition, domain-specific requirements may consider different levels of consistency and even their change at runtime.

Instead of relying on fixed strategies, the MOOs design and development will profit from an approach that allows the customization of contextual solutions by the tuning and composition of predefined reusable components. Even if there are several systems providing solutions for the information sharing support, few of these systems have the required flexibility to adapt to the applications' particular requirements. This paper intends to offer a solution to a better protocol composition for the application requirements.

2.3   Configuration Requirements

Each virtual environment with its particular objects places different requirements on the information sharing support system. In this section we will introduce a very simple example that shows the complexity of the configuration
requirements usually found in MOO systems.

Lets consider a simple game, a MUD (Multi-User Dungeon). In this type
of game, each player personifies an animal that moves in a virtual universe,
searching for food. Each user is represented by an *avatar*, implemented as a
shared object with three attributes: its appearance, its geographical position and
the direction it is facing; and a single action: eat. The appearance is influenced
by the amount of food consumed. In the following example we will consider the
scenario in which there are two users that interact in a virtual shared space
composed of a single virtual room with a cooling fan and a food container. The
cooling fan position is fixed and pre-defined so its only relevant attribute, in
terms of changing information sharing, is its rotation speed. The food container
has two relevant attributes: position and number of items within. The users must
approach the food container and eat one or more items. This must reflect in their
avatars' appearance.

It should be pointed out that if two users try to take the last item, only
one of them should succeed. This requires that some order on these concurrent
actions should be established. The system must also guarantee that the order
in which the attributes are changed respects causal order. For instance, if the
number of items in the container diminishes an appearance change must be made
because of their ingestion. On the other hand, changes to the cooling fan state
are independent of the changes made to other objects.

In the following section, we describe different ways to configure the communication protocols in a setup were in each user node there is a replica of each
object in the application. In this setup, users must be informed of all operation
that change object attributes. In the following discussion we will use the term
channel to describe a composition of communication protocol components. The
quality of service offered by the channel depends on the protocols that compose
a channel. For instance, one may build a communication channel that supports
ordered and reliable point-to-point communication (typically supported by a
TCP/IP protocol stack). Later in Section 3.1, we will provide a more precise
definition of a channel in the context of the *Appia* system.

Independent communication channels. A possible protocol composition
for the information sharing in the virtual room just mentioned, is to use an
independent communication channel for each attribute, as depicted in Figure 1.
This architecture has the advantage that allows each attribute to use a particular
quality of service. For example, to disseminate cooling fan speed changes it would
use a reliable communication channel without any particular order. On the other
hand, to disseminate state changes to the food container it would use a total-
order protocol, to enforce that all nodes see the changes in a coherent order.
The disadvantage of this alternative is that it is not possible to use a shared

communication component to enforce that causal order is maintained between the changes made to different attributes. For instance, it would be impossible to causally order updates to the number of items in the food contained and updates to the appearance of who has eaten them (therefore, it would be possible to observe changes in the appearance before observing its cause, the removal of a food item).

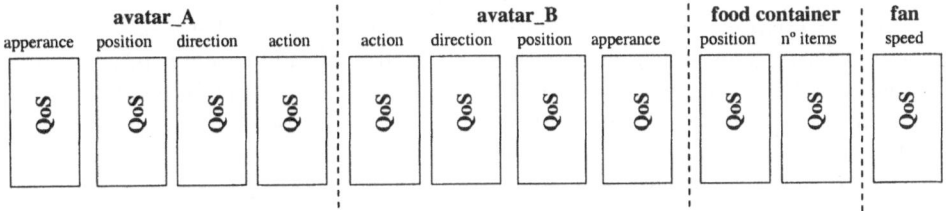

Fig. 1. Independent Channels

A single shared channel. A frequent solution to the coherence problems raised by the previous architecture is to use a single channel that is shared among all attributes, as illustrated in Figure 2. This channel must satisfy the strongest order required by the shared objects. In the example it would be total-order. The drawback of this solution is that the communication among all attributes would use total-order, when only a small subset of the attributes demanded it. Since dissemination protocols that provide total-order are typically less efficient than those that only provide causal-order, or even no order at all (for the speed of the cooling fan), the use of strong total order might be an overkill, for those attributes not requiring it, leading to possible degradation of performance.

	avatar_A				**avatar_B**			**food container**		**fan**
apperance	position	direction	action	action	position	direction	apperance	position	nº items	speed
					Total Order					
					Causal Order					
					Reliable Multicast					

Fig. 2. Global Channels

Shared channel with inter-channel dependencies. As just shown, neither the use of a single independent channel for each attribute, nor the use of a single channel shared among all attributes fully satisfies the requirements in our example. A solution is to create a protocol composition in which some attributes share some ordering properties, without forcing all attributes to share those properties.

In our example, all attributes would use a reliable information dissemination channel. This would be the quality of service strictly required for the dissemination of the cooling fan speed. Therefore this attribute would not use any additional ordering protocol. The remaining attributes would share a common causal order, to enforce the relations between attributes, as previously mentioned. Finally, a stronger ordering protocol, total order, would be shared among avatars and only be used for the avatars' actions. Since there is a certain predictability in the avatar's displacement it would be possible to reduce network traffic by extrapolating its movement. This could be achieved by another protocol, dead-reckoning, that does movement prediction and only propagates position updates when the forecast deviation is above a certain threshold. As this prediction potentially generates minor inconsistencies between the position of an avatar and what other users perceive, and it is a requirement that an avatar *must* be near the food container in order to be able to eat, the avatar's actions would need a new protocol, called force-proximity, that guarantees that when an eat action is disseminated every user accurately sees the avatar near the basket. The resulting protocol composition is depicted in Figure 3.

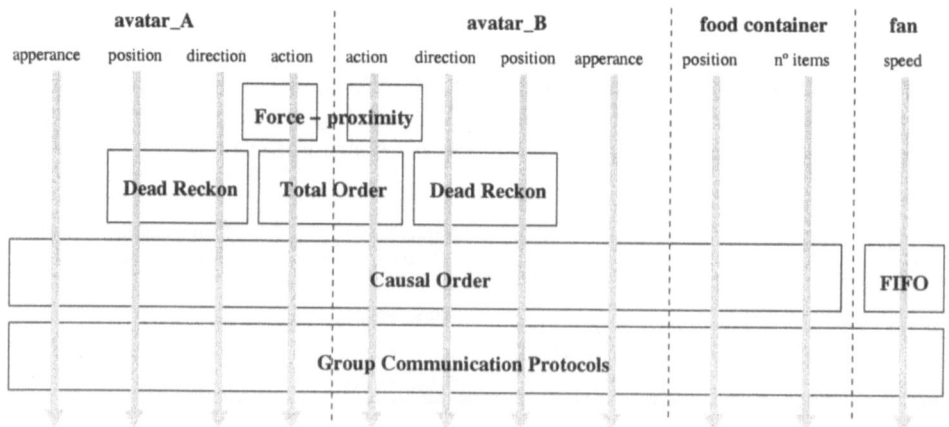

Fig. 3. Shared Channels

In the following section we will describe a configurable communication system that allows the implementation of such adaptation.

3   A Configurable Communication System

3.1   The *Appia* Protocol Composition Framework

Appia [11] is a protocol composition and communication framework that allows communication channels, each with its own *QoS*, to be integrated in a coherent multi-channel protocol stack. Using *Appia*, the application designer can specify the protocol stack that meets her/his QoS requirements through the composition of micro-protocols.

In the previous sections, we have identified the need for inter-channel coordination to support MOO applications. For instance, we have identified the need to preserve causal order across different channels. Similar examples have been identified by other research teams [14,4]. A powerful feature of *Appia* is that it provides the mechanisms to express inter-channel coordination.

Stack composition in *Appia* relies on a clear separation between two related concepts: *layers* and *sessions*. We define a *layer* as the implementation of a protocol. All protocols implement the same *event interface*, which defines the types of events each layer is able to consume and produce. The format and semantics of these events is irrelevant to our exposition. Typical examples of events are data transmission requests, indications and confirmations. Examples of layers are "datagram transport", "positive acknowledgment", "total order", "checksum", etc. Examples of relevant layers and events in the context of fault-tolerant applications can be found in [8].

An ordered set of layers (protocols) defines a quality of service. When a new quality of service is defined, *Appia* gathers the event types that each layer is able to produce and consume and uses that information for:

Performance improvement. *Appia* defines event routes for each event type that will flow in a composition. Each event route keeps a reference to the protocols that are interested in receiving that event type. When an event travels a protocol composition, it will only be delivered to the protocols in his corresponding event route. We have shown elsewhere that this feature improves *Appia* performance [11].

Incoherent composition detection. To be able to behave correctly, most protocols rely on the services provided by other protocols in the composition. One example of incoherent compositions are those where one service fundamental for one protocol is not provided by any other. In *Appia*, protocols can only communicate by the exchange of events. Layers are free to declare event types that must be provided by some other protocol in the composition. When creating a protocol composition, the *Appia* runtime throws an exception if it is found that one event type required by one protocol is not provided by any other.

As in *x*-kernel, we define a *session* as an instance of a layer [9]. The session maintains state that is used by the protocol code to process events. A protocol that implements ordering may keep a sequence number or a vector clock as part of the session state. In connection oriented protocols, the session also maintains information about the endpoints of the connection. Note that it is often useful to maintain several active sessions for the same layer even when they share the same endpoints: for instance, one might want to have different FIFO channels for different priority streams.

We can now provide a precise definition of a *channel* in the *Appia* system. A channel is defined as an ordered sequence of sessions. Sessions are used as a composition mechanism to implement coordination among channels. If needed, different channels may share the same session at one or more layers. The common session stores state that is shared by all channels and can implement the desired coordination. Each channel is modeled on a previously defined quality of service. Channels inherit the event routes defined by qualities of service mapping layers of the latter on sessions of the former. However, *Appia* does not require that two or more channels sharing at least one session are modeled by the same quality of service. In fact, the quality of service and the number of simultaneous channels where a session is being used may be transparent for the session. This is an innovative feature of *Appia* that, to the extent of our knowledge, can not be found in other composition frameworks.

Figure 4 shows how three protocols named *Proto 1*, *Proto 2* and *Proto 3* can be used in the definition of two channels. Layers are grouped for the definition of two independent qualities of service (QoSs). Each of these QoSs can be used for the definition of any number of channels. In this example, protocols 1 and 2 have each one session created, while protocol 3 has two sessions created. Sessions are then used for defining the channels. Note that each channel uses one session for each layer declared on his corresponding QoS. However, when the channels are defined, the same session of protocol 2 is shared between both channels. Protocol 3, in turn, uses one separate session for each channel.

3.2   Defining Channels with Shared Sessions

As noted in Section 2.3, users may share a set of objects and their respective attributes from the virtual environment. When one of the attributes is changed, its new state must be disseminated to all the processes that share the corresponding object. This dissemination must respect the consistency criteria defined by the application. With *Appia* the consistency criteria is mapped to a communication channel that offers the desired protocol composition. Therefore, for each attribute, a different communication channel is created: each channel is composed by the protocols required to provide the desired quality of service. Channels may have independent or shared sessions. When one wants to coordinate the activity of the channels at a certain protocol level, shared sessions should be used.

Applying this model to our previous example should result in the configuration depicted in Figure 3. Each attribute has its own channel to disseminate its own changes. But these channels are not independent. At the bottom of the stack, all channels share the set of protocols necessary to provide reliable

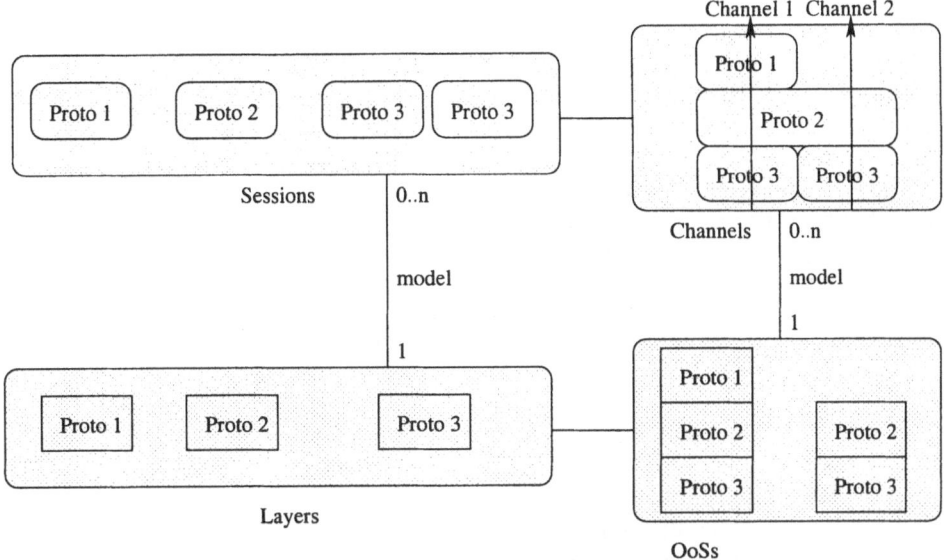

Fig. 4. Relation between the basic concepts of *Appia*

group communication[1]. The channel used to disseminate the cooling fan speed only needs one more FIFO layer, whose state is preserved in a private session. All the remaining channels share a causal order session. The channels used to disseminate the position and direction of each avatar share a session of a dead-reckoning protocol. Finally, the two channels used to disseminate the eat action of the avatars also share a session of a total order protocol and each channel has its own session of a force-proximity protocol.

3.3   The Configuration Process

In the previous Section, we have shown how it is possible to use the *Appia* composition model to build a multi-channel protocol stack. In this section we show how the user can specify a configuration fitting her/his consistency requirements, for instance, to build the communication stack illustrated in Figure 3.

The XML language is appropriate for specifying the users' configuration. Using this language, the user can define a set of rules to build a well formed and structured file. These rules must be defined in a grammar (DTD Document Type Definition), that will be followed to define the file. Those files will be easily built and understood due to its organization.

The user defines an XML file for each object he/she wants to create. Although nothing prevents this file from being created in run-time, in our current prototype

---

[1] Actually, it could be possible to refine even further the example and consider the use of best-effort communication protocols in some channels but we omit such optimizations to maintain the exposition simpler.

```
<!ELEMENT configuration (attribute+)>
<!ATTLIST configuration object CDATA #REQUIRED>
<!ELEMENT attribute (name, QoS)>
<!ELEMENT QoS (micro-protocol+)>
<!ELEMENT micro-protocol (name, sessionname?, initParameters*, mode)>
<!ELEMENT name (#PCDATA)>
<!ELEMENT sessionname (#PCDATA)>
<!ELEMENT initParameters (parameter+)>
<!ELEMENT parameter (#PCDATA)>
<!ELEMENT mode (#PCDATA)>
```

Fig. 5. System's grammar

we use exclusively specifications that are made prior to the execution. However, as we will describe, a single file can be used for each class of objects (for instance, for all avatars), thus allowing the creation of new objects in run-time.

The configuration file must follow the grammar rules that the system is ready to interpret, as presented in Figure 5. Selected portions of the XML configuration file for the avatar objects is presented in Figure 6 and the corresponding file for the fan is depicted in Figure 7. We will refer to these files to give concrete examples of some configuration features.

According to the grammar specification this file must have: the name of the object, the name of each attribute, for each attribute the declaration of the stack of protocols that implement the target consistency criteria, an identifier of the sessions to be used. Each channel is composed of a sequence of layers: the order in which they are listed corresponds to the order by which they appear in the communication stack. The configuration file for each object is parsed when the user places the object into the virtual environment to build the associated communication channel. When an object is shared, the configuration file of the channel is disseminated along with the object state, such that remote processes can create the corresponding communication channel in their local nodes.

Both protocols and sessions are identified by textual names in the configuration file. The session declaration has an attribute called `initParameters` that are used to configure the session. These parameters are passed to the session in an initialization event. For instance, in the definition of the dead-reckoning session this parameter is used to defined the threshold used to trigger an update. Each session is also characterized by an attribute called *mode* with the following meaning:

- If the session cannot be shared with other attributes, mode should be set to `localAttribute`. Such session does not need to be named as a unique name is assigned automatically in run-time using the object's name and the name of the attribute. An example of a session with this characteristic is the session of the Force-proximity protocol, which is used exclusively by the channel of the action attribute of each object.

```
<configuration object="avatar">              <name>
  <attribute>                                     Force-proximity
    <name>                                        </name>
      apperance                                   <mode> localAttribute </mode>
    </name>                                     </micro-protocol>
    <QoS>                                       <micro-protocol>
      <micro-protocol>                            <name>
        <name>                                      Total Order
          Causal Order                            </name>
        </name>                                   <sessionname>
        <sessionname>                               total session
          causal session                          </sessionname>
        </sessionname>                            <mode> shared </mode>
        <mode> shared </mode>                   </micro-protocol>
      </micro-protocol>                         <micro-protocol>
      <micro-protocol>                            <name>
        <name>                                      Causal Order
          Reliable group communication            </name>
        </name>                                   <sessionname>
        <sessionname>                               causal session
          group session                           </sessionname>
        </sessionname>                            <mode> shared </mode>
        <mode> global </mode>                   </micro-protocol>
      </micro-protocol>                         <micro-protocol>
    </QoS>                                         <name>
  </attribute>                                      Reliable group communication
                                                  </name>
  ...                                             <sessionname>
                                                    group session
                                                  </sessionname>
  <attribute>                                     <mode> global </mode>
    <name>                                       </micro-protocol>
      action                                  </QoS>
    </name>                                  </attribute>
    <QoS>                                   </configuration>
      <micro-protocol>
```

Fig. 6. Avatar XML configuration file (partial)

- If a session is to be shared by more than one attribute of the same object, but not with attributes of other objects, the mode should be set to localObject. As before, the name of the session is automatically assigned in run-time using the name of the object. An example of such a session is the dead-reckoning protocol that controls the dissemination of the position and direction attributes of each avatar: for each object a different session is created that is shared among these two attributes.
- If a session is to be shared among different objects, the mode should be set to shared. In this case the user must identify the name of the session to be shared. This allows objects from different types to share different sessions of

```
<configuration object="fan">              </micro-protocol>
   <attribute>                             <micro-protocol>
      <name>                                  <name>
         speed                                   Reliable group communication
      </name>                                 </name>
      <QoS>                                   <sessionname>
         <micro-protocol>                        group session
            <name>                            </sessionname>
               FIFO Order                     <mode>global</mode>
            </name>                        </micro-protocol>
            <mode>                       </QoS>
               localAttribute            </attribute>
            </mode>                   </configuration>
```

Fig. 7. Fan XML configuration file

the same protocols. In our example, the total order and causal sessions are shared sessions.

- If one knows *a priori* that, due to some global consistency criteria, all objects should share a given session, the mode should be set to `global`. In this case, the run-time ensures that no other attribute may create a new session of that protocol. In our example, all attributes share a single session of the group communication protocols.

The use of modes allows to create configuration files that can be applied to several objects of the same type. In our example, all avatars may use the configuration file of Figure 6. Thus, this sort of fine-grain configuration does not restrict the number of avatars than can be created in run-time.

4   Performance

The system has been implemented as a set of extensions and new layers to the *Appia* system [11]. A companion prototype multi-user cooperative application, that demonstrates the the operation of the system was also developed.

To illustrate the comparative performance of the different configurations, we have measured the round-trip delay associated with the propagation of updates in shared attributes. We have considered the "position" and "action" attributes, since these have quite different requirements in terms of communication protocols. We have measure the values obtained with three different configurations for the supporting communication channels: *i)* independent channels, where each channel offers different properties but where it is impossible to enforce inter-channel constraints; *ii)* a single shared channel enforcing the strongest requirement of both attributes, in this case, total order; *iii)* channels that enforce distinct properties but where inter-channel dependencies are expressed using the notion of shared sessions.

	Independent channels	Shared channel	Shared sessions
position	68	145	74
action	71	150	147
inter-channel consistency	no	yes	yes

Fig. 8. Comparative performance

The results are depicted in Figure 8 (all values are in milliseconds). It can be observed that the configuration that uses independent channels offers the best round-trip delays but does not allow to enforce inter-channel constraints (order across different attributes). If such constraints need to be enforced, the use of shared sessions is more beneficial than to use a single channel, since in this case, total order does not need to be used when dissemination updates to the position attribute. It can be also observed that the degradation in performance for the configuration using shared sessions is not significant when compared with the degradation of performance incurred by a solution that requires the use of a single shared channel.

5 Related Work

All existing MOO systems, such as [2,6,13], provide support for information sharing. DIVE [6] and SPLINE [2] use a replicated database approach: all interaction is performed through the replicated database. Although they offer a clean separation between the application and the replicated database, applications have little control over the replication issues. In particular, none of these systems allow the application developer to specify customized algorithms. Furthermore, from the point of view of communications support, existing MOO systems are usually tied to a single quality of service. For instance, NPSNET [10] only uses unreliable communication while DIVE only use reliable communication. SPLINE support both reliable and unreliable with ordering for messages regarding the same object. However in some situations it could be useful to force message ordering for a particular set of objects. In all existing systems there is no support for quality of service adaptation that takes into consideration application specific requirements. As result of their monolithic structure these systems are restricted to a single user model.

In recent years, there has been a significant progress in the development of group communication infrastructures. The latest systems offer a very impressive range of configuration facilities. For instance, Horus [15] allows communication stacks to be changed in runtime; BAST [7] allows different protocols to be selected to implement the same services under different usage patterns. Coyote [3] allows the same message to be processed by different protocols in parallel. However, these systems lack built-in mechanisms to implement inter-channel coordination. Although presenting different composition models, none of these frameworks is able to support inter-channel coordination while hiding the final composition schema from the programmer of the protocols to be shared. Previous support for these kind of features has always been limited to particular cases, typically for performance improvement. This is the case of the Horus's FAST protocol [15].

Frameworks explicitly supporting inter-channel constraints lack generality. The work of CCTL [14] uses independent communication channels which are managed by a single control channel. The quality of service of each channel must be chosen by the application programmer from one of a predefined set available at the framework. Another example is the Maestro [4] system, that illustrates the difficulties of maintaining consistent failure detection when channels with diverse characteristics are used concurrently.

6   Discussion

The main advantage of the proposed architecture is that the user is able to configure a communication stack that satisfies the consistency requirements of the set of shared objects used by the application. A specialized communication channel can be assigned to each object attribute and the different channels can be coordinated thanks to the concept of configurable shared sessions. This and the possibility to access domain-specific information from a session allowed for different protocols, not just related to communication but with general consistency required for replication, another important aspect of MOO applications. This is illustrated, for instance, by the dead-reckoning protocol whose threshold value can be configured by the user depending on the object being shared. Supporting both concerns under the same infrastructure while still maintaining the separation of concerns allows to define coherent consistency from the network-level up to application-level and yet allow for separate development and reasoning.

The composition model offered by *Appia* is a step forward with regard to previous approaches to support MOO applications. However, the current system still exhibits some limitations. A disadvantage of the configuration procedure is that it requires the use of a global name space for the sessions. When two channels need coordination, the same session name must be used in configuring the channels. Thus, in practice, the user is forced to have a global view of the configuration of all channels. The provision of *local* and *global* modes mitigates this disadvantage, as a single configuration file can be used for all objects that share a given protocol composition. Therefore, the object has not to consider the configuration of channels on an object by object basis, but in terms of classes of objects.

One of the challenges raised by the model is the development of multi-channel communication protocols. Although session sharing is provided by *Appia* since its inception, several protocols developed for it do not consider this capability. This is due to two main reasons. One is concerned with programming discipline. Since the concept of shared sessions is unusual, programmers do not consider this case unless directly requested to do so. Another reason is that the complexity of coding a protocol that accepts multi-channel sessions is highly variable. Some protocols, such as FIFO protocols are very simple to implement but others are more complex.

To illustrate the difficulty of building multi-channel protocol we give the example of the total order protocol used in our MOO. The protocol is a sequencer-based protocol: a given member of the group of replicas is elected to assign sequence number to all messages exchanged in the group. In a multi-channel implementation, a single sequence of sequence numbers is used across all channels that share the same session. However, the protocol designer has to decide if it creates an additional channel just to exchange control information (such as the sequence numbers) or if it used one of the data channels and, in the later case, which one to use. Since different channels may have different properties (protocols), some introspection may be required to select the most appropriate channel.

7 Conclusions

This article presents a configurable communication architecture that satisfies the complex requirements raised by interactive multi-user applications. This architecture is based on the vertical and horizontal composition of protocols. Vertical composition enables the configuration of the protocols that compose the channels used for update dissemination. Horizontal composition enables to respect dependencies between attributes through the use of shared sessions. The configuration may be performed during the application deployment phase, without being fixed into the code. This allows the configuration to be adapted not only to the properties of the shared objects, but also to the environment in which the system is running.

Acknowledgements. The authors are grateful to the anonymous reviewers for their comments on an earlier version of this paper.

References

1. M. Antunes and A. Silva. Using separation and composition of concerns to build multiuser virtual environments. In *Proceedings of the 6th International Workshop on Groupware - CRIWG'2000*, Madeira, Portugal, 2000. IEEE.
2. J. Barrus, R. Waters, and D. Anderson. Locales: Supporting Large Multiuser Virtual Environments. In *IEEE Computer Graphics and Applications*, pages 16(6):50–100, Nov. 1996.
3. N. Bhatti, M. Hiltunen, R. Schlichting, and W. Chiu. Coyote: A system for constructing fine-grain configurable communication services. *ACM Transactions on Computer Systems*, 16(4):321–366, November 1998.
4. K. Birman, R. Friedman, and M. Hayden. The maestro group manager: A structuring tool for applications with multiple quality of service requirements. Technical report, Cornell University, Ithaca, USA, February 1997.
5. S. Evans. Building blocks of text-based virtual environments. Technical report, Computer Science University, University of Virginia, April 1993.

6. E. Frécon and M. Stenius. Dive: A Scalable Network Architecture for Distributed Virtual Environments. In *Distributed systems Engineering Journal(Special Issue on Distributed Virtual Environments)*, number Vol. 5, No 3, pages 91–100, September 1998.

7. B. Garbinato and R. Guerraoui. Flexible protocol composition in Bast. In *Proceedings of the 18th International Conference on Distributed Computing Systems (ICDCS-18)*, pages 22–29, Amsterdam, The Netherlands, May 1998. IEEE Computer Society Press.

8. M. Hayden. *The Ensemble System*. PhD thesis, Cornell University, Computer Science Department, 1998.

9. N. Hutchinson and L. Peterson. The x-Kernel: An architecture for implementing network protocols. *IEEE Trans. on Software Engineering*, 17(1):64–76, January 1991.

10. M. Macedonia, M. Zyda, D. Pratt, D. Brutzman, and P. Barham. Exploiting Reality with Multicast Groups. In *IEEE Computer Graphics and Applications*, pages 15(5):38–45, September 1995.

11. H. Miranda, A. Pinto, and L. Rodrigues. Appia, a flexible protocol kernel supporting multiple coordinated channels. In *Proceedings of the 21st International Conference on Distributed Computing Systems*, pages 707–710, Phoenix, Arizona, April 2001. IEEE.

12. MOOSCo. Multi-user Object-Oriented environments with Separation of Concerns. Home Page URL:http://www.esw.inesc.pt/moosco/.

13. J. Pubrick and C. Greenhalg. Extending Locales: Awareness Management in MASSIVE-3. In *URL:http://www.crg.cs.nott.ac.uk/research/systems/MASSIVE-3*, September 1999.

14. I. Rhee, S. Cheung, P. Hutto, and V. Sunderam. Group communication support for distributed collaboration systems. In *Proceedings of the 17th International Conference on Distributed Computing Systems*, pages 43–50, Balitmore, Maryland, USA, May 1997. IEEE.

15. R. van Renesse, K. Birman, and S. Maffeis. Horus: A flexible group communications system. *Communications of the ACM*, 39(4):76–83, April 1996.

Distributed Component System Based on Architecture Description: The SOFA Experience

Tomáš Kalibera and Petr Tůma

Charles University
Faculty of Mathematics and Physics,
Department of Software Engineering
Malostranské náměstí 25, 118 00 Prague 1,
Czech Republic
kalibera@nenya.ms.mff.cuni.cz   petr.tuma@mff.cuni.cz

Abstrakt In this paper, the authors share their experience gathered during the design and implementation of a runtime environment for the SOFA component system. The authors focus on the issues of mapping the SOFA component definition language into the C++ language and the integration of a CORBA middleware into the SOFA component system, aiming to support transparently distributed applications in a real-life environment. The experience highlights general problems related to the type system of architecture description languages and middleware implementations, the mapping of the type system into the implementation language, and the support for dynamic changes of the application architecture.

Keywords. Architecture description languages, ADL, component definition languages, CDL, middleware, CORBA, language mapping, dynamic architectures.

1 Introduction

The notion of components enjoys significant interest in the software engineering community. Components are considered to be useful *units of code sharing and reuse*, as well as useful *building blocks of software architectures*. While the former view is supported by practical component systems [15,19,24], the latter view appears to be lagging behind. The current trend of modeling software architectures using UML is criticized as being inadequate [8], and while the research in component systems based on architecture description languages (ADL component systems) cites inarguable benefits of such systems [1,5,13,14,23], the described projects rarely get past research prototypes.

The discrepancy between the cited benefits of ADL component systems and the lack of their practical employment leads us to believe that there are unresolved issues that prevent this employment. In order to investigate these issues, we have designed and implemented a runtime environment for the SOFA ADL component system [21] (SOFA environment).

R. Meersman, Z. Tari (Eds.): CoopIS/DOA/ODBASE 2002, LNCS 2519, pp. 981–994, 2002.

Our chief goal in the design and implementation of the SOFA environment is to support development of transparently distributed applications. The development centers around a hierarchical description of the application architecture. This description is gradually refined from a coarse granularity level, where components correspond to implementation modules, to a fine granularity level, where components correspond to implementation objects. These components are then mapped to implementation objects using a standardized language mapping, with the architecture description defining the interconnection of these objects into the component application. When the application is run, its components can be deployed onto several network hosts. The components that share a host are interconnected through linking and run in one address space. The components that run on different hosts are interconnected through connectors.

The SOFA environment describes the application architecture using the SOFA component definition language [10,21] (SOFA CDL). SOFA CDL is mapped into C++, which is used to implement the components. The connectors are built using CORBA [18]. The SOFA environment also allows interfacing the application with GNOME [26] to provide user interface support. The choice of GNOME as a representative of a component framework and CORBA as a representative of an off-the-shelf middleware allows us to evaluate how the SOFA environment supports real-life applications in a real-life environment.[1]

The paper continues by a brief introduction of the SOFA component model and SOFA CDL in Sect. 2. The description of the design and implementation of the SOFA environment follows in Sect. 3. Our experience with the CDL to C++ mapping and the integration of CORBA, as well as the ability of the SOFA environment to support applications, is evaluated and generalized for a broad class of ADL component systems in Sect. 4. Section 5 relates this paper to other work in the field of ADL component systems. The paper is concluded in Sect. 6.

2   SOFA Component Model and SOFA CDL

The SOFA component model [21] views an application as a hierarchy of nested software components. A component is an instance of a component *template*, which consists of a component *frame* and a component *architecture*. The frame lists all interfaces that the component *requires* and *provides*. The architecture implements the operations of the provided interfaces, relying only on the operations of the required interfaces. A frame can be implemented by several architectures.

An architecture is either *composed* or *primitive*. A composed architecture defines a *composed component* as built from *subcomponents* by listing the frames of the subcomponents and the *ties* between the interfaces of the component and the subcomponents. A primitive architecture defines a *primitive component* as implemented in an implementation language outside the scope of the component model.

---

[1] The SOFA ADL component system also includes a Forte IDE and a Java runtime. These are outside the scope of this paper.

A tie between the interfaces of a component and its subcomponents can be of three types. *Binding* denotes connecting a required interface of a subcomponent to a provided interface of a subcomponent. *Delegating* denotes connecting a provided interface of a component to a provided interface of its subcomponent. *Subsuming* denotes connecting a required interface of a subcomponent to a required interface of its component.

An example of the interface, frame and architecture definitions in SOFA CDL is in Fig. 1. The example defines a variation of the ubiquitous "Hello World" application that prints a greeting. The application is an instance of a component with the `ApplicationArch` architecture, which implements the `ApplicationFrame` frame. The `Message` subcomponent provides the greeting to be displayed, the `Display` subcomponent provides the functionality to display a message, the `HelloWorld` subcomponent uses the two other subcomponents to display the greeting. The application defined by the example will be used in other examples throughout the paper.

```
interface MessageIface { string message (); };
interface DisplayIface { void print (in string message); };

frame MessageFrame { provides: MessageIface MessageProv; };
frame DisplayFrame { provides: DisplayIface DisplayProv; };

frame HelloWorldFrame {
  requires: MessageIface MessageReq; DisplayIface DisplayReq;
  provides: ApplicationIface ApplicationProv;
};

architecture MessageArch implements MessageFrame primitive;
architecture DisplayArch implements DisplayFrame primitive;
architecture HelloWorldArch implements HelloWorldFrame primitive;

architecture ApplicationArch implements ApplicationFrame {
  inst MessageFrame Message;
  inst DisplayFrame Display;
  inst HelloWorldFrame HelloWorld;
  bind HelloWorld:MessageReq to Message:MessageProv;
  bind HelloWorld:DisplayReq to Display:DisplayProv;
  delegate ApplicationProv to HelloWorld:ApplicationProv;
};
```

Fig. 1. A SOFA CDL definition of an application architecture.

SOFA CDL can also specify semantics of interfaces and frames using behavior protocols [22] and employ complex connectors [3,4]. These are outside the scope of this paper.

3   SOFA Environment

The SOFA environment defines and implements a mapping of SOFA CDL into C++ used to map components to implementation objects, implements a deployment mechanism used to deploy the components onto network hosts and to interconnect the components, and implements the connector generator used to produce connectors between components that run on different hosts. These three parts of the SOFA environment are described in this section.

3.1   Mapping SOFA CDL into C++

The CDL to C++ mapping is based on the IDL to C++ mapping of CORBA [16]. Similar to CORBA IDL, the type system of SOFA CDL is independent of the implementation languages of components and has a standardized mapping into these languages. Making the type system independent on the implementation language makes it easier to generate connectors and potentially also to support multiple implementation languages of components.

The mapping of the types that SOFA CDL shares with CORBA IDL follows the IDL to C++ mapping. The types original to SOFA CDL, namely frames and architectures, are mapped into the frame and architecture classes that follow the approach used to map interfaces with attributes.

A frame class has accessor methods for the provided and required interfaces of the frame, which are represented as protected references to the classes that map the interfaces. An example of a generated frame class is in Fig. 2. To allow substitution of components with the same frame but different architectures, the frame class is a virtual base class that is inherited by architecture classes of the architectures implementing the frame.

```
class HelloWorldFrame : virtual public FrameBase {
  public:
    // Accessor methods generated for provided and required interfaces
    inline virtual ApplicationIface_ptr ApplicationProv () {
      return (ApplicationIface::_duplicate (pApplicationProv)); };
    inline virtual void ApplicationProv (const ApplicationIface_ptr value) {
      pApplicationProv = ApplicationIface::_duplicate (value); };
  protected:
    ApplicationIface_ptr pApplicationProv;
    ...
};
```

Fig. 2. A generated C++ mapping of HelloWorldFrame.

The implementation of an architecture class differs for composed and primitive architectures. An architecture class of a composed architecture has accessor methods for the subcomponents of the architecture, which are represented as private references to the frame classes of the frames of the subcomponents. The architecture class also contains code that allows to set up the ties between interfaces as defined by the **bind**, **delegate** and **subsume** clauses in the architecture definition.

For performance reasons, the code does not interconnect the interfaces of the composed component with the interfaces of its subcomponents directly. Instead, it allows propagating references to the provided interfaces of primitive components along the ties of the architecture definition by the **createBindingsAndDelegates** and **createSubsumes** methods. The required interfaces of primitive components are thus tied directly to the provided interfaces, with the composed components whose boundaries the ties cross adding no overhead to the invocations of methods accessible through these ties.

An example of a generated composed architecture class is on Fig. 3.

```
class ApplicationArch :
  virtual public ApplicationFrame, virtual public ArchitectureBase
{
  public:
    // Methods generated for setting up the ties between interfaces
    virtual void createBindingsAndDelegates () {
      iHelloWorld->MessageReq (iMessage->MessageProv ());
      iHelloWorld->DisplayReq (iDisplay->DisplayProv ());
      pApplicationProv = iHelloWorld->ApplicationProv (); };
    virtual void createSubsumes () {
      iMessage->createSubsumes ();
      iDisplay->createSubsumes ();
      iHelloWorld->createSubsumes (); };
  private:
    HelloWorldFrame_ptr iHelloWorld;
    . . .
};
```

Fig. 3. A generated C++ mapping of ApplicationArch.

An architecture class of a primitive architecture is a virtual base class that the implementation of the primitive component inherits from. An example of an implementation of a primitive component is on Fig. 4. The example uses nested classes to implement the provided interfaces, and demonstrates how both the provided and the required interfaces of a frame are accessed by the implementation of the primitive component.

The frame and architecture classes also inherit from base classes that define methods for generic access to the provided and required interfaces of the frame and the subcomponents and the ties of the architecture. These methods are required by the deployment mechanism.

```
class HelloWorld : public virtual HelloWorldArch {
  public:
    // Implementation of the ApplicationIface interface
    class Application : public virtual ApplicationIface {
      public:
        Application (HelloWorld *frame) { me = frame; };
        // Displaying the greeting using the other subcomponents
        virtual Short run (const StringSequence& args) {
          char *message = me->MessageReq()->message ();
          me->DisplayReq()->print (message);
          return 0;
        };
      private:
        HelloWorld *me;
    };
    // Initialization of the HelloWorldArch architecture
    virtual void initialize () {
      HelloWorldArch::initialize ();
      ApplicationProv (new Application (this));
    };
};
```

Fig. 4. A C++ implementation of HelloWorldArch.

3.2   Deploying Application Components

The deployment is configured by a deployment descriptor. For each frame, the deployment descriptor specifies the architecture that the component will use and the host where the component will run. The deployment is controlled from a single place and expects each host to run a simple server that allows remote instantiation of components. The initialization and interconnection methods of the component are then invoked remotely on the component itself.

The control flow of the deployment mechanism follows the hierarchical architecture of the application being deployed. The architecture forms a tree with each node representing a component. Nodes representing composed components are parents of nodes representing their subcomponents. Nodes representing primitive components are leaves. The references to provided and required interfaces are attributes of each node.

At the beginning of the deployment process, the references to provided interfaces are stored in the attributes of nodes representing primitive components. The references are then propagated toward the root of the tree along the bind and delegate ties in one tree traversal pass, and toward the leaves of the tree along the subsume ties in another traversal pass. The process uses the create-BindingsAndDelegates and createSubsumes methods defined by the language mapping of the component architectures.

typedef sequence<string> StringSequence;
interface ApplicationIface { **short** run (**in** StringSequence args); };
frame ApplicationFrame { **provides:** ApplicationIface ApplicationProv; };

Fig. 5. The application frame.

The deployment expects the application to implement a standardized frame in Fig. 5. After the application is deployed, the run method of `Application-Iface` provided by the application is invoked to launch the application.

3.3   Generating Connectors Using CORBA

Connectors are used to interconnect components that run on different network hosts by delivering remote method invocations to the components. As the hosts where components should run are only known at deployment time, the connectors have to be generated and dynamically loaded at deployment time.

Although the SOFA environment does not place any principal restrictions on the middleware used to implement connectors, we have focused on connectors that are generated by off-the-shelf CORBA middleware. The connector generator is flexible enough to support a number of CORBA middleware implementations.

CORBA middleware generates connectors from a CORBA IDL definition of the interfaces that the connector delivers invocations to. An IDL compiler accepts the CORBA IDL definition of an interface as input and generates C++ source code of the stub and skeleton parts of the connector as output. Both parts need to be compiled, the stub part of the connector is then called by the components that require the interface, the skeleton part of the connector then calls the components that provide the interface.

A development environment that includes both an IDL compiler and a C++ compiler is needed to generate a connector. To avoid the need of having this environment available at deployment time, the SOFA environment pregenerates a set of connectors for all interfaces of an application.

For each interface, a CORBA IDL file that contains the definition of the interface and includes the definitions of all types that the interface relies on is generated by the SOFA environment. The file is compiled by the IDL compiler to yield the C++ source code of the stub and skeleton parts of the connector. The SOFA environment also generates C++ source code of the connectors that uses the code generated by the IDL compiler and interfaces it with the components. The C++ source code is compiled into a pregenerated connector. At deployment time, the pregenerated connectors are dynamically linked with the components.

The SOFA environment can be configured at deployment time to use several middleware implementations. All connectors of a single middleware implementation are managed by a single connector manager. The task of the connector manager is to provide access to the listening loop of the middleware and to enable creation of stub and skeleton parts of a connector in a middleware independent manner.

```
class ConnectorManager {
  public:
    virtual ObjectBase_ptr loadStubPart (const char *reference) = 0;
    virtual char *loadSkeletonPart (ObjectBase_ptr servant) = 0;
    virtual void startListening () = 0;
    virtual void stopListening () = 0;
};
```

Fig. 6. The connector manager interface.

The interface of the connector manager is in Fig. 6. The `loadSkeletonPart` method creates the skeleton part of a connector, returning a stringified reference of the target interface. The `loadStubPart` method creates the stub part of a connector, accepting this stringified reference. The `startListening` and `stopListening` methods control the listening loop of the middleware.

4   Experience in Retrospective

4.1   Shareable Language Mapping

The initially most visible feature of the SOFA environment was the CDL to C++ mapping, based on the IDL to C++ mapping of CORBA [16]. The CDL to C++ mapping of the data and interface types, which SOFA CDL shares with CORBA IDL, is almost as complex as the IDL to C++ mapping of these types. In addition to the data and interface types, the CDL to C++ mapping also supports the frame and architecture types. Considering the size of the IDL to C++ language mapping, over 170 pages of specification at this time, the CDL to C++ language mapping is obviously far from trivial.

The complexity of the mapping can introduce extra cost in terms of code size and runtime overhead. In principle, the extra cost of a mapping designed solely for use by the component code does not have to exceed the extra cost introduced by other libraries that provide useful types in the C++ environment, such as STL [11]. The problem particular to the CDL to C++ mapping, and a language mapping used by any other component system that aspires to employ off-the-shelf middleware to build connectors, is that the mapping is used both by the component system and by the middleware. A typical situation in this case is that the mapping used by the component system is not compatible with the mapping used by the middleware, prompting the need for deep copying at best, and deep copying and data conversion at worst, of all data passed through the middleware. Given the performance of contemporary middleware implementations [25], the copying and conversion might be acceptable in an explicitly distributed application that employs the middleware in a few carefully selected points, but not in a transparently distributed application that relies on the middleware for interconnecting its components at fine granularity levels, where components correspond to implementation objects.

The problem of compatibility of the language mappings used by the component system and the middleware implementations employed to build connectors can be solved by sharing the mapping among the component system and the middleware implementations. In most cases, this requires extending the language mappings of contemporary middleware implementations.

A language mapping of a contemporary middleware implementation is typically designed to make it possible to write applications that are portable across middleware implementations. The mapping is defined so that the application employing the middleware can easily access the mapped types, but it does not define how the middleware itself accesses the mapped types.

A language mapping that is to be shared among a component system and middleware implementations has to extend the contemporary mappings by defining how the middleware itself accesses the mapped types. Such a language mapping makes it possible not only to write applications that are portable across middleware implementations, but also to write middleware implementations that can share language mappings and thus coexist in a single application without incurring extra cost in terms of code size and runtime overhead. A step in this direction are the ORB portability interfaces in the IDL to Java mapping of CORBA [17].

4.2   Connectors Built Using CORBA

The separation of development and deployment phases of the application lifecycle implies a need to postpone the decision on what connectors to employ from the development time to the deployment time. This goes contrary to the typical usage of off-the-shelf middleware, where the connectors are generated and integrated into the application at the development time.

Although it is theoretically possible to use off-the-shelf middleware to generate connectors at deployment time, such an approach runs into a number of practical difficulties. First, it is unusual to require the development system of the middleware to be available at deployment time. Second, the development system of the middleware is often interactive and thus hard to integrate into the component system.

Alternatively, a set of connectors for all interfaces of an application can be pregenerated at the development time. Only those pregenerated connectors that are actually employed will be used at the deployment time. Our experience demonstrates that while feasible, this approach runs against the typical usage of off-the-shelf middleware, where connectors for multiple interfaces are generated from a single CORBA IDL file.

When connectors for multiple interfaces are generated from a single CORBA IDL file, the middleware produces a monolithic module that contains the marshalling code together with the mapping of all types used by the connectors. When used to generate the connectors for one interface at a time, the middleware produces modules that are largely redundant in mapping of those types that are shared by the connectors. Even though the redundancy can be removed during function level linking, the time spent generating and compiling redundant code is prohibitive even for relatively small number of types and interfaces.

To avoid the problems of redundancy when employed in a component system, an off-the-shelf middleware should provide features that allow for separated generation of the marshalling code and the mapping of the types used by the connectors. Provided that the mapping of the types could be shared among the component system and the middleware implementations, this would allow for generating the mapping of the types at development time, and generating the marshalling code on demand at deployment time.

4.3   ADL Type System Not Suitable

In retrospect, the most constraining decision with respect to the usability of the component system was basing the SOFA type system on the CORBA type system. The type system of CORBA is tailored to suit the underlying remote procedure call mechanism, which is acceptable because a CORBA application uses IDL interfaces in a few carefully selected points. When carried over to SOFA, the type system becomes much more restrictive because a SOFA application uses CDL interfaces for interconnecting its components at fine granularity levels, where components correspond to implementation objects.

Looking at the differences between the type system of C++, which is normally used in the environment we consider, and the type system of SOFA, we can see that C++ relies heavily on reference and pointer types that may not have a counterpart in the SOFA type system.

Reference and pointer types that are used to pass data by reference, whether merely for sake of efficiency or to allow modification of the data, have a good match in the SOFA types used to pass the same data in one of the in, out or inout directions.

Reference and pointer types that are used to build dynamic data structures do not have a good match in the SOFA types. Even if the dynamic data structure happens to match the SOFA sequence or value types, the sharing semantics applied by C++ will not match the copy semantics applied by SOFA. The sharing semantics of the reference and pointer types is difficult to mimic in a component system that supports transparently distributed applications. When building dynamic data structures, it is therefore better to employ high level tools such as containers and iterators rather than low level tools such as references and pointers.

A component system can provide containers and iterators modeled after STL [11] or another well tested framework. These can be employed to build dynamic data structures without having to associate a specific sharing or copy semantics with the type, which would be difficult to implement when the type is used both by C++ and by SOFA.

Reference and pointer types that are used to denote objects may appear to have a good match in the SOFA object reference type. Instances of both types give their holder the ability to invoke methods on an object. Implementation of a component system that employs this similarity is possible, although not without difficulties [3]. Reference and pointer types that are used to denote functions represent a similar case.

4.4   Need Anticipated Dynamic Changes

From the architectural point of view, passing references that denote objects has the effect of creating new ties between components. Together with the ability to instantiate components, this provides a mechanism for dynamically changing the architecture of the application. The mechanism is similar to the one normally employed by object oriented applications to introduce dynamic changes by creating and linking objects. This similarity makes it well suited for supporting anticipated dynamic changes of the architecture of component applications. The flexibility and ease of use of the mechanism supersedes that of many contemporary component systems with architecture description languages [5,14].

The downside of the mechanism is that the new connections and components are not reflected in the architecture description. This makes the architecture description lose its relevancy to the application architecture it is to describe. This problem exists in most component systems that employ architecture description languages, where the architecture description is either static [5,23], or expressed in a way that does not lend itself to describing anticipated dynamic changes [2, 12].

Anticipated dynamic changes of the application architecture appear to be of fundamental importance, much more so than the unanticipated dynamic changes the software architecture research community focuses on. If the architecture description is to be used in a component system at fine granularity level, it is necessary to extend the architecture description language to support such changes. Following the approach suggested for building dynamic data structures, the dynamic architectures could be described as dynamic collections of components.

4.5   Legacy Components and Connectors

Integrating the component system with CORBA and GNOME gave rise to the need of supporting legacy components, especially the components of GNOME used to build the user interface. Besides running into problems with the type system outlined earlier, we also encountered problems related to legacy distribution mechanisms.

The graphical user environment of GNOME runs on top of the X Window System [20], which relies on its own distribution mechanism. The legacy components of GNOME use X resource identifiers as references. The distribution mechanism of the X Window System should therefore be regarded a middleware and X protocol connectors should be introduced to interconnect X components. This would have the advantage of using the X protocol, which is more efficient than the protocols of general purpose middleware. More work needs to be done to design a mechanism for cooperation between multiple types of middleware.

5   Related Work

Although a number of ADL component systems exists, most share the basic architectural concepts related to components and connectors. The component model of SOFA is no exception, being similar to the component model of Darwin [13]. It also fits well into the ACME framework [9] and the xADL toolkit [7], which provide a basis for sharing and manipulating architectural information.

What distinguishes our work on SOFA from that carried out on other component systems is the close integration of our SOFA implementation with CORBA and GNOME. To our knowledge, few other ADL component systems come close to this level of implementation. The notable exceptions are the C2 [14] and Rapide [12] projects, both exerting effort to support real-life applications in real-life settings. Neither project, however, aims at supporting transparently distributed applications.

With its design and implementation, the SOFA environment is also close to component systems that are not based on formal architecture description, such as Microsoft COM [15] or Sun EJB [24]. Besides the lack of the architecture description itself, these systems differ from the SOFA environment also by omitting the explicit specification of interfaces required by components, which is needed for rigorous assembly of components.

Although also lacking the formal architecture description, more similar to the SOFA environment is the CORBA Component Model [19], which provides a definition of components with explicit specification of provided and required interfaces. We believe that the need for shareable language mapping, identified in this paper, also concerns the CORBA Component Model.

Also related to our work is the development in middleware implementations, especially in the area of reflective middleware. Reflective middleware implementations are generally more modular and thus lend themselves better to integration with a component system. Reflective middleware can also employ the formal architecture description for its configuration [6].

6   Conclusion

We have presented the design and implementation of a runtime environment for the SOFA component system. The implementation is integrated with GNOME and CORBA as representatives of a contemporary component framework and a distributed middleware.

The SOFA environment features a CDL to C++ mapping, a deployment mechanism and a connector generator. The language mapping is easy to use, introduces little overhead per se, and enables component substitution. The deployment mechanism is configurable and supports both single-host and distributed deployment transparent to the application. The connector generator produces connectors independent of the application and can integrate several CORBA middleware implementations.

The SOFA environment meets our goals of supporting real-life applications in real-life settings, vital to discover the limitations of ADL component systems with respect to applications. The paper further highlights our findings in this respect, related to the type system of architecture description languages and middleware implementations, the mapping of the type system into the implementation language, and the support for dynamic changes of the application architecture.

We argue that the type system of the architecture description languages needs to be enriched to support building of dynamic data structures without having to resort to the low level tools such as references and pointers, which do not lend themselves well to transparent distribution.

We point out that the mapping of the type system used by contemporary off-the-shelf middleware needs to be extended to define those features of the mapped types that the implementations of the middleware rely upon. This allows sharing the language mapping among the component system and the middleware implementations used to build the connectors. For efficiency reasons, the middleware should generate the marshalling code and the mapping of the types separately.

We also emphasize that the dynamic changes of the application architecture should be allowed through a mechanism similar to the one normally employed by applications to introduce dynamism, such as creating and linking objects. The architecture description languages should reflect this mechanism and provide support for anticipated dynamic changes.

We believe that our findings are not constrained to the particular design and implementation of the SOFA environment we have described, but can be generalized to cover the broad class of component systems that employ architecture description languages or other forms of formal architecture description.

The implementation of the SOFA environment is available for download at http://nenya.ms.mff.cuni.cz.

Acknowledgments. The authors would like to thank František Plášil, Stanislav Višňovský nd Adam Buble for valuable comments, and all the members of the Distributed Systems Research Group at Charles University for their work on the SOFA project.

Reference

1. Allen R. J.: A Formal Approach to Software Architecture, Doctoral thesis at Carnegie Mellon University, USA, 1997
2. Allen R. J., Douence R., Garlan D.: Specifying and Analyzing Dynamic Software Architectures, Proceedings of FASE 1998, Portugal, 1998
3. Bálek D.: Connectors in Software Architectures, Doctoral thesis at Charles University, Czech Republic, http://nenya.ms.mff.cuni.cz, 2002
4. Bálek D., Plášil F.: Software Connectors and Their Role in Component Deployment, Proceedings of DAIS 2001, Poland, 2001
5. Bellissard L., Ben Atallah S., Boyer F., Riveill M.: Distributed Application Configuration, Proceedings of ICDCS 1996, Hong Kong, 1996

6. Blair G., Blair L., Issarny V., Tùma P., Zarras A.: The Role of Software Architecture in Constraining Adaptation in Component-based Middleware Platforms, Proceedings of Middleware 2000, USA, 2000

7. Dashofy E. M., van der Hoek A., Taylor R. N.: An Infrastructure for the Rapid Development of XML-based Architecture Description Languages, Proceedings of ICSE 2002, USA, 2002

8. Garlan D., Kompanek A.: Reconciling the Needs of Architectural Description with Object-Modeling Notations, Proceedings of UML 2000, United Kingdom, 2000

9. Garlan D., Monroe R., Wile D.: ACME: An Architecture Description Interchange Language, Proceedings of CASCON 1997, Canada, 1997

10. Hnětynka P., Mencl V.: Managing Evolution of Component Specifications using a Federation of Repositories, Technical report 2001/2, Department of Software Engineering, Charles University, Czech Republic, 2001

11. International Organization for Standardization: C++ Programming Language, ISO/IEC standard 14882, 1998

12. Luckham D. C., Kenney J. J., Augustin L. M., Vera J., Bryan D., Mann W.: Specification and Analysis of System Architecture Using Rapide, IEEE Transactions on Software Engineering 21(4), 1995

13. Magee J., Tseng A., Kramer J.: Composing Distributed Objects in CORBA, Proceedings of ISADS 1997, Germany, 1997

14. Medvidovic N., Taylor R. N., Whitehead E. J.: Formal Modeling of Software Architectures at Multiple Levels of Abstraction, Proceedings of CSS 1996, USA, 1996

15. Microsoft: Component Object Model Specification 0.9, http://www.microsoft.com, 1995

16. Object Management Group: C++ Language Mapping Specification, formal/99-07-41, ftp://ftp.omg.org/pub/docs/formal/99-07-41.pdf, 1999

17. Object Management Group: Java Language Mapping Specification, formal/99-07-53, ftp://ftp.omg.org/pub/docs/formal/99-07-53.pdf, 1999

18. Object Management Group: Common Object Request Broker: Architecture and Specification, CORBA 2.6.1, formal/02-05-08, ftp://ftp.omg.org/pub/docs/formal/02-05-08.pdf, 2002

19. Object Management Group: CORBA Component Model Specification, ptc/01-11-03, ftp://ftp.omg.org/pub/docs/ptc/01-11-03.pdf, 2001

20. Open Group: X Windows System, http://www.x.org, 2002

21. Plášil F., Bálek D., Janeèek R.: SOFA/DCUP: Architecture for Component Trading and Dynamic Updating, Proceedings of ICCDS 1998, USA, 1998

22. Plášil F., Višňovský S.: Behavior Protocols for Software Components, IEEE Transactions on Software Engineering 28(9), 2002

23. Shaw M., DeLine R., Klein D. V., Ross T. L., Young D. M., Zelesnik G.: Abstractions for Software Architecture and Tools to Support Them, IEEE Transactions on Software Engineering 21(4), 1995

24. Sun Microsystems: Enterprise JavaBeans Specification 2.0, http://www.microsoft.com, 2002

25. Tůma P., Buble A.: Open CORBA Benchmarking, Proceedings of SPECTS 2001, USA, 2001.

26. GNOME Documentation Project, http://developer.gnome.org/projects/gdp, 2002

On Components with Explicit Protocols Satisfying a Notion of Correctness by Construction*

Andrés Farías and Mario Südholt

Département Informatique,
Ecole des Mines de Nantes,
4, rue Alfred Kastler – BP 20722
F-44307 Nantes Cedex 3, France
http://www.emn.fr/{farias,sudholt}

Abstract. Component-based programming, which promises to facilitate the construction of large-scale applications, relies to a large degree on interfaces. Interfaces on most component models only declare types and sets of services that components implement, and are not expressive enough to formulate structural and behavioral properties of components. In this paper we show how to integrate one important class of behavioral properties: constraints on the sequentialization of services. We are interested in operators for the construction of components, satisfying a correctness property, allowing a component to be substituted by another one. We define a set of protocol composition operators satisfying the correctness property, we provide a first step toward the integration of additional abstract state information into protocols, and we apply our theory to two widely-used component models: JavaBeans and Enterprise JavaBeans.

1 Introduction

Component-based programming promises to facilitate the construction of large-scale applications by supporting the composition of simple building blocks into complex applications. Frequently, several characteristics are accepted as being fundamental to components, in particular explicit interfaces. Interfaces are intended to impose strong restrictions on components: they should make explicit all the means to use components, such as communication and transfer of control between components. Interfaces of traditional component platforms, such as Sun's Enterprise JavaBeans (EJB) [1], define the (Java) type of a component and the types of the services, i.e., methods, provided by a component. More elaborate behavioral specifications are often expressed using separate methodologies, such as UML [2] and State Charts [3] for object interactions. In the case of EJB, concerns such as security and persistence, are — in part — declaratively configured by means of deployment descriptors, which are text files separating such behavioral descriptions from the business code. This way, an EJB can be configured by the bean deployer without intervening on the code.

---

* This work has been partially funded by the EU project "EASYCOMP" (www.easycomp.org), no. IST-1999-014191

R. Meersman, Z. Tari (Eds.): CoopIS/DOA/ODBASE 2002, LNCS 2519, pp. 995–1012, 2002.

An important behavioral property of components is sequencing constraints that components must obey when calling services one another. Consider the following example that shows the dynamic dependencies regarding service availability in the context of a chat server application. The figure below presents a suitable component-based client-server architecture of a chat server application for broadcasting messages among several clients. Components are represented by boxes and their services by small squares at their border. The `ChatServer` component, for example, offers services for clients to log in and to log out, to broadcast messages to all logged clients and to search for a posted message. The Component `ChatServer` relays the services of its two collaborators `Login` and `MessageBoard` through its interface, e.g. `login()`, or uses them to implement its own services, e.g. `posting()`.

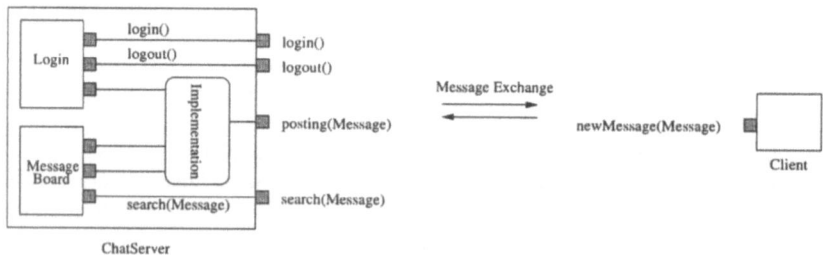

Obviously, the availability of the services of the chat server depends on its runtime state and potentially on the state of its clients or collaborators. Messages, for instance, can only be posted by clients who have previously logged in. The availability of the chat server's services may also depend on the identity of components with which the interaction takes place. This is the case of the posting service: it depends both on a call to the login service and the identities of the components having logged in.

Following work on object-oriented languages, explicit protocols in component interfaces have been proposed [4,5,6] to facilitate the concise definition of sequencing constraints. We explore two enhancements of such techniques. First, we define component composition operators for explicit protocols, such as concatenation and union of protocols. We investigate an important correctness property, substitutability, for such operators. This property can be checked at application-assembly time. We show that it does not hold for some straightforward operator definitions and we propose a technique to solve this problem. Second, we consider the addition of state information to protocols, which restricts protocol transitions according to the identity of collaborating components. We apply our research to the JavaBeans model and show how its implicit protocols can be made explicit. Finally, we show how protocols can be used to define access-control security policies that cannot be defined in the EJB's security model.

The paper is structured as follows: we define our notion of components with explicit protocols in Section 2. Protocol operators, their properties and how components are composed are presented in Section 3. An application to JavaBeans is presented in Section 4. We show an extension to the EJB's security model that can benefit from our technique in Section 5. Related work is discussed in Section 6 and conclusions are given in Section 7.

2   Components with Explicit Protocols

Components encapsulate implementations of services which are exposed in their interfaces: Interfaces should make explicit all the means by which interaction can be performed among components. We consider components as software units providing an interface consisting of a set of method declarations, one protocol, and a set of lists of identities of collaborating components that are used by the protocol to control the reception and sending of methods calls. There are many ways to associate protocols to services, e.g., one protocol per service or one protocol per component. We choose to associate one protocol to a component, because we are interested in expressing sequencing constraints. This solution is not less expressive than having several protocols by component: we can merge, for example, per-service protocols into one protocol using the techniques we present.

Informally, the semantics of interfaces is the following: the method declarations define the services a component offers, the protocol defines sequences of possible interactions (receiving and sending ones) by means of transitions of a finite-state system, and the collaborator lists provide information to restrict protocol transitions based on component identities. The figure on the right illustrates this for the chat component introduced earlier. The provided services include login(), the protocol includes a sequencing constraint between login and logout, and a collaborator list records logged-in clients.

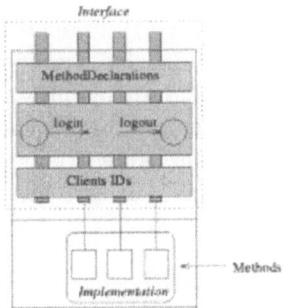

2.1   Component Protocols

We consider protocols formalized in terms of finite-state machines. We are interested in describing sequencing constraints that let a component specify the order in which services can be requested as well as constraints on possible Clients. Transition labels should include information of the direction of interactions (a message sent or a message received) and constraints about the identity of the caller or receiver. Transitions are labeled with directed service requests which enable expressions of two kinds of service request: requests by other components to the one considered (denoted by the direction label '−') and requests to the services of other components by the one considered (direction '+'). Transition labels may also include identity constraint terms, which are lists of component identities. In this case, transitions are triggered only if the corresponding service is requested by a component whose identity is in the list denoted by the identity constraint term. There are four operations on transition labels which can occur in transition labels:

- l+: Add to list l the identity of the component which performs the request corresponding to the current transition.
- l!: Enable transitions only for components whose identity is in l.

- l–: Enable transitions only for components in l and remove the identity of the component requesting the current service.
- $l*$: Sequence of transitions consisting of one transition for each identity in l. This term can be defined as follows. Let l be a list with n components then $l* \ : \ + \ \texttt{m()}$ is equivalent to the following set of transition sequences:

$$\{\langle s_i :: l_{p_i}!\rangle \, m() + s_{i+1}\rangle_i \mid (p_1, \ldots, p_n) \in permutations(l), \ i \in \{1, \ldots, n\}\}$$

The figure on the right shows a protocol definition of a basic behavioral description for the chat server example. The initial state *Stable* has three transitions repre-

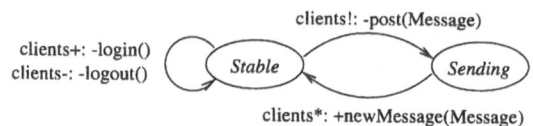

senting service requests provided by the server (denoted by the direction '–') to add a client (`login()`), to remove a client (`logout()`) and to post a message (`post()`). The transitions labeled with identity constraints record added and removed identity clients and thus ensure that messages are posted by clients that are currently logged in to all clients that have been added but not removed. Once a client has successfully posted a message the protocol transits to the *Sending* state from which the server broadcasts a `newMessage(Message)` message to every client that are logged in.

2.2 Properties: Protocol Substitutability and Compatibility

Explicit protocol information in interfaces, in particular protocols based on finite-state systems, is intended to enable the automatic verification of composition properties and adaptation properties. Existing approaches to explicit protocols for objects and components [7,4,6] provide a number of suitable properties and verification procedures. Two kinds of property are of foremost importance: *compatibility* and *substitutability*. The former is concerned with the problem of traces, i.e., the set of acceptable sequences of service requests of one protocol that match the traces of one another. In other words, it says whether one component can satisfy the requirements of a second component for any sequence of service requests. Satisfaction of the latter property enables one protocol to be substituted for another. Informally, a protocol replacing another one must accept at least the same sequences of service requests and cannot refuse more service requests than the protocol it replaces. Moreover, if a protocol q is substitutable for protocol p, then protocol q is compatible with every protocol compatible with p [7].

We strongly believe that substitutability is a key property in the development of component-based and distributed applications because it allows one to determine whether an extended server is still compatible with its clients. In this paper we consider substitutability properties of the protocol composition operators in some detail and discuss compatibility briefly. To treat substitutability formally, we choose Nierstrasz' notion of request substitutability [7] and the corresponding notion of substitutability between protocols.

3   Composition

We consider component composition as the basic relation that enables a component to use the services provided by another one. In the context of components with explicit protocols, component composition naturally involves composition of protocols. We propose five protocol composition operators to support component composition:

- *Union at state.* Merge a protocol into another at a given state.
- *Union.* Merging a protocol into one at their initial state.
- *Concatenation.* Append a protocol at the end of another one.
- *Insertion.* Insertion of a protocol into another one.
- *Identity constraint propagation.* Propagation of an identity constraint from one protocol to another.

These operators are useful for combining protocols. For example, it is possible to construct a protocol which behaves first at one protocol and then a second one using the Concatenation operator. While the first four operators, Union at state, Union, Concatenation and Insertion are structural operators, the last operator, Identity constraint propagation, is an operator for the manipulation of the abstract state, i.e., lists of component identities, associated with protocols. Although the structural operator are not original by themselves (see [7,4] for example), no study of their properties, in particular substitutability, has been conducted. One of the main contributions of this article is to analyze the relations between the operand protocols and the resulting protocol while trying to focus on the *substitutability* property previously studied in [7].

These protocol operators then give rise to corresponding component operators as follows. Let a component be denoted as $((d, p, s), i)$ where d is a set of method declarations, p a protocol, s a state associated to a protocol, and i a set of method implementations. Given one of the composition operators introduced above (denoted op), the composition of two components c_1, c_2 can be defined as:

$$((d_1 \cup d_2, p_1 \ op \ p_2, s_1 \cup s_2), i_1 \cup i_2)$$

3.1   Protocol Composition

We formally define the protocol operators using the well-known definition of finite-state systems as 5-tuples $p = (Q, \Sigma, \delta, i^p, F)$ [8]. Q is the set of states of the component protocol. Σ is the alphabet of valid labels consisting of service requests, i.e. method signatures, directions, and identity constraints. $\delta \subseteq Q \times \Sigma \times Q$ is the transition relation, i^p is the initial state and F the set of final states. For the sake of simplicity, we make two assumptions: first, operand protocols in a composition are defined using disjoint sets of states. Second, the set of final states of all protocols is $F = \{s \in Q \mid (s, t, s') \in \delta : s = s'\}$, i.e., all states from which no other state except itself can be reached. We choose a mathematical notation for representing protocols principally because it is more appropriate than a simple graphical representation for making proofs about the preservation of properties, in particular substitutability.

Protocol operators are subject to a recurring problem with regard to substitutability: operators may introduce non-determinism in protocols, which then violate this property.

We propose a technique to solve this problem in some important cases: we can construct a new protocol which preserves request substitutability by merging specific protocol states. Along the definition of the protocol operators, we illustrate them with small abstract examples and we provide concrete applications later in the paper.

Union at state. We define next a general protocol operator that merges a protocol into another one at a specific state. This operator is useful, for example, to merge different protocols, which are each associated to a different service into one protocol at different states of a main protocol. The resulting protocol has the same structure as the first operand and from the target state accepts any sequences that are accepted from the initial state of the second operand protocol.

Considering that the structure of the left operand protocol is not modified we can expect that the resulting protocol is substitutable for its first operand. However, this is not always the case because the resulting protocol can fail after executing a sequence of service requests when a constituent protocol does not fail. This is due to the non-determinism introduced by inserting the second operand in the target state of the first operand protocol. Consider protocols p and q defined in Figure 1, the union of protocol q at the state p_2 of protocol p is represented by the protocol u_1. After accepting the service request $a.a$, protocol p is in state p_1 and protocol u_1 may be in either state p_1 or q_2, and in q_2 it may refuse a service request a, while protocol p in state p_1 cannot. Protocol u_1 may fail to execute the sequence $a.a.a$, while protocol p cannot fail for the same sequence which makes protocol u_1 non substitutable for protocol p.

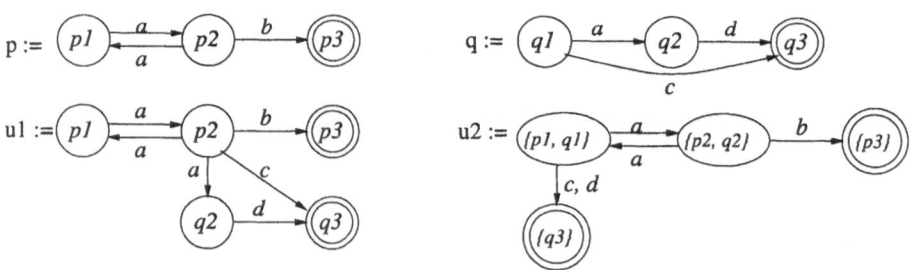

Fig. 1. Protocols p and q, and two versions, a correct and an incorrect one, of a unification of q into p at state p_2

To preserve substitutability, we must avoid introducing non-deterministic transitions in the resulting protocol if they introduce failures not present in the corresponding constituent protocols. We must consider states reached by common sequences of service requests from the target state (p_2 in the previous example). The problem arises if the outgoing transitions of the states reached by such a sequence in the two protocols are different. In such a case, we propose to merge the concerned states into a new state: every transition ending in one of the old states is redirected to the new one, and transitions starting from one of the old states now start from the new state. In this way, different failures of states reachable by common traces are eliminated.

We can characterize two states as problematic with respect to the substitutability property in the sense above by means of two relations, denoted by $\uparrow^s$ and $\Uparrow^s$, where s is the state where the union takes place. Let p and q be protocols, $x \in Q^p$, $y \in Q^q$, and $i \overset{t}{\Longrightarrow} x$ denote that x is reachable via trace t from i. Then:

$$(s, i^q) \overset{def}{\in} \uparrow^s$$

$$x \uparrow^s y \overset{def}{\Leftrightarrow} \exists t : (s \overset{t}{\Longrightarrow} x \wedge i^q \overset{t}{\Longrightarrow} y) \wedge initials(x) \neq initials(y)$$

where $initals(x)$ denotes the outgoing transitions of state x. $\uparrow^s$ relates two states which can be reached by at least one common trace from their respective initial state and which have differently-labeled outgoing transitions. We denote the reflexive, transitive closure of $\uparrow^s$ by $\Uparrow^s$ defined as follows:

$$x \Uparrow^s y \overset{def}{\Leftrightarrow} (x = y) \vee (x \uparrow^s y) \vee \exists \langle a_1, \ldots, a_n \rangle \subseteq (Q^p \cup Q^q)^n : x \uparrow^s a_1 \ldots a_n \uparrow^s y \tag{1}$$

The relation $\Uparrow^s$ is an equivalence relation (i.e., reflexive, symmetric and transitive; the proof can be found in [9]). We denote its equivalence classes by $[x]^{\Uparrow^s}$.

Based on these definitions, the union operator can then be defined as follows:

Definition 1 (Union at state, $\oslash$). *Let p and q be two protocols, the union of protocol q at state s of protocol p, written $p \oslash^s q$, is defined as the protocol $r = (Q^r, \Sigma^r, \delta^r, [i^p]^{\Uparrow^s}, F^r)$:*

$$Q^r = \{[x]^{\Uparrow^s} \mid x \in (Q^p \cup Q^q)\}$$
$$\Sigma^r = \Sigma^p \cup \Sigma^q$$
$$\delta^r = \{(s_1, m, s_2) \mid (x, m, y) \in (\delta^p \cup \delta^q) : s_1 = [x]^{\Uparrow^s} \wedge s_2 = [y]^{\Uparrow^s}\}$$

This definition merges states by means of the relation $\Uparrow^s$. This operator definition represents an important contribution of this paper because it ensures by construction that the protocol resulting of the union at a given state of two protocols can safely substitute its left operand protocol. The proof of this substitutability property relies on the fact that the resulting protocol inherits all the traces from its operands and thus can accept all the sequences that its operands may accept. Moreover, the states of the resulting protocol are created in such a way that it cannot fail to serve a request after a given sequence s of requests if the first operand is able to serve the request after s. (The formal proof can be found in [9].) Unifying protocols p and q of the previous example with this definition yields the protocol u_2 shown in Figure 1. This time, the resulting protocol will never refuse the sequence $a.a.a$.

Union. A particular case of the *union at state* operator unifies two protocols at their initial state to result in a protocol that accepts any sequence accepted by its parent protocols. This particular union is useful, for example, to merge different per-service protocols into one protocol and has the property that the resulting protocol is substitutable for both of its operand protocols.

Definition 2 (Union operator, $\oplus$). *Let p and q be two protocols, the* union operator *preserving substitutability, written $p \oplus q$, is defined as the protocol r:*

$$r = p \oslash^{i^p} q$$

The particularity of this operator is that it ensures that the resulting protocol can be substituted for any of its operand protocols (the proof can be found in [9]). Applied to the two example protocols p and q shown in Figure 1, the union operator yields the protocol shown in Figure 2a.

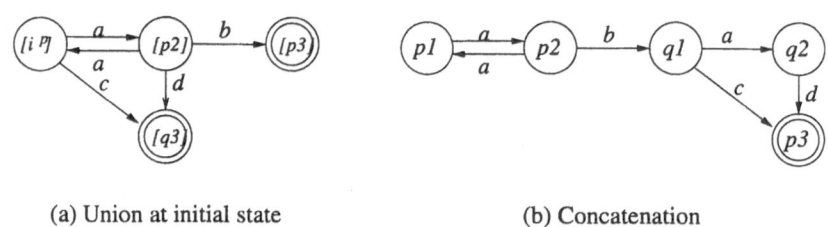

(a) Union at initial state   (b) Concatenation

Fig. 2. Applying different operators to p and q

Concatenation. The concatenation of two protocols consists in appending one protocol to another. The resulting protocol behaves initially as the first constituent protocol but once the protocol reaches any of its final states, it starts behaving as the second protocol. We define this operator as a restricted variant of the union at state operator to get immediate benefit of its substitutability property.

Definition 3 (Concatenation operator, $\mapsto$). *Let p and q be two protocols and $F^p = \{f_1, f_2, \cdots, f_n\}$ the set of p's final states. The concatenation of protocol q to protocol p, written $p \mapsto q$, is defined as follows:*

$$p \mapsto q := ((p \oslash^{f_1} q) \oslash^{f_2} q) \cdots \oslash^{f_n} q$$

Figure 2b shows the resulting protocol from concatenating protocol q to protocol p. Regarding substitutability, the resulting protocol can safely substitute its left operand: $p \mapsto q$ is protocol substitutable for protocol p but not for protocol q.

Insertion. The last structural operator considered in this paper is a very general protocol operator that allows the insertion of a protocol into another one at an arbitrary state, say s, by specifying explicitly redirection of transitions to and from s. Reconsider protocols p and q shown in Figure 1. Inserting q in protocol p at state p_2 and replacing states q_2, q_3 with p_2, p_3, respectively, yields the protocol shown in Figure 3.

In general, such an insertion depends on four parameters: the two protocols, the target state t where insertion should take place and an identification mapping $I : Q^q \to Q^p$,

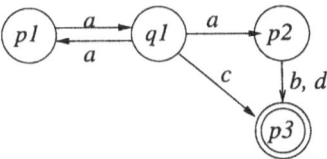

Fig. 3. Inserting q at p: $p \odot^{p2}_{\{(q_2,p_2),(q_3,p_3)\}} q$

which defines states of q that have to be replaced by states from p. The insertion operation can be defined as consisting of two steps. First, every transition starting from t is replaced by an analogous transition starting from q's initial state (i^q). Second, the identification mapping is processed. For each pair $(s_p, s_q) \in I$, all transitions going to s_q are redirected to s_p and all transitions going out from s_q start at s_p, instead.

This operator is not very natural in terms of protocol programming, but its main purpose is to express any protocol as the protocol composition of the four first protocols presented previously. Let us define the insertion protocol operator more formally:

Definition 4 (Insertion operator, $\odot$). *Let p and q be two protocols, $t \in Q^p$, $I : Q^q \longrightarrow Q^p$ such that $\exists y \in Q^q : I(y) = t$. The insertion of q into p at t, written $p \odot^t_I p$, is defined by the protocol $r = (Q^r, \Sigma^r, \delta^r, i^p, F^r)$, where:*

$$Q^r = Q^p \cup Q^q - Dom(I)$$
$$\Sigma^r = \Sigma^p \cup \Sigma^q$$
$$\begin{aligned}
\delta^r = \ & \{(x, m, y) \mid (x', m, y') \in (\delta^p \cup \delta^q) : \\
& (x' = I(x) \vee x = x') \wedge (y' = y \vee y' = I(y)) \wedge (y = t \Rightarrow x = t)\} \\
& \cup \{(x, m, i^q) \mid (x, m, t) \in \delta^p, x \neq t\} \cup \{(t, m, t) \in \delta^p\}
\end{aligned}$$

This definition constructs an automaton preserving the states of both automata except for unified states, i.e., states in $Dom(I)$. In the resulting automaton, the transitions of q et p are preserved if they do not involve states mapped by I and the target state t. Transitions involving states mapped by I are translated to the corresponding transitions involving mapped states. Transitions from other states to t originate from i^q after insertion and self edges on t are preserved.

Obviously, the insertion operator does not preserve substitutability property w.r.t. its constituent protocols. This is due to its generality, in particular the structural changes induced by the identification mapping.

Identity constraint propagation operator. The operators defined previously are structural operators because they are defined only in terms of states and transitions representing service requests. Our protocols also include state information to record identities of collaborating components and restrict transitions based on identities. Protocols can therefore be combined to manipulate this state information. In this section we present such an operator that propagates identity constraints among protocols. One operator for identity constraint propagation may label all its transitions with an identity constraints. This operator can be defined as follows:

Definition 5 (Identity constraint propagation operator, $\lfloor$). *Let p be a protocol and X an identity constraint term. The* identity constraint propagation *constraining p by X, written $p\lfloor_X$, is defined as the protocol $r = (Q^p, \Sigma^r, \delta^r, i^p, F^r)$ where:*

$$\Sigma^r = \{Z : \pm m \mid Z = (Y \cap X), Y : \pm m \in \Sigma^p\}$$
$$\delta^r = \{(x, Z : \pm m, y) \mid Z = (Y \cap X), (x, Y : \pm m, y) \in \delta^p\}$$

This operator does not preserve the substitutability property by itself but there are state-specific laws guaranteeing the preservation of substitutability for parts of the result, for example, where $Y \subseteq X$.

This operation can be combined with the other operators. A specialized concatenation operator of protocols, for example, may propagate an identity constraint from final transitions of the first protocol to the second one in addition to concatenation. More precisely, let p and q be two protocols such that every transition leading to a final state of p is constrained by the same component term X. The result of propagating the constraint X of p to q in $p \mapsto^X q$ can be defined as:

$$r = (p \mapsto q) \lfloor_X$$

4   Making JavaBeans' Implicit Protocols Explicit

JavaBeans [10] is a white-box component model based on Java, which adheres to the publish-subscribe paradigm [11], permitting components to register for notification (through broadcast) of events. The mechanisms for event-based communication can be seen as defining implicit protocols (because they are not explicitly declared in the JavaBeans' interface) between communicating JavaBeans. Basically, two implicit protocols are supported: *bound properties* represent values for which the modification is notified through a broadcast event to all registered components; *constrained properties* are values for which the modification is subject of a veto emitted (possible) by any registered component. These particular kinds of properties are used as a composition mechanism, specially in GUI interfaces, where, for instance, buttons and other graphics elements are plugged together to conform to a new interface entity. In this section, we render these protocols explicit using the notions introduced previously and we show how we can define JavaBeans declaratively. This enable us to apply our operators and reasoning about their substitutability properties in a concrete example.

4.1   Basic Event Management

Events are used to propagate information from a source bean to a set of collaborating beans, called listeners. Event objects encapsulate information about the state change of an *event source* bean. The event source bean must implement two methods for adding and removing listeners.

The event mechanism can be represented as a protocol between an event source and one or more event listeners (see the figure on the

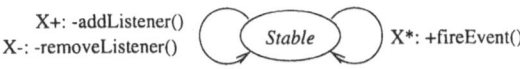

right). The protocol is defined by one state with three transitions constrained by identity constraints. The transition labeled with addListener() allows any component to call the service for subscribing as event listener and to add its identity to the variable X. The transition labeled removeListener() allows a component to request its removal from the list of listeners provided that it has been previously registered. Finally, the transition labeled fireEvent() describes the source sending an event to all registered listeners.

4.2 Bound Properties

A *bound property* is an instance variable of a JavaBean satisfying two characteristics. First, other beans can access a bound property only through its accessors methods for getting and setting its value. Second, the beans owning the bound property keeps a list of subscribed listeners that are notified with a suitable event each time that the bound variable changes.

This protocol can be represented explicitly as shown in the figure on the right. Basically, bound properties reuse

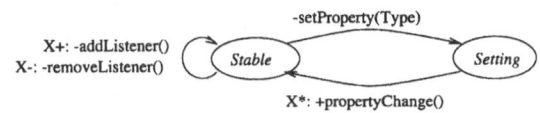

the protocol for basic event management and add one state which is reached by setting the property. Once the property has been set, the protocol transits to its initial state by broadcasting an appropriate event to all listeners.

4.3 Constrained Properties

In the case of *constrained properties*, the source bean keeps, in general, two lists of listeners: one list of beans listening to changes of the constrained property and another list of beans that can veto a change to the property value. Once a change has been requested, the bean broadcasts an event to the beans in the second list which can veto or not the proposed change. If a bean disagrees with the change, it throws an exception of type PropertyVetoException. Otherwise, the value is changed and a changeProperty event is broadcast to the registered listeners for notification.

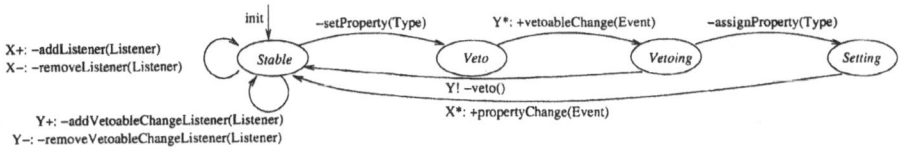

Fig. 4. Component protocol of a constrained property.

The protocol of constrained properties can be made explicit as shown in Figure 4. Compared to the protocol for bound properties, this protocol features an intermediate state *Vetoing* that allows beans to emit a veto, in which case no change occurs. Otherwise the protocol transits to the *Setting* state from where the bean fires a `changeProperty` event to every listener registered for change notification.

This discussion suggests that constrained properties can be seen as an extension of bound properties. Because it is possible to express these protocols explicitly in our framework, we can define the relationship between the two protocols precisely. The protocol on the right captures the veto-part of the protocol for the constraint property. In state `Veto` the bean notifies

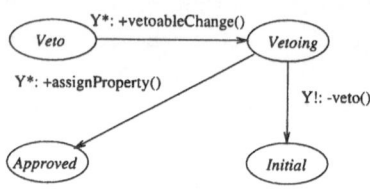

all beans registered in `Y` of the change proposal. Then, in state `Vetoing`, two transitions can be taken. Either an `assignProperty` message is sent to every component in `Y` and the `Approved` state is reached. Or the change is vetoed by one of the listeners that is represented by the message `veto`.

Then, the constrained protocol can be written as a protocol composition between the bound protocol and the `Veto` protocol by inserting the `Veto` protocol after the state *Stable* and redirecting transitions as follows:

$$ConstrainedProtocol = BoundProtocol \odot^{Setting}_{\{(Approved,Setting),(Vetoed,Stable)\}} Veto$$

We can formally proof the correctness of this construction by equational reasoning; (see [9] for the proof).

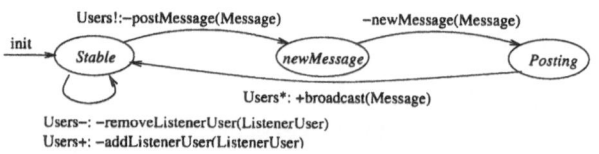

Fig. 5. The posting protocol.

To demonstrate the application of the proposed formalism, consider the use of bound and constrained protocols as part of the chat server application. Sometimes, a special chat session may require one or more moderators to refuse the broadcasting of an inadequate message. This can be implemented by constraining the messages to be sent with the vetos of moderators. Figure 5 shows the protocol for posting (broadcasting) messages. From an initial state, it is possible to either add or remove users who can request to post a message that is broadcasted afterward to every registered user. Figure 6 shows the protocol for moderation of messages using a constrained property. From an initial state, moderators can be added or removed and their approval is requested whenever a message is posted. If no moderator disagrees the message is posted.

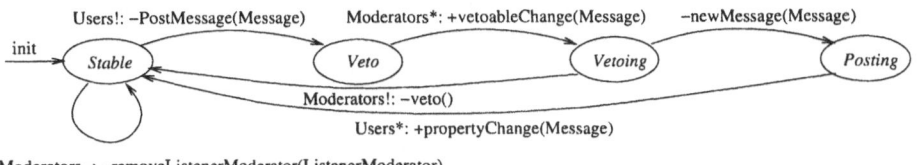

Fig. 6. The moderator protocol.

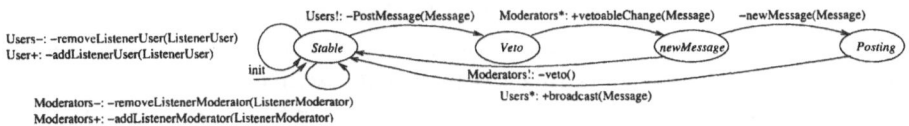

Fig. 7. The resulting protocol.

The moderated version of the posting protocol can be composed from protocols a) and b) as shown in Figure 7. The protocol composition essentially consists in inserting the moderator protocol into the posting protocol by binding their initial and posting states. Let $l = \{(Stable_M, Stable_P), (Posting_M, Posting_P)\}$ be an identification mapping. The complete protocol can be defined as a composition:

$$MederatedPosting = Posting \odot_l^{Stable} Moderator$$

A chat server protocol, which provides a monitored posting service and a message board search facility, can then be defined by the following expression:

$$Chat = ModeratedPosting \oplus SearchMessage \qquad (2)$$

The protocol $Chat$ is substitutable for both protocols and can therefore safely replace any server providing only one of these. Finally, we can require clients and moderators to log in first using the protocol shown on the right and then define the whole Chat server protocol as in the equation 3 shown below. These examples show that our operators can be used to define certain common compositions quite concisely and declaratively.

$$SecureChat = Login \mapsto^X Chat \qquad (3)$$

5   Extending the EJB Security Model

Enterprise JavaBeans (EJB) [1] is an industrial-strength component model, which supports the development, deployment, and management of transactional business systems, using distributed components implemented in Java. In this section, we discuss several limitations of the security model of EJB and we show how we can use explicit protocols to improve expression of access-control policies at the interface level.

5.1   The EJB Security Model and Its Limitations

The EJB security model is a role-based access-control model that permits deployers to configure and to parameterize security in a *black box* fashion. An EJB server can authenticate a client (using an authentication service, such as the JAAS service, for example) and then authorize the client to call certain of its services. The authorization process is based on a mechanism that maps a set of identities to a role with associated authorizations, are declaratively specified in the *deployment descriptor* file. At runtime a bean is subject to security checks performed on the server side by the bean container, which has been configured based on the deployment descriptor.

During bean development, the bean provider can implement security-related code directly within the bean, effectively working in a *white box* fashion. To this end, the EJB component model provides some methods in the `EJBContext` class to query the container about security-related information, such as the identity of the caller of a method (`getCallerPrincipal()`) or to check whether a caller belongs or not to a given role (`isCallerInRole(String)`). One of the main goals of the EJB's security model is to provide a mechanism for specifying policies at deployment time and to avoid the insertion of security-related code into the bean after the bean development phase. This way, providers are encouraged to develop beans without mixing security policies with the business logic and the application of security policies is left to the deployer of an application.

The EJB security model is well suited for the expression of security policies to control method calls according to the caller's identity. This is appropriate for implementing many security policies for distributed resources. However, we argue that more complex policies break down the overall goal of separating the security logic from the bean code. Explicit protocols enable three natural extensions of the EJB security model that allows more flexible security policies to be defined while respecting the goal of separation:

1. Explicit protocols enable access to be controled on the basis of information about sequences of methods. For example, in EJB it is possible to authorize identities belonging to a role X to execute methods m_1 and m_2, but it is not possible to restrict access of an identity to call m_2 only if it has already called method m_1 (which can be expressed using explicit protocols as $X! : -m_1 - m_2$). This limitation does not allow programmers to specify a policy such as *a client must first get the value to increment later*.

2. EJB does not provide support for specifying the interaction between roles when calling a sequence of services. Suppose, for example, that a role X can call methods m_1 and m_2 and role Y can call method n. There is no explicit support for stating policies such that role X calls method m_1, then role Y calls n and, finally, X calls method m_2 (using explicit protocols: $X! : -m_1; Y! : -n; X! : -m_2$).

3. Roles are static in the sense that it is not possible to add or to remove dynamically identities from roles. This is because roles and identities are associated at deployment time.

This three extensions directly put at work the definition of identity constraints terms presented in section 2.1. To illustrate how explicit protocols can be used to overcome the three these limitations while preserving a black-box model of access control, let us have another look at the example of the distributed chat server. Consider the collaboration of two different entities belonging to different roles: clients and moderators, where a client may create a forum and become moderator of that forum. Let the forum creation be supported by the chat server through the following services: askForForum(Forum), which allows a client to propose the creation of a forum; verifyRequest(), which is used to validate requests with respect to some criteria; and openForum(Forum), which allows the instantiation of a forum. We assume that clients have two methods: accepted(Forum) and refused(Forum), which are invoked to inform a client if a forum-related request has been accepted or refused. We would like to state the following *forum-related policies* over that set of services:

1. Limit the invocation of askForForum(Forum) and openForum(Forum) to *clients*, and access to askForForum(Forum) to clients that have already called openForum(Forum).
2. Limit calls to verifyRequest() to moderators and additionally ensure that verifyRequest() is executed after askForForum(Forum) is performed.
3. Require that accepted(Forum) and refused(Forum) are called only on clients that have requested the creation of a forum.

The EJB security model is not appropriate to implement these policies. For the first and second policies, it is possible to restrict the call of the methods to authenticated entities that belong to the corresponding roles (Client and Moderator). This can be done in a declarative way by specifying the identities belonging to each role in the deployment descriptor. However, it is not possible to specify in the deployment descriptor constrains over sequential executions of methods. To implement the second and third policies, in EJB, it is necessary to make an analysis of previous methods calls with respect to the current method by introducing code for managing sequences of methods calls.

5.2 Using Protocols to Enhance the EJB Security Model

Figure 8 shows a protocol implementing the three forum-related policies, governing the creation of new forums. The server restricts the execution of the method askForForum(Forum) to the same client c that afterwards requests openForum(Forum). The protocol limits requests verifyRequest() to moderators (represented by the identity term M) and expresses that a client must have requested the creation of a forum before. Only after the request verifyRequest(), is allowed the server to send an answer to the client who has requested the forum's creation. Finally, only after the reception of an acceptance notification from the server, the client can request the initialization of the forum by the server.

Once again, we can show how to extend the chat server protocol by unifying the secured version of the chat server, defined in Equation 3, at the state *Stable*, with the new service protocol:

$$NewChat = SecureChat \oslash^{Stable} ForumCreation$$

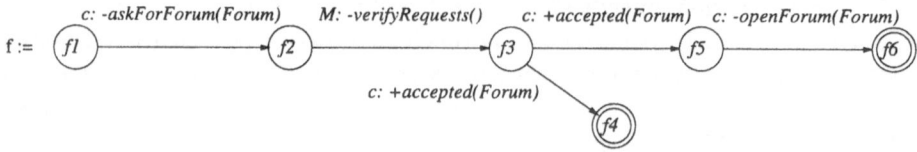

Fig. 8. Protocol of a Forum creation request

By construction, substitutability w.r.t. the secured chat server protocol holds, and we can thus conclude that existing clients are still compatible with this new version of the server.

We have given evidence that component with explicit protocols can provide a better solution for the implementation of sophisticated security policies. First, protocols are expressed at the interface level and security policies can be expressed separately from code of the client and the server beans and their expression can be done in the deployment descriptor, thus not breaking the EJB security model. Second, protocols allow us to describe sequencing constraints between methods and roles. Third, protocols allow a more flexible treatment of identities and roles, such as adding and removing identities from roles dynamically. Finally, the construction operators and associated substitutability property are also useful within a black-box component model: unnecessary generation of adaptors and modification of the client/server code is avoided.

6   Related Work

There are many approaches to the specification of sequencing constraints in many different fields. In the following we only consider approaches concerned with explicit protocol specifications based on finite-automata in components or object-oriented systems.

Objects and protocols. Nierstrasz uses regular types [7] to investigate service availability of objects using CSP [12] as a basis. He defines notions for compatibility and substitutability of protocol-enhanced objects. Our work can be seen as an extension of his work to components. PROCOL [13] is a parallel C-based object-oriented language with explicit per-objects protocols. Protocols describe the sequencing and synchronization constraints between an object and its collaborators. PROCOL is intended to be a general programming language and does not provide support for the automatic verification of properties. In contrast to our work, neither of these approaches considers construction operators and state separated from the protocol.

Component and protocols. Plazil *et al.* from the SOFA project at Charles University in Prague propose an enhanced architectural description language for component behavior with explicit protocols. They investigate protocol composition operators similar to regular expressions [6]. However, they do not consider property preservation of such operators. Yellin and Strom [4] also integrate explicit protocol into components. Their work is genuine in that it considers automatic generation of adapter code among component protocols in order to satisfy compatibility. However, they do not consider construction operators. Finally, these approaches do not consider separated state information associated to protocols.

Separated component specifications. There are numerous approaches supporting specifications of component-related properties that are separated from the underlying component model itself. UML [2], for instance, has been applied to the specification of components. Similarly, Message Sequence Charts [14] is a trace language used to describe interactions among components based on finite-state systems. Architectural description languages, such as Wright [15], have also been used for similar purposes. In contrast to our work, few of these approaches have considered construction operators and none of them explores the separation of state information from the protocol.

7 Conclusion

Extending previous work on finite-state based protocols for objects and components, we proposed three main contributions. First, a set of four composition operators for components with explicit protocols and discussed the impact of existing notions of protocol correctness, in particular substitutability. We showed, in particular, that they do not hold for some operator definitions when non deterministic transitions are introduced in the resulting protocol, and we presented a technique to solve this problem. Second, we considered the addition of state information to protocols to restrict protocol transitions based on the identity of collaborating components. Finally, we validated the use of the proposed techniques by applying them to Sun's component models, JavaBeans and Enterprise JavaBeans. We were able to make explicit the implicit protocols of JavaBeans components. As to EJB, we have shown that explicit protocols at the interface level allow the declarative formulation of more flexible access-control policies while preserving EJB's black-box properties.

Future work. There are many topics for future research based on the work presented in this paper. The current set of protocol constructors should be enlarged to make protocol construction more flexible. Furthermore, our investigation of separated state information only constitutes a first step on this concept and should be pursued. Finally, we plan to test our ideas with real-life EJB applications.

References

[1] DeMichiel, L., Yalçinalp, L., Krishnan, S.: Enterprise JavaBeans^{TM} Specification. SUN Microsystems. (2001) Version 2.0, Final Release.
[2] Rumbaugh, J., Jacobson, I., Booch, G.: The Unified Modeling Language Reference Manual. 1 edn. Addison-Wesley, Reading, Massachusetts, USA (1999)
[3] Harel, D.: Statecharts: A visual formalism for complex system. Science of Computer Programming **8** (1987) 231–274
[4] Yellin, D.M., Strom, R.E.: Protocol specifications and component adaptors. ACM Transactions of Programming Languages and Systems **19** (1997) 292 – 333
[5] Wydaeghe, B.: PACOSUITE, Component Composition Based on Composition Patterns and Usage Scenarios. PhD thesis, Vrije Universiteit Brussels (2001)
[6] Plasil, F., Visnovsky, S.: Behavior protocols for software components. In: Transactions on Software Engineering, IEEE (2002)

[7] Nierstrasz, O.: Regular types for active objects. In Nierstrasz, O., Tsichritzis, D., eds.: Object-Oriented Software Composition. Prentice Hall (1995) 99–121

[8] Hopcroft, J.E., Motwani, R., Ullman, J.D.: Introduction to Automata Theory, Languages, and Computation. Second edn. Addison Wesley (2001)

[9] Farias, A., Südolt, M.: A component model with explicit protocols. Technical Report 02/4/INFO, Ecole des Mines de Nantes (2002)

[10] Hamilton, G.: Java beans API specification. Technical report, Sun Microsystems (1997)

[11] Eugster, P., Guerraoui, R., Damm, C.: On objects and events. In: Proceedings OOPSLA. (2001)

[12] Brookes, S.D., Hoare, C.A.R., Roscoe, A.W.: A theory of communicating sequential processes. Journal of the ACM **31** (1984) 560–599

[13] Van Den Bos, J., Laffra, C.: PROCOL: a parallel object language with protocols. ACM SIGPLAN Notices **24** (1989) 95–102

[14] Rudolph, E., Graubmann, P., Grabowski, J.: Tutorial on Message Sequence Charts. Computer Networks and ISDN Systems **28** (1996) 1629–1641

[15] Allen, R.J.: A Formal Approach to Software Architecture. Ph.D. thesis, School of Computer Science, Carnegie Mellon University, Pittsburgh (1997)

Well-Founded Optimism: Inheritance in Frame-Based Knowledge Bases*

Guizhen Yang and Michael Kifer

Department of Computer Science
Stony Brook University
Stony Brook, NY 11794, U.S.A.
{guizyang,kifer}@CS.StonyBrook.EDU

Abstract. F-logic is a popular formalism for knowledge-intensive applications and, especially, for ontology management in Semantic Web. However, the original F-logic's semantics for inheritance suffers from a number of anomalies when inheritance and deduction closely interact.

This work rectifies this problem and develops a natural model-theoretic semantics for inheritance in frame-based knowledge bases, which supports inference by inheritance as well as inference via rules. Inference by inheritance supports a multitude of features, such as overriding and nonmonotonic multiple inheritance, meta programming, and dynamic inheritance hierarchies — the features that are fundamental to advanced knowledge management. This semantics has been effectively implemented in the Flora-2 system which is extensively used in a number of projects.

To the best of our knowledge, this work is the only model-theoretic semantics for nonmonotonic multiple inheritance that applies to general, unrestricted frame-based knowledge bases and has several independent characterizations, which testifies to its naturalness and robustness.

The problems discussed in this paper are inherent in any logic-based system that supports inheritance and deductive rules and our techniques apply to such systems. In particular, they apply to DAML+OIL extended with rules and inheritance.

1 Introduction

F-logic (Frame Logic) [21,22] is a formalism that unifies the deductive and object-oriented programming paradigms. Since then several implementations have been made available, such as FLORID[1], SiLRI[2], FLORA[3], and TFL[4]. Some of these systems have served as critical components in projects ranging from data integration in neuroscience [16], to processing semistructured and semantic information

---

* This work was supported in part by NSF grants INT-9809945 and IIS-0072927.
[1] http://www.informatik.uni-freiburg.de/~dbis/florid/
[2] http://ontobroker.semanticweb.org/silri/
[3] http://flora.sourceforge.net/
[4] http://www.dsic.upv.es/~pcarsi/tfl/

on the Web [11,9], to information mediation [15], to commercial and research prototypes of Web information management systems [8,10,30].

The use of F-logic for ontology management was pioneered by the Ontobroker project [30,10] and since then it has become one of the primary contenders to provide formalization and inference mechanism for the various aspects of Semantic Web. In [9], F-logic was advocated as an inference service for RDF and later an F-logic based language, TRIPLE, was developed specifically for this purpose [29]. The ability to handle RDF also exists in FLORA-2 [33,34], a powerful system for programming knowledge-based applications, which is built around the semantics of F-logic, HiLog [6], and Transaction Logic [2].

Inheritance is one of the key aspects in frame-based knowledge representation and it has been extensively studied both in the AI and database literature (see [31,3,5,1,4,25,22,19,20] just to name a few). Unfortunately, as pointed out in [22], integration of inference by inheritance into rule-based deductive systems presents serious semantic and computational difficulties. Although F-logic, as described in [22], resolved many semantic and proof-theoretic issues in frame-based knowledge systems, nonmonotonic multiple inheritance was handled in an ad hoc, nonlogical way. In fact, the semantics proposed in [22] was known to yield questionable results in many cases. Subsequent works by a number of authors [24,4,25,1,19,20] tried to either "justify" this flawed (in our opinion) semantics or propose new ones, which worked by extensively restricting the syntax of F-logic and eliminating some of the desired features (like meta-programming, virtual class definitions, etc.).

In this paper, we solve all these problems and develop a natural model-theoretic semantics for nonmonotonic multiple inheritance in F-logic. We also describe its implementation in Flora-2 [33,34], which is based on the top-down tabling inference engine of XSB[5]. While the original fixpoint procedure [22] for computing inheritance in F-logic was inherently bottom-up, the new semantics can be implemented either bottom-up, using an extended alternating fixpoint, or top-down, using XSB's realization of the SLG resolution [7].

We should note that the problems discussed in this paper are *inherent* in logic-based systems that support inheritance and deductive rules. Our techniques apply to such systems and, in particular, to DAML+OIL [17] when it is extended with rules and inheritance.

We now briefly survey the literature on inheritance. To make our comparison concrete, we first list the main features of inheritance that, in our opinion, must be supported by a frame-based knowledge base system:

- implicit inference by inheritance, as well as explicit inference via rules
- overriding by intermediate superclasses
- dynamic class hierarchies, *i.e.*, the ability to define both ISA membership and subclass relationship via rules
- nonmonotonic inheritance from multiple superclasses that are incomparable with respect to the subclass relationship
- meta-programming, by which variables can range over class and method names

---

[5] http://xsb.sourceforge.net

There is a large body of work based on Touretzky's framework of Inheritance Nets [31]. On one hand, the overriding mechanism in this framework is more sophisticated than what is typically considered in the knowledge base context. On the other hand, this framework supports neither deductive inference via rules nor dynamic class hierarchies, which makes it too weak for many applications of knowledge bases. We will not discuss this framework any further.

Abiteboul et al. [1] propose a framework for implementing inheritance that is based on program rewriting using Datalog with negation. In spirit, this implementation is close to our implementation in Flora-2. However, [1] is not based on a formal, model-theoretic formalization. On the practical side, this framework excludes nonmonotonic multiple inheritance and makes strong assumptions, such as that programs must have a total (two-valued) well-founded model. This property is undecidable without far-reaching syntactic restrictions.

Bugliesi and Jamil [4] propose a model-theoretic semantics for inheritance with overriding which bears close resemblance to two-valued stable models [14]. However, their semantics applies only to negation-free programs (a severe limitation in practice) and does not handle multiple inheritance conflicts properly. More importantly, [4] is not backed by an algorithm.

May et al. [25] apply the ideas behind the well-founded semantics to F-logic. However, inheritance is still dealt with in the same way as in the original F-logic. Apart from being ad hoc, this semantics is known to produce counter-intuitive results when dynamic class hierarchies interact with overriding and multiple inheritance (cf. Section 2).

In [19,20], Jamil introduces a series of techniques to tackle the inheritance problem. Among these, the ideas of *locality* and *context*, which were proposed to resolve code inheritance and encapsulation in the language Datalog^{++}, have influenced our approach the most. However, these works do not define a model-theoretic inheritance semantics and support neither dynamic class hierarchies nor meta-programming. In [19] the inheritance semantics is defined by program rewriting while in [20] the approach is proof-theoretic.

In contrast to all these previous works, we propose a comprehensive framework and develop a natural model theory for nonmonotonic multiple inheritance in knowledge base systems. We adopt the well-founded semantics [13,12] and extend it with the ideas of locality and context [19]. In order to capture the common intuition behind overriding and conflict resolution in multiple inheritance, we formalize locality and context in the setting of *three-valued* models and introduce the concept of *inheritance candidacy*. We then formally define the *inheritance postulates*, which embody the common intuition and the main principles behind nonmonotonic multiple inheritance. To the best of our knowledge, this intuition has not been formalized before. We treat the inheritance postulates as the minimum requirements for an *object model* of a program. To further tighten the semantics, we apply the principle of *well-founded optimism* and develop the notion of a *unique* canonical model, called *optimistic object model*, which exists for any program. "Optimism" here means that we apply the closed world assumption with a bias towards undefinedness rather than falsehood.

The new optimistic object model semantics satisfies all the aforementioned desiderata for inheritance, produces intuitively satisfactory results in all known "benchmark" cases, does not impose syntactic restrictions on the programs (beyond requiring them to be rule-based), and has been effectively implemented in the Flora-2 system. The proposed semantics is *robust* in the sense that it can be characterized in at least three different ways: as the least fixpoint of an extended alternating fixpoint operator, as a minimal object model (with respect to truth ordering), and as the intersection of all *three-valued stable* object models.

The paper is organized as follows. Section 2 introduces the basic F-logic syntax, defines its three-valued semantics, and illustrates the main challenges in dealing with nonmonotonic multiple inheritance in the presence of deductive rules and dynamic class hierarchies. Section 3 describes our model theory for nonmonotonic multiple inheritance and Section 4 provides an alternating fixpoint computation for the optimistic object model of any F-logic program. The properties of optimistic object models are discussed in Section 5. Section 6 describes an implementation of our semantics by translation to general logic programs, which can be executed by any deductive engine that supports the well-founded semantics for negation, and formally proves that this implementation is correct. The data complexity of computing optimistic object models is discussed in Section 7. Section 8 concludes the paper.

Limitation of space does not allow us to present the proofs and expand on the relationship between optimistic object models and three-valued stable object models. However, it can be shown that, similarly to [27], three-valued stable object models that obey all inheritance postulates can be defined and the optimistic object model is the least among these models.

All proofs and a detailed account of the theoretical development of the optimistic object model semantics can be found in a technical report available at http://www.cs.sunysb.edu/~guizyang/papers/inheritance.ps

2   Preliminaries

2.1   Basic Syntax

To simplify the exposition, we focus on a subset of F-logic, which includes only two kinds of atoms: those that represent the subclass relationships and those that represent inheritable multivalued method specifications. An atom of the form $s :: c$ says that s is a subclass of c, while $s[m \twoheadrightarrow v]$ [6] specifies that s has an inheritable multivalued method, m, whose return value is a set, and v is one of the members in that set. The symbols s, c, m, and v in the above atomic formulas are first-order terms, which represent the ID of an object, a class, a method, and a value of the method, respectively. Moreover, the terms that represent these entities in a program can contain variables and, thus, they can represent multiple objects, one per variable instantiation. This design makes meta-programming in F-logic as natural as querying.

Let A be any atom. A literal of the form A is called a *positive* literal while a literal of the form $\neg A$ is called a *negative* literal. An F-logic program is a

---
[6] To reduce clutter, we slightly depart from the syntax of F-logic and Flora-2 and use $\twoheadrightarrow$ instead of $\star\twoheadrightarrow$ to represent inheritable multivalued methods.

finite set of rules where all variables are universally quantified. An F-logic rule has the following form: $\forall(H \leftarrow L_1 \wedge \dots \wedge L_n)$ where $n \geq 0$, H is a positive literal, and L_i $(1 \leq i \leq n)$ is either a positive or a negative literal. H is called the *head* of the rule, and the *conjunction* of L_i's is called the *body* of the rule. The symbol $\forall$ indicates that all variables are universally quantified. Following the standard convention, we will omit universal quantifiers in the rules and simply write $H \leftarrow L_1, \dots, L_n$. We will also use uppercase names to denote variables and lowercase names to denote constants. A rule with an empty body is called a *fact*. When writing down the facts, we will omit the implication symbol and simply show the head.

2.2   Motivating Examples

We now illustrate some of the main issues that arise from the interaction among deduction, inheritance, and dynamic class hierarchies. These issues were first explored in [22].

In the following examples, a solid arrow from a node c_1 to another node c_2 means that c_1 is a subclass of c_2. All examples in this section are discussed informally. The formal treatment will be given in Sections 3 and 4.

$$c_1 :: c_2.$$
$$c_2[m \twoheadrightarrow a].$$
$$c_2[m \twoheadrightarrow b] \leftarrow c_1[m \twoheadrightarrow a].$$

Fig. 1. Inheritance through Context

Consider the program in Figure 1. Without inheritance, this program has a unique model, which consists of the first two facts. According to the common intuition behind inheritance, c_1 ought to inherit $m \twoheadrightarrow a$ from c_2. However, just adding the fact $c_1[m \twoheadrightarrow a]$ will not make the resulting set a model, since the last rule is no longer satisfied: The least model that contains the inherited fact should also include $c_2[m \twoheadrightarrow b]$. However, this begs the question as to whether c1 should inherit $m \twoheadrightarrow b$ from c_2 as well. The intuition suggests that the intended model should be "stable" with respect to not only deduction but inheritance as well. Therefore $c_1[m \twoheadrightarrow b]$ also should be in that model. This problem was recognized in [22], but the proposed solution was not stable in the above sense, because it was not based on semantic principles but rather on an ad hoc definition of a plausible fixpoint computation.

$$c_1 :: c_2.$$
$$c_2[m \twoheadrightarrow a].$$
$$c_1[m \twoheadrightarrow b] \leftarrow c_1[m \twoheadrightarrow a].$$

Fig. 2. Interaction between Derived and Inherited Facts

Now consider the program in Figure 2, which is the same as the program in Figure 1 except for the head of the last rule. Again, the intuition suggests that $c_1[m \twoheadrightarrow a]$ ought to be inherited, and $c_1[m \twoheadrightarrow b]$ be derived to make the resulting set of facts into a model in the conventional sense. This, however, leads to the following observation. The method m of c_1 now has one value, a, which is inherited, and another value, b, which is derived via a rule. Although the traditional frameworks for inheritance were developed without deduction in mind, it is clear that derived facts like $c_1[m \twoheadrightarrow b]$ are akin to "local" method definitions and so should be treated similarly. In particular, local definitions always override inheritance. The conclusion is that although derivation is done "after" inheritance, its existence undermines the original reason for inheritance. This is similar to the known phenomenon where a reasoner rejects an assumption when it leads to the derivation of a contradiction. Again, the framework presented in this paper, which is based on semantic principles, differs from the ad hoc computation in [22] (which keeps both derived and inherited facts).

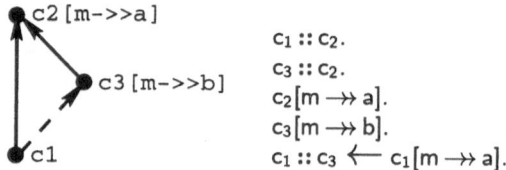

$c_1 :: c_2.$
$c_3 :: c_2.$
$c_2[m \twoheadrightarrow a].$
$c_3[m \twoheadrightarrow b].$
$c_1 :: c_3 \leftarrow c_1[m \twoheadrightarrow a].$

Fig. 3. Interaction between Inheritance and Derived Intervening Superclass

The example in Figure 3 shows a case where inheritance changes the class hierarchy, which creates conditions that undermine the original reason for inheritance. Initially, c_3 is not known to be a superclass of c_1. So, it seems that c_1 can inherit $m \twoheadrightarrow a$ from c_2. However, this makes the fact $c_1[m \twoheadrightarrow a]$ true, which in turn causes $c_1 :: c_3$ to be derived by the last rule of the program. Since this makes c_3 a more specific superclass of c_1 than c_2, it appears that c_1 ought to inherit $m \twoheadrightarrow b$ from c_3 rather than $m \twoheadrightarrow a$ from c_2. However, this would make the fact $c_1 :: c_3$ unsupported. Either way, the deductive inference enabled by the original inheritance undermines the support for the inheritance itself. Unlike [22], a logically correct solution in this case would be to leave both $c_1 :: c_3$ and $c_1[m \twoheadrightarrow a]$ undefined. The dashed arrow from c_1 to c_3 represents the undefinedness of $c_1 :: c_3$.

2.3 Three-Valued Semantics

The above examples show that inheritance candidacy can be invalidated by a subsequent derivation, which suggests the use of the stable model semantics [14] or the well-founded semantics [13]. In this paper we adopt the latter. Since well-founded models are three-valued and the original F-logic models were two-valued [22], we define a suitable three-valued semantics for F-logic programs first.

The Herbrand universe $\mathcal{HU}_P$ of an F-logic program P consists of all the *ground* (*i.e.*, variable-free) terms constructed using the function symbols and constants found in the program. The *Herbrand instantiation* of an F-logic program P, denoted $ground(P)$, is the set of rules obtained by consistently substituting all the terms in $\mathcal{HU}_P$ for all variables in every rule of P. Although the program P is finite, its Herbrand instantiation may well be infinite. In this paper, we consider only the Herbrand instantiation of a program.

The Herbrand base $\mathcal{HB}_P$ of an F-logic program P consists of two sorts of atoms: $s :: c$ and $s[m \twoheadrightarrow v]/c$, where s, m, v, and c are terms from $\mathcal{HU}_P$. A *three-valued* interpretation $\mathcal{I}$ of an F-logic program P is a pair $\langle T; U \rangle$, where T and U are *disjoint* subsets of the Herbrand base $\mathcal{HB}_P$ of P. The set T contains all atoms that are *true* in $\mathcal{I}$ and U contains all atoms that are *undefined* in $\mathcal{I}$. The set F of all atoms that are *false* in $\mathcal{I}$ is defined as $F = \mathcal{HB}_P - (T \cup U)$. A three-valued interpretation $\mathcal{I} = \langle T; U \rangle$ is called *two-valued* if $U = \emptyset$.

Following [26], we define the valuation functions for atoms, literals, and rules. The atoms in $\mathcal{HB}_P$ can take one of the three values: **t**, **f**, and **u**. The ordering among truth values is as follows: $\mathbf{f} < \mathbf{u} < \mathbf{t}$. Given an interpretation $\mathcal{I} = \langle T; U \rangle$ of an F-logic program P, for any atom A from $\mathcal{HB}_P$ we can define a truth valuation function $\mathcal{I}$ as follows: (i) $\mathcal{I}(A) = \mathbf{t}$, if $A \in T$; (ii) $\mathcal{I}(A) = \mathbf{u}$, if $A \in U$; (iii) Otherwise, $\mathcal{I}(A) = \mathbf{f}$. Moreover, for any $A_i \in \mathcal{HB}_P$, $1 \leq i \leq n$: $\mathcal{I}(A_1 \wedge \ldots \wedge A_n) = min\{\mathcal{I}(A_i) \,|\, 1 \leq i \leq n\}$.

We can extend the truth valuation function $\mathcal{I}$ to all rules in the Herbrand instantiation of P, $ground(P)$. The intuitive reading of a rule is as follows: the head of the rule functions as a *local definition* while the body of the rule functions as a *query*. In particular, if $s[m \twoheadrightarrow v]$ is in the head of a rule and the body of the rule is satisfied, it means that $m \twoheadrightarrow v$ is *locally defined* for s. If $s[m \twoheadrightarrow v]$ appears in the body of a rule, it is a query that tests whether s has a local definition of $m \twoheadrightarrow v$, or s inherits $m \twoheadrightarrow v$ from some superclass. In an interpretation of an F-logic program, atoms of the form $s[m \twoheadrightarrow v]/s$ capture the idea that $m \twoheadrightarrow v$ is locally defined at s, and atoms of the form $s[m \twoheadrightarrow v]/c$, where $s \neq c$, capture the idea that s inherits $m \twoheadrightarrow v$ from c. Therefore, the truth valuation of an F-logic literal may be different depending on whether it appears in a rule head or in a rule body. The following definitions make the above discussion precise.

Definition 1. *Given an interpretation $\mathcal{I}$ of an F-logic program P, the* truth *valuation functions $\mathcal{V}_\mathcal{I}^h$ and $\mathcal{V}_\mathcal{I}^b$ (h stands for* head *and b for* body*) on ground F-logic literals are defined as follows:*

$$\mathcal{V}_\mathcal{I}^h(s :: c) = \mathcal{I}(s :: c) \qquad \mathcal{V}_\mathcal{I}^h(c[m \twoheadrightarrow v]) = \mathcal{I}(c[m \twoheadrightarrow v]/c)$$

$$\mathcal{V}_\mathcal{I}^b(s :: c) = \mathcal{I}(s :: c) \qquad \mathcal{V}_\mathcal{I}^b(s[m \twoheadrightarrow v]) = max\{\mathcal{I}(s[m \twoheadrightarrow v]/c) \,|\, c \in \mathcal{HU}_P\}$$

Let L and L_i ($1 \leq i \leq n$) be variable-free literals. Then

$$\mathcal{V}_\mathcal{I}^b(\neg L) = \neg \mathcal{V}_\mathcal{I}^b(L) \qquad \mathcal{V}_\mathcal{I}^b(L_1 \wedge \ldots \wedge L_n) = min\{\mathcal{V}_\mathcal{I}^b(L_i) \,|\, 1 \leq i \leq n\}$$

where $\neg \mathbf{f} = \mathbf{t}$, $\neg \mathbf{u} = \mathbf{u}$, and $\neg \mathbf{t} = \mathbf{f}$.

Definition 2. *Given an interpretation $\mathcal{I}$ of an F-logic program P, the truth valuation function $\mathcal{I}$ on a rule, $H \leftarrow B$, in $ground(P)$, is defined as follows:*

$$\mathcal{I}(H \leftarrow B) = \begin{cases} \mathbf{t}, & \text{if } \mathcal{V}_\mathcal{I}^h(H) \geq \mathcal{V}_\mathcal{I}^b(B); \\ \mathbf{f}, & \text{otherwise.} \end{cases}$$

The truth valuation function $\mathcal{I}$ on a fact, $\mathsf{H} \in ground(\mathrm{P})$, is defined as follows:

$$\mathcal{I}(\mathsf{H}) = \begin{cases} \mathbf{t}, \text{ if } \mathcal{V}_{\mathcal{I}}^{\mathsf{h}}(\mathsf{H}) = \mathbf{t}; \\ \mathbf{f}, \text{ otherwise.} \end{cases}$$

Definition 3 (Program Satisfaction). *A three-valued interpretation $\mathcal{I}$ satisfies an F-logic program P, if for every rule R in $ground(\mathrm{P})$, $\mathcal{I}(\mathsf{R}) = \mathbf{t}$.*

3   Nonmonotonic Multiple Inheritance

Program satisfaction, as in Definition 3, does not necessarily mean that an interpretation $\mathcal{I}$ is an intended *object model* of an F-logic program P, because $\mathcal{I}$ must also include facts that are derived by inheritance. An F-logic program specifies only the class hierarchy and method definitions — what needs to be inherited is not explicitly stated. In fact, as we saw in Section 2.2, defining exactly what should be inherited is a subtle issue. In our framework, it is the job of the *inheritance postulates*, which embody the common intuition behind nonmonotonic multiple inheritance. The purpose of this section is to develop these postulates and the associated notion of an object model.

Note that although the intuition behind these postulates is commonly accepted, these postulates have never been formalized before in a general framework where inheritance and deduction coexist. Our contribution is in showing that these postulates can form a foundation for a semantics that is both mathematically robust and intuitively satisfactory.

Intuitively, $\mathsf{c}[\mathsf{m} \twoheadrightarrow \mathsf{v}]$ is an *inheritance context* for s, which has no local definition for the method m, if c is a superclass (but not necessarily an immediate superclass) of s, and $\mathsf{m} \twoheadrightarrow \mathsf{v}$ is locally defined at c, *i.e.*, $\mathsf{c}[\mathsf{m} \twoheadrightarrow \mathsf{v}]$ is defined as a fact or derived via a program rule. Inheritance context is necessary for inheritance to take place, but is not sufficient. Indeed, inheritance of $\mathsf{m} \twoheadrightarrow \mathsf{v}$ from c might be overridden by a more specific inheritance context that sits below c along the inheritance path. If an inheritance context is not overridden by any other inheritance context, then we call it an *inheritance candidate*. Intuitively, inheritance candidates represent potential sources for inheritance. But there must be exactly one inheritance candidate for inheritance to take place — having more just leads to a multiple inheritance conflict.

The various concepts defined below come in with two flavors: *strong* or *weak*. The "strong" flavor of a concept requires that all relevant facts must be positively established; the "weak" flavor allows some or all facts to be undefined.

Definition 4 (Local Context). *Given an interpretation $\mathcal{I}$, $\mathsf{s}[\mathsf{m} \twoheadrightarrow \mathsf{v}]$ is a strong local context for s in $\mathcal{I}$, if $\mathcal{I}(\mathsf{s}[\mathsf{m} \twoheadrightarrow \mathsf{v}]/_\mathsf{s}) = \mathbf{t}$. Similarly, $\mathsf{s}[\mathsf{m} \twoheadrightarrow \mathsf{v}]$ is a weak local context for s in $\mathcal{I}$ if $\mathcal{I}(\mathsf{s}[\mathsf{m} \twoheadrightarrow \mathsf{v}]/_\mathsf{s}) = \mathbf{u}$.*

Definition 5 (Inheritance Context). *Given an interpretation $\mathcal{I}$, $\mathsf{c}[\mathsf{m} \twoheadrightarrow \mathsf{v}]$ is a strong inheritance context for s in $\mathcal{I}$, if $\mathsf{c} \neq \mathsf{s}$[7], $\mathcal{I}(\mathsf{s} :: \mathsf{c} \wedge \mathsf{c}[\mathsf{m} \twoheadrightarrow \mathsf{v}]/_\mathsf{c}) =$*

---

[7] $\mathsf{c} \neq \mathsf{s}$ means that c and s are distinct terms.

t, and $\mathcal{I}(s[m \twoheadrightarrow x]/_s) = \mathbf{f}$ *for all* x. *(i.e.,* s *is a proper subclass of* c, $m \twoheadrightarrow v$ *is locally defined at* c, *and* s *has neither strong nor weak local context on the method* m *). Similarly,* $c[m \twoheadrightarrow v]$ *is a weak inheritance context for* s *in* $\mathcal{I}$ *if* $c \neq s$, $\mathcal{I}(s :: c \wedge c[m \twoheadrightarrow v]/_c) = \mathbf{u}$, *and* $\mathcal{I}(s[m \twoheadrightarrow x]/_s) \neq \mathbf{t}$ *for all* x *(i.e.,* s *has no strong local context on the method* m *).*

Definition 6 (Overriding). *Given an interpretation* $\mathcal{I}$, *the class* o *strongly overrides* $c[m \twoheadrightarrow v]$ *for* s *in* $\mathcal{I}$, *if* $o \neq c$, $\mathcal{I}(o :: c) = \mathbf{t}$, *and there is* x *such that* $o[m \twoheadrightarrow x]$ *is a strong inheritance context for* s.

The class o *weakly overrides* $c[m \twoheadrightarrow v]$ *for* s *in* $\mathcal{I}$ *if the above conditions are relaxed by allowing* $o :: c$ *to be undefined and/or allowing* $o[m \twoheadrightarrow x]$ *to be a weak context. Formally this means that either*

(1) $\mathcal{I}(o :: c) = \mathbf{t}$ *and there is* x *such that* $o[m \twoheadrightarrow x]$ *is a weak inheritance context for* s; *or*

(2) $\mathcal{I}(o :: c) = \mathbf{u}$ *and there is* x *such that* $o[m \twoheadrightarrow x]$ *is either a weak or a strong inheritance context for* s.

Definition 7 (Inheritance Candidate). *Given an interpretation* $\mathcal{I}$, $c[m \twoheadrightarrow v]$ *is a strong inheritance candidate for* s *in* $\mathcal{I}$, *denoted* $c[m \twoheadrightarrow v] \stackrel{s}{\leadsto}_{\mathcal{I}} s$, *if* $c[m \twoheadrightarrow v]$ *is a strong inheritance context for* s, *and there is no* o *that strongly or weakly overrides* $c[m \twoheadrightarrow v]$ *for* s.

$c[m \twoheadrightarrow v]$ *is a weak inheritance candidate for* s *in* $\mathcal{I}$, *denoted* $c[m \twoheadrightarrow v] \stackrel{w}{\leadsto}_{\mathcal{I}} s$, *if the above conditions are relaxed by allowing* $c[m \twoheadrightarrow v]$ *to be a weak inheritance context and/or allowing weak overriding. Formally, this means that there is no* o *that strongly overrides* $c[m \twoheadrightarrow v]$ *for* s, *and either*

(1) $c[m \twoheadrightarrow v]$ *is a weak inheritance context for* s; *or*

(2) $c[m \twoheadrightarrow v]$ *is a strong inheritance context for* s *and there is* o *that weakly overrides* $c[m \twoheadrightarrow v]$ *for* s.

As an example, consider an interpretation $\mathcal{I} = \langle \mathrm{T}; \mathrm{U} \rangle$, where $\mathrm{T} = \{c_1 :: c_2,$ $c_1 :: c_4, c_1 :: c_5, c_2 :: c_4, c_3 :: c_5, c_2[m \twoheadrightarrow a]/_{c_2}, c_3[m \twoheadrightarrow b]/_{c_3}, c_4[m \twoheadrightarrow c]/_{c_4}, c_5[m \twoheadrightarrow d]/_{c_5}\}$ and $\mathrm{U} = \{c_1 :: c_3\}$. $\mathcal{I}$ is shown in Figure 4, where solid and dashed arrows represent true and undefined subclass relationships, respectively.

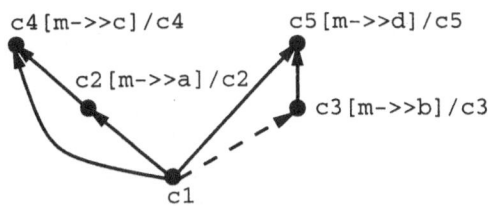

Fig. 4. Inheritance Context, Overriding, and Inheritance Candidate

In $\mathcal{I}$, $c_2[m \twoheadrightarrow a]$, $c_4[m \twoheadrightarrow c]$, and $c_5[m \twoheadrightarrow d]$ are strong inheritance contexts for c_1. On the other hand, $c_3[m \twoheadrightarrow b]$ is a weak inheritance context for c_1. The class c_2 strongly overrides $c_4[m \twoheadrightarrow c]$, while c_3 weakly overrides $c_5[m \twoheadrightarrow d]$. The context $c_2[m \twoheadrightarrow a]$ is a strong inheritance candidate for c_1, while $c_3[m \twoheadrightarrow b]$ and $c_5[m \twoheadrightarrow d]$ are both weak inheritance candidates for c_1, and $c_4[m \twoheadrightarrow c]$ is neither a strong nor a weak inheritance candidate for c_1.

For convenience, we use $c[m \twoheadrightarrow v] \rightsquigarrow_{\mathcal{I}} s$ in situations where it does not matter whether $c[m \twoheadrightarrow v]$ is a strong or a weak inheritance candidate. Now we are ready to introduce our postulates for nonmonotonic multiple inheritance.

Definition 8 (Positive ISA Transitivity). *An interpretation $\mathcal{I}$ satisfies the* positive ISA transitivity constraint *if the positive part of the class hierarchy is transitively closed, formally, for all s, c: if there is o such that $\mathcal{I}(s::o) = t \wedge \mathcal{I}(o::c) = t$, then $\mathcal{I}(s::c) = t$.*

Definition 9 (Context Consistency). *An interpretation $\mathcal{I}$ satisfies the* context consistency constraint, *if the following two conditions hold:*

(1) for all c, m, v: if $\mathcal{I}(c[m \twoheadrightarrow v]/_c) = \mathbf{f}$, then $\mathcal{I}(s[m \twoheadrightarrow v]/_c) = \mathbf{f}$ for all s;

(2) for all s, m: if there is v such that $\mathcal{I}(s[m \twoheadrightarrow v]/_s) = t$, then $\mathcal{I}(s[m \twoheadrightarrow x]/_c) = \mathbf{f}$ for all x, c, such that $c \neq s$,

The context consistency constraint captures the implications of locality and specificity. The first condition states that if $m \twoheadrightarrow v$ is not locally defined for c, then no class should inherit $m \twoheadrightarrow v$ from c. The second condition states that if $m \twoheadrightarrow v$ is locally defined for s, then this definition should prevent s from inheriting any information about m from other classes.

The following constraint captures the meaning of nonmonotonic multiple inheritance. Intuitively, we want our semantics for inheritance to have the property that if inheritance is allowed, then it should take place from a *unique* source.

Definition 10 (Unique Source Inheritance). *An interpretation $\mathcal{I}$ satisfies the* unique source inheritance constraint, *if the following two conditions hold:*

(1) for all c, s, m, and v: if $c[m \twoheadrightarrow v] \rightsquigarrow_{\mathcal{I}} s$, then $\mathcal{I}(s[m \twoheadrightarrow x]/_o) = \mathbf{f}$ for all x, o, such that $o \neq c$;

(2) for all m, v, c, and s, such that $s \neq c$: $\mathcal{I}(s[m \twoheadrightarrow v]/_c) = t$ iff

    (i) $c[m \twoheadrightarrow v] \rightsquigarrow_{\mathcal{I}} s$; and

    (ii) there are no o, y, such that $o \neq c$ and $o[m \twoheadrightarrow y] \rightsquigarrow_{\mathcal{I}} s$.

The first condition above states that if a strong inheritance candidate, c, exists then inheritance cannot take place from any other source (because this would be a multiple inheritance conflict). However, inheritance might take place from c, if there are no other inheritance candidates. The second condition specifies when "definite" inheritance takes place: s *must* inherit $m \twoheadrightarrow v$ from c if and only if: (i) $c[m \twoheadrightarrow v]$ is a strong inheritance candidate for s; and (ii) there are no other inheritance candidates — weak or strong — from which s could inherit the method m.

Definition 11 (Object Model). *An interpretation $\mathcal{I}$ of an F-logic program P is called an* object model *of P if $\mathcal{I}$ satisfies P plus the three postulates defined in this section: the positive ISA transitivity constraint, the context consistency constraint, and the unique source inheritance constraint.*

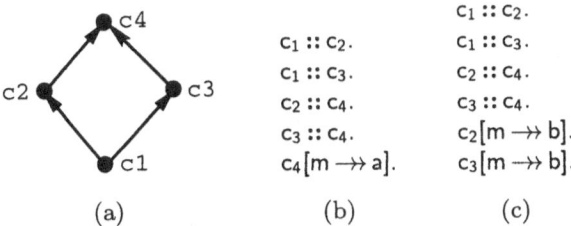

$$c_1 :: c_2.$$

$$c_1 :: c_2. \qquad c_1 :: c_3.$$

$$c_1 :: c_3. \qquad c_2 :: c_4.$$

$$c_2 :: c_4. \qquad c_3 :: c_4.$$

$$c_3 :: c_4. \qquad c_2[m \twoheadrightarrow b].$$

$$c_4[m \twoheadrightarrow a]. \qquad c_3[m \twoheadrightarrow b].$$

(a)   (b)   (c)

Fig. 5. Unique Source Inheritance

Consider the two programs in Figure 5(b) and Figure 5(c) which share the same class hierarchy as shown in Figure 5(a). Let $C = \{c_1 :: c_2,\ c_1 :: c_3,\ c_2 :: c_4,$ $c_3 :: c_4\}$ and $\mathcal{I}_1 = \langle T_1; U_1 \rangle$ be an interpretation for the program in Figure 5(b) where $T_1 = C \cup \{c_4[m \twoheadrightarrow a]/_{c_4},\ c_2[m \twoheadrightarrow a]/_{c_4},\ c_3[m \twoheadrightarrow a]/_{c_4},\ c_1[m \twoheadrightarrow a]/_{c_4}\}$ and $U_1 = \emptyset$. One can verify that $\mathcal{I}_1$ is an object model for the program in Figure 5(b). From $\mathcal{I}_1$ we can see that $c_4[m \twoheadrightarrow a]$ is the *unique* strong inheritance candidate for c_2, c_3, and c_4, which all inherit $m \twoheadrightarrow a$ from c_4.

Let C be the same set of ISA atoms as before and consider the interpretation $\mathcal{I}_2 = \langle T_2; U_2 \rangle$ for the program in Figure 5(c) where $T_2 = C \cup \{c_2[m \twoheadrightarrow b]/_{c_2},$ $c_3[m \twoheadrightarrow b]/_{c_3},\ c_1[m \twoheadrightarrow b]/_{c_2},\ c_1[m \twoheadrightarrow b]/_{c_3}\}$ and $U_2 = \emptyset$. Clearly, $\mathcal{I}_2$ satisfies the program in Figure 5(c). But it is not an object model — the presence of each one of $c_1[m \twoheadrightarrow b]/_{c_2}$ and $c_1[m \twoheadrightarrow b]/_{c_3}$ in $\mathcal{I}_2$ violates the first condition of the unique source inheritance constraint, because both $c_2[m \twoheadrightarrow b]$ and $c_3[m \twoheadrightarrow b]$ are strong inheritance candidates for c_1 and $c_1 \neq c_2 \neq c_3$.

It is worth pointing out the difference between *source-based* and *value-based* approaches to multiple inheritance. Suppose $c_2[m \twoheadrightarrow x]$ and $c_3[m \twoheadrightarrow y]$ are both strong inheritance candidates for c_1, where $c_1 \neq c_2 \neq c_3$. In the source-based approach c_1 has a multiple inheritance conflict on the method m regardless of the values of x and y. On the contrary, in the value-based approach, no conflict would occur if m returns the *same* set of values in both classes c_2 and c_3. For instance, the above interpretation $\mathcal{I}_2$ for the program in Figure 5(c) would be an object model under the value-based approach, since m returns the same set of values, $\{b\}$, in c_2 and c_3. However, value-based nonmonotonic multiple inheritance requires higher-order reasoning and is expensive to compute. In this paper we consider only source-based inheritance.

The constraints introduced so far capture the intuition behind the "definite" part of an object model, *i.e.*, the true and the false components. We view them as *core postulates* that any reasonable object model must obey. However, we still need to assign a meaning to the undefined part of an object model. Since "undefined" means possibly true or possibly false, we intuitively want the conclusions drawn from undefined facts to remain undefined. In other words, the semantics should be "closed" with regard to undefined facts. Thus, although it might seem tempting to "jump" to negative conclusions from undefined facts in some cases (*e.g.*, if there are multiple weak inheritance candidates), our semantics is biased towards undefined conclusions, which is why we call it "optimistic."

Definition 12 (Optimistic ISA Transitivity). *An interpretation $\mathcal{I}$ satisfies the* optimistic ISA transitivity *constraint if the undefined part of the class hierarchy is transitively closed, formally, for all s, c: if there is o such that $\mathcal{I}(s :: o \land o :: c) = \mathbf{u}$ and $\mathcal{I}(s :: c) \neq \mathbf{t}$, then $\mathcal{I}(s :: c) = \mathbf{u}$.*

Definition 13 (Optimistic Inheritance). *An interpretation $\mathcal{I}$ satisfies the* optimistic inheritance *constraint if the following condition is true: for all m, v, c, and s, such that $s \neq c$: $\mathcal{I}(s[m \twoheadrightarrow v]/_c) = \mathbf{u}$ iff*

   (i) $c[m \twoheadrightarrow v] \rightsquigarrow_{\mathcal{I}} s$; and
   (ii) there are no o, y, such that $o \neq c$ and $o[m \twoheadrightarrow y] \overset{\centerdot}{\rightsquigarrow}_{\mathcal{I}} s$; and
   (iii) $\mathcal{I}(s[m \twoheadrightarrow v]/_c) \neq \mathbf{t}$.

The optimistic inheritance constraint captures the intuition behind multiple inheritance based on undefined knowledge. Indeed, s *optimistically* inherits $m \twoheadrightarrow v$ from c if and only if: (i) $c[m \twoheadrightarrow v]$ is either a strong or a weak inheritance candidate for s; (ii) there are no other strong inheritance candidates that can *invalidate* inheritance from c (by the unique source inheritance constraint); and (iii) s cannot *positively* inherit $m \twoheadrightarrow v$ from c.

4   Optimistic Object Model

In this section we define a particular object model, called *optimistic object model*, which exists for *any* F-logic program and has certain desirable properties. First, it satisfies all the postulates of the previous section, including the two "optimistic" postulates at the end. Second, it has several independent characterizations. This section presents a procedural characterization, which can be used to compute such models bottom-up.

First we need to extend the definition of an interpretation in Section 2 to include book-keeping information used by the computation. The book-keeping information is projected out when the final model is produced. The *extended Herbrand base* of an F-logic program P, denoted $\widehat{\mathcal{HB}}_P$, consists of atoms from $\mathcal{HB}_P$ and *auxiliary* atoms of the form $c[m \twoheadrightarrow v] \rightsquigarrow s$, where c, m, v, and s are terms from $\mathcal{HU}_P$. During the computation, we use the auxiliary atoms to approximate the inheritance candidates. An *extended atom set* is a subset of $\widehat{\mathcal{HB}}_P$. In the sequel, we will use symbols with a hat (*i.e.*, $\widehat{\mathrm{I}}$) to denote extended atom sets. The *projection* of an extended atom set $\widehat{\mathrm{I}}$, denoted $\pi(\widehat{\mathrm{I}})$, is $\widehat{\mathrm{I}}$ with the auxiliary atoms removed.

It is easy to extend the definitions of the valuation functions in Section 2 to extended atom sets, since the auxiliary atoms do not occur in F-logic programs. Formally, given an extended atom set $\widehat{\mathrm{I}}$, let $\mathcal{I} = \langle \pi(\widehat{\mathrm{I}}); \emptyset \rangle$. We define: (i) $val_{\widehat{\mathrm{I}}}^{\mathrm{h}}(\mathrm{H}) \overset{\mathrm{def}}{=} \mathcal{V}_{\mathcal{I}}^{\mathrm{h}}(\mathrm{H})$, for a ground rule head H; (ii) $val_{\widehat{\mathrm{I}}}^{\mathrm{b}}(\mathrm{B}) \overset{\mathrm{def}}{=} \mathcal{V}_{\mathcal{I}}^{\mathrm{b}}(\mathrm{B})$, for a ground rule body B; and (iii) $val_{\widehat{\mathrm{I}}}(\mathrm{R}) \overset{\mathrm{def}}{=} \mathcal{I}(\mathrm{R})$, for a ground rule R.

The computation process for the optimistic object model, defined below, extends the alternating fixpoint computation in [12]. The new element here is the book-keeping mechanism for recording the inheritance information.

Definition 14. *Given a ground literal* L *of an F-logic program* P *and an atom* A ∈ $\mathcal{HB}_P$, *we say that* L *matches* A, *if either* L = s::c *and* A = s::c; *or* L = s[m↠v] *and* A = s[m↠v]$_{\!/s}$.

Definition 15 (Rule Consequence). *The* rule consequence operator, $\mathbf{RC}_{P,\widehat{I}}$, *is defined for an F-logic program* P *and an extended atom set* $\widehat{I}$. *It takes as input an extended atom set,* $\widehat{J}$, *and generates a new extended atom set,* $\mathbf{RC}_{P,\widehat{I}}(\widehat{J})$, *as follows:*

$$
\left\{ A \;\middle|\; \begin{array}{l} \textit{There is } H \leftarrow L_1, \ldots, L_n \textit{ in ground}(P), \textit{ such that } H \textit{ matches } A, \\ \textit{and for every literal } L_i \;\; (1 \leq i \leq n)\text{:} \;\; (i) \textit{ if } L_i \textit{ is positive, then} \\ val_{\widehat{J}}^{\mathbf{b}}(L_i) = \mathbf{t}; \;\; \textit{and (ii) if } L_i \textit{ is negative, then } val_{\widehat{I}}^{\mathbf{b}}(L_i) = \mathbf{t}. \end{array} \right\}
$$

This operator is adopted from the usual alternating fixpoint computation; it derives new facts from the rules in the program.

Definition 16 (Inheritance Blocking). *The* inheritance blocking operator, **IB**, *takes as input an extended atom set,* $\widehat{I}$, *and generates the set,* $\mathbf{IB}(\widehat{I})$, *which is the* union *of the following three sets of atoms:*

$$
\left\{ lc(\mathsf{s,m}) \;\middle|\; \exists \mathsf{v}, \textit{ such that } \mathsf{s}[\mathsf{m}↠\mathsf{v}]_{\!/\mathsf{s}} \in \widehat{I} \right\}
$$

$$
\left\{ mc(\mathsf{c,s,m}) \;\middle|\; \exists \mathsf{o,v}, \textit{ such that } \mathsf{o} \neq \mathsf{c} \textit{ and } \mathsf{o}[\mathsf{m}↠\mathsf{v}]\rightsquigarrow\mathsf{s} \in \widehat{I} \right\}
$$

$$
\left\{ ov(\mathsf{c,s,m}) \;\middle|\; \exists \mathsf{o,v}, \textit{ such that } \mathsf{o} \neq \mathsf{c}, \mathsf{o} \neq \mathsf{s}, \textit{ and } \mathsf{s::o, o::c,} \; \mathsf{o}[\mathsf{m}↠\mathsf{v}]_{\!/\mathsf{o}} \in \widehat{I} \right\}
$$

This is an auxiliary operator used in defining the inheritance consequence operator below. It returns the book-keeping information that is needed in deciding which facts can be inherited and which ones are the inheritance candidates. Intuitively, $lc(\mathsf{s,m})$ means that the method m is locally defined at s; $mc(\mathsf{c,s,m})$ means that inheritance of method m from c to s is not possible due to a multiple inheritance conflict (as manifested by the existence of an inheritance candidate at o); $ov(\mathsf{c,s,m})$ means that any inheritance of the method m from c to s would be overridden by another class (o) that lies between s and c in the class hierarchy.

Definition 17 (Inheritance Consequence). *The* inheritance consequence operator, $\mathbf{IC}_{\widehat{I}}$, *where* $\widehat{I}$ *is an extended atom set, takes as input an extended atom set,* $\widehat{J}$, *and generates a new extended atom set as follows:*

$$
\mathbf{IC}_{\widehat{I}}(\widehat{J}) \stackrel{\text{def}}{=} \mathbf{IC}^s(\widehat{J}) \cup \mathbf{IC}^c_{\widehat{I}}(\widehat{J}) \cup \mathbf{IC}^i_{\widehat{I}}(\widehat{J})
$$

$$
\mathbf{IC}^s(\widehat{J}) = \left\{ \mathsf{s::c} \;\middle|\; \exists \mathsf{o}, \textit{ such that } \mathsf{s::o, o::c} \in \widehat{J} \right\}
$$

$$
\mathbf{IC}^c_{\widehat{I}}(\widehat{J}) = \left\{ \mathsf{c}[\mathsf{m}↠\mathsf{v}]\rightsquigarrow\mathsf{s} \;\middle|\; \begin{array}{l} \mathsf{s::c} \in \widehat{J}, \mathsf{c} \neq \mathsf{s}, \mathsf{c}[\mathsf{m}↠\mathsf{v}]_{\!/\mathsf{c}} \in \widehat{J}, \\ lc(\mathsf{s,m}) \notin \mathbf{IB}(\widehat{I}), \textit{ and } ov(\mathsf{c,s,m}) \notin \mathbf{IB}(\widehat{I}) \end{array} \right\}
$$

$$
\mathbf{IC}^i_{\widehat{I}}(\widehat{J}) = \left\{ \mathsf{s}[\mathsf{m}↠\mathsf{v}]_{\!/\mathsf{c}} \;\middle|\; \mathsf{c}[\mathsf{m}↠\mathsf{v}]\rightsquigarrow\mathsf{s} \in \widehat{J}, \textit{ and } mc(\mathsf{c,s,m}) \notin \mathbf{IB}(\widehat{I}) \right\}
$$

At each step this operator derives newly inherited facts as well as inheritance candidates.

Definition 18 (Program Completion). *The* program completion operator, $\mathbf{T}_{P,\widehat{I}}$, *where P is an F-logic program and $\widehat{I}$ an extended atom set, takes as input an extended atom set, $\widehat{J}$, and generates a new extended atom set as follows:* $\mathbf{T}_{P,\widehat{I}}(\widehat{J}) \stackrel{\text{def}}{=} \mathbf{RC}_{P,\widehat{I}}(\widehat{J}) \cup \mathbf{IC}_{\widehat{I}}(\widehat{J}).$

In other words, $\mathbf{T}_{P,\widehat{I}}$ derives new "local" facts (via the rules), inherited facts, plus inheritance candidacy information that is used to decide which facts to inherit in the future.

Lemma 1. $\mathbf{RC}_{P,\widehat{I}}$ *is monotonic when P and $\widehat{I}$ are fixed.* $\mathbf{IB}$ *is monotonic.* $\mathbf{IC}^s$ *is monotonic.* $\mathbf{IC}^c_{\widehat{I}}$, $\mathbf{IC}^i_{\widehat{I}}$, *and* $\mathbf{IC}_{\widehat{I}}$ *are monotonic when $\widehat{I}$ is fixed.* $\mathbf{T}_{P,\widehat{I}}$ *is monotonic when P and $\widehat{I}$ are fixed.*

Let P be an F-logic program. The set of all subsets of the extended Herbrand base $\widehat{\mathcal{HB}}_P$ constitutes a complete lattice where the partial ordering is defined by set inclusion. Therefore, any monotonic operator, Φ, defined on this lattice has a unique least fixpoint lfp(Φ) [23].

Definition 19 (Alternating Fixpoint). *The* alternating fixpoint operator, Ψ_P, *for an F-logic program P takes as input an extended atom set, $\widehat{I}$, and generates a new extended atom set as follows:* $\Psi_P(\widehat{I}) \stackrel{\text{def}}{=} lfp(\mathbf{T}_{P,\widehat{I}}).$

Definition 20 (F-logic Fixpoint). *The* F-logic fixpoint operator, $\mathbf{F}_P$, *where P is an F-logic program, takes as input an extended atom set, $\widehat{I}$, and generates a new extended atom set as follows:* $\mathbf{F}_P(\widehat{I}) \stackrel{\text{def}}{=} \Psi_P(\Psi_P(\widehat{I})).$

Lemma 2. *When P is fixed, Ψ_P is antimonotonic and $\mathbf{F}_P$ is monotonic.*

Definition 21 (Optimistic Object Model). *The* optimistic object model, $\mathcal{M}$, *of an F-logic program P is defined as follows:* $\mathcal{M} = \langle T; U \rangle$, *where $T = \pi(lfp(\mathbf{F}_P))$ and $U = \pi(\Psi_P(lfp(\mathbf{F}_P))) - \pi(lfp(\mathbf{F}_P))$. Here π is the projection operator defined earlier. It removes the auxiliary atoms of the form $c[m \twoheadrightarrow v] \leadsto s$, which are used for book-keeping during computation.*

We illustrate the computation of optimistic object models using the following example. Consider the F-logic program P in Figure 3. Let $T = \{c_1 :: c_2, c_3 :: c_2, c_2[m \twoheadrightarrow a]/_{c_2}, c_3[m \twoheadrightarrow b]/_{c_3}\}$ and $U = \{c_1 :: c_3, c_1[m \twoheadrightarrow a]/_{c_2}, c_1[m \twoheadrightarrow b]/_{c_3}\}$. Then we have lfp($\mathbf{F}_P$) $= T$ and $\Psi_P(lfp(\mathbf{F}_P)) = T \cup U \cup \{c_2[m \twoheadrightarrow a] \leadsto c_1, c_3[m \twoheadrightarrow b] \leadsto c_1\}$. So $\langle T; U \rangle$ is the optimistic object model for the program in Figure 3.

Theorem 1. *The optimistic object model $\mathcal{M}$ of an F-logic program P is an object model of P. In addition, this model satisfies the optimistic ISA transitivity constraint, and the optimistic inheritance constraint.*

5   Minimal Object Model

Since the introduction of the Closed World Assumption [28], comparing different models of a program based on the amount of "truth" contained in those models has become a common technique. Typically, the true component of a model is minimized and the false component is maximized. However, in F-logic we also deal with inheritance, which complicates the matters somewhat, because the truth value of a fact may depend on inheritance. This can create object models that look similar but actually are incomparable. This issue is illustrated by an example that follows the definition of minimality below. The solution is to minimize not only the set of true atoms of an object model, but also the amount of positive inheritance information implied by the object model.

Definition 22. *Given two object models,* $\mathcal{I}_1 = \langle P_1; Q_1 \rangle$ *and* $\mathcal{I}_2 = \langle P_2; Q_2 \rangle$, *of an F-logic program P, we write* $\mathcal{I}_1 \leq \mathcal{I}_2$ *if and only if* $P_1 \subseteq P_2$, $P_1 \cup Q_1 \subseteq P_2 \cup Q_2$, *and* $c[m \rightarrow v] \overset{s}{\leadsto}_{\mathcal{I}_1} s$ *implies* $c[m \rightarrow v] \overset{s}{\leadsto}_{\mathcal{I}_2} s$, *for all c, m, v, s.*

Definition 23 (Minimal Object Model). *An object model* $\mathcal{I}$ *is* minimal *iff there exists no object model* $\mathcal{I}'$ *such that* $\mathcal{I}' \leq \mathcal{I}$ *and* $\mathcal{I}'$ *is different from* $\mathcal{I}$.

The above definitions minimize the number of strong inheritance candidates implied by an object model *in addition to* the usual minimization of truth and maximization of falsehood. This is needed because increasing the number of false facts might inflate the number of strong inheritance candidates, which in turn might unjustifiably inflate the number of facts that are derived by inheritance.

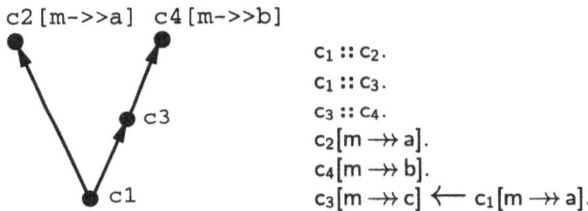

$c_1 :: c_2.$
$c_1 :: c_3.$
$c_3 :: c_4.$
$c_2[m \rightarrow a].$
$c_4[m \rightarrow b].$
$c_3[m \rightarrow c] \leftarrow c_1[m \rightarrow a].$

Fig. 6. Minimal Object Model

Consider the program in Figure 6 and the following two object models of the program: $\mathcal{I}_1 = \langle P_1; Q_1 \rangle$, where $P_1 = \{c_1 :: c_2, c_1 :: c_3, c_3 :: c_4, c_2[m \rightarrow a]/_{c_2}, c_4[m \rightarrow b]/_{c_4}\}$, $Q_1 = \emptyset$, and $\mathcal{I}_2 = \langle P_2; Q_2 \rangle$, where $P_2 = P_1$, $Q_2 = \{c_1[m \rightarrow a]/_{c_2}, c_3[m \rightarrow c]/_{c_3}\}$. $\mathcal{I}_1$ and $\mathcal{I}_2$ both agree on the atoms that are true. But in $\mathcal{I}_1$ both $c_1[m \rightarrow a]/_{c_2}$ and $c_3[m \rightarrow c]/_{c_3}$ are false, whereas in $\mathcal{I}_2$ they are both undefined. Clearly, $\mathcal{I}_1$ carries more false atoms than $\mathcal{I}_2$ and so with the usual notion of minimality we would say $\mathcal{I}_1 \leq \mathcal{I}_2$. However, $\mathcal{I}_1$ is not as "tight" as it appears, because the additional false atoms in $\mathcal{I}_1$ are not automatically implied by the program under our optimistic object model semantics. Indeed, although $c_4[m \rightarrow b]$ is a strong inheritance candidate for c_1 in $\mathcal{I}_1$, it is only a weak inheritance candidate in $\mathcal{I}_2$. We can see that it is due to this extra positive information about inheritance candidates that $\mathcal{I}_1$ is able to increase the number of false atoms while keeping the true atoms intact. This anomaly is eliminated by the inheritance minimization built into Definition 22, which renders the two models incomparable, *i.e.*, $\mathcal{I}_1 \not\leq \mathcal{I}_2$.

Theorem 2. *The optimistic object model $\mathcal{M}$ of an F-logic program P is minimal among the object models of P that satisfy the optimistic ISA transitivity constraint and the optimistic inheritance constraint.*

6   Implementation

It turns out that the optimistic object model of an F-logic program P can be computed as the well-founded model [13,12] of a certain general logic program with negation. Given an F-logic program P, we first rewrite P into a general logic program P^{wf}. Then we show that the well-founded model of P^{wf} is isomorphic to the optimistic object model of P.

Definition 24. *Given an F-logic program P, let L be a literal in P. The functions ρ^h and ρ^b for rewriting head and body literals in P, respectively, are defined as follows:*

$$\rho^h(L) = \begin{cases} sub(s, c), & \text{if } L = s :: c \\ locmvd(s, m, v), & \text{if } L = s[m \twoheadrightarrow v] \end{cases}$$

$$\rho^b(L) = \begin{cases} sub(s, c), & \text{if } L = s :: c \\ mvd(s, m, v), & \text{if } L = s[m \twoheadrightarrow v] \\ \neg (\rho^b(G)), & \text{if } L = \neg G \end{cases}$$

Let $R \equiv H \leftarrow L_1, \ldots, L_n$, $n \geq 0$, be a rule in P. The function ρ for rewriting the rules in P is defined as follows: $\rho(R) = \rho^h(H) \leftarrow \rho^b(L_1), \ldots, \rho^b(L_n)$.

$$
\begin{aligned}
mvd(S, M, V) &\leftarrow locmvd(S, M, V). \\
mvd(S, M, V) &\leftarrow inhmvd(S, M, V, C). \\
sub(S, C) &\leftarrow sub(S, O), sub(O, C). \\
inhmvd(S, M, V, C) &\leftarrow candidate(C, M, V, S), \neg multiple(C, S, M). \\
candidate(C, M, V, S) &\leftarrow sub(S, C), locmvd(C, M, V), C \neq S, \\
&\qquad \neg local(S, M), \neg override(C, S, M). \\
local(S, M) &\leftarrow locmvd(S, M, V). \\
multiple(C, S, M) &\leftarrow candidate(O, M, V, S), O \neq C. \\
override(C, S, M) &\leftarrow sub(O, C), sub(S, O), locmvd(O, M, V), O \neq C, O \neq S.
\end{aligned}
$$

Fig. 7. Trailer Rules for Well-Founded Rewriting

Definition 25 (Well-Founded Rewriting). *The well-founded rewriting of an F-logic program P, denoted* P^{wf}, *is a general logic program constructed by the following steps:*

(1) *For every rule R in P, add its* rewriting $\rho(\mathrm{R})$ *into* P^{wf}.

(2) *Include the* trailer *shown in Figure 7 to* P^{wf} *(note that uppercase letters denote variables in the trailer rules).*

Definition 26. *Let* P^{wf} *be the well-founded rewriting of an F-logic program P,* $\mathcal{HB}_{\mathrm{P}^{wf}}$ *be the Herbrand base of* P^{wf}, $\mathcal{HB}_{\mathrm{P}}$ *be the Herbrand base of P,* I^{wf} *be a subset of* $\mathcal{HB}_{\mathrm{P}^{wf}}$, *and* I *be a subset of* $\mathcal{HB}_{\mathrm{P}}$, *we say that* I^{wf} *is isomorphic to* I, *if all of the following conditions are true:*

(1) *for all* s *and* c: $sub(\mathsf{s},\mathsf{c}) \in \mathrm{I}^{wf}$ *iff* $\mathsf{s} :: \mathsf{c} \in \mathrm{I}$

(2) *for all* s, m, *and* v: $locmvd(\mathsf{s},\mathsf{m},\mathsf{v}) \in \mathrm{I}^{wf}$ *iff* $\mathsf{s}[\mathsf{m} \twoheadrightarrow \mathsf{v}]/_{\mathsf{s}} \in \mathrm{I}$

(3) *for all* s, m, v, *and* c, *such that* $\mathsf{s} \neq \mathsf{c}$: $inhmvd(\mathsf{s},\mathsf{m},\mathsf{v},\mathsf{c}) \in \mathrm{I}^{wf}$ *iff* $\mathsf{s}[\mathsf{m} \twoheadrightarrow \mathsf{v}]/_{\mathsf{c}} \in \mathrm{I}$

Let T^{wf} *and* U^{wf} *be disjoint sets of true and undefined atoms in* $\mathcal{HB}_{\mathrm{P}^{wf}}$, *respectively,* $\mathcal{M}^{wf} = \langle \mathrm{T}^{wf}; \mathrm{U}^{wf} \rangle$ *be the well-founded model of* P^{wf}, *and* $\mathcal{M} = \langle \mathrm{T}; \mathrm{U} \rangle$ *be the optimistic object model of P. We say that* $\mathcal{M}^{wf}$ *is isomorphic to* $\mathcal{M}$, *if* T^{wf} *is isomorphic to* T *and* U^{wf} *is isomorphic to* U.

Theorem 3. *Given the well-founded rewriting* P^{wf} *of an F-logic program P, the well-founded model of* P^{wf} *is isomorphic to the optimistic object model of P.*

7 Data Complexity

In general, the optimistic object model of an F-logic program is not necessarily recursively enumerable. However, for function-free F-logic programs, the Herbrand universe is finite and thus the optimistic object model can be effectively constructed. In this section we discuss data complexity for such programs.

Since in this paper we only consider a subset of F-logic, which contains only two kinds of atoms, $\mathsf{s} :: \mathsf{c}$ and $\mathsf{s}[\mathsf{m} \twoheadrightarrow \mathsf{v}]$, any ground atomic query must have one of these two forms, where s, c, m, v are constants.

As for Datalog programs, we can divide any F-logic program, P, into two disjoint parts: an *intensional* database (IDB), $\mathrm{P_R}$, which consists of all rules in P and no facts, and an *extensional* database (EDB), $\mathrm{P_F}$, which contains only the facts in P. We can think of $\mathrm{P_R}$ as a function that maps any EDB, $\mathrm{P_F}$, to the optimistic object model of the combined F-logic program $\mathrm{P_R} \cup \mathrm{P_F}$. Following [32], we have the following definition of data complexity.

Definition 27 (Data Complexity). *Given an IDB* $\mathrm{P_R}$ *and an EDB* $\mathrm{P_F}$, *the data complexity of* $\mathrm{P_R}$ *is defined as the computational complexity of deciding the truth value of any ground atomic query in the optimistic object model of* $\mathrm{P_R} \cup \mathrm{P_F}$, *as a function of the size of* $\mathrm{P_F}$.

Given an F-logic program $\mathrm{P} = \mathrm{P_R} \cup \mathrm{P_F}$ and its well-founded rewriting P^{wf}, let $\mathrm{P_R}^{wf}$ be the IDB of P^{wf}, and $\mathrm{P_F}^{wf}$ be the EDB of P^{wf}. By Definitions 24 and 25, $\mathrm{P_R}^{wf}$ consists of the trailer shown in Figure 7 plus the rewritings of all rules in P_R. The EDB P_F^{wf} consists of the rewritings of all facts in P_F. Because the rewriting of an F-logic rule is linear and the size of the trailer is a constant, the size of P_R^{wf} is linear in the size of P_R and the size of P_F^{wf} is also linear in the size of P_F.

By Theorem 3, the well-founded model of P^{wf} is isomorphic to the optimistic object model of P. Therefore, the data complexity of the optimistic object model semantics reduces to the data complexity of the well-founded semantics.

Because the rewriting does not introduce new function symbols, the rewriting of a function-free F-logic program is a function-free Datalog program. Since data complexity of the well-founded semantics for function-free programs is polynomial time [13], we have the following corollary.

Corollary 1. *The data complexity of the optimistic object model semantics for function-free F-logic programs is polynomial time.*

8   Conclusion and Future Work

We developed a new model theory for nonmonotonic multiple inheritance in frame-based knowledge bases. Unlike previous attempts, this new semantics is rooted in well-defined postulates, which formalize the commonly accepted intuition behind nonmonotonic multiple inheritance in frame-based languages, and extend this intuition to handle the interaction between deduction and inheritance. Although we chose F-logic as a framework for presenting our results, the problem described here is *inherent* in any logic-based system that supports both inheritance and rules. Our solution applies to such systems and, in particular, to extensions of DAML+OIL [17] which permit deductive rules and inheritance.

We should note that the kind of inheritance considered here is known as *value inheritance*, which is commonly used in AI systems. However, it has been shown that value inheritance can also simulate *code inheritance* that is traditionally used in object-oriented programming [22]. Therefore, our results apply to code inheritance as well.

In addition to the inheritance semantics, our formalization of the concepts of locality, context, inheritance candidacy, and the inheritance postulates sets the stage for a framework in which *programmable* inheritance policies can be defined formally. It has been argued in the past that along with the "default" semantics for inheritance, tools for programming inheritance-like deduction in an ad hoc way can benefit certain applications. For instance, discretionary access control and trust management can benefit from a variety of inheritance-based strategies, such as most-specific-definition-based overriding [18] (similar to the semantics developed here), path-based overriding [18], inflating inheritance [20], and null inheritance [20]. We are currently working on extensions of our framework to allow users to specify their inheritance strategies *declaratively*. Such a system can be part of an infrastructure for advanced knowledge base systems.

References

1. S. Abiteboul, G. Lausen, H. Uphoff, and E. Waller. Methods and rules. In *ACM SIGMOD Conference on Management of Data*, pages 32–41, 1993.

2. A. J. Bonner and M. Kifer. An overview of transaction logic. *Theoretical Computer Science*, 133:205–265, October 1994.
3. G. Brewka. The logic of inheritance in frame systems. In *International Joint Conference on Artificial Intelligence*, pages 483–488, San Francisco, CA, 1987. Morgan Kaufmann.
4. M. Bugliesi and H. M. Jamil. A stable model semantics for behavioral inheritance in deductive object oriented languages. In *International Conference on Database Theory*, pages 222–237, 1995.
5. L. Cardelli. A semantics of multiple inheritance. *Information and Computation*, 76(2):138–164, February 1988.
6. W. Chen, M. Kifer, and D. S. Warren. HiLog: A foundation for higher-order logic programming. *Journal of Logic Programming*, 15(3):187–230, February 1993.
7. W. Chen and D. S. Warren. Tabled evaluation with delaying for general logic programs. *Journal of ACM*, 43(1):20–74, 1996.
8. H. Davulcu, G. Yang, M. Kifer, and I.V. Ramakrishnan. Design and implementation of the physical layer in webbases: The XRover experience. In *First International Conference on Computational Logic, DOOD'2000 Stream*, July 2000.
9. S. Decker, D. Brickley, J. Saarela, and J. Angele. A query and inference service for RDF. In *QL'98 - The Query Languages Workshop*, December 1998.
10. D. Fensel, S. Decker, M. Erdmann, and R. Studer. Ontobroker: Or how to enable intelligent access to the WWW. In *Proceedings of the 11th Banff Knowledge Acquisition for Knowledge-Based Systems Workshop*, Banff, Canada, 1998.
11. J. Frohn, R. Himmeröder, G. Lausen, W. May, and C. Schlepphorst. Managing semistructured data with FLORID: A deductive object-oriented perspective. *Information Systems*, 23(8):589–613, 1998.
12. A. Van Gelder. The alternating fixpoint of logic programs with negation. In *ACM Symposium on Principles of Database Systems*, pages 1–10, 1989.
13. A. Van Gelder, K. Ross, and J. S. Schlipf. The well-founded semantics for general logic programs. *Journal of ACM*, 38(3):620–650, July 1991.
14. M. Gelfond and V. Lifschitz. The stable model semantics for logic programming. In R. A. Kowalski and K. Bowen, editors, *Proceedings of the Fifth International Conference on Logic Programming*, pages 1070–1080. The MIT Press, 1988.
15. C. H. Goh, S. Bressan, S. E. Madnick, and M. D. Siegel. Context interchange: Representing and reasoning about data semantics in heterogeneous systems. Technical report, MIT, School of Management, 1996.
16. A. Gupta, B. Ludäscher, and M. E. Martone. Knowledge-based integration of neuroscience data sources. In *12th International Conference on Scientific and Statistical Database Management (SSDBM)*, Berlin, Germany, July 2000. IEEE.
17. I. Horrocks. DAML+OIL: A description logic for the Semantic Web. *IEEE Bulletin of the Technical Committee on Data Engineering*, 25(1), March 2002.
18. S. Jajodia, P. Samarati, M. L. Sapino, and V. S. Subrahmanian. Flexible support for multiple access control policies. *ACM Transactions on Database Systems*, 26(2):214–260, June 2001.
19. H. M. Jamil. Implementing abstract objects with inheritance in Datalog^{neg}. In *International Conference on Very Large Data Bases*, pages 56–65, 1997.
20. H. M. Jamil. A logic-based language for parametric inheritance. In A. G. Cohn, F. Giunchiglia, and B. Selman, editors, *KR2000: Principles of Knowledge Representation and Reasoning*, pages 611–622, San Francisco, 2000. Morgan Kaufmann.
21. M. Kifer and G. Lausen. F-Logic: A higher-order language for reasoning about objects, inheritance and schema. In *ACM SIGMOD Conference on Management of Data*, pages 134–146, New York, 1989. ACM.

22. M. Kifer, G. Lausen, and J. Wu. Logical foundations of object-oriented and frame-based languages. *Journal of ACM*, 42:741–843, July 1995.

23. J. W. Lloyd. *Foundations of Logic Programming*. Springer Verlag, 1984.

24. W. May and P. Kandzia. Nonmonotonic inheritance in object-oriented deductive database languages. *Journal of Logic and Computation*, 11(4), 2001.

25. W. May, B. Ludäscher, and G. Lausen. Well-founded semantics for deductive object-oriented database languages. In *International Conference on Deductive and Object-Oriented Databases*, pages 320–336. Springer Verlag LNCS, 1997.

26. T. C. Przymusinski. Every logic program has a natural stratification and an iterated least fixed point model. In *ACM Symposium on Principles of Database Systems*, pages 11–21, 1989.

27. T. C. Przymusinski. The well-founded semantics coincides with the three-valued stable semantics. *Fundamenta Informaticae*, 13(4):445–464, 1990.

28. R. Reiter. On closed world databases. In H. Gallaire and J. Minker, editors, *Logic and Databases*, pages 55–76. Plenum Press, New York, 1978.

29. M. Sintek and S. Decker. TRIPLE – An RDF query, inference, and transformation language. In *Deductive Databases and Knowledge Management (DDLP'2001)*, October 2001.

30. S. Staab, J. Angele, S. Decker, M. Erdmann, A. Hotho, A. Maedche, H.-P. Schnurr, R. Studer, and Y. Sure. AI for the Web — Ontology-based community web portals. In *9-th International World Wide Web Conference (WWW9)*, Amsterdam, The Netherlands, May 2000.

31. D. S. Touretzky. *The Mathematics of Inheritance*. Morgan-Kaufmann, Los Altos, CA, 1986.

32. M. Vardi. The complexity of relational query languages. In *ACM Symposium on Theory of Computing*, pages 137–145, 1982.

33. G. Yang and M. Kifer. Implementing an efficient DOOD system using a tabling logic engine. In *First International Conference on Computational Logic, DOOD'2000 Stream*, July 2000.

34. G. Yang and M. Kifer. Flora-2: User's manual. http://flora.sourceforge.net/, June 2002.

A Defeasible Ontology Language

S. Heymans and D. Vermeir

Dept. of Computer Science
Free University of Brussels, VUB
{sheymans,dvermeir}@vub.ac.be

Abstract. We extend the description logic $\mathcal{SHOQ}(\mathbf{D})$ with a preference order on the axioms. With this strict partial order certain axioms can be overruled, if defeated with more preferred ones. Furthermore, we impose a preferred model semantics, thus effectively introducing nonmonotonicity into $\mathcal{SHOQ}(\mathbf{D})$. Since a description logic can be viewed as an ontology language, or a proper translation of one, we obtain a defeasible ontology language. Finally, we argue that such a defeasible language may be usefully applied for learning and integrating ontologies.

1 Introduction

The "Semantic Web" [8] seeks to improve on the current World Wide Web, making knowledge not only viewable and interpretable by humans, but also by software agents. Ontologies play a crucial role in the realization of this next generation web, by providing a "shared understanding" [29] of certain domains.

In order to describe ontologies, one needs ontology languages, such as DAML+OIL or OIL [6,11,12]. For example the OIL language is built on three roots [18]:

- frame-based systems provide the basic modeling primitives: frames (classes) with attributes;
- by mapping the language to a suitable description logic (DL), one obtains a precise semantics and associated inference procedures; and
- the concrete syntax is based on web languages such as XML and RDF [23,10].

A description logic is used to express the formal semantics of an ontology written in an ontology language like OIL, but it also provides some basic reasoning services such as checking whether an instance is of a certain type, whether classes are subclasses of other classes, . . . [2,21].

In particular the DL $\mathcal{SHIQ}$ corresponds to the ontology language OIL [17]. As explained in [19] this mapping is incomplete with respect to *concrete data types* and *named individuals*, two features that are present in current ontology languages. A DL that overcomes these two deficiencies is $\mathcal{SHOQ}(\mathbf{D})$[19], which includes support for data types ($\mathbf{D}$) and named individuals ($\mathcal{O}$, see also [28] and [20] for reasoning with individuals), however, it doesn't support inverse roles.

In this paper we further extend the DL $\mathcal{SHOQ}(\mathbf{D})$ with a preference order, as in [16]. This order indicates whether a certain axiom is more preferred than another and

R. Meersman, Z. Tari (Eds.): CoopIS/DOA/ODBASE 2002, LNCS 2519, pp. 1033–1046, 2002.

thus may defeat the meaning of that axiom. For example, we could be tempted to assume that, in general, movie stars are bright people. If we came to the discovery that movie stars residing in Hollywood are actually not that clever, we would not be able to retain this information consistently. However by *defeating* the rule saying that movie stars are clever with the rule saying they are not if they are Hollywood stars, we can still retain a consistent knowledge base (KB).

In addition to adding a preference order on axioms, implementing the notion of defeat, we restrict the semantics of [16], by introducing an order on the models of such a description logic knowledge base, taking into account the order on the axioms. Nonmonotonicity is then introduced by preferring models that defeat as few axioms as possible, and if defeat cannot be avoided, we select those models that defeat less preferred axioms.

Nonmonotonic reasoning in description logics is not new: e.g. [4] and [5] introduce defaults in description logic. Our approach is different, however, as it is based on an explicit ordering of defeasible axioms, as in ordered logic programming, see e.g. [14, 13,22]. Besides being often more intuitive, we also do not restrict ourselves to just the object names in an Abox, thus staying closer to the "open world assumption" spirit of description logics. [26] also works with preferred models, and thus nonmonotonicity, but axioms are just split up in defeasible and not defeasible axioms, while our approach allows not only to express defeasible knowledge but also some gradation in defeasibility, i.e. some axioms are more preferred or less defeasible than others.

Often, new ontologies are constructed starting from (a combination of) existing ontologies, adding refinements that correspond to specialized knowledge. Both integration of ontologies and ontology refinement may lead to inconsistencies. We argue that a description logic with a preference order may prove useful when integrating ontologies, since conflicting rules may be defeated.

The remainder of this paper is organized as follows: Section 2 extends $\mathcal{SHOQ}(\mathbf{D})$ to ordered $\mathcal{SHOQ}(\mathbf{D})$ (denoted $\mathcal{OSHOQ}(\mathbf{D})$) by providing a strict partial order on the axioms, indicating a preference for certain axioms over others. Section 3 provides a nonmonotonic semantics for $\mathcal{OSHOQ}(\mathbf{D})$, effectively modeling this preference relation. Applications such as an algorithm that learns the preference order from examples and a discussion of ontology integration with $\mathcal{OSHOQ}(\mathbf{D})$ can be found in Sect. 4. Finally, Sect. 5 contains conclusions and directions for further research.

2   Extending $\mathcal{SHOQ}(\mathbf{D})$ with a Preference Order

2.1   An Example

In order to obtain some intuition, consider the following example from the field of law, adapted and modified from [15]. According to the law, if you steal something, you normally will be punished, i.e.

$$TP : \mathit{Thief} \sqsubseteq \mathit{Punished}$$

where we use *Thief* to denote the concept of people that have stolen something and *Punished* for people that have received a sentence.

Instantiating this small conceptual schema with a particular individual *Bill* that was caught stealing, denoted as

$$BT : \{Bill\} \sqsubseteq Thief \ ,$$

we can deduce, from our schema and basic reasoning, that Bill must be punished ($\{Bill\} \sqsubseteq Punished$).

Now assume that, according to the law, minors (i.e. people younger than 18) do not get punished for committing crimes:

$$MP : Minors \sqsubseteq \neg Punished$$

Additionally assuming that Bill is a minor

$$BM : \{Bill\} \sqsubseteq Minors$$

leads to a problem. On the one hand we can deduce, using BM and MP, that Bill should not be punished (because he is a minor) while on the other hand, according to BT and TP, he should be punished.

To solve this contradiction, we will make explicit our tacit assumption that TP should be read as a *default*, i.e. "Thieves should be punished unless there are overriding concerns that prohibit this". By stating that MP **defeats** TP, we indicate that MP ("Minors should not be punished") is such an overriding concern. Informally, this means that it is acceptable to not "apply" TP as long as the defeating rule MP is applied, e.g. Bill need not be punished (no need to apply TP for Bill) if he is a minor (MP is applied for Bill).

Note that we might obtain a similar effect by refining TP to

$$TP' : Thief \sqcap \neg Minors \sqsubseteq Punished$$

("Thieves that are not minors should be punished.") which is consistent with MP, BP and BT. However, this approach does not scale well since each addition of an "exception" will make the default rule more complex and less intuitive. Humans tend not to think about exceptions when considering the truth of a general rule such as TP; only the confrontation with an actual exception such as MP will prohibit the application of the general rule. Not having to modify default rules also allows for modular specifications, where one can concentrate on adding pieces of knowledge independently, and relating them via possible defeat relationships later.

We briefly formalize the above using the description logic $\mathcal{OSHOQ}(\mathbf{D})$ [16], an extension of the DL $\mathcal{SHOQ}(\mathbf{D})$ [19].

2.2 $\mathcal{OSHOQ}(\mathbf{D})$

We assume that we have a set of data types $\mathbf{D}$ and associate with each $d \in \mathbf{D}$ a set $d^{\mathbf{D}} \subseteq \Delta_{\mathbf{D}}$, where $\Delta_{\mathbf{D}}$ is the domain of all data types (the *concrete domain*, see [3]).

Let $\mathbf{C}$ be the set of *concept names*, $\mathbf{R}$ the disjoint union of *abstract role names* $\mathbf{R}_A$ and *concrete role names* $\mathbf{R}_{\mathbf{D}}$. A *role box* $\mathcal{R}$ is a finite set of *role axioms* $R \sqsubseteq S$ where

$R, S \in \mathbf{R}_A$ or $R, S \in \mathbf{R}_\mathbf{D}$ and *transitivity axioms* $\mathsf{Trans}(R)$ for $R \in \mathbf{R}_A$. An abstract role R is called *transitive* if $\mathsf{Trans}(R) \in \mathcal{R}$. A *simple role* R for a role box $\mathcal{R}$ is a role that is not transitive nor does it have any transitive subroles. Let $\mathbf{I}$ be a set of *individual names*. $\mathbf{C}, \mathbf{R}$ and $\mathbf{I}$ are mutually disjoint. The set of $\mathcal{SHOQ}(\mathbf{D})$-*concept expressions* is defined such that every concept name $A \in \mathbf{C}$ is a concept expression and for every $o \in \mathbf{I}$, $\{o\}$ is a concept expression. Moreover, for C and D concept expressions, $R \in \mathbf{R}_A$, $T \in \mathbf{R}_\mathbf{D}$, S a simple role and $d \in \mathbf{D}$, the constructors in Table 1 can be used to form complex concept expressions.

Table 1. Syntax and semantics of $\mathcal{SHOQ}(\mathbf{D})$-concept expressions

construct name	syntax	semantics
atomic concept $\mathbf{C}$	A	$A^{\mathcal{I}} \subseteq \Delta^{\mathcal{I}}$
abstract role $\mathbf{R}_A$	R	$R^{\mathcal{I}} \subseteq \Delta^{\mathcal{I}} \times \Delta^{\mathcal{I}}$
concrete role $\mathbf{R}_\mathbf{D}$	T	$T^{\mathcal{I}} \subseteq \Delta^{\mathcal{I}} \times \Delta_\mathbf{D}$
nominals $\mathbf{I}$	$\{o\}$	$\{o\}^{\mathcal{I}} \subseteq \Delta^{\mathcal{I}}, \#\{o\}^{\mathcal{I}} = 1$
data types $\mathbf{D}$	d	$d^\mathbf{D} \subseteq \Delta_\mathbf{D}$
	$\neg d$	$(\neg d)^\mathbf{D} = \Delta_\mathbf{D} \setminus d^\mathbf{D}$
conjunction	$C \sqcap D$	$(C \sqcap D)^{\mathcal{I}} = C^{\mathcal{I}} \cap D^{\mathcal{I}}$
disjunction	$C \sqcup D$	$(C \sqcup D)^{\mathcal{I}} = C^{\mathcal{I}} \cup D^{\mathcal{I}}$
negation	$\neg C$	$(\neg C)^{\mathcal{I}} = \Delta^{\mathcal{I}} \setminus C^{\mathcal{I}}$
exists restriction	$\exists R.C$	$(\exists R.C)^{\mathcal{I}} = \{x \mid \exists y : (x, y) \in R^{\mathcal{I}} \text{ and } y \in C^{\mathcal{I}}\}$
value restriction	$\forall R.C$	$(\forall R.C)^{\mathcal{I}} = \{x \mid \forall y : (x, y) \in R^{\mathcal{I}} \Rightarrow y \in C^{\mathcal{I}}\}$
atleast restriction	$\geq nR.C$	$(\geq nR.C)^{\mathcal{I}} = \{x \mid \#\{y \mid (x, y) \in R^{\mathcal{I}} \text{ and } y \in C^{\mathcal{I}}\} \geq n\}$
atmost restriction	$\leq nR.C$	$(\leq nR.C)^{\mathcal{I}} = \{x \mid \#\{y \mid (x, y) \in R^{\mathcal{I}} \text{ and } y \in C^{\mathcal{I}}\} \leq n\}$
data type exists	$\exists T.d$	$(\exists T.d)^{\mathcal{I}} = \{x \mid \exists y : (x, y) \in T^{\mathcal{I}} \text{ and } y \in d^\mathbf{D}\}$
data type value	$\forall T.d$	$(\forall T.d)^{\mathcal{I}} = \{x \mid \forall y : (x, y) \in T^{\mathcal{I}} \Rightarrow y \in d^\mathbf{D}\}$

A *Tbox* $\mathcal{T}$ is a finite set of *terminological axioms* $C \sqsubseteq D$ with C and D $\mathcal{SHOQ}(\mathbf{D})$-concept expressions.

Traditionally, a description logic consists of a Tbox and an Abox, where the Abox is used for assertional statements like $C(a)$ (or $R(a, b)$) which intuitively means that the individual a is an instance of C (a is related to b by means of the role R). However, in $\mathcal{SHOQ}(\mathbf{D})$ we have named individuals together with the $\{\}$-constructor ($\mathcal{O}$ in [28]) and we can simulate the Abox assertions with Tbox axioms:

$$C(a) \Leftrightarrow \{a\} \sqsubseteq C$$
$$R(a, b) \Leftrightarrow \{a\} \sqsubseteq \exists R.\{b\}$$

For simplicity, we will consider the role box to be empty in the remainder of this paper, and consider only terminological axioms. It is straightforward to extend the results to knowledge bases with nonempty role boxes.

We define the defeat relation, by means of a strict[1] partial order on the Tbox axioms. Intuitively, $a_1 < a_2$, represents a preference for a_1 over a_2, i.e. a_1 defeats a_2.

Definition 1. *An $\mathcal{OSHOQ}(\mathbf{D})$-knowledge base is a tuple[2] $\langle \mathcal{T}, < \rangle$ where $\mathcal{T}$ is a Tbox, and $<$ is a strict partial order between axioms of $\mathcal{T}$. For a pair $a_1 < a_2$, a_2 is said to be **defeasible** while a_1 is a (possible) **defeater** of a_2. We use $\mathcal{T}_s$ to denote the set of **strict** axioms in $\mathcal{T}$, i.e. those axioms that have no defeaters (are minimal w.r.t. $<$).*

The semantics of $\mathcal{OSHOQ}(\mathbf{D})$ is defined using an interpretation $\mathcal{I} = (\Delta^{\mathcal{I}}, \cdot^{\mathcal{I}})$, where $\Delta^{\mathcal{I}}$ is a nonempty domain (the *abstract domain*) and $\cdot^{\mathcal{I}}$ is an interpretation function, defined on concept expressions and roles as in Table 1.

The notion of defeat is formalized in the following definition.

Definition 2. *Let $\Sigma = \langle \mathcal{T}, < \rangle$ be an $\mathcal{OSHOQ}(\mathbf{D})$-knowledge base and $\mathcal{I} = (\Delta^{\mathcal{I}}, \cdot^{\mathcal{I}})$ an **interpretation** of Σ. A terminological axiom $A \sqsubseteq B \in \mathcal{T}$ is*

- *applicable w.r.t. $x \in \Delta^{\mathcal{I}}$ and $\mathcal{I}$[3] iff $x \in A^{\mathcal{I}}$.*
- *applied w.r.t. $x \in \Delta^{\mathcal{I}}$ iff it is applicable w.r.t. x and $x \in B^{\mathcal{I}}$.*
- *classically satisfied[4] w.r.t. $x \in \Delta^{\mathcal{I}}$ iff it is applied w.r.t. x whenever it is applicable w.r.t. x.*
- *defeated w.r.t. $x \in \Delta^{\mathcal{I}}$ iff $\exists C \sqsubseteq D < A \sqsubseteq B$ such that $C \sqsubseteq D$ is applied w.r.t. x. In this case, we say that $C \sqsubseteq D$ **defeats** $A \sqsubseteq B$ w.r.t. x.*

*$\mathcal{I}$ satisfies an axiom $A \sqsubseteq B$ from $\mathcal{T}$ if for each x for which $A \sqsubseteq B$ is applicable, $A \sqsubseteq B$ is either applied or defeated, $\mathcal{I}$ is a **model** of Σ if it satisfies all the axioms in Σ.*

Essentially, the above definition allows a less preferred (larger according to the order $<$) axiom $C \sqsubseteq D$ to not be classically satisfied w.r.t. an individual x, provided that it is defeated by a more preferred applied axiom $A \sqsubseteq B < C \sqsubseteq D$ w.r.t. the same domain element x.

The earlier example, without defeat, can then be formulated as the $\mathcal{OSHOQ}(\mathbf{D})$-knowledge base

$$\Sigma = \langle \{ \textit{Thief} \sqsubseteq \textit{Punished}, \textit{Minors} \sqsubseteq \neg\textit{Punished},$$
$$\{\textit{Bill}\} \sqsubseteq \textit{Thief}, \{\textit{Bill}\} \sqsubseteq \textit{Minors} \}, < \rangle$$

Note that the order $<$ is empty, since we did not yet impose a preference order on the axioms. That there was a problem with this knowledge base, can now formally be stated as "the knowledge base is inconsistent", i.e. there does not exist a model for it. Indeed, assume that, on the contrary, there exists a model $\mathcal{I}$ of Σ with $\{\textit{Bill}\}^{\mathcal{I}} = \{\textit{Bill}^{\mathcal{I}}\}$. Then it can easily be deduced that $\textit{Bill}^{\mathcal{I}}$ would have to be both in $\textit{Punished}^{\mathcal{I}}$ and

---

[1] A strict partial order $<$ on a set X is a binary relation on X that is antisymmetric, anti-reflexive and transitive. Note that this relation is also well-founded, i.e. no infinite chain $\ldots < x_n < \ldots < x_1$ exists, since the Tbox is finite.

[2] For the sake of brevity, we omit the concept names **C**, role names **R**, data types **D** and individual names **I** from the notation.

[3] In the following we will only mention $\mathcal{I}$ if it is not clear from the context.

[4] We omit the "classically" qualification if it is clear from the context.

$(\neg Punished)^{\mathcal{I}}$, which is impossible. Our solution was to defeat $Thief \sqsubseteq Punished$ with $Minors \sqsubseteq \neg Punished$, i.e. allowing a thief not to be punished if he is a minor. Formally, we add to the order $<$

$$Minors \sqsubseteq \neg Punished < Thief \sqsubseteq Punished$$

expressing precisely this intuition, yielding models such as $\mathcal{I}$, with $Thief^{\mathcal{I}} = \{Bill^{\mathcal{I}}\}$, $Minors^{\mathcal{I}} = \{Bill^{\mathcal{I}}\}$ and $Punished^{\mathcal{I}} = \emptyset$, e.g. Bill is a stealing minor who is not being punished, thus effectively bypassing the rule TP with the rule MP.

Continuing the example, we add a recent development (in Belgium) where it has been proposed that committing a serious crime leads to punishment, even if the criminal is a minor. Hence the rule

$$CP : Criminal \sqsubseteq Punished$$

where the concept $Criminal$ stands for "people that have committed a serious crime". Clearly, we would again have a contradiction if Bill is a minor and a known criminal, MP saying Bill should not be punished and CP saying that Bill should in fact be punished. However, the intention is that the CP law has precedence over MP, and thus we add CP **defeats** MP to the knowledge base (note that we do not assert that Bill is a criminal).

$$\Sigma = \langle\{ Thief \sqsubseteq Punished, Minors \sqsubseteq \neg Punished, Criminal \sqsubseteq Punished,$$
$$\{Bill\} \sqsubseteq Thief, \{Bill\} \sqsubseteq Minors\}, <\rangle$$

with $<$ generated by

$$Criminal \sqsubseteq Punished < Minors \sqsubseteq \neg Punished$$
$$\text{and } Minors \sqsubseteq \neg Punished < Thief \sqsubseteq Punished$$

Table 2. Two example models

	Minors	Thief	Criminal	Punished
$\mathcal{I}_1$	$\{bill\}$	$\{bill\}$	$\{bill\}$	$\{bill\}$
$\mathcal{I}_2$	$\{bill\}$	$\{bill\}$	$\emptyset$	$\emptyset$

Definition 2 now yields two kinds of models (see Table 2, page 1038): those such as $\mathcal{I}_1$ where Bill is assumed to be a criminal (and thus should be punished) and those, like $\mathcal{I}_2$, where Bill is not a criminal and thus should not be punished ($\mathcal{I}_1$ and $\mathcal{I}_2$ share the interpretation $bill$ for Bill).

Intuitively, the second type of model, exemplified by $\mathcal{I}_2$, is to be preferred since there is no reason to assume that Bill is a criminal and thus MP should not be defeated.

More precisely, we can base our preference on the fact that $\mathcal{I}_2$ (classically) satisfies more preferred rules than $\mathcal{I}_1$ does: indeed, $\mathcal{I}_2$ satisfies (w.r.t. *bill*) $\{CP, MP, BT, BM\}$ while $\mathcal{I}_1$ satisfies $\{CP, TP, BT, BM\}$. Thus, while, unlike $\mathcal{I}_1$, $\mathcal{I}_2$ does not satisfy TP, it does satisfy the more preferred MP, which is not satisfied by $\mathcal{I}_1$.

Since, for $\mathcal{I}_1$, we need to defeat a more preferred rule than we do for $\mathcal{I}_2$ ($MP < TP$), it is natural to prefer $\mathcal{I}_2$ as a model that better respects the preference order.

We formalize this intuition by defining the notion of "support" for a model as the set containing the domain elements and the axioms they satisfy, i.e. the set of "instantiated axioms" that are classically satisfied by the model.

Definition 3. *The **support** for a model $\mathcal{I}$ of $\Sigma = \langle \mathcal{T}, < \rangle$ is the set*

$$\mathcal{S}^{\mathcal{I}} = \{(x, A \sqsubseteq B) \mid x \in \Delta^{\mathcal{I}}, A \sqsubseteq B \in \mathcal{T} \text{ is (classically) satisfied w.r.t. } x \text{ and } \mathcal{I}\}$$

Whether one model is preferred over another, is then a matter of checking the supports for the models.

Definition 4. *A model $\mathcal{I}$ of a knowledge base Σ is **preferred** over a model $\mathcal{J}$ of Σ, denoted $\mathcal{I} \preceq \mathcal{J}$, if*

$$\forall (x, A \sqsubseteq B) \in \mathcal{S}^{\mathcal{J}} \setminus \mathcal{S}^{\mathcal{I}} \cdot \exists (x, C \sqsubseteq D) \in \mathcal{S}^{\mathcal{I}} \setminus \mathcal{S}^{\mathcal{J}} \cdot C \sqsubseteq D < A \sqsubseteq B$$

We use $\mathcal{I} \prec \mathcal{J}$ just when $\mathcal{I} \preceq \mathcal{J}$ and $\mathcal{S}^{\mathcal{I}} \neq \mathcal{S}^{\mathcal{J}}$ (note that $\mathcal{I} \preceq \mathcal{J}$ whenever $\mathcal{S}^{\mathcal{J}} \subseteq \mathcal{S}^{\mathcal{I}}$).

Intuitively, this means that $\mathcal{I}$ is preferred over $\mathcal{J}$ if all elements that support $\mathcal{J}$ and not $\mathcal{I}$ are countered by more preferred element that supports $\mathcal{I}$ and not $\mathcal{J}$. For the models $\mathcal{I}_1$ and $\mathcal{I}_2$ of the Bill-example (we use the names for the axioms), we have that

$$\mathcal{S}^{\mathcal{I}_1} = \{(bill, CP), (bill, BT), (bill, BM), (bill, TP)\}$$
$$\mathcal{S}^{\mathcal{I}_2} = \{(bill, CP), (bill, BT), (bill, BM), (bill, MP)\}$$

and thus, $(bill, TP) \in \mathcal{S}^{\mathcal{I}_1} \setminus \mathcal{S}^{\mathcal{I}_2}$, is countered by (note that $MP < TP$) $(bill, MP) \in \mathcal{S}^{\mathcal{I}_2} \setminus \mathcal{S}^{\mathcal{I}_1}$, yielding that $\mathcal{I}_2 \prec \mathcal{I}_1$, which fits our intuition.

The preference order $\prec$ is itself a strict partial order.

Theorem 1. *Let $\Sigma = \langle \mathcal{T}, < \rangle$ be an $\mathcal{OSHOQ}(\mathbf{D})$-knowledge base. $\prec$ defines a strict partial order on the models of Σ.*

The definition of preferred models is straightforward.

Definition 5. *A model $\mathcal{I}$ of $\Sigma = \langle \mathcal{T}, < \rangle$ is a **preferred model** of Σ if there is no model $\mathcal{I}'$ of Σ, such that $\mathcal{I}' \prec \mathcal{I}$, i.e. $\mathcal{I}$ is minimal w.r.t. $\prec$.*

In the sequel, we make the following extra assumption [1], basically to make sure that e.g. $\{Bill\}^{\mathcal{I}_1}$ does not mean something else than $\{Bill\}^{\mathcal{I}_2}$ does.

- The *Common Domain Assumption* assumes that every interpretation is defined over the same abstract domain Δ, i.e. $\Delta^{\mathcal{I}} = \Delta$ for all interpretations $\mathcal{I}$.
- The *Rigid Term Assumption* assumes a fixed function $\gamma : \mathbf{I} \to \Delta$, such that, for any individual name a and interpretation $\mathcal{I}$, $\{a\}^{\mathcal{I}} = \{\gamma(a)\}$. Thus named individuals have a fixed interpretation.

Intuitively, the above conditions restrict our attention to a single UoD (Universe of Discourse) corresponding to the knowledge base.

3   Nonmonotonic Reasoning with $\mathcal{OSHOQ}(D)$

While description logics can be given a user-friendly interface for designing and maintaining ontologies (see e.g. [7]), their main use lies in their reasoning capabilities. Using a description logic representation, one may for example answer the questions below.

- Given an individual o, what is its type, what classes does it belong to?
- Given a new class with certain properties, what is its place in the ontology's taxonomy? What are its sub- and super classes?
- Is a class subsumed by another class?
- Is a class satisfiable, i.e. can there exist instances of this class?
- Is the ontology consistent, i.e. does it have models?

E.g. subsumption and consistency can then be stated in $\mathcal{OSHOQ}(D)$ (and in other DLs, see e.g. [2,21]) as in the following definition.

Definition 6. *A $\mathcal{SHOQ}(D)$-concept expression C is **satisfiable** w.r.t. an $\mathcal{OSHOQ}(D)$ knowledge base Σ if there exists a model $\mathcal{I}$ of Σ such that $C^{\mathcal{I}} \neq \emptyset$. C is **subsumed by** a concept expression D w.r.t. Σ (notation: $\Sigma \models C \sqsubseteq D$) if $C^{\mathcal{I}} \subseteq D^{\mathcal{I}}$ for each model $\mathcal{I}$ of Σ. Furthermore, we call Σ **consistent** iff there exists a model $\mathcal{I}$ of Σ.*

Focusing on subsumption, we alter the definition to take into account preferred models instead of models.

Definition 7. *Let Σ be an $\mathcal{OSHOQ}(D)$ knowledge base, C and D concept expressions. C is **defeasibly subsumed by** D, denoted, $\Sigma \mathrel{\vert\!\approx} C \sqsubseteq D$, iff $C^{\mathcal{I}} \subseteq D^{\mathcal{I}}$ for each preferred model $\mathcal{I}$ of Σ.*

Defeasible subsumption ($\mathrel{\vert\!\approx}$) is "strictly weaker" than classical subsumption ($\models$), in the sense that if $\Sigma \models C \sqsubseteq D$ then $\Sigma \mathrel{\vert\!\approx} C \sqsubseteq D$, but not the other way around.

Moreover, $\models$ is monotonic, while $\mathrel{\vert\!\approx}$ is not.

Theorem 2 ($\models$ **is monotonic**). *Let $\langle \mathcal{T}, < \rangle$ be an $\mathcal{OSHOQ}(D)$ knowledge base and let A and B be concept expressions. If $\langle \mathcal{T}, < \rangle \models A \sqsubseteq B$ then $\langle \mathcal{T} \cup \mathcal{T}', < \rangle \models A \sqsubseteq B$ where $\mathcal{T}'$ is a finite set of terminological axioms.*[5]

Thus, extending a knowledge base preserves earlier subsumption conclusions. This does not hold for defeasible subsumption, $\mathrel{\vert\!\approx}$, as illustrated by the knowledge base

$$\Sigma = \langle \{P \sqsubseteq B, P \sqsubseteq \neg F, \{Tweety\} \sqsubseteq B, B \sqsubseteq F\}, < \rangle$$

with $<$ generated by $P \sqsubseteq \neg F < B \sqsubseteq F$. According to Σ, birds (B) tend to fly (F), penguins (P) don't fly, penguins are birds and $Tweety$ is a bird. The rule that birds tend to fly may be defeated by the more specialized rule saying that penguins don't fly.

Note that, $\Sigma \not\models \{Tweety\} \sqsubseteq F$ since we can easily construct a model $\mathcal{I}$ where $\{Tweety\}^{\mathcal{I}} = P^{\mathcal{I}} = B^{\mathcal{I}} = \{t\}$ while $F^{\mathcal{I}} = \emptyset$, which does not satisfy $\{Tweety\} \sqsubseteq F$.

---

[5] Note that $\langle \mathcal{T} \cup \mathcal{T}', < \rangle$ may actually be inconsistent, i.e. it may not have any models. However, it is easy to verify that, for an inconsistent knowledge base, all subsumptions hold, and thus the theorem remains valid.

Still, in the absence of other information, in particular if we have no evidence that *Tweety* might be a penguin, it is common sense to tentatively conclude that *Tweety* flies, i.e. $\{Tweety\} \sqsubseteq F$. It is precisely this intuition that is captured by defeasible subsumption. Indeed, there exists another model $\mathcal{J}$ with $\{Tweety\}^{\mathcal{J}} = F^{\mathcal{J}} = B^{\mathcal{J}} = \{t\}$ and $P^{\mathcal{J}} = \emptyset$. Clearly, $\mathcal{J}$, unlike $\mathcal{I}$, classically satisfies all axioms of Σ and therefore $\mathcal{J} \prec \mathcal{I}$ and $\mathcal{I}$ is not a preferred model (but $\mathcal{J}$ is). In fact, it is easy to verify that all preferred models satisfy $\{Tweety\} \sqsubseteq F$ and therefore $\Sigma \mathrel{\mapstochar\sim} \{Tweety\} \sqsubseteq F$.

If, however, we extend Σ to Σ' by adding a fresh axiom $\{Tweety\} \sqsubseteq P$, i.e. *Tweety* is a penguin, $\mathcal{J}$ ceases to be a model and $\mathcal{I}$ becomes a preferred model of Σ'. Thus, while $\Sigma \mathrel{\mapstochar\sim} \{Tweety\} \sqsubseteq F$, $\Sigma' \mathrel{\not\mapstochar\sim} \{Tweety\} \sqsubseteq F$, which shows that $\mathrel{\mapstochar\sim}$ is nonmonotonic.

The following characterization shows that the definition of defeasible subsumption follows our intuition: C is defeasibly subsumed by D just when, for any new individual a, if all we know about a is that it belongs to C, then it also (defeasibly) belongs to D.

Theorem 3. *Let* $\Sigma = \langle \mathcal{T}, < \rangle$ *be an* $\mathcal{OSHOQ}(\mathbf{D})$ *knowledge base, C and D concept expressions and a a new individual, not appearing in Σ, then*

$$\langle \mathcal{T}, < \rangle \mathrel{\mapstochar\sim} C \sqsubseteq D \iff \langle \mathcal{T} \cup \{\{a\} \sqsubseteq C\}, < \rangle \mathrel{\mapstochar\sim} \{a\} \sqsubseteq D$$

In view of the role of DLs as providing the basic reasoning mechanisms for ontologies, an important requirement is that the reasoning procedures are decidable. We can extend the $\mathcal{SHOQ}(\mathbf{D})$ tableau algorithm, deciding satisfiability and subsumption [19], to incorporate the preference order and the notion of preferred models.

Theorem 4. *Let* Σ *be an* $\mathcal{OSHOQ}(\mathbf{D})$ *knowledge base, C and D concept expressions.* $\Sigma \mathrel{\mapstochar\sim} C \sqsubseteq D$ *is a decidable problem.*

4 Applications

4.1 Ontology Learning

However convenient the preference order may be, when designing an ontology for a certain application domain, the ontology engineer may not be aware of the preferences amongst axioms. He will, however, almost certainly be confronted with conflicts or inconsistencies during the design process, e.g. as a result of the DLs reasoning procedures. Inconsistencies may have various causes, like the designer wrongly assuming an axiom to be universally valid.

As an example, suppose the aim is to design an ontology regarding the nature of sports. Having seen a live coverage of a bowling game, the designer believes that in general "sports (S) is an exciting pastime (P)". However, since the next show he saw was a cricket game, he added the belief that "English sports (E) are boring (B)". This leads to the knowledge base

$$\Sigma = \{S \sqsubseteq P, E \sqsubseteq B, E \sqsubseteq S, P \sqsubseteq \neg B, \{cricket\} \sqsubseteq E\}$$

additionally saying that "English sports are sports", "an exciting pastime is not boring" and "cricket is an English sport".

The DLs reasoning procedures will tell the designer that this is an inconsistent knowledge base. However, they will not tell him that defeating one axiom with another is a possible solution for the inconsistency. We propose an order-learning algorithm for extending the order of an inconsistent knowledge base $\langle \mathcal{T}, < \rangle$ to a consistent version $\langle \mathcal{T}, <' \rangle$ where $< \subseteq <'$, i.e. if we denote $<$ and $<'$ as two subsets $\mathcal{O}$ and $\mathcal{O}'$ of $\mathcal{T} \times \mathcal{T}$, $\mathcal{O} \subseteq \mathcal{O}'$.

This algorithm [16], based on the candidate elimination algorithm of [24], will provide the ontology designer with a choice of extensions to the current order on his inconsistent knowledge base. The decision of which order to take, remains the responsibility of the designer and should correspond with the underlying UoD, however, every order he picks is guaranteed to solve the inconsistency.

The algorithm in Table 3 is initialized with the order $<$ of the original knowledge base (viewed as a subset $\mathcal{O}$ of $\mathcal{T} \times \mathcal{T}$). By adding real-world examples (a training set E) which represent the knowledge that must be satisfied by the the resulting ontology, we minimally extend $\mathcal{O}$ as to make $\langle \mathcal{T} \cup E, \mathcal{O}' \rangle$ consistent. Additionally, we can restrict the range of possible orders by forcing certain axioms to be "strict" (as in Def. 1), and not allowing the order to defeat strict axioms. In our sports ontology we can clearly assume $E \sqsubseteq S, P \sqsubseteq \neg B$ and $\{cricket\} \sqsubseteq E$, to be strict (English sports are always sports, an exciting pastime is never a boring pastime, and cricket is an English sport).

Table 3. "Candidate elimination" algorithm

1. Start with $S = \{\mathcal{O}\}$ where $\mathcal{O}$ is the set representing the original relation, and $\Sigma = \langle \mathcal{T}_0 = \mathcal{T}, < \rangle$ is the original KB, and examples $E = \{\{a_1\} \sqsubseteq K_1, \ldots, \{a_n\} \sqsubseteq K_n\}, i = 1$.
2. Consider an example $\{a_i\} \sqsubseteq K_i$ from E.
3. For each $\mathcal{O} \in S$ such that $\langle \mathcal{T}_{i-1} \cup \{\{a_i\} \sqsubseteq K_i\}, \mathcal{O} \rangle$ is not consistent
   a) Remove $\mathcal{O}$ from S.
   b) Add to S all generalizations $\mathcal{O}' \supset \mathcal{O}$ ($\mathcal{O}'$ formed with axioms from Σ, to be a generator of a strict partial order such that no strict axiom is defeated) of $\mathcal{O}$ such that
      i. $\langle \mathcal{T}_{i-1} \cup \{\{a_i\} \sqsubseteq K_i\}, \mathcal{O}' \rangle$ is consistent, and
      ii. $\mathcal{O}'$ is minimal, i.e. $\forall \mathcal{O}'', \mathcal{O} \subset \mathcal{O}'' \subset \mathcal{O}' \cdot \langle \mathcal{T}_{i-1} \cup \{\{a_i\} \sqsubseteq K_i\}, \mathcal{O}'' \rangle$ is not consistent.
4. $\mathcal{T}_i = \mathcal{T}_{i-1} \cup \{\{a_i\} \sqsubseteq K_i\}; i \leftarrow i + 1$
5. Continue from 2. until either $S = \emptyset$, in which case the algorithm fails, or all examples in E have been considered and $S \neq \emptyset$. In the latter case, the algorithm succeeds and the learned orders are in S.

Formally we have the result,

Theorem 5. *Let* $\Sigma = \langle \mathcal{T}, < \rangle$ *be an* $\mathcal{OSHOQ}(\mathbf{D})$ *knowledge base and let* $E = \{\{a_1\} \sqsubseteq K_1, \ldots, \{a_n\} \sqsubseteq K_n\}$, *be a set of examples. If the algorithm from Table 3 succeeds with non-empty solution set S, then $<' \in S$ iff $\langle \mathcal{T}, <' \rangle$ is a minimal order-extension ($< \subseteq <'$) of Σ such that $\langle \mathcal{T} \cup E, <' \rangle$ is consistent.*

Going back to our game of cricket, we wish to learn which minimal orders will solve the inconsistency. We provide the algorithm with the knowledge we have about cricket

$$\{cricket\} \sqsubseteq B \ .$$

We pick-up the learning algorithm after have seen this example. Our result set S of learned orders then becomes

$$S = \{\{E \sqsubseteq B < S \sqsubseteq P\},$$
$$\{E \sqsubseteq S < S \sqsubseteq P\},$$
$$\{\{cricket\} \sqsubseteq E < S \sqsubseteq P\}\}$$

The designer then has three corresponding choices. He probably should not choose the third order, since this involves defeating the rule with a single fact, which may not be general enough. The choice between the first and the second is a matter of a taste. In both cases a sport that is not exciting must be an English sport. The second choice adds nothing, being an English sport is enough for not being exciting, while the first choice would amount to not only having an English sport but also a boring sport.

4.2 Ontology Integration

We describe integration of ontologies as the problem of merging two ontologies into a single unified ontology. In addition to representing the information from both ontologies, the integrated ontology should also describe the relationships between them.

In practice, merging ontologies is a complex multi-layered and difficult to automate task. Possible problems include [9], for example, two terms with the same name in different ontologies, but actually representing different concepts. E.g. in one ontology, the term *President* may mean "president of a country", while in the other it may be used to express "president of a company". Another related problem is two different terms that represent the same concept in different ontologies: *Mafia* and *Mob* can both represent a large organized group of criminals. Although these and other problems are crucial to ontology integration, we assume here a simplified setting where different terms in different ontologies represent different concepts, and terms have a single common meaning.

In this setting, we attempt to integrate two consistent ontologies (expressed as DL knowledge bases) in a new ontology. The basic procedure is then, assuming all necessary pre-processing has taken place, to take the union of the two knowledge bases. Clearly, this new ontology may not be consistent. A typical action would be, as the SMART algorithm for merging and aligning ontologies indicates [25], to put the conflict on a conflict list together with actions that remedy the inconsistency.

This is where $\mathcal{OSHOQ}(\mathbf{D})$ becomes useful. While there may be several reasons for having an inconsistency, it could well be that an inconsistency arose because of the fact that a certain axiom is in general more preferred than another one, or because an axiom applies in a general ontology while it has exceptions in a more specific ontology, or, in the most extreme case, an axiom in one ontology may just be wrong, and it should be defeated by another one. All the foregoing problems can be relatively easily solved by placing a preference order on some axioms of the ontologies.

The ontology learning algorithm in Table 3 can, when encountering an inconsistency, suggest several orders that remedy the inconsistency. It is then up to the designer to decide which order to choose according to the UoD he is modeling. As in the SMART algorithm, the designer should be able to adapt some parameters as to (partially) automate this behavior. For example, when integrating two ontologies where one of them has greater authority (e.g., it comes from a trusted source), axioms of this preferred ontology should always be preferred.

To make things more explicit we take a look at a toy example. Consider two little ontologies, one representing the knowledge that quakers are pacifists and that Nixon is a quaker, while the other acknowledges the fact that republicans are not pacifists and that Nixon is a republican.

$$\mathcal{O}_1 = \langle\{quakers \sqsubseteq pacifists, \{Nixon\} \sqsubseteq quakers\}\rangle$$

and

$$\mathcal{O}_2 = \langle\{republicans \sqsubseteq \neg pacifists, \{Nixon\} \sqsubseteq republicans\}\rangle$$

While both ontologies are consistent in their own right, when one attempts to unite the knowledge in a new ontology

$$\mathcal{O} = \langle\{quakers \sqsubseteq pacifists, \{Nixon\} \sqsubseteq quakers,$$
$$republicans \sqsubseteq \neg pacifists, \{Nixon\} \sqsubseteq republicans\}\rangle$$

one ends up with an inconsistent knowledge base. More specifically, Nixon can be shown to be both a pacifist and a non-pacifist.

However if, for some reason, ontology $\mathcal{O}_2$ is more preferred than $\mathcal{O}_1$, for example because $\mathcal{O}_2$ was released by the government and $\mathcal{O}_1$ by some unauthorized Nixon website, we have the means to incorporate this preference in $\mathcal{OSHOQ}(\mathbf{D})$ by simply defining a preference order $<$ on $\mathcal{O}$, such that $a < b$ for every axiom a in $\mathcal{O}_2$ and b in $\mathcal{O}_1$, claiming that axioms from the authorized source are preferred. From this new $\mathcal{OSHOQ}(\mathbf{D})$ ontology

$$\mathcal{O} = \langle\{quakers \sqsubseteq pacifists, \{Nixon\} \sqsubseteq quakers,$$
$$republicans \sqsubseteq \neg pacifists, \{Nixon\} \sqsubseteq republicans\}, <\rangle$$

we can deduce, with the preferred model semantics, that Nixon is not a pacifist.

5   Conclusion and Directions for Further Research

We provided a nonmonotonic extension for the $\mathcal{SHOQ}(\mathbf{D})$ description logic, by imposing a strict partial order on the axioms. In this way we were able to express that not all knowledge can be caught in rigid rules since rules may be valid in a general situation but have exceptions where more preferred rules override the general case. The preferred model semantics provides a natural way to express such situations.

We discussed an order learning algorithm that, given an inconsistent knowledge base, can suggest orders to solve the inconsistency. While $\mathcal{OSHOQ}(\mathbf{D})$ does not claim to solve the ontology integration problem as such, it can however be a helpful instrument for removing inconsistencies from the merged ontology, by suggesting (or automatically enforcing) a preference on axioms.

For the future, it would be interesting to see how $\mathcal{OSHOQ}(\mathbf{D})$ exactly relates to other nonmonotonic description logics, for example to the general framework in [26]. Also other approaches, like the ordered theory presentation of [27] may provide useful insights.

References

[1] F. Baader, D.L. McGuinness, D. Nardi, and P.F. Patel-Schneider, editors. *Description Logic Handbook*, chapter 2, pages 47–100. Cambridge University Press, 2002.

[2] F. Baader and U. Sattler. Tableau algorithms for description logics. In R. Dyckhoff, editor, *Proceedings of the International Conference on Automated Reasoning with Tableaux and Related Methods (Tableaux 2000)*, volume 1847 of *Lecture Notes in Artificial Intelligence*, pages 1–18, St Andrews, Scotland, UK, 2000. Springer-Verlag.

[3] Franz Baader and Philipp Hanschke. A scheme for integrating concrete domains into concept languages. Technical Report RR-91-10, Deutsches Forschungszentrum für Künstliche Intelligenz GmbH, 1991.

[4] Franz Baader and Bernhard Hollunder. Embedding defaults into terminological knowledge representation formalisms. In Bernhard Nebel, Charles Rich, and William Swartout, editors, *KR'92. Principles of Knowledge Representation and Reasoning: Proceedings of the Third International Conference*, pages 306–317, San Mateo, California, 1992. Morgan Kaufmann.

[5] Franz Baader and Bernhard Hollunder. How to prefer more specific defaults in terminological default logic. In Ruzena Bajcsy, editor, *Proceedings of the Thirteenth International Joint Conference on Artificial Intelligence*, pages 669–674, San Mateo, California, 1993. Morgan Kaufmann.

[6] S. Bechhofer, C. Goble, and I. Horrocks. DAML+OIL is not enough. In *Proceedings of the First Semantic Web Working Symposium (SWWS'01)*, pages 151–159. CEUR, 2001.

[7] Sean Bechhofer, Ian Horrocks, Carole Goble, and Robert Stevens. OilEd: a reason-able ontology editor for the semantic web. In *Proceedings of KI2001, Joint German/Austrian conference on Artificial Intelligence*, number 2174 in Lecture Notes in Computer Science, pages 396–408, Vienna, September 2001. Springer-Verlag.

[8] T. Berners-Lee, J. Hendler, and O. Lassila. The Semantic Web. *Scientific American*, pages 34–43, May 2001.

[9] A. Borgida and R. Küsters. What's not in a name: Some Properties of a Purely Structural Approach to Integrating Large DL Knowledge Bases. In F. Baader and U. Sattler, editors, *Proceedings of the International Workshop on Description Logics (DL2000)*, number 33 in CEUR-WS, 2000.

[10] S. Decker, F. van Harmelen, J. Broekstra, M. Erdmann, D. Fensel, I. Horrocks, M. Klein, and S. Melnik. The Semantic Web - on the respective roles of XML and RDF. *IEEE Internet Computing*, September-October 2000.

[11] D. Fensel, I. Horrocks, F. van Harmelen, S. Decker, M. Erdmann, and M. Klein. OIL in a Nutshell. In R. Dieng et al., editor, *Knowledge Acquisition, Modeling, and Management, Proceedings of the European Knowledge Acquisition Conference (EKAW-2000)*, Lecture Notes in Artificial Intelligence. Springer-Verlag, 2000.

[12] D. Fensel, F. van Harmelen, I. Horrocks, D. McGuinness, and P. F. Patel-Schneider. OIL: An ontology infrastructure for the semantic web. *IEEE Intelligent Systems*, 16(2):38–45, 2001.

[13] D. Gabbay, E. Laenens, and D. Vermeir. Credulous vs. sceptical semantics for ordered logic programs. In *Proceedings of the Second International Conference on Principles of Knowledge Representation and Reasoning*, pages 208–217. Morgan Kaufmann, 1991.

[14] P. Geerts and D. Vermeir. Defeasible logics. In D. M. Gabbay and P. Smets, editors, *Handbook of defeasible reasoning and uncertainty management systems*, volume 2, pages 175–210. Kluwer Academic Press, 1998.

[15] J.C. Hage, H.B. Verheij, and A.R. Lodder. Reason Based Logic; a Logic that Deals with Rules and Reasons. In J.M. Akkermans and J.A. Breuker, editors, *Working Papers NAIC '93*, pages 293–304. 1993.

[16] S. Heymans and D. Vermeir. Using Preference Order in Ontologies. 2002. To appear.

[17] I. Horrocks. A denotational semantics for Standard OIL and Instance OIL. http://www.ontoknowledge.org/oil/downl/semantics.pdf, 2000.

[18] I. Horrocks, D. Fensel, J. Boekstra, S. Decker, M. Erdmann, C. Goble, F. Van Harmelen, M. Klein, S. Staab, R. Studer, and E. Motta. The ontology inference layer OIL. http://www.cs.vu.nl/~dieter/oil/Tr/oil.pdf, 2000.

[19] I. Horrocks and U. Sattler. Ontology reasoning in the $\mathcal{SHOQ}(\mathbf{D})$ description logic. In B. Nebel, editor, *Proc. of the 17th Int. Joint Conf. on Artificial Intelligence (IJCAI-01)*, pages 199–204. Morgan Kaufmann, 2001.

[20] I. Horrocks, U. Sattler, and S. Tobies. Reasoning with individuals for the description logic $\mathcal{SHIQ}$. In David MacAllester, editor, *Proc. of the 17th Int. Conf. on Automated Deduction (CADE-17)*, number 1831 in Lecture Notes In Artificial Intelligence, pages 482–496. Springer-Verlag, 2000.

[21] Ian Horrocks, Ulrike Sattler, and Stephan Tobies. Practical reasoning for expressive description logics. In Harald Ganzinger, David McAllester, and Andrei Voronkov, editors, *Proceedings of the 6th International Conference on Logic for Programming and Automated Reasoning (LPAR'99)*, number 1705, pages 161–180. Springer-Verlag, 1999.

[22] E. Laenens and D. Vermeir. A Logical Basis for Object Oriented programming. In J. Siekmann, editor, *Logics in AI*, number 478 in Lecture notes in Artificial Intelligence, pages 317–332. Springer-Verlag, September 1990.

[23] Ora Lassila and Ralph R. Swick. Resource description framework (RDF) model and syntax specification. W3C Recommendation – http://www.w3.org/TR/1999/REC-rdf-syntax-19990222/, February 1999.

[24] Tom Mitchell. *Machine Learning*. McGraw-Hill, 1997.

[25] N.F. Noy and M.A. Musen. SMART: Automated Support for Ontology Merging and Alignment. In *Proceedings of the Twelfth Workshop on Knowledge Acquisition (KAW'99)*, Banf, Canada, 1999.

[26] J.J. Quantz and M. Ryan. Preferential Default Description Logics. KIT 110, Technische Universität Berlin, 1993.

[27] Mark Ryan. Representing Defaults as Sentences with Reduced Priority. In Bernhard Nebel, Charles Rich, and William Swartout, editors, *KR'92. Principles of Knowledge Representation and Reasoning: Proceedings of the Third International Conference*, pages 649–660. Morgan Kaufmann, San Mateo, California, 1992.

[28] Andrea Schaerf. Reasoning with individuals in concept languages. *Data Knowledge Engineering*, 13(2):141–176, 1994.

[29] Mike Uschold and Michael Grüninger. Ontologies: principles, methods, and applications. *Knowledge Engineering Review*, 11(2):93–155, 1996.

On the Semantics of Anonymous Identity and Reification[*]

Guizhen Yang and Michael Kifer

Department of Computer Science
Stony Brook University
Stony Brook, NY 11794, U.S.A.
{guizyang,kifer}@CS.StonyBrook.EDU

Abstract. Reification and anonymous resources are two of the more interesting features of RDF — an emerging standard for representing semantic information on the Web. Ironically, when RDF was standardized by W3C over three years ago [18], it came without a semantics. There is now growing understanding that a Semantic Web language without a semantics is an oxymoron, and a number of efforts are directed towards giving RDF a precise semantics [12,10]. In this paper we propose a simple semantics for reification and anonymous resources in F-logic [17] — a frame-based logic language, which is a popular formalism for representing and reasoning about semantic information on the Web [22,9,11,8,7].
The choice of F-logic (over RDF) as a basis for our semantics is motivated by the fact that F-logic provides a comprehensive solution for the problem of integrating frames, rules, and deduction, and it has been shown to provide an effective inference service for RDF [8,21].

1 Introduction

RDF [18] was proposed as a standard for representing semantic information on the Web. Ironically, the specification of RDF did not formally define a semantics. Fortunately this peculiar situation is currently being rectified by a number of efforts [12,10].

While much of the RDF syntax is first-order in nature, *reification* (which is involved in expressing statements like "Tom believes that Alice said that RDF is a good idea") is not.[1] Related to this is the issue of anonymous resources, which in RDF are invoked to express statements such as "A person, called Ora Lassila, is the creator of RDF." In this paper, we propose a simple model-theoretic semantics for both of these issues using F-logic [17] as the underlying formalism.

The choice of F-logic is motivated by several considerations. First, it has been a popular vehicle for information mediation and representing semantic information on the Web whenever complex inference is required [14,16,22,9,11,7]. As such applications grow in complexity, the need for an inferencing service will increase. For instance, [8] envisions F-logic precisely as such a service for RDF.

---

[*] This work was supported in part by NSF grant IIS-0072927.

[1] In fact, when left to its own devices, reification can lead to logical paradoxes [20].

R. Meersman, Z. Tari (Eds.): CoopIS/DOA/ODBASE 2002, LNCS 2519, pp. 1047–1066, 2002.

Our contention is that a model theory for RDF must be considered as part of a more general framework, because experience shows that semantics developed for a limited language like RDF might not generalize. For instance, rules and inheritance are some of the issues whose subtle influence is not apparent in the restricted setting of RDF [25]. In fact, we argue that the current proposal for the RDF model theory [10] has several weaknesses, such as *non-compositionality*, which might cause problems down the road. We also point out that there are at least two different useful notions of entailment for RDF graphs, but only one is currently reflected in the RDF model theory document [10].

The idea of embedding RDF into a larger theory is, of course, not new. Embedding RDF into F-logic was proposed in [8], and in [12] the same was done for KIF [13]. Both proposals are incomplete, however, as they do not address reification and anonymous resources. The embedding into F-logic *would have been* complete if F-logic, as described in [17], had support for these two features. We are rectifying this situation in the present work. Our proposed semantics is conceptually very simple[2] and is inspired by HiLog [6] — a logic language that provides a foundation for tractable higher-order logic programming — and by the treatment of anonymous object identities in $\mathcal{F}$LORA-2 [23,24] — a powerful frame-based language for knowledge representation and reasoning, which is based on F-logic, HiLog, and Transaction Logic [2,3]. Therefore, by incorporating reification into the F-logic model theory we provide a model theory for reification in RDF and extend it with powerful meta-programming and inferencing capabilities, which F-logic is known for.

Embedding into F-logic also provides an immediate practical benefit. There are already F-logic based systems, such as $\mathcal{F}$LORA-2 [23,24] and TRIPLE [21], which support reification and have RDF handling capabilities. In particular, $\mathcal{F}$LORA-2 implements the proposed semantics and provides full support for frame-based representation, rules, inheritance, meta-programming, database updates, and more — all in a clean logical fashion. It has already been used in a number of projects ranging from data integration in neuroscience [15] to processing semistructured and semantic information on the Web [7].

This paper is organized as follows. Section 2 surveys the necessary background from F-logic and HiLog. Section 3 motivates the proposed extension to F-logic from the point of view of modeling RDF. Section 4 formally treats the semantics of the proposed extensions. Sections 5 and 6 discuss the properties of the semantics introduced in Section 4 and point out some problems with the current proposal for the RDF model theory [10]. Section 7 concludes the paper.

2   Preliminaries

In this section we review the main ideas behind F-logic [17] and HiLog [6] — the two formalisms that form the basis for our proposed semantics.

---

[2] While it is simple, it is not obvious, as a number of authors believed that F-logic does not generalize to deal with reification directly [4,8,21].

2.1   F-logic

F-logic is an extension of classical predicate logic which allows frame-based (or object-oriented) syntax, and has a natural model-theoretic semantics, and sound and complete proof theory.

F-logic uses Prolog *ground* (*i.e.*, variable-free) terms to represent object identities (abbr., oids), *e.g.*, john and father(mary). Objects can have functional (single-valued), multivalued, or Boolean attributes, for example:

mary[spouse → john, children ⤀ {alice, nancy}].
mary[children ⤀ jack].

Here spouse → john is a *single-valued* attribute specification; it says that mary has a attribute spouse, whose value is a singleton oid john. The specification children ⤀ {alice, nancy} says that children is a *multivalued* attribute; its value in the context of the object mary is a set that *includes* the oids alice and nancy. We emphasize "includes" because a set does not need to be specified all at once. For instance, the second fact above says that mary has one additional child, jack. Note also that we usually omit the braces while specifying a singleton set.

While some attributes of an object can be specified explicitly as facts, other attributes can be defined using inference rules. For instance, we can derive john[children ⤀ {alice, nancy, jack}] with the help of the following inference rule:

X[children ⤀ {C}] :− Y[spouse → X, children ⤀ {C}].

Here we adopt the usual Prolog convention that capitalized symbols denote variables, while symbols beginning with a lowercase letter denote constants.

F-logic objects can also have *methods*, *i.e.*, functions that return a value or a set of values when appropriate arguments are provided. For instance,

john[grade(cs305,f2002) → 100, courses(f2002) ⤀ {cs305, cs306}].

says that john has a single-valued method, grade, whose value on the arguments cs305 and f2002 is 100, and a multivalued method courses, whose value on the argument f2002 is a set of oids that contains cs305 and cs306. As attributes, methods can also be defined using rules.

In addition, *class memberships* (*e.g.*, john : student), *subclass relationships* (*e.g.*, student :: person), *types* (*e.g.*, person[name ⇒ string]), and many other things can also be specified — both statically, as facts, and dynamically, via rules.

In the sequel, we will consider only multivalued attributes and ignore the rest of the features — the results of this paper extend straightforwardly to include class membership, subclass relationship, methods, types, etc.

2.2   HiLog

HiLog was introduced in [5,6] to provide a convenient syntax and tractable model theory to higher-order logic programming. The main highlights of this language are the variables that can range over both function and predicate symbols and a complete elimination of the barrier between predicate formulas and first-order terms. In this way, HiLog provides a natural syntax and semantics for reification: a statement can be a formula and an object at the same time.

We illustrate HiLog through examples. The simplest yet most unusual one is the definition of the standard Prolog meta-predicate call:

    call(X) :− X.

In this example, HiLog does not distinguish between function terms and atomic formulas: the same variable can range over both. Therefore, one can reify statements and reason about them in the same language. For instance, we can state that Bob believes that Mary likes RDF (and possibly other beliefs) as follows:

    believes(bob,likes(mary,rdf)).

and then state that whatever Bob believes is true:

    X :− believes(bob,X).

Variables can also range over function symbols, as in $X(Y, a)$. A query of the form ?− p(X), X, X(Y, X) is well within the boundaries of HiLog. The syntax for HiLog terms also extends that of classical logic. For instance, $g(X)(f(a, X), Y)(b, Y)$ is perfectly fine. Of course, such powerful syntax should be used sparingly, but people have found many important uses for these features. For instance, the following simple program defines transitive closure of *any* binary relation. The program defines a higher-order predicate constructor closure, which takes a binary predicate as a parameter and yields a first-order predicate:

    closure(Pred)(X,Y) :−   Pred(X,Y).
    closure(Pred)(X,Y) :−   Pred(X,Z), closure(Pred)(Z,Y).

Here Pred is a variable that ranges over predicate symbols. When it is bound to a particular symbol, say parent, the above program would compute the relation closure(parent), *i.e.*, the ancestor relation. More examples of this kind of programming are found in [6].

When combined with F-logic, HiLog enables powerful meta-programming features [17,23,24]. For instance, we can define an attribute, methods, whose value for any object is the set of the names of unary and binary single-valued methods defined for that object:

    X[methods ↠ {M}] :−   X[M(A) → V].
    X[methods ↠ {M}] :−   X[M(A1,A2) → V].

Since the main focus of this paper is reification and anonymous identity, in the rest of this paper we will consider only the subset of HiLog that enables reification and combine it with F-logic. Indeed, the use of HiLog to enhance meta-programming in F-logic was discussed in [17,23], but its use for supporting reification has not been considered.

3 Supporting RDF in F-logic

It was argued in [8] that F-logic is a natural formalism to provide semantics and inference service for RDF(S) [18]. However, some important aspects, such as anonymous resources, containers, and reification were left out because the original F-logic [17] did not support them. In this section we illustrate on a number of examples that all these features can be supported by slightly extending the logic with *anonymous ID symbols* and *reified statements*. Formal treatment of this extension is given in Section 4.

First, we briefly recall the RDF data model. An RDF document is a finite set of statements of the form {predicate, subject, object}, where predicate is a *property*, subject is a *resource*, and object is a resource or a literal.

A resource describes a real or conceptual entity (*e.g.* "John Doe"). Typically, resources are represented as URIs. But they can also be *anonymous* (*e.g.* "someone"). For instance, the URI http://www.w3.org/TR/REC-rdf-syntax represents the abstract concept of RDF itself. A property is a predicate that specifies a binary relationship (*e.g.* "works for"). In RDF, properties form a subset of resources and are also represented by URIs. Finally, literals are constants in some primitive data types, such as a string or number.

A set of RDF statements can be viewed as a *directed labeled graph*, where the vertexes are the resources and the literals, and a triple {p, s, o} represents an arc from s to o, labeled by p.

3.1 Anonymous Object Identity

Representation of RDF statements with named resources in F-logic is straightforward. For instance, the following sentence

> *Thomas Edison is the inventor of the bulb (represented by a resource with the URI* http://foo.org/TheBulb).

can be represented as a triple

> {inventor, [http://foo.org/TheBulb], "Thomas Edison"}

where the notation [ref] denotes the resource identified by the URI ref and a string enclosed by double quotes denotes a literal. In F-logic, the same statement is written like this:

> 'http://foo.org/TheBulb'[inventor $\twoheadrightarrow$ 'Thomas Edison'].

One difficulty arises in translating RDF statements that include *anonymous resources*, *i.e.*, resources that are not named explicitly. This kind of resources are involved in expressing statements such as

> *Someone, named Thomas Edison, born in 1847, is the inventor of the resource* http://foo.org/TheBulb.

The intent here is to make a structured resource *without a known object ID* and state that it has two properties, name and born, with the above values. In RDF, this sentence would be represented using the triple syntax as follows:

```
{name, [X], 'Thomas Edison'}
{born, [X], 1847}
{inventor, [http://foo.org/TheBulb], [X]}
```

Here [X] represents an anonymous resource.

Objects with anonymous IDs were not envisioned in the original work on F-logic [17], but were introduced in $\mathcal{F}$LORA-2 [24,23] — our implementation of F-logic that extends it with many additional concepts. To represent such objects, $\mathcal{F}$LORA-2 uses a special symbol, _#, called an *unnumbered anonymous ID symbol*, and another countable set of symbols, _#1, _#2, ..., etc., called *numbered anonymous ID symbols*. The intended meaning (which is formalized in Section 4) is that each occurrence of _# denotes a distinct object ID that does not occur anywhere else in the program. All occurrences of the same numbered anonymous ID symbol, *e.g.* _#1, within the same scope are treated as representing the same object ID, but this ID is distinct from any other ID used elsewhere in the program (including the occurrences of _#1 in a different scope). The notion of scope is formalized in Section 4, but for our current purposes let us assume that the scope of numbered anonymous ID symbols extends over the entire clause (where each clause is terminated with a "." and comma represents the conjunction). Thus, the above statement can be represented in $\mathcal{F}$LORA-2 as follows:

```
'http://foo.org/TheBulb'[inventor ↠ _#1],
_#1[name ↠ 'Thomas Edison', born ↠ 1847].
```

Note that here the two occurrences of _#1 are within the same clause and thus the same scope. So they refer to the same object. If we want to state that *someone invented the bulb and someone called Thomas Edison was born in 1847*, then we could write

```
'http://foo.org/TheBulb'[inventor ↠ _#],
_#[name ↠ 'Thomas Edison', born ↠ 1847].
```

Here we use unnumbered anonymous ID symbols and, even though they occur within the same scope, they represent different objects.

Anonymous resources are also frequently used to represent *containers* in RDF. For example, the following sentence

The committee of Fred, Wilma, and Dino approved the resolution.

can be expressed using the *Bag* container of RDF and would be written in the RDF syntax as follows:

```
<rdf:RDF>
    <rdf:Description about="http://xyz.org/resolution">
        <approvedBy>
            <rdf:Bag>
                <rdf:li resource="http://xyz.org/members/Fred" />
                <rdf:li resource="http://xyz.org/members/Wilma" />
                <rdf:li resource="http://xyz.org/members/Dino" />
            </rdf:Bag>
        </approvedBy>
    </rdf:Description>
</rdf:RDF>
```

In $\mathcal{F}$LORA-2, the same sentence can be represented as follows:

```
_#1[
    'rdf:type' → 'rdf:Bag',
    'rdf:_1' → 'http://xyz.org/members/Fred',
    'rdf:_2' → 'http://xyz.org/members/Wilma',
    'rdf:_3' → 'http://xyz.org/members/Dino'
],
'http://xyz.org/resolution'[approvedBy ↠ _#1].
```

Again, here the two occurrences of _#1 are within the same scope and thus represent the same object. The first occurrence represents a *Bag* object and the second occurrence refers to this object.

3.2   Reified Statements

Reification in RDF is used to make statements about statements. Since statements are formulas, making statements about them means that formulas must be somehow treated as objects. To represent the following statement

> *Someone named John Doe believes that a person, called Thomas Edison, invented the bulb (resource* http://foo.org/TheBulb*).*

using the RDF triple syntax one would have to write a rather cumbersome document as follows:

```
{type, [X], [RDF:Statement]}
{predicate, [X], [inventor]}
{subject, [X], [http://foo.org/TheBulb]}
{object, [X], [Y]}
{name, [Y], "Thomas Edison"}
{name, [Z], "John Doe"}
{believes, [Z], [X]}
```

Here a new, anonymous resource X is used as a *referent* to the following reified statement

A person, called Thomas Edison, invented the bulb.

This is expressed by the first four triples, which say that: (1) X represents an RDF statement; (2) its predicate is inventor; (3) its subject is the URI http://foo.org/TheBulb; and (4) its object is another anonymous object Y. In the fifth triple we say that this latter object has property name with the value "Thomas Edison". The sixth statement says that there is an anonymous object Z with property name whose value is "John Doe". Finally, the last statement says that object Z has property believes with value X — the anonymous resource that represents the reified statement that *a person, called Thomas Edison, invented the bulb.*

In our extension to F-logic this statement can be modeled in the following much more natural way:

```
_#[
  name →» 'John Doe',
  believes →»
     'http://foo.org/TheBulb'[inventor →» _#[name →» 'Thomas Edison']]
].
```

Note that here the formula 'http://foo.org/TheBulb'[inventor →» _#1] *itself* is an object — not some other object ID that refers to this formula. We will argue in Section 6 that this syntax and its corresponding semantics is superior to that of the current proposal for RDF model theory [10]. It also permits more interesting reasoning to be easily performed over reified statements (see Section 6).

We should note that the above syntax is *not* the actual syntax of ℱLORA-2 [24]. It is also quite different from the F-logic syntax as described in [17]. We do so to avoid introducing additional features of F-logic and ℱLORA-2 and to simplify the formal development of the model theory in Section 4. In fact, the actual syntax of ℱLORA-2 is much richer, which allows to write the above and the earlier sentences more succinctly:

```
_#[
  name →» 'John Doe',
  believes →»
     ${'http://foo.org/TheBulb'[inventor →» _#[name →» 'Thomas Edison]]}
].
```

That is, in the actual ℱLORA-2 syntax, reification is specified using the ${...} construct and the statement inside of ${...} is a shorthand for the conjunction of two F-logic statements: 'http://foo.org/TheBulb'[inventor →» _#1] and _#1[name →» 'Thomas Edison']. The interested reader is referred to [24] for details.

In Section 4, we discuss the notions of RDF graph entailment and equivalence and show that there are at least two such notions, both useful, but only one is currently considered by the RDF model theory proposal [10].

4 Formal Syntax and Semantics

In this section we formally define the syntax and semantics of an F-logic language extended with anonymous identity and reification. We will continue to call this extension "F-logic" in order to avoid introducing yet another name.

To simplify the exposition, we focus on a subset of the new F-logic syntax. The only kind of atoms we consider here is in the form of o[m $\twoheadrightarrow$ v], which specifies that the object o has a multivalued method, m, whose return value is a set that contains v as a member. The symbols o, m, and v are F-logic terms (to be defined below); they represent the ID of an object, a method, and a value of the method, respectively. In a program, these terms can contain variables in which case they would represent a parameterized collection of objects — one object per variable instantiation. This design makes meta-programming in F-logic as natural as querying.

An F-logic language $\mathcal{L}$ consists of a set of *constants*, $\mathcal{C}$; a set of *variables*, $\mathcal{V}$; an *unnumbered anonymous ID* symbol, _#; *numbered anonymous ID* symbols, _#1, _#2, ... (for each positive integer); *connectives* including ¬, ∨, ∧, and ←; *quantifiers* including ∃ and ∀; and *auxiliary symbols*, such as comma, parentheses, and brackets. While defining semantics for F-logic programs, we will always *fix* an F-logic language $\mathcal{L}$.

Intuitively, an occurrence of an unnumbered anonymous ID symbol implies a *distinct* object that is different from any object represented by any other term. Moreover, two occurrences of _# represent two distinct objects. Numbered anonymous ID symbols are essentially the same but slightly different. Different occurrences of _#N and _#M, where N ≠ M, represent distinct objects. However, different occurrences of _#N (with the same number N) within *the same scope* refer to the same object. This intended meaning will be made precise later when we give a formal semantics.

Formally, F-logic *terms* and *atoms* are constructed inductively as follows. The idea of this construction is borrowed from HiLog [5,6] and is extended to accommodate reification of F-logic atoms (statements).

Definition 1 (Terms and Atoms). *Given an F-logic language $\mathcal{L}$, the terms and atoms are defined inductively as follows:*

- *Any constant c ∈ $\mathcal{C}$ is a term.*
- *Any variable X ∈ $\mathcal{V}$ is a term.*
- *Any unnumbered or numbered ID symbol, _#, _#1, _#2, ..., is a term.*
- *If t is a term and $t_1, ..., t_n$ are terms, then $t(t_1, ..., t_n)$ is a term.*
- *Any term in any of the above forms is called a HiLog term or a HiLog atom.*
- *If o, m, and v are terms, then o[m $\twoheadrightarrow$ v] is a term, also called an F-logic term or an F-logic atom.*
- *If $A_1, ..., A_n$ are terms, then their conjunction, $A_1 \wedge ... \wedge A_n$, is a term.*

Note that both F-logic and predicate terms (or, more precisely, HiLog terms) are atomic formulas in our language. In this way, both relational and object-oriented programming are supported. The last two cases in the above Definition 1 indicate that atomic formulas as well as their conjunctions are terms and so first-class objects in the language. In particular, as we shall see, variables can range over such formulas. This makes the syntax higher-order and provides support for reification. However, the semantics needs to be carefully defined so as to stay tractable and first-order in the sense of [5,6].

Definition 2 (Flat Formula). *Any HiLog atom or F-logic atom is an atomic flat formula. If ϕ and ψ are flat formulas, then so are*

- *$\neg \phi$*
- *$\phi \vee \psi$ and $\phi \wedge \psi$*
- *$\phi \leftarrow \psi$, which is defined to be just a shortcut for $\phi \vee \neg \psi$*
- *$\exists X \phi$ and $\forall X \phi$, where $X \in \mathcal{V}$ is a variable.*

Now we will define interpretations, *i.e.*, the semantic structures that give meanings to F-logic formulas and programs. Our definitions follow the standard convention except that we need to take special care of the anonymous ID symbols and reified statements. To this end, we first have to define the domain of interpretations. In classical logic programming, the domain is typically the set of all ground terms in the language, which is called the Herbrand universe. In our case, however, the domain must also include the constants that are used to interpret the anonymous ID symbols. This idea is formalized next.

Definition 3 (Augmented Herbrand Universe). *Let $\mathcal{L}$ be an F-logic language, $\mathcal{C}$ be the set of constants in $\mathcal{L}$, and $\mathcal{D}$ be a countable set of constants that is disjoint from $\mathcal{C}$. We shall call $\mathcal{D}$ an anonymous domain, since it will be used to interpret the anonymous ID symbols. The augmented Herbrand universe of $\mathcal{L}$ with respect to $\mathcal{D}$, denoted $\mathcal{HU}(\mathcal{D})$, is the set of all terms (see Definition 1) constructed using the constants in $\mathcal{C} \cup \mathcal{D}$. In other words, variables and anonymous ID symbols are excluded. Such variable-free terms are called ground.*

Definition 4 (Interpretation). *Given an F-logic language $\mathcal{L}$, an interpretation $\mathcal{I}$ is a pair $(\mathcal{D}, \mathcal{S})$, where*

- *$\mathcal{D}$ is an anonymous domain, i.e., a countable set of constants that is disjoint from $\mathcal{C}$ (the set of all constants in $\mathcal{L}$).*
- *$\mathcal{S}$ is a subset of $\mathcal{HU}(\mathcal{D})$, the augmented Herbrand universe of $\mathcal{L}$ with regard to $\mathcal{D}$. Intuitively, $\mathcal{S}$ represents "what is true" in $\mathcal{I}$.[3]*

The above definition differs from those used in classical logic programming, HiLog, and the original F-logic in its use of the anonymous domain. One significant impact of this domain is that the Herbrand universes of different models

---

[3] Observe that in classical logic programming an interpretation would contain a subset of the *Herbrand base* — a set of atomic formulas (which is distinct from the set of terms that comprises the Herbrand universe). However, in our case (as in HiLog), atomic formulas are reified and thus the Herbrand base and the Herbrand universe are the same.

are different when they use different anonymous domains. To be more precise, the ground terms that are constructed using the constants in C are the same in all Herbrand universes, but the terms that involve the constants from anonymous domains may not be shared. In classical theory of logic programming all interpretations have the same domain — the Herbrand universe. Our definitions reduce to classical ones when there are no anonymous ID symbols and thus no anonymous domains.

Since interpretations can have different domains, there are many ways to compare interpretations. One is by set inclusion. But it makes sense only for interpretations over the same domain. Another way involves domain mappings and domain isomorphisms. Formally, we have the following definitions.

Definition 5 (Domain Mapping). *Let $\mathcal{D}_1$ and $\mathcal{D}_2$ be two anonymous domains with regard to an F-logic language $\mathcal{L}$, C be the set of constants in $\mathcal{L}$. Then a function $\tau\colon \mathcal{D}_1 \to \mathcal{D}_2$ is called an anonymous domain mapping. And a function $\lambda\colon \mathcal{D}_1 \to \mathcal{D}_2 \cup C$ is called an augmented domain mapping.*

For any $\mathsf{t} \in \mathcal{HU}(\mathcal{D}_1)$, $\tau(\mathsf{t})$ is a term obtained from t by simultaneously replacing every constant $\mathsf{d} \in \mathcal{D}_1$ with $\tau(\mathsf{d})$ and leaving the constants in C intact. For any $\mathcal{S} \subseteq \mathcal{HU}(\mathcal{D}_1)$, $\tau(\mathcal{S}) = \{\tau(\mathsf{x}) \mid \mathsf{x} \in \mathcal{S}\}$. $\lambda(\mathsf{t})$ and $\lambda(\mathcal{S})$ are defined similarly.

Definition 6 (Ordering and Isomorphism). *Let $\mathcal{D}_1$ and $\mathcal{D}_2$ be two anonymous domains, and $\mathcal{I}_1 = (\mathcal{D}_1, \mathcal{S}_1)$ and $\mathcal{I}_2 = (\mathcal{D}_2, \mathcal{S}_2)$ be two interpretations.*

- *We write $\mathcal{I}_1 \preceq \mathcal{I}_2$ iff there is an 1-1 anonymous domain mapping $\tau\colon \mathcal{D}_1 \to \mathcal{D}_2$ such that $\tau(\mathcal{S}_1) \subseteq \mathcal{S}_2$. We will write $\mathcal{I}_1 \prec \mathcal{I}_2$ if $\tau(\mathcal{S}_1) \subsetneq \mathcal{S}_2$.*
- *$\mathcal{I}_1$ is isomorphic to $\mathcal{I}_2$, denoted $\mathcal{I}_1 \simeq \mathcal{I}_2$, iff $\mathcal{I}_1 \preceq \mathcal{I}_2$ and $\mathcal{I}_2 \preceq \mathcal{I}_1$.*

Before we can give semantics to formulas that contain anonymous ID symbols, we need to introduce one more notion, the *scoped formulas*. Recall from Section 3 that the intended meaning of a numbered anonymous ID symbol is that two different occurrences of the same symbol within the scope of the same rule denote the same object; otherwise, they potentially refer to different objects. The notion of scoped formulas allows us to extend this idea to more general types of formulas.

Definition 7 (Scoped Formula).

- *If ϕ is a flat formula, then $\{\, \phi \,\}$ is a scoped formula.*
- *If ψ and ξ are scoped formulas, then so are $\psi \vee \xi$ and $\psi \wedge \xi$.*

Note that our definition of scoped formulas is such that the scoping braces, $\{\ldots\}$, always and only apply to the top level conjuncts and disjuncts. For instance, $\{\, \_\#1[\mathsf{loves} \twoheadrightarrow \mathsf{mary}] \,\} \wedge \{\, \exists X(\_\#1[\mathsf{child} \twoheadrightarrow X]) \,\}$ is a valid scoped formula whereas $\{\, \_\#1[\mathsf{loves} \twoheadrightarrow \mathsf{mary}] \,\} \wedge \exists X(\_\#1[\mathsf{child} \twoheadrightarrow X])$ is not. Although we could define even more general scoping rules, including nested scoping, this is probably not useful in practice and so we shall not introduce it in this paper.

An *F-logic program* is a finite collection of *scoped rules* where all variables are universally quantified. A rule has the following form:

$$\{ \forall(A_1 \wedge \ldots \wedge A_m \leftarrow B_1 \wedge \ldots \wedge B_n) \}$$

where $m \geq 1, n \geq 0$, A_i $(1 \leq i \leq m)$ and B_j $(1 \leq j \leq n)$ are atoms and only the atoms in the rule head (the A_i's) are allowed to have anonymous ID symbols. Note that each rule is a scoped formula where the scope is the entire rule. Thus an F-logic program can be thought of as a scoped formula formed by conjoining all the scoped formulas corresponding to the rules.

Following the standard convention, we will omit universal quantifiers in the rules and since the scope is the entire rule we will omit the scoping braces as well. Thus, rules will be simply written as follows:

$$A_1, \ldots, A_m \leftarrow B_1, \ldots, B_n$$

We will continue to use the convention from Section 2 whereby uppercase names denote variables and lowercase names denote constants. A rule with an empty body is called a *fact*. When writing down the facts, we will omit the implication symbol and simply show the head.

Definition 8 (Skolemization). *Let ϕ be a scoped formula and $\mathcal{D}$ be an anonymous domain. A skolemization of ϕ with regard to $\mathcal{D}$, denoted $\Pi_{\mathcal{D}}(\phi)$, is a formula obtained as follows:*

- *If $\phi = \psi \vee \varphi$, then $\Pi_{\mathcal{D}}(\phi) = \Pi_{\mathcal{D}}(\psi) \vee \Pi_{\mathcal{D}}(\varphi)$.*
- *If $\phi = \psi \wedge \varphi$, then $\Pi_{\mathcal{D}}(\phi) = \Pi_{\mathcal{D}}(\psi) \wedge \Pi_{\mathcal{D}}(\varphi)$.*
- *If $\phi = \{ \psi \}$, where ψ is a flat formula, then $\Pi_{\mathcal{D}}(\phi) = \mathsf{skolem}(\mathcal{D}, \psi)$, where $\mathsf{skolem}(\mathcal{D}, \psi)$ is defined as follows:*
  - *Every occurrence of the unnumbered anonymous ID symbol, _#, in ψ is mapped to a distinct constant in $\mathcal{D}$; and*
  - *Every different numbered anonymous ID symbol in ψ is mapped to a distinct constant in $\mathcal{D}$.*

Note that, in a flat formula, each occurrence of the *unnumbered* anonymous ID symbol _# is mapped to a different element of $\mathcal{D}$, but all occurrences of the same *numbered* anonymous ID symbol, say _#1, are mapped to the same distinct element of $\mathcal{D}$. Also observe that two occurrences of the same numbered ID symbol, say _#1, under different scopes are mapped to different elements. For instance, consider a scoped formula $\{ \phi \} \wedge \{ \psi \}$. Then occurrences of _#1 in ϕ are going to be skolemized differently from those in *psi*.

Another way of looking at $\Pi_{\mathcal{D}}(\phi)$ is that it is just like a flat formula, with no scope and no anonymous ID symbols, but some of the symbols in that formula might come from the anonymous domain $\mathcal{D}$. The following example illustrates skolemization.

Let $\mathcal{D} = \{o1, o2, o3, o4, \ldots\}$ be an anonymous domain and P be the following simple F-logic program:

_#[_# →» _#1], _#1[name →» mary].
_#1[name →» 'Ora Lassila'], 'RDF'[creator →» _#1].

Note that according to our definition of F-logic programs, the above program is a shortcut for the following scoped formula:

$$\{ \; \_\#[\_\# \;\twoheadrightarrow\; \_\#1] \;\wedge\; \_\#1[name \;\twoheadrightarrow\; mary] \; \}$$
$$\wedge$$
$$\{ \; \_\#1[name \;\twoheadrightarrow\; 'OraLassila'] \;\wedge\; 'RDF'[creator \;\twoheadrightarrow\; \_\#1] \; \}$$

If we map the first occurrence of _# to o1, its second occurrence to o4, both occurrences of _#1 in the first rule to o2, and both occurrences of _#1 in the second rule to o3, then we obtain the following skolemization $\Pi_{\mathcal{D}}(P)$:

o1[o4 →» o2], o2[name →» mary].
o3[name →» 'Ora Lassila'], 'RDF'[creator →» o3].

A different way of mapping anonymous ID symbols to the constants in $\mathcal{D}$ (*e.g.*, where the first occurrence of _# is mapped to o4 and the second to o1) would lead to a different skolemization of P. Both mappings are valid skolemizations, however, as they satisfy the conditions of Definition 8.

We can now define what it means to be a model of a given scoped formula.

Definition 9 (Model). *Let $\mathcal{I} = (\mathcal{D}, \mathcal{S})$ be an interpretation and ϕ be a scoped formula. Then $\mathcal{I}$ is a model of ϕ, denoted $\mathcal{I} \models \phi$, if and only if there is a skolemization, $\psi = \Pi_{\mathcal{D}}(\phi)$, of the formula ϕ such that $\mathcal{I} \models \psi$, where $\mathcal{I} \models \psi$ is defined in the classical sense:*

- *If ψ is an atom, then $\mathcal{I} \models \psi$ iff $\psi \in \mathcal{S}$.*
- *If $\psi = \neg\varphi$, then $\mathcal{I} \models \psi$ iff it is not the case that $\mathcal{I} \models \varphi$.*
- *If $\psi = \varphi \vee \xi$, then $\mathcal{I} \models \psi$ iff either $\mathcal{I} \models \varphi$ or $\mathcal{I} \models \xi$.*
- *If $\psi = \varphi \wedge \xi$, then $\mathcal{I} \models \psi$ iff $\mathcal{I} \models \varphi$ and $\mathcal{I} \models \xi$.*
- *If $\psi = \exists X\varphi$, then $\mathcal{I} \models \psi$ iff there is $t \in \mathcal{HU}(\mathcal{D})$ (a term in the augmented Herbrand universe) such that $\mathcal{I} \models \psi[X/t]$, where $\psi[X/t]$ denotes the formula obtained from ψ by substituting t for all free occurrences of the variable X.*
- *If $\psi = \forall X\varphi$ then $\mathcal{I} \models \psi$ iff for all $t \in \mathcal{HU}(\mathcal{D})$, $\mathcal{I} \models \psi[X/t]$.*

Lemma 1. *If $\mathcal{I} \models \phi$ and $\mathcal{I} \simeq \mathcal{J}$, then $\mathcal{J} \models \phi$. Thus, the set of models of a formula is closed under the equivalence.*

We can now develop a fixpoint model theory analogously to the classical theory of logic programming. This would provide one computational model for the proposed semantics. Let P be an F-logic program. We will show that it has a property similar to the least model property of logic programs. Of course, given that different models of P can have different anonymous domains, this assertion should not be taken literally.

Definition 10 (Initial Model). *Given an F-logic program P and an interpretation $\mathcal{I}$, $\mathcal{I}$ is an initial model of P, iff*

– $\mathcal{I}$ *is a model of* P, *i.e.*, $\mathcal{I} \models$ P; *and*
– $\mathcal{I}$ *is minimal, i.e., there is no* $\mathcal{J} \models$ P *such that* $\mathcal{J} \prec \mathcal{I}$.

To construct initial models, we will adapt the classical fixpoint theory for Horn programs to the case of F-logic programs with anonymous ID symbols and reified statements. Namely, we will define a program consequence operator whose least fixpoint computes an initial model of a given F-logic program.

Definition 11 (Program Consequence Operator). *Let* P *be an F-logic program,* $\mathcal{D}$ *be an anonymous domain, and* $\Pi_{\mathcal{D}}(P)$ *be a skolemization of* P *with regard to* $\mathcal{D}$. *Similarly to [19], we can define a program consequence operator,* $\mathcal{T}_{\Pi_{\mathcal{D}}(P)}$, *which maps an interpretation,* $\mathcal{I} = (\mathcal{D}, \mathcal{S})$, *over* $\mathcal{D}$ *to another interpretation over* $\mathcal{D}$ *as follows:* $\mathcal{T}_{\Pi_{\mathcal{D}}(P)}(\mathcal{I}) = \mathcal{J}$, *where* $\mathcal{J} = (\mathcal{D}, \mathcal{R})$ *and* $\mathcal{R}$ *is the following set of terms:*

$$
\left\{
A
\;\middle|\;
\begin{array}{l}
\text{There is a ground instance } A_1, \ldots, A_m \leftarrow B_1, \ldots, B_n \\
\text{of a rule in } \Pi_{\mathcal{D}}(P) \text{ such that:} \\[4pt]
- A = A_i, \text{ for some } 1 \leq i \leq m; \text{ and} \\
- B_j \in \mathcal{S} \text{ for all } B_j, 1 \leq j \leq n.
\end{array}
\right\}
$$

Let $\mathcal{I} = (\mathcal{D}, \mathcal{S})$ and $\mathcal{J} = (\mathcal{D}, \mathcal{R})$ be two interpretations. We write $\mathcal{I} \subseteq \mathcal{J}$ iff $\mathcal{S} \subseteq \mathcal{R}$. Thus $\subseteq$ defines a partial order among all interpretations on the same anonymous domain. It follows from the standard results in logic programming [19] that $\mathcal{T}_{\Pi_{\mathcal{D}}(P)}$ is monotonic and so has a *unique* least fixpoint, denoted $\mathrm{lfp}(\mathcal{T}_{\Pi_{\mathcal{D}}(P)})$.

Theorem 1. *Let* P *be an F-logic program,* $\mathcal{D}$ *be an anonymous domain, and* $\Pi_{\mathcal{D}}(P)$ *be a skolemization of* P. *Then* $\mathrm{lfp}(\mathcal{T}_{\Pi_{\mathcal{D}}(P)})$ *is an initial model of* P.

Of course, a program can have different initial models, since there can be different anonymous domains and different skolemizations. However, all initial models are isomorphic.

Corollary 1. $\mathcal{I} = (\mathcal{D}, \mathcal{S})$ *is an initial model of an F-logic program* P *iff there is a skolemization,* $\Pi_{\mathcal{D}}(P)$, *of* P *such that* $\mathcal{I} = \mathrm{lfp}(\mathcal{T}_{\Pi_{\mathcal{D}}(P)})$.

Corollary 2. *All initial models of an F-logic program are isomorphic.*

To answer queries and to reason about logical statements we need to define the notion of *logical entailment* of one scoped formula by another. The definition is identical to the one used in classical logic.

Definition 12 (Entailment). *Let* ϕ *and* ψ *be two scoped formulas. We write* $\phi \models \psi$ *iff for every model* $\mathcal{I} \models \phi$ *it is the case that* $\mathcal{I} \models \psi$.

This definition has expected properties, *e.g.*, if $\phi \models \psi$ then $\phi \models \psi \vee \xi$, and if $\phi \models \psi \wedge \xi$ then $\phi \models \psi$ and $\phi \models \xi$. As a special case, if ϕ represents an RDF graph, *i.e.*, ϕ is just a conjunction of scoped atomic F-logic formulas, and ψ represetns a subgraph of ϕ, then $\phi \models \psi$. This property is analogous to the one exhibited by the current proposal for the RDF model theory [10]. However, the difference is that the entailment relationship here does not hold between a *proper instance*[4] of an RDF graph and the graph itself. For instance, { john[likes $\twoheadrightarrow$ food] } is a proper instance of both { _#[likes $\twoheadrightarrow$ food] } and { john[likes $\twoheadrightarrow$ _#] }, but

$$\{ \text{john}[\text{likes} \twoheadrightarrow \text{food}] \} \not\models \{ \_\#[\text{likes} \twoheadrightarrow \text{food}] \}$$
$$\{ \text{john}[\text{likes} \twoheadrightarrow \text{food}] \} \not\models \{ \text{john}[\text{likes} \twoheadrightarrow \_\#] \}$$

Indeed, when applied to RDF graphs, the notion of entailment defined above corresponds to isomorphic embedding of graphs (the entailed graph is the one that is embedded). In isomorphic embedding, named resource nodes in one graph are mapped to identically named nodes in another graph, while blank nodes are mapped to blanked nodes. Moreover, this mapping is 1-1.

In contrast, the notion of entailment defined in the proposed RDF model theory [10] corresponds to a more relaxed notion of embedding — one where blank nodes can be mapped to anything. In this notion, two blank nodes can even be spliced into the same node.

It turns out that this second notion of entailment can be easily captured in our framework. Namely, we can define the following notion of entailment, denoted $\approx$.

Definition 13 (Embedding). *Let* P *and* Q *be two F-logic programs over a language* $\mathcal{L}$, $\mathcal{C}$ *be the set of constants in* $\mathcal{L}$, $\mathcal{D}_1$ *and* $\mathcal{D}_2$ *be two anonymous domains, and* $\mathcal{I} = (\mathcal{D}_1, \mathcal{R})$ *and* $\mathcal{J} = (\mathcal{D}_2, \mathcal{S})$ *be the initial models of* P *and* Q, *respectively. We say that* Q *can be embedded into* P, *denoted* P $\approx$ Q, *iff there is an augmented domain mapping* $\lambda \colon \mathcal{D}_2 \to \mathcal{D}_1 \cup \mathcal{C}$ *such that* $\lambda(\mathcal{S}) \subseteq \mathcal{R}$.

Note that in Definition 13 the choices of the initial models for P and Q are not important, since by Corollary 2 all initial models of an F-logic program are isomorphic.

Lemma 2. *Let* P *and* Q *be two F-logic programs. If* P $\models$ Q *then* P $\approx$ Q.

Theorem 2. *Given two F-logic prgrams* P *and* Q, *if* Q *represents an RDF graph, i.e., a conjunction of scoped atomic F-logic formulas, and* P *is a proper instance of* Q, *then* P $\approx$ Q.

Revisiting the previous example where { john[likes $\twoheadrightarrow$ food] } is a proper instance of both { _#[likes $\twoheadrightarrow$ food] } and { john[likes $\twoheadrightarrow$ _#] }, we have

$$\{ \text{john}[\text{likes} \twoheadrightarrow \text{food}] \} \approx \{ \_\#[\text{likes} \twoheadrightarrow \text{food}] \}$$
$$\{ \text{john}[\text{likes} \twoheadrightarrow \text{food}] \} \approx \{ \text{john}[\text{likes} \twoheadrightarrow \_\#] \}$$

---

[4] A proper instance of an RDF graph is obtained by replacing one or more anonymous resources with arbitrary named resources [10].

We should note that it is not clear which notion of entailment, $\models$ or $\approx\!$, is more appropriate for RDF graph entailment. Perhaps, both should be used, as they give rise to different notions of equivalence for these graphs. We say that $P \equiv Q$ iff $P \models Q$ and $Q \models P$. Similarly, $P \cong Q$ iff $P \approx\! Q$ and $Q \approx\! P$. It is easy to show that if $P \equiv Q$ then the initial models of P and Q are isomorphic and in a well-defined sense they correspond to the RDF graph represented by these programs. In contrast, even if $P \cong Q$, P and Q can still have non-isomorphic initial models and their RDF graphs can be different. For instance, if P has only one fact, { $a[b \twoheadrightarrow c]$ }, and Q is { $a[b \twoheadrightarrow c], a[b \twoheadrightarrow \_\#]$ }, then $P \cong Q$. However, the RDF graph of P has only one arc and two nodes, while the graph of Q has three nodes and two arcs. But each graph can be (non-isomorphically) embedded into the other.

It turns out, however, that if Q is a formula that does not use anonymous ID symbols then the two notions of entailment are the same.

Theorem 3. *Let P and Q be F-logic programs such that Q does not involve anonymous ID symbols. Then $P \models Q$ iff $P \approx\! Q$.*

5   Compositionality of Semantics

It is our contention that a logic language for the Web should have the *compositionality* property. Intuitively, this means that the result of putting together, say, two RDF documents should be another valid RDF document. Intuitively, from the point of view of semantics this means that if P_1 and P_2 are two RDF documents then each model of $P_1 \cup P_2$ should be some sort of a union of the models of P_1 and P_2 separately.

It turns out that the F-logic language with anonymous ID symbols presented in the previous section satisfies this requirement, whereas the N3 notation for RDF and the current proposal for the RDF model theory [10] do not. To make this requirement precise, we first need to define what we mean by the "union" of two interpretations.

First, we recall the notion of a disjoint union of sets. Let $\mathcal{D}_1$ and $\mathcal{D}_2$ be two sets. Their *disjoint union*, denoted $\mathcal{D}_1 \uplus \mathcal{D}_2$, is obtained by "renaming apart" the common elements of $\mathcal{D}_1$ and $\mathcal{D}_2$ (thus making the sets disjoint) and then taking the union. The set $\mathcal{D}_1 \uplus \mathcal{D}_2$ has the following properties:

- There are 1-1 mappings $\iota_1 : \mathcal{D}_1 \to \mathcal{D}_1 \uplus \mathcal{D}_2$ and $\iota_2 : \mathcal{D}_2 \to \mathcal{D}_1 \uplus \mathcal{D}_2$;
- $\mathcal{D}_1 \uplus \mathcal{D}_2 = \iota_1(\mathcal{D}_1) \cup \iota_2(\mathcal{D}_2)$; and
- $\iota_1(\mathcal{D}_1) \cap \iota_2(\mathcal{D}_2) = \emptyset$.

Definition 14 (Disjoint Union of Interpretations). *Let $\mathcal{I}_1 = (\mathcal{D}_1, \mathcal{S}_1)$ and $\mathcal{I}_2 = (\mathcal{D}_2, \mathcal{S}_2)$ be two interpretations. A disjoint union of $\mathcal{I}_1$ and $\mathcal{I}_2$, denoted $\mathcal{I}_1 \uplus \mathcal{I}_2$, is an interpretation of the form $(\mathcal{D}_1 \uplus \mathcal{D}_2, \iota_1(\mathcal{S}_1) \cup \iota_2(\mathcal{S}_2))$, where ι_1 and ι_2 are the 1-1 embeddings $\iota_1 : \mathcal{D}_1 \to \mathcal{D}_1 \uplus \mathcal{D}_2$ and $\iota_2 : \mathcal{D}_2 \to \mathcal{D}_1 \uplus \mathcal{D}_2$ that are associated with $\mathcal{D}_1 \uplus \mathcal{D}_2$. In other words, a disjoint union of two interpretations makes sure that anonymous constants that happen to occur in both anonymous* *domains $\mathcal{D}_1$ and $\mathcal{D}_2$ are renamed apart (both in these domains and in $\mathcal{S}_1$ and $\mathcal{S}_2$) prior to taking the union.*

We can now state the following simple result:

Theorem 4. *Let P_1 and P_2 be two F-logic programs, $\mathcal{I}_1$ and $\mathcal{I}_2$ be the initial models of P_1 and P_2, respectively. Suppose that both P_1 and P_2 represent an RDF graph (i.e., a conjunction of scoped atomic formulas). Suppose also that P_1 and P_2 use disjoint vocabularies, i.e., the sets of named constants that occur in P_1 and P_2 are disjoint. Then $\mathcal{I}_1 \uplus \mathcal{I}_2$ is an initial model of $P_1 \cup P_2$.*

It appears that the current proposal for the RDF model theory does not have the compositionality property. To see this, consider the sentence *someone loves Mary* represented using the RDF triple syntax:

{loves, [X], [Mary]}

Let P_1 denote this document. Let P_2 denote the document that represents the sentence *someone invented the bulb*:

{inventor, [X], [Bulb]}

By composing the two documents, we get $P_1 \cup P_2$:

{loves, [X], [Mary]}
{inventor, [X], [Bulb]}

Although the interpretation { {loves, [John], [Mary]} } is a model for the document P_1 and { {inventor, [ThomasEdison], [Bulb]} } is a model for P_2, their (disjoint) union, { {loves, [John], [Mary]}, {inventor, [ThomasEdison], [Bulb]} } is *not* a model of $P_1 \cup P_2$. This problem can be rectified by adding the notion of scope, as introduced in this paper, to N3 and the RDF model theory.

6   Properties of Reification

In this section we discuss some properties of reification in F-logic and compare them to the current proposal for RDF model theory [10].

One important difference is that in F-logic reified statements are themselves objects, whereas in the RDF model theory they are referred to by names. In particular, one can give two names to the same statement and these would be completely unrelated objects. In our opinion, such a semantics is too week. To illustrate the problem, consider again the statement from Section 3 that *John believes that Thomas Edison (this time a known resource) invented the bulb*:

{type, [X], [RDF:Statement]}
{predicate, [X], [inventor]}
{subject, [X], [http://foo.org/TheBulb]}
{object, [X], [http://foo.org/ThomasEdison]}
{believes, [http://xyz.com/John], [X]}

In the RDF triple syntax, one can add another reference to the reified statement:

{type, [Y], [RDF:Statement]}
{predicate, [Y], [inventor]}
{subject, [Y], [http://foo.org/TheBulb]}
{object, [Y], [http://foo.org/ThomasEdison]}

However, the objects referred to via X and Y would have nothing to do with each other. For instance, John believes X but not Y. Likewise, stating that X is a true statement or that it was made by Encyclopedia Britannica does not imply that the same holds for Y. In contrast, in F-logic we can state

('http://foo.org/TheBulb'[inventor ⟶ 'http://foo.org/ThomasEdison'])
[veracity ⟶ true, authority ⟶ 'http://www.britannica.com/'].

So anyone who believes this statement would be believing a statement whose veracity attribute has the value true and which is believed to be authorized by Britannica. In fact, we can even go further and specify the rule

Statement ⟵ Statement[veracity ⟶ true].

which will make any statement whose veracity property is "true" into a true statement in every model. Thus, for example, Mary, who also believes this statement and who might even be defined in a different document, would be believing a true assertion.

Note that in our semantics conjunctions of atomic formulas are terms and thus can be treated as objects. In fact, this idea can be further extended to allow reification of more general statements. We will show some simple uses of reified conjunctions. First, for some properties, such as beliefs, it is reasonable to assume that conjunctions can be broken apart, because if someone believes in a combined statement then she is likely to believe in all of its parts. This can be expressed by the following rule:

X[believes ⟶ S1], X[believes ⟶ S2] ⟵ X[believes ⟶ (S1 ∧ S2)].

On the other hand, in some contexts reified conjuncted statements cannot be broken up. For instance, the following might be considered as a true statement

(john[likes ⟶ sally] ∧ sally[likes ⟶ john]) [statementAbout ⟶ friendship].

But (john[likes ⟶ sally]) [statementAbout ⟶ friendship] is not necessarily a true statement.

An important advantage of our semantics is that it is developed in a general framework, which enables reasoning about reified statements — not only stating them as facts. We have already shown how one can state that certain beliefs are actually true. However, there are many more possibilities for non-trivial reasoning. For instance, *Bob always believes when Alice says that some statement is made by a third party*. This knowledge can be encoded using the following rule:

'http://xyz.com/Bob'[believes ⟶ Statement[authority ⟶ A]] ⟵
        'http://xyz.com/Alice'[says ⟶ Statement[authority ⟶ A]].

In fact, one can express a number of belief systems using rules and then combine them with reification to derive useful conclusions about beliefs that are expressed as reified statements.

7   Conclusion

In this paper we presented an extension of F-logic that supports anonymous objects and reification. Such an extension makes F-logic a suitable foundation for Semantic Web languages, such as RDF. The language has a simple and natural semantics and a proof theory and has been implemented in the $\mathcal{F}$LORA-2 system [24]. In particular, our semantics rectifies a number of drawbacks of the current proposal for the RDF model theory [10]: non-compositional semantics and weaker than necessary treatment of reification. We also pointed out that there are at least two different (and useful) meanings for the notion of RDF graph entailment. On top of this, our semantics is much more general than [10], as it is given in the framework of an expressive rule-based and frame-based language, which opens up many possibilities for encoding knowledge.

Anonymous object identity and reification have uses outside of the Semantic Web context. In fact, they were originally introduced in $\mathcal{F}$LORA-2 to satisfy database-specific needs. For instance, anonymous object identities are related to the so-called *pure values* in object-oriented databases [1,17] and they are also very convenient for object-oriented modeling of XML documents. In addition, they turned out to be valuable from the software engineering point of view. Reification was introduced in $\mathcal{F}$LORA-2 to provide a clean semantics (and an implementation) for aggregate operators in $\mathcal{F}$LORA-2, which take a query (*i.e.*, a reified formula) as an argument and perform summarization operations over the set of answers to the query.

References

1. F. Bancilhon, C. Delobel, and P. Kanellakis, editors. *Building an Object-Oriented Database System: The Story of O2*. Morgan Kaufmann, San Francisco, CA, 1990.
2. A.J. Bonner and M. Kifer. An overview of transaction logic. *Theoretical Computer Science*, 133:205–265, October 1994.
3. A.J. Bonner and M. Kifer. A logic for programming database transactions. In J. Chomicki and G. Saake, editors, *Logics for Databases and Information Systems*, chapter 5, pages 117–166. Kluwer Academic Publishers, March 1998.
4. J. Broekstra, C. Fluit, and F. van Harmelen. The state of the art on representation and query languages for semistructured data. Technical report, Administrator, Nederland BV, August 2000. http://www.aidministrator.nl/publications/otk-del8.pdf.
5. W. Chen, M. Kifer, and D.S. Warren. HiLog: A first-order semantics for higher-order logic programming constructs. In *North American Conference on Logic Programming*, Cambridge, MA, October 1989. MIT Press.
6. W. Chen, M. Kifer, and D.S. Warren. HiLog: A foundation for higher-order logic programming. *Journal of Logic Programming*, 15(3):187–230, February 1993.

7. H. Davulcu, G. Yang, M. Kifer, and I.V. Ramakrishnan. Design and implementation of the physical layer in webbases: The XRover experience. In *First International Conference on Computational Logic, DOOD'2000 Stream*, July 2000.
8. S. Decker, D. Brickley, J. Saarela, and J. Angele. A query and inference service for RDF. In *QL'98 - The Query Languages Workshop*, December 1998.
9. S. Decker, M. Erdmann, D. Fensel, and R. Studer. Ontobroker: Ontology based access to distributed and semi-structured information. In R. Meersman et al., editor, *Database Semantics, Semantic Issues in Multimedia Systems*, pages 351–369. Kluwer Academic Publisher, Boston, 1999.
10. P. Hayes (editor). RDF Model Theory. Technical report, W3C, April 2002. http://www.w3.org/TR/rdf-mt/.
11. D. Fensel, S. Decker, M. Erdmann, and R. Studer. Ontobroker: Or how to enable intelligent access to the WWW. In *Proceedings of the 11th Banff Knowledge Acquisition for Knowledge-Based Systems Workshop*, Banff, Canada, 1998.
12. R. Fikes and D.L. McGuinness. An axiomatic semantics for RDF, RDF Schema, and DAML+OIL. Technical Report KSL-01-01, Knowledge Systems Laboratory, Stanford University, October 2001.
13. M.R. Genesereth. Knowledge interchange format. Technical Report NCITS.T2/98-004, Knowledge Systems Laboratory, Stanford University, 1998. Draft proposed American National Standard, http://logic.stanford.edu/kif/dpans.html.
14. C. H. Goh, S. Bressan, S. E. Madnick, and M. D. Siegel. Context interchange: Representing and reasoning about data semantics in heterogeneous systems. Technical report, MIT, School of Management, 1996.
15. A. Gupta, B. Ludäscher, and M. E. Martone. Knowledge-based integration of neuroscience data sources. In *12th International Conference on Scientific and Statistical Database Management (SSDBM)*, Berlin, Germany, July 2000. IEEE.
16. G.-J. Houben. HERA: Automatically generating hypermedia front-ends for ad hoc data from heterogeneous and legacy information systems. In *Engineering Federated Information Systems*, pages 81–88. Aka and IOS Press, 2000.
17. M. Kifer, G. Lausen, and J. Wu. Logical foundations of object-oriented and frame-based languages. *Journal of ACM*, 42:741–843, July 1995.
18. O. Lasilla and R.R. Swick (editors). Resource description framework (RDF) model and syntax specification. Technical report, W3C, February 1999. http://www.w3.org/TR/1999/REC-rdf-syntax-19990222/.
19. J. W. Lloyd. *Foundations of Logic Programming*. Springer Verlag, 1984.
20. D. Perlis. Languages with self-reference i: Foundations. *Artificial Intelligence*, 25:301–322, 1985.
21. M. Sintek and S. Decker. TRIPLE – An RDF query, inference, and transformation language. In *Deductive Databases and Knowledge Management (DDLP'2001)*, October 2001.
22. S. Staab, J. Angele, S. Decker, M. Erdmann, A. Hotho, A. Maedche, H.-P. Schnurr, R. Studer, and Y. Sure. AI for the Web — Ontology-based community web portals. In *9-th International World Wide Web Conference (WWW9)*, Amsterdam, The Netherlands, May 2000.
23. G. Yang and M. Kifer. Implementing an efficient DOOD system using a tabling logic engine. In *First International Conference on Computational Logic, DOOD'2000 Stream*, July 2000.
24. G. Yang and M. Kifer. Flora-2: User's manual. http://flora.sourceforge.net/, March 2002.
25. G. Yang and M. Kifer. Well-founded optimism: Inheritance in frame-based knowledge bases. Submitted for publication, 2002.

Extending Datatype Support in Web Ontology Reasoning

Jeff Z. Pan and Ian Horrocks

Information Management Group
Department of Computer Science
University of Manchester
Oxford Road, Manchester M13 9PL, UK
{pan,horrocks}@cs.man.ac.uk

Abstract. The Semantic Web is a vision of the next generation Web, in which semantic markup will make Web resources more accessible to automatic processes. Description Logics (DLs) are of crucial importance to the development of the Semantic Web, where their role is to provide formal underpinnings and automated reasoning services for Semantic Web ontology languages such as DAML+OIL. In this paper, we show how the description logic $\mathcal{SHOQ}(\mathbf{D})$, which has been designed to provide such services, can be extended with n-ary datatype predicates and qualified number restrictions with n-ary datatype predicates, to give $\mathcal{SHOQ}(\mathbf{D_n})$, and we present an algorithm for deciding the satisfiability of $\mathcal{SHOQ}(\mathbf{D_n})$ concepts, along with a proof of its soundness and completeness. The work is motivated by the requirement for n-ary datatype predicates and qualified number restrictions with n-ary predicates in relation to "real world" properties in semantic Web ontologies and applications.

1 Introduction

The Semantic Web [2] is a vision of the next generation Web, in which the current rendering markup, which specifies how to display Web resources for human consumption, will be enhanced with so called "semantic" markup, which will specify the meaning of web resources so as to make them more accessible to automatic processes.

Description Logics (DLs) are of crucial importance to the development of the Semantic Web, where their role is to provide formal underpinnings and automated reasoning services for semantic Web ontology languages [3, 11] such as DAML+OIL[1] [7, 12]. Significant effort has already been devoted to the investigation of suitable DLs—in particular, [8] have presented the $\mathcal{SHOQ}(\mathbf{D})$ DL, along with a sound and complete algorithm for deciding concept satisfiability, a basic reasoning service for DLs and ontologies.

A key feature of $\mathcal{SHOQ}(\mathbf{D})$ is that, like DAML+OIL, it supports *datatypes* [1, 8, 9] (e.g., string, integer) as well as the usual abstract concepts

---

[1] http://www.daml.org/

R. Meersman, Z. Tari (Eds.): CoopIS/DOA/ODBASE 2002, LNCS 2519, pp. 1067–1081, 2002.

(e.g., animal, plant). $\mathcal{SHOQ}(\mathbf{D})$, however, supports a very restricted form of datatypes, i.e., it can only deal with unary datatype predicates. While this is quite close[2] to the requirements of the *current version* of the DAML+OIL language, it is not enough for (even the current version of) DAML+OIL and some semantic Web ontologies and applications.

An approach of extending DL with datatypes was first introduced by [1], who described a datatype ($\mathcal{D}$) extension of the well known $\mathcal{ALC}$ DL. [1] have shown that although the satisfiability of $\mathcal{ALC}(\mathcal{D})$ is decidable, if $\mathcal{ALC}(\mathcal{D})$ is extended with transitive closure of features, the satisfiability problem is undecidable. Lutz [9] proved that reasoning with $\mathcal{ALC}(\mathcal{D})$ and general TBoxes is undecidable. In order to extend *expressive* DLs with concrete domains, Horrocks and Satler [8] proposed a simplified approach on concrete domain and applied this approach on the $\mathcal{SHOQ}(\mathbf{D})$ DL. Pan [10] investigated the simplifying constraints of $\mathcal{SHOQ}(\mathbf{D})$ w.r.t. datatypes, and showed how these could be relaxed in order to extend $\mathcal{SHOQ}(\mathbf{D})$ with n-ary datatype predicates. We should mention that, similar to Baader and Hanschke [1]'s approach, Haarslev et al. [5] extended the $\mathcal{SHN}$ DL with restricted concrete domain $(\mathcal{D})^-$ and gave the $\mathcal{SHN}(\mathcal{D})^-$ DL, which supports n-ary datatype predicates without qualified number restrictions.

In this paper, we extend our work in [10] and add qualified number restrictions with n-ary predicates to give the $\mathcal{SHOQ}(\mathbf{D_n})$ DL, and we present a sound and complete decision procedure for deciding concept satisfiability and subsumption in this logic. The rest of the paper is organised as follows. In Section 2, we introduce some basic concepts of datatypes and give some concrete examples to demonstrate why n-ary datatype predicates, as well as qualified number restrictions with n-ary datatype predicates, are often necessary in semantic Web ontologies and applications. Section 3 briefly compares the two approaches to extend description logics with datatypes. In Section 4, we introduce $\mathcal{SHOQ}(\mathbf{D_n})$, which supports the n-ary datatype predicates and qualified number restrictions with n-ary datatype predicates. In Section 5, we give a tableau algorithm for $\mathcal{SHOQ}(\mathbf{D_n})$ and its decidability proof. Section 6 is a brief discussion of possible future work.

2   Datatypes in the Semantic Web

Datatypes are important in semantic Web ontologies and applications, because most of which need to represent, in some way, various "real world" properties such as size, weight and duration, and some other complex user defined datatypes. Reasoning and querying over datatype properties are important and necessary if these properties are to be understood by machines.

Before we go further, we introduce the following basic concepts (about datatype), which we will use in this paper:

---

[2] DAML+OIL supports unary datatype predicates *and* qualified number restrictions with unary datatype predicates.

- *Datatype* is a declaration of the kind of data, i.e. integer and string. The datatype determines which constraints/operations can be performed on such data values.
- *Datatype properties* can be used to represent "real world" properties, i.e. size, weight and duration. They have data values, which belong to certain datatypes.
- *Datatype predicates* represent constraints over a list of datatype properties. Usually we call them "n-ary datatype predicates" if the constraints are defined over n datatype properties.

Currently DAML+OIL supports only unary datatype predicates and qualified number restrictions on unary datatype predicates, e.g. you can define a `less than 21 years old` predicate over datatype property *age*. Many people think it is not enough, while n-ary datatype predicates and qualified number restrictions on n-ary predicates are often necessary. Here are some concrete examples:

Example 1 E-ontologies may need to classify items according to their sizes, and to reason that an item which has *height* `less than 5cm` and `the sum of` *length* and *width* `less than 10cm` is a kind of items for which no shipping costs are charged. Here *height,length* and *width* are datatype properties and `the sum of ... less than 10cm` is an n-ary datatype predicate.

Example 2 Let's go back to the *age* example. Suppose in an ontology we define a class Person with a datatype property *age*. If one of its instance is John, and John has age 20, then John's age satisfies the predicate `less than 21 years old`. This may be true *now*, but what about in 10 years—is it still true? Of course not, because our ages change every year. One solution is to define three datatype properties *birth-year*, *current-year* and *real age* and to define a `minus` predicate over them, which is 3-ary, so that we can calculate the *real age* by *birth-year* and *current-year*.

Example 3 E-ontologies may need to classify customers according to the numbers of their friends' email addresses they provide, and decide that those who provide (1) at least 10 *friends' e-addresses*, (2) among them at least 5 *friends' e-addresses* are `from` UK (e.g. man.ac.uk), (3) and at least 5 *friends' e-addresses* `have the same domain` (e.g. hotmail.com) as *their e-addresses* can have 5% cash back during promotion. Here *friends' e-addresses* and *their e-addresses* are datatype properties, and `have the same domain as` is an n-ary datatype predicate. Qualified number restrictions with n-ary predicates are also used in this example. They are very expressive in the sense that they force restrictions on the numbers of the tuples of data values that satisfy the datatype predicate, instead of on the numbers of a certain datatype property. Therefore they are quite different from the qualified number restrictions that we have in the $\mathcal{SHOQ}(\mathbf{D})$ DL and become new challenges to DL reasoners. (See section 5 to find out how we solve this problem.)

From these examples, we can see n-ary datatype predicates and qualified number restrictions with n-ary predicates are very important and useful in semantic Web ontologies and applications. On the one hand, it is very desirable to express business rules [4] or constraints for datatype properties in semantic Web ontologies and applications. On the other hand, too expressive rules and constraints could easily introduce undecidability. In this paper, we prove that adding n-ary datatype predicates as well as qualified number restrictions with n-ary predicates to the $\mathcal{SHOQ}(\mathbf{D})$ DL, which is quite suited to the provision of reasoning support for DAML+OIL, does not change the decidability property of the $\mathcal{SHOQ}(\mathbf{D})$ DL. Thus we suggest that future versions of DAML+OIL, or OWL[3] can include these extended datatype constructs without worrying the decidability problem.

3   Description Logics and Datatypes

For many knowledge representation application, it is essential to integrate reasoning about datatype properties with reasoning about knowledge represented at the abstract level. One theoretically well-founded approach, first described by Baader and Hanschke [1] is to extend a DL with *concrete domains*. Concrete domains were defined as follows:

Definition 1 *A* concrete domain *is a pair* $(\Delta_\mathcal{D}, \Phi_\mathcal{D})$, *where* $\Delta_\mathcal{D}$ *is a set called the* domain *and* $\Phi_\mathcal{D}$ *is a set of predicate names. Each predicate name* P *is associated with an arity* n, *and an n-ary predicate* $P^\mathcal{D} \subseteq dom(\mathcal{D})^n$. *A concrete domain is called* admissible *iff*

1. *the set of its predicate names is closed under negation and contains a name* $\top_\mathcal{D}$ *for* $\Delta_\mathcal{D}$, *and*
2. *the satisfiability problem for an expression of the form* $P_1^\mathcal{D} \cap \ldots \cap P_n^\mathcal{D}$ *is decidable.*

In order to extend *expressive* DLs with concrete domains, Horrocks and Sattler [8] proposed a simplified approach on concrete domain and give the $\mathcal{SHOQ}(\mathbf{D})$ DL. Pan [10] investigated the simplifying constraints introduced in [8] and extend the $\mathcal{SHOQ}(\mathbf{D})$ DL with n-ary predicates. One of the simplifying constraints about concrete datatype is that $\Delta_\mathbf{D}$ is defined as the domain of *all* concrete datatypes, instead of any *specific* concrete domain $\Delta_\mathcal{D}$.

Here we give a formal definition of (some of) the concepts we introduced in Section 2.

Definition 2 $\Delta_\mathbf{D}$ *is the* datatype domain *covering all concrete datatypes. A set of datatypes* $d_1 \ldots, d_m$ *can be defined in* $\Delta_\mathbf{D}$, *whose domain are subsets of the datatype domain,* $\forall i : 1 \leq i \leq m, d_i^\mathbf{D} \subseteq \Delta_\mathbf{D}$. *Datatype predicates* $P_1, \ldots, P_r$ *can be defined over these datatypes, and each predicate* P_j *is associated with an arity* n_j, *where* $\forall j : 1 \leq j \leq r, P_j^\mathbf{D} \subseteq d_{j1}^\mathbf{D} \times \ldots \times d_{jn_j}^\mathbf{D} \subseteq \Delta_\mathbf{D}^{n_j}$.

Each such datatype predicate $P_j(v_1, \ldots, v_{n_j})$ *is a boolean function, where* $v_1, \ldots, v_{n_j}$ *are its input variables. It returns true iff there exists a tuple of data values* $t_1, \ldots, t_{n_j}$ *in* $\Delta_\mathbf{D}$, *s.t.* $\forall i : 1 \leq i \leq n_j, v_i^\mathbf{D} = t_i$ *and* $\langle t_1, \ldots, t_{n_j} \rangle \in P_j^\mathbf{D}$.

---

[3] http://www.w3.org/2001/sw/WebOnt/

The negation of datatype predicate $P_j(v_1, \ldots, v_{n_j})$, i.e. $\neg P_j(v_1, \ldots, v_{n_j})$, is also a boolean function. It returns true iff. $P_j(v_1, \ldots, v_{n_j})$ returns false.

An example of datatype is INT+, which has the set of nonnegative integers as its domain. A binary predicate $\geq$ and a unary predicate $\geq_n$ are defined over INT+.

Definition 3 *A set of datatypes $d_1 \ldots, d_m$ is conforming if*

1. *the datatype domain $\Delta_{\mathbf{D}}$ is disjoint with the object domain $\Delta^{\mathcal{I}}$, and*
2. *a required binary inequality-checking predicate $\neq_i \in \{P_1, \ldots, P_r\}$, is defined for each datatype d_i, and*
3. *there exists a sound and complete decision procedure for checking if a set of tuples of data values satisfy a set of related datatype predicates $P_1, \ldots, P_r$.*

The datatype INT+ is not conforming, since it doesn't have a built-in binary inequality-checking predicate $\neq$. Thus any set of datatypes which has INT+ as its member is not conforming due to the second condition in Definition 3. Please note that according to Definition 2, datatype predicates can be defined over different datatypes, and Definition 3 requires that each conforming datatype have a built-in binary inequality-checking predicate $\neq$.

In the simplified approach, *type systems* are introduced to define datatypes and datatype predicates, including the built-in binary inequality-checking predicates for all supported data- types. Type systems are used with DL reasoners, and can answer boolean questions, e.g. to check if a set of tuples of data values satisfy a set of predicates simultaneously. With type systems, we can deal with an arbitrary conforming set of datatypes and predicates without compromising the compactness of the concept language or the soundness and completeness of our decision procedure [8].

Another main difference between the two approaches, besides the definition of the datatype domain, is that in the new approach, datatype properties are roles instead of features (functional roles), which makes it possible to have qualified number restrictions on n-ary predicates—while with features, the number restriction is already set as less than or equal to 1.

In next section, we will give the definition of the $\mathcal{SHOQ}(\mathbf{D_n})$ DL. Please note that in DLs, "classes" are usually called "concepts", "properties" are often called "roles", and "datatype properties" are also called "concrete roles".

4 $\mathcal{SHOQ}(\mathbf{D_n})$

Definition 4 *Let $\mathbf{C}$, $\mathbf{R} = \mathbf{R}_A \uplus \mathbf{R_D}$, $\mathbf{I}$ be disjoint sets of concept, abstract and concrete role and individual names. For R and S roles, a role axiom is either a role inclusion, which is of the form $R \sqsubseteq S$ for $R, S \in \mathbf{R}_A$ or $R, S \in \mathbf{R_D}$, or a transitivity axiom, which is of the form $\mathsf{Trans}(R)$ for $R \in \mathbf{R}_A$. A role box $\mathcal{R}$ is a finite set of role axioms. A role R is called* simple *if, for $\sqsubseteq^*$ the transitive reflexive closure of $\sqsubseteq$ on $\mathcal{R}$ and for each role S, $S \sqsubseteq^* R$ implies $\mathsf{Trans}(S) \notin \mathcal{R}$.*

The set of concept terms of $\mathcal{SHOQ}(\mathbf{D_n})$ is inductively defined. As a starting point of the induction, any element of $\mathbf{C}$ is a concept term (atomic terms). Now let C and D be concept terms, o be an individual, R be a abstract role name, $T_1, \ldots, T_n$ be concrete role names, P be an n-ary datatype predicate name. Then the following expressions are also concept terms:

1. *$\top$ (universal concept) and $\top_D$ (universal datatype),*
2. *$C \sqcup D$ (disjunction), $C \sqcap D$ (conjunction), $\neg C$ (negation), and $\{o\}$ (nominals),*
3. *$\exists R.C$ (exists-in restriction) and $\forall R.C$ (value restriction),*
4. *$\geqslant m R.C$ (atleast restriction) and $\leqslant m R.C$ (atmost restriction),*
5. *$\exists T_1, \cdots, T_n.P_n$ (datatype exists) and $\forall T_1, \cdots, T_n.P_n$ (datatype value),*
6. *$\geqslant m T_1, \ldots, T_n.P_n$ (datatype atleast) and $\leqslant m T_1, \ldots, T_n.P_n$ (datatype atmost),*
7. *$\geqslant m T$ (concrete role atleast), $\leqslant m T$ (concrete role atmost).*

$\mathcal{SHOQ}(\mathbf{D_n})$ extends $\mathcal{SHOQ}(\mathbf{D})$ by supporting n-ary datatype predicates P_n. The interpretations of datatype constructs are listed in Figure 1. Note that concrete role atleast (atmost) is only a special form of datatype atleast (atmost, respectively) where $n = 1$ and $P_n = \top_D$.

To illustrate the use of $\mathcal{SHOQ}(\mathbf{D_n})$-concept, let's go back to the examples we used in Section 2:

1. Items with height less than 5cm, and the sum of their length and width less that 10cm can be defined as a $\mathcal{SHOQ}(\mathbf{D_n})$-concept

    $$Item \sqcap = 1 height. <_{5cm} \sqcap = 1 length \sqcap = 1 width \sqcap \forall length, width.\mathbf{sum} <_{10cm}$$

    where "=1" is a shortcut for "$\leqslant 1 \sqcap \geqslant 1$", and *height, length* and *width* are concrete roles, $<_{5cm}$ is a unary datatype predicate and $\mathbf{sum} <_{10cm}$ is a binary predicate. Note that $<_{5cm}$ and $\mathbf{sum} <_{10cm}$ are datatype predicates, rather than datatype atmost.

2. Persons who are younger than 21 years old can be defined as a $\mathcal{SHOQ}(\mathbf{D_n})$-concept

    $$Person \sqcap = 1 birth - year \sqcap = 1 current - year \sqcap = 1 age. <_{21} \sqcap \forall birth - year, current - date, age.\mathbf{minus}$$

    where $\mathbf{minus}$ is a trinary datatype predicate, which can be defined in the type system as lambda expression $\lambda(x, y, z)(z = y - x)$.

3. Customers in example 3 can be defined as a $\mathcal{SHOQ}(\mathbf{D_n})$-concept

    $$Customer \sqcap \geqslant 10 friends - eaddress \sqcap \geqslant 5 friends - eaddress.\mathbf{from} - \mathbf{UK} \sqcap$$
    $$\geqslant 5 friends - eaddress, eaddress.\mathbf{same} - \mathbf{domain}$$

    where $\geqslant 10 friends - eaddress$ is a concrete role atleast, and $\geqslant 5 friends - eaddress.\mathbf{from} - \mathbf{UK}$ and $\geqslant 5 friends - eaddress, eaddress.\mathbf{same} - \mathbf{domain}$ are datatype atleast.

Now we define a tableau for $\mathcal{SHOQ}(\mathbf{D_n})$. For ease of presentation, we assume all concepts to be in *negation normal form* (NNF). We use $\sim C$ to denote the NNF of $\neg C$. Moreover, for a concept D, we use $cl(D)$ to denote the set of all sub-concepts of D, the NNF of these sub-concepts, and the (possibly negated) datatypes occurring in these (NNF of) sub-concepts.

Construct Name	Syntax	Semantics
universal datatype	$\top_D$	$\top_D^D = \Delta_D$
datatype exists	$\exists T_1, \cdots, T_n.P_n$	$(\exists T_1, \cdots, T_n.P_n)^{\mathcal{I}} = \{x \in \Delta^{\mathcal{I}} \mid \exists y_1 \cdots y_n.$ $\langle x, y_1 \rangle \in T_1^{\mathcal{I}} \wedge \cdots \wedge \langle x, y_n \rangle \in T_n^{\mathcal{I}} \wedge \langle y_1, \cdots y_n \rangle \in P_n^D\}$
datatype value	$\forall T_1, \cdots, T_n.P_n$	$(\forall T_1, \cdots, T_n.P_n)^{\mathcal{I}} = \{x \in \Delta^{\mathcal{I}} \mid \forall y_1 \cdots y_n.$ $\langle x, y_1 \rangle \in T_1^{\mathcal{I}} \wedge \cdots \wedge \langle x, y_n \rangle \in T_n^{\mathcal{I}} \rightarrow \langle y_1, \cdots y_n \rangle \in P_n^D\}$
datatype atleast	$\geqslant m T_1, \ldots, T_n.P_n$	$(\geqslant m T_1, \ldots, T_n.P_n)^{\mathcal{I}} = \{x \in \Delta^{\mathcal{I}} \mid \sharp\{\langle y_1 \cdots y_n \rangle \mid$ $\langle x, y_1 \rangle \in T_1^{\mathcal{I}} \wedge \cdots \wedge \langle x, y_n \rangle \in T_n^{\mathcal{I}} \wedge \langle y_1, \cdots y_n \rangle \in P_n^D\} \geq m\}$
datatype atmost	$\leqslant m T_1, \ldots, T_n.P_n$	$(\leqslant m T_1, \ldots, T_n.P_n)^{\mathcal{I}} = \{x \in \Delta^{\mathcal{I}} \mid \sharp\{\langle y_1 \cdots y_n \rangle \mid$ $\langle x, y_1 \rangle \in T_1^{\mathcal{I}} \wedge \cdots \wedge \langle x, y_n \rangle \in T_n^{\mathcal{I}} \wedge \langle y_1, \cdots y_n \rangle \in P_n^D\} \leq m\}$
concrete role atleast	$\geqslant m T$	$(\geqslant m T)^{\mathcal{I}} = \{x \in \Delta^{\mathcal{I}} \mid \sharp\{y \in \Delta_D \mid \langle x, y \rangle \in T\} \geq m\}$
concrete role atmost	$\leqslant m T$	$(\leqslant m T)^{\mathcal{I}} = \{x \in \Delta^{\mathcal{I}} \mid \sharp\{y \in \Delta_D \mid \langle x, y \rangle \in T\} \leq m\}$

Fig. 1. Datatype constructs in $\mathcal{SHOQ}(\mathbf{D_n})$

Definition 5 *If D is a $\mathcal{SHOQ}(\mathbf{D_n})$-concept in NNF, $\mathcal{R}$ a role box, and $\mathbf{R}_A^D$, $\mathbf{R}_D^D$ are the sets of abstract and concrete roles occurring in D or $\mathcal{R}$, a tableau $\mathcal{T}$ for D w.r.t. $\mathcal{R}$ is defined as a quadruple $(\mathbf{S}, \mathcal{L}, \mathcal{E}_A, \mathcal{E}_D)$ such that: $\mathbf{S}$ is a set of individuals, $\mathcal{L} : \mathbf{S} \to 2^{cl(D)}$ maps each individual to a set of concepts which is a subset of $cl(D)$, $\mathcal{E}_A : \mathbf{R}_A^D \to 2^{\mathbf{S} \times \mathbf{S}}$ maps each abstract role in $\mathbf{R}_A^D$ to a set of pairs of individuals, $\mathcal{E}_D : \mathbf{R}_D^D \to 2^{\mathbf{S} \times \Delta_D}$ maps each concrete role in $\mathbf{R}_D^D$ to a set of pairs of individuals and concrete values, and there is some individual $s \in \mathbf{S}$ such that $D \in \mathcal{L}(s)$. For all $s, t \in \mathbf{S}$, $C, C_1, C_2 \in cl(D)$, $R, S \in \mathbf{R}_A^D$, $T, T', T_1, \ldots, T_n \in \mathbf{R}_D^D$, n-ary predicate P_n and*

$$S^T(s, C) := \{t \in \mathbf{S} \mid \langle s, t \rangle \in \mathcal{E}_A(S) \text{ and } C \in \mathcal{L}(t)\},$$
$$T_1 T_2 \ldots T_n^T(s, P_n) := \{\langle y_1, \ldots, y_n \rangle \in P_n^D \mid \langle s, y_1 \rangle \in \mathcal{E}_D(T_1), \ldots, \langle s, y_n \rangle \in \mathcal{E}_D(T_n)\},$$
$$DC^T(s, T_1, \ldots, T_n, y_1, \ldots, y_n, P_n) := \begin{cases} true & \text{if } \langle s, y_i \rangle \in \mathcal{E}_D(T_n)(1 \leq i \leq n) \text{ and} \\ & \langle y_1, \ldots, y_n \rangle \in P_n^D \\ false & \text{otherwise} \end{cases}$$

it holds that:

(P1) *if $C \in \mathcal{L}(s)$, then $\neg C \notin \mathcal{L}(s)$,*

(P2) *if $C_1 \sqcap C_2 \in \mathcal{L}(s)$, then $C_1 \in \mathcal{L}(s)$ and $C_2 \in \mathcal{L}(s)$,*

(P3) *if $C_1 \sqcup C_2 \in \mathcal{L}(s)$, then $C_1 \in \mathcal{L}(s)$ or $C_2 \in \mathcal{L}(s)$,*

(P4) *if $\langle s, t \rangle \in \mathcal{E}_A(R)$ and $R \sqsubseteq S$, then $\langle s, t \rangle \in \mathcal{E}_A(S)$,*
     if $\langle s, t \rangle \in \mathcal{E}_D(T)$ and $T \sqsubseteq T'$, then $\langle s, t \rangle \in \mathcal{E}_D(T')$,

(P5) *if $\forall R.C \in \mathcal{L}(s)$ and $\langle s, t \rangle \in \mathcal{E}_A(R)$, then $C \in \mathcal{L}(t)$,*

(P6) *if $\exists R.C \in \mathcal{L}(s)$, then there is some $t \in \mathbf{S}$ such that $\langle s, t \rangle \in \mathcal{E}_A(R)$ and $C \in \mathcal{L}(t)$,*

(P7) *if $\forall S.C \in \mathcal{L}(s)$ and $\langle s, t \rangle \in \mathcal{E}_A(R)$ for some $R \sqsubseteq S$ with $\mathsf{Trans}(R)$, then $\forall R.C \in \mathcal{L}(t)$,*

(P8) *if $\geqslant n S.C \in \mathcal{L}(s)$, then $\sharp S^T(s, C) \geqslant n$,*

(P9) *if $\leqslant n S.C \in \mathcal{L}(s)$, then $\sharp S^T(s, C) \leqslant n$,*

(P10) *if $\{\leqslant n S.C, \geqslant n S.C\} \sqcap \mathcal{L}(s) \neq \emptyset$ and $\langle s, t \rangle \in \mathcal{E}_A(S)$, then $\{C, \sim C\} \sqcap \mathcal{L}(t) \neq \emptyset$,*

(P11) *if $\{o\} \in \mathcal{L}(s) \cap \mathcal{L}(t)$, then $s = t$,*

(P12) if $\forall T_1, \cdots, T_n.P_n \in \mathcal{L}(s)$ and $\langle s, t_1 \rangle \in \mathcal{E}_{\mathbf{D}}(T_1), \cdots, \langle s, t_n \rangle \in \mathcal{E}_{\mathbf{D}}(T_n)$, then $DC^{\mathcal{T}}(s, T_1, \ldots, T_n,$
       $t_1, \ldots, t_n, P_n) = true,$

(P13) if $\exists T_1, \cdots, T_n.P_n \in \mathcal{L}(s)$, then there is some $t_1, \cdots, t_n \in \Delta_{\mathbf{D}}$ such that
       $\langle s, t_1 \rangle \in \mathcal{E}_{\mathbf{D}}(T_1), \cdots,$
       $\langle s, t_n \rangle \in \mathcal{E}_{\mathbf{D}}(T_n), DC^{\mathcal{T}}(s, T_1, \ldots, T_n, t_1, \ldots, t_n, P_n) = true,$

(P14) if $\geqslant m T_1, \ldots, T_n.P_n \in \mathcal{L}(s)$, then $\sharp T_1 T_2 \ldots T_n^{\mathcal{T}}(s, P_n) \geqslant m,$

(P15) if $\leqslant m T_1, \ldots, T_n.P_n \in \mathcal{L}(s)$, then $\sharp T_1 T_2 \ldots T_n^{\mathcal{T}}(s, P_n) \leqslant m,$

(P16) if $\{\leqslant m T_1, \ldots, T_n.P_n, \geqslant m T_1, \ldots, T_n.P_n\} \cap \mathcal{L}(s) \neq \emptyset$ and $\langle s, t_1 \rangle \in$
       $\mathcal{E}_{\mathbf{D}}(T_1), \quad \ldots, \quad \langle s, t_n \rangle \in \quad \mathcal{E}_{\mathbf{D}}(T_n), \quad then \quad for \quad 1 \quad \leq \quad i \quad \leq \quad n,$
       we have either $DC^{\mathcal{T}}(s, T_1, \ldots, T_n, t_1, \ldots, t_n, P_n) = true,$ or
       $DC^{\mathcal{T}}(s, T_1, \ldots, T_n, t_1, \ldots, t_n, \neg P_n) = true.$

Lemma 1. *A* $\mathcal{SHOQ}(\mathbf{D_n})$-*concept* D *in NNF is satisfiable w.r.t. a role box* $\mathcal{R}$ *iff* D *has a tableau w.r.t.* $\mathcal{R}$.

Proof: For the *if* direction, if $\mathcal{T} = (\mathbf{S}, \mathcal{L}, \mathcal{E}_A, \mathcal{E}_{\mathbf{D}})$ is a tableau for D, a model $\mathcal{I} = (\Delta^{\mathcal{I}}, \cdot^{\mathcal{I}})$ of D can be defined as: $\Delta^{\mathcal{I}} = \mathbf{S}, \mathsf{CN}^{\mathcal{I}} = \{s \mid \mathsf{CN} \in \mathcal{L}(s)\}$ for all concept names CN in $\mathrm{cl}(D)$, if $R \in \mathbf{R_+}, \mathbf{R}_A^{\mathcal{I}} = \mathcal{E}_A(R)^+$, otherwise $\mathbf{R}_A^{\mathcal{I}} = \mathcal{E}_A(R) \cup \bigcup\limits_{P \not\sqsubseteq R, P \neq R} P^{\mathcal{I}},$
$\mathbf{R}_{\mathbf{D}}^{\mathcal{I}} = \mathcal{E}_{\mathbf{D}}(R)$, where $\mathcal{E}_A(R)^+$ denotes the transitive closure of $\mathcal{E}_A(R)$. $D^{\mathcal{I}} \neq \emptyset$ because $s_0 \in D^{\mathcal{I}}$. Here we only concentrate on (P14) to (P15); the remainder is similar to the proofs found in [10][4].

1. $E = \geqslant m T_1, \ldots, T_n.P_n$. According to (P14), $E \in \mathcal{L}(s)$ implies that $\sharp T_1 T_2 \ldots T_n^{\mathcal{T}}$ $(s, P_n) \geqslant m$. By the definition of $T_1 T_2 \ldots T_n^{\mathcal{T}}(s, P_n)$, we have $s \in \{x \in \Delta^{\mathcal{I}} \mid$ $\sharp\{\langle t_1, \ldots, t_n \rangle \mid \langle x, t_1 \rangle \in \mathcal{E}_{\mathbf{D}}(T_1) \wedge \ldots \wedge \langle x, t_n \rangle \in \mathcal{E}_{\mathbf{D}}(T_n) \wedge \langle t_1, \ldots, t_n \rangle \in P_n^{\mathbf{D}}\} \geqslant$ $m\}$, Since $\mathcal{E}_{\mathbf{D}}(T_i) = T_i^{\mathcal{I}}$, we have $s \in (\geqslant m T_1, \ldots, T_n.P_n)^{\mathcal{I}}$. Similarly, if $E = \leqslant m T_1, \ldots, T_n.P_n$, we have $s \in (\leqslant m T_1, \ldots, T_n.P_n)^{\mathcal{I}}$.

For the converse, if $\mathcal{I} = (\Delta^{\mathcal{I}}, \cdot^{\mathcal{I}})$ is a model of D, then a tableau $\mathcal{T} = (\mathbf{S}, \mathcal{L}, \mathcal{E}_A, \mathcal{E}_{\mathbf{D}})$ for D can be defined as: $S = \Delta^{\mathcal{I}}$, $\mathcal{E}_A(R) = R_A^{\mathcal{I}}$, $\mathcal{E}_{\mathbf{D}}(R) = R_{\mathbf{D}}^{\mathcal{I}}$, $\mathcal{L}(s) = \{C \in \mathrm{cl}(D) \mid s \in C^{\mathcal{I}}\}$. It only remains to demonstrate that T is a tableau for D: $\mathcal{T}$ satisfies (P14) to (P16) as a direct consequence of the semantics of datatype constructs. $\square$

5 A Tableau Algorithm for $\mathcal{SHOQ}(\mathbf{D_n})$

Form Lemma 1, an algorithm which constructs a tableau for a $\mathcal{SHOQ}(\mathbf{D_n})$-concept D can be used as a decision procedure for the satisfiability of D with respect to a role box $\mathcal{R}$.

---

[4] Note that in this paper, we mainly focus on the proof of the number restriction on concrete roles, the remainder is similar to the proofs found in [10].

Definition 6 *Let $\mathcal{R}$ be a role box, D a $\mathcal{SHOQ}(\mathbf{D_n})$-concept in NNF, $\mathbf{R}_A^D$ the set of abstract roles occurring in D or $\mathcal{R}$, and $\mathbf{I}^D$ the set of nominal occurring in D. A tableaux algorithm works on a* completion forest *for D w.r.t. $\mathcal{R}$, which is a set of trees F. Each node x of the forest is labelled with a set*

$$\mathcal{L}(x) \subseteq \mathtt{cl}(D) \cup \{\uparrow (R, \{o\}) \mid R \in \mathbf{R}_A^D \text{ and } \{o\} \in \mathbf{I}^D\},$$

and each edge $\langle x, y \rangle$ is labelled with a set of role names $\mathcal{L}(\langle x, y \rangle)$ containing roles occurring in cl(D) or $\mathcal{R}$. A node x is either an abstract node or a concrete node, the latter one represents a data value, and is always a leaf of F. Additionally, we keep track of inequalities between nodes of the tree with a symmetric binary relation $\neq$, which can be used between two abstract nodes, or between two tuples of concrete nodes of F. Inequality relations between tuples of concrete nodes can be mapped to inequality-checking predicates provided by the type systems[5]. For each $\{o\} \in \mathbf{I}^D$ there is a distinguished node $x_{\{o\}}$ in F such that $\{o\} \in \mathcal{L}(x)$. The algorithm expands the forest either by extending $\mathcal{L}(x)$ for some node x or by adding new leaf nodes.

  Given a completion forest, a node y is called an R-successor of a node x if, for some R' with $R' \sqsubseteq^* R$, either y is a successor of x and $R' \in \mathcal{L}(\langle x, y \rangle)$, or $\uparrow (R', \{o\}) \in \mathcal{L}(x)$ and $y = x_{\{o\}}$. Ancestors and roots are defined as usual. For an abstract role S and a node x in F we define $S^{\mathsf{F}}(x, C)$ by

$$S^{\mathsf{F}}(x, C) := \{y \mid y \text{ is an } S\text{-successor of } x \text{ and } C \in \mathcal{L}(y)\}.$$

  Given a completion forest, concrete nodes $t_1, \ldots, t_n$ are called $T_1 T_2 \ldots T_n$-successors of a node x if, for some concrete roles $T_1', \ldots, T_n'$ with $T_i' \sqsubseteq T_i$, $t_1, \ldots, t_n$ are successors of x and $T_i' \in \mathcal{L}(\langle x, t_i \rangle), 1 \leq i \leq n$. For a node x, its $T_1 T_2 \ldots T_n$-successors $\langle t_1, \ldots, t_n \rangle$, n-ary datatype predicate P_n, we define a set DC^{F} by

$$DC^F = \{< DCelement >\}$$

where DC^{F} is a set of DCelements, which have the form

$$< DCelement >= \{x, \langle T_1, \ldots, T_n \rangle, \langle t_1, \ldots, t_n \rangle, P_n\}$$

DC^{F} is initialised as an empty set. DC^{F} is is satisfied *iff. (i) there exists value : $N_C \to \Delta_{\mathbf{D}}$, where N_C is the set of all concrete nodes, s.t. for all $\{x, \langle T_1, \ldots, T_n \rangle, \langle t_1, \ldots, t_n \rangle, P_n\} \in DC^{\mathsf{F}}$, $\langle value(t_1), \ldots, value(t_n) \rangle \in P_n^{\mathbf{D}}$ are true; (ii) the inequality relations between tuples of concrete nodes are satisfied. In order to retrieve the set of all the $T_1 T_2 \ldots T_n$-successors of x, which satisfy a certain predicate P_n, we define $DCSuccessors^{\mathsf{F}}(x, P_n)$ by*
$DCSuccessors^{\mathsf{F}}(x, T_1, \ldots, T_n, P_n) := \{\langle t_1, \ldots, t_n \rangle \mid \{x, \langle T_1, \ldots, T_n \rangle, \langle t_1, \ldots, t_n \rangle, P_n\} \in DC^{\mathsf{F}}\}$
In order to retrieve the set of datatype predicates, which are satisfied by $T_1 T_2 \ldots T_n - successors\ t_1, \ldots, t_n$ of x, we define $DCPredicates^{\mathsf{F}}(x, T_1, \ldots, T_n, t_1, \ldots, t_n)$ by

---

[5] See the definition of conforming datatypes in section 3

$\forall_P$-rule:	if 1. $\forall T_1, \cdots, T_n.P_n \in \mathcal{L}(x)$, x is not blocked, and
	2. there are $T_1 T_2 \ldots T_n$-successors $\langle t_1, \ldots, t_n \rangle$ of x
	with $P_n \notin DCPredicates^F(x, T_1, \ldots, T_n, t_1, \ldots, t_n)$,
	then $DC^F \longrightarrow DC^F \cup \{x, \langle T_1, \ldots, T_n \rangle, \langle t_1, \ldots, t_n \rangle, P_n\}$.
$\exists_P$-rule:	if 1. $\exists T_1, \cdots, T_n.P_n \in \mathcal{L}(x)$, x is not blocked, and
	2. there are no $T_1 T_2 \ldots T_n$-successors $\langle t_1, \ldots, t_n \rangle$ of x,
	with $P_n \in DCPredicates^F(x, T_1, \ldots, T_n, t_1, \ldots, t_n)$,
	then 1. create $T_1 T_2 \ldots T_n$-successors $\langle t_1, \cdots, t_n \rangle$ with $\mathcal{L}(\langle x, t_i \rangle) = \{Ti\}$
	for $1 \le i \le n$ and
	2. $DC^F \longrightarrow DC^F \cup \{x, \langle T_1, \ldots, T_n \rangle, \langle t_1, \ldots, t_n \rangle, P_n\}$.
$\geqslant_P$-rule:	if 1. $\geqslant m T_1, \cdots, T_n.P_n \in \mathcal{L}(x)$, x is not blocked, and
	2. there is no m $T_1 T_2 \ldots T_n$-successors $\langle t_{11}, \ldots, t_{1n} \rangle, \cdots, \langle t_{m1}, \ldots, t_{mn} \rangle$,
	such that $\{x, \langle T_1, \ldots, T_n \rangle, \langle t_{j1}, \ldots, t_{jn} \rangle, P_n\} \in DC^F$, and
	$\langle t_{j1}, \ldots, t_{jn} \rangle \ne \langle t_{k1}, \ldots, t_{kn} \rangle$, for all $1 \le j < k \le m$
	then 1. create m $T_1 T_2 \ldots T_n$-successors $\langle t_{11}, \ldots, t_{1n} \rangle, \cdots, \langle t_{m1}, \ldots, t_{mn} \rangle$,
	with $\mathcal{L}(\langle x, t_{ji} \rangle) \longrightarrow \{Ti\}$, and
	2. $DC^F \longrightarrow DC^F \cup \{x, \langle T_1, \ldots, T_n \rangle, \langle t_{j1}, \ldots, t_{jn} \rangle, P_n\}$ and
	3. set $\langle t_{j1}, \ldots, t_{jn} \rangle \ne \langle t_{k1}, \ldots, t_{kn} \rangle$, for all $1 \le i \le n$, $1 \le j < k \le m$.
$\leqslant_P$-rule:	if 1. $\leqslant m T_1, \cdots, T_n.P_n \in \mathcal{L}(x)$, x is not blocked, and
	2. $\sharp DCSuccessors^F(x, T_1, \ldots, T_n, P_n) > m$ and
	3. there exist $j \ne k$, s.t. $\langle t_{j1}, \ldots, t_{jn} \rangle, \langle t_{k1}, \ldots, t_{kn} \rangle \in DCSuccessors^F(x,$
	$T_1, \ldots, T_n, P_n)$ but not $\langle t_{j1}, \ldots, t_{jn} \rangle \ne \langle t_{k1}, \ldots, t_{kn} \rangle, 1 \le j < k \le m+1$,
	then 1. $\mathcal{L}(\langle x, t_{ki} \rangle) \longrightarrow \mathcal{L}(\langle x, t_{ki} \rangle) \cup \mathcal{L}(\langle x, t_{ji} \rangle)$, and
	2. $DC^F \longrightarrow DC^F[\langle t_{j1}, \ldots, t_{jn} \rangle / \langle t_{k1}, \ldots, t_{kn} \rangle] \mid_{x, T_1, \ldots, T_n, P_n}$, and
	3. add $u \ne \langle t_{k1}, \ldots, t_{kn} \rangle$ for each tuple u with $u \ne \langle t_{j1}, \ldots, t_{jn} \rangle$, and
	4. remove all t_{ji} where t_{ji} isn't in any tuples of $DCSuccessors^F(x, *, *)$ and
	remove all edges leading to these t_{ji} from F.
$choose_P$-rule:	if 1. $\{\leqslant m T_1, \cdots, T_n.P_n, \geqslant m T_1, \cdots, T_n.P_n\} \cap \mathcal{L}(x) \ne \emptyset$, x is not blocked, and
	2. $\langle t_1, \ldots, t_n \rangle$ are $T_1 T_2 \ldots T_n$-successors of x, and
	then either $DC^F \longrightarrow DC^F \cup \{x, \langle T_1, \ldots, T_n \rangle, \langle t_1, \ldots, t_n \rangle, P_n\}$,
	or $DC^F \longrightarrow DC^F \cup \{x, \langle T_1, \ldots, T_n \rangle, \langle t_1, \ldots, t_n \rangle, \neg P_n\}$.

$DCPredicates^F(x, T_1, \ldots, T_n, t_1, \ldots, t_n) := \{P_n \mid \{x, \langle T_1, \ldots, T_n \rangle, \langle t_1, \ldots, t_n \rangle, P_n\} \in DC^F\}$
Note that we can use * *as parameter in* $DCSuccessors^F$ *and* $DCPredicates^F$,
e.g. $DCSuccess - ors^F(x, *, *)$ *means all the concrete successors of node* x.

A node x *is* directly blocked *if none of its ancestors are blocked, and it has
an ancestor* x' *that is not distinguished such that* $\mathcal{L}(x) \subseteq \mathcal{L}(x')$. *We call* x' *blocks*
x. *A node is* blocked *if it is directly blocks or if its predecessor is blocked.*

If $\{o_1\}, \cdots, \{o_l\}$ *are all individuals occurring in D, the algorithm initialises
the completion forest* F *to contain* $l + 1$ *root nodes* $x_0, x_{\{o_1\}}, \cdots, x_{\{o_l\}}$ *with*
$\mathcal{L}(x_0) = \{D\}$ *and* $\mathcal{L}(x_{\{o_i\}}) = \{\{o_i\}\}$. *The inequality relation* $\ne$ *is initialised
with the empty relation.* F *is then expended by repeatedly applying the* expansion
rules, *listed in Figure 5* [6], *stopping if a* clash *occurs in one of its nodes.*

For a node x, $\mathcal{L}(x)$ *is said to contain a* clash *if:*

1. *for some concept name* $A \in N_C$, $\{A, \neg A\} \subseteq \mathcal{L}(x)$, *or*
2. *for some role* S, $\leqslant S.C \in \mathcal{L}(x)$ *and there are* $n + 1$ S-*successors* $y_0, \cdots, y_n$
of x *with* $C \in \mathcal{L}(y_i)$ *for each* $0 \le i \le n$ *and* $y_i \ne y_j$ *for each* $0 \le i < j \le n$,
or
3. DC^F *isn't satisfied;*

---

[6] Figure 5 only lists the rules about datatypes, other rules can be found in [10].

4. *for some concrete roles* $T_1, \ldots, T_n$, *n-ary datatype predicate* P_n, $\leqslant m T_1, \ldots, T_n$.
$P_n \in \mathcal{L}(x)$, *we have* $\sharp DCSuccessors^F(x, T_1, \ldots, T_n, P_n) \geqslant m + 1$, *or*

5. *for some* $\{o\} \in \mathcal{L}(x), x \neq x_{\{o\}}$.

The completion forest is complete *when, for some node* x, $\mathcal{L}(x)$ *contains a* clash, *or when none of the expansion rules is applicable. If the expansion rules can be applied in such a way that they yield a complete, clash-free completion forest, then the algorithm returns "D is* satisfiable *w.r.t.* $\mathcal{R}$*", and "D is* unsatisfiable *w.r.t.* $\mathcal{R}$*" otherwise.*

Lemma 2. (Termination) *When started with a* $\mathcal{SHOQ}(\mathbf{D_n})$*-concept* D *in NNF, the tableau algorithm terminates.*

Proof: Let $d = |cl(D)|$, $k = |\mathbf{R}_A^D|$, n_{max} the maximal number in atleast number restrictions as well as datatype atleast, and $\ell = |\mathcal{I}^D|$. Here we mainly concentrate on rules about number restriction on concrete roles. Note that the set of datatypes used is conforming, so we don't have to worry about the checking on concrete nodes. Termination is a consequence of the following properties of the expansion rules:

1. Each rule but the $\leqslant$-, $\leqslant_P$- or the **O**-rule strictly extends the completion forest, by extending node labels or adding nodes, while removing neither nodes nor elements from node.

2. New nodes are only generated by the $\exists$-, $\exists_P$-, $\geqslant$-rule or the $\geqslant_P$-rule as successors of a node x for concepts of the form $\exists R.C$, $\exists T_1, \cdots, T_n.P_n$, $\geqslant nS.C$ and $\geqslant m T_1, \cdots, T_n.P_n$ in $\mathcal{L}(x)$. For a node x, each of these concepts can trigger the generation of successors at most once—even though the node(s) generated was later removed by either the $\leqslant$-, $\leqslant_P$- or the **O**-rule. For the $\geqslant_P$-rule: If $T_1 T_2 \ldots T_n$-successors $\langle t_{11}, \cdots, t_{1n} \rangle, \cdots, \langle t_{m1}, \cdots, t_{mn} \rangle$ were generated by an application of the $\geqslant_P$-rule for a concept $(\geqslant m T_1, \cdots, T_n.P_n)$, then $\langle t_{j1}, \cdots, t_{jn} \rangle \neq \langle t_{k1}, \cdots, t_{kn} \rangle$ holds for all $1 \leq i \leq n$ and $1 \leq j < k \leq m$. This implies there will always be m $T_1 T_2 \ldots T_n$-successors $\langle t_{11}, \cdots, t_{1n} \rangle, \cdots, \langle t_{m1}, \cdots, t_{mn} \rangle$ of x with $P_n(i) \in \mathcal{L}(t_i)$ and $\langle t_{j1}, \cdots, t_{jn} \rangle \neq \langle t_{k1}, \cdots, t_{kn} \rangle$ holds for all $1 \leq i \leq n$ and $1 \leq j < k \leq m$, since the $\leqslant$-, **O**- and $\leqslant_P$-rule can never merge them, and, whenever an application of the $\leqslant_P$-rule sets some $\mathcal{L}(t_{ji})$ to $\emptyset$, then there will be some $T_1 T_2 \ldots T_n$-successors $\langle t_{k1}, \cdots, t_{kn} \rangle$ of x with $P_n(i) \in \mathcal{L}(t_{ki})$ and $\langle t_{k1}, \cdots, t_{kn} \rangle$ "inherits" all inequalities from $\langle t_{j1}, \cdots, t_{jn} \rangle$. Hence the out-degree of the forest is bounded by $d \cdot n_{max}$.

3. Nodes are labelled with subsets of $cl(D) \cup \{\uparrow(R, \{o\}) \mid R \in \mathbf{R}_A^D \text{ and } \{o\} \in \mathcal{I}^D\}$, and the concrete value nodes are always leaves, so there are at most $2^{d+k\ell}$ different node labellings. Therefore, if a path p is of length at least $2^{d+k\ell}$, then, from the blocking condition above, there are two nodes x, y on p such that x is directly blocked by y. Hence paths are of length at most $2^{d+k\ell}$. $\square$

Lemma 3. (Soundness) *If the expansion rules can be applied to a $\mathcal{SHOQ}(\mathbf{D_n})$-concept D in NNF and a role box $\mathcal{R}$ such that they yield a complete and clash-free completion forest, then D has a tableau w.r.t. $\mathcal{R}$.*

Proof: Let F be the complete and clash-free completion forest constructed by the tableaux algorithm for D. To cope with cycle, an individual in **S** corresponds to a *path* in F. Due to qualifying number restrictions, we must distinguish different nodes that are blocked by the same node. We refer the readers to [10] for the definitions of path and related concepts. We can define a tableau $\mathcal{T} = (\mathbf{S}, \mathcal{L}, \mathcal{E}_A, \mathcal{E}_\mathbf{D})$ with: $\mathbf{S} = \texttt{Paths}(F)$, $\mathcal{L}(p) = \mathcal{L}(\texttt{Tail}(p))$, $\mathcal{E}_A(R_A) = \{\langle p, q\rangle \in \mathbf{S} \times \mathbf{S} \mid q = [p|(x, x')]$ and x' is an R_A-successor of $\texttt{Tail}(p),\} \ \mathcal{E}_\mathbf{D}(R_\mathbf{D}) = \{\langle p, value(t)\rangle \in \mathbf{S} \times \Delta_\mathbf{D} \mid t$ is an $R_\mathbf{D}$-successor of $\texttt{Tail}(p)\}$.

We have to show that $\mathcal{T}$ satisfies (P14) to (P16) from Definition 5.

- (P14): Assume $\geqslant m T_1, \ldots, T_n.P_n \in \mathcal{L}(p)$. This implies that in F there exist m $T_1 T_2 \ldots T_n$-successors $\langle t_{11}, \ldots, t_{1n}\rangle, \ldots, \langle t_{m1}, \ldots, t_{mn}\rangle$ of $\texttt{Tail}(p)$, s.t. $\langle t_{j1}, \cdots, t_{jn}\rangle \neq \langle t_{k1}, \cdots, t_{kn}\rangle$ and $\{p, \langle T_1, \ldots, T_n\rangle, \langle t_{j1}, \ldots, t_{jn}\rangle, P_n\} \in DC^\mathsf{F}$ for all $1 \leq j < k \leq m$ (otherwise, $\geqslant_P$-rule was still applicable). We claim that, for each of these concrete nodes, according to the construction of $\mathcal{E}_\mathbf{D}$ above, we have $\langle p, value(t_{ji})\rangle \in \mathcal{E}_D(T_i)$ and $\langle value(t_{j1}), \ldots, value(t_{jn})\rangle \in P_n^\mathbf{D}$ for all $1 \leq i \leq n$ and $1 \leq j \leq m$. According to the satisfiability of DC^F and definition of $T_1 T_2 \ldots T_n^\mathcal{T}(p, P_n)$, this implies $\sharp T_1 T_2 \ldots T_n^\mathcal{T}(p, P_n) \geqslant m$.
- (P15): Assume (P15) doesn't hold. Hence there is some $p \in \mathbf{S}$ with $(\leqslant m T_1, \ldots, T_n.P_n) \in \mathcal{L}(p)$ and $\sharp T_1 T_2 \ldots T_n^\mathcal{T}(p, P_n) > m$. According to the definition of $T_1 T_2 \ldots T_n^\mathcal{T}(p, P_n)$, this implies that there exist $\langle t_{11}, \ldots, t_{1n}\rangle, \ldots, \langle t_{m+1,1}, \ldots, t_{m+1,n}\rangle$ such that $\langle p, value(t_{ji})\rangle \in \mathcal{E}_D(T_i)$, and $\{p, \langle T_1, \ldots, T_n\rangle, \langle t_{j1}, \ldots, t_{jn}\rangle, P_n\} \in DC^\mathsf{F}$, for all $1 \leq i \leq n$ and $1 \leq j < k \leq m + 1$. Since the $m + 1$ tuples of data values aren't equal to each other, so the $m + 1$ tuples of concrete nodes aren't equal to each other. Thus $DCSuccessors^\mathsf{F}(x, T_1, \ldots, T_n, P_n) \geqslant m + 1$, which fires a clash. Thus the assumption $\sharp T_1 T_2 \ldots T_n^\mathcal{T}(p, P_n) > m$ is false. So we have $\sharp T_1 T_2 \ldots T_n^\mathcal{T}(p, P_n) \leqslant m$.
- (P16): Assume $\{\leqslant m T_1, \cdots, T_n.P_n, \geqslant m T_1, \cdots, T_n.P_n\} \cap \mathcal{L}(p) \neq \emptyset$, $\langle p, t_i\rangle \in \mathcal{E}_\mathbf{D}(T_i), 1 \leq i \leq n$, thus $\langle t_1, \ldots, t_n\rangle$ is a $T_1 T_2 \ldots T_n$-successors of $\texttt{Tail}(p)$. Let $value(t_i)$ be the value of t_i: (1) if $\{p, \langle T_1, \ldots, T_n\rangle, \langle t_1, \ldots, t_n\rangle, P_n\} \in DC^\mathsf{F}$, we have $DC^\mathcal{T}(p, T_1, \ldots, T_n, value(t_1), \ldots, value(t_n), P_n) = true$; (2) if $\{p, \langle T_1, \ldots, T_n\rangle, \langle t_1, \ldots, t_n\rangle, \neg P_n\} \in DC^\mathsf{F}$, we have $DC^\mathcal{T}(p, T_1, \ldots, T_n, value(t_1), \ldots, value(t_n), \neg P_n) = true$.

$\square$

Lemma 4. (Completeness) *If a $\mathcal{SHOQ}(\mathbf{D_n})$-concept D in NNF has a tableau w.r.t. $\mathcal{R}$, then the expansion rules can be applied to D and $\mathcal{R}$ such that they yield a complete, clash-free completion forest.*

Proof: Let $\mathcal{T} = (\mathbf{S}, \mathcal{L}, \mathcal{E}_A, \mathcal{E}_\mathbf{D})$ be a tableau for D w.r.t. a role box $\mathcal{R}$. We use $\mathcal{T}$ to guide the application of the non-deterministic rules. We define a function π, mapping the nodes of the forest F to $\mathbf{S} \cup \Delta_\mathbf{D}$ such that

$\mathcal{L}(x) \subseteq \mathcal{L}(\pi(x))$; $\langle \pi(x), \pi(y) \rangle \in \mathcal{E}_A$ if: 1. $\pi(y) \in \mathbf{S}$ and y is an R_A-successor of x, or 2. $\uparrow (R, \{o\}) \in \mathcal{L}(x)$ and $y = x_{\{o\}}$; $\langle \pi(x), \pi(y) \rangle \in \mathcal{E}_D$ if $\pi(y) \in \Delta_\mathbf{D}$ and y is an $R_\mathbf{D}$-successor of x; abstract nodes $x \neq y$ implies $\pi(x) \neq \pi(y)$; while tuples of concrete nodes $\langle y_{j1}, \ldots, y_{jn} \rangle \neq \langle y_{k1}, \ldots, y_{kn} \rangle$ implies $\langle \pi(y_{j1}), \ldots, \pi(y_{jn}) \rangle \dot{\neq} \langle \pi(y_{k1}), \ldots, \pi(y_{kn}) \rangle$. (*)

We only have to consider the various rules about number restriction on datatypes.

- The $\geqslant_P$-rule: If $\geqslant m T_1, \ldots, T_n . P_n \in \mathcal{L}(x)$, then $\geqslant m T_1, \ldots, T_n . P_n \in \mathcal{L}(\pi(x))$. Since $\mathcal{T}$ is a tableau, (P14) of Definition 5 implies that $\sharp T_1 T_2 \ldots T_n^\mathcal{T}(\pi(x), P_n) \geqslant m$. Hence there are m tuples of data values $\langle t_{11}, \ldots, t_{1n} \rangle, \ldots, \langle t_{m1}, \ldots, t_{mn} \rangle$, such that $\langle \pi(x), t_{ji} \rangle \in \mathcal{E}_D$, $\langle t_{j1}, \ldots, t_{jn} \rangle \neq \langle t_{k1}, \ldots, t_{kn} \rangle$, and $DC^\mathcal{T}(\pi(x), T_1, \ldots, T_n, t_{j1}, \ldots, t_{jn}, P_n) = true$, for $1 \leq i \leq n$ and $1 \leq j < k \leq m$. The $\geqslant_P$-rule generates m new $T_1 T_2 \ldots T_n$-successors $\langle y_{11}, \ldots, y_{1n} \rangle, \ldots, \langle y_{m1}, \ldots, y_{mn} \rangle$. By setting $\pi' := \pi[y_{ji} \mapsto t_{ji}](1 \leq i \leq n, 1 \leq j < k \leq m)$, one obtains a function π' that satisfies (*) for the modified forest.
- The $\leqslant_P$-rule: If $\leqslant m T_1, \ldots, T_n . P_n \in \mathcal{L}(x)$, then $\leqslant m T_1, \ldots, T_n . P_n \in \mathcal{L}(\pi(x))$. Since $\mathcal{T}$ is a tableau, (P15) of Definition 5 implies $\sharp T_1 T_2 \ldots T_n^\mathcal{T}(\pi(x), P_n) \leqslant m$. If the $\leqslant_P$-rule is applicable, we have $\sharp DCSuccessors^F(x, T_1, \ldots, T_n, P_n) > m$, which implies that there are at least $m + 1$ $T_1 T_2 \ldots T_n$-successors $\langle y_{11}, \ldots, y_{1n} \rangle, \ldots, \langle y_{m+1,1}, \ldots, y_{m+1,n} \rangle$ such that $\{x, \langle T_1, \ldots, T_n \rangle, \langle y_{j1}, \ldots, y_{jn} \rangle, P_n\} \in DC^\mathbf{F}$, for $1 \leq j \leq m + 1$. Thus, there must be two $\langle y_{j1}, \ldots, y_{jn} \rangle$ and $\langle y_{k1}, \ldots, y_{kn} \rangle$ among the $m+1$ $T_1 T_2 \ldots T_n$-successors such that $\langle \pi(y_{j1}), \ldots, \pi(y_{jn}) \rangle = \langle \pi(y_{k1}, \ldots, \pi(y_{kn}) \rangle$ (otherwise $\sharp T_1 T_2 \ldots T_n^\mathcal{T}(\pi(x), P_n) > m$ would hold). This implies $\langle y_{j1}, \ldots, y_{jn} \rangle \dot{\neq} \langle y_{k1}, \ldots, y_{kn} \rangle$ cannot hold because of (*). Hence the $\leqslant_P$-rule can be applied without violating (*).
- The $choose_P$-rule: If $\{\leqslant m T_1, \cdots, T_n . P_n, \geqslant m T_1, \cdots, T_n . P_n\} \cap \mathcal{L}(x) \neq \emptyset$, we have $\{\leqslant m T_1, \cdots, T_n . P_n, \geqslant m T_1, \cdots, T_n . P_n\} \cap \mathcal{L}(\pi(x)) \neq \emptyset$, and if there are $T_1 T_2 \ldots T_n$-successors $\langle y_1, \ldots, y_n \rangle$ of x, then $\langle \pi(x), \pi(y_i) \rangle \in \mathcal{E}_D, 1 \leq i \leq n$, due to (*). Since $\mathcal{T}$ is a tableau, (P16) of Definition 5 implies either $DC^\mathcal{T}(\pi(x), T_1, \ldots, T_n, \pi(y_1), \ldots, \pi(y_n), P_n) = true$, or $DC^\mathcal{T}(\pi(x), T_1, \ldots, T_n, \pi(y_1), \ldots, \pi(y_n), \neg P_n) = true$. Hence the $choose_P$-rule can accordingly either set $DC^\mathbf{F} \longrightarrow DC^\mathbf{F} \cup \{x, \langle T_1, \ldots T_n \rangle, \langle y_1, \ldots, y_n \rangle, P_n\}$, or set $DC^\mathbf{F} \longrightarrow DC^\mathbf{F} \cup \{x, \langle T_1, \ldots, T_n \rangle, \langle y_1, \ldots, y_n \rangle, \neg P_n\}$.

Whenever a rule is applicable to F, it can be applied in a way that maintains (*), and, from Lemma 2, we have that any sequence of rule applications must terminate. Since (*) holds, any forest generated by these rule-applications must be clash-free. This can be seen from the condition described in [8] plus the following:

- If F does not satisfy DC^F, there must be some concrete nodes from which no values mapping satisfies all the relevant predicates, and therefore there can be no values satisfying all of properties (P12) to (P16).
- F cannot contain a node x with $\leqslant m T_1, \ldots, T_n.P_n \in \mathcal{L}(x)$, and $m + 1$ $T_1 T_2 \ldots T_n$-successors $\langle t_{11}, \ldots, t_{1n} \rangle$, $\ldots$, $\langle t_{m+1,1}, \ldots, t_{m+1,n} \rangle$ of x with $\langle t_{j1}, \ldots, t_{jn} \rangle \neq \langle t_{k1}, \ldots, t_{kn} \rangle$ and $\{x, \langle T_1, \ldots, T_n \rangle, \langle t_{j1}, \ldots, t_{jn} \rangle, P_n\} \in DC^F$, for all $1 \leq i \leq n, 1 \leq j < k \leq m + 1$, because $\leqslant m T_1, \ldots, T_n.P_n \in \mathcal{L}(\pi(x))$, and, since $\langle t_{j1}, \ldots, t_{jn} \rangle \neq \langle t_{k1}, \ldots, t_{kn} \rangle$ implies $\langle \pi(t_{j1}), \ldots, \pi(t_{jn}) \rangle \neq \langle \pi(t_{k1}), \ldots, \pi(t_{kn}) \rangle$, $\sharp T_1 T_2 \ldots T_n^{\mathcal{T}}(\pi(x), P_n) > m$ would hold which contradicts (P15) of Definition 5. □

As an immediate consequence of Lemmas 2,4,5 and 6, the completion algorithm always terminates, and answers with "D is satisfiable w.r.t. $\mathcal{R}$" iff. D has a tableau T. Next, subsumption can be reduced to (un)satisfiability. Finally, $\mathcal{SHOQ}(\mathbf{D_n})$ can internalise general concept inclusion axions [6]. However, in the presence of nominals, we must also add $\exists O.o_1 \sqcap \cdots \sqcap \exists O.o_l$ to the concept internalising the general concept inclusion axioms to make sure that the universal role O indeed reaches all nominals O_i occurring in the input concept and terminology. Thus, we can decide these inference problems also w.r.t. terminologies.

Theorem 7 *The tableau algorithm presented in Definition 6 is a decision procedure for satisfiability and subsumption of $\mathcal{SHOQ}(\mathbf{D_n})$-concepts w.r.t. terminologies.*

6   Discussion

As we have seen, unary datatype predicates are usually not enough, while n-ary datatype predicates as well as qualified number restrictions with n-ary datatype predicates are often necessary when modelling the "concrete properties" of real world entities in semantic Web ontologies and applications. Therefore, we have extended $\mathcal{SHOQ}(\mathbf{D})$ with n-ary datatype predicates and qualified number restrictions with n-ary predicates to give the $\mathcal{SHOQ}(\mathbf{D_n})$ DL. We have shown that the decision procedure for concept satisfiability and subsumption is still decidable in $\mathcal{SHOQ}(\mathbf{D_n})$. An implementation based on the FaCT system is planned, and will be used to test empirical performance.

With its support for nominals, n-ary datatype predicates and qualified number restrictions with n-ary datatype predicates, $\mathcal{SHOQ}(\mathbf{D_n})$ is well suited to provide reasoning support for ontology languages in general, and semantic Web ontology languages in particular. Therefore, we think that future versions of Web ontology languages, e.g. DAML+OIL and OWL, can include n-ary datatype predicates and qualified number restrictions with n-ary datatype predicates. As future work, it is interesting to study how the extended datatype support introduced in the paper can help to express various business rules required in semantic Web ontologies and applications. Secondly, it is also important to extend current optimisation techniques to cope with nominals used in the $\mathcal{SHOQ}(\mathbf{D_n})$ DL.

Acknowledgements. We would like to thank Ulrike Sattler, since the work presented here extends the original work on $\mathcal{SHOQ}(\mathbf{D})$. Thanks are also due to Carsten Lutz and Volker Haarslev for their helpful discussion on concrete datatypes.

References

1. F. Baader and Philipp Hanschke. A Scheme for Integrating Concrete Domains into Concept Languages. In *IJCAI-91*, pages 452–457, 1991.
2. Tim Berners-lee. Semantic Web Road Map. W3C Design Issues. http://www.w3.org/DesignIssues/Semantic.html, Oct. 1998.
3. J. Broekstra, M. Klein, S. Decker, D. Fensel, F. can Harmelen, and I. Horrocks. Enabling knowledge representation on the Web by extending RDF Schema, Nov. 2000.
4. Benjamin N. Grosof and Terrence C. Poon. Representing Agent Contracts with Exceptions using XML Rules, Ontologies, and Process Descriptions. In *Proceedings of International Workshop on Rule Markup Languages for Business Rules on the Semantic Web*, Jun 2002.
5. Volker Haarslev, Ralf Möller, and Michael Wessel. The Description Logic AL-CNHR+ Extended with Concrete Domains: A Practically Motivated Approach. In *Proceedings of International Joint Conference on Automated Reasoning, IJCAR'2001, R. Goré, A. Leitsch, T. Nipkow (Eds.),Siena, Italy, Springer-Verlag, Berlin.*, pages 29–44, Jun. 2001.
6. I. Horrocks, U. Sattler, and S. Tobies. Practical Reasoning for Expressive Description Logics. In H. Ganzinger, D. McAllester, and A. Voronkov, editors, *Proceedings of the 6th International Conference on Logic for Programming and Automated Reasoning (LPAR'99)*, number 1705 in Lecture Notes in Artificial Intelligence, pages 161–180. Springer-Verlag, 1999.
7. Ian Horrocks and Peter F. Patel-Schneider. The Generation of DAML+OIL. Aug. 2001. The 2001 International Workshop on Description Logics.
8. Ian Horrocks and U. Sattler. Ontology Reasoning for the Semantic Web. In *In B. Nebel, editor, Proc. of the 17th Int. Joint Conf. on Artificial Intelligence (IJCAI'01), Morgan Kaufmann*, pages 199–204, 2001.
9. C. Lutz. NExpTime-complete Description Logics with Concrete Domains. LuFG Theoretical Computer Science, RWTH Aachen, Germany, 2000.
10. Jeff Z. Pan. Web Ontology Reasoning in the SHOQ(Dn) Description Logic. In *Proceedings of the Methods for Modalities 2 (M4M-2)*, Nov 2001. ILLC, University of Amsterdam, URL
    http://www.cs.man.ac.uk/ panz/Zhilin/download/Paper/Pan-shoqdn-2001.pdf.
11. Jeff Z. Pan and Ian Horrocks. Metamodeling Architecture of Web Ontology Languages. In *Proceeding of the Semantic Web Working Symposium (SWWS)*, July 2001. URL
    http://www.cs.man.ac.uk/ panz/Zhilin/download/Paper/Pan-Horrocks-rdfsfa-2001.pdf.
12. Frank van Harmelen, Peter F. Patel-Schneider, and Ian Horrocks. A Model-Theortis Semantics of DAML+OIL (March 2001). Mar. 2001.

A Conceptual Modeling Approach for Semantics-Driven Enterprise Applications

Boris Motik, Alexander Maedche, and Raphael Volz

FZI Research Center for Information Technologies at the University of Karlsruhe,
D-76131 Karlsruhe, Germany
{motik,maedche,volz}@fzi.de

Abstract. In recent years ontologies – shared conceptualizations of some domain – are increasingly seen as the key to further automation of information processing. Although many approaches for representing and applying ontologies have already been devised, they haven't found their way into enterprise applications. In this paper we argue that ontology-based systems lack critical technical features, such as scalability, reliability, concurrency and integration with existing data sources, as well as the support for modularization and meta-concept modeling from the conceptual modeling perspective. We present a conceptual modeling approach that balances some of the trade-offs to more easily integrate into existing enterprise information infrastructure. Our approach is implemented within KAON, the Karlsruhe Ontology and Semantic Web tool suite.

1 Introduction

The application of ontologies[1] – shared conceptualizations of some domain – is increasingly seen as key to enable semantics-driven information access. There are many applications of such an approach, e.g. automated information processing, information integration or knowledge management, to name just a few. Especially after Tim Berners-Lee coined the vision of the Semantic Web[2], where Web pages are annotated by ontology-based meta-data, the interest in ontology research increased, in hope of finding ways to off-load large-volume information processing from the human user to autonomous agents. Many ontology languages have been developed, each aimed at solving particular aspects of conceptual modeling. Some of them, such as RDF(S) [20,6], are simple languages offering elementary support for ontology modeling for the Semantic Web. There are other, more complex languages with roots in formal logic, focused around inference – ways to automatically infer facts not explicitly present in the model. For example, the F-logic language[18] (implemented, among others, in the OntoBroker system [10]) is based on an object-oriented extension of Prolog. On the other hand, various classes of description logic languages (e.g. OIL [12]) are mainly concerned with finding an appropriate subset of first-order logic with decidable and complete inference procedures (implemented, among others, in highly-optimized systems such as FaCT [16]).

---

[1] An ontology is a conceptual model shared between autonomous agents in a specific domain.
[2] http://www.gca.org/attend/2000_conferences/XML_2000/knowledge.htm#lee

R. Meersman, Z. Tari (Eds.): CoopIS/DOA/ODBASE 2002, LNCS 2519, pp. 1082–1099, 2002.
© Springer-Verlag Berlin Heidelberg 2002

Despite a large body of research in improving ontology management and reasoning, features standardized and widely adopted in the database community (such as scalability or transactions) must be adapted and re-implemented for logic-based systems. Relational databases have been developed over the past 20 years to a maturity level unparalleled with that of ontology-based systems, incorporating features critical for business applications, such as scalability, reliability and concurrency support.

Further, integration of existing information sources into ontology-based systems isn't easy. Databases cannot be replaced with ontology-based systems, because of the number of existing applications that depend on them. Hence, complicated and error-prone replication strategies are typically devised. Finally, ontology modularization is not provided in available systems. Because of these problems, up until today there hasn't been a large number of successful enterprise application of ontology technologies.

On the other hand, database technologies alone are not appropriate for handling information based on ontologies. This is mainly due to the fact that in databases systems first the conceptual model of the model is developed (e.g. using entity-relationship modeling [9]), but for actual implementation it is transformed into the logical model. After the transformation, the structure and the intent of the original model are not obvious. Therefore, the conceptual and the logical model tend to diverge. Further, operations that are natural within the conceptual model, such as navigation between objects, are not straightforward within the logical model.

Contribution of the paper. In this paper we present a conceptual modeling approach suitable for business-wide applications, designed based on the requirements analysis of several applications we are working on. We adjust the expressiveness of traditional logic-based languages to sustain tractability. As a side effect this makes realization of enterprise-wide ontology-based system using existing and well-established technologies, such as relational databases, possible. Other critical features are modularization and modeling meta-concepts with well-defined semantics. Our goal is to allow expressing and accessing conceptual models in a natural and easily understandable way, with a low gap between model conceptualization and its implementation in the system. We present the current status of the implementation of our approach within KAON[3] – Ontology and Semantic Web tool suite used as basis for our research and development. Finally, we discuss the possibilities of integration of ontology systems with existing information sources.

2 Requirements

In this section we discuss the requirements gathered during our work on various projects.

Unambiguous Semantics. The primary motivation for using ontologies over other modeling approaches is to enrich the information with semantics. For example, the notion that a class should be understood as a set of instances is defined by the semantics of an ontology modeling language.

---

[3] http://kaon.semanticweb.org/

The absence of clear a clear semantics may led to diverging interpretations of intended meaning, for example, with RDFS [13,15,7,23] and UML [5]. Thus, a clear semantic description of an ontology modeling language is an important requirement.

Object-oriented Paradigm. In the last decade the object-oriented paradigm has become prevalent for conceptual modeling. A wide adoption of UML [14,11] as syntax for object-oriented models has further increased its acceptance.

Object-oriented modeling paradigm owes its success largely to the fact that it is highly intuitive. Its constructs match well with the way people think about the domain they are modeling. Object-oriented models can easily be visualized, thus making them easily understandable. Thus, any successful conceptual modeling approach should incorporate the object-oriented paradigm.

Meta-concepts. In real-world conceptual models, it is often unclear whether some element should be represented as a concept or as an instance. An excellent example in [25] demonstrates problems with meta-concept modeling. While developing a semantics-driven image retrieval system, it was necessary to model the relationship between notions of species, apes and particular apes. Most natural conceptualization is to say that there is a concept SPECIES (representing the set of all species), with instances such as APE. However, APE may be viewed as a set of all apes. It may be argued that APE may be modeled as a subconcept of SPECIES. However, if this is done, other irregularities arise. Since APE is a set of all apes, SPECIES, being a superconcept of APE, must contain all apes as their members, which is clearly wrong. Further, when talking about the APE species, there are many properties that may be attached to it, such as habitat, type of food etc. This is impossible to do if APE is a subconcept of SPECIES, since concepts cannot have properties. There are other examples where meta-concept modeling is necessary:

- Ontology mapping is a process of mapping ontology entities in different ontologies in order to achieve interoperability between information in both ontologies. As described in [21], it is useful to represent ontology mapping as a meta-ontology that relates concepts of the ontologies being mapped.
- It is beneficial to represent ontology changes by instantiating a special evolution ontology [22]. Evolution (meta-)ontology consists of concepts reflecting various types of changes in an ontology.

Modularization. It is a common engineering practice to extract a well-encapsulated body of information in a separate module, that can later be reused in different contexts. However, modularization of conceptual models has some special requirements: both instances and schematic definitions may be subjected to modularization.

For example, a concept CONTINENT will have exactly seven instances. In order to include information about continents in some ontology, it is not sufficient to include the CONTINENT concept – one must include its instances as well to be able to talk about particular continents, such as Europe. The shared nature of ontology implies reuse. We consider modularization – on both ontologies and instances – to be an important aspect of reuse.

Lexical Information. Many applications, such as semantics-driven web content management, extensively depend on lexical information about entities in an ontology, such as labels for ontology entities in different languages. Hence, consistent way of associating lexical information with ontology entities is mandatory.

Root Concept. Although not a semantically critical issue, from the methodological point of view, the necessity to explicitly classify a concept into the hierarchy forces the modelers to think about the proper characterization of the concept in the hierarchy. Further, including a root concept from which all other concepts are derived results in more elegant and manageable conceptual models. For example, a property is made applicable to instances of any concept by specifying the root concept as the property domain. If there were no root concept, the case with no domain should be treated specially, thus resulting in a slightly more complicated system. Many systems – e.g. all description logic systems or Protege-2000 – include some form of a root concept.

Light-weight Inferences. Inference mechanisms for deduction of information not explicitly asserted is an important characteristic of ontology-based systems. However, systems with very general inference capabilities often do not take into account other needs, such as scalability and concurrency.

Based on our experience, we observed that while rules in conceptual modeling are important, they are often used in some well-defined patterns. Hence, instead of building a system based on a general reasoning paradigm, we introduce the notion of light-weight inferences based on axiom patterns [26] – predefined types of rules that sustain scalability and tractability. The list of axiom patterns is currently limited to common patterns in ontology structure, such as symmetric, transitive and inverse relations.

Technical Issues . In order to be applicable for real-world enterprise applications, our conceptual modeling approach must make it easy fulfill technical requirements such as scalability, concurrency support, reliability and easy integration with existing data sources.

3 Conceptual Modeling Approach

In this section we present the mathematical definition of our modeling language. Next the denotational semantics is presented in standard Tarski style. Finally, several examples are presented.

3.1 Mathematical Definition

We present our approach on an abstract, mathematical level that defines the structure of our models[4]. We may support this structure with several different syntaxes. Further, in enterprise systems the structure of model is much more important, since this structure must be reflected in the systems for information storage and retrieval.

---

[4] The definition is based on previous work as described in [4]

Definition 1 (OI-model Structure). *An OI-model (ontology-instance-model) structure is a tuple OIM := (E, INC) where:*

- *E is the set of entities of the IO-models,*
- *INC is the set of included OI-models.*

An OI-model represents a self-contained unit of structured information that may be reused. Elements in an OI-model are entities. An OI-model may include a set of other OI-models (represented through the set INC). Definition 5 lists the conditions that must be fulfilled when an OI-model includes another model.

Definition 2 (Ontology Structure). *An ontology structure associated with an OI-model is a 10-tuple $O(OIM) := (C, P, S, T, INV, H_C, H_P, domain, range, mincard, maxcard)$ where:*

- $C \subseteq E$ *is a set of concepts,*
- $P \subseteq E$ *is a set of properties,*
- $S \subseteq P$ *is a subset of symmetric properties,*
- $T \subseteq P$ *is a subset of transitive properties,*
- $INV \subseteq P \times P$ *is a symmetric relation that relates inverse properties, if $(p_1, p_2) \in INV$, then p_1 is an inverse property of p_2,*
- $H_C \subseteq C \times C$ *is an acyclic relation called concept hierarchy, if $(c_1, c_2) \in H_C$ then c_1 is a subconcept of c_2, c_2 is a superconcept of c_1,*
- $H_P \subseteq P \times P$ *is an acyclic relation called property hierarchy, if $(p_1, p_2) \in H_P$ then p_1 is a subproperty of p_2, p_2 is a superproperty of p_1,*
- *function domain : $P \rightarrow 2^C \setminus \{\emptyset\}$ gives the set of domain concepts for some property $p \in P$,*
- *function range : $P \rightarrow (2^C \setminus \{\emptyset\}) \cup \{L\}$ gives the set of range concepts for some property $p \in P$,*
- *function $mincard : C \times P \rightarrow N_0$ gives the minimum cardinality for each concept-property pair,*
- *function $maxcard : C \times P \rightarrow (N_0 \cup \{\infty\})$ gives the maximum cardinality for each concept-property pair.*

Each OI-model has an ontology structure associated with it, consisting of a set definitions regulating how instances should be constructed. An ontology consists of concepts (sets of elements) and properties (specification how objects may be connected). Each property must have at least one domain concept, while its range may either be a literal, or a set of at least one concept. Domain and range concept restrictions are treated conjunctively – all of them must be fulfilled for each property instantiation. Some properties may be marked as transitive, and it is possible to say that two properties are inverse of each other. For each class-property pair it is possible to specify the minimum and maximum cardinalities, defining how many times a property may be specified for instances of that class. Concepts and properties can be arranged in a hierarchy, as specified by the H_C (H_P) relation. This relation relates directly connected concepts (properties), whereas its transitive closure follows from the semantics, as defined in the next subsection.

Definition 3 (Instance Pool Structure). *An instance pool associated with an OI-model is a 4-tuple $IP(OIM) := (I, L, instconc, instprop)$ where:*

- $I \subseteq E$ *is a set of instances,*
- L *is a set of literal values,* $L \cap E = \emptyset$,
- *function* $instconc : C \to 2^I$ *relates a concept with a set of its instances,*
- *partial function* $instprop : P \times I \to 2^{I \cup L}$ *assigns to each property-instance pair a set of instances related through given property.*

Each IO-model has an instance pool associated with it. Instance pool is constructed by specifying instances of different concepts and by establishing property instantiation between instances. Property instantiations must follow the domain and range constraints, and must obey the cardinality constraints.

Definition 4 (Root OI-model Structure). *Root OI-model is defined as a particular, well-known OI-model with structure* $ROIM := (\{ROOT\}, \emptyset)$. $ROOT$ *is the root concept, each other concept must subclass* $ROOT$ *(it may do so indirectly).*

Each other OI-model must include ROIM and thus gain visibility to the root concept. This is similar to object-oriented languages approaches – for example, in Java every class extends java.lang.Object class.

Definition 5 (Modularization Constraints). *If OI-model OIM imports some other OI-model* OIM_1 *(with elements are marked with subscript 1), that is, if* $OIM_1 \in INC(OIM)$ *must satisfy following modularization constraints:*

- $R_1 \subseteq R$, $C_1 \subseteq C$, $P_1 \subseteq P$, $T_1 \subseteq T$, $INV_1 \subseteq INV$, $H_{C1} \subseteq H_C$, $H_{P1} \subseteq H_P$,
- $\forall p \in P_1$ $domain_1(p) \subseteq domain(p)$,
- $\forall p \in P_1$ $range_1(p) \subseteq range(p)$,
- $\forall p \in P_1, \forall c \in C_1$ $mincard_1(c, p) \geq mincard(c, p)$,
- $\forall p \in P_1, \forall c \in C_1$ $maxcard_1(c, p) \leq maxcard(c, p)$,
- $I_1 \subseteq I$, $L_1 \subseteq L$,
- $\forall c \in C_1$ $instconc_1(c) \subseteq instconc(c)$,
- $\forall p \in P_1, i \in I_1$ $instprop_1(p, i) \subseteq instprop(p, i)$.

If an OI-model imports some other OI-model, it contains all information – no information may be lost. Modularization constraints just specify structural consequences of importing an OI-model. This is independent from the implementation – imported OI-models may be physically duplicated, whereas in other cases they may be linked.

Definition 6 (Meta-concepts and Meta-properties). *In order to introduce meta-concepts, the following constraint is stated:* $C \cap I$ *may, but does not need to be* $\emptyset$. *Also,* $P \cap I$ *may, but does not need to be* $\emptyset$.

The same element may be used as a concept and as an instance, or as a property and as an instance in the same OI-model.

Definition 7 (Lexical OI-model Structure). *Lexical OI-model structure LOIM is a well-known OI-model with the structure matching that presented in the Figure 1[5].*

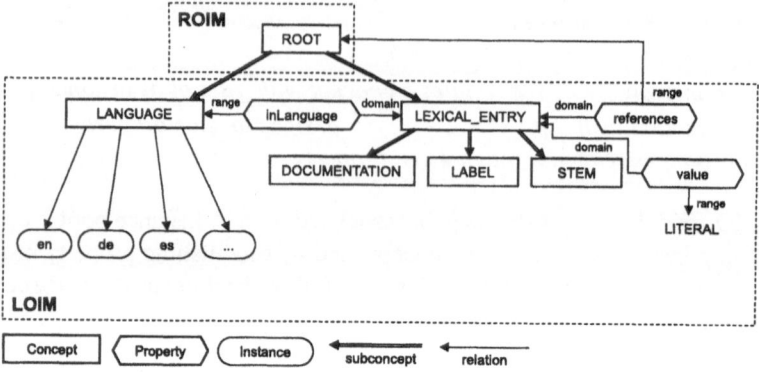

Fig. 1. Lexical OI-Model Structure

Lexical entries (instances of the LEXICAL ENTRY concept) reflect various lexical properties of ontology entities, such as a label, stem or textual documentation. There is an n : m relationship between lexical entries and instances, established by the property $references$. Thus, the same lexical entry may be associated with several elements (e.g. jaguar label may be associated with an instance representing a Jaguar car or a jaguar cat). The value of the lexical entry is given by property $value$, whereas the language of the value is specified through the $inLanguage$ property. Concept LANGUAGE represents the set of all languages, and its instances are defined by the ISO standard 639.

A careful reader may have noted that LOIM defines the references property to have the $ROOT$ concept as the domain. In another words, this means that each instance of $ROOT$ may have a lexical entry. This excludes concepts from having lexical entries – concepts are not instances, but are subclasses of root. However, it is possible to view each concept as an instance of some other concept (e.g. the $ROOT$ concept), and thus to associate a lexical value with it.

3.2   Denotational Semantics

Definition 8 (OI-model Interpretation). *An interpretation of an OI-model OIM is a structure* $I = (\Delta^I, C^I, L^I, I^I, P^I)$ *where:*

- Δ^I *is the domain set,*
- $C^I : C \to 2^{\Delta^I}$ *is a concept interpretation function that maps each concept to a subset of the domain set,*
- $L^I : L \to \Delta^I$ *is a literal interpretation function that maps each literal to a single element of a domain,*
- $I^I : I \to \Delta^I$ *is an instance interpretation function that maps each instance to a single element in a domain,*
- $P^I : P \to 2^{\Delta^I \times \Delta^I}$ *is a property interpretation function that maps each property into a relation over the domain set.*

---

[5] Instead a formal definition, we present a graphical view of LOIM because we consider it to be more informative.

An interpretation is a model of OIM if it satisfies the following properties:

- $\forall c \in C, i \in I \;\; i \in instconc(c) \Rightarrow I^I(i) \in C^I(c)$,
- $\forall c_1, c_2 \in C \;\; (c_1, c_2) \in H_C \Rightarrow C^I(c_1) \subseteq C^I(c_2)$,
- $\forall c \in C \;\; C^I(c) \subseteq C^I(ROOT)$,
- $\forall p_1, p_2 \in P \;\; (p_1, p_2) \in H_P \Rightarrow P^I(p_1) \subseteq P^I(p_2) \wedge$

$$\bigcup_{c_1 \in domain(p_1)} C^I(c_1) \subseteq \bigcup_{c_2 \in domain(p_2)} C^I(c_2) \wedge$$

$$\bigcup_{c_1 \in range(p_1)} C^I(c_1) \subseteq \bigcup_{c_2 \in range(p_2)} C^I(c_2),$$

- $\forall p \in P, i \in I \;\; instprop(p, i) \text{ is defined} \Rightarrow \forall c \in domain(p) \;\; I^I(i) \in C^I(c)$,
- $\forall p \in P, i_1, i_2 \in I \;\; i_2 \in instprop(p, i_1) \Rightarrow range(p) \neq L \wedge$
  $(I^I(i_1), I^I(i_2)) \in P^I(p) \wedge \forall c \in range(p) \;\; I^I(i_2) \in C^I(c)$,
- $\forall p \in P, i \in I, l \in L \;\; l \in instprop(p, i) \Rightarrow range(p) = L \wedge$
  $(I^I(i), L^I(l)) \in P^I(p)$,
- $\forall p \in P, c \in C \;\; mincard(c, p) \leq |\{\, y \mid (x, y) \in P^I(p) \wedge x \in C^I(c)\,\}| \leq$
  $maxcard(c, p)$,
- $\forall s \in S \;\; P^I(s) \text{ is a symmetric relation}$,
- $\forall p, ip \in P \;\; (p, ip) \in INV \Rightarrow P^I(ip) \text{ is an inverse relation of } P^I(p)$,
- $\forall t \in T \;\; P^I(t) \text{ is a transitive relation}$.

OIM is unsatisfiable it is doesn't have a model. Following information can be inferred from OIM, since it is true in all models of OIM:

- $H_C^* \subseteq C \times C$ *is the transitive closure of the concept hierarchy and is defined by*
  $C^I(c_1) \subseteq C^I(c_2) \Leftrightarrow (c_1, c_2) \in H_C^*(c_1, c_2)$,
- $H_P^* \subseteq P \times P$ *is the transitive closure of the property hierarchy and is defined by*
  $P^I(p_1) \subseteq P^I(p_2) \Leftrightarrow (p_1, p_2) \in H_P^*(p_1, p_2)$,
- $instprop^* : P \times I \rightarrow 2^{I \cup L}$ *is a partial function assigning to each property-instance pair a set of related instances or literals and is defined by*
  $i_2 \in instprop^*(p, i_1) \Leftrightarrow (I^I(i_1), I^I(i_2)) \in P^I(p)$ *and*
  $l \in instprop^*(p, i) \Leftrightarrow (I^I(i), L^I(l)) \in P^I(p)$.

This definition of semantics has the following interesting consequences:

- H_C, H_P and instprop represent explicit (ground) information in an OI-model. From this ground information and an interpretation, it is possible to infer H_C^*, H_P^* and instprop*, thus supporting the light-weight inference requirement.
- A subproperty of some property may add additional domain and range restrictions, but cannot remove existing ones.
- An interpretation is not associated with entities, but with concepts, instances and properties. As stated by the definition 6, it is possible for a single entity to be a concept and an instance at the same time. However, such an entity has two different interpretations – once an interpretation as a set (through function C^I), and once as an instance (through function I^I). These interpretations map concept resp. instance to completely different domain objects. The notion of spanning object unifies these different interpretations.

Definition 9 (Spanning Object). *Under interpretation I, for each entity $e \in E$ the spanning object is defined as a triple $SO(e) := (C^I(e), P^I(e), I^I(e))$ that combines different interpretations of the entity e.*

Returning to the example presented in section 2, information about species, ape species and apes may be modeled as in the Figure 2. In this model element APE plays a dual role. Once it is treated as a concept, in which it has the semantics of a set, and one can talk about the members of the set, such as ape1. However, the same object may be treated as an instance of the (meta-)concept SPECIES, thus allowing information such as the type of food to be attached to it. Both interpretations of the element SPECIES are connected by the spanning object.

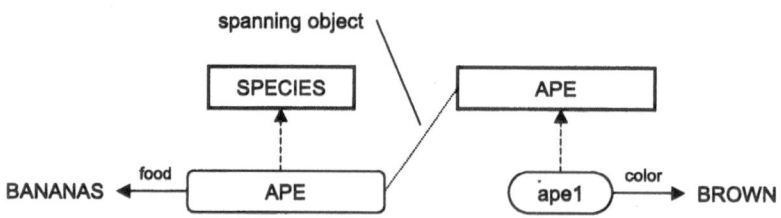

Fig. 2. Spanning Object Example

In [28] the problems of considering concepts as instances are well explained. A solution proposed in the paper is to isolate different domains of discourse. What is an concept in one domain, may become an instance in a higher-level domain. Elements from two domains are related through so called spanning objects. Our approach builds on that, however, without explicit isolation of domains of discourse.

This has subtle consequences on how an OI-model should be interpreted. It is not allowed to ask what does entity e represent in my model. Instead, one must ask a more specific question: what does e represent if it is considered as either a concept, a property or an instance. Before interpreting a model, the interpreter must filter out a particular view of the model – it is not possible to consider multiple interpretations simultaneously. However, it is possible to move from one interpretation to another – if something is viewed as a concept, it is possible to switch to a different view and to look at the same thing as an instance.

This approach is similar to the approach from F-Logic. In F-Logic it is possible to use the same symbol to denote the concept and an instance. Two occurrences are mutually independent, unless an explicit rule is created.

In [24] RDFS has been criticized for its infinite meta-modeling architecture that may under some circumstances cause Russell's paradox. A fixed four-layer meta-modeling architecture called RDFS(FA) has been proposed that introduces a strict separation between concepts and instances. Concepts are part of the ontology layer, whereas instances are part of the instance layer.

In our proposal we are less restrictive, as each entity may be assigned several different interpretations, but the modeling architecture is fixed to three layers (meta-model, ontology, instances). Thus, with the added flexibility in creation of models similar to that of RDFS, the Russell's paradox cannot happen.

3.3 Example

In this section we present an example OI-model. A common problem in knowledge management systems is to model documents classified into various topic hierarchies. We base the conceptualization of the domain on the DOCUMENT concept whose instances represent individual documents. Topics are modeled as instances of the TOPIC concept and the subtopic transitive property specifies that a topic is a subtopic of another topic. The has-author property between a document and an author determines the author of a document, and the has-written property is inverse to it. The has-topic property between a document and a topic determines the topic of the document. Individual persons are members of the PERSON concept. Two roles – RESEARCHER and AUTHOR – are subconcepts of the PERSON concept.

The hierarchy of topics is self-contained unit of information, so to allow its reuse, it is factored out into a separate OI-model called TOPICS. Similarly the personnel information is separated into OI-model called HR, and the document information is separated into OI-model called DOCUMENT. Within a company it doesn't make sense to reuse just the ontology of HR – all information about people is centralized in one place. Therefore, HR OI-model will contain both ontology definitions as well as instances. Similar arguments may be made for other OI-models.

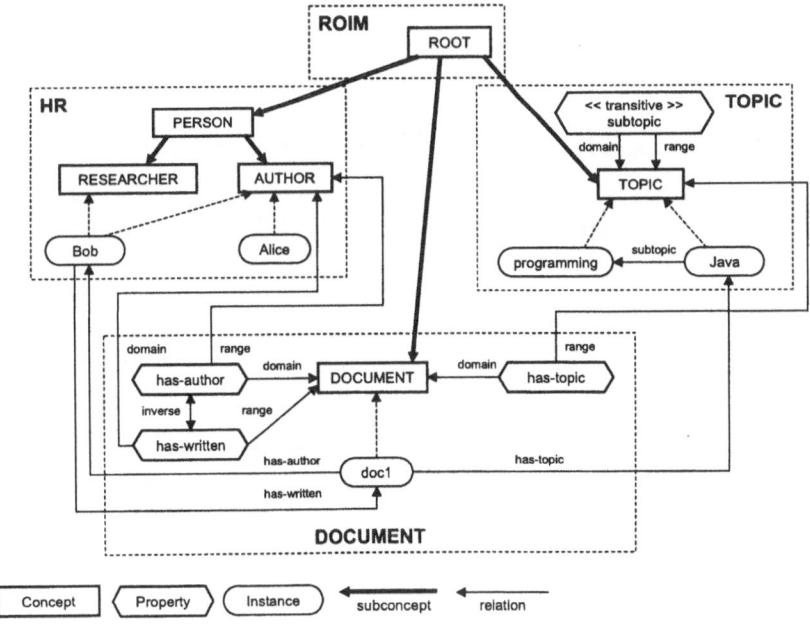

Fig. 3. Example Domain Ontology

Figure 3 shows the information graphically. In this figure the boxes represent concepts, rounded boxes represent instances, and hexagonal boxes represent property definitions. Please note that property instances are members of the OI-model that contains their label (e.g. has-author between doc1 and Bob is member of the DOCUMENT OI-model). Transitivity of the subtopic property has been specified by the ≪ transitive ≫ stereotype.

4   Implementation

In this section we present how our conceptual modeling approach is applied to KAON – a platform for developing and deploying semantics-driven enterprise applications.

4.1   KAON API within KAON Architecture

Our conceptual modeling approach defines the data model of KAON. The manipulation of the data model is performed through KAON API, a set of interfaces offering access and manipulation of ontologies and instances. A UML view of the KAON API is shown in figure 4.

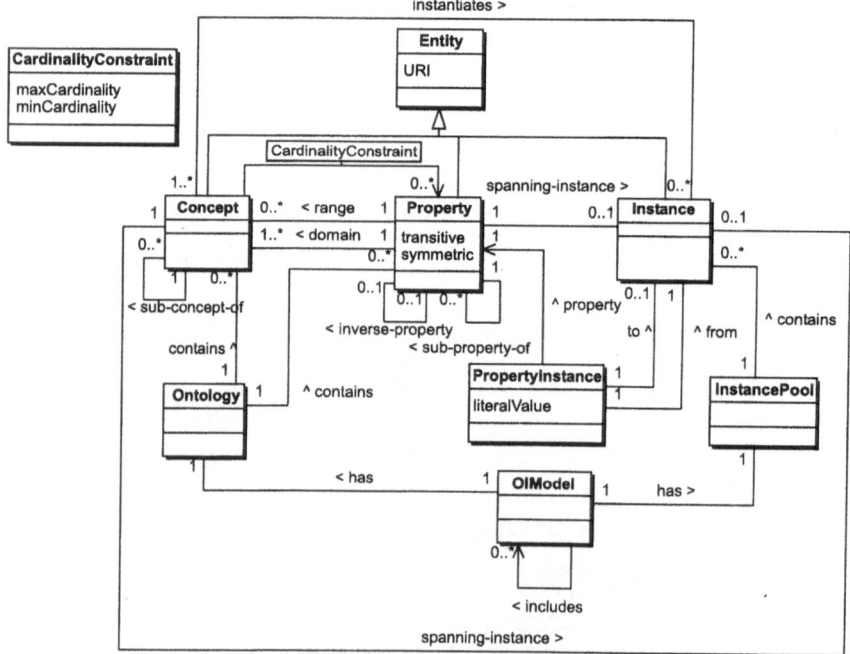

Fig. 4. UML View of KAON API

The API closely follows the definitions presented in 3.1. For example, an OI-model from definition 1 is represented as an OIModel object, that may include other OI-models according to modularization constraints from definition 5. Ontology and instance pool objects are associated with each OI-model.

KAON API is realized on top of the Data and Remote Services layer that is responsible for realizing typical business-related requirements, such as persistence, reliability, transaction and concurrency support. The layer is realized within an EJB application server and uses relational databases for persistence. Apart from providing abstractions for accessing ontologies, KAON API also decouples actual sources of ontology data by offering different API implementations for various data sources. Following API implementations may be used:

Implementation optimized for ontology engineering. A separate implementation of KAON API may be used for ontology engineering. This implementation provides efficient implementation of operations that are common during ontology engineering, such as concept adding and removal in a transactional way. The schema for this API implementation is described in the next subsection.

Implementation for RDF repository access. An implementation of KAON API based on RDF API[6] may be used for accessing RDF repositories. This implementation is primarily useful for accessing in-memory RDF models under local, autonomous operation mode. However, it may be used for accessing any RDF repository for which RDF API implementation exists. KAON RDF Server is such a repository that enables persistence and management of RDF models.

Implementation for accessing any database. An implementation of KAON API may be used to lift existing databases to the ontology level. To achieve that, one must specify a set of mappings from some relational schema to the chosen ontology, according to principles described in [27]. E.g. it is possible to say that tuples of some relation make up a set of instances of some concept, and to map foreign key relationships into instance relationships. After translations are specified, a OI-model is generated. When accessed, the model will translate the request into native database queries, thus fulfilling most requests directly within the database itself. Similarly, the OI-model will will translate ontology update requests to a series of updates to the underlying database. In such way the persistence of ontology information is obtained, while reusing well-known database mechanisms such as transactional integrity.

4.2   Database Schemas for Storing Conceptual Models

In previous section we discussed how KAON API isolates applications from actual data sources by offering various API implementations. In this section we describe possible database organizations for these API implementations.

---

[6] We adapted and reengineered Sergey Melnik's RDF API for our purposes, see http://www-db.stanford.edu/ melnik/rdf/api.html.

Generic Schema for Ontology Engineering. Ontology engineering is a cooperative consensus building process, during which several ontology modelers experiment with different modeling possibilities. As a result, concept adding, removal, merging and splitting of concepts are operations whose performance is most critical. Further, since several people are working on the same data set at once, it is important to support transactional ontology modification. At the same time, accessing efficiently large data sets is not so critical during ontology engineering. In order to support such requirements, a generic database schema, presented in Figure 5, is used. The schema is a straightforward translation of the definitions 1, 2 and 3 into relational model.

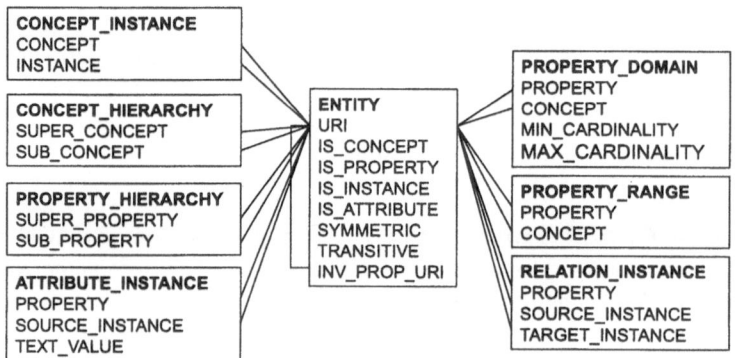

Fig. 5. Generic KAON Schema

The schema is organized around the ENTITY table, whose single row represents a concept, instance and property attached to a single URI. This structure has been chosen due to the presence of meta-class modeling – by keeping all information within one table it is possible to access all information about an entity at once.

Our schema design differs from the schema of RDF Query Language (RQL) [17] in one significant point. In the RQL implementation, to each concept an unary table is assigned whose rows identify the instances of some concept. Clearly, such schema will offer much better performance, but has a significant drawback – adding (removing) a concept requires creating (removing) a table in the database. Such operations are quite expensive and are not performed within a transaction. However, our goal is to design a system supporting users in cooperative ontology engineering, where creation and removal of concepts is quite common and must be transactional, while run-time performance is not critical.

Schema Optimized for Instance Storage. While it is possible to use the generic schema for run-time ontology storage and access as well, typically this will result in suboptimal performance. This is especially true for accessing instance data – joins are required for accessing a value of an instance property. After ontology engineering is finished and if it may be assumed that the ontology will not to change significantly, an optimized schema for storing concept extensions may be automatically generated. Such schema can then be accessed using the KAON API implementation for accessing any database. The process of optimized schema generation is inspired by well-known approaches for mapping objects to relational databases (e.g. [1]), and may be performed through following steps:

- For each concept c, create a table c_{EXT} for the extension of c and include a primary key equal to the instance URI.
- For each property p and $c \in$ domain(p), if maxcard(c, p) $\leq t$, where t is some predefined threshold, add attributes $p_1, ..., p_{maxcard}$ to c_{EXT} for storing values of the property. Attributes $p_1, ..., p_{mincard}$ mark as not nullable, others mark as nullable. If range(p) $\neq LITERAL$, create a foreign key constraint from each p_i to t_{EXT}, for each $t \in$ range(p).
- If maxcard(c, p) $> t$, where t is some predefined threshold, create a table p_{EXT} for the extension of p. Create a foreign key constraint from SOURCE_URI to s_{EXT} for each $s \in$ domain(p). If range(p) $= LITERAL$, include an attribute VALUE, otherwise an attribute TARGET_URI with a foreign key constraint to t_{EXT} for each $t \in$ range(p).
- If concept c is a subconcept of a, then create a foreign key constraint on URI from c_{EXT} to a_{EXT}.

Figure 6 shows the schema obtained through by applying the algorithm to example in Figure 3. For illustration purposes we assume that a single document can have at most one topic.

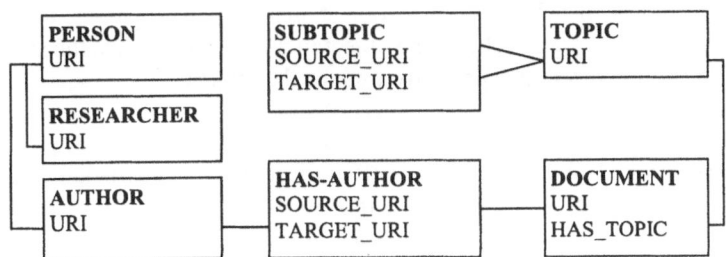

Fig. 6. Optimized KAON Schema

5   Related Work

In this section we discuss how our approach differs from other conceptual modeling approaches and tools available.

Entity-Relationship and Relational Modeling. Entity-relationship models are a tool for conceptual design of databases. Before implementation ER models are transformed into a logical model – nowadays this is the relational model. Evolving and implementing such models is more complex than if only one paradigm were used, since the conceptual and logical perspective must be kept in synchrony.

In our approach we isolate the mapping of the conceptual model to the logical one into a separate step, thus making the logical model hidden from the ontology user. The users of the ontology should use ontology in an ontology-natural way, while enjoying the benefits of relational database technology for information storage and management.

RDF and RDFS. It has been argued by many (e.g. [24]) that the definition of RDFS is very confusing, because RDFS modeling primitives are used to define the RDFS language itself. Currently there is no specification for modularization of RDF models. The handling of lexical information is very messy – languages can be attached to RDF model using XML attributes. Further, only 1:m relationships between lexical entries with elements of the ontology are possible.

UML. There have been proposals for using UML as an ontology modeling language (e.g. [8]). However, the reader may note that there are significant, but subtle, differences in standard object-oriented and ontology modeling. Classes of an object-oriented model are assigned responsibilities, which are encapsulated as methods. Often fictitious classes are introduced to encapsulate some responsibility (also known as pure fabrications [19]). On the other hand, ontologies don't contain methods so responsibility analysis is not important.

The fact that UML is targeted for modeling of software systems containing methods is far-reaching. For instance, an object cannot be an instance of more than one class and, if an object is created as an instance of some class, it is impossible for it to later become an instance of some other class. The class of an object is determined at the point when object is created.

In our conceptual modeling paradigm, however, these statements do not hold. Membership of an object in a class is often interpreted as statement that some unary predicate is true for this object. If properties of an object change as time passes, then the object should be reclassified. Membership of an object in different classes at the same time has the notion that some different aspects are true for that object.

Frame-based Languages. The ideas of object-oriented modeling paradigm on ontology modeling has resulted in creation of so called frame-based knowledge modeling languages, and F-logic [18] is one example. In F-logic, the knowledge is structured into frames (analogous to classes) that have different value slots (analogous to attributes). Frames may be instantiated, in which case slots are filled with values. F-logic introduces other advanced modeling constructs, such as expressing meta-statements about classes. Also it is possible to define Horn-logic rules for inferring new not explicitly present information.

Although F-logic is an expressive modeling language, the application of axioms makes F-logic often intractable and therefore unpractical for many of the aforementioned applications. Implementing inference procedures for Horn logic requires special data structures that are incompatible with data structures typically found in relational databases. In comparison, our conceptual model approach introduces the notion of lightweight inferences, which are intended to be easily implementable with existing systems.

Description Logics. A large body of research has been devoted to a subclass of logic-based languages, called description logics (a good overview is presented in [3]). Although description logics are founded on a well-research theory, as mentioned in [2], they have proven to be difficult to use due to the non-intuitive style of modeling. This is due to the mismatch between with predominant object-oriented way of thinking. For example, a common knowledge management problem is to model a set of documents that have topics chosen from a topic hierarchy. A typical solution is to create a DOCUMENT concept acting as a set of individual documents. However, modeling a topic hierarchy is not so straightforward, since it is not clear whether topics should be modeled as concepts or as individuals.

In object oriented systems it is not possible to relate instances of classes with classes. Therefore, a possible approach is to model all topics as members of the concept TOPIC, and to introduce subtopic transitive relation between topic instances. To an experienced object-oriented modeler, this solution will be intuitive.

On the other hand, in description logic systems, since topics are arranged in a hierarchy, the preferred modeling solution is to arrange all topics in a concept hierarchy to rely on the subsumption semantics of description logics[7]. Thus, each topic will be a subtopic of its superconcepts. However, two problems arise:

- If topics are sets, what are the instances of this set? Most users think of topics as fixed entities, and not as (empty and abstract) sets.
- How to relate some document, e.g. d1, to a particular topic, e.g. t1? Documents will typically have a role has-topic that should be created between d1 and topic instance. But, t1 is a concept, and there are no instances of t1. The solution is exists, but is not intuitive – we do not specify exactly with which instance of t1 is d1 related, but to say that it is related to "some" instance of t1. In the syntax of CLASSIC[8] description logic system, this is expressed as

$$(createIndividual\ d1\ (some\ \text{has-topic}\ t1)).$$

OIL. Another important ontology modeling language is OIL [12]. This language combines the intuitive notions of frames, clear semantics of description logics and the serialization syntax of RDF embedded within a layered architecture[9]. Core OIL defines constructs that equal in expressivity to RDF schema without the support for reification. Standard OIL contains constructs for ontology creation that are based on description logics. However, the syntax of the language hides the description logics background and presents a system that seems to have a more frame-based "feel". However, standard OIL doesn't support creation of instances. Instance OIL defines constructs for creation of instances, whereas heavy OIL is supposed to include the full power of description logics (it hasn't been defined yet). Despite its apparent frame-based flavor, OIL is in fact a description logic system, thus our comments about description logics apply to OIL as well. Although it supports ontology modularization, it doesn't have a consistent strategy for management of lexical information.

6   Conclusion

In this paper we present a conceptual modeling approach, currently being developed within KAON. Our main motivation is to come up with an conceptual modeling approach that can be used to build scalable enterprise-wide ontology-based application

---

[7] Thanks to Ian Horrocks for discussion on this topic.

[8] http://www.bell-labs.com/project/classic/

[9] http://oil.semanticweb.org/

using existing, well established technologies. In the paper we argue that existing approaches for conceptual modeling lack some critical features, making them unsuitable for application within enterprise systems. From the technical point of view, these features include scalability, reliability, concurrency and support for integration with existing data sources. From the conceptual modeling point of view, existing approaches lack the support for modularization and concept meta-modeling.

Based on the motivating usage scenarios, a set of requirements has been elicited. A mathematical definition of the ontology language has been provided, along with a denotational semantics. Finally, we have presented the current status of the implementation in the form of the KAON API – an API for management of ontologies and instances. Finally, we have shown how our conceptual modeling approach fulfills the requirements for integration with existing data sources.

In future, a query language for conceptual models is needed, perhaps based on paradigms found in description logics. Next, we want to investigate how to extend the set of axiom patterns (e.g. by allowing some form of free Horn-logic rules), by keeping required performance levels. Finally, we want to test the adequacy of the conceptual modeling approach and its implementation by testing its suitability and performance in our target applications.

References

1. S. W. Ambler. Mapping objects to relational databases: What you need to know and why. http://www-106.ibm.com/developerworks/library/mapping-to-rdb/, July 2002.
2. S. Bechhofer, C. Goble, and I. Horrocks. DAML+OIL is not Enough. In *SWWS-1, Semantic Web working symposium*, Stanford (CA), July 29th-August 1st 2001.
3. A. Borgida. Description logics are not just for the FLIGHTLESS-BIRDS: A new look at the utility and foundations of description logics. Technical Report DCS-TR-295, Department of Computer Science, Rutgers University, 1992.
4. E. Bozak, M. Ehrig, S. Handschuh, A. Hotho, A. Maedche, B. Motik, D. Oberle, R. Studer, G. Stumme, Y. Sure, S. Staab, L. Stojanovic, N. Stojanovic, J. Tane, and V. Zacharias. KAON – Towards An Infrastructure for Semantics-based E-Services. In *Proceedings of the 3rd International Conference on Electronic Commerce and Web Technologies - EC-Web 2002*, Aix-En-Provence, France, 2002. Springer-Verlag.
5. R. Breu, U. Hinkel, C. Hofmann, C. Klein, B. Paech, B. Rumpe, and V. Thurner. Towards a Formalization of the Unified Modeling Language. In *Proceedings of ECOOP'97 - Object-Oriented Programming, 11th European Conference*, LNCS 1241, Finland, June 1997. Springer Verlag.
6. D. Brickley and R.V. Guha. RDF Vocabulary Description Language 1.0: RDF Schema, http://www.w3.org/TR/rdf-schema/.
7. W. Conen and R. Klapsing. A Logical Interpretation of RDF. In *Journal of Electronic Transactions on Artificial Intelligence (ETAI), Area: The Semantic Web (SEWEB)*, volume 5, 2000.
8. S. Cranefield and M. Purvis. UML as an ontology modelling language. In *Proceedings of the Workshop on Intelligent Information Integration, 16th International Joint Conference on Artificial Intelligence (IJCAI-99)*, 1999.
9. C. Davis, S. Jajodia, P. Ng, and Eds. R. Yeh. Entity-Relationship Approach to Software Engineering. In *Proceedings of the International Conference on Entity-Relationship Approach*, North-Holland, 1983.

10. S. Decker, M. Erdmann, D. Fensel, and R. Studer. Ontobroker: Ontology Based Access to Distributed and Semi-Structured Information. In *Database Semantics - Semantic Issues in Multimedia Systems, Proceedings TC2/WG 2.6 8th Working Conference on Database Semantics (DS-8)*, Rotorua, New Zealand, January 1999.

11. A. Evans and A. Clark. Foundations of the unified modeling language. In *In 2nd Northern Formal Methods Workshop, Ilkley, electronic Workshops in Computing*. Springer-Verlag, 1998.

12. D. Fensel, I. Horrocks, F. van Harmelen, S. Decker, M. Erdmann, and M. Klein. OIL in a Nutshell. In *Knowledge Acquisition, Modeling, and Management, Proceedings of the European Knowledge Acquisition Conference (EKAW-2000)*, pages 1–16. Springer-Verlag, October 2000.

13. R. Fikes and D. McGuinness. An Axiomatic Semantics for RDF, RDF-S, and DAML+OIL (March 2001), http://www.w3.org/TR/daml+oil-axioms.

14. M. Fowler and K. Scott. *UML Distilled: A Brief Guide to the Standard Object Modeling Language (2nd Edition)*. Addison-Wesley Pub Co., August 1999.

15. P. Hayes. RDF Model Theory, http://www.w3.org/TR/rdf-mt/.

16. I. Horrocks. FaCT and iFaCT. In *Proceedings of the International Workshop on Description Logics (DL'99)*, pages 133–135, 1999.

17. G. Karvounarakis, S. Alexaki, V. Christophides, D. Plexousakis, and M. Scholl. RQL: A Declarative Query Language for RDF. In *Proceedings of The Eleventh International World Wide Web Conference (WWW'02)*, Hawaii, May 2002.

18. M. Kifer, G. Lausen, and J. Wu. Logical Foundations of Object-Oriented and Frame-Based Languages. *Journal of the ACM*, 42:741–843, July 1995.

19. C. Larman. *Applying UML and Patterns: An Introduction to Object-Oriented Analysis and Design and the Unified Process (2nd Edition)*. Prentice Hall, July 2001.

20. O. Lassila and R. R. Swick. Resource Description Framework (RDF) Model and Syntax Specification, http://www.w3.org/TR/REC-rdf-syntax/.

21. A. Maedche, B. Motik, N. Silva, and R. Volz. MAFRA — An Ontology MApping FRAmework in the Context of the Semantic Web. In *Workshop on Ontology Transformation at ECAI - 2002*, Lyon, France, July 2002.

22. A. Maedche, B. Motik, L. Stojanovic, R. Studer, and R. Volz. Managing Multiple Ontologies and Ontology Evolution in Ontologging. In *Proceedings of the Conference on Intelligent Information Processing, World Computer Congress 2002*, Montreal, Canada, 2002. Kluwer Academic Publishers.

23. W. Nejdl, H. Dhraief, and M. Wolpers. O-Telos-RDF: A Resource Description Format with Enhanced Meta-Modeling Functionalities based on O-Telos. In *Workshop on Knowledge Markup and Semantic Annotation at the First International Conference on Knowledge Capture (K-CAP'2001)*, Victoria, B.C., Canada, October 2001.

24. J. Pan and I. Horrocks. Metamodeling architecture of web ontology languages. In *Proceedings of the Semantic Web Working Symposium*, pages 131–149, July 2001.

25. G. Schreiber. Some challenge problems for the Web Ontology Language, http://www.cs.man.ac.uk/ horrocks/OntoWeb/SIG/challenge-problems.pdf.

26. S. Staab, M. Erdmann, and A. Maedche. Engineering Ontologies using Semantic Patterns. In *Proceedings of the IJCAI-2001 Workshop on E-Business & Intelligent Web*, Seattle, August 2001.

27. N. Stojanovic, L.Stojanovic, and R. Volz. A reverse engineering approach for migrating data-intensive web sites to the Semantic Web. In *Proceedings of the Conference on Intelligent Information Processing, World Computer Congress*, Montreal, Canada, 2002. Kluwer Academic Publishers.

28. C. A. Welty and D. A. Ferrucci. What's in an instance? Technical report, RPI Computer Science, 1994.

Towards Ontological Foundations for UML Conceptual Models

Giancarlo Guizzardi[1], Heinrich Herre[2], and Gerd Wagner[3]

[1] Centre for Telematics and Information Technology, Univ. of Twente
Enschede, The Netherlands
guizzard@cs.utwente.nl
[2] Institut fur Informatik, Univ. Leipzig and
Institute for Formal Ontology and Medical Information Science (IFOMIS)
herre@informatik.uni-leipzig.de
[3] Eindhoven Univ. of Technology, Faculty of Technology Management,
G.Wagner@tm.tue.nl,
http://tmitwww.tm.tue.nl/staff/gwagner

Abstract. UML class diagrams can be used as a language for expressing a conceptual model of a domain. We use the General Ontological Language (GOL) and its underlying upper level ontology, proposed in [1], to evaluate the ontological correctness of a conceptual UML class model and to develop guidelines for how the constructs of the UML should be used in conceptual modeling. In particular, we discuss the UML metaconcepts of classes and objects, power-types, association and aggregation/composition from an ontological point of view. We make some proposals of how to extend version 1.4 of the UML in order to obtain a more satisfactory treatment of aggregation.

1 Introduction

Conceptual modeling is concerned with identifying, analyzing and describing the essential concepts and constraints of a domain with the help of a (diagrammatic) modeling language that is based on a small set of basic meta-concepts (forming a meta-model). Ontological modeling, on the other hand, is concerned with capturing the relevant entities of a domain in an ontology of that domain using an ontology specification language that is based on a small set of basic, domain-independent ontological categories (forming an upper level ontology). While conceptual modeling languages are evaluated on the basis of their successful use in (the early phases of) information systems development, ontology specification languages and their underlying upper level ontologies have to be rooted in principled philosophical theories about what kinds of things exist and what are their basic relationships with each other.

Recently, it has been proposed that UML should be used as an Ontology Representation Language [2,3]. Moreover, in [2] it is argued that although UML lacks a precise definition of its formal semantics, this difficulty shall be overcome with the current

R. Meersman, Z. Tari (Eds.): CoopIS/DOA/ODBASE 2002, LNCS 2519, pp. 1100–1117, 2002.
© Springer-Verlag Berlin Heidelberg 2002

developments made by the precise UML community [4, 5]. We believe, however, that defining UML constructs only in terms of its mathematical semantics, although essential, it is not sufficient to make it a suitable ontology representation language. The position defended here is that, in order to model reality, a conceptual modeling language should be founded on formal upper-level ontologies. In other words, it should have both, formal and ontological semantics.

In this paper we use the General Ontological Language (GOL) and its underlying upper level ontology, proposed in [1], to evaluate the ontological correctness of a conceptual UML class model and to develop guidelines that assign well-defined ontological semantics to UML constructs.

Due to space limitations we cannot examine all UML constructs here. This paper discusses, in particular, the ontological meaning of the UML metaconcepts of *classes and objects*, *powertypes*, *association* and *part-whole* relations (*aggregation/composition*). The UML metaconcepts of *abstract classes* and *datatypes* are addressed in a companion paper [6].

In addition we propose some extensions to version 1.4 of the UML in order to obtain a more satisfactory treatment of *part-whole* relations. Section 2 introduces the basic elements that form the upper level ontology of GOL. Section 3 uses this upper level ontology to define the real-world semantics for UML class diagrams for the purpose of conceptual modeling. Section 4 discusses some related work. Finally, section 5 presents some conclusions.

2 Basic Elements of the Upper Level Ontology of GOL

The basic elements of the upper level ontology of GOL can be visually described by means of the UML class diagram shown in Figure 1.

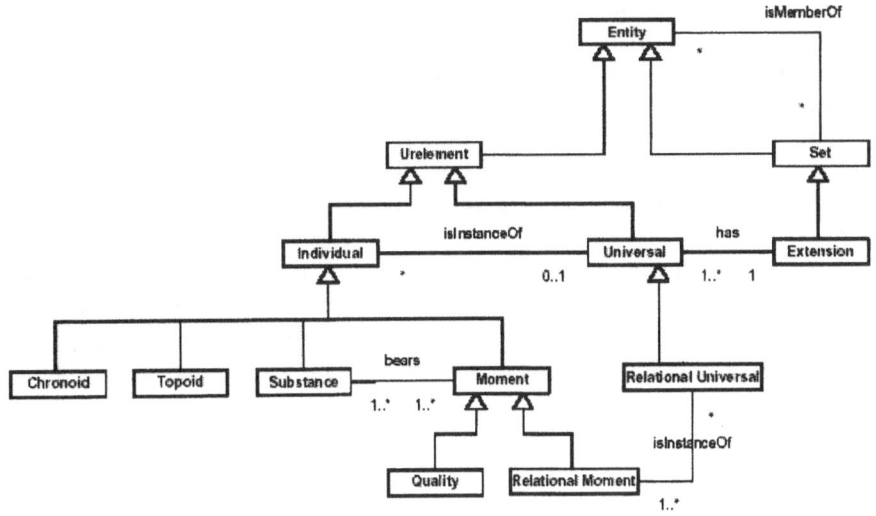

Fig. 1. A UML Class Diagram describing the basic concepts of GOL.

2.1 Urelements and Sets

The main distinction of the GOL-ontology is between *urelements* and *sets*. We assume the existence of both urelements and sets in the world and presuppose that both the impure sets and the pure sets constructed over the urelements belong to the world. This implies, in particular, that the world is closed under all set-theoretical constructions. Urelements are entities which are not sets. They form an ultimate layer of entities without any set-theoretical structure in their build-up. Neither the membership relation nor the subset relation can unfold the internal structure of urelements. In GOL, urelements are classified into two main categories: individuals and universals. There is no urelement being both an individual and a universal. This is expressed in GOL by the following axioms:

$$\forall x \ (Ur(x) \leftrightarrow Ind(x) \lor Univ(x)) \tag{U1}$$

$$\neg \exists x \ (Ind(x) \land Univ(x)) \tag{U2}$$

2.2 Individuals

Individuals may be substances, moments, chronoids, or topoids.

Substances and Moments. A *substance* is that which can exist by itself, or does not need another entity in order to exist. Typical examples of substances are: an individual person, a house, the moon, a car. Every substance is founded on matter. Substances come into existence because the matter is formed in various ways which give rise to pieces separated in more or less stable ways from their surroundings and possessing qualities of different sorts.

A *moment*[1] is an individual which can only exist in other individuals (in the way in which, for example an electrical charge can exist only in some conductor). Typical examples of moments are: a color, a connection, a purchase order. Moments have in common that they are all dependent on substances. Some moments are one-place qualities, for example color or temperature. But there are also *relational moments* – for example flight connections or purchase orders – which depend on several substances.

The inherence relation i – sometimes called ontic predication – glues moments to the substances which are their bearers. For example it glues your smile to your face, or the charge in a specific conductor to the conductor itself. Substances must bear moments, and moments must inhere in substances. This is axiomatically expressed as follows:

---

[1] The origin of the notion of moment lies in the theory of individual accidents developed by Aristotle in his Metaphysics and Categories. An accident is an individualized property, event or process which is not a part of the essence of a thing. We here use the term "moment" in a more general sense and do not distinguish between essential and inessential moments.

$$\textbf{Subst(x)} \rightarrow \exists y \; (\textbf{Mom(y)} \wedge i(y,x)) \tag{SM1}$$

$$\forall x \; (\textbf{Mom(x)} \rightarrow \exists y \; (\textbf{Subst(y)} \wedge i(x,y))) \tag{SM2}$$

Chronoids and Topoids. Chronoids and topoids are instances of the universals *Time* and *Space*, respectively. Chronoids can be understood as temporal durations, and topoids as spatial regions having a certain mereotopological structure. On one version of the theory chronoids and topoids have no independent existence; they depend for their existence in every case on the situations which they frame. Every substance x has a certain maximal temporal extent, a chronoid which we denote by *lifetime(x)*. The substance x exists during *lifetime(x)*. Also, every moment m inhering in x has a *lifetime*, which is such that *lifetime(m)* $\leq$ [2] *lifetime(x)*. Moreover, if n is a relational moment connecting substances $x_1,..., x_k$, then *lifetime(n)* $\leq$ *lifetime(x_i)*, for i ranging from 1 to k.

2.3 Universals

A universal is an entity that can be instantiated by a number of different individuals which are similar in some respect. Following Aristotle, we assume that the universals exist in the individuals (*in re*) but not independently from them. As a consequence, in order to exist, universals must possess instances.

For every universal U there is a set *Ext(U)*, called its extension, containing all instances of U as elements. It is, however, not the case that every set is the extension of a universal (there is no such axiom in GOL).

There are two kinds of universals that are of particular interest: **quality universals**, such as color and weight, and **relational universals**, such as flight connection ('...is connected with...') or purchase ('...purchases...from...'). Every universal has an intension which, in GOL, is captured by means of an axiomatic specification, i.e., a set of axioms that may involve a number of other universals representing its essential features. A particular form of such a specification of a universal U, called elementary specification, consists of a number of universals $U_1,...,U_n$ and corresponding functional relations $R_1, ...,R_n$ which attach instances from the U_i to instances of U, expressed by the following axiom:

$$\forall a \; (a::U \rightarrow \exists e_1...\exists e_n \bigwedge_{i \leq n} (e_i ::U_i \wedge R_i(a,e_i)))$$

The universals $U_1,...,U_n$ used in an elementary specification are called features. A special case of an elementary specification is a quality specification where $U_1,...,U_n$ are quality universals and the instances of U are substances.

---

[2] In context of this article, the symbols $<$ and $\leq$ represent the *part-of and reflexive part-of* relations, respectively. These relations are discussed in section 2.5.

Humans, as cognitive subjects, grasp universals by means of concepts that are in their head and cannot capture the universals completely, but only as approximate views.

Meta-universals of Finite Order. Ordinary universals are universals of first order and the instances of universals of (n+1)-th order are universals of n-th order. Instantiation relations of n-th order are denoted by $::_n$, and the relation $::_1$ is also notated as $::$. Since no universal is a set, it follows that all universals (of whatever order) are urelements.

2.4 Relations and Relational Universals

Relations are entities which glue together other entities. Without relations the world would fall into many isolated pieces. Every relation has a number of relata or arguments which are connected or related by it. The number of a relation's arguments is called its arity. Relations can be classified according to the types of their relata. There are relations between sets, between individuals, and between universals, but there are also cross-categorical relations for example between urelements and sets or between sets and universals.

We divide relations into two broad categories, called material and formal, respectively. The relata of a material relation are mediated by individuals which are called relators. Relators are individuals with the power of connecting entities; a flight connection, for example, is a relator that connects airports.

A formal relation is a relation which holds between two or more entities directly – without any further intervening individual. Examples of formal relations are: 5 *is greater than* 3, this day is *part-of* this month, and N *is subset of* Q.

Holding Relation and Facts. One important formal relation is called the holding relation. If r is a relator connecting the entities $a_1,...,a_n$, $n \geq 1$, then we say that r, $a_1,...,a_n$ (in this order) stand to each other in the holding relation, symbolically $h(r, a_1,...,a_n)$. The fact that h holds directly success to block the obvious regress which would arise if a new material relation were needed to tie h to r, $a_1,...,a_n$, and so on. Holding holds directly.

If r connects (holds of) the entities $a_1,...,a_n$, then this yields a new individual which is denoted by $\langle r: a_1,...,a_n \rangle$. Individuals of this latter sort are called *material facts*.

A material fact $\langle r: a_1,...,a_n \rangle$ has a duration, which depends on the lifetime of the relator r. We write $\langle r: a_1,...,a_n ; t \rangle$ if t is a chronoid which is a part of the lifetime of r, i.e. this fact exists at least during the chronoid t.

Relator Universals. A relator universal is a universal whose instances are relators. For every relator universal R there exists a set of facts, denoted by *facts(R)*, which is defined by the instances of R and their corresponding arguments. We assume the axiom that for every relator universal R there exists a factual universal $F = F(R)$ whose extension equals the set *facts(R)*. Take, for example, the relator universal *Conn* whose instances are individual flight connections. Then we may form a factual universal *F(Conn)* having the meaning 'An airport X is connected to an airport Y' whose instances are all facts of the form $\langle c{:}a,b \rangle$, where c is an individual connection and a, b are individual airports.

Formal Relations. A formal relation is a relation which holds between two or more entities directly – without any further intervening individual. A formal relation may be either an extensional relation (i.e. a set) or it may be given by a relational universal (having an intension and an extension). If R is a formal relation and $[a,b]{:}R$ then $\langle R{:}a,b \rangle$ is called a formal fact.

2.5 Basic Ontological Relations

We can distinguish a number of basic ontological relations which form an important part of the upper level ontology of GOL. The first and most familiar one is set-theoretic membership, denoted by $\in$. Further basic relations include:

- the proper and reflexive part-of relations, denoted by $<$ and $\leq$
- the contextual part-of relation, denoted by $<_U$, where the universal U denotes the context
- the holding relation h
- the inherence relation, denoted by i
- the instantiation relation, denoted by $::$
- the relational instantiation, denoted by $:$

We discuss some of these basic ontological relations in more detail.

Instantiation. The symbol $::$ denotes the instantiation relation. Its first argument is an individual, and its second a universal. If $x{::}u$, then u is a certain time- and space-independent pattern of features and x is an individual in which this pattern of features is realized. x might be, for instance, a molecule of DNA, u a pattern of features shared by all exactly similar molecules, where the notion of exact similarity is determined by the granularity and point of view of genetic science. The symbol $:$ denotes the relational instantiation. Its first argument is a list of entities, and its second a relation universal. Note, that the components of the instantiating list are not necessarily individuals.

Part-Whole Relation. There are many different part-whole relations between individuals. They can be classified by means of the axioms they satisfy. All part-whole relations are asymmetric and transitive. In addition to formal part-whole relations, there are also material part-whole relations. Part-whole relations may be either proper (denoted by $<$) or reflexive (denoted by $\leq$). We use the following definitions:

$$ov(x,y) =_{df} \exists z \, (z \leq x \wedge z \leq y) \qquad \textbf{(overlap)}$$

$$x \leq y =_{df} (x = y \vee x < y) \qquad \textbf{(reflexive part-whole)}$$

A proper part-whole relation $<$ is a strict partial order, that is, it satisfies the following axioms:

$$\neg \, x < x \qquad \textbf{(irreflexivity)}$$

$$x < y \rightarrow \neg y < x \qquad \textbf{(asymmetry)}$$

$$x < y \wedge y < z \rightarrow x < z \qquad \textbf{(transitivity)}$$

In addition, it may satisfy some of the following axioms:

$$x < y \rightarrow \exists z \, (z \leq y \wedge \neg ov(z,x)) \qquad \textbf{(weak supplementation)}$$

$$\neg x \leq y \rightarrow \exists z \, (z \leq x \wedge \neg ov(z,y)) \qquad \textbf{(supplementation)}$$

$$(z < x \wedge z < y) \rightarrow (x \leq y \vee y \leq x) \qquad \textbf{(exclusivity)}$$

Contextual Part-Whole Relation. The contextual part-whole relation $x <_U y$ has the meaning: "U is a universal and x is a part of y in the context of U". Briefly, if x is a U-part of y in this sense, then x and y are parts of instances of U and $x \leq y$. But more is involved, since again the notions of granularity and point of view are an issue. We propose the following axiom: for every universal U there are universals $U_1,...,U_n$ such that $x <_U y$ implies that x, y are instances of one of the U_i's and every instance of one of the U_i's is part of an instance of U.

Consider the following example, taken from the domain of biology. Let T be the biological universal whose instances are those organisms called trees. Then $x <_T y$ describes the part-whole relation based on the granularity of the context of whole trees. A biologist is interested in describing the structure of trees only in terms of parts of a certain minimal size. He is not interested in atoms or molecules. There is a finite number of universals $\{U_1,...,U_n\}$ by which the biologically relevant parts of trees are demarcated. All such parts of trees are either instances of some U_i, $1 \leq i \leq n$, or they can be decomposed into a finite number of parts, each of which satisfies this condition. Examples of universals U_i within the granularity of the tree context would be branch of a tree, leaf of a tree, trunk of a tree, root of a tree, and so on.

We have the following axioms:

$$\forall xyU \, (x <_U y \rightarrow Univ(U) \wedge x < y) \qquad \textbf{(CPW1)}$$

$$\forall xyzU \, (x <_U y \wedge y <_U z \rightarrow x <_U z) \qquad \textbf{(CPW2)}$$

3 Ontological Foundations of the UML

In the sequel, we refer to the *OMG UML Specification 1.4*, when we cite text in italics using page references in the form of [p.2-31].

For simplicity, we simply say *conceptual model* when we mean a conceptual model of a domain in the form of a *UML class model*. Whenever the context is clear, we omit the name space prefix UML and simply say 'object', 'class', etc., instead of 'UML object', 'UML class', etc.

3.1 Classes and Objects

In the UML, "an object represents a particular instance of a class. It has identity and attribute values." While in the UML objects are instances of classes, individuals are instances of universals in GOL.

A *"Class describes a set of Objects sharing a collection of Features, including Operations, Attributes and Methods, that are common to the set of Objects."* [p.2-26] *"The model is concerned with describing the intension of the class, that is, the rules that define it. The run-time execution provides its extension, that is, its instances."* [p.3-35] Attributes come with associated data types. Since in conceptual modeling, the behavior of objects is normally not taken into consideration, we exclude the 'operations' and 'methods' of an object from our discussion.

We may observe a direct correspondence between universals and classes of a certain kind, as stated in the following principles.

Principle 1 (Class) In a conceptual model, any universal U of the domain may be represented as a concrete class C_U. Conversely, for all concrete classes (of a conceptual model of the domain) whose instances are basic objects or links (representing individuals), there must be a corresponding first-order universal in the domain.

Principle 2 (Attribute) If there is an elementary specification for a universal U, then any feature of it may be represented as an attribute of the corresponding class C_U in a conceptual model of the domain.

In a conceptual model, any individual of the domain that is an instance of a universal may be represented as an object (or link) of the class representing the universal. Notice that classes are not sets. In general, two classes C_1 and C_2 with identical extensions, $Ext(C_1) = Ext(C_2)$, even if they have the same set of attributes, are not equal, $C_1 \neq C_2$.

3.2 Powertype

"A Powertype is a user-defined metaelement whose instances are classes in the model." A powertype is a special class, designated with the stereotype 'powertype'. It

represents a higher-order universal of order n whose instances are universals of order $n-1$. Unfortunately, the UML does not provide higher-order '*isInstanceOf*' relationships.

Figure 2 shows an example of a *powertype* represented in UML. In this figure, a Pigeon is a first-order universal whose instances are particular pigeons. However, individual breeds of birds, such as Pigeon and Peafowl, are also instances of the second-order universal Breed. In GOL, these two instantiation relations can be represented as $x::Pigeon::_2Breed$, where x is a particular pigeon.

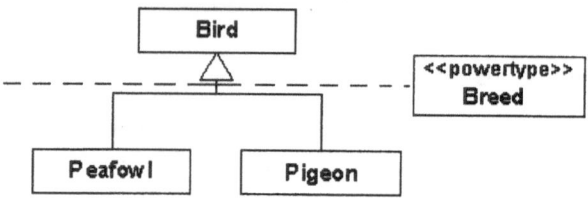

Fig. 2. Example of a second-order universal *Breed* represented in UML as a powertype.

3.3 Association

In the UML, the ER concept of a relationship type is called association. *"An association defines a semantic relationship between classifiers. The instances of an association are a set of tuples relating instances of the classifiers. Each tuple value may appear at most once."* [p. 2-19] *"An instance of an Association is a Link, which is a tuple of Instances drawn from the corresponding Classifiers."* [p. 2-20]

The OMG UML Specification is somehow ambiguous in defining associations. An association is primarily considered to be a 'connection', but, in certain cases (whenever it has 'class-like properties'), an association may be a class: *"An association class is an association that is also a class. It not only connects a set of classifiers but also defines a set of features that belong to the relationship itself and not any of the classifiers."* [p.2-21]

An association A between the classes $C_1,...,C_n$ of a conceptual model can be understood in GOL as a relation R between the corresponding universals $U_1,...,U_n$ induced by the relational universal whose extension consists of all relational moments corresponding to the links of A. Let $\phi(a_1,...,a_n)$ denote a condition on the individuals $a_1,...,a_n$. Then

$$[a_1...a_n]: R_A\,(U_1...U_n) \leftrightarrow \bigwedge_{i \leq n} aj::Ui \wedge \phi\,(a_1...a_n)$$

An association is called *material* if there is a relator universal F such that the condition ϕ is obtained from F as follows:

$$\phi(a_1...a_n) \leftrightarrow \exists k\,(k::F \wedge h(k,a_1...a_n))$$

An example of a ternary material association is *purchFrom* corresponding to a relator universal *Purchase* whose instances are individual purchases. These individual purchases connect three individuals: a *person*, say *John*, an individual *good*, e.g. the book *Speech Acts by Searle*, and a *shop*, say *Amazon*. Thus,

$$[\text{John, SpeechActsBySearle, Amazon}]:R_{\text{purchFrom}}(\text{Person, Good, Shop})$$

since *John::Person*, *SpeechActsBySearle::Good* and *Amazon::Shop*, and there is a specific purchase event *p::Purchase* such that

$$h(\text{p, John, SpeechActsBySearle, Amazon}).$$

We obtain the following definition for the triple $[a_1, a_2, a_3]$ being a link of the association *purchFrom* between *Person*, *Good* and *Shop*:

$$[a_1, a_2, a_3]:R_{\text{purchFrom}}(\text{Person, Good, Shop}) \leftrightarrow a_1::\text{Person} \wedge a_2::\text{Good} \wedge a_3::\text{Shop}$$
$$\wedge \exists p \ (p::\text{Purchase} \wedge h(\text{p}, a_1, a_2, a_3))$$

3.4 Aggregation and Composition

"An association may represent an aggregation; that is, a whole/part relationship. In this case, the association-end attached to the whole element is designated, and the other association-end of the association represents the parts of the aggregation. Only binary associations may be aggregations. Composite aggregation is a strong form of aggregation, which requires that a part instance be included in at most one composite at a time and that the composite object has sole responsibility for the disposition of its parts. This means that the composite object is responsible for the creation and destruction of the parts. In implementation terms, it is responsible for their memory allocation. If a composite object is destroyed, it must destroy all of its parts. It may remove a part and give it to another composite object, which then assumes responsibility for it. If the multiplicity from a part to composite is zero-to-one, the composite may remove the part, and the part may assume responsibility for itself, otherwise it may not live apart from a composite." [p.2–66]

"A shareable aggregation denotes weak ownership; that is, the part may be included in several aggregates and its owner may also change over time. However, the semantics of a shareable aggregation does not imply deletion of the parts when an aggregate referencing it is deleted. Both kinds of aggregations define a transitive, antisymmetry relationship; that is, the instances form a directed, non-cyclic graph. Composition instances form a strict tree (or rather a forest)." [p.2–67]

A part-whole relation is by default expressed as an aggregation in the UML. Otherwise, if the parts in the part-whole relation are non-shareable, then the relation is expressed as a composition (black-diamond) – the use of composition implies the maximum cardinality of 1 w.r.t. the whole. An example of part-whole relation with shareable parts is the relation between researchers and research groups (researchers can be part of several research groups) – figure 2(a) Conversely, the relation between a person and one of his organs is an instance of a non-shareable part-whole relation (a human organ cannot be shared by more than one human body).

3.4.1 Mandatory Aggregates and Mandatory Parts

Asides from the distinction between shareable and non-shareable parts, UML allows to express the distinctions between mandatory and optional aggregates and between mandatory and optional parts.

A *mandatory aggregate* refers to whether a part can exist without being part of an aggregate of certain class. This is the case, for instance, of a human heart that must be attached to a human body but not necessarily the same body forever. This is represented in UML by a minimum cardinality of (at least) *1* in the aggregate side. This example also depicts the notion of *mandatory parts*: refers to whether a whole can exist without having a part of a certain class – a human body must have a human heart but not necessarily the same heart for the entire life. This is represented in UML by a minimum cardinality of (at least) *1* in the part side of the relation. Figure 3(b) depicts this example as a non-shareable part-whole relation with mandatory aggregate and mandatory part.

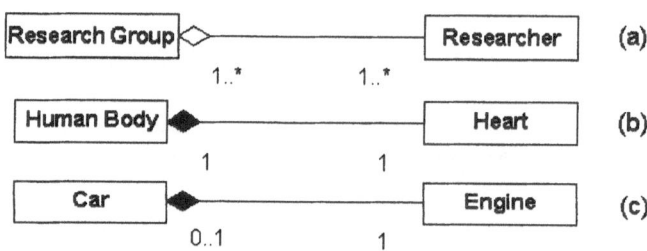

Fig. 3. A part-whole relation with sharable part; Fig 3.b part-whole relation with non-sharable and mandatory part and mandatory whole; Fig 3.c part-whole relation with non-sharable and mandatory part and optional whole.

3.4.2 Inseparable and Essential Parts

The concept of Inseparable parts refers to whether an object can exist without being part of a particular whole. UML is quite imprecise when dealing with the difference between Inseparable Parts and Mandatory aggregates. The specification prescribes that "*the composite object is responsible for creation and destruction of its parts*" and that, "*if the composite is destroyed if must destroy all its parts*". Let w be a whole and p be one of its parts, this means that, *lifetime(p) ≤ lifetime(w)* and that the destruction of whole implies the destruction of the part.

Lifetime dependency is a characteristic of part-whole relations with inseparable parts – i.e. parts that are dependent always on the same whole. In this sense, we disagree with examples such as the one used in [7] to justify the existence of separable parts but that share same destruction as the whole: "*a car wheel is independent of the car but if the wheel is in the car during the car's destruction then it is also destroyed*". In this case, the wheel is clearly separable from the car, it just happened to be the same event that caused the destruction of both objects (if the wheel was separated from the car the car's destruction would not propagate to the wheel). Nonetheless, the UML specification also states *"it [the whole] may remove a part and give it to another composite object, which then will be responsible for it"* which give us the clearly impression that the composition notation with one-to-one cardinality refers to mandatory wholes but not to inseparable parts. This is confirmed by the statement *"if the multiplicity from the part to composite is zero-to-one, the composite may remove the part, and the part may assume responsibility for itself, otherwise it may not live apart from a composite"*. In sum, the UML composition notation means: (i) zero-to-one cardinality – non-shareable separable parts with optional aggregate – figura 3.c; (ii) one-to-one cardinality: non-shareable separable parts but with mandatory aggregate – figura 3.b; In both cases, there is no necessary relation between the chronoids *lifetime(p)* and *lifetime(w)*.

We can conclude that in its current form (version 1.4), UML does not allow to express the distinctions between *separable* and *inseparable* Parts. Likewise, it also does not allow expressing the distinctions between *essential* and *nonessential* parts. The concept of *essential* part refers to whether an object can exist without having a particular object as a part. An example is relation between the car and its chassis. The removal of the car chassis breaks the identity criteria of the car. The human brain in the relation with a Person is an example of an essential part (actually this is an example of both essential and inseparable part) – figure 4.

In order to represent these two important ontological distinctions we therefore propose to extend UML by adding two Boolean-valued tags for the part association-end of an aggregation: *inseparable* and *essential*.

Proposal 1 (Aggregation with Inseparable and Essential Parts). UML 1.4 has to be extended by adding two predefined Boolean-valued tags for the part association end of an aggregation: *inseparable* and *essential*, whose default value is false.

A lifetime dependency between a part and a whole, referred to in the sentence *"If a composite object is destroyed, it must destroy all of its parts"* [p.2-66], is only in effect in the case of an inseparable part. In the case of a merely mandatory aggregate, it would be admissible to reassign the part when the mandatory aggregate is destroyed.

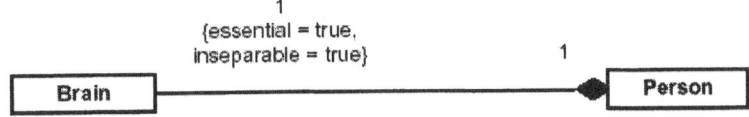

Fig. 4. An example of a composition with parts that are inseparable and essential.

According to the notation we propose, a composition with parts that are inseparable and essential would be expressed as in Fig. 4. As this example seems to suggest, one may be inclined to assume that an inseparable part is always non-shareable. But this is not the case, as the example in Fig. 5 shows.

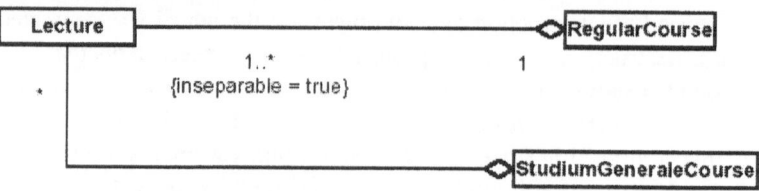

Fig. 5. An example of an aggregation with shareable parts that are inseparable: although a specific lecture of a regular course is an inseparable part of that course, it may be shared with any number of studium generale courses.

3.4.3 The Scope of Transitivity

Among the primary characteristics of part-whole relations, the most discussed one is transitivity. In the domain of philosophy and mathematics there is almost a consensus that transitivity should be included in the basic axiomatization of a part-whole theory [1,8,9]. Likewise, in Object Oriented modeling, several authors propose transitivity as a primary characteristic of aggregation [10]. More specifically, In UML, *"both kinds of aggregations define a transitive, antisymmetric relationship"*. We can say, for example, that the hand is part of the arm, the arm is part of the human body, ergo, the hand is part of the human body. However, there are also various authors who claim that transitivity does not always hold. As an example, the brain is part of person, this person is part of a Research Group but it sounds strange to state that the person's brain is part of the Research Group.

On the basis of linguistic and cognitive studies, Winston, Chaffin and Herrmann (WCH) proposed a distinction among various sorts of part-whole relationships, with the aim to overcome these apparent transitivity paradoxes [11]. The main idea was capture the different ways in which parts contribute to the structure of the whole. This framework has been further refined in [12] by isolating three basic kinds of wholes: *masses*, *collections* and *complexes* (whose parts are respectively called quantities, members and components). *Masses* are homogeneous aggregates which are similar to its quantities (*homeromeous*) – e.g. an amount of sugar. *Complexes* are characterized by structural (configurational) relationships among the parts – e.g. the human body and its parts. Finally, in *collections* a part is regard not to have an essential role w.r.t. the whole – e.g. a tree is part of forest, a person is part of research group [7].

In [10], it is claimed, *"as long as we are careful to keep a single sense of part, it seems that the part-whole relation is always transitive. However, when we inadvertently mix different meronymic relations problems with transitivity arise"*. In [7], Henderson-Sellers and Barbier disagree with this statement showing the following counter-example: *"I am member of a club (collection) and my club is a member of an International body (collection). However, it does not follow that I am a member of this International body since this only has clubs as members, not individuals"*.

In the example given above, a *research group* is a sort of social system, i.e. an instance of whole whose parts comprise a set of socially linked persons. The *brains* of such individuals are parts of the latter but do not qualify as members or components of a social system because they do not enter independently in social relations: only entire persons can enter independently in those type of social relations. In other words, the set of parts of a *research group* is not the collection of all its parts but the collection of its atoms, i.e. the collection of those parts that are *socially coupled*. This particular notion of atomic composition is expressed in GOL in terms of the contextual part-whole relation. In this case, if x is part of y in context of a *research group*, then either x is an instance of the universal *Person* or x can be decomposed in finite parts that are instances of *Person* (e.g. a subgroup is composed of members which are instances of Person, thus, a subgroup can be considered a part of a research group).

In [1] and in [13], a distinction is made between a formal part-whole relation that is unrestrictedly transitive and material part-whole relations whose transitivity is scoped to a certain context. Moreover, according to [13], absolute transitivity is a characteristic that only makes sense in a mathematical perspective, for the axiomatic definition of the theory. In the ontological and cognitive sense, part-whole relations should only be interpreted w.r.t. a certain context.

The distinction between formal and material (contextual) part-whole relations seems to be a much more elegant solution to the apparent transitivity paradox – transitivity always holds for contextual part-whole relations (axiom *CPW2*). We therefore propose to add the concept of a contextual part-whole relation, as described in section 2.5, to the UML. For defining the context of such a relation, we propose to use the UML construct of a *package*.

Proposal 2 (Contextual Aggregation). UML 1.4 has to be extended by adding a contextual aggregation construct. Such an aggregation is defined within a package, and any part class participating in it must also be in that package. Transitivity, then, only holds between the contextual aggregations within a package, but not across packages.

4   Related Work

The upper level ontology of GOL is under development at the Institute for Formal Ontology and Medical Information Science at the University of Leipzig, Germany. The project is a collaboration between philosophers, linguists and other cognitive scientists and computer and information scientists. For a comparison between GOL an other upper-level ontologies, such as the IEEE Standard Upper Ontology [14], KIF [15], Sowa [16], Russel and Norvig [17] and LADSEB [18,19], one should refer to [1].

The goal of this paper is to use the upper level ontology of GOL to analyze the ontological correctness of a conceptual UML class models and to develop guidelines that assign well-defined ontological semantics to UML constructs. For this reason, we limit our discussion of related work w.r.t. this point .

The approach found in the literature that is closest to the one presented here is the approach by Evermann and Wand [20] and, Weber, Storey and Weber [21]. In these two articles, the authors report their results in mapping common constructs of conceptual modeling to an upper level ontology. Their approach is based on the BWW ontology, a framework created by Wand and Weber on the basis of the original meta-physical theory developed by Mario Bunge in [8] and [13].

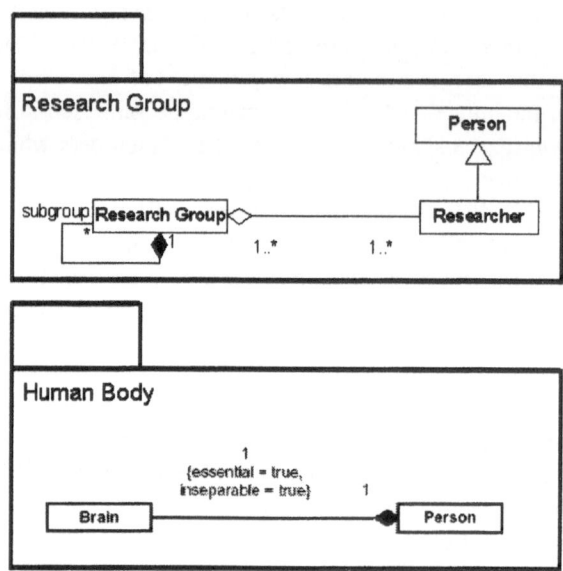

Fig. 6. The same individual researcher participating in different contextual part-whole relations.

The concepts of substance (in GOL) and of thing in BWW are both based on the Aristotelian idea of substance: (i) an essence which makes a thing what it is; (ii) that which remains the same through changes; (iii) that which can exist by itself, i.e., which does not need a 'subject' in order to exist. In [20], it is proposed that *"only substantial entities in the world are modeled as objects"* (Rule 1). As a direct conse-quence, classes in UML should only represent universals that denote substances. Con-versely, in our approach, concrete classes can represent any type of universals. In [20], instantiation relations of higher-order are not considered, therefore, no guideline for the UML concept of *powertype* is provided.

In BWW, a thing has necessarily at least one property. Likewise, a property exists only in connection with things. A property whose existence depends only on a single thing is called an intrinsic property (e.g. the height of a person). A property that de-pends on two or more things is called a mutual property (e.g. being a student is a mu-tual property between a person and an educational institution). Again the concepts of BWW's intrinsic and mutual properties can be directly related to the concepts of qual-ity and relational moments in GOL. Nevertheless, in BWW only things possess prop-erties. As a consequence, a property cannot have properties. This dictum leads to the following modeling principle: *"Associations should not be modeled as classes"*, (Rule 7) in [20]. Contrary to this principle, GOL allows associations, representing relational universals, to have attributes and to participate in second or higher-order associations.

Thus, while the BWW approach prohibits to use association classes in conceptual modeling, they are allowed in GOL.

In [22], Opdahl et al. uses BWW ontology as a foundation for a conceptual framework defining a taxonomy of part-whole relations in terms of its primary (e.g. reflexivity, asymmetry and transitivity), secondary (shareability, mutability, separability, etc...) and consequent properties (e.g. ownership, propagation of operations, encapsulation). Moreover, the article analyses the different kinds of part-whole relations in terms of ontological expressiveness, i.e., if the proposed concepts are meaningful in terms of real-world semantics. Finally, some UML stereotypes are proposed in order to provide syntactical representations to the proposed ontological distinctions.

In our approach we are interested on those properties that have meaning in terms of ontological correspondence. For that reason, we have chose to ignore properties that are relevant only in terms of implementation decision (e.g. ownership, propagation of operations, encapsulation, by-value or by-reference, used or not used). In terms of the primary characteristics of part-whole relations there are two points of disagreement between the two proposals:

Transitivity: Opdahl et. al. claim that transitivity is valid only for certain types of relation and, thus, should not be considered as a primary characteristic. As we have discussed in section 3.4, proposal 2, both in the ontological and cognitive sense, part-whole relations should only be interpreted w.r.t. a certain context. Moreover, contextual part-whole relations are always transitive. In our approach we, thus, consider transitivity w.r.t. a certain context as a primary characteristic of part-whole relations.

Emergent and Resultant properties: both in [21] and [22] it is proposed that a thing should only be modeled as an aggregate if we are interested in modeling its emergent and resultant properties. In [22], it is presented a UML class diagram with the classes *Department* and *Employee*. In this example they state that in the problem domain all *Departments* are aggregates of *Employees*. However, it is claimed unacceptable to add a part-whole between these two classes since the diagram would comprise no resultant/emergent property of Department relative to Employee. We strongly disagree with this view and we thing that this restriction arises from a misinterpretation of Bunge's ontology. According to Bunge, every aggregate will certainly have emergent and resultant properties. However, it is important to notice that his Ontology makes explicit the distinction between the properties possessed by a thing and the representations of these properties, namely attributes. According to Bunge, there are no bare individuals, i.e., things without properties: a thing posses at least one substantial property, even if we humans are not or cannot be aware of them. Humans get in contact with the properties of things exclusively via the things attributes, i.e. via a chosen representational view of its properties. In sum, we agree that emergent/resultant properties are basic characteristics of part-whole relations, in the sense they are present in all of them. What we do not agree is to use the existence of resultant/emergent attributes as a criteria for representation of part-whole relationships. In other words, these properties will always exist but we do not have always to be interested in them and sometimes we cannot even be aware of them. Additionally, we think that the representation of these attributes is not a necessary condition for one to benefit from the representation of part-whole relations in terms of communicability, understanding and problem-solving.

5 Conclusions

The development of a well-grounded, axiomatized upper level ontology is an important step towards the definition of real-world semantics for conceptual modeling diagrammatic languages. In this paper we use the General Ontological Language (GOL) and its underlying upper level ontology to evaluate the ontological correctness of UML as a conceptual modeling language. Moreover, we develop guidelines that assign well-defined ontological semantics to UML constructs. In particular, we have focused on the UML metaconcepts of *classes and objects*, *powertypes*, *association* and *part-whole* relations (*aggregation/composition*).

Except from the distinction between shareable and non-shareable parts, the UML allows to express the distinctions between mandatory and optional aggregates and between mandatory and optional parts. However, in its current form (UML 1.4), it does not allow to express the distinctions between separable and inseparable parts, and between essential and nonessential parts. We therefore propose some extensions to version 1.4 of the UML in order to obtain a more satisfactory treatment of *part-whole* relations. Additionally, we define in terms of *GOL's contextual part-whole relation*: (i) a solution to the transitivity paradox of part-whole relations; (ii) a representation of contextual part-whole relations in UML.

Acknowledgements. We are grateful to Barbara Heller and João Paulo Andrade Almeida for fruitful discussions and for providing valuable input to the issues of this article.

References

1. Degen, W., Heller B., Herre H., Smith, B.: GOL: Towards an axiomatized upper level ontology. In Barry Smith and Nicola Guarino, editors, Proceedings of FOIS'01, Ogunquit, Maine, USA, October 2001. ACM Press.
2. Cranefield, S., Purvis M.: UML as an ontology modelling language, Proceedings of the Workshop on Intelligent Information Integration, 16th International Joint Conference on Artificial Intelligence (IJCAI-99), Germany, University of Karlsruhe (1999) 46-53.
3. Baclawski K. et al.: Extending UML to Support Ontology Engineering for the Semantic Web, Fourth International Conference on the Unified Modeling Language: UML 2001, Toronto, Canada, 2001.
4. Overgaard G.: A formal approach to relationships in the Unified Modeling Language. In Manfred Broy, Derek Coleman, Tom S. E. Maibaum, and Bernhard Rumpe, editors, Proceedings PSMT'98 Workshop on Precise Semantics for Modeling Techniques. Technische Universitat Munchen, TUM-I9803, 1998.

5. Evans A., France R., Lano K., Rumpe B.: Developing the UML as a formal modelling notation. In Pierre-Alain Muller and Jean Bezivin, editors, Proceedings of UML'98 International Workshop, Mulhouse, France, June 3 - 4, 1998, pages 297–307. ESSAIM, Mulhouse, France, 1998.
6. Guizzardi, G., Herre, H., Wagner G.: On the General Ontological Foundations of Conceptual Modeling. In Proceedings of 21th International Conference on Conceptual Modeling (ER 2002). Springer-Verlag, Berlin, Lecture Notes in Computer Science.
7. Henderson-Sellers, B., Barbier F.: What Is This Thing Called Aggregation, proceedings of Technology of Object-Oriented Languages and Systems Europe'99, Nancy, France, IEEE Computer Society Press, pp. 236-250, June 7-10, 1999 (ISBN: 0-7695-0275-X)
8. Bunge M.: Treatise on Basic Philosophy. Vol. 3. Ontology I. The Furniture of the World. D. Reidel Publishing, New York, 1977.
9. Varzi. A.C.: Parts, wholes, and part-whole relations: The prospects of mereotopology. J. of Data and Knowledge Engineering, 20:259–286, 1996.
10. Artale A., Franconi E., Guarino N., Pazzi L.: 1996. Part-Whole Relations in Object-Centered Systems: an Overview. Data and Knowledge Engineering, 20(3): 347-383.
11. Winston M.E.; Chaffin R.; Herrman D.: A taxonomy of part-whole relations, Cognitive Science 11 (1987), pp.417-444.
12. Iris M.; Litowitz B.; Evens M.: Problems of the part-whole relation. In M.Evens (Ed.) Relational Models of the Lexicon, Cambridge University Press (1988), pp.261-288.
13. Bunge M.: Treatise on Basic Philosophy, vol. 4: Ontology II: A World of Systems, Reidel Publishing Company, Dordrecht, Holland, 1979.
14. SUO: http://suo.ieee.org.
15. Genesereth, M. R., Fikes, R.E.: Knowledge Interchange Format, Version 3.0, Reference Manual, Logic Group Report Logic-92-1, Computer Science Department, Stanford University.
16. Sowa J.F.: Knowledge Representation: Logical, Philosophical, and Computational Foundations, Brooks Cole Publishing Co., Pacific Grove, CA, 1999.
17. Russell, S., Norvig, P.:Articial Intelligence, Prentice Hall, 1995.
18. Gangemi, A., Guarino, N., Masolo, C., Otramari, A.: Understanding Top-Level Ontological Distinctions. Technical Report 04/2001,LADSEB-CNR.
19. Guarino, N.: Formal Ontology and Information Systems, in: N. Guarino (ed.) Formal Ontology in Information Systems Proceedings of FOIS' 98, Trento, Italy, Amsterdam, IOS-Press.
20. Evermann J., Wand Y.: Towards ontologically based semantics for UML constructs. In H.S. Kunii, S. Jajodia, and A. Solvberg, editors, Proceedings of ER 2001, pages 354–367. Springer-Verlag, 2001.
21. Wand Y.,Storey V.C., Weber R.: An ontological analysis of the relationship construct in conceptual modeling. ACM Transactions on Database Systems, 24(4):494–528, December 1999.
22. Opdahl A., Henderson-Sellers, B., Barbier F.: Ontological Analysis of whole-part relationships in OO-models, Information and Software Technology 43 (2001), pp. 387-399.

Towards Secure Object Oriented Database Systems

Yun Bai

School of Computing and Information Technology
University of Western Sydney
Locked Bag 1797
Penrith South DC NSW 1797, Australia
ybai@cit.uws.edu.au

Abstract. In this paper, we propose a formal approach for securing object oriented database systems. We combine the specification of object oriented database with security policies and provide its formal syntax and semantics. The properties in the inheritance of authorizations in object oriented database system is also investigated in detail.

Keywords: Intelligent systems, logical reasoning, object oriented database security, security policy

1 Introduction

The object oriented database system is one of the active trends of today's database systems. Hence data protection in object oriented databases has became an active research area recently. In this paper, we address authorization specification for securing object oriented database system from a formal logic point of view. Our formalization characterizes the model-theoretic semantics of object oriented databases and authorizations associated with them. A direct advantage of this approach is that we can formally specify and reason about authorizations on data objects without loosing inheritance and abstraction features of object oriented databases.

In the rest of the paper, we first propose a logic language $\mathcal{L}^o$ for specifying object oriented database and then extend it to $\mathcal{L}^{oa}$ to include authorizations associated with it. These languages have a high level syntax and their semantics shares some features of Kifer *et al*'s F-logic [4]. The semantics of the language is defined in such a way that both the inheritance property in an object oriented database (OODB) and authorization rules among different data objects can be formally justified. Then we investigate some properties in the inheritance of authorizations on objects, Finally we present the conclusions of the paper.

2 A Formal Specification for Object Oriented Database

Now we propose a language $\mathcal{L}^o$ for specifying object oriented database and its syntax and semantics [1].

R. Meersman, Z. Tari (Eds.): CoopIS/DOA/ODBASE 2002, LNCS 2519, pp. 1118–1131, 2002.

2.1   Syntax of $\mathcal{L}^o$

We use a language $\mathcal{L}^o$ to specify object oriented database. The *vocabulary* of $\mathcal{L}^o$ consists of:

1. A finite set of *object variables* $\mathcal{OV} = \{o, o_1, o_2, \cdots\}$ and a finite set of *object constants* $\mathcal{OC} = \{O, O_1, O_2, \cdots\}$. We will simply name $\mathcal{O} = \mathcal{OV} \cup \mathcal{OC}$ as *object set*.
2. A finite set $\mathcal{F}$ of function symbols as *methods* where each $f \in \mathcal{F}$ takes objects as arguments and maps to an object or a set of objects[1]. The set of *object constructors* are included in $\mathcal{F}$ since *object constructors* are a special kind of *method*.
3. Auxiliary symbols $\Rightarrow$ and $\mapsto$.

An *object proposition* is an expression of the form

$$O \text{ has method } f_1(\cdots) \Rightarrow \Pi_1,$$
$$\cdots,$$
$$f_m(\cdots) \Rightarrow \Pi_m,$$
$$f_{m+1}(\cdots) \mapsto \Pi_{m+1},$$
$$\cdots,$$
$$f_n(\cdots) \mapsto \Pi_n. \tag{1}$$

In (1) O is an object from $\mathcal{O}$ and $f_1, \cdots, f_m, \cdots, f_n$ are function symbols (as object constructors). Each function symbol f takes objects as arguments and maps to some Π that is an object or a set of objects.

In an object proposition, a method of the form $f(\cdots) \Rightarrow \Pi$ indicates that the arguments of f represent the types of actual objects that should be taken in any instance of this object proposition, and f returns a set of types of the resulting object/objects. It is important to note that in our context, the type of an object is also an object. We should also mention that as a special case, if a function symbol is 0-arity, then this function just presents a simple attribute of the associated object. On the other hand, a method of the form $f(\cdots) \mapsto \Pi$ indicates that f takes actual objects as arguments and returns an actual object or a set of objects. For example, the following is an object description about a PhD student:

$$PhDStd \text{ has method } name \Rightarrow String,$$
$$area(Staff) \Rightarrow String,$$
$$firstdegree \mapsto \text{'}Bachelor\text{'},$$

where $name \Rightarrow String$ represents that the type of name is a string, and method $area$ takes type $Staff$ (i.e. another object, eg. the student's supervisor) as a parameter and returns a type of string to indicate the research field, while $firstdegree \rightarrow \text{'}Bachelor\text{'}$ simply expresses that every PhD student should hold

---

[1] For the sake of simplicity, we also call an element in $\mathcal{O}$ as an *object*.

a Bachelor degree. An object proposition is called *ground* if there is no object variable occurrence in it.

An *isa proposition* of $\mathcal{L}^o$ is an expression of one of the following two forms:

$$O \text{ isa member of } C, \tag{2}$$

$$O \text{ isa subclass of } C, \tag{3}$$

where O and C are objects from $\mathcal{O}$, i.e., O and C may be object constants or variables. Clearly, *isa propositions* (2) and (3) explicitly represent the hierarchy relation between two objects. An isa proposition without containing any object variables is called *ground isa proposition*.

We call an object or isa proposition a *data proposition*. A data proposition is *ground* if there is no object variable occurrence in it. If the detail of a data proposition is not interested in the context, we usually use notation ϕ to denote the data proposition. We assume that any variable occurrence in a data proposition is universally quantified.

A *constraint proposition* is an expression of the form

$$\phi \text{ if } \phi_1, \cdots, \phi_k, \tag{4}$$

while $\phi, \phi_1, \cdots, \phi_k$ are data propositions. A constraint proposition represents some relationship among different data objects. The intuitive meaning of (4) is that if $\phi_1, \cdots, \phi_k$ are present in the current database state, then so is ϕ. With this kind of proposition, we can represent some useful deductive rules of the domain in our database. This will be illustrated later using some examples. A *database proposition* is an object proposition, isa proposition, or constraint proposition.

Now we can formally define our object oriented database as follows.

Definition 1. *An* object oriented database *(or simply called a database)* Σ *is a triplet* (Γ, Δ, Ω), *where* Γ *is a finite set of ground object propositions,* Δ *is a finite set of ground isa propositions, and* Ω *is a finite set of constraint propositions.*

Example 1. Consider a simplified domain about research people in a computer science department. The structure of such domain is illustrated in Figure 1.

In Figure 1, line arrows indicate subclass relations while dotted line arrows indicate membership relations in the database.

Using language $\mathcal{L}^o$, the database $\Sigma = (\Gamma, \Delta, \Omega)$ is specified as follows:
(1) the set of ground object propositions Γ consists of:

$$ResPeople \textbf{ has method } name \Rightarrow String,$$
$$age \Rightarrow Integer,$$
$$firstdegree \mapsto \text{'}Bachelor\text{'}, \tag{5}$$
$$Postgraduate \textbf{ has method } id \Rightarrow Integer,$$
$$degree \Rightarrow String,$$
$$area(Staff) \Rightarrow String, \tag{6}$$

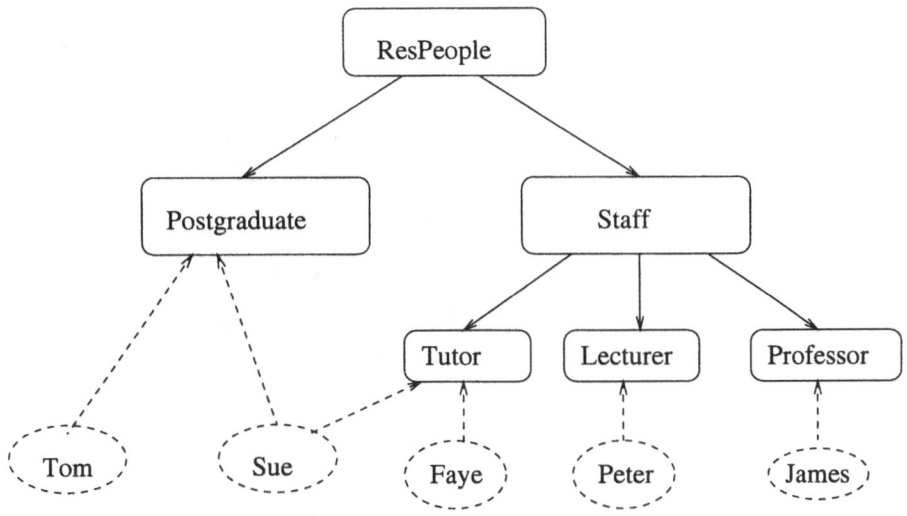

Fig. 1. A research people database.

$$Staff \textbf{ has method } research \Rightarrow \{String, \cdots, String\},$$
$$teaching \Rightarrow \{String, \cdots, String\},$$
$$salary \Rightarrow String, \qquad (7)$$
$$Tutor \textbf{ has method } topsalary \mapsto \text{ '\$45,000'}, \qquad (8)$$
$$Lecturer \textbf{ has method } topsalary \mapsto \text{ '\$58,000'}, \qquad (9)$$
$$professor \textbf{ has method } topsalary \mapsto \text{ '\$85,000'}, \qquad (10)$$
$$Tom \textbf{ has method } name \mapsto \text{ 'Tom'},$$
$$age \mapsto 21,$$
$$id \mapsto 96007,$$
$$degree \mapsto \text{ 'Master'},$$
$$area(Peter) \mapsto \text{ 'Database'}, \qquad (11)$$
$$Sue \textbf{ has method } name \mapsto \text{ 'Sue'},$$
$$age \mapsto 24,$$
$$id \mapsto 95012,$$
$$degree \mapsto \text{ 'PhD'},$$
$$area(James) \mapsto \text{ 'Security'},$$
$$salary \mapsto \text{ '\$38,000'}, \qquad (12)$$
$$Faye \textbf{ has method } name \mapsto \text{ 'Faye'},$$
$$age \mapsto 30,$$
$$research \mapsto \{\text{ 'Networking'}\},$$
$$teaching \mapsto \{\text{ 'CS1', 'CS2'}\},$$

$$salary \mapsto \text{ '\$43,000'}, \qquad (13)$$

$$\textit{James } \textbf{has method } name \mapsto \text{ 'James'},$$
$$age \mapsto 42,$$
$$research \mapsto \{\text{ 'Security', 'Networking'}\},$$
$$Teaching \mapsto \{\text{ 'Networking'}\},$$
$$salary \mapsto \text{ '\$78,000'}, \qquad (14)$$

(2) the set of ground isa propositions Δ consists of:

$$\textit{Tom } \textbf{isa member of } \textit{Postgraduate}, \qquad (15)$$
$$\textit{Sue } \textbf{isa member of } \textit{Postgraduate}, \qquad (16)$$
$$\textit{Sue } \textbf{isa member of } \textit{Tutor}, \qquad (17)$$
$$\textit{Faye } \textbf{isa member of } \textit{Tutor}, \qquad (18)$$
$$\textit{Ann } \textbf{isa member of } \textit{Lecturer}, \qquad (19)$$
$$\textit{James } \textbf{isa member of } \textit{Professor}, \qquad (20)$$
$$\textit{Postgraduate } \textbf{isa subclass of } \textit{ResPeople}, \qquad (21)$$
$$\textit{Staff } \textbf{isa subclass of } \textit{ResPeople}, \qquad (22)$$
$$\textit{Tutor } \textbf{isa subclass of } \textit{Staff}, \qquad (23)$$
$$\textit{Lecturer } \textbf{isa subclass of } \textit{Staff}, \qquad (24)$$
$$\textit{Professor } \textbf{isa subclass of } \textit{Staff}, \qquad (25)$$

and (3) Ω consists of two constraint propositions:

$$y \textbf{ isa member of } \textit{Staff}$$
$$\textbf{if } x \textbf{ isa member of } \textit{Postgraduate},$$
$$x \textbf{ has method } area(y) \mapsto z, \qquad (26)$$
$$y \textbf{ has method } research \mapsto \{..., z, ...\}$$
$$\textbf{if } x \textbf{ isa member of } \textit{Postgraduate},$$
$$x \textbf{ has method } area(y) \mapsto z, \qquad (27)$$

where x, y and z are object variables, and notation $\{..., z, ...\}$ means that set $\{..., z, ...\}$ includes element z which is of interest.

In database Σ, we assume that objects $Integer$ and $String$ be *primitive* object constants and do not require explicit descriptions. That is, we omit isa propositions like 21 **isa member of** $Integer$ and $'Tom'$ **isa member of** $String$ from our database.

Our database also presents necessary inheritance properties among different objects. For instance, since object Tom is a member of $Postgraduate$, it should inherit method $firstdegree \mapsto 'Bachelor'$. The semantics of inheritance will be described in next subsection. Finally, in Σ, Γ and Δ represent *explicit* data object descriptions and hierarchical relations among these objects, while Ω describes constraints of the domain which characterize some *implicit* data objects and their properties. By using these rules in Ω and facts in $\Gamma \cup \Delta$, we actually can derive new data objects with some clear properties. For instance, in the above database, we do not give explicit description about object *Peter*. But from propositions (11) and (15) about object *Tom*, we can derive the facts that *Peter* is a member of *Staff* and has a research field *'Database'*.

Due to space limit, the semantics of $\mathcal{L}^o$ will not be described in here, it can be referred at [1].

3   Inheritance Properties of Object Oriented Database

In this section, we explore inheritance properties of object oriented databases under our framework. First, from the specification [1], it is easy to prove the *method projection* and *method aggregation* with respect to an object.

Proposition 1. *(Method Projection) Let I be a structure of $\mathcal{L}^o$ and ϕ a ground object proposition with the form:*

$$O \text{ has method } f_1(\cdots) \hookrightarrow \Pi_1,$$
$$\cdots,$$
$$f_n(\cdots) \hookrightarrow \Pi_n,$$

where $\hookrightarrow$ is a symbol for $\Rightarrow$ or $\mapsto$. Then $I \models \phi$ implies that $I \models O$ has method $f_1(\cdots) \hookrightarrow \Pi_1, \cdots, I \models O$ has method $f_n(\cdots) \hookrightarrow \Pi_n$.

Proposition 2. *(Method Aggregation) Let I be a structure of $\mathcal{L}^o$ and ϕ_1 and ϕ_2 be ground object propositions with forms:*

$$O \text{ has method } f_1(\cdots) \hookrightarrow \Pi_1,$$
$$\cdots,$$
$$f_n(\cdots) \hookrightarrow \Pi_n,$$

and

$$O \text{ has method } f_1'(\cdots) \hookrightarrow \Pi_1',$$
$$\cdots,$$
$$f_m'(\cdots) \hookrightarrow \Pi_m',$$

respectively, where $\hookrightarrow$ is a symbol for $\Rightarrow$ or $\mapsto$. Then $I \models \phi_1$ and $I \models \phi_2$ imply that $I \models \phi$, where ϕ is a ground object proposition of the form:

$$O \text{ has method } f_1(\cdots) \hookrightarrow \Pi_1,$$
$$\cdots,$$
$$f_n(\cdots) \hookrightarrow \Pi_n,$$
$$f_1'(\cdots) \hookrightarrow \Pi_1',$$
$$\cdots,$$
$$f_m'(\cdots) \hookrightarrow \Pi_m'.$$

Although the above two properties are quite obvious, they are actually useful for our reasoning about object methods. Method projection allows us to focus on some particular method of an object when needed, while method aggregation allows us to get an object proposition associated with all of its methods.

Theorem 1. *(Subclass Inclusion) If $I \models O$ isa member of C_1, and $I \models C_1$ isa subclass of C_2, then $I \models O$ isa member of C_2.*

Theorem 2. *(Subclass Type Inheritance) The following results hold.*

(i) *If $I \models O$ has method $f(Q_1, \cdots, Q_k) \Rightarrow S$ and $I \models R$ isa subclass of O, then $I \models R$ has method $f(Q_1, \cdots, Q_k) \Rightarrow S$.*

(ii) *If $I \models O$ has method $f(Q_1, \cdots, Q_i, \cdots, Q_k) \Rightarrow S$ and $I \models Q_i'$ isa subclass of Q_i, then $I \models O$ has method $f(Q_1, \cdots, Q_i', \cdots, Q_k) \Rightarrow S$.*

(iii) *If $I \models O$ has method $f(\cdots) \Rightarrow S$ and $I \models S$ isa subclass of R, then $I \models O$ has method $f(\cdots) \Rightarrow R$.*

In Theorem 2, (i) and (ii) follow directly from the anti-monotonicity constraint on mapping $\Rightarrow_I$ and (iii) follows from the upward-closure of $\Rightarrow_I$ as defined in Definition 2. The following two propositions directly follow from the specification [1].

Proposition 3. *(Subclass Value Inheritance) If $I \models O$ isa subclass of C and $I \models C$ has method $f(\cdots) \mapsto \Pi$, then $I \models O$ has method $f(\cdots) \mapsto \Pi$.*

Proposition 4. *(Membership Type and Value Inheritance) The following results hold.*

(i) *If $I \models O$ isa member of C and $I \models C$ has method $f(\cdots) \Rightarrow \Pi$, then $I \models O$ has method $f(\cdots) \Rightarrow \Pi$.*

(ii) *If $I \models O$ isa member of C and $I \models C$ has method $f(\cdots) \mapsto \Pi$, then $I \models O$ has method $f(\cdots) \mapsto \Pi$.*

Example 2. Let us return to the research people domain example described earlier. From previous propositions and theorems, it is easy to verify that every class and object inherits all of the type and value methods from all of its superclasses. For instance, we have the following results:

$\Sigma \models Tom$ **has method** $firstdegree \mapsto$ *'Bachelor'*,
$\Sigma \models Sue$ **has method** $topsalary \mapsto$ *'\$45,000'*, and
$\Sigma \models Tutor$ **has method** $name \Rightarrow String$.

Also note that object *Peter* is only implicitly described in Σ. But from constraint propositions (26) and (27), we can further derive

$\Sigma \models Peter$ **isa member of** $Staff$, and
$\Sigma \models Peter$ **has method** $research \mapsto \{\cdots, \text{'Database'}, \cdots\}$.

4   Authorization Specification in Object Oriented Database

In this section, we will extend our formal language $\mathcal{L}^o$ to $\mathcal{L}^{oa}$ which is used in the specification of authorization in object-oriented databases. First let us consider the following requirements in the specification of access policies in object oriented databases.

1. If a subject (user) has an access right to a complete object (class), then this should imply that this subject has the same access right to *every* method of the object (class). That means, we should allow *default authorization policy* in our system. But there are some exceptions. For example, an administration officer usually can access every method (attribute) of a postgraduate. But if a postgraduate student is also a tutor, this officer should not be able to access the postgraduate's salary record.

2. If a subject has an access right to a class, there may be a need that this subject should be generally allowed to access all of its subclasses. Again, some exceptions should be taken into account. For example, a general research officer can access all the research records of the class Staff except that of the class Professor. A similar requirement is also needed for memberships.

3. We also need to represent *causal* or *conditional* authorization policies. For instance, an access policy such as "if subject A can access object O then subject B can also access O" is very useful in certain applications. For instance, "if the member of a team can access the Budget object, then the team leader can also access the Budget object".

4. Sometimes it is also necessary to represent negative authorizations in our system. For instance, a subject S can access all methods (attributes) of class Postgraduate except *salary*.

4.1   Syntax of $\mathcal{L}^{oa}$

Now we present the syntax of $\mathcal{L}^{oa}$. Again its semantics is omitted due to space limit. Refer to [1] for the semantics of $\mathcal{L}^{oa}$.

The *vocabulary* of $\mathcal{L}^{oa}$ includes the vocabulary of $\mathcal{L}^o$ together with the following additions:

1. A finite set of *subject variables* $\mathcal{SV} = \{s, s_1, s_2, \cdots\}$ and a finite set of *subject constants* $\mathcal{SC} = \{S, S_1, S_2, \cdots\}$. We denote $\mathcal{S} = \mathcal{SV} \cup \mathcal{SC}$.

2. A finite set of *access-rights variables* $\mathcal{AV} = \{r, r_1, r_2, \cdots\}$ and a finite set of *access-right constants* $\mathcal{AC} = \{R, R_1, R_2, \cdots\}$. We denote $\mathcal{A} = \mathcal{AV} \cup \mathcal{AC}$.

3. A ternary predicate symbol *holds* taking arguments subject, access-right, and object/method respectively.

4. Logic connectives $\wedge$ and $\neg$.

In language $\mathcal{L}^{oa}$, a fact that a subject S has access right R for object O is represented using a ground atom $holds(S, R, O)$. A fact that S has access right R for object O's method $f(\cdots) \hookrightarrow \Pi^2$ is represented by ground atom $holds(S, R, O|f)$.

In general, we define an *access fact* to be an atomic formula $holds(s, r, o)$ (or $holds(s, r, o|f)$, where $o|f$ indicates a method associated with object o.) or its negation. A ground access fact is an access fact without any variable occurrence. We view $\neg\neg F$ as F. An *access fact expression* in $\mathcal{L}^{oa}$ is defined as follows: (i) each access fact is an access fact expression; (ii) if ψ is an access fact expression and ϕ is an isa or object proposition, then $\psi \wedge \phi$ is an access fact expression; (iii) if ψ and ϕ are access fact expressions, then $\psi \wedge \phi$ is an access fact expression. A ground fact expression is a fact expression with no variable occurrence in it. An access fact expression is *pure* if it does not have an isa proposition occurrence in it.

Based on the above definition, the following are access fact expressions: $holds(S, R, O) \wedge O$ **isa subclass of** C, $\neg holds(S, R, o) \wedge o$ **isa member of** C, where o is an object variable.

Now we are ready to define propositions in language $\mathcal{L}^{oa}$. Firstly, $\mathcal{L}^{oa}$ has the same types of database propositions as $\mathcal{L}^o$, i.e. object proposition, isa proposition and constraint proposition. It also includes the following additional type of *access proposition*:

$$\psi \text{ implies } \phi \text{ with absence } \gamma, \tag{28}$$

where ψ is an access fact expression, and ϕ and γ are pure access fact expressions. Note that ψ, ϕ and γ may contain variables. In this case, as before, (28) will be treated as a set of access propositions obtained by replacing ψ, ϕ and γ with their ground instances respectively.

As an example, consider the following access proposition

$$holds(S, Read, Tutor|salary) \wedge Sue \text{ isa member of } Tutor$$
$$\text{implies } holds(S, Read, Sue|salary)$$
$$\text{with absence } \neg holds(S, Read, Sue|salary),$$

Intuitively, this expression says that if subject S can read tutor's salary record and Sue is a member of tutor, then S can also read Sue's salary record if the fact that S cannot read Sue's salary does not currently hold.

A special form of access proposition (28) occurs when γ is empty. In this case, we can rewrite (28) as

$$\psi \text{ provokes } \phi, \tag{29}$$

which is viewed as a *causal* or *conditional* relation between ψ and ϕ. For instance, we may have an access proposition like:

$$holds(s, r, c) \wedge o \text{ isa subclass of } c$$
$$\text{provokes } holds(s, r, o).$$

---

[2] Recall that symbol $\hookrightarrow$ indicates symbol $\Rightarrow$ or $\mapsto$.

This access proposition expresses that for any subject s, access right r and objects o and c, if s has access right r on c and o is a subclass of c, then s also has access right r on o. This is also an example of access inheritance.

On the other hand, there is also another special form of (28) when ψ is also empty. In this case, we can rewrite (28) simply as

$$\textbf{always } \phi. \tag{30}$$

For example, we can express a fact that the database administrator (DBA) should have any access right on any object as follows:

$$\textbf{always } holds(DBA, r, o).$$

4.2   Databases with Associated Authorizations

In the previous subsection, we have introduced language $\mathcal{L}^{oa}$ which is augmented from language $\mathcal{L}^{o}$. It is clear that our access propositions (28), (29) and (30) provide flexibility to express different types of authorization policies on objects. However, to ensure the proper inheritance of access policies on different objects, some specific types of access policies are particularly important for database systems. The set of these kinds of authorization policies is referred to as the *generic authorization scheme* for databases.

Consider

$$holds(s, r, o) \textbf{ implies } holds(s, r, o|f)$$
$$\textbf{with absence } \neg holds(s, r, o|f), \tag{31}$$

Intuitively, (31) says that if s has access right r on object o, then s also has access right r on each of its methods under the assumption that $\neg holds(s, r, o|f)$ is not present.

We also have the following two generic access propositions:

$$holds(s, r, c) \wedge o \textbf{ isa subclass of } c$$
$$\textbf{implies } holds(s, r, o)$$
$$\textbf{with absence } \neg holds(s, r, o), \tag{32}$$

and

$$holds(s, r, c|f) \wedge o \textbf{ isa subclass of } c$$
$$\textbf{implies } holds(s, r, o|f)$$
$$\textbf{with absence } \neg holds(s, r, o|f). \tag{33}$$

(32) and (33) guarantee the proper inheritance of access policies on subclasses.

Finally, the following two propositions ensure the membership inheritance of access policies.

$$holds(s, r, c) \wedge o \textbf{ isa member of } c$$
$$\textbf{implies } holds(s, r, o)$$
$$\textbf{with absence } \neg holds(s, r, o), \tag{34}$$

and

$$holds(s, r, c|f) \wedge o \text{ isa member of } c$$
$$\text{implies } holds(s, r, o|f)$$
$$\text{with absence } \neg holds(s, r, o|f). \tag{35}$$

Now we can formally define our database with associated authorizations as follows. We will refer to this kind of database as *extended object oriented database*.

Definition 2. *An* extended object oriented database *in $\mathcal{L}^{oa}$ is a pair $\Lambda = (\Sigma, \Xi)$, where $\Sigma = (\Gamma, \Delta, \Omega)$ is the database as defined in Definition 1, and $\Xi = GA \cup A$ is an* authorization description *on Σ where GA is a collection of generic authorization propositions (31) - (35), and A is a finite set of user-defined access propositions.*

4.3   Research People Database Revisited

In this subsection, we revisit the research people database domain discussed in Example 1. We consider a set of authorizations on objects in this database and show how our approach can be used to reason about authorizations in this object oriented database environment.

Example 3. **Research people database domain revisited**. Consider an extended research people database $\Lambda = (\Sigma, \Xi)$, where Σ is specified to be the database described in Example 1, and Ξ is a set of authorization policies on Σ. We assume that in this domain, there are three layers of subjects:

(i) A super user called a database administrator DBA, who can read and update class *ResPeople* and all its subclasses and members through inheritance;

(ii) A student administrator $StdAdm$ who can read and update class *Postgraduate* and all its members through the inheritance. An academic administrator $AcaAdm$ who can read and update class $Staff$ and all its subclasses and members through inheritance.

(iii) Five individual users named T, S, F, P and J indicating people Tom, Sue, Faye, Peter and James respectively, who can read their own objects $Tom, Sue, Faye, Peter$ and $James$.

The structure of this extended database is shown in Figure 2.

Now we can specify Ξ as follows. Let $\Xi = GA \cup A$, where GA is a collection of (31) - (35) (i.e. generic authorization scheme). Based on the above descriptions (i), (ii) and (iii), clearly A should include the following access propositions:

$$\text{always } holds(DBA, Read, ResPeople), \tag{36}$$
$$\text{always } holds(DBA, Update, ResPeople), \tag{37}$$
$$\text{always } holds(StdAdm, Read, Postgraduate), \tag{38}$$
$$\text{always } holds(StdAdm, Update, Postgraduate), \tag{39}$$
$$\text{always } holds(AcaAdm, Read, Staff), \tag{40}$$

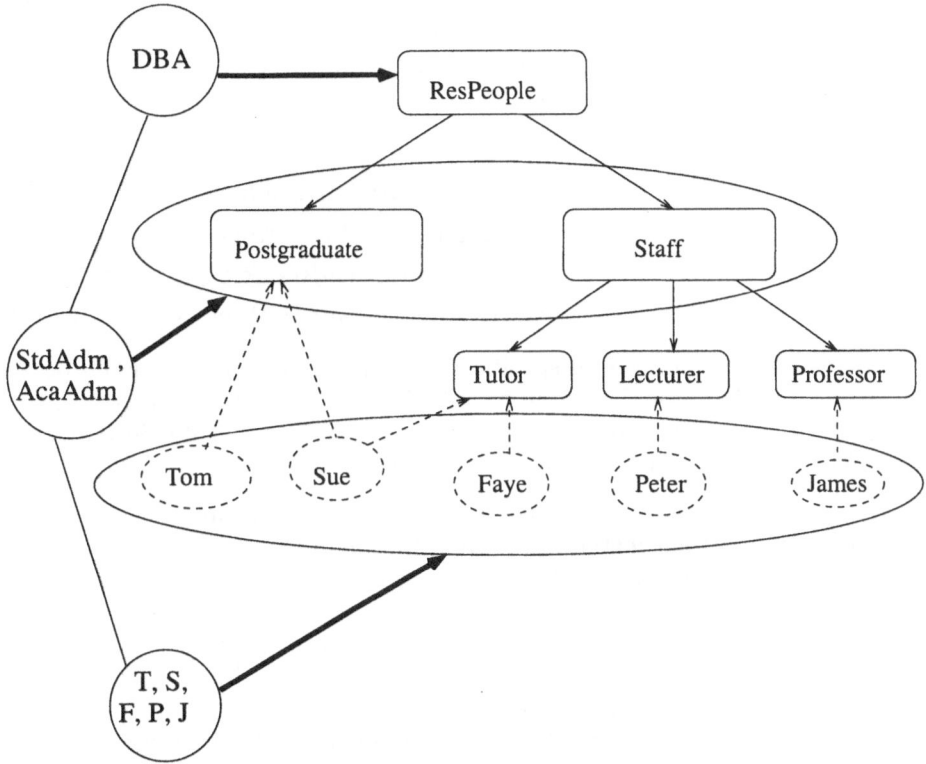

Fig. 2. A complex research people database.

$$\mathbf{always}\ holds(AcaAdm, Update, Staff), \tag{41}$$

$$\mathbf{always}\ holds(T, Read, Tom), \tag{42}$$

$$\mathbf{always}\ holds(S, Read, Sue), \tag{43}$$

$$\mathbf{always}\ holds(F, Read, Faye), \tag{44}$$

$$\mathbf{always}\ holds(P, Read, Peter), \tag{45}$$

$$\mathbf{always}\ holds(J, Read, James). \tag{46}$$

(iv) Observing our database structure, it is also clear that *Sue* belongs to two different classes *Postgraduate* and *Tutor*. Due to the membership authorization inheritance property, it turns out that subject *StdAdm* can read and update all methods of *Sue* that are inherited from classes *Staff* and *Tutor*. Clearly, this is not our expectation since intuitively, a student administrator is not usually allowed to access some staff's information (e.g. salary). This problem can be avoided easily by including the following proposition in *A*:

$$o\ \mathbf{isa\ member\ of}\ Staff\ \mathbf{implies}$$
$$\neg holds(StdAdm, r, o|salary). \tag{47}$$

(v) Furthermore, if some staff is the supervisor of a postgraduate student, this staff should be able to read all information about his/her student unless there is an explicit declaration denying this. So A also includes one more access proposition:

$$holds(s, read, o') \land o' \text{ isa member of } Staff \, \land$$
$$o \text{ isa member of } Postgraduate \, \land$$
$$o \text{ has method } area(o') \mapsto \Pi$$
$$\textbf{implies } holds(s, Read, o)$$
$$\textbf{with absence } \neg holds(s, Read, o). \tag{48}$$

Now we have completed all specifications for this extended research people object oriented database. It can be proved that this databases is well-specified. That is, Λ has a unique model. The following results show that Λ indeed presents the desired authorization policies on objects in the database.

(a) DBA can read and update every postgraduate student and staff members' objects and all their methods inherited from all of their superclasses, i.e.
  $\Lambda \models_\lambda holds(DBA, Read/Update, O)^3$, and
  $\Lambda \models_\lambda holds(DBA, Read/Update, O|f)$,
  where O is any object constant in Λ and f is any method associated with O.

(b) $StdAdm$ can read and update every student member object, i.e.
  $\Lambda \models_\lambda holds(StdAdm, Read/Update, O)$,
  where O is Tom or Sue, which also implies that $StdAdm$ can also read and update all methods of Tom and Sue inherited from their superclasses $ResPeople$ and $Postgraduate$, i.e.
  $\Lambda \models_\lambda holds(StdAdm, Read/Update, O|f)$.
  But $StdAdm$ cannot read and update Sue's salary which is inherited from class $Staff$:
  $\Lambda \models_\lambda \neg holds(StdAdm, Read/Update, Sue|salary)$.

(c) $AcaAdm$ can read and update staff members $Faye$ and $James$, i.e.
  $\Lambda \models_\lambda holds(AcaAdm, Read/Update, Faye)$, and
  $\Lambda \models_\lambda holds(AcaAdm, Read/Update, James)$,
  which also imply that $AcaAdm$ can also read and update all methods of $Faye$ and $James$. Note that since there is no explicit description about object $Peter$, $AcaAdm$ cannot access every method of $Peter$.

(d) For every individual user (i.e. T, S, F, P and J), he/she can read his/her corresponding object and all its methods inherited from all its superclasses, i.e.
  $\Lambda \models_\lambda holds(T, Read, Tom)$,
  $\Lambda \models_\lambda holds(T, Read, Tom|f)$,
  $\cdots$,
  $\Lambda \models_\lambda holds(J, Read, James)$,
  $\Lambda \models_\lambda holds(J, Read, James|f)$,
  where f denotes the any method associated with the corresponding object.

---

[3] It denotes $holds(DBA, Read, O)$ and $holds(DBA, Update, O)$.

(e) Every supervisor can read his/her student object's all methods, i.e.
$$\Lambda \models_\lambda holds(P, Read, Tom|f) \text{ and}$$
$$\Lambda \models_\lambda holds(J, Read, Sue|f'),$$
where f and f' denotes any method of Tom and Sue respectively. Note that $\Lambda \models_\lambda holds(P, Read, Tom|f)$ is derived from the fact that $\Sigma \models Peter$ **isa member of** $Staff$.

5   Conclusions

In this paper, we have proposed a logic formalization for specifying authorizations in object oriented databases. Our work consisted of two steps: the first step involved a formal language $\mathcal{L}^o$ to formalize object oriented databases within a logic framework. We provided a high level language to specify an object oriented database and defined a precise semantics for it. Our semantics of $\mathcal{L}^o$ shares some features of Kifer $elt.$'s F-logic for specifying object oriented databases. But our database specification is more succinct and intuitive, and hence it has been possible to extend this by combining it with authorization structures. The second step of our work was to extend $\mathcal{L}^o$ to language $\mathcal{L}^{oa}$ by representing different types of authorizations in the database. It has been shown that the types of authorizations in our formalism are quite flexible and can be used to reason about complex authorizations compared with other approaches.

References

1. Y. Bai, On Formal Specification of Authorization Policies and Their Transformations, Ph.D. Thesis, School of Computing and Information Technology, University of Western Sydney Nepean, 2000.
2. Y. Bai and V. Varadharajan, A Logical Formalization for Specifying Authorizations in Object Oriented Databases, *Proceedings of IFIP Working Conference on Database Security*, pp. 259–269, 1999.
3. M. Gelfond and V. Lifschitz, Classical Negation in Logic Programs and Disjunctive Databases. *New Generation Computing*, 9: pp. 365–385, 1991.
4. M. Kifer, G. Lausen, J. Wu, Logical Foundations of Object-oriented and Frame-based Languages. *Journal of ACM*, Vol. 42, No. 4 (july), pp. 741–843, 1995.
5. S.Y.W. Su and L. Raschid, Incorporating Knowledge Rules in a Semantic Data Model: An Approach to Integrated Knowledge Management, *Proceedings of AI Applications Conference*, 1985.

Information-Flow-Based Ontology Mapping

Yannis Kalfoglou[1] and Marco Schorlemmer[2]*

[1] Advanced Knowledge Technologies (AKT)
Department of Electronics and Computer Science
University of Southampton
[2] Advanced Knowledge Technologies (AKT)
Centre for Intelligent Systems and their Applications
The University of Edinburgh

Abstract. As ontologies become ever more important for semantically-rich information exchange and a crucial element for supporting knowledge sharing in a large distributed environment, like the Web, the demand for sharing them increases accordingly. One way of achieving this ambitious goal is to provide mechanised ways for mapping and merging ontologies. This has been the focus of recent research in knowledge engineering. However, we observe a dearth of mapping methods that are based on a strong theoretical ground, are easy to replicate in different settings, and use semantically-rich mechanisms for performing ontology mapping. In this paper, we aim to fill in these gaps with a method we propose for Information-Flow-based ontology mapping. Our method draws on the proven theoretical ground of Information Flow and channel theory, and we provide a systematic and mechanised methodology for deploying it on a distributed environment to perform ontology mapping among a variety of different ontologies. We applied our method at a large-scale experiment of mapping five ontologies modelling Computer Science departments in five UK Universities. We elaborate on a theory for ontology mapping, analyse the mechanised steps of applying it, and assess its ontology mapping results.

1 Introduction

One of the aspects in ontology sharing is to perform some sort of mapping between ontology constructs. That is, given two ontologies, one should be able to map concepts found in one ontology onto the ones found in the other. Further, some research suggest that we should also be able to merge ontologies where the product of this merge will be, at the very least, the intersection of the two given ontologies. These are the dominant approaches and have been studied and applied in a variety of systems (see, for example, [31]).

There are, however, some drawbacks that prevent engineers benefiting from such systems. Firstly, the assumptions made in making these mappings and performing merging are not always exposed to the community and no technical

---

* Last names of authors are in alphabetical order.

R. Meersman, Z. Tari (Eds.): CoopIS/DOA/ODBASE 2002, LNCS 2519, pp. 1132–1151, 2002.

details are disclosed. Secondly, the systems that perform ontology mapping are often either embedded in an integrated environment for ontology editing or are attached to a specific formalism. Thirdly, in most cases mapping and merging are based on heuristics that mostly use syntactic clues to determine correspondence or equivalence between ontology concepts, but rarely use the meaning of those concepts, a.k.a. their semantics. Fourthly, most, if not all approaches, do not treat ontological axioms or rules often found in formal ontologies. Finally, ontology mapping as a term has a different meaning in different works merely due to the lack of a formal account of what ontology mapping is. There is an observed lack of theory behind most of the works in this area.

Motivated by these drawbacks we worked on a method and a theory for ontology mapping and merging. We were determined to tackle these drawbacks so our approach draws heavily on a proven theoretical ground but at the same time we are providing a systematic approach for ontology mapping and mechanised methodological steps. In particular, in this paper we propose an Information-Flow-based method for ontology mapping (hereafter, IF-Map). We are mostly interested in mapping ontologies, but we can extend the approach to merge them, too. IF-Map draws on the works of Schorlemmer [34] on using Information Flow (hereafter, IF) theory to align ontologies and the heuristics defined by Kalfoglou (in [21], pp.95–97), to analyse prospective mappings between ontologies. On the theoretical side, our method draws on the IF theory described by Barwise and Seligman [3] and the work of Kent on the IF Framework [23] for the IEEE standardisation activity and his proposed methodology for merging ontologies [22]. The methodological part of IF-Map has also been influenced by the work of Stumme and Maedche on the FCA-Merge method [35].

We describe a scenario for ontology mapping and the architecture we built to perform ontology mapping in Section 2. We briefly provide mathematical preliminaries on IF and channel theory in Section 3, before we proceed to describe our ontology mapping method in Section 4, together with an example case of its use. In Section 5 we do an evaluation of our method and elaborate on scalability issues. We discuss related work in Section 6 and summerise the paper in Section 7.

2   An Architecture for Ontology Mapping

In Figure 1 we illustrate our approach to ontology mapping. In particular, the focus is on the use of IF as the underpinning mathematical foundation for establishing mappings between two ontologies. We shall formalise these mappings in terms of *logic infomorphisms*, which we introduce in Section 3. Actually, this figure clearly resembles Kent's proposed two-step process in ontology sharing [22], but it has differences in its implementation. The solid rectangular line surrounding Reference ontology, Local ontology 1 and Local ontology 2 denotes the existing ontologies. We assume that Local ontology 1 and Local ontology 2 are ontologies used by different communities and populated with their instances, while Reference ontology is an agreed understanding for favouring knowledge sharing, and is not supposed to be populated. The dashed rectangular line sur-

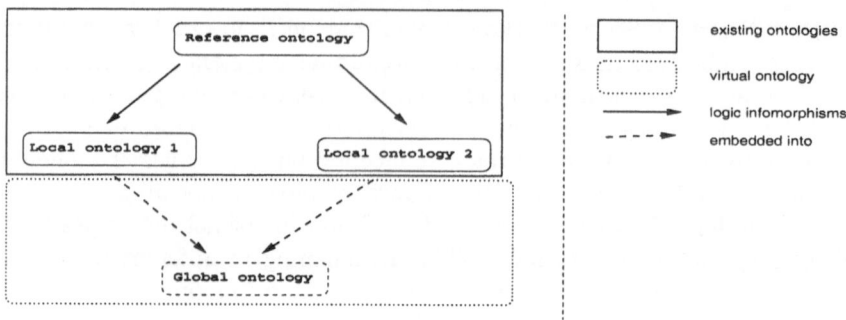

Fig. 1. The scenario for ontology mapping.

rounding `Global ontology` denotes an ontology that does not exist yet, but will be constructed "on the fly" for the purpose of alignment. This is similar to Kent's "virtual ontology of community connections" [22]. The solid arrow lines linking `Reference ontology` with `Local ontology 1` and `Local ontology 2` denote IF between these ontologies formalised as logic informorphisms. In this paper we present the methodology to generate these logic infomorphisms. The dashed arrow lines denote the embedding from `Local ontology 1` and `Local ontology 2` into `Global ontology`. This latter is the sum of the local ontologies *modulo* `Reference ontology` and the generated logic infomorphisms. As we mentioned earlier, this extension would be the merging part of IF-Map.

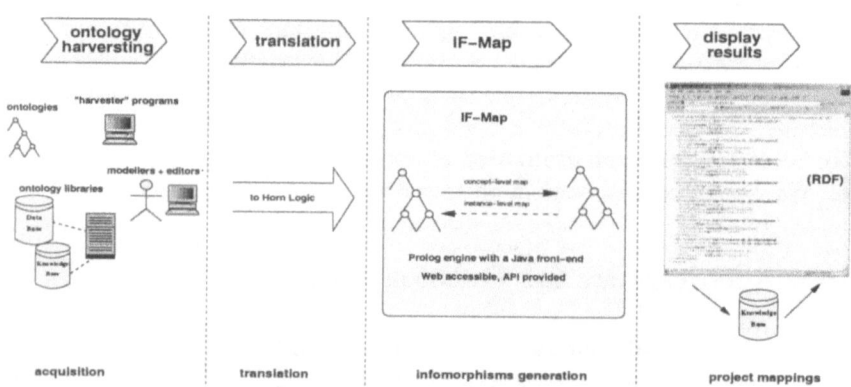

Fig. 2. The IF-Map architecture.

In Figure 2 we illustrate the process of IF-Map. We have built a step-wise process that consists of four major steps: (a) ontology harvesting, (b) translation, (c) infomorphisms, and (d) display results. In the ontology harvesting step we perform our acquisition. We acquire ontologies by using a variety of methods: use existing ontologies, download them from ontology libraries (for example, from Ontolingua [11] or WebOnto [9] servers), edit them in ontology editors (for example, in Protégé [18]), or harvest them from the Web. The latter is ongoing research in the AKT project (http://www.aktors.org) where we are writing scripting programs to crawl the Web and harvest RDF-encoded resources for semi-automatically construct and populate ontologies. We will not expand on this topic here as it is peripheral to our theme of ontology mapping. As a result of our versatile ontology acquisition step, we have to deal with a variety of ontology-language formats ranging from KIF [17] and Ontolingua to OCML [30], RDF [26], Prolog, and native Protégé knowledge bases.

This introduces the second step in our process, that of translation. As we have declaratively specified the IF-Map method in Horn logic and execute it with the aim of a Prolog engine, we partially translate the above formats to Prolog clauses. Our translator programs are either written in-house, or whenever available, use public translators. For example, there are public RDF to Prolog translators[1] as well as Ontolingua to Prolog. In most of the cases though, we found it practical to write our own translators. We did that to have a partial translation, customised for the purposes of ontology mapping. Furthermore, as it has been reported in a large-scale experiment with publicly available translators [6], the Prolog code produced is not elegant or even executable. Our own translators are customised to translate — from KIF, Ontolingua, and Protégé knowledge bases into Prolog clauses — those constructs that are needed for IF-Map: class taxonomy, relations and representative instances for classes. Thus, we deliberately neglect constructs such as documentation slots, separation of own-slots and template-slots and other object-oriented modelling primitives used in Ontology languages (such as KIF or Ontolingua[2]) as they are not useful for IF-Map and their absence from the translated Prolog code does not invalidate their meaning. For Protégé knowledge bases we used the built-in Java API to obtain the constructs we wanted, and for RDF we used publicly available RDF to Prolog translators. The issue of a full-blown translation from one formalism to another is a knotty problem, and recent research from Corrêa da Silva and colleagues [6] offer an account on the effort involved.

The next step in our process is the main mapping mechanism: the IF-Map method, which we describe in Section 4. We have written a Java front-end to the Prolog-written IF-Map program so that we can access it from the Web, and we are currently in the process of writing a Java API to enable external calls to it from other systems. This step will find logic infomorphisms, if any, between the two ontologies under examination, and in the last step of our process we display them in RDF format. This step involves translating back from Prolog clauses to RDF triples with the aim of an intermediary Java layer, where RDF is being produced using the Jena RDF API [27]. Finally, we store the results in a knowledge base for future reference and maintenance.

---

[1] Like the one from Wielemaker downloadable from http://www.swi-prolog.org/packages/rdf2pl.html

[2] We briefly describe the principles we used to partially translate from Ontolingua to Prolog in [21], pp.105–107.

Before proceeding to an example case of deploying this architecture we shall introduce the theoretical background of IF-Map. In the next section We expand on channel theory and logic informorphisms, and give a formal account of ontology mapping.

3   Theoretical Preliminaries

In order to give an formal characterisation of ontology mapping we start from the assumption that mapping ontologies presupposes flow of information, and that we need to base any formal notion of ontology mapping on a sound mathematical theory of information and information flow. There is no such theory of information yet, but there have been several efforts in establishing one [10,2,7, 3].

3.1   Channel Theory

Channel theory has been developed based on the understanding that information flow results from regularities in a distributed system, and that it is by virtue of regularities among the connections that information of some components of a system carries information of other components; furthermore it is the particular instances that carry information, so that information flow crucially involves both types (i.e., the terminology to describe components) and instances.

Central to channel theory is the idea of a *local logic*. Separate interacting communities will typically use different vocabularies, i.e., they will use different systems of *types*, and the *instances* that these communities manage will be *classified* according to these types in quite different ways. In addition, each community will have its own particular *constraints* that describe the local behaviour of their instances with respect to their system of types. A *local logic* brings all these ideas together:

Definition 1. *A local logic is a quadruple* $\mathcal{L} = (I, T, \models, \vdash)$, *where*

1. *I is a set of instances;*
2. *T is a set of types;*
3. *$\models$ is a classification relation, a binary relation between elements of I and T;*
4. *$\vdash$ is a consequence relation, a binary relation between subsets of T;*

There are two parts of a local logic that are of particular importance in the channel-theory framework. The first one is the triple $(I, T, \models)$, and is called the *classification* of the local logic, because the binary relation $\models$ determines a classification of instances in I with respect to types in T. Thus, $x \models a$ means that instance $x \in I$ is classified as of type $a \in T$.

The second important part is the pair $(T, \vdash)$, which is called the *theory* of the local logic. This theory is specified by a set of *sequents* $\langle \Gamma, \Delta \rangle$, i.e., pairs where $\Gamma, \Delta \subseteq T$. The set of types Γ is to be interpreted conjunctively, the set Δ disjunctively, so that an instance $x \in I$ *satisfies* a sequent $\langle \Gamma, \Delta \rangle$ provided that, if x is of *every* type in Γ, then x is of *some* type in Δ. Sequents that belong to the theory of a logic are called *constraints* and denoted $\Gamma \vdash \Delta$. Theories of local logics must satisfy the following conditions of *regularity*[3]:

1. Identity: $a \vdash a$, for all $a \in T$;
2. Weakening: If $\Gamma \vdash \Delta$ then $\Gamma, \Gamma' \vdash \Delta, \Delta'$, for all $\Gamma, \Gamma', \Delta, \Delta' \subseteq T$;
3. Global Cut: If $\Gamma, T_0' \vdash \Delta, T_1'$ for each partition[4] $\langle T_0', T_1' \rangle$ of any $T' \subseteq T$, then $\Gamma \vdash \Delta$, for all $\Gamma, \Delta \subseteq T$.

There is an additional element in local logics that we have deliberately left out in Definition 1. Ideally, instances of a local logic adhere to its constraints, although, we cannot pressupose this in general, and exceptions may occur. Local logics also distinguish a subset $N \subseteq I$ of *normal instances* that must satisfy all constraints of the local logic. The idea of normal instance is needed if we want to model reasonable but unsound flow of information. For the purposes of IF-Map, though, we shall assume that all instances are normal. Such logics are said to be *sound*.

For information to flow between separate components of a distributed system, we need to link local logics that characterise components in a sensible way. This will essentially affect the system of classifications and its associated theory, but in a way that allows the information to flow. This latter is captured with the idea of a *logic infomorphism*:

Definition 2. *A logic infomorphism* $f : \mathcal{L} \rightleftarrows \mathcal{L}'$ *from local logic* $\mathcal{L} = (I, T, \models, \vdash)$ *to local logic* $\mathcal{L}' = (I', T', \models', \vdash')$ *is a contravariant pair of functions* $f = \langle f^*, f_\star \rangle$, *where* $f^* : T \to T'$ *and* $f_\star : I' \to I$, *such that,*

1. *for* $x \in I'$ *and* $a \in T$, $f_\star(x) \models a$ *if and only if* $x \models' f^*(a)$;
2. *for* $\Gamma, \Delta \subseteq T$, *if* $\Gamma \vdash \Delta$, *then* $f^*[\Gamma] \vdash' f^*[\Delta]$[5].

The restriction of logic infomorphisms to the classification part of local logics are called *infomorphisms*.

3.2   Ontologies and Ontology Morphisms

For the purposes of IF-Map described in this paper, we adopt a definition of ontology that includes some of the core components that are usually part of an ontology: *concepts* of an *is-a hierarchy*, which we caputre with a partial order relation '$\leqslant$'; *relations* defined over these concepts; and notions of *disjointness* of

---

[3] Regularity arises from the observation that, given a classification of instances to types, the set of all sequents that are satisfied by all instances do fulfill these properties.

[4] A partition of T' is a pair $\langle T_0', T_1' \rangle$ of subsets of T', such that $T_0' \cup T_1' = T'$ and $T_0' \cap T_1' = \emptyset$; T_0' and T_1' may themselves be empty (hence it is actually a quasi-partition).

[5] $f^*[\Gamma]$ and $f^*[\Delta]$ denote the set images of sets Γ and Δ along function f^*, respectively.

two concepts — when no instance can be considered of both concepts — and *coverage* of two concept — when all instances are covered by two concepts.[6]

Disjointness and coverage are typically specified by means of ontological axioms. IF-Map takes these kind of axioms into account including disjointness and coverage into the hierarchy of concepts by means of two binary relations '$\perp$' and '$|$', respectively. In a future, we plan do extend IF-Map to cope with full first-order axioms.

Definition 3. *An* ontology *is a tuple* $\mathcal{O} = (C, R, \leqslant, \perp, |, \sigma)$ *where*

1. C *is a finite set of concept symbols;*
2. R *is a finite set of relation symbols;*
3. $\leqslant$ *is a reflexive, transitive and antisymmetric relation on* C *(a partial order);*
4. $\perp$ *is a symmetric and irreflexive relation on* C;
5. $|$ *is a symmetric relation on* C; *and*
6. $\sigma : R \to C^+$ *is the function assigning to each relation symbol its arity; the functor* $(-)^+$ *sends a set* C *to the set of finite tuples whose elements are in* C.

When discarding binary relations $\perp$ and $|$, this definition is equivalent to that of a *core ontology* in [35].

When an ontology $\mathcal{O} = (C, R, \leqslant, \perp, |, \sigma)$ is used in some particular application domain, we need to populate it with instances. First, we will have to classify objects of a set X according to the concept symbols in C by defining a binary classification relation $\models_\mathbf{C}$. This will determine a classification $\mathbf{C} = (X, C, \models_\mathbf{C})$. Next, we will have to specify over which instances the relations represented by the symbols in R are to hold, thus classifying finite tuples of objects of X to the relation symbols in R by defining a binary classification relation $\models_\mathbf{R}$. This will determine a classification $\mathbf{R} = (X^+, R, \models_\mathbf{R})$. Both classifications will have to be defined in such a way that the partial order $\leqslant$, the disjointness $\perp$, the coverage $|$, and the arity function σ are respected:

Definition 4. *A populated ontology is a tuple* $\widetilde{\mathcal{O}} = (\mathbf{C}, \mathbf{R}, \leqslant, \perp, |, \sigma)$ *such that* $\mathbf{C} = (X, C, \models_\mathbf{C})$ *and* $\mathbf{R} = (X^+, R, \models_\mathbf{R})$ *are classifications and* $\mathcal{O} = (C, R, \leqslant, \perp, |, \sigma)$ *is an ontology; we say the ontology is* sound *when, for all* $x, x_1, \ldots, x_n \in X$, $c, d \in C$, $r \in R$, *and* $\sigma(r) = \langle c_1, \ldots, c_n \rangle$,

1. *if* $x \models_\mathbf{C} c$ *and* $c \leqslant d$, *then* $x \models_\mathbf{C} d$;
2. *if* $x \models_\mathbf{C} c$ *and* $c \perp d$, *then* $x \not\models_\mathbf{C} d$;
3. *if* $c \mid d$, *then* $x \models_\mathbf{C} c$ *or* $x \models_\mathbf{C} d$;
4. *if* $\langle x_1, \ldots, x_n \rangle \models_\mathbf{R} r$ *then* $x_i \models_\mathbf{R} c_i$, *for all* $i = 1, \ldots, n$.

Notice that we write $\widetilde{\mathcal{O}}$ for a populated ontology and $\mathcal{O}$ for the respective unpopulated one.

---

[6] Both disjointness and coverage can easily be extended to more than two concepts, although we stay with binary relations, for the ease of presentation.

Transformations of mathematical structures that preserve the structure that characterises them are usually described with homomorphism (or morphisms, for short). Thus, we study the mapping of ontologies through the morphisms of those mathematical structures we have defined for ontologies in Definition 3. The concept of 'populated ontology' is central to our approach to ontology mapping, and we shall use it later in Proposition 1 in order to justify the following definition of an ontology morphism:

Definition 5. *Given two ontologies* $\mathcal{O} = (C, R, \leqslant, \perp, |, \sigma)$ *and* $\mathcal{O}' = (C', R', \leqslant', \perp', |', \sigma')$, *an ontology morphism* $\langle f^{\star}, g^{\star} \rangle : \mathcal{O} \to \mathcal{O}'$ *is a pair of functions* $f^{\star} : C \to C'$ *and* $g^{\star} : R \to R'$, *such that, for all* $c, d \in C$, $r \in R$, *and* $\sigma(r) = \langle c_1, \ldots, c_n \rangle$,

1. *if* $c \leqslant d$, *then* $f^{\star}(c) \leqslant' f^{\star}(d)$;
2. *if* $c \perp d$, *then* $f^{\star}(c) \perp' f^{\star}(d)$;
3. *if* $c \mid d$, *then* $f^{\star}(c) \mid' f^{\star}(d)$;
4. *if* $\sigma'(g^{\star}(r)) = \langle c'_1, \ldots, c'_n \rangle$, *then* $c'_i \leqslant' f^{\star}(c_i)$, *for all* $i = 1, \ldots, n$.

3.3   Information Flow between Ontologies

Our approach to ontology mapping is built upon the assumption that, in the context of channel theory, local logics characterise ontologies.

Hence, a populated ontology $\widetilde{\mathcal{O}} = (\mathbf{C}, \mathbf{R}, \leqslant, \perp, |, \sigma)$ determines a local logic $\mathcal{L} = (X, C, \models_{\mathbf{C}}, \vdash)$ whose theory $(C, \vdash)$ is given by the smallest regular consequence relation (i.e., the smallest relation closed under Identity, Weakening, and Global Cut) such that, for all $c, d \in C$

$$
\begin{array}{lll}
c \vdash d & \text{iff} & c \leqslant d \\
c, d \vdash & \text{iff} & c \perp d \\
\vdash c, d & \text{iff} & c \mid d
\end{array}
$$

The characterisation of an ontology as a local logic justifies the IF-Map method presented in next section, which stems from our intention — explained in Section 2 — to map an unpopulated ontology $\mathcal{O} = (C, R, \leqslant, \perp, |, \sigma)$ to a populated one $\widetilde{\mathcal{O}}' = (\mathbf{C}', \mathbf{R}', \leqslant', \perp', |', \sigma')$, by looking at the information flow. For this reason we "formally" populate the concept types given in C and the relation types given in R to obtain classifications $\mathbf{C} = (Y, C, \models_{\mathbf{C}})$ and $\mathbf{R} = (Z, R, \models_{\mathbf{R}})$ (notice that, unlike a populated ontology, the instances of R need not to be finite tuples of instances of C), and further establish infomorphisms $f : \mathbf{C} \rightleftarrows \mathbf{C}'$ and $g : \mathbf{R} \rightleftarrows \mathbf{R}'$, such that their type-level components $f^{\star}$ and $g^{\star}$ constitute an ontology morphism; because in that case we know that the populated ontology $\widetilde{\mathcal{O}}'$ will be a *sound extension* of $\mathcal{O}$, in the sense that the images of $\widetilde{\mathcal{O}}'$'s instances conform to $\mathcal{O}$, as stated in the following proposistion:

Proposition 1. *Let* $\mathcal{O} = (C, R, \leqslant, \perp, |, \sigma)$ *be an (unpopulated) ontology, and let* $\widetilde{\mathcal{O}}' = (\mathbf{C}', \mathbf{R}', \leqslant', \perp', |', \sigma')$ *be a populated ontology with classifications* $\mathbf{C}' = (X', C', \models_{\mathbf{C}'})$, $\mathbf{R}' = (X'^{+}, R', \models_{\mathbf{R}'})$. *Let* $\mathbf{C} = (Y, C, \models_{\mathbf{C}})$ *and* $\mathbf{R} = (Z, R, \models_{\mathbf{R}})$

be two classifications whose types are the concept and relation types of $\mathcal{O}$. If $\tilde{\mathcal{O}}'$ is sound and $f : \mathbf{C} \rightleftarrows \mathbf{C}'$ and $g : \mathbf{R} \rightleftarrows \mathbf{R}'$ are informorphisms, such that $(f^\star, g^\star) : \mathcal{O} \to \mathcal{O}'$ is an ontology morphism, then, for all $x, x_1, \ldots, x_n \in X$, $c, d \in C$, $r \in R$, and $\sigma(r) = \langle c_1, \ldots, c_n \rangle$,

1. *$f_\star(x) \models_{\mathbf{C}} c$ and $c \leqslant d$ imply $f_\star(x) \models_{\mathbf{C}} d$;*
2. *$f_\star(x) \models_{\mathbf{C}} c$ and $c \perp d$ imply $f_\star(x) \not\models_{\mathbf{C}} d$;*
3. *$c \mid d$ implies $f_\star(x) \models_{\mathbf{C}} c$ or $f_\star(x) \models_{\mathbf{C}} d$;*
4. *$g_\star(\langle x_1, \ldots, x_n \rangle) \models r$ implies $f_\star(x_i) \models c_i$, for all $i = 1, \ldots, n$.*

Proof.

1. Suppose $f_\star(x) \models_{\mathbf{C}} c$ and $c \leqslant d$. Since f is an infomorphism, $x \models_{\mathbf{C}'} f^\star(c)$. Furthermore, $c \leqslant d$ implies $f^\star(c) \leqslant' f(d)$ because $\langle f^\star, g^\star \rangle$ is an ontology morphism; consequently, $x \models_{\mathbf{C}'} f^\star(d)$. Finally, since f is a infomorphism, $f_\star(x) \models_{\mathbf{C}} d$.
2. Analogous to 1.
3. Analogous to 1.
4. Suppose $g_\star(\langle x_1, \ldots, x_n \rangle) \models r$. Because g is an infomorphism, $\langle x_1, \ldots, x_n \rangle \models g^\star(r)$. Let $\sigma(g^\star(r)) = \langle c_1', \ldots, c_n' \rangle$. By the soundness of $\tilde{\mathcal{O}}'$, $x_i \models c_i'$, for all $i = 1, \ldots, n$, and since $\langle f^\star, g^\star \rangle$ is an ontology morphism, $x_i \models f^\star(c_i)$, for all $i = 1, \ldots, n$. Consequently, and because f is a infomorphism, $f_\star(x_i) \models c_i$, for all $i = 1, \ldots, n$.

In the next section we describe the ontology mapping method based on the above characterisation of ontologies as local logics, and ontology morphisms as logic infomorphisms.

4   The IF-Map Method

We propose a method for mapping ontologies that draws on the mathematical foundations of information-flow, and we shall use a small easy-to-follow example to illustrate the core parts of IF-Map.

4.1   Reference and Local Ontology

Let us assume that we want to map two ontologies, a reference ontology with a local ontology. We follow the scenario given in Section 2 and assume that the reference ontology has no instances defined, just concept types and constraints over those types. The local ontology, however, has instances classified under its concept types according to a classification relation.

Let Reference be the ontology $\mathcal{O} = (C, R, \leqslant, \perp, |, \sigma)$, with

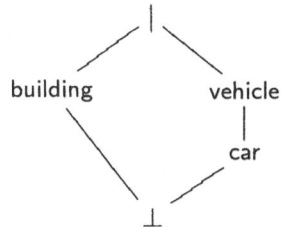

- concepts $C = \{\text{building,vehicle,car}\}$;
- relations $R = \{\text{hasParkingSpaceFor}\}$;
- arities $\sigma(\text{hasParkingSpaceFor}) =$
  $\langle \text{building}, \text{vehicle} \rangle$; and
- partial order $\leqslant$, disjointness $\perp$, and coverage $|$
  as defined by the given lattice.

Let the Local be the ontology $\mathcal{O}' = (C', R', \leqslant', \perp', |', \sigma')$, with

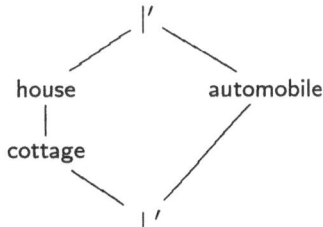

- concepts $C' = \{\text{house,cottage,automobile}\}$;
- relations $R' = \{\text{hasGarageFor,hasShelterFor}\}$;
- arities $\sigma'(\text{hasGarageFor}) = \langle \text{house, automobile} \rangle$,
  $\sigma'(\text{hasShelterFor}) = \langle \text{cottage, automobile} \rangle$; and
- partial order $\leqslant'$, disjointness $\perp'$, and coverage
  $|'$ as defined by the given lattice.

Local, unlike Reference, is populated with instances $X = \{cabrio, bcn,$ $4wd, mall, skye, coupe\}$, which are classified as follows,

$\models_{\mathbf{C}'}$	house	cottage	automobile
cabrio	0	0	1
bcn	1	0	0
4wd	0	0	1
mall	1	1	0
skye	1	1	0
coupe	0	0	1

This table contains the following information: *cabrio*, *4wd* and *coupe* are automobiles, *bcn* is a house in Barcelona, *mall* and *skye* are specific kinds of house, cottages in Mallorca and the Isle of Skye, respectively. It specifies the classification $\mathbf{C}' = (X, C', \models_{\mathbf{C}'})$.

4.2   Characterisation as Local Logics

In order to automatically find mappings between Reference and Local that conform to the definition of ontology morphism given in Definition 5, we will need to look for logic infomorphisms between the local logics that characterise these ontologies. First we shall concentrate on the concepts symbols and leave the relation symbols for Section 4.4.

Reference, which is not populated, is characterised by the following local logic. Its regular theory $(C, \vdash)$ has concept symbols as types, and $\vdash$ is the smallest consequence relation closed by Identity, Weakening, and Global Cut that includes the following constraints:

$$\text{building,vehicle} \vdash \emptyset \qquad \text{car} \vdash \text{vehicle} \qquad \emptyset \vdash \text{building,vehicle}$$

Recall that the comma on the left-hand side of these constraints has conjunctive force whereas on the right-hand side it has disjunctive force. Following this, we can give a declarative reading of the above constraints: nothing is both a building and a vehicle; all cars are vehicles; and everything is either a building or a vehicle.

We will need to provide the theory with a set of instances and a classification of these instances with respect to the types. Now, every regular theory determines a classification as follows:

1. We take as instances Y all those sequents $\langle \Gamma, \Delta \rangle$ that
   - form a partition of the set of concepts ($\Gamma \cup \Delta = C$ and $\Gamma \cap \Delta = \emptyset$); and
   - are *not* constraints of the theory ($\Gamma \not\vdash \Delta$)

   For the theory given above, these sequents are $\langle \{\text{vehicle,car}\}, \{\text{building}\} \rangle$, $\langle \{\text{building}\}, \{\text{vehicle,car}\} \rangle$, and $\langle \{\text{vehicle}\}, \{\text{building,car}\} \rangle$.
2. We then classify these instances according to the concepts that occur in the left-hand side component of the sequent:

$\models_C$	building	vehicle	car
$\langle \{\text{vehicle,car}\}, \{\text{building}\} \rangle$	0	1	1
$\langle \{\text{building}\}, \{\text{vehicle,car}\} \rangle$	1	0	0
$\langle \{\text{vehicle}\}, \{\text{building,car}\} \rangle$	0	1	0

The local logic that characterises **Reference**, i.e., the ontology given by $\mathcal{O}$, is $\mathcal{L} = (Y, C, \models_C, \vdash)$. The generation of instances by means of sequents and their classification may not seem obvious, but it turns out that classifications generated in this way satisfy a fundamental Representation Theorem (see [3]) stating that a local logic that is generated from the structure given in a classification is equivalent to the local logic constructed from its theory as described above.

Local is populated, and hence has already instances and a classification relation. We only need to derive the theory of the local logic that characterises its concept hierarchy as specified in the lattice above. Therefore, its regular theory $(C', \vdash')$ has concept symbols as types, and $\vdash'$ is the smallest consequence relation closed by Identity, Weakening, and Global Cut that includes the following constraints:

$$\text{house,automobile} \vdash' \emptyset \qquad \text{cottage} \vdash' \text{house} \qquad \emptyset \vdash' \text{house,automobile}$$

The local logic that characterises **Local** is, thus, $\mathcal{L}' = (X, C', \models_{C'}, \vdash')$.

4.3   Generation of Ontology Morphisms via Infomorphisms

To map the ontologies, we must find an ontology morphism from $\mathcal{O}$ to $\mathcal{O}'$, which means that there must exist a logic infomorphism $f = \langle f^*, f_* \rangle$ from local logic $\mathcal{L}$ to local logic $\mathcal{L}'$. This amounts to first look for an infomorphism between their respective classifications:

– a map of concepts $f^* : C \rightarrow C'$ (concept-level);
– a map f_* from instances *cabrio*, . . . , *coupe* to the formally created instances of the reference ontology (instance-level);

Note that an ontology morphism, as defined in Definition 5, only captures the concept-level of the infomorphism, i.e. f^*. But f^* has to map the concepts in a way that it respects the hierarchy. One possible way would be:

$$f^*(\text{building}) = \text{house} \qquad f^*(\text{vehicle}) = \text{automobile} \qquad f^*(\text{car}) = \text{automobile}$$

However, we should point out that the automatic generation of these maps is growing exponentially. But we can use the constraint that the map has to respect the concept hierarchy and limit the number of possible maps. Once the map is fixed, there is at most one acceptable way to map the instances in order for f to be an infomorphism.

We do that by building the following table that represents an infomorphism[7]: we label rows by the instances in $X = \{cabrio, . . . , coupe\}$ of Local, and columns by Reference's concepts $C = \{\text{building,vehicle,car}\}$. We put under each of these concepts the values of the column of Local's classification table that corresponds to the image along the map of ontologies f^* (i.e., under building we put the column of house):

	building	vehicle	car
cabrio	0	1	1
bcn	1	0	0
4wd	0	1	1
mall	1	0	0
skye	1	0	0
coupe	0	1	1

Each row should identify (taking into account the classification table of Reference) the formal instances to which each local instance should be mapped onto. Hence, we have the following instance-component of our infomorphism:

$$\begin{aligned}
f_*(cabrio) &= \langle\{\text{vehilce,car}\}, \{\text{building}\}\rangle \\
f_*(bcn) &= \langle\{\text{building}\}, \{\text{vehilce,car}\}\rangle \\
f_*(4wd) &= \langle\{\text{vehilce,car}\}, \{\text{building}\}\rangle \\
f_*(mall) &= \langle\{\text{building}\}, \{\text{vehilce,car}\}\rangle \\
f_*(skye) &= \langle\{\text{building}\}, \{\text{vehilce,car}\}\rangle \\
f_*(coupe) &= \langle\{\text{vehilce,car}\}, \{\text{building}\}\rangle
\end{aligned}$$

We can also interpret the above table (and its resulting mapping of instances) as that: *cabrio* is classified as both a vehicle and a car, according to Reference. No other classification is possible without violating the definition of infomorphism. If *cabrio* was a vehicle but not a car, Local would have been classifying its instances in a way that does not conform to Reference and the fixed map of concepts.

---

[7] Infomorphisms can themselves be represented by means of classification tables; this draws on theoretical work based on Chu spaces [19,1,32].

4.4   Relations and Their Arities

In order to constrain the search space when infomorphisms are generated in an automated way, we use ontological relations to guide the classification process that will result in the ontology mapping, namely by looking for infomorphisms $g : \mathbf{R} \to \mathbf{R}'$ in a similar fashion as before. So, in our example case, we have the following relation defined in Reference:

$$\text{hasParkingSpaceFor : building} \times \text{vehicle}$$

that is, the binary relation hasParkingSpaceFor holds over building and vehicle. Similarly, in Local we have the following two binary relations:

hasGarageFor : house × automobile   hasShelterFor : cottage × automobile

These Local relations could be used to classify pairs of local instances:

	hasShelterFor	hasGarageFor
$\langle bcn, cabrio \rangle$	0	0
$\langle bcn, 4wd \rangle$	0	0
$\langle bcn, coupe \rangle$	1	1
$\langle mall, cabrio \rangle$	1	0
$\langle mall, 4wd \rangle$	0	0
$\langle mall, coupe \rangle$	1	0
$\langle skye, cabrio \rangle$	0	0
$\langle skye, 4wd \rangle$	1	0
$\langle skye, coupe \rangle$	0	0

That is, the house in Barcelona has a garage (also considered a shelter) only for a coupe, the cottage in Mallorca has a shelter for a cabrio and a coupe, and the cottage in the Isle of Skye has shelter for a 4wd. We then take these pairs and classify them according to the concepts of Reference to determine the mapping of these ontologies:

1. Generate a classification of the above pairs with respect to Reference's relation, by taking any of the two columns of the table above; this gives us two possibilities to explore, suppose we choose:

	hasParkingSpaceFor
$\langle bcn, cabrio \rangle$	0
$\langle bcn, 4wd \rangle$	0
$\langle bcn, coupe \rangle$	1
$\langle mall, cabrio \rangle$	1
$\langle mall, 4wd \rangle$	0
$\langle mall, coupe \rangle$	1
$\langle skye, cabrio \rangle$	0
$\langle skye, 4wd \rangle$	1
$\langle skye, coupe \rangle$	0

This   is   the   column   corresponding   to   hasShelterFor,   hence $g^*(\text{hasParkingSpaceFor}) = \text{hasShelterFor}$.

2. The arity of relation hasParkingSpaceFor forces to classify the instances as in Figure 3 (a).
3. Then we need to complete the table according to the definition of infomorphism. This is done as follows: columns have to correspond to columns of Local's classification table. The only possible completion is shown in Figure 3 (b).

   Hence, f^*(building) = house and f^*(vehicle) = automobile. Rows have to correspond to rows of Reference's classification table. The only possible completion is shown in Figure 3 (c).

	building	vehicle	car
cabrio		1	
bcn	1		
4wd		1	
mall	1		
skye	1		
coupe		1	

(a)

	building	vehicle	car
cabrio	0	1	
bcn	1	0	
4wd	0	1	
mall	1	0	
skye	1	0	
coupe	0	1	

(b)

	building	vehicle	car
cabrio	0	1	1
bcn	1	0	0
4wd	0	1	1
mall	1	0	0
skye	1	0	0
coupe	0	1	1

(c)

Fig. 3. Completing the classification table.

Hence, f^*(car) = automobile, which completes one possible valid ontology mapping.

The steps described above constitute the core part of the IF-Map method. We complement it with heuristic-based techniques to help us kick-start the infomorphism generation.

4.5   Kick-Start for the IF-Map Method

Our definition of ontology morphism (Definition 5) enforces an arity-compatibility check to ensure that the local instances are mapped onto appropriate reference types. When automating this step though, we have to be careful for undesired assignments. These arise when the prospective relations to be mapped share the same types but do not have the same semantics. For instance, assume that Reference has relation hasJobTitle defined over concepts employee and string and Local has relation authoredBy defined over string and employee[8]. The infomorphism generation will map Local's employee to Reference's string and Local's string to Reference's employee, which will inevitably map hasJobTitle relation to authoredBy by virtue of sharing the same types.

To tackle this problem we are thinking of two possible ways: (a) we provide a partial map of concepts from one ontology to concepts of the other or (b) classify some representative instances from the Local to their Reference counterparts.

---

[8] Note that here Reference and Local do not denote the same ontologies used in the mapping example.

This way, we can say that Reference's employee maps onto Local's employee and Reference's string maps onto string and only this mapping between these types is possible. This will constrain the infomorphism generation and the offending infomorphisms will not appear. To do this partial mapping automatically we employ a set of heuristics (originally described in [21], pp.95–97). In particular, these heuristics are working on a purely syntactic match fashion but they use the *is-a* hierarchy and type checking to find types that are shared by relations in both ontologies. The algorithm goes like that:

1. find relation names from both ontologies that are syntactically equivalent (i.e., publishedBy from Reference matches publishedBy from Local);
2. check if their argument types match (since we are dealing with binary relations, both argument types have to match, for instance employee for Reference and Local; paper for Reference and Local);
3. use these types to fix a partial map to start the infomorphism generation;
4. if 2 fails, then use the *is-a* hierarchy to traverse the hierarchy of types and find syntactically common types that subsume or are subsumed by the common relations' argument types (we traverse the *is-a* hierarchy in both directions: we check for parent and child nodes of the starting node);
5. those that are found syntactically equivalent will be used as in 3 for partially fixing the initial map of the two ontologies;
6. if step 2 yields only one argument type match, use it and do 4 for the other argument type;

Note that this algorithm relies on the existence of common relation names in both ontologies. This is based on the assumption that, since the role of reference ontologies within a community is to favour the sharing of knowledge expressed by means of different local ontologies, many of the names of concepts and relations used to express the reference ontology are syntactically equivalent to the ones used in the local ontologies to express the same (or similar) concepts and relations.

In case this fails, the algorithm cannot be initiated and then we turn to the second solution proposed above, which is to let the knowledge engineer classify representative instances manually. This solution though, requires familiarisation of the engineer with both the reference and local ontologies.

5 Evaluation of IF-Map

We applied the algorithmic steps described in the illustrative example of Section 4 in a large-scale experiment that we conducted in the context of the AKT project. We have not finished our experiments yet, but we have done enough to assess IF-Map. The setting of the experiment is as follows: in the AKT project, five participating universities are contributing their own ontologies representing their own important concepts in the domain of computer-science departments in the UK. There is also a reference ontology, AKT Reference, which was built collaboratively by interested participants from all five sites. So, we had to deal

with five local ontologies and a reference ontology. The local ontologies were populated whereas the reference ontology was not. That is in-line with the IF-Map
scenario as we described in Section 4. Furthermore, since local ontologies are
maintained locally, by five different sites, it anticipated to use a variety of formalisms and tools for ontology design, development, and deployment. IF-Map's
architecture (see Section 2) allows for different formalisms to be used as input.

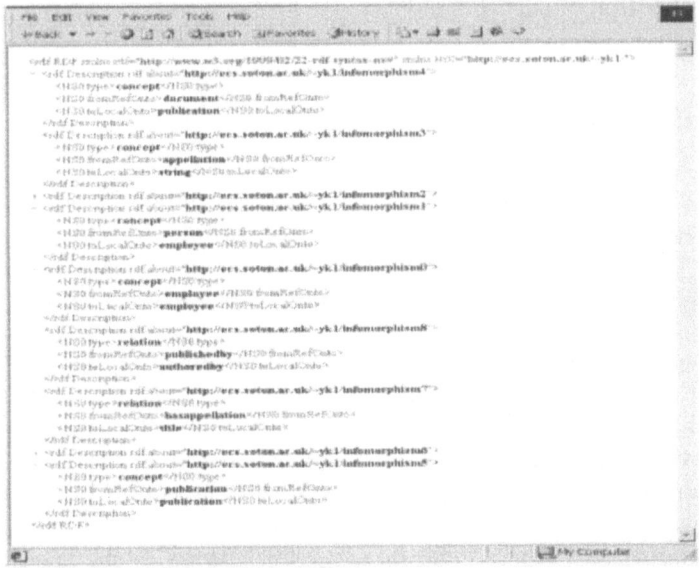

Fig. 4. Results of ontology mapping in Web accessible RDF format.

We applied IF-Map to map `AKT Reference` to Southampton's and Edinburgh's local ontologies. These local ontologies are populated with a few thousand instances (ranging from 5k to 18k) and a few hundreds of concepts. There
are a few axioms defined, and both have relations. The `AKT Reference` ontology
is more compact, it has no instances and approximately 65 concepts with 45 relations. There are a few axioms defined as well. In Figure 4 we include a screenshot
of our Web accessible RDF results page for some relations and concepts. In this
page, we show a small fraction of the results from mapping concepts and relations from `AKT Reference` to to their counterparts in Southampton's ontology.
As we can see, apart from mapping concepts, like `AKT Reference`'s document
to Southampton's publication we also map relations: `AKT Reference`'s hasap-
pellation to Southampton's title. The arities of these relations allow this sort
of mapping, whereas in other ontologies this would have been inappropriate,
when for example title refers to title of a paper. These mappings were generated
automatically; IF-Map initiated these experiments with the semantically-rich
heuristics we described in 4.5.

The algorithms we have implemented so far are of exponential complexity in the number of concepts. Although the implementation of IF-Map as it currently stands can still be improved by using more sophisticated algorithms for ontology morphism generation, we are basing the IF-Map method on an incremental construction of ontology morphisms, in order to tackle large-scale ontologies: first, only certain manageable fragments of the ontologies are mapped, and next, these fixed maps are used to guide the generation of larger fragments, in the manner explained in Section 4. We are currently investigating heuristics for the automatic identification of such fragments.

6   Related Work

IF-Map, amid its well-defined purpose of ontology mapping and, extensionally, merging, taps on a number of areas and uses techniques discussed in diverse communities. Therefore, it is impossible to compile an exhaustive list of references to related work but we have deliberately expanded the scope of references to cover as many representative works as possible. At the same time though, we were careful to identify works that are related somehow with IF-Map's core characteristics: use of formal definitions of ontology mapping, use of Information Flow theory, expressed in a declarative and executable language in a domain and tool independent manner, applied as a method and as a theory for ontology mapping, and being — under circumstances — fully automatic. Not all of the references we cite here meet these criteria; some provide features that IF-Map does not support and others focus on a single criterion of the list given above. Nevertheless, the diversity of works reported in this section demonstrates the importance of the topic in a number of communities. Space reasons and this paper's scope prevents us from getting into great detail when describing related work hereinafter, but we aim to give a flavour of the current landscape in ontology mapping research across different communities.

Among the few formal approaches in ontology mapping and merging is that of FCA-Merge [35]. It is based on Formal Concept Analysis [16] and it is aimed, mainly, at merging ontologies, hence, FCA-Merge. Its developers, Stumme and Maedche, incorporate natural language techniques in their FCA-based method to derive a lattice of concepts. The lattice is then explored manually by a knowledge engineer who will build the merged ontology with semi-automatic guidance from FCA-Merge. In particular, FCA-Merge works as follows: the input to the method are a set of documents from which concepts will be extracted and the ontologies that will be merged. These documents should be representative of the domain at question and be related to the ontologies. They also have to cover all concepts from both ontologies as well as separating them well enough. These strong assumptions have to be met in order to obtain good results from the FCA-Merge. Once the concepts will be extracted, the authors construct the concepts lattice and from there provide semi-automatic support for knowledge engineers to derive the final merged ontology.

Formal Concept Analysis has also been used by the database community in their federated databases domain. In particular, Schmitt and Saake employ Formal Concept Analysis techniques to assist database schema integration [33]. The focus of their work is to merge different inheritance hierarchies by decomposing overlapping class extensions into base extensions and use Formal Concept Analysis techniques to inform algorithms for integrating the databases schemata. In the Scalable Knowledge Composition (SKC) project, Jannink and colleagues [20] presented the use of a rule-based algebra for encapsulating and composing ontologies. Ontologies are clustered in contexts, and the authors use a rule-based algebra to define interfaces to link the extracted contexts with the original ontologies.

Fridman Noy and Musen have developed two systems for performing ontology merging and alignment in the Protégé-2000 [18] ontology development environment: SMART [13] and its successor PROMPT [14]. These tools use linguistic similarity matches between concepts for initiating the merging or alignment process and then use the underlying ontological structures in Protégé-2000 environment (classes, slots, facets) to inform a set of heuristics for identifying further matches between the ontologies. A similar tool has been developed by McGuinness and colleagues for the Ontolingua ontology editor: Chimaera [28]. As in PROMPT, this tool is interactive and the engineer is in charge of making decisions that will affect the merging.

From the machine learning perspective we report the works of Lacher and Groh [25] and Doan and colleagues [8] where their systems employ machine learning algorithms in conjunction with similarity measures to yield prospective mappings between ontology concepts. Other works worth citing here are Chalupsky's OntoMorph [5] translation system for symbolic knowledge, Kiryakov and colleagues' OntoMap portal [24] for mapping linguistic ontologies, the OBSERVER system [29] by Mena and colleagues for information integration, Gangemi and colleagues' [15] ONIONS methodology for medical ontologies, Visser and Tamma's heterogeneity categorisation [36], and the reports from Pinto and colleagues [31] and Fridman Noy and Hafner in [12].

7 Summary

In this paper we presented a novel method and a theory for ontology mapping. We formalised the notion of ontology, ontology morphism, ontology mapping and linked them to the formal notions of local logic and logic infomorphism stemming from IF theory. We then applied them in a mechanised manner, IF-Map, to map diverse ontologies. The first results are promising for the application of IF-Map in large-scale ontology mapping efforts and are continue researching fruitful extensions of it, such as, ontology merging, reasoning about ontology evolution, and inclusion of ontological axioms.

Acknowledgements. This work is supported under the Advanced Knowledge Technologies (AKT) Interdisciplinary Research Collaboration (IRC), which is sponsored by the UK Engineering and Physical Sciences Research Council under grant number GR/N15764/01. The AKT IRC comprises the Universities of Aberdeen, Edinburgh, Sheffield, Southampton and the Open University.

References

1. M. Barr. The Chu construction. *Theory and Applications of Categories*, 2(2):17–35, 1996.
2. J. Barwise and J. Perry. *Situations and Attitudes*. MIT Press, 1983.
3. J. Barwise and J. Seligman. *Information Flow: the Logic of distributed systems.* Cambridge Tracts in Theoretical Computer Science 44. Cambridge University Press, 1997.
4. T. Berners-Lee, J. Hendler., and O. Lassila. The Semantic Web. *Scientific American*, May 2001.
5. H. Chalupksy. OntoMorph: A Translation System for Symbolic Knowledge. In *Proceedings of the 17th International Conference on Knowledge Representation and Reasoning (KR-2000), Colorado, USA*, April 2000.
6. F. Corrêa da Silva, W. Vasconcelos, D. Robertson, V. Brilhante, A. de Melo, M. Finger, and J. Agustí. On the insufficiency of ontologies: problems in knowledge sharing and alternative solutions. *Knowledge Based Systems*, 15(3):147–167, 2002.
7. K. Devlin. *Logic and Information*. Cambridge University Press, 1991.
8. A. Doan, J. Madhavan, P. Domingos, and A. Halevy. Learning to map between ontologies on the Semantic Web. In *Proceedings of the 11th International World Wide Web Conference (WWW 2002), Hawaii, USA*, May 2002.
9. J. Domingue. Tadzebao and WebOnto: Discussing, Browsing, and Editing Ontologies on the Web. In *Proceedings of the 11th Knowledge Acquisition, Modelling and Management Workshop, KAW'98, Banff, Canada*, April 1998.
10. F. Dretske. *Logic and the Flow of Information*. MIT Press, 1981.
11. A. Farquhar, R. Fikes, and J. Rice. The Ontolingua Server: a tool for collaborative ontology construction. *International Journal of Human-Computer Studies*, 46(6):707–728, June 1997.
12. N. Fridman Noy and C.D. Hafner. The State of the Art in Ontology Design: A Survey and Comparative Review. *AI Magazine*, 18(3):53–74, 1997.
13. N. Fridman Noy and M. Musen. SMART: Automated Support for Ontology Merging and Alignment. In *Proceedings of the 12th Workshop on Knowledge Acquisition, Modelling and Management (KAW'99), Banff, Canada*, October 1999.
14. N. Fridman Noy and M. Musen. PROMPT: Algorithm and Tool for Automated Ontology Merging and Alignment. In *Proceedings of the 17th National Conference on Artificial Intelligence, (AAAI'00), Austin, TX, USA*, July 2000.
15. A. Gangemi, D. Pisanelli, and G. Steve. Ontology Integration: Experiences with Medical Terminologies. In N. Guarino, editor, *Proceedings of the 1st International Conference on Formal Ontology in Information Systems, FOIS'98, Trento, Italy*, pages 163–178, June 1998.
16. B. Ganter and R. Wille. *Formal Concept Analysis: mathematical foundations.* Springer, 1999.
17. R. Genesereth and R. Fikes. *Knowledge Interchange Format*. Computer Science Dept., Stanford University, 3.0 edition, 1992. Technical Report, Logic-92-1.
18. W. Grosso, H. Eriksson, R. Fergerson, J. Gennari, S. Tu, and M. Musen. Knowledge Modelling at the Millennium (The Design and Evolution of Protege-2000). In *proceedings of the 12th Knowledge Acquisition, Modelling, and Management(KAW'99), Banff, Canada*, October 1999.

19. V. Gupta. *Chu Spaces: A Model of Concurrency*. PhD thesis, Stanford University, 1994.
20. J. Jannink, S. Pichai, D. Verheijen, and G. Wiederhold. Encapsulation and Composition of Ontologies. In *Proceedings of the AAAI'98 Workshop on Information Integration, Madison, WI, USA*, July 1998.
21. Y. Kalfoglou. *Deploying Ontologies in Software Design*. PhD thesis, Department of Artificial Intelligence, University of Edinburgh, June 2000.
22. R. Kent. The Information Flow Foundation for Conceptual Knowledge Organization. In *Proceedings of the 6th International Conference of the International Society for Knowledge Organization (ISKO), Toronto, Canada*, August 2000.
23. R. Kent. The IFF Foundation Ontology, v.1.0. In *Proceedings of the IJCAI'01 Workshop on the IEEE Standard Upper Ontology, Seattle, WA, USA*, August 2001.
24. A. Kiryakov, K. Simov, and M. Dimitrov. OntoMap: Portal for Upper-Level Ontologies. In *Proceedings of the 2nd International Conference on Formal Ontology in Information Systems (FOIS'01), Ogunquit, Maine, USA*, October 2001.
25. M. Lacher and G. Groh. Facilitating the exchange of explicit knowledge through ontology mappings. In *Proceedings of the 14th International FLAIRS conference, Key West, FL, USA*, May 2001.
26. O. Lassila and R. Swick. Resource Description Framework (RDF) Model and Syntax Specification. W3C recommendation, W3C, February 1999.
27. B. McBride. Jena: Implementing the RDF model and syntax specification. Technical report, HP Labs at Bristol, UK, December 2001. Semantic Web Activity, http://www.hpl.hp.com/semweb/.
28. D. McGuinness, R. Fikes, J. Rice, and S. Wilder. An Environment for Merging and Testing Large Ontologies. In *Proceedings of the 17th International Conference on Principles of Knowledge Representation and Reasoning (KR-2000), Colorado, USA*, April 2000.
29. E. Mena, V. Kashyap, A. Illarramendi, and A. Sheth. Domain Specific Ontologies for Semantic Information Brokering on the Global Information Infrastructure. In N. Guarino, editor, *Proceedings of the 1st International Conference on Formal Ontology in Information Systems (FOIS'98), Trento, Italy*, pages 269–283. IOS Press, June 1998.
30. E. Motta. *Reusable Components for Knowledge Models: Case Studies in Parametric Design Problem Solving*, volume 53 of *Frontiers in Artificial Intelligence and Applications*. IOS Press, 1999.
31. S. Pinto, A. Gómez-Pérez, and J. Martins. Some Issues on Ontology Integration. In *Proceedings of the IJCAI-99 Workshop on Ontologies and Problem-Solving Methods (KRR5), Stockholm, Sweden*, August 1999.
32. V. R. Pratt. The Stone gamut: A coordination of mathematics. In *Logic in Computer Science*, pages 444–454. IEEE Computer Society Press, 1995.
33. I. Schmitt and G. Saake. Merging Inheritance Hierarchies for Database Integration. In *Proceedings of the 3rd International Conference on Cooperative Information Systems (CoopIS'98), New York, USA*, August 1998.
34. M. Schorlemmer. Duality in Knowledge Sharing. In *Proceedings of the 7th International Symposium on Artificial Intelligence and Mathematics, Fort Lauderdale, Florida, USA*, January 2002.
35. G. Stumme and A. Maedche. Ontology Merging for Federated Ontologies on the Semantic Web. In *Proceedings of the International Workshop for Foundations of Models for Information Integration (FMII-2001), Viterbo, Italy*, September 2001.
36. P. Visser and V. Tamma. An experiment with ontology-based agent clustering. In *Proceedings of the IJCAI-99 Workshop on Ontologies and Problem-Solving Methods, Stockholm, Sweden*, August 1999.

The Semantics of Semantic Annotation

Sean Bechhofer[1], Leslie Carr[2], Carole Goble[1], Simon Kampa[2], and
Timothy Miles-Board[2]

[1] Information Management Group
Department of Computer Science, Kilburn Building
University of Manchester, Oxford Road, Manchester M13 9PL
http://img.cs.man.ac.uk
seanb@cs.man.ac.uk
[2] Intelligence, Agents, Multimedia Group
Department of Electronics & Computer Science
University of Southampton, Highfield, Southampton SO17 1BJ
http://www.iam.ecs.soton.ac.uk

Abstract. Semantic metadata will play a significant role in the provision of the Semantic Web. Agents will need metadata that describes the content of resources in order to perform operations, such as retrieval, over those resources. In addition, if rich semantic metadata is supplied, those agents can then employ reasoning over the metadata, enhancing their processing power. Key to this approach is the provision of annotations, both through automatic and human means. The semantics of these annotations, however, in terms of the mechanisms through which they are interpreted and presented to the user, are sometimes unclear. In this paper, we identify a number of candidate interpretations of annotation, and discuss the impact these interpretations may have on Semantic Web applications.

1 Introduction

The Semantic Web (SW) vision, as articulated by Tim Berners-Lee [2], is of a Web in which resources are accessible not only to humans, but also to automated processes, e.g., automated "agents" roaming the web performing useful tasks such as improved search (in terms of precision) and resource discovery, information brokering and information filtering. The automation of tasks depends on elevating the status of the web from machine-readable to something we might call machine-understandable. The key idea is to have data on the web defined and linked in such a way that its meaning is explicitly interpretable by software processes rather than just being implicitly interpretable by humans.

To realise this vision, it will be necessary to associate *metadata* (i.e., data describing content/functionality) with web resources. One mechanism for associating such metadata is annotation. In particular, we may wish to annotate resources with *semantic* metadata that provides some indication of the content of a resource. This is a further step along the way from simple textual annotations, as the intention within the SW context is that this information will be

R. Meersman, Z. Tari (Eds.): CoopIS/DOA/ODBASE 2002, LNCS 2519, pp. 1152–1167, 2002.

accessible not only to humans but also to software agents. In order to do this we require languages which will support the representation of semantic metadata.

Standardisation proposals for metadata languages have already been submitted to the World Wide Web Consortium (W3C), in particular the Resource Description Framework (RDF) and RDF Schema (RDF(S)) – see [8] for a discussion of the roles of these languages and of XML/XML Schema. However, such annotations will be of limited value to automated processes unless they share a common understanding as to their meaning. Ontologies (which have already proved their usefulness in a range of application domains [28,23,26] can help to meet this requirement by providing a "representation of a shared conceptualisation of a particular domain" and a shared, controlled vocabulary that can be communicated across people and applications [11,12].

In addition to the requirement for representation languages that support the sharing and exchange of semantic information between applications, we must also have a common understanding of the annotation process. Schemas to support annotation have been developed [19], but these do not explicitly provide support for this understanding. What does it mean when we make an annotation, and what are the implicit tasks that are being performed? Within the SW context, confusion reigns as to the interpretation of the annotation task. In order to support the use of automated agents (a central tenet to the Semantic Web vision), we must be *explicit* about the assumptions that we make and the context within which such annotations should be interpreted. Note that our use of the phrase "the *semantics* of semantic annotation" refers to the provision of a consistent interpretation of the task, but we do not intend to present here a formal semantics, such as that provided for languages like DAML+OIL [27].

The paper is structured as follows. We first give a brief introduction to the COHSE project and the approach being adopted there. This gives an overview of our motivation and some context for the following discussions. We then discuss annotation and provide a classification of annotation tasks along with their intended semantics. We discuss the related issue of identification and finally conclude with some remarks concerning future directions and recommendations. References to existing and related work are made throughout the paper.

2   The COHSE Project

Our interest in annotation here is within the context of the COHSE (Conceptual Open Hypermedia Service) project [3]. COHSE aims to bring together an open hypermedia architecture (in particular the Distributed Links Service [4] or DLS) with ontological services in order to provide an architecture for the Semantic Web [10].

Detailed descriptions of the COHSE system can be found in [3,10]. Put briefly, the COHSE approach consists of a *COHSE agent* (along with supporting services such as an *ontology service* and *annotation service*) that augments documents with links based on the semantic content of those documents. The system em-

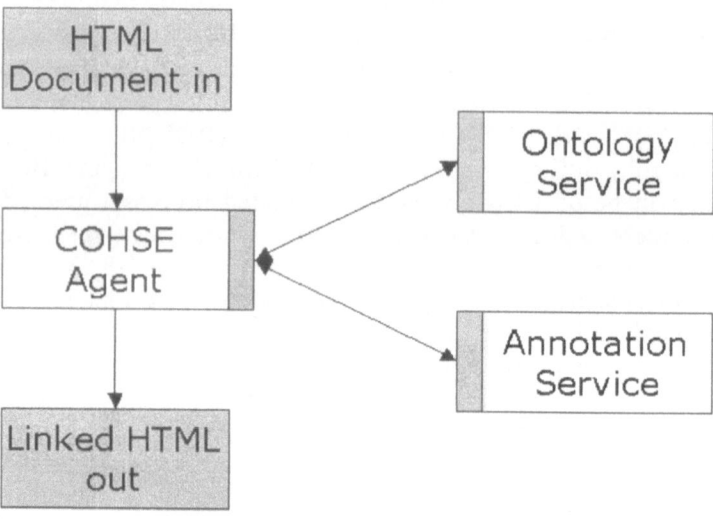

Fig. 1. COHSE Architecture

ploys either a specialist browser (based on Mozilla[1]) or a proxy through which all http requests are routed. The words and terms that appeared in a document are used as entry points to an ontology. The relevant concepts in the ontology can then be used to determine appropriate targets for links out of the given resource. Key to the novelty of the COHSE approach is the provision of an *editorial component* within the agent. This component uses information within the ontology (such as hierarchical classification) in order to determine whether the links are suitable or to perhaps expand or cull the set of possible targets. Figure 1 shows a simplified view of the basic architecture of the system.

Figure 2 shows a page taken from Sun's Java Tutorial web site. In Figure 3, we see the same page augmented by the COHSE agent. A number of link anchors (signified by the small "L" icon) have been added to the page. One of these has been opened up, and we see a collection of possible targets which have been annotated as being "about" the particular concept selected – in this case the concept of byte.

In addition to using the words and phrases that appear in the documents, the COHSE agent can also use explicit metadata applied to the resources (rather than relying solely on mappings from words and terms). This approach relies on the ability to annotate resources with semantic metadata – where by semantic metadata we mean the explicit binding of concepts to resources rather than the use of terms and words as simple proxies for the concepts. The explicit annotations can then help guide the editorial component in its linking strategy. For example, if a passage in a web page has been annotated as being about a particular subject, say programming datatypes, the editorial component may

---

[1] http://www.mozilla.org

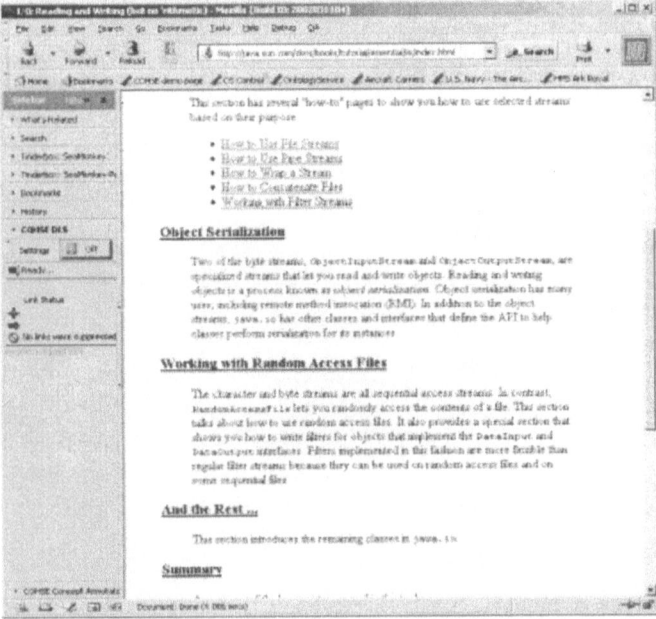

Fig. 2. Before COHSE Linking

know that there are certain terms that should be focused on within the context of that annotation (say the terms int or float) – an example of an agent using semantic information to make decisions as to its behaviour.

2.1   Produce and Consume

The situation has parallels with the underlying motivation for the use of rich languages for representing content on the Semantic Web. Languages like DAML+OIL [6] are being proposed as mechanisms which provide "machine-processable" semantic information. They provide an explicit representation of the relationships between terms and concepts which can then be used by reasoners or software agents to interpret those terms and concepts. The vision is one of providing shared conceptualizations, which then allow communities to share and exchange information unambiguously.

Within COHSE (or indeed other SW systems), there are two complementary strands, with annotation *providers* enriching content and annotation *consumers* using those annotations to process, organise and present information to end users. The consumer could be a sophisticated ontological search process or portal, or alternatively document enrichment through the addition of links as used by COHSE. It is key within this relationship, however, that consumer and provider *share underlying assumptions* about the annotations. Part of this sharing is provided by the use of concept models or ontologies, part of it is provided by

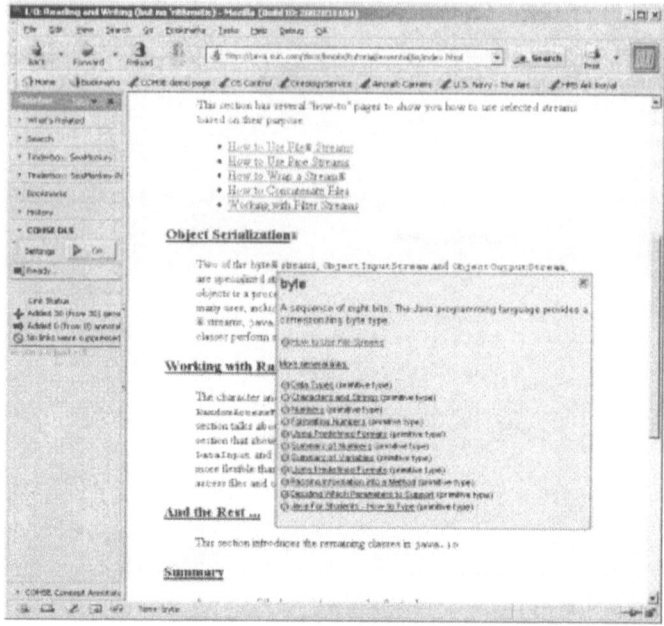

Fig. 3. After COHSE Linking

shared assumptions about the way these terms are to be used. If we build rich models, and then use them in a haphazard fashion, we are in some way selling ourselves short.

2.2 Linking as Annotation

The provision of dynamic linking as used by the COHSE project can be seen as a kind of annotation – in this case hypertext links are being provided rather than some textual annotation. This will be discussed in further detail below (as an example of **Link Annotation**), but we introduce the notion here as it has relevance to the description of COHSE.

Koivunen et al. [18] discuss approaches to Web annotations and categorise systems as, in the main, either **proxy-based** or browser-based. In a proxy-based approach, the annotations and document are merged by the proxy, with the browser seeing only the merged documents. In a browser-based approach, a specialist browser application will merge the annotations with the original documents while browsing. Annotations can be stored separately and provided via some annotation service (or kept within the proxy itself).

COHSE has two implementations, as either proxy or browser – the proxy having the advantage that no specialist browsing software is required, and delivery can be targeted at a number of platforms (e.g. mobile devices).

Within COHSE, the purpose of annotation is twofold: to populate a knowledge base for retrieval, and to provide anchors for links as the annotations are used to derive outward links from resources. At its simplest, then, annotation within COHSE can be seen as a mechanism that allows the user to specify possible link anchors within a document, with the anchor being associated with a conceptual description. This description will then be used to determine appropriate links at read-time. Simultaneously, the annotations are being used to provide link targets (as is the case in other, resource-discovery based, systems).

2.3 Extending Simple Annotation

COHSE's current implementation adopts a basic approach to the interpretation of annotation – an annotation simply associates a resource with a concept and no attempt is made to disambiguate the relationship between the concept and resource. This simple approach has served us well and allows us to extend and enrich the hypertext. An experiment based on Sun's Java Tutorial site[2] has been conducted and an evaluation of the resulting hypertext structure produced by the COHSE agent shows promising results[3].

A possible extension to this situation is to provide further information that describes in more detail the relationship between the resource and the annotation concept. This then has an impact in two ways:

- it can affect the way that the agent presents the link anchor;
- it can affect the way that possible link targets are found or displayed.

This leads us to a desire to classify and categorise the different ways in which this association between resource and concept could be made. The remainder of the paper proposes a number of different interpretations of the annotation process and discusses how those interpretations could affect the behaviour of systems such as COHSE.

3 Annotation

> **annotation** noun. A note by way of explanation or comment added to a text or diagram.   *New Oxford Dictionary of English*

Annotation takes many forms and there are a number of what we could term "popular" ideas of annotation. Marshall [21] writes that "[annotation] has been construed in many ways: as link making, as path building, as commentary, as marking in or around existing text, as a decentering of authority, as a record of reading and interpretation, or as community memory". Here we briefly present a rough classification of annotation types. We will return to this in more detail in the later section on semantics.

Textual Annotation is the process whereby notes or commentaries are added to resources. Annotations of this kind have been used for many years in

---

[2] http://java.sun.com/tutorial

[3] See http://cohse.semanticweb.org/evaluation for preliminary findings.

communities such as biology. For example the SWISS-PROT database [24] contains protein sequence information along with annotations describing functions, structure, domains, sites and so on. Within a database like SWISS-PROT, the annotations are first-class citizens, and are, in effect, the data. Although some use is made of controlled vocabularies such as GO [25], the hand-crafted and hand-curated annotations are primarily aimed at human readers.

This is the kind of activity supported by Annotea [17,29,18]. Extensions to the basic schema allow the use of richer annotation types [5] (for example commentaries can be marked as replies or gathered into threaded discussions), but a principle characteristic of this approach is that it is primarily aimed at human readers (and authors).

Systems such as the Distributed Links Service (DLS) [4] or 3rd Voice [20], allow the addition of links to arbitrary documents (including those in control of a third party). This **Link Annotation** extends the textual annotation notion, where here the content of the annotation is given, not by some text, but by a link destination (and possibly associated behaviour). Again, link annotation can be seen to be an activity primarily targeted at human readers.

Finally, we can consider what might be called **Semantic Annotation**, where the content of the annotation consists of some rich semantic information[4]. This idea of semantic annotation has been pursued in both the Ontobroker [7] and SHOE [16] projects and more recently in COHSE [3]. In both Ontobroker and SHOE, specialised markup was inserted into web pages – this markup contained semantic information drawn from an ontology providing richer descriptions of resource content. In COHSE, a more open annotation framework following the DLS philosophy is in use, allowing the decoration of arbitrary resources without the necessity to control the original document. Semantic Annotation is targeted not only at human readers of resources, but also at software agents – this does bring with it the requirement that relationships are explicitly represented. The use of semantic information taken from well defined ontologies will allow agents to make decisions based on those resource descriptions (for example the COHSE editorial component as described above).

Returning to Marshall [21], a number of different axes or dimensions are identified that reflect the forms of annotation. Included in these are a notion of *formal* vs. *informal*. Informal includes personal notes written in the margin while reading an article. Formal is deemed to be metadata following structural standards and assigned values using conventional naming authorities. The use of semantic annotation, drawing on conceptual models represented using well-defined knowledge representation languages can be seen to sit at the extreme end of the formal spectrum, perhaps even more so than Marshall's original intension of formality. Also of interest is the identification of *explicit* vs. *tacit* annotation. According to Marshall, many personal annotations are tacit – they are telegraphic and incomplete and rely on contextual information for their interpretation. For example, a bookmark, highlighted sentence or the annotation

---

[4] Of course Textual Annotations can also contain rich semantic information, but in general this is not accessible to machine-processing.

"No!" are examples of tacit annotation as we need extra information about the annotator, or the history of the annotation process in order to interpret them. An explicit annotation will carry sufficient information for its interpretation. As Marshall says, the dimension of explicit vs. tacit is crucially related to intelligibility – in the context of the provision of markup intended for software agents or processes the requirement of explicitness is particularly strong as such agents will not possess the real world knowledge, reading history, cultural background and so on, of human readers.

4   Semantics of Annotation

Here we present a classification of possible uses of annotation. This can be seen as a classification of the possible semantics of the annotation relationship (where here we use the term semantics in a loose fashion). For the purposes of this discussion, we consider the following situation. A web page with the URL U is being viewed and a region of the document corresponding to an XPointer expression X has been selected. This is to be annotated with a concept expression C.

What does it now mean to annotate resource U\#X with concept C? Table 1 lists a number of what we might call use cases regarding this action. For each class described in the table, we discuss the ideas in more detail using simple concrete examples to illustrate the differences.

Note that the distinction between these different annotation types introduced in Section 3 can become blurred. For example, semantic annotation (e.g. the association of a resource fragment with a machine-processable concept description as discussed here) may result in the addition of a link if the resource is viewed using the COHSE agent. The **Type** column of Table 1 gives an idea of the annotation type in terms of Section 3.

Decoration is the Annotea view of the world, where annotations are seen as commentaries on resources. In the simple annotation scheme used by Annotea, the body of a resource is a chunk of HTML, which simply provides the (textual) content of the annotation. Other approaches (such as COHSE [1]) may extend this schema, however, to provide annotations of other types.

Linking (or possibly *Transclusion*, to borrow Ted Nelson's term) provides a simple COHSE view – annotations are simply a mechanism that provides link anchors. If the content of that annotation happens to be a complex conceptual description that then enables a client agent to support "better" linking, then all to the good.

Instance Identification makes a strong assertion about the resource U\#X, i.e. that it is an instance of a particular class. For example, the resource http://www.w3.org/TR/xptr is a CandidateRecommendation of the W3C. The situation here is clear in part, because in this case, the object about which the assertion is being made (the XPointer Recommendation) is clearly accessed by the given URI. Dereferencing the URI provides exactly the object that the assertion is about.

Table 1. Possible Uses of Annotation. U is a URL, X is an XPointer expression and C is a concept

Name	Usage	Type
Decoration	When the user views U, the concept C will decorate the resource fragment referred to by U\#X.	link/textual
Linking	When the user views U, links about C will appear with the source anchor being the fragment U\#X.	link
Instance Identification	We are making an assertion that there is some individual x in the world, such that x is an instance of the concept C, and the url U\#X identifies x.	kb population
Instance Reference	We are making an assertion that there is some individual x in the world, such that x is an instance of the concept C, and the url U\#X in some way refers to x.	kb population
Aboutness	The resource fragment U\#X is "about" C.	textual
Pertinence	For any x such that x is an instance of C, the information in the resource fragment U\#X is pertinent to x.	textual

For annotations of class **Instance Reference**, the situation is less clear. The resource http://www.mcfc.co.uk/player.asp?PLAYER=1191 is about Shaun Goater the Manchester City football (soccer) player. We could annotate this resource with the concept Footballer, but the intended interpretation here is that there is an object in the world (Shaun Goater) that is an instance of Footballer and which is referred to or referenced by the given URI rather than a statement that the URI is an instance of the concept Footballer. A human reader seeing such an annotation would implicitly assume that the assertion was being made about the subject of the page (e.g. Shaun Goater), as the idea of a web page being a Footballer is nonsensical – to make this inference, however, requires background and world knowledge.

This distinction between **Instance Identification** and **Instance Reference** and the mechanisms that may be used to support the difference is discussed in the later section on Identification.

Aboutness gives a rather loose notion of annotation. In contrast to **Instance Identification** and **Instance Reference**, there is no assertion of the existence of a specific instance of the concept C. Instead there is a loose association of the resource with the concept. As an example of this, the page http://www.nczooeletrack.org/ is about Elephants. It does not discuss a particular elephant, nor does it contain information that applies about the class of elephants (see discussion of **Pertinence** below).

Pertinence gives what we might call a kind of weak ontological extension. It allows us to make assertions about the classes and concepts within the ontology without actually explicitly enocoding or embedding that information within the

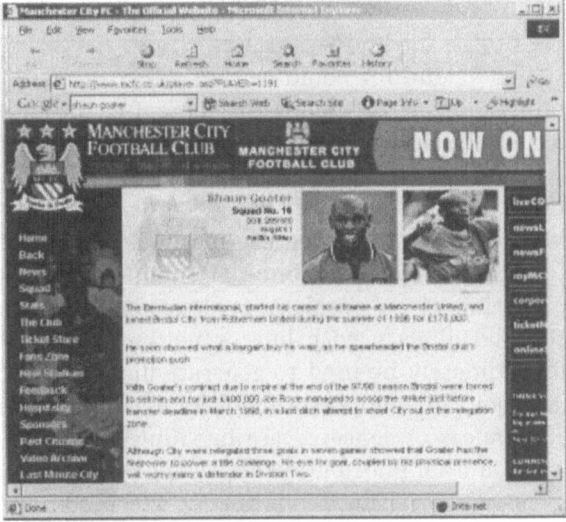

Fig. 4. Page about Shaun Goater

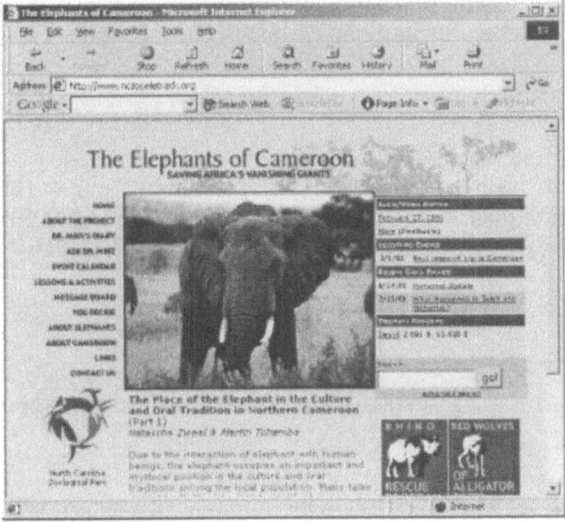

Fig. 5. Page about Elephants

ontology. Of course this means that the information may not be readily available to reasoning agents, but it may be that the information is not appropriate for a reasoner. For example, the EPSRC (Engineering and Physical Sciences Research Council) web site may have pages which contain useful information relating to Researchers such as employment opportunities, pay scales and the like. This is not necessarily information we would wish to model directly within the ontology, but is, in the main, of interest to researchers. An annotation of such a resource could be considered to be in the **Pertinence** class.

Aboutness and **Pertinence** could be considered as examples of textual annotation as introduced above – although the content of the annotation may have some richer structure, the annotation is essentially a note or commentary on the resource. We can consider **Decoration** and **Linking** as enabling mechanisms for the construction of hypertexts, in other words link annotation (although **Decoration** is also a kind of commentary mechanism). In contrast, **Instance Identification** and **Instance Reference** are about knowledge base construction, i.e. the population of an ontology or conceptual schema with instances and do not correspond directly with link or textual annotation (although the information could ultimately be used to generate links).

The OntoMat tool [14] supports annotation corresponding to **Instance Identification**. Instances of concepts are introduced and have fillers for their relationships harvested from information appearing on the web page being annotated. In the current version, annotations are not anchored to particular resource fragments, but are instead stored as markup within the web page being annotated. The new instances have generated identifiers which are based on the URI of the page being annotated. This could be extended to use external storage of the annotations (for example using an annotation service or RDF repository) along with an XPointer mechanism.

5   Instance vs. Aboutness and Identification

A key question to address when we consider annotation is that of *instance-of* vs. *aboutness*. RDF has a built in property `rdf:type` that allows us to make assertions about individual resources. For example, take the RDF statement shown in Figure 6.

```
<rdf:Description rdf:about="http://www.w3.org/TR/xptr/">
 <rdf:type rdf:resource=
 "http://cohse.semanticweb.org/ontologies/docs#W3C_Candidate_Recommendation"/>
</rdf:Description>
```

Fig. 6. XPointer spec is a Candidate Recommendation

This says that the resource `http://www.w3.org/TR/xptr/` is an instance of the class `W3C_CandidateRecommendation`. RDF is well set up to deal with such assertions. However, there may often be situations where we want to make an assertion that a particular resource is *about* a particular concept (in terms of its content), rather than saying it is an instance of it. This relates to annotations of kind **Instance Reference** as discussed above.

The instance vs. aboutness issue is closely related to the problem of **identification** of objects within the Semantic Web. In a fully-fledged implementation of the SW, we would expect to be able to make assertions not only about web resources, but also about objects, for example being able to assert information about Sean Bechhofer the person, not just about the URIs `http://www.cs.man.ac.uk/~seanb` or `mailto:seanb@cs.man.ac.uk`. In order to do this we need mechanisms that allow us to refer to objects that may not directly have an explicitly dereferenceable URI. Mechanisms such as **tdb** [22] or existential quantification over DAML+OIL `uniqueProperties` [15] have been proposed which allow us to refer to "the thing described by x" or "the thing with property x".

These mechanisms will then allow us to support interpretations such as **Instance Reference** as discussed above. For instance, in our example of Shaun Goater, we can now say that `tdb:20011030:http://www.mcfc.co.uk/player.asp?PLAYER=1191` has `rdf:type` `Footballer`, in other words the thing described by the given URI (i.e. Shaun Goater) is a footballer.

Note that we should not confuse RDF's **rdf:about** attribute with "aboutness" as discussed here. Within RDF, **rdf:about** is really a syntactic mechanism that relates a resource to RDF statements concerning it, rather than describing the content of some resource.

The CREAM framework [13] distinguishes different roles that correspond to the treatment of an annotation. **Quotation** copies an excerpt from a resource (such as the string "Shaun Goater"). This is a rather loose association, similar to **Instance Reference** as described above – the copied string is referring to some object in the world. **Reference** allows the metadata to use a pointer to a resource fragment – the example given uses a pointer to a particular place at `http://www.whitehouse.gov` in order to refer to the current U.S. president. If the actual president changes, the metadata will continue to refer to "the president". In this example, this is again an **Instance Reference** as the URL is not the president, but is a reference to the president.

The Annotea [19] schema[5] contains properties which link the Annotation to the resource which it is annotating – `annotates` refers to the enclosing URI and `context` provides the precise location, say using XPointer [9]. The schema also contains a `body` property which provides a link to the body of the annotation. The schema, however, remains agnostic as to the exact semantics of the annotation (in terms of our classification above). All that the annotation asserts is that the selected resource has an annotation which consists of the selected concept. There is no direct instance-of assertion and it is up to the application using the annotations to decide on the appropriate interpretation.

This is weak, and we suggest that extensions to the schema are needed in order to record and represent what the intended semantics of the annotation are. As an example of this approach, the COHSE annotations employed an extension of the W3C Annotea schema, with a property `http://cohse.semanticweb.org/annotation-ns\#concept` being used to indicate that the content of the annotation is a concept. This property is a specialisation of the `http://www.w3.org/2000/10/annotation-ns\#body` prop-

---

[5] `http://www.w3.org/2000/10/annotation-ns`

erty from the Annotea schema. In addition, approaches such as **tdb** [15] give us the machinery to represent the differing interpretations of annotation, The **tdb** namespace provides [22] "...a space which is useful for describing entities, concepts, abstractions, and other items which are not themselves network accessible resources, but have been at some point described by network accessible resources. The "tdb" namespace designates the "thing described by" a resource at a given URI at the given time."

We must ensure, however, that tools provide adequate support for users during the process of annotation.For example, we may expect to be offered different options corresponding to the class or category of annotation being made. This can be seen as a requirement for *explicitness* in the process. We cannot make assumptions about what the intended semantics of the annotation should be.

6   Application Behaviour

What might the effects of the different uses be on the behaviour of applications? We use COHSE as an example of an application making use of semantic annotations in the following discussion, although this topic is relevant to many other SW applications.

Consider the distinction between Instance Identification, Instance Reference and Aboutness as introduced above. The first states that a resource R is an instance of concept C, the second states that R refers to some instance of C and the third states that the resource R is about the concept C (where aboutness is itself a rather loose notion). If this information is included in the annotation, we can make use of it in the following possible ways.

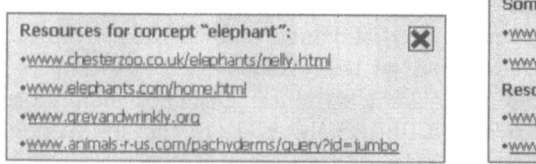 

Fig. 7. Result Presentation depending on annotation type

The information can affect what happens when the agent tries to find link targets for the concept C, when C has been identified as the concept associated with a source anchor. The classification of the annotations may help the application in organising and presenting the links to the user. For example, rather than simply displaying a list of targets, the targets could be grouped according to whether they are deemed to be actual instances of the concept, or simply "about" the concept. Figure 7 gives an example of what the popup link menu might look like in the COHSE application with the left hand side showing the bare list and the right hand the reorganised list.

In our Java tutorial example[6], an example of where this behaviour could help the user would be if we are dealing with a concept such as Java Servlet Engine. The user may want to find out more information about Java Servlet Engines (for example API documentation or an overview of what a Servlet Engine is). In this case pages described as being about the concept may be useful. Alternatively, the user may actually want to go and get a Java Servlet Engine, in which case an Instance Reference or Identification annotation will be of more relevance. The issue here is very much concerned with how information can be organised and presented to the user.

The scenario described above could, of course, hold true of any resource discovery agent – for example this extra information could be of benefit for search engines in ranking and presenting information.

If the annotation has been used to derive a source anchor for a link, this may then affect the way that possible link targets are found. If the user is looking at a resource R which has been annotated as being about some concept C, a sensible option for the agent would be to present links with targets which are instances of C. Alternatively, if the resource being viewed is described a being an instance of C, then it may be more appropriate to display resources about C first (providing me with some more context) rather than other instances of the the concept. Of course, such behaviour is strongly application dependent, and may also depend on factors such as user preferences. However, the presence of the extra information associated with the annotation allows the agent to make more informed choices about the way that results are presented to the user.

7   Concluding Remarks

Semantic metadata is set to play a major part in the implementation of the Semantic Web and annotation will be a primary mechanism for supplying the metadata which will then be used by agents as they retrieve information. In this paper we have presented a number of different interpretations for the process of semantic annotation. Current annotation mechanisms do not support this distinction, or if they do it is in an implicit rather than explicit fashion. Extensions to existing annotation schemas (such as Annotea) can provide some support, but must be done in an agreed fashion to ensure a shared understanding.

It is clear that even without an agreement on the precise interpretation, annotation information can be of use to applications, as is demonstrated by the current COHSE system. Without an agreement on the underlying assumptions behind the use of semantic annotation, however, software agents within the SW will be unable to perform their tasks in a truly consistent fashion. The consistent interpretation of notions such as Instance Identification and Aboutness will help SW applications to present and use information in ways that will further benefit users. Key to the provision of workable semantic annotation is a need for *explicitness*. We require explicitness of **context** to allow us to determine how

---

[6] http://cohse.semanticweb.org/evaluation

to interpret the conceptual content of the annotations. In addition, we require that the intended **semantics** of the annotation be made explicit in order that agents which use the annotations can process and interpret them consistently.

Acknowledgements. This work was supported by EPSRC Grant GR/M75426. The authors would like to thank Bernard Horan of Sun Microsystems for his comments on the paper.

References

1. S. Bechhofer, I. Horrocks, C. Goble, and R. Stevens. OilEd: a Reason-able Ontology Editor for the Semantic Web. In *Proceedings of KI2001, Joint German/Austrian conference on Artificial Intelligence*, Vienna, September 2001.
2. T. Berners-Lee. *Weaving the Web*. Orion Business Books, 1999.
3. L. Carr, S. Bechhofer, C. A. Goble, , and W. Hall. Conceptual Linking: Ontology-based Open Hypermedia. In *Proceedings of WWW10, Tenth World Wide Web Conference*, Hong Kong, May 2001.
4. L. Carr, D. De Roure, W. Hall, , and G. Hill. The Distributed Link Service: A Tool for Publishers, Authors and Readers. *World Wide Web Journal*, 1(1):647–656, 1995.
5. P. Cross, L. Miller, and S. Palmer. Using RDF to Annotate the (Semantic) Web. In *K-Cap Workshop on Knowledge Markup and Semantic Annotation*, Victoria,B.C., Canada, October 2001.
6. DAML+OIL. `http://www.daml.org/language`.
7. S. Decker, M. Erdmann, D. Fensel, , and R. Studer. Ontobroker: Ontology Based Access to Distributed and Semi-Structured Information. In R. Meersman, Z. Tari, , and S. Stevens, editors, *Semantic Issues in Multimedia Systems. Proceedings of DS-8*, pages 351–369. Kluwer Academic Publishers, 1999.
8. S. Decker, F. van Harmelen, J. Broekstra, M. Erdmann, D. Fensel, M. Klein I. Horrocks, , and S. Melnik. The Semantic Web — on the Respective Roles of XML and RDF. *IEEE Internet Computing*, 2000.
9. S. DeRose, E. Maler, and R. Daniel Jr. XML Pointer Language (XPointer) Version 1.0. W3C Candidate Recommendation. `http://www.w3.org/TR/xptr/`, September 2001.
10. C. A. Goble, S. Bechhofer, L. Carr, D. De Roure, , and W. Hall. Conceptual Open Hypermedia = The Semantic Web? In *SemWeb2001 The Second International Workshop on the Semantic Web*, Hong Kong, May 2001.
11. T. R. Gruber. Towards principles for the design of ontologies used for knowledge sharing. In *Proceedings of International Workshop on Formal Ontology*, 1993.
12. N. Guarino. Formal Ontology and Information Systems. In *Proceedings of FOIS-98.*, 1998.
13. S. Handschuh and S. Staab. Authoring and Annotation of Web Pages in CREAM. In *Proceedings of WWW2002, Eleventh World Wide Web Conference*, Honolulu, Hawaii, May 2002.
14. S. Handschuh, S. Staab, and A. Maedche. CREAM - Creating relational metadata with a component-based, ontology-driven annotation framework. In *Proceedings of K-CAP 2001, First International Conference on Knowledge Capture*, Victoria, B.C. Canada, October 2001.

15. S. Hawke. How We Identify Things (on the Semantic Web)?
    http://www.w3.org/2001/03/identification-problem/.
16. J. Heflin, J. Hendler, , and S. Luke. SHOE: A Knowledge Representation Language
    for Internet Applications. Technical Report CS-TR-4078 (UMIACS TR-99-71),
    Department of Computer Science, University of Maryland, 1999.
17. J. Kahan, M.-R. Koivunen, E. Prud'Hommeaux, and R. Swick. Annotea: An Open
    RDF Infrastructure for Shared Web Annotations. In *Proceedings of the Tenth
    International World Wide Web Conference*, Hong Kong, May 2001.
18. M.-R. Koivunen, D. Brickley, J. Kahan, E. Prud'Hommeaux, and R. R. Swick.
    The W3C Collaborative Web Annotation Project ... or how to have fun while
    building an RDF infrastructure.
    http://www.w3.org/2000/02/collaboration/annotation/papers/annotation
    infrastructure, May 2000.
19. M.-R. Koivunen and Ralph Swick. Metadata Based Annotation Infrastructure
    offers Flexibility and Extensibility for Collaborative Applications and Beyond. . In
    K-Cap Workshop on Knowledge Markup and Semantic Annotation, Victoria, B.C.,
    Canada, October 2001.
20. M. Margolis and D. Resnick. Third Voice: Vox Populi Vox Dei? *First Monday*,
    4(10), 1999. http://www.firstmonday.dk/issues/issue4_10/margolis/.
21. C.C. Marshall. Towards an ecology of hypertext annotation. In *Proceedings of
    HT98, ACM Conference on Hypertext*, pages 40–49, Pittsburgh PA, USA, 1998.
22. L. Masinter. "duri" and "tdb": URN Namespaces based on dated URIs. IETF
    Internet-Draft, http://larry.masinter.net/duri.html, April 2002.
23. D. L. McGuinness. Ontological issues for knowledge-enhanced search. In *Proceedings of FOIS-98*, 1998.
24. SWISS-PROT Annotated Protein Sequence Database. http://www.expasy.org.
25. The Gene Ontology Consortium. Gene Ontology: a tool for the unification of
    biology. *Nature Genetics*, 25:25–29, 2000.
26. M. Uschold and M. Grüninger. Ontologies: Principles, methods and applications.
    Knowledge Engineering Review, 11(2):93–136, 1996.
27. F. van Harmelen, P.F. Patel-Schneider, and I. Horrocks. A Model-Theoretic Semantics for DAML+OIL.
    http://www.daml.org/2001/03/model-theoretic-semantics.html.
28. G. van Heijst, A. Schreiber, , and B. Wielinga. Using explicit ontologies in KBS
    development. *International Journal of Human-Computer Studies*, 46(2/3):183–292,
    1997.
29. World Wide Web Consortium. Annotea Project.
    http://www.w3.org/2001/Annotea.

A User Behavior-Based Agent for Improving Web Usage

Francesco Buccafurri*, Gianluca Lax, Domenico Rosaci, and Domenico Ursino

DIMET – Università "Mediterranea" di Reggio Calabria
Via Graziella, Località Feo di Vito, 89060 Reggio Calabria, Italy
{bucca,lax,rosaci,ursino}@ing.unirc.it

Abstract. Designing applications for supporting the user activity on accessing Web information sources is one of the most appealing challenges for researchers in the area of Artificial Intelligence. The agent paradigm represents a natural way of facing this problem, mainly because of the autonomy and reactivity properties which these applications should have. In this paper we design an agent capable of both creating and managing a personal ontology as well as of exploiting it for discovering navigation paths potentially interesting for the user. The agent, during the navigation of a site, provides the user with a set of recommendations and, at the same time, *learns* her/his preferences by updating the ontology. The power of the approach is based on the capability of the ontology model (called *concept-graph*) of representing user-behavior dependent relationships among concepts and, importantly, dealing with structural and semantic heterogeneity of Web sources.

1   Introduction

The exponential growth of accessible information sources, mainly due to the very fast expansion of the Web and its permeating information system architectures, has determined the necessity of adequately supporting the user activity for driving her/his actions in a so large and composite universe. E-commerce is certainly one of the most evident case in which such a need strongly arises, since a frequent reason of low profit is the confusion of customers in front of a large offer landscape. In this case, automatic techniques, based on the construction of personal *ontologies*, may allow the reduction of the search space, by identifying the portion of the offers of interest for the customer. Similar considerations can be done in many other Web application contexts. To face this problem, one immediately thinks to adopt agent-based solutions, since the above requirements lead to software systems that autonomously react to user actions and continuously learn, from her/his behavior, new knowledge which is then exploited for supporting her/his activity. But, one of the main difficulty we have to overcome concerns with the inherently heterogeneous nature of the Web. Heterogeneity in the sense of multiplicity of data formats (HTML, XML, text, images, etc.), but

---

* Corresponding author

R. Meersman, Z. Tari (Eds.): CoopIS/DOA/ODBASE 2002, LNCS 2519, pp. 1168–1185, 2002.

also semantic, as, for instance, that originated by the presence of terminological, structural and semantic differences on terms [2]. Consider, for an instance, an agent which should support the navigation, through an e-shop site, of the user John Smith, who is a *sommelier*. Even if the site contains a section named *Ferrari*, selling gadgets of the famous Italian car, it should be undesirable that the agent drives the user into this section, only because the word *Ferrari* appears in the profile of Smith. In fact, *Ferrari* is also the name of a famous Italian "spumante" wine.

There are many recent proposals in the context of user modeling [18,7,23,20, 17,13,1,19,15]. However, conceptual models used in these cases take into account only *lexical* and *syntactic* (i.e., *structural*) information and, thus, they are not capable of capturing the *semantics* underlying each concept as well as semantic relationships among concepts.

The problem of dealing with heterogeneity, even semantic, has been deeply investigated in the field of Cooperative Information Systems (CIS, for shortly) [3,9,10,12,8,21,14,11,22]. As a consequence, an interesting research direction is studying how the integration of CIS with agent-based solutions for user modeling can be profitably exploited for designing models and applications for supporting Web usage. The purpose of this approach is that of obtaining the capability of representing user profiles describing her/his preferences at conceptual level (that is, interest of the user for a given concept, relationships felt by the user among concepts, and so on) and, thus, necessarily, the capability of dealing with all the above mentioned forms of heterogeneity.

In this paper we give a contribution in such a context. Indeed, we propose a framework for supporting Web usage, which exploits recent results in the field of Cooperative Information Systems [21]. In particular, we design an agent capable of creating and managing the user ontology and exploiting it for supporting the user activity. Construction and updating of the user ontology is done by taking into account information about the *structure* of the visited information sources. The agent, during the navigation of a site, carries out, at the same time, two activities: the first is providing the user with a set of recommendations for supporting her/his navigation, and the second is monitoring the user behavior for *learning* her/his preferences and encoding such a new knowledge into the ontology. A key issue which has to be faced concerns with the model used for representing the user ontology, that should be capable of embedding both concepts of interest for her/him and the correlations she/he perceives. For this purpose, we define a conceptual model, which we call *concept-graph* (*c-graph*, for short). Since ontologies are built by the agent on the basis of user Web navigation, we exploits results of [21] for providing the model with the capability of representing structural properties of information sources with different formats (i.e., HTML and XML documents, OEM graphs, E/R schemes) and dealing with inter-source heterogeneity. Moreover, c-graphs allow us also to give a temporary representation of the site navigation, embedding both the structure of the site and the dynamics of the user behavior expressing her/his preferences. Such a temporary representation is then used, at the end of the visit, for updating the user ontology.

The paper is organized as follows. Related work are discussed in Section 2. Section 3 describes the concept-graph model, and, together with Section 4, illustrating how inter-source heterogeneity is solved, gives the basis for constructing the agent model. This is presented in Section 5, where the two tasks performed by the agent are described. For updating ontology (that is the second agent task) an integration process between two c-graph is needed: Section 6 illustrates technical details of c-graph integration. A brief section of conclusion and future work closes the paper.

2   Related Work

In the context of models dealing with heterogeneity we cite [12] describing the conceptual model associated with Lore which appears well suited for handling OEM graphs and XML documents. In [5] a graph-based conceptual model managing a series of different formats is also given. The Description Logic based model $\mathcal{DLR}$, allowing a designer to represent and reason about the content of information sources, is described in [8]. A conceptual model capable of uniformly handling both relational and E/R and object oriented information sources is presented in [16] and is adopted also in [9]; it can be seen as a relational model augmented with object oriented features. In [3] a model, called ODL_{I^3}, is proposed for representing and handling relational and object oriented databases, as well as XML documents. [21] present a graph-based conceptual model, called SDR network; the authors provide rules for translating OEM graphs, XML documents and E/R schemes into this model. Recently, integration and cooperation tasks have been supported by some intelligent agent systems, for making them semi-automatic; as an example, in InfoSleuth [14] a network of cooperating agents is exploited for supporting information retrieval and processing in ever-changing networks of sources. Analogously, in [11], an agent-based integration approach, particularly suited for operating in an e-commerce environment, is described; in the same paper the authors provide a formal semantics for information integration able of coping with distributed, autonomous, partial and redundant information. [4] proposes an approach based on mobile agents in the context of an infrastructure for semi-automatic information integration of heterogeneous information sources. In [22], a structure of multiple shared agent ontologies for integrating heterogeneous information sources is presented. From the side of user profiles, a large number of proposals has been recently presented. In this context, the existing techniques are based on the computation of simple statistic indicators; conceptual models used in these cases are purely structural and, thus, not suited for dealing with semantic heterogeneity. Some example of these approaches are cookies [18] and Web logs [7,23]. Recently, in the agent community, a great attention has been posed on approaches for constructing the profiles of users on the basis of their past behavior on accessing various sites [20, 17,13,1]. Basically, these approaches work as follows: a user, possibly supported by an agent, chooses a site to visit. On the basis of the visited sites, another agent tries to guess the topics of her/his interest; this task can be carried out by exploiting various techniques such as text filtering, keyword searching and so on. Particularly interesting is the approach described in [19], where a way of modeling user interests is presented and the user model is exploited for effective information retrieval and filtering. A system based on this model "watches over the shoulders" of a user while she/he is surfing on the Web and the visited pages are characterized by some behavioral parameters such as the length of the pages and the time spent thereon. Although such parameters are very useful for representing the perception of the user w.r.t. the pages she/he has visited, they do not characterize the perception of the various concepts, i.e., it is impossible to derive the user behavior at a conceptual level. In [15] an approach that makes use of the embedded structural information of the documents frequently accessed by the user for deriving a personalized concept categorization (i.e., an ontology) and for identifying user preferences concerning document accesses, is presented. This approach allows to group documents having similar structure, and the behavior of the user in accessing documents is exploited as a feed-back for suitably ranking and sorting the various categories.

3   The Framework for Representing User Ontologies

In this section we describe the framework used for representing user ontologies. It is based on a graph of concepts with labeled arcs. Labels encode knowledge about both structure and semantics of visited sites and past user behavior. A synthetic function elaborating all components (both structural and behavioral) provides a user-behavior dependent metrics for quantifying closeness of concepts.

3.1   The Concept-Graph

In this section we present the concept-graph model utilized in the following for representing the user ontology.

The atomic elements of our model are *instances* belonging to a given universe $\mathcal{U}$. Instances are used for representing different kinds of objects, depending on the data format we refer (that is, they can be XML instances, or relational tuples, etc.). Since our model is Web oriented, we assume that instances are accessible by the user by means of Web documents.

A *concept* is a pair $\langle c, name(c) \rangle$ where c is a set of instances and $name(c)$ is a string (with prefixed maximum length). For example, an element of the DTD of a XML site represents a concept whose name is the name of the element and instances are the instances of this element.

We denote by $\mathcal{C} = 2^{\mathcal{U}} \times \Sigma^*$ the set of all possible concepts named with strings in the alphabet Σ. Often, with a little abuse of notation, we denote a concept just as a set of instances, not by a pair (according to definition above). So, we could say that, a given set of instances s is a concept with name $name(s)$.

The concept-graph, which we next formally introduce, is defined for a given user and a given set of concepts with different names. It contains an explicit representation of membership of instances to such concepts, as well as the semantic relationships among them. Moreover, information about accesses of the user is included. From a physical point of view, user accesses occur only on instances since concepts do not correspond to physical objects. But we say that a user *accesses a concept* every time she/he accesses one of its instances. In order to discover useful information about the relationships among concepts, as well as the user preference for an instance w.r.t. the other ones of the same concept, we need to distinguish *internal* accesses from *external* ones. An access to an instance t of a concept s is internal if the user comes from another instance of the same concept s. A user may access an instance t of a concept s by an external access if she/he comes from an instance of a concept s' distinct from s.

We define now the *concept-graph* (*c-graph*, for short). Given a subset of concepts $N \subseteq C$ such that no two concepts with same name occur in it and an instance may belong only to one concept., and a user u, a *c-graph* (for u on N) is a rooted labeled direct graph $C\_Graph(N, u) = \langle N, A \rangle$, where N is the set of nodes and $A \subseteq N \times N$ is the set of arcs. Informally, N represents the set of concepts of interest for the user u. Arcs encode semantic relationships among concepts. Their labels define a number of properties associated to relationships of $C\_Graph(N, u)$ containing also the dependency of the model on the user u. More precisely, an arc (s, t) is provided with a label $label(s, t) = \langle d_{st}, r_{st}, h_{st}, \tau_{st} \rangle$, where both d_{st} and r_{st} are real numbers ranging from 0 to 1, h_{st} is a non negative integer, and τ_{st} is a non negative real number. The four *label coefficients* above encode different properties, and their definition, which we next provide, clarifies why our graph is directed. In particular:

- d_{st} is the *(semantic) independence coefficient*. It is inversely related to the contribution given by the concept t in characterizing the concept s. As an example, in an E/R scheme, for an attribute t of an entity s, d_{st} will be smaller than $d_{s't}$, where s' is another entity related to s by a relationship. Analogously, in an XML document, a pair element, sub-element (s, t) will have an independence coefficient d_{st} smaller than $d_{s't}$, where s' is another element which s refers to through an $IDREF$ attribute.
- r_{st} is the *(semantic) relevance coefficient*, indicating the fraction of instances of the concept s whose complete definition requires at least one instance of the concept t. The relevance plays a role similar to the *support* defined for data mining association rules: it gives a measure (in terms of instances) of how much the concept t characterizes the concept s. Such a coefficient is necessary since c-graph is used for representing also semi-structured information.
- h_{st} is the *hit coefficient*, counting the number of hits which u carries out on t (i.e., on some instance of t) coming from s (i.e., coming from some instance of s).
- τ_{st} is *(no-idle) time coefficient*, defined as $\sum_{i=1}^{h_{st}} \frac{t_i}{q_i}$, where t_i the effective total time spent by u at the i-th hit for consulting the concept t (i.e., instances of

t) coming from s (i.e., coming from some instance of s) and q_i is the size of the relative accessed page.[1]

Similarly to the relationship between concepts, also the membership of instances to concepts is weighed by labeling. In particular, for each pair (s,t) such that s is a node of the graph and t is an instance belonging to s, we define $label(s,t) = \langle h_{st}, \tau_{st} \rangle$, where h_{st}, called *hit coefficient*, and τ_{st}, called *(no-idle) time coefficient*, are defined in obvious way, coherently with the corresponding coefficients presented above. The only difference here is that the instance which the user comes from is either another instance of the concept s or an instance of another concept. In other words, while hit and time coefficients for pairs of concepts regard only external accesses, the corresponding coefficients in case of pairs concept-instance sum both internal and external accesses to instances. For taking into account the locality principle, we assume that, periodically, h_{st} and τ_{st} are suitably automatically reduced (if greater than 0) in order to gives less importance to old accesses.

The c-graph is used for representing the user ontology. The construction and management of the user ontology is a task of our agent and will be explained in detail in Section 5. As we shall see, the agent first extracts from visited sources concepts and structural information (kept in independence and relevance coefficients). The user behavior is then monitored in order to capture user preferences: hit and time coefficients allow to keep memory of user actions. For extracting structural information, it is necessary to define how, given an information source, a *static* c-graph (that is, a c-graph with hit and time coefficients set to 0), can be automatically built. This is the first step which the agent performs at the beginning of each new visit in order to have a temporary c-graph on which the user behavior is marked up. At the end of the visit, such a temporary c-graph will be exploited for updating the user ontology.

For facing the non-trivial problem of constructing the static c-graph of an information source (which may be represented by means of different data formats), we exploit results obtained in the field of Cooperative Information System, and, in particular, the techniques defined in [21]. In these papers, a conceptual model called SDR network is proposed which basically coincides with the notion of c-graph deprived of the instances associated to each node and the hit and time coefficients. Thus, for the construction of a static c-graph we follow an approach similar to that used for SDR networks [21]. The algorithm is rather technical and elaborated, therefore we do not report it in detail. We just note that such a computation depends on the format of the involved information sources. The reader may found in [6] the case of XML format as well as the translation rules from other kinds of information sources.

We conclude this section by showing an example of a simple user ontology.

Example 1. In Figure 1 a c-graph representing the ontology of a user, named *John Smith*, is reported. Labels of arcs are 4-tuples listing, in order, indepen-

---

[1] Throughout the paper, for simplicity, we assume that all pages have size 1.

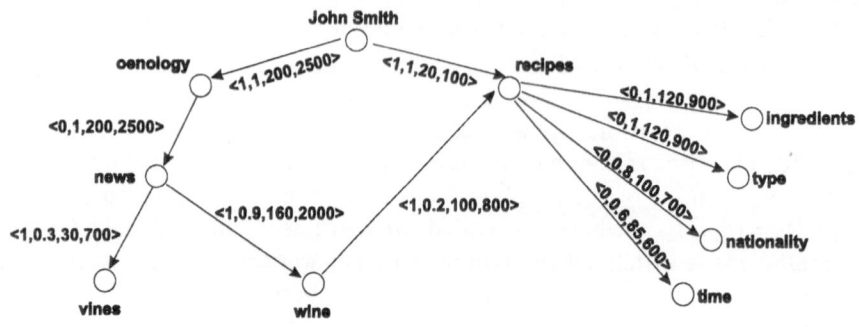

Fig. 1. The ontology of John Smith

dence, relevance, hit and time coefficients. For simplicity, we do not represent instances.

John Smith is a sommelier, very interested in wine as well as in optimal combination between food and wine. For simplicity, we assume that the navigation history of John Smith consists of just a number of visits to two XML sites, one regards wine, the other gastronomy. The DTD of the first site contains the elements *oenology*, *wine* and *vines*. The element *oenology* has a sub-element *news*, and such a sub-element has one IDREFS attribute. An instance of *oenology* collects general news about wine; such news may contain links to particular wines or to information about vines. An instance of *wine* is a particular wine, and it may contain links to external instances belonging to the second site concerning recipes – the structure of the second site will be explained in the following. The second site regards recipes, and its DTD contains the element *recipes*, which has the attributes *ingredients*, *type*, *nationality* and (preparation) *time*.

The topology of the c-graph representing the Smith's ontology (see Figure 1), reflects the structure of the visited documents. This is true also for structural coefficients, that is, independence and relevance coefficients. For instance, consider the arc (*wine, recipes*): the independence coefficient is 1 (that is, the maximum value). This is rather intuitive, since an IDREF attribute just represents a link between the two concepts but not the composition of one concept in terms of the other one, as, for instance it occurs for XML sub-elements. Conversely, for the arc (*recipes, ingredients*) the independence coefficient is 0, since *ingredients* is an attribute of *recipes*, and it gives an high contribution in characterizing the concept *recipes*. The relevance coefficient measures how much instances support relationships. For instance, for the arc (*recipes, time*), the relevance coefficient is 0.6, meaning that the 60% of recipes visited by Smith reports the preparation time. Behavioral coefficients (that is, hit and time coefficients), keep memory of actions performed by Smith. For instance, from the label of the arc (*wine, recipes*) it results that Smith has moved from an instance of wine to an instance of recipes for 100 many times, summarizing 800 seconds for consulting such instances of recipes.   □

3.2   Measuring Concept Closeness

The four coefficients composing labels of a c-graph need to be elaborated in order to become really interpretable.

First examine independence and relevance coefficients. Consider given a pair of concepts s and t. As remarked above, they express structural semantic closeness. In particular, having $(1-d_{st})$ and r_{st} close to 1 means that t strongly characterizes s. r_{st} has the role of support for such a relationship. Indeed, dealing with semi-structured information, it may happen that only a fraction of instances witnesses such a relationship. A reasonable way for merging the information arising from the two coefficients is using the relevance coefficient as a reducing factor of $(1-d_{st})$. Thus, we define the function $\psi(s,t)$, called *s(tructural)-closeness* as:

$$\psi(s,t) = (1 - d_{st}) \cdot r_{st}$$

for giving a synthetic measure of the structural dependence of the concept s from t.

Also hit and time coefficients have to be elaborated in order to express, in a synthetic way, usable information about the user behavior. Consider given a pair (s,t) where s is a concept and t is either a concept or an instance of s.

First we define the function θ, giving a measure of the "interest" the user u has for t when she/he accesses t through s. θ is defined as:

$$\theta(s,t) = h_{st} + \lfloor \tfrac{\tau_{st}}{q} \rfloor$$

where q is a suitably set parameter allowing us to modulate the importance of the effective access time w.r.t. the number of hits. Indeed, for high values of q the interest measures just how many times the user contacted t. On the contrary, a small q cancels the effect of contact actions. The value q could be set taking into account several variables, like the connection bit rate, the expertise of the user and so on. For instance, in a search strategy tree, an inexpert user typically stands in a fail node for a lot of time before realizing she/he is not interested in it. Thus, in this case, the effective time spent in each contact cannot give us information about the real interest of the user (i.e., q should be set to an high value). The contrary happens in the case of an expert user.

Then, we define the function ρ, representing the preference the user u gives to t w.r.t. all the other concepts (in case t is a concept) or instances (in case t is an instance) reachable in just one step by s. The preference is computed as a fraction of the overall interest. More precisely, ρ is:

$$\rho(s,t) = \frac{\theta(s,t)}{\sum_{t' \in A(s)} \theta(s,t')}$$

where $A(s)$ is either the set of nodes adjacent to s, in case t is a concept, or s itself, in case t is an instance.

At this point we have two synthetic functions, that are ψ and ρ, the former encoding the structural closeness, the latter the user preference. In order to have a unique synthetic information summarizing both structural and behavioral components we define the function γ, measuring the "subjective" semantic closeness of two concepts, where by subjective we mean that the user preference function ρ is used for modulating structural semantic closeness. γ, called *u-closeness*, is defined as

$$\gamma(s,t) = k \cdot \psi(s,t) + (1-k) \cdot \rho(s,t)$$

where $0 \le k \le 1$ is a parameter modulating the importance of behavioral information versus the structural one (a small k reduces the importance of the structural component).

Example 2. Consider the ontology of John Smith of Example 1. Again, consider the arc $(wine, recipes)$. The independence coefficient of the arc is 1. As observed in Example 1, this correctly reflects the structure of the sites visited by Smith. As a consequence, the function $\psi(wine, recipes)$, measuring how much the concept *recipes* structurally characterizes the concept *wine*, takes the value 0. However, under the perspective of Smith, who is interested in food and wine combination, the two concepts are strongly related each other and this is proved by the high values of behavioral coefficients of the arcs $(wine, recipes)$. The function γ encodes this knowledge. Assuming the parameter k is set to 0.25 (thus, in a case in which the behavioral component is considered more important than the structural one), we obtain that $\gamma(wine, recipes) = 0.75$, denoting a high degree of semantic closeness. □

The function γ allows us to define the notion of *neighborhood* of a given concept s. Informally, it consists of the set of concepts that are sufficiently (i.e., up a suitable threshold) "close" (according to the function γ) to the concept s. This is done by extending the function γ to the paths of the c-graph.

More formally, let s and t be a pair of nodes and π be a path in a c-graph $C\_Graph(N, u)$ from s to t. The *p-closeness* of t w.r.t. s by π, denoted by $\gamma_{path}(s, t, \pi)$, is the sum of the γ values associated to the arcs of π. Let s and t be two nodes such that there exists a path in $C\_Graph(N, u)$ from s to t. The *closeness* of t from s, denoted by $\Gamma(s,t)$, is defined as $min\{\gamma_{path}(s,t,\pi) \mid \pi$ is a path in $C\_Graph(N, u)$ from s to $t\}$. Given a c-graph $C\_Graph(N, u)$, a positive integer number k and a concept $t \in N$, the *k-neighborhood* of t in $C\_Graph(N, u)$ is the set of nodes $\{s' \in N \mid \Gamma(s,t) \le k\}$.

Example 3. Consider the c-graph of Example 1 and its concept *wine*. The 1-neighborhood of *wine* is the set of concepts $\{recipes, time\}$ since $\Gamma(wine, recipes) = 0.5$, $\Gamma(wine, time) = 0.9$. Moreover, the 2-neighborhood of *wine* is $\{recipes, time, ingredients, nationality, type\}$ since $\Gamma(wine, nationality) = 1.01$, $\Gamma(wine, type) = \Gamma(wine, ingredients) = 1.14$. □

4   Solving Semantic Heterogeneity

In order to use the c-graph for representing the user ontology, and design an agent capable of exploiting such an ontology for supporting the user, we have to be able to deal with structural and semantic heterogeneity. Indeed, for instance, the agent must be able to discover that a given concept of the user ontology coincides with a concept of a visited site, even if they have a different name. In some cases, different names corresponding to two coinciding concepts are simply lexical synonymes and available dictionaries on the Web may be used for detecting them. But sometimes, synonymies can be detected only by means of techniques based on semantic approaches. Another possible case is that two concepts with the same name have actually a different meaning, that is, they are homonym. We have to discover also such cases, since, clearly, they may cause erroneous agent actions.

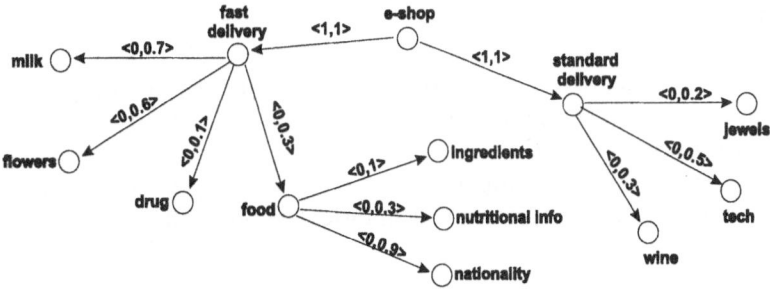

Fig. 2. The e-shop site

Example 4. Consider the ontology of John Smith introduced in Example 1. Suppose John Smith visits a XML e-shop site whose associated c-graph (built according to translation rules rules) is depicted in Figure 2. The site, among others, contains a category called *food*. On the basis of the interests of Smith, it would be desirable that the agent is able to conduct the user into the section of the site corresponding to *food*. But, in the Smith's ontology, it appears neither a concept named as *food* nor some lexical synonym. Indeed, it appears only the concept *recipes*. We can argue that such a synonymy cannot be discovered only by means of dictionaries. This is a case of a semantic synonymy.   □

The issue of detecting semantic heterogeneity has been deeply investigated in the field of Cooperative Information Systems [3,12,8]. Most of the approaches for solving synonymies and homonymies proceed by analyzing the *context* of concepts. Two concepts are detected as synonyms, if their contexts are sufficiently similar, while two concepts are homonymous if they have the same name but their contexts are sufficiently different. In our case, the semantics of a given concept c can be captured by analyzing concepts which are sufficiently close to c. Closeness, in this case, is only structural, and thus computed on the basis of independence and relevance coefficients (that is, assuming that c-graphs are static). For such a reason, the approach we follow for detecting synonyms and homonyms is similar to that proposed in [21]. The *context* of a concept is captured by adapting the notion of neighborhood defined in Section 3 to the static case: this is obtained simply by giving to the function ψ the role played by the function γ. We call this new notion *structural neighborhood*. Further, given two c-graphs B_1 and B_2, for any pair of concepts s and t belonging to B_1 and B_2, respectively, we determine a real coefficient, called *similarity coefficient*, ranging from 0 to 1, expressing how much concepts s and t are similar. Once two suitable thresholds for the similarity are dynamically computed , say th_1 and th_2, two concepts s and t are synonymous if both (1) they have different name and (2) their similarity coefficient is greater than th_1. Conversely, s and t are homonyms if both (1) they have the same name and (2) their similar coefficient is smaller than th_2. The complete procedure is rather complex and, for the sake of presentation, we do not include it in the paper. The reader may refer to [6] for further details.

Example 5. Consider the c-graph of Example 1 and the c-graph of Figure 2. Let denote by B_1 be the first c-graph and by B_2 the second one. Consider the concept *recipes* of B_1 and the concept *food* of B_2. By applying translation rules, it can be verified that the similarity coefficient of the pair (*food,recipes*) is 0.74 showing that such a concepts are (semantic) synonymous (for any reasonable fixed threshold).   □

5   The Agent Model

User activity is thought as an iterative process consisting of accesses to different sites. We design an agent for supporting such an activity based on handling a user ontology. The ontology represents the profile of the user in terms of preferences and semantic relationships learnt by monitoring the history of her/his activity. To recent history is given a more important role than the past (thanks to the automatic reduction of behavioral coefficients), in order to take into account the *locality* of user interests.

The agent carries out two tasks: the first one is supporting the user in the navigation of each site, by providing her/him with a set of recommendations; the second one concerns with the ontology management (that is, its construction and updating). Ontology update concerns with new user actions: knowledge coming from new accesses to (possibly already exploited) information sources has to be incorporated into the ontology. This is also periodically pruned, in order to eliminate what can be considered just as noise. Pruning can be done on the basis of the function γ, by using a suitable thresholding. For simplicity, we have not described in this paper the pruning process (the reader may refer to [6] for details).

The user ontology, denoted by O, is a c-graph, initially empty and updated after each new visit. Suppose now the user visits a new site, say IS. First of all, the c-graph $S(IS)$, representing the structure of the site, is automatically built by the agent. Observe that this is a "static" c-graph in the sense that behavioral coefficients (that is, hit and time coefficients) are set to 0. From a practical point of view, the feasibility of such an initial step depends on the presence of some kind of cooperation between client and server sides. Cooperation could be implemented by using mobile agents, for instance, or agents working on both sides (client and server) and exchanging data. Of course, such design decisions could be adopted only after that a precise application setting (like, for instance, e-commerce) is chosen. However, we have intentionally presented the model in the most general context, with the purpose of concentrating on the description of its features. Thus, a deep analysis of the above considerations, as well as of other implementation issues is outside of the scope of this paper.

Now we describe the two agent activities, that are supporting the user navigation and ontology management.

5.1 Supporting User Navigation

By exploiting $S(IS)$ and the user ontology O, the user is supported during the visit by providing her/him with a set of recommended links to concepts (corresponding to collections of URLs) of the site. For each visited page, the user receives new recommendations. Such recommendations are obtained by identifying in $S(IS)$ those concepts which belong also to the user ontology. Suggested links are obtained by considering relationships among such concepts occurring in the user ontology. Thus, recommendations take into account user preferences. As noted in the previous section, in order to discover concepts of $S(IS)$ which belong also to O, semantic heterogeneity has to be solved. Indeed, a certain concept of $S(IS)$ can appear in O as (either lexical or semantic) synonym (even not trivially lexical), and this can be detected by using the already described technique. Moreover, a concept of $S(IS)$ can be an homonym of a concept of O, and thus could be erroneous considered belonging to O.

Once synonymies and homonymies have been detected and homonymous nodes in $S(IS)$ are renamed, the agent is able to select the concepts of the site (i.e., occurring in $S(IS)$) of interest for the user, by finding in $S(IS)$ the concepts such that there exists at least a synonymous concept appearing in O (hereafter in this section, we say that two concepts are synonymous also if they have the same name). Let C_I be such a set of concepts. For each concept c of C_I the agent builds the collection of the URLs of all the pages containing instances of c in the site IS. At this point, the agent builds a graph, say $R(IS, O)$, with set C_I of nodes. For each pair s and t of concepts in C_I an arc (s, t) occurs in $R(IS, O)$ if there exists in O an arc (s', t') such that s' and s are synonymous and t' and t are synonymous. This graph, called the *recommendation graph*, is exploited for supporting the user visit in the following way: Initially the agent suggests to the user the page collections associated to C_I, as starting points of the visit. Then, when the user visits a page corresponding to an instance of some concept of C_I, say c, the agent extracts from $R(IS, O)$ all adjacent concepts, and, for each of them, a link to the corresponding collection is suggested to the user. Observe that, in a suggested URL collection associated to a concept c of O, the agent may identify the URLs leading to instances detected as sufficiently similar (by text matching techniques) with the k−first instances of c ordered by decreasing user preference, determined by means of the function ρ (see Section 3), where k

is a given fixed parameter. Note that suggested links might not be actual links of the site, but they could only derive from the past behavior of the user, encoded into her/his ontology, and representing the semantic closeness among concepts she/he perceives. Thus, the user can be driven by the agent through paths not directly provided by the site but (probably) appearing as "natural" for the user.

Example 6. Consider the user John Smith of Example 1 having the ontology O reported in Figure 1. Suppose the user visits the e-shop site, called here IS, of Example 2. Again, assume that Smith prefers red wines and, thus, he recently and many times accessed instances of *wine* regarding red wines. Consequently, Smith frequently consulted meat based recipes. Thus, it results that the 10-first instances of wine ordered by preference contain the word "red" and the 10-first instances of *recipes* ordered by preference contain the word "meat".

Denote by $S(IS)$ the c-graph, reported in Figure 2 of the site. In this example we show how the agent supports the navigation of Smith in the site IS. First, semantic heterogeneity is solved: The agent, by computing similarity coefficients, discovers that, besides lexical synonyms, concepts *recipes* of O and *food* of $S(IS)$ can be considered as synonyms (as shown in Example 5). Thus, the set C_I of concepts of $S(IS)$ appearing also in O is $\{wine, food\}$. Therefore, for the concept *wine*, the agent builds a collection of URLs of pages containing the instances of this concept in IS, and carries out the same task for the concept *food*.

At this point the agent builds the *recommendation graph $R(O, IS)$*, which has as nodes the concepts of C_I (to which the corresponding URL collections are associated). Arcs are copied from O, by considering corresponding nodes. The graph $R(O, IS)$ so obtained is composed of just two nodes, namely *wine* and *food* and there is only one arc directed from *wine* to *food*. As a first suggestion the agent submits to the user the list of URL collections associated to concepts *wine* and *food*. Due to the preferences of Smith, among all the URL associated to *wine*, the agent selects red wines as favourite (because of the occurrence of the word "red" in the favourite instance of Smith). Suppose now Smith chooses to visit the page *Brunello di Montalcino* (that is a famous Italian red wine) following one of the links appearing in the URL collection associated to the concept *wine*, suggested by the agent. On this page, the agent provides the user with a set of suggested links extracted from the recommendation graph $R(O, IS)$ by considering all concepts adjacent to *wine*. In this case, there is only one concept adjacent to *wine*, that is *food*. Therefore, the agent shows to the user a link to the URL collection associated to the concept *food*. Moreover, exploiting the most user favourite instances of *recipes* (that is, the concept corresponding to *food* in the user ontology), the agent selects, among the above URLs, those corresponding to the instances containing the word "meat". This way, the user, who is expert in combination between wine and food, is correctly driven to the section of the site regarding meat dishes, as the chosen wine is red, even if the site is not provided with such a direct link (see Figure 2) (actually the two sections of the site are quite far each other). We remark that such a useful recommendation can be generated only by exploiting the history of the user behavior (showing that the user sees a strong relation between concepts *wine* and *recipes*), embedded in his ontology, and, importantly, the capability of the model of dealing with semantic heterogeneity, allowing the agent to discover the semantic correspondence between the concept *recipes* of the user ontology and the concept *food* of the site. Thus, this example shows how the (apparently too complex) features of the model, are actually needed for effectively dealing with practical situations.   □

5.2   Ontology Management

The second task of the agent, transparent for the user, concerns with the ontology management. Each new visit, updates the user ontology, in such a way that the behavior history of the user is recorded in it. Clearly, for privacy reasons, the user is allowed to disable the visit monitoring.

For updating the user ontology, the user dynamically builds a c-graph $B(IS)$ during the visit and, at the end, incorporates the knowledge encoded in $B(IS)$ into the user ontology O by integrating the two c-graphs. At the beginning of the visit, $B(IS)$ is empty. During the visit $B(IS)$ changes, as all concepts accessed by u, as well as their neighborhoods in $S(IS)$, are recorded in $B(IS)$ by inserting new nodes and new arcs. Moreover, hit and time coefficients are recomputed at each step according to their definition. Independence and relevance coefficients are taken from corresponding arcs in $S(IS)$. At the end of the visit, $B(IS)$ is a representation of the portion of IS, visited by u in this session, containing also information about the user behavior, thanks to hit and time coefficients. By considering also neighborhoods (in $S(IS)$) of visited concepts, the agent autonomously discovers potentially interesting concepts for the user and includes them in $B(IS)$. More formally, given a concept s, we denote by $nbh(s)$ its k-neighborhood. In obvious way, we define as $arcs(nbh(s))$ the set of arcs induced by the k-neighborhood of a concept s. Thus, for each access a to an instance t of a concept s:

- if a is the first access of the visit, then the node s is inserted into $B(IS)$ with only the instance t belonging to it. h_{st} and τ_{st} are updated (in this case h_{st} is set to 1).
- if s is accessed for the first time, a is not the first access, and, thus, the user comes from an instance of another concept, say s', then the node s is inserted into $B(IS)$ with only the instance t belonging to it, and an arc (s', s) is also added. h_{st} and $h_{s's}$ are set to 1, τ_{st} and $\tau_{s's}$ are set to the same measured value. Independence and relevance coefficients of the arc (s', s) are set to the corresponding values occurring in $S(IS)$.
- if a is an external access coming from a concept s' but s was already accessed, then the arc (s', s) is added in $B(IS)$ if not already present. h_{st} and $h_{s's}$ are increased of 1; τ_{st} and $\tau_{s's}$ are equally updated.
- if a is an internal access and it is not the first one, then h_{st} is increased and τ_{st} is updated.
- for every kind of access a, nodes of $nbh(s)$ and arcs of $arcs(nbh(s))$ are inserted into $B(IS)$, if not already occurring in it. Independence and relevance

coefficients of inserted arcs are taken from the corresponding arcs of $S(IS)$. Hit and time coefficients are set to 0.

At this point, before handling the choice of a new information source, the knowledge encoded in $B(IS)$ has to be incorporated into the ontology O, updating it. This is done by *integrating* the two c-graphs. Integration is described in Section 6. After the update of O, $B(IS)$ is not useful anymore, since the memory of such a visit of IS is kept into the ontology. Now, O must be pruned, in order to eliminate all concepts and instances with low interest for the user u. O now can be exploited for supporting next user visits.

6   Integration of Two C-Graphs

In this section we describe how two c-graphs are merged into a global c-graph. Informally, this merge consists of a "union" of the two c-graphs executed after that synonymies and homonymies are eliminated: by computing the similarity coefficients between all possible pairs of nodes (a node belonging to the first c-graph, the other belonging to the second c-graph), synonyms and homonyms are first detected, and then, synomnym nodes are renamed giving the same name and homonym nodes are renamed in such a way that they assume distinct names. The union of the two "normalized" c-graphs is done by suitably averaging labels of arcs.

Let $B_1 = \langle N_1, A_1 \rangle$ and $B_2 = \langle N_2, A_2 \rangle$ be two c-graphs. The *union* of B_1 and B_2, denoted by $U(B_1, B_2)$, is a directed labeled graph with set of nodes:

$$N = \{s \in N_1 \mid \nexists t \in N_2 \ s.t. \ name(s) = name(t)\} \cup$$
$$\{s \in N_2 \mid \nexists t \in N_1 \ s.t. \ name(s) = name(t)\} \cup$$
$$\{x \in \mathcal{C} \mid x = s \cup t, s \in N_1 \wedge t \in N_2 \wedge name(s) = name(t) = name(x)\}$$

and set of arcs

$$A = \{(s,t) \mid \exists(s_1, t_1) \in A_1 \ s.t. \ name(s) = name(s_1) \wedge name(t) = name(t_1)\} \cup$$
$$\{(s,t) \mid \exists(s_1, t_1) \in A_2 \ s.t. \ name(s) = name(s_1) \wedge name(t) = name(t_1)\}$$

Nodes are obtained by copying nodes of each c-graph with name not appearing in the other c-graph and by merging nodes with common name into a node with equal name including all the instances of the original nodes. Arcs are obtained in obvious way. Now we define how labels are determined. Let (s,t) be an arc belonging to A. Its label is the 4-tuple $\langle d_{st}, r_{st}, h_{st}, \tau_{st} \rangle$ defined as follows:

(a) $d_{st} = d_{s_1 t_1}, r_{st} = r_{s_1 t_1}, h_{st} = h_{s_1 t_1}, \tau_{st} = \tau_{s_1 t_1}$
    if $\exists(s_1, t_1) \in A_i \ s.t. \ name(s) = name(s_1) \wedge name(t) = name(t_1) \wedge \nexists s_2 \in N_j \ s.t. \ name(s) = name(s_2)$.

(b) $d_{st} = d_{s_1 t_1}, r_{st} = f(r_{s_1 t_1}, |s_2|), h_{st} = h_{s_1 t_1}, \tau_{st} = \tau_{s_1 t_1}$
    if $\exists(s_1, t_1) \in A_i \ s.t. \ name(s) = name(s_1) \wedge name(t) = name(t_1) \wedge \exists s_2 \in N_j \ s.t. \ name(s) = name(s_2) \wedge \nexists(s_2, t_2) \in A_j \ s.t. \ name(t_1) = name(t_2)$.

(c) $d_{st} = \frac{|s_1| \cdot d_{s_1 t_1} + |s_2| \cdot d_{s_2 t_2}}{|s_1| + |s_2|}, r_{st} = f(r_{s_1 t_1}, |s_2|), h_{st} = h_{s_1 t_1} + h_{s_2 t_2}, \tau_{st} = \tau_{s_1 t_1} + \tau_{s_2 t_2}$

if $\exists (s_1, t_1) \in A_i$ s.t. $name(s) = name(s_1) \wedge name(t) = name(t_1) \wedge \exists s_2 \in N_j$ s.t. $name(s) = name(s_2) \wedge \exists (s_2, t_2) \in A_j$ s.t. $name(t_1) = name(t_2)$.

where $i = 1, 2$, $j = 1, 2$, $i \neq j$, and by $f(r_{s_1 t_1}, |s_2|)$ we denote the function for re-computing the relevance coefficient of the arc (s_1, t_1) when the cardinality of the node s_1 is increased by $|s_2|$ (recall that the relevance coefficient depends on the number of instances of the source node).

With a little abuse, we assume that $U(B_1, B_2)$ is a c-graph. Note that this is not necessarily true since $U(B_1, B_2)$ might not to be rooted. However, in this case, a dummy root can be added to make $U(B_1, B_2)$ a c-graph.

In absence of lexical and semantic heterogeneity, the integration of two c-graphs would correspond to the union defined above. Unfortunately, the correspondence between names of concepts on which the union is based does not take into account the possibility of occurrence of synonymies and homonymies. Thus, before applying the union operation, we have to solve such a heterogeneity as shown in Section 4.

Let $T = \{(s, t) \mid s \in N_1 \wedge t \in N_2 \wedge name(s) \neq name(t) \wedge sim(s, t) \geq th_1\}$, where, $sim(s, t)$ is the similarity coefficient of the pair (s, t) and th_1 is the threshold computed for detecting synonymies (see Section 4). T represents the set of all pairs of candidate synonyms. Any subset $\bar{T}$ of T such that both (1) $(s, t) \in \bar{T}$ implies that there is no $(s, t') \in \bar{T}$ and $t \neq t'$ and (2) $(s, t) \in \bar{T}$ implies that there is no $(s', t) \in \bar{T}$ and $s \neq s'$, is an *admissible synonym set*, that is a set of pairs of candidate synonyms such that a concept of N_1 (N_2, resp.) is involved at most once. We require this last condition since we intend to solve synonyms by renaming candidates pairs of concepts assigning the same name. Thus, the above condition guarantees that, after this operation, there are no two nodes in B_1 (in B_2, resp.) with the same name (according to definition of c-graph). Among all admissible synonym sets, we choose a set with maximum value of the *global similarity*, where, for global similarity of an admissible set $\bar{T}$ we mean the sum of all the similarity coefficients of the pairs belonging to $\bar{T}$. Such a set, called S, represents the set of the detected synonyms. Now, the set of homonyms is determined. It results $O = \{(s, t) \mid s \in N_1 \wedge t \in N_2 \wedge name(s) = name(t) \wedge sim(s, t) \leq th_2\}$. Note that, a concept s of N_1 (N_2, resp.) can appear in O once at most. At this point S and O can be used for solving synonymies and homonymies in B_1 and B_2. In particular, for each pair $(s, t) \in S$, the concept t is renamed in such a way that $name(t) = name(s)$, and, for each pair $(s, t) \in O$, the concept t is renamed in such a way that $name(t) \neq name(s)$. Let denote by $\bar{B}_1$ and $\bar{B}_2$ the two c-graphs so obtained. The integration of B_1 and B_2 is then obtained by computing the c-graph $U(\bar{B}_1, \bar{B}_2)$.

7   Conclusion and Future Work

This paper deals with the problem of modeling Web users by means of personal ontologies. Our approach is based on a semantic representation of the user activity, which takes into account both the structure of visited sites and the way the user navigates them. The model appears promising, mainly because of its capability of dealing with semantic inconsistency occurring in the Web. This is shown by examples in the paper, by simulating the execution of an agent-based application exploiting the user ontology for supporting the user navigation. Thus, the paper gives the formal framework as well as the design guidelines for building an agent system and providing experiments as further validation of the model. This is matter of current and future work.

References

1. M. Balabanovic, Y. Shoham. Fab: Content-based, collaborative recommendation. *Communications of the ACM, 40(3)*, 4(3), 1997.
2. C. Batini, M. Lenzerini. A methodology for data schema integration in the entity relationship model. *IEEE Trans. on Software Eng.*, 10(6):650–664, 1984.
3. S. Bergamaschi, S. Castano, M. Vincini, D. Beneventano. Semantic integration and query of heterogeneous information sources. *Data & Knowledge Eng.*, 36(3):215–249, 2001.
4. S. Bergamaschi, G.Cabri, F. Guerra, L. Leonardi, M. Vincini, and F. Zambonelli. Supporting information integration with autonomous agents. In *International Workshop on Cooperative Information Agents (CIA'01)*, pages 88–99, Modena, Italy, 2001. Lecture Notes in Artificial Intelligence.
5. P. Buneman, S. Davidson, M. Fernandez, and D. Suciu. Adding structure to unstructured data. In *Proc. of International Conference on Database Theory (ICDT'97)*, pages 336–350, Delphi, Greece, 1997. Lecture Notes in Computer Science, Springer-Verlag.
6. F. Buccafurri, G. Lax, D. Rosaci, D. Ursino. The c-graph model. *DIMET Techn. Report 2002*, available from the authors.
7. A.G. Buchner and M.D. Mulvenna. Discovering internet marketing intelligence through online analytical web usage mining. *SIGMOD Record*, 27(4):54–61, 1998.
8. D. Calvanese, G. De Giacomo, M. Lenzerini, D. Nardi, R. Rosati. Description logic framework for information integration. In *Proc. of International Conference on Principles of Knowledge Representation and Reasoning (KR'98)*, pages 2–13, Trento, Italy, 1998. Morgan Kaufman.
9. S. Castano, V. De Antonellis, and S. De Capitani di Vimercati. Global viewing of heterogeneous data sources. *Transactions on Data and Knowledge Engineering*, 13(2), 2001.
10. A. Doan, P. Domingos, and A. Halevy. Reconciling schemas of disparate data sources: A machine-learning approach. In *Proc. of International Conference on Management of Data (SIGMOD 2001)*, Santa Barbara, California, USA, 2001. ACM Press.
11. C. Ghidini, L. Serafini. Information integration for electronic commerce. In *Proc. of International Workshop on Agent Mediated Electronic Trading 1998 (AMET'98)*, pages 189–206, Minneapolis, USA, 1998. Lecture Notes in Artificial Intelligence, Springer Verlag.
12. R. Goldman, J. McHugh, J. Widom. From semistructured data to XML: Migrating the lore data model and query languages. In *Proc. of International Workshop on the Web and Databases (WebDB'99)*, pages 25–30, Philadelphia, USA, 1999.

13. T. Joachims, D. Freitag, T.M. Mitchell. Web watcher: A tour guide for the world wide web. In *Proc. of International Joint Conference on Artificial Intelligence (IJCAI 97)*, pages Vol. 1, 770–777, Montreal, Canada, 1997. Morgan Kaufmann.

14. R. J. Bayardo Jr., B. Bohrer, R. S. Brice, A. Cichocki, J. Fowler, A. Helal, V. Kashyap, T. Ksiezyk, G. Martin, M. H. Nodine, M. Rashid, M. Rusinkiewicz, R. Shea, C. Unnikrishnan, A. Unruh, D. Woelk. Infosleuth: Semantic integration of information in open and dynamic environments. In *Proc. of International Conference on Management of Data (SIGMOD'97)*, 195–206, Tucson, USA, 1997. ACM Press.

15. S. Kim, W. Hall, A. Keane. Using document structures for personal ontologies and user modeling. In *User Modeling 2001: 8th International Conference LNCS 2109*, pages 240–242, Sonthofen, Germany, 2001. Springer-Verlag.

16. A. Levy, A. Rajaraman, and J. Ordille. Querying heterogeneous information sources using source descriptions. In *Proc. of International Conference on Very Large Data Bases (VLDB'96)*, pages 251–262, Bombay, India, 1996. Morgan Kaufmann.

17. H. Lieberman. Letizia: An agent that assists web browsing. In *Proc. of International Joint Conference on Artificial Intelligence (IJCAI 95)*, pages Vol. 1, 924–929, Montreal, Quebec, Canada, 1995. Morgan Kaufmann.

18. J.S. Park and R.S. Sandhu. Secure cookies on the web. *IEEE Internet Computing*, 4(4):36–44, 2000.

19. A. Pretschner, S. Gauch. Ontology based personalized search. In *IEEE International Conference on Tools with Artificial Intelligence*, pages 391–398, Chicago, 1999.

20. G. Somlo, A. E. Howe. Incremental clustering for profile maintenance in information gathering web agents. In *Proc. of International Conference on Autonomous Agents 2001*, pages 262–269, Montreal, Canada, 2001. ACM Press.

21. G. Terracina, D. Ursino. Deriving synonymies and homonymies of object classes in semi-structured information sources. In *Proc. of International Conference on Management of Data (COMAD 2000)*, pages 21–32, Pune, India, 2000. McGraw Hill.

22. P.R.S. Visser, V.A.M. Tamma. An experience with ontology-based agent clustering. In *IJCAI-99 Workshop on Ontologies and Problem-Solving Methods (KRR5)*, pages 12–1–12–13, Stockolm, Sweden, 1999.

23. O. Zaiane, M. Xin, and J. Han. Discovering web access patterns and trends by applying olap and data mining technology on web logs. In *IEEE Advances in Digital Libreries Conference (ADL'98)*, pages 19–29, Santa Barbara, California, USA, 1998. IEEE Computer Society Press.

Usage-Oriented Evolution of Ontology-Based Knowledge Management Systems

Nenad Stojanovic[1] and Ljiljana Stojanovic[2]

[1]Institute AIFB, University of Karlsruhe,
76128 Karlsruhe, Germany
nst@aifb.uni-karlsruhe.de
[2]FZI – Research Center for Information Technology at the University of Karlsruhe,
Haid-und-Neu-Str. 10-14, 76131 Karlsruhe, Germany
Ljiljana.Stojanovic@fzi.de

Abstract. In this paper, we present a novel approach for the management of the ontology-based knowledge management system. It extends our previous work in the ontology evolution by taking into account the usage of the ontology in the knowledge management system. The approach is mainly based on the analysis of the users' behaviour in two phases of a knowledge management cycle: (i) in providing knowledge by analysing the quality of annotations and (ii) in searching for knowledge by analysing users' queries and the responses from the knowledge repository. This analysis results in the recommendations for changes in the underlying ontology, the annotations and/or the knowledge repository in order to make the whole system more efficient. We present two short case studies.

1 Introduction

Successful knowledge management is the key to many areas of corporate growth, including a successful creation of new electronic commerce strategies and businesses. But a successful implementation of a knowledge management strategy entails much more than just high-level strategic understanding and establishment of knowledge-sharing policies. Foremost, it requires a successful delivery of relevant knowledge to people who need it, when they need it [1]. In fact, the effectiveness of a knowledge management strategy rests on the effectiveness of searching, which can be illustrated through the statement of a leading automotive manufacturer [2]: "if our people saved just 10 minutes a day in wasted search time, our company would see savings of $100m per year". Consequently, if someone can't find the knowledge she seeks, then the knowledge management system had failed to meet user's expectation and it doesn't fulfil its purpose.

However, the focus of searching is not only to find knowledge, but also to find knowledge easily, since a user prefers to get only a few highly relevant knowledge resources that will help in resolving the problem at hand. This requires the methods for decreasing information overload, which is the most frequently occurring problem in the knowledge management practice. The well-known trade-off between precision and recall makes resolving this problem very difficult.

R. Meersman, Z. Tari (Eds.): CoopIS/DOA/ODBASE 2002, LNCS 2519, pp. 1186–1204, 2002.

From the knowledge management point of view, the task of achieving efficient searching for knowledge can be decomposed into two subtasks:

- how to enable that the content of the knowledge repository reflects knowledge needs of users, e.g. the knowledge repository contains knowledge resources which users are interested in;
- how to support efficient finding[1] of such knowledge resources, e.g. to ensure the retrieval of the highly relevant resources.

Knowledge needs of the users can be defined as requirements for the delivery of the knowledge resources, which might help users in solving tasks they are working on. Knowledge needs are related to the concrete users and concrete problems, which means that for each organisation they have to be designed separately. Moreover, they are dynamic categories and they have to be changed according to the preferences of users, new employees, new style of the learning on-the-site. Consequently, an efficient knowledge repository should reflect knowledge needs of users and adapt continually its content to evolving users' preferences. For example, when a lot of users are interested in two topics together (e.g. debug and java) and there is no knowledge resource relevant to this need, then an efficient knowledge management system should generate a requirement to "import" in the knowledge repository one or more new knowledge resources about the combination of these topics (e.g. a document about how to perform debugging of a java code). Moreover, the further analysis of this requirement can result in learning actions, such as the creation of a new course about these topics (e.g. a course about methods for debugging java programs) or in better understanding of the problem domain (e.g. the java-debugging is a knowledge-intensive task, it can be error-prone and a constraint in the java-software development, it requires an especial experience etc).

Even when the knowledge repository contains resources which a user is interested in, it remains the question how to support the efficient finding of such resources. Since the searching for resources is organised as a process of going through "index" space of these resources, the crucial factor for a more efficient searching is the way in which indexes are organised. One of the most promising approaches is the organisation of indexes based on the conceptual model of a domain, i.e. ontologies, providing substantial improvements to traditional search systems [3]. In a knowledge management system ontologies are used as a conceptual backbone for providing information about knowledge resources and for accessing to the knowledge resources [4]. More precisely, in an ontology-based knowledge management system ontologies support the process of "indexing" content of a knowledge resource – so called semantic annotation [5] and the navigation through the knowledge repository – so called conceptual navigation [6]. However, ontologies, as a conceptual model for the given business domain, should react to all changes in the business environment. This includes accounting the modification in the application domain or in the business strategy; incorporating additional functionality according to changes in the users' needs; organizing information in a better way etc. If the underlying ontology is not

---

[1] In the context of this paper the term "efficient finding" is related to the high precision of the information retrieval system.

For the given request and the system's response, the following numbers can be determined: r = number of relevant documents in database, n = number of documents retrieved, nr = number of relevant documents retrieved. Assuming $n, r > 0$ than recall = nr/r and precision = nr/n

up-to-date or the annotation of knowledge resources is inconsistent, redundant or incomplete, then the reliability, accuracy and effectiveness of the system decrease significantly [7]. In order to avoid these real problems, ontology-based applications have to be supported by a very efficient mechanism for the discovering of these changes, analysing and resolving them in a consistent way [8].

Summarising the previous discussion, it can be concluded that an efficient ontology-based knowledge management system requires a management component that will be able to cope with the frequent changes in user's preferences as well as in business environment. However, although the importance of such management component is demonstrated in the industrial praxis [9], as known to the authors, methods and tools supporting this complex activity are still missing.

In this paper we present a usage-oriented approach for the management of an ontology-based knowledge management system, which is based on our previous research in the dynamic knowledge management [7] and ontology evolution [8]. The approach is oriented toward the analysis of the users behaviour in two phases of a knowledge management cycle [10]: (i) in providing knowledge by analysing the quality of annotations and (ii) in searching for knowledge by analysing users' queries and the responses from the knowledge repository. We assume that the searching procedure itself is realised as an ontology-based inferencing mechanism, which already proved its efficiency [11]. The analyses result in the recommendations for changes in the underlying ontology, the annotations and/or knowledge repository in order to make the process of searching for knowledge more efficient. Moreover, the approach results not only in the increasing the precision of the knowledge retrieval system by making the annotations more optimal, but also in the overall guidelines how to avoid potential knowledge overload or gap in the system. These guidelines are dynamically adapted to the changes in users' needs, which are not explicitly stated but discovered from the data. Consequently, our approach leads to a self-evolving knowledge management system, which can discover changes in its environment autonomously and reacts on them accordingly.

The paper is organised as follows: In the second section we propose the conceptual architecture of the management component in an ontology-based knowledge management system, whereas in the section 3 more details about two main modules, namely Ontology Evolution and KM Change Discovery, are given. Section 4 contains two evaluation studies. After a discussion of related work in the section 5, concluding remarks summarize the importance of the presented approach.

2 Conceptual Architecture

As mentioned in the introduction, the management of an ontology-based knowledge management system is a complex problem and requires dealing with frequent changes in user's needs as well as business environment. In this section we present a novel framework for the management, which includes mechanisms for tracking users' behaviour and ontology evolution. The conceptual architecture is given on the Fig. 1.

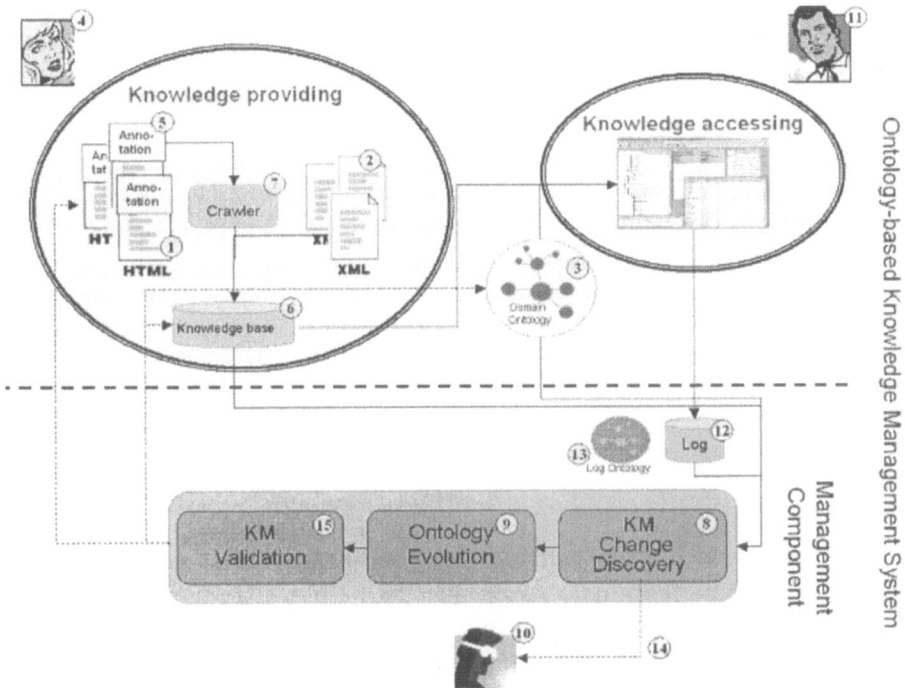

Fig. 1. Conceptual architecture for the management of the knowledge management systems

In order to be found efficiently, the content of knowledge resources (cf. 1 and 2 in Fig. 1) is described by several topics, which are related to the underlying domain ontology (3). Due to the great importance of the "quality" of annotation to the efficiency of a knowledge management, we consider manual annotation of knowledge resources, which can be supported by an annotation tool [5]. Though not perfect, manual annotation is currently the most appropriate, since the expert on the domain subject provides annotation in a way, which facilitates the search process [12].

The annotation can be the task either of the author of the knowledge resources or a specialist, i.e. knowledge annotator (4). Annotations can be explicitly added to the knowledge resources, e.g. in the form of XML comments (5), or may be placed in a separate knowledge repository with the reference to the original source (6). In the first case, such annotations are crawled (7) into the knowledge repository, thus the analysis remains the same for both cases.

Since the annotations are "interfaces" to knowledge resources, their structure should be analysed in order to resolve problems, which can arise in the searching for knowledge, e.g. knowledge gap or knowledge overload. The analysis of annotations is performed in the KM Change Discovery component (8). It results in the set of recommendation for changes in the annotations and/or domain ontology, which are processed in the ontology evolution component (9). The knowledge engineer (10) accepts or rejects such recommendations. The ontology evolution component ensures that the ontology and all dependent artefacts remain in the consistent stage after resolving changes [8].

The information whether and how the knowledge repository reflects knowledge needs of end-users (11) can be obtained by analysing the users' interaction with the system, e.g. which topics are searched for, how many results are delivered, which documents are retrieved etc. This data is captured in the log file (12) in the form of the instances of the log-ontology (13) (see the Section 3.2.2). The log file is also proceeded in the KM Change Discovery module (8). In contrast to the analysis of annotations, the log-file analysis might result in requirements for the update in the knowledge repository or in suggestions for revision of the knowledge strategy (14).

However, the changes derived from the user's behaviour are application-oriented and, after applying these changes, the system should improve its performances. The task of the KM Validation module (15) is to restore the original state of the whole system (the ontology, annotations and the knowledge repository) in the case of decreasing performances. This feature is very useful in situations when some fine-tuning is needed and there are several possibilities to resolve the changes.

In the next section, we describe the main modules in more details.

3 Management Component in the Ontology-Based Knowledge Management System

The management component in the ontology-based knowledge management system should take into consideration (i) the ontology as a domain model that might underpin different applications or can be used for many purposes and (ii) the usage of the ontology in the knowledge management system. Consequently, the corresponding management component contains two essential parts:

- the ontology evolution component as a basic component that enables the timely adaptation of an ontology, as well as the consistent management/propagation of the ontology changes to dependent elements [8];
- the knowledge management extensions of the basic component that incorporates context in which the ontology and its instances are used.

In the rest of this section, we present the above-mentioned components and indicate their significance for the improving of a knowledge management system.

3.1 Ontology Evolution

Based on our experience in building ontologies and using them in several applications (e.g. [6]), we have formulated the following set of design requirements for ontology evolution:

1. It has to (i) enable resolving the given ontology changes and [8] (ii) ensure the consistency of the underlying ontology and all dependent artefacts [7];
2. It should be supervised allowing the user to manage changes more easily [13];
3. It should offer advice to the user for continual ontology refinement [14].

The first requirement is the essential one for any ontology evolution approach – after applying a change to a consistent ontology, the ontology should remain in a consistent state. However, there are many ways to achieve consistency after a change request. A mechanism that enables users to manage changes which result not in an arbitrary consistent state, but in a consistent state fulfilling the user's preferences, is described in [8].

The second requirement complements to the first one by presenting the user with information needed to control changes and make appropriate decisions. When working on an ontology collaboratively, different knowledge engineers may have different ideas about how the ontology should be changed. Further, the knowledge engineer may fail to understand the actual effect of the change and approve the change that shouldn't be performed. Moreover, it may be desired to change the ontology for experimental purposes. Thus, ontology evolution has to enable undoing changes at the user's request.

The last requirement states that potential changes improving the ontology may be discovered semi-automatically. An ontology may be in a consistent state, but it may contain some redundant entities or can be better structured with respect to the domain. For example, multiple users may be working on different parts of an ontology without enough communication. They may be deleting subconcepts of a common concept at different points in time to fulfil their immediate needs. As a result, it may happen that only one subconcept is left. Since classification with only one subclass beats the original purpose of classification, we consider such ontology to have a suboptimal structure. To aid users in detecting such situations, we investigated the possibilities of applying the self-adaptive system principles and proactively making suggestions for *ontology refinements* – changes to the ontology with the goal of improving ontology structure, making the ontology easier for understanding and cheaper for modifying.

A more careful analysis of these requirements (e.g. the changes have to be captured, analysed, applied and validated by the user) implies the necessity to consider the ontology evolution problem as a composition of several subproblems realized in a determined sequence. This sequence of activities is called the ontology evolution process. Due to lack of space we omit the detailed description of the phases of the ontology evolution process, which can be found in [8].

3.2 KM Change Discovery

Some changes in the domain are implicit, reflected in the behaviour of the system, and can be discovered only through the analysis of its behaviour. In contrast to the ontology refinement phase [15] in the ontology evolution component that is based on the analysis of the structure of an ontology and its instances, the KM Change Discovery component (cf. 8 in Fig. 1) takes into account the usage of the ontology in a knowledge management system. Its goal is to generate recommendations for the improvement of the ontology-based knowledge management system, from the point of view of the efficiency of searching for knowledge. Our approach for change discovery is usage-oriented and it is based on the analysis of the results of the user's activities in knowledge providing and knowledge accessing phases of the knowledge management process. Since the annotations are results of the knowledge providing phase, their analysis can discover ambiguity in the description of the content of the knowledge resources. The ambiguity is the main factor that decreases precision in the knowledge retrieval. Considering the knowledge accessing phase, we analyse the user's queries and the response of the knowledge repository, which are reflections of the user's needs and the "response factor" (see 3.2.2) of the knowledge repository, respectively.

In the rest of this section, we discuss both analyses we perform in order to discover the changes in a knowledge management system:

– the analysis of the knowledge resources annotations' quality;
– the analysis of the users' interaction during the search in the knowledge management system.

3.2.1 Changes Discovered from the Annotations

The experience from the information retrieval research shows that the "quality" of annotations is crucial for the retrieval of relevant knowledge resources. Our primary objective was not only to monitor the quality of annotations over time, but also to suggest how to adapt them or the underlying ontology, in order to enhance the whole system. Indeed, we developed an approach (and corresponding tools) that guides the knowledge engineer through the update process, rather than requiring them to find what has to be modified and how. In this way we alleviate the modification process, but we don't perform the modification, since the knowledge engineer has to decide whether she wants to apply the suggestions or not.

We define the quality of annotations[2] according to two assessment criteria:

- *Validity*   – if metadata in annotation is inconsistent with the domain ontology, then the metadata is not treated in the knowledge sharing;
- *Optimality*   – if metadata in the annotation is redundant, inaccurate or incomplete, then it can seriously damage the users' confidence in the system;

To note that assessment is performed on the annotation level, and the ontology structure is the basis for all measures. From the point of view of the information retrieval, the analysis of the first criterion enables increasing of the recall of the system, whereas the second criteria ensures enhancing of the precision. While the main problem in the sharing of knowledge in a knowledge management system is the huge percent of irrelevant information (i.e. low precision), in the rest of this section we elaborate only the secondly mentioned annotation quality criteria. Moreover, we explain how this assessment can help a knowledge engineer to refine and improve the annotation and/or ontology, in order to support searching for knowledge. The analysis of first assessment criteria is given in [15].

Optimality

In order to emphasise the real need of the optimal annotation, we use examples from the MEDLINE[3] database, which represents the state-of-the-art in human indexing. However, our experiments with MEDLINE show that there are many possibilities to optimise the annotations.

To estimate the optimality of an annotation, we introduce the following three criteria that are important from the knowledge management point of view:

---

[2] An annotation consists of a set of ontology instances. We use term metadata as a synonym for an ontology instance.
[3] www.ncbi.nlm.nih.gov/PubMed/

1. Compactness – A semantic annotation is incompact or redundant if it contains more metadata than is needed and desired to express the same "idea". In order to achieve compactness (and thus to avoid redundancy), the annotation has to comprise the minimal set[4] of the metadata without exceeding what is necessary or useful. The repetition of the metadata or the usage of several metadata with the same meaning only complicate maintenance and decrease the system performance.

Concept hierarchy and property hierarchy from the domain ontology are used to check this criterion. The first example in Fig. 2 represents the incompact annotation, because the knowledge resource is annotated, after all, with the concept **Person** and its subconcept **Female**. When someone searches for all knowledge resources about **Person**, she searches for the resources about all its subconcepts (including **Female**) as well. Consequently, she gets this resource (minimum) twice. Moreover, such annotation introduces an ambiguity in the understanding of the content of a knowledge resource, which implies problems in knowledge sharing. Let us examine the meaning of the annotation of a medical document using the set of metadata **Person, Female, Aspirin, Complications**. Does it mean that the document is about complications in using aspirin only in females, or in all persons? When the second answer is the right one, then this document is also relevant for the treatment of male persons with aspirin. This implies new questions: is the annotation using metadata **Female** an error, or the metadata **Male** is missing? Anyway, there is an ambiguity in annotations, which can be detected and resolved by using our approach.

In order to prevent this, a knowledge resource should be annotated using as special metadata as possible (i.e. more specialised sub-concepts). In this way, the mentioned ambiguities are avoided. Moreover, the maintenance of the annotations is also alleviated, because the annotation is more concise and only changes linked to the concept **Female** (first example in Fig. 2) can provoke changes in the annotation.

2. Completeness – An annotation is incomplete if it is possible to extend the annotation only by analysing existing metadata in the annotation, in order to clarify its semantic. It means that the annotation is not finished yet, and requires that some additional metadata have to be filled up.

This criterion is computed based on the structure of the domain ontology. For example, one criterion is the existence of a dependency in the domain ontology between the domain entities, which are already used in the annotation. The second example in Fig. 2 contains concepts with many relationships between them (e.g. properties "*cures*" and "*causes*" exist between concepts **Therapy** and **Disease**). The interpretation is ambiguous, e.g. are the knowledge resources about how a disease (i) can be cured by a therapy, or (ii) caused by a therapy. In order to constrain the set of possible interpretations, the annotation has to be extended with one of these properties.

This problem is especially important when the knowledge repository contains a lot of resources annotated with the same concepts, because the search for knowledge retrieves irrelevant resources that use certain concepts in a different context. Consequently, the precision of the system is decreased.

---

[4] An annotation is not minimal if excluding metadata results in the same retrieval for the same query i.e. precision and recall remain the same.

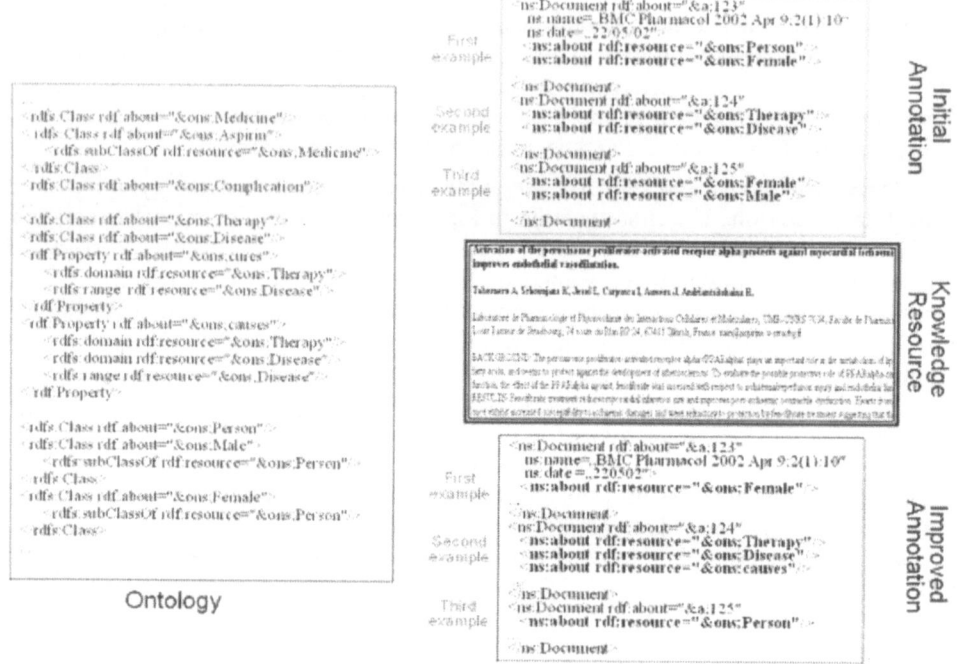

Fig. 2. Annotation refinement based on the analysis the ontology structure and the existing annotations. The ontology is depicted in the left part. The right part shows downward the initial annotation, corresponding knowledge resource and the improved semantic annotation.

3. Aggregation – An annotation is aggregative if it contains a set of metadata that can be replaced with semantically related metadata in order to achieve a shorten annotation, but without producing any retrieval other than the original annotation. For example, this pattern for the annotation refinement occurs when a resource is described with all subconcepts of one concept (concepts **Female** and **Male** in third example in Fig. 2). From the searching for knowledge point of view, it is the same whether a resource is annotated using the combination of concepts (e.g. **Female** and **Male**) or using only the parent concept (e.g. **Person**). It is obvious that the second case of annotation makes the management much easier. Moreover, since the standard approaches for the ranking results of querying [6] exploit conceptual hierarchies, for example in a querying for persons a resource annotated using **Female** and **Male** will be placed at the same level as a resource annotated using only one of these concepts. It has to be ranked on the top level (level of concept **Person**), because it covers all subtypes of concept **Person**.

3.2.2   Changes Discovered from the End-Users' Activities

The task of a knowledge management system is to deliver the right knowledge in the right moment (at the right place). Interpreted on the level of the searching for knowledge, it means that a user has the opportunity to easily find relevant knowledge resources for the topics which are important for the problem she solves. In other words, the list of retrieved knowledge resources for a user query should not be empty, and should also contain only highly relevant sources.

It implies that the management component of a knowledge management system should track the interests of users, as well as the list of answers for the posted queries. In order to support this task, our system records the user's interaction with the knowledge management system. The prerequisite for the meaningful analysis is that this log information is properly organized and interpreted. In order to use as much as possible of the existing mechanism for storage and query, we introduced the log ontology. The role of the log ontology is to model what happens, and why, when, by whom, how it is performed. Indeed, the structure of the log ontology is determined in order to enable reasoning about accessibility, usability and numerousness of knowledge resources, as well as domain knowledge. Each user's activity is captured in a log file in the form instances of the log ontology. Fig. 3 shows a part of the log ontology and the corresponding log metadata.

Log Ontology	Log metadata

Event::Root[
  date=>Date;
  relatedTo=>Interest;
  performedBy=>User;
  previousEvent=>Event;
  numOfResults=>Number;
  resultsIn=>Result;
].
  Access::Event.
  Query::Access.
  Browse::Access.
  Read::Access.
    ReadResource::Read.
    ReadMetadata::Read.
  Provide::Event.
...
	Query100:Query[
	  date->220502;
	  relatedTo->InterestX;
	  numOfResults->22;
	  resultsIn->ResultY
	].
	InterestX:Interest[
	  relatedTo->>dom#Aspirin;
	  relatedTo->>dom#Disease
	].
	ResultY:Result[
	  includes->>ks#doc101;
	  ...
	  includes->>ks#rule234
	].
	...

Fig. 3. Log ontology and log metadata. The conceptual structure of the log ontology is represented in the left part. The right part shows several log entries in the form of metadata generated as a response to the user's request for knowledge resources about Aspirin and Disease.

To note that the presented log file tracks only the interaction which is related to the knowledge management task, i.e. each user's activity is modeled through the hierarchy of the concept Event. We assume that only a knowledge engineer has privileges to modify the domain ontology, and the end users search for knowledge resources or provide a new knowledge resource. Thus, the log ontology doesn't contain events regarding the development/evolution of the domain ontology.

Each event has one or more data elements that are specific to that event. For all events, the model includes a timestamp, user, previous event etc. In the current realization, this information has only a documentation purpose. For our analysis, the most important parts of the log ontology are those related to (i) representing the user's interest (concept **Interest** in Fig. 3), (ii) number of answers (property **numOfResults**) provided by the system and (iii) answers themselves (concept **Result**). In the rest of the section, we perform the following analyses:

1) the analysis of the users' interests – the frequency of a topic's occurrence in the users' queries[5];

2) the analysis of the knowledge repository response factor – the capability of the knowledge repository to satisfy the users' interests in an efficient manner.

The Analysis of the Users' Interests

We define the rate of interest IRate(E) of users for an ontology entity E as:

$$IRate(E) = IFrequency(E) \cdot Clarity(E) \tag{1}$$

IFrequency(E) represents the users' interest in ontology entity E, and it is calculated as a ratio between the numbers of the users' interactions with the system related to the ontology entity E and the total number of the interactions. Indeed, we use the formula:

$$IFrequency(E) = \frac{Q(E)}{Q}$$

whereas Q(E) is the number of queries that contains entity E, and Q is the total number of queries.

The clarity factor represents the uncertainty to determine the user's interest in a posted query. For example, when a user makes a query using a concept **Person**, which contains two subconcepts **Female** and **Male**, it could be matter of discussion: whether she is interested in the concept **Person** or in its subconcepts, but she failed to express it in a clear manner. Our experiences show that users who are not familiar with the given ontology used to use a more general concept in searching for knowledge resources, instead of using more specific concepts. In other words, the clarity factor makes the calculation of the users' interest more sensitive to the structure of the ontology by accounting possible "errors" in the query formulation.

The formula for the clarity factor depends on the entity type:

$$Clarity(E) = \begin{cases} k(E) \cdot \dfrac{1}{numSubConcepts(E)+1} & E \quad is \quad a \quad concept \\[2em] k(E) \cdot \dfrac{1}{numSub\Pr opeties(E)+1} \cdot \dfrac{1}{numDomains(E)} & E \quad is \quad a \quad propetry \end{cases}$$

whereas numSubConcepts(E) is the number of subconcepts of a concept E, numSubProperties(E) is the number of subproperties of a property E and numDomains(E) is the number of domains defined for the property E.

The coefficient k is introduced in order to favour the frequency of the usage. It is calculated using the following formula:

$$k(E) = numLevel(E) + 1$$

where numLevel(E) is the depth of the hierarchy of the entity E.

Our primary goal is to decrease the impact of the non-leaf concepts, since they represent the common view to the set of their subconcepts, as described above. The similar strategy is applied to the properties and their hierarchy. However, the unclearness of reasons for a property usage can also arise when multiple domains for

---

[5] According to the glossary for the information retrieval [http://www.cs.jhu.edu/~weiss/glossary.html#infoneed] information need represents what the user really wants to know and a query is an approximation to the information need.

a property are defined. Thus, in order to clarify the context of a property usage, we require the explicit specification of the domain of that property, or otherwise we decrease its clarity factor.

The IRate value is calculated for all entities, and two extreme cases are analysed: the frequently used and unused entities. The first extreme corresponds to the entities with the highest rates that should be considered for changes. The formula (1) expresses our experience that the frequent usage of an entity in queries can be a consequence of the bad modelling of the hierarchy of that entity, i.e. in modelling that entity, the hierarchy is not explored in details. For example, in a medical domain the concept **Person** is not split into concepts **Male** and **Female**, although there are a lot of differences between medical treatment of male and female patients. In end effect, any time the user wants to find knowledge resources related to either the male or female patients, she has to make a query with the concept **Person** and consequently the number of retrieved queries is huge. Therefore, our analysis can suggest that the concept **Person** should be divided into several subconcepts. The knowledge engineer decides whether and how to do that. If the considered concept already has a hierarchy, then its suitability (probability) for change is decreased by the clarity factor. The similar strategy is applied to the properties, too.

In the case that nobody is interested in an entity, i.e. the rate of interest for that entity is equal 0, then the entity should be considered for deleting from the ontology and consequently from annotations. However, the problem arises when the knowledge repository contains a lot of resources annotated with that entity. It can be interpreted in various ways, including that the topic is interesting for the community, but not used in past projects, or that employees are very familiar to this topic, etc.

The previous analysis takes into consideration only one entity. The recent analyses show that web users typically submit very short queries to search engines and the average length of web queries is less than two "words" [16]. For an enterprise portal we suppose making of queries containing 3-4 searching topics, which implies some extension in the calculation of the clarity factor. This analysis is out of scope of this paper and can be found in [15].

The Analysis of the Content of the Knowledge Repository

The previous analysis makes the recommendations only for the changes in the ontology and the annotation by considering the user's interests. In this section, we extend it by analysing the users' interaction during the search in the knowledge management system. Indeed, in order to estimate the usefulness of the repository to the user's needs, we analyse the number of retrieved knowledge resources for a query. This value represents the response factor, and can be expressed as:

$$RFactor(E) = IRate(E) \cdot \frac{KR}{KR(E)} \qquad (2)$$

whereas KR(E) is the number of knowledge resources retrieved for the entity E and KR is the total number of resources in the repository.

The formula (2) reflects the situation in which a problem arises when knowledge resources related to an entity are frequently requested, but the repository is very rarely filled by such resources. This problem is known as the knowledge vacancy. Its occurrence can be a signal to the knowledge engineer to incorporate new resources for the entities with the high IRate and low RFactor into the knowledge repository or at least to analyse why this knowledge vacancy has arisen. The most critical case is when RFactor(E) is equal to 0, which means that the knowledge repository doesn't contain the resources related to the entity E, although there are interests for that entity. One of the interpretations is the knowledge gap – an empty knowledge space.

Moreover, it is possible to make the complement analysis for the high value of RFactor and low value of IRate. It means that there are a lot of knowledge resources related to an entity, since they are annotated with that entity. However, that entity is very rarely used in queries. The knowledge engineer has to decide whether it is necessary to refine the knowledge repository or to change annotations of resources.

The high value of the response factor indicates the potential knowledge overload. Since this factor is estimated based on the rate of interest and the annotation frequency, the resolving of the knowledge overload can be achieved by resolving the clarity of the queries or by improving the quality of the annotation (see Section 3.2.1).

4 Evaluation

In order to prove the validity of our research, we conducted two case studies, one for each of the proposed strategies for changes discovery: (i) changes discovered from the annotations and (ii) changes discovered from the end-users' activities.

4.1 Analysis of Annotations in MEDLINE

MEDLINE is one of the largest index and abstract databases of medical journal articles, which contains over 11 million references to articles from 4,600 worldwide journals in life sciences. It is maintained by the U.S. National Library of Medicine, which has developed a sophisticated controlled vocabulary called the Medical Subject Headings[6], used in the indexing of articles. The assignment of MeSH topics to articles, from the MEDLINE database, represents the state-of-the-art in human indexing; the professional indexers who perform this task train for at least 1 year. Ten to twelve topics in the form MainHeading/Qualifier are associated to the each article, which can be interpreted as the concept-relation relationship. Although such annotations help in searching for articles, MEDLINE suffers from the overload of information. For example, searching the MEDLINE using the MeSH topic "common cold"[7] yields over 1,400 articles written in the last 30 years. Finding a relevant article might take 20-30 minutes.

In order to prove whether our approach can discover some inconsistencies in MEDLINE annotations, which lead to the decreasing of the precision of the system, we analysed a corpus of MEDLINE articles and corresponding annotations regarding criteria we mentioned in the section 3.2.1. About 200 articles are randomly selected from the MEDLINE database and the results are presented in Table 1.

---

[6] MeSH (http://www.nlm.nih.gov/pubs/factsheets/mesh.html) is so-called medical ontology
[7] The example is taken from http://www.ovid.com.

Table 1. The result of the analysis of the MEDLINE annotations (to note that in some articles two or more inconsistencies were found)

Criteria	Optimality		
	Compactness	**Completeness**	**Aggregation**
Inconsistences found in % **of documents**	80	43	10

Discussion:

The rate of compactness is very small – High-frequent occurrence of this inconsistence can be explained by the format of the annotations itself. Since all metadata in an annotation are assigned separately to the corresponding knowledge resource and are not grouped according to the context, the concept-subconcept pairs occur very often in the annotations (e.g. Human and Female).

Completeness is small – A part of the problem lies in the format of annotations itself: articles are annotated using topics and not relation metadata [5]. Consequently, it is not possible to express any relationship between medical concepts. Therefore, in lots of annotations the meaning of used topics has to be specified by adding a property, or the range of the property.

Aggregation is high – The small number of cases we found are related to the explanation given for the Compactness.

4.2 Analysis of Users' Queries in a Semantic Portal

The Semantic Portal (SEAL) [6] is an ontology-based application, which provides a "single-click" access to the almost all information related to the organisation, people, researches and projects of our Institute. It is widely used by our research and administrative staff as well as by our students. One of the most usable features is the possibility to search for people, research areas and projects on the semantic basis, i.e. using corresponding Institute Ontology. The portal provides a very user-friendly interface, which enables formation of arbitrary queries using entities from the underlying ontology. The search is performed as an inference through metadata, which is crawled from Portal pages. As the inference mechanism we use the Ontobroker [11].

Since the installation of the new version of the portal three months ago, the information about users' activities, regarding querying the portal, are logged in a file. The primary goal was to test the stability of the used version of inference engine. However, we reused the log file in order to evaluate our methods for discovering changes in the ontology. We set up a "what-if" experiment concerning this log file as follows:

1. We rewrote 1000 randomly selected queries under following hypothetical conditions:

    a) The hierarchy of the concept **Person** that originally had five levels is shorten to only one level including the sub-concepts **Researcher** and **Student**;

b)   The hierarchy of the concept **Project** that originally had two levels is deleted;

The hierarchy of the concept **ResearchArea** is shorten to the first level only. Consequently, we use 20 subconcepts instead of 80 subconcepts in the original hierarchy

The hypothetical conditions given above are used for query rewriting. For example, from the original query in the form of (**Professor, pastProject, Knowledge_Acquisition**), meaning that a user is interested in information about professors whose past project was related to the knowledge acquisition, one gets the rewritten query in the form (**Researcher, Project, Knowledge_Based_Systems**).

2.   We started searching (inferencing) using these queries.

3.   We calculated interesting rate IRate (formula 1 in the section 3.2.2) for concepts **Person, Researcher, Project** and research areas **Knowledge_Based_System** and **E-Commerce**. In order to simplify the analysis, for the coefficient k we used the value 1. Table 2 shows the result of our analysis.

Table 2. The result of the interesting rate analysis

Concept	Researcher	Project	Knowledge_ Based_ System	E- Commerce	Person
IRate Value	(202/1000)*(1) = 0,202	(100/1000)*(1) = 0,1	(10/1000)*(1) = 0,01	(2/1000)*(1) = 0,002	(4/1000)* (1/2) = 0,002

Discussion:

We made a hypothetical situation in which the ontology is badly modelled and some hierarchies are not explored at all. A user can select only some restricted, higher-level concepts and for each specialisation she has to use one of higher-level concepts (e.g. for the query about professors she has to use the concept **Researcher**). In such a way we modelled the situation in which **the underlying ontology did not correspond to the users' needs**. The task of our method was to recognize which of badly modelled hierarchies do not reflect users' needs. We discuss several results:

The concept Researcher has the highest IRate - it should be considered firstly - This is the right decision while a lot of queries contain concept **Researcher** and it has no hierarchy in the hypothetical situation. It means that we could conclude that concept **Researcher** is used as a replacement for the users' need to search for some specialisations of researchers.

The concept Knowledge_Based_Systems should be considered before the concept E-Commerce - In our experiment the both hierarchies are shorten. However, in the original ontology the first one was larger and therefore should be firstly considered for a change. The number of queries, which contain topic "knowledge-based system", reflects users' needs for more specialised areas of the knowledge-based system.

The concept Person has the lowest IRate - This is the right estimation, since the concept **Person** has one level of the hierarchy, which satisfies users' needs regarding this concept.

5   Related Work

In this section we give an overview of the researches related to our approach. We divide this overview into three parts regarding three research communities: the knowledge management, the digital library and the ontology evolution.

Knowledge Management

As mentioned in the introduction, the area of maintaining knowledge management systems is rather seldom explored in the research community, although the practical importance is elsewhere announced [9]. The part of the problem lies in the gap between real industrial knowledge management projects, which are oriented to one-shoot results and, consequently, resolve the management in an ad-hock manner and research projects, which try to analyse the essence of the managerial problem and to result in the sound and reusable solutions. Indeed, several (partial) solutions for the management of knowledge management systems can be found in industrial praxis. For example, in [17] authors describe the approach performed in the VTT Electronics, the Technical Research Centre of Finland. The approach is based on the process model and one of five main knowledge processes, named knowledge update, deals with changes in the business environment. This process has several sub-processes (identification of changes, evaluation of change impact, etc.) and for each of them a worksheet is defined. The users should fill the requests for changes and someone than calculates the impacts etc. However, the approach is nor based on a conceptual model of domain (such as an ontology) neither the changes are resolved systematically (as in our change propagation phase of the ontology evolution component).

Further, from the research's perspective, the interesting study of managing changes in a knowledge management system is given in [9]. The authors consider two types of changes: (i) functional changes that are about new KM-systems in the organization, new versions of a KM-system and new features in one KM-system and (ii) structural changes that deal with new business models, new subsidiaries and new competencies in the organisation. The results of the study show that managing the evolution of KM-systems on an ad hoc basis can lead to unnecessary complexity and KM-systems failures and that KM research has paid little attention to the evolution of KM-systems.

Digital Library

Analysing one of the most popular definition of digital libraries, given in [18], that a digital library is an environment that brings together "collections, services, and people in support of the full life cycle of creation, dissemination, use, and preservation of data, information, and knowledge", we concluded that this research community can be very useful source of information regarding management of knowledge repositories. Indeed, the problem of repositories' management was recognised on the high level. The separate service, named collection management or collection maintenance, is introduced in the architecture. However, as in knowledge management community, no systematic realisation of such service was found. It seems that each of institutions has its own "collection management policy" when a resource should be removed or a new one added to the library collection, as for example in the [19].

Regarding to information retrieval component, which is one of constitutive elements of a digital library, we found a lot of similarities to our analysis. More precisely, the evaluation of a digital library only in the system-centered way, so called quantitative evaluation, which is based on the traditional information retrieval measures such as precision and recall, is not enough for the estimation whether the users are satisfied with the library system [20]. It is needed to perform a user-centered analysis [21], so-called qualitative evaluation in terms of user's needs, tasks, goals, which partially correspond to our analysis of user's queries.

Ontology Evolution

In the last decade, there has been much active research in the area of ontology-based systems. However, there are very few approaches investigating the problems of changing in the ontologies.

Heflin [22] points out that ontologies on the Web will need to evolve and he provides a new formal definition of ontologies for the use in dynamic, distributed environments. Although good design may prevent many ontological errors, some errors will not be realized until the ontology is put to use. However, this problem as well as the problem of the change propagation are not treated in the work of Heflin. Moreover, the user cannot customize the way of performing the change and the problem of the identification of the change is not analysed.

In contrast to the ontology evolution that allows access to all data only through the newest ontology, ontology versioning allows access to data through different versions of the ontology. Thus, ontology evolution can be treated as a part of the ontology versioning mechanism that is analysed in [23]. Authors provide an overview of causes and consequences of the changes in the ontology. However, the most important flaw is the lack of a detailed analysis of the effect of specific changes on the interpretation of data which is a constituent part of our work.

Other research communities also have influenced our work. The problem of schema evolution and schema versioning support has been extensively studied in relational and database papers [24]. In [25] authors discuss the differences that steam from different knowledge models and different usage paradigms. Moreover, research in ontology evolution can also benefit from the many years of research in knowledge-based system evolution. The script-based knowledge evolution [13] that identifies typical sequences of changes to knowledge base and represents them in a form of scripts, is similar to our approach. In contrast to the knowledge- scripts that allow the tool to understand the consequences of each change, we go step further by allowing the user to control how to complete the overall modification and by suggesting the changes that could improve the ontology.

6 Conclusion

In this paper, we present a novel approach for the evolution of an ontology-based knowledge management system. The approach is based on the analysis of the user's interaction with the system in providing annotations for knowledge resources, as well as in the process of accessing the knowledge by querying the knowledge repository. Our previous work in ontology evolution is used as a basis for this research. We defined several assessment criteria to estimate the quality of annotations, the user's needs and the quality of a knowledge repository from the point of view of the knowledge management. These criteria result in the recommendations for the continual system improvement. The benefits of the proposed approach are manifold:

dynamic adaptation of the system to the changes in the business environment, dynamic analysis of the user's needs and the usefulness of particular knowledge resources and the organisation of the knowledge repository to fulfil these needs, to name but a few.

The evaluation experiments show that our approach can be applied in the real-world applications successfully. We find that it represents a very important step in the achievement of a self-adaptive knowledge management system, which can discover some changes from the user's interactions with the system automatically and evolves its structure correspondingly.

References

1.   Woods, W.: Knowledge Management Needs Effective Search Technology, Sun Journal, March (1998)
2.   Wordmap – the platform for consistent naming and description throughout the enterprise, white-paper, Wordmap Ltd, UK, http://www.wordmap.com/ downloads/wordmap_whitepaper.pdf, (2002)
3.   Guarino, N., Masolo, C., Vetere, G.: OntoSeek: Content-Based Access to the Web, IEEE Intelligent Systems, 14(3) (1999) 70-80
4.   Staab, S., Schnurr, H.-P., Studer, R., Sure, Y.: Knowledge Processes and Ontologies, IEEE Intelligent Systems, 16(1) (2001)
5.   Handschuh, S., Staab, S.: Authoring and Annotation of Web Pages in CREAM, Proceedings of the Eleventh International World Wide Web Conference WWW-2002, Hawaii, (2002)
6.   Stojanovic, N., Maedche, A., Staab, S., Studer, R., Sure, Y.: SEAL — A Framework for Developing SEmantic PortALs, ACM K-CAP 2001, Vancouver, October, (2001)
7.   Stojanovic, N., Stojanovic, L.:   Evolution in ontology-based knowledge management systems, ECIS 2002 - The European Conference on Information Systems, Gdańsk, Poland (2002)
8.   Stojanovic, L., Maedche, A., Motik, B., Stojanovic, N.: User-driven Ontology Evolution Management, Proceedings of the 13th European Conference on Knowledge Engineering and Knowledge Management EKAW, Madrid, Spain, (2002)
9.   Hardless, C., Lindgren, R., Nulden, U., Pessi, K.: The Evolution of knowledge management system need to be managed, http://www.viktoria informatik.gu.se/ groups/ KnowledgeManagement/Documents/kmman.pdf, (2000)
10. Probst, G., Raub, R., Romhardt, K., Doughty, H.: Managing Knowledge: Building Blocks for Success, Prentice Hall (1999)
11. Decker, S., Erdmann, M., Fensel, D., and Studer, R.: Ontobroker: Ontology Based Access to Distributed and Semi-Structured Information. In R. Meersman et al., (eds.): Database Semantics: Semantic Issues in Multimedia Systems, Kluwer Academic Publisher (1999) 351-369
12. Kobayashi, M., Takeda, K.: Information retrieval on the Web, IBM Research Report, RT0347, April (2000)
13. Tallis, M., Gil, Y.: Designing Scripts to Guide Users in Modifying Knowledge-based Systems, AAAI/IAAI (1999) 242-249
14. Foo, N.: Ontology Revision, In Conceptual Structures; Third International Conference, 16-31. Berlin: Springer-Verlag (1995)
15. Maedche, A., Stojanovic, L., Stojanovic, N.: A Framework for Change Discovery in Ontology-based Systems. Second International Workshop on Evolution and Change in Data Management (ECDM 2002), held in conjunction with the 21st International Conference on Conceptual Modelling, ER 2002, Tampere, Finland

16. Wen, J.-R., Nie, J.-Y. and Zhang, H.-J.: Clustering User Queries of a Search Engine. WWW10, May 1-5, Hong Kong (2001)

17. Kusza, T.: Knowledge Management Process Model, Espoo'01, Technical Research Centre of Finland, VTT Publications 455, (2001)

18. NSF Planning Workshop on Distributed Knowledge Work Environments: Digital Libraries, March 9-11, Santa Fe, New Mexico (1997)

19. SOSIG Internet Catalogue Social Science Information Gateway Collection Management Policy, http://www.sosig.ac.uk/desire/collect.html

20. Hersh, W., Elliot, D., Hickam, D., Wolf, S., Molnar, A., Leichtenstien, C.: Towards New Measures of Information Retrieval Evaluation, SIGR1995, (1995) 164-170

21. Saracevic, T.: Digital Library Evaluation: Toward Evolution of Concepts, Library Trends, 49, (2) Special issue on Evaluation of Digital Libraries (2000) 350-369

22. Heflin, J.: Towards the Semantic Web: Knowledge Representation in a Dynamic, Distributed Environment, Ph.D. Thesis, University of Maryland, College Park, (2001)

23. Klein, M., Fensel, D.: Ontology versioning for the Semantic Web, Proc. International Semantic Web Working Symposium (SWWS), USA, July, (2001)

24. Franconi, E., Grandi, F., Mandreoli, F.: A semantic approach for schema evolution and versioning in object-oriented databases, Proc. CL2000, (2000)

25. Noy, N.F., Klein, M.: Ontology Evolution: Not the Same as Schema Evolution, SMI technical report, SMI-2002-0926, (2002)

OntoEdit: Guiding Ontology Development by Methodology and Inferencing

York Sure[1], Juergen Angele[2], and Steffen Staab[1,2]

[1] Institute AIFB, University of Karlsruhe, 76128 Karlsruhe, Germany
{sure,staab}@aifb.uni-karlsruhe.de
http://www.aifb.uni-karlsruhe.de/WBS/
[2] Ontoprise GmbH, Haid-und-Neu-Str. 7, 76131 Karlsruhe, Germany,
angele@ontoprise.de
http://www.ontoprise.de/

Abstract. Ontologies now play an important role for many knowledge-intensive applications for which they provide a source of precisely defined terms. The terms are used for concise communication across people and applications. OntoEdit is an ontology editor that has been developed keeping five main objectives in mind: 1. Ease of use. 2. Methodology-guided development of ontologies. 3. Ontology development with help of inferencing. 4. Development of ontology axioms. 5. Extensibility through plug-in structure. This paper is about the first four of these items.

1 Introduction

Ontologies now play an important role for many knowledge-intensive applications for which they provide a source of formally defined terms. They aim at capturing domain knowledge in a generic way and provide a commonly agreed understanding of a domain, which may be reused, shared, and operationalized across applications and groups. However, because of their size, their complexity and their formal underpinnings ontologies are still far from being a commodity.

This urgent need motivated researchers in recent years to support the ontology engineering process. Mainly, we have seen three directions. Firstly, several seminal proposals for guiding and supporting the ontology development process have been proposed [UK95,LGPSS99,GW02]. Secondly, a considerable number of tools that support the ontology engineering process [DSW+99,NFM00,ACFLGP01,Dom98] have been developed. Third, inferencing mechanisms for large ontologies have been developed and implemented (cf., e.g., [Hor98]). However, only few of these seminal works have worked towards integrating these aspects.

OntoEdit is an ontology editor that is rather unique in its kind as it is based on a recent methodology for ontology development and as it makes comprehensive use of inferencing. In particular, OntoEdit focuses on three main steps for ontology development (as described in [SSSS01]), viz. requirements specification, refinement and evaluation[1].

---

[1] In a recently accepted companion paper [SEA+02], we have described how OntoEdit supports collaborative ontology engineering.

R. Meersman, Z. Tari (Eds.): CoopIS/DOA/ODBASE 2002, LNCS 2519, pp. 1205–1222, 2002.

First, all requirements of the envisaged ontology are collected. Typically an ontology engineer captures domain and goal of the ontology, design guidelines, available knowledge sources (e.g. reusable ontologies and thesauri etc.), potential users and use cases and applications supported by the ontology. Output of this phase is a semi-formal description of the ontology. Second, during the refinement phase the semi-formal description is extended and completely formalized into an appropriate representation language. The language is chosen according to the requirements for the ontology, e.g. identified applications that will be supported by the ontology. Output of this phase is a mature ontology (aka. "target ontology"). Third, the target ontology needs to be evaluated according to the requirement specifications and formal evaluation criteria (as proposed in the OntoClean methodology, cf. [GW02]). Typically this phase serves as a proof for the usefulness of developed ontologies.

Support for these development steps is a crucial objective that must be merged with the conflicting needs for ease of use and the construction of complex ontology structures.

In the following, we will first present a brief, real-life case study on configuration management that motivates our examples given thereafter. Section 3 explains theoretical and practical issues of the inference engine that constitutes the internal knowledge model of OntoEdit. The Sections 4 to 6 correspond to the core steps of the ontology development methodology sketched above. In particular, they elucidate how inferencing is used for supporting methodology-based ontology construction and evaluation and how this support is clad into a user-friendly environment.

2 Case Study: Configuration Management

We have developed an ontology based configuration tool OnKo for the German Telecom. It represents a set of IT components together with their complex interrelationships. It supports an interactive configuration process of such components to IT systems and IT landscapes. It contains intelligent search and retrieval of already existing IT systems with similar functionality and thus integrates already existing experience of the company.

The ontology is exploited for navigation purposes. The user can switch between different views, i.e. *specialization view*, *part-of view* etc. to the available components and thus the user is able to choose the best presentation for the current configuration task. These views are represented as hierarchical trees and additional links between the nodes enabling a simple interactive search within the available IT components. By this way the user subsequently searches for components and adds them to the current configuration. In each step the interrelationships of the components of the current configuration are checked for consistency and feed back is delivered. Thus upcoming dead ends of configurations which would not work are recognized early. The system automatically derives new knowledge and makes further suggestions about possible extensions of the current configuration which therefore must not be specified by the user. This "mixed initiative intelligence" strategy enables the development of a configuration in close cooperation with the user and thus supports the user without telling him what to do.

In Figure 1 a screenshot of OnKo is shown. In the left frame the user navigates within an is-a hierarchy of the components. This view may be switched to a part-of hierarchy. The attribute values of a selected component are editable in a form in the middle frame.

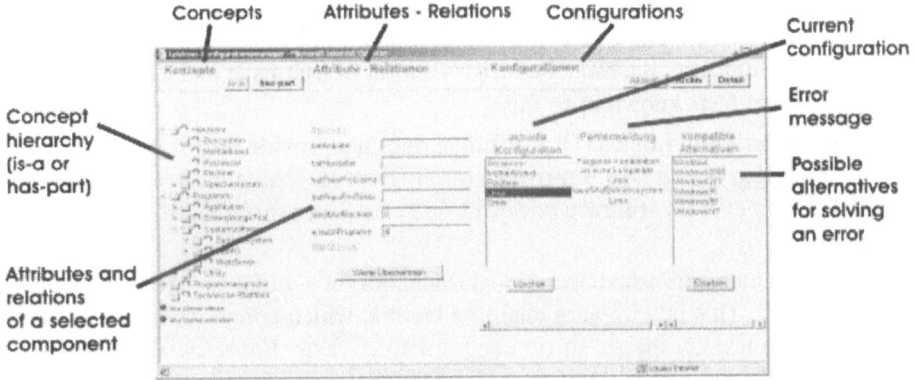

Fig. 1. OnKo an interactive configuration tool for the German Telecom

The selected component together with its attribute values are used to derive attribute values of dependent components, i.e. the frequency of the processor is propagated upwards in the part-of hierarchy to the frequency of the entire computer. The current configuration with all its components is shown in the right frame. If a configuration contains inconsistent components which is checked by applying consistency rules, appropriate error and warning messages are immediately given and alternatives for a selected component are presented to the user which make the configuration consistent. In each step the current configuration may be compared to similar existing configurations in the company. This makes existing experience transparent to the user compiling a new configuration.

In our screenshot the current configuration contains two incompatible components: "Omni" does not work on "Linux". To solve this incompatibility, the system suggests to use "Windows" or "Windows2000" or ... etc. instead of "Linux". A user may now replace incompatible components to get a valid configuration for a computer system.

In the following, we will show some examples derived from the experiences in this case study.

3   Inferencing — Theoretical and Practical Issues

Theoretical Issues. In order to provide a clearly defined semantics to the knowledge model of OntoEdit, the knowledge structures of OntoEdit correspond to a well-understood logical framework, viz. F-Logic [KLW95] ("F" stands for "Frames").

F-Logic allows for concise definitions with object oriented-like primitives (classes, attributes, OO-style relations, instances) that fit very nicely with the OntoEdit GUI. Furthermore, it also has PL-1 like primitives (predicates, function symbols). Furthermore, F-Logic allows for axioms that further constrain the interpretation of the model. Axioms may either be used to describe constraints or they may define rules, e.g. in order to define a relation R by the composition of two other relations S and Q.

F-Logic rules have the expressive power of Horn-Logic with negation and may be transformed into Horn-Logic rules. The semantics for a set of F-Logic statements is defined by the well-founded semantics[GRS91]. This semantics is close to first-order semantics. In contrast to first order semantics not all possible models are considered but one "most obvious" model is selected as the semantics of a set of rules and facts. It is a three valued logic, i.e. the model consists of a set of true facts and a set of unknown facts and a set of facts known to be false.

Unlike Description Logics (DL), F-Logic does not provide means for subsumption [Hor98], but (also unlike DL) it provides for efficient reasoning with instances and for the capability to express arbitrary powerful rules, e.g. ones that quantify over the set of classes.

The most widely published operational semantics for F-Logic is the alternating fixed point procedure. This is a forward chaining method which computes the entire model for the set of rules, i.e. the set of true and unknown facts. For answering a query the entire model must be computed (if possible) and the variable substitutions for the query are then derived. In contrast, our inference engine Ontobroker performs a mixture of forward and backward chaining based on the dynamic filtering algorithm [KL86] to compute (the smallest possible) subset of the model for answering the query. In most cases this is much more efficient than the simple evaluation strategy. These techniques stem from the deductive data base community and are optimized to deliver all answers instead of one single answer as e.g. resolution does.

Within our F-Logic compiler F-Logic statements are translated to normal programs. Normal programs are horn programs where rules may contain negated literals in their bodies. Horn logic is turing complete, thus F-Logic programs are not decidable in principle. The semantics defined for these normal programs is the wellfounded semantics [Gel93]. In contrast to the stratified semantics the wellfounded semantics is also applicable for rules which depend on cycles containing negative rule bodies. Because F-Logic is very flexible, during the translation to normal programs such negative cycles often arise. In [GRS91] the alternating fixpoint has been described as a method to operationalize such logic programs. This method has been shown to be very inefficient. Therefore our inference engine realizes dynamic filtering [KL86] which combines top-down and bottom-up inferencing. Together with an appropriate extension to compute the wellfounded semantics this method has been proven to be very efficient compared to other horn based inference engines.

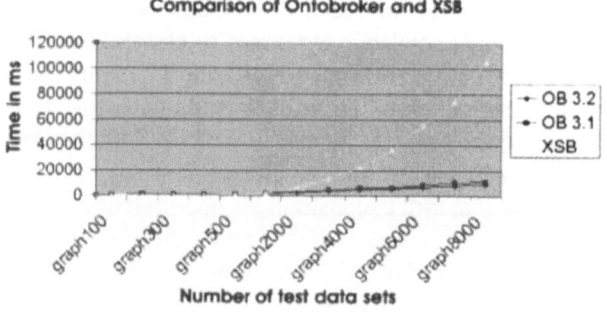

Fig. 2. Comparison of Ontobroker and XSB

We have shown this for test cases where all paths in large graphs are computed. The results are shown in Figure 2. We measured the time in milliseconds Ontobroker (versions 3.1 and 3.2) and XSB[2] needed for computing all paths of a certain number of graphs given. XSB is a "Logic Programming and Deductive Database system for Unix and Windows" and is a comparable inference engine to Ontobroker. XSB needs exponentially more time for computation when data sets rise and therefore does not scale up very well. Both Ontobroker versions have almost a linear growth of time, Ontobroker therefore scales up very nicely for this scenario. However, this test is not exhaustive at all and therefore only provides limited information about the scale ratio of the two systems.

Practical Issues. Our inference engine Ontobroker (cf. [DEFS99]) comes with several features that makes it adequate as a backbone for an ontology editor. In particular, it provides:

- A namespace mechanism: Thus, several ontologies (or ontology parts) may be syntactically split into modules and processed by different inference engines.
- Switch-off: It is possible to switch of (possibly singleton) sets of definitions. Thus, one may test interactions and easily distinguish between modules.
- DB Connectors: Thus, one may easily map db tables into predicates via JDBC.
- User-definable built-Ins: Besides of standard built-ins like "multiply", the user may define his own ones for special purposes.
- An extensive API: Thus, one may remotely connect to the inference engine and one may also import and export several standards (e.g., RDF(S)).

The use of all but the last of these items will be explained in more details subsequently.

4   Requirements Specification

Like in software engineering and as proposed by [LGPSS99], we start ontology development with collecting requirements for the envisaged ontology. By nature this task is performed by a team of experts for the domain accompanied by experts for modeling. The outcome of this phase is (i) a document that contains all relevant requirement specifications (domain and goal of the ontology, design guidelines, available knowledge sources, potential users and use cases and applications supported by the ontology) (ii) a semi-formal ontology description, i.e. a graph of named nodes and (un-)named, (un-)directed edges, both of which may be linked with further descriptive text.

To operationalize a methodology it is desirable to have a tool that reflects and supports all steps of the methodology and guides users step by step through the ontology engineering process. Along with the development of the methodology we therefore extended the core functionalities of OntoEdit by two plug-ins to support first stages of the ontology development, viz. OntoKick and Mind2Onto[3].

OntoKick targets at (i) creation of the requirement specification document and (ii) extraction of relevant structures for the building of the semi-formal ontology description.

---

[2] Available at http://xsb.sourceforge.net/.

[3] Describing the plug-in framework is beyond the scope of this paper, it is described in [Han01]. In a nutshell, one might easily expand OntoEdit's functionalities through plug-ins.

Mind2Onto targets at integration of brainstorming processes to build relevant structures of the semi-formal ontology description. As computer science researchers we were familiar with software development and preferred to start with a requirement specification of the ontology, i.e. OntoKick. People who are not so familiar with software design principles often prefer to start with "doing something". Brain storming is a good method to quickly and intuitively start a project, therefore one also might begin the ontology development process with Mind2Onto.

OntoKick. OntoKick is an OntoEdit plug-in that extends the functionality of OntoEdit by support for requirements specification (describing the plug-in structure itself is beyond the scope of this paper). OntoKick allows for describing important aspects of the ontology, viz.: the domain and the goal of the ontology, the design guidelines, the available knowledge sources (e.g. domain experts, reusable ontologies etc.), the potential users, the use cases, and the applications supported by the ontology. OntoKick stores these descriptions with the ontology definitions.

As proposed by [UK95], we use competency questions (CQ) to define requirements for an ontology. Each CQ defines a query that the ontology should be able to answer and therefore defines explicit requirements for the ontology. Typically, CQs are derived from interviews with domain experts and help to structure knowledge. We take further advantage of using them to create an initial version of the semi-formal description of the ontology. Based on the assumption that each CQ contains valuable information about the domain of the ontology we extract relevant concepts and relations (see example below). Furthermore, OntoKick establishes and maintains links between CQs and concepts derived from them. This allows for better traceability of the origins of concept definitions in later stages.

We illustrate the usage of CQs by an example from our case study. Figure 3 shows a screenshot of our ontology environment OntoEdit presenting the configuration management ontology. In the left column, one may recognize an excerpt of the *is-a* hierarchy of concepts from our case study ontology. One concept is selected, i.e. highlighted, ("Bussysteme" which is the German word for bus systems of microprocessors), in the right column all relations and attributes for the selected concept are shown. A context menu for the selected concept offers possibilities for typical modification (e.g. id, external representations and documentations in multiple languages etc.) including the feature to show corresponding competency questions.

The methodology is supported as follows. First, the ontology engineer has interviewed an expert in configuration management. Thereby they have identified CQs, e.g. "Which bus systems are available for the AS400?" (English equivalent of the CQ shown in Figure 3). Based on these CQs the ontology engineer has created the semi-formal description of the ontology. He has identified relevant concepts and relations from of the above-mentioned CQ, e.g. "Bussysteme". After capturing CQs and modeling the ontology with OntoEdit the ontology engineer has been able to retrieve the corresponding CQ for each concept and relation, helping him to identify the context in which they were modelled.

Mind2Onto is a plug-in for supporting brainstorming and discussion about ontology structures. Especially during early stages of projects in general, brainstorming methods are commonly used to quickly capture pieces of relevant knowledge. A widely used

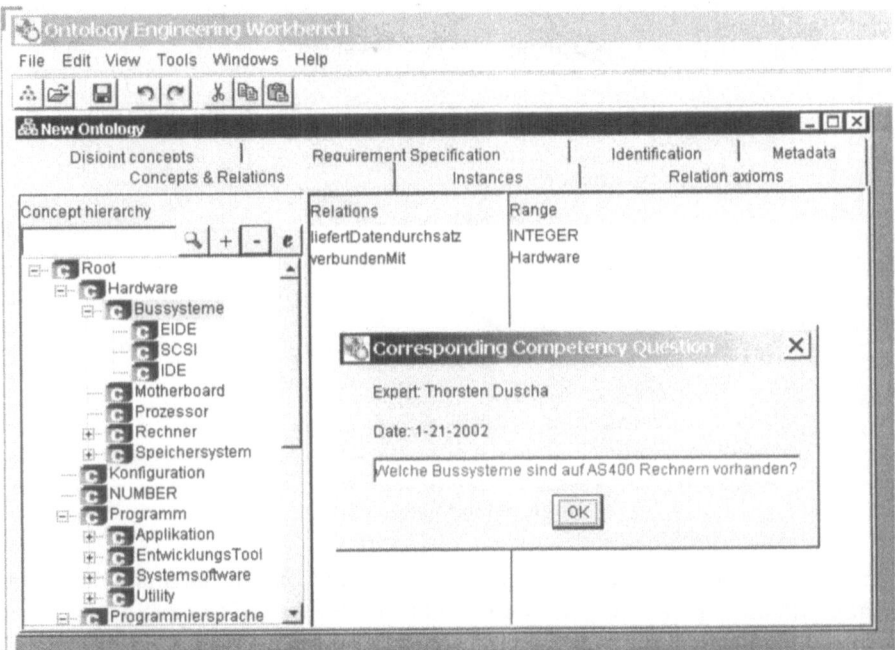

Fig. 3. A Competency Question (CQ) in the Ontology Engineering Environment OntoEdit

method are mind maps™ [Buz74], they were originally developed to support more efficient learning and evolved to a management technique used by numerous companies. In general, a mind map™ provides information about a topic that is structured in a tree. Each branch of the tree is typically named and associatively refined by it's subbranches. Icons and pictures as well as different colors and fonts might be used for illustration based on the assumption that our memory performance is improved by visual aspects. There already exist numerous tools for the electronically creation of mind maps™. Many people from academia and industry are familiar with mind maps™ and related tools – including potential ontology engineers and domain experts. Therefore the integration of electronic mind maps™ into the ontology development process is very attractive (cf. e.g. [LS02]).

We relied on a widely used commercial tool[4] for the creation of mind maps™. It has advanced facilities for graphical presentations of hierarchical structures, e.g. easy to use copy&paste functionalities and different highlighting mechanisms. It's strength but also it's weakness lies in the intuitive user interface and the simple but effective usability, which allows for quick creation of mind maps™ but lacks of expressiveness for advanced ontology modeling. By nature, mind maps™ have (almost) no assumptions for it's semantics, i.e. branches are somehow "associatively related" to each other. This assumption fits perfectly well during early stages of ontology development for quick

---

[4] MindManager™ 2002 Business Edition, cf. http://www.mindjet.com

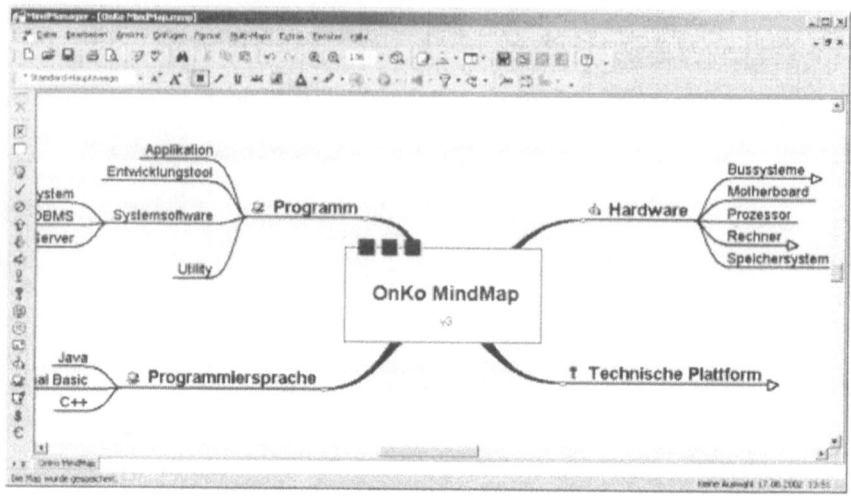

Fig. 4. Mind Map for OnKo

and effective capturing of relevant knowledge pieces and makes the mind map™ tool a valuable add-on. Figure 4 shows a draft mind map™ for the OnKo system.

Mind2Onto integrates the mind map™ tool into the ontology engineering methodology. Currently OntoEdit and the mind map™ tool interoperate through import and export facilities based on XML.

5   Ontology Refinement

In the ontology refinement phase the semi-formal description of the ontology is extended and completely formalized in order to make it machine understandable and processable. In this phase we take advantage of the inferencing capabilities of OntoEdit for several purposes.

Reuse by semantic integration. Reuse in the refinement phase comes in two flavors. First, we may exploit existing thesauri, e.g. ones that are stored in databases by semantically integrating them into the inferencing model. As in general information integration [WG97], this involves two steps. The first step concerns the mapping onto a common data model. For this purpose, we take advantage of the inference engine's capabilities, viz. to read in RDF(S) [W3C99], to connect to relational databases, to provide further built-ins (e.g. for connection to XML repositories). The outcome of this step are data in F-Logic structures, but with some rather arbitrary semantics. In the second step, we build rules to map the outcome of the first step into the desired categories. For instance, we may map a database table-like structure into a target structure of sub- and superconcepts. An example may be given with a database table that contains WordNet hyponyms and synonyms. Our example is based on a locally installed mySQL database system that contains a 'wordnet-db' database.

1. In the first step we map this table into an equivalent predicate HYPONYM:
   FORALL C, D HYPONYM$(C, D) \leftarrow$

DBACCESS(hyponym, F('sub', C, 'super', D), 'mySQL', 'wordnet-db', 'localhost').

2. In the second step, we define the objects of the predicted hyponym to be subconcepts of *Computer* if it is known that one of their superconcepts is a subconcept of *Computer*:
   FORALL C, D $C :: D \leftarrow$ HYPONYM(C, D) AND $D ::$ *Computer*.

   Taken the two steps together, this means: "Specify every C to be a subclass of D if in the mySQL database called 'wordnet-db' on my local machine the table called hyponym there is a row with attribute 'sub' being C and 'super' being D and simultaneously D is already known to be a subclass of *Computer*."

Combining such a query for hyponyms with search for synonyms yields about 100 terms, not all of which are obvious and which may be considered for inclusion in the ontology. Thus, one may easily reuse existing thesauri or database schema in order to generate a large number of concepts fast.

Reusing axioms integrating them into the ontology. Secondly, one may reuse axioms definitions from a library of ontology modules that are distinguished by namespace mechanism. A set of axiom definitions specified in one domain is reusable in another domain by the inference engine's capability to store and load axioms from a library to and into different namespaces in a way that is reusable for another domain.

For instance, *partonomic role propagation* may be given for a medical ontology (cf. [HSR99] for a comprehensive description and appendix A for an illustrating example), but it has been reused for describing properties of computer systems. The underlying idea of partonomic role propagation is that some properties of parts of a system are propagated to the whole. For instance, the clock frequency of the CPU is frequently used as being descriptive of the overall computer system — while others like frequency rates of the bus system are not used for that abstracting purpose.[5]

We specify an axiom library by a meta-predicate. In this current example, this predicate is named PARTONOMICROLEPROPAGATION. This meta-predicate takes four input parameters (cf. the formal specification in Table 1):

1. The relation that is propagated (FREQUENCYOF), because not every relation is propagated from a part to a whole.
2. The relation that is propagating (PHYSICALPARTOF), because not every relation thay may be propagated is propagated along all part-whole relations.
3. The whole up to which the relation is maximally propagated (*ComputerSystem*), because propagation may be stopped (e.g. FREQUENCYOF should not be propagated to a car that the computer system is a part of).
4. The concept for the instances of which the relation may be propagated (e.g., a (here fictitious) *WheelFrequency* might not be propagated), because not every class is treated the same.

---

[5] Similarly, the color of the car body is typically equated with the color of the car. This is not true for the color of the seats, though seats and car body are both parts of the car.

Table 1. Partonomic Role Propagation

0	PARTONOMICROLEPROPAGATION(FREQUENCYOF, PHYSICALPARTOF, *ComputerSystem*, *ClockFrequency*)
1	$\forall x, y, z, R, S, C, D\ x[R \twoheadrightarrow z] \leftarrow$ PARTONOMICROLEPROPAGATION(R, S, C, D) AND $x : D$ AND $x[R \twoheadrightarrow y]$ AND $y[S \twoheadrightarrow z]$ AND PARTINSTANCEOF(z, C, S).
2	$\forall z, C, S$ PARTINSTANCEOF$(z, C, S) \leftarrow$ $\exists E\ z : E$ AND PARTOFALONG(E, C, S).
3	$\forall C, S$ PARTOFALONG(C, C, S).
4	$\forall E, C, S$ PARTOFALONG$(E, C, S) \leftarrow$ $\exists F$ PARTOFALONG(E, F, S) AND $\exists Q\ F[Q \twoheadrightarrow C]$ AND $Q :: S$.
5	$\forall x, y, S, R\ x[S \twoheadrightarrow y] \leftarrow R :: S$ AND $x[R \Rrightarrow y]$.

Reusing axioms applying them to the ontology. Besides of integrating axioms from a library into the ontology, one may apply axioms in order to enforce constraints on the ontology. We distinguish three major types:

1. **Axioms of F-Logic:** They are an integral part of the F-Logic definition. However, not all of them are needed for inferencing during the usage of the ontology. For instance, type coercion at the conceptual level:

   FORALL $C, D, E, A, T\ E :: T \leftarrow C[A \Rrightarrow T]$ AND $D :: C[A \Rrightarrow E]$.

   "Specify E as a subclass of T if some concept C has an attribute A of type T and a subclass D of C has an attribute A with type E."

2. **Axioms for domain-specific consistency:** They enforce consistency constraints at building time. E.g., they may enforce that the domain specific relation HASPHYSICALPART is without cycles:

   NONCYCLIC(HASPHYSICALPART).

   FORALL X, R UNDEFINED $\leftarrow$ NonCyclic(R) AND $X[A \twoheadrightarrow X]$.

   "HASPHYSICALPART is of type NONCYCLIC. Indicate consistency violation if an attribute A is of type NonCyclic and X is related via A to itself."

3. **Axioms enforcing modeling policies:** Such axioms do not add to the semantic description, but they are applied in order to enforce semiotic constraints, e.g. that no subconcept should have more than n subconcepts, that no hierarchy should be deeper than m, or that every attribute symbol should begin with a lower case letter:

   FORALL A UNDEFINED $\leftarrow$

   EXISTS $X, Y\ X[A \Rrightarrow Y]$ AND NOT regexp('^$[a - z]$', A).

   "Indicate consistency violation if there is an attribute symbol A between some classes X, Y and it does not match with a string beginning with lowercase alphabetical letters."

The three types of axioms just described are not integrated into the ontology, because once the ontology is fixed and remains unchanged they are not violated anyway. Still, switching them off improves performance, because they need not be revisited and checked again.

6   Evaluation

The last step in ontology development is about evaluating the formal ontology.

Analysis of Typical Queries. For this purpose, the Ontology engineer may interactively construct and save instances and axioms into modules. OntoEdit contains a simple instance editor that the ontology engineer can use to create test sets. The test set can be automatically processed and checked for consistency. Once, the ontology goes into the evolution phase and needs changes to remain up-to-date, these test sets may be re-used for checking validity of the ontology.

For instance, one may create a test case for partonomic role propagation (test case cf. Table 2, the partonomic role propagation is explained in Appendix A or, more detailed, in [SEM01]), viz. an instance CPU1 of CPU with a clock frequency of 1600MHz (line 1), an instance PC1 of PC which has a MB456 (line 2) that is of type Motherboard and that has the CPU1 on board (line 3).

The test case is completed by the query that asks for all clock frequencies of all PCs. This query is reformulated as a rule (line 4), in order to allow for comparison with an intended set of result tuples (line 5), by a generally applicable rule (lines 6 – 8).

Table 2. Formalizing Test Cases

Test instances
1 CPU1:CPU[hasClockFrequency$\twoheadrightarrow$'1600MHz'].
2 PC1:PC[hasPhysicalPart$\twoheadrightarrow$MB456].
3 MB456:Motherboard[hasPhysicalPart$\twoheadrightarrow$CPU1].
Query formulated as test query
4 FORALL X, Y test1$(X, Y) \leftarrow X$:CPU[hasClockFrequency$\twoheadrightarrow Y$].
Intended set of result tuples
5 test2(CPU1,'1600MHz').
General rule for comparing query results with intended resuls
6 FORALL X, Y Undefined $\leftarrow$
7 (test1(X, Y) AND NOT test2(X, Y)) OR
8 (test2(X, Y) AND NOT test1(X, Y)).

In this small example, we have provided only one result tuple for testing, but the specification is modular and general enough to easily integrate sets of test cases.

Error Avoidance and Location. While the generation and validation of test cases allows for detection of errors, it does not really support the localization of errors. The set of all axioms, class and instance definitions express sometimes complex relationships and axioms often interact with other axioms when processed. Thus it is frequently very difficult to overview the correctness of a set of axioms and detect the faulty ones.

In principle there exist three types of problems with axioms:

- Axioms contain typing errors like variables not specified by a quantifier, typos in concept names or relationship names etc.

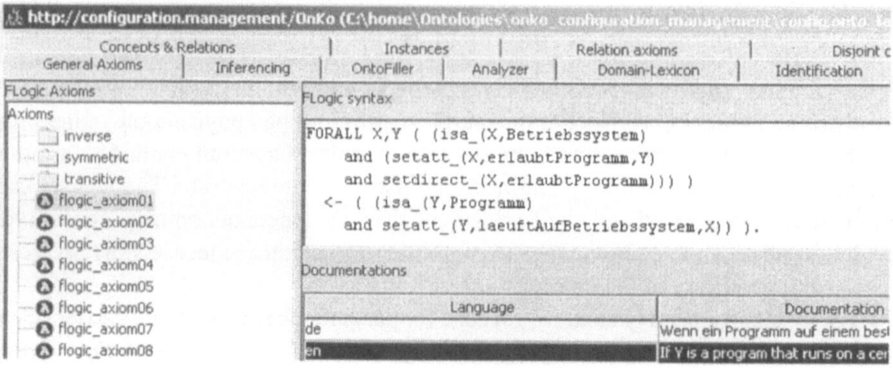

Fig. 5. Specifying F-Logic axioms in OntoEdit

- Axioms contain semantic errors, i.e. the rules do not express the intended meaning.
- Performance issues, like axioms defined such that evaluation needs a lot of time, which is not always easily recognizable by the user.

In order to avoid problems, OntoEdit offers several means:

1. Some axiom definitions may be generated by asserting through clicks that relations or concepts belong to particular types. OntoEdit allows for defining several properties of relationships by clicking on the GUI, viz. symmetry, transitivity and composition of relations. Database connections as shown above in Section 5 need not be specified in F-Logic, but can be composed by drag-and-drop.
2. For other types of axioms a graphical rule editor is available which avoids syntactical errors, delivers axioms which are optimal in their performance (as seen in isolation from other axioms) and supports users not familiar in F-Logic.
3. Third, there are axioms that cannot be specified by either 1. or 2. For them, OntoEdit provides at least syntax highlighting in order to support the user avoiding syntactical errors.

In order to locate problems, OntoEdit takes advantage of the inference engine Ontobroker itself, which allows for introspection and also comes with a debugger. Axioms are operationalized by posing queries (e.g. on the test cases specified as seen above). Based on queries one may pursue several alternatives:

First, a very simple but effective method to test axioms with test cases is to switch off and switch on axioms or parts of the axiom premises. The different answers from Ontobroker then allow to draw conclusions about possible errors.

Second, for a given query the results and their dependencies on existing test instances and intermediate results may be examined by visualizing the proof tree. This proof tree shows graphically which instances or intermediate results are combined by which rules to the final answers. Thus the drawn inferences may be traced back to the test instances and semantic errors in rules may be discovered.

Third, the inference engine may be "observed" during evaluation. A graphical presentation of the set of axioms as a graph structure indicates which axiom is evaluated at the moment and also shows which intermediate results have already been created up to

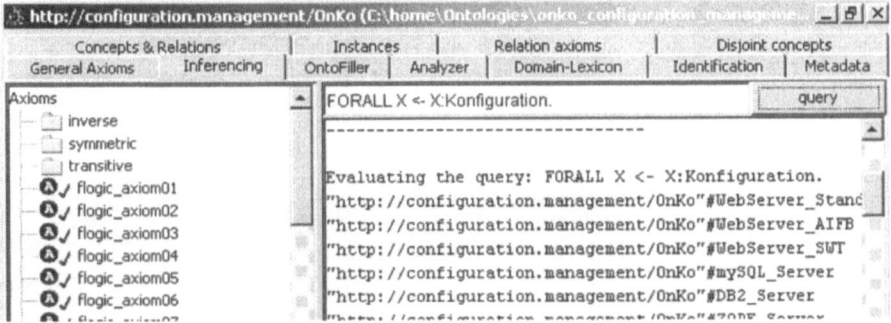

Fig. 6. Inferencing with Ontobroker in OntoEdit

now and thus "have flown" in the axiom graph to other axioms. This also gives the user a feeling how much time it is needed to evaluate special rules.

An example is given by the two Figures 5 and 6. The former illustrates how F-Logic axioms can be specified in OntoEdit in the "General Axioms" plugin (the more advanced graphical rule editor is near completion). On the left side are listed all specified axioms, on the right side one may see a selected F-Logic axiom as well as its documentation in different languages. The latter shows the GUI of the "Inferencing" plugin for OntoEdit, that integrates Ontobroker into OntoEdit. On the left side each previously specified axiom can be switched on or off. On the right side on may enter an F-Logic query (here: give me all instances of the concept "Konfiguration") which is subsequently answered by Ontobroker. The results are presented below the query, here one might see that for each result item the name of an instance includes the corresponding namespace.

In the future, it is planned to take more care about the efficient construction of efficiently handable ontologies. For this purpose, OntoEdit will provide a profiler that will deliver statistics about evaluation times.

Formal Evaluation with OntoClean. Beside the above mentioned process oriented and pragmatic evaluation methods, there exist also formal evaluation methodologies for ontologies. One of the most prominent is the OntoClean methodology (cf., e.g., [GW02]), which is based on philosophical notions. It focuses on the cleaning of taxonomies and e.g. is currently being applied for cleaning the upper level of the WordNet taxonomy (cf. [GGOB02]). Core to the methodology are the four fundamental ontological notions of *rigidity*, *identity*, *unity* and *dependence*. By attaching them as meta-relations to concepts in a taxonomy they are used to represent the behavior of the concepts. I.e. these meta-relations impose constraints on the way subsumption is used to model a domain (cf. [GW00]). We can only briefly and simplified sketch the methodology (please note that *property* is used here in our sense of "concept"):

Rigidity is defined based on the idea of essence. A *property* is essential to an individual if and only if necessarily holds for that individual. Thus, a *property* is rigid (+R) if and only if is necessarily essential to all its instances. A *property* is non-rigid (-R) if and only if it is not essential to some of its instances, and anti-rigid (~R) if and only if it is not essential to all its instances. An **identity** criterion (IC) is carried by a *property* (+I) if and only if all its instances can be (re)identified by means of a suitable "sameness"

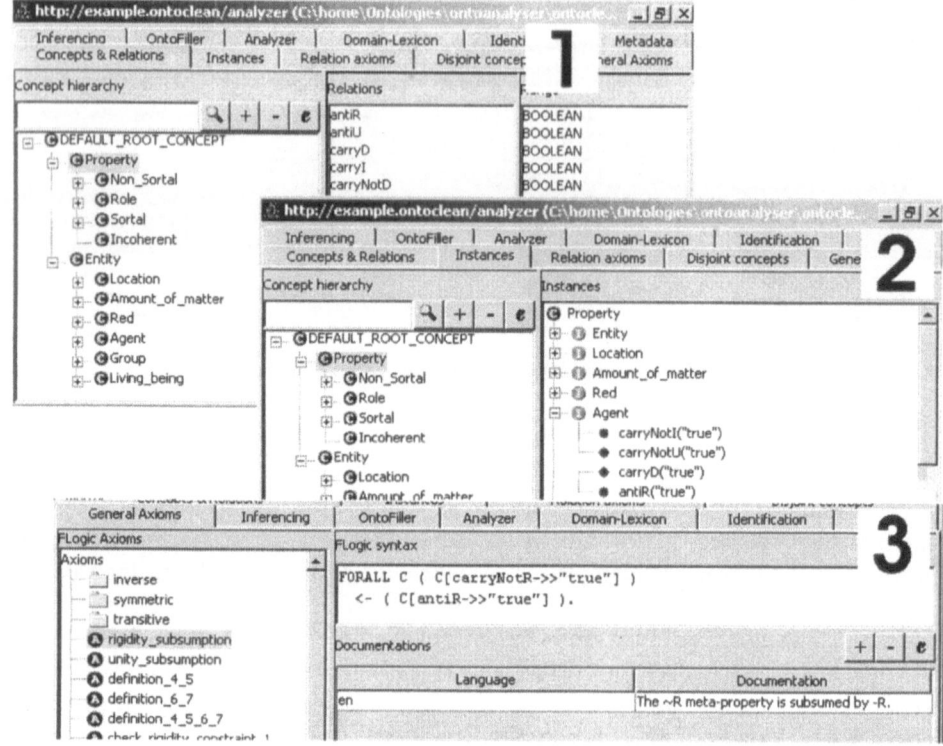

Fig. 7. Implementation of OntoClean in OntoEdit

relation. A *property* supplies an identity criterion (+O) if and only if such criterion is not inherited by any subsuming *property*. An individual *X* is constantly **dependent** on *Y* if and only if, at any time, *X* cannot be present unless *Y* is fully present, and *Y* is not part of *X*. A *property* is constantly dependent if and only if, for all its instances, there exists something they are constantly dependent on. **Unity** is defined by saying that an individual is a whole if and only if it is made by a set of parts unified by a relation *R*. A *property P* is said to carry unity (+U) if there is a common unifying relation R such that all the instances of *P* are wholes under *R*. A *property* carries anti-unity (∼U) if all its instances can possibly be non-wholes.

Based on these meta-relations OntoClean classifies concepts into categories (Sortal, Non-sortal, Role etc.). E.g., a concept that is tagged with "+O +I +R" is called a "Type". Beside these meta-relations OntoClean contains rules that can be applied to evaluate the correctness of a given taxonomy. For instance, a rule suggested in OntoClean is "a property carrying anti-unity has to be disjoint of a property carrying unity". As a consequence, "a property carrying unity cannot be a subclass of a property carrying anti-unity" and "a rigid property and an anti-rigid property are ever disjoint", to name but a few.

To implement the OntoClean methodology in OntoEdit[6], we formalized the meta-relations and classifications as a "meta ontology" that can be used to classify concepts of an ontology. We modelled both, the "meta ontology" and an example ontology (the example is taken from [GW02], we started to implement the methodology but did not yet apply it) that has to be evaluated, in OntoEdit and specified each concept of the regular ontology, i.e. all subconcepts of "Entity", as an instance of the top-level concept "Property" of the meta ontology through an axiom:

FORALL A A : $Property \leftarrow A :: Entity.$

Figure 7 shows the subsequent steps: (1) model the ontologies, (2) fill the meta relations with values (i.e. tag the concepts with "carryR" (+R) etc.) and (3) specify the definitions and constraints from OntoClean as axioms. Like shown in Figure 6 one can now ask queries to find inconsistencies according to the OntoClean methodology.

7   Related Work

There exist various ontology engineering environments, which we divide into two categories: *with* and *without* inferencing support.

A good overview, viz. a comparative study of existing tools up to 1999, is given in [DSW+99]. Typically the internal knowledge model of ontology engineering environments is capable of deriving is-a hierarchies of concepts and attached relations. On top of that we provide facilities for axiom modeling and debugging. Naturally, it could not fully consider the more recent developments, e.g. Protégé [NFM00], and WebODE [ACFLGP01].

About WebODE, [ACFLGP01] mentions that it offers inferencing services (developed in Prolog) and an axiom manager (providing functionalities such as an axiom library, axiom patterns and axiom parsing and verification), but the very brief mentioning of these functionalities is too short to assess precisely.

A system well-known for it's reasoning support is OilEd in combination with the description logics (DL) reasoner FaCT [BHGS01]. Their focus is to use reasoning to check class consistency and to infer subsumption relationships which are typical DL tasks. We may not provide subsumption, but we provide extensive reasoning on instances — in particular rules — or axioms that specify user-definable consistency constraints. Furthermore, we support the whole methodology cycle for developing ontologies.

Environments like Protégé [NFM00] or Chimaera [MFRW00] offer sophisticated support for ontology engineering and merging of ontologies. Protégé has also a flexible plugin-structure, that allows for modular extension of the functionalities. However, they do not provide comprehensive methodological support for ontology engineering and it is also difficult to assess the extent that they exploit reasoning capabilities.

---

[6] There is also the group from the Artificial Intelligence Laboratory of the Technical University of Madrid (UPM) working on the integration of the philosophically oriented OntoClean [GW02] methodology with the process oriented METHONTOLOGY [LGPSS99] by extending the WebODE [ACFLGP01] ontology development environment (cf. http://www.ontoweb.org/workshop/ontoweb2/slides/ontocleansig3.pdf)

8 Conclusion

In this paper we have presented OntoEdit, a sophisticated ontology editor that supports methodology-based ontology construction and that takes comprehensive advantage of its inferencing capabilities. OntoEdit also has some features that could not be presented here in full detail, e.g. an extremely capable plug-in structure (cf. [Han01]), a lexicon component and support for collaborative engineering of ontologies (cf. [SEA$^+$02]).

Obviously, there are a large number of ontology construction tools now available and many of them offer very intriguing features that are not in OntoEdit. However, according to our experiences the combination of a methodological basis with comprehensive reasoning on class and instance definitions with Ontobroker is a very powerful paradigm that has not been exploited to the extent that OntoEdit does.

For the future, OntoEdit is planned to be developed in several directions: (1) new im- and exports will be developed and (2) the integration of ontology construction with requirements specification documents will be generalized by means of semantic document annotation, (3) stronger support for the integration of mind maps™ into the ontology development process, (4) finish the OntoClean implementation and apply it, to name but a few.

Acknowledgements. We thank especially our colleagues Alexander Maedche (now: Research Center FZI, Research Group WIM, Karlsruhe, Germany) and Dirk Wenke (now: chief developer of OntoEdit at Ontoprise GmbH, Karlsruhe, Germany). Together they initiated the development of OntoEdit, which is now being continued by the constant efforts of Dirk. We also thank Siggi Handschuh (Institute AIFB, University of Karlsruhe) for his plug-in framework OntoMat. Research for this paper was partially funded by EU in the project IST-1999-10132 "On-To-Knowledge".

References

[ACFLGP01]   J.C. Arprez, O. Corcho, M. Fernandez-Lopez, and A. Gomez-Perez. WebODE: a scalable workbench for ontological engineering. In *Proceedings of the First International Conference on Knowledge Capture (K-CAP) Oct. 21-23, 2001, Victoria, B.C., Canada*, 2001.

[BHGS01]   S. Bechhofer, I. Horrocks, C. Goble, and R. Stevens. OilEd: A reason-able ontology editor for the semantic web. In *KI-2001: Advances in Artificial Intelligence*, LNAI 2174, pages 396–408. Springer, 2001.

[Buz74]   T. Buzan. *Use your head.* BBC Books, 1974.

[DEFS99]   S. Decker, M. Erdmann, D. Fensel, and R. Studer. Ontobroker: Ontology based access to distributed and semi-structured information. In R. Meersman et al., editor, *Database Semantics: Semantic Issues in Multimedia Systems.* Kluwer Academic, 1999.

[Dom98]   J. Domingue. Tadzebao and WebOnto: Discussing, browsing, and editing ontologies on the web. In *Proceedings of the 11th Knowledge Acquisition for Knowledge-Based Systems Workshop, April 18th-23rd. Banff, Canada*, 1998. http://ksi.cpsc.ucalgary.ca/KAW/KAW98/KAW98Proc.html.

[DSW+99] A. J. Duineveld, R. Stoter, M. R. Weiden, B. Kenepa, and V. R. Benjamins. Wondertools? A comparative study of ontological engineering tools. In *Proc. of the Twelfth Workshop on Knowledge Acquisition, Modeling and Management. Banff, Alberta, Canada. October 16-21, 1999*, 1999. http://sern.ucalgary.ca/KSI/KAW/KAW99/papers.html.

[Gel93] A. Van Gelder. The alternating fixpoint of logic programs with negation. *Journal of Computer and System Sciences*, 47(1):185–221, 1993.

[GGOB02] A. Gangemi, N. Guarino, A. Oltramari, and S. Borgo. Cleaning-up WordNet's top-level. In *Proc. of the 1st International WordNet Conference*, January 2002.

[GRS91] A. Van Gelder, K. A. Ross, and J. S. Schlipf. The well-founded semantics for general logic programs. *Journal of the ACM*, 38(3):620–650, July 1991.

[GW00] N. Guarino and C. Welty. A formal ontology of properties. In R. Dieng and O. Corby, editors, *Knowledge Engineering and Knowledge Management: Methods, Models and Tools. 12th International Conference, EKAW2000*, pages 97–112. Springer Verlag, 2000.

[GW02] N. Guarino and C. Welty. Evaluating ontological decisions with OntoClean. *Communications of the ACM*, 2(45):61–65, 2002.

[Han01] Siegfried Handschuh. Ontoplugins – a flexible component framework. Technical report, University of Karlsruhe, May 2001.

[Hor98] I. Horrocks. Using an expressive description logic: Fact or fiction? In *Proceedings of KR 1998*, pages 636–649. Morgan Kaufmann, 1998.

[HSR99] U. Hahn, S. Schulz, and M. Romacker. Part-whole reasoning: A case study in medical ontology engineering. *IEEE Intelligent Systems*, 14(5):59–67, 1999.

[KL86] M. Kifer and E. Lozinskii. A framework for an efficient implementation of deductive databases. In *Proceedings of the 6th Advanced Database Symposium*, pages 109–116, Tokyo, August 1986.

[KLW95] M. Kifer, G. Lausen, and J. Wu. Logical foundations of object-oriented and frame-based languages. *Journal of the ACM*, 42:741–843, 1995.

[LGPSS99] M. F. Lopez, A. Gomez-Perez, J. P. Sierra, and A. P. Sierra. Building a chemical ontology using Methontology and the Ontology Design Environment. *Intelligent Systems*, 14(1):37–45, January/February 1999.

[LS02] T. Lau and Y. Sure. Introducing ontology-based skills management at a large insurance company. In *Proc. of the Modellierung 2002*, Tutzing, Germany, March 2002.

[MFRW00] D. McGuinness, R. Fikes, J. Rice, and S. Wilder. An environment for merging and testing large ontologies. In *Proceedings of KR 2000*, pages 483–493. Morgan Kaufmann, 2000.

[NFM00] N. Fridman Noy, R. Fergerson, and M. Musen. The knowledge model of Protégé-2000: Combining interoperability and flexibility. In *Proceedings of EKAW 2000*, LNCS 1937, pages 17–32. Springer, 2000.

[SEA+02] Y. Sure, M. Erdmann, J. Angele, S. Staab, R. Studer, and D. Wenke. OntoEdit: Collaborative ontology development for the semantic web. In *Proc. of the International Semantic Web Conference 2002 (ISWC 2002), June 9-12 2002, Sardinia, Italia.*, 2002.

[SEM01] S. Staab, M. Erdmann, and A. Maedche. Ontologies in RDF(S). *ETAI Journal – Section on Semantic Web (Linkoeping Electronic Articles in Computer and Information Science)*, 9(6), 2001.

[SSSS01] S. Staab, H.-P. Schnurr, R. Studer, and Y. Sure. Knowledge processes and ontologies. *IEEE Intelligent Systems, Special Issue on Knowledge Management*, 16(1), Jan/Feb 2001.

[UK95]   M. Uschold and M. King. Towards a methodology for building ontologies. In *Workshop on Basic Ontological Issues in Knowledge Sharing, held in conjunction with IJCAI-95*, Montreal, Canada, 1995.

[W3C99]   W3C. RDF Schema specification. http://www.w3.org/TR/PR-rdf-schema/, 1999.

[WG97]   G. Wiederhold and M. Genesereth. The Conceptual Basis for Mediation Services. *IEEE Expert / Intelligent Systems*, 12(5):38–47, September/October 1997.

A   Example of Partonomic Role Propagation

Partonomic role propagation is about propagating particular property values from parts to wholes. For instance, if the engine of my car is defunct, the whole car is defunct ("defunct" being propagated from the part "engine" to the whole "car"). However, if the rear window is broken, it might be less safe to drive the car, but it would be strange to consider it defunct.

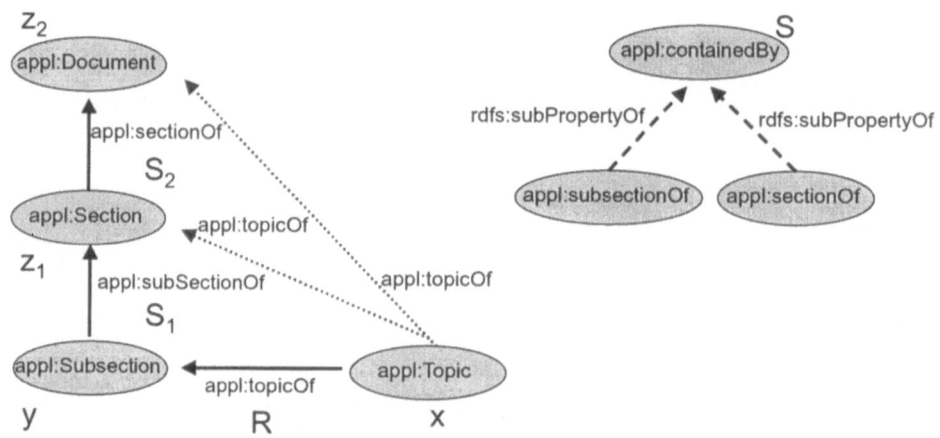

Fig. 8. Partonomic Role Propagation

Figure 8 depicts an example that propagates topics from subparts of documents to superparts (using the graphical notion of RDF(S), cf. [W3C99]). It takes four input parameters:

1. The relation that is propagated (TOPICOF in Figure 8), because not every relation is propagated from a part to a whole.
2. The relation that is propagating (CONTAINEDBY in Figure 8), because not every relation that may be propagated is propagated along all part-whole relations.
3. The whole up to which the relation is maximally propagated (*Document* in 8, because propagation may be stopped (e.g. TOPICOF may be considered to be not propagated to an additional Library).
4. The concept for the instances of which the relation may be propagated (e.g., *Topic* in Figure 8), because not every class is treated the same (cf. [HSR99a] for comprehensive examples).

Open Mind Common Sense: Knowledge Acquisition from the General Public

Push Singh[1], Thomas Lin[1], Erik T. Mueller[2], Grace Lim[1],
Travell Perkins[1], and Wan Li Zhu[1]

[1] MIT Media Laboratory, 20 Ames Street, Cambridge, MA 02139 USA
{push, glim, tlin, markt, wlz}@mit.edu,
travell_perkins@yahoo.com
[2] IBM Thomas J. Watson Research Center, P.O. Box 704,
Yorktown Heights, NY 10598, USA
etm@us.ibm.com

Abstract. Open Mind Common Sense is a knowledge acquisition system designed to acquire commonsense knowledge from the general public over the web. We describe and evaluate our first fielded system, which enabled the construction of a 450,000 assertion commonsense knowledge base. We then discuss how our second-generation system addresses weaknesses discovered in the first. The new system acquires facts, descriptions, and stories by allowing participants to construct and fill in natural language templates. It employs word-sense disambiguation and methods of clarifying entered knowledge, analogical inference to provide feedback, and allows participants to validate knowledge and in turn each other.

1 Introduction

We would like to build software agents that can engage in commonsense reasoning about ordinary human affairs. Examples of such commonsense-enabled agents are:

- SensiCal, which reminds a user not to take a vegetarian friend to a steakhouse [1],
- the Cyc team's image retrieval program, which retrieves a photo of a grandmother with her grandchild given the query "happy person" [2], and
- REFORMULATOR, which searches for local veterinarians when a user enters "my cat is sick" [3].

Few such common-sense agents currently exist, and those that do have only been demonstrated to work on select examples to demonstrate the promise of applying common sense. However, as perceptive environments emerge and software becomes more context-aware, the need for reasoning about the ordinary human life will only increase.

What is holding back the development of such applications? While there has been much work on developing representations and reasoning methods for commonsense domains [4], and on the logical underpinnings for commonsense reasoning [5], there

R. Meersman, Z. Tari (Eds.): CoopIS/DOA/ODBASE 2002, LNCS 2519, pp. 1223–1237, 2002.

has been far less work on finding ways to accumulate the knowledge to do so in practice. The most well-known attempt has been the Cyc project [6] which contains 1.5 million assertions built over 15 years at the cost of several tens of millions of dollars. Knowledge bases this large require a tremendous effort to engineer. With the exception of Cyc, this problem of scale has made efforts to study and build commonsense knowledge bases nearly non-existent within the artificial intelligence community.

2   Turning to the General Public

In this paper we explore a possible solution to this problem of scale, based on one critical observation: *Every ordinary person has the common sense we want to give our machines.* The advent of the web has made it possible for the first time for thousands of people to collaborate to construct systems that no single individual or team could build. Projects based on this idea have come to be known as *distributed human projects.* An early and very successful example was the Open Directory Project, a Yahoo-like directory of several million web sites built by tens of thousands of topic editors distributed across the web. The very difficult problem of organizing and categorizing the web was effectively solved by distributing the work across thousands of volunteers across the Internet.

It is now possible for smaller groups within the artificial intelligence community to build systems that require large amounts of knowledge by engaging the general public. What are the issues that are raised when knowledge acquisition systems turn to the general public, employing thousands of people instead of just a few? The Open Mind Initiative [7] was formed with the goal of studying this issue and applying these kinds of distributed approaches to the problems faced by AI researchers. As part of this initiative, we began the *Open Mind Common Sense* project. The goal was to study whether a relatively small investment in a good collaborative tool for knowledge acquisition could support the distributed construction of a commonsense database by many people in their free time. In this paper we report on our progress so far.

This paper is organized as follows. In the first section we review the first version of the Open Mind Common Sense knowledge acquisition system, present an evaluation of the database accumulated by the system, and describe some applications that have been built using this database. In the second section we present the more sophisticated second-generation version of the system under development and soon to be deployed. The new system uses strict natural language templates, lets participants design those templates, employs word-sense disambiguation and methods of clarifying entered knowledge, engages in analogical inference to provide feedback, and allows participants to validate knowledge and in turn each other.

3 Open Mind Common Sense

The original Open Mind Common Sense system[1] (OMCS-1) is a commonsense knowledge acquisition system targeted at the general public. It is a web site that gathers facts, rules, stories, and descriptions using a variety of simple elicitation activities [3]. Some of the items collected include:

- *Every person is younger than the person's mother*
- *A butcher is unlikely to be a vegetarian*
- *People do not like being repeatedly interrupted*
- *If you hold a knife by its blade then it may cut you*
- *If you drop paper into a flame then it will burn*
- *People pay taxi drivers to drive them places*
- *People generally sleep at night*

OMCS-1 has been running on the web since September 2000. As of August 2002 we have gathered 456,195 pieces of commonsense knowledge from 9296 people. Thousands of people, many with no special training in computer science or artificial intelligence, have participated in building the bulk of the database.

There have been a number of efforts in recent years to develop knowledge acquisition systems that can acquire knowledge from people with no formal training in computer science [8]. One of the key problems such systems address is that end users do not know formal languages. We had considered using the Cyc representation for our project, but it was clear that few members of the general public would be willing to spend the time to learn CycL or the thousands of terms in the Cyc ontology. Some approaches deal with the problem by finding a way to present a constrained natural language interface to the system. One method is to use pull down menus from which the user can select English forms consistent with the underlying representation [9]. Another method is to develop a subset of English which is restricted enough to be easily parsed into first-order logic [10].

We were concerned with overly restricting our users by imposing our own ontological preconceptions, so we took a different approach, which was to allow users to supply knowledge in free-form natural language. We constructed a variety of activities for eliciting this knowledge. One activity was to present the user with a simple story and ask for knowledge that would be helpful in understanding that story. For example, given the story *"Bob had a cold. Bob went to the doctor."*, the user might enter the following:

- *Bob was feeling sick*
- *Bob wanted to feel better*
- *The doctor made Bob feel better*
- *People with colds sneeze*
- *The doctor wore a stethoscope around his neck*
- *A stethoscope is a piece of medical equipment*

---

[1] http://www.openmind.org/commonsense

- *The doctor might have worn a white coat*
- *A doctor is a highly trained professional*
- *You can help a sick person with medicine*
- *A sneezing person is probably sick*

In choosing to acquire knowledge in free-form natural language, we shifted the burden from the knowledge acquisition system to the methods for using the acquired knowledge. We have taken two approaches:

1. Use the English items directly for reasoning. We describe some experiments in reasoning with English syntactic structures in [3]. A few other systems have used natural-language-like representations as an underlying representation, such as the Pathfinder causal reasoning system [11].

2. Use information extraction techniques to convert English items into more standard knowledge representations. There has been significant progress in the area of information extraction from text [12] in recent years, due to improvements in syntactic parsing and part-of-speech tagging. A number of systems are able successfully to extract facts, conceptual relations, and even complex events from text.

This latter approach is a very different way to think about how to go about building a commonsense database. Rather than directly engineering the knowledge structures used by the reasoning system, we instead encourage people to provide information clearly in natural language and then extract from that more usable. As a knowledge acquisition method it is closer in spirit to approaches that apply learning and induction techniques to learn rules from examples supplied by users [13].

We have developed extraction patterns to mine hundreds of types of knowledge out of the database into simple frame representations. Some examples include:

[a | an | the] N1 (is | are) [a | an | the] [A1] N2
- *Dogs are mammals*
   Hurricanes are powerful storms

a person [does not] want[s] to V1 A1
- *A person wants to be warm*
   A person wants to be attractive

N1 requires [a | an] [A1] N2
- *Writing requires a pen*
   Bathing requires water

4 Evaluating the Accumulated Database

Evaluation is difficult but important for any knowledge acquisition effort. A manual evaluation was performed on the OMCS-1 database to assess its quality and composition. 3245 unique items were collected (about 1% of the database of 432,552 items). Of these, 236 (7.3%) nonstandard items were automatically discarded. Nonstandalone items are those requiring additional materials such as images and stories in order to make sense. The remaining 3009 items were distributed among 7 judges. Of these, 370 (12.3%) were marked by the judges as being garbage. Examples of garbage were:

- *it has a meaning*
- *gone to lunch*
- *you are*

The remaining 2639 items were rated on a scale from 1 to 5 for the following attributes: generality (1=specific fact, 5=general truth), truth (1=false, 5=true), neutrality (1=biased, 5=neutral), and sense (1=makes no sense, 5=makes complete sense).

Results are shown in Fig. 1 (NA=no answer). The average rating for generality was 3.26, reflecting the fact that items of common sense may range from the specific to the general. Sample items rated 5 for generality were:

- *Birds often make nests out of grass.*
- *Dew is wet*
- *Round objects roll with greater ease than other shapes*

Sample items rated 1 for generality were:

- *Eritrea is part of Africa*
- *Tom Smothers knows how to play with yo-yo's*

The average rating for truth was 4.28, with 75% of items rated 4 and higher. 67% of items were rated 5, reflecting the presence of exceptions in many statements of common sense. Sample items rated 5 for truth were:

- *An outfit is something that might have buttons.*
- *houses have many kinds of roofs*
- *Legal matters can be confusing to most humans.*

Sample items rated 4 for truth were:

- *a person wants to be successful.*
- *Small cars are uncomfortable*

Sample items rated 1 for truth are:

- *someone can be at infinity*
- *time flys like an arrow; fruit flies like a banana*

The average rating for neutrality was 4.42, with 82% of items rated 4 and higher, indicating that the database is judged to be relatively unbiased. Sample items rated 1 for neutrality are:

- *Idiots are obsessed with star trek.*
- *Men should do the laundry*

The average rating for sense was 4.55, with 85% of items rated 4 and higher. Sample items rated 1 for sense are:

- *There are limits to how English words may be spelled.*
- *cows can low quietly*

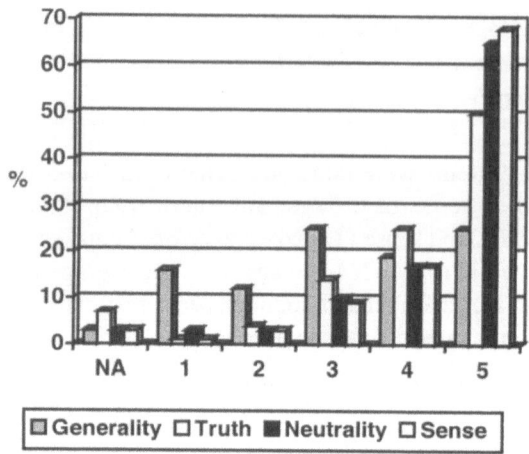

Fig. 1. Manual evaluation of database sample

Judges were also asked to rate sentences for age level. Results are shown in Fig. 2. Most (84%) items were at the grade school or high school level, indicating that the database consists mostly of items that most people know.

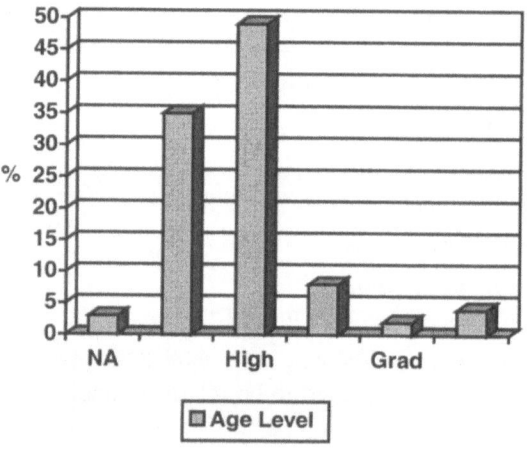

Fig. 2. Contributions by age level

In the next version the users themselves judge the quality of the data, which, of course, requires that they also judge each other.

5   Commonsense-Based Applications

The database we have accumulated has proven useful in prototyping a number of commonsense-based applications. Our database has been used to build search engines that can reason about users' goals. Novice search engine users naturally express search goals rather than topic keywords. Both REFORMULATOR [3] and GOOSE (goal-oriented search engine) [14] use common sense to infer the query that can most effectively satisfy the search goal. For example, when the user enters "my cat is sick", the system makes the inference that because people care about their pets, to care about something means you want it to be in good health, and that veterinarians can heal sick animals, that the search engine should search for a veterinarian.

A second application that has been developed is the ARIA program, which manages people's personal photos [15]. ARIA uses a spreading activation network of 50,000 sentences from OMCS-1 –statements about object classifications, spatial relations, object purposes, causal relations between events, and emotions resulting from experiencing objects and events –to improve the retrieval of annotated photos. For example, given the information "Susan is Jane's sister", the system can use the fact "in a wedding, the bridesmaid is often the sister of the bride" to retrieve a photo annotated with the text "Susan and her bridesmaids".

A third application is being developed to provide feedback to documentary videographers during shooting process. In the Cinematic Commonsense project [16] OMCS-1 relations and scripts relevant to the documentary subject domain are retrieved to assist the filmmaker in filming content for a documentary subject and recognizing story threads that emerge as content is gathered. After a shot is recorded, metadata is created by the videographer in natural language and submitted as a query to the OMCS-1 database. For example, the shot metadata "a street artist is painting a painting" would yield the shot suggestions such as "the last thing you do when you paint a painting is clean the brushes" and "red paint is expensive." Knowledge about the order of typical events in the painting domain can also be retrieved to create a framework for a sequence of shots.

6   Open Mind Common Sense 2

We have found enough applications and interest that we have begun work on a next-generation version of the system, OMCS-2. While this version has not yet been launched to the general public, we report here on our results so far. The design of OMCS-2 was driven by the lessons learned from the first system, and we will introduce each feature as a way to correct a deficiency in the first system. We learned the following from our experience with OMCS-1:

1. Different participants prefer to enter different types of knowledge.
2. The template activities were the most efficient and most usable form of knowledge.
3. The participants wanted the interaction to be more engaging and provide a sense of utility.

4. The participants wished they could assess, clarify and repair the knowledge.
5. Participants wished they could do more to organize the entered knowledge.

7 Workflow Model for Acquisition

A major difference between acquiring knowledge from the general public and acquiring it from experts or end users is that the general public is likely to leave as soon as they encounter something difficult. But this does not mean that there should be nothing painful or tedious in the system. Different people like to do different things. Some like to enter new items. Others like to evaluate items. Others like to refine items.

Our system is therefore based on a *distributed workflow* model where the different stages of knowledge acquisition, as in the elicitation, refinement, and restructuring stages of [13], may be performed separately by different participants. The output of the workflow is a *finalized* piece of knowledge, one that has its word senses tagged, clarified, validated, and can participate in some inference. This also gives the participants greater control over their experience.

OMCS-2 allows both template-based input and free-form input. One workflow sequence for template-based entry is as follows:

1. The user browses items in the database until finding an item associated with a template the user is interested in. This frees the user from having to learn the ontology of templates. Instead, a template is located by example.
2. The user then clicks on the template and is given a new input form for that template, along with example items based on that template.
3. After the user enters an item, inferences that result from the item are presented.
4. The user is then given the option of accepting or rejecting those inferences. The accepted and rejected inferences, along with the rules that produced the inferences, are all tagged as accepted or rejected and added to the database. Thus a single interaction supplies many different types of knowledge.

Entered items are also spell checked, tagged for part of speech, and disambiguated as to word sense.

The user may also enter a free-form sentence. The user is informed if the sentence matches an existing template. A template editor may also be brought up, enabling the user to create a new template through variabilization of the entered sentence.

When the user clicks on an item, the user is presented with various activities for criticizing and refining that item.

We now discuss aspects of OMCS-2 in more detail.

8 Templates for Knowledge Entry

The most useful items gathered by OMCS-1 were those for which we could write information extraction procedures. OMCS-2 therefore encourages knowledge to be supplied using templates rather than as free-form English text. We did not want to use templates in OMCS-1 because we were worried that we would not ourselves be able to design a sufficiently large and fully encompassing set of templates, and we wanted to learn an ontology of relations from our users, instead of imposing one upon them. But since we have now collected several hundred thousand free-form facts from which we can extract templates, we no longer feel we are imposing an ontology on our users. Further, we allow our users to extend the template library themselves.

These templates can extend across multiple lines, so the user can enter descriptions and simple stories extending across multiple sentences. From these we hope to extract larger causal and temporal constraints between states and events, which lets us build structures such as frames and scripts, which we believe are critical for commonsense reasoning. This type of knowledge has not been extensively accumulated in previous commonsense acquisition efforts. Mueller compared several systems and found that most systems were acquiring facts and rules, and not cases and stories against which analogical reasoning could be performed [17]. Examples of these templates include:

> *?N1 is ?ADJ*
> *?N1 ?V [a] ?N2*
> *?N1 is not ?ADJ*
> $\rightarrow$ *Bob is hungry*
> *Bob eats a sandwich*
> *Bob is not hungry*

The initial set of OMCS-2 templates is based on the templates we extracted from the OMCS-1 database.

9 Feedback through Inference

OMCS-1 participants complained that there was no interesting feedback upon entering an item. They wanted some evidence the system could use the item, to feel that they were contributing to the construction of a "thinking machine" and not just a static database. In OMCS-2 we have incorporated several inference mechanisms into the acquisition cycle. The system induces inference rules from the knowledge that people have supplied, and these rules are used immediately to feed back inferences on entered items.

OMCS-2 engages in three types of inference. These methods are simple and fast, and while they do not necessarily produce accurate rules, this is less of a problem since the user is in the loop. The inference depends on the knowledge in the database being stored as instances of templates. The database is a graph of concepts and n-ary relations indexed for retrieval by concept or relation or both. The graph is much larger version of that shown in Fig. 3.

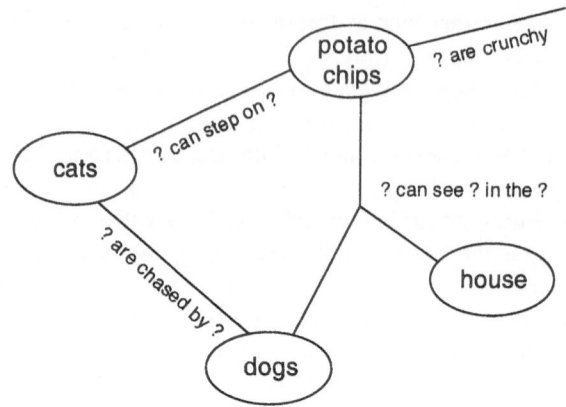

Fig. 3. In this graph, nodes are the "concepts" and links are the "relations." Notice that a relation can connect any number of concepts.

9.1   Method 1: Analogies over Concepts

The first method finds analogies over concepts:

1. A user enters "A mother can have a baby" as an instance of the template "A ? can have a ?" with the concepts "mother" and "baby."
2. The program finds all other items in the database relating "mother" and "baby," such as "A mother can hold her baby."
3. Each such item is an instance of a template. In this case, "A mother can hold her baby" is an instance of the template "A ? can hold her ?" with the concepts "mother" and "baby."
4. Then it finds all other instances of this template, such as "A small girl can hold her small dog."
5. For each one, it instantiates the original template with the concepts. In our example, it yields "A small girl can have a small dog," which is fed back to the user.

9.2   Method 2: Analogies over Relations

The second method finds analogies over relations:

1. A user enters "A mother can have a baby" as an instance of the template "A ? can have a ?" with the concepts "mother" and "baby."
2. The program finds all other sets of concepts involved in instances of this template, such as "A child" and "goldfish" in "A child can have a goldfish."
3. For each such set of concepts, the program finds other instances of templates involving the concepts. For example, "child" and "goldfish" are also involved in "A child can take care of a goldfish," an instance of the template "A ? can take care of a ?."

4. Each of these templates is then instantiated with the original concepts. Here, we get "A mother can take care of a baby," which is fed back to the user.

Using this system, the program has used "Hawks eat rabbits" to infer "There is more rabbits than there are hawks" by relating (hawks, rabbits) to (cows, grass) and finding "There is more grass than there are cows."

9.3   Method 3: Analogies as Inference Rules

The third method performs analogical inference by first generating a list of inference rules. This is achieved by identifying cycles in the graph in which 3 binary relations connect three concepts, such as that shown in Fig. 4.

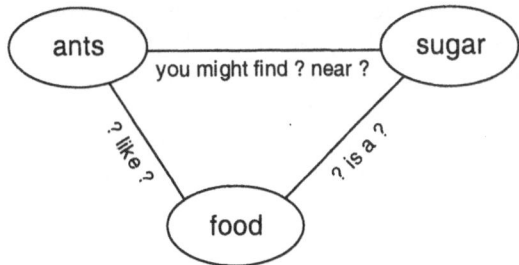

Fig. 4. In this graph, "ants," "sugar," and "food" are in a cycle. The three original sentences are: "You might find ants near sugar," "Ants like food," and "Sugar is a food."

Whenever the program finds such a cycle, it produces a new inference rule. When run on the original OMCS-1 database, 1,860,182 such inference rules are automatically extracted by this method. Inference rules are currently judged as "better" if they match more occurrences in the original database. For each such rule, the program can identify other places in the graph where any two of the three elements in the inference rule can be instantiated. The program then pieces together what a third element must look like to be consistent with the first two, and presents it as an inference.

If the user enters "Bats like darkness" and "You might find bats near cave interiors" is already in the database, then the program matches: ?a = "bats," ?b = "darkness," and ?c = "cave interiors" to infer "Cave interiors is a darkness." While this new sentence is not syntactically correct, it expresses the new idea that "Cave interiors are dark" which was not originally in the database.

Using this system, the program has used "The piano is in the lake" to infer "If you want to go to the piano, then you should take a boat." It has also used "The Christmas Tree has candy canes" to infer "The Christmas Tree is covered mostly by sugar."

These are of course the examples where the method succeeds.

We are presently extending these techniques to allow the system to hypothesize not just inference rules, but also chains of stories. This allows for some limited forms of temporal reasoning by finding analogies between stories. Narratives and stories are unified into a single template representation in which either facts, descriptions, or stories may be expressed.

10 Clarification

It is important to develop techniques to simplify and disambiguate the contributed knowledge.

10.1 Restricting Vocabulary

OMCS-1 participants often entered expert rather than commonsense knowledge. One way to make it more likely for participants to enter commonsense knowledge is to encourage the use of common English words. We formed a set of common words by ranking words in OMCS-1 by number of occurrences. In OMCS-2, we encourage the use of common words by suggesting replacements for uncommon words used in entered items. Replacements are suggested through the use of a synonym and hypernym dictionary such as WordNet. The user may accept or reject the replacements.

10.2 Word Sense Disambiguation

OMCS-1 participants were asked to enter items in "simple English." Though this produced items easy to parse syntactically, it also resulted in items that were difficult to disambiguate since common words are the most polysemous! Word-sense disambiguation is a well-known problem in natural language processing, and a variety of automated and semi-automated methods exist for dealing with the problem. To date the best automated methods achieve about 70% accuracy [18].

The Open Mind Word Expert web site [19] was recently launched as an experiment in gathering word sense information from the general public. Similarly, OMCS-2 introduces word-sense disambiguation into the workflow. Participants are not required to tag the sense of every word in every sentence. Rather, automated methods are used to suggest sense tags, which may be corrected by the user. Further, given that the user has disambiguated some of the words, the system should be able to disambiguate the rest of the words automatically. The user should only have to disambiguate one or two words out of every sentence to pin down the meanings of the other words.

11 Organization

OMCS-1 participants wished they could organize the database to make browsing easier, and application developers using the database wished they could quickly acquire knowledge on particular topics.

We ask users to supply not only knowledge items, but ways to index and organize those items to facilitate retrieval and application. To do this we have our users build *topic vectors*, sets of concepts that are related to a given topic. These are initially built automatically by looking at the words that are correlated with the topic word. Users can then increase and decrease the probability of membership of individual concepts, and add new concepts as well. Topic vectors are commonly used in knowledge retrieval to cast a wider net in order to retrieve all knowledge relevant to a topic. These might also be used as a dynamic way of generating reasoning contexts. In Cyc every assertion belongs to a fixed microtheory and this requires the user to know all the microtheories. In our system the user only has to build topic vectors, and never has to manually arrange the knowledge into particular microtheories.

12   Validation and Repair

In a large collaborative effort it is important to assess user honesty. Our present set of participants is relatively small and so it has been fairly easy to filter troublesome users manually. But if the system grew by an order of magnitude, manually filtering users would become too time-consuming. OMCS-2 incorporates mechanisms for peer review, enabling users to judge each other by judging samples of each other's knowledge. By giving users "trust" ratings, the judgments of users with higher trust ratings are given greater weight. We also employ catch trials, as described in [20], in which a fixed set of pre-validated sentences are presented to users from time to time in order to assess their truthfulness.

In order to suggest items for review, we use plausibility measures. If words appear together in ways that are implausible statistically, the system raises an alarm and posts that item for review.

OMCS-2 enables reviewed items to be corrected, subject to further review.

13   Conclusion

We have built the second largest database of commonsense knowledge, after Cyc. In this paper we presented Open Mind Common Sense, a system for acquiring commonsense knowledge from the general public. We described our experiences with the first system OMCS-1 and how they motivated the design of OMCS-2. We presented a manual evaluation of the quality of the database produced by OMCS-1 and discussed several prototype applications built with the database using various inferencing techniques.

What issues arise when knowledge acquisition systems turn to the general public, using thousands of people instead of, as is typical, just a few? Participants should be able to enter many forms of knowledge for commonsense reasoning. Participants should be able to enter knowledge using a friendly interface that seems invisible. Individuals like to do certain things, and they will not necessarily be careful about all aspects of the knowledge they enter. Therefore participants should be able to organize and repair each other's pieces of knowledge, and validate each other. Participants should be able to teach more intricate things such as inference rules by example. Participants should feel after entering an item that the system can use it. Motivation is critical.

What future work is suggested by our approach? We wish to absorb more of the powerful ideas that have been developed by the knowledge acquisition community such as methods for acquiring procedural knowledge by example [21], using knowledge acquisition scripts for coordinating changes to the database [22], and turning to more reflective architectures [23] that can understand and detect problems in the knowledge that users have put in, and pose them back to other users for clarification and repair. We wish to allow artificial intelligence researchers to map templates onto logical formulas and to existing ontologies. We wish to give participants a greater degree of control regarding inferencing and procedural knowledge. Our approach has yet to deal with many of the hardest issues in commonsense reasoning such as contexts, exceptions, combining narratives, elaboration tolerance, and others.

Open Mind Common Sense is the first attempt at realizing the idea that we might distribute the problem of constructing a system with common sense. We are excited because we believe that work on building commonsense databases is no longer only the domain of multi-million-dollar "Manhattan projects", and can now be pursued by the distributed artificial intelligence community as a whole and by turning to the general public to achieve what is too difficult and expensive to be achieved by any one group. There is a goldmine of opportunity for people who are willing to accept that there are countless people out there who would be willing to participate as volunteers in the effort to help artificial intelligence researchers build databases larger than any one group could build.

Acknowledgements. We extend our thanks to David Stork for organizing the larger Open Mind effort, and the many thousands of members of the general public who contributed their knowledge to our database. This project was supported by the sponsors of the MIT Media Lab.

References

1. Mueller, E. T. 2000. A calendar with common sense. In Proceedings of the 2000 International Conference on Intelligent User Interfaces, 198-201. New York: Association for Computing Machinery.
2. Guha, R.V. and Lenat, D. B. 1994. CYC: Enabling agents to work together. Communications of the ACM 37(7): 127-142.
3. Singh, P. 2002. The public acquisition of commonsense knowledge. In Proceedings of AAAI Spring Symposium: Acquiring (and Using) Linguistic (and World) Knowledge for Information Access. Palo Alto, CA, AAAI.
4. Davis, E. 1990. Representations of commonsense knowledge. San Mateo, Calif.: Morgan Kaufmann.
5. Shanahan, M. 1997. Solving the frame problem. Cambridge, Mass.: MIT Press.
6. Lenat, D.B. 1995. CYC: A large-scale investment in knowledge infrastructure. Communications of the ACM 38(11): 33-38.

7. Stork, D. 1999. The OpenMind Initiative. IEEE Intelligent Systems 14(3):19-20.
8. Blythe, J.; Kim, J.; Ramachandran, S.; and Gil, Y. 2001. An integrated environment for knowledge acquisition. In Proceedings of the 2001 International Conference on Intelligent User Interfaces, 13-20.
9. Blythe, J. and Ramachandran, S. 1999. Knowledge acquisition using an English-based method editor. In Proceedings of the Twelfth Knowledge Acquisition for Knowledge-Based Systems Workshop, Banff, Alberta.
10. Fuchs, N. E. and Schwitter, R. 1996. Attempto Controlled English (ACE). CLAW 96, First International Workshop on Controlled Language Applications, University of Leuven, Belgium.
11. Borchardt, G. C. 1992. Understanding Causal Descriptions of Physical Systems. In Proceedings of the Tenth National Conference on Artificial Intelligence, San Jose, CA, 2-8.
12. Cardie, C. 1997. Empirical Methods in Information Extraction, AI Magazine, 65-79.
13. Bareiss, R.; Porter, B.; and Murray, K. 1989. Supporting start-to-finish development of knowledge bases. Machine Learning 4, 259-283.
14. Liu, H., Lieberman, H., Selker, T. 2002. GOOSE: A Goal-Oriented Search Engine With Commonsense. Proceedings of the 2nd International Conference on Adaptive Hypermedia and Adaptive Web Based Systems, (AH2002) Malaga, Spain.
15. Lieberman, H. and Liu. H. 2002. Adaptive Linking between Text and Photos Using Common Sense Reasoning. In Proceedings of the 2nd International Conference on Adaptive Hypermedia and Adaptive Web Based Systems, (AH2002) Malaga, Spain.
16. Barry, B. & Davenport. G. 2002. *Why Common Sense for Video Production?* (Interactive Cinema Technical Report #02-01). Media Lab, MIT.
17. Mueller, E. T. 1999. A database and lexicon of scripts for ThoughtTreasure. CogPrints ID cog00000555 http://cogprints.soton.ac.uk/
18. Ide, N. and Véronis, J. (Eds.) 1998. Special Issue on Word Sense Disambiguation. Computational Linguistics, 24(1).
19. Chklovski, T. and Mihalcea, R. 2002. Building a Sense Tagged Corpus with Open Mind Word Expert. In Proceedings of the Workshop on "Word Sense Disambiguation: Recent Successes and Future Directions", ACL 2002.
20. Stork, D. 2001. Toward a Computational Theory of Data Acquisition and Truthing. In Proceedings of Computational Learning Theory (COLT 01), David Helmbold (editor), Springer Series in Computer Science, 2001.
21. Cypher, A. 1993. Bringing programming to end users. In Watch What I Do: Programming by Demonstration. Cambridge, Mass: MIT Press.
22. Tallis, M. and Gil, Y. 1999. Designing scripts to guide users in modifying knowledge-based systems. In Proceedings of the Sixteenth National Conference on Artificial Intelligence. AAAI Press.
23. Gil, Y. 1994. Knowledge refinement in a reflective architecture. In Proceedings of the Twelfth National Conference on Artificial Intelligence.

Formal Ontology Engineering in the DOGMA Approach

Mustafa Jarrar and Robert Meersman

VUB STARLab
Vrije Universiteit Brussel
Pleinlaan 2 – B-1050 Brussels, Belgium
{mjarrar, meersman}@vub.ac.be

Abstract. This paper presents a specifically database-inspired approach (called DOGMA) for engineering *formal ontologies*, implemented as shared resources used to express agreed formal semantics for a real world domain. We address several related key issues, such as knowledge reusability and shareability, scalability of the ontology engineering process and methodology, efficient and effective ontology storage and management, and coexistence of heterogeneous rule systems that surround an ontology mediating between it and application agents. Ontologies should represent a domain's semantics *independently* from "language", while any process that *creates* elements of such an ontology must be entirely rooted in some (natural) language, and any *use* of it will necessarily be through a (in general an agent's computer) language.
To achieve the claims stated, we explicitly decompose ontological resources into *ontology bases* in the form of simple binary facts called *lexons* and into so-called *ontological commitments* in the form of description rules and constraints. Ontology bases in a logic sense, become "representationless" mathematical objects which constitute the range of a classical *interpretation mapping* from a first order language, assumed to lexically represent the commitment or binding of an application or task to such an ontology base. Implementations of ontologies become database-like on-line resources in the model-theoretic sense. The resulting architecture allows to materialize the (crucial) notion of commitment as a separate layer of (software agent) services, mediating between the ontology base and those application instances that *commit* to the ontology. We claim it also leads to methodological approaches that naturally extend key aspects of database modeling theory and practice. We discuss examples of the prototype **DOGMA** implementation of the ontology base server and commitment server.

1 Motivation, Context, and Overview of Related Work

What are Ontologies. Computer science (re-)defines ontology as a branch of knowledge engineering, where agreed semantics of a certain domain is represented formally in a computer resource, which then enables sharing and interoperation between information systems (IS). Representing the formal semantics for a certain domain implies *conceptualizing* the domain objects and their interrelationships in a

R. Meersman, Z. Tari (Eds.): CoopIS/DOA/ODBASE 2002, LNCS 2519, pp. 1238–1254, 2002.

declarative way. Ontologies should therefore support formal and agreed so-called *ontological commitments* (for definitions, see below) needed for new open application environments (e.g. electronic commerce, B2B, semantic web). In an open environment autonomous applications possibly developed without *a priori* knowledge about each other, need to communicate to exchange data in order to make transactions interoperate.

For the time being and for mental imagery's sake, picture such an ontology as a set of object (type-)s and their conceptual relationships expressing possible facts in a domain (an EER or ORM diagram labeled with natural language terms will do fine), plus first order theory expressing rules, constraints, ... involving the concepts over this domain. For an example, see fig. 2. A correct understanding of ontologies must however reconcile that they are repositories of (in principle) language- and task-independent knowledge, while any effective use by e.g. software agents naturally requires interaction with *some necessarily lexical* representation.. Also the creation of ontologies as (sets of) agreements about structure and semantics of a domain requires the use of —usually natural— language, leading to interesting research issues on methodology.

Information systems (in any broad sense, especially web-based ones) are expected to benefit substantially from the use of ontologies as externalized resources of agreed knowledge. To a database engineer the following parallel may perhaps be enlightening: implementations of ontologies will in a real sense permit a form of *"semantics independence"* for such information- and knowledge based systems. Just like database schemas achieved *data independence* by making the specification and management of stored data elements external to their application programs, ontologies now will allow to specify and manage domain semantics external to those programs as well.

Ontologies are Shared Computer-Based Resources. The fundamentally *a-priori-shared* nature of an ontology makes it important to understand that ontology engineering, while similar to data modeling, is substantially more than that, even when the data modeling methodology takes business rules into account [6]. Representing formal semantics in the domain of "air travel" is more than designing, or collecting, a set of data models for a number of airline reservation systems. Existing data models likely would have been autonomously specified for optimal use within an individual organization or company. Thus, an ontology needs to be even more *generic*, across tasks and even task types, than a data model is for a number of given applications. Just adding a mere *"is_a"*- taxonomy of terms is not sufficient, as the literature sometimes seems to suggest. An ontology needs to include (the meaning of) a much richer set of relationships, such as *instance_of, part_of, ...,* which depending on the domain all might deserve a "generic semantics".

Ontologies must be Scalable Resources. As the main purpose of an ontology is to be a shared and agreed semantic resource over a wide range of agents, building scalable ontologies will effectively be a group effort, with ontologies growing over time [19]. In particular, they will need a form of consensus about the conceptualizations to be adopted. In [12] such a consensus is the result of a mental process, assisted by exemplifying, testifying, investigating etc, while [24] proposes a so-called Adequacy

Search. Any such process will inevitably be oriented to *tasks* to be carried out, and are likely to be influenced also by personal taste and even may reflect fundamental disagreements [2]. Several conceptualizations could be adopted for the same domain [15], especially in large-scale and multi-domain ontologies, which may lead to potentially "locally" inconsistent (and incomplete) ontologies. Notice that difficulties and disagreements in the conceptualization process normally appear at a "deeper" level of abstraction, i.e. as a result of conceptual heterogeneity and difficulties in ontology integration [14]. (This level is dubbed the "Detail Level" by [31].) Rules constrain the structure and interrelationships of the concepts. More specifically other words, *constraints, rules and procedures* are essential to achieve an understanding about a domain's semantics, but agreement about them in general is difficult and nearly always specific to a context of application. Note that from an ontology's *application point of view* constraints will likely be there to limit updates of data stores that exist entirely *within* that application's realm, the actual consistency of which will *not* be the ontology's responsibility. For example it is easy to agree that "person has a blood-pressure", while disagreement might on whether the actual value of this pressure is (too) high *in a given context*. People could agree on "a book has ISBN" but might disagree whether *for a given application* that ISBN value is a mandatory property for the book to have, or that "person has age", but disagree on the value range. In general database design methodology has shown that people agree fairly easily about the basic facts in a domain than about the "lower level" details of and constraints on these facts.

Knowledge reusability is another important goal of building ontologies ([18] [34] [23] [13] [11]). As a result of a conceptualization process, an ontological theory will stand as a formal resource of knowledge. Reusing such resources means sharing the same conceptualization. Ontologies may only need to be reused partially: for example, when building a "Manufacturing" ontology, one may wish to reuse the "Customers" aspects from an existing "Shopping" ontology, if they are assumed to share a same conceptualization about a certain set of axioms. The ability to share a partial conceptualization (as a result of partial agreement) across two ontologies depends on the degree of abstraction that can be applied by ontology engineers to their respective concepts. To improve knowledge reusability, several researchers from the problem-solving area (e.g. Chandrasekaran and Johnson [3], Clancey [4], or Swartout and Moore [32]) have proposed the idea of structuring the knowledge into different levels of abstractions, where Steels in [30] proposed a componential framework that decomposes a knowledge level into reusable components. In addition to the level of abstraction, several issues related to the reusability of knowledge are outlined and discussed in [27] such as the importance of context, the need for more knowledge, etc.

It seems plausible that building large knowledge bases will only be possible if efforts are combined (Neches et al in [26]). This translates into a requirement for a unified framework that enables and maximizes knowledge reusability. Such a framework must be scalable and allow connecting of ontological theories in spite of the diversity of ontology languages and their representation models.

The above aspects and considerations translate within DOGMA into a model and associated architecture that explicitly separates "base" facts in a domain from constraints, rules, identification, derivation etc that occur to support an application's *use* of an ontology.

Methodology by Transition and Growth. *Knowledge management* is the corporate control of an organization's business data and metadata and of their use in applications that are increasingly connected to "external" business domain knowledge. From the above it should not surprise that effective corporate knowledge management is becoming dependent on the availability of semantic information resources. Most likely the most immediate business applications of ontologies will lie in this area ([9]). As an organization's information typically resides in its (large) databases, data dictionaries, websites, documents, and in its people, this implies not just scalability and knowledge reusability but also a *methodological* approach to the "ontologization" of information resources at the individual organization level, one that is geared towards current information paradigms. Methodology implies *teachability* and *repeatability*, in general will be aimed at the involvement of *non-computer experts*, and therefore must be based on sound, easy to understand and broadly accepted principles. Naturally, any good methodology will closely reflect the architecture of the resulting system. For instance, the separation of facts and constraints indicated above allows a "database-style" architecture for ontologies and their use in information systems, which in turn leads to familiar techniques for the creation, deployment and maintenance phases in their lifecycles.

Structure of this Paper: In section 2 we discuss fundamental challenges and goals for engineering ontologies, and introduce and discuss these in our "DOGMA" framework. By examples, Section 3 illustrates this framework for building, (re)using, ontologies. Section 4 briefly discusses aspects of the important issue of ontological consistency and versioning that emerge while engineering an ontology. Section 5 overviews design and implementation consequences for ontology tools (in particular the ontology base and commitment servers) under development as part of the DOGMA System at VUB STARLab. Section 6 then lists early conclusions and maps ongoing and future work.

2 The DOGMA Approach to Ontology Engineering

According to Gruber [11] an ontology is "an explicit specification of a conceptualization", referring to an *extensional* ("Tarski-like") notion of a conceptualization as found e.g. in [15]. Guarino and Giaretta [12] pointed out that this definition *per se* does not adequately fit the purposes of an ontology. They argue correctly that a conceptualization benefits from invariance under changes that occur at the instance level by transitions between merely different "states of affairs" in a domain, and thus should not be extensional. Instead, they propose a conceptualization as an *intensional* semantic structure i.e. abstracting from the instance level, which encodes *implicit* rules constraining the structure of a piece of reality. In other words an ontology becomes a logical theory which possesses a conceptualization as an explicit, partial model.

While we arrived at it independently from a database-inspired perspective [21], in the DOGMA framework we embrace this viewpoint but unlike [12] and subsequent work by Guarino et al, we also pursue this idea to arrive at concrete software architectural and engineering conclusions. In the following sections we treat the fundamental issues for engineering and deploying ontologies that follow from this in more detail.

While the limited scope of this paper does not allow a fully detailed exposition of DOGMA's formalism, in what follows we will refer to existing related literature and illustrate largely by example its —somewhat simplified— formal structure model for ontology engineering. The illustrations derive from a prototype ontology modeler-/server-/mining-/alignment environment currently under development in the authors' lab. It will permit us to make hopefully explicit most of the key issues in ontology organization, engineering, scalability and methodology listed above, starting from familiar database design principles.

2.1 Model Theoretic Database Inspiration for Ontologies: The Ontology Base

By adopting agreement as pragmatic basis for the formal semantics of information systems (see [20] for an early position on this) we claim that classical, i.e. model-theoretic database technology and methodologies become suitable for "reuse" in an ontology context, and therefore perhaps is an interesting new research subject in its own right.

Suppose we want to build a system to support the running of scientific conferences such as ODBASE'02, but in such a way that its domain knowledge (its *ontology* of course) is *a priori* maximally accessible, reusable, and "understood" by —as yet— unidentified software agents. The openness of this environment prohibits us from prescribing a single definitive set of concepts, but instead we need to provide for an extensible set of alternative plausible worlds from which agents can "choose" and to which they can "commit". In DOGMA we will split these knowledge components into a set of *lexons*, grouped into abstract contexts, and into a layer of commitments. For the Scientific Conferences Domain, some lexons could be

```
(Organization-ContextID)
    Person      IsMemberOf  Committee
    Person      Chairs      Committee
    Committee   ChairedBy   Person
    Reviewer    SubtypesOf  Person
    Author      SubtypesOf  Person
    Reviewer    Reviews     Paper
    Paper       ReviewedBy  Reviewer
    Paper       WrittenBy   Author
    Author      Presents    Paper
    Paper       Has    PaperTitle
    Paper       Has    PaperNumber
  {...}
(ResearchAreas-ContextID)
```

```
Representation_and_Storage SuperAreaOf Ontology_Languages
Representation_and_Storage SuperAreaOf Semi-Structured_Data
Applications_and_Evaluation SuperAreaOf Semantic_Web
Applications_and_Evaluation SuperAreaOf Media_Archives
{...}
```

As an example of one *commitment* (-fragment), for instance by an application that wishes to access, or register submitted papers, consider

```
(ConferenceAdmin Commitment)
  <Each Committee ChairedBy at most one Person>
  <Each Person who chairs a Committee must also IsMemberOf that Committee>
  <Each Reviewer Reviews at least one Paper>
  <Each Paper which is WrittenBy a Person must not ReviewedBy with that Person>
  {...}     (Rules are verbalized in a suitable pseudo-NL syntax)
```

Commitment[1] implies the choice of, and/or adherence to, a set of rules, constraints, derivations that will in general depend on the task to be performed: rules that hold in one commitment need not do so in another, but will nevertheless need to be formally *interpreted* (in a first-order logic sense) in terms of the lexons in the same or "related" contexts.

It could be noted at this point that most recent ontology research, and the resulting formalisms and languages [25] are based on versions of earlier *description logics* [1] [10] and in general correspond more closely with the proof-theoretic view of database [28] with its natural implementations with Datalog and deductive databases in general. Although the proof-theoretic paradigm (arguably) is the more elegant and "general" one, and although the relationship between the model- and proof-theoretic views is well-understood since [28] ff., it is undeniably so that the model-theoretic view of databases gave rise to a technology, scalable *par excellence* and a successful industry of high-performance DBMS, tools and applications. By bringing to ontology engineering a precisely defined analogue to the model-theoretic paradigm of databases we find that important methodological and productivity advantages are obtained as well as technological ones, such as scalability, performance and a "familiar" transition path from existing database environments. For the latter statement, early evidence emerges in that even the prototypical DOGMA approach, while limited in other respects, is perceived by database practitioners and domain experts as fairly intuitive.

According to this well-tried model-theoretic database methodological principle, in the DOGMA framework we therefore decompose an ontology formally into an *ontology base*, a set of context-specific binary fact types which we call *lexons* (see example below), and instances of their explicit *ontological commitments*; the latter in our architecture become reified as a separate layer mediating between the ontology base and the instances of applications that commit to the ontology, see Fig.1.

Any computer *representation* of an ontology, albeit *by definition different* from the ontology itself, obviously must be lexically rendered (see Sowa's discussion about

---

[1] We will return to this example in more detail in Section 3.

ontologies and semiotics [29]). It must also at least provide correct contextual identification of its concepts (possibly to be negotiated by its application instances) through some language. To maximize the "conceptual gain" of the interpretation mapping, the formalism for specifying a conceptualization, as an ontology(-base), should be as simple as possible, e.g. just objects and relationships in the mathematical sense as intended by Tarski [15]. Thus our ontology base is a set of (binary, even) conceptual relationships, while other domain knowledge and its formal semantics will be "approximately" specified in a *commitment layer*. To accommodate alternative "models" of reality, or even versions as knowledge about the world evolves e.g. through observations, the ontology base may contain many different conceptualizations (defined in DOGMA in terms of *ontological contexts*, see below, and we in fact shall use the terms interchangeably) even about the same real world domain. In summary we have

Definition. An *ontology base* is
- A set of context-specific binary fact types, called *lexons*. Notation: <γ: Term$_1$, Role, Term$_2$>. Here $\gamma \in \Gamma$ is just an abstract *context identifier* chosen from a set, (more about this below). The lexical terms (Term$_1$, Role, Term$_2$) are constructed from a given alphabet;
- For each $\gamma \in \Gamma$, and each term T occurring in a lexon, the pair (γ, T) specifies exactly a *unique concept*.

Remarks. Lexons are thus assumed to express a binary conceptual relationship that is agreed to hold within a given context (among "all" the parties involved in the ontology, using some given metalanguage). Note only one of its two roles is used. The requirement of uniqueness for the specified concepts translates into a strong condition on the notion of contexts. Contexts may also be used to accommodate different alternative, "plausible" conceptualizations in one ontology base. See the Note on Contexts below.

A Note on Contexts. Contexts have been and are the subject of occasionally intense study notably in AI; examples are [22], specifying them as higher-order theories [29]. [27] reports on research effort under way for adding contexts into KIF in order to facilitate the translation of facts from one context to another. Also, large KBS such as CYC require context to be captured in order to applying knowledge for different domains.

In DOGMA contexts only provide internal organization of an ontology into contextual knowledge components, i.e. context identifiers are used, intuitively and informally, to "group" lexons that are "related" in an intended conceptualization of a domain. In the DOGMA lexon structure (for the purpose of this paper) therefore they appear merely as abstract identifiers. At this stage their only formal "semantics" or interpretation within DOGMA is defined as a *mapping* from Γ to a *collection of sources* (not further defined, but for example a corpus of documents) each assumed to contain an intended conceptualization together with its implicit assumptions. Turning again to intuition, lexons are assumed (by an outside cognitive agent such as a human understanding that document) to be "true within that context's source". In the Note on

Formal Semantics below we shall return to this informal ":interpretation" of an ontology base as a set of "true facts".

Clearly there is a lot more than meets the eye here; in particular expressing relationships between concepts (as is needed when *aligning* or integrating ontologies) from different contexts cannot be done without e.g. a notion of *context calculus* in which to define the relationships (predicate formulas) that are permitted or assumed to hold between contexts. This notion is not explored further in this paper. Also, the extraction of lexons from a context's source is a research topic in its own right of course, involving NL parsing and understanding in the case of ontology mining from documents [8]. For this paper however we assume that these extractions "are done" and merely provide an architecture with a repository that allows to store and manages the result of this process.

2.2 The Commitment Layer

The commitment layer is organized as a set of *ontological commitments,* each responds to an explicit *instance* of an (intensional) first-order *interpretation* of application it terms of ontology base; each commitment is a consistent set of rules (/axioms) in a given syntax that constrains to a particular aspect of reality, or also: *commits it ontologically.*

The ontological commitments may be seen as a set of reusable knowledge components. Such components may interoperate since they share the same ontology base. In practice "similar" applications reuse or inherit commitments from each other, which should facilitate new applications to commit to and use the ontology. (Also, successful commitments in certain domains and applications likely will become "popular" (i.e. serve a more general purpose) and a *de facto* trusted resource in their own right for achieving interoperability, or just compatibility between applications.

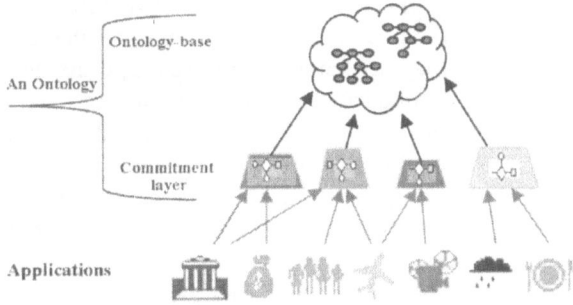

Fig. 1. Knowledge Organization in DOGMA Framework

A Note on Ontology as a Formal Semantics. An ontology base in DOGMA is the range of the (first-order) commitments (seen as interpretation mappings) of the application software agents, which for formal convenience we shall assume to be expressed in a first order language. "Real" interpretations, which thus actually are the definition of semantics, are truth-preserving mappings from the application to the "real world domain", usually called models. It is fundamental to realize that this formalism implies that to the application agents, the ontology (i.e. the ontology base plus the agent's commitment to a part of it) *is* the real world, nothing more nor less. Lexons in a DOGMA ontology base are always "true", i.e. free of further "interpretation". Alternative truths, or partial ones as typically emerge during the engineering process have to be provided in separate conceptualizations or contexts (see the Note on Contexts above). Contexts that specify improbable or impossible (contradictory) worlds are possible, especially in the early stages of engineering an ontology, but in practice will have few or no applications that can commit to them. Incidentally note also that (some of) the actual instances of a real world may or may not be part of a given conceptualization. For instance, the notion described by the term "November" may refer to an instance in some conceptualizations, and to an ontological concept in others. This yields another reason why ontologies behave not quite the same as data models, although it suffices in this particular case to formally specify customized interpretations of an "is_instance_of" relationship in the relevant commitments... The ontological commitments above are merely part of the specification of this mapping, namely they specify the intensional interpretations of an application in terms of the ontology base.

Naturally there is a trade-off between complexity and size that lies in the requirements to (a) manage the (huge) size and (organizational) complexity of the lexon base, (b) map nearly all application assumptions to the terms and relations of the lexons in the ontology, and (c) develop, link and manage (even index) the domain-specific commitment packages (e.g. in the form of sets of constraints and functions). With the design of the DOGMA commitment Server discussed further in this paper we attempt to provide at least an initial solution to some of these problems.

The alert reader may have noted incidentally that our approach appears motivated —at least in part— by earlier experience with successful "semantical" database (-schema) modeling methodologies used in practice (ORM, Object-Role Modeling [17] and NIAM, aN Information Analysis Method [35], also "Nijssen's-" or "Natural"-IAM). This indeed allows identifying and analyzing some of the essential differences between database- and ontology modeling. While we stated that formal ontologies are best thought of as abstract, mathematical entities, any use of them must be through a (lexical, application) language. ORM and especially NIAM have strong methodological roots for handling this distinction. However, the principal modeling feature of ORM/NIAM, the adoption of an explicit separation between lexical (term-) and non-lexical (concept-) knowledge, partly disappears in an ontology context, all knowledge being lexical. In fact the precise ontological relevance of the "bridge" between the lexical and non-lexical knowledge base for the "ontology proper" is as yet not fully studied and understood (it forms part of the ontological commitment) and is the subject of ongoing research.

3 Example: A Simple Ontology in the DOGMA Framework

The following example, with its necessary simplicity, shows part of a Trivial Conference ontology, used by two different *kind of* conference applications. Fig. 2 shows the graphical representation of this ontology in an ORM diagram. Notice that the ontology in this example is not the aim of the paper itself, and is *supposed* to be specified at the knowledge level[2], i.e. it is more than a data model for the application instances. Applications that commit to this ontology may retain their internal data models[3].

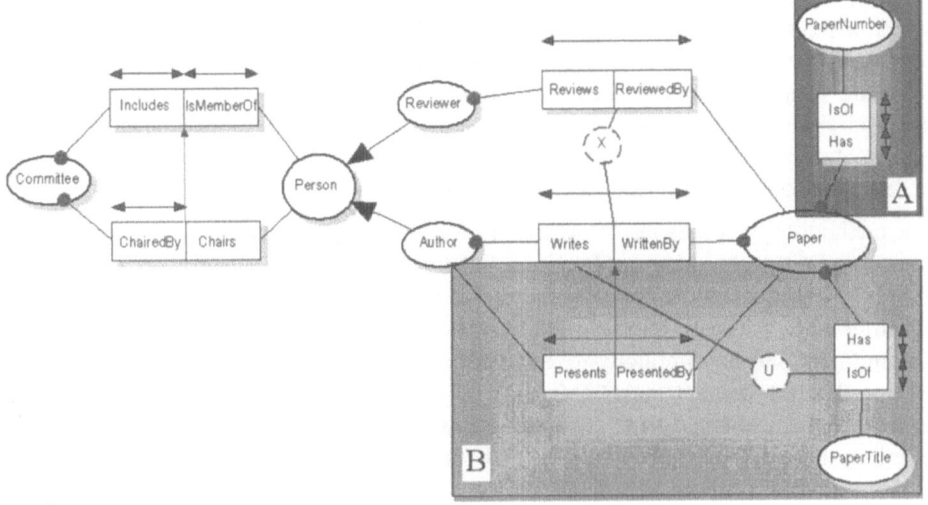

Fig. 2. Trivial Scientific Conference Ontology[4]

Each kind of conference application in general will have certain rules that do not necessarily agree with those of other kinds; application B for example agrees with application A on all lexons and rules, except those grouped as "A" in Fig. 2. Likewise application A agrees with everything except those rules grouped as "B". For instance, application A identifies a Paper by Paper_Number, while application B instead identifies the same paper by the combination of Paper_Title and a reference to its Author. Also in application B, the Person who presents a Paper must be the Author of this Paper, while in application A this rule does not hold.

Building such ontologies by allowing only partial agreement about the conceptualization of a domain obviously is difficult and complex, but realistic. As discussed before, in such cases, which are common in open environments as Semantic

---

[2] The Knowledge Level is a level of description of the knowledge of an agent that is independent of the symbol-level representation used internally by the agent [11]

[3] Note that the commitments may be more than *integrity constraints* (to be committed by an application), such as derivation or reasoning rules that may help to enrich or filter queries.

[4] If the reader is not familiar with reading ORM schemas, he can find its representation in Table 1 and Table 2.

Web: (1) the completeness of an ontology should be considered and managed, and (2) applications might not commit to an ontology because they do not agree about the ontology's interpretation. For the sake of reusability we believe that such issues should not be ignored —as they cannot be avoided— but instead be *managed*.

In Fig 2 and Table 1 below we represent the Scientific Conference ontology base both as link types in an ORM-style diagram and as lexons in a "database" format. Next, in Table 2 we define the ontological commitments. The representation of the rules in the commitment layer is not restricted to a particular ontology language or standard, but we adopt a notational convention to specify which rule system/standard is used, in the form of a rule prefix. For example, the prefix "ORM." is used in Table 2 for rules which are intended to be interpreted as "standard" ORM ([17]) by "standard ORM" tools. Furthermore, each ontological commitment should define an ontological *view*, i.e. state which lexons are used and constrained in that particular commitment. For simplicity we allow the use of rule numbers 1, 5, and 12 to show that the symbolic representation of those lexons is constrained and is visible as they are defined in the ontology base.

For methodological reasons of organization and management that ruses knowledge of these commitments, new applications must be able to easily commit to (selected contexts of) the ontology. We therefore group the rules into commitments, as illustrated in Table 2. Notice that any rule can be used within more than one commitment, but for simplicity we have not exploited this in this particular example.

Notice that we present the ORM rules in Table 2 by *verbalizing* them into fixed-syntax English sentences (i.e. generated from agreed templates parameterized over the ontology base content). We believe that this allows non-experts to (help to) check, validate or build the commitment rules and will simplify the commitment modeling process. For ORM, verbalizations may eventually be replaced by RIDL Constraint Language expressions ([35], [7]) or expressed in another formalism as ORM Markup Language [6].

Fig. 3 shows that the application "Conference A" using two commitments (V1, V2), while application "Conference B" uses commitments (V1, V3). This implies that each of the commitments (V1, V2) and (V1, V3) must be consistent, as will be discussed in section 4.

4 Establishing Ontological Consistency

What is consistent for one application may be inconsistent for another, this depends on the interpretation of reality, but of course applications that do not share a common consistent commitment cannot communicate or interoperate with each other in a meaningful way. By definition, the ontology base as a "substitute for a plausible real world" must *always* be assumed to be consistent, although multiple *seemingly* incompatible alternatives may simultaneously coexist in it (but not within the same context, though). It is quite literally "a matter of interpretation" which model an

Table 1. The Ontology Base

Ontology Base (Lexons)				
LNo	**Context**	**Term1**	**Role**	**Term2**
1	Organization	Person	IsMemberOf	Committee
2	Organization	Committee	Includes	Person
3	Organization	Person	Chairs	Committee
4	Organization	Committee	ChairedBy	Person
9	Organization	Reviewer	SubtypesOf	Person
10	Organization	Person	Types	Reviewer
11	Organization	Author	SubtypesOf	Person
12	Organization	Person	Types	Author
13	Organization	Reviewer	Reviews	Paper
14	Organization	Paper	ReviewedBy	Reviewer
15	Organization	Author	Writes	Paper
16	Organization	Paper	WrittenBy	Author
17	Organization	Author	Presents	Paper
18	Organization	Paper	PresentedBy	Author
19	Organization	Paper	Has	PaperTitle
20	Organization	PaperTitle	IsOf	Paper
21	Organization	Paper	Has	PaperNumber
22	Organization	PaperNumber	IsOf	Paper

application commits to. It is indeed the responsibility of this application's interpretation, *not* that of the ontology base, to maintain its own internal consistency. Note however that by working in this way we tend to maximize the independence between the ontology and the applications, which consequently increases the

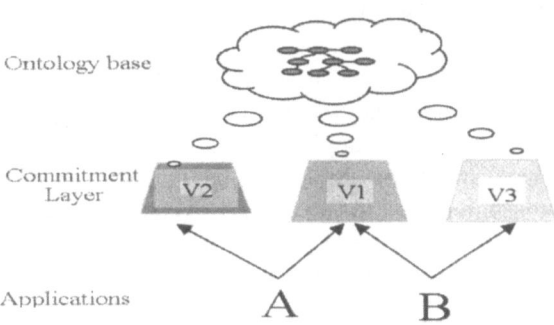

Fig. 3. Organization of the Interpretation Layer

Table 2. The Commitment Layer

RuleID	Rule Definition	CID
1	DOGMA. Visible Lexons to this commitment are {$$L21 .. $$L22}	V2
2	ORM.Mandatory(Each Paper Has at least one PaperNumber)	V2
3	ORM.InternalUniqueness(Each Paper Has at most one PaperNumber)	V2
4	ORM.InternalUniqueness(Each PaperNumber IsOf at most one Paper)	V2
5	DOGMA. Visible Lexons to this commitment are {$$L17 .. $$L20}	V3
6	ORM.Mandatory(Each Paper Has at least one PaperTitle)	V3
7	ORM.InternalUniqueness(Each Paper Has at most one PaperTitle)	V3
8	ORM.InternalUniqueness(Each PaperTitle IsOf at most one PaperTitle)	V3
9	ORM.ExternalUniqueness(Each (Author, PaperTitle) as a combination refers to at most one Paper)	V3
10	ORM.InternalUniqueness(It is disallowed that the same Author Presents the same paper more than once, and it is disallowed that the same Paper PresentedBy the same Author more than once)	V3
11	ORM.SubSet(Each Author who Presents a Paper must also Writes that Paper)	V3
12	DOGMA. Visible Lexons to this commitment are {$$L1 .. $$L16}	V1
16	ORM.InternalUniqueness(Each Person Chairs at most one Committee)	V1
17	ORM.Mandatory(Each Committee Includes at least one Person)	V1
18	ORM.InternalUniqueness(Each Committee Includes at most one Person)	V1
19	ORM.InternalUniqueness(Each Committee ChairedBy at most one Person)	V1
20	ORM.Mandatory(Each Committee ChairedBy at least one Person)	V1
21	ORM.Exclusion (Each paper which is WrittenBy a Person must not ReviewedBy with that Person)	V1
22	ORM.SubSet(Each Person who chairs a Committee must also IsMemberOf that Committee)	V1
24	ORM.Mandatory(Each Reviewer Reviews at least one Paper)	V1
25	ORM.InternalUniqueness(It is disallowed that the same Reviewer Reviews the same paper more than once, and it is disallowed that the same Paper ReviewedBy the same Reviewer more than once)	V1
26	ORM.Mandatory(Each Author Writes at least one Paper)	V1
27	ORM.Mandatory(Each Paper WrittenBy at least one Author)	V1
28	ORM.InternalUniqueness(It is disallowed that the same Author Writes the same paper more than once, and it is disallowed that the same Paper WrittenBy the same Author more than once)	V1

reusability of the knowledge involved. Applications can safely interoperate among each other and exchange data and transactions where they share "the same" ontological commitments [34]. For example, the two Scientific Conference applications A and B in Example 1 can interoperate over the commitment V1, the intersection of (V1, V2) and (V1, V3).

A note on Ontology Versioning. Ontologies are not static; at least while they are being engineered they grow (and are modified) over time or domain. Therefore versioning mechanisms normally adopted to deal with changes may cause consistency problems for the applications that commit to the ontology, as noted already in [19]. Adopting our approach, the need for an ontology versioning mechanism is simplified: (a) lexons can be added to the ontology base without any effect to the ontological commitments; and (b) lexons cannot be deleted or modified if they are in use (see rules 1, 5 and 12 in Table2). Adding or modifying rules in the ontological commitments also becomes easier to manage for a versioning mechanism, as the number of applications committing to a given ontological commitment in general is less than those committing to the whole ontology, therefore reducing the impact of changes to be controlled.

In the DOGMA architecture (see the note on semantics in Section 2.2) each ontological commitment necessarily must be a consistent theory, as it is a possible interpretation of a domain, i.e. forms a set of rules that constrain, interpret, or rather commit to a particular aspect of reality as specified in a conceptualization. On the other hand, it is allowed in our approach that an application can commit to more than one commitment, therefore we must require that a set of ontological commitments that are used by one application must be consistent with each other. The meaning in such case is that all commitments together form one *complete* interpretation [11] for such applications.

The complexity of establishing consistency strongly depends on the language that is used to explicitly express the commitments. Adopting a given well-defined set of rule types, i.e. adopting a particular description logic, helps analyzing the consistency and evaluating the ontology. To give two examples, a formal toolkit for ontological analysis is introduced in [16] to help check the ontological consistency of taxonomies, and in [7] RIDL-A was defined as consistency analyzer for the well-circumscribed NIAM/ORM rules system [17], easily mapable to a subset of first order logic.

Nothing in the definition prevents different ontological commitments even on the same ontology base to be expressed in a mix of languages (e.g. in different rule systems). Of course this implies that a consistency analyzer must be able to map between them.

5 Implementation and Tools: the DOGMAModeler for Ontology Engineering

This section briefly outlines the tools and projects that are implemented and based on the approach described in this paper.

The kernel of the system is formed by the *DOGMA Server* which stores and serves up the ontology base and the commitment layer. The most recent active version of the prototype implementation design for both commitment layer and ontology base may be downloaded[5]. The main components in the prototype implementation design are the storage module and the API. Storage is in a vanilla database system, currently Microsoft SQL Server that just implements efficient serving of the ontology base and interpretations. The API (JAVA JDK 1.3) provides a unified access to the basic functionality of the ontology server, and is designed to be accessible from any high level programming language.

DOGMAModeler is a suite of ontology engineering tools, including ontology browser, editor, manager, and mining tools. It supports functionality for modeling both ontology base and commitments. It supports derivative of ORM as graphical notation, and its cross-bonding ORM-ML [6] that is easy to exchange, as well as the verbalizations of ontological commitments into pseudo natural language[6].

---

[5] http://www.starlab.vub.ac.be/research/dogma/OntologyServer.htm
[6] http://www.starlab.vub.ac.be/research/dogma/dogmamodeler/

Some of the principles underlying the DOGMA approach are and were illustrated (not to say refined or even developed as desirable side effects) in a number of projects such as HyperMuseum (EU Telematics-3088), where simplified ontologies in a digital-library-type query application were deployed, using an earlier version of the DOGMA ontology server to develop WordNet-based ontological support [33]. In NAMIC (IST-1999-12392) it is intended to assist news agencies and journalists in authoring news items. The DOGMA ontology base model is used for storage of the ontology, which is then provided as a service to a query module. A commitment layer built on top of this ontology base as a JAVA API provides support for NAMIC-specific features such as profiles [5]. These profiles are in fact defined as query specifications on the ontology; for instance, the user profile of sports journalists would be based around a commitment that contains sports-related lexons in the ontology. Annotation of the incoming news stream could then be used to match the news content with the different users' preferences or views[7].

OntoWeb is an EU thematic network (IST-2000-29243) for the support of semantic web and related research. A DOGMA-based ontology (among others) and its ontology-based query system are being developed as part of the server infrastructure underlying the semantically annotated web portal and websites of the network[8]. In *OntoBasis*, a Flemish government-funded long-term project, we explore the development and use of "practical" ontologies stored in the DOGMA Server for the knowledge management and advanced applications in a variety of business environments, as part of the future semantic Web[9].

6 Conclusion

In this paper we have presented a architecture for ontologies that includes an ontology base and a commitment layer to mediate between the ontology base and applications. The ontology base is intended to be a computer-rendering of sets of simple, easy to agree on facts about possible "domains", to be accessed though an application's language. We have tried to analyse the dependency between the applications and the ontology, inspired by related research in database semantics, and discussed the benefits that could be achieved. The DOGMA project aims at implementing a proof of concept for this approach, in order to simplify building, deployment and (re)use of ontologies for semantics in a multi- domain environment.

Acknowledgements. The authors are grateful to the other members of the STARLab team, for stimulating discussions and criticism. Partial support for the reported work from t EC FP5 IST project NAMIC (IST-1999-12392) and the EC FP5 Thematic Network OntoWeb (IST-2000-29243) is hereby also gratefully acknowledged.

---

[7] www.hltcentral.org/projects/namic

[8] http://www.ontoweb.org

[9] http://www.starlab.vub.ac.be/research/ontobasis

References

1. Bechhofer S., Horrocks I., Patel-Schneider P.F., Tessaris S.: A Proposal for a Description Logic Interface. In: Lambrix, P.: Proceedings of the International Workshop on Description Logics, et al (eds.) (1999) 33-36
2. Bench-Capon T.J.M., Malcolm G.: Formalizing Ontologies and Their Relations. In: Proceedings of DEXA'99 (1999) 250-259
3. Chandrasekaran B., and Johnson T.R.: Generic Tasks and Task Structures: History, Critique and New Directions. In David J.M., Krivine J.P., and Simmons R. (Eds.): Second Generation Expert Systems, Springer-Verlag, London (1993) 233-272
4. Clancey W.J.: Model construction operators. *Artificial Intelligence* 53(1) (1992) 1-115
5. De Bo J., Jarrar M., Majer Ben., Meersman R.: Ontology-based author profiling of documents. In: Towards Improved Evaluation Measures for Parsing Systems Workshop, Third International Conference on Language Resources and valuation, (2002)
6. Demey, J., Jarrar, M. & Meersman, R.: A Conceptual Markup Language that supports interoperability between Business Rule modeling systems, Proceedings of the Tenth International Conference on Cooperative Information Systems (CoopIS 2002).
7. De Troyer, O.M.F., Meersman, R., Verlinden, P.: RIDL* on the CRIS Case: A Workbench for NIAM. In: Olle T.W., Verrijn-Stuart A.A., Bhabuta L.(eds.): Computerized Assistance during the Information Systems Life Cycle, North-Holland/IFIP Amsterdam (1988) 375—459
8. Daelemans W., Buchholz S., Veenstra J.: Memory-based shallow parsing. In: Proceedings of CoNLL-99, Bergen (1999)
9. Fensel, D.: Ontologies: Silver Bullet for Knowledge Management and Electronic Commerce, Springer Verlag (2001)
10. Fensel D., Horrocks I., van Harmelen F. et al.: OIL in a Nutshell. In: Proceedings of EKAW 2000, Springer-Verlag (2000)
11. Gruber T.R.: Toward principles for the design of ontologies used for knowledge sharing, International Journal of Human-Computer Studies, 43(5/6) (1995)
12. Guarino, N. and Giaretta, P.: Ontologies and Knowledge Bases: Towards a Terminological Clarification. In: Mars, N. (ed.): Towards Very Large Knowledge Bases: Knowledge Building and Knowledge Sharing, IOS Press, Amsterdam (1995) 25-32
13. Gomez-Perez, A., Benjamins, R.: Overview of Knowledge Sharing and Reuse Components: Ontologies and Problem-Solving Methods. In: Proceedings of the IJCAI-99 Workshop on Ontologies and Problem-Solving Methods (KRR5), Morgan-Kaufmann (1999)
14. Gangemi A., Pisanelli D., Steve G.: Ontology Integration: Experiences with Medical Terminologies. In: Guarino, N.: Formal Ontology in Information Systems, (ed.), IOS Press (1998)
15. Genesereth, M.R., Nilsson, N.J.: Logical Foundation of Artificial Intelligence. Morgan Kaufmann, Los Altos, California (1987)
16. Guarino, N., Welty, C.: Identity, Unity, and Individuality: Towards a Formal Toolkit for Ontological Analysis. In: Werner, H. (ed.): Proceedings of ECAI-2000, IOS Press, Berlin (2000) 219-223
17. Halpin, T.: Information Modelling and Relational Databases. 3rd edn. Morgan-Kaufmann (2001)
18. Iwasaki I., Farquhar A., Fikes, R., Rice, J.: A Web-Based Compositional Modeling System for Sharing of Physical Knowledge. In: Proceedings of IJCAI'97 Conference, Morgan-Kaufmann (1997) 494-500
19. Klein, M., Fensel, D.: Ontology Versioning on the Semantic Web. In: First International Semantic Web Working Symposium (SWWS-1) (2001)

20. Meersman, R.A.: Some Methodology and Representation Problems for the Semantics of Prosaic Application Domains. In: Ras, Z.W., Zemankova, M. (eds.): Methodologies for Intelligent Systems (ISMIS-94), Springer LNAI, Heidelberg (1994)
21. Meersman, R.: Semantic Ontology Tools in Information Systems Design. In: Ras, Z., Zemankova, M. (eds.): Proceedings of the ISMIS'99 Conference. LNCS, Springer Verlag, (1999)
22. McMacrthy, J. "Notes on Formalizing Context". In: Proceedings of IJCAI'93, Morgan-Kaufmann, (1993).
23. Motta, E., Fensel, D., Gaspari, M. and Benjamins, R.,: Specifications of Knowledge Components for Reuse. In: Proceedings of the 11th International Conference on Software Engineering and Knowledge Engineering. KSI Press, Kaiserslautern Germany (1999) 36-43
24. Da Nobrega G.M., Castro E., Malbos P., Sallantin J., Cerri S.A.: A framework for supervised conceptualizing. In: ECAI'00. (2000) 17.1-17.4
25. http://www.ontoweb.org
26. Patil R.S., Fikes R.E., Patel-Schneider P.F., McKay D., Finin T., Gruber T., Neches R.: The DARPA Knowledge Sharing Effort: Progress Report. In: Proc. of Knowledge Representation and Reasoning (1992) 777-788
27. Richards. D.: The Reuse of Knowledge: A User-Centered Approach, *International Journal of Human Computer Studies* (2000)
28. Reiter, R.: Towards a Logical Reconstruction of Relational Database Theory. In: Mylopoulos, J., Brodie, M.L. (eds.): Readings in AI and Databases. Morgan Kaufman (1988)
29. Sowa, J.F.: Ontology, metadata, and semiotics. In: Ganter, B., Mineau, G.W., (eds): Conceptual structures: logical, linguistic and computational issues: 8th international conference on conceptual structures. ICCS 2000, Darmstadt Germany, August 2000 (Lecture Notes in Artificial Intelligence, 1867), Springer-Verlag Berlin (2000) 55-81
30. Steels, L.: The componential framework and its role in reusability. In: David, J.-M., Krivine, J.-P., Simmons,R. (eds.): Second Generation Expert Systems. Springer-Verlag Berlin (1993) 273-298
31. Steve G., Gangemi A., Pisanelli D.M.: Integrating Medical Terminologies with the ONIONS Methodology. In: Kangassalo H., Charrel J.P. (eds.): Information Modelling and Knowledge Bases VIII. IOS Press Amsterdam (1998)
32. Swartout, W.R., Moore, J.D.: Explanation in Second Generation Expert Systems. In:David, J.-M., Krivine, J.-P., Simmons, R. (eds): Second Generation Expert Systems. Springer-Verlag Berlin (1993)
33. Stuer, P., Meersman, R., De Bruyne, S.: The HyperMuseum Theme Generator System: Ontology-based Internet support for the active use of digital museum data for teaching and presentation. In Bearman, D. & Trant, J. (eds.): Museums and the Web 2001. Selected Papers, Archives & Museum Informatics, pp.127-137, (2001)
34. Uschold, M. and Gruninger, M.: Ontologies: principles, methods and applications, The Knowledge Engineering Review, vol. 11, no. 2, June (1996).
35. Verheyen, G., van Bekkum, P.: NIAM, An Information Analysis Method. In: Olle, T.W., Sol, H., Verrijn-Stuart,A. (eds.): IFIP Conference on Comparative Review of Information Systems Methodologies. North-Holland (1982).

A Dynamic Model for Mapping XML Elements in a Object-Oriented Fashion

Francesco Garelli and Carlo Ferrari

Department of Information Engineering
University of Padua
via Gradenigo 6/a
garelli@dei.unipd.it, carlo@dei.unipd.it

Abstract. XML is becoming a wide used standard both for data management and application interoperability in web services. This fact promotes further analyses and the development of new methods for creating, modifying and retrieving all the information that is encoded in a XML fashion. This paper presents a XML data binding technique that aims to unify, in a single solution, the benefits from design-time and run-time data binding. In order to reach this goal, we introduce an abstract representation for XML elements. This representation shows to be very effective and makes easy a simple data binding with XML documents. The effectiveness of the model has been analyzed by developing a library for XML management, in the Python language.

Keywords: Data binding, Python, Web Services, XML

1 Introduction

XML is usually considered a well-suited mark-up language for data storage and communication because of its simplicity and its flexibility. Anyway, its diffusion is not related to its inner features, but it depends on an evident fact: XML is being proposed as universal standard for managing and distributing data. When a technology is able to broaden out as a standard, it has a value added apart from its real characteristics. This is because it has a wide support from software companies, because it can be easily reused, and because it guarantees a good interoperability with legacy and future applications.

Hence XML is becoming the authoritative solution for any information management problem, even thought a different or proprietary format could fit better or could be applied more quickly. Very often new applications adopt XML as format for configuration files, even thought a simpler format could be expressive and concise enough. An other important example deals with middleware for distributed application: XML-based protocols (e.g. SOAP) are serious competitors of traditional solutions, such as CORBA and DCOM, at least over the Internet, because of their wide acceptance in the computer science community.

R. Meersman, Z. Tari (Eds.): CoopIS/DOA/ODBASE 2002, LNCS 2519, pp. 1255–1272, 2002.
© Springer-Verlag Berlin Heidelberg 2002

Hence in the next future, XML will be probably used in many different environments and both the developers and the researchers will have to cope with some language limitations. Actually some of the more appreciated XML properties, are its human readability and its descriptive nature. In fact the content and the meaning of a document are usually comprehensible not only for very skilled people but also for less expert ones. Unluckily, when XML must be managed in a traditional programming environment, these properties show to be really unhandy. Usual programming environments are conceived on imperative and procedural languages that fit quite badly with descriptive and typeless data, like XML documents. Moreover in traditional programming languages there is not a data structure that resembles a XML element. Even though an XML element is an object that can contain items of different types (strings, other elements with different tags) and that could be described by a C struct or an equivalent construct, the number of contained items is not fixed, and this feature is a list property. Hence an XML element looks similar to an array of heterogeneous types. But again this model is not enough, because a XML element can have also attributes and it can appears as a class instance in a object oriented language. Finally a XML element is a strange hybrid between a struct, an array and an object. Moreover XML documents have often a large and deep structure that applications must split in small parts so that the information can be dealt with. As consequence, there is not a single solution for XML data treatment but many technologies are available according to the problem that must be faced; we refer to these technologies as to the XML data binding methods.

This paper introduces a model and a related technology for XML management, that aims to offer a simple and rationale approach. Our model takes many features from existing solutions and tries to unify them in a coherent architecture inside a powerful and dynamic language, such as Python [21][22]. The next section presents a brief description of existing solutions. The next paragraph describes a composite data type for representing structured information, and it suggests a related data binding with XML. The remaining of the paper introduces a Python library to manage XML data in an easy and effective fashion.

1.1 XML Data Binding to Date

In this paper, XML data binding concerns with all models that figure any aspect of XML in traditional programming languages constructs. To date, these models can be categorized in two groups, the former includes all those that deal with data binding during the application development, the latter includes the others that solve the data binding at run-time.

All the approaches that need some information about the XML structure, such as the tags and the attributes of the documents they have to manage, belong to the former category; this information is usually named a XML schema [16]. The most used format for describing schemas is the XML schema language [11], although many other solutions have been proposed [12]. An appropriate compiler can analyze the schema and produce a library for an object oriented language, such as Java, C++, C# or Visual Basic (figure 1).

The developer uses the functions and the objects that the library supplies, to read, modify and write XML documents. As the library is customized to a particular XML dialect, the developer can benefit from an appropriate and natural API when accessing a document. Moreover if the schema provides enough information, the developer can verify that the document complies with the schema rules (validation).

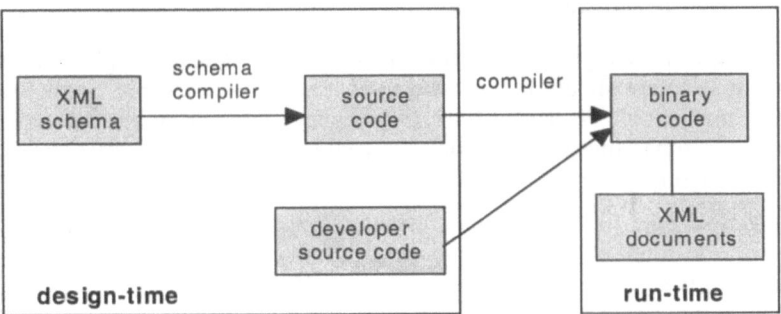

Fig. 1. Design-time XML data binding

Many technologies for design-time binding are under development. The most notable ones are the Java Architecture for XML Binding (JAXB) [13][14][18], and the Microsoft XSD Compiler [19][20]. Anyway there are many other available solutions, both from industry and academic environments [9]. Unluckily all can process documents only when a schema has been analyzed during the development process. The main limitation in design-time binding is that it is not applicable when a schema is not available or it is available just at run-time.

In this case, the only suitable alternative is a model where all knowledge about XML is not encoded in a class or a type, but it is loaded at run-time in the application variables. In fact a XML document has some items that describe the document structure, such as tags or attributes names, and some items that describes the effective information, such as elements content, attributes values, and elements position. In the design-time binding, the former items are encoded in a new type and the latter ones are stored in variables. Instead in the run-time binding, all items must be stored in variables. As consequence the developer must deal with both the structure and the information; obviously, as soon as documents are large or complex, this XML managing interface becomes unhandy and slow. Anyway run-time data binding has been the first available method for managing XML, and it is surely the most used one. The two most notable approaches are the SAX and DOM interfaces. SAX[3] is a callback based API. A SAX library parses a XML document at run-time and it generates different callbacks in correspondence of elements and simple text. Unluckily the callbacks are not related to elements tag.

Instead DOM [5] is an API for a tree based representation. A DOM library generates a tree structure starting from the XML document. As DOM aims to be platform and language independent, it provides a complex API, which doesn't use the environment peculiarities. An API similar to DOM, that takes advantage of the Java environment, is JDOM [4]. In fact JDOM is simpler than the standard Java implementation for DOM, but it is not as natural as JAXB, the Java solution for design-time binding.

To sum up, current solutions for XML data binding are either design-time or run-time. The former ones provide an easy and effective API for managing supported documents, while the latter ones are applicable to any document.

This paper presents a XML data binding technique that aims to unify, in a single solution, the benefits from the two different approaches. This unified approach requires some properties that are often available in weak-typed object-oriented languages. In particular two issues are critical:

- *the language must support reflection.* In order to assure a simple interface, the document structure should be encoded in abstract data types, but, as this structure could be unavailable at design-time, the language must allow the creation of new types at run-time. Indeed this property is common also in modern strong-typed object oriented languages.

- *full dynamic binding.* Pure object oriented languages, such as Smalltalk, select attributes and methods according to string identifiers only at run-time: when an attribute has been used or a method has to be called, the related object virtual table is browsed looking for the related identifier. As a result, the developer can code a correct program with references to attributes and methods that are not available at design-time. Other object oriented languages, such as C++ or Java, support a partial dynamic binding for methods: that is, at compile-time they translate each method identifier to an index, and at run-time they bind this index to the method code. This approach guarantees good performances, but all methods and attributes have to be declared before compilation because of the mapping between string identifiers and numbers. Unluckily when schema is not available at design-time, this condition is false.

These properties are usually provided by object oriented environments with weak-typing. In particular for the technique we study, we take advantage of the Python [21][22] programming language and its run-time environment. Python looks an appropriate choice because it is very simple, it has a rich native library, it is widely used, and it support both reflection and full dynamic binding.

To sum up, our goal is to explore powerful and easy methods for XML managing, in particular in the Python environment. Actually some solutions have been already developed. In particular the library *xml_objectify* [17] is an interesting approach for mapping XML documents to Python objects at run-time.

Thanks to the environment features, the run-time binding is natural as if it were realized at design-time: both XML elements and attributes are mapped to objects attributes. In particular a XML attribute for a particular tag is represented as a string, while XML elements are represented as items in a list; there is a different list for each different tag, and the list identifier is the same as the tag. In python, objects attributes are accessible with the usual operator '.' and lists items with the selector '[]'.

Figure 2 shows a very simple XML document that describes a zoo, and some Python code that manages the object-oriented representation.

```
<zoo>

  <tiger name="leo">

    <diet>beefsteak</diet>

    <diet>chicken</diet>

  </tiger>

  . . .
```

```
1: from xml_objectify import *

2: d = XML_Objectify('z.xml')

3: obj = d.make_instance()

4: first_tiger = obj.tiger[0]

5: tname = first_tiger.name
```

Fig. 2. xml_objectify data binding

The library *xml_objectify* offers an interesting approach to XML data binding, but it suffers from some important limitations. The first one deals with a still immature implementation; in fact the tool that binds XML to python objects, is able neither to handle XML namespaces, nor to create new documents, nor to save a modified document. There are other limitations that depend on the binding model, and that can't be faced by a different implementation.

In fact, as both XML elements and attributes are bound to the same python construct (the object attribute), there is an identifier overlap when an element owns a XML attribute and a XML sub-element with the same identifier. In this case *xml_objectify* can't distinguish between them. The choice of mapping elements to object attributes implies an other problem. In fact, as there is not any order between the attribute of a object, any order relationship between XML elements is lost during the mapping to the object-oriented representation. This is not a problem when elements order is meaningless, but it makes the binding not applicable otherwise.

To overcome these limitations, the next paragraph introduces a different binding model.

2 The Binding Model

In the introduction, we noted that no usual programming language construct (and hence python constructs), is able to represent a XML element by oneself. That is because a XML element behaves as a hybrid between an array, a list and an object. Starting from this idea, we can introduce a new data type that has all the required properties. Such a data type is a composite data structure that unifies the list properties and the object properties; we call it a *xlist* or *eXtended list*.

A xlist has both the operations related to a list and the capability of getting and setting attributes. In this paper, we talk of *xlist attributes* when we are referring to the object interface, and we talk of *xlist items* when we are referring to the list interface.

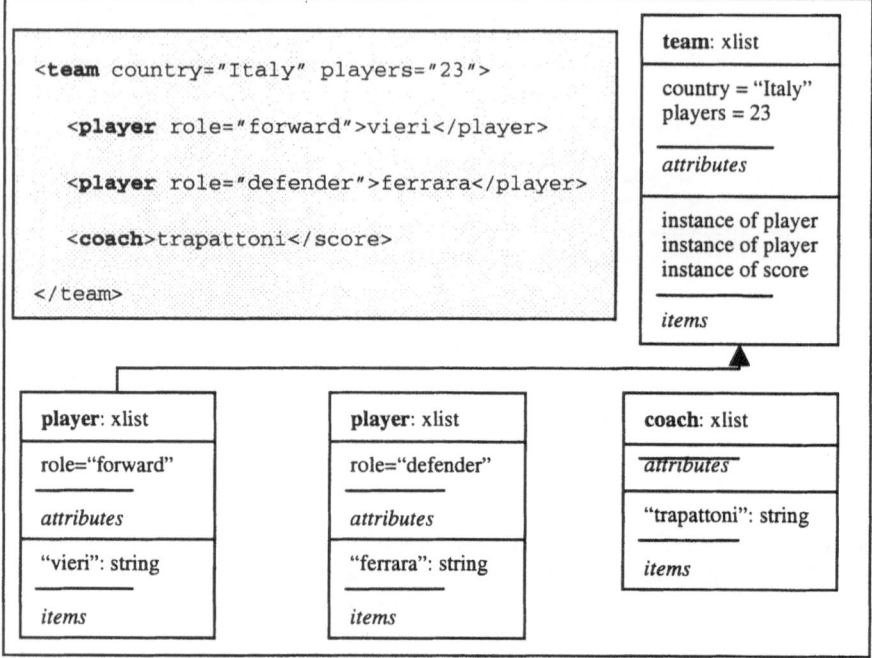

Fig. 3. xlists that describe the Italian soccer team

A *xlist* offers the following operations:

- append(item): add a new item to a xlist. The item can be both an other xlist or a simple type (e.g. a string, a number,...)
- remove(item): remove an item from the xlist
- view(criteria): return a subview according to some criteria (template match, sorting...). Any change to the subview modifies also the xlist.
- typeCheck(value): enable or disable the type check feature
- iter(): return an iterator that provides a sequential access to the items.
- operator '.': set or get a xlist attribute

Figure 3 shows how xlists represent some information about a soccer team, the Italian national team. The team is described both by simple attributes, such as the team country and size, and complex attributes, such as the players and the coach. The first ones can be stored as xlist attributes because they are simple types. Indeed, the second ones have to be saved in other xlists. The players and the coach names could be represented either with an attribute or an item; in the example they are xlist items.

Besides operations, a xlist has five object fields that characterize its behavior. Most of these are shared between many xlists. The first two are:

- *tag*. It is an identifier that group all xlist describing the same object. For instance in the figure 3, all xlists that represent players has to share the value "player" in their attribute *tag*.
- *uri*. It is an identifier for all xlist that share the same space of concepts. For instance all the xlists that represent a soccer team objects (i.e. teams, players and coaches) belong to a single space.

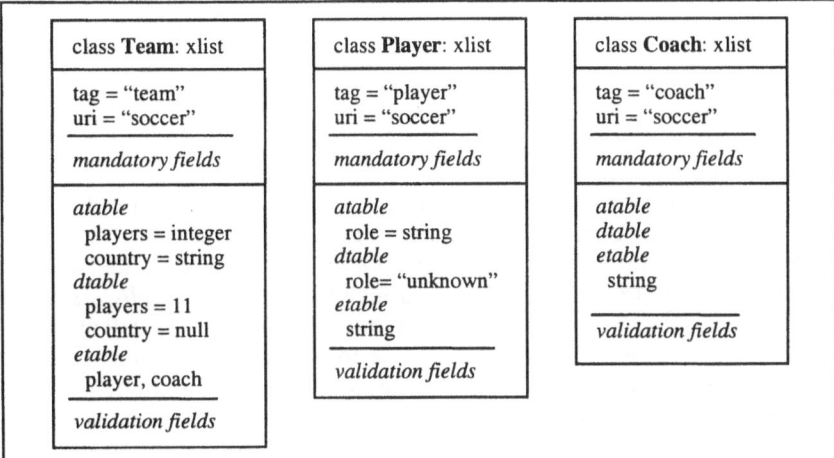

Fig. 4. xlists classes describe a soccer team

These fields are mandatory. The other three provide useful information about the valid values for attributes and items; hence they define a data validation infrastructure for the xlists content. As we assume to work in a weak-typed language, they are optional. They are:

- *atable*. It is map between each xlist attribute identifier (e.g. *country* or *players* in figure 4) and a type.
- *dtable*. It is map between each xlist attribute identifier and a default value.
- *etable*. It is a list of types

These fields constrain the content of a xlist both as regard the attributes and the items. In particular the field *atable* defines the correct type for each possible attribute. When data validation is on (it is handled through the xlist operation *typeCheck*), any attempt to assign an attribute with a wrong type should raise either a conversion or an exception. The field *dtable* defines the default value for each attribute, i.e. the value after the xlist creation. Finally the field *etable* lists all the types that can be possible items. Any attempt to insert an object with an unsupported type raises an exception. All fields, but *uri*, are shared by xlists that describe the same object. In the object oriented paradigm the set of all variables that deals with the same object is a class. This fact suggests an easy consideration: *tag, atable, dtable, etable* are class fields, that is they shared by all instances of a class. Indeed the field *tag* is a class identifier; hence it should be useless, because it is equivalent to the class name. Actually in most programming languages, a class name can't be any string identifier because some tokens are reserved. On the other hand we want to avoid any limitation, and, although the field *tag* is usually a class name, it could be any word.

The fields *uri* has not a class scope, but it deals with a set of correlated classes. Hence it is very similar to the package construct, but for the same argument of *tag,* it is a required field.

To sum up, in a object oriented environment, xlists are objects that exhibit a list interface and that belong to many different classes. All xlists, that represent the same entity, share some fields and belong to the same class.

Figure 4 shows the fields for the xlists that describe a soccer team. The team is defined by three entities, the team, the players and the coach. As a result, for each entity there is a different class with xlist properties defined by different fields. For instance, as regard a player, the related xlist is a class *player* with an homonymous field *tag*. The team is described by the belonging country, the cardinality, the players and the coach. The variable *country* is a string and the variable *players* is an integer; as they are both simple type instances, they can be xlist attributes. Instead both the players and the coach are complex entities, and they must be items.

The validation fields provide a strong-type facility. In figure 4, the class *team* constrain the attribute *players* and *country* through the field *atable*: *players* has to be an integer while *country* is a string. The field *dtable* set instead the default value for the two attributes; as there is not a default value for the attribute *country*, the neutral value null is used. Finally the class *team* constrains also the possible items; the field *etable* imposes that any item must be either a player instance or a coach instance.

This paragraph present xlists like a concrete model for representing complex elements that behave both as lists and as objects. The next section aims to represent XML documents through this model.

In order to reach this result, we need a binding between XML content and xlists: we are going to prove that this binding exists and that there is reversible mapping between an XML element and an xlist.

2.1 XML Data Binding

In order to produce a comprehensive XML data binding, there must be an appropriate relation between each concept that defines a XML element, and a corresponding xlist concept. An XML element is an entity that is defined by few items:
1. a tag
2. some attributes and their values
3. some children, either other elements or strings
4. a namespace, specified as a URI

Figure 5 shows a simple XML fragment that describes a very simple address-book entry; it provides information about a person name and his phone numbers.

The first binding we face, deals with the XML tags in the document. A tag function is to identify the element attributes and their values range; in the example, the tag *person* implies the two attributes *firstname* and *surname* and the element *phone*. The tag doesn't constrain the attributes values, because it is a property shared by many elements. In particular it is a property shared by all elements that describe the same entity, such as a person.

In the previous paragraph we have seen that, in a similar fashion, xlists with the same field *tag* represent the same entity. Hence there is a natural binding between a XML tag and the field *tag* in a class that implements the xlist interface, because they both deal with a real object. Moreover this binding suggests a further correspondence: like a XML tag accords with the field *tag*, a XML element accords with a xlist.

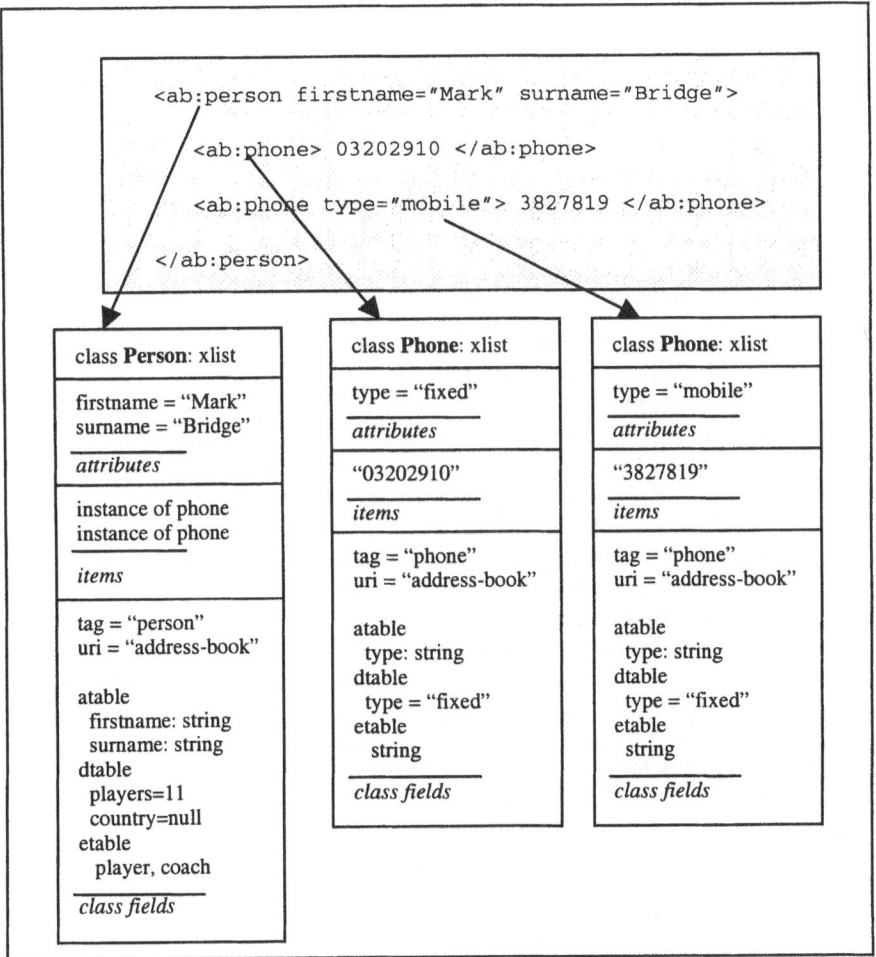

Fig. 5. XML data binding with xlists

In the figure 5 the three XML elements map three different xlists. The outer element in the fragment, i.e. ab:person, is bound to an xlist that has "person" as field *tag*. Similarly the two XML elements with tag *phone*, correspond to two different xlist belonging to the class *Phone* and with field *tag* "phone". Moreover the class can have also some information about the valid content for an element with a particular tag. In fact, the fields *atable*, *dtable* and *etable*, constrain the xlist attributes and items, like a XML schema constrains the attributes names, the attributes types and the valid content for each different tag. Actually a XML schema often provides also some other information (e.g. the order between the element sub items) that our model doesn't take into account.

This restriction is a good thing in order to make the model as simple as possible, and anyway it doesn't limit the documents that can be represented, but just the XML validation process.

In XML, the element attributes are a set of unordered identifiers with a related value. Hence a XML can be easily mapped to a xlist attribute, with the same identifier and value. Anyway, in order to guarantee a correct binding with XML, we need a comprehensive binding between the types specified in the attribute tables and the XML datatypes [10]. These types are specific to the language where the xlist model is implemented. Quite all programming languages provides a type system not as complete as the XML one. In the next paragraph we present a possible binding for the Python environment. With regards to the XML content, a XML document allows to nest elements inside other elements. Also it lets you to insert sequences of characters between the elements. These sub items show two relevant properties:

1. Their cardinality is (usually) variable
2. Their order is (sometimes) meaningful

The xlist attributes are entities that don't exhibit these properties, because they are atomic and fix; also their order is not relevant. Instead xlist items have not a fixed cardinality and they provide a order relationship according to the xlist iterator. Hence they are appropriate entities for representing the XML element children. For example, in figure 5, the element *person* contains two XML elements with tag *phone*. The corresponding xlist with tag person, has two items that are xlists with tag *phone*.

On the other hand, the content of an XML element can be also any XML datatype; the related xlist has items whose type is in accordance with the XML datatype. In the example a phone number is the content of a XML element with tag *phone*. The related xlist has a single item that is a string.

The last member that defines a XML element is its namespace. A namespace groups all the elements that share the same context. For example all elements that define XHTML items belong to the same namespace. As it can be considered a collection of tags, the natural binding for a namespace is a collection of classes, that is all classes constraining the xlist data type and with the field *uri*.

As there is an appropriate binding for each entity that defines a XML element, the XML data binding is complete. Moreover it is also reversible, because any object oriented representation of a XML document contains all the information required to rebuild the original document.

3 Implementation

The presented model has been used to project and develop a library for the Python language, called *Satine*. Satine extends the Python language, adding a new type *xlist* with the operators and properties defined in the proposed model. The library is based on different modules that provide many features, but actually the basic one is *satine.kernel*. This module is the data binding engine; it provides the type xlist and few methods for managing it or the classes derived from it. The module is particular also because it is not written in Python, but in C. This choice was mandatory both for assuring good performances and for some Python limits. In fact, although Python is very flexible, it does not allow developing a new type that complies all the xlist properties we need. In particular Python does not permit defining a method and an attribute with the same identifier, while a XML attribute name can be any string and hence it can be an existing method identifier too. Moreover Python does not permit to define as attribute identifier, something different from a string. Instead when a XML attribute has a namespace different from its owner element, its identifier is a couple of strings. These issues can be faced just defining a new native type by an extension of the Python language.

An other important module is *satine.dt*. It defines many new classes that extend the Python native types in order to support a correct binding with the XML datatypes. They provide interesting features, such as range constraints for numeric types and enumerations for string types. As these classes are derived from Python native types, they can be used in legacy environments in place of native ones.

Following there are many examples that explain better our implementation. All examples are coded in the Python programming language because, at the moment, Python is the only environment we use for the current experimentation. Indeed, quite all arguments apply as well to any other object-oriented language with weak typing.

The upper panel in figure 6 shows how to code the classes *Team* and *Player*, introduced in the figure 4. Line 1 declares the class *Team* by extending the class *satine.kernel.xlist*. The lines from 2 to 6 initialize the class fields. Line 2 set the tag value; usually this identifier is the same as the class name. Line 3 assignes the field *uri*, the same for the other two classes too. Line 4 joins each attribute to a class from the module *satine.dt*: in particular country is declared to be a *dt.string* and players a *dt.integer*. Line 5 defines the default values for the attributes when a new instance is created. Finally, line 6 defines what types are allowed to be items; in this case the classes Player and Coach, both derived from *satine.kernel.xlist*. Anyway an item can be also any class from the module *satine.dt*. For instance the class *Player* declare its item to be an instance of *dt.string* (line 12).

The lower panel in figure 6 shows the use of classes *Team*, *Player* and *Coach*. The code defines the Italian soccer team according to the information in figure 3. Line 1 creates a new instance of *Team*. As the constructor has no parameters, the object is initialized with default values: hence, *country* is None and *players* is 11. Lines 2 and 3 overwrite the default values with respectively the string "italy" and the integer 23.

Line 4 appends an item to the list; this item is an instance of *Player*. The line shows also how to initialize a xlist with constructor parameters. In Python any constructor accepts both named and unnamed parameters. The *satine.kernel.xlist* constructor consider all the unnamed parameters as items and the named ones as attributes. As a result the line 4 creates a new object of class *Player*, it sets the attribute *role* to "forward" and it appends the string "vieri" to the object.

Lines 5 and 6 behave in a similar fashion: the former appends an other instance of *Player* with different data, the latter appends an instance of *Coach*.

Once a xlist contains the information, the iterator allows to visit its items. In the example (lines from 7 to 9), the variable *i* iterates over *team* in order to print all players names. In particular line 8 prints the name only if the item has a field *tag* equal to "player"[1]. Evidently the iterator deals with items only, and it doesn't browse through the attributes.

---

[1] The function *satine.kernel.tag* returns the tag of its argument. It returns None if the argument is not an xlist

```
1:   class Team(xlist):

2:    tag = "team"

3:    uri = "http://localhost/ns/soccer"

4:    atable = {country: dt.string, players: dt.integer}

5:    dtable = {country: None, players: 11}

6:    etable = [Player, Coach]

7:   class Player(xlist):

8:    tag = "player"

9:    uri = "http://localhost/ns/soccer"

10:   atable = {role: dt.string }

11:   dtable = {role: None}

12:   etable = [dt.string]
```

```
1: team = Team()

2: team.country = "italy"

3: team.players = 23

4: team.append(Player("vieri", role="forward"))

5: team.append(Player("ferrara", role="defender"))

6: team.append(Coach("trapattoni"))

7: for i in team:

8:    if kernel.tag(i) == "player":

9:           print 'player name', i[0]
```

Fig. 6. Python code that describes the Italian soccer team

```
<ab:person firstname="Mark" surname="Bridge">

  <ab:phone> 03202910 </ab:phone>

  <ab:phone type="mobile"> 3827819 </ab:phone>

</ab:person>
```

```
1: [Person(firstname="Mark",surname="Bridge"),

2: Phone(),

3: 03203910,

4: None,

5: Phone(type="mobile"),

6: 3827819,

7: None,

8: None]
```

Fig. 7. XML binding for a data source

3.1 Streams

In the previous sections we talked about XML without any reference to the technology for its storage. On the other hand, documents storage is an important issue because of the increasing use of XML as a data management format. At the moment the documents are quite always stored in a traditional text file, although other supports are possible, such as binary files or relational databases.
Despite the different possible sources for XML structured information, a single abstract interface to access to any data source would be a simple and effective solution. This interface should be independent of the technical details that distinguish, for example, a text file from a relational database.

In general, when XML data binding is available, the most natural and simple interface is a function that loads the XML from a data source and returns an object representing it. That is a single function that acts as a filter. For this reason, many XML data binding tools, such as *xml_objectify*, adopt this solution. Unluckily in many cases it shows to be very inefficient.

In fact, until the data size is small, a complete data binding is very handy, but when the XML documents are large enough (few Megabytes are usually sufficient), this approach can be prohibitive both for the large memory required and for the time spent in converting XML to objects. Actually this problem was present also in the DOM API: often SAX is preferred to DOM just because of the documents size. Anyway our intention is not to relay on SAX; we would like an abstract model, more powerful than SAX and more flexible then a single data binding function. After some attempts, we realized that a very good model was a *xlist*. Although it looks curious, an xlist is not only an appropriate abstraction for a XML element but also it is a perfect model for a data source. In order to prove this statement, it is better to analyze the typical XML data source, a text file. A XML document is just a sequence of three different kinds of items, XML start tags, characters sequences, XML end tags. A xlist can contain all these items, if a suitable binding for them is available. Indeed the binding required exists and it is a simple variation of XML data binding we described in the previous paagraph. In fact XML start tags are just XML elements without nested items; hence we can bind a start tag to an empty xlist. Characters sequences can be mapped to simple Python strings as usual. Finally a binding for end tags is still required. Evidently, in order to avoid any overlapping, the Python construct for the binding can be neither a xlist nor a string; indeed a good construct is the Python object None, the Python construct for representing a NULL reference. The object None does not allow storing either the tag or its namespace, but this information is not required because it can be retrieved from the previous items in the xlist. In fact for each object None, a previous xlist must be present, because a corresponding start tag must be in the XML document; moreover the related xlist is the last one that has not yet a corresponding object None. Figure 7 shows a XML fragment and the corresponding binding. Line 4 contains the first object None; the related xlist is Phone on line 2. The same statement is valid for lines 7 and 5. In these two cases, the object None corresponds to the immediately previous xlist. Instead line 8 contains an object None that does not correspond to the nearest previous xlist but to Person on line 1, because both the xlist Phone on lines 2 and 5 are yet linked to an appropriate object None. All these items can be contained in a single xlist that represents the data source.

Satine provides some streams that support the xlist interface and that embed different data sources. When a stream loads a start tag from a data source, it looks for a class that supports the tag and its namespace. If the class is not available, the stream creates at run-time a completely new class with the required tag and uri. Thanks to the advanced reflection provided by Python, this technique unifies in a single solution design-time and run-time data bindings. Moreover Satine offers a further facilities when a XML schema for the data is available: it provides a XML schema compiler that generates all the Python classes for managing and validating documents. Although all information stored in the data source is represented as a single xlist, it must not be all loaded in memory; in fact a stream loads data only when it is needed according to the position of the xlist iterator.

Moreover all streams defines two new operations, *seek* and *tell*, that permit to move the xlist iterator to a random location. At the moment Satine offers two important stream: *xmlReader* and *odbcStream*. The former provides access to the XML in text files; it uses a C-based xml tokenizer, which we developed from expat, for fast reading and search. The latter embeds a XML data into a relational database that support the ODBC interface.

```
1: root = xlist()

2: current = root

3: for item in stream:

4:   if item is xlist:

5:     current.append(item)

6:     current = item

7:   else if item is None:

8:     current = owner of current

9:   else:

10:     current.append(item)
```

Fig. 8. Algorithm for xlist deserialization

3.2 Serialization

The simplest way to use streams is to iterate over their content, in case moving their iterator. Applications that search through a stream looking for an element or a string, needs exactly a sequential access: it is very fast and requires little memory but it is not flexible in all situations.

There are applications that visit a XML document as a tree of elements and nested elements. These applications benefit from information representations that are based on a tree structure. The composite list model, which we proposed in the previous sections, offers exactly a structure conforming these requirements: xlists can contain other xlists, such as XML elements contain other XML elements.

Moreover there is a simple and fast function for generating a xlist tree starting from a stream. All is required is to visit the stream sequentially and follows the steps of algorithm in figure 8. Line 1 and 2 prepare the root xlist. Then, starting from line 3 the algorithm iterates over the stream and at each loop it retrieves an item. If the item is a xlist, it is appended to the current xlist (line 5) and it is set as the current composite list (line 6). Indeed if the item is the object None, it indicates that the next items belong no more to the current xlist but to its owner; hence it change the current xlist (line 8). Finally if the item is a simple type, it is inserted in the current xlist without further actions.

This simple algorithm builds a tree representation from a serial representation; hence actually it is a deserialization function. A mutual and easy algorithm provides the corresponding serialization.

To sum up, we designed a model for XML documents that relays on composite lists, we developed a similar model with empty lists for XML data sources, and finally we noted that the two models are linked by a serialization procedure.

Satine provides two functions *roll* and *unroll,* for serialization and deserialization respectively. Interestingly, these functions operate also on fragments of XML documents. Hence it is possible to mix the two approaches, the stream and the tree representations, according to the required performances. For example, a sequential access can find the first element with a relevant tag or attribute. Then the *unroll* function can create a tree representation just for the found element.

Moreover the *unroll* function provides a further important feature: it supports some call-back functions called during the deserialization. The function accepts as parameter a map between some matching rules and some corresponding functions. Each time that a item is retrieved from the stream, the algorithm looks for the rule that match the item and its branch in the tree. For each matching rules, the algorithm calls the associated function. This technique provides a call-back feature very similar to a SAX parser but also much more powerful. In fact the matches take into account not just the item nature, as in SAX, but also its properties and its location in the tree.

3.3 Performances Comparison

The library Satine has not reached a mature stage, because it lacks some minor features and it has some performance bottlenecks. Anyway the current implementation shows already interesting results with respect to other XML data binding solutions.

During some tests we performed, Satine prove to be always faster than xml_objectfy, the other available solution for XML data binding in Python.

Table 1 show some impressive results as regard the analysis of two XML documents with different structure. The first document, *jungle.xml,* is the transcription in XML format of the novel "The Jungle Book" by Rudyard Kipling. It is a large document (over 300 Kbytes) with a lot of text, but, on the other hand, it has a simple structure. The second document, *xhtml.xsd,* is a XML schema for the XHTML format; it is shorter than 40 Kbytes but it has a rich structure with many nested elements.

The test lies in two steps:

1. The document is read from the file and it is converted into an object oriented representation in Python
2. A recursive algorithm visits all the information in the object oriented representation of the document

For each action, the table shows the required time in seconds. In any cases Satine proves to be very fast, at least three times faster that xml_objectfy. In particular it performs very well with complex documents with little text, where the module *satine.kernel,* coded in C, speeds up the computation.

Such good results are not comparable with the DOM library for Java, provided in JAXP. In fact a Java DOM application, which performs the same operations, shows to be an order of magnitude faster. Further efforts are required to understand better the reasons of the large gap.

Table 1. Performance comparison

XML Document	jungle.xml binding	jungle.xml visit	xhtml.xsd binding	xhtml.xsd Visit
satine (in sec.)	0.7309	0.0199	0.2009	0.0099
xml_objectify (in sec.)	6.1590	0.0700	2.2029	0.0600
performance ratio xml_objectify/satine	8.4254	3.5000	10.9602	6.0000
Java DOM (in sec.)	0.07141	0.0009	0.0289	0.0007

4 Conclusion

This paper introduces an interesting model for managing XML documents or any information that is stored in XML fashion. Thanks to composite lists, i.e. *xlists*, the proposed model succeeds in representing in a single paradigm the characteristic properties from the many approaches in literature. The XML data binding problem was faced by unifying in a single solution two traditional far approaches to data binding, the design-time one and the run-time one. Moreover our paradigm offers a composite access to XML data sources; it provides both stream and tree representations, and it allows to mix them according to the developer's needs.

Also the model has been useful for developing a Python library for XML management. Satine provides a simple and effective environment for managing complex data structures that can be represented in XML fashion. Some small test-bed applications seems to confirm the flexibility of this library, that, unlike other tools for Python, takes advantage of the enhanced run-time features of the Python environment.

An interesting open issue regards the flexibility of composite lists. Their capability to represent data sources, suggests that xlists are a good model in other computer science contexts. In the current release of Satine, we are testing the use of composite lists to represent file systems and we are studying a possible binding for other resources, such as web services and web servers.

Acknowledgement. This work has been developed under the support of the young researchers project "Message-based Comunication Models for Distributed Systems" at University of Padua.

References

1.   Apache Group. *Xerces Java Parser Readme*. http://xml.apache.org/xerces-j/index.html.
2.   Bray, T., Paoli, J., Sperberg-McQueen, C. M., Maler, *E.Extensible Markup Language (XML) 1.0 (Second Edition)*. http://www.w3.org/TR/2000/REC-xml-20001006
3.   DeRose, S., Maler, E. and Orchard, D., eds. *XML Linking Language (XLink) Version 1.0*. http://www.w3.org/TR/xlink
4.   JDom.org. *JDOM*. http://www.jdom.org/

5. Le Hors, A., ed. *Document Object Model (DOM) Level 3 Core Specification.*
    http://www.w3.org/TR/2001/WDDOM-Level-3-Core-20010126/.
6. Megginson Technologies. *SAX 2.0: The Simple API for XML.*
    http://www.megginson.com/SAX/.
7. D. E. Perry and A. L.Wolf. Foundations for the Study of Software Architectures. *ACM SIGSOFT Software Engineering Notes*, October 1992.
8. Sall, K. and St. Laurent, S. DTDs vs. XML Schemas for Datacentric JavaTM Technology-based Applications. http://www.cen.com/ng-html/xml/schema/
9. Eric M. Dashofy. *Issues in Generating Data Bindings for an XML Schema-Based Language.* Proceedings of the Workshop on XML Technologies and Software Engineering (XSE2001), Toronto, ONT, Canada.
10. Biron, P. and Malhotra. *XML Schema Part 2: Datatypes.*
    http://www.w3.org/TR/xmlschema-2/.
11. Thompson, H., Beech, D., Maloney, M. and Mendelsohn, N., eds. XML Schema Part 1: Structures. http://www.w3.org/TR/xmlschema-1/.
12. Dongwon Lee and Wesley W.Chu. Comparative analysis of six xml schema languages. ACM SIGMOD record, 29(3), 2000.
13. Code Fast, Run Fast with XML Data Binding by Eric Armstrong for Sun Microsystems, Inc. URL: http://java.sun.com/xml/jaxp/dist/1.0.1/docs/binding/DataBinding.html
14. Brett McLaughlin. *Data binding from XML to Java applications.*
15. Didier, Marting, et al. *Professional XML.* Wrox Press Ltd. 2000
16. Ashvin Radiya, Vibha Dixit. *The basics of using XML Schema to define elements.*
    http://www-106.ibm.com/developerworks/xml/library/xml-chema/index.html?dwzone=xml
17. David Mertz, Data Masseur. *On the Pythonic Treatment of XML Documents As Objects.*
    http://gnosis.cx/publish/programming/xml_matters_1.txt,
    http://gnosis.cx/publish/programming/xml_matters_2.txt
18. Sun Microsystem. *The Java™ Architecture for XML Binding. User's Guide.* May 2001.
    http://java.sun.com/xml/jaxb/jaxb-docs.pdf
19. Microsoft. *XSD Compiler, .NET Development.* http://msdn.microsoft.com
20. Jason Masterman and Chris Predeek. *XML Code Generator: Generating Visual Basic Classes from XML Schemas.*
    http://msdn.microsoft.com/xml/articles/generat.asp
21. Mark Lutz, David Ascher. *Learning Python.* April 1999. O'Reilly
22. Christopher A. Jones, Fred L. Drake. *Python & XML.* December 2001. O'Reilly

KF-Diff+: Highly Efficient Change Detection Algorithm for XML Documents

Haiyuan Xu, Quanyuan Wu, Huaimin Wang, Guogui Yang, and Yan Jia

Laboratory 613, School of Computer Science, National University of Defense Technology,
Changsha, Hunan, P.R. China
hyxu@nudt.edu.cn

Abstract. Most previous work in change detection on XML documents used the ordered tree, with the best complexity of O(nlogn), where n is the size of the document. The best algorithm we had ever known for unordered model achieves polynomial time in complexity. In this paper, we propose a highly efficient algorithm named KF-Diff+. The key property of our algorithm is that the algorithm transforms the traditional tree-to-tree correction into the comparing of the key trees which are substantially label trees without duplicate paths with the complexity of O(n), where n is the number of nodes in the trees. In addition, KF-Diff+ is tailored to both ordered trees and unordered trees. Experiment shows that KF-Diff+ can handle XML documents at extreme speed.

1 Introduction

Data publication on the web is constantly increasing. The web constitutes the largest body of information accessible to any individual throughout the history of humanity and keeps growing at a healthy pace [14]. It should be pointed that change monitoring is becoming very popular on the web. Users are often not only interested in the current values of documents and query answers but also in changes. They want to see changes as information that can be used to learn about the evolution of the web.

One of the key challenges for building a large-scale web based change monitoring system is that it must scale to large number of sources and subscriptions, since that in the Internet environment, where huge volumes of input data and large numbers of users are typical, efficiency and scalability are key concerns. In our XFDS project [12], a partly implemented prototype system designed to monitor the fetching of millions of XML [13] documents per day where supporting millions of subscriptions, we are lead to compute the difference between the millions of documents obtained each day and previous version of these documents. This motivates the study of an extremely efficient change detection algorithm for tree data. Usually, the change detection algorithm will determine whether or not the two versions are identical. If not, then tries to match each element in the old version with every one in the new version to know the difference of the two versions. Since we focus on deltas, as opposed to other ap-

R. Meersman, Z. Tari (Eds.): CoopIS/DOA/ODBASE 2002, LNCS 2519, pp. 1273–1286, 2002.
© Springer-Verlag Berlin Heidelberg 2002

proaches that might focus on snapshots or object history, and delta data is usually much smaller than the original data, query evaluation will be much faster.

Since XML documents can be represented as trees, the change detection problem is related to the problem of change detection on trees. Algorithms to compute the difference between trees can be divided into two categories depending on whether they deal with ordered or unordered trees. An ordered tree is one in which both the ancestor relationship and the left-to-right ordering among siblings are significant. An unordered tree is one in which only ancestor relationships are significant, where the left-to-right order among siblings is not significant. Change detection on unordered trees has been shown to be NP-Complete in general case and is substantially harder than that on ordered trees. For unordered trees, we term two trees isomorphic if they are identical except for the orders among siblings. We considers two trees are equivalent if they are isomorphic. In this paper, we introduce some notions (e.g., key path), which are used to compute the difference between two trees. Based on these notions, we propose a highly efficient algorithm named KF-Diff+. The key property of our algorithm is that the algorithm transforms the traditional tree-to-tree correction into the comparing of the key trees which are substantially label trees without duplicate paths. Thus, our algorithm achieves high efficiency with the complexity of $O(n)$, where n is the number of nodes in the trees. In addition, KF-Diff+ is tailored to both ordered trees and unordered trees, which is also a significant difference compared with previous work. KF-Diff+ has two kinds of forms named algorithm 1 and algorithm 2 respectively. Algorithm 1 has the complexity of $O(n)$ by using hash tables, which usually consumes much more time than algorithm 2. Algorithm 2 usually achieves better performance with the complexity estimated of $O(n\log\lambda)$, where λ is the average out-degree of nodes in the document. Experiments shows that KF-Diff+ can handle XML documents at extreme speed, which is significant to the large scale applications.

The remainder of the paper is organized as follows. Related work is contained in Sect. 2. In Sect. 3, we formulate the problem and give an overview of our approach. Sect. 4 presents the details of KF-Diff+ with complexity analysis. Sect. 5 gives some preliminary performance results. Our conclusions and future research directions are contained in Sect. 7.

2 Related Work

Some previous work in change detection has focused on computing differences between flat files, e.g. GNU diff and CVS. They cannot be generalized to handle structured data because they do not understand the hierarchical structure information contained in such data sets. The AT&T Internet Difference Engine [6] uses HtmlDiff [1] to determine the differences between two HTML pages. This method cannot be applied to XML documents because markups in XML data provide context, and contents within different markups cannot be matched. Since XML documents can be represented as trees, it is a natural idea to utilize tree-to-tree correction techniques to detect changes in XML documents. Zhang and Shasha proposed a fast algorithm to find the minimum cost editing distance between two ordered labeled trees [9]. Given two ordered trees T_1 and T_2, in which each node has an associated label, their algorithm finds an optimal edit script in time $O(|T_1| \times |T_2| \times \min \{depth(T_1), leaves(T_1)\} \times \min \{depth(T_2), leaves(T_2)\})$, which is the best known result for the general tree-to-tree correction problem.

Recently, Sun released an XML specific tool named DiffMK [4] that computes the difference between two XML documents. This tool is based on the unix standard diff algorithm, and uses a list description of the XML document, thus losing the benefit of tree structure of XML. [2, 5, 3, 11, 8] deal with the problem on hierarchically structured documents. However, LaDiff [2] is limited by its assumption and not guaranteed to generate the optimal result. MH-Diff [5] provides an efficient heuristic solution based on transforming the problem to the edge cover problem, with a worst case cost in $O(n^2 logn)$, where n is the total number of nodes. XMLTreeDiff [3] use DOMHash [7] and Zhang's algorithm [9]. Since the former conflicts with the later, this method may not generate an optimal result. [11] proposed XyDiff, an algorithm for detecting changes in XML documents. This algorithm achieves $O(nlogn)$ complexity in execution time where n is the size of the document and generates fairly good results in many cases. However, XyDiff cannot guarantee any form of optimal or near-optimal result because of the greedy rules used in the algorithm. The major difference between [8] and [2, 5, 3, 11] is that the former is designed to handle unordered trees, where the later for ordered trees. [8] presents an algorithm named X-Diff for computing the difference between two versions of an XML document, which achieves polynomial time in complexity. Since X-Diff can only reduce the size of tree by removing equivalent second-level subtrees, the filtering is not efficient. Besides, in some case, X-Diff may not satisfy uses' needs. In this paper, we propose a highly efficient algorithm named KF-Diff+. The key property of our algorithm is that the algorithm transforms the traditional tree-to-tree correction into the comparing of the key trees which are substantially label trees without duplicate paths.

3   Preliminaries

3.1   Tree Representation of XML Documents

Definition 1. Assume a countably infinite set E of element labels (tags), a countably infinite set A of attribute names, and a symbol S indicating text (e.g., PCDATA in XML). Assume that E, A and {S} are pairwise disjoint. An XML (document) tree [10] T is defined to be (V, lab, Ele, att, val, r), where V is a set of *vertices* (*nodes*); lab is a function from V to $E \cup A \cup \{S\}$; Ele is a partial function from V to sequences of V vertices such that for any $v \in V$, if Ele(v) is defined then lab(v)$\in$ E; att is a partial function from V×A to V such that for any $v \in V$ and $l \in A$, if att(v,l) = v' then lab(v)$\in$ E and lab(v') = l; val is a partial function from V to string values such that for any node $v \in V$, val(v) is a string iff either lab(v) = S or lab(v)$\in$ A ; r is a distinguished vertex in V and is called the root of T. Without loss of generality, assume lab(r) = r , and that there is a unique node in T labeled r.

Definition 2. A (simple) *path* is a sequence of node labels, syntactically defined as follows: $\rho \equiv \varepsilon \,|\, 1 \,.\, \rho$ where ε is the empty path, node label $1 \in E \cup A \cup \{S\}$, and "." is the concatenation operator. Intuitively, a path represents the sequence of node labels in a parent-child path in an XML tree. More precisely, let T be an XML tree, v_1, v_2 be nodes in T and ρ be a path. We say that there is a path from v_1 to v_2, denoted by $T \models \rho(v_1, v_2)$, if there is a parent-child path from v_1 to v_2 whose sequence of node labels is ρ.

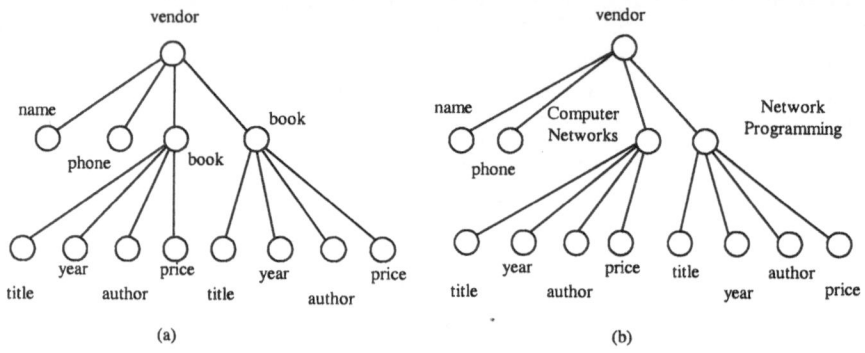

Fig. 1. (a) Tree representation for an XML document, (b) An example of Key tree

3.2 Key Field and Key Path

As mentioned before, many previous work utilize tree-to-tree correction techniques to detect changes in XML documents. However it is still a problem that how to compare the nodes which have the same path. For instance, as shown in Figure 1(a), there are two book elements with the same path in the tree. For unordered model, a naïve way is to compare them each other, which is obviously not efficient. For ordered model, the left-to-right ordering can help to discriminate among these nodes. However, if these nodes are compared directly according to the ordering, the quality of the result can not be guaranteed. So, can we discriminate those nodes in the instinctive features of the XML document? To answer the question, we introduce the notion of the key constraint [10] (see Sect. 3.3) in order to support such a discrimination. That is, we want to substitute the value of the key constraint, denoted by *key value*, for the label of the nodes. For example, suppose a vendor has many books which each has an unique name, thus we can use the name of book as the value of the key constraint corresponding to the path "vendor/book". Suppose the name of the two books are "Network Programming" and "Computer Networks" respectively, we will see the tree changed in Fig. 1(b). It should be pointed that we need not to change all the labels of the elements. It is another question that what's kind of nodes should be changed. To answer the question, we introduce the notion of Multi-Instance node. A set of the Multi-Instance nodes is substantially the set of nodes that have the same father node and the same label.

Definition 3. A set of *Multi-Instance* nodes, denoted by MI, is defined as follows: Suppose v is a node in a tree T, If there is a node v′ in T, v ≠ v′, lab(v) = lab(v′), and there is another node n in T, and have $v' \in Ele(n) \wedge v \in Ele(n)$, then $MI(v) = \{ v' | lab(v) = lab(v'), \exists\ n \in V\ (v' \in Ele(n) \wedge v \in Ele(n))\}$, otherwise MI(v) = ϕ, where ϕ denotes empty set. That is, MI is meaningful only when it has at least two satisfied nodes.

To explain the relation between MI and the set of nodes which have the same path, we give the following theorem.

Theorem 1. Suppose v, v′ are different nodes with the same path ρ in T, $(e_1, e_2, \ldots, e_k)$ are the nodes from r to v along ρ, and $(e_1', e_2', \ldots, e_k')$ are the nodes from r to v′ along ρ (obviously, $e_1 = e_1' = r$, $e_k = v$ and $e_k' = v'$), we have that there is one and only one MI, denoted by S, which makes the following true:

$(\exists\ i \in [1, k])(e_i \in S \wedge e_i' \in S \wedge e_{i-1} = e_{i-1}')$.

Proof is omitted here. Theorem 1 shows that for any two nodes that have same path, we can find such a MI, and then substitute the labels of two nodes (such as e_i and e_i' described above, or two book elements in Fig. 1(a)) for the different values. Intuitively, after we handle all the MIs in the tree, it seems there is no elements that have same path (as shown in Figure 1(b)). We will proof it in the theorem 2. Since the value used to take the place of the label of node v in the MI comes from the subtree rooted at v, the relative path (from v to the leaf node which contain the value) is called a *key field*. We next present the definition of the *key field*.

Definition 4. A MI is substantially a set that consists of the sibling nodes with the same label. To describe the difference of the nodes in the MI, we introduce the notion of *key field*, denoted by KF, which is defined as follows: If MI (v) ≠ ϕ, then KF (v) = $\{\rho \mid \rho$ is a relative path expression, and $\forall (e_1, e_2 \in MI(v))((e_1 \neq e_2) \rightarrow (\exists (k_1, k_2 \in V) (T \models \rho(e_1, k_1) \wedge T \models \rho(e_2, k_2) \wedge val(k_1) \neq val(k_2))))\ \}$. Obviously, ρ can be ε, in which case that v is a leaf node. It should be pointed that the definition above is a simple form. In some case, there may be no such a satisfied key field. To solve the problem, we give an extended definition described as following: KF (v) = {P | P is a set of relative paths from v to the leaf nodes in the subtree rooted at v, and have

$\forall (e_1, e_2 \in MI(v))((e_1 \neq e_2) \rightarrow NOT(\bigwedge_{1 \le i \le k} (\exists (k_1, k_2 \in V) (\rho_i \in P \wedge T \models \rho_i (e_1, k_1) \wedge T \models \rho_i (e_2, k_2) \wedge val(k_1) = val(k_2)))))$, where k is the total number of paths in P. The extended definition is tailored to almost all kinds of XML documents because in the case that there is no such an extended key field, there must be two nodes in the MI which are value equal (see Sect. 3.3), where such nodes need not to be discriminated at all. In this case, we can neglect those nodes which are value equal because they do not change the correctness of the algorithm. Due to the space limitation, we only discuss the simple form of the definition in the paper, which is usually enough in practice.

As mentioned above, KF is a notion relates to MI. For each node v in the MI, it shows where to find the key value in the subtree rooted at v. The key property of KF is that given a MI and associated KF, any two different nodes in the MI should not have the same value corresponding to the KF. As mention before, some elements's labels should be changed in the tree, where others not. Thus, in the key tree, as shown in Figure 1(b), the notion of the label is changed. We next give the notion of *key label*. Intuitively, the *key label* of an unchanged element is exactly the original label of the element, where the *key label* of an changed element is not. Here is the definition.

Definition 5. The notion of *key label* of node v, denoted by KLab, is defined as follows: 1) If MI (v) = ϕ, then KLab(v) = lab(v) ; 2) Otherwise, suppose p is one of the paths of KF(v) and $T \models p(v , k)$, then KLab(v) = val(k). We also define *key path*, denoted by KPath, as follows: KPath(v) = KLab(e_1) ... KLab(e_k) . KLab(v), where (e_1, e_2, . . ., e_k, v) are nodes from r to v. The tree consists of KLabs is denoted by *key tree*.

Notice that KF (v) may has many satisfied paths, in theory, we can use any of them to obtain a key value. In practice, we utilize some criterions to select better key values. For example, we much prefer to select the key value that is less likely be modified. The detail is omitted here. In this paper, to be more precisely presented, definition 5 is based on assumption 1.

Assumption 1. Given any $v \in V$ and MI (v) $\neq \phi$, for any different sibling element v' of v, we have KLab(v) $\neq$ KLab(v').

Observe that this assumption is usually satisfied. In addition, in our implementation, we have some special ways to deal with the case encountered that the assumption is not satisfied. The detail is out of the scope of the paper.

Now, we transform the tree-to-tree correction into the comparing of the key trees. We expect that the key path is unique in the key tree. So we give the following theorem.

Theorem 2. Suppose e_1, e_2 are nodes in the T, KPath(e_1) = KPath(e_2) iff $e_1 = e_2$.
Here we give a brief proof for Theorem 2.
Proof: $\Leftarrow$ is obvious.
$\Rightarrow$ Given KPath(e_1) = KPath(e_2), then by definition 5, there must exist nodes (x_1, x_2, ..., x_k, e_1) from r to e_1, and (y_1, y_2, ..., y_k, e_2) from r to e_2, and KLab(x_1) ... KLab(x_k) . KLab(e_1) = KLab(y_1) ... KLab(y_k) . KLab(e_2). Since x_1, y_1 are both the root of T, we have $x_1 = y_1 = r$. Now we consider the case i = 2, suppose $x_2 \neq y_2$, thus we have that x_2 and y_2 are sibling nodes. Since KLab(x_2) = KLab(y_2), this contradicts the assumption 1. Similarly, we can proof for all i $\in$ [1, k], we have $x_i = y_i$, and similarly, we have $e_1 = e_2$. Theorem 2 shows that there is no case that two different elements have same key path in the key tree, which is the foundation of our algorithm.

Now the question is how to obtain the key value of MI. To answer the question, we need to introduce the notion of key constraint. First, we give the notion of value equal which is central to a definition of *key constraint*. In relational databases, this is not a problem: one needs only to compare values of atomic types when checking the satisfaction of a key. An XML tree has a hierarchical structure and it is no longer trivial to compare the values of two XML trees (subtrees). Intuitively, we need a definition of equality on the values of XML trees such that if two trees are *value equal*, then the two XML documents represented by the two trees are the same. Here is the definition of *value equal*.

3.3 Selection of the Key Field

Definition 6. We say that v and v′ are *value equal* [10] denoted by $v =_v v'$, iff the following conditions are satisfied: 1) lab(v) = lab(v′); 2) if lab(v) = S or lab(v) ∈ A then val (v) = val (v′); 3) if lab(v)∈ E, then for any l∈ A, att(v, l) is defined iff att(v′, l) is defined, and val (att(v, l)) = val (att(v′, l)); if Ele(v) = [e_1 , e_2, ..., e_k], then Ele(v′) = [e_1', e_2', ..., e_k'] and for all i∈ [1, k], $e_i =_v e_i'$. In short, $v =_v v'$ iff their substrees are isomorphic by an isomorphism that is the identity on string values.

In relational databases, to define a key we specify the name of a relation (a set of tuples) and a set of attributes of the relation that uniquely identifies tuples in the relation. Along the same lines, to define a *key constraint* φ for XML data we specify a form $(Q,\{P_1,..., P_k\})$, where Q is a path called the target path of φ ; P_1, ..., P_k are path expressions called the feature paths of φ with k≥1. We use [[Q]] to denote the set of nodes in T that is reachable by following Q from the root r, and use n[[P]] to denote the set of nodes reachable form n by following P. An XML tree T satisfies φ, denoted by $T \vDash φ$, iff $\forall e_1 , e_2 \in [[Q]] (\underset{1 \le i \le k}{\wedge} \exists x \in e_1[[P_i]] \exists y \in e_2[[P_i]](x =_v y) \rightarrow e_1 = e_2)$

There are two forms of *keys* are important for hierarchically structured data. The first is *absolute key*. Similar to relational database keys, an *absolute key* identifies a unique node x in [[Q]] with the values of nodes in the subtree rooted at x. The second is *relative key*, which is analogous to a key for a weak entity in a relational database. In this paper, we only consider the former. Now, it is time for answering the question. Intuitively, the *feature paths* in the *key constraint* are the satisfied paths in the *key field*. It should be pointed that the condition of the *feature paths* are stronger than that of the *key field*. Thus, we relax the satisfaction of the keys by follows: given *key* φ = { Q, $\{P_1,..., P_k\}$}, we say $T \vDash φ$, iff for each MI that is reachable by following Q from the root r, $\forall e_1 , e_2 \in MI (\underset{1 \le i \le k}{\wedge} \exists x \in e_1[[P_i]] \exists y \in e_2[[P_i]](x =_v y) \rightarrow e_1 = e_2)$. This means that we only discuss the satisfaction inside the MI, which can significantly reduce the cost of finding keys. Due to the space limitation, we only consider the *keys* that have just one feature path in this paper.

Let Σ be a finite set of *key constraints*, given a MI, corresponding *key field* can be obtained as one of the follows: i) utilizing the ID attribute in the DTD of the documents; ii) utilizing the index of *keys*; iii) by experience. For instance, some labels such as "title", "name", "id", "ssn", etc, usually fit for key field; iv) computing directly. Since the number of nodes in the MI usually is not very large, the time cost will not be very much. In addition, usually we can get keys before computing the difference between trees, so, the cost of finding keys does not change the performance of the algorithm in most case.

4 Change Detection with KF-Diff+

In this section we propose KF-Diff+, a highly efficient algorithm which need not to compute the hash signatures of all the nodes in the documents. As mentioned before, the key property of KF-Diff+ is that the algorithm transforms the traditional tree-to-tree correction into the comparing of the *key trees*. Since any two different nodes in the key tree should not have the same *key path*, the comparing between two trees will be more efficient.

There are two steps in KF-Diff+ as follows: 1). Parsing. KF-Diff+ parses DOC_1 and DOC_2 into trees T_1 and T_2. During the parsing process, KF-Diff+ will find out all MIs and compute the *key paths* associated. 2).Matching. The goal of this step is to find a minimum-cost matching between T_1 and T_2. Due to the space limitation, the generating of the edit scripts [15] is omitted here.

Input: DOC_1, DOC_2
Output: T_1, T_2 , HT[ ] (HT[i] is a hash table)
Initialize: $T_1 = T_2 = NULL$, HS[i] =NULL, i∈ (2, DEPTH),
                 where DEPTH is the maximal depth of the DOC_1.
for each element v in the DOC_1 **do**
    Assign v a ID denoted by EID(v); Construct T_1;
    Find out whether the node belongs to a MI, and if so,
       look for the associated key field and compute the KLab(v);
for each element v in the DOC_2 **do**
    Assign v EID(v); Construct T_2;
    Find out whether the node belongs to a MI, and if so,
       look for the associated key field and compute the KLab(v).
    if v is not the root of T_2 Put <KPath(v), EID(v)> into HT [depth(v)]
return T_1, T_2 , HT[ ]

Fig. 2. Preprocessing phase of Algorithm 1

4.1 Algorithm 1

Parsing. The parsing phase, as shown in Fig. 2, is the preprocessing step in KF-Diff+. Two input XML documents, DOC_1 and DOC_2, are parsed into trees first. Since DOM tree contains much unnecessary information and consumes more memory, we just construct a simple tree by using SAX programming interface. Notice that during the parsing process, KF-Diff+ will find out all MIs and compute the key paths associated, which will be used directly by the later step.

Matching. The algorithm is shown in Fig. 3. According the theorem 2, KPath(x) $\neq$ KPath(y) iff x $\neq$ y. Thus, in the matching algorithm, we compare T_1 with T_2 directly by using key paths of nodes.

Input: T_1, T_2, HT[ ] (obtained by previous step)
Output: DeletedNodes, InsertedNodes, UpdatedNodes
Initialize: Suppose = Root(T_1), r_2 = Root(T_2), TempSet$_1$ = TempSet$_2$ = { },
                    DeletedNodes = InsertedNodes = UpdatedNodes = { };
First Step: **if** lab(r_1) $\neq$ lab(r_2)   **return** NULL
                    else TempSet$_1$ = Children(r_1), TempSet$_2$ = Children(r_2)
        /* Children(v) is the function that returns all the child nodes of v*/
Second Step: Call MatchFunc(TempSet$_1$, TempSet$_2$)
return DeletedNodes, InsertedNodes, UpdatedNodes
MatchFunc(TempSet$_1$, TempSet$_2$)
{ **for** each element v in TempSet$_1$ **do**
        Look for KPath(v) in the hash table HT[depth(v)]
            if the result is NULL move v to DeletedNodes
            else let v' denotes the corresponding node in T_2 we get
                Remove v' from TempSet$_2$
                if v is a leaf node
                    if val(v) $\neq$ val(v')   add <v, val(v') > to UpdatedNodes
                else call MatchFunc(Children(v), Children(v'))
        if v is the last element in TempSet$_1$
            Add all unprocessed nodes in TempSet$_2$ to InsertedNodes
}

Fig. 3. Matching of Algorithm 1

Algorithm Analysis. Obviously, the complexity of parsing is $O(|T_1| + |T_2|)$, and the complexity of matching is also $O(|T_1| + |T_2|)$, without considering the hashing cost. Thus the complexity of algorithm 1 is $O(n)$, where n is the total number of the nodes in the trees.

4.2 Algorithm 2

Parsing. The parsing is similar to the one of algorithm 1. The difference is algorithm 2 do not use hash tables.

Matching. The algorithm is shown in Fig. 4. Similarly, algorithm 2 compares T_1 with T_2 directly by using key paths. The difference is that algorithm use set oriented techniques instead of hash tables.

Algorithm Analysis. Similarly, the complexity of parsing is $O(|T_1| + |T_2|)$. Suppose there are N matching pairs between T_1 and T_2, thus the cost of matching is bounded by $\sum_{i=1}^{N} O(\max\{\deg(x_i), \deg(y_i)\} \times \log(\max\{\deg(x_i), \deg(y_i)\}))$, where deg(x) denote the out-degree of node x in the trees. Consider the case that every element has the same out-degree, denoted by λ. Thus we have that the number of non-leaf elements is

Input: T_1, T_2 (obtained by previous step)
Output: DeletedNodes, InsertedNodes, UpdatedNodes
Initialize: Suppose r_1 = Root(T_1), r_2 = Root(T_2), TempSet$_1$ =TempSet$_2$=M = { },
               DeletedNodes = InsertedNodes = UpdatedNodes = { };
First Step: **if** lab(r_1) $\neq$ lab(r_2) **return** NULL;
               else TempSet$_1$ = Children(r_1), TempSet$_2$ = Children(r_2);
Second Step: Call MatchFunc(TempSet$_1$, TempSet$_2$);
return DeletedNodes, InsertedNodes, UpdatedNodes
MatchFunc(TempSet$_1$, TempSet$_2$)
{ TempSet = { } /* local variable */
   Sort the elements in TempSet$_1$ according KLab;
   Sort the elements in TempSet$_2$ according KLab;
   Compare TempSet$_1$ with TempSet$_2$ according KLab; /* sort merge */
   for each matching pair <v, v'> **do**
      /* v belongs to TempSet$_1$, v' belongs to TempSet$_2$ */
      Remove v from TempSet$_1$, Remove v' from TempSet$_2$
      Add <v, v'> to M
        if v is a leaf node
           if val(v) $\neq$ val(v') add <v, val(v') > to UpdatedNodes
        else add v to TempSet
   Add remainder nodes in TempSet$_1$ to DeletedNodes
   Add remainder nodes in TempSet$_2$ to InsertedNodes
   For each element v in TempSet do
      Get corresponding v' in M
      Call MatchFunc (Children(v), Children(v'))
}

Fig. 4. Matching of Algorithm 2

less than $(1/\lambda) \times n$, where n is the total number of the nodes in the trees. Since the out-degree of the leaf node is zero, the cost of matching is less than $O((1/\lambda) \times n \times \lambda \log \lambda)$ = $O(n \log \lambda)$. Note that $O(n \log \lambda)$ is only an estimate of the complexity. In the case that $\lambda \leq 2$, the complexity of the matching is $O(n)$. In the worst case that all other nodes are the child nodes of the root, that is λ= n-1, the complexity of algorithm 2 is $O((n-1)\log(n-1))$.

4.3 KF-Diff+ for Ordered Trees

The algorithms mentioned above can easily be tailored to handle ordered trees which the left-to-right ordering among siblings are significant. The main differences are as follows. 1) Ordering of the nodes are considered; 2) Move operations are considered. It should be pointed that the algorithms presented in this paper only support limited detection of move operations. That is to say, we can only detect the case that nodes are moved within the sibling nodes, and in other case, such a move operation will be detected into one delete operation plus one insert operation. Notice that in practice, the most move operations occur within the sibling nodes. Of course, we can adapt our algorithms to detect more move operations. However, it is beyond the scope of the present paper.

5 Implementation and Performance

5.1 Implementation

We have implemented KF-Diff+ in C and C++. It takes two XML documents as input. We implement a workload generator that, according to a workload specification, emits XML documents modified to the system. The workload generation task ran as a separate process on the another PC. The parameters(e.g., average number of change rate) may be set in the workload specification. We implement a faster XML parser based on the SAX interface. To reduce the time cost, we store the logic trees instead of the original XML documents. Thus, we need not to parse the old document and compute the key tree again. Since our data structure is very simple, it nearly does not take additional space cost. It should be pointed that the structure contains some information associated with key paths in the tree which can be directly used by the change detecting algorithm, so as to save the time for recomputing. To reduce the cost of disk I/O, we implement some cache strategies in order to preload the data of the previous version. For more detail about logical storage of the document and cache strategies, please refer to [12], a partly implemented prototype system based on the KF-Diff+. Notice that KF-Diff+ does not require two XML documents to conform the same schema.

5.2 Performance

In this section, we study the performance of KF-Diff+. Since XyDiff is the best algorithm for ordered tree that we had ever known, and algorithms for unordered trees usually perform worse than those for ordered trees, we compare KF-Diff+ with XyDiff in this paper. Due to the space limitation, we only show some preliminary performance results.

We use a PC with a PIII 850 CPU and 512M RAM operating under Linux. Let C denotes the average change ratio of the documents, λ denotes the average out-degree of the documents.

First, we evaluate the execution time of the three algorithms, XyDiff, algorithm 1 and algorithm 2, on documents of different sizes. In Fig. 5(a), given $\lambda = 3.1$, C = 35%, the figure shows that execution times of the three algorithms are almost linear in the size of the document. Notice that algorithm 2 is much faster than algorithm 1, although the complexity of algorithm 2 is higher than algorithm 1, where algorithm 1 is faster than XyDiff. The reason mainly lies in that algorithm 1 uses hash table which consumes more time.

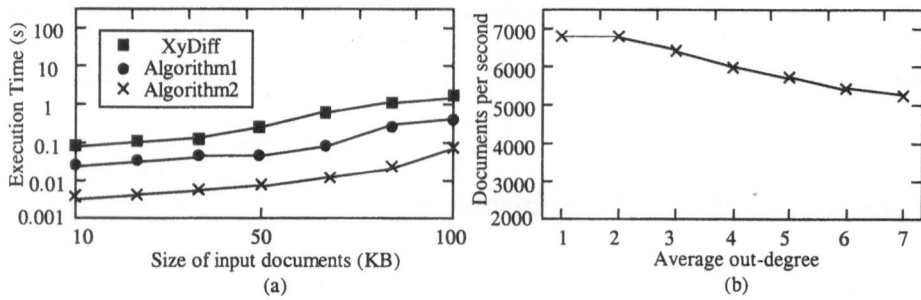

Fig. 5. (a) Execution time of the algorithms, (b) Documents per second with varying out-degree

Given C = 50%, workload parameters are fixed as follows: Each generated XML document has a maximal depth of 16, and average depth of 4.4 and an average number of 29.4 elements. Fig. 5(b) shows that how many documents can be handled per second by algorithm 2, as the average out-degree of the documents varies. Observe that the absolute execution time of the algorithm increase significantly when the average out-degree of the document increases. This is consistent with our analyse which demonstrates that the complexity of the algorithm 2 increases as the out-degree increases. Notice also that the algorithm 2 is highly efficient as the out-degree is small, and can process nearly 7000 documents per second, which is very important for large scale applications.

Given $\lambda = 4.1$, Fig. 6(a) shows the average processing time for various change rates of the XML documents. This Figure shows that: the execution time almost has no change when change ratio increases. This is because KF-Diff+ does not filter the equivalent part of the two versions.

Given $\lambda = 3.5$, C = 80%, Fig. 6(b) shows the processing time per document of KF-Diff+ when the ratio of the modify operation varies. The result shows that KF-Diff+ is effected by the percentage of the modify operations. Observe that given a fixed change rate, the more insert and delete operations are in the delta, the higher the performance is. This is because that for the nodes inserted or deleted, we do not need to compare their descendants.

Given $\lambda = 4.1$, Fig. 7 shows that the result obtained by running KF-Diff+ (algorithm 1 and algorithm 2 generate exactly the same result), is close to the optimal difference. One reason that KF-Diff+ generates non-optimal results is that it can not detect the move operations that do not occur within the sibling nodes, in which case each move operation can be detected into one delete operation plus one insert operation. Notice that in practice, such kind of move operations are not occur often. Another reason is that the key fields may be modified (although not occur often), in which case the modify operation can be detected into one delete operation plus one insert operation. However we can adapt the system to minimize the problem in practice.

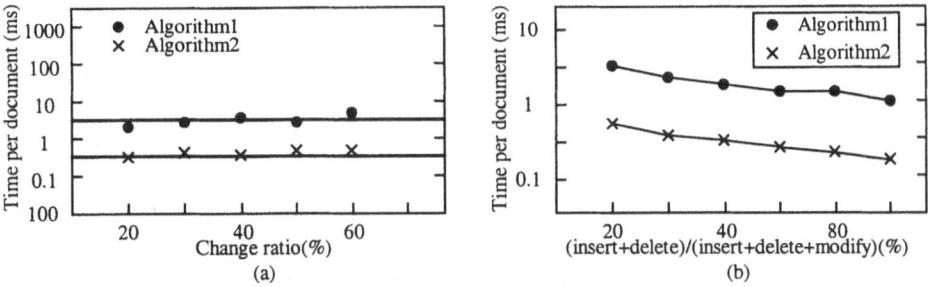

Fig. 6. (a) Varying change ratio (b) Varying ratio of insert and delete operation

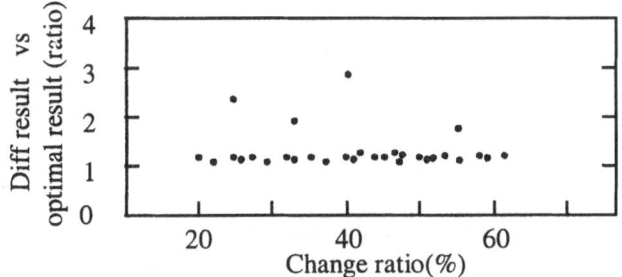

Fig. 7. Quality of diff result

5.3 Contribution of Key Path

The main contribution of the paper is that we transforms the traditional tree-to-tree correction into the comparing of the key trees, which are substantially label trees without duplicate paths, so that our algorithm achieves high efficiency with linear complexity. In addition, KF-Diff+ is tailored to both ordered trees and unordered trees, which is also a significant difference compared with previous work.

6 Summary and Future Work

KF-Diff+ is motivated by the problem of efficiently detecting changes to XML documents on the web. Most previous work in change detection on XML or other hierarchically structured data used the ordered trees. In this paper, we propose a highly efficient algorithm named KF-Diff+. The key property of our algorithm is that the algorithm transforms the traditional tree-to-tree correction into the comparing of the key trees which are substantially label trees without duplicate paths. Thus, our algorithm achieves high efficiency with the complexity of O(n), where n is the total number of nodes. In addition, KF-Diff+ is tailored to both ordered trees and unordered trees, which is also a significant difference compared with previous work. We analyze the algorithm, and give some preliminary performance results.

Many issues may be further investigated. For instance, we plan to continue the study of the feature of the key fields on real web data. Other aspects of the actual implementation could be improved for a different trade-off in quality over performance.

Acknowledgements. We would like to thank Yanli Diao, Brain Cooper, Prasan Roy, and Louiqa Raschid for the valuable comments they provided.

References

1. Berk, E.: HtmlDiff: A Differencing Tool for HTML Documents. Student Project, Princeton University
2. Chawathe, S., Rajaraman, A. Garcia-Molina, H.: Change Detection in Hierarchically Structured Information. Proceedings of the ACM SIGMOD International Conference on Management of Data, Montreal, June 1996.
3. Curbera, F. P.: Fast Difference and Update of XML Documents. XTech'99, San Jose, March 1999.
4. Microsystems, S.: Making all the difference. http://www.sun.com/xml/developers/diffmk/.
5. Chawathe, S., Garcia-Molina, H.: Meaningful change detection in structured data. In Proceedings of the ACM SIGMOD International Conference on Management of Data, Tuscon, Arizona, May 1997.
6. Douglis, F., Ball,T., Chen,Y. F., Koutsofios, E.: The AT&T Internet Difference Engine: Tracking and Viewing Changes on the Web. World Wide Web, 1(1): 27-44, January 1998.
7. Maruyama, H., Tamura, K., Uramoto, R.: Digest values for DOM (DOMHash) proposal. IBM Tokyo Research Laboratory, http://www.trl.ibm.co.jp/projects/xml/domhash.htm, 1998.
8. Wang, Y., DeWitt, D. J., Cai, J.: X-Diff: A Fast Change Detection Algorithm for XML Documents. http://www.cs.wisc.edu/~yuanwang/xdiff.html.
9. Zhang , K., Shasha, D.: Simple Fast Algorithms for the Editing Distance between Trees and Related Problems. SIAM Journal of Computing, 18(6): 1245-1262, 1989.
10. Fan, W., Schwenzer, P., Wu, K.: Keys with Upward Wildcards for XML. Database and Expert Systems Applications, 657-667, 2001.
11. Cobéna, G., Abiteboul, S., Marian, A.: Detecting Changes in XML Documents. ICDE, Feb, 2002.
12. Xu, H., Wu, Q., Wang, H., Yang, G., Jia, Y.: XFDS: Efficient Monitoring and Filtering of XML Information on the Web. submitted to publication, 2002.
13. World Wide Consortium. Extensible markup language (xml) 1.0. http://www.w3.org/TR/REC-xml, 2000.
14. The internet archive. http://www.archive.org/
15. Zhang, K.: A New Editing based Distance between Unordered Labeled Trees. Combinatorial Pattern Matching, 1: 254 – 265, 1993.

Naming in XML Documents

Ramon Lawrence

IDEA Lab, Department of Computer Science, University of Iowa
Iowa City, IA, USA, 52242
ramon-lawrence@uiowa.edu
http://www.cs.uiowa.edu/~rlawrenc/

Abstract. XML is now an established standard for data communication and representation. There has been considerable work on XML querying, modeling, and type definition. However, one of the most important aspects of XML, standardized tag naming for conveying semantics, has been almost ignored by the research community. This paper argues that the naming aspects of XML are important to consider and presents a naming methodology for XML tags that captures increased context information. Using semantic tag names opens up the possibility of semantic querying of XML documents, which simplifies query formulation by reducing the reliance on path expressions. A semantic query facility allows XML documents with similar semantics, but organized using different DTDs, to be queried without modifying the original query formulation. Finally, we demonstrate an algorithm for converting semantic queries to structural queries by disambiguating incomplete path expressions.

1 Introduction

As XML becomes a *de facto* standard for data communication and representation, research has focused on XML querying, modeling, and type definition. However, there has been little focus on the naming challenge of XML. Without the ability to define unique tag sets for XML documents, XML as a modeling language is very similar to the hierarchical model [11] of years past. XML provides the ability to model and query semistructured data. Its usefulness as an integration and communication tool is founded on the ability to define tags with standardized meaning. Consequently, **semantics**, not just structure, may be communicated.

Unfortunately, name construction for XML tags has devolved into the often poor naming characteristics used in the database community where it is not uncommon to build names for attributes and relations by various combinations of abbreviation, concatenation, and hyphenation. The result are names that although concise, are often ambiguous, especially when extracted from surrounding context. Exploiting algorithmic naming has beneficial properties for documentation, human readability, and simplifying querying. Our contribution is a semantic naming methodology that can be applied to existing XML DTDs. After enumerating some of the challenges of XML modeling and naming in Section 2, a naming model is presented in Section 3. A major benefit of the model

R. Meersman, Z. Tari (Eds.): CoopIS/DOA/ODBASE 2002, LNCS 2519, pp. 1287–1303, 2002.
© Springer-Verlag Berlin Heidelberg 2002

is that the tag names become *context independent* in that they encode sufficient context information that their semantic meaning can be determined regardless of surrounding context. Further, a major advantage of exploiting the naming model is that semantic querying can be performed on XML DTDs. Semantic querying provides the ability to re-arrange XML documents and DTDs without re-writing queries, and simplifies XML querying by reducing the reliance on path expressions. Section 4 overviews an algorithm that maps a semantic query to a structural query on a particular DTD. The algorithm uses the naming of DTD elements to determine a complete path expression. The paper closes with future work and conclusions.

2   Modeling Challenges in XML

Despite its wide-spread adoption, XML is actually not a very powerful modeling language. An XML document has a hierarchical structure based on the nesting of elements. Without considering the use of ID/IDREF linking within a document or XLink [10] or XPath [7] between documents, the DTD for an XML document is very similar to the original hierarchical model [11] in that it can only model tree structured data.

A working example used throughout this paper is based on the automobile XML DTDs originally proposed in [16]. For this paper, the two DTDs from separate organizations will be combined into one source, while preserving most of the original elements and semantics. We only examine querying from a single source, although the work may be extended to handle querying across sources (XML documents)[1]. An ER-model for the combined information is given in Figure 1.

Construction of a DTD modeling the information in the ER diagram requires a decision on a hierarchical ordering of the information. Thus, there are multiple possible DTDs that can be used to encode the exact same semantic information present in the ER model. Each of these DTDs can be considered as a view of the original model. Two possible DTDs are given in Figure 2. DTD1 selects a hierarchical representation from the manufacturer perspective listing manufacturer, then model, then vehicle. DTD2 is from the vendor perspective and lists vendors, then vehicles with their associated manufacturer and model information. Note that there are both minor naming differences in the DTDs (option versus op-name) and structural differences besides nesting. For example, manufacturer is represented as a composite object in DTD1, and as a simple attribute in DTD2. In most cases DTD2 is a suboptimal choice because of the duplication of manufacturer and model information. However, DTD2 is just as valid as DTD1.

After the hierarchical ordering of elements in a DTD is selected, the nesting of XML elements has ambiguous semantics. A nesting relationship between two XML elements may encode: a specialization/generalization (IS-A) relationship,

---

[1] The two XML documents can be considered as views of a global schema as given by the ER diagram.

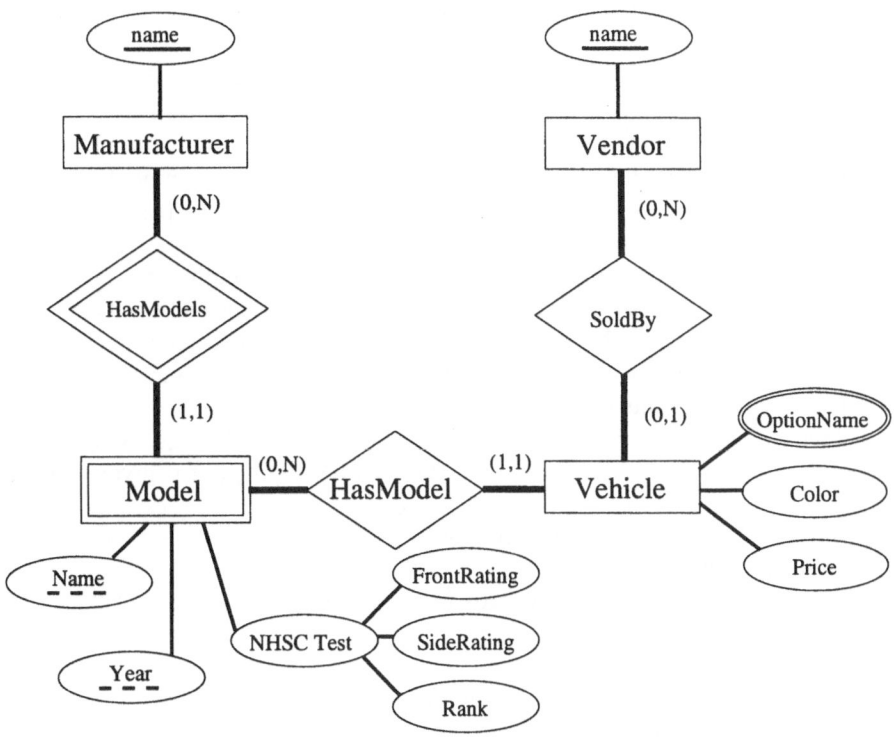

Fig. 1. ER Diagram for XML Example

DTD1

<!ELEMENT list-manufacturer (manufacturer+)>
<!ELEMENT manufacturer (mn-name, model+)>
<!ELEMENT mn-name #PCDATA>
<!ELEMENT model (mo-name, year, front-rating
                         side-rating, rank, vehicle+)>
<!ELEMENT mo-name #PCDATA>
<!ELEMENT year #PCDATA>
<!ELEMENT front-rating #PCDATA>
<!ELEMENT side-rating #PCDATA>
<!ELEMENT rank #PCDATA>
<!ELEMENT vehicle (color, price, vendorName, option+)>
<!ELEMENT color #PCDATA>
<!ELEMENT price #PCDATA>
<!ELEMENT vendorName #PCDATA>
<!ELEMENT option #PCDATA>

DTD2

<!ELEMENT list-vendor (vendor+)>
<!ELEMENT vendor (vendorName, vehicle+)>
<!ELEMENT vendorName #PCDATA>
<!ELEMENT vehicle (color, price, op-name,
                         mn-name, model)>
<!ELEMENT color #PCDATA>
<!ELEMENT price #PCDATA>
<!ELEMENT op-name #PCDATA>
<!ELEMENT mn-name #PCDATA>
<!ELEMENT model (mo-name, year, front-rating
                         side-rating, rank)>
<!ELEMENT mo-name #PCDATA>
<!ELEMENT year #PCDATA>
<!ELEMENT front-rating #PCDATA>
<!ELEMENT side-rating #PCDATA>
<!ELEMENT rank #PCDATA>

Fig. 2. Two different DTDs for the same ER Model

a meronym/holonym (PART-OF/HAS-A) relationship, an ordering/grouping of elements, or a general relationship (join). Thus, given only the structure of an XML document without considering the tag name semantics, it is impossible to determine the relationship between nested elements. Further, structural ambiguity is present when attributes are used to encode information instead of just elements. For this paper, only elements are used to encode information.

XML query languages [4] rely on the structure of the document (DTD) for querying. XML queries are specified by providing path expressions that navigate through the document to retrieve the appropriate elements. A parallel can be drawn between path expressions and navigating through records in hierarchical databases. Although path expressions can be given declaratively in SQL syntax, the formulation of the query is so intertwined with document structure that structural transparency is not achieved. Consider the query: *"Return the manufacturer name and vehicle price for all vehicles with price < 30,000, and the vehicle model is in the top 10 for safety tests"*. [16] The query specified in the Lorel [2] query language for DTD1 (Q_1) and DTD2 (Q_2) is given below:

> **select** M.mn-name, M.model.vehicle.price
> **from** list-manuf.manufacturer M
> **where** M.model.rank $\leq$ 10 **and** M.model.vehicle.price < 30000   (Q_1)

> **select** V.manufacturer.mn-name, V.price
> **from** list-vehicles.vehicle V
> **where** V.manufacturer.model.rank $\leq$ 10 **and** V.price < 30000   (Q_2)

Notice that despite both DTDs modeling exactly the same information, the hierarchical nature of XML causes considerably different queries to obtain an identical answer. Although it is possible to create a single query that functions over both XML DTDs (see Q_3), the complexity of such a query is clearly undesirable. The addition of the selection operator ("|") and the Kleene closure operator ("*") unnecessarily complicate the query formulation and add to possible interpretation ambiguity for the user.

> **select** T._*.mn-name, T._*.vehicle.price
> **from** (list-vehicles | list-manufacturer).(vendor | manufacturer) T
> **where** T._*.model.rank $\leq$ 10 **and** T._*.vehicle.price < 30000   (Q_3)

Further, the naming in each DTD demonstrates some undesirable properties. In both cases, an outer tag name (list-vehicles or list-manufacturers) must be defined and used in querying to group elements in the document. Second, naming for a common concept such as a name of an entity is not systematic. For instance, mn-name and mo-name are concatenated abbreviations for manufacturer name and model name. Given these two tag names out-of-context of the DTD or original document[2], it is extremely difficult to determine their semantics. The `vendor` tag stores a name attribute, but that information can only be determined by examining the actual values in the XML document and using domain knowledge to recognize them as names.

From this brief overview, it should be apparent that modeling and naming in XML are complicated issues. The goal of this work is to present a systematic naming mechanism for XML DTDs. We then define a canonical semi-structured model that allows queries to be posed on semantically equivalent DTDs without query re-formulation. Given a particular DTD and a semantic query, a mapping algorithm translates the semantic query into a structural query for the DTD.

3   XML Naming Model

Every element in a DTD is associated with a tag name. For example, some of the tag names in DTD1 (see Figure 2) are: {`list-manufacturer`, `manufacturer`, `mn-name`, `year`, ...}. Let N_x be the tag name set for a given DTD x. Each tag name $tn \in N_x$ is selected during the design of the DTD to represent the semantics of the element it is naming. Typically, an element's semantics can be adequately captured by selecting a term t from some ontology D. This term t "captures" the appropriate semantics based on its standard usage in the language. For example, the term `manufacturer` has a defined meaning that can be determined using a database of lexical relations such as WordNet [17].

The complexity in naming arises when a single term t cannot adequately convey the semantics of an element. In this case, a set of terms T can be used to provide the additional semantic information. Each $t_i \in T$ has a unique definition in the ontology D. Given a set of terms T the challenge is to combine these terms appropriately to preserve the intended semantics of the element. Common techniques include selecting the most representative term[3] t_i of T and discarding the other terms, or selecting some set $S \subseteq T$ and applying to each $t_i \in S$ the operators of abbreviation and concatenation. Concatenation may be performed with or without using separators such as underscore ("_"), hypen ("-"), or changes in capitalization.

Naming schemes are already used in the naming of classes, variables, and methods in programming languages. We present a naming scheme for XML elements that preserves semantic information to an arbitrary degree of accuracy.[4] Further, the systematic naming scheme allows for the construction of unique tag names as required by XML.

---

[2] Determining semantics of tag elements out-of-context is not a rare occurrence. Consider an XML query that extracts only the manufacturer name and model name from the original document to produce a new document.

[3] The most representative term is determined by the user.

[4] Increased accuracy is achieved by using more terms.

3.1   Constructing XML Tag Names

Given a set of concepts C to be modeled in an DTD x, each concept $c_i \in C$ must be associated with a tag name $tn_i \in N_x$. The structure of each tag name tn_i is as follows:

$$tag\_name ::= [CT\_Term] \mid [CT\_Term].PN$$
$$CT\_Term ::= CT \mid CT \, ; CT\_Term \mid CT \, , CT\_Term$$
$$CT ::= < context\ term >$$
$$PN ::= < property\ name >$$

The *context term(s)* and *property name* are selected from some ontology D. We will not discuss the actual construction of the ontology. The ontology may be considered as a "light-weight ontology"[5] that defines a concept hierarchy using IS-A and HAS-A relationships and provides terms and definitions for the modeled concepts. A database such as WordNet [17] may be used, but in small domains, custom-built concept hierarchies are also practical. For our purposes, the ontology provides terms that have an *accepted meaning* to a human user.

A tag name consists of one or more context terms and an optional property name term. Context terms are related by either IS-A or HAS-A relationships (represented using "," or ";" respectively). In general, tag names are not assigned based on the nesting of elements, but rather the semantics of the element they represent. The following rules dictate the naming for a concept c_i to produce a tag name tn_i:

- The XML document root element (view root) is always assigned a name V.
- Every tag name must have at least one context term.
- A tag name for a composite element has only context terms.
- An atomic element name (#PCDATA) or attribute name must always have a property name that represents the semantics of the attribute. The tag name must also contain all the context terms from its associated entity.
- A weak entity contains the context terms of its parent entity.
- A non-weak entity is named based on its semantics independent of its structural representation and nesting in the document.
- Additional context terms can be added for clarity, but then they must always be used consistently.

The above rules dictate a naming methodology for the construction of tn_i, but not an exact algorithm. There are two major degrees of freedom that are not restricted by the naming method:

- The selection of the ontology D, and the individual terms chosen from D to represent each concept.
- The number of context terms chosen for a tag name. Additional terms can be used to capture various levels of semantic precision.

---

[5] The term "light-weight ontology" is used to differentiate between knowledge base ontologies which in addition to a concept hierarchy also define a rule-base to relate concepts.

It is these two degrees of freedom that complicate naming. The first dictates that it may be impossible to create a single ontology D to name all concepts precisely in any domain. The English language is full of ambiguity and multiple terms with similar meaning. The tag names chosen may differ between designers if different ontological terms are chosen. That is, two different designers may select two different term sets E_1, E_2 where $E_1 \subset D$, $E_2 \subset D$, and $E_1 \neq E_2$. Applying the name construction rules will result in two tag names tn_1 and tn_2 where $tn_1 \neq tn_2$. This degree of freedom can be limited in a given domain by reducing ontology size and the choice of terms.

The second degree of freedom relates to the fact that there is no "one correct way" to capture semantics in a name. Any name we chose will miss some of the related semantics. When assigning names, a designer must make the trade-off between adding more context terms to improve the semantic description and increasing the size of the tag name. One example of this is the decision to introduce the term `NHSC Test` into DTD1 (see Figure 3) to provide more semantics to the model rating statistics. This is an optional addition that improves human readability.

The naming methodology, and later the semantic query facility built on top of it, is not significantly hindered by these two degrees of freedom. One of the reasons for this is the names are defined for a given domain. Given prior agreement on naming in the domain, conflicts may be minimized.[6] Note however that it is the existence of these degrees of freedom that make integration of structures and ontologies between domains so complex. We will not consider integration and querying between domains in this work.

Assigning semantic names to DTD1 gives the resulting DTD in Figure 3. DTD2 is similar. Note that since tag names in an XML document cannot contain the characters `"["`,`"]"`, `";"`, and `","` the semantic names when represented in a DTD have been translated such that: `"["` and `"]"` are removed, and the relationship characters (`";"`, `","`) are substituted with the valid characters (`"-"`, `"_"`) respectively. Finally, the `"."` used to separate the property name is replaced with `"--"`, and spaces within a term are removed. For clarity of presentation in the text, the tag names use the original format presented.

An important difference between regular DTDs and those with semantic naming is that the semantics of every tag name can be determined without examining the nesting inherent in the DTD. That is, given a tag name, we can uniquely determine its semantics. Further, inconsistent naming issues such as the tag names for manufacturer name, model name, and vendor name are avoided. Thus, this methodology contributes by reducing the ambiguity inherent in XML naming by systematically combining additional context terms.

Constructing semantic names for elements increases the string length of the tag name without modifying the document structure. This may be an issue when typing queries or even in the physical size of the resulting XML documents.[7] These issues are discussed in a following section.

---

[6] Effectively, the term sets E_i for each concept c_i are agreed upon *a priori*.

[7] XML compression algorithms exist to reduce document sizes.

```
<!ELEMENT V (Manufacturer+)>
<!ELEMENT Manufacturer (Manufacturer--Name, Manufacturer-Model+)>
<!ELEMENT Manufacturer--Name #PCDATA>
<!ELEMENT Manufacturer-Model (Manufacturer-Model--Name, Manufacturer-Model--Year,
      Manufacturer-Model-NHSCTest--FrontRating, Manufacturer-Model-NHSCTest--SideRating,
      Manufacturer-Model-NHSCTest--Rank, Vehicle+>
<!ELEMENT Manufacturer-Model--Name #PCDATA>
<!ELEMENT Manufacturer-Model--Year #PCDATA>
<!ELEMENT Manufacturer-Model-NHSCTest--FrontRating #PCDATA>
<!ELEMENT Manufacturer-Model-NHSCTest--SideRating #PCDATA>
<!ELEMENT Manufacturer-Model-NHSCTest--Rank #PCDATA>
<!ELEMENT Vehicle (Vehicle--Color, Vehicle--Price, Vendor--Name, Vehicle-Option--Name+)>
<!ELEMENT Vehicle--Color #PCDATA>
<!ELEMENT Vehicle--Price #PCDATA>
<!ELEMENT Vendor--Name #PCDATA>
<!ELEMENT Vehicle-Option--Name #PCDATA>
```

Fig. 3. DTD1 with Semantic Naming

4   Semantic Querying

Although systematic naming captures increased semantics in XML names, many users would see the increased size of the XML document and tag size as sufficiently negative to avoid systematic naming. However, by exploiting systematic naming it is possible to define a semantic query facility that reduces the negative features of longer semantic names and the need for path expressions in XML querying.

A *path expression* in XML querying is a sequence of edge labels starting from the root that enumerates a set of nodes. Complex path expressions may contain regular expressions both on the edge label strings or on the path itself. Operators such as selection ("|") and Kleene closure ("*") can be used.

Path expressions often complicate querying by focusing on the structure of the document rather than realizing the semantics of the query. The frustration users encounter with joins in the relational model is magnified considerably with XML querying where their required awareness of the structure of the document is increased further. In effect, the structure of the XML document **impedes** user querying as simple queries may be unnecessarily complicated by path expressions. Even graphical query languages such as XML-GL [8] focus on structural querying of documents rather than semantic data extraction. Our query language uses the semantic names assigned during systematic naming to produce a canonical query tree that is later mapped to the exact structure of a specific XML document.

Although we exploit the previously presented semantic naming system, semantic querying can be performed with any naming system as long as it has two important properties:

- A tag (semantic) name must be uniquely identifiable by a human user without presenting surrounding structure or names.

– The same tag name must be used consistently to represent the identical concept even though the concept may be organized using different structural representations in various DTDs.

The combination of these two naming features allows the construction of an algorithm that dynamically searches structural representations for particular concepts by name.

An XML document can be modeled as an edge-labeled tree [1] where the label of each edge is the tag name. We will use an edge-labeled tree to model a DTD. Formally, a DTD $x = (N_x, L_x, E_x, v_x)$ where N_x is a set of nodes, L_x is a set of edge labels, $E_x \subset N_x \times N_x \times L_x$, and v_x is the root node of the tree. For our purposes, we will initially consider DTDs with no ID or IDREF attributes (i.e. those XML documents that can be modeled as a tree). The two example DTDs modeled as trees are given in Figure 4 with leaf nodes represented as empty circles, and interior nodes as filled circles.

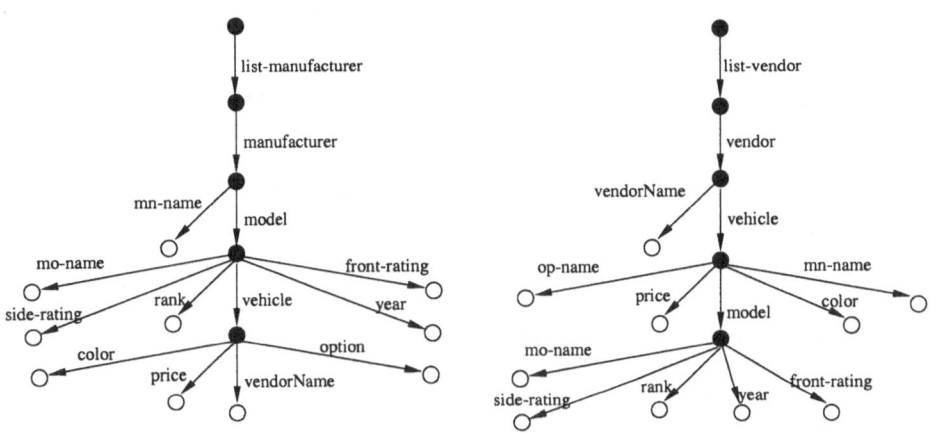

Fig. 4. Tree representations of DTDs

By examining the tree structures, it is apparent why the two DTDs require different XML queries: path expressions denote paths from the root to target nodes. Hence, re-organizing the tree changes the path expressions. Now, consider a canonical tree structure of the same data given in Figure 5. This canonical tree structure is built by extracting the semantic tag names from the DTDs and nesting them according to the term nesting in each tag. For the following discussion, the term semantic name is used interchangeably for tag name.

Definition 1 *Define a* **context view** $CV = (N_v, L_v, E_v, v_0)$ *as a rooted, edge-labeled graph that consists of a set of nodes N_v, a set of edge labels L_v, and a set of edges $E_v \subset N_v \times N_v \times L_v$, and a distinguished root $v_0 \in N_v$. CV can be built algorithmically given DTD x by using the tag set N_x. The root node v_0 is referred to as V or the* view root *in the text.*

Given the canonical form of the context view (see Figure 5), users specify their query on the context view. Note that to simplify presentation the
edge label only displays the *term at depth*. The full edge label is constructed
by constructing the path expression from root to node and concatenating the
edge labels. For example, the tag name `Year` under `Model` has an edge label of
`[Manufacturer;Model].Year`.

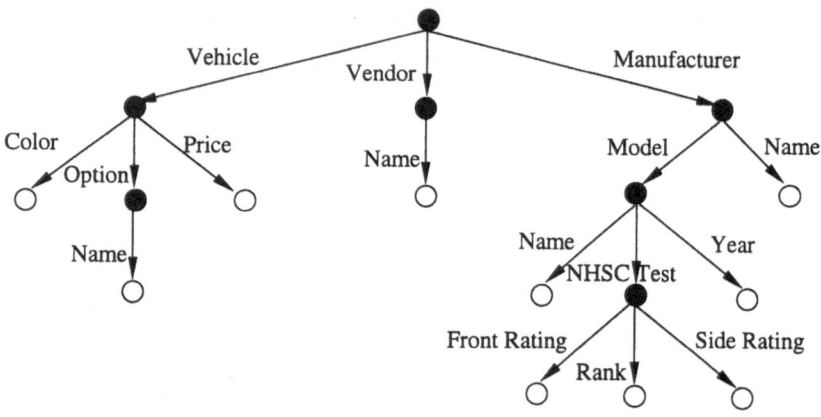

Fig. 5. Context view

The query procedure is straight-forward:

- The user is given the context view $CV = (N_v, L_v, E_v, v_0)$ in tree form.
- The user selects a set of edges $E' \subseteq E_v$ for inclusion into their query either
  as conditions (WHERE) or selection clauses. Each edge $e = (u, v, tn) \in E'$
  has a unique tag name tn.
- Given the actual DTD $x = (N_x, L_x, E_x, v_x)$ and the edge set E' selected by
  the user, the system attempts to match each edge $e = (u, v, tn) \in E'$ with
  an edge $f = (u', v', tn') \in E_x$ where $tn = tn'$.
- This matching produces a set of edges $E'_x \subseteq E_x$. Each edge $f \in E_x$ has a
  unique path from the root. The path replaces the tag name to produce a
  structural query.

The example query posed on the context view is in Figure 6. The canonical
query does not need a FROM clause in this case. In general, the introduction of
a FROM clause is not required if the query can be answered using a single query
iterator variable. Notice how path expressions are removed from the query. Thus,
the query will be correct even if the DTD changes.

To map from a canonical query to an XML query requires that each element
referenced in the query be converted into the appropriate path expression for
the DTD. For a tree-structured DTD with no internal linking, this mapping can
be easily achieved by performing a breadth-first search from the DTD root to

select [Manufacturer].Name, [Vehicle].Price
where [Vehicle].Price < 30000 and [Manufacturer;Model;NHSC Test].Rank ≤ 10 (Q_4)

Fig. 6. Semantic Query on Context View

```
<!ELEMENT V (Vendor+, Manufactuer-Model+)>
<!ELEMENT Vendor (Vendor--Name, Vehicle+)>
<!ELEMENT Vendor--Name #PCDATA>
<!ELEMENT Vehicle (Vehicle--Color, Vehicle--Price, Vehicle-Option--Name+,
                   Vehicle-Manufacturer-Model)>
<!ELEMENT Vehicle--Color #PCDATA>
<!ELEMENT Vehicle--Price #PCDATA>
<!ELEMENT Vehicle-Option--Name #PCDATA>
<!ELEMENT Vehicle-Manufacturer-Model #EMPTY>
    <!ATTLIST Vehicle-Manufacturer-Model Vehicle-Manufactuer-Model--Id IDREF #IMPLIED>
<!ELEMENT Manufacturer-Model (Manufacturer--Name,Manufacturer-Model--Name,
    Manufacturer-Model--Year, Manufacturer-Model-NHSCTest--FrontRating,
    Manufacturer-Model-NHSCTest--SideRating, Manufacturer-Model-NHSCTest--Rank)>
    <!ATTLIST Manufacturer-Model Manufacturer-Model--Id ID #REQUIRED>
<!ELEMENT Manufacturer--Name #PCDATA>
<!ELEMENT Manufacturer-Model--Name #PCDATA>
<!ELEMENT Manufacturer-Model--Year #PCDATA>
<!ELEMENTManufacturer-Model-NHSCTest--FrontRating #PCDATA>
<!ELEMENT Manufacturer-Model-NHSCTest--SideRating #PCDATA>
<!ELEMENT Manufacturer-Model-NHSCTest--Rank #PCDATA>
```

Fig. 7. DTD with ID/IDREF Attributes

the appropriate tag names. Since the DTD is a tree structure, there is a unique path from root to tag name for each tag, and there is a single path that relates all concepts.

4.1 Advanced Querying

Although simple XML documents can be modeled as tree structures, linking between XML elements is possible using ID and IDREF attributes. The ID attribute is used to assign a unique key to an element, and IDREF is used to reference an ID of another element. This allows data to be hierarchically organized in the base XML document, but also include cross-links between elements to model other relationships in which they participate. ID and IDREF attributes can be easily modeled in the context view by introducing ID and IDREF nodes. Consider modifying DTD2 to produce DTD3. DTD3 contains IDs for models so that they may be listed separately and eliminate duplication. The modification to the DTD results in an attribute ID added to model element, and attribute IDREF added to vehicle element (see Figure 7). The context view now becomes a canonical graph structure with directed links between ID and IDREF nodes (see Figure 8).

There are several new challenges when introducing links via ID/IDREF. The first challenge is naming the IDREF values appropriately. In the exam-

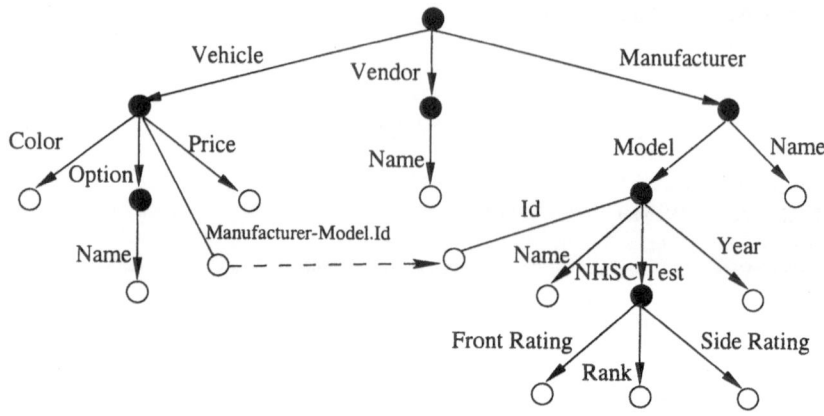

Fig. 8. Context View with Linking

ple, we could not use the tag name Model to refer to both the model element itself, and the sub-element introduced under vehicle to provide a link to the actual model element. In our system, the standard name for IDREF attributes is the name of the parent element ([Vehicle]) plus the name of the linked element ([Manufacturer;Model]) plus the generic term Id. Thus, the name for the IDREF attribute for vehicle is [Vehicle;Manufacturer;Model].Id. This guarantees unique IDREF attribute naming.

The second challenge is handling path ambiguity now that we have a canonical graph. For example, querying for [Manufacturer;Model].Name now has two potential paths:

- A semantically direct path of [Manufacturer;Model].Name that corresponds to model names whether or not there is a vehicle in the XML document with that model. The particular path for DTD3 is
  V.Manufacturer-Model.Manufacturer-Model--Name.
- A semantically indirect path through [Vehicle] with the constraint that we only want model names if there is a vehicle in the XML document with that model. This path is [Vehicle;Manufacturer;Model].Name, and the physical path in DTD3 is V.Vendor.Vehicle.Vehicle-Manufacturer-Model then linked to V.Manufacturer-Model.Name using ID/IDREF.

The first semantic path is a direct path in the canonical graph. The second semantic path represents a derived tag name by linking [Vehicle] and [Manufacturer;Model]. The user can select the derived path by giving its full derived tag name. The system resolves path ambiguity by selecting the path that reflects the hierarchical organization of the document (avoids using ID/IDREF) if possible. A full discussion of semantic querying in the presence of ID/IDREF is beyond the scope of this paper. Further, we have not considered links between documents using XLink [10] or XPath [7], although the context view model could be extended to handle them.

Most XML query languages allow path expressions to contain wild cards such as: selection ("a | b"), match one edge ("_"), Kleene closure ("*"), at least one occurrence ("+"), and optional occurrence ("?"). Although such wild card operators give path expressions more flexibility to hide some of the structure of the document, they do not provide the same flexibility as the context view. Further, the context view can be queried using the same wild card operators.

4.2   Mapping Algorithm

This section overviews the mapping algorithm that converts a semantic query S expressed on the context view CV to an XML query Q on a given DTD x. The element tag names for x are defined according to the ontology used to define CV. DTD x may contain linking via ID/IDREF. Query translation is performed by mapping every semantic name to a path expression for x. The algorithm performs the following steps:

– Perform a breadth-first traversal of DTD x starting from the root to build a mapping table T.
– Each entry in the mapping table contains a semantic tag name tn and an associated set of path expressions P. Each path expression $p \in P$ provides a path in DTD x to an element with tag name tn.
– If DTD x is a tree, then each tag name tn has only one path, and replacing a semantic name in the query with a path expression is a 1:1 mapping.
– If DTD x is a graph, there may be multiple possible paths $p_1, p_2, ..., p_n$ to tn. The multiple mappings can be used to return the union of all paths, or the possible paths can be given to the user to select one.
– After a set of mappings to path expressions have been determined, the system must verify that the path expressions are connected. A set of path expressions is *connected* if it is possible to build a minimal spanning tree with a defined root connecting all nodes involved in the query **after** the root node of DTD x is removed.
  • DTDs with no linking always have a connected spanning tree for all queries.
  • DTDs with ID/IDREF linking many have more than one possible spanning tree for certain queries. The system enumerates the possibilities and has the user select one.

The performance of the algorithm is primarily determined by the cost to perform the mappings. The cost to construct the mapping table is $O(|E_x|)$ where $|E_x|$ is the number of edges in the graph representing DTD x. However, this cost can be amortized across multiple queries by pre-computing the mapping table. At query time, the query processor must only lookup the appropriate mappings in the table which can be performed quite efficiently. If the mappings yield a set of paths that is not connected, the system must search for connections to produce a spanning tree.

For example, the query in Figure 6 is translated for DTD1 by searching for $E' = \{$ `[Manufacturer].Name`, `[Manufacturer;Model;NHSC Test].Rank`, `[Vehicle].Price`$\}$. Parsing the DTD gives a path to `[Manufacturer].Name` as `V.Manufacturer.Manufacturer--Name`. The path for `[Vehicle].Price` is `V.Manufacturer.Manufacturer-Model.Vehicle.Vehicle--Price`. Searching for the rank attribute is similar. Note that once the first attribute is found (in this case `[Manufacturer].Name`) all other attributes contain as part of their path, a path through the parent node of the first attribute. Performing substitution of semantic tag names for paths results in a Lorel query. The parent node of the first attribute found is used to define a variable in the FROM clause. In this case, this produces `FROM V.Manufacturer M`, and then `M` is used to specify relative paths to the remaining elements.

The same query on DTD3 results in two possible paths for several tag names, including `[Manufacturer].Name`, that can be accessed through a direct path or through an indirect path using the IDREF under the `Vehicle` element. In this case, there is only one mapping for `[Vehicle].Price`, so this mapping is chosen. This selection forces the mapping for `[Manufacturer].Name` to use the IDREF mapping, so there is no ambiguity. Using the IDREF mapping produces a spanning tree with `Vendor` as the root element. Note that if the query just specified `[Manufacturer].Name` then the mapping selected would be the one without using IDREF. For cases where multiple IDREF links are possible, the user must chose a correct mapping (method of relating the individual trees of the forest) to produce a single spanning tree.

5 Related Work

There has been a comparison [4] between the numerous XML query languages. All the query languages studied, including graphical query languages such as XML-GL [8] focus on extracting data based on structural path expressions. Although this is sufficient for users with intimate knowledge of XML querying and the DTD itself, it is challenging for users with less domain and structural DTD knowledge to formulate queries. We have proposed a semantic query facility built on top of systematic naming of XML elements. The user queries a canonical view, and the system translates semantic tags to path expressions on the actual DTDs. Further, after semantic naming of the document, it is still possible to query the document using normal XML query languages. Thus, the semantic naming can be considered as a virtual, overlay semantics on top of the original structure.

Related work on XML querying includes the MIX system [3], integrating keyword search into XML query processing [12], and the definition of a meet operator [20]. These systems allow simpler user querying by allowing navigation of XML documents, allowing imprecise queries by using keyword search, or by relating concepts in a document by structure. Our work improves on these systems by providing a general, semantic querying layer on top of existing XML structure that hides the entire structure from the user. Further, the semantic layer can be browsed independently of the XML documents, and queries can be formulated graphically over the context view [14]. XML Namespaces [23] can be used to create unique tag names, but there is no requirement for their systematic usage. Further, comparing semantics of names across namespaces encapsulates many of the challenges in system integration. This work presents a methodology for naming that does not rely on the construction of namespaces, and the use of XML namespaces is mostly orthogonal to this work.

One of the motivations for our work is that XML documents (views) allow access to a relational database [21] by multiple parties. In these cases, it is beneficial for users to be able to graphically browse and semantically query information stored in XML documents without in-depth detail of its organization.

Others areas of similar work include integration and querying using ontologies such as Ontobroker [9]. At its basis, semantic naming relies on an ontology (the canonical view) for naming XML elements. However, the ontology defined for this work does not formally encode axioms or relationships between elements. This is a design decision as the relationships can be dynamically realized by matching element names. The Ontobroker ontology is more powerful than the one we use for semantic querying. However, it does not provide a naming system for entities, nor was it designed for structure-independent querying.

In the relational database world, there has been extensive work in the development of graphical query tools [5,22] to aid in the formulation of SQL queries, query languages such as query by example (QBE) [24], and semantic query approaches [15,18] to reduce the semantic burden on users. Systems such as Query-by-Example (QBE) [24] and Kaleidoscope [6] allow users to query relational databases without using SQL. There also have been examples of semantic query languages for the relational model such as SemQL [15], SemanticAccess [19], and conceptual query language (CQL) [18]. Our approach works on XML as well as the relational model, and does not require wrappers or advanced database knowledge. For less experienced users, querying using names is simple due to is similarity with keyword searching. Further, we have implemented a graphical query tool [13] that allows querying by context and provides an easy-to-use query interface.

6   Future Work and Conclusions

In conclusion, we have presented a semantic naming methodology to construct element tag names for XML DTDs. The semantic naming procedure produces names with regular structure that contain sufficient context to identify element semantics. Systematic naming allows for increased human readability and documentation. Given a semantically named DTD, it is possible to build a canonical context view for semantic querying. Semantic queries are then mapped to structural queries on specific DTDs and ambiguity is resolved by exploiting the hierarchical structure of the document itself. Since the document structure is unchanged, regular structural queries can still be performed, albeit with longer tag names. The drawback of longer tag names is mitigated by graphical user interfaces for querying and browsing the context view, and by lessening the requirement for path expressions which are automatically determined for semantic queries. This work represents one of the first attempts at providing systematic naming and querying without specifying path expressions.

Future work includes developing a formal query algebra for semantic queries and mapping semantic queries to relational and object-oriented models.

References

1. S. Abiteboul, P. Buneman, and D. Suciu. *Data on the Web: From Relations to Semistructured Data and XML*. Morgan Kaufmann Publishers, 2000.
2. S. Abiteboul, D. Quass, J. McHugh, J. Widom, and J. Wiener. The Lorel query language for semistructured data. *International Journal on Digital Libraries*, 1(1):68–88, 1997.
3. C. Baru, A. Gupta, B. Ludascher, R. Marciano, Y. Papakonstantinou, P. Velikhov, and V. Chu. XML-Based Information Mediation with MIX. In *Proceedings of the 1999 ACM SIGMOD International Conference on Management of Data*, pages 597–599, 1999.
4. A. Bonifati and S. Ceri. Comparative analysis of five XML query languages. *SIGMOD Record*, 29(1):68–79, 2000.
5. T. Catarci and G. Santucci. Query by Diagram: A Graphical Environment for Querying Databases. *SIGMOD Record*, 23(2):515–515, June 1994.
6. S. Cha and G. Wiederhold. Kaleidoscope Data Model for An English-like Query Language. In *17th International Conference on Very Large Data Bases*, pages 351–361, 1991.
7. J. Clark and S. DeRose. XML Path Language (XPath), November 1999.
8. S. Comai, E. Damiani, and P. Fraternali. Computing Graphical Queries over XML Data. *ACM Transactions on Information Systems*, 19(4):371–430, 2001.
9. S. Decker, M. Erdmann, and R. Studer. ONTOBROKER: Ontology based access to distributed and semi-structured information. In *Database Semantics - Semantic Issues in Multimedia Systems*, volume 138, 1998.
10. S. DeRose, E. Maler, and D. Orchard. XML Linking Language: XLink, 1995.
11. R. Elmasri and S. Navathe. *Fundamentals of Database Systems*. Addison-Wesley, 2000.
12. D. Florescu, D. Kossmann, and I. Manolescu. Integrating keyword search into XML query processing. *WWW9 / Computer Networks*, 33(1-6):119–135, 2000.
13. R. Lawrence and K. Barker. Integrating Relational Database Schemas using a Standardized Dictionary. In *SAC'2001- ACM Symposium on Applied Computing*, March 2001.
14. R. Lawrence and K. Barker. Using Unity to Semi-Automatically Integrate Relational Schema. In *18th International Conference on Data Engineering (ICDE 2002)*, pages 329–330, March 2002.
15. J. Lee and D. Baik. SemQL: A Semantic Query Language for Multidatabase Systems. In *Proceedings of the 8th International Conference on Information Knowledge Management (CIKM'99)*, pages 259–266, Kansas City, MO, November 1999.
16. D. Maier. Database desiderata for an XML query language, 1998.
17. G. Miller, R. Beckwith, C. Fellbaum, D. Gross, and K. Miller. Five Papers on Word-Net. Technical Report CSL Report 43, Cognitive Systems Laboratory, Princeton University, 1990.

18. V. Owei and S. Navathe. Enriching the conceptual basis for query formulation through relationship semantics in databases. *Information Systems*, 26(6):445–475, 2001.

19. N. Rishe, J. Yuan, R. Athauda, S. Chen, X. Lu, X. Ma, A. Vaschillo, A. Shaposhnikov, and D. Vasilevsky. Semantic Access: Semantic Interface for Querying Databases. In *VLDB 2000, Proceedings of 26th International Conference on Very Large Data Bases*, pages 591–594, 2000.

20. A. Schmidt, M. Kersten, and M. Windhouwer. Querying XML Documents Made Easy: Nearest Concept Queries. In *Proceedings of the 17th International Conference on Data Engineering*, pages 321–329. IEEE Computer Society, 2001.

21. J. Shanmugasundaram, J. Kiernan, E. Shekita, C. Fan, and J. Funderburk. Querying XML views of relational data. In *VLDB 2001, Proceedings of 27th International Conference on Very Large Data Bases*, pages 261–270, 2001.

22. M. Stonebraker, J. Chen, N. Nathan, C. Parson, A. Su, and J. Wu. Tioga: A Database-Oriented Visualization Tool. In *Proceedings of the Visualization '93 Conference*, pages 86–93, San Jose, CA, October 1993.

23. T.Bray, D. Hollander, and A. Layman. Namespaces in XML, January 1999.

24. M. Zloof. Query-by-Example: the Invocation and Definition of Tables and Forms. In *Proceedings of the International Conference on Very Large Data Bases*, pages 1–24. ACM, 1975.

Reasoning with Ontologies by Using Knowledge Conjunction in Conceptual Graphs

Dan Corbett

Advanced Computing Research Centre
School of Computer and Information Science
University of South Australia
Adelaide, South Australia 5095

Abstract. This paper discusses automated reasoning over ontologies represented as Conceptual Graphs. We discuss a tool which has been implemented using Conceptual Graphs as its underlying knowledge structure. The significance of this work is that we demonstrate that the power of logic as implemented in Conceptual Graphs, and the tools available in Conceptual Graph Theory can be used as powerful ontology reasoning tools in a real-world domain. We show that ontologies can be constrained and unified using efficient methods, and that these methods provide the basis for an automated reasoning system. The Conceptual Graph techniques of concept join, partial order and subsumption are all exploited to create these reasoning tools.

We discuss the implementation of these ideas, and demonstrate the software tool created in two domains: building architecture and defence. Examples show that the system can reason over these domains and assist the users in their tasks.

1 A Brief Overview of Conceptual Graphs

Conceptual Structures (or Conceptual Graphs, or „CGs") are a knowledge representation scheme, inspired by the existential graphs of Charles Sanders Peirce and further extended and defined by John Sowa [2, 3]. Informally, CGs can be thought of as a formalization and extension of Semantic Networks, although the origins are different. They are labeled graphs with two types of nodes: concepts (which represent objects, entities or ideas) and relation nodes, which represent relations between the concepts. As an example, Figure 1 shows a Conceptual Graph which represents the knowledge that „The cat Felix is sitting on the mat which is known as mat 47."

Every concept or relation has an associated type. A concept may also have a specific referent or individual. A concept in a CG may represent a specific instance of that type (e.g., *Felix* is a specific instance, or individual, of type *cat*) or we may choose only to specify the type of the concept. That is to say that a concept may simply represent a generic concept for a type, such as *mammal* or *room*, or a concept

Fig. 1. A Simple CG.

R. Meersman, Z. Tari (Eds.): CoopIS/DOA/ODBASE 2002, LNCS 2519, pp. 1304–1316, 2002.

may represent a specific object or idea, such as *my cat* or *the kitchen at the Smith's house*. In the former case, the concepts in Figure 1 would be shown as „cat: * " and „mat: * " indicating non-specified entities of types *cat* and *mat*. In the standard canonical formation rules for Conceptual Graphs, unbound concepts are existentially quantified.

A relation may have zero or one incoming arcs, and one or more outgoing arcs. The type of the relation determines the number of arcs allowed on the relation. The arcs always connect a concept to a relation. Arcs cannot exist between concepts, or between relations.

A canon in the sense discussed here is the set of all CGs which are well-formed, and meaningful in their domain. Canonical formation rules specify how CGs can be legally built and guarantee that the resulting CGs satisfy „sensibility constraints." The sensibility constraints are rules in the domain which specify how a CG can be built, for example that the concept *eats* must have a theme which is *food*. Note that canonicity does not guarantee validity. A CG may be well-formed in the canononical formation rules for the domain, but still be false.

Sowa discusses his original definitions in [2] but our work follows the further formalized and refined versions of Sowa's original ideas presented by Willems [4], by Chein and Mugnier [5, 6] and by Corbett [7, 8] .

A type hierarchy is established for both the concepts and the relations within a canon. This hierarchy is expressed by a subsumption or generalization-order on types.

Formally, we define Conceptual Graphs as follows:

Definition 1. Canon. A canon is a tuple $(T, I, \leq, ::)$ where:

T is the set of types. We will further assume that T contains two disjunctive subsets T_C and T_R containing types for concepts and relations.

I is the set of individuals. I includes all possible instances, as well as the generic marker *.

$\leq \subseteq T \times T$ is the subtype relation. It is assumed to be a lattice (so there are types $\top$ and $\bot$ and operations $\wedge$ and $\vee$).

$:: \subseteq I \times T$ is the conformity relation. The conformity relation relates type labels to individual markers. This is essentially the relation which enforces that the typing of the concepts makes sense in the domain.

Definition 2. Conceptual Graph. A Conceptual Graph with respect to a canon is a tuple $G = (C, q, R, type, referent, arg_1, \ldots, arg_m)$ where

C is the set of concepts, $type : C \to T$ indicates the type of a concept, and *referent* : $C \to I$ indicates the referent marker of a concept. The referent marker is either a pointer to an individual or a generic marker, which indicates that the individual is of the type indicated, but is existentially quantified.

T is the set of types. We will further assume that T contains two disjunctive subsets T_C and T_R containing types for concepts and relations.

I is the set of individuals.

q is a distinguished member of C, the head or root node of the graph.

R is the set of conceptual relations, *type* : $R \rightarrow T$ indicates the type of a relation, and each $arg_i : R \rightarrow C$ is a partial function where $arg_i(r)$ indicates the i-th argument of the relation *r*. The argument functions are partial as they are undefined for arguments higher than the relation's arity.

2 Types and Inheritance

The set of types discussed in Definition 2 is arranged into a type hierarchy, ordered according to the specificity of each type. A type hierarchy is established for both the concepts and the relations within a canon. A type hierarchy is based on the intuition that some types subsume other types, for example, every instance of *cat* would also have all the properties of *mammal*. This hierarchy is expressed by a subsumption or generalization order on types. A type *t* is said to be more specific than a type *s* if *t* specializes some of the concepts from *s*.

An example of a relation type hierarchy is shown in Figure 2. In one domain that

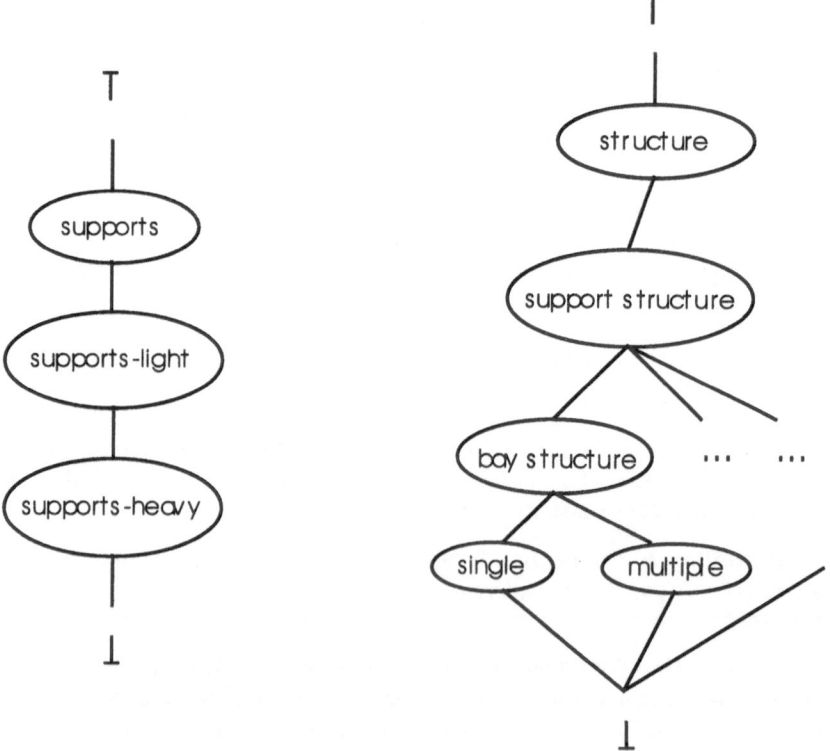

Fig. 2. A relation type hierarchy.   **Fig. 3.** A concept type hierarchy.

we have worked in, building architecture, we may wish to represent that one structure supports another structure. We may further want to represent that any type of support structure which supports a heavy load will also support a light load. This relationship is expressed in the hierarchy. In this manner, some constraints on the relations between concepts can be represented.

Similarly, an example type hierarchy for concepts is shown in Figure 3. The universal type is shown at the top of the hierarchy, and is represented by T. The absurd type is shown at the bottom of the graph, and is represented by ⊥. Here we see that a support structure is a specialization of a structure, and that a bay structure specializes support structure. Using these type hierarchies, it is possible to show, for example, that the multiple-bay structure will support a heavy load, by using concepts for multiple-bay structure, and a relation of the type supports-heavy.

The definitions of unification, consistency and type subsumption in this paper are based on formal concepts of projection and lower bounds. Carpenter [9] defines each of these operators as a morphism. We have modified Carpenter's definitions to work with the properties of Conceptual Graphs. A morphism is then a mapping from the set of nodes of one Conceptual Graph to the set of nodes of another that preserves the order of relation arguments and the values of those arguments. In a morphism, all of the connections and arguments are preserved. The following definition of projection is the standard definition used in recent Conceptual Graph literature [4, 6, 7, 10, 11].

Definition 3. Projection.
$G = (C, R, type, referent, arg_1, \ldots, arg_m)$ subsumes $G' = (C', R', type',$
$referent', arg'_1, \ldots, arg'_m)$, $G \geq G'$, if and only if there is a pair of morphisms h_C:
$C \rightarrow C'$ and h_R: $R \rightarrow R'$, such that:

$$\forall c \in C \text{ and } \forall c' \in C', h_C(c) = c' \text{ only if } type(c) \geq type'(c'), \text{ and}$$
$$referent(c) = * \text{ or } referent(c) = referent(c')$$
$$\forall r \in R \text{ and } \forall r' \in R', h_R(r) = r' \text{ only if } type(r) \geq type'(r')$$
$$\forall r \in R, arg'_i(h_R(r)) = h_C(arg_i(r)),$$

Willems also includes the following non-emptiness condition in his definition of projection in [4]:

$$\forall c \in C \text{ there is a concept } c' \in C', \text{ such that } h_C(c) = c'$$

This non-emptiness condition guarantees that all the concepts present in the more general graph are also present in the more specific graph, although they may be in a more specific state. Willems' definition allows for the more specific graph to have concepts of a more specific type, or for a generic referent to be replaced by a specific individual. The definition used here also includes the non-emptiness condition.

This definition of projection then gives us a formal definition for subtype and *supertype and for subsumption* on the partial order of the type hierarchy. All of these operations are now simply applications of the projection operator. Finding types which are compatible (i.e. that can be unified) is now a matter of finding a common subtype (or *join*) between the two types. If the only common subtype is $\perp$ then there can be no unification.

3 Unification as Reasoning

In early pioneering work on the unification of first-order terms, Reynolds [12] used the natural lattice structure of first-order terms, which was a partial ordering based on subsumption of terms [13] . Many terms (or types in our case) are not in any subsumption relation, for example *cat* and *dog*, or *wood* and *mammal*. Unification corresponds to finding the greatest lower bound of two terms in the lattice [14] . The bottom of any lattice, which is represented with the symbol $\perp$, is the type to which all types can unify, and represents inconsistency. The top of the lattice, represented by $\top$, is the type to which all pairs of types can generalize, and is called the universal type. Every type is a subtype of $\top$. Inheritance hierarchies can be seen as lattices that admit unification and generalization [14] . The common specialization of two Conceptual Graphs, s and t, is known as a join. The common generalization of the two graphs is known as a meet.

The process of unifying Conceptual Graphs includes the process of finding the most general subtypes for pairs of types of concepts, which depends on the two types in question being consistent. We also allow constraints on the concepts in the graphs, which are processed during the unification and resolution process. Unification (by projection) is the mechanism we use to find the solution of the constraints. In our work, unification is a tool which performs the work of identifying two structures using subsumption, where the elements of the structure can be constrained.

Until very recently, CGs have had no formalism for constraining real values in the referent of a concept. The standard method for representing and validating constraints has been to use type subsumption to specify which concept types (or subsumed subtypes) are valid in a system. One could constrain values in a knowledge representation system by forcing the concepts to conform to a specified type, or else to be subsumed by that type. A similar method applies to relations. For example, the concept *eats* is specified to occur only between an agent which is an *animal* and a theme which is a *food*. Any individual used in the animal concept must conform to the *animal* type, which means that it must either be *animal*, or be subsumed by *animal*, such as *cat* or *reptile*.

One generalization of unification constraints is the use of ordering constraints, i.e., constraints of the form $s \leq t$ where s and t are terms. Depending on the application, the ordering $\leq$ may have different interpretations. A concept may unify by subsumption with another concept if one of the concepts is a more general expression of the other, as defined in the partial order. There are also constraint approaches in logic programming where constraints are not interpreted over a single structure.

An example for such an approach is H. Aït-Kaci's Login [1] , where first-order terms are replaced by feature terms. In the ψ-terms of Aït-Kaci [1, 15] subterms are labeled symbolically, rather than by argument position, and there is no fixed arity.

The novel contribution of ψ-terms is in the use of type inheritance information. Aït-Kaci's view of unification was as a filter for matching partial structures, using functions and variables as the „filters." Aït-Kaci disagreed with the philosophy of Feature Structure unification [9], where two structures with different functors can never unify [14, 15]. Aït-Kaci relaxed this requirement for his ψ-terms by allowing type information to be attached to functions and variables. Then, his unification technique uses information from a taxonomic hierarchy to achieve a more gradual filtering.

An example from Knight [14] illustrates this gradual filtering technique. Assume that we have the following inheritance information, as illustrated in Figure 4: Birds and fish are animals; a fish-eater is an animal; a trout is a fish; and a pelican is both a bird and a fish-eater. Then unifying the following ψ-terms:

fish-eater (likes → trout)
bird (color → brown; likes → fish)

will yield the new ψ-term:

pelican (color → brown; likes → trout)

Unification does not fail on comparing *fish-eater* to *bird*, or *trout* to *fish*. Instead, the conflict is resolved by finding the greatest lower bound on each of the two pairs of items in the taxonomic hierarchy, in this case *pelican* and *trout*, respectively. In this manner, Aït-Kaci's system naturally extends the information-merging (or *knowledge conjunction*) nature of unification.

The formal definition of unification for Conceptual Graphs is set out in [7, 16] however, it is essential to clarify the difference between the „join" operator and the general concept of unification. The difference between these two operators can be illustrated in the following way. In the standard canonical formation rules for Conceptual Graphs, unbound concepts are existentially quantified. We take for our example the two graphs in Figure 5, which can be interpreted as „Felix is on some object," and „There is some animal sitting on that particular mat." Joining these two graphs is not possible under the standard canonical formation rule for external

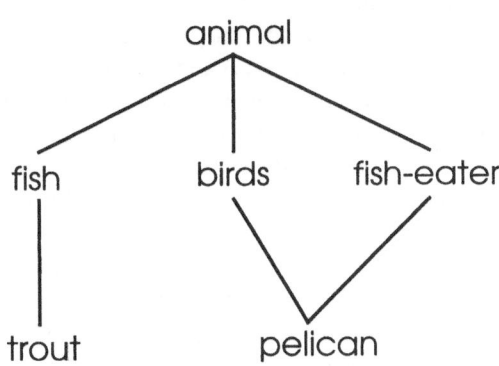

Fig. 4. An example type hierarchy from Aït-Kaci's work [1].

join because there's no projection from one graph to the other. However, there are

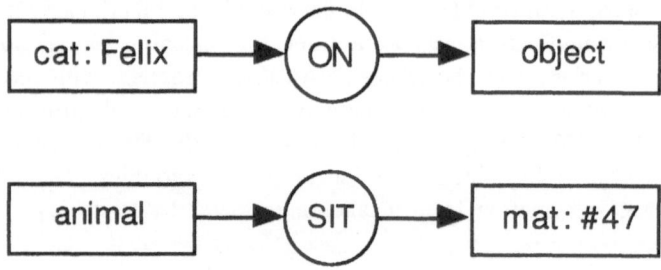

Fig. 5. Is Felix on the mat?

individual concepts which can be joined, such as the concept that „Felix is a cat" and „animal." However, as discussed in previous sections, true unification is the knowledge conjunction of the two graphs. The unification of these two Conceptual Graphs would be similar to the unification of ψ-terms presented by Aït-Kaci [1] . The unification is therefore „Felix sat on mat number 47," as shown in Figure 6. Here, the more general concepts of „animal," „on," and „object" have been replaced by their more specific instances. This illustrates that unification is more than an external join, and is composed of several operations, including join.

4 Knowledge Conjunction

Unification is somewhat more complicated, and also more interesting and useful than merely an extension of the join operation. The unification of two graphs contains neither more nor less information than the two graphs being unified. Figure 6 shows that the unification of the two graphs in Figure 5 still retains all the information of the original two graphs. This is the idea behind knowledge conjunction.

The main thrust of the research described in this paper is the unification of Conceptual Graphs in terms of conjoining the knowledge contained in two different graphs. While this may involve term substitution (or the Conceptual Graphs equivalent - instantiation, subsumption, variable binding, etc.) and constraint solving, our research is more concerned with knowledge conjunction. Carpenter defines unification as a system in which two pieces of partial information can be combined into a single unified whole [9]. In our case, these pieces of partial information are represented by Conceptual Graphs. Carpenter refers to this idea as information conjunction, but in our work, it is *knowledge conjunction* that is more important to us. We want to be able to combine the expert knowledge of a system, or even combine knowledge from different sources, not merely gather additional information. Unification here is the combining of pieces of knowledge in a domain, represented as Conceptual Graphs. We define unification as an operation that simultaneously

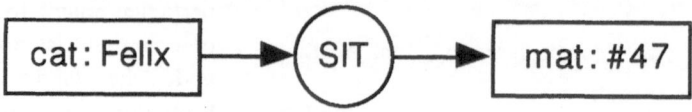

Fig. 6. Felix is on the mat.

determines the consistency of two pieces of partial or incomplete knowledge, and if they are consistent, combines them into a single result.

When an ontology is represented by the use of Conceptual Graphs constructed in this way, subsumption can be used to combine, refine and reuse the knowledge contained in the graphs. This further allows us to perform reasoning over the knowledge in the graphs as concepts. Reasoning is not limited to objects, classes or libraries, but can also be applied to generic concepts in the knowledge. We demonstrate reasoning over generic concepts in the next section.

One major advantage that Conceptual Graphs have over other representation schemes is that Conceptual Graphs which contain existentially quantified concepts can still be unified. In Feature Structures theory [9] for example, it is important to know whether one is attempting to unify the *intensions* or the *extensions* of two Feature Structures (FS). Essentially, the intension of a Feature Structure is all of the attributes (or properties, or *features*) of a construct. The extension of a Feature Structure is the actual object being represented, with the attributes specified, even if only partially. In Feature Structures theory, one must decide whether the Feature Structures being unified are of the same *intensional* type, or the same *extensional* type, and then seek to identify the two FSs under that type. The unification of two FSs under their extensional type is simply the identification of all their values for their features (similar to type labels and individual markers for the concepts in CGs). There is no way to derive identities of intensional types of two Feature Structures, as there are no values to be compared.

Mineau uses Conceptual Graphs to represent the semantics behind web agents in [17]. Mineau shows that the main advantages of Conceptual Graphs in this regard is that they are highly expressive, formal, easy to use and easy to understand. He shows that the use of CG-based agents as Knowledge Servers increases the interoperability between objects in the ontology. Knowledge conjunction extends this capability by providing a formal, efficient model for reasoning over ontologies.

5 The Air Operations Officer

The results discussed in this section are those recorded from the application of the knowledge conjunction reasoning tool operating over the defense domain. The domain knowledge is represented as Conceptual Graphs with constraints on either the structure of the graph or on the values in the concepts [7]. Here, we discuss the idea behind the reasoning mechanism by employing order sorted unification and constraints within the domain of architectural design. The concepts discussed previously were implemented in Allegro Common Lisp on a Sun Workstation.

An Air Operations Officer (usually known as an OPSO) is the defense officer responsible for deciding the appropriate defensive response to an air threat. A study of the Operations Officer decision-making methods was recently conducted, using a cognitive modeling technique [18, 19] . The study was used to show the usefulness of cognitive modeling in deriving rules from expert knowledge. In this section, we only make use of the rules which resulted from the study; the cognitive modeling technique is not discussed here.

In the domain of the Operations Officer, the magnitude of the response to an air threat is in proportion to the threat itself. So, if the opposing aircraft are very close, or if the aircraft is of a type which can cause a great deal of damage (known as a *strike* aircraft), then the response is large. If the threat is smaller, then the response is smaller. For example, Figure 7 shows a rule in this domain. (We have borrowed the style of Cao [20] to express the rule, although we do not employ Cao's fuzzy reasoning here.) This graph expresses the rule that if a fighter aircraft (small threat) is between 400 and 500 nautical miles distant, then assert a threat level of „alert 60" (the lowest level of alert, in which response fighters must be ready to take off within sixty minutes), and a single fighter is assigned to deal with this threat.

The assertion shown in Figure 7 unifies with the „if" portion of this rule, since the aircraft is certainly a fighter, and there is a join on the intervals of the distance concepts. A join exists here because we define interval concepts on an interval type hierarchy. Informally, the lattice is ordered on interval inclusion, such that two intervals have a join if there is some other interval which is in the „overlap" area of the two intervals. Formal definitions and discussions on interval type hierarchies are described in [21] and [7]. The „then" portion of the rule represents the response to the situation, and it is asserted into the current world knowledge. In this manner, we can represent the decision-making capabilities of the Operations Officer.

The rule shown in Figure 8 is used for a bigger and more impending threat. Any threat aircraft which is closer than 400 nautical miles is considered an immediate threat, and a response squadron must be ready very quickly. Further, a strike aircraft is one which can inflict a great deal of damage, and is therefore dealt with more severely than a fighter aircraft.

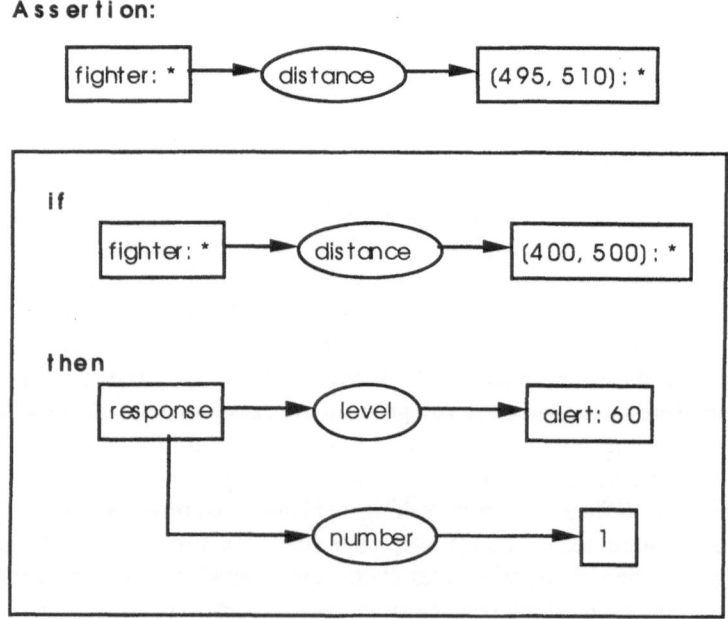

Fig. 7. A rule in the defense domain.

Assertion:

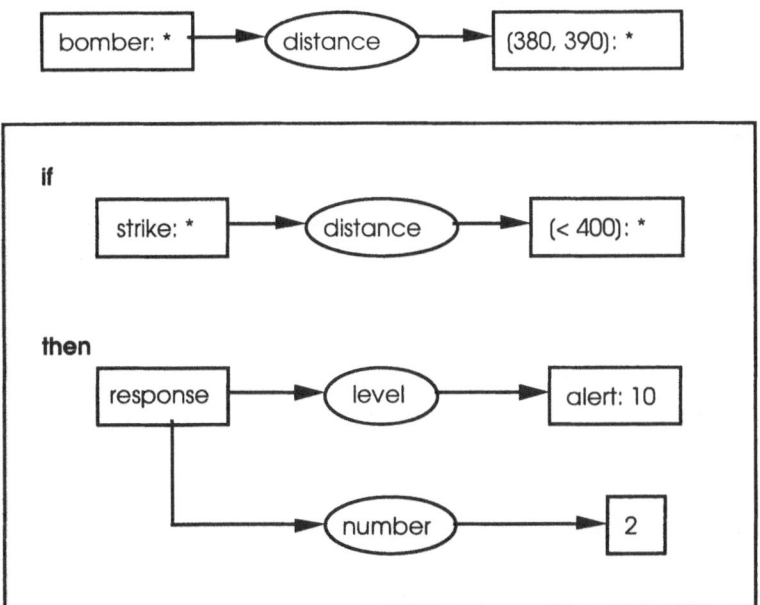

Fig. 8. Another rule from the same domain.

The assertion shown in Figure 8 states that a bomber is known to be between 380 and 390 nautical miles distant. Our type hierarchy indicates that a bomber is a type of strike aircraft. Because of the proximity of the threat, the response aircraft are put on „alert 10" status. Because of the enormity of the threat, two fighters are assigned to deal with the target aircraft. Again, the assertion unifies with the „if" portion of the rule, causing the „then" portion of the rule to be asserted.

6 Results and Discussion: The Air Operations Officer

Conceptual Graphs and knowledge conjunction can be used to efficiently represent a set of rules in the domain of the Air Operations Officer. The use of Conceptual Graphs is an efficient method for representing the complete ontology of the OPSO, not only in the rules, but also in the exploration and use of the knowledge of types of aircraft and responses. General rules can be represented as Conceptual Graphs, and then specialized dynamically to match the current situation and describe an appropriate response.

7 Architectural Design Tool

The results discussed in this section are those recorded from the application of the knowledge conjunction reasoning tool operating over the domain of architectural design. The point of automated search for the designer is to use computer media that engage designers in exploring design modifications. The design user may want to create new designs, or index, compare or adapt existing designs. This type of user requires efficient representations for the designs and states (of designs) in a symbol system [22]. The designer needs to be able to represent spaces of possibilities which are both relevant to the language and knowledge of design and lend themselves to tractable computations.

Consider a design for the kitchen of a custom-made house. In this design, the architect has specified some of the lighting design and that the floor area must be greater than 20 square meters. The architect has also retrieved an old design, which specifies the remainder of the lighting design. The knowledge conjunction software discussed above combines these two graphs into a single result which represents neither more nor less knowledge than the original graphs. In this graph, all the original knowledge of the first two graphs has been preserved, and the values in the concepts have been joined as specified.

8 Results and Discussion: Architectural Design Tool

Conceptual Graphs can be used to efficiently represent a building design ontology. The use of Conceptual Graphs is an efficient method for representing not only the designs, but also constraints on the designs and knowledge conjunction of designs. The system described in this paper allows general designs to be represented as concepts, and also allows values to be constrained by specifying real-valued constraints as intervals.

The three main areas where the architects want the contribution of Knowledge Conjunction are in type subsumption, knowledge-level reasoning, and pattern matching. First, architects want to be able to use type subsumption to make statements such as, „An office (or kitchen, or corridor) is a kind of room. All the properties which apply to one should apply to its specializations." This is distinct from the object-oriented objective of objects inheriting all the properties of a class of objects. The essential difference is in treating a kitchen as you would any generic room. A generic room can be placed, occupy space, and have attributes like color and number of doors. A *class* of rooms will have attributes, but cannot be said to occupy a space or have specific dimensions, or have a specific count or placement of doors.

The knowledge conjunction model that we developed give this ability to the architects. The algorithm allows the user to specialize designs by matching (unifying) previous designs with the current design problem. Since all characteristics, attributes and constraints are carried along in the unification, the specialization represents all of the design concepts included in the more generic design. Further, and more importantly, there is no real separation between generic and specific, since all points in between can be represented. Conceptual Graphs combined with the ability to specialize using unification are the ideal tool for the knowledge conjunction approach and the constructive nature of architectural design.

The second major concern of architectural designers was the ability to have knowledge-level reasoning. That is, they want to be able to speak in the language of the architect, not the language of the computer (or CAD system). The user wants to be able to refer to the „North Wall" or „door" without resorting to discussing geometric coordinates in space. The user wants to depart from previous CAD-based data-level processing, and work at the knowledge level in the architecture domain.

This is certainly another area where Conceptual Graphs and unification combine to bring a solution to this domain. While spatial coordinates (and their constraints) can be stored in a graphical representation of a room, there is no need for the user to bother with using them. The graph can be manipulated as a whole, and treated as a room, rather than a square in a diagram. The completed system will not deal with lines and boxes, but rather with specializing entire designs for rooms (or houses, or office buildings). This approach frees the architect from dealing with data-level concerns of numbers and coordinates, and allows the architect instead to deal with the architectural design.

Finally, the users want to be able to start with a high-level, generic description of a building, and then make queries such as, „Can this bay structure be used in the support structure?" or, „Do the constraints match up adequately for a particular technology to be used? If yes, tell me the constraints under which it is usable."

Once again, the work presented in this paper meets the requirements of the architects. A query is represented as a Conceptual Graph. The user can specify a type of structure for support, and make the query by attempting to unify the structure with the more generic design. If the unification fails, then the user knows that the proposed structure does not meet the constraints of the design problem. If the graphs unify, then the resulting graph will contain the constraints which must be met in order to make the design work.

Overall, the system of unification over constraints on Conceptual Graphs presented in this paper gives a set of tools to the designer. The ability to use knowledge conjunction with constraints to handle objects at the knowledge level greatly leverages the ability of the designer to work efficiently.

9   Conclusions

We have demonstrated a method for automated reasoning on ontologies, using Conceptual Graphs to represent the underlying ontology. Type hierarchies and the canonical formation rules efficiently specialize graphs into concrete instances. A simple unification operation, using join and type subsumption, is used to perform knowledge conjunction of the concepts represented as graphs. The significance of our work is that the previously static knowledge representation of ontology is now a dynamic, functional reasoning system.

References

1. Aït-Kaci, H. and R. Nasr, *LOGIN: A Logic Programming Language with Built-in Inheritance*. Journal of Logic Programming, 1986. **3**.
2. Sowa, J.F., *Conceptual Structures: Information Processing in Mind and Machine*. 1984, Reading, Mass: Addison-Wesley.

3. Sowa, J.F., *Conceptual Graphs Summary*, in *Conceptual Structures: Current Research and Practice*. 1992, Ellis Horwood: Chichester, UK.
4. Willems, M. *Projection and Unification for Conceptual Graphs*. in *Proc. Third International Conference on Conceptual Structures*. 1995. Santa Cruz, California, USA: Springer-Verlag.
5. Chein, M. and M.-L. Mugnier, *Conceptual Graphs: Fundamental Notions*. Revue d'Intelligence Artificielle, 1992. **6**(4): p. 365-406.
6. Mugnier, M.-L. and M. Chein, *Représenter des Connaissances et Raisonner avec des Graphes*. Revue d'Intelligence Artificielle, 1996. **10**(6): p. 7-56.
7. Corbett, D.R., *Conceptual Graphs with Constrained Reasoning*. Revue d'Intelligence Artificielle, 2001. **15**(1): p. 87-116.
8. Corbett, D.R. and R.F. Woodbury. *Unification over Constraints in Conceptual Graphs*. in *Proc. Seventh International Conference on Conceptual Structures*. 1999. Blacksburg, Virginia, USA: Springer-Verlag.
9. Carpenter, B., *The Logic of Typed Feature Structures*. 1992, Cambridge: Cambridge University Press.
10. Leclère, M. *Reasoning with Type Definitions*. in *Proc. Fifth International Conference on Conceptual Structures*. 1997. Seattle, Washington, USA: Springer-Verlag.
11. Müller, T. *Conceptual Graphs as Terms: Prospects for Resolution Theorem Proving*. Masters Thesis, Department of Computer Science, Vrije Universiteit Amsterdam. Amsterdam, Netherlands, 1997.
12. Reynolds, J.C., *Transformational Systems and the Algebraic Structure of Atomic Formulas*. Machine Intelligence, 1970. **5**.
13. Davey, B.A. and H.A. Priestley, *Introduction to Lattices and Order*. 1990, Cambridge: Cambridge University Press.
14. Knight, K., *Unification: A Multidisciplinary Survey*. ACM Computing Surveys, 1989. **21**(1): p. 93-124.
15. Aït-Kaci, H., *An Algebraic Semantics Approach to the Effective Resolution of Type Equations*. Theoretical Computer Science, 1986. **45**(3): p. 293-351.
16. Corbett, D.R. *A Framework for Conceptual Graph Unification*. in *Proc. Eighth International Conference on Conceptual Structures*. 2000. Darmstadt, Germany: Shaker Verlag.
17. Mineau, G. *A First Step Toward the Knowledge Web: Interoperability Issues Among Conceptual Graph Based Software Agents, Part I*. in *Proc. International Conference on Conceptual Structures*. 2002. Borovets, Bulgaria: Springer.
18. Mitchard, H. *Cognitive Model of an Operations Officer*. Honours Thesis, Computer and Information Science, University of South Australia. Adelaide, South Australia, 1998.
19. Mitchard, H., J. Winkles, and D.R. Corbett. *Development and Evaluation of a Cognitive Model of an Air Defence Operations Officer*. in *Proc. Fifth Biennial Conference of the Australasian Cognitive Science Society*. 2000. Adelaide, South Australia.
20. Cao, T.H., P.N. Creasy, and V. Wuwongse. *Fuzzy Unification and Resolution Proof Procedure for Fuzzy Conceptual Graph Programs*. in *Proc. Fifth International Conference on Conceptual Structures*. 1997. Seattle, Washington, USA: Springer-Verlag.
21. Older, W.J., *Involution Narrowing Algebra*. Constraints, 1997. **2**: p. 113-130.
22. Woodbury, R., S. Datta, and A.L. Burrow. *Erasure in Design Space Exploration*. in *Proc. Artificial Intelligence in Design*. 2000. Worcester, Massachusetts, USA.

Natural Language Annotations for the Semantic Web

Boris Katz[1], Jimmy Lin[1], and Dennis Quan[2]

[1] MIT Artificial Intelligence Laboratory
200 Technology Square
Cambridge, MA 02139
{boris,jimmylin}@ai.mit.edu
[2] IBM Internet Technology Division
1 Rogers Street
Cambridge, MA 02142
dennisq@us.ibm.com

Abstract. Because the ultimate purpose of the Semantic Web is to help users locate, organize, and process information, we strongly believe that it should be grounded in the information access method humans are most comfortable with—natural language. However, the Resource Description Framework (RDF), the foundation of the Semantic Web, was designed to be easily processed by computers, not humans. To render RDF friendlier to humans, we propose to augment it with natural language annotations, or metadata written in everyday language. We argue that natural language annotations are not only intuitive and effective, but can also accelerate the pace with which the Semantic Web is being adopted. We demonstrate the use of natural language annotations from within Haystack, an end user Semantic Web platform that also serves as a testbed for our ideas. In addition to a prototype Semantic Web question answering system, we describe other opportunities for marrying natural language and Semantic Web technology.

1 Introduction

The vision of the Semantic Web [2] is to convert information on Web sites into a more machine-friendly form, with the goal of making the Web more effective for its users. This vision grew out of the recognition that although a wealth of information readily exists today in electronic form, it cannot be easily processed by computers due to a lack of external semantics.

Fundamentally, we interpret Semantic Web research as an attempt to address the problem of information access: building programs that help users locate, collate, compare, and cross-reference content. As such, we strongly believe that the Semantic Web should be motivated by and grounded in the method of information access most comfortable to users—natural language. We believe that natural language is the best information access mechanism for humans; it is intuitive, easy to use and rapidly deployable, and requires no specialized training. In our

R. Meersman, Z. Tari (Eds.): CoopIS/DOA/ODBASE 2002, LNCS 2519, pp. 1317–1331, 2002.

vision, the Semantic Web should be equally accessible by computers using specialized languages and interchange formats, and humans using natural language. The vision of being able to ask a computer "when was the president of Taiwan born?" or "what's the cheapest flight to the Bahamas this month?" and getting back "just the right information" is very appealing.

Because the first step to building the Semantic Web is to transform existing sources (stored as HTML pages, in legacy databases, etc.) into a machine-understandable form (i.e., RDF), it is sometimes at odds with a human-based natural language view of the world. Although the general framework of the Semantic Web includes provisions for natural language technology, the actual deployment of such technology remains largely unexplored.

Exactly what synergistic opportunities exist between natural language technology and the Semantic Web? State of the art natural language systems are capable of providing users intuitive access to a wealth of textual data using ordinary language. However, such systems are often hampered by the knowledge engineering bottleneck; knowledge bases are difficult, and often time consuming, to craft. This is where the Semantic Web comes in: Semantic Web research is concerned with constructing, integrating, packaging, and exporting segments of knowledge to be usable by the entire world. We believe that natural language technology can tap into this knowledge framework, and in return provide natural language information access for the Semantic Web.

To illustrate the potential opportunities that lie on the intersect between natural language and the Semantic Web, we describe a prototype question answering system capable of retrieving relevant information from a repository of RDF triples in response to user queries formulated in natural language. We draw our inspiration from two existing systems: START, the first question answering system available on the World Wide Web, and Haystack, an end user Semantic Web platform that aggregates all of a user's information into a unified repository.

2   The START Natural Language System

The use of metadata is a common technique for rendering information fragments more tenable to processing by computer systems. We believe that using natural language itself as metadata presents several advantages and opportunities: it preserves human readability and encourages non-expert users to engage in metadata creation. To this end, we have developed natural language annotations [7], which are machine-parsable sentences and phrases that describe the content of various information segments. These annotations serve as metadata that describe the kinds of questions a particular piece of knowledge is capable of answering. We have implemented natural language annotation technology in the START Natural Language System[1] [6,7].

To illustrate how our system works, consider the following paragraph about Joseph Brodsky, which may contain images and other non-textual elements:

---

[1] http://www.ai.mit.edu/projects/infolab/

"For an all-embracing authorship, imbued with clarity of thought and poetic intensity," Joseph Brodsky was awarded the 1987 Nobel Prize in Literature.

This paragraph may be annotated with the following English sentences and phrases:

Joseph Brodsky was awarded the Nobel Prize for Literature in 1987.
1987 Nobel Prize for Literature

START parses these annotations and stores the parsed structures (called embedded ternary expressions [9,6]) with pointers back to the original information segments. To answer a question, the user query is compared against the annotations stored in the knowledge base. Because this match occurs at the level of syntactic structures, linguistically sophisticated machinery such as synonymy/hyponymy, ontologies, and structural transformation rules are all brought to bear on the matching process. Linguistic techniques allow the system to achieve capabilities beyond simple keyword matching, for example, handling complex syntactic alternations involving verb arguments. If a match is found between ternary expressions derived from annotations and those derived from the query, the segment corresponding to the annotations is returned to the user as the answer. For example, the annotations above allow START to answer the following questions (see Figure 1):

What prize did Brodsky receive in 1987?
Who was awarded the Nobel Prize for Literature in 1987?
Tell me about the winner of the 1987 Nobel Prize for Literature.
To whom was the Nobel Prize for Literature given in 1987?

An important feature of natural language annotations is that any information segment can be annotated: not only text, but also images, multimedia, and even procedures!

Since it came online in December, 1993, START has engaged in millions of exchanges with hundreds of thousands of users all over the world, supplying them with useful knowledge. Currently, our system can answer millions of natural language questions about places (e.g., cities, countries, lakes, coordinates, weather, maps, demographics, political and economic systems), movies (e.g., titles, actors, directors), people (e.g., birthdates, biographies), dictionary definitions, and much, much more.

In order to give START uniform access to semistructured resources on the Web, we have created Omnibase [8], a virtual database system that integrates a multitude of Web sources under a single query interface. To actually answer user questions, the gap between natural language questions and structured Omnibase queries must be bridged. Natural language annotations serve as the enabling technology that allows the integration of START and Omnibase. Since annotations can describe arbitrary fragments of knowledge, there is no reason why they cannot be employed to describe Omnibase queries. In fact, annotations can be parameterized, i.e., they can contain symbols representative of an entire

Fig. 1. START answering the question "Who won the Nobel Prize for Literature in 1987?"

class of objects. For example, the annotation "a person wrote the screenplay for imdb-movie" can be attached to an Omnibase procedure that retrieves the writers for various movies from the Internet Movie Database (IMDb). The symbol imdb-movie serves as a placeholder for any one of the hundreds of thousands of movies about which IMDb contains information; when the annotation matches the user question, the actual movie name is instantiated and passed along to the Omnibase query. After Omnibase fetches the correct answer, START performs additional postprocessing, e.g., natural language generation, to present the answer.

3 Haystack

We are constantly investigating new systems whose integration with START will provide synergy. In this way, Haystack [5] provides a wealth of opportunities from both a research and a practical standpoint. Haystack is a system that aggregates all of a user's information, including e-mail, documents, calendar, and

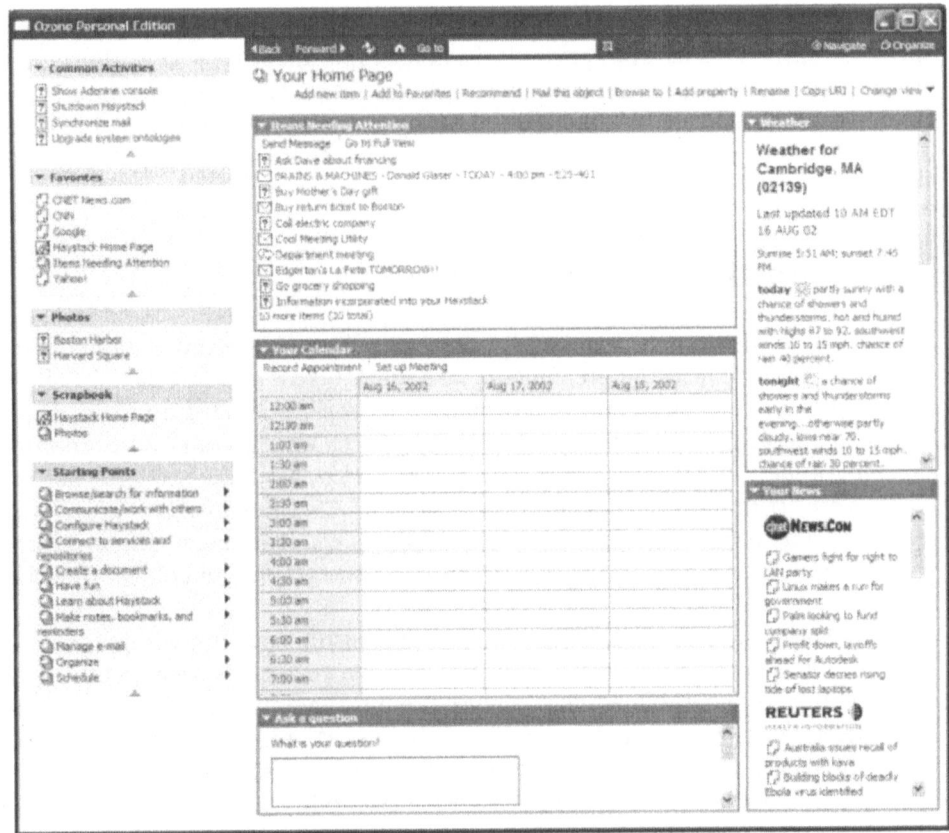

Fig. 2. Screenshot of Haystack

web pages, into a unified repository. This information is described using RDF, which makes it easy for agents to access, filter, and process this information in an automated fashion. As a motivating example, consider a query such as "show me the letter from the woman I met with last Tuesday from Human Resources." Current information technology allows our computers to store all of the information necessary to answer this question. However, it is scattered amongst multiple systems; an agent resolving this query would need to be able to communicate with an e-mail client, a calendar, the filesystem, and a directory server. By reducing the protocol barriers to information—standardizing on RDF as a common model for information—agents are free to mine the semantics of a user's various data sources and not be bogged down by syntactic barriers.

Figure 2 shows a screenshot of Haystack. In this scene, a user's Haystack "home page" is depicted, in which the user is given a snapshot of her e-mails and to-do items, her calendar, applicable weather and news reports, and access to a question answering service.

In addition to being an end-user application for managing information, Haystack also serves as a powerful platform for experimenting with various information retrieval and user interface research problems. By incorporating natural language search capabilities into Haystack, we are able to both demonstrate the usefulness of natural language search and show its applicability to the Semantic Web in general.

4   Towards Human-Friendly RDF

RDF [10,3] is the lingua franca of the Semantic Web, providing a standardized data model for allowing interchange of metadata across the Internet. In short, it is a portable representation of a semantic network, a labeled directed graph. Nodes in the graph fall into two classes: resources and literals. Resources are concrete objects or abstract concepts such as `http://www.cnn.com/` or a person. Literals are string values used for defining primitive properties of resources, such as names. The basic unit of information in RDF is the statement, consisting of a triple of subject (a resource), predicate (an arc in the graph), and object (another resource or a literal).

In its original form, RDF was meant for consumption by computers, not humans. Our central idea for bridging this gap between the core Semantic Web data model and natural language revolves around the application of the natural language annotations technology employed by START. In essence, we propose to "tag" fragments of RDF with language to facilitate access.

Suppose we want to endow Haystack with the ability to answer the following "family" of questions about various attributes (e.g., state bird, state flower, state motto, population, area, etc.) of states:

> What is the state bird of California?
> Tell me what the state motto of Massachusetts is.
> Do you know Colorado's population?
> What is the capital of Kentucky?

Fortunately, the data necessary to answer such questions can be easily found on the Web.[2] However, in order for this data to be usable by any Semantic Web system, it must be restructured in terms of the RDF model.[3]

Ordinarily, RDF data is written in XML syntax; however, as it was designed for machine-to-machine interchange, this syntax tends to be cumbersome and difficult for humans to read. In order to facilitate frequent manipulation of RDF data, Haystack provides a programming language called Adenine specifically suited for these purposes. Adenine incorporates features of Lisp, Python, and Notation3 [1]. A full specification of Adenine's syntax and semantics is beyond the scope of this paper (for more information, please refer to [5]), but a brief overview is presented here. Adenine's basic data unit is the RDF triple. RDF

---

[2] `http://www.50states.com/`
[3] That is, until Web sites start exporting the contents of their sites in RDF.

triples are enclosed in curly braces {} and are expressed in subject-predicate-object order. A semicolon denotes that the following predicate-object pair is to assume the last used subject. URIs can be specified either in fully canonical form using angle brackets (e.g., <http://www.w3.org/>) or using prefix notation (e.g., rdf:Property). RDF literals are written as strings in double quotes. Finally, DAML+OIL[4] lists (i.e., Lisp-style lists) are written with an at sign followed by parentheses @(...).

In this paper we will use Adenine syntax for expressing RDF data. The following Adenine code declares the :State class and the :bird property as well as some basic information about the state of Alabama.

```
@prefix dc: <http://purl.org/dc/elements/1.1/>
@prefix :   <http://www.50states.com/data#>

add { :State
      rdf:type          rdfs:Class ;
      rdfs:label        "State"
}

add { :bird
      rdf:type          rdf:Property ;
      rdfs:label        "State bird" ;
      rdfs:domain       :State
}

# ... more property declarations

add { :alabama
      rdf:type          :State ;
      dc:title          "Alabama" ;
      :bird             "Yellowhammer" ;
      :flower           "Camellia" ;
      :population       "4447100"

      # ... more information about Alabama and other states
}
```

Adenine also supports imperative functions, called "methods", that can take parameters and return values. A unique feature of Adenine is that methods compile into RDF, i.e., each Adenine instruction is encoded as a node in the RDF graph, and a sequence of instructions is expressed by adenine:next arcs between these instruction nodes. As a result, data and procedures can be embedded within the same RDF graph and can thus be distributed together.

Adenine uses tabbing to denote block structure as Python does. Function calls and instructions are expressed in prefix notation; for example, = x 1 assigns the value 1 to the variable x.

---

[4] http://www.daml.org/2001/03/daml+oil-index.html

Given this description of Adenine, we can now express the connection between the RDF schema and the natural language annotations in a *natural language schema*, as follows:

```
@prefix nl: <http://www.ai.mit.edu/projects/infolab/start#>

add { :stateAttribute
      rdf:type           nl:NaturalLanguageSchema ;

      # This annotation handles cases like "[state bird] of [Alabama]"
      # and "[population] of [Maine]".
      nl:annotation    @( :attribute "of" :state ) ;

      # Code to run to resolve state attribute
      nl:code           :stateAttributeCode
}

add { :attribute
      rdf:type                nl:Parameter ;
      nl:domain               rdf:Property ;
      nl:descriptionProperty rdfs:label
}

add { :state
      rdf:type                nl:Parameter ;
      nl:domain               :State ;
      nl:descriptionProperty dc:title
}

# The identifier [state] will be bound to the value of the named
# parameter :state. The identifier [attribute] will be bound to the
# value of the named parameter :attribute.
method :stateAttributeCode :state = state :attribute = attribute
       # Ask the system what the [attribute] property of [state] is
       return (ask %{ attribute state ?x })
```

The definition of :attribute restricts the resource representing the attribute to be queried to have type rdf:Property; furthermore, the rdfs:label property should be used to resolve the actual literal, e.g., "State bird" or "population". Similarly, :state restricts the resource to have type :State and to have the resolver dc:title. In short,

```
@( :attribute "of" :state )
```

is a stand-in for any natural language phrase such as *state bird of Alabama, population of Maine, area of California*, etc.

Given this natural language schema, Haystack and START can now answer questions about various natural attributes of states. The process of answering a question such as "what is the state bird of Alabama?" is as follows:

1. START parses the question and determines that :stateAttribute is the relevant natural language schema to invoke.
2. START extracts the natural language bindings of :attribute and :state, which are "state bird" and "Alabama", respectively. This is further resolved into the RDF resources :bird and :alabama.
3. As a response to the question, the method :stateAttributeCode is invoked with named parameter :attribute bound to :bird and named parameter :state bound to :alabama.
4. The invoked method performs a query into Haystack's RDF store, which returns "Yellowhammer", the state bird of Alabama.

Because the user query is parsed by START, a single natural language annotation is capable of answering a wide variety of questions:

What is the state bird of California?
Tell me what the state motto of Massachusetts is.
Do you know Colorado's population?
What is the capital of Kentucky?

For example, START knows that a possessive relation can also be expressed as an *of* prepositional phrase. In addition, START is capable of normalizing different methods for requesting the same information, e.g., imperative ("Tell me..."), interrogative ("What is..."). As another example, consider the following natural language schema:

```
add { :stateAttribute
      rdf:type         nl:NaturalLanguageSchema ;
      nl:annotation    @( :state " has the largest " :comparisonAttribute ) ;
      nl:code          :maxComparisonAttributeCode
}

method :maxComparisonAttributeCode :comparisonAttribute = attribute
       return (ask %{
                   rdf:type ?x :State ,
                   adenine:argMax ?x ?y 1 xsd:int %{
                       :attribute ?x ?y
                   }
       } @(?x))
```

Instead of a simple request for information, the method invoked by the natural language schema queries the RDF store for the resource of type :State that contains the maximal integer value for the property given by :comparisonAttribute. As a result, this schema would allow a system to answer the following questions:

Which state has the largest population?
Do you know what state has the largest area?

We have built a prototype implementing the natural language schemata described above. The system is currently limited in the types of questions that

it can answer and the domain; in fact, START can easily handle the types of
questions discussed above. However, we believe that the system is a proof of
concept that demonstrates a viable method of marrying natural language with
the Semantic Web. Naturally, more development of our system is required to
validate our approaches.

In our vision of the Semantic Web, natural language schemata, such as the
ones presented above, would co-exist alongside RDF metadata. These schemata
could be distributed (e.g., embedded directly into web pages) or centralized; either way, a software agent would compile these schemata into a question answering system capable of providing natural language information access to users.

5   Further Integration

In addition to our working prototype of natural language schemata, we have
further explored other methods of integrating natural language technology with
the Semantic Web. Specifically, we propose two additional opportunities for the
integration of natural language technology with the Semantic Web.

5.1   Adding Language to RDF Properties

We have noticed a striking similarity, both in form and in spirit, between RDF
triples and START's ternary expression representation of natural language [9,6].
To support a seamless integration of the two technologies, we propose to hook
natural language annotations directly into rdf:Property definitions.

To illustrate our proposed approach, consider this fragment of an ontology
modeling an address book entry in Haystack:

```
add { :Person
      rdf:type          rdfs:Class
}

add { :homeAddress
      rdf:type          rdf:Property ;
      rdfs:domain       :Person ;
      rdfs:range        xsd:string ;

      nl:annotation     @( nl:subject " lives at " nl:object ) ;
      nl:annotation     @( nl:subject "'s home address is "
                          nl:object ) ;
      nl:annotation     @( nl:subject "'s apartment" ) ;

      nl:generation     @( nl:subject "'s home address is "
                          nl:object )
}
```

The :homeAddress is a property specifying a user's home address. Our annotation expresses this connection concretely in natural language, via the nl:annotation

property. For example, the phrase "`nl:subject` lives at `nl:object`" is linked to every RDF statement involving the `:homeAddress` property, where `nl:subject` is shorthand for indicating the subject (domain) of the relation, and `nl:object` is shorthand for the object (range) of the relation. From this, a natural language-aware software agent could answer the following English questions:

> Where does John live?
> What's David's home address?
> Tell me where Bob's apartment is.

In addition, the `nl:generation` property specifies a natural language rendition of the knowledge, allowing software agents to present meaningful, natural sounding responses to users:

> *Question:* Where does Jimmy live?
> Jimmy's home address is 200 Technology Square.

By "hooking" natural language annotations directly into RDF property definitions, we can not only ensure that our triples "make sense" to a user, but also provide natural language question answering capabilities simultaneously with minimal cost to the knowledge engineer.

5.2   Natural Language Plans

Consider the question "how do I get from Dave's apartment to John's apartment?" A person faced with this question would first lookup the address of Dave's apartment, i.e., from the user's personal address book, and then find the address of John's apartment using the same method. Given the two address, the user would probably then use a mapping service, e.g., MapQuest, to obtain directions from one address to the other. People generally have no difficulty describing in natural language a "plan" for answering questions that require multiple operations from different sources. Could humans "teach" such plans to a computer directly? Currently, the answer is no, because existing mechanisms of knowledge acquisition require familiarity with precise ontologies, something that cannot be realistically expected for all users. Despite having plenty of common sense, most users cannot become effective knowledge engineers. We propose to utilize natural language annotations to address this difficulty in imparting knowledge to computers.

We propose to capture human-like question answering knowledge in "natural language plans," which can dramatically simplify the task of knowledge engineering:

```
add { :directionsPlan
      rdf:type          nl:NaturalLanguagePlan ;

      nl:annotation     @( "directions from " :location1
                           " to " :location2 ) ;
```

```
         nl:annotation        @( "getting from " :location1
                                  " to " :location2 ) ;

         nl:plan              @(
             ${  nl:annotation  @( "What is the address of "
                                      :location1 "?" ) ;
                 nl:result      :address1
             }
             ${  nl:annotation  @( "What is the address of "
                                      :location2 "?" ) ;
                 nl:result      :address2
             }
             ${  nl:annotation  @( "How do I get from "
                                      :address1 " to " :address2 "?" ) ;
                 nl:result      :directions
             }
         ) ;
         nl:action            :displayDirections
     }

method :displayDirections :directions = directions
     # Some code to display this information
     print directions
```

Instead of directly manipulating RDF, which would require knowledge of domain-specific ontologies, we could use natural language itself to describe the process of answering a question. The answer plan (nl:plan) reflects the user's thought process expressed in natural language: first find the respective addresses of the desired locations, and then obtain directions. In the fragment above, the ${} operator denotes an RDF anonymous node whose properties are given by the predicate-object pairs within the curly braces {}.

This method of specifying schemata essentially serves to capture the intuitive thought patterns of a human, and allows ordinary users to "teach" a computer knowledge using natural language.

5.3   Hiding the Details

Ultimately, the actual details of natural language annotations should be hidden from the user behind GUI authoring tools, so that she need not come into direct contact with XML or RDF. Haystack's user interface was specifically designed with these needs in mind. Additionally, an authoring tool could pre-parse the natural language annotations and store those representations (essentially triples themselves) alongside the annotations.[5] With both natural language and parsed

---

[5] Without an authoring tool, such a scheme would not be feasible because we cannot expect humans to manually generate parse structures. Note also that keeping natural language annotations makes it possible for them to be re-analyzed later as more powerful parsers become available.

representations at their disposal, software agents would have even greater flexibility in manipulating metadata.

6 Deploying the Semantic Web

We believe that natural language annotations are not only an intuitive and helpful extension to the Semantic Web, but will also assist in the deployment and adoption of the Semantic Web itself. The primary barrier to the success of the Semantic Web is a classic chicken-and-egg problem: people will not spend extra time marking up their data unless they perceive a value for their efforts, and metadata will not be useful until a "critical mass" has been achieved. Although researchers have been focusing on ontology editors to reduce barriers to entry, such initiatives may not be sufficient to overcome the hurdles. As James Hendler [4] remarks, lowering markup cost is not enough; for many users, the benefits of the Semantic Web should come for free.

Haystack takes a relatively unique approach to bringing the Semantic Web to the average computer user: Semantic markup should be a by-product of normal computer use. The act of organizing documents, entering contact information, or replying to e-mails in Haystack all result in the creation of semantic markup. In addition to the relatively structured information that can be entered with graphical user interfaces, natural language descriptions can be used as an alternative input modality for entering information. This markup then serves as a rich source of semistructured information that can then be queried by advanced natural language question answering systems such as the one described here.

By providing "natural" means for creating and accessing information on the Semantic Web, we can dramatically lower the barrier of entry to the Semantic Web. Natural language support gives users a whole new way of interacting with any information system, and from a knowledge engineering point of view, natural language technology divorces the majority of users from the need to understand formal ontologies and precisely defined vocabularies.

Furthermore, just as RDF schemata can be shared on the Semantic Web, natural language schemata, also being expressed in RDF, can be shared in the same fashion. Clients such as Haystack will be able to interact with global ontology directories and download both the RDF schema and the natural language schema for any data types encountered by the user. On the flip side, new data types invented by the user can be uploaded to these directories. Our technology of information access schemata provides a system for creating these annotations suitable for different levels of user experience. Novices to the Semantic Web merely have to tag resources with a short natural language description in order to access to those resources later on using natural language. For more advanced users, the ability to access RDF directly and manipulate it using Adenine allows finer-tuned control, greater flexibility, and more concise descriptions.

By facilitating the creation, display, retrieval, and sharing of natural language schemata, we are enabling users to interact with information on the Semantic

Web in an intuitive fashion. We believe that these benefits go a long way in advancing the concept of the Semantic Web.

7   Patterns of Information Requests

Now that we have addressed the question, "are natural language annotations a good idea?" let us turn to the question, "are they enough?" Specifically, can information access schemata achieve broad enough knowledge coverage to be useful? We believe the answer is yes.

Natural language annotations can serve as more than metadata; they can capture generalized patterns of information access. As shown in the previous sections, our annotations can be parameterized to encompass entire classes of questions. For example, our prototype can answer questions about half a dozen attributes of any state, which translates into hundreds of possible questions. A schema about the CIA Factbook in which the properties and countries are parameterized can answer tens of thousands of potential questions. The cost of writing schemata is not proportional to the number of class instances but rather to the complexity of the class itself. A single schema to the Internet Movie Database, for example, could grant the user natural language access to over three hundred thousand titles! Furthermore, because a natural language engine analyzes the questions, simple grammatical alternations would be handled automatically without requiring additional annotations.

It is our empirical experience that people ask the same types of questions frequently [11,8]. Thus, information access schemata are an effective way of achieving broad knowledge coverage at reasonable costs.

8   The Future

Much like the development of the Semantic Web itself, early efforts to integrate natural language technology with the Semantic Web will no doubt be slow and incremental. However, we believe that our prototype system demonstrates a step in the right direction, and that our proposals sketch out a path for future developments. By weaving natural language annotations into the basic fabric of the Semantic Web, we can begin to create an enormous network of knowledge easily accessible by both machines and humans alike. Furthermore, we believe that natural language querying capabilities will be a key component of any future Semantic Web system.

Acknowledgements. Special thanks to David Karger for his insightful comments on drafts of this paper. Thanks to David Huynh and Vineet Sinha for numerous conversations about the Semantic Web, as well as reading earlier drafts of this paper. This research is funded by DARPA under contract number F30602-00-1-0545, the MIT-NTT collaboration, a Packard Foundation fellowship, IBM, and MIT Project Oxygen.

References

1. Tim Berners-Lee. Primer: Getting into RDF and Semantic Web using N3, 2000.
2. Tim Berners-Lee, James Hendler, and Ora Lassila. The Semantic Web. *Scientific American*, 284(5): 34–43, 2001.
3. Dan Brickley and R.V. Guha. RDF vocabulary description language 1.0: RDF Schema. W3C Working Draft, World Wide Web Consortium, April 2002.
4. James Hendler. Agents and the Semantic Web. *IEEE Intelligent Systems*, 16(2):30–37,2001.
5. David Huynh, David Karger, and Dennis Quan. Haystack: A platform for creating, organizing and visualizing information using RDF. In *Proceedings of the Eleventh World Wide Web Conference Semantic Web Workshop*, 2002.
6. Boris Katz. Using English for indexing and retrieving. In *Proceedings of the 1st RIAO Conference on User-Oriented Content-Based Text and Image Handling (RIAO '88)* 1988.
7. Boris Katz. Annotating the World Wide Web using natural language. In *Proceedings of the 5th RIAO Conference on Computer Assisted Information Searching on the Internet (RIAO '97)* 1997.
8. Boris Katz, Sue Felshin, Deniz Yuret, Ali Ibrahim, Jimmy Lin, Gregory Marton, Alton Jerome McFarland, and Baris Temelkuran. Omnibase: Uniform access to heterogeneous data for question answering. In *Proceedings of the 7th International Workshop on Applications of Natural Language to Information Systems (NLDB 2002)*, 2002.
9. Boris Katz and Patrick H. Winston. Parsing and generating English using commutative transformations. AI Memo 677, MIT Artificial Intelligence Laboratory, 1982.
10. Ora Lassila and Ralph R. Swick. Resource Description Framework (RDF)model and syntax specification. W3C Recommendation, World Wide Web Consortium, February 1999.
11. Jimmy J.Lin. The Web as a resource for question answering: Perspectives and challenges. In *Proceedings of the Third International Conference on Language Resources and Evaluation (LREC-2002)*, 2002.

A Metadata Integration Assistant Generator for Heterogeneous Distributed Databases

Young-Kwang Nam[1], Joseph Goguen[2], and Guilian Wang[2]

[1] Dept. of Computer Science, Yonsei University, Wonjoo, Republic of Korea
yknam@dragon.yonsei.ac.kr,
[2] Dept. of Computer Science and Engineering, UCSD, La Jolla, CA 92093
{goguen, guilian}@cs.ucsd.edu

Abstract. This paper describes a metadata interchange approach for semi-automated integration of heterogeneous distributed databases. Our system prototype uses distributed metadata to generate a GUI tool for a meta-user (who does the metadata integration) to describe mappings between master and source databases by assigning index number and specifying conversion function names; the system uses Quilt as its XML query language. The queries for the local databases being transparent for users are generated, which is based on the metadata built semi-automatically. An experiment testing feasibility is reported in which 3 different publishers' databases are integrated.

1 Introduction

It is often required to integrate and analyze data from multiple sources, e.g., in ecology, sociobiology, medicine, and electronic commerce. As stated in [23,25], increasing standardization or adoption of ad hoc standards, such as Dublin Core [5], as well as metadata standards in domains such as bibliography [4], space, astronomy, geography, environmental science [13], and ecology [24], have achieved system, syntactic, structural, and limited semantic interoperability. Unfortunately, it is unrealistic to expect that integration can be done entirely through standardization. The major difficulty is that the data at different sources tends to be formatted in changing and incompatible ways, and even worse, represented under changing, incompatible and often implicit assumptions. For example, the bibliographical databases of different publishers may use different units of prices, different formats for author and editor names (e.g., full name or separated first name and last name), and the publisher name may be only implicit. Moreover, some data values in one schema may correspond to database or schema labels in another. Even worse, the same word may have a different meaning, and the same meaning may have different names. This implies that syntactical data and meta-data can not provide enough semantics for all potential integration purposes. As a result, the data integration process is often very labor-intensive and demands more computer expertise than most application users have. Therefore, semi-automated schemes seem the most promising, where mediation engineers

R. Meersman, Z. Tari (Eds.): CoopIS/DOA/ODBASE 2002, LNCS 2519, pp. 1332–1344, 2002.
© Springer-Verlag Berlin Heidelberg 2002

are given an easy tool to describe mappings between the global (global and master are used interchangely in this paper) schema and local schemas, to produce a uniform view over the local databases.

Our approach, called DDXMI (for Distributed Database XML Metadata Interface), builds on that of XMI [28]. The master DDXMI file includes database or XML document name or location information, table column or XML path information, semantic information about table column or XML elements and attributes. A system prototype has been built that generates a tool for meta-users to do the meta-data integration, producing a master DDXMI file, which is then used to generate queries to local databases from master queries, and to integrate the results. This tool parses local DTDs, generates a path for each element, and produces a convenient GUI. The mappings assign indices to match local elements to corresponding master elements and to names of conversion functions. These functions can be built-in or user-defined in Quilt [9], which is our XML query language. The DDXMI is then generated based on the mappings by collecting over index numbers. User queries are processed by Quilt according to the generated DDXMI, by generating an executable query for each relevant local database.

This system is simple, since some of the most complex issues are handed off to Quilt, and it is easy to use, due to its simple GUI. The system is also flexible: users can get any virtual integrated database they want from the same set of data sources, and different users can have different virtual databases supporting their own applications.

2 Related Work

Many diverse solutions to data integration have been developed, although most of them are based on a common mediator architecture [27]. Mainly, they can be classified into structural approaches and semantic approaches. In structural approaches, the mediation engineer's knowledge of the application specific requirements and local data sources are assumed as a crucial but implicit input. The integration is obtained through a virtual global schema that characterizes the underlying data sources. On the other hand, semantic approaches assume that enough domain knowledge for integration is contained in the exported conceptual models, or "ontologies" of each local database. This requires a common ontology among the data source providers, and it assumes that everything of importance is explicitly described in the ontologies; however, these assumptions are often violated in practice.

Tsimmis [26], MedMaker [22] and MIX [2] are structural approaches. A common data model is used, e.g., OEM (Object Exchange Model) in Tsimmis and MedMaker, and XML in MIX. A view definition language is provided for the mediation engineer to define an integrated view that specifies how local data sources are integrated to the system, e.g., MSDL in Tsimmis and MedMaker and XMAS in MIX. MSDL and XMAS also act as query languages. All of these take a global-as-view approach. According to the integrated view definition, at query time, the mediator resolves the user query into sub-queries to suitable wrappers that translate between the local languages, models and concepts, and global concepts, and then integrates the information returned from the wrappers.

In some other systems with structural approaches, users are given a language or graphical interface to specify only the mappings between the global schema and local schemas. The system will then generate the view definition based on these mappings. In Information Manifold (IM) [19,26], description logic CARIN is used to specify local database contents and capabilities. IM has a mediator that is independent of applications, since queries over the global schema are rewritten to sub-queries over the local databases (defined as views over the global schema) using the same algorithm for different combinations of queries and sources. The most important advantage of local-as-view approaches is that it allows an integrated system built this way easily handles dynamic environments. Clio [14, 20] introduced an interactive schema-mapping paradigm in which users are released from the manual definition of integrated views in a different way from IM. A graphical user interface allows users to specify value correspondences, that is, how the value of an attribute in the target schema is computed from values of the attributes in the source schema. Based on the schema mapping, the view definition is computed using traditional DBMS optimization techniques. In addition, Clio has a mechanism allowing users to verify correctness of the generated view definition by checking example results. However, Clio transforms data from a single legacy source to a new schema; it remains a challenge to employ this paradigm for virtual data integration of multiple distributed data sources. Xyleme [8] provides a mechnism for view definitions through path-to-path mappings in its query language, assuming XML data.

Recently, in order to realize semantic interoperability in the sense of allowing users to integrate data and query the system at a conceptual level, many efforts are being made to develop semantic approaches, including RDF (Resource Description Framework) [2], Knowledge Sharing Effort [16], Intelligent Integration of Information [15], the Digital Library Initiative [10], and Knowledge-based Integration [12,17]. Several ontology languages have been developed for data and knowledge representation, and reasoning formalism to help data integration from semantic perspective, such as F-Logic [12,17,18], Ontolingua [11], XOL [4], OIL and DLR [7,6]. But despite some optimistic projections to the contrary, the representation of meaning in anything like the sense that humans use that term, is far beyond current technology. The meaning of a document often involves a deep understanding of its social context, including how it is used, its role in organizational politics, its relation to other documents, its relation to other organizations, and much more, depending on the particular situation. Moreover, these contexts may be changing at a rather rapid rate, as may the documents themselves. These complexities mean it is unrealistic to expect any single semantics written in a special ontology language to adequately reflect the meaning of documents for every purpose. Ontology mediation approaches can be frustrating to users, due to the difficulty of discovering, communicating, formalizing and updating all the necessary contextual information

3   System Architecture

The overall architecture of the DDXMI distributed database system is shown in Figure 1. We assume that all databases are in XML, either directly or through wrapping. The basic idea is that a query to the integrated system, called a master query, is automatically rewritten to sub-queries, called local queries, which fit each local database format using the information stored in DDXMI by the query generator. The DDXMI contains the path information and functions to be applied to each local database, along with identification information such as author, date, comments, etc. The paths in a master query are parsed by the query generator and replaced by corresponding paths of each local document, by consulting the DDXMI if there are paths for the master query. If not, a null query is generated for the corresponding path in the local query, which means that this query cannot be applied to that local database. Each local query generated will be sent to its corresponding local database engine, which will process the query and return the result for the master query. Of course, there may be duplicated answers, and/or the results of some of local queries may need to be joined. Such issues will be handled by the database engine in a future prototype.

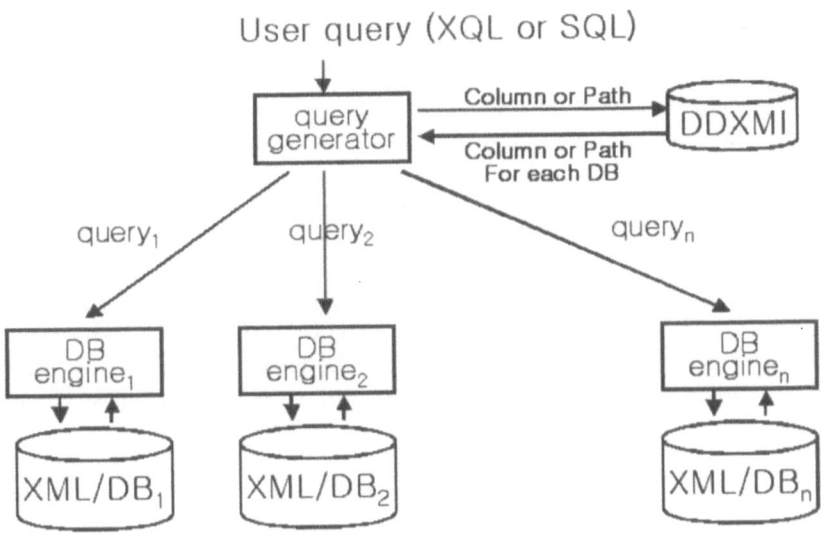

Fig. 1. System architecture

4   Distributed Database XML Interface (DDXMI)

4.1   DDXMI DTD

The DDXMI is an XML document, containing meta-information about relationships of paths among databases, and function names for handling semantic and structural discrepancies. The DTD for DDXMI documents is shown in Figure 2. Elements in the master database DTD are called source elements, while cor-

```
<!ELEMENT DDXMIA (DDXMI.header, DDXMI.isequivalent, documentspec)>
<!ELEMENT DDXMI.header (documentation,version,date,authorization)>
<!ELEMENT documentation (#PCDATA)>
<!ELEMENT version (#PCDATA)>
<!ELEMENT date (#PCDATA)>
<!ELEMENT authorization (#PCDATA)>
<!ELEMENT DDXMI.isequivalent (source,destination*)*>
<!ELEMENT source (#PCDATA)>
<!ELEMENT destination (#PCDATA)>
<!ELEMENT documentspec (document, (elementname, shortdescription,
                         longdescription, operation)*)*>
<!ELEMENT document (#PCDATA)>
<!ELEMENT elementname (#PCDATA)>
<!ELEMENT shortdescription (#PCDATA)>
<!ELEMENT longdescription (#PCDATA)>
<!ELEMENT operation (#PCDATA)>
```

Fig. 2. DDXMI DTD

responding elements in local database DTDs are called destination elements. When the query generator finds a source element name in a master query, if its corresponding destination element is not null, then paths in the query are replaced by paths to the destination elements to get a local query. (We will see that these may be more than one destination element.) For example, consider there are several book databases at different sites. The 'author' field in the master database may be represented as 'author', 'author-name', 'name', 'auth' element, etc. in different local databases. Then in the DDXMI, the 'author' source element matches with the destination element 'author', 'author-name', 'name', or 'auth' appropriate in each local database. More complex cases are discussed below.

4.2   How to Generate a DDXMI

Since each database is in XML format, each document has its own DTD file. We assume that elements in local DTDs do not contain attributes. This implies that DTDs can be represented as n-ary trees. Our approach involves mapping paths in the master DTD to (sets of) paths in the local DTDs, though we often speak of nodes instead of the paths that lead to these nodes. We match a node in the master DTD with nodes in local database DTDs, through numbering each node in the master DTD tree and then assigning these numbers to the node(s) with the same meaning in the local DTD trees. Hence nodes with the same number are involved with the same meaning. By collecting all nodes with the same numbers, the source and destination paths can be generated automatically, and the DDXMI can be easily constructed. An especially convenient special case is where an element in the master DTD matches one in a local database DTD, in that its field has the same meaning as the one in the master DTD. Elements in local databases should not appear in the DDXMI file if their meaning does not relate to any element in the DDXMI. The possible number of elements in the master DTD is the union of those in all the local database DTDs.

```
<!ELEMENT bib   (book* )>
<!ELEMENT book  (title,  (author+ | editor+ ), publisher, price )>
<!ATTLIST book  year CDATA  #REQUIRED >
<!ELEMENT author  (last, first )>
<!ELEMENT editor  (last, first, affiliation )>
<!ELEMENT title  (#PCDATA )>
<!ELEMENT last  (#PCDATA )>
<!ELEMENT first  (#PCDATA )>
<!ELEMENT affiliation  (#PCDATA )>
<!ELEMENT publisher  (#PCDATA )>
<!ELEMENT price  (#PCDATA )>
```

Fig. 3. Book1.DTD file

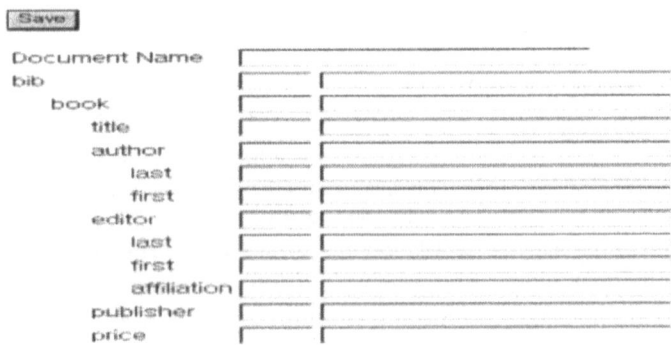

Fig. 4. Tree for Book1.DTD

For example, Figure 4 is generated from the parsed form of the Book1.DTD in Figure 3. The first column of Figure 4 is for entering indices for database DTDs. Then by collecting all nodes with the same index, the DDXMI source and destination elements are generated. Nodes without an index are not included in the master database. The document name is for the name of the local data document. The second column is for names of functions to resolve semantic issues.

Because local databases may have different structures for the same element, we have to provide some mechanism to handle such cases. For example, a local document may represent author's names as full names, while the master document separates the first and last names. In that case, the answer from the local document must be separated if a query is to retrieve the first name of the author. We classify such cases according to the mapping cardinality in the following subsections.

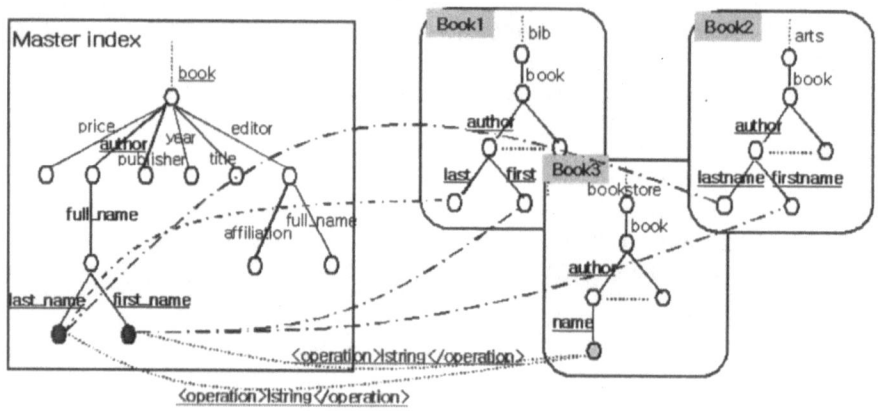

Fig. 5. N to one mapping example

N to one mapping. If two or more nodes of the master DTD correspond to one node in a local database, then the node in the local DTD will have more than one index numbers. For example, the first_name and last_name nodes in the master DTD tree in Figure 5 are mapped to the full name node in the Book3.DTD tree. In this figure, only the Book3.DTD has full names; the others use separated first name and last name. The separation function names, fstring and lstring, are included in the DDXMI file for the full name node of the Book3.DTD. A portion of DDXMI for handling this mapping is shown in Figure 6.

One to N mapping. Another case is where one node in the master DTD is mapped to several nodes in a local document. For example, the editor name in the master DTD may be represented separately in a local document, Book1, as in Figure 7. Here the function con is used to concatenate the first and the last element to get the full name.

One to One with semantic functions. As mentioned earlier, conflicts may be caused by using different reference systems. For example, the price field in Figure 4 may use the dollar currency, but the Book3.DTD in Figure 8 may use

```
<source>/book/author/full_name/first_name</source>
        <destination>/bookstore/book/author/name</destination>
<source>/book/author/full_name/last_name</source>
        <destination>/bookstore/book/author/name</destination>
<documentspec>
        <document>book.xml</document>
                <elementname>/book/author/full_name/first_name</elementname>
                        <operation>lstring</operation>
                <elementname>/book/author/full_name/last_name</elementname>
                        <operation>fstring</operation>
```

Fig. 6. A portion of DDXMI for N to one mapping case

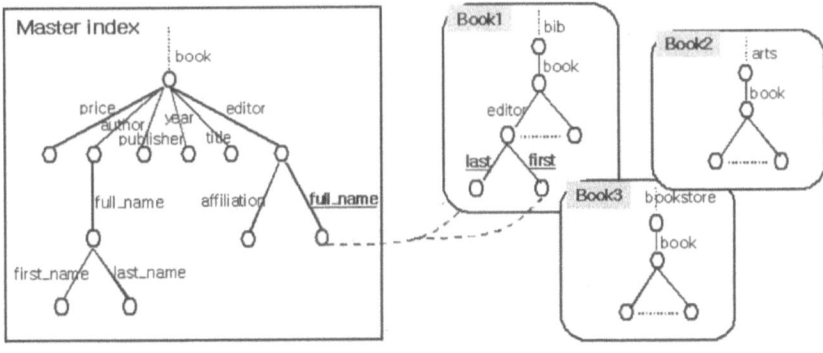

```
<source>/book/editor/full_name</source>
        <destination>/bib/book/editor/last,/bib/book/editor/first</destination>
```

Fig. 7. One to N mapping case example

Canadian currency or be represented in cents. Some mechanism is required to translate such representations. For the price element, when the query is parsed, it is replaced by the function price/100 in order to get the dollar unit answer.

4.3 Replacing Paths in a Query

In XML query languages, there are two kinds of paths, relative and absolute. A path name after '/' means an absolute path, and one after '//' means a relative path. Every master element has a corresponding path name with local element names if it has the same index number. But some elements in the master DTD may have a longer path name in the local query. When assigning the index number, some nodes in the middle of the tree may be skipped without assigning a number. Then the node in that path will include the skipped node name in the path. In Figure 9, the price node in the master DTD and in a local DTD have the same node name, but the index number is not assigned in the price_info

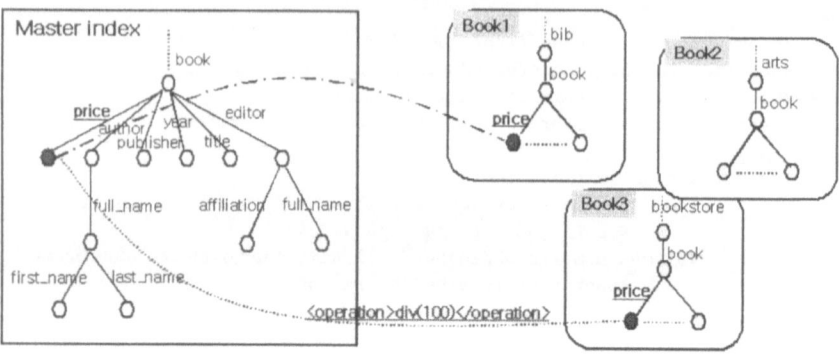

Fig. 8. An example for one to one mapping with a function

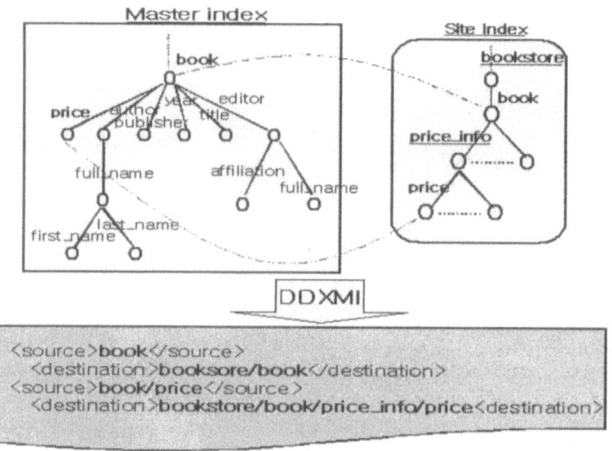

Fig. 9. An example for getting path name

node in the local DTD, so that the price element in the query is replaced by the
"/price_info/price" path.

5   DDXMI Generation Example

Assume we are going to build a library master database consisting of DTD paths
as shown in Figure 10. Figure 11 shows three indexed DTD trees. The same
index number is given to elements that have the same meaning, and each index
sequence is different. Some nodes in the DTD tree have no number, since the
master index does not include it. Book1.DTD and Book3.DTD have a 'price'
node but Book2 DTD doesn't. If some query includes the 'price' element, then
no query would be generated for Book2.XML since Book3.DTD doesn't have a
price element. Based on the Figure 10 index assignment, the DDXMI file will
be generated automatically by collecting paths with the same numbers. Using

```
0      book.xml
1      /book
11     /book/price
12     /book/author
121    /book/author/full_name
1211   /book/author/full_name/first_name
1212   /book/author/full_name/last_name
13     /book/title
14     /book/year
15     /book/publisher
16     /book/editor
161    /book/editor/affiliation
162    /book/editor/full_name
```

Fig. 10. A Master Library database DTD paths with the index numbers

[Book1.Index]

0	Book1.xml
1	/bib/book
11	../price
12	../author
1211	../author/first
1212	../author/last
13	../title
15	../publisher
16	../editor
161	../editor/affiliation
162	../editor/last
162	../editor/first

[Book2.Index]

0	Book2.xml
1	/arts/book
12	../author
1211	../author/firstname
1212	../author/lastname
13	../title
15	../publisher

[Book3.Index]

0	Book3.xml
1	/bookstore/book
11	../price div(100)
12	
1211	../name fstring
1212	../name lstring
13	../title

Fig. 11. The indexed DTD tree for Book1.DTD, Book2.DTD, and Book3.DTD tree.

this file, users can modify or update the DDXMI file easily, or the file can be re-generated by reassigning the index numbers.

6 Query Generation and Execution Examples

Quilt is the XML query language of our prototype implementation. For the above three XML documents, three query generation and execution examples are given. Kweelt, developed in University of Washington, is used as a query engine to execute quilt queries. In our system, when a user enters a query name and pushes the enter button, then the local queries are generated. Figure 12 and 13 show examples of Quilt queries with their generated local queries and their executions for 2 mapping cases.

```
FOR    $a IN  document("book1.xml") //book//author
RETURN <author > $a/last,  $a/first</author>
```
exec

```
FOR    $a IN  document("book2.xml") //book//author
RETURN <author > $a/lastname,  $a/firstname</author>
```
exec

```
{ split(" ",$str)[1]}
FUNCTION lstring($str)
{ split(" ",$str)[2]}
FOR    $a IN  document("book3.xml") //book//author
RETURN <author> fstring($a/name),  lstring($a/name)</author>
```
exec

```
<?xml version="1.0"?>
<author>  Benjamin  Franklin</author>
<author>  Herman  Melville</author>
<author>  Plato  Joon</author>
<!-- end of document -->
```

Fig. 12. The query generation and execution in case of one to N mapping

```
FOR $edi IN document("book1.xml")//book/editor
RETURN <editor>$edi/last/text(),$edi/first/text()</editor>
```
exec

```
There is no matched query!!!!!
```
exec

```
There is no matched query!!!!!
```
exec

```
<?xml version="1.0"?>
<editor>  Kent  Tamura</editor>
<editor>  Gerbarg  Darcy</editor>
<!-- end of document -->
```

Fig. 13. The query generation and execution in case of N to one mapping

7 Conclusion and Remaining Issues

We have proposed a system for resolving both structural and semantic conflicts in a distributed database system using a GUI tool for generating a file called DDXMI that contains information about data semantics. DTD trees are generated automatically, allowing a metadata engineer to assign the same index number to nodes with the same meaning and to name any necessary semantic functions for resolving representational differences. Then the DDXMI file is generated by collecting the index numbers. A master query from an end-user is then translated to queries to local databases by looking up corresponding paths in the DDXMI. Finally the results from local databases are integrated, using the named semantic functions.

Our DDXMI system has been implemented for the NT operating system under Java servlet server and JavaCC compiler. Any databases or documents represented in XML can be handled without rebuilding or changing the databases. The only requirement for users to employ this approach to integration is to be familiar with the XML data model.

However some issues remain to be investigated. First, if there are attributes in some DTD elements, they might correspond to just elements in other databases. This makes it difficult to generate queries for local databases. Helping users to handle redundancy will also be considered in our next prototype. In addition, we plan to migrate to XML schemas, instead of DTDs.

References

1. C. Baru, A. Gupta, B. Ludascher, R. Marciano, Y. Papakonstantinou, P. Velikhov, V. Chu. XML-Based Information Mediation with MIX. Exhibition program, ACM Conf. on Management of Data, SIGMOD'99, Philadelphia, 1999.
2. D. Brickley, R. Guha, eds. Resource Description Framework (RDF) Schema Specification. W3C Proposed Recommendation. March 1999.
   http://www.w3.org/1999/TR/PR-rdf-schema.
3. K. Beard, T. Smith. A framework for meta-information in digital libraries. In Sheth A, Klas W (eds) Multimedia Data Management: Using Metadata to Integrate and Apply Digital Media. McGraw Hill: 341-365. 1998.
4. V. K. Chaudhri, A. Farquhar, et al. OKBC: Open Knowledge Base Connectivity 2.0. Technical report KSL-98-06, Knowledge System Laboratory, Stanford, July 1997.
5. Online Computer Library Center, Inc 1997 Dublin Core Metadata Element Set: Reference Description. 1997. Office of Research and Special Projects, Dublin, Ohio. http:// www.oclc.org:5046/research/dublin_core/
6. D. Calvanese, G. Giacomo, and M. Lenzerini. Ontology of Integration and Integration of Ontologies. Proc. of the 2001 Description Logic Workshop (DL 2001). 2001.
7. D. Calvanese, G. Giacomo, M. Lenzerini, D. Nardi, R. Rosati. Description Logic Framework for Information Integration. In Proc. of Principles of Knowledge Representation and Reasoning (KR'98), pages 2–13, 1998.
8. S. Cluet, P. Veltri and D. Vodislav. Views in a Large Scale XML Repository. 27th International Conference on Very Large Data Bases (VLDB 2001), Roma, Italy, 2001.

9. D. Chamberlin, J. Robie and D. Florescu. Quilt: An XML Query Language for Heterogeneous Data Sources. Proceedings of WebDB 2000 Conference, in Lecture Notes in Computer Science, Springer-Verlag, 2000.
10. Digital Library Initiative. http://www.cise.nsf.gov/iis/dli_home.html.
11. A. Farquhar, R. Fikes and J. Rice. The Ontiliqua Server: A Tool for Collaborative Ontology Construction. International Journal of Human-Computer Studies, 46:707-728, 1997.
12. A. Gupta, B. Ludascher, M. E. Martone. Knowledge-Based Integration of Neuroscience Data Sources, 12th Intl. Conference on Scientific and Statistical Database Management (SSDBM), Berlin, Germany, IEEE Computer Society, July, 2000.
13. O. Gunther, A. Voisard. Metadata in geographic and environmental data management. In Sheth A, Klas W (eds) Multimedia Data Management: Using Metadata to Integrate and Apply Digital Media. McGraw Hill: 57–87. 1998.
14. L. M. Haas, R. J. Miller, B. Niswonger, M. Tork Roth, P. M. Schwarz and E. L. Wimmers. Transforming Heterogeneous Data with Database Middleware: Beyond Integration. Bulletin of IEEE Computer Society Technical Committee on Data Engineering. 1999.
15. Intelligent Integration of Information. http://mole.dc.isx.com/I3.
16. Knowledge Sharing Effort. http://www-ksl.stanford.edu/knowledge-sharing.
17. B. Ludascher, A. Gupta, M. E. Martone. Model-Based Mediation with Domain Maps. 17th Intl. Conference on Data Engineering (ICDE), Heidelberg, Germany, IEEE Computer Society, April 2001.
18. B. Ludascher, R. Himmeroder, G. Lausen, W. May, and C. Schlepphorst. Managing Semistructured Data with FLORID: A Deductive Object-Oriented Perspective. Information Systems, 23(8):589 -613, 1998.
19. A. Y. Levy, A. Rajaraman, J. J. Ordille: Querying Heterogeneous Information Sources Using Source Descriptions. In Proc. of VLDB. pp. 251–262, Bombay, India, 1996.
20. R. J. Miller, L. M. Haas and M. A. Hernandez. Schema Mapping as Query Discovery. Proceedings of the 26th VLDB Conference. Cairo Egypt, 2000.
21. R. J. Miller. Using Schematically Heterogeneous Structures. SIGMOD '98 Seattle WA, USA. ACM 0-89791-995-5. 1998.
22. Y. Papakonstantinou, H. Garcia-Molina, J. Ullman. MedMaker: A Mediation System Based on Declarative Specifications. Data Engineering (ICDE). 1996.
23. C. Parent and S. Spaccapietra. Issues and Approaches of Database Integration. Communications of the ACM, 41(5):166-178, 1998.
24. O. Reichman, J. Brunt, J. Helly, M. Jones, M. Willig. A Knowledge Network for Biocomplexity: Building and Evaluating a Metadata-based Framework for Integrating Heterogeneous Scientific Data. http://www.nceas.ucsb.edu/
25. A. P. Sheth. Changing focus on interoperability in information systems: from system, syntax, structure to semantics. In M F Goodchild, M J Egenhofer, R Fegeas and C A Kottman (eds), Interoperating Geographic Information Systems. Kluwer. 1998.
26. J. D. Ullman. Information Integration Using Logical Views 6th Int. Conference on Database Theory, LNCS 1186, 1997.
27. G. Wiederhold. Mediators in the Architecture of Future Information System. IEEE Computer 25:3, pp. 38-49, 1992.
28. XML Metadata Interchange (XMI). http://www-4.ibm.com/software/ad/library/standards/xmi.html.

Intelligent Web Search via Personalizable Meta-search Agents

Larry Kerschberg[1], Wooju Kim[2], and Anthony Scime[3]

[1]E-Center for E-Business, George Mason University
4400 University Drive, Fairfax, VA 22030, USA
kersch@gmu.edu
[2]Department of Industrial Engineering, Chonbuk National University
664-14 Deokjin, Chonju, Chonbuk, 560-756, Korea
wjkim@chonbuk.ac.kr
[3]Department of Computer Science, State University of New York College at Brockport
350 New Campus Drive, Brockport, NY 14420, USA
ascime@brockport.edu

Abstract. This paper addresses several problems associated with the specification of Web searches, and the retrieval, filtering, and rating of Web pages in order to improve the relevance, precision and quality of search results. A methodology and architecture for an agent-based system, WebSifter is presented, that captures the semantics of a user's search intent, transforms the semantic query into target queries for existing search engines, and ranks resulting page hits according to a user-specified, weighted-rating scheme. Users create personalized search taxonomies, in the form of a Weighted Semantic-Taxonomy Tree. Consultation with a Web-based ontology agent refines the terms in the tree with positively- and negatively-related terms. The concepts represented in the tree are then transformed into queries processed by existing search engines. Each returned page is rated according to user-specified preferences such as semantic relevance, syntactic relevance, categorical match, and page popularity. Experimental results indicate that WebSifter improves the precision of Web searches, thereby leading to better information.

1   Introduction

The World Wide Web [1] has become an essential tool to search for information. Yet, so much information is now available that people must sift and winnow through a plethora of accessible information in order to obtain meaningful information.

Typically, users initiate a keyword-based Web search by using a search engine to find documents that refer to the desired subject. Unfortunately, because of the limited ability of Web search engines to capture and interpret the user's *information needs*, many of the retrieved results may be irrelevant. There is a *semantic gap* between the user's perception of the search domain and the results provided by search engines.

If the search is approached as a decision-making problem in which the user must select a Web page that satisfies his information need, criteria are needed on which to base the selection. These criteria need to be user determined based on the user's previous experience with the domain of the search.

R. Meersman, Z. Tari (Eds.): CoopIS/DOA/ODBASE 2002, LNCS 2519, pp. 1345–1358, 2002.
© Springer-Verlag Berlin Heidelberg 2002

To improve upon the search results obtained from Web queries, we have developed a community of search agents that result in a user-determined and experience-driven ranking of Web pages.

This is motivated by several shortcomings in available search engines:

1. There is a *semantic gap* between the user's perceived problem, and the keyword-based search engines;

2. Ranking algorithms are considered *proprietary*, so a user cannot personalize the ranking mechanism; and

3. Users cannot provide feedback regarding the relevance of returned pages to allow the search agent to learn user preferences.

The approach in this paper addresses these shortcomings by allowing users to specify queries as taxonomies of concepts to a meta-search agent which then enhances the terms with synonyms and antonyms, transforms the queries into formats accepted by search engines, and then performs post-processing of the returned hits along several *relevancy components*. In addition, users may indicate whether the ranked pages are relevant to their decision-making situation.

2   Related Work

Most current Internet search engines suffer from *Recall* and *Precision* problems. The relatively low coverage of individual search engines led to the concept of meta-search engines, such as MetaCrawler [2], SavvySearch [3], NECI Metasearch Engine [4], and Copernic (http://www.Copernic.com), so as to improve the recall of a query [2]. Although coverage may improve by using a meta-search engine, the precision problem remains. Increased coverage does not necessarily imply increased precision.

Research on precision may be categorized into three major themes: content-based, collaborative, and domain-knowledge. The content-based approaches first represent a user's explicit preferences and then evaluate Web page relevance in terms of its content and user preferences. Some research takes into account Web page content and its structure to evaluate relevance [5, 6].

The collaborative approach determines information relevancy based on similarity among users rather than the similarity of information itself. There are hybrids that incorporate both above approaches. Example systems are Firefly and Ringo [7], and CiteSeer [8]. The third category is the domain knowledge approach that uses domain knowledge to improve the relevancy of search results. Yahoo! uses domain knowledge to classify pages and provides a pre-defined taxonomy path. The automatic classification of Web pages into a pre-defined or a dynamically created taxonomy [9] is a related issue. Domain knowledge may be represented as a set of user-provided example Web pages [10] or as a taxonomy [11].

Another related research category is the ontology-based approach, where domain-specific ontologies are being developed for knowledge-based search. OntoSeek [12], On2Broker [13], GETESS [14], and WebKB [15] are examples of such systems. The Semantic Web [16] may eventually provide a semantically rich ontology and associated meta-tagging tools [17], enabling more powerful indexing, searching, and services [18]. At present, however, there is no common agreement on the representation of the ontology, nor the query language or reasoning mechanisms. Even so, the precision problem remains due to the huge amount of the information on the Web [19].

3   The Web Search Decision-Making Process

WebSifter II incorporates a user-centric information relevancy evaluation scheme, which complements the above approaches. It permits the user to create a taxonomy representing his individual search intention. This taxonomy provides a context for the Web search. The taxonomy is populated with Web pages found by searches conducted using multiple search engines.

Web page rating can be viewed as a decision-making problem, where a decision maker (a user) must evaluate various alternatives (Web pages) on selected criteria (evaluation components) for his/her problem (user's Web search intention). Web page evaluation and ranking is completed using decision analytic techniques on six user-weighted evaluation components that represent different evaluation criteria.

Web page evaluation and ranking is completed using decision analytic techniques on six evaluation components weighted by the user. The *Semantic* component represents a Web page's relevance with respect to its content. The *Syntactic* component represents the value of a page independent of the current search. A *Categorical Match* component measures the similarity between the structure of user-defined problem and category information provided by search engines. A *Search Engine* component accounts for the user's biases toward and confidence in specific search engine results. An *Authority/Hub* component represents the level of authoritativeness other users and sites attribute to a page or a site by virtue of referencing that site. The *Popularity* component represents the user's preference for sites popular with other users. Web page rating can itself be viewed as a decision-making problem, where a decision maker (a user) must evaluate various alternatives (Web pages) on selected criteria (evaluation components) for his/her problem (user's Web search intention).

Considering the Web search process as a decision-making process, the user identifies a problem for which information is required to determine a solution. The specification of objectives, parameters, and probabilities; the retrieval and management of data; and the generation of decision alternatives are important steps. The selection of search keywords and the creation of a problem hierarchy provides a specification of the problem's objectives and parameters from the user's viewpoint.

The selection of Web pages involves information gathering and results analysis. The user formulates a query to yield candidate solution pages. He then uses decision methods to rank the query results to select a solution. Figure 1 shows the decision process undertaken by a web-searcher to find and select Web pages meeting the web-searcher/decision-maker's problem understanding.

The various activities in the model are:

Problem Identification: The decision-maker determines there is a problem. Problem definition is based on the biases, priorities, and goals of the decision-maker.

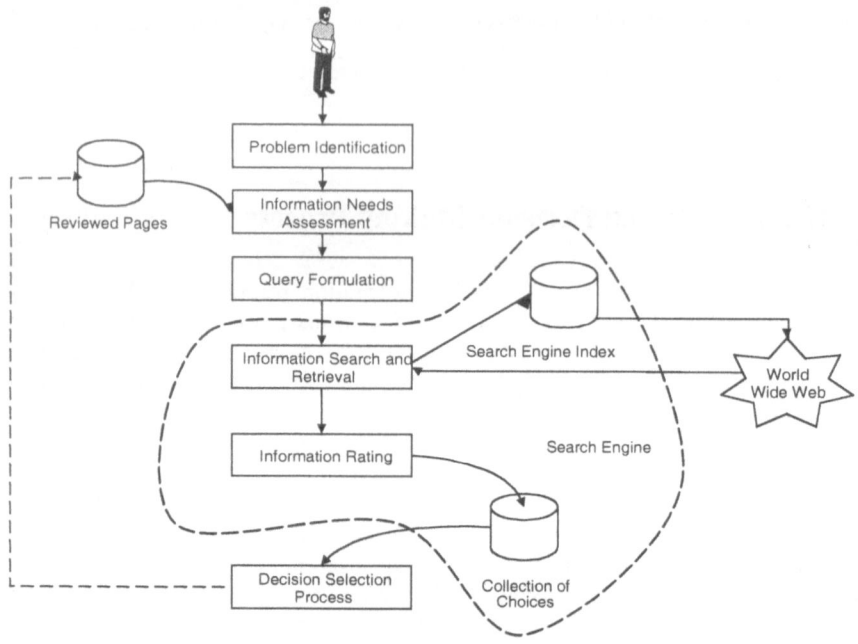

Fig. 1. Web Search Activity Model

Information Needs Assessment: The decision-maker determines what information is required to assist in the determining the solution to the problem.

Query Formulation: The decision-maker creates a set of queries to retrieve the information needed.

Information Search and Retrieval: The queries are used to search the indices of Web search engines and return Web page meta-data (hits).

Search Engine: The available Web search engines are searched for matches to the individual queries.

Information Rating: The hits returned are evaluated and ranked by the search engine.

Collection of Choices: The hits are stored in rank order for review by the decision-maker.

Decision Selection: The decision-maker reviews the list of hits from the top ranked hit to the lower ranked ones, as much as time allows, selecting and reviewing the information to assist in the solution to the problem. Therefore ordering of the list of hits is very important in decision quality with limited decision time. Feedback is also given to help users in future queries

Reviewed Pages: The information gathered and knowledge obtained influences the user during future problem identification and information needs assessments.

We now proceed to show how WebSifter II supports the Web Search Activity Model.

3.1   Defining the User's Search Intention

The user places his information need in a context, by specifying a Weighted Semantic Taxonomy Tree (WSTT). The WSTT provides a simple ontological representation of the user's search intent. The taxonomy tree approach is already being used to classify pages in search engines such as Google and Yahoo! We have devised a tree-based search representation model that allows users to present their search intention by defining their own taxonomy topology. We call this the *Weighted Semantic Taxonomy Tree* (WSTT) model. The method to build such a tree is very similar to the approach in a conventional AHP approach, which has been shown to be a convenient way for a general user to describe his decision criteria in Decision Science. To build a WSTT model, a user defines a broad concept term that includes the term he seeks. Then he continues to refine that concept, specializing it by adding child nodes with more specific concept terms. At the same time he is assigning the relative importance levels to each concept term between sibling nodes. Through this procedure, users can build their own hierarchical taxonomy tree, and assign importance levels to each term within the context of their antecedent terms. In the context of organizational ontologies, we note that organizations can specify focused ontologies that can be used by users to formulate search requests. They may also extend the organizational terms by specializing the terms as discussed above.

Assume that a person has started a new business and needs office equipment. He wants to search for information on the web. Suppose he wants information about chairs, so he might build a query using a single term, „chair". A more skilled user of search engines, might build a query using two terms, „office" and „chair" to obtain more precise results. In this case, the term „office" provides added context for the search. This is depicted in Figure 2 and in the top-right pane of Figure 6.

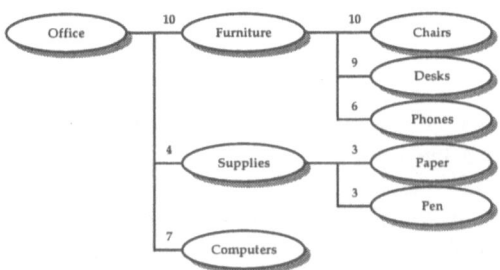

Fig. 2. WSTT for Office Equipment Search Intention.

One drawback to using terms for keywords is that the terms may have multiple meanings. This is one of the major reasons that search engines return irrelevant search results. To address this limitation, WebSifter II allows the user to expand and refine the context using WordNet [20]. For example, chair may have any one of four meanings, each with different synonyms:

1.   {chair, seat} – a seat for one person, with a support for the back,
2.   {professorship, chair} – the position of professor, or a chaired professorship,

3. {president, chairman, chairwoman, chair, chairperson} – the officer who presides at the meetings of an organization,
4. {electric chair, chair, death chair, hot seat} – an instrument of death by electrocution that resembles a chair.

The user chooses meanings to represent each WSTT concept. It is assumed that the remaining concepts are not of interest, thereby obtaining both positive and negative indicators (*Positive Concept Terms* (pct) and *Negative Concept Terms* (nct)) of the user's intent. In the example, the positive concept terms are chair and seat while the others constitute the negative terms. In the example, the positive concept terms are chair and seat and the negative concept terms are professorship, president, chairman, chairwoman, chairperson, electric chair, death chair, hot seat. The internal representation of the user's search intention, represented by the WSTT augmented by positive and negative terms, is shown in Figure 3. This figure also shows positive and negative terms for the other concepts in the WSTT. The user, however, sees the WSTT of Figure 2.

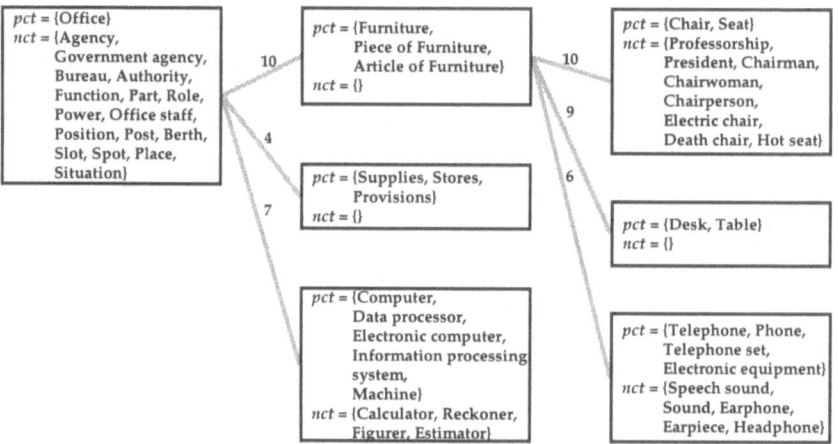

Fig. 3. Internal Representation of User's Search Intention

The WSTT schema, is translated into Boolean queries expanded by the positive concept terms. The leaf nodes of the tree denote the terms of interest to the user, and the antecedent nodes for each node form the search context. The entire tree is transformed into a set of separate queries. For the leaf path {Office, Furniture, Chair} six queries are constructed:

1. „Office" AND „Furniture" AND „Chair",
2. „Office" AND „Furniture" AND „Seat",
3. „Office" AND „Piece of Furniture" AND „Chair",
4. „Office" AND „Piece of Furniture" AND „Seat",
5. „Office" AND „Article of Furniture" AND „Chair",
6. „Office" AND „Article of Furniture" AND „Seat".

Using the AND operator provides more precision in the results. The number of queries generated from term combinations provides for coverage of possible results. Query results are stored for further processing.

3.2   Web Information Rating and Ranking Mechanism

WebSifter II's ranking of Web search hits by users involves the evaluation of multiple attributes, which reflect user preferences and their conception of the information need. Ranking is approached as a multi-attribute decision problem. Using Multi-attribute Utility Technology (MAUT) the Web pages most likely to satisfy the user's search intent are brought to the top of the results list. MAUT permits the evaluation of the hits on criteria weighted in importance by the user. Search results provided by multiple search engines are ranked according to decision criteria using MAUT [21], Repertory Grid [22], Dimensional Analysis [23], and Analytic Hierarchy Process (AHP) [24] techniques on six components. The computed relevance values of each component are combined into a single measure of relevance. Figure 4 shows the various components of the user's evaluation preferences. The weights assigned to each component indicate the user's evaluation of its perceived importance to the overall relevancy computation.

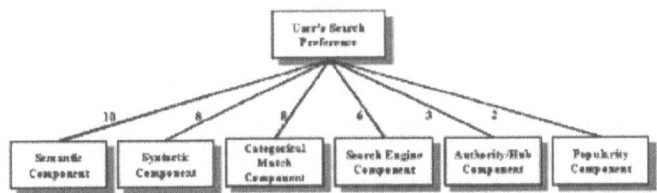

Fig. 4. Conceptual Model of User's Preference Representation Scheme

Semantic Component. The semantic component represents relevancy of a Web page to a user's search intent with respect to its content. The semantic relevance value of a Web page to a query is computed by counting the number of times a term appears on the page with respect to the number of terms in the associated query. Negative concepts offset the semantic relevance by adjusting for irrelevant terms on a page.
Syntactic Component. The syntactic component measures the structural aspects of the page as a function of the role of that page within the structure of a Web site. This permits an evaluation of the page independently of the specific search underway. The approach takes into account the location of the document, its role, and the well formedness of its URL [25].

Since a Web page might be classified into more than one class, we synthesize by averaging multiple matches into one measure.

We define three types of Web pages for which the user may assign weight values.
- *Direct-Hit* – the page may be a home page or a page with significant content within its domain.
- *Directory-Hit* – this page has links to other pages in the domain of the Web site.
- *Page-Hit* – these pages contain partial information about the domain of the Web site.

Categorical Match Component. The categorical match component represents the similarity measure between the structure of the user-created taxonomy and search engine category information for the retrieved Web page. Many popular search engines, for example Yahoo! and Google, respond to user's queries not only with a list of URLs but also with categorical information for each Web page. Although different search engines associate different category information to the same Web page, such categorical information helps users filter out some of the returned search results without actually visiting the URL. The categorical match component is designed to provide the benefits of manual filtering by automatic means; this is accomplished by comparing the WSTT terms with the categorical information provided by search engines.

Search Engine Component. The Search Engine component represents the user's biases toward and confidence in a search engine's results. A user preference value is assigned to each search engine. Dimensional analysis is used to discriminate between a second place rank by a search engine with 10 ranked page hits and a second place ranking among 5 page hits. To obtain a composite search engine relevance value of a Web page for a term combination, we adopt a weighted average method based on user's search engine preference and then consider the path length from the root of the WSTT to the leaf concept.

Authority/Hub Component. The Authority/Hub component represents the level of user preference for *Authority* or *Hub* sites and pages. At present, no such authority or hub ranking service exists on the Web. Therefore, we have not incorporated this component into our proof-of-concept prototype.

Popularity Component. The number of requests for the specific page measures popularity. There are several publicly available popularity services, which are accessed by the popularity component, such as www.yep.com. The popularity measure is propagated to the root of the WSTT for each Web page. The computed relevance values of each component are combined into a single measure of relevance.

Finally, after results are returned the user may review the ranked pages and indicate page relevance to the WTTS. Relevancy selection drives a feed-forward neural network mechanism learning more about the search intent, dynamically re-rating and re-ranking the results list [26].

4   WebSifter II System Architecture

WebSifter II is a semantic taxonomy-based personalizable meta-search agent system. shows the overall architecture of WebSifter II. The WSTT elicitor guides the user in building the taxonomy tree, assigning weights on each node, and choosing node meanings found by the ontology agent. The WSTT is stored in XML format. The stemming agent transforms terms in a concept Web page content into stemmed terms. The search preference elicitor captures the user's search preferences. The user expresses his search preference by assigning preference weights to each of the preference components, syntactic classes, and search engines.

The search broker interprets the WSTT to generate query statements. It queries information from popular search engines and stores the results.

The page request broker obtains the content of a specific URL. The Web page rater evaluates Web pages and displays ranked results to the user. The user profile-learning agent allows the user to provide feedback on the relevancy of the proposed Web page hits, learns about user's search preferences, and updates the user profile.

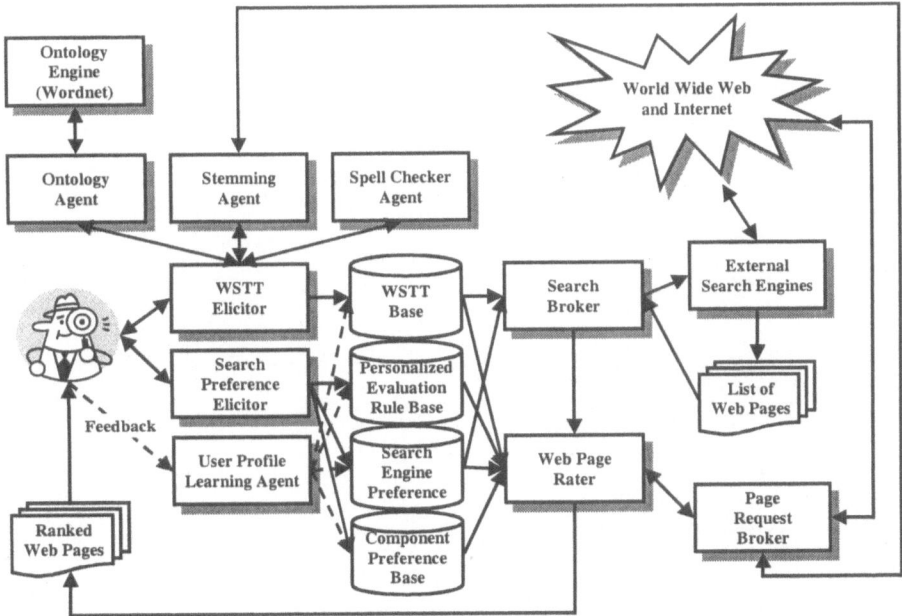

Fig. 5. System Architecture for WebSifter II

4.1   Implementation

WebSifter II is implemented as a working Java prototype, except for the spell checker. Figure 6 shows the main screen and illustrative results for a search query. The top-left pane contains specified WSTT queries with „Office Problem" highlighted. The top-right pane shows the Weighted Semantic Taxonomy Tree constructed by the user for this search.

The bottom pane shows results ranked by Total Relevance. The bottom pane left-most column is provided to obtain user feedback regarding page relevance to the search.

4.2   Experimental Results

Results from three experiments demonstrate the individual effects of facets of WebSifter. Results of expanding the search through positive and negative concepts are shown in Table 1. The page hits retrieved by WebSifter II for the search of a just a single term, „chair" together with the selected concept terms of seat for a person. In this table, the WebSifter ranking of Web pages appears in the first column.

The five columns on the right compare the WebSifter ranking to those of various search engines. Note that many of WebSifter's highly-ranked pages do not appear in the top-twenty rankings of other search engines; this is due to WebSifter's use of *semantic concepts* from WordNet to enhance the search terms. The relevancy decisions are based on the user's subjective assessment as to whether the corresponding Web page is relevant to a real chair. WebSifter found six relevant Web pages.

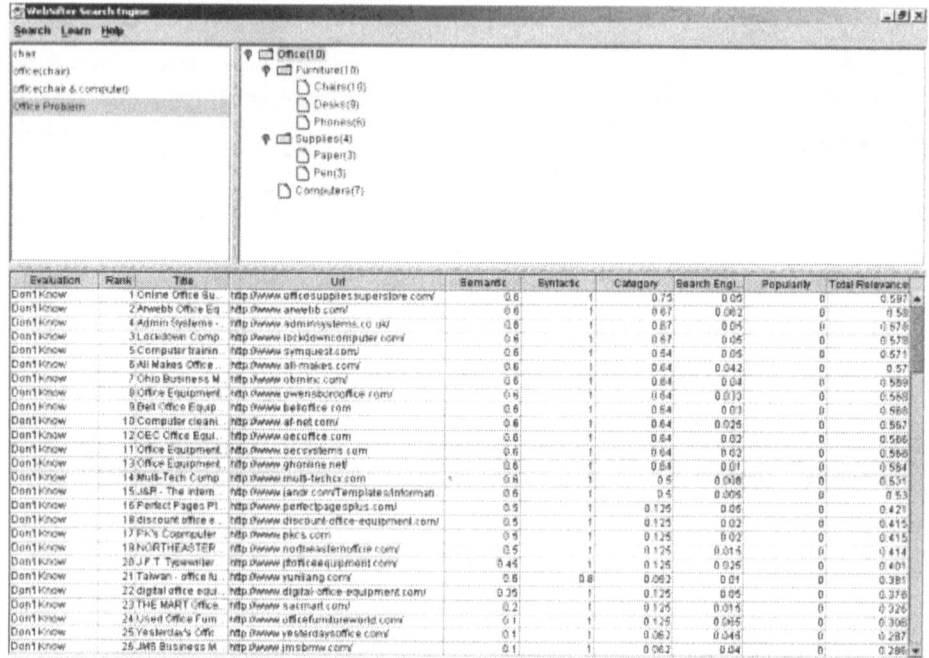

Fig. 6. A Screen Shot of Web Page Rater Results

Tables 2 and 3 show the retrieved page-hits when the taxonomy is extended to „Office and Chair". In Table 2 WebSifter has a 95%-hit ratio with the only irrelevant page-hit ranked 20th. This is due to the influence of the category match component, and the 'w/o Categ' column shows the corresponding WebSifter ranking with the category match component suppressed.

Table 3 of Figure 7 shows the WebSifter retrieved page-hits and their ranks for the case where the categorical match is turned off initially. The right-most column labeled 'with Categ' shows what the WebSifter ranking would have been were the category match component activated. Note that the non-relevant page hits would have been ranked 20th and below. The results in the three tables indicate that the concept taxonomy and the categorical match component affect considerably the resulting rankings. The category match component provides a 15% performance improvement in the precision to the concept taxonomy.

5   Conclusions

We have presented a methodology and architecture for a semantic taxonomy-based personalizable meta-search agent. WebSifter II achieves two important and comple-

Table 1. Results from WebSifter for the Query *Chair* and Search Engine Comparison.

Rank	URL	Relevancy	Copernic	Alta Vista	Google	Yahoo	Excite
1	www.countryseat.com	Y	-	-	-	-	-
2	www.infant-car-seat.com/	N	-	-	-	-	-
3	www.chairmaker.co.uk/	Y	-	-	-	19	-
4	www.convertible-car-seat.com/	N	-	-	-	-	-
5	www.booster-car-seats.com/	N	-	-	-	-	-
6	www.booster-seats-online.com/	N	-	-	-	-	-
7	www.booster-car-seat.com/	N	-	-	-	-	-
8	www.podiatrychair.com/	N	-	-	-	-	9
9	www.carolinachair.com/	Y	-	-	-	9	-
10	www.chairdancing.com/	N	-	-	-	-	-
11	www.massage-chairs-online	N	-	-	-	-	13
12	www.panasonic-massage-	N	-	-	-	-	14
13	www.fairfieldchair.com/	Y	-	-	15	-	-
14	www.gasserchair.com/	Y	-	16	-	-	-
15	www.chairtech.com/	Y	-	18	-	-	-
16	www.snugseat.com/	N	-	-	-	-	-
17	www.seat.com/	N	-	-	-	-	-
18	www.fifthchair.org/	N	3	2	5	8	3
19	www.painted-	N	19	-	9	-	-
20	www.jeanmonnetprogram.org/	N	5	1	1	-	5

Notes:
Y – relevant   N – irrelevant
Numbers indicate rank order from search engine
'-' denote pages ranked lower than 20ᵗʰ or were not found by the search engine

mentary goals: it allows users more expressive power in formulating their Web searches, and it improves the relevancy of search results based on the user's real intent. In contrast to previous research, we have focused not only on the search problem itself, but also on the decision-making problem that motivates users to search the Web.

The Weighted Semantic Taxonomy Tree provides a mechanism for users to specify the context and intent of domain-specific terms related to the search problem. User may also state their preferences and weights for the five components by which a Web page is evaluated: semantic relevance, syntactic relevance, categorical match, search engine preference, and page popularity.

To improve the precision of the retrieved information, WebSifter uses a hybrid rating scheme that considers both the user's search intent as represented by the WSTT and the user's search preference represented by preferences associated with the relevance components.

Experimental results indicate that this approach improve the precision of the search results, and allows users to control the search terms as well as the overall ranking

Table 2. Office Chair Taxonomy with Categorical Match

Rank	URL	Rele-vancy	w/o Categ
1	www.seatingvfm.com/	Y	1
2	www.officechair.co.uk/	Y	2
3	www.AmericanErgonomics.com/	Y	9
4	www.ompchairs.com/	Y	22
5	www.klasse.com.au/	Y	4
6	www.cyberchair.com/	Y	46
7	www.leap-chair.com	Y	47
8	www.seizaseat.com/	Y	50
9	www.zackback.com	Y	49
10	www.fairfieldchair.com	Y	2
11	www.chair-ergonomics.com/	Y	5
12	www.buy-ergonomic-chairs.com/	Y	6
13	www.jfainc.com/	Y	7
14	www.chairtech.com/	Y	8
15	www.plasticfoldingchairs.com/	Y	13
16	www.kneelsit.com/	Y	10
17	www.home-office-furiniture-store.com/	Y	11
18	www.home-office-furniture-site.com/	Y	12
19	www.amadio.it/uk/	Y	19
20	www.newtrim.co.uk/	N	15

Table 3. Office Chair Taxonomy without Categorical Match

Rank	URL	Rele-vancy	with Categ
1	www.seatingvfm.com/	Y	1
2	www.fairfieldchair.com	Y	10
3	www.officechair.co.uk/	Y	2
4	www.klasse.com.au/	Y	5
5	www.chair-ergonomics.com/	Y	11
6	www.buy-ergonomic-chairs.com/	Y	15
7	www.jfainc.com/	Y	13
8	www.chairtech.com/	Y	14
9	www.AmericanErgonomics.com/	Y	3
10	www.kneelsit.com/	Y	16
11	www.home-office-furiniture-store.com/	Y	17
12	www.home-office-furniture-site.com/	Y	18
13	www.plasticfoldingchairs.com/	Y	15
14	www.office-interior-plans.com/	N	21
15	www.newtrim.co.uk/	N	20
16	www.oa-chair.com/	N	23
17	www.buy-ergonomic-chair.com/	Y	24
18	www.countryseat.com/	Y	26
19	www.amadio.it/uk/	Y	19
20	www.mobile-office-desk.com/	N	28

process. This approach could be augmented with ontologies developed by organizations to provide taxonomies for employees to use in knowledge-directed searches. This is a topic of ongoing research by the WebSifter group.

Acknowledgements. This research was sponsored, in part, by grants from the Virginia Center for Innovative Technology, webMethods, and other sponsors of the E-Center for E-Business, http://eceb.gmu.edu, at George Mason University. The authors wish to acknowledge Hanjo Jeong and Srikala Kanumuru for their Java-based implementation of the WebSifter II prototype.

References

1. T. Berners-Lee, R. Cailliau, A. Loutonen, H. F. Nielsen, and A. Secret, „The World-Wide Web," *Communications of the ACM*, vol. 37, pp. 76–82, 1994.
2. E. Selberg and O. Etzioni, „The MetaCrawler Architecture for Resource Aggregation on the Web," *IEEE Expert*, vol. 12, pp. 11-14, 1997.
3. A. E. Howe and D. Dreilinger, „Savvy Search: A Metasearch Engine that Learns which Search Engines to Query," *AI Magazine*, vol. 18, pp. 19-25, 1997.
4. S. Lawrence and C. L. Giles, „Context and Page Analysis for Improved Web Search," *IEEE Internet Computing*, vol. 2, pp. 38-46, 1998.
5. S. Chakrabarti, B. Dom, and P. Indyk, „Enhanced Hypertext Categorization using Hyperlinks," presented at Proceedings of ACM SIGMOD International Conference on Management of Data, Seattle, Washington, 1998.
6. Y. Li, „Toward a Qualitative Search Engine," *IEEE Internet Computing*, vol. 2, pp. 24-29, 1998.
7. P. Maes, „Agents that reduce work and information overload," *Communications of the ACM*, vol. 37, pp. 30-40, 1994.
8. K. D. Bollacker, S. Lawrence, and L. Giles, „Discovering Relevant Scientific Literature on the Web," *IEEE Intelligent Systems*, vol. 15, pp. 42-47, 2000.
9. H. Chen and S. Dumais, „Bringing Order to the Web: Automatically Categorizing Search Results," presented at Proceedings of the CHI 2000 conference on Human factors in computing systems, The Hague Netherlands, 2000.
10. Y. Aridor, D. Carmel, R. Lempel, A. Soffer, and Y. S. Maarek, „Knowledge Agent on the Web," presented at Proceedings of the 4th International Workshop on Cooperative Information Agents IV, 2000.
11. S. Chakrabarti, M. v. d. Berg, and B. Dom, „Focused Crawling: A New Approach to Topic-Specific Web Resource Discovery," presented at Proceedings of the Eighth International WWW Conference, 1999.
12. N. Guarino, C. Masolo, and G. Vetere, „OntoSeek: Content-based Access to the Web," *IEEE Intelligent Systems*, vol. 14, pp. 70-80, 1999.
13. D. Fensel, J. Angele, S. Decker, M. Erdmann, H.-P. Schnurr, S. Staab, R. Studer, and A. Witt, „On2broker: Semantic-Based Access to Information Sources at the WWW," presented at Proceedings of the World Conference on the WWW and Internet (WebNet 99), Honolulu, Hawaii, USA, 1999.
14. S. Staab, C. Braun, I. Bruder, A. Dusterhoft, A. Heuer, G. Neumann, B. Prager, J. Pretzel, H.-P. Schnurr, R. Studer, and H. Uszkoreit, „A System for Facilitating and Enhancing Web Search," presented at Proceedings of IWANN '99 - International Working Conference on Artificial and Natural Neural Networks, Berlin, Heidelberg, 1999.
15. P. Martin and P. W. Eklund, „Knowledge Retrieval and the World Wide Web," *IEEE Intelligent Systems*, vol. 15, pp. 18-25, 2000.
16. J. Hendler, „Agents and the Semantic Web," *IEEE Intelligent Systems*, vol. March/April 2001, pp. 30-37, 2001.
17. N. F. Noy, M. Sintek, S. Decker, M. Crubézy, R. W. Fergerson, and M. A. Musen, „Creating Semantic Web Contents with Protégé-2000," *IEEE Intelligent Systems*, vol. March/April 2001, pp. 60-71, 2001.
18. S. A. McIlraith, T. C. Son, and H. Zeng, „Semantic Web Services," *IEEE Intelligent Systems*, vol. March/April 2001, pp. 46-53, 2001.
19. E. J. Glover, S. Lawrence, M. D. Gordon, W. P. Birmingham, and C. L. Giles, „Web Search – Your Way," *Communications of the ACM*, vol. 44, pp. 97-102, 2001.
20. G. A. Miller, „WordNet a Lexical Database for English," *Communications of the ACM*, vol. 38, pp. 39-41, 1995.
21. D. A. Klein, Decision-Analytic Intelligent Systems: Automated Explanation and Knowledge Acquisition: Lawrence Erlbaum Associates, 1994.

22. J. H. Boose and J. M. Bradshaw, „Expertise Transfer and Complex Problems: Using AQUINAS as a Knowledge-acquisition Workbench for Knowledge-Based Systems," *Int. J. Man-Machine Studies*, vol. 26, pp. 3-28, 1987.
23. M. E. Martin, *Analysis and Design of Business Information Systems*. Englewood Cliffs, NJ: Prentice hall, 1991.
24. T. L. Saaty, *The Analytic Hierarchy Process*. New York: McGraw-Hill, 1980.
25. A. Scime and L. Kerschberg, „WebSifter: An Ontology-Based Personalizable Search Agent for the Web," presented at International Conference on Digital Libraries: Research and Practice, Kyoto Japan, 2000.
26. W. Kim, L. Kerschberg, and A. Scime, „Personalization in a Semantic Taxonomy-Based Meta-Search Agent," presented at International Conference on Electronic Commerce 2001 (ICEC 2001), Vienna, Austria, 2001.

Defining Information System Components

Thang Le Dinh and M. Leonard

Centre Universitaire d'Informatique, University of Geneva
24 Général Dufour, CH 1211 Geneva 4, Switzerland
{Thang, Leonard}@cui.unige.ch

Abstract. This paper introduces an overview of a component-based develop-ment (CBD) approach based on the concept of *Information System component* that aims to be conformed to the nature of information system (IS) and handles components at the earlier phases of the development process.

1   Summary

In our viewpoint, components in the context of information system (IS) must be concerned with *the nature of information system* that has a great deal of differences compared with software systems. In case of enterprise-wide information systems, it is indispensable to deal with the most fundamental challenges of IS engineering such as the interactions with the organizational environment, the information overlaps among components and the evolution of IS.

An *Information System component* is a reusable artifact of an IS part that represents adequate characteristics of an information system. *The content of an IS component* must be constituted by all fundamental aspects of an IS such as the static, the dynamic and the integrity rule aspects.

The context of an IS component deals with the environment in which the component is designed to interact. It has formed from: i) the interactions of an IS component with the organizational environment through the activities and the responsibility zone; and ii) the interactions among IS components through the information overlaps.

On the other hand, the *development process* of the IS component-based approach includes two distinct phases: design for reuse and design by reuse. The *design for reuse* concerns with the production of reusable components including the tasks of extraction, representation and organization of components. The *design by reuse* concerns with the selection, adaptation and integration of components to develop new information systems.

In brief, the IS component-based approach has tried to respond to the challenges above by providing certain independences and the ability to coordinate with the organizational environment. The benefit of these responds is to be conformed to the nature of IS by improving its adaptability, flexibility and evolution.

The perspective of this work is to provide an effective CBD that would be best suited for the conception, the implementation as well as the evolution of enterprise wide information systems.

R. Meersman, Z. Tari (Eds.): CoopIS/DOA/ODBASE 2002, LNCS 2519, p. 1359, 2002.
© Springer-Verlag Berlin Heidelberg 2002

Discovering Resources in the Semantic Web

Luis Anido, Judith Rodríguez, Manuel Caeiro, and Juan Santos

Departamento de Ingeniería Telemática,
ETSI Telecomunicación,
Universidad de Vigo, Spain
{lanido,jestevez,mcaeiro,jsgago}@det.uvigo.es

Abstract. Present day brokerage systems rely on customized or standardized (meta)data models. Although this approach partially solves interoperability problems at data-level, software-level interoperability problems still remain. The Semantic Web paradigm, envisioned by Tim Berners-Lee, and its related technologies (e.g. RDF, WSDL, ontologies, etc.) provide us a new point of view to face this kind of problems. In this poster we outline the main features of our proposal for the definition of a complete set of software services to build Web-based educational brokerage systems in the upcoming Semantic Web framework.

1 Poster Topics

Some of the most outstanding features of our proposal for educational brokerage systems are summarized next:

- Definition of ontologies for educational resources and services. For this task we are taking advantage of the previous standardization efforts carried out by the main European and American institutions (e.g. LTSC, IMS, etc).
- Identification and definition of common brokerage services. In that topic we are using the *Web Services Description Language* (WSDL) to describe service characteristics. This specification together with other ones in progress, such as the *Universal Description, Discovery and Integration* (UDDI), allow dynamically discovering and binding services. In such way, software components or agents can be programmed to dynamically achieve the goals they have been designed for.
- Definition of common brokerage services compositions (e.g. discover, order and deliver). To accomplish this task we will use XML-based languages as the *Web Services Flow Language* specification.

In order to develop our proposal we are following a strict and systematic methodology for domain-specific service specification that follows the guidelines established in the "*Model Driven Architecture*" document by the Object Management Group (OMG). This methodology allows us to obtain an underlying model that is independent from the further chosen development technologies.

Although some questions are still open in our proposal since Semantic Web related specifications are not stable, we have already established the root basis of the proposal and changes in those specifications will mean minor modifications in our work.

R. Meersman, Z. Tari (Eds.): CoopIS/DOA/ODBASE 2002, LNCS 2519, p. 1360, 2002.
© Springer-Verlag Berlin Heidelberg 2002

Geodata Interoperation via Semantic Correspondences

Anastasiya Sotnykova

EPFL, Swiss Federal Institute of Technology in Lausanne, Database Laboratory,
1015 Lausanne, Switzerland

Extended Abstract. With the expansion of the information space and constant increase in the volume of the available data, semantics becomes one of the most important aspects for data description and collaborative usage. Semantics is an implementation independent feature of data, which requires a clear separation of the conceptual level from other levels of information systems design.

Our work aims at developing an integration method for spatio-temporal data that focuses on conceptual level specifications. It's position is somehow in between the highly abstract methods using formal ontologies to resolve data heterogeneity, as in [1], and the real-world instance based methods, as in [3]. The core part of our method is the set of semantic correspondences that are formulated for element pairs of the database schemas that model related real-world objects. As the common data model we employ the MADS [2] conceptual data model, which was designed to fulfill the requirements for modeling of spatial and temporal data.

Evolving from the relationships between real world sets of related objects our method takes into account the relativism of conceptual representation and employs the notion of the multiple instantiation class sets. Our method is intended for geodata, and it supports correspondences between objects' spatial and temporal features. For the integrity issue of interoperable systems we propose an algorithm for consistency checking. Semantic correspondences that are established for the source data sets are checked for compatibility against the integrity constraints imposed on the same data. To ensure a meaningful integrated solution even for the cases of greatly diverse representations of related data, we employ a multi-representation solution that consistently preserves the initial representations on the integrated level.

References

1. Farshad Hakimpour and Andreas Geppert. Global schema generation using formal ontologies. In *Proceedings of the 21st International Conference on Conceptual Modeling (ER2002)*, Tampere, Finland, October, 8–10 2002.
2. Cristine Parent, Stefano Spaccapietra, and Esteban Zimanyi. Spatio-temporal conceptual models: Data structures + Space + Time. In *7th ACM Symposium on Advances in GIS*, Kansas City, Kansas, November 5–6 1999.
3. Mark W.W. Vermeer and Peter M.G. Apers. The role of integrity constraints in database interoperation. In *Proceedings of the 22nd VLDB Conference*, Mumbai, India, 1996.

R. Meersman, Z. Tari (Eds.): CoopIS/DOA/ODBASE 2002, LNCS 2519, p. 1361, 2002.
© Springer-Verlag Berlin Heidelberg 2002

Extending Datatype Support in Web Ontology Reasoning

Jeff Z. Pan and Ian Horrocks

Department of Computer Science, University of Manchester, UK
{pan,horrocks}@cs.man.ac.uk

The Semantic Web is a vision of the next generation Web, which aims at machine understandability. "Semantic" markup will be added to Web resources, specifying their meanings so as to make them more accessible to software agents. Markups will use ontologies for shared understanding within certain domain. DAML+OIL [van Harmelen *et al.*, 2001] is a Web ontology language, which is compatible with existing Web standards, i.e. RDF. It is formally specified and have adequate expressive power—on the one hand, it is much more expressive than RDF, while on the other hand, it is believed to be still decidable.

DAML+OIL is in fact a Description Logic (DL). Significant efforts have already been devoted to the investigation of suitable DLs to provide reasoning support for DAML+OIL—in particular, [Horrocks and Sattler, 2001] have presented the $\mathcal{SHOQ}(\mathbf{D})$ DL, which is a good candidate, along with a sound and complete algorithm for deciding concept satisfiability, a basic reasoning service for DLs and ontologies.

A key feature of $\mathcal{SHOQ}(\mathbf{D})$ is that, like DAML+OIL, it supports *datatypes*(e.g., string, integer) as well as the usual abstract concepts (e.g., animal, plant). $\mathcal{SHOQ}(\mathbf{D})$, however, only supports unary datatype predicates. While this is quite close to the requirements of the *current version* of the DAML+OIL language, it is not enough for (even the current version of) DAML+OIL and some semantic Web ontologies and applications.

E.g., ontologies used in e-commerce may need to classify different customers according to the numbers of their friends' email addresses they provide, and to reason that a customer who provides at least 10 *friends' email addresses*, and at least 5 of them are from UK, at least 5 of them have the same domain as the *customer's email address*, e.g. hotmail.com, is a kind of customers who are entitled to have 5% cash back during the promotion. Here "*friend's email address*" and "*customer's email address*" have concrete values (string). "From UK (*friends' email address*)" is a unary datatype predicate, and "the same domain as (*friends' email address,customer's email address*)" is a binary predicate. As shown above, unary predicates are *not enough*, while n-ary predicates, as well as qualified number restrictions with n-ary predicates, are often necessary in (Web) ontology applications.

[Baader and Hanschke *et al.*, 1991] extended the well known $\mathcal{ALC}$ DL with concrete domain. Though $\mathcal{ALC}(\mathcal{D})$ is proved decidable, $\mathcal{ALC}(\mathcal{D})$ with general TBox is found undecidable. In order to extend *expressive* DLs with concrete domains, [Horrocks and Sattler, 2001] proposed a simplified approach on concrete domain and gave the $\mathcal{SHOQ}(\mathbf{D})$ DL. [Pan, 2001] investigated the simplifying constraints introduced in [Horrocks and Sattler, 2001]. One of the main differences between the two approaches is that the latter one uses concrete roles, instead of features.

R. Meersman, Z. Tari (Eds.): CoopIS/DOA/ODBASE 2002, LNCS 2519, pp. 1362–1363, 2002.

We extend the $\mathcal{SHOQ}(\mathbf{D})$ DL with n-ary datatype predicates and qualified number restrictions on n-ary predicates, to give the $\mathcal{SHOQ}(\mathbf{D_n})$ DL. The kind of customers described in the above example can be a $\mathcal{SHOQ}(\mathbf{D_n})$-concept

$$customer \sqcap \geqslant 10 friends - email \sqcap \geqslant 5 friends - email.$$
$$\texttt{from} - \texttt{uk} \sqcap \geqslant 5 friends - email, email.\texttt{same} - \texttt{domain}$$

where *friends-email* and *email* are concrete roles, from-uk is unary datatype predicate and same-domain is binary datatype predicate.

We prove that the tableau algorithm we give is a *decision procedure* for concept satisfiability and subsumption of the $\mathcal{SHOQ}(\mathbf{D_n})$-concept w.r.t. terminologies. With its support for both nominals and n-ary datatype predicates, $\mathcal{SHOQ}(\mathbf{D_n})$ is well suited to provide reasoning support for ontology language in general, and Semantic Web ontology language in particular, e.g. DAML+OIL and suggests that *future version* of DAML+OIL can have n-ary datatype predicates and qualified number restrictions with n-ary datatype predicates. As future work, we plan to work out a framework for reasoning with both ontologies and datatypes in DLs.

References

[van Harmelen *et al.*, 2001] Frank van Harmelen and Peter F. Patel-Schneider and Ian Horrocks. *A Model-Theoretic Semantics of DAML+OIL(March 2001)*.

[Horrocks and Sattler, 2001] Ian Horrocks and Ulrike Sattler. Ontology Reasoning for the Semantic Web. In *Proc. of the 17th Int. Joint Conf. on Artificial Intelligence (IJCAI'01)*,2001.

[Baader and Hanschke, 1991] F. Baader and P. Hanschke. A Scheme for Integrating Concrete Domains into Concept Languages. In *Proceedings of IJCAI-91*, 1991.

[Pan, 2001] Jeff Z. Pan. Web Ontology Reasoning in the SHOQ(Dn) Description Logic. In *Proceedings of the Methods for Modalities 2 (M4M-2)*, ILLC, University of Amsterdam, 2001.

Author Index

Lecture Notes in Computer Science

For information about Vols. 1–1234

please contact your bookseller or Springer-Verlag